Law, Business, and Society

Eleventh Edition

Tony McAdams
University of Northern Iowa

Kiren Dosanjh Zucker
California State University, Northridge

Nancy Neslund
University of New Hampshire School of Law

Kristofer Neslund
Ashland University

Mc
Graw
Hill
Education

LAW, BUSINESS, AND SOCIETY, ELEVENTH EDITION

Published by McGraw-Hill Education, 2 Penn Plaza, New York, NY 10121. Copyright © 2015 by McGraw-Hill Education. All rights reserved. Printed in the United States of America. Previous editions © 2012, 2009, and 2007. No part of this publication may be reproduced or distributed in any form or by any means, or stored in a database or retrieval system, without the prior written consent of McGraw-Hill Education, including, but not limited to, in any network or other electronic storage or transmission, or broadcast for distance learning.

Some ancillaries, including electronic and print components, may not be available to customers outside the United States.

This book is printed on acid-free paper.

1 2 3 4 5 6 7 8 9 0 DOC/DOC 1 0 9 8 7 6 5 4

ISBN 978-0-07-802386-6
MHID 0-07-802386-6

Senior Vice President, Products & Markets: *Kurt L. Strand*
Vice President, General Manager, Products & Markets: *Marty Lange*
Vice President, Content Production & Technology Services: *Kimberly Meriwether David*
Brand Manager: *Kathleen Klehr*
Managing Director: *Tim Vertovec*
Director of Development: *Ann Torbert*
Development Editor: *Gail Korosa*
Product Developer: *Jaroslaw Szymanski*
Marketing Manager: *Michelle Nolte*
Director, Content Design & Delivery: *Terri Schiesl*
Content Project Manager: *Lisa Bruflodt*
Buyer: *Michael McCormick*
Cover Image: *Pawel Gaul/Getty Images*
Compositor: *MPS Limited*
Typeface: *10/12 Times LT Std*
Printer: *R. R. Donnelley*

All credits appearing on page or at the end of the book are considered to be an extension of the copyright page.

Library of Congress Cataloging-in-Publication Data

Law, business, and society / Tony McAdams, University of Northern Iowa, Nancy Neslund, University of New Hampshire School of Law, Kiren Dosanjh Zucker, California State University, Northridge, Kristofer Neslund, Ashland University. — Eleventh edition.
   p. cm.
  Includes index.
  ISBN 978-0-07-802386-6 (alk. paper)
  1. Business enterprises—Law and legislation—United States. 2. Trade regulation—United States. 3. Business ethics—United States. 4. Industries—Social aspects—United States. I. McAdams, Tony, author. II. Neslund, Nancy, author. III. Zucker, Kiren Dosanjh, author. IV. Neslund, Kristofer, author.
  KF1355.M28 2014
  346.73'065—dc23

                           2014022614

The Internet addresses listed in the text were accurate at the time of publication. The inclusion of a website does not indicate an endorsement by the authors or McGraw-Hill Education, and McGraw-Hill Education does not guarantee the accuracy of the information presented at these sites.

www.mhhe.com

About the Authors

Tony McAdams

Tony McAdams is a Professor of Management at the University of Northern Iowa. He earned a BA in History from the University of Northern Iowa, a JD from the University of Iowa, and an MBA from Columbia University. Professor McAdams's primary teaching interests include government regulation of business, business and society, and employment law. Professor McAdams's research interests include managerial accountability, business ethics, and employment law. His scholarly articles have appeared in such journals as *The Harvard Business Review, The Academy of Management Review, The Journal of Business Ethics,* and *The American Business Law Journal.* Professor McAdams has received the Iowa Board of Regents Award for Faculty Excellence, the Distinguished Teacher of the Year Award from the student government at the University of Kentucky, and the University of Northern Iowa College of Business Administration Excellence in Teaching Award.

Kiren Dosanjh Zucker

Kiren Dosanjh Zucker, author of Chapters 4, 6, 7, 12, 13, and 14, is a Professor of Accounting and Information Systems at California State University, Northridge (CSUN). She earned a BA in Political Science from Syracuse University and a JD from the University of Michigan. A member of the State Bar of California, she has served on its Committee of Bar Examiners and Committee on Professional Responsibility and Conduct. Her teaching and research interests focus primarily on employment law, pedagogy, and accounting ethics. In 2001, she was selected as a Master Teacher by the Academy of Legal Studies in Business, and in 2004 she received the Outstanding Faculty Award from CSUN's Students with Disabilities Resources. In 2004 and 2006, she also received a CSUN University Ambassadors' Polished Apple Award. In 2014, CSUN Accounting students named her the Harvey A. Bookstein Accounting Professor of the Year.

Nancy Neslund

During the preparation of this edition, Nancy Neslund, author of Chapters 16, 17, and 18, was a visiting professor at the Ohio Northern University Pettit College of Law in Ada, Ohio. She earned a BA in Economics from Willamette University, a JD from Columbia University, and an LLM from New York University. Prior to entering academia, she was a lawyer in private practice for 14 years. During the academic year 2004 to 2005, she was a visiting professor on the law faculty of Europa Universität Viadrina, in Germany on its border with Poland. She teaches business organizations, business planning, financial literacy, and tax law. Her research interests include the social benefit business entities, transnational tax issues, and digital currencies.

Kristofer Neslund

Kristofer Neslund, author of Chapter 9, is Associate Professor of Accounting at Ashland University. He holds a DBA from Kent State University, a JD from Lewis and Clark College, and an LLM in taxation from New York University. He is a CPA and a member of the Oregon bar. Prior to entering academia, he was a tax partner in two law firms, as well as the CFO of a telecommunications company operating in three western states. During the academic year 2004 to 2005, he was a visiting professor in the Master of Professional Accountancy program at UNITEC in New Zealand, and a visiting professor of law at the Europa Universität Viadrina in Germany and La Trobe University in Australia. Dr. Neslund has more recently been a visiting professor of law at the University of New Hampshire and Roger Williams University. He has been selected for a Fulbright Scholarship in Accounting at the University of Iceland for 2015. His research interests are corporate governance, the regulation of the accounting profession, securities regulation, and taxation. He is presently the President of the Tri-State Academy of Legal Studies in Business and President-Elect of Region 4 of the Accreditation Council for Business Schools and Programs.

Preface

Broadly, our adjustments for this eleventh edition were designed to refresh the book and achieve increased reader interest, but more specifically this edition is directed to the nation's ongoing debate about how much government we need in our lives, particularly in our business lives. Although the general structure and philosophy of the book are unchanged, we have made significant revisions.

WHAT'S NEW

Chapter 1, a survey of the economic continuum from capitalism to collectivism and their various mutations, has been thoroughly rewritten and updated to reflect the striking economic developments of recent years in the United States and around the world.

Chapter 1 includes discussions of the subprime mortgage fallout and the law's response, as well as the critics' views of big banks and their treatment as being "too big to fail." Recent Wall Street alleged abuses are also discussed, and new data on the wealth gap, poverty, and overall quality of life in the United States are offered. China's ongoing balance between the free market and state oversight is also explored.

Chapter 2 explores the recent financial crisis as an ethics scandal and legal challenge. Various new vignettes, anecdotes, questions, and other features aid this exploration.

Chapter 3 offers a critical view of expanding corporate power addressing tax avoidance, state incentives, and politics. Corporate social responsibility issues such as guns and gun sales are explored, along with the Toyota sudden acceleration case, and fast-food labor issues, which are explored from a legal perspective in subsequent chapters as well.

Chapter 4 includes a discussion of the Rutgers University cyberbullying case and questions that will elicit student discussion on the controversial sentence, as well as antibullying legislation. "Stand your ground," the George Zimmerman trial for the killing of Trayvon Martin, and the "Castle Doctrine" are the subject of a Practicing Ethics box. Critics' views of the Roberts Court are updated, along with discussion of the Walmart class action aftermath, firms' billing practices, and access to justice. Service of process through social media and the use of small claims to sue big corporations is also explored, along with an updated look at the Japanese practice of law.

Chapter 5's discussion of the ongoing Federalism debate is updated, and its analysis of free speech has been simplified and clarified, and the takings debate is revisited. Along with a new search and seizure case discussion, changes in the law governing gay and lesbian rights, including marriage, are discussed.

Chapter 6 offers updates on the Facebook ownership and Huffington Post blogger pay disputes, a clarified example of unjust enrichment, and questions on recent cases such as the *Modern Family* cast's contract dispute. Also covered are the recent claims against Lance Armstrong by his former sponsors following his television admissions of wrongdoing. Further, the Uniform Electronic Transactions Act (UETA) and websites' terms of sale are added subjects.

Chapter 7 includes updates and an accompanying question regarding the Walmart trampling death for the opening Practicing Ethics section, as well as an update on the battery charge against a Valdosta State University professor for shutting a laptop on a student's fingers. A discussion of the 2014 jury verdict in a defamation lawsuit stemming from Yelp postings, and a 2013 negligence case involving an assault in a bowling alley parking lot have also been added. The closure of Blitz, the red gasoline can maker, is discussed to raise the larger question of whether litigation or corporate greed are to blame for the pressures facing high-risk businesses. The recent legal issues raised by video game makers' use of college football players' images are discussed in light of recent developments. The Toyota saga as it extends to electric throttle systems is also discussed.

Chapter 8 explores the 2012 U.S. Supreme Court decision in *National Federation of Independent Business v. Sebelius,* and its view of the commerce clause versus taxation power of the U.S. Congress. A new case on indecency is included. TARP and Dodd–Frank developments are reviewed.

Chapter 9 includes discussion of "distorporations," as well as discussions of the SEC's recent social media guidance on Regulation FD, its approach to settlements, its lift on the ban to advertise for unregistered securities, and new approach to settlements. Recent white-collar criminal cases against SAC and Goldman Sachs' Rajat Gupta are also discussed, as is Delaware's attempt to gain exclusive jurisdiction over incorporation.

Chapter 10 includes a recent Robinson–Patman case: The intersection between antitrust and intellectual property is further explored and clarified.

Chapter 11 updates antitrust developments with Apple, Google, and Microsoft and provides an overview of recent legal scrutiny applied to mergers.

Chapter 12's drug testing sections are reorganized for clarity and flow, and a new "privacy at work" case highlights personal privacy in the small, private-sector workplace. Recent legal developments are highlighted, such as updated discussions on the 2010 Patient Protection and Affordable Care Act, the EEOC 2012 criminal background check guidelines, and a recent case raising questions on the utility of such pre-employment measures in preventing workplace violence, a 2012 U.S. Supreme Court decision impacting the FMLA rights of state workers, updated examples including a new example of constructive discharge, as well as more recent surveys and statistics.

Chapter 13 includes the U.S. Supreme Court's recent decisions impacting retaliation and employers' affirmative defense for sexual harassment, which is, in turn, highlighted by a 2014 federal case. An updated discussion on sexual-orientation discrimination protections that includes the Spring 2014 social-media-fueled, successful campaign to oust a CEO who had contributed to an anti-gay marriage political group, as well as the EEOC's GINA Enforcement Guidance, is offered. Updates on the cases against A&F found in the opening Practicing Ethics discussion, as well as updated survey results and statistics, are offered. The discussion of the EEOC's "right to sue" letters is clarified as well.

Chapter 14's discussion of unfair labor practices in management is reorganized to include a fuller discussion of recent applications of the NLRA, to, for example, at-will employment clauses, dress codes, and social media postings. The good-faith bargaining explanation has been clarified and updated, as well as the Boeing dispute.

Chapter 15 offers a discussion of the consumer protection issues associated with for-profit schools. Legal and ethical issues raised by payday loans operations are also explored.

The ongoing struggles at the governing agencies such as FDA, CFPB, and CPSC are also discussed.

Chapter 16 offers an updated discussion of free speech, encompassing social media and Internet service providers. Emerging issues of effective regulation of multinational enterprises are discussed, as well as the SEC's extraterritorial powers under the Dodd–Frank Act. Updates on accounting standards, including the status of the convergence project between IFRS and GAAP and the PCAOB on the global stage, are also included.

Chapter 17 sheds light on the complexity of environmental issues through current examples, such as the impact of burning of forests in Indonesia to accommodate palm oil plantations on air pollution levels in Singapore and southern Malaysia. Cap-and-trade programs, tax incentives, "green growth" examples, and updated statistics and enforcement settlements are also discussed.

Chapter 18 updates include cybersecurity, the digital divide, the FCC's recent rules on net neutrality, legal issues stemming from "revenge porn" websites, price discrimination, cross-device tracking, market response to the use of copyrighted material, top-level domain name sales (TLDS) as an ethical issue, and the effort to make state sales tax uniform to support interstate, online sales transactions.

OVERVIEW

This text is directed to courses at both the upper-division undergraduate and masters levels in the legal environment of business, government and business, and business and society. Authors of textbooks in these areas often rely on a single discipline (for example, law, economics, or management) as the foundation for their efforts. In this text we take an interdisciplinary approach, using elements of law, political economy, international business, ethics, social responsibility, and management. This large task necessarily requires certain trade-offs, but we hope the product will more accurately capture the fullness of the business environment.

Our primary goal is to produce an interesting, provocative reading experience. Naturally, accuracy and reasonable comprehensiveness cannot be sacrificed. Our feeling, however, is that a law text can be both intellectually and emotionally engaging without sacrificing substantive ends. To meet our objective we have presented the bulk of the book in the form of contemporary legal and ethical conflicts emerging from today's news. We have provided scholarly results, surveys, polls, data, anecdotes, and other specific details that lend credibility, immediacy, and interest to the reading experience.

The book is divided into five units, as follows:

Unit I—Business and Society.   We do not begin with the law. Rather, in Chapter 1 (Capitalism and the Role of Government), Chapter 2 (Business Ethics), and Chapter 3 (The Corporation and Public Policy: Expanding Responsibilities), we describe some of the economic and social forces that shape our legal system.

The goals of Unit I are to (a) enhance student awareness of the many societal influences on business, (b) establish the business context from which government regulation arose, and (c) explore the roles of the free market, government intervention, and individual and corporate ethics in shaping business behavior.

The student must understand not merely the law but the law in context. What forces have provoked government intervention in business? What alternatives to our current "mixed economy" might prove healthy? These considerations help the students respond to one of the critical questions of the day: To what extent, if any, should we regulate business?

Unit II—Introduction to Law.   Chapter 4 (The American Legal System) and Chapter 5 (Constitutional Law and the Bill of Rights) survey the foundations of our legal system. Here we set out the "nuts and bolts" of law, combining cases and narrative. Then with Chapter 6 (Contracts) and Chapter 7 (Business Torts and Product Liability), we examine the foundations of business law.

Unit III—Trade Regulation and Antitrust.   Chapter 8 (Government Regulation of Business) raises the book's central policy inquiry: When should the government intervene in business practice? Chapter 9 (Business Organizations and Securities Regulation), Chapter 10 (Antitrust Law—Restraints of Trade), and Chapter 11 (Antitrust Law— Monopolies and Mergers) survey the core of government oversight of business.

Unit IV—Employer–Employee Relations.   Chapter 12 (Employment Law I: Employee Rights), Chapter 13 (Employment Law II: Discrimination), and Chapter 14 (Employment Law III: Labor–Management Relations) are intended not only to survey the law in those areas, but also to introduce some of the sensitive and provocative social issues that have led to today's extensive government intervention in the employment relationship.

Unit V—Selected Topics in Government–Business Relations.   Two of the closing chapters of this book—Chapter 15 (Consumer Protection) and Chapter 17 (Environmental Protection)—emphasize the dramatic expansion of the public's demands for socially responsible conduct in business. Chapter 16 (International Ethics and Law) provides an overview of the legal and ethical issues emerging from global business practice, and Chapter 18 (Internet Law and Ethics) surveys some cyberlaw and ethics problems.

ACCREDITATION

Our text conforms to Association to Advance Collegiate Schools of Business (AACSB) International accreditation standards.

Two chapters are devoted exclusively to ethics, and ethics themes emerge throughout the book. The chapter on employment discrimination should be quite helpful in aiding students' understanding of diversity issues.

Furthermore, as required by the rapidly changing nature of commerce and as recommended by the AACSB, the text devotes extensive attention to legal and ethical issues arising from international business. Various topics throughout the text (for example, comparative economic systems, the Foreign Corrupt Practices Act, and global pollution) afford the student a sense of the worldwide implications of American business practice, and Chapter 16 is entirely devoted to international themes.

PHILOSOPHY.

As noted, our primary goal is to provoke student thought. To that end, we place heavy emphasis on analysis. We consider the questions we ask more important than the answers to those questions. We introduce the student to existing policy in the various substantive areas, to encourage understanding and retention, as well as careful thought about the desirability of those policies.

Our book takes a strong public policy orientation. Attention in Unit I to political economy and ethics is a necessary foundation on which the student can build a logical understanding of the regulatory process. Thereafter, those business and society themes persist throughout the book. In virtually every chapter, we look beyond the law itself to other social and environmental forces. For example, in the antitrust chapters economic philosophy is of great importance. Antitrust is explored as a matter of national social policy. We argue that antitrust has a good deal to do with the direction of American life generally. Law is at the heart of the fair employment practices section, but we also present material from management, sociology, history, and popular culture to treat fair employment as an issue of public policy rather than as a series of narrower technical legal disputes. These multidimensional approaches characterize most chapters as we attempt to examine the various topics as a whole and in context. At the same time, the law remains the core of the book.

KEY FEATURES/DEPARTURES

Approximately 150 "boxes" and ethics vignettes place the law in a practical context and offer many provocative opportunities for discussion.

Ethics and social responsibility are at the heart of the text rather than an afterthought to meet accreditation standards.

International issues receive extensive attention.

Law cases are long enough to clearly express the essence of the decision while challenging the reader's intellect.

The law is studied in the economic, social, and political context from which it springs.

Critics of business values and the American legal system receive attention.

Approximately 200 selected websites, including suggested online videos, appear in this edition, and each chapter includes at least one Internet Exercise.

Perhaps the key pedagogical tactic in the book is the emphasis on questions rather than on answers.

INSTRUCTOR'S MANUAL

A package of supplementary materials is included in the instructor's manual. Those materials include (1) chapter outlines, (2) general advice regarding the goals and purposes of the chapters, (3) summaries of the law cases, (4) answers for the questions raised in the text, and (5) a test bank.

TEST BANK

Instructors can test students using a vast bank of test questions divided by chapter.

POWERPOINTS

This edition's revised PowerPoints contain an easy-to-follow lecture outline summarizing key points for every chapter.

ACKNOWLEDGMENTS

Completion of the eleventh edition of this book depended, in significant part, on the hard work of others.

The authors are pleased to acknowledge the contributions of these good people: Tim Vertovec, Managing Director; Lisa A. Bruflodt, Content Project Manager; Gail Korosa, Senior Product Developer; Jaroslaw (Jarek) Szymanski, Product Developer; and Dheeraj Chahal, Full Service Project Manager.

The authors also thank the reviewers from past editions.

SUGGESTIONS

The authors welcome comments and feedback from all readers.

Kiren Dosanjh Zucker

Brief Contents

Contents

Chapter 5
Constitutional Law and the Bill
of Rights   188

Chapter 6
Contracts   231

Chapter 7
Business Torts and Product Liability   277

Chapter 10
Antitrust Law—Restraints of Trade   434

Chapter 11
Antitrust Law— Monopolies and Mergers   467

UNIT FOUR
EMPLOYER–EMPLOYEE
RELATIONS   501

Chapter 12
Employment Law I: Employee
Rights   502

UNIT FIVE
SELECTED TOPICS IN GOVERNMENT–BUSINESS RELATIONS   645

Chapter 15
Consumer Protection   646

Chapter 16
International Ethics and Law 685

Chapter 17
Environmental Protection   736

Chapter 18
Internet Law and Ethics   779

Links to Brief Videos for Classroom Use

The following video links appear in the body of the text in conjunction with the subject matter of the videos.

Chapter 1

Trailer *Atlas Shrugged* documentary movie [**http://www.youtube.com/watch?v=Tv29SXnd2dk&feature=related**].

Trailer *Inside Job* documentary movie. Oscar winner 2011 [**http://www.youtube.com/watch?v=FzrBurlJUNk**].

Steve Croft, "The Case Against Lehman Brothers," 60 Minutes, CBS News, April 22, 2012, at **www.cbsnews.com/video/watch/?id=7406224n**

Martin Smith, "The Untouchables," Frontline, PBS, January 22, 2013, at [**www.pbs.org/wgbh/pages/frontline/untouchables/**]

Chapter 2

2009 Harvard MBA Ethics Oath, *The Daily Show with John Stewart* [**http://www.thedailyshow.com/watch/wed-august-12-2009/mba-ethics-oath**].

Trailer, "The Company Men" **http://www.youtube.com/watch?v=xa5qg7cB1ZQ**

Trailer, Wall Street: Money Never Sleeps, at [**http://www.youtube.com/watch?v=HcMFA2SHES4**]

Chapter 3

Vermont Senator Bernie Sanders, "A scandal" (a Senate speech criticizing corporate tax loopholes) [**http://www.youtube.com/watch?v=Sknt-UBRhxo**].

Trailer *Wal-Mart: The Corporation* [**http://www.thecorporation.com/index.cfm?page_id=46**] *The High Cost of Low Price* documentary movie [**http://www.walmartmovie.com**].

Chapter 4

"What Is Mediation?" (a brief overview of mediation and arbitration) [**https://www.youtube.com/watch?v=KLdia39awl0**]. (The final two characters in this URL are a lower case l, as in law, and a zero.)

Chapter 5

"1967 ABC News Report on Loving Case" (application of due process and equal protection principles to Virginia anti-miscegenation statute) [**http://abcnews.go.com/video/playerIndex?id=3278653**](upper case I in Index).

Chapter 6

A video of the Pepsi ad that was the basis of the *Leonard v. Pepsico* lawsuit [**http://www. youtube.com/watch?v=ZdackF2H7Qc**].

Chapter 7

Susan Saladoff, "Hot Coffee" documentary movie trailer [**http://hotcoffeethemovie.com/**].

InjuryBoard, "Mr. Fancy Pants" (a video defense of the tort system) [**http://www.youtube. com/watch?v=h85j1vNxd8A**].

Chapter 8

Cato Institute, "There Are Too Many Bureaucrats and They Are Paid Too Much" [**http:// www.youtube.com/watch?v=5xzd3puYmiM**].

Video, "IJ's Jeanette Petersen Explains Three Reasons You Can't Get a Cab" [**www.you-tube.com/watch?v=Oq-hPuESJng**].

Chapter 9

ChinaForbiddenNews, NTDTV.COM, "Insider Trading 'Rats'" [**http://www.youtube.com/ watch?v=IT3FAr0eIEo**] (capital I as in Iowa, T3FAr, zero, e, capital I as in Iowa, Eo).

"Billionaire Convicted of Insider Trading," *Boston.com,* May 11, 2011 (Raj Rajaratnam) [**http://www.clicker.com/web/bostoncom-featured-necn-video/billionaire-convicted-of-insider-trading-1768946/**].

Chapter 10

The Informant! movie trailer [**http://www.traileraddict.com/trailer/the-informant/trailer**].

Chapter 11

Stephen Colbert, "Mega-Mergers," 2007 [**http://www.businessinsider.com/stephen-colbert-att-2011-3**].

Chapter 12

Inland Valley Daily Bulletin and The San Bernardino Sun, "A Special Report on Immigration" ("Smuggler's Gulch") 2005 [**http://lang.dailybulletin.com/socal/beyondborders/ video/121805_smugglers_gulch_video.asp**].

Chapter 13

Sheryl Sandberg, "In her own words," discussing her 2013 book: "Lean In: Women, Work, and the Will to Lead" [**http://leanin.org/book/**]

American Civil Liberties Union, "New Video Shows the Need for a Transgender-Inclusive ENDA"

[**http://www.aclu.org/lgbt-rights_hiv-aids/new-aclu-video-shows-need-transgender-inclusive-enda**].

Chapter 14

Fox News discussion of NLRB—Boeing Conflict [**http://www.youtube.com/watch?v= j_JvA6yKB_M**].

Chapter 15

A Consumer Financial Protection Bureau video explaining the Bureau's mission [**http://www.consumerfinance.gov/the-bureau/**].

2011 ABC News Visit to Consumer Product Safety Commission Testing Lab [**http:// abcnews.go.com/GMA/video/consumer-product-safety-commission-test-lab-13827984**].

Chapter 16

2004 John Stossel "20/20" overview of sweatshop protests followed by Stossel's defense of low-wage jobs [**http://www.youtube.com/watch?v=0VaHmgoB10E**]. (Both large 0 symbols are zeros.)

Chapter 17

2011 Bill McKibben/Stephen Thompson video editorial about the alleged causal relationship between climate change and recent "extreme weather events" in America and around the world [**http://www.grist.org/climate-change/2011-06-11-the-most-powerful-climate-video-youll-see-all-week**].

Chapter 18

Video Essay: "What Is the 'Digital Divide?'" [**http://www.youtube.com/watch?v= fCIB_vXUptY**]. (In CIB, the middle letter is a capital I, as in Iowa.)

Business and Society

CHAPTER ONE

Capitalism and the Role of Government

After completing this chapter, students will be able to:

1. Describe capitalism and its relationship to individual rights.

2. Compare and contrast capitalism and collectivism.

3. Differentiate between communism and socialism as collectivist philosophies.

4. Evaluate arguments regarding government's proper role in the global, technology-based economy.

5. Describe the primary characteristics of a "mixed economy."

6. Analyze the impact of capitalism on equality, fairness, and community in American and global society.

7. Discuss the theory and practice of privatization.

8. Discuss the current state of capitalism in China and Russia.

9. Describe the income and wealth gaps in America.

Part One—Introduction

Are you a capitalist?

Are you a capitalist? If so, what role, if any, should the law play in your business life? How much government does America need? These themes, examining the relationship between government and business in America, are the core of this text. Since the fall of the Soviet Union and the general decline of communist influence, free market reasoning has dominated worldwide economic discourse. Indeed, noted theorist Francis Fukuyama argued that capitalism and Western democracy had so thoroughly proven their worth that the capitalism/collectivism debate was over.[1] Democracy and markets, Fukuyama claimed, were so clearly triumphant that no new forms of civilization are likely to emerge. Thus, he said, we are at the end of history. Events, however, have challenged Fukuyama's bold thesis. The Great Recession, including the subprime mortgage crisis, the stunning power of the Wall Street banks, and the continuing turmoil of globalization have raised grave doubts about the economic reliability of capitalism. Likewise, government's failure to send corrupt bankers off to jail, rampant greed, and the Occupy Wall Street movement have magnified longstanding doubts about the morality of capitalism.

Capitalism Challenged: Economics

We will briefly examine the economic and moral turmoil of contemporary American capitalism, but more detail on most of these topics will be provided in subsequent chapters.

The Great Recession

In late 2008, America's financial markets seemed near collapse. Lending had essentially frozen. A powerful Wall Street bank, Lehman Brothers, went broke while Bear Stearns and Merrill Lynch, also Wall Street titans, faced failure and were sold. American and global financial markets panicked and appeared unable to correct themselves. Fearing a Great Depression as occurred in the 1930s, the federal government had, during both the George W. Bush and Barack Obama administrations, essentially flooded the market with cash, took on much of the debt held by endangered banks, and, through its Troubled Asset Relief Program (TARP), bailed out failing giants such as Goldman Sachs, General Motors, and Chrysler: companies that were deemed "too big to fail." Additional stimulus measures included tax reductions, bond sales, infrastructure and "green" projects, and enhanced unemployment benefits. Depending on how the word *stimulus* is defined, government expenditures to prop up the endangered economy ranged from perhaps $1.7 trillion[2] to $4.7 trillion[3] or more. Most of the TARP money has been repaid, but economists differ both on the need for the stimulus efforts and on their success.

Subprime Mortgages

The nation's housing bubble burst.

The financial community's near collapse had been most directly ignited by the subprime mortgage crisis; a situation in which the nation's housing bubble burst and millions of Americans were no longer able to pay their home mortgages. Instead of continuing their sometimes meteoric rise in value, those homes had plunged in price and much of the total real estate market had essentially imploded. The resulting mountain of bad debt could not be managed by the American financial institutions that were holding it; fear paralyzed the lending markets, and the government felt obliged to step in to prevent a greater financial tragedy. Whereas greed and inept management were instrumental in the subprime debacle, the role of financial fraud remains unclear. Some big civil penalties have been imposed, and criminal investigations undertaken.

[For a critical examination of the 2008 financial meltdown, see the trailer for the 2011 Oscar-winning best documentary, Inside Job, at **http://www.youtube.com /watch?v=FzrBurlJUNk**]

Big Banks

America's biggest banks were deemed "too big to fail."

America's biggest banks, including the five largest—JPMorgan Chase, Bank of America, Citigroup, Wells Fargo, and Goldman Sachs—were deemed "too big to fail" during the subprime mortgage crisis, and they remain a grave threat should the economy falter again. In 2001, the assets of the five biggest American banks totaled about 25 percent of all U.S. bank assets whereas today that number exceeds 50 percent.[4] The Dodd–Frank Wall Street Reform and Consumer Protection Act (see Chapter 8) includes provisions designed to reduce the likelihood of big bank failures, but implementation of the new law has been troubled. Federal regulators in 2013 proposed requiring the biggest banks to increase their capital on hand substantially to guard against unexpected losses and reduce the risk to the American economy.

Globalization

Globalization represents the international flowering of capitalism; the power of free markets has been embraced, enthusiastically or reluctantly, almost everywhere on Earth. That power raised new threats, of course, including the spread of America's corporate influence and values around the globe (see Chapter 3). Now, however, globalization seems to be entering a new phase. In a "hyper-connected," "flat" world, we are all linked together in an economic and cultural intimacy scarcely imaginable a few decades back, but new evidence suggests that a period of "de-globalization" may be emerging. International trade and money flows are slowing or actually declining.[5] Globalization has succeeded in raising wages significantly in emerging powers such as China and India. As a result, manufacturing jobs are returning to America in surprising numbers. Of course, globalization is not vanishing, but its economic advantages are shifting and new nationalistic urges threaten to slow the pace of global linkages.

Capitalism Challenged: Morality

Beyond fears about capitalism's economic performance, particularly its instability and harshness, critics point to capitalism's indecencies.

Wall Street Abuses

> Many Americans are angered by the government's inability to criminally punish the big banks and bankers.

Certainly many Americans are puzzled, if not angered, by the government's inability to criminally punish the big banks and bankers who profited so handsomely in the events that led to the nation's economic collapse and who, in several cases, had to be bailed out with public money following the collapse. (For more, see Chapter 2.) Those same bankers have not only escaped jail, but they continue to earn stunning sums of money. Responding, however, to harsh publicity, among other factors, some of the big banks have either cut or curbed executive pay. In 2013, at Goldman Sachs and JPMorgan Chase, compensation costs were falling and Morgan's high-profile CEO, Jamie Dimon, took a 2012 pay cut of 50 percent, down to $11.5 million. The cut, at least in part, served as a signal to regulators and investors that the board of directors was in charge following a troubled year that included a $6 billion trading loss.[6]

Greed

CEO salaries for the top 200 U.S. corporations (not limited to bankers) rose 16 percent in 2012. Among those top 200 CEOs, the average income was 273 times the income of the average worker—up from a 20 to 1 ratio in 1965.[7] The average CEO's *daily* salary at those 200 biggest firms now exceeds the average *annual* salary of their workers.[8] Actual salaries have often remained limited or flat in recent years, but stock-based pay has fueled an overall rise.

Congress showed its concern about CEO pay in a Dodd-Frank provision requiring the Securities and Exchange Commission to give shareholders a "say on pay" by writing new rules requiring periodic shareholder voting on executive compensation. At this writing, "say on pay" seems to have encouraged attention to CEO pay, but a shareholder backlash has not yet materialized.[9]

Anger with corporate greed and perceived abuse of power led to a grassroots global protest movement labeled Occupy Wall Street. Hundreds of peaceful protesters (mostly young, often college-educated and jobless) camped in New York's financial district in **Occupy Wall Street** late 2011 to "restore democracy" while denouncing the "greed" and "corruption" of the "upper 1 percent." The movement then spread to many other American cities and around the globe. Occupy Wall Street gained enormous publicity as a leftist assault on corporate America and the wealthy, but the movement sputtered—perhaps for want of a clear, coherent message. Occupy Wall Street continues its efforts, but at least for the present, the attention of the broader American public has been lost. (See **occupy.org.**)

[For an overview of the Lehman Brothers banking collapse and a critique of the government's regulatory oversight, see Steve Croft, "The Case Against Lehman Brothers," *60 Minutes,* CBS News, April 22, 2012, at **www.cbsnews.com/video /watch/?id=7406224n**]. [For an investigation of "why no Wall Street execs have been prosecuted for the financial crisis," see Martin Smith, "The Untouchables," *Frontline,* PBS, January 22, 2013, at **www.pbs.org/wgbh/pages/frontline/untouchables/**].

Questions

1. Thomas Hoenig, a member of the board of directors of the Federal Deposit Insurance Corporation, observed: "[Americans] realize that more must be done to address a threat that remains increasingly a part of our economy: financial institutions that are 'too big to fail.'"[10] Do you agree that our concentrated financial sector is a threat that must be addressed? Explain.

2. Journalist/lecturer Richard Doak laments what he believes to be unfair and excessive pay to executives: "Executive greed has perverted risks, rewards. . . . The American system has been rigged to over-enrich those at the top."[11] What do you think? Is greed the culprit? Has the system been "rigged," or can we continue to count on the market to properly distribute pay? Explain.

Capitalism Challenged: America in Decline?

The economic and moral challenges to our capitalist system, the rise of China, and the ongoing political dysfunction in Washington, DC, have combined to shake our faith in America's future. When asked in a 2013 Gallup Poll if the nation's best days are ahead of us or behind, Americans were split with 47 percent seeing the best as yet to come whereas 50 percent said we have already witnessed our peak.[12] Some critics attribute the nation's problems to fundamental flaws in capitalism and in the American character. Michael

Moore's 2009 documentary movie, *Capitalism: A Love Story*, assails capitalism as "evil."[13] Moore was questioned about his movie:

> *Wall Street Journal:* Why call the movie "Capitalism: A Love Story?" You don't seem to love very much about capitalism. Mr. Moore: It is a love story about the well-to-do. They happen to love their money very much. Now they love our money and they want all our money and our homes. It's about their love.[14]

Capitalism drags us into decadence.

Political scientist Benjamin Barber believes that capitalism drags us into decadence by encouraging us to buy as many unnecessary products as we can manage, thus replacing historical principles of hard work and deferred gratification with infantile hungers for anything that might promise comfort. In America's version of capitalism, as Barber sees it, we find liberty in commerce. We can buy whatever we want; therefore, we are free.[15] But that undemanding vision of liberty means we have no sense of obligation for social and political ideals greater than self-satisfaction.[16] Asking no more of us than unbridled consumption may undermine democracy itself, as columnist Rod Dreher argues:

> Democracy requires virtue. So does a healthy capitalism. A nation that cannot govern its own appetites will, in time, be unable to govern itself. An economy that divorces economic activity from the restraining virtues that make for good stewardship will implode.[17]

Vast Resources

Although America has been grievously shaken by the terrorist attacks of 9/11 and the Great Recession, shouldn't we find encouragement in the nation's extraordinary strengths and resources? We remain dominant in economic, military, and international affairs, and, as Goldman Sachs recently told its clients, we should recognize "the key economic institutional, human capital and geopolitical advantages the U.S. enjoys over other economies."[18] In particular, Goldman pointed to America's attractiveness as a location for investment, the nation's vast natural resources (especially arable land, oil, and gas), a workforce that is younger and more energetic than those of our chief rivals, and our continuing leadership in innovation.[19] Commentator David Brooks says that America is merely in one of its periodic economic pauses, but he is sure that: "The gospel of success will recapture the imagination."[20] Brooks summarized our fundamentally commercial nature:

> Walt Whitman got America right in his essay, "Democratic Vistas." He acknowledged the vulgarity of the American success drive. He toted up its moral failings. But in the end he accepted his country's "extreme business energy," its "almost maniacal appetite for wealth." He knew that the country's dreams were all built upon that energy and drive, and eventually the spirit of commercial optimism would always prevail.[21]

Questions

British Labour Party leader Ed Miliband asked in 2012 if 20th century capitalism is failing 21st century society.

1. What did he mean?
2. Answer his question. See Ed Miliband, "At Davos, Debating Capitalism's Future," *New York Times,* January 26, 2012 [**http://www.nytimes.com/**].

Purpose: What Do We Hope to Accomplish?

Until this point, we have provided a brief reminder of some of the big challenges facing America's capitalist system. The balance of this chapter more carefully examines the philosophical nature of free market capitalism, introduces some alternatives to the free market, and asks where America's political economy is headed. Chapter 1 thereby serves as a foundation for the book's detailed investigation of the following questions:

1. What is the proper ethical/social role of business in American life?
2. How much, if any, government regulation of business is necessary to secure that role?

Markets and Governments

We certainly cannot understand America's system of laws without a firm appreciation for the principles of capitalism from which those laws spring. We have embraced an evolving capitalist, democratic approach to life. Other cultures have placed less faith in the market and more in government planning.

In this chapter we will explore the full economic spectrum, moving from a laissez-faire, free market approach on the extreme right to a brief reminder of command economy principles on the far left. The bulk of our attention, however, will rest where the world is at this moment. Most nations are practicing varying combinations of markets and rules that we can label *mixed economies*.

The pure free market approach assumes that we can operate our business system and our society at large free of all but foundational legal mechanisms such as contract and criminal law. The wisdom of the market—our individual judgments, in combination with our individual consciences—would "regulate" American life. Most forms of government including regulatory agencies, consumer protection, environmental rules, occupational licensure, zoning restrictions, antitrust law, and all but the most basic government services would be eliminated.

Of course, today's global debate is not so much about capitalism versus communism as about the mixed economy—that is, about what combination of capitalism and government best serves the needs of America and the world. Substantially open markets have shown themselves to be the stronger vehicle for productivity, efficiency, and personal freedom. Are open markets also the stronger vehicle for improving living conditions for all citizens, for maximizing democracy, for discouraging crime and corruption, and for building strong communities? Are America and the world best served by the speed and efficiency of largely unrestrained markets, or do we still need the "civilizing" influence of government rules?

Law

Finally, this chapter should be read as a platform for the study of law that commences in Chapter 4. Once a society settles on some broad political and economic principles, it employs the law as a primary method of social control. So to understand the law, we need to understand its roots in the economic, political, and social preferences of America and the world.

Questions—Part One

1. The John Templeton Foundation recently asked a number of prominent thinkers the following question: "Does the free market corrode moral character?" Answer that question. [See **www.templeton.org/market**]

2. Former Iranian President Mahmoud Ahmadinejad in 2009 said a "new era is starting" after the "definite defeat of capitalism."[22] Is capitalism dead (or dying)? Explain.

3. Scholar Robert Skidelsky applauds capitalism for overcoming scarcity, organizing production, and lifting many out of poverty, but he thinks capitalism, at least in rich countries like the United States, has also produced a culture where our main occupation has become the production and consumption of unnecessary goods. He asks whether capitalism can succeed if it continues to produce "more of the same, stimulating jaded appetites with new gadgets, thrills, and excitements? . . . Do we spend the next century wallowing in triviality?"[23] What do you think?

Part Two—Capitalism: Reduce Government?

Capitalism in America was built on the strong philosophical foundation of personal freedom and private property rights. Our great natural resources and personal ambition led to extraordinary prosperity. Monopolistic abuse followed, however, and government grew to curb the power of big business. Thus, America's substantially free market was gradually constrained by government regulation. The proper balance between open markets and government intervention remains perhaps the central public policy debate in American life.

Should we consider a return to a purer form of capitalism; largely free of government oversight? Can we, in large measure, do without government regulation of business? The controversial philosopher and novelist Ayn Rand was an uncompromising advocate of free market principles. She believed the necessary categories of government were only three in number: the police, the armed services, and the law courts. Rand's philosophy of Objectivism contends that the practice of free market principles is necessary for a rational, moral life. Rand's views and the quality of her writing are heavily criticized, but she has been cited as a powerful influence by some of America's leading corporate and political figures. Her books, including *Atlas Shrugged* and *The Fountainhead,* are among the best-selling novels of all time. Indeed, *Atlas Shrugged* is one of the most influential business books in history, and according to a national survey, has been read by over 8 percent of American adults.[24]

[For the trailer of a 2011 documentary treatment of *Atlas Shrugged,* see **http://www .youtube.com/watch?v=Tv29SXnd2dk&feature=related**]

> Big business leaders are the great heroes of Rand's writing.

Big business leaders, who so often are the villains of contemporary American life, are the great heroes of Rand's writing, in which she championed "the virtue of selfishness" and rejected self-sacrifice. Commentator Stephen Moore explained Rand's core theme in *Atlas Shrugged*:

Politicians invariably respond to crises—that in most cases they themselves created—by spawning new government programs, laws and regulations. These, in turn, generate more havoc and poverty, which inspires the politicians to create more programs . . . and the downward spiral repeats itself until the productive sectors of the economy collapse under the collective weight of taxes and other burdens imposed in the name of fairness, equality and do-goodism.[25]

[See the Center for the Moral Defense of Capitalism at **http://www.moraldefense.com**] [For a brief look at major league baseball player Orlando Cabrera's devotion to *Atlas Shrugged* and a journalist's criticism of Rand's admirers, see **http://hardballtalk.nbcsports.com /2011/06/23/orlando-cabrera-is-john-galt/**]

READING   # Man's Rights

Ayn Rand

If one wishes to advocate a free society—that is, capitalism— one must realize that its indispensable foundation is the princi- ple of individual rights. If one wishes to uphold individual rights, one must realize that capitalism is the only system that can uphold and protect them.

* * * * *

Every political system is based on some code of ethics. The dominant ethics of mankind's history were variants of the altruist-collectivist doctrine which subordinated the individual to some higher authority.

* * * * *

Under all such systems, morality was a code applicable to the individual, but not to society. Society was placed *outside* the moral law, and the inculcation of self-sacrificial devotion to social duty was regarded as the main purpose of ethics in man's earthly existence.

Since there is no such entity as "society," since society is only a number of individual men, this meant, in practice, that the rulers of society were exempt from moral law; subject only to traditional rituals, they held total power and exacted blind obedience—on the implicit principle of "The good is that which is good for society . . ."

This was true of all statist systems, under all variants of the altruist-collectivist ethics. . . . As witness: the theocracy of Egypt, with the Pharaoh as an embodied god—the unlimited majority rule or *democracy* of Athens—the welfare state run by the Emperors of Rome—the Inquisition of the late Middle Ages—the absolute monarchy of France—the welfare state of Bismarck's Prussia—the gas chambers of Nazi Germany—the slaughterhouse of the Soviet Union.

All these political systems were expressions of the altruist- collectivist ethics—and their common characteristic is the

fact that society stood above the moral law. . . . Thus, politi- cally, all these systems were variants of an *amoral* society.

The most profoundly revolutionary achievement of the United States of America was *the subordination of society to moral law.*

The principle of man's individual rights represented the ex- tension of morality into the social system—as a limitation on the power of the state . . . The United States was the first *moral* society in history.

All previous systems had regarded man as a sacrificial means to the ends of others, and society as an end in itself. The United States regarded man as an end in himself, and so- ciety as a means to the peaceful, orderly, *voluntary* coexist- ence of individuals. All previous systems had held that man's life belongs to society, that society can dispose of him in any way it pleases, and that any freedom he enjoys is his only by favor, by the *permission* of society, which may be revoked at any time. The United States held that man's life is his by *right*, that a right is the property of an individual, that society as such has no rights, and that the only moral purpose of a government is the protection of individual rights.

A "right" is a moral principle defining and sanctioning a man's freedom of action in a social context. There is only *one* fundamental right (all the others are its consequences or cor- ollaries): a man's right to his own life . . .

America's inner contradiction was the altruist-collectivist ethics. Altruism is incompatible with freedom, with capitalism, and with individual rights . . .

It was the concept of individual rights that had given birth to a free society. It was with the destruction of individual rights that the destruction of freedom had to begin.

A collectivist tyranny dare not enslave a country by an out- right confiscation of its values, material or moral. It has to be done by a process of internal corruption. . . . The process entails such a growth of newly promulgated "rights" that people do not notice the fact that the meaning of the concept is being reversed . . .

The Democratic Party platform of 1960 summarizes the switch boldly and explicitly. It declares that a democratic administration "will reaffirm the economic bill of rights which Franklin Roosevelt wrote into our national conscience 16 years ago."

Bear clearly in mind the meaning of the concept of *rights* when you read the list which that platform offers:

1. The right to a useful and remunerative job in the industries or shops or farms or mines of the nation.

2. The right to earn enough to provide adequate food and clothing and recreation.

3. The right of every farmer to raise and sell his products at a return which will give him and his family a decent living.

4. The right of every businessman, large and small, to trade in an atmosphere of freedom from unfair competition and domination by monopolies at home and abroad.

5. The right of every family to a decent home.

6. The right to adequate medical care and the opportunity to achieve and enjoy good health.

7. The right to adequate protection from the economic fears of old age, sickness, accidents, and unemployment.

8. The right to a good education.

A single question added to each of the above eight clauses would make the issue clear: *At whose expense?*

Jobs, food, clothing, recreation (!), homes, medical care, education, etc. do not grow in nature. These are man-made values—goods and services produced by men. *Who* is to provide them?

If some men are entitled *by right* to the products of the work of others, it means that those others are deprived of rights and condemned to slave labor.

* * * * *

Observe, in this context, the intellectual precision of the Founding Fathers: they spoke of the right to *the pursuit* of happiness—*not* of the right to happiness. It means that a man has the right to take the actions he deems necessary to achieve his happiness; it does *not* mean that others must make him happy . . .

Property rights and the right of free trade are man's only "economic rights" (they are, in fact, *political* rights)—and there can be no such thing as "an *economic* bill of rights." . . .

And while people are clamoring about "economic rights," the concept of political rights is vanishing . . .

Such is the state of one of today's most crucial issues: *political* rights versus "*economic*" rights." It's either-or. One destroys the other. But there are, in fact, no "economic rights," no "collective rights," no "public-interest rights." The term *individual rights* is a redundancy: there is no other kind of rights and no one else to possess them.

Those who advocate laissez-faire capitalism are the only advocates of man's rights.

Source: From *The Virtue of Selfishness* by Ayn Rand. Copyright © 1961, 1964 by Ayn Rand. Copyright, © 1962, 1963, 1964 by the Objectivist Newsletter, Inc. Reprinted by arrangement with New American Library, New York, New York, and with permission of the Estate of Ayn Rand. [For more information about Ayn Rand and objectivism, see **http://www.aynrand.org**]

Questions

1. *a.* Columnist E. J. Dionne Jr. recently examined the question, "Why are there no libertarian countries?" (countries operated on free market/personal freedom principles like those advocated by Ayn Rand). Answer his question.

   b. Of all the nations of the world, does the United States enjoy the greatest level of economic freedom? Explain. [See the Index of Economic Freedom at **www.heritage.org/index/**]

2. *a.* Sandy Banks, writing in the *Los Angeles Times:*

   > The boys' faces brightened when they got to the front of the line. We're next! They'd been waiting to say it. But their smiles faded when another family was ushered in from the sidelines and slid into "their" Legoland ride. We'd been waylaid by the Premium Play Pass, Legoland's wristband version of the front-of-the-line pass.[26]

   Banks asked her readers what they thought of the fairness of paying to jump to the front of the line. Some said it was no different than flying first class or choosing to drive on a toll road. One thought the kids received a good lesson in the competitiveness of capitalism. Legoland, in Carlsbad, California, said they sell only about 65 of the Premium Play wristbands daily, but those who buy them value the time saved.

What do you think of the fairness of paying to jump to the head of the line at amusement parks?

b. Do you think that drivers who pay more should be entitled to drive in a faster lane? Explain.[27]

c. Addressing his state's budget problems, 2010 candidate for Nevada governor, Eugene DiSimone, proposed allowing people to pay extra to drive up to 90 miles per hour on designated highways.[28] What do you think?

3. Elementary schools often ban tag, dodge ball, touch football, kickball, and other vigorous games from the playgrounds. One school banned touching altogether. Administrators fear physical injuries, reduced self-esteem, and lawsuits. As the *Los Angeles Times* editorialized, "It's hard sometimes to tell whether schools are graduating students or growing orchids."[29] Ayn Rand argued for reduced rules in life, thus relying on the market to address virtually all problems.

a. From Rand's free market point of view, explain why we should reduce playground rules as much as possible, even at the risk of children being hurt.

b. Would you follow the rules approach or Rand's free market approach in managing a playground? Explain.

Free Market Solution to the Baby Shortage?

The following ad appeared in the *Stanford Daily* (Stanford University):

> EGG DONOR WANTED $35,000 (PLUS ALL EXPENSES) Ivy League Professor and High-Tech CEO seek one truly exceptional woman who is attractive, athletic, under the age of 29. GPA 3.5+, SAT: 1400+.

Experts estimate that about 10,000 babies annually are born from "donated" eggs and about $38 million is spent on those eggs. Fees range from a few thousand dollars to $50,000 or more. The fertility industry is lightly regulated by the federal Centers for Disease Control and Prevention. A few states are considering their own rules. Most industrial nations have banned paid "donations."

Questions

1. Harvard Business School professor Debora Spar says, "We are selling children."
   a. Is she correct?
   b. Should we be doing so? Explain.

2. a. Does capitalism encourage us to treat people as products?
   b. Are people, in fact, products? Explain.

3. Should we more closely regulate the fertility industry? Explain.

4. Would you favor the increased use of surrogate mothers? Explain. [See Thomas Frank, "Rent-a-Womb Is Where Market Logic Leads," *The Wall Street Journal,* December 10, 2008, p. A17.]

5. Asian egg donors typically earn two to four times as much for their eggs as do those of other ethnicities.

   a. Why do you think Asian eggs are worth more in the market?

   b. In your judgment, does that price differential constitute unlawful discrimination? Explain. See Shan Li, "Asian Women Command Premium Prices for Egg Donation in the U.S.," *latimes.com,* May 3, 2012 [**http://www.latimes.com/**].

Source: Jim Hopkins, "Egg-Donor Business Booms on Campus," *USA TODAY,* March 16, 2006, p. 1A.

Capitalism in Practice—"Privatization" in America and Abroad

Championed in the 1980s by President Ronald Reagan in the United States and Prime Minister Margaret Thatcher in Great Britain, nations across the globe along with many American states and cities have turned to privatization both to address financial problems and to satisfy ideological preferences for smaller governments.

Most commonly, privatization follows two patterns: (1) contracting out where government, in effect, turns over a portion of its duties, such as garbage collection, to a private firm; and (2) the sale or lease of public assets, such as an airport, to a private party. Privately operated prisons, now rather common across America, are a primary example of the privatization movement. Of course, privatization also brings worries about job losses, reduced services, reduced responsiveness to consumers, corruption, and so on.

Price-driven, free market solutions range from highly pragmatic cost savings to exotic proposals for changing long-standing traditions. Greece, currently the most visible privatization example, faces a collapsing economy and an unemployment rate exceeding 25 percent. Desperate for cash, Greece has been forced by its lenders to begin selling public property such as land, ports, airports, roads, water utilities, the national lottery, and banks to receive a multibillion euro bailout. At this writing in 2013, Greece's privatization plan faces legal and operational difficulties, and fears have erupted that Greek oligarchs along with Chinese and Russian interests will buy many of the nation's prized assets.

Struggling American governments likewise see privatization as a solution for financial distress. At this writing, the state of Louisiana has privatized four formerly state-operated hospitals and plans to do the same with five of the six public hospitals that remain. Several thousand hospital workers have lost their jobs, although many are expected to be rehired by the private firms that took over operations. Of course, wages and benefits may be lower in the privatized arrangement. State officials say the privatization plan will save millions of dollars while improving medical care.

Citing free market efficiency and personal freedom while challenging moral conventions, privatization supporters envision major changes to daily life. For example, some doctors and others are arguing for lifting the federal ban on organ sales as a way of addressing the current donor shortage. The resulting increase in supply would save many lives, but others fear the privatized approach would exploit the poor and vulnerable and discourage altruistic donors.[30] Professor Stephanie Coontz pushes the free market argument further by challenging the need for the state's permission to marry. For most of Western history, marriage was a private contract, and Coontz wonders if the time has come to let couples, gay or straight, decide entirely on their own if they want to join together to assume the protections and obligations of a committed relationship.[31] In each of these examples, the underlying idea is that the market can make decisions more efficiently and effectively than government while also maximizing personal freedom. [For a large database supportive of privatization, see **http://reason.org/areas/topic/privatization**]

Space Travel

Trying to save money while emerging from the Great Recession, the U.S. government has retired its shuttle rockets and will encourage the continuing development of private-sector rockets that are expected to carry on space exploration and travel in cooperation with the government. Presumably, space will be "commercialized" with companies hauling space travel customers and exploiting vast mineral resources that may lead to a new "gold rush." SpaceX, a pioneer in the industry, carried supplies to the International Space Station in 2012. Several other private firms are seeking space contract work and at least one is selling tickets to the moon. Critics, however, think the private sector is unlikely to be able to meet the enormous safety and financial hurdles involved in sustained space travel.[32]

Room for Big Ideas

SpaceX founder Elon Musk (the cocreator of PayPal and the founder of Tesla, the electric car company) recently said he is working on a vertical liftoff passenger jet as well as a project called a Hyperloop, a tube that would be capable of moving people from San Francisco to Los Angeles in 30 minutes.

Question

Is a market-based culture of freedom and daring necessary to the creation and sustenance of these very big ideas, or is a blend of the market and government necessary? Explain. See David Brooks, "Temerity at the Top," *The New York Times*, September 20, 2012 [**http://www.nytimes.com/**].

Toll Roads, Parking Meters, and Congestion Pricing

Should users pay fees for access to highways? Private companies are building, maintaining, and operating new toll roads in places such as northern Virginia and suburban San Diego to the Mexican border. Taking the privatization movement a step further, state and local governments are selling or leasing existing roads to private companies. Indiana, for example, leased its 157-mile Indiana East–West Toll Road to an international group for $3.8 billion for 75 years. The new operators can raise tolls each year by 2 percent, the inflation rate, or the increase in GDP; whichever is higher.[33]

Critics worry, however, about declining service, excessive tolls, too much profit for the investors, pricing poorer drivers out of access to the roads, and trading secure government jobs with benefits for low-wage private-sector jobs without benefits.[34] Nonetheless, increasing government revenue problems suggest that transportation privatization will continue. [For labor union opposition to privatization, see **http://www.afscme.org/issues/76.cfm**]

The privatization movement is extending beyond toll roads to other infrastructure resources. Chicago sold control of its parking garages to Morgan Stanley for $563 million[35] and entered a 75-year, $1.15 billion lease arrangement with private investors who control and manage its 36,000 parking meters.[36] A 2012 report concludes that Chicago's parking cost in the downtown Loop will be about $6.50 per hour in 2013, the highest rate in the United States.[37] Many believe the parking deal has turned out to be a financial disaster for the city.[38]

While adding to and upgrading infrastructure through privatization, governments and their agents are also turning to pricing/market mechanisms to reduce demand for that infrastructure. One expanding initiative is congestion pricing that involves making a service more expensive at times of peak demand in order to curb that demand. Employing new technology and the law of supply and demand, San Francisco is experimenting with a plan that may raise on-street parking to as much as $6 per hour in high-demand areas during busy hours of the day while lowering prices in less congested areas and during less frantic hours. At least 10 metropolitan areas have in place or are contemplating so-called HOT lanes or Lexus Lanes where, for a fee, drivers can move to an express lane with reduced traffic and higher speeds. In some locales, those lanes are also available without charge to motorists in car pools, motorcyclists, buses, and hybrid vehicles.

Questions

1. Author Joan Didion referred to our highways as America's only communion. Would it be a social/ethical wrong to adopt widespread "congestion fees," privately operated toll roads, and "Lexus Lanes" that would permit those with money to avoid the democracy of the highways? Explain.

2. *Governing Magazine* labeled golf courses "perhaps the most non-essential of the non-essential public services."[39] Studies show that payrolls for city-operated golf courses are about 13 percent higher than for privately operated courses.[40] Why do we subsidize golf, and should we continue doing so? Explain.

3. *a.* The U.S. Postal Service currently loses a few billion dollars annually. Should we privatize the postal service?

   b. Would UPS, for example, want to assume responsibility for delivery to every home in America? Explain.

Schools

Is capitalism the answer to poor school performance? The idea was unthinkable a few decades ago, but some increasingly frustrated parents and school boards have adopted a free market "fix." Schools are experimenting with market-based approaches such as for-profit web-based classes, open enrollment (students attend the school of their choice regardless of their place of residence), charter schools (funded by taxes but freed of much government oversight), and vouchers (students "spend" their taxpayer-provided dollars on the school of their choice). The hope is that competition will push all schools to higher achievement levels, but a 2010 evaluation of Milwaukee, Wisconsin's Parental Choice Program, the biggest and oldest voucher and charter school experiment in America, found that achievement growth rates were about the same as in the public schools, a result that is consistent with a number of other studies.[41] In Dallas, Worcester, Massachusetts, and other districts, direct payments to students of $100 to $500 per year for improved test performance have produced some success. Although experts believe the payments alone do not lift results, but when combined with tutoring and other support tactics, learning may be strengthened.[42]

> Direct payments to students for improved test performance.

Privatize Higher Education?

The Anderson School of Management at the University of California at Los Angeles (UCLA) received permission in 2013 to substantially privatize its prestigious MBA program. The program will be allowed to raise tuition, keep most of its income, and spend that income on attracting yet more skilled professors and students thus raising its academic profile to better compete with Harvard University, Stanford University, and the like. Anderson leaders also believe the self-sufficiency/privatization decision will allow them to raise more money in contributions, some of which are contingent on the change. Tuition, currently over $96,000 for the two-year program, is projected to rise to "market rates" for top-tier schools (e.g., nearly $130,000 for Stanford). A few other UCLA programs were already privatized and the University of Virginia's Darden School of Business became self-sufficient in 2002.

Those opposing Anderson's privatization fear that UCLA's responsibilities for the general welfare may be replaced by the more self-interested goals of those running the program, its donors, and the business community. Perhaps, for example, a privatized MBA program would be more likely to allow admission to a major donor's child, shape its research agenda to conform to the interests of corporate donors, diminish its attention to community needs or eventually replace merit-based admission with an auction allowing space to the highest bidders. Of course, the long-term interest of the Anderson School is in taking only those steps that strengthen the school's performance and reputation in a highly competitive MBA market, and even in its self-sufficient/privatized mode, the Anderson School continues to be a part of UCLA and the University of California system.

Questions

1. *a.* If it is not already, should your college or university become a for-profit institution?
   b. How would your education change?
   c. How would you change?
2. Would our current system of higher education benefit from aggressive private-sector competition or is the current competition among schools sufficient? Explain.

Privatization a Success?

Privatization often brings substantially reduced costs and improved expertise, but sometimes the transition does not work well. Fury might be the best word to describe consumer reaction to the higher rates and poor service that accompanied Chicago's parking meter privatization, but Indiana has used the money from its toll road leases to fund a popular, 10-year highway improvement program.[43] Some privatization efforts, such as Florida's plan to lease its "Alligator Alley" toll road, fail because of an absence of private-sector bids.[44] Some projects do not generate the anticipated savings. Although more than 30 states contract with private prisons, a 2011 study in Arizona found little or no savings in doing so even though private prisons often "cherry pick" the least expensive prisoners.[45]

Firefighters Watch a House Burn

Obion County, Tennessee, firefighters drew national attention in 2010 and 2011 when they allowed two rural family homes to burn to the ground because the families had not paid their $75 annual subscription fee to the city-operated fire department in nearby South

Fulton. Apparently, no one was seriously injured in either fire. The homeowner in the 2010 blaze, Gene Cranick, said that he offered to pay the fee on the spot, but the fire department declined and engaged the fire only to the extent necessary to protect the property of a neighbor who had paid the fee.

Questions

1. *a.* Why did the fire department decline Cranick's money at the time of the fire?
   b. Do you think the fire department should have extinguished the fire even though Cranick had not paid? Explain.

2. In 2012, South Fulton decided to respond to all reported fires and bill nonsubscribers $3,500 for the response. Do you think the new policy is an improvement over the original? Explain.

3. Should fire service be privatized across the nation? Explain.

Source: Jason Hibbs, "Firefighters Watch as Home Burns to the Ground," *WPSD Local 6 – News, Sports, Weather,* Paducah, KY, September 30, 2010 [**http://www.wpsdlocal6.com/**]; Timothy W. Martin, "Putting Out Fires for a Fee," *Wall Street Journal,* March 12, 2012 [**http://online.wsj.com/news/articles/SB1000142405297020396120457 7269591267553530?mg=reno64-wsj**].

Questions—Part Two

1. From the capitalist viewpoint, why is the private ownership of property necessary to the preservation of freedom?

2. Ayn Rand argued, "Altruism is incompatible with freedom, with capitalism, and with individual rights."
   a. Define altruism.
   b. Explain why Rand rejected altruism.

3. In describing life in aggressively commercialized Hong Kong, Alvin Rabushka praised the "single-minded pursuit of making money" and the "emphasis on the material things in life." Rabushka admitted to finding "Hong Kong's economic hustle and bustle more interesting, entertaining, and liberating than its lack of high opera, music, and drama." See Alvin Rabushka, *Hong Kong: A Study in Economic Freedom* (Chicago: University of Chicago Press, 1979), pp. 83–86.
   a. Although it is often criticized in America, is materialism the most certain and most interesting path to personal happiness? Explain.
   b. Would "sophisticated" culture (such as opera and drama) substantially disappear in America without government support? Explain.
   c. If so, how may we justify that support? If not, how may we justify that support?

4. Assume the federal government removed itself from the purchase and maintenance of its parks.
   a. Left to the private sector, what sorts of parks would develop under the profit incentive?
   b. Would Yellowstone, for example, survive in substantially its present state? Explain.
   c. Make the argument that the federal parks are an unethical, undemocratic expropriation of private resources.

5. Assume the abolition of the federal Food and Drug Administration. How would the free market protect the citizenry from dangerous food and drug products?

6. Puritan leaders felt concern over the morality of merchants selling goods for "more than their worth." That concern was particularly grave when the goods were scarce or in great demand.
   a. Should our society develop an ethic wherein goods are to be sold only "for what they are worth"? Explain.
   b. Can a seller make an accurate determination of worth? Explain.
   c. Does a product's worth differ from the price that product will bring in the market-place? Explain.
   d. Personalize the inquiry: Assume you seek to sell your Ford car for $10,000. Assume you know of several identical Fords in a similar state of repair that can be purchased for $9,000. Assume you find a buyer at $10,000. Will you unilaterally lower your price or direct the purchaser to the other cars? Explain.
   e. If not, have you acted justly? Explain.

7. Critics of our capitalist system contend that ability and effort often are less responsible for one's success than "unearned" factors such as family background, social class, luck, and willingness to cheat.

   Do you agree? Explain.

8. Gregg Williams, former defensive coordinator for the New Orleans Saints National Football League (NFL) team, was suspended for one year by the League as punishment for his alleged role in establishing a bounty system that paid players for injuring other players. Allegedly many NFL teams had employed similar schemes. Williams has apologized for his "previous actions" and was hired for the 2013/2014 season to be a defensive assistant for the Tennessee Titans. In a free market, rewards for performance are helpful as an incentive and just as a measure of contribution. Do you think bonuses for injuring opposing players should be permissible in the NFL? Explain.

9. Professor Robert E. Lane argued that the person who is motivated by needs for affiliation, rather than by needs for achievement, does less well in the market. Such a person is not rewarded so well as autonomous, achievement-oriented people.
   a. Is Lane correct? Explain.
   b. Is capitalism, in the long run, destructive of societal welfare in that achievement is better rewarded than affiliation? Explain. See generally, Robert E. Lane, *The Loss of Happiness in Market Democracies* (New Haven: Yale University Press, 2000).

10. How would poor people be cared for in a free market society?

11. Critic William Deresiewicz said, "Wall Street is capitalism in its purest form, and capitalism is predicated on bad behavior." Do you agree that capitalism is built on bad behavior? Explain. See William Deresiewicz, "Capitalist and Other Psychopaths," *The New York Times,* May 12, 2012 [**http://www.nytimes.com/**].

12. Using private money, New York City experimented from 2007 to 2010, with a program that paid poorer residents for practicing good life habits such as holding a job ($150 per month), going to the dentist ($100), regular school attendance ($25 to $50 per month), and passing certain examinations ($600). The average family received about $3,000. Would you expect this program to be an effective encouragement to improved life habits? Explain. See Associated Press, "N.Y.C. Pays Poor for Good Habits . . .," *The Des Moines Register,* March 31, 2010, p. 10A.

Part Three—Collectivism: Increase Government?

The term *collectivism* embraces communism and socialism and similar philosophies on the left side of the political/economic spectrum. Collectivist systems feature economic cooperation and varying degrees of centralized control as contrasted with capitalism's economic individualism and political freedom.

Communism

Although China, Cuba, North Korea, Vietnam, and a few other nations continue to practice communism, the balance of the world has clearly rejected Marxist-Leninist totalitarianism. China is rapidly and enthusiastically embracing free market practices, with continuing state direction; a strategy that some label *state capitalism,* as discussed below. Chinese enthusiasm for elements of free market practice should not be misunderstood, however. The communist state remains firmly in charge.

Fidel Castro's departure from the Cuban presidency in favor of his brother Raul has resulted in initial free market reforms. For the first time in 50 years, Cubans are now allowed to buy and sell houses freely as well as used cars. Cubans can own cell phones and other electronic de-

> Cubans can own
> cell phones.

vices, some state land is being distributed for private farming, and some private cabs are being licensed. Some 400,000 people now hold private-sector jobs such as scooter repair, barber, and produce vendor in the 180 government-approved employment categories. Restaurants, snack bars, and other small shops are springing up. However, the bureaucratic pace is extremely slow, and Cuba remains firmly communist/socialist. Most of the 11 million Cubans continue to lead a spare, government-supported existence, and political liberty is nonexistent.

Communist Vietnam is also embracing elements of capitalism. Nike, Samsung, and smartphone component suppliers for Apple are among the manufacturers drawn to Vietnam for its relatively low wages and stable political environment. *New York Times* reporter Keith Bradsher says that many Asian executives and some in America, believe that communism encourages the societal stability they value.[46] Perhaps America's investment presence in Vietnam, our enemy in a fierce war of the 1970s, is encouraging evidence of the healing power of international trade? More cynically, perhaps host-country political practices don't trouble foreign investors unless those practices threaten the bottom line?

Communist Principles

Despite the decline of communism, we need to briefly remind ourselves of some Marxist fundamentals, among which the core promise of economic justice for all remains a particularly powerful motivator. Lenin, not Marx, created the communist dictatorship in Russia. Lenin and the other communist totalitarians, most notably Stalin in the Soviet Union and Mao in China, did horrific damage. However, Marx, along with Freud and Einstein, is among the thinkers who most profoundly shaped the 20th century. For our purposes, Marx's central message concerns the severe abuses that can accompany unrestrained capitalism. Marx was particularly concerned about the growing imbalance between rich and poor. Moreover, he felt that the pursuit of wealth and self-interest would erode society's moral core. More broadly, Marx built an economic interpretation of history, arguing that "the mode of production in material life determines the general character of the social, political, and spiritual processes of life."[47] [For an introduction to Marxist thought, see **http://www.cla.purdue.edu/English/theory/marxism**]

Communism to Capitalism: A Bumpy Road

People in former communist nations in Eastern Europe, including Romania, Poland, Hungary, the Czech Republic, and Russia, report mixed feelings as they look back on the years following the fall of the Berlin Wall and the end of the Cold War between the former Soviet Union and the Western European/American allies. When dictatorships were replaced by democracy, the initial reaction was euphoria, but in subsequent years some nostalgia for the certainties of communism has emerged. A Czech professor summarized the current feelings of disappointment: "People here admired the freedom and prosperity of the Western world. Now what they see is materialism, corruption, inflation, lawlessness—and they can't find spiritual or material prosperity."[48] High unemployment, poverty, and harsh cuts in public spending have dashed the high hopes for post-communist prosperity. Many in Eastern Europe yearn for the comfort of state-provided health care and education and state-subsidized goods and services, but the evidence suggests they tend to forget about the poor quality of those goods and services, state censorship, the absence of freedom, and fear of the state.

Question

1. Do you think capitalism, by its nature, is unfair to ordinary people? Explain.

Sources: Michael J. Jordan, "After the Berlin Wall, Nostalgia for Communism Creeps Back," *The Christian Science Monitor,* November 8, 2009 [**http://www.csmonitor.com/2009/1109/p11s01-woeu.html**]; and Rossen Vassilev, "The Tragic Failure of 'Post-Communism' in Eastern Europe," *Global Research,* March 8, 2011 [**http://www.globalresearch.ca/the-tragic-failure-of-post-communism-in-eastern-europe/23616**]

Socialism

Communism appears to have run its course philosophically and pragmatically, but the problems that generated its appeal—poverty, oppression, the rich-poor gap, and so on—remain. Hence government intervention in the market continues to be needed. The question is: How much government is appropriate? Socialists provide one answer by rejecting communist totalitarianism and embracing democracy while calling for aggressive government intervention to correct economic and social ills. Historically, socialism has often been associated with democratic governments and peaceful change, whereas communism has been characterized by totalitarianism and violent revolution.

Socialists aim to retain the benefits of industrialism while abolishing the social costs often accompanying the free market. The government is likely to be directly involved in regulating growth, inflation, and unemployment. In the contemporary Western world, Austria, Norway, Denmark, Sweden, South Africa, Finland, and France are among the nations where socialist principles have retained a significant presence. Those nations have now embraced free markets, but socialist welfare concerns remain influential.

Socialist Goals

A critical distinction between socialists and capitalists is that the former believe a society's broad directions should be carefully planned rather than left to what some take to be the whimsy of the market. Furthermore, socialists are convinced that problems of market failure (inadequate information, monopoly, externalities, public goods, and so on—see Chapter 8) mean that the free market is simply incapable of meeting the needs of all segments of society. The socialist agenda includes these elements:[49]

1. **Liberty.** To the capitalist, socialism appears to harshly restrain individual freedom. To the socialist, the freedoms of capitalism are largely an illusion, accessible only to the prosperous and powerful.

2. **Social welfare.** Socialists reserve much of their concern for the condition of the lower class—poverty, exploitation, cultural deprivation, and so on. Socialists believe that the economy must be directed toward the general interest rather than left free to multiply the welfare of successful capitalists. Hence, socialists advocate income supports, free education, free health care, generous sick pay, family planning, and the like to correct the failures of capitalism.

3. **Fulfilling work.** Socialists object to the harshness of working life where a large segment of society is chained to degrading labor.

> Socialists seek a communitarian approach to life.

4. **Community.** Socialists seek a communitarian approach to life where the excessive individualism of capitalism is muted by a concern for the welfare of all.

5. **Equality.** Class distinctions are anathema to the socialist. All humans are equally meritorious, and distinctions among them are inherently unjust.

6. **Rationality.** Socialists fear the "irrationality" of a society based on competition and unrestrained pursuit of industrial growth.

As explained in the account that follows, poverty and claims of corporate exploitation have allowed socialism to regain a tentative foothold in parts of South America.

Socialism in South America

Recently deceased President of Venezuela Hugo Chavez hoped to build a "21st century socialism" in South America that would elevate the poor—forgotten by "savage capitalism"—while leading his country and neighbors, including Bolivia, Ecuador, Honduras, and Nicaragua away from American dominance. He wanted to destroy what he saw as centuries of plundering, humiliation, and discrimination against indigenous people by monied interests, particularly American multinationals. Chavez said that world power is shifting from America:

> The uni-polar world has collapsed. The power of the U.S. empire has collapsed. Everyday, the new poles of world power are becoming stronger. Beijing, Tokyo, Tehran. . . . It's moving toward the East and toward the South.[50]

Chavez nationalized many companies, drove out ExxonMobil and ConocoPhillips, and redistributed land from the government and private owners to the poor. While Chavez said he would "bury" Venezuelan capitalism, the private sector continues to control about two-thirds of the Venezuelan economy.

With strong oil prices, Chavez had a steady and generous revenue stream that allowed him to dramatically increase state funding of social projects. The government claims to have cut poverty in half, and Chavez inspired many Venezuelans to engage in civic life and to feel a new concern for the nation's welfare. Critics say he stifled dissent, took control of almost every government institution, and subjected the nation to double-digit inflation, food and power shortages, a devalued currency, and a murder rate that has doubled in recent years.

At this writing in 2013, Chavez has been succeeded by former Vice President Nicolas Maduro, who seems to share Chavez's ideology. Ecuador's popular leftist president, Rafael Correa, easily won reelection in 2013. At the same time, Mexico, Brazil, Chile, and other South American nations are governed by market-based regimes.

Sources: Associated Press, "Chavez Asserts: We'll Bury Capitalism," *The Des Moines Register*, July 19, 2010, p. 10A; Editorial, "The State Department Responds to Repression by Hugo Chavez," *The Washington Post*, January 4, 2011[**http://www.washingtonpost.com**]; Juan Forero, and "Venezuela Tries to Create Its Own Kind of Socialism."

Coping with Capitalism—China and Russia

China—Economics

China and some other nations practice what is sometimes labeled "state capitalism" in which the government is the dominant economic force as it intervenes in and shapes the market to further the state's political goals. The result has been something of an economic miracle as China has blended its large but shrinking system of state-owned enterprise with the explosive power of the free market (guided by the government) to sprint ahead of Japan and become in 2010 the globe's second ranking economy as measured by gross national product.

China's new president, Xi Jinping, has indicated that his nation of 1.3 billion people must boost market-based competition, but at the same time, he appears resolute in his commitment to the Communist Party. With economic growth slowing, labor shortages, pollution and corruption mounting, and the transition from a middle- to high-income economy in the offing, China's leadership generally recognizes that adjustments are necessary. Entrenched interests, however, make change difficult.

State-owned firms control about 30 percent of the Chinese economy with about 120 giants controlled by the central government and about 150,000 smaller, state-owned companies.[51] Huge sectors of the economy are dominated by government entities, as explained by the *Los Angeles Times:*

> Need a cellphone plan? Choose from the trio of state-owned giants: China Mobile, China Telecom and China Unicom. Looking to fly? You're most likely to take one of the three major state carriers: Air China, China Southern and China Eastern. Upset about gas prices? They're determined by a government duopoly of PetroChina and Sinopec.[52]

Problems

As noted, China faces many problems, particularly as it attempts to balance its export-led economy with increased domestic consumer spending. Stunning levels of environmental pollution; stock market manipulation; dangerous foods and drugs; rampant piracy of software, movies, and music; and government corruption are among those difficulties. Basic social support structures like affordable access to health care, unemployment insurance, and pensions remain inadequate. More broadly, China's income gap between rich and poor is estimated to be among the world's largest, although China has reduced the disparity in recent years.[53] Furthermore, China has instituted new environmental rules, corruption crackdowns, and social service initiatives.

Changing Labor Markets

Low wages, often difficult working conditions, and a rapidly shrinking supply of young laborers (the result of strict family planning policies) have caused unrest among workers leading to occasional strikes and some increase in wages, although those wages remain low relative to the economy's overall health. China's reliance on cheap labor to drive its economy is threatened as other nations are able to undercut the Chinese advantage. Despite China's renewed global prominence and its stunning economic advances, record numbers of professionals reportedly leave annually. Well-paid in her job at a multinational, Chen Kuo, age 30, explained why she had decided to leave China for Australia:

> It's very stressful in China—sometimes I was working 128 hours a week for my auditing company. . . . And it will be easier raising my children as Christians abroad. It is more free in Australia.[54]

China—Politics

Freedom   Of course, China remains a dictatorship governed by the Communist Party. Repression is common. The government controls the media as evidenced by censorship battles between the Chinese government and Internet news sources such as Google, *The New York Times,* and *Bloomberg,* each of which has been blocked at times. China uses its "Great Firewall" of Internet censors to filter search results, particularly those addressing politically sensitive themes such as official corruption, democracy, Tibetan freedom, Taiwan, and the 1989 Tiananmen Square crackdown (during which troops killed hundreds of protesters during prodemocracy demonstrations in Beijing). An estimated 30,000 to 50,000 regulators monitor the web in China with certain sites such as Facebook, YouTube, and Twitter blocked from public access.[55]

> China uses its "Great Firewall" of Internet censors to filter search results.

Reforms   Even as China has rejected calls to guarantee freedom of speech and move toward democracy, the Communist Party leadership recognizes the need for gradual change. In a bid to stimulate a slowing economy, China announced in late 2013 that it would open state industries to greater private-sector competition while also easing some limits on foreign investment. Further, the government has announced plans to abolish its system of "reeducation" through forced labor, and to ease its one-child per family policy. The rule of law is increasingly powerful in Chinese life as the number of lawyers in China more than doubled from 1997 to 2008.[56] Still Communist Party bosses use the law as a means of social control, repression remains common, and governance by the rule of law, where no person or political party is above the law, is not yet the case in China.[57] [For the latest Chinese news, see **http://thebeijingnews.net**]

> The number of lawyers in China more than doubled.

Visit Mom and Dad

"The son has forgotten the mother," 78-year-old Li Lanyu said recently in a Chinese court where she complained about her 60-year-old son's failure to visit her regularly and bring needed grain and cooking oil.[58] China's Buddhist heritage commands extraordinary respect for parents, but effective July 1, 2013, a new Chinese law requires attention to parents 60 and older and living on their own. Family members "should often visit or send regards to their parents," and they must attend to their parents' "spiritual needs" and must not "overlook" or "neglect" them. The law does not specifically define those new expectations. Some Chinese are troubled that their nation may have reached the point where it must force filial piety by law, but others suspect the state is simply looking for a way to sustain a swelling elderly population as the workforce shrinks, in part as a consequence of the official "one child" population control policy.

At this writing, a judgment in Li's lawsuit has not been rendered, but in a similar case, a judge recently ordered a woman to visit her 77-year-old mother every two months and on major holidays.

Sources: Michelle FlorCruz, "China Enacts Law Requiring Adult Children to Visit Their Elderly Parents, but Can It Be Enforced?" *International Business Times*, July 1, 2013 [**http://www.ibtimes.com/**]; and Julie Makinen, "China's 'Visit Your Parents' Law Weighs on Many in One-Child Nation," *latimes.com*, July 29, 2013 [**http://www.latimes.com/**].

Question

Technology entrepreneur and academic Vivek Wadhwa, in assessing emerging economic trends, asked, "Does China own the future—or does the United States?"[59] Answer Wadhwa's question.

Russia—Economics

A Western visitor to modern Moscow must be hard-pressed to imagine that this thriving, consuming, competitive place was once the global center of communism, the dour capital of the Union of Soviet Socialist Republics, and the home of America's nuclear enemy. After the fall of the USSR and the ideological defeat of communism, Moscow embraced consumer capitalism, a change described by *The Christian Science Monitor*:

> The heavy, block buildings of Russia's capital are no longer covered in banners of Lenin, Marx, and Engels. Instead, enormous billboards advertise watches, cars, clothing—items unimaginable in Soviet times. Capitalism has taken hold with a vengeance.[60]

Russia remains a developing nation with a total economy about one-eighth the size of the U.S economy.[61] Nonetheless, Russia's economic performance since the late 1990s has been impressive. With only a brief bump during the Great Recession, Russia has used its vast natural resources (Russia leads the world in oil production and is second in natural gas) to buy increased prosperity and achieve a balanced budget with near full employment. At this writing in 2013, however, growth has slowed and Russian president, Vladimir Putin, has proposed borrowing from Russian pension reserves to modernize the famous Trans-Siberian Railway, build a superhighway around Moscow, and build a 500-mile high-speed rail line between Moscow and Kazan, a regional capital.[62] Putin's economic plan also includes a slowdown in the planned privatization of state-owned banks, utilities, oil companies, and other enormous assets. The Russian government controls about 50 percent of the nation's economy,[63] a presence that many economists believe must be reduced if Russia is to encourage foreign investment and maintain a vibrant economic future.

A big threat to Russia's long-term economic welfare and national stability is its aging population, now at about 143 million and growing slightly, but projected to decline to 116 million by 2050.[64] Life expectancy declined to 69.7 years in 2012 (as compared with 78 in the United States and 83 in Japan).[65] Russia's population dilemma is at least significantly attributable to a national culture of drinking and smoking that has contributed to a life expectancy for Russian men of only 60 years.[66]

Russia—Politics

Russia's future economic success is intimately tied, of course, to its political processes. The state needs to win over foreign multinational investors who fear political tyranny and domestic corruption. Maplecroft, the British political risk consulting firm, in 2011 ranked Russia 186th out of 196 countries in political risk to business (1 being least risky) and according to *Transparency International,* Russia is the world's most corrupt major economy, ranking 154th out of 178 countries (1 being least corrupt).[67]

The Russian government's centralization of economic power has been accompanied by tightened control over politics, courts, activists, and the mass media. A 2012 law imposes a $9,000 fine on those taking part in unsanctioned demonstrations that damage people or property.[68] At this writing in 2013, hundreds of Russian civil organizations (e.g., supporting voting rights) have been subjected to "inspections" for "political activity."[69] Recent legislation bans the "propaganda of nontraditional sexual relations" and imposes fines for holding gay pride rallies or providing information about the gay community to minors.[70] The Russian people, nonetheless, express strong support for President Putin, even as they acknowledge a wide gap between what is and what should be in Russian elections, judicial systems, free press, and the like.[71] Critics question whether state capitalism as practiced in Russia can succeed in the face of political repression, routine corruption, and abuse of the rule of law.[72]

> Propaganda of nontraditional sexual relations

Questions

1. China wants to curb its population growth, while Russia has sought to increase its number of children. China's government allows each couple to have only one child, although exceptions are permitted for those living in rural areas and for minorities. Heavy fines may be imposed on those who violate the rules. In Russia, then President Dmitri Medvedev, in his 2010 State of Russia speech, called for a baby bonus, better health care, and free land for women who will have a third child. Why would governments make commands on childbearing practices? Is this acceptable? Explain.

2. Can China maintain its closed, centrally controlled political system while enjoying the benefits of its somewhat open economic markets? Explain.

3. In 2014, in response to Russian military action in Ukraine, the United States imposed sanctions—travel bans and asset freezes—on several Russian government officials as well as business executives and companies. What impact might these sanctions have? Should such sanctions be a part of an international response to a government's actions? Explain.

Part Four—Middle Ground? A Mixed Economy (The Third Way)

Communism has failed. Socialist principles, to the extent that they require central planning, bloated bureaucracies, and restraints on personal freedom, are discredited. An era has passed, but the shape of the future is unclear. The state capitalism of China, Russia, and other nations has little appeal in America and Western Europe and yet America's brand of free market capitalism has lost a great deal of luster in the recent financial collapse and the ongoing Great Recession. Some middle ground in free market and welfare state principles may be the next step, but the appropriate mixture is proving elusive. For years, the Nordic states of Sweden, Norway, Denmark, and Finland practiced their market socialism or social democracy with such success that it was labeled a "Third Way" between the harsher extremes of capitalism and communism. Their welfare states provided healthy economic growth with cradle-to-grave social care for all in a system emphasizing the collective welfare over individual preferences.

Sweden

Life expectancy in Sweden is 81.28 years, as compared with about 78.62 years in the United States.[73] The government provides education, health care, child care, maternity and paternity leave, unemployment protection, and more. Government incentives promote preferred behaviors. For example, the Swedish government will pay 80 percent of a parent's salary (capped at $65,000) for up to 13 months of parental leave from work. Fathers are required to take at least two months of that leave time to receive government benefits. Some employers, such as the international clothing retailer H&M, make up the difference in pay if the salary of the parent on leave exceeds the government's payment. H&M favors the parental leave policy as an opportunity for employees to try out new jobs, and each H&M employee has a designated substitute should leave be needed. Overall, the parental leave policy has contributed to Sweden's standing as a world leader in gender equality. About 72 percent of working-age Swedish women work at least part time.[74]

> H&M favors the parental leave policy.

Gender Equality

Sweden aggressively encourages gender equality. Believing boys have an unfair edge, eradication of gender stereotypes has become a key ingredient in Swedish education. At Stockholm's "Egalia" (equality) preschool, for example, the staff avoids using the words "him" or "her" and addresses all children as "friends." Children's books often feature homosexual couples, single parents, or adopted children and classics like *Cinderella* are shunned. Egalia's methods are controversial, even in Sweden.

Source: John Tagliabue, "A School's Big Lesson Begins with Dropping Personal Pronouns," *The New York Times,* November 14, 2012, p. A8.

Taxes   To pay for its cradle-to-grave welfare benefits, Sweden takes about 45 percent of its national income (gross domestic product-GDP) in taxes, while the United States, in contrast, has one of the developed world's lowest total tax burdens at about 27 percent of GDP in recent decades, but down to about 24 percent during the recession.[75] In order to keep its economy healthy, Sweden has followed a policy of comparatively low total corporate taxes (22 percent[76] as compared with a U.S. rate of 39.2 percent, federal and state combined, although with loopholes included, the U.S. effective rate is an estimated 29.2 percent.[77] As a result, Sweden's economic performance over the past 20 years has been among the strongest in the world, supporting, for example, a health care system that exceeds U.S. health care on almost all performance measures but costs less than half as much per person (although waiting times for some nonemergency services might be considerably longer in Sweden).[78] Even so, the pressure of globalization has been felt in Sweden where a more moderate and somewhat right-center government has pushed aside the left-leaning Social Democrats and has significantly lowered taxes, privatized some state-dominated companies, and reduced unemployment by encouraging work over welfare. Business regulations have been dramatically reduced, and tens of thousands of long-term unemployed welfare recipients have been pushed back into the labor market. Sweden hopes to maintain its core welfare commitment in combination with an entrepreneurial spirit more like America's. The result is an economy of relatively low unemployment, low inflation, and high GDP growth.[79]

One expert attributes the Third Way success to "lavish" spending on research and development and higher education.[80] Thus, for Sweden and the other Scandinavian states, wise government spending is a key ingredient in a successful market-based economy. We should remember, of course, that Sweden is a small, homogeneous nation. Replicating its policies in the United States would be difficult. And the Swedes are, of course, not free from difficulties. Angry, youths rioted in Stockholm and other communities in 2013 protesting lack of jobs in their communities and discrimination. At this writing, the disturbances have quieted.

Speeding Ticket

Ferrari-driving millionaire, "Roland S." was fined $290,000 in 2009 for speeding 60 miles per hour through a small village in Switzerland where the speed limit was 30. In their verdict, which was subject to appeal, judges labeled the driver a "traffic thug." The fine reflected a 2007 Swiss law allowing judges to hand down fines in certain misdemeanor cases based on personal income and wealth. "Roland S." was worth some $20 million, and he was a repeat offender. The maximum Swiss fine is $1 million, while Germany permits as much as a $16 million fine. France, Austria, and the Nordic nations also permit punishments based on personal wealth.

Question

Would you favor penalties in America based on income and wealth? Explain.

Source: Frank Jordans, "Rich Driver Hit with $290,000 Speeding Ticket," *The Des Moines Register,* January 11, 2010, p. 1A.

American Capitalism in Europe?

Does the European Union—ranging broadly from the Scandinavian Third Way to Germany's cooperative, but increasingly aggressive capitalism—have a better long-term vision for personal and societal welfare than the United States? Is America's more libertarian "cowboy capitalism" better adapted to the globe's demands than the "coordinated, stakeholder capitalism" characteristic of much of Europe? The evidence is mixed. In building entrepreneurial spirit, personal freedom, and personal wealth and income, the United States is the clear world leader, but the EU's very powerful, 28 nation, over 500 million person bloc generates a gross national product slightly larger than the United States and more than three times that of India or Japan.[81] For Europeans, however, quantity seems to be less important than quality. Europeans choose to work less than Americans, and as they see it, enjoy life more. Their economy is less flexible than ours and typically produces fewer jobs, but it is also less harsh.[82] Universal health care, job protection, and strong unemployment benefits are part of the European identity.

Welfare Reform   Europe's warmer, more communal values and practices are inviting, but the ongoing recession has resulted in a EU unemployment rate of more than 12 percent (as compared with about 7 percent in the United States) and the need for Eurozone economic bailouts of nearly bankrupt economies in Ireland, Greece, Spain, and Portugal. Youth (age 15–24) unemployment at over 23 percent for the EU generally[83] and nearing 60 percent in Spain and Greece has produced something approaching a "lost generation"[84] in some countries. In Italy more than 40 percent of 25- to 34-year-olds continue to live at home.[85]

These struggles have also sharpened the divide between the more prosperous northern European nations (Germany's unemployment rate is about 5.4 percent) and the struggling south (unemployment in Greece and Spain exceeds 26 percent).[86] Austerity, that is, higher taxes and sharp cutbacks in government spending, has been implemented in the struggling nations. In France, for example, dramatic government spending cuts in 2013 and beyond may challenge the nation's generally comfortable lifestyle. Public spending amounting to about 57 percent of GDP had produced a protected population with strong family support, low poverty, and generous pensions, but for the present at least the French government has concluded that it simply cannot afford that approach. Social programs will not be dismembered but painful cutbacks seem to be unavoidable.[87]

Germany, on the other hand, has been able to balance a rather generous social safety net (long-term care, vacations, pensions, etc.) with a very robust and highly skilled manufacturing sector, and an effective government to produce job security and a comfortable life. Germany has managed its budget carefully, adopted reforms such as an increased retirement age, and maintained a strong market-based economy to support its social programs.[88]

EU Failure?   The Great Recession has shaken the European Union—so much so that Yale professor Nicholas Sambanis recently asked in *The New York Times,* "Has 'Europe' Failed?"[89] He argued that the European Union's problems extend beyond economics to its very identity. Can the union remain united or will its citizens, particularly in the wealthier nations, identify more with their native homeland than with the EU? Compounding their economic challenges, many European nations are struggling to assimilate immigrants and to become comfortable with growing Muslim populations, as pointedly noted by German chancellor Angela Merkel:

> This multicultural approach, saying that we simply live side by side and live happily with each other, has failed. Utterly failed.[90]

Contrasting Values

Obviously, both Europe and America are struggling in this troubled time, but which vision of life seems most promising over the long term? American commentator and social activist Jeremy Rifkin contrasted the American and European "Dreams":[91]

American Dream	vs.	European Dream
Wealth/Individual success	vs.	Quality of life
Growth	vs.	Sustainable development
Property/Civil rights	vs.	Social/Human rights
Live to work	vs.	Work to live
Religiosity/Piety	vs.	Declining faith
Strong military	vs.	Build peace

Rifkin thinks the European strategy is the better one. What do you think? Which of those two lists of values is more comfortable and inspiring for you? Which is more likely to meet the demands of the ongoing global competition and evolution? [For an argument that the United States is better positioned than either the European Union or China for the long-term economic future, see Ian Bremmer and Nouriel Roubini, "Whose Economy Has It Worst?" *The Wall Street Journal,* November 12–13, 2011, p. C3].

Is the Welfare State a Key to Personal Happiness?

Denmark turns out to be the happiest place on Earth, according to a 2013 United Nations study of global happiness in 156 countries. The top of the happiness list includes: 1. Denmark, 2. Norway, 3. Switzerland, 4. The Netherlands, and 5. Sweden, all northern European states with strong welfare principles. The United States ranks 17th on the list, ahead of the United Kingdom (22), France (25), and Japan (43). Most of the various happiness studies find the Scandinavian countries at or near the top of the list. Why? One theory, according to researchers, is that basic needs are satisfied in those countries to a higher degree than elsewhere.

What matters most? Broadly, good health, education, freedom, and wealth are associated with happiness, but wealth seems to increase happiness only up to a point. According to a 2010 study, happiness basically peaks at about $75,000 in the United States, but life satisfaction keeps rising with increasing income. Another 2010 study found that getting richer, in and of itself, does not make a nation happier in the long run. Simply "hanging out" with friends and family seems to be critical to the Danes' being first in the world level of happiness. Ninety-two percent of Danes belong to some kind of social club, and the government encourages these get-togethers by helping to pay for them. Likewise, while Danes value nice things, they are said to be a "post-consumerist" society where consumption is not a high priority. Their extraordinarily high taxes (around 50 percent of income) may also play a role in the happiness quotient in that income is substantially leveled, allowing careers to be chosen more on the basis of interest rather than money and also allowing everyone to "hold his/her head high" regardless of occupational status. Finally, experts point particularly to the Danes' very high quotient of trust, which may be a product of the cradle-to-grave security provided by the government. For example, mothers often leave their babies unattended in strollers outside shops and restaurants. Of course, Denmark has the advantage of being a small, homogenous nation largely free of America's worldwide responsibilities.

Purpose? A 2011 *Wall Street Journal* survey of happiness research raised a cautionary note by drawing a distinction between a purposeful life and a happy life. Mounting evidence suggests that people who focus on a meaningful life, while sometimes sacrificing happiness feelings in the moment, may be healthier, live longer, and have a greater sense of well being over time than people who focus on short-term feelings of happiness by eating a good meal, going to a movie, enjoying a big game, etc. Noting that symptoms of depression, paranoia, and psychopathology steadily increased in American college students from 1938 to 2007, San Diego State University researchers have offered as a plausible explanation America's increasing emphasis on pleasure, materialism, and status and decreasing attention to community and meaning in life. For noted scholar and consultant Michael Porter's *Social Progress Index,* a measure of "the extent to which countries provide for the social and environmental needs of their citizens," see **www.socialprogressimperative.org/**.

Questions

For several decades, tiny Himalayan nation of Bhutan has sought to measure itself, not by Gross Domestic Product (GDP), but by Gross National Happiness (GNH), calculated from the nation's "four pillars" of sustainable development, environmental protection, cultural preservation, and good governance, each of equal importance. Alternatives to GDP measurement have captured global attention, although Bhutanese leaders have cautioned that pursuit of GNH should not distract from addressing problems of unemployment, poverty, and corruption.

1. Would the United States be a better nation if we sought GNH rather than GDP?
2. Would pursuit of GNH produce a winner in today's fierce global competition? Explain.

Sources: Brook Larmer, "Bhutan's Enlightened Experiment," *National Geographic Magazine*, March 2008 [**http://ngm.nationalgeographic.com/2008/03/bhutan/larmer-text**]; Dylan Matthews, "Yes, Money Can Buy Happiness," *The Washington Post,* April 29, 2013 [**http://www.washingtonpost.com**]; Alok Jha, "Happiness Doesn't Increase with Growing Wealth of Nations, Study Finds," *guardian.co.uk,* December 13, 2010 [**http://www .guardian.co.uk/science/2010/dec/13/happiness-growing-wealth-nations-study**]; Kim Painter, "Smile: USA Ranks 17th among World's Happiest Countries," *USA Today,* September 9, 2013 [**http://www.usatoday.com/**]; Shirley Wang, "Is Happiness Overrated?" *The Wall Street Journal,* March 15, 2011, p. D1; and Bill Weir and Sylvia Johnson, "Denmark: The Happiest Place on Earth," *ABC News,* January 8, 2007 [**http://abcnews.go.com/2020 /story?id=40860928page=1**].

Questions—Parts Three and Four

1. Billionaire investor George Soros, in his book *Open Society,* sees "market fundamentalism as a greater threat to open society today than communism."[92] Soros fears contemporary capitalism's extreme commitment to self-interest, which results, he says, in our greatest challenge today: "to establish a set of fundamental values."[93]
   a. What does Soros mean?
   b. Do you agree with him? Explain.

2. Americans feel a great deal of faith in the free market. Explain some of the weaknesses in the market. That is, where is the free market likely to fail?

3. Writing in *Dissent,* Joanne Barkan says, "[A]lmost all Swedes view poverty, extreme inequalities of wealth, and the degradation that comes with unemployment as unacceptable."[94]
   a. Do you agree with the Swedes? Explain.
   b. Why are Americans more tolerant of those conditions than are the Swedes?

4. Scholars Daron Acemoglu, James A. Robinson, and Thierry Verdier have argued that the United States would hurt world growth if it adopted the "cuddly capitalism" of Scandinavia. For the United States to maintain its vital role of chief global innovator, Acemoglu and Verdier say that America must maintain an economic system that generously rewards successful innovators which "implies greater inequality and greater poverty (and a weaker safety net) for a society encouraging innovation."[95] Do you agree? Explain.

5. *a.* Should an American citizen's primary duty be to herself or himself or to all other members of society? Explain.
   b. Should all humans be regarded as of equal value and thus equally worthy of our individual support? Explain.
   c. Can social harmony be achieved in a nation whose citizens fail to regard the state as a "superfamily"? Explain.

6. *a.* In your view, is an individual's possession of extravagant wealth a moral wrong?
   b. Would economic justice require that we treat "being rich" as a social wrong? Explain.
   See George Scialabba, "Asking the Right Questions," *Dissent,* Spring 1988, p. 114.

7. In questioning Oakland Athletics general manager Billy Beane, *The Wall Street Journal* described professional football as "socialist" and baseball as "capitalist":

   > The NFL (National Football League) has been successful as a socialist league, equally divvying up the league's revenue among all the teams. Major league baseball, on the other hand, is a capitalist league, with a clear divide between big-market and small-market teams.[96]

   a. Do you think some of major league baseball's financial rules have to be changed to better balance the playing field?
   b. Is "socialism" or "capitalism" the better system for professional sports? Explain.

8. In 2011, Denmark sought to improve citizen health by imposing a "fat tax" based on the amount of saturated fat in foods. The tax raised the price of a hamburger, for example, by about 40 cents.[97] The tax failed and was soon repealed. Explain why the fat tax failed.

Part Five—America's Economic Future: Where Are We Going?

How Much Government? Should we expand our faith in free market capitalism, or do we need to move our present mixed economy a bit closer to the welfare state model, which itself is under great pressure? Or must a new model emerge? In sum, how much government do we need? To think further about those questions, let's briefly examine some of the key indicators of America's economic and social health.

Good News   Of course, Americans have a great deal to be proud of. We enjoy extraordinary material comfort along with healthy, generally safe lives. As the *Los Angeles Times* reported, since 1980 the percentage of those earning $100,000 or more, in today's dollars, has doubled, the average size of our homes has doubled in the past 50 years to about 2,200 square feet, and the total hours spent working have declined steadily for over 150 years.[98] We are inventive, adventuresome, free, and zealously democratic. Roughly half of all patents are earned by Americans, minorities now hold high-ranking political office, and more women than men are earning college degrees.[99] Much of the world strives to achieve America's blend of entrepreneurial capitalism along with intellectual and pop culture leadership. And we should not forget that capitalist America is among the most generous of global cultures. Indeed, recent polling data ranked the United States first among the nations of the world in helping others (donations, volunteering, and aiding strangers).[100]

> Americans have a great deal to be proud of.

The American Dream at Risk?

America is strong but struggling. Globalization and new technology, in the short run at least, have chipped away at our job market. Labor unions have lost much of their power. Our multinational giants seem to be more interested in investing abroad than in America.

The core of America—the middle class—and the very idea of the American Dream seem at risk. From the time the Great Recession hit bottom in mid-2009 to mid-2012, a period of recovery, median household income in America *fell* about 5 percent[101] and new data show that the size of the middle class (annual household incomes in 2010 between $39,000 and $118,000 for a family of three) *fell* from 61 percent of all adults in 1971 to 51 percent of all adults in 2010.[102] (A portion of that change reflected Americans moving to the upper class.) The middle class struggle has been particularly damaging to those younger than 35, whose net worth, for the typical family, fell by 68 percent between 1984 and 2009, after adjusting for inflation.[103]

In a broad sense, should we have doubts about the top-to-bottom fairness of our American system? Let's examine some concerns.

Overall Quality of Life

According to a United Nations 2013 report on overall quality of life (based on income, life expectancy, etc.), we are doing very well, ranking third behind Norway (1st) and Australia (2nd),[104] but when the scores are adjusted for inequality in health, education, and income the United States ranks 16th in the world in overall human development behind Norway(1st), Australia (2nd), and Sweden (3rd), among others.[105] One score of particular note was America's 22nd place ranking in gender equality where limited female roles in politics and relatively poor maternal health reduce the American performance.[106]

> America's 22nd place ranking in gender equality.

In general, the United States ranks well on standard economic measures and not so well on standard social measures. Our 2012 estimated GDP per capita of $50,700 ranked 14th in the world behind smaller, more specialized economies such as Qatar (1st at $103,900 and

Norway (9th at $55,900) and well ahead of our chief industrial rivals such as Germany (29th at $39,700) and Japan (38th at $36,900).[107]

In 2013 estimated life expectancy, on the other hand, the United States ranked 51st at an estimated 78.62 years while Japan, for example, ranked 3rd at an estimated 84.19 years.[108] Among the most discouraging U.S. performances is in the category of infant mortality (the probability of dying between birth and age one per 1,000 live births) where 50 nations do a better job of keeping babies alive than we do.[109] For some years, the United States has led the world in producing prisoners, but the U.S. prison population declined in 2012 for the third straight year.[110] On the other hand, violent crime rose in 2012 for the first time since 2006.[111]

> The United States has led the world in producing prisoners.

Some trends portend a worrisome future. The United States ranks fifth in the world in total spending for education, but young adult college completion rates have fallen to 14th globally, national K–12 test scores are only middling by international norms, and just half of 3-year-olds are enrolled in preschool (as compared with 90 percent in France, Italy, and Norway).[112] Family structures are changing dramatically. A record 40 percent of households with children under 18 include a mother who is either the sole or primary source of income with two-thirds of those being single mothers.[113] Marriage itself is in decline, particularly among those who are not well educated.[114] The economically and socially productive institution of marriage with children apparently is becoming a sort of luxury item for growing numbers of middle Americans.[115]

Poverty

Four out of five U.S. adults, for at least a part of their lives, are on welfare, unemployed, or facing near poverty, according to a 2013 study.[116] Fifteen percent of Americans fall below the official government poverty line ($23,021 for a family of four in 2011), but that number understates the magnitude of the problem.[117] Economic insecurity is spreading throughout the country, increasingly reaching white families and pressing even those in the upper half of America's income stream as median debt levels have increased and median net worth has fallen.[118] America's children are particularly at risk. A 2013 United Nations study of the well-being (material goods, education, etc.) of children in 29 of the world's "rich" countries ranked the United States 26th, just ahead of Lithuania, Latvia, and Romania with northern European countries at the top of the list.[119] The result of these dismal economic conditions is that poor people, as commentator Paul Krugman explained, live in a separate America:

> Living in or near poverty has always been a form of exile, of being cut off from the larger society. . . . To be poor in America today, even more than in the past, is to be an outcast in your own country.[120]

Of course, America's poorer people live better than the bulk of the citizens of the world, but the struggle is quite real, nonetheless. Even those who are employed often live a perilous life on the edge of collapse, as *BusinessWeek* explained:

> [M]ost (of the working poor) labor in a netherworld of maximum insecurity, where one missed bus, one stalled engine, one sick kid means the difference between keeping a job and getting fired, between subsistence and setting off the financial tremors of turned-off telephones and $1,000 emergency-room bills. . . .[121]

Historically we have accepted difficulties for a significant share of the population in the belief they would move up if they worked hard. Unfortunately, those prospects seem to be dimming. As *Forbes* recently reported, many of the fastest growing jobs (e.g., health aid, tradespeople, assistants/helpers) do not pay well and most do not require a college education.[122] Thus, many Americans lead surprisingly harsh lives, and their prospects for the future are not as bright as the American Dream suggests.

> Most do not require a college education.

Pets or People?

We may not take the best care of our disadvantaged fellow Americans, but we seem to be unstinting in generosity toward our pets. Americans in 2011 spent nearly $61 billion on their pets, a sum that exceeds the gross domestic product of all but about 70 nations.

Question

Would our money for pets be more wisely spent on impoverished children? Explain.

Sources: Danielle Kurtzleben, "Americans Spend $61 Billion on Pets," *US News and World Report,* May 22, 2013 [**http://www.usnews.com/**]; and "GDP—Official Exchange Rate 2013 Country Ranks," Countries of the World] [**http://www.photius.com/rankings/economy/gdp_official_exchange_rate_2013_0.html**]

The Gaps

Extravagant wealth, side-by-side with punishing poverty, is perhaps the greatest disappointment and injustice, from the critics' point of view, in the global advance of capitalist principles.

The wealthiest 1 percent of Americans now have a greater collective net worth than the bottom 90 percent.[123] The six heirs of Walmart founder, Sam Walton, have as much wealth as the bottom 100 million Americans.[124] The wealth gap is not surprising when we note that the incomes of the upper 1 percent of households rose nearly 20 percent in 2012 compared to a 1 percent increase for the bottom 99 percent.[125] Income inequality in the United States is the largest among Western industrialized countries.[126] Furthermore, although many Americans do move up and down the income and wealth ladders, the odds of climbing are now lower in the United States than in almost all developed nations.[127] We should note, however, that the rich–poor gap has been growing in most industrial nations, including the Scandinavian states.[128]

Average CEO pay has risen from about 20 times the average worker's pay in 1965 to about 273 times today (down from a high of 383 in 2000).[129] Hedge fund manager John Paulson earned an estimated $5 billion in 2010, perhaps the biggest investment killing in history.[130] To put his stunning income in perspective, $5 billion would allow him, for example, to nearly pay the full operating costs for the Chicago public schools (with more than 41,000 employees and over 400,000 students) for a year.[131] [For a discussion of recent research challenging the mainstream findings on income inequality, see Thomas B. Edsall, "What If We're Looking at Inequality the Wrong Way?" *The New York Times,* June 26, 2013 at **http://opinionator.blogs.nytimes.com/**]

PRACTICING ETHICS — The Moral Decline of White Working-Class America?

What forces have caused the growing income and wealth gaps in America? Libertarian scholar Charles Murray in his controversial book, *Coming Apart: The State of White America, 1960–2010* looks at the blue-collar, white working class for some answers. He points to declining moral values in that group as a crucial factor in American inequality and reduced mobility. He provides evidence of an alarming fall in white working-class social capital (neighborliness and civic engagement) prompted by decreasing industry, community, religion, and marriage. Murray does not ignore similar problems in the black working class, but his focus is on white people.

Questions

1. Do you agree with Murray that the erosion of traditional middle-class morals/values helps explain inequality in contemporary America?

2. What other forces might have contributed to increasing inequality in American life?

3. Based on your personal sense of fairness, is a large and growing gap in income and wealth in America an ethical wrong? Explain.

Sources: Charles Murray, *Coming Apart: The State of White America, 1960–2010* (New York: Crown Forum, 2012); and Thomas B. Edsall, "What to Do about 'Coming Apart'," *The New York Times,* February 12, 2012 [http://campaignstops.blogs.nytimes.com/].

Community

Thus we see that American capitalism, despite its extraordinary success, is criticized for problems of poverty, inequality, and unfairness, among others. Perhaps the more interesting concern, however, is mounting evidence that our lives are increasingly solitary, distant, alone, and unshared. The market is driven by and rewards individual achievement. Could that struggle for success be depriving us of the full satisfaction of our humanity? A 2006 study found that even trivial exposure to money changes our goals and behaviors such that our sense of self-sufficiency is elevated and our social interests may decline,[132] whereas a 2008 study showed that how people spend their money may be just as important in happiness as how much money they have. Specifically, the study demonstrated that spending money on others rather than on oneself produced greater levels of happiness.[133]

> Spending money on others rather than on oneself produced greater levels of happiness.

Whether a product of capitalist impulses or not, we do have evidence of declining social connections. Only 30 percent of Americans, according to a 2008 study, report a close confidant at work, down from nearly 50 percent in 1985, and workers in many other nations are much more likely to have close friends at work than are Americans. American workers report inviting 32 percent of their "close" colleagues to their homes, while Polish and Indian workers report inviting more than double that percentage.[134] More worrisome perhaps are findings from a 2011 study where Americans reported an average of only two discussion confidants in their lives, down from a mean of three in 1985. That decline, however, could reflect a shrinking in those whom we classify as suitable for an important discussion rather than an actual reduction in our number of close friends.[135]

> Americans reported only two discussion confidants in their lives.

Declining Social Capital?

In his now famous book, *Bowling Alone,* Robert Putnam meticulously documented the decline of what he labeled social capital, the community and commitment bonds that seem to emerge in a culture where people regularly interact with one another.[136] Putnam's book explains that virtually every measure of social interaction, from voting to picnics to playing cards, to church attendance, to membership in social clubs fell significantly from roughly 1975 to 2000. The most vivid example was a decline of 40 percent in league bowling from 1980 to 2000 although the total number of bowlers increased by about 10 percent; thus the notion of "bowling alone." Even the tradition of inviting others to visit one's home as dinner guests fell by about 40 percent. Criticism of Putnam's thesis was abundant with many saying he focused too much on "older" activities such as social clubs and not enough on emerging interests such as Internet groups.[137]

Putnam's more recent research has produced no convincing evidence of rising community engagement among adults, but he acknowledges they are reaching one another in different ways from the past, principally through social media.[138] In contrast to Putnam's discouraging assessment, Americans say they trust their neighbors (76 percent) and talk with them frequently (44 percent); these self-reported measures of neighborliness have been rising recently.[139]

An Opportunity Gap and Declining Community?

Putnam has for the last few years been collecting data about the growing gap in opportunities among socioeconomic classes of American children. In decades past, parents with high school educations invested money and time in their children at much the same level as college-graduate parents, but today a large gap has grown in both resources, favoring, of course, the more affluent families. Specifically, the more comfortable class of children receive about one hour per day more time with their parents than do less advantaged children. A generation ago, Putnam says, participation in extracurricular activities varied little by social class, but today participation has risen sharply for affluent children while falling sharply among those less well-off. One of the results of this opportunity divide is that children of the well-off express increasing trust in those around them while that trust has "collapsed" among the less well-off children.[140]

Likewise, young products of affluent America have steadily deepened their community engagement (going to church more, better connecting to their parents, volunteering) while the less affluent young whites have withdrawn or never undertaken that engagement. That disparity in involvement is not present among young blacks, but the overall engagement gap between whites and blacks is wide.[141]

Questions

1. Is Putnam correct about (a) declining social capital in America and (b) a growing opportunity gap between affluent and less well-off children? Explain.

2. American Dan Lawton commenting on his first trip to Africa:

   In Ghana, I have danced, eaten, and spoken with more strangers in six weeks than I would have in America in six years, And this paradox—that despite its material wealth and technological might America is so standoffish and lonely—has been burning a hole in my head.[142]

a. Do you agree that Americans are "standoffish and lonely"?

b. If so, do you have any explanation for that condition?

PRACTICING ETHICS   Technology and Loneliness

Since publishing *Bowling Alone*, Robert Putnam has said we need to develop new kinds of connections when old ones die. Electronic links often are considered part of the problem, but he believes they could also be part of the solution. Indeed, a 2008 survey of American adults found 60 percent saying that new technologies had not affected the closeness of their families and a 2011 study found that self-reported feelings of empathy were higher among college students the more time they spent on Facebook. On the other hand, a 2009 Pew report found that social networking users are 26 percent less likely than others to turn to their neighbors for companionship. MIT professor Sherry Turkle says we have sacrificed conversation for "mere connection":

> We've become accustomed to a new way of being "along together." Technology-enabled, we are able to be with one another, and also elsewhere, connected to wherever we want to be. We want to customize our lives. We want to move in and out of where we are because the thing we value most is control over where we focus our attention."[143]

Questions

1. In your view, is Turkle correct? Explain.

2. How might our ethical standards and performances be affected by excessive reliance on social technology?

Sources: Charles M. Blow, "Friends, Neighbors and Facebook," *The New York Times*, June 11, 2010 [http://www.nytimes.com]; Shirley S. Wang, "Could Those Hours Online Be Making Kids Nicer?" *The Wall Street Journal,* August 16, 2011, p. D1; and Donna St. George, "Internet, Cell Phones May Strengthen Family Unit, Study Finds," **washingtonpost.com**, October 20, 2008, p. A07.

Too Much Capitalism? Or Too Little?

Has America placed too much faith in the market and too little in government? Is the alleged decline in community in some sense a product of capitalism itself? Are poverty, inequality, crime, and the Wall Street collapse inevitable by-products of a "selfish, greedy" market? Even some conservatives are concerned:

> "What I'm concerned about is the idolatry of the market," says conservative intellectual William Bennett, a former education secretary and author of *The Book of Virtues*. He worries particularly that the market for popular music and movies with sexual or violent content has a corrosive effect. "Unbridled capitalism . . . may not be a problem for production and for expansion of the economic pie, but it's a problem for human beings. It's a problem for . . . the realm of values and human relationships."[144]

> "Capitalism is more efficient . . . But it is not more fair."

The dilemma, in brief, was expressed by a 20-year-old Cuban student and communist organizer: "Capitalism is more efficient . . . But it is not more fair."[145]

Can robust capitalism be sustained if it produces not just efficiency and growth but also extreme income and wealth gaps, corruption, and injustice? Can we tolerate capitalism's collapses and injustices? Can we improve the market through judicious regulation? Or must we look for new answers?

A "Remix" Needed?

Clearly, we have had at least a free market detour in the United States. The government has stepped in to bail out a failing economy. Does that shift to the left signal the sharp decline of markets? Almost certainly not. According to a 2013 nationwide Marist Poll, 55 percent of Americans favor free enterprise and fear expanded government regulation of business.[146] Perhaps some form of "re-mix" is needed. Journalist Anatole Kaletsky reminds us that capitalism is adaptive, reinventing itself through crises.[147] Scholar Robert Skidelsky, in reviewing Kaletsky's 2010 book, *Capitalism 4.0: The Birth of a New Economy,*[148] summarized Kaletsky's view of the evolution of capitalism:

> Laissez-faire Capitalism 1.0, inspired by Adam Smith, lasted from the Napoleonic wars to the First World War, the Russian Revolution and the mass unemployment of the 1930s. Then came the Capitalism 2.0 of John Maynard Keynes, Franklin D. Roosevelt's New Deal and the welfare state, which eventually provoked Capitalism 3.0 in the 1970s in reaction to rising inflation. Capitalism 3.0, a modified return to laissez-faire, has just self-destructed, leaving the door open to Capitalism 4.0.[149]

Kaletsky thinks his Capitalism 4.0 should involve smaller, smarter governments, less reliance on theory, and greater recognition of the need for pragmatic change.

A New World Consensus?

Notwithstanding Kaletsky's hope for a more rational market–government balance, other thinkers say the world is already reshaping itself into two conflicting forms of capitalism.

In his book *The End of the Free Market,*[150] political scientist Ian Bremmer says capitalism may have established its claim as the best economic system, but the world is still in conflict over whether Western capitalism is the best political-social-economic system. As *New York Times* columnist David Brooks explained in reviewing Bremmer's work, the world now seems to be divided into a pair of general camps. *Democratic capitalism* in the United States, Japan, Denmark, and other nations favors business to create wealth and government to regulate as needed. *State capitalism* in countries such as China, Russia, and Saudi Arabia employ the market to build wealth, which, in turn, is controlled and distributed by the state for its political purposes. As we saw in our discussion above of China and Russia, state capitalism varies in its practices across nations, but private enterprise, state-owned corporations, and sovereign wealth funds (huge aggregations of capital controlled by the government for investment purposes) all may play a role. The two systems trade with each other for mutual advantage but are economic and political rivals.[151]

We do not know what comes next, of course, but Oxford University professor Timothy Garton Ash sees the likelihood, in the short term at least, of a fractured, somewhat conflicted world:

> The result? Not a uni-polar world, converging on a single model of liberal democratic capitalism, but a no-polar world, diverging toward many different national versions of often illiberal capitalism. Not a new world order but a new world disorder. . . .[152]

Individualism Up, Morality Down?

Scholars now have access to a giant Google database of 5.2 million books published between 1500 and 2008. They can type in a word and see how frequently it has been used over the years. One study looking at 1960 to 2008 found individualistic words (e.g., self, standout, unique) were used more frequently over those 48 years whereas communal words (e.g., collective, common good, band together) declined in use. Another study found that general moral terms (e.g., virtue, decency, conscience) and words associated with moral excellence (e.g., honesty, patience, compassion) receded in use over the course of the 20th century.

Questions

1. Do you see a link between increasing attention to individualism and declining attention to morality? Explain.
2. Do you think government can or should do anything about these changing social conditions and the link between them, if it does exist? Explain.

Source: David Brooks, "What Our Words Tell Us," *The New York Times,* May 20, 2013 [**http://www.nytimes.com/**].

Questions—Part Five

1. As you see it, is Western democratic capitalism or state capitalism more likely to prevail over the long term? Explain.
2. Roger Cohen, writing in *The New York Times*, made the interesting point that India, as of 2010, had more cell phones than toilets; 563.7 million people connected to modern communication, but only 366 million had access to modern sanitation. He says this imbalance could be seen as "skewed development" favoring private goods over public necessities. In India and in America, he sees a kind of schizophrenia where we are increasingly autonomous, wanting to be left alone; our technology connecting us, allowing us to feel no need for government until a crisis, like the recent meltdown, arrives. Then many desperately plead for the government to save us.[153]
   a. Are we giving too much attention to private needs and too little, via government and taxes, to public goods? Explain.
   b. Can we have an autonomous, free market culture, substantially contemptuous of government, and still maintain a stable, healthy, and fair national and global community? Explain.
3. a. Is America deliberately seeking to convert the balance of the globe to American, free market, democratic values?
   b. Would all nations be well served if they adopted American, free market, democratic values? Explain.
4. In what ways might American culture be viewed as offensive and threatening to Muslims and others around the globe?

Internet Exercise

The Global Policy Forum provides a broad overview of the globalization movement. Go to the Forum's "Globalization of Law" page [**http://www.globalpolicy.org/globalization/globalization-of-law.html**]. Explain how globalization is changing international legal systems.

Chapter Questions

1. The gravestone of the late baseball great Jackie Robinson is inscribed with this advice: "A life is not important except in the impact it has on other lives." Will your life be meaningful only if you contribute to the well-being of others? Explain.

2. Commenting in *Newsweek,* economist Robert Samuelson said, "The . . . pervasive problem of capitalist economies is that almost no one fully trusts capitalists."[154]
   a. Do you agree? Why?
   b. Do you think free market capitalism is the best economic system? Explain.
   c. Do you think that multinational companies have more power than national governments? Explain.

3. a. In your mature years, do you expect to be as wealthy as your parents, or more so? Explain.
   b. Do you think you deserve to be as wealthy as your parents, or more so, or less so? Explain.

4. According to a 2011 Congressional Budget Office study, the share of government benefits going to the bottom fifth of Americans has declined from 54 percent in 1979 to 36 percent in 2007.[155] According to the conservative Tax Foundation, in 2010, 60 percent of Americans were receiving more in government benefits than they paid in taxes.[156] (Of course, many of those people paid higher taxes in subsequent years.)
   a. Other than aid to those who are poor, disabled and/or aged, what government benefit programs are you aware of that provide support to working and middle-class Americans?
   b. Do you think it is "fair" that more than half of Americans receive more in government benefits than they pay in taxes? Explain.

5. a. Noted economist Lester Thurow argued that the economic demands of the market are destroying the traditional two-parent, nuclear family. Explain his argument.
   b. Child development authority Benjamin Spock likewise blamed capitalism for the "destruction of the American family," but his reasoning differed from Thurow's:

   > The overriding problem is excessive competition and our glorification of it. It may contribute to our rapid technological advancement, but it has done so at a great price. We are taught to be rugged individualists, and we are obsessed with getting ahead. The family gets lost in this intense struggle. In a healthy society, family should come first, community second, and our outside jobs third. In this country, it is the other way around.[157]

   Comment.
   c. If Spock was correct, how did we reach this condition?

6. Scholar Donna Wood points to America's poor showing in Gallup's emotional well-being polls of 150 countries that find the United States 68th in sadness, 75th in anger,

89th in worry, and 145th in stress (150th being the lowest ranking). Wood also points to America's poor showing in health and other measures of social well-being and asks why America scores so poorly on these measures.[158] What do you think?

7. We often read that many college professors actively criticize capitalism and support welfare state principles.

   a. Has that been your experience? Explain.

   b. If that assessment is accurate, how do you account for the leftist inclinations among intellectuals?

8. Should we reduce the government's presence throughout our lives? Consider a couple of possibilities.

   a. Facing severe financial problems, the state of Nevada was thinking of expanding legal prostitution from its current rural areas to the gambling centers, Las Vegas and Reno. Do you think legal prostitution managed by the market but subject to reasonable health and safety regulation would be a good policy for your state or any state? Explain.

   b. The bitter, ongoing debate about same-sex marriage raises the question of whether the state's role in marriage should be eliminated. Explain why the state should or should not be involved in regulating marriage. See "Why Do We Need the State's Permission to Get Married Anyway?" *The Wall Street Journal,* January 14, 2010 [**http://blogs.wsj.com/2010/01/14/why-do-we-need-to-ask-the-state-for-permission -to-get-married-anyway/**].

9. If we are fundamentally selfish, must we embrace capitalism as the most accurate and, therefore, most efficient expression of human nature? Explain.

10. About 57 percent of college students are female. In 2010, 36 percent of women in their late 20s had earned a bachelor's degree, as compared with about 27.8 percent of males of the same age.[159] How do you explain those gaps and what, if anything, do they portend for the future of America?

11. *New York Times* columnist Nicholas Kristof wrote what he called a "blunt" and "politically incorrect truth" about global poverty:

    > It's that if the poorest families spent as much money educating their children as they do on wine, cigarettes and prostitutes, their children's children's prospects would be transformed.[160]

    He told about one Congolese family that is eight months behind on its $6 per month rent and is unable to pay for mosquito netting ($6 each) or the $2.50 per month school tuition for each of their three school-age children. But the parents do spend $10 per month on cell phone expenses, and the father does drink several times weekly at a cost of about $1 per night.[161]

    a. What solutions would you suggest to protect children from the ill-advised financial choices of their fathers and mothers?

    b. Do you think poor parental choices are a significant feature of child suffering in the United States? Explain.

    c. Do you think reduced government in the United States would likely lead to increased personal responsibility? Explain.

12. Commentator Thomas Friedman reflects on the Islamic terrorists' hatred for America:

> Their constant refrain is that America is a country with wealth and power but "no values." The Islamic terrorists think our wealth and power is unrelated to anything in the soul of this country. . . . Of course, what this view of America completely misses is that American power and wealth flow directly from a deep spiritual source—a spirit of respect for the individual, a spirit of tolerance for differences of faith or politics, a respect for freedom of thought as the necessary foundation for all creativity, and a spirit of unity that encompasses all kinds of differences. Only a society with a deep spiritual energy, that welcomes immigrants and worships freedom, could constantly renew itself and its sources of power and wealth.[162]

    a. Do you agree that the "spiritual source" Friedman cites is the foundation for American success? Explain.

    b. Is America without a meaningful "soul"? Explain.

13. *a.* Make the argument that America's free market economy is better for children than the welfare state approach in northern Europe.

    b. Do you think that argument is correct? That is, do you think children are better off in America's free market or in northern Europe's welfare state? Explain.

14. The intellectual Adolph Berle once said, "A day may come when national glory and prestige, perhaps even national safety, are best established by a country's being the most beautiful, the best socially organized, or culturally the most advanced in the world."[163]

    a. Is government intervention necessary to achieving Berle's goal? Explain.

    b. If faced with a choice, would most Americans opt for Berle's model or for a nation preeminent in consumer goods, sports, and general comfort? Explain.

15. Marketing research firm GfK Roper and policy advisor Simon Anholt annually rank the 50 most admired nations globally. The United States has ranked at the top of that list in recent years. Their research shows that we can think of countries as being either primarily useful (competent, efficient, smart) or primarily decorative (stylish, sexy, attractive) or both.[164]

    a. List some nations that you take to be primarily useful and some that you believe to be primarily decorative. Which do you prefer?

    b. Do you regard the United States as primarily useful or primarily decorative or both? Explain.

16. Benjamin Barber, writing in *The Atlantic,* saw two possible political futures, which he labeled the "forces of Jihad" and the "forces of McWorld":

> The first is a retribalization of large swaths of humankind by war and bloodshed . . . culture is pitted against culture, people against people, tribe against tribe—a Jihad in the name of a hundred narrowly conceived faiths against every kind of interdependence. . . . The second is being borne in on us by the onrush of economic and ecological forces that demand integration and uniformity and that mesmerize the world with fast music, fast computers, and fast food—with MTV, Macintosh, and McDonald's pressing nations into one commercially homogeneous global network: One McWorld tied together by technology, ecology, communications, and commerce.[165]

    a. Does either of these scenarios make sense to you? Explain.

    b. Which would you prefer? Explain.

17. Critics argue that socialism requires a uniformity, a "sameness" that would destroy the individuality Americans prize.
    a. Are Americans notably independent and individualistic? Explain.
    b. Explore the argument that socialism would actually enhance meaningful individualism.

18. Hilda Scott wrote a book to which she affixed the provocative title *Does Socialism Liberate Women?*
    a. Answer her question. Explain.
    b. Are minority oppression and oppression of women inevitable by-products of capitalism? Explain.

19. In Wisconsin, members of the Old Order Amish religion declined to formally educate their children beyond the eighth grade. The U.S. Supreme Court held that their First Amendment right to freedom of religion was violated by the Wisconsin compulsory education statute, which required school attendance until the age of 16. Chief Justice Burger explained:

    > They object to the high school, and higher education generally, because the values they teach are in marked variance with Amish values and the Amish way of life; they view secondary school education as an impermissible exposure of their children to a "worldly" influence in conflict with their beliefs. The high school tends to emphasize intellectual and scientific accomplishments, self-distinction, competitiveness, worldly success, and social life with other students. Amish society emphasizes informal learning-through-doing; a life of "goodness," rather than a life of intellect; wisdom, rather than technical knowledge; community welfare, rather than competition; and separation from, rather than integration with, contemporary worldly society.[166]

    a. Have the Amish taken the course we should all follow? Explain.
    b. Could we do so? Explain.

20. Distinguished economist Gary Becker argued for a free market approach to America's immigration difficulties:

    > In a market economy, the way to deal with excess demand for a product or service is to raise the price. This reduces the demand and stimulates the supply. I suggest that the United States adopt a similar approach to help solve its immigration problems. Under my proposal, anyone willing to pay a specified price could enter the United States immediately.[167]

    Comment.

21. Management scholars Rabindra Kanungo and Jay Conger remark that "'Altruism' is a word rarely associated with the world of business," but they ask, "Does altruism have a place in our business lives? And does it make good economic sense?"[168] Answer their questions.

Notes

1. Francis Fukuyama, "Are We at the End of History?" *Fortune,* January 15, 1990, p. 75.
2. Kathy Ruffing and Joel Friedman, "Economic Downturn and Legacy of Bush Policies Continue to Drive Large Deficits," *Center on Budget and Policy Priorities*, February 28, 2013 [**http://www.cbpp.org/cms/?fa=view&id=3849**].

3. "The Stimulus Tracker," *CNNMoney* [**http://money.cnn.com/news/specials/storysupplement /stimulus-tracker/**].

4. David Wessel, "Decoding New Rules for Banks," *The Wall Street Journal,* October 17, 2012 [**http://online.wsj.com/**].

5. Robert J. Samuelson, "Can Globalization Survive 2013?" *The Washington Post,* December 30, 2012 [**http://articles.washingtonpost.com/**].

6. Jessica Silver-Greenberg, "JPMorgan's Board Uses a Pay Cut as a Message," *The New York Times Dealbook,* January 16, 2013 [**http://dealbook.nytimes.com/**].

7. Richard Smallteacher, "Daily CEO Pay Now Exceeds U.S. Workers Annual Salary," *Corp-Watch,* June 30, 2013 [**http://www.corpwatch.org/**].

8. Ibid.

9. Randall S. Thomas, "Dodd-Frank's Say on Pay: Will It Lead to a Greater Role for Shareholders in Corporate Governance?" *The Legal Workshop,* April 16, 2013 [**http://legalworkshop .org/**].

10. Thomas M. Hoenig, "Too Big to Succeed," *The New York Times,* December 1, 2010 [**http://www.nytimes.com/**].

11. Richard Doak, "Can Capitalism Survive? Sorry, It Already Died," *Des Moines Register,* June 21, 2009, p. 10P.

12. Frank Newport, "Americans Unsure If Best Times for U.S. Are Past or to Come," *Gallup Poll,* January 2, 2013 [**http://www.gallup.com/**].

13. Michael Corkery, "Capitalism, Love and Mr. Moore," Deal Journal, *The Wall Street Journal,* September 23, 2009, p. C3.

14. Ibid.

15. Benjamin R. Barber, *Consumed: How Markets Corrupt Children, Infantilize Adults, and Swallow Citizens Whole* (New York: W.W. Norton & Company, 2007).

16. Rod Dreher, "Big Business Can Be as Dangerous a Threat as Big Government," *The Waterloo/ Cedar Falls Courier,* July 23, 2007, p. A6.

17. Ibid.

18. Robert J. Samuelson, "Is America in Decline?" *The Washington Post,* January 27, 2013 [**http://www.washingtonpost.com/**].

19. Ibid.

20. David Brooks, "The Commercial Republic," *The New York Times,* March 17, 2009 [**http: //www.nytimes.com/**].

21. Ibid.

22. Scott Peterson, "Iran's Ahmadinejad: Capitalism Is Dead," *The Christian Science Monitor,* November 9, 2009 [**http://www.csmonitor.com/**].

23. Robert Skidelsky, "Life After Capitalism," *Project Syndicate,* January 19, 2011 [**http://www .skidelskyr.com/site/article/life-after-capitalism/**].

24. "Zogby Poll: *Atlas Shrugged* by Ayn Rand Read by 8.1 Percent," *PRWeb,* October 17, 2007 [**http://www.prweb.com/releases/1969/12/prweb561836.htm?tag=poll**].

25. Stephen Moore, "*Atlas Shrugged:* From Fiction to Fact in 52 Years," *The Wall Street Journal,* January 9, 2009, p. W11.

26. Sandy Banks, "When Money Talks to Kids," *latimes.com,* April 17, 2010 [**http://www .latimes.com/**].

27. See "Should Drivers Who Pay More Get a Faster Lane?" *Parade,* October 19, 2008, p. 22.

28. "Nevada Candidate: Let People Pay to Legally Go 90 MPH," *The Des Moines Register,* September 5, 2010, p. 2A.

29. Editorial, "Tag—You're Illegal," *Los Angeles Times,* October 28, 2006 [**http://www.latimes.com/news/opinion/la-ed-tag28oct28,0,59791.story?coll=la=opinion-leftrail**].

30. Laura Meckler, "Kidney Shortage Inspires a Radical Idea: Organ Sales," *The Wall Street Journal,* November 13, 2007, p. A1.

31. Stephanie Coontz, "Taking Marriage Private," *The New York Times,* November 26, 2006 [**http://www.nytimes.com/2007/11/26/opinion/26coontz.html**].

32. Peter Diamandis, "Space: The Final Frontier of Profit?" *The Wall Street Journal,* February 13–14, 2010, p. W3.

33. Brad Plumer, "More States Privatizing Their Infrastructure. Are They Making a Mistake?" *The Washington Post,* March 31, 2012 [**http://www.washingtonpost.com**].

34. Emily Thornton, "Roads to Riches," *BusinessWeek,* May 7, 2007, p. 50.

35. Thornton, "Roads to Riches," p. 50.

36. Susan Saulny, "Long a Driver's Curse, Chicago Parking Gets Worse," *The New York Times,* May 30, 2009 [**http://www.nytimes.com/**].

37. Associated Press, "Chicago Parking Meters Will Be Most Expensive in U.S.," *Waterloo/Cedar Falls Courier,* December 27, 2012, p. A4.

38. Ibid.

39. Charles Mahtesian, "Revenue in the Rough," *Governing,* October 1997, pp. 42–44.

40. Editorial, "City-Owned Golf Courses Cannot Be Sacred Cows," *Waterloo/Cedar Falls Courier,* July 13, 2003, p. C7.

41. Charles Murray, "Why Charter Schools Fail the Test," *The New York Times,* May 5, 2010 [**http://www.nytimes.com**].

42. Sam Dillon, "Incentives for Advanced Work Let Pupils and Teachers Cash In," *The New York Times,* October 2, 2011 [**http://www.nytimes.com/**].

43. Leslie Wayne, "Politics and the Financial Crisis Slow the Drive to Privatize," *The New York Times,* June 5, 2009 [**http://www.nytimes.com/**].

44. Leslie Williams Hale, "Poll: State Receives No Bids for Alligator Alley Lease," *naplesnews.com,* May 18, 2009 [**http://www.naplesnews.com/**].

45. Richard A. Oppel, Jr., "Private Prisons Found to Offer Little in Savings," *The New York Times,* May 18, 2011 [**http://www.nytimes.com/**].

46. Keith Bradsher, "Investors Seek Asian Options to Costly China," *The New York Times,* June 18, 2008 [**http://www.nytimes.com**].

47. Henry Myers, "His Statues Topple, His Shadow Persists: Marx Can't Be Ignored," *The Wall Street Journal,* November 25, 1991, p. A1.

48. Michael J. Jordan, "After the Berlin Wall, Nostalgia for Communism Creeps Back," *The Christian Science Monitor,* November 8, 2009 [**http://www.csmonitor.com/2009/1109/p11s01-woeu.html**].

49. Elements of this list are drawn from Agnes Heller and Ferenc Feher, "Does Socialism Have a Future?" *Dissent,* Summer 1989, p. 371.

50. Associated Press, "Chavez in China Touts 'New World Order,'" *The Wall Street Journal,* April 8, 2009 [**http://online.wsj.com/article/SB123917904370300585.html**].

51. David Pierson and Don Lee, "World Bank Tells China to Reform State Sector to Ensure Stability," *latimes.com,* February 27, 2012 [**http://www.latimes.com/**].

52. Ibid.

53. Associated Press, "China Figures Show Wide Income Gap," *The New York Times,* January 18, 2013 [**http://www.nytimes.com/**].

54. Ian Johnson, "Wary of Future, Professionals Leave China in Record Numbers," *The New York Times,* October 31, 2012 [**http://www.nytimes.com/**].

55. Michael Kan, "Google CEO: China's Internet Censorship Will Fail in Time," *IDG News Service,* November 4, 2010 [**http://www.computerworld.com/**].

56. Geoffrey A. Fowler, Sky Canaves, and Juliet Ye, "Chinese Seek a Day in Court," *The Wall Street Journal,* July 1, 2008, p. A12.

57. Editorial Board, "The Rule of Law Proves Elusive in China," *The Washington Post,* September 28, 2012 [**http://www.washingtonpost.com/**].

58. Julie Makinen, "China's 'Visit Your Parents' Law Weighs on Many in One-Child Nation," *latimes.com,* July 29, 2013 [**http://www.latimes.com/**].

59. Vivek Wadhwa, "Does China Own the Future—Or Does the U.S.?" *The Washington Post,* December 13, 2012 [**http://www.washingtonpost.com/**].

60. Melanie Stetson Freeman, "In Moscow, Capitalism Now in Full Fashion," *The Christian Science Monitor,* February 21, 2008 [**http://www.csmonitor.com/2008/0221/p13s01-woeu.html**].

61. "GDP Ranking—Gross Domestic Product 2012," *World Bank Data,* 2013 [**http://data .worldbank.org/**].

62. David M. Herszenhorn and Andrew E. Kramer, "Putin Puts Pensions at Risk in $43 Billion Bid to Jolt Economy," *The New York Times,* June 21, 2013 [**http://www.nytimes.com/**].

63. Scott Rose and Olga Tanas, "Russia Scales Down Asset Sales as Medvedev Bemoans Delays," *Bloomberg,* June 27, 2013 [**http://www.bloomberg.com/**].

64. Oliver Bullough, "The Russians Are Shrinking," *The Wall Street Journal,* May 4–5, 2013, p. C3.

65. Ibid.

66. Kathy Lally, "Russia Tries to Improve Life Expectancy with Laws Curbing Drinking, Smoking," *The Washington Post,* February 21, 2013 [**http://articles.washingtonpost.com/**].

67. Andrew E. Kramer, "Russia Seeks Foreign Investment to Fill Budget Gap," *The New York Times,* January 24, 2011 [**http://www.nytimes.com/**].

68. "Russia, Soviet Style," *The New York Times,* June 12, 2012 [**http://www.nytimes.com/**].

69. Editorial Board, "Putin Continues Witch Hunt of Civil Society Groups," *The Washington Post,* May 11, 2013 [**http://www.washingtonpost.com/**].

70. Associated Press, "Irked with Russia, U.S. Gays Target Vodka and Sochi," *The Moscow Times,* July 31, 2013 [**http://www.themoscowtimes.com/**].

71. Will Englund, "In Poll, Russians See Wide Gap between Democratic Ideals and Reality," *The Washington Post,* May 22, 2012 [**http://www.washingtonpost.com/**].

72. Paul Roderick Gregory, "Leading Economist Gives Up on Putin's Russia," *Forbes,* May 30, 2013 [**http://www.forbes.com/**].

73. Central Intelligence Agency, *The World Factbook 2013* [**https://www.cia.gov/library /publications/the-world-factbook/**].

74. Jens Hansegard, "For Paternity Leave, Sweden Asks if Two Months Is Enough," *The Wall Street Journal,* August 1, 2012, p. D1.

75. "The U.S. Continues to Be One of the Least Taxed of the Developed Countries," *Citizens for Tax Justice,* April 8, 2013 [**http://ctj.org/**].

76. "Corporate and Capital Income Taxes 2000–2013," *OECD Tax Database* [**http://www.oecd.org/**].

77. Chris Isidore, "U.S. Corporate Tax Rate: No. 1 in the World," *CNNMoney,* March 27, 2012 [**http://money.cnn.com/**].

78. Robert H. Frank, "What Sweden Can Tell Us about Obamacare," *The New York Times,* June 15, 2013 [**http://www.nytimes.com/**].

79. Anne Jolis, "The Swedish Reform Model, Believe It or Not," *The Wall Street Journal,* May 19–20, 2012, p. A15.

80. Jeffrey Sachs, "The Social Welfare State, Beyond Ideology," *Scientific American* 295, Issue 5 (November 2006), p. 42.

81. Central Intelligence Agency, "Country Comparison: GDP (Purchasing Power Parity)," *The World Factbook 2012* [**https://www.cia.gov/library/publications/the-world-factbook/**].

82. Roger Cohen, "For Europe, A Moment to Ponder," *The New York Times,* March 25, 2007, sec. 4, p. 1.

83. "Unemployment Statistics," *Eurostat,* June 2013 [**http://epp.eurostat.ec.europa.eu/statistics_explained/**].

84. Daniel Bosque Homs, "Spain's 'Lost Generation': Youth Unemployment Hits 57 Percent," *HuffPost World,* May 28, 2013 [**http://www.huffingtonpost.com/**].

85. Alessandra Galloni, "The Nonna State," *The Wall Street Journal,* June 16–17, 2012, p. C1.

86. "Youth Unemployment," *Eurostat,* July 12, 2013 [**http://epp.eurostat.ec.europa.eu/statistics_explained/**].

87. David C. Unger, "Europe's Social Contract, Lying in Pieces," *The New York Times,* June 8, 2013 [**http://www.nytimes.com/**].

88. Don Lee, "Germany Has the Economic Strengths America Once Boasted," *latimes.com,* January 21, 2012 [**http://www.latimes.com/**].

89. Nicholas Sambanis, "Has 'Europe' Failed?" *The New York Times,* August 26, 2012 [**http://www.nytimes.com/**].

90. Associated Press, "Multicultural Society Has Been Failure, Merkel Says," *Des Moines Register,* October 18, 2010, p. 8A.

91. Jeremy Rifkin, "Why the European Dream Is Worth Saving," *SpiegelOnline,* July 28, 2005 [**http://www.spiegel.de/international/0,1518,druck-366940,00.html**].

92. Adrian Karatnycky quoting Soros in "The Merits of the Market, the Perils of 'Market Fundamentalism,'" *The Wall Street Journal,* January 9, 2001, p. A20.

93. Ibid.

94. Joanne Barkan, "Not Yet in Paradise, But . . .," *Dissent,* Spring 1989, pp. 147, 150.

95. Thomas B. Edsall, "Why Can't America Be Sweden?" *The New York Times,* May 29, 2013 [**http://opinionator.blogs.nytimes.com/**].

96. Jim Chairusmi, "Winning with Smaller Pockets," *The Wall Street Journal,* October 18, 2004, p. R2.

97. Karen Kaplan, "Fat Tax in Denmark: Why They Have It; Could It Happen in U.S.?" *latimes.com,* October 3, 2011 [**http://www.latimes.com/**].

98. Michael Shermer, "Life Has Never Been So Good for Our Species," *latimes.com,* April 30, 2010 [**latimes.com/news/opinion/la-oe-shermer-20100430,0,2676540.story**].

99. David Gergen, "Cheer Up, America," *Parade,* April 11, 2010, p. 26.

100. *The Chronicle of Philanthropy,* "Americans Are the Most Generous, Global Poll Finds," *The Christian Science Monitor,* December 21, 2011 [**http://www.csmonitor.com/**].

101. Harold Meyerson, "Workers Face an Economic Power Gap," *The Washington Post,* September 2, 2012 [**http://www.washingtonpost.com/**].

102. Rebecca Trunson, "Eroding Middle Class Falls to 51%, Survey Finds," *latimes.com,* August 23, 2012 [**http://www.latimes.com/**].

103. Mark Trumbull, "Wealth Gap between Young and Old Is Wider Than Ever," *The Christian Science Monitor,* November 7, 2011 [**http://www.csmonitor.com/**].

104. United Nations Development Program, "The Rise of the South: Human Progress in a Diverse World," *2013 Human Development Report* [**http://hdr.undp.org/en/**].

105. Ibid.

106. Ibid.

107. Central Intelligence Agency, "Country Comparison: GDP—Per Capita," *The World Factbook 2013* [**https://www.cia.gov/library/publications/the-world-factbook/rankorder/2004rank .html**].

108. Central Intelligence Agency, "Country Comparison: Life Expectancy at Birth," *The World Factbook 2013* [**https://www.cia.gov/library/publications/the-world-factbook /rankorder/2102rank.html**].

109. Central Intelligence Agency, "Country Comparison: Infant Mortality Rate," *The World Factbook 2013* [**https://www.cia.gov/library/publications/the-world-factbook /rankorder/209/rank.html**].

110. Erica Goode, "U.S. Prison Populations Decline, Reflecting New Approach to Crime," *The New York Times,* July 25, 2013 [**http://www.nytimes.com/**].

111. Timothy Williams, "Violent Crime in U.S. Rises for First Time Since 2006," *The New York Times,* June 3, 2013 [**http://www.nytimes.com/**].

112. Stephanie Simon, "U.S. Spends Big on Education, but Results Lag Many Nations: OECD," *Reuters,* June 25, 2013 [**http://www.reuters.com/**].

113. Wendy Wang, Kim Parker, and Paul Taylor, "Breadwinner Moms," *Pew Research Social and Demographic Trends,* May 29, 2013 [**http://www.pewsocialtrends.org/**].

114. Kay Hymowitz, W. Bradford Wilcox, and Kelleen Kaye, "The New Unmarried Moms," *The Wall Street Journal,* March 15, 2013 [**http://online.wsj.com/**].

115. Ibid.

116. Hope Yen, "80 Percent of U.S. Adults Face Near-Poverty, Unemployment: Survey," *HuffPost Business,* July 28, 2013 [**http://www.huffingtonpost.com/**].

117. Ibid.

118. Paul Buchheit, "Half of Americans Below or Near Poverty Line," *Salon.com,* May 30, 2013 [**http://www.saloncom/**].

119. UNICEF Office of Research, "Child Well-Being in Rich Countries," *Innocenti Report Card 11,* 2013 [**www.unicef-irc.org/publications/pdf/rc11_eng.pdf**].

120. Paul Krugman, "Poverty Is Poison," *The New York Times,* February 18, 2008 [**http://www .nytimes.com/2008/02/18/opinion/18krugman.html?em**].

121. Michelle Conlin and Aaron Bernstein, "Working . . . and Poor," *BusinessWeek Online,* May 31, 2004 [**http://www.businessweek.com/print/magazine/content/04_22/b3885 . . .**].

122. Pascal-Emmanuel Gobry, "The Jobs of the Future Don't Require a College Degree," *Forbes,* May 7, 2013 [**http://www.forbes.com/**].

123. Nicholas D. Kristof, "Equality, a True Soul Food," *The New York Times*, January 1, 2011 [**http://www.nytimes.com**].

124. Nicholas D. Kristof, "Why Let the Rich Hoard All the Toys?" *The New York Times*, October 3, 2012 [**http://www.nytimes.com/**].

125. Paul Wiseman, "Top 1% Took Record Share of 2012 U.S. Income," *The Des Moines Register*, September 11, 2013, p. 3A.

126. Joseph Stiglitz, "The Price of Inequality," *Project Syndicate*, June 5, 2012 [**http://www.project-syndicate.org/**].

127. Edward Luce, "The Crisis of Middle Class America," *FT.com*, July 30, 2010 [**http://www.ft.com/**].

128. Associated Press, "Rich-Poor Gap Found to Grow Around Globe," *The Des Moines Register*, October 22, 2008, p. 4A.

129. Lydia DePillis, "Congrats, CEOs! You're Making 273 Times the Pay of the Average Worker," *The Washington Post*, June 26, 2013 [**http://www.washingtonpost.com/**].

130. Svea Herbst-Bayliss, "John Paulson's $5 Billion Payout Shocks, Raise (sic) Questions," *Reuters*, January 28, 2011 [**http://www.huffingtonpost.com/**].

131. Chicago Public Schools, "Stats and Facts," 2013 [**http://www.cps.edu/about_cps/at-a-glance/pages/stats_and_facts.aspx**].

132. Kathleen Vohs, Nicole L. Mead, and Miranda R. Goode, "The Psychological Consequences of Money," *Science* 314, no. 5802 (November 17, 2006), p. 1154.

133. Elizabeth W. Dunn, Lara B. Aknin, Michael I. Norton, "Spending Money on Others Promotes Happiness," *Science* 319, no. 5870 (March 21, 2008), p. 1687.

134. "Do Co-Workers Engage or Estrange after Hours," University of Michigan [**http://www.bus.umich.edu/NewsRoom/ArticleDisplay.asp?news_id=11931**].

135. Matthew E. Brashears, "Small Networks and High Isolation? A Reexamination of American Discussion Networks," *Social Networks* 33, no. 4 (October 2011), p. 331.

136. Robert Putnam, *Bowling Alone* (New York: Simon& Schuster, 2000).

137. For a critique of Putnam's declining social capital research, see Garry Wills, "Putnam's America," *The American Prospect*, November 30, 2002 [**http://www.prospect.org/cs/articles?article=putnams_america**].

138. Thomas H. Sander and Robert D. Putnam, "Still Bowling Alone? The Post-9/11 Split," 21 *Journal of Democracy* 11, no. 1 (January 2010), p. 9.

139. Sharon Jayson, "Americans Mostly Trust, Help Neighbors," *USA Today*, December 12, 2012, p. 3A.

140. David Gergen, Charles Murray, and Robert D. Putnam, "Are We Really Coming Apart?" *Aspen Ideas Festival 2012* [**http://www.aspenideas.org/session/are-we-really-coming-apart#**].

141. Sander and Putnam, "Still Bowling Alone?" 2010.

142. Dan Lawton, "In Ghana, No One Is a Stranger for Long," *The Christian Science Monitor*, November 9, 2009 [**http://www.csmonitor.com/2009/1109/p18s01-hfes.html**].

143. Sherry Turkle, "The Flight from Conversation," *The New York Times*, April 21, 2012 [**http://www.nytimes.com/**].

144. David Wessel and John Harwood, "Capitalism Is Giddy with Triumph; Is It Possible to Overdo It?" *The Wall Street Journal*, May 14, 1998, p. A1.

145. Associated Press, "A Threat to Castro," *The Des Moines Register*, August 30, 1994, p. 8A.

146. Mark Tapscott, "Majority of Millenials Favor Free Enterprise, Say More Regulation Will Harm Economy, Marist Poll Finds," *San Francisco Examiner,* August 16, 2013 [**http://www .sfexaminer.com/**].

147. Anatole Kaletsky, "Capitalism 4.0," *OECD Observer,* no. 279 (May 2010) [**http://www .oecdobserver.org/**].

148. Anatole Kaletsky, *Capitalism 4.0: The Birth of a New Economy* (New York: Public Affairs/ Perseus, 2010).

149. Robert Skidelsky, "For a New World, New Economics," *New Statesman,* August 30, 2010 [**http://www.newstatesman.com/**].

150. Ian Bremmer, *The End of the Free Market* (New York: Portfolio/Penguin, 2010).

151. David Brooks, "The Larger Struggle," *The New York Times,* June 14, 2010 [**http://www .nytimes.com/**].

152. Timothy Garton Ash, "A New World Disorder," *latimes.com,* January 28, 2011 [**latimes.com /news/opinion/**].

153. Roger Cohen, "Toilets and Cellphones," *The New York Times,* May 24, 2010 [**http://www .nytimes.com/**].

154. Robert Samuelson, "Economics Made Easy," *Newsweek,* November 27, 1989, p. 64.

155. Binyamin Appelbaum and Robert Gebeloff, "Even Critics of Safety Net Increasingly Depend on It," *The New York Times,* February 11, 2012 [**http://www.nytimes.com/**].

156. Brad Plumer, "Who Receives Government Benefits, in Six Charts," *The Washington Post,* September 18, 2012 [**http://www.washingtonpost.com/**].

157. Carla McClain, "Dr. Spock: Restore the Family," *The Des Moines Register,* November 7, 1993, p. 3E.

158. Donna Wood, "Don't Give Up on Chance at Happiness," *Waterloo/Cedar Falls Courier,* October 24, 2010, p. F1.

159. David Wessel and Stephanie Banchero, "Education Slowdown Threatens U.S.," *The Wall Street Journal,* April 26, 2012, p. A1.

160. Nicholas D. Kristof, "Moonshine or the Kids?" *The New York Times,* May 22, 2010 [**http://www.nytimes.com/**].

161. Ibid.

162. Thomas L. Friedman, "Foreign Affairs; Eastern Middle School," *The New York Times,* October 2, 2001. [**http://www.nytimes.com**].

163. Adolph Berle, *Power* (New York: Harcourt Brace Jovanovich, 1969), pp. 258–59.

164. John Nylander, "Sweden 10th 'Most Admired Country Globally,'"*swedishwire.com,* October 18, 2010 [**http://www.swedishwisre.com/nordic/6755-sweden-10th-most-admired -country-globally**].

165. Benjamin Barber, "Jihad v. McWorld," *The Atlantic* 269, no. 3 (March 1992), p. 53.

166. *Wisconsin v. Yoder,* 406 U.S. 205, 210–11 (1972).

167. Gary Becker, "Why Not Let Immigrants Pay for Speedy Entry?" *BusinessWeek,* March 2, 1987, p. 20.

168. Rabindra Kanungo and Jay Conger, "Promoting Altruism as a Corporate Goal," *The Academy of Management Executive* 8, no. 3 (August 1993), p. 37.

CHAPTER TWO

Business Ethics

After completing this chapter, students will be able to:

1. Describe some of the ethics issues associated with America's recent banking and finance crisis.

2. Discuss America's current moral climate.

3. Discuss the leading ethical decision-making theories.

4. Distinguish between teleological and deontological ethical systems.

5. Distinguish utilitarianism and formalism.

6. Describe Kohlberg's theory of moral development.

7. Describe some of the forces that encourage unethical behavior in the workplace.

8. Explain the general purpose of ethics codes in the workplace.

9. Explain the general requirements of the Foreign Corrupt Practices Act.

10. Discuss some of the risks and rewards of whistle-blowing.

Part One—Introduction to Ethics

Can we count on self-regulation (ethics) as a useful means of controlling managerial/corporate behavior? Put another way, can we count on the free market as discussed in Chapter 1, along with managerial and corporate ethics, to guide business conduct such that government regulation (law) can be significantly reduced?

This chapter will examine the ethical climate of business and the role of ethics in business decision making. Our goal here is not to teach morality but to sensitize the reader to the vital role honor plays in building a sound career and a responsible life.

PRACTICING ETHICS   Baseball Bats Encourage Subprime
                                 Loan Approvals

Maggie Hardiman cringed as she heard the salesmen knocking the sides of desks with a baseball bat as they walked through her office. Bang! Bang "'You cut my [expletive] deal!'" she recalls one man yelling at her. "'You can't do that.'" Bang! The bat whacked the top of her desk.[1]

Hardiman was an appraiser for New Century Financial in 2004 and 2005. Her job was to weed out bad mortgage applications. She says most of the applications she reviewed had problems, but if she turned them down, "all hell would break loose" and "her bosses often overruled her and found another appraiser to sign off on it." She says the pressure to approve loans was immense: "The stress in the place was ungodly. It was like selling your soul." Hardiman says she was fired for refusing to approve weak loans.[2]

New Century was the nation's leading specialized subprime mortgage lender in 2006 with $51.6 billion in loans. To achieve that volume, New Century and others often sold subprime mortgages with "teaser" adjustable rates to Americans with poor credit. Then when housing values began to fall and adjustable rates went up, many new homeowners were unable to make their payments. New Century filed for bankruptcy protection in 2007, laid off over 5,000 employees, and admitted it underreported the number of bad loans it had made.[3]

Question

Do you think the pressure to produce—to approve weak loan applications in this instance—that Maggie Hardiman says she faced is routine in American business practice, or was this episode an exception to the norm? Explain.

The Financial Crisis: A Corporate Scandal?

Corporate misconduct has been a staple of the news in this 21st century. The nation's (and the world's) ongoing financial crisis, the most threatening since the Great Depression, appears to have been the product of a variety of forces including inadequate government regulation, dangerously easy credit, overextended borrowers, real estate speculation, greed, and a collapsed housing market (for more, see Chapter 8). The facts may never be fully clear, but the International Monetary Fund has estimated that worldwide losses attributable to the U.S. residential and commercial real estate market collapse at about one trillion dollars or $142 per person in the entire world.[4] The larger financial recession that accompanied the real estate collapse resulted in additional trillions in losses in the United States alone.[5] The portion of those losses attributable to fraudulent and unethical transactions produced, in part, by the kind of pressure that Maggie Hardiman faced will never be known. Of course, no law is broken when lenders merely show poor judgment or borrowers are unable to pay, but the subprime collapse allegedly involved intentionally fraudulent schemes.

Too Big to Jail?

As of this writing in 2013, one of the continuing frustrations of the 2008 financial meltdown and the widespread financial misconduct of recent years is the fact that America's big banks have been largely untouched by *criminal prosecution*. Money laundering, mortgage fraud, foreclosure fraud, big rigging, and more have been discovered, but prosecutions have not followed. In fairness we note that tens of billions of dollars in *settlements* and *civil penalties* have been achieved. For example, in 2013, JPMorgan Chase agreed to pay $13 billion to settle federal civil charges directed to questionable mortgage practices including allegations that the bank had failed to tell investors what it knew of the risks associated with some of its mortgage-backed securities. The settlement is the largest sum a single firm has ever agreed to pay the government, but it amounts to only about one-half of Chase's profits for a year, and the bank says over half of the settlement will be tax deductible. The bank did not admit to a violation of the law, and criminal charges are yet possible.

At this writing, however, criminal action against the big banks has not been broadly achieved. Why? Proving criminal wrongdoing "beyond a reasonable doubt"— and particularly proving the required intent to commit a crime—are daunting burdens. Thus, the government often leaves the wrongdoing to regulators who can pursue civil causes of action with their more modest standard of proof. Bigger policy considerations, however, are also influencing the government's policy. U.S. Attorney General Eric Holder may have recently revealed the reasons behind the federal government's seeming reluctance to act:

> I am concerned that the size of some of these institutions becomes so large that it does become difficult for us to prosecute them when we are hit with indications that if we do prosecute—if we do bring a criminal charge—it will have a negative impact on the national economy, perhaps even the world economy. . . . I think that is a function of the fact that some of these institutions have become too large.[6]

Holder later said he had been misconstrued and that no bank is too big to prosecute. In any case, the government moves very carefully against giants in banking and industry. Indeed, the lesson of Arthur Andersen, the venerable public accounting firm that was put out of business on obstruction of justice charges during the Enron bankruptcy of the early 2000s, is made more sobering by the 28,000 jobs that were lost. Most of those who lost their jobs at Arthur Andersen had nothing to do with the alleged wrongdoing, and the Arthur Andersen conviction was later overturned by the U.S. Supreme Court. Of course, the government can and does pursue individuals engaging in Wall Street fraud. Powerful financiers such as Bernie Madoff, Allen Stanford, and Raj Rajaratnam have been sentenced to long jail terms, and the government has become increasingly aggressive in some areas of prosecution such as insider trading (see Chapter 9). Still, some sense of justice unfulfilled accompanies the continuing economic pain of the financial collapse.

Nonetheless, Wall Street's ethical reputation, if not its criminal record, clearly has been undermined. Nearly 70 percent of Americans say "most" of those on Wall Street would be willing to break the law to make "a lot of money" if they felt they could get away with it.[7] Warren Buffet's long-time investments partner, Charlie Munger, was particularly condemnatory in his assessment of Wall Street: "The whole damn industry lost its moral moorings."[8]

"The whole damn industry lost its moral moorings."

A Conscience at Goldman Sachs?

"It makes me ill how callously people still talk about ripping off clients," mid level Goldman Sachs executive Greg Smith wrote in *The New York Times* as he was resigning from the firm in 2012. Smith's commentary, "Why I Am Leaving Goldman Sachs," claimed that the Goldman Sachs culture had become "toxic," and that the "interests of the client continue to be sidelined in the way the firm operates and thinks about making money." Smith, 33, a Stanford graduate and finalist for a Rhodes scholarship, wrote that he was once proud of Goldman Sachs's culture of teamwork, integrity, humility, and concern for clients, but that spirit, he said, had been lost.

Goldman Sachs says that regular employee feedback contradicts Smith's characterizations. Critics say Smith was angry because he had been denied a promotion and raise prior to his departure. Others simply saw Smith as naïve. One Goldman client told *The New York Times* that the company had traded against its clients for years. "Come on, that is what they do and they are good traders, so I do business with them." And a *Bloomberg* editorial satirized Smith's view that the firm was too concerned about making money:

> If you want to dedicate your life to serving humanity, do not go to work for Goldman Sachs. That's not its function, and it never will be. Go to work for Goldman Sachs if you wish to work hard and get paid more than you deserve even so. . . .

Questions

1. A friend of Smith's characterized his resignation and public condemnation of Goldman Sachs as the "ultimate act of loyalty." What did he mean?

2. *a.* What did Smith mean when he spoke of Goldman Sachs's "culture"?

   b. In seeking a job after graduation, will you be looking for a company whose "culture" matches your values? Explain.

   c. Do you think you would give up the approximately $500,000 per year that Smith reportedly was making because your employer's culture was not consistent with your values? Explain.

3. *a. Should* Goldman Sachs's purpose be service to humanity?

   b. Would that approach work in the marketplace? Explain.

Sources: Susanne Craig and Landon Thomas Jr., "Public Rebuke of Culture at Goldman Opens Debate," *The New York Times*, March 14, 2012 [**http://dealbook.nytimes.com/**]; Editorial, "Yes, Mr. Smith, Goldman Sachs Is All about Making Money: View," *Bloomberg*, March 14, 2012 [**www.bloomberg.com/**]; Greg Smith, "Why I Am Leaving Goldman Sachs," *The New York Times*, March 14, 2012 [**www.nytimes.com**].

A Pattern of Abuse

Of course, the subprime mortgage crisis was not the first instance of morally unhinged corporate conduct. We give lengthier attention to corporate crime later in the chapter, but for now we should put the subprime scandal in context by remembering some of the most prominent corporate and white-collar missteps of recent years. The subprime scandal is reminiscent of the savings and loan crisis of the 1980s when $150 billion evaporated, in part because of criminal behavior. The corporate greed of the Enron era played out on worldwide televisions as some of the great titans of American commerce shuffled off to prison. Tyco Chief Executive Officer Dennis Kozlowski is infamous for his $2 million birthday bash for his wife on Sardinia and his $6,000 shower curtain. Kozlowski, currently serving up

His $6,000 shower curtain.

to 25 years in prison on charges of looting millions from Tyco, reportedly begged in 2012 for parole but was denied.[9] Most breathtaking was Bernard Madoff's colossal Ponzi scheme that stole as much as $65 billion (in paper gains) before Madoff was caught and sent to prison in 2009 on a sentence of 150 years. [For a comprehensive archive of the Enron story, see **http://archive.wn.com/2007/12/23/1400/enronfiles**]

Of course, we should not condemn the American business community based on the misconduct of some. The problems are serious, but former General Electric CEO Jack Welch and his wife, Suzy, remind us that the business community is the source of much of America's greatness:

> Business is a huge source of vitality in the world and a noble enterprise. Thriving, decent companies are everywhere, and they should be celebrated. They create jobs and opportunities, provide revenue for government, and are the foundation of a free and democratic society. . . .[10]

Ethics Survey

We can see that executive wrongdoing has been a significant problem in recent years, but what about questionable employee behavior? Should some commonplace worker practices be considered unethical? The Ethics Officer Association and the Ethical Leadership Group sampled a cross section of workers at large companies nationwide. How would you respond?

1. "Is it wrong to use company e-mail for personal reasons?"
2. "Is it wrong to play computer games on office equipment during the workday?"
3. "Is it OK to take a $100 holiday food basket?"
4. "Due to on-the-job pressure, have you ever abused or lied about sick days?"

Source: "The Wall Street Journal Workplace-Ethics Quiz," *The Wall Street Journal,* October 21, 1999, p. B1.

America's Moral Climate

Perhaps more than ever, Americans are questioning the nation's moral health. Spectacular corporate corruption as noted above, steroid use by professional athletes, an economy seemingly permanently tilted toward the rich, government officials paying more attention to reelection than to the general welfare, sexual abuse of children by clerics and teachers, and so on cause us to question our decency as a society. Gallup's 2012 poll of American values and beliefs found 73 percent of respondents saying that our moral values are deteriorating and a 2013 NBC poll showed that 43 percent of Americans believe "a decline in moral values" is the number-one source of our problems as a nation (50 percent said that economic pressures are the principal source of our problems as a nation).[11]

Sociologist David Callahan's book *The Cheating Culture: Why More Americans Are Doing Wrong to Get Ahead* argues that we are a society in moral decline.[12] The result of this winner-take-all ethos, Callahan thinks, is a nation increasingly falling into two groups: a "winning class" who cheated their way to the top and an "anxious class" who fear falling behind if they too do not cheat.[13]

Cheating, in one form or another, does seem to be routine in American life. But we find a glimmer of good news in scholar Dan Ariely's 2012 book *The (Honest) Truth about Dishonesty: How We Lie to Everyone—Especially Ourselves*, which shows, through a serious of experiments, that almost all of us cheat, but most of us cheat only a little.[14] We may be further pleased to learn that wealthier people, according to a 2012 study, cheat more than poorer people as revealed in a series of experiments:

> People driving expensive cars were more likely than other motorists to cut off drivers and pedestrians at a four-way-stop intersection in the San Francisco Bay area, . . . researchers observed. Those findings led to a series of experiments that revealed that people of higher socioeconomic status were also more likely to cheat to win a prize, take candy from children and say they would pocket extra change handed to them in error rather than give it back.[15]

The study also found that wealthier people were more likely to condone unethical conduct and to value greed. We should note, however, that the study has been criticized for alleged methodological problems.[16]

Do you think Callahan is correct: Is America in moral decline? Or are we basically good people who tend to cheat only a little, as Ariely found? [For the Josephson Institute of Ethics, see **http://www.josephsoninstitute.org**]

Sex or Cell Phone?

Cell phone practices may offer some insights about what we value most in life. Consider these recent study results:

- A 2013 survey found more than twice as many Americans were willing to give up sex for a week as to give up their cell phones. Men ages 18 to 34 were least willing to give up sex; five times less likely than women of the same age. The latter favored their cell phones.[17]

- Twelve percent of U.S. mothers between the ages of 18 and 35 ("Millennial moms") admit to having used their cell phones while having sex.[18]

- Fourteen percent of cell phone users in 15 nations (15 percent of Americans) admit to having interrupted sex to answer their cell phones. Almost half of those responding worldwide and about one-third of Americans thought their cell phones said as much about them as their cars.[19]

College Students

In perhaps the largest cheating scandal in school history, about 125 Harvard University undergraduates were investigated for collaborating on a 2012 take-home examination in a course on government. More than half of those students were forced to withdraw from school and others were placed on probation.[20] Certainly we should not be surprised about the Harvard episode because cheating appears to be epidemic. Business students seem to be particularly suspect. A large 2006 survey found 56 percent of graduate students in business admitted to cheating at least once in the previous year, the largest percentage of any discipline surveyed.[21] Among nonbusiness graduate students, 47 percent admitted cheating.[22]

Ninety-five percent of 3,000 undergraduate business students polled in 31 universities admit they cheated in high school or college, although only 1 to 2 percent admit having done so "frequently."[23] Academic ethics expert Donald McCabe's surveys find about 75 percent of college students cheating on either a test or a paper at some point, with business majors, fraternity and sorority members, and male students being among those most likely to cheat.[24] The cheating evidence is discouraging, but some evidence of change should also be noted. High school students who said they had cheated on an examination in the past year declined from 59 percent in 2010 to 51 percent in 2012.[25] Harvard MBA students have received a great deal of attention for their voluntary campaign to sign "The MBA Oath," a pledge that Harvard MBAs will act ethically, "serve the greater good," and avoid advancing their own "narrow ambitions" at the expense of others.[26] Now an international oath project pledges higher standards of integrity and service by business leaders. [See **www.theoathproject.org**]

[For a video of *The Daily Show's* treatment of the MBA Oath, see **http://www.thedailyshow .com/watch/wed-august-12-2009/mba-ethics-oath**] This clip contains profanity and violent rhetoric. [For the "Top 10 Cheating Scandals in College History," see **http://collegetimes.us /top-10-cheating-scandals-in-history/**]

Questions

1. If you were to sign an ethics oath as a student, do you think your behavior as a student and thereafter would improve? Explain.

2. Do you think ethics instruction, religious commitment, or higher natural intelligence would reduce academic cheating? Explain. See James M. Bloodgood, William H. Turnley, and Peter Mudrack, "The Influence of Ethics Instruction, Religiosity, and Intelligence on Cheating Behavior," *The Journal of Business Ethics* 82, no. 3 (2008), p. 557.

3. Professor Robert A. Prentice argues: "Those who choose to attend business school on the assumption that an MBA will help them change jobs, make more money, and therefore be happier are very likely misinformed." Do you agree? Explain. See Robert A. Prentice, "What's an MBA Worth in Terms of Happiness?" *The Chronicle of Higher Education,* November 8, 2009 [**http://chronicle.com/article /Whats-an-MBA-Worth-in/49056/**].

Changing Values?

Contemporary cheating behaviors offer a stark and unflattering contrast to the views of a 1928 Princeton University freshman writing home:

> Father, you suggest that the greatest benefit from college is to be found in . . . habits of intellectual diligence and application. I am nonetheless putting my chief emphasis on the study of right and wrong.[27]

UCLA's annual survey of college first-year students provides further evidence of changing values among young people. Responding to the 2012 survey, a record 81 percent of first-year students valued wealth as a goal, but only 46 percent sought a "meaningful philosophy of life." That result is essentially a reversal of the 1971 survey when 37 percent of freshmen identified being "very well off financially" as an essential or very important objective, and 73 percent felt the same about "developing a meaningful philosophy of life."[28] The college experience, however, seems to strengthen some important ethical values. A 2010 UCLA study found that students were more likely as juniors than as freshmen to say that "they wanted to develop a meaningful philosophy of life, seek beauty, become a more loving person, and attain inner harmony."[29] Broadly, as compared with their freshmen attitudes, college juniors are more likely to be engaged in a spiritual quest and more likely to be "caring" persons.[30] On the other hand, *The Atlantic* in 2013 reported on a growing body of evidence claiming we are in the midst of a "narcissism epidemic."[31] One study based on the Narcissistic Personality Inventory of college students nationwide, responding to such statements as "I think I am a special person," concluded that the average college student today is about 30 percent more self-absorbed than the average student in 1982.[32] One of the study leaders, Jean Twenge of San Diego State University, remarked: "We need to stop endlessly repeating 'you're special,' . . . Kids are self-centered enough already."[33] [The UCLA freshmen survey website: **http://www.heri.ucla.edu/cirpoverview.php**] [Professor Twenge's website: **http://www.jeantwenge.com/**]

> "We need to stop endlessly repeating, 'you're special.'"

Questions

1. Do you think you and your college friends are excessively narcissistic and insufficiently empathetic? Explain.
2. Why might empathy be declining among college students? [To measure your own level of empathy and to compare it with the average empathy level of college students, see **http://umichisr.qualtrics.com/SE/?SID=SV_bCvraMmZBCcov52&SVID**].

Too Little Studying = Cheating?

According to the 2011 National Survey of Student Engagement, business majors spend less time studying than students in any other broad field. Nearly half of senior business majors say they study fewer than 11 hours per week outside of class. According to the Collegiate Learning Assessment national essay test, business majors in their first two years of college improve their writing and reasoning skills less than any other major.

Questions

1. Can you explain why business majors apparently study less, on average, than students in other majors?
2. Can you explain why business students' writing and reasoning skills apparently increase less than those of any other major during the first two years of college?
3. The evidence, as noted above, indicates that business students cheat more than those majoring in other fields. What relationship, if any, do you see between student study patterns and student cheating patterns? Put another way, do you think cheating in business schools would decline if students studied more? Explain.
4. Do you think that studying ethics, as you are assigned to do in this chapter and in this book, is likely to materially improve the ethical quality of your professional life following graduation? Explain.

Source: David Glenn, "Business Educators Struggle to Put Students to Work," *The Chronicle of Higher Education*, April 14, 2011 [**http://chronicle.com/**].

Part Two—Analyzing Ethical Dilemmas

Ethics Theories

We have looked in a preliminary way at some business ethics issues and at America's moral climate. Now we turn to an overview of the primary philosophical theories employed in examining ethics problems. Ethics, of course, involves judgments as to good and bad, right and wrong, and what ought to be. Business ethics refers to the measurement of business behavior based on standards of right and wrong, rather than relying entirely on principles of accounting and management. (In this discussion, the word morals will be used interchangeably with the word ethics. Distinctions certainly are drawn between the two, but those distinctions are not vital for our purposes.)

Finding and following the moral course is not easy for any of us, but the difficulty may be particularly acute for the businessperson. The pressure to produce is intense, and the temptation to cheat may be great. Although the law provides very useful guides for minimum comportment, clear moral answers frequently do not exist. Therefore, when the businessperson faces a difficult decision, a common tactic is simply to do what he or she takes to be correct at any given moment. Indeed, in one survey of ethical views in business, 50 percent of the respondents indicated that the word ethical meant "what my feelings tell me is right."[34]

Philosophers have provided powerful intellectual support for that approach. Existentialists, led by the famed Jean-Paul Sartre, believe standards of conduct cannot be objectively discovered or rationally justified via ethical theory and reasoning. No actions are inherently right or wrong. Thus, each person may reach his or her own choice about ethical principles. Personal freedom is the defining characteristic of every person. Each of us is, therefore, fully and exclusively responsible for our own moral decisions.[35] That view finds its roots in the notion that humans are only what we will ourselves to be. If God does not exist, there can be no human nature, because there is no one to conceive that nature.

Existence precedes essence. In Sartre's famous interpretation, existence precedes essence. First humans exist; then we individually define what we are—our essence. Therefore, each of us is free, with no rules to turn to for guidance. Just as we all choose our own natures, so must we choose our own ethical precepts. Moral responsibility belongs to each of us individually.

Responsibility

Indian spiritual, political, and civil rights leader, Mahatma Gandhi, viewed moral responsibility quite differently from Sartre. Gandhi's view: "All humanity is one undivided and indivisible family, and each one of us is responsible for the misdeeds of all the others."[36] Whose view makes more sense to you?

Universal Truths?

Have we then no rules or universal standards by which to distinguish right from wrong? Have we no absolutes? Philosophers seek to provide guidance beyond the uncertainties of ethical relativism. We will survey two ethical perspectives, teleology and deontology, which form the core of the philosophical approach to ethical analysis. Before proceeding to those theories, we will note the important role of religion in ethics and take a brief look at two additional formulations—libertarianism and virtue ethics—that have been increasingly influential in contemporary moral analysis.

1. **Religion.** Judeo–Christian beliefs, Islam, Confucianism, Buddhism, and other faiths are powerful ethical voices in contemporary life. They often feature efforts such as the Golden Rule to build absolute and universal standards. Scholarly studies indicate that most American managers believe in the Golden Rule and take it to be their most meaningful moral guidepost. From a religious point of view, the deity's laws are absolutes that must shape the whole of one's life, including work. Faith, rather than reason, intuition, or secular knowledge, provides the foundation for a moral life built on religion. [For worldwide coverage of ethics issues, see **http://www.bbc. co.uk/ethics**]

Spirituality at Work

Many businesses directly practice Christian principles in the workplace. Hobby Lobby, for example, closes its 525 stores on Sunday, donates Christian counseling services, and buys holiday ads promoting the Christian faith. The top boss of the family-owned business, David Green, says, "We're Christians and we run our business on Christian principles."[37] Responding to employees' personal and spiritual needs and sometimes fulfilling the religious convictions of the owners, many U.S. companies provide on-the-job chaplains.

We should note, however, that the growing spirituality movement in business often does not involve religion at all. Rather, managers may see spirituality as an expression of the whole person and a part of the broader search for meaning in life. Business, they think, must acknowledge the soul to maximize performance.

Questions

1. Do you think corporate America must now make room for spirituality and the soul in the workplace to maximize success? Explain.

2. Must we believe in God to be moral? Explain.

3. The Affordable Care Act (Obamacare; see Chapter 8) requires companies with 50 or more full-time employees to provide health insurance—including birth control coverage—for employees or pay a fine. Hobby Lobby and its owners sued the federal government for an exemption from that law. In 2014, the U.S. Supreme Court held that requiring family-owned corporations like Hobby Lobby to pay for insurance coverage for contraception violates the federal Religious Freedom Restoration Act of 1993. The law aside, do you think that corporations and owners should be excused, on religious grounds, from providing contraception coverage? Explain.

Sources: Cathy Lynn Grossman, "Survey: Number of Religious 'Nones' Hits Nearly 20 Percent," *Des Moines Register,* July 23, 2012, p. 6A; Bill Keller, "The Conscience of a Corporation," *The New York Times,* February 10, 2013 [**http://www.nytimes.com**]; Adam Liptak, "Supreme Court Rejects Contraceptives Mandate for Some Corporations," *The New York Times,* July 1, 2014 [**http://www.nytimes.com**].

---

2. **Libertarianism.** Contemporary philosopher Robert Nozick (1938–2002) built an ethical theory rooted in personal liberty. For him, morality coincided with the maximization of personal freedom. Justice and fairness, right and wrong are measured not by equality of results (such as wealth) for all, but from ensuring equal opportunity for all to engage in informed choices about their own welfare. Hence Nozick took essentially a free market stance toward ethics.

3. **Virtue ethics.** In recent years, an increasing number of philosophers have argued that the key to good ethics lies not in rules, rights, and responsibilities but in the classic notion of character. As Plato and Aristotle argued, our attention should be given to strategies for encouraging desirable character traits such as honesty, fairness, compassion, and generosity. Aristotle believed that virtue could be taught much as any other skill. Virtue ethics applauds the person who is motivated to do the right thing and who cultivates that motivation in daily conduct. A part of the argument is that such persons are more morally reliable than those who simply follow the rules but fail to inspect, strengthen, and preserve their own personal virtues. [For an overview of virtue ethics, see **http://plato.stanford.edu/entries/ethics-virtue/**]

Teleology or Deontology—An Overview

Religion, libertarianism, and virtue provide crucial ethical lessons. Philosophers have further clarified ethical theory by defining two broad analytical systems, *teleology* and *deontology,* that capture much of our current understanding about how to engage in careful ethical analysis.

Teleological ethical systems (often referred to as *consequentialist ethical systems*) are concerned with the consequences, the results, of an act rather than the act itself. A teleological view of life involves ends, goals, and the ultimate good. Duty and obligation are subordinated to the production of what is good or desirable. For the teleologist/consequentialist, the end is primary and that end or result is the measure of the ethical quality of a decision or act.

To the deontologist, on the other hand, principle is primary and consequence is secondary or even irrelevant. Maximizing right rather than good is the deontological standard. The deontologist might well refuse to lie, as a matter of principle, even if lying would maximize good.

Deontology, derived from the Greek word meaning *duty,* is directed toward what ought to be, toward what is right. Similarly, deontology considers motives. For example, why a crime was committed may be more important than the actual consequences of the crime. Relationships among people are important from a deontological perspective primarily because they create duties. A father may be bound by duty to save his son from a burning building, rather than saving another person who could do more total good for society.

The distinction here is critical. Are we to guide our behavior by rational evaluation of the consequences of our acts, or according to duty and principle—that which ought to be? Let's take a closer look at *utilitarianism,* the principal teleological ethical theory, and *formalism,* the principal deontological ethical theory.

Teleology

Utilitarianism   In reaching an ethical decision, good is to be weighed against evil. A decision that maximizes the ratio of good over evil for all those concerned is the ethical course. Jeremy Bentham (1748–1832) and John Stuart Mill (1806–1873) were the chief intellectual forces in the development of utilitarianism. Their views and those of other utilitarian philosophers were not entirely consistent. As a result, at least two branches of utilitarianism have developed. According to *act-utilitarianism,* our goal is to identify the consequences of a particular act to determine whether it is right or wrong. *Rule-utilitarianism* requires us to follow those rules that generate the greatest value for society. Thus the rule-utilitarian may be forced to shun a particular act that would result in greater immediate good (punishing a guilty person whose constitutional rights have been violated) in favor of upholding a broader rule that results in the greater total good over time (maintaining constitutional principles by freeing the guilty person). In sum, the principle to be followed for the utilitarian is the greatest good for the greatest number. [For an extensive database exploring utilitarianism, see **http://www.hedweb.com /philsoph/utillink.htm**]

Deontology

Formalism   The German philosopher Immanuel Kant (1724–1804) developed perhaps the most persuasive and fully articulated vision of ethics as measured not by consequences (teleology) but by the rightness of rules. In this formalistic view of ethics, the rightness of an act depends little (or, in Kant's view, not at all) on the results of the act. Kant believed in the key moral concept of "the goodwill." The moral person is a person of goodwill, and that person renders ethical decisions based on what is right, regardless of the consequences of the decision. Moral worth springs from one's decision to discharge one's duty. Thus the student who refuses to cheat on exams is morally worthy if his or her decision springs from duty, but morally unworthy if the decision is merely one born of self-interest, such as fear of being caught.

How does the person of goodwill know what is right? Here Kant propounded the *categorical imperative,* the notion that every person should act on only those principles that he or she, as a rational person, would prescribe as universal laws to be applied to the whole of humankind. A moral rule is "categorical" rather than "hypothetical" in that its prescriptive force is independent of its consequences. The rule guides us independent of the ends we seek. Kant believed that every rational creature can act according to his or her categorical imperative because all such persons have "autonomous, self-legislating wills" that permit them to formulate and act on their own systems of rules. To Kant, what is right for one is right for all, and each of us can discover that "right" by exercising our rational faculties.

Questions

1. Fifty-year-old Wesley Autry, waiting with his two young daughters in January 2007 at a New York City subway station, saw a man collapse and fall off the passenger platform into the space between the train rails. The headlight of a train appeared. Mr. Autry immediately jumped on top of the fallen man holding him down while the train passed over them, inches above Autry's head. Asked later why he jumped to the rescue, Autry said: "I did what I felt was right."[38] What form of ethical reasoning did Autry seem to employ in making his courageous decision?

2. British priest Tim Jones caused a big stir by telling his congregation in 2009 that shoplifting is sometimes morally permissible for desperate people. In a sermon, Jones said

that shoplifting can be justified when a person is in real need, is not greedy and takes only what is necessary to get by. Later Jones said: "The point I'm making is that when we shut down every socially acceptable avenue for people in need, then the only avenue left is the socially unacceptable one."[39]

a. Was Jones arguing from a teleological/consequentialist or a deontological/formalist point of view? Explain.

b. Do you agree with Jones? Explain.

3. In March 2013 as Tiger Woods's golf game was recovering from a long period of poor performance (by his standards), Nike released an ad with Woods's picture and the caption "Winning Takes Care of Everything," a remark Woods reportedly made many times in reference to his golfing performance. Critics attacked Woods and Nike saying the ad implied that golf victories would cancel out the shortcomings and misconduct of Woods's past, including his failed marriage, repeated infidelities and generally perceived arrogant, rude behavior.

a. Is the ad an example of consequentialist or formalist thinking? Explain.

b. In assessing the moral quality of an individual's life, can we properly weigh exemplary productivity against extensive wrongdoing? Consider cyclist Lance Armstrong, who has acknowledged having cheated by engaging in forbidden doping measures. Can we, nonetheless, consider Armstrong a "good person" in light of the enormous contribution he has made as an advocate for cancer research and as an inspiration to those who suffer from cancer? Explain.

c. In your view, was Nike wrong to run the "Winning Takes Care of Everything" ad? Explain.

Using Ethical Reasoning: Two Cases

Obviously, ethical theory does not provide magical answers to life's most difficult questions. Those theories are useful, however, in identifying and sorting the issues that lead to better decision making. Apply those theories to the Toyota and Malden Mills cases that follow, as you think about when layoffs are ethical.

Are Layoffs Unethical? Case One—Toyota

Despite its highly publicized product defect problems and the global financial crisis, Toyota has tried to continue its half-century-old policy of not laying off permanent employees. When Toyota halted production in some of its U.S. plants in 2008, the 4,500 idled workers were kept on with full pay and benefits at a cost estimated at more than $50 million. Toyota executive Norm Bafunno said the retention decision was easy because the company used the economic slowdown as an opportunity to retrain its team members. Bafunno said Toyota used a shared sacrifice approach:

> During these times, we suspended all overtime, we suspended all variable compensation (bonuses), we suspended pay raises, and in addition, for our senior leadership team . . . base pay was reduced . . . everyone needs to sacrifice together.

As Latondra Newton, general manager of Toyota's Team Member Development Center in Erlanger, Kentucky said: "We're not just keeping people on the payroll because we're nice. At the end of all this, our hope is that we'll end up with a more skilled North American workforce."

Despite its protective policies, Toyota has laid off thousands of temporary workers and in 2010, its Fremont, California plant was shut down leaving 4,700 workers without jobs. Toyota's lifetime employment policy suffered another jolt in 2012 when 8 percent of its workforce at its Melbourne, Australia, factory reportedly were laid off owing to declining demand for some models.

Questions

1. Do you share Toyota's vision that all workers should sacrifice in order to avoid layoffs for permanent workers?

2. If so, are you a "socialist"?

3. If not, are you selfish?

4. Broadly, is shared sacrifice a moral wrong? Explain.

Sources: Norm Bafunno, "2010 Management Briefing Seminar," August 2, 2010 [**http://pressroom.toyota .com/pr/tms/2010-management-briefing-seminar-165965.aspx**]; Lindsay Chappell, "Toyota Idles Factories but Can't Lay Anybody Off," *Workforce Management*, August 18, 2008 [**http://www.workforce.com/section/00 /article/25/71/62.php**]; and Hans Greimel, "Toyota's 'Lifetime Employment' Takes a Hit with Australian Layoffs," *Automotive News*, January 30, 2012 [**www.autonews.com/**].

Are Layoffs Unethical? Case Two (Part I)—Aaron Feuerstein and Malden Mills

Fabric manufacturer Malden Mills of Lowell, Massachusetts, provided 3,100 high-paid manufacturing jobs in the Boston area when a 1995 fire destroyed most of the plant. The next morning Aaron Feuerstein, CEO of the family-controlled mill, announced that the business would be rebuilt and all employees would retain their jobs. Feuerstein said that keeping all of the workers through the rebuilding process was "the right thing to do and there's a moral imperative to do it, irrespective of the consequences." Apparently, Feuerstein was significantly influenced by his Jewish heritage. In his youth, Feuerstein reportedly memorized in Hebrew the Leviticus passage: "You are not permitted to oppress the workingman because he is poor and needy."

The new plant was designed to expand production of the company's patented and very successful Polartec fabric. Following the fire, makeshift production lines were developed in warehouses and about 85 percent of the employees returned to work with the remaining 400 workers or so remaining idle but paid. The new plant, machinery, and business losses cost Feuerstein some $300 million, much of which was covered by insurance. Feuerstein was convinced that the big investment would pay in the long run and since he had a highly successful, patent-protected product and since the company was family-owned and thus under no immediate pressure to perform, he felt he could afford to do what his long-time family investment in the community and workers seemed to require. Professor Michael Useem, commenting on Feuerstein's commitment to his workers, said that the idea had appeal: "The thinking is: employees can be seen as an ultimate competitive advantage. If you treat them well, they'll pay you back in really hard work later on."

Questions

1. Aaron Feuerstein became something of an overnight national hero by protecting his workers. Feuerstein said, "It was the right thing to do and there's a moral imperative to do it, irrespective of the consequences."

   a. Was Feuerstein employing utilitarian or formalist reasoning? Explain.

   b. In your view, was he correct to say that the consequences, in this instance, did not matter? Explain.

2. Commenting on Feuerstein's approach to his employees' needs, Wharton School professor Michael Useem said, "The thinking is: employees can be seen as an ultimate competitive advantage. If you treat them well, they'll pay you back in really hard work later on."[40]

   a. Was Useem expressing formalist or utilitarian reasoning?

   b. In a 1986 pastoral letter, the U.S. Catholic bishops argued that "every economic decision and institution must be judged in light of whether it protects or undermines the dignity of the human person."[41] Does the thinking summarized by Useem undermine that dignity and as such require rejection under either utilitarian or formalist reasoning? Explain.

3. If you were a successful entrepreneur with the flexibility of Aaron Feuerstein, would you operate your business like an extended family? Explain.

Source: Richard Lorant, Associated Press, *The Chicago Tribune,* December 10, 1996, p. 8, and Mary McGrory, "Tale of Two Bankruptcies," *Pittsburgh Post-Gazette,* December 22, 2001, p. A15.

 [For a film treatment of corporate downsizing/layoffs, see "The Company Men" trailer at **http://www.youtube.com/watch?v=xa5qg7cB1ZQ**]

Are Layoffs Unethical? Case Two (Part 2)—Aaron Feuerstein, Malden Mills, and Bankruptcy

In November 2001, Malden Mills was forced to enter Chapter 11 bankruptcy proceedings (see Chapter 15) for the purpose of reorganizing its finances under court protection. At the time, Malden Mills was bearing a $140 million debt load. Lenders demanded the bankruptcy action as a condition for extending an additional $20 million to keep the company afloat. In late 2003, Malden Mills emerged from bankruptcy. Creditors controlled the board of directors with Aaron Feuerstein occupying the family's one seat. Malden's precarious financial position was the product of a variety of forces: Customers were lost during the rebuilding after the fire, cheaper fleece substitutes entered the market, the company took on substantial debt in rebuilding and in keeping on its employees following the fire, and the company probably overbuilt following the fire. As a result, the Malden Mills workforce shrunk to 1,200 employees. Then in 2007, Malden Mills was once again forced into bankruptcy and was purchased by Chrysalis Capital partners, a private-equity firm that renamed the company Polartec LLC. Aaron Feuerstein's association with the company ended with the sale.

Questions

1. *The Wall Street Journal* raised the question, "Are layoffs moral?"[42]

   a. Should we establish a universal, formalist rule forbidding layoffs of all hard-working, competent employees, or should we rely on utilitarian reasoning, libertarian thought, virtue theory, or religious beliefs to answer that question? Explain.

   b. Is morality irrelevant to the question of when layoffs are necessary? Explain.

2. Do you think it would be accurate and fair to say that Feuerstein's ethical choice to protect his employees led to the decline of his business? Explain.

3. Did Feuerstein make an error in judgment in relying on an absolute principle—that is, the protection of his workers at all costs? Explain.

4. How might Feuerstein's workers have benefited by being laid off immediately following the fire?

5. John MacKenzie, in a letter to *The New York Times,* said he had a duty to help Aaron Feuerstein and Malden Mills: "Of course I have an ethical obligation to buy from Malden Mills if I have a choice and if my purchase can make a difference. It would reward Mr. Feuerstein for what he has done and what he is trying to do, and the system needs more of that."[43] Do you have a duty to buy only from the most ethically responsible sellers? Explain.

See "Articles about Aaron M. Feuerstein," *The New York Times* [**topics.nytimes.com /topics/refrence/timestopics/people/f/aaron_m_feuerstein/index.html**].

[For another view of the Malden Mills facts, as well as an analysis of the wisdom of Feuerstein's decision, see David W. Gill, "Was Aaron Feuerstein Wrong?" June 25, 2011, available at **ethix.org/2011/06/25/was-aaron-feuerstein-wrong**]

Part Three—Managerial Misconduct?

Corporate Ethical Climate

Given the subprime mortgage crisis, a strong sense of misconduct on Wall Street, and our ongoing recession-related problems, we should not be surprised that public attitudes toward big business are not positive. A global survey of 30,000 people in 2012 found only 18 percent of the public trusts business leaders to tell the truth. Unfortunately, government leaders scored even lower at 13 percent.[44] In Gallup's 2012 poll of confidence in major institutions only 21 percent of Americans expressed a "great deal" or "quite a lot" of confidence in big business and in banks. For some perspective, we should note that Congress ranked last among the 16 institutions surveyed by Gallup with only 13 percent of Americans expressing a great deal or quite a lot of confidence.[45]

Mistrust of the American business community is supported by ample evidence of corporate misconduct, but some new evidence is more encouraging. According to a large 2011 national survey, 45 percent of for-profit employees witnessed misconduct at work (lying to employees, misuse of company resources, etc.), but that number compares with 49 percent in 2009 and 55 percent in 2007. Thirty-four percent of employees reported a negative view of their supervisors' ethics.[46]

> Ethical behavior in business is, in many ways, at an historical high.

In assessing America's corporate ethical climate, we should keep in mind ethicist Chris MacDonald's reminder that ethical behavior in business is, in many ways, at an historical high.

Businesses, he argues, are more transparent and more accountable than ever before, and, as he says: "Workplaces, while still far from perfect, are less sexist, less racist, and generally more civilized and humane than at any time in history" (in considerable part as a response to government oversight and public pressure).[47] [For "The Business Ethics Blog," see **http://businessethicsblog.com/**]

Questions

At this writing in 2013, British Petroleum (BP) is on trial in New Orleans to assign blame for the massive 2010 *Deepwater Horizon* oil spill in the Gulf of Mexico. The spill threatened marine life while also severely damaging the Gulf's economic, recreational, and aesthetic contributions to American life. The Gulf appears to be healing itself more quickly than expected and the economic consequences have been mitigated by BP payments. Although the company continues to carry a stigma in the American market, it seems fair to say that media attention and public concern have abated.

Soon after the 2010 spill, a critic at a locally owned Des Moines, Iowa, BP station berated customers and the station owner by saying: "Do you realize you're buying from a company that's polluting the Earth?"

1. Should we blame local BP station owners for the Gulf spill? Explain.
2. Should we boycott those stations? Explain.
3. Several years have passed. BP has been brought to trial and has made significant reparations. For how long, if at all, should our purchasing decisions be shaped by corporate misconduct as damaging as the Gulf spill? Explain.

See Marc Hansen, "Local BP Retailers Want You to Know They Are Not the Bad Guys," *The Des Moines Register,* June 29, 2010, p. 1A.

Why Do Some Managers Cheat?

Moral Development

Scholars argue that some individuals are better prepared to make ethical judgments than others. Psychologist Lawrence Kohlberg built and empirically tested a comprehensive theory of moral development in which he claimed that moral judgment evolves and improves primarily as a function of age and education.

Kohlberg, via interviews with children as they aged, was able to identify moral development as movement through distinct stages, with the later stages being improvements on the earlier ones. Kohlberg identified six universal stages grouped into three levels:

1. **Preconventional level:**

   Stage 1: Obey rules to avoid punishment.

   Stage 2: Follow rules only if it is in own interest, but let others do the same. Conform to secure rewards.

2. **Conventional level:**

   Stage 3: Conform to meet the expectations of others. Please others. Adhere to stereotypical images.

   Stage 4: Doing right is one's duty. Obey the law. Uphold the social order.

3. **Postconventional or principled level:**

Stage 5: Current laws and values are relative. Laws and duty are obeyed on rational calculations to serve the greatest number.

Stage 6: Follow self-chosen universal ethical principles. In the event of conflicts, principles override laws.[48]

At Level 3 the individual is able to reach independent moral judgments that may or may not conform with conventional societal wisdom. Thus the Level 2 manager might refrain from sexual harassment because it constitutes a violation of company policy and the law. A manager at Level 3 might reach the same conclusion, but his or her decision would be based on independently defined universal principles of justice.

Kohlberg found that many adults never pass beyond Level 2. Consequently, if Kohlberg was correct, many managers may behave unethically simply because they have not reached the upper stages of moral maturity.

Kohlberg's model is based on extensive longitudinal and cross-cultural studies over more than three decades. For example, one set of Chicago-area boys was interviewed at 3-year intervals for 20 years. Thus the stages of moral growth exhibit "definite empirical characteristics" such that Kohlberg was able to claim that his model had been scientifically validated.[49] Although many critics remain, the evidence, in sum, supports Kohlberg's general proposition. [For a link to an overview of moral development and moral education, see **http://www.davidsongifted.org/db/Resources_id_11335.aspx**]

Feminine Voice   One of those lines of criticism requires a brief inspection. Kohlberg colleague Carol Gilligan contends that our conceptions of morality are, in substantial part, gender-based.[50] She claims that men typically approach morality as a function of justice, impartiality, and rights (the ethic of justice), whereas women are more likely to build a morality based on care, support, and responsiveness (the ethic of care). Men, she says, tend to take an impersonal, universal view of morality as contrasted with the feminine "voice" that rises more commonly from relationships and concern for the specific needs of others. Gilligan criticizes Kohlberg because his highest stages, 5 and 6, are structured in terms of the male approach to morality while the feminine voice falls at stage 3. Furthermore, Kohlberg's initial experimental subjects were limited to young males. The result, in Gilligan's view, is that women are underscored. Of course, a danger in the ethic of care is that it might be interpreted to restore and legitimize the stereotype of women as care giving subordinates not deserving of moral autonomy.[51] Subsequent research both challenges[52] and supports[53] Gilligan's view.

Reason or Emotion?

Controlled or automatic? We have seen that Kohlberg and Gilligan (and most moral philosophers) take the position that moral decision making is the controlled product of analysis, deliberation and experience. In recent years, however, new psychological and neuroscience evidence has supported an alternative theory of morality that involves decision making by emotion or intuition. The emotion/intuition approach claims that moral decision making is an automatic, nonreflective process in which our minds, when confronted with a moral question, instantaneously generate feelings of approval or disapproval.[54]

Brain-scanning experiments have provided support for the automatic emotion/intuition hypothesis.[55] Some scientists speculate that controlled moral reasoning may be little more than an after-the-fact method of justifying conclusions already reached automatically via emotions/intuitions.

Moral theorist Marc Hauser extends the emotion/intuition thesis in his book *Moral Minds*.[56] He claims that our brains are biologically endowed with a moral faculty that has evolved over eons and is designed to reach very rapid judgments about right and wrong based on unconscious processes that are involuntary and universal. Thus, when we judge an action to be morally right or wrong, Hauser says we are doing so instinctively, using our inborn moral faculty. Even babies seem to make moral judgments. Experiments show that

> Even babies seem to make moral judgments.

6- and 10-month-old infants overwhelmingly prefer helping characters (objects manipulated like puppets in helping/hindering situations) over neutral characters and neutral characters are preferred over those who actively hinder others.[57]

The emotion/intuition/ biological theory provides a stern challenge to Kohlberg and to our faith in moral reasoning generally. Psychologist Jonathan Haidt compares the intuitive, moral machinery of the brain with an elephant and conscious moral reasoning with a small rider on the elephant's back.[58] Other scholarly evidence, however, continues to support a very robust role for rational moral decision making,[59] and reasoning may at times override intuitions, as Haidt himself acknowledges.[60] Overall, moral decision making may be the product of a dual process system employing both automatic emotions (produced deep in the brain in its older structures) and controlled reasoning (produced in the newer, frontal lobes of the brain.[61] [For more, see the website **YourMorals.org**, where Haidt and his colleagues invite you to "learn about your own morality, ethics, and/or values, while also contributing to scientific research."]

Moral Identity?

The moral development story does not end with an understanding of moral reasoning and moral emotion. Neither of those forces, according to current research, adequately explains why some among us are moved, after reaching a moral judgment, to take moral action.[62] Early evidence suggests that a critical feature in total moral development, including the will to act, involves what is labeled *moral identity*. In general, moral identity involves the degree to which moral concerns are central to our sense of self. As Professor Sam Hardy explains it, a person might have a stronger sense of moral identity if that identity is centered more on moral virtue than on amoral virtues such as creativity.[63] Some studies find that those with stronger moral identities are more likely to engage in good behaviors such as volunteering or showing respect for members of "out-groups."[64] Remember, however, that the moral identity evidence remains quite tentative.

Organizational Forces

Obviously, individual character influences corporate misconduct, but organizational culture is also important.[65] Unfortunately, only 10 percent of American companies demonstrate the characteristics that are associated with a "strong ethical culture," according to a 2007 Ethics Resource Center study.[66] Similarly, Ethisphere Institute, in its 2012 ranking of the world's most ethical companies, reviewed 5,000 nominees and identified 145 (102 of which were American) that met its standards. Ethisphere bases it rankings on what it calls an Ethics Quotient derived from nominees' codes of ethics, regulatory and legal infractions, sustainable investment policies, corporate citizenship, and more.[67] [For the Business Roundtable Institute for Corporate Ethics, see **http://www.corporate-ethics.org/**]

Pressure to cheat is often cited as evidence of an organization's ethical culture. A near-record 13 percent of American for-profit workers "perceived pressure to compromise standards in order to do their jobs," according to the 2011 National Business Ethics Survey.[68] Thirty graduates of the Harvard Business School agreed to in-depth interviews about their on-the-job ethics experiences, including the pressure to cheat felt by their bosses:

> I really feel for people who are middle management, with a wife and four kids, under financial strain. . . . You see it happen all the time, that people are indicted for fraud or larceny. You can empathize with their situation. The world is changing fast. And a lot of people have been blindsided by it—so they've done things that they don't like. I can't say that will never happen to me. It's easy for me as a single person. . . but when you're desperate, you're desperate. [My boss] was not willfully unethical. It was the pressure of the time. . . .
>
> I have no idea what pressures were on him to drive the project. It probably wasn't [his] initiative to fudge the numbers. There may have been a good intention at some point in the organization. But as it got filtered through the organization, it changed. Some executive may have said, "This is an interesting project." Unfortunately this got translated as, "The vice president really wants this project." This sort of thing can happen a lot. Things start on high. As they go down they are filtered, modified. What was a positive comment several levels above becomes "do this or die" several levels down.[69] [For a variety of business ethics links, see **http://www.ethics.ubc.ca/resources/business/**]

> "[My boss] was not willfully unethical. It was the pressure of the time."

The Boss

Top corporate bosses have hit a particularly rough patch in American life. Many have been disgraced by various scandals, and a number of them are in jail. Wall Street executives are accused of bringing the economy to near collapse while continuing to collect big bonuses. Although business leaders often blame these trust woes on a "few bad apples," the 2013 Edelman Trust Barometer (a survey of 26,000 people in 26 countries) found that only 18 percent of respondents "would trust a business leader to tell the truth in a complex situation."[70]

Notwithstanding the current cynicism, we know that bosses are crucial in setting the ethical climate in an organization. *The Wall Street Journal* reviewed retired corporate chief Herb Baum's leadership book:

> In *The Transparent Leader,* Herb Baum argues that a climate of integrity is crucial to the success of a public company and that it begins at the top.
>
> Mr. Baum . . . is at the top himself, but he drives a VW Beetle to work, he tells us, and doesn't have a reserved parking space. Not that he minds: He arrives at 5 AM, ahead of the crowd. He espouses straight talk, solid values, and hiring literally good people—as opposed to people who are merely good at their jobs. His catchall term for this ethos is "transparency."

How to create it? Mr. Baum rightly insists that it has to come from the chief executive's office. He emphasizes valuing people by keeping an open door, communicating honestly, listening carefully, and making sure that integrity permeates every aspect of the company. Hypocrisy is anathema: "A lot of CEOs, including me, are overpaid," he says bluntly—and at one point he distributed his annual bonus to Dial's lowest-paid employees.[71]

 [For a film treatment of ethical issues in the business community, see the trailer *Wall Street: Money Never Sleeps,* at **http://www.youtube.com/watch?v=HcMFA2SHES4**]

Bill Hawkins: A Tough Decision

Bill Hawkins, CEO at Medtronic ($14.6 billion, Minneapolis-based medical device maker), faced a critical ethical decision-making moment in 2007 when he learned that Medtronic's Sprint Fidelis leads might have been malfunctioning at an unacceptably high rate. Leads are very thin wires that connect implanted heart defibrillators to the heart thus allowing a shock to be delivered from the defibrillator to the heart muscle. Sprint Fidelis leads (Sprint was the brand name for Medtronic's leads and Fidelis was the particular model of lead) were the company's newest, and thinnest, model. Medtronic began receiving reports of fractures in the Sprint Fidelis leads. Those fractures might prevent a needed shock from reaching the heart, or patients might receive random shocks.

Hawkins had been with Medtronic for about five years and had been serving as president and chief operating officer for about two months when he learned in March 2007 that one hospital was reporting problems with the leads. According to Hawkins, Medtronic's internal experts and an independent physician advisory board investigated and the company concluded that monitoring should continue but the leads should not be removed from the market. In October 2007, when Hawkins had been CEO for two months, he received new data showing that the Fidelis lead's resistance to fracture was 97.7 percent versus 99.1 for the previous model; a statistically insignificant difference, but a gap that would become statistically significant over time if the fracture rates remained constant. After consultation with other company officers and an independent physician advisory board, Hawkins felt that the Fidelis was displaying a negative trend, but he wanted more deliberation. Various Medtronic leaders met for discussion, as did the physicians. The next day they met again by teleconference and after 90 minutes of discussion, the decision was reached to voluntarily recall the Sprint Fidelis.

The leads had been on the market for about 38 months and 268,000 had been implanted. The day the recall was announced, Medtronic had its worst day on the stock market in 23 years with a 12 percent decline and its market share in the category fell from 51 to 47 percent. By March 2009, Medtronic's physician panel had identified 13 deaths that might have been associated with the lead fractures. Within two years, however, Medtronic had largely recovered from the episode, a software package had been developed that would alert patients that a lead might be fracturing, and a favorable U.S. Supreme Court decision was offering Medtronic substantial shelter from lawsuits.

Hawkins described how Medtronic's culture influenced him and his company:

Our founder wrote in 1960 that the purpose of our company is to "alleviate pain, restore health, and extend life." I am not being coy when I say that I take this very personally and that our company is strongly influenced by this sense of mission. During the course of our Fidelis discussions, not once did we talk about what might happen to the stock price or market share if we suspended distribution. The conversation was about our responsibility to do the right thing.[72]

Questions

1. Beyond market share and stock market prices, what considerations would have influenced Hawkins's decision?

2. Some critics have said that Hawkins's decision could not be considered difficult because lives were at risk. Do you agree that Hawkins's decision was, in fact, easy? Explain.

Sources: Bill Hawkins, as told to Cait Murphy, "Bill Hawkins: How I Made the Toughest Call of My Career," BNET, October 5, 2009 [**http://www.bnet.com/**]; Cait Murphy, "The Price Medtronic Paid," BNET, October 5, 2009 [**http://www.bnet.com/**]; and Chris MacDonald, "Can Life-Saving Decisions Really Be 'Tough Calls'?" *The Business Ethics Blog,* October 15, 2009 [**http://www.businessethics.ca/blog/**].

Bank Robber to Boardroom

Some bosses go wrong but correct their lives—none more dramatically than James Joseph Minder, 74-year-old former chairman of Smith & Wesson Holding Corp. In his twenties, Minder was the notorious "Shotgun Bandit" of Michigan. He committed dozens of armed holdups, some while a student at the University of Michigan. On one occasion he terrorized employees before stealing $53,000 from a branch of Manufacturers National Bank. He served time in prison and was free of trouble, he says, after 1965. After release from prison in 1969, he spent 20 years successfully setting up group homes and programs for troubled children and young adults. After retiring in the 1990s, Minder got involved in the gun industry and eventually became chairman of handgun manufacturer, Smith & Wesson. Then in 2004 a reporter came to his home asking about his past, a life he had not hidden but one he had not advertised either. At first he denied he was the "Bandit," but he reconsidered and decided, "I had better tell the truth." He later told the other members of the Smith & Wesson board, and resigned as chairman.

Source: Vanessa O'Connell, "How Troubled Past Finally Caught Up with James Minder," *The Wall Street Journal,* March 8, 2004, p. A1.

Questions—Part Three

1. *a.* Do you think it is important for our character development to have heroes in our lives? Explain.

   b. Do you think we have fewer heroes today than in the past? Explain.

   c. Do you have a hero? Explain.

2. A Business & Media Institute study entitled *Bad Company* looked at the top 12 television dramas from May and November 2005, including shows like *CSI* and *Desperate Housewives*. Thirty-nine episodes featured business-related plots, and among those

shows, 77 percent projected unfavorable images of business. The *Law & Order* episodes, for example, had businessmen committing almost 50 percent of the felonies—mostly murders.

  a. Do you think those unfavorable depictions of business are unfair? Explain.

  b. Do you think those depictions significantly harm the image of the business community? Explain. See Editorial, "TV's Killer Capitalists," *The Wall Street Journal,* July 14, 2006, p. W9.

3. Does a corporation have a conscience? Explain. See Kenneth Goodpaster and John B. Matthews, Jr., "Can a Corporation Have a Conscience?" *Harvard Business Review,* January–February 1982, p. 136.

4. "You are being considered for a promotion. Would you flirt with your boss or someone else who can help you get the job?" *Money Magazine* asked this and other ethics questions in a national poll of 1,000 adults. Answer the flirting question, then go online to see how your answer compared with the poll response: "Money and Ethics: How You Stack Up," *CNNMoney.com* [**http://money.cnn.com/galleries/2007/moneymag/0705/quiz.money_ ethics.moneymag/3.html?score=2**]

5. Kansas City Royals pitcher Gil Meche, 32 years old and troubled by a shoulder injury, decided in 2011 to retire from baseball. The decision would not be considered particularly newsworthy beyond the sports pages except that Meche passed up the $12 million final year of his contract by doing so. Others in similar situations have reported to spring training, gone through the motions and collected their big paychecks. Meche said, "When I signed my contract, my main goal was to earn it. Once I started to realize I wasn't earning my money, I felt bad." Meche thought he had already earned enough from the Royals: "Making that amount of money from a team that's already given me over $40 million for my life and for my kids, it just wasn't the right thing to do."

  a. Would you do the same as Meche if you were similarly situated? Explain.

  b. Have you ever spurned money for reasons of principal?

  c. Why did you do so?

  d. Was Meche employing utilitarian or formalist reasoning? Explain. See Tyler Kepner, "Pitcher Spurns $12 Million, to Keep Self-Respect," *The New York Times,* January 26, 2011 [**http://www.nytimes.com**].

6. Boris Siperstein, 38, of Austin, Texas, bikes to meetings for his private-equity firm and estimates that he has saved the firm several thousand dollars because he takes his folding bike on business trips and uses it in place of cabs. Siperstein has also slept on the floor of the company's former Manhattan headquarters rather than exceed his personal limit of $200 for a hotel room. David Payne, 41, a trainer for a Brooklyn, New York, software firm, often washed his clothing in the bathtub while on the road. Now he travels with detergent and uses local laundromats, thus saving, he estimates, $30 to $40 off hotel service.[73]

  a. Will you impose frugal spending limits on yourself when you are on a company expense account? Explain.

  b. Is frugality morally required? Explain.

  c. Do employers value frugal employees? Explain.

Part Four—Business Ethics in Practice

Introduction: Corporate/White-Collar Crime

Having established a general foundation in ethical climate and theory, we turn now to corporate misconduct in practice. Forty-five percent of U.S. respondents to Pricewaterhouse-Coopers' (PwC) 2011 economic crime survey reported that their organization had suffered fraud in the previous 12 months.[74] Presumably reflecting increasing workforce participation and increasing opportunities, women in the United States constituted 40 percent of the perpetrators in internal fraud cases as opposed to 19 percent in other nations.[75] Ernst & Young's 2013 survey of officers and employees in 36 nations in Europe, Africa, the Middle East, and India found 42 percent of senior managers and directors knew of instances of accounting fraud in their organizations during the previous 12 months.[76]

The U.S. government struggles to curb corporate crime, but in 2012, corporate payments to the government to settle fraud charges reached a record total of about $8 billion.[77] Critics are not satisfied, however, partly because, as a *New York Times* headline said, "Corporate Fraud Cases Often Spare Individuals."[78] With notable exceptions, including Ponzi master Bernie Madoff and numerous insider trading cases (see Chapter 9), the government has often been slow to go after bosses. As we noted previously in this chapter, that tendency has been particularly evident in the case of the big banks and their bosses, but we need to remember that the task of linking particular people to instances of wrongdoing can be extremely difficult and expensive.

Because of those difficulties and expenses, the government has recently turned with frequency to what are called "deferred prosecution" or "nonprosecution" agreements with corporations and individuals. *The New York Times* explained:

> Deferred and non-prosecution agreements are contracts with the government in which a company (or individual) undertakes specified actions in exchange for charges being dismissed or not filed altogether. The terms usually require payment of a fine, continued cooperation with any investigations or trials and a commitment to enhance internal controls.[79]

Deferring charges is a common prosecution practice, especially in alcohol and drug cases, and deferrals avoid destroying corporations and the jobs they provide. Critics of corporate crime deferrals, however, say "it is the rare case when senior management pays any price."[80]

Is Theft Sometimes OK?

A shopper wrote a letter to the editor explaining how he felt after observing what appeared to be a theft:

> [A]t Wal-Mart I saw a person try to put an item in their jacket. At first I thought this person was a jerk. . . . But after I returned home, I became convinced that it was OK to steal. . . . When I compare the theft of a $15 item to the grand larceny by corporate America, which ran Enron into the ground, which reaps record oil

profits,. . . which occupies the seats of government and takes bribes, I now see the act of stealing a small gift . . . as heroic.

Questions

1. What do you think the letter writer meant when he applied the label "heroic" to the apparent theft?
2. Should we be more aggressive in pursuing corporate fraud? Explain.

Source: Greg Wilcox, "It's All Relative," *The Des Moines Register*, December 12, 2005, p. 6A.

Prevention or Enhanced Punishment

Responding to public outrage over Enron, WorldCom, and other stunning and destructive corporate scandals, Congress and the president approved the 2002 Sarbanes–Oxley Act (SOX) to attack corporate crime by publicly traded companies. Among its provisions, the bill:

- Establishes an independent board to oversee the accounting profession.
- Requires corporate executives to personally certify the accuracy of their financial reports.
- Creates new crimes and raises penalties.
- Requires publicly traded companies to establish internal control systems designed to assure the accuracy of financial information.
- Requires publicly traded companies to disclose whether they have adopted an ethics code for senior financial management, and if not, why not.

SOX is often criticized as a drain on company resources and an impediment to economic growth, but most organizations seem to have settled in to the SOX requirements and often praise its effects. In a 2010 survey of 400 business executives, 87 percent said SOX is good for private enterprise,[81] and a 2009 Securities and Exchange Commission study concluded that the benefits of SOX exceeded its costs.[82] Worrisome, perhaps, is the apparent underutilization of SOX in response to our financial crisis as reported by *The Wall Street Journal* in 2012:

> As the Sarbanes–Oxley Act turns 10 years old, the law's biggest hammer—the threat of jail time for corporate executives who knowingly certify inaccurate financial reports—is going largely unused.[83]

Over the past decade, the government has applied the false certification provisions of SOX to at least 200 individuals, but no executive from any of the big banks suspected of misleading the public during the financial crisis has been prosecuted under SOX.

Of course, these cases are difficult to win, but critics such as University of San Diego law and finance professor Frank Partnoy are skeptical:

> Could it really be the case that the number of high-level criminal actions at Wall Street firms over the last decade is zero? Could the firms really be that clean?[84]

Sentencing

Federal sentencing guidelines, issued by the U.S. Sentencing Commission, provide ranges (e.g., 10–12 months imprisonment) within which judges are advised to impose sentences. Relying on the crime's "offense level" and the defendant's criminal history, the punishment range for each category of both white-collar and street crime is established. The guidelines are designed to provide greater predictability and consistency in punishment. Companies must develop programs to prevent and detect crime, provide ethics training, and monitor the success of compliance efforts. Companies involved in crimes may receive reduced penalties if they have effective compliance programs in place. Responsibility for compliance rests explicitly with the board of directors and top-level executives. Directors and officers complying with the guidelines may receive leniency while those engaging in aggravating behaviors such as a leadership role in crime may face increased punishment. Of course, the challenges of maintaining close, effective compliance in extended, complex giants such as Enron and McDonald's are formidable.[85]

Recent Supreme Court decisions have diminished the power of the guidelines by significantly restoring federal judges' authority to deviate from them. Judges who follow the guidelines are presumed to have acted reasonably, but departures from the guidelines are now permissible on a case-by-case basis.

Too Lenient?

Federal judge Sandra Beckwith in Ohio stretched sentencing latitude to the maximum in her 2011 sentencing of Michael E. Peppel, former chair and CEO of technology firm MCSi. Peppel pleaded guilty to fraud resulting in estimated damages of $18 million. The sentencing guidelines called for 8 to 10 years of incarceration, but the judge handed down a sentence of seven days in jail and three years of supervised release. The judge had responded to evidence of Peppel's 100 letters of support, strong role in the community, business expertise, five children, and other family needs. On appeal, however, the Sixth Circuit ruled that Judge Beckwith had abused her discretion. The appeals court specifically rejected the reasoning that Peppel's professional skills and capacity to contribute to society justified a lighter sentence. Following the appeals decision, Judge Beckwith sentenced Peppel to two years in prison, three years of court supervision, and a $5 million fine.

Question

Critics of increased government activism regard the free market as the best protection against corporate misconduct. They see SOX, the sentencing guidelines, and aggressive prosecution as government-inflicted drags on the economy. Do you agree? Explain. [For more on white-collar crime, see **http://www.fbi.gov/about-us/investigate/white-collar/whitecollarcrime**]

Source: For an overview of Peppel's sentencing, see Walter Pavlo, "6th Circuit to Michael Peppel 'You Need More Prison Time,'" *Forbes*, February 18, 2013 [**http://www.forbes.com**].

Global Bribery

Esteemed clothier Ralph Lauren Corp. reportedly bribed Argentine customs officials with about $600,000 worth of perfume, dresses, and cash from 2004 to 2009 to facilitate passage of company products into the country. Lauren officials say they reported the misconduct as soon as they learned of it. Lauren agreed in 2013 to pay $1.6 million in fines to resolve federal bribery charges and entered into a nonprosecution agreement with the government.[86]

In many cultures, the payment of bribes—*baksheesh* (Middle East), *huilu* (China), *vzyatku* (Russia), *mordida* (South America), or *dash* (Africa)—is accepted as a necessary and, in some cases, a lawful way of doing business. American firms and officers wishing to succeed abroad have faced great pressure to engage in practices that are illegal and unethical in the American culture.

The Foreign Corrupt Practices Act (FCPA), the chief federal weapon against bribery abroad, was enacted in 1977 in response to disclosure of widespread bribery by American firms. In brief, the FCPA provides that U.S. nationals and businesses acting anywhere in the world, foreign nationals and companies acting in U.S. territory, and foreign companies listed on a U.S. stock exchange are engaging in criminal conduct if they offer or provide money or anything of value to foreign government officials to obtain or retain business or otherwise secure "any improper advantage." In addition, the FCPA requires rigorous internal accounting controls and careful recordkeeping to ensure that bribes cannot be concealed via "slush funds" and other devices. The act does not forbid "grease" payments to foreign officials or political parties where the purpose of the payments is "to expedite or to secure the performance of a routine governmental action," such as processing papers (like visas), providing police protection, and securing phone service. Likewise a "small gift or token of esteem or gratitude" ordinarily is permissible. And those accused may offer the affirmative defense that the alleged payoff was lawful in the host country or was a normal, reasonable business expenditure directed to specific marketing and contract performance activities. Criminal penalties include fines of up to $2 million for companies, while individuals may be fined $250,000 and imprisoned for as long as five years. The U.S. Justice Department has recently shown some leniency in FCPA cases where alleged violators have strong ethics and compliance programs in place. [For a summary of the FCPA, see **http://fcpaenforcement.com/explained/explained.asp**]

Controversy

The FCPA has been controversial from the outset. Some businesspeople see it as a blessing both because it is an honorable attempt at a firm moral stance and because it is often useful for an American businessperson abroad to say, "No, our laws forbid me from doing that." On the other hand, some consider the act damaging to our competitiveness. Now other nations are recognizing that corruption is a great risk to the global economy. Once believing that bribery aided the poor, most industrial countries are now moving toward the zero tolerance view held by the United States. In addition to the FCPA, the United States also participates in several other anticorruption initiatives including the U.N. Convention against Corruption, the OECD Anti-Bribery Convention, and the Inter-American Convention. [For details on the OECD Anti-Bribery Convention, see **www.oecd.org**]

United States Corruption   Total corporate sanctions under the FCPA reached a record $1.7 billion in 2011.[87] Corporate titans such as Pfizer and Tyco have recently agreed to pay penalties totaling tens of millions of dollars. Microsoft reportedly is under investigation in connection with alleged bribery schemes in China, Italy, and Romania.[88] By far the most publicized FCPA news, however, involves ongoing investigations of Walmart's alleged bribes in Mexico designed to win approval for new stores, including one near ancient pyramids. A *New York Times* 2012 report headlined "How Wal-Mart Used Payoffs to Get Its Way in Mexico"[89] has generated ongoing investigations by Congress, the federal Securities and Exchange Commission, the Justice Department, and Walmart itself. Even as the facts continue to be revealed, the *Times* has reported that 19 stores in Mexico were associated with bribes and that Walmart was often the aggressor in these alleged deals:

> The *Times*'s examination reveals that Wal-Mart de Mexico was not the reluctant victim of a corrupt culture that insisted on bribes as the cost of doing business. Nor did it pay bribes merely to speed up routine approvals. Rather, Wal-Mart de Mexico was an aggressive and creative corrupter, offering large payoffs to get what the law otherwise prohibited. It used bribes to subvert democratic governance—public votes, open debates, transparent procedures. It used bribes to circumvent regulatory safeguards that protect Mexican citizens from unsafe construction. It used bribes to outflank rivals.[90]

> The United States ranked only 19th in Transparency International's 2012 Corruption Perceptions Index.

The United States ranked only 19th in Transparency International's 2012 Corruption Perceptions Index, which aggregates data provided by experts and business leaders to assess the perceived level of public sector corruption around the globe. The countries perceived to be least corrupt were Denmark, New Zealand, and Finland. Most of northern and Western Europe as well as Canada were perceived to be less corrupt than the United States. France (22), China (80), and Russia (133) were among the nations ranking lower than the United States.[91]

Bribery in Daily Life

Bribery seems to be a routine cost of living in some countries:

> Nikolai can't even count the number of bribes he has paid in his life.

Like many Russians, Nikolai can't even count the number of bribes he has paid in his life. He remembers the big ones, like the $1,000 he paid to avoid mandatory military service or the $1,200 he gave his wife's obstetrician to ensure her a place at one of Moscow's state-run maternity hospitals. But the small ones, like the dozens of $10 to $20 bribes he's handed to traffic police over the years, are instantly forgotten.

Whether it's getting your child into a good school, passing your driving test or even making sure you get medical treatment, there are few areas of life in Russia where a well-placed bribe isn't essential. Experts say corruption in Russia is endemic, especially in the corporate world—where big companies, both domestic and foreign, often have to shell out hundreds of thousands of dollars to get permission for a project or win a government contract.[92]

Russian think tank INDEM estimates that, on average, Russian businesses spend 7 percent of their budgets on bribes.[93] Interestingly, Russia has recently strengthened its antibribery laws. China executed the former head of its food and drug agency in 2007 for allegedly accepting $850,000 in bribes from Chinese pharmaceutical companies, but bribery continues to be a routine feature of business practice in China. The World Bank estimates that bribes to government officials globally total $1 trillion annually.[94] Frustration with routine, petty bribery expectations in India led to the establishment of an online site [**ipaidabribe .com**] where bribes can be reported anonymously, offering both a place to vent frustration and a venue for collecting information that will help in implementing reforms.

> China executed the former head of its food and drug agency for allegedly accepting $850,000 in bribes.

PRACTICING ETHICS   Bribe the Terrorists?

Banadex, a subsidiary of Cincinnati-based Chiquita Brands International, paid bribes to Colombian rebels over a period of years, including $1.7 million from 1997 to 2004 to the AUC (Autodefensas Unidas de Colombia), a right-wing Colombian terrorist group. Chiquita, one of the world's leading banana producers with operations in 70 nations, learned of the payments in 2000, but allowed them to continue. Reliable reports indicated that thousands of people had been killed, tortured, raped, or "disappeared" by the AUC (now disbanded). At the time, terrorists in Colombia were holding Americans for ransom or killing some of them, and years earlier four Chiquita employees had been killed by left-wing guerillas. The bribes, then lawful under American and Colombian law, were thought necessary to protect employees and company property at Chiquita's Colombian operations.

In 2003, Chiquita allegedly "stumbled across" news that the AUC had in 2001 been designated a "foreign terrorist organization" by the U.S. government, which meant payments thereafter were unlawful. The payments continued, however, despite warnings from outside counsel to discontinue them or face the risk of felony charges. Chiquita said that stopping the payments would have endangered its employees. By 2003, Chiquita's operations in Colombia were its most profitable. The bribe payments were stopped in 2004 when a new CEO arrived. Chiquita soon sold its Colombian interests. Chiquita had earned

about $50 million in profits from the time AUC was designated a terrorist organization until the period when the payments ceased.

In 2007, Chiquita entered a guilty plea to the felony of engaging in transactions with terrorists. A federal judge sentenced Chiquita to $25 million in fines and five years probation. Some evidence suggests Chiquita may have delayed its decision to stop payments by nearly one year as it waited for the U.S. government to review the security implications of a Chiquita withdrawal from Colombia. U.S. Justice Department officials denied that claim, and in 2007 they concluded their investigation by deciding not to bring criminal charges against former Chiquita officials.

Families of Colombians killed or tortured by the terrorists along with human rights groups have filed several civil lawsuits against Chiquita for supporting the terrorists who allegedly used the bribe money to buy weapons. During the period of Chiquita payments to AUC, some 4,000 Colombians were killed in the banana-growing region of Colombia. An Organization of American States investigation concluded that 3,000 Central American rifles and millions of rounds of ammunition reached the terrorists after allegedly being unloaded at a Colombian port by Banadex. Colombian officials argue that Chiquita was not a victim of extortion and that the company knew AUC was using the bribery proceeds to attack peasants, union workers, and various rival groups.

Questions

1. Chiquita argued that the safety of its employees required payment of the bribes, even after learning of their illegality. What would you have done, had you been in charge? Explain.

2. Should Chiquita's corporate officers have been prosecuted by the U.S. government? Explain.

Sources: Sibylla Brodzinsky, "Chiquita Case Puts Big Firms on Notice," *The Christian Science Monitor*, April 11, 2007 [**http://www .csmonitor.com/2007/0411/p01s03-woam.html**]; Laurie P. Cohen, "Chiquita Ex-Officials Won't Face Charges," *The Wall Street Journal*, September 12, 2007, p. B2; Carol D. Leonnig, "In Terrorism-Law Case, Chiquita Points to U.S.," *Washington Post*, August 2, 2007, p. A01; David J. Lynch, "Murder and Payoffs Taint Business in Colombia," *USA TODAY*, October 30, 2007, sec. Money, p. 1B; and Sue Reisinger, "Blood Money Paid by Chiquita Shows Company's Hard Choices," *Corporate Counsel*, November 26, 2007 [**http://www .law.com/jsp/ihc/PubArticleFriendlyIHC.jsp?id= 1195639472310**].

Whistle Blowing

Whistle blower Bradley Birkenfeld was awarded a $104 million government payment in 2012 for telling the Internal Revenue Service how his employer, Swiss bank UBS, helped thousands of Americans evade taxes. Birkenfeld's inside information helped the U.S. government crack open Swiss banking secrecy. As a result, at least 33,000 Americans have voluntarily disclosed their offshore accounts, resulting in perhaps $5 billion in revenue for the Internal Revenue Service.[95] UBS avoided prosecution by paying $780 million and disclosing useful information to the federal government. Birkenfeld had been sentenced in 2009 to 40 months in prison for fraud in withholding information from federal investigators, but he was released early. Birkenfeld reportedly also told a court that he had smuggled diamonds for a client in a tube of toothpaste.[96] Despite those alleged misdeeds, the government decided to make the big payment to Birkenfeld to avoid discouraging other potential whistle blowers.[97]

> **Whistle-blower Bradley Birkenfeld was awarded $104 million.**

Many federal statutes include whistle blower provisions and the federal False Claims Act rewards those who help stop fraud involving government contracts. Whistle blowers typically are entitled to 10 to 30 percent of the recovery from the wrongdoer. Whistle blowing appears to be on the rise following the passage of the 2010 Dodd–Frank Wall Street Reform and Consumer Protection Act (see Chapter 8) which includes a cash reward for those whose information regarding federal securities law violations leads to a recovery exceeding $1 million. The Securities and Exchange Commission received about 3,000 tips in the first year of the program.[98] [For an overview of whistle blower activity and protections, see **http://www.whistleblowers.org/** and for a law firm dedicated to representing whistle blowers as well as their stories, see **http://www .phillipsandcohen.com/**]

Retaliation

Despite expanded legal protection, whistle-blowers often pay a high price for exercising their consciences. Americans have long deplored "squealing," and we tend to ignore

> Americans have long deplored "squealing."

violations, partly out of fear of retribution. A recent survey found that 73 percent of full-time American employees observed wrongdoing on the job, but only about 36 percent of those employees actually reported that wrongdoing to bosses.[99]

James Nordgaard, a hedge fund trader, said his former employer, Paradigm Capital, "embarked on a campaign of retaliation" against him after he blew the whistle on what he says were "trading violations." Nordgaard says he was removed from his trading desk, isolated in a room "with little ventilation" and subsequently demoted.[100] Dodd–Frank expressly forbids discharge, demotion, and other forms of retribution against securities law whistle-blowers; other federal laws, such as Sarbanes–Oxley, provide varying degrees of protection in some other areas of enforcement.

Questions

1. Why is the role of "squealer" or whistle-blower so repugnant to many Americans?
2. *a.* How would you feel about a classmate who blew the whistle on you for cheating on an examination?
   b. Would you report cheating by a classmate if it came to your attention? Explain.

Ethics Codes

Most big companies have voluntarily developed ethics codes; some providing rather detailed "dos and don'ts" about employee conduct and others consisting of more generalized statements of principles. Section 406 of Sarbanes–Oxley—specifically requires publicly traded companies to adopt a code of ethics for senior financial officers or to explain why they have not done so. Section 406 defines a code of ethics as written standards that are reasonably designed to deter wrongdoing and to promote such behaviors as honest conduct, full disclosure in reports, compliance with all applicable laws and rules, prompt reporting of violations, and methods for conforming to the code's expectations. [For the Ethics Officers Association, see **http://www.eoa.org**]

Responding to SOX and other pressures, an increasing number of companies have prepared more detailed codes, displayed them more prominently, required employees to read and sign the codes, and created training methods to more firmly integrate ethical expectations into company decision making. Companies that can show well-developed ethical systems, including codes of conduct and compliance with those codes, may receive more sympathetic treatment from the justice system if criminal problems emerge. [For the Ethics Resource Center, see **http://www.ethics.org/**]

Are codes effective in practice? Research on that question is mixed, although a 2011 study of 392 international companies found a positive relationship between the quality (topics covered, tone, commitment to corporate values, nonretaliation provisions, etc.) of codes of conduct and ethical performance. Companies that maintained high-quality codes of conduct were found to rank highly in corporate citizenship, sustainability, ethical behavior, and public perception of the firm.[101] [For information on global corporate governance and citizenship, see **http://www.conference-board.org/**]

Assuring an Ethical Culture at Raytheon

Jay Stephens, general counsel, and Patti Ellis, vice president for business ethics and compliance, at defense contractor Raytheon, outlined some strategies for building an ethical commitment throughout a complex organization:

- **Aim High.** The Board of Directors and top leaders must set the ethics tone and push it down through the company.
- **Keep Learning.** Raytheon's 70,000 employees are regularly educated about ethics.
- **Discuss.** Talking about ethics builds trust in the organization.
- **Keep It Real.** Each year employees receive four ethics videos featuring dilemmas that may be encountered on the job.
- **Step Back.** Don't be driven to wrongdoing by deadlines. If not sure what to do, employees are encouraged to pause and think.

Questions

1. Do you think ethics training is likely to have a significant impact on managerial and corporate misconduct? Explain.
2. Do you think companies with reputations for high ethical quality would have an edge in recruiting employees? Explain.

Source: Steve Watkins, "Regular Ethics Training Gets Employees Talking," *Investors.com,* March 15, 2012 [**http://news.investors.com/**].

Internet Exercise

Can ethics be taught? Many people say no. Experts at the Markkula Center for Applied Ethics at Santa Clara University explored that question. Look for their answer at [**http://www.scu.edu/ethics/practicing/decision/canethicsbetaught.html**].

a. Explain their conclusion.
b. Do you agree? Explain.

Chapter Questions

1. *Business Ethics* magazine reported the following ethical dilemma submitted by an anonymous reader:

    Mary had only a few days to earn $1,000 in sales that would allow her to reach the $1 million sales plateau where she would receive a $10,000 bonus allowing her to finance the dream home she had found. The sales climate was tough, but she had one remaining prospect, inner-city Lincoln School, which could make especially good use of new educational materials. Lincoln had no budget for discretionary purchases, but Mary considered "donating" $1,000 to the school in return for which they would make the purchases that would put her over the top. She knew her donation would help disadvantaged students and herself, but her conscience was troubled.[102] What should she do? Explain.

2. Psychologists Jean Twenge and W. Keith Campbell say that we are in the midst of a "narcissism epidemic."[103]
   a. Have you observed any evidence that supports their conclusion? Explain.
   b. Do you agree with their conclusion? Explain.

3. a. Would you say that female undergraduate business students are more ethically inclined than their male counterparts? Explain.
   b. Would you say that religious commitment correlates with a stronger ethical inclination among undergraduate business students? Explain.

4. a. In her book *Lying,*[104] Sissela Bok argues that lying by professionals is commonplace. For example, she takes the position that prescribing placebos for experimental purposes is a lie and immoral. Do you agree with her position? Explain.
   b. Is the use of an unmarked police car an immoral deception? Explain.
   c. One study estimates that Americans average 200 lies per day if one includes "white lies" and inaccurate excuses. On balance, do you believe Americans approve of lying? Explain.

5. A group of 12 employees at a real estate office in south Florida chipped in $20 each toward the purchase of lottery tickets for a March 2013 Powerball drawing. One employee, Jennifer Maldanado, an administrative assistant who had been working in the office for only two weeks had not even received her first paycheck yet, so she declined to join the pool. The group of 12 won $1 million, which came to over $83,000 each. Laurie Finkelstein Reader, the team leader in the office, said that winning was not going to be as much fun for the group without Maldanado, so she texted the other winners, and they all agreed to give a portion (undivulged) of their winnings to Maldanado.[105]
   a. Morally speaking, is sharing winnings more commendable than keeping all for oneself? Explain.
   b. Could this real estate office operate effectively if workers shared their earnings as well as their lottery winnings? Explain.
   c. Morally speaking, would sharing earnings be the more commendable approach to the office's pay policies? Explain.
   d. Most of the office workers who shared with Maldanado were women. Do you think women are more inclined to share than men? If so, are women more worthy of moral approval than are men? Explain.

6. The following quote and questions are drawn from Leonard Lewin's "Ethical Aptitude Test."

   > As with other goods and services, the medical care available to the rich is superior to that available to the poor. The difference is most conspicuous in the application of new and expensive lifesaving techniques.[106]

   a. Is ability to pay an acceptable way to allocate such services? Explain.
   b. If not, how should such services be apportioned?
   c. Many lifesaving drugs can be tested effectively only on human beings. But often subjects are exposed to such dangers that only those who feel they have nothing to lose willingly participate. Are there any circumstances in which it would be right

to conduct such tests without ensuring that the persons tested clearly understood the risks they were taking? Explain.

  d. How much in dollars is the average human life worth?

7. *The Los Angeles Times* recently headlined a story: "Getting Brilliant Students to Seek Jobs beyond Wall Street."[107] The article examined the movement at some of the nation's top universities to encourage the brightest graduates to broaden their job search beyond high-paying Wall Street opportunities. An online campaign labeled "Stop the Brain Drain" gathers signatures and pushes for changes in campus recruiting practices. The prestigious Massachusetts Institute of Technology has created an entrepreneurship center to provide support for students seeking work with start-ups and other smaller ventures. Bill Aulet, who heads the center, explained some of his reasoning: "Once it became clear that financial instruments were a big cause of the [financial] crisis, and that's what our incredibly intelligent students were being used for, we thought, 'Boy, can't they be used to do more useful things?'"[108]

  a. Would we be better off as a nation if more of our brighter students shunned Wall Street jobs? Explain.

  b. What will you do? Explain.

8. A pharmacist in Lexington, Kentucky, refused to stock over-the-counter weight reducers. His reasons were (1) the active ingredient is the same as that in nasal decongestants; (2) he feared their side effects, such as high blood pressure; and (3) he felt weight reduction should be achieved via self-discipline.[109] Assume the pharmacist manages the store for a group of owners who have given him complete authority about the products stocked. Was his decision ethical? Explain.

9. When *Business and Society Review* surveyed the presidents of 500 large U.S. companies, 51 responded with their reactions to hypothetical moral dilemmas. One question was this:

  > Assume that you are president of a firm that provides a substantial portion of the market of one of your suppliers. You find out that this supplier discriminates illegally against minorities, although no legal action has been taken. Assume further that this supplier gives you the best price for the material you require, but that the field is competitive. Do you feel that it is proper to use your economic power over this supplier to make them stop discriminating?[110]

  Respond to this question.

10. *a.* Do you think taking office supplies home from work for personal use is unethical? Explain.

  b. Are employers committing a serious ethics breach when they monitor their employees' e-mail? Explain.

11. Commentator Robert Scheer asked, "What does it mean that a whopping 70 percent of Americans, according to a recent *New York Times–CBS News* poll, believe that mass culture is responsible for debasing our moral values?"[111]

  a. Answer Scheer's question.

  b. Scheer went on to say;

  > Worse, these national moralists—dominated these days by evangelical Christians—politicize the issue by blaming "liberal Hollywood" for what deregulation and the free

market have wrought. Never mind that Arnold Schwarzenegger made all those violent movies, it is the Democrats and their ilk who are corrupting youth by promulgating our "relativistic" morality. But that's just bunk.[112]

Do you agree with Scheer's "that's just bunk" position? If not, why? If so, who is to blame for our arguable moral decay?

12. In general, does the American value system favor "cheaters" who win in life's various competitions over virtuous individuals who "lose" with regularity? Explain.

13. If you were an executive about to hire a new manager, which of the following qualities would you consider most important/least important: verbal skills, honesty/ integrity, enthusiasm, appearance, sense of humor? Explain.

14. Noted University of Sydney psychologist Vince Cakic has warned that students are increasingly using drugs to enhance performance on examinations and papers.
    a. Is the use of drugs to enhance school performance unfair/wrong/immoral in your view? Explain.
    b. Would you advocate urine testing as a means of identifying those using brain-boosting drugs in examination situations? Explain.

15. *a.* Rank the following occupations as to your perception of their honesty and ethical quality: bankers, lawyers, doctors, college teachers, engineers, police officers, car salespeople, stockbrokers, clergy, and journalists.
    b. In general, do you find educated professionals to be more ethical than skilled but generally less educated laborers? Explain.
    c. Can you justify accepting an occupation that is not at or near the top of your ethical ranking? Explain how your ranking affects your career choices.

16. Can businesspeople successfully guide their conduct by the Golden Rule?

17. Comment on the following quotes from Albert Z. Carr:

    [M]ost bluffing in business might be regarded simply as game strategy—much like bluffing in poker, which does not reflect on the morality of the bluffer.

    I quoted Henry Taylor, the British statesman who pointed out that "falsehood ceases to be falsehood when it is understood on all sides that the truth is not expected to be spoken"—an exact description of bluffing in poker, diplomacy, and business.

    * * * * *

    [T]he ethics of business are game ethics, different from the ethics of religion.

    * * * * *

    An executive's family life can easily be dislocated if he fails to make a sharp distinction between the ethical systems of the home and the office—or if his wife does not grasp that distinction.[113]

18. Is lying a routine ingredient in American sales practice? Explain.

19. Assume you are working as manager of women's clothing in a large department store. You observe the manager of equivalent rank to you in men's clothing performing poorly in that she arrives late for work, she keeps records ineptly, and she is rude to customers. Her work, however, has no direct impact on your department.

    a. Do you have any responsibility either to help her or to report her poor performance? Explain.

    b. If the store as a whole performs poorly, but you have performed well, do you bear any personal responsibility for the store's failure in that you confined your efforts exclusively to your own department even though you witnessed mismanagement in the men's clothing department? Explain.

20. We are often confronted with questions about the boundaries of our personal responsibilities.

    a. How much money, if any, must you give to satisfy your moral responsibility in the event of a famine in a foreign country? Explain.

    b. Would your responsibility be greater if the famine were in America? Explain.

Notes

1. David Cho, "Pressure at Mortgage Firm Led to Mass Approval of Bad Loans," *The Washington Post,* May 7, 2007, p. A01.

2. Ibid.

3. Ibid.

4. Katalina Bianco, "The Subprime Lending Crisis: Causes and Effects of the Mortgage Meltdown," *CCH,* 2008 [**www.business.cch.combanking/finance/focus/. . ./Subprime_WP_rev.pdf**].

5. PEW Economic Policy Group, "The Cost of the Financial Crisis: The Impact of the September 2008 Economic Collapse," *Financial Reform Project,* April 28, 2010 [**http://www.pewfr.org/project_reports_detail?id=0033**].

6. "Eric Holder Admits Some Banks Are Just Too Big to Prosecute," *HuffPost Business,* March 6, 2013 [**www.huffingtonpost.com/**].

7. Carl Hausman, "Most Doubt the Integrity of Wall Street," *Ethics Newsline,* March 15, 2010 [**http://www.globalethics.org/newsline/**].

8. Scott Patterson and Susan Pulliam, "Buffett Is Expected to Fire at Will," *The Wall Street Journal,* April 30, 2010, p. C1.

9. Kevin McCoy, "Ex-Tyco CEO Begs, but Parole Board Says No." *USA TODAY,* April 12, 2012, P. 3B.

10. Jack and Suzy Welch, "The Welch Way," *BusinessWeek,* June 12, 2006, p. 100.

11. "Americans Negative about United States' Moral Values, Poll," *HuffPost Religion,* May 19, 2012 [**http://www.huffingtonpost.com**] and "U.S. Problems about More than 'Moral Values': NBC/WSJ Poll," *CNBC.com* [**http://www.cnbc.com**].

12. David Callahan, *The Cheating Culture: Why More Americans Are Doing Wrong to Get Ahead* (New York: Harcourt, 2004).

13. Eriq Gardner, "Cheat Sheet," *Corporate Counsel,* June 2004, p. 131.

14. For a commentary on Ariely's book, see David Brooks, "The Moral Diet," *The New York Times*, June 7, 2012 [**http://www.nytimes.com**].

15. Eryn Brown, "Wealthy, Motivated by Greed, Are More Likely to Cheat, Study Finds," *latimes.com*, February 27, 2012 [**latimes.com/news/science/la-sci-0228-greed-20120228,0,5965885.story**].

16. Chris McDonald, "Social Class and Unethical Behavior," *Canadian Business,* March 1, 2012 [**http://www.canadianbusiness.com/**].

17. SaintPetersBlog, "Poll: More Americans Would Give Up Sex Before Smartphone," *The Daily Kos,* April 12, 2013 [**http://www.dailykos.com/**].

18. Olivia Fleming, "Is This the Ultimate Multi-Tasking?" *MailOnline*, May 10, 2012 [**http://www.dailymail.co.uk/**].

19. Bill Hoffman, "Cell Users Put Sex on Hold," *New York Post,* April 12, 2005 [**nypost.com**].

20. Jennifer Levitz, "Harvard Punishes Dozens of Students for Cheating," *The Wall Street Journal,* February 1, 2013 [**http://online.wsj.com/**].

21. Donald L. McCabe, Kenneth D. Butterfield, and Linda Klebe Trevino, "Academic Dishonesty in Graduate Business Programs: Prevalence, Causes, and Proposed Action," *Academy of Management Learning & Education* 5, no. 3 (2006), p. 294.

22. Ibid.

23. Lee Berton, "Business Students Hope to Cheat and Prosper, New Study Shows," *The Wall Street Journal,* April 25, 1995, p. B1.

24. Susan C. Thomson, "Internet Helps Swell E-Cheating on Campuses," *The Washington Post,* March 14, 2004, p. A08.

25. Cathy Payne, "High School Students Cheating Less, Survey Finds," *USA TODAY,* November 25, 2012 [**http://www.usatoday.com/**].

26. Leslie Wayne, "A Promise to Be Ethical in an Era of Immorality," *The New York Times,* May 30, 2009 [**www.nytimes.com**].

27. Mary Rourke, "What Happened to America's Moral Climate?" *Los Angeles Times,* April 26, 2001, p. E1.

28. John H. Pryor et al., "The American Freshman: National Norms Fall 2012," Cooperative Institutional Research Program at the Higher Education Research Institute at UCLA [**www.heri.ucla.edu/monographs/TheAmericanFreshman2012.pdf**].

29. Beckie Supiano, "How Spiritual Traits Enhance Students' Lives—And Maybe Their Grades," *The Chronicle of Higher Education,* November 16, 2010 [**http://chronicle.com/**].

30. News Release, "Students Experience Spiritual Growth During College," December 18, 2007 [**www.spirituality.ucla.edu**].

31. Bill Davidow, "The Internet 'Narcissism Epidemic'," *The Atlantic, March,* 2013 [**http://www.theatlantic.com/**].

32. "The Most-Praised Generation Goes to Work," *The Wall Street Journal,* April 20, 2007, p. W1.

33. Jonah Goldberg, "Our Centers of the Universe," *latimes.com,* August 7, 2007 [**http://www.latimes.com/news/opinion/la-oe-goldberg7aug07,0,692285.column?coll=la-tot-opinion&track=ntottext**].

34. Raymond Baumhart, *Ethics in Business* (New York: Holt, Rinehart & Winston, 1968), p. 10.

35. For more about existentialism, see Andrew West, "Sartrean Existentialism and Ethical Decision-Making in Business," *Journal of Business Ethics* 81 (2008), p. 15.

36. Carl Hausman, "Responsibility," *Ethics Newsline,* September 28, 2009 [**http://www.globalethics.org/newsline/2009/09/28/responsibility/**].

37. Mark Oppenheimer, "The Rise of the Corporate Chaplain," *BusinessWeek,* August 23, 2012 [**http://www.businessweek.com/**].

38. Cara Buckley, "Man Is Rescued by Stranger on Subway Tracks," *The New York Times,* January 3, 2007 [**http://www.nytimes. com/2007/01/03/nyregion/03life.html**].

39. Associated Press, "British Priest: Shoplifting Is Sometimes OK," *Waterloo/Cedar Falls Courier,* December 23, 2009, p. 3A.

40. Richard Lorant, "Rebuilding Corporate Compassion—Oath to Millworkers May Pay Off," *Seattle Times,* December 11, 1996 [**community.seattletimes.nwsource.com/**].

41. Timothy Schelhardt, "Are Layoffs Moral? One Firm's Answer: You Ask, We'll Sue," *The Wall Street Journal,* August 1, 1996, p. A1.

42. Ibid.

43. John P. MacKenzie, "Lending a Hand If a Company Asks," *The New York Times,* February 3, 2002, Sec. 3, p. 11.

44. Antonia Van De Velde, "Trust in Business Leaders at Low as Davos Begins," *CNBC.com*, January 22, 2013 [**http://www.cnbc.com/100396721**].

45. "Confidence in Institutions," *Gallup Historical Trends*, June 7–10, 2012 [**www.gallup.com /poll/1597/confidence-institutions.aspx**].

46. "Survey Sees Less Misconduct but More Reporting and Retaliation," *The Wall Street Journal*, January 5, 2012 [**http://blogs.wsj.com/**].

47. Chris MacDonald, "The Golden Age of Ethical Business," *The Business Ethics Blog,* March 15, 2010 [**http://businessethicsblog.com/**].

48. For an elaboration of Kohlberg's stages, see, for example, W.D. Boyce and L.C. Jensen, *Moral Reasoning* (Lincoln, NE: University of Nebraska Press, 1978), pp. 98–109.

49. Lawrence Kohlberg, "The Cognitive–Development Approach to Moral Education," *Phi Delta Kappan* 56 (June 1975), p. 670.

50. Carol Gilligan, "In A Different Voice: Women's Conceptions of Self and Morality," *Harvard Educational Review* 47, no. 4 (November 1977), p. 481.

51. For an overview of the justice versus care debate, see Grace Clement, *Care, Autonomy, and Justice* (Boulder, CO: Westview Press, 1996).

52. James Weber and David Wasieleski, "Investigating Influences on Managers' Moral Reasoning," *Business & Society* 40, no. 1 (March 2001), pp. 79, 83.

53. Diana Robertson et al., "The Neural Processing of Moral Sensitivity to Issues of Justice and Care," *Neuropsychologia* 45 (2007), pp. 755, 763.

54. For a description of the moral intuition argument, see Jonathan Haidt, "The Emotional Dog and Its Rational Tail: A Social Intuitionist Approach to Moral Judgment," *Psychological Review* 108, no. 4 (2001), p. 814.

55. See Joshua Greene & Jonathan Haidt, "How (and Where) Does Moral Judgment Work?" *Trends in Cognitive Science* 6 (2002), p. 517.

56. Marc Hauser, *Moral Minds* (New York: HarperCollins Publishers, 2006).

57. Paul Bloom, "The Moral Life of Babies," *The New York Times,* May 3, 2010 [**http://www .nytimes.com**].

58. Nicholas Wade, "Is 'Do Unto Others' Written into Our Genes?" *The New York Times,* September 18, 2007 [**http://www.nytimes.com/2007/09/18/science/18mora.html?**].

59. See, e.g., David Pizarro and Paul Bloom, "The Intelligence of the Moral Intuitions Comment on Haidt," *Psychological Review* 110, no. 1 (2003), p. 193.

60. David Brooks, "The End of Philosophy," *The New York Times,* April 7, 2009 [**http://www .nytimes.com/**].

61. Benedict Carey, "Study Finds Brain Injury Changes Moral Judgment," *The New York Times,* March 21, 2007 [**http://www.nytimes.com/**].

62. Sam A. Hardy, "Identity, Reasoning, and Emotion: An Empirical Comparison of Three Sources of Moral Motivation," *Motivation and Emotion* 30 (2006), p. 207.

63. Ibid.

64. Ruodan Shao, Karl Aquino, and Dan Freeman, "Beyond Moral Reasoning: A Review of Moral Identity Research and Its Implications for Business Ethics," *Business Ethics Quarterly* 18, no. 4 (2008), p. 513.

65. Edwin M. Hartman, "Can We Teach Character? An Aristotelian Answer," *Academy of Management Learning & Education* 5, no. 1 (2006), p. 68.

66. "2007 National Business Ethics Survey," *Ethics World,* December 31, 2010 [**http://www.ethicsworld.org/ethicsandemployees/nbes.php**].

67. Jacquelyn Smith, "The World's Most Ethical Companies," *Forbes*, March 15, 2012 [**www.forbes.com/**].

68. Michael Connor, "Survey Forecasts 'Looming Ethics Downturn' in Corporate America," *Business Ethics,* January 5, 2012 [**business-ethics.com/**].

69. Joseph L. Badaracco, Jr., and Allen P. Webb, "Business Ethics: A View from the Trenches," *California Management Review 37,* no. 2 (Winter 1995), pp. 8, 12.

70. Richard Edelman, "Denial in the Corner Office," *The Conference Board CEO Challenge 2013,* May 9, 2013 [**www.edelman.com/p/6-a-m/denial-in-the-corner-office/**].

71. Daniel Akst, "Room at the Top, for Improvement," *The Wall Street Journal,* October 26, 2004, p. D8.

72. Bill Hawkins, as told to Cait Murphy, "Bill Hawkins: How I Made the Toughest Call of My Career," BNET, October 5, 2009 [**http://www.bnet.com**].

73. Lauren Weber, "Expense-Account Tightwads Take the Road Less Expensive," *The Wall Street Journal*, March 30, 2012, p. A1.

74. Pricewaterhouse Coopers, "Global Economic Crime Survey 2011," November 2011 [**http://www.pwc.com/**].

75. Ibid.

76. Floyd Norris, "A Troubling Survey on Global Corruption," *The New York Times*, May 17, 2013 [**http://www.nytimes.com/**].

77. Michael S. Schmidt and Edward Wyatt, "Corporate Fraud Cases Often Spare Individuals," *The New York Times*, August 7, 2012 [**http://www.nytimes.com**].

78. Ibid.

79. Peter Henning, "Deferred Prosecution Agreements and Cookie-Cutter Justice," *The New York Times*, September 17, 2012 [**http://dealbook.nytimes.com/**].

80. Ibid.

81. News Editor, "Sarbanes–Oxley Compliance Benefits Outweigh Costs, Companies Say," *EDGAROnline*, June 28, 2010 [**http://www.edgar-online.com/**].

82. Lora Bentley, "SEC Study: Benefits of Sarbanes–Oxley Compliance Outweigh Cost," *ITBusinessEdge*, October 16, 2009 [**http://www.itbusnessedge.com**].

83. Michael Rapoport, "Law's Big Weapon Sits Idle," *The Wall Street Journal*, July 29, 2012 [**http://online.wsj.com/**].

84. Ibid.

85. Portions of this paragraph relied on Robert G. Morvillo and Robert J. Anello, "White-Collar Crime, Corporate Compliance Programs: No Longer Voluntary," *New York Law Journal*, December 7, 2004, p. 3.

86. Chad Bray, "Perfume, Dresses and Cash in Ralph Lauren Bribe Scheme," *The Wall Street Journal*, April 22, 2013 [**http://online.wsj.com/**].

87. Shearman and Sterling, "FCPA Digest: Recent Trends and Patterns in the Enforcement of the Foreign Corrupt Practices Act," January 2012 [**www.shearman.com**].

88. Nick Wingfield, "U.S. Said to Look into Microsoft Bribery Allegations," *CNBC.com,* March 20, 2013 [**http://www.cnbc.com**].

89. David Barstow and Alejandra Xanic von Bertrab, "How Wal-Mart Used Payoffs to Get Its Way in Mexico," *The New York Times*, December 17, 2012 [**http://www.nytimes.com**].

90. Ibid.

91. Transparency International, "2012 Corruption Perceptions Index," [**www.transparency.org /cpi2012/**].

92. Michael Mainville, "Bribery Thrives as Big Business in Putin's Russia," *SFGate.com*, January 2, 2007 [**http://www.sfgate.com/cgi-bin/article.cgi?file=/c/a/2007/01/02/MNG8QNBCTN1 .DTL**].

93. Ibid.

94. Leslie Wayne, "Hits, and Misses, in a War on Bribery," *The New York Times*, March 10, 2012 [**http://www.nytimes.com**].

95. Tom Schoenberg and David Voreacos, "UBS Whistle-Blower Secures $104 Million Award from IRS," *Bloomberg*, September 11, 2012 [**http://www.bloomberg.com/**].

96. David Kocieniewski," Whistle-Blower Awarded $104 Million by I.R.S.," *The New York Times*, September 11, 2012 [**www.nytimes.com**].

97. Ibid.

98. LeClair Ryan and Michael Volkov, "The Whistleblower Era," *Lexology*, November 20, 2012 [**http://www.lexology.com/**].

99. Pallavi Gogoi, "The Trouble with Business Ethics," *BusinessWeek*, June 22, 2007 [**www .businessweek.com/**].

100. Ben Protess and Nathaniel Popper, "Hazy Future for Thriving S.E.C. Whistle-Blower Effort," *The New York Times*, April 23, 2013 [**dealbook.nytimes.com/**].

101. Patrick Erwin, "Corporate Codes of Conduct: The Effects of Code Content and Quality on Ethical Performance," *Journal of Business Ethics* 99 (2011), pp. 535–548.

102. Shel Horowitz, "Should Mary Buy Her Own Bonus?" *Business Ethics*. Submitted by Anonymous, August 1, 2007 [**http://www.business-ethics.com/node/65**].

103. Bill Davidow, "The Internet 'Narcissism Epidemic,'" *The Atlantic*, March 2013 [**http://www .theatlantic.com/**].

104. Sissela Bok, *Lying: Moral Choice in Public and Private Life* (New York: Vintage Books, 1999).

105. Maria Camila Bernal, "Lucky Lady: She Opted Out of Powerball Pool, but Gets a Cut of $1 Million Anyway," *The Miami Herald*, March 26, 2013 [**http://www.miamiherald.com/**].

106. Leonard C. Lewin, "Ethical Aptitude Test," *Harper's*, October 1976, p. 21.

107. Nathaniel Popper, "Getting Brilliant Students to Seek Jobs beyond Wall Street," *latimes.com*, November 4, 2011 [**www.latimes.com**].

108. Ibid.

109. Reported on WKYT TV, Channel 27, Evening News, Lexington, Kentucky, May 12, 1980.

110. "Business Executives and Moral Dilemmas," *Business and Society Review*, no. 13 (Spring 1975), p. 51.

111. Robert Scheer, "The Invisible Hand Holds the Remote," *Los Angeles Times*, November 30, 2004, p. B13.

112. Ibid.

113. Albert Z. Carr, "Is Business Bluffing Ethical?" *Harvard Business Review* 46, no. 1 (January–February 1968), pp. 143–52.

CHAPTER THREE

The Corporation and Public Policy: Expanding Responsibilities

After completing this chapter, students will be able to:

1. Recognize the interdependent relationship between business and the larger society.

2. Discuss whether business should play a more or less active role in politics, education, and other public-sector activities.

3. Discuss concerns about globalization.

4. List some of the critics' primary complaints about the alleged abuse of corporate power in contemporary America.

5. Make a tentative assessment regarding the proper role of business in society.

6. Explain the concept of corporate social responsibility.

7. Discuss whether socially responsible business is "good business."

8. Explain the triple bottom-line/sustainability approach to corporate citizenship.

9. Contrast the stakeholder and shareholder approaches to corporate social responsibility.

PRACTICING ETHICS Yvon Chouinard and Patagonia

Outdoor adventurer Yvon Chouinard and his wife, Ellen Pennoyer, in 1972, founded Patagonia, Inc., the sports clothing and outdoor gear retailer. Privately owned, Ventura, California-based Patagonia with annual revenues that recently reached $540 million is the product of entrepreneurial drive and a corporate culture practicing "green" business and "management by absence."

Chouinard, was an early advocate of doing business in an environmentally friendly way, including for example, placing notes in Patagonia catalogs encouraging customers to buy only what they need. Chouinard's 2005 memoir, *Let My People Go Surfing,* explains his commitment to a workplace where capitalism, ethics, and fun can coexist. Chouinard minimizes workplace monitoring, believing lightly supervised employees will complete their work responsibly. Good surf and fresh snow are embraced at Patagonia where employees are free to take breaks for fun. Patagonia is often recognized as one of the best companies to work for in America.

Chouinard has become famous for his sense of social responsibility and his leadership in the environmental movement. Since 1985, Patagonia has donated 1 percent of its annual sales to environmental groups. Chouinard's 2012 book, *The Responsible Company,* details methods for making money while avoiding undue societal damage.

Chouinard threatened to leave Patagonia in 1994 when he learned that the cotton bought by the company often was produced by industrial farming that used toxic chemicals and was having, he felt, a devastating effect on the Earth. That cotton figured in 20 percent of the company's sales, but Patagonia changed over to organic cotton and persuaded others such as Nike and Timberland to begin to do the same. Chouinard said that Patagonia went a year without making a profit while the company found organic suppliers, overcame bankers' resistance, and found new gins and mills. The bigger point is that the switch was profitable and the right thing to do, a concept often missed by corporate America, he said.

Patagonia clothing is made in China, Thailand, Vietnam, and a number of other countries along with limited production in the United States. In establishing ties with a new manufacturing partner, Patagonia's Social and Environmental Responsibility team does a comprehensive analysis and follows up with constant audits, visits, and corrective measures to assure a safe, healthy, environmentally sound operation. Patagonia refuses to contract with companies employing workers under the age of 15, the minimum age acceptable to the International Labor Organization. All workers must be paid "a legal minimum wage," but Patagonia admits to falling short of its goal of a "living wage" for all those who make its products. [For more detail about Chouinard and Patagonia, see, e.g., Seth Stevenson, "America's Most Unlikely Corporate Guru," *The Wall Street Journal Magazine,* May 2012, p. 86.]

Questions

1. Is Chouinard correct that companies can treat workers well, respect the environment, and still make money? Explain.

2. If he is correct, why aren't all companies following the Patagonia model?

Sources: Keith Garber, "Yvon Chouinard: Patagonia Founder Fights for the Environment," *U.S. News & World Report,* October 22, 2009 [http://www.usnews.com/news/best-leaders/articles/2009/10/22]; Brad Wieners, "The Gospel of Yvon," *Men's Journal,* July 2007, p. 51, "Employees Who March to Their Own Music," *BusinessWeek,* December 19, 2005, p. 81; and Hugo Martin, "Outdoor Retailer Patagonia Puts Environment Ahead of Sales Growth," **latimes.com**, May 24, 2012 [latimes.com/].

Introduction

The Yvon Chouinard/Patagonia story expresses the central mission of this chapter; the examination of the corporation's duties, if any, beyond providing the best products and services at the lowest price. We ask in this chapter whether the corporation must make a broad contribution to the general societal welfare beyond the performance required by the market. Put another way, must the corporation fulfill the role of citizen with all of the responsibilities that corporate wealth and power suggest? Clearly, tomorrow's leaders must understand the increasingly complex and interdependent relationship between business and the larger society. We explore the changing nature of that relationship in four parts: (1) criticism of corporate America, (2) the emergence of the expectation of corporate social responsibility, (3) the management of social responsibility, and (4) the examination of some specific business and society issues.

Part One—Corporate Power and Corporate Critics

Corporate critics have long argued that the public interest has not been well served by America's big corporations. We recognize that colossal size and the economies of scale that accompany it have been critical to American competitiveness in today's tough global market. At the same time, that very size, the critics say, permits continuing abuse of the American public. Of course, we recognize that big companies are a fixture of the American landscape. However, a reminder of the specifics may be useful. (This chapter's examination of corporate America is limited to the critics' objections to corporate conduct. The legal standards governing corporate practice are addressed primarily in Chapter 9.)

Walmart is now the largest company in America (see Table 3.1) and the first service company to hold the top spot. Walmart is, by a wide margin, America's number-one employer with some 2.2 million workers globally, 1.4 million of whom work in the United States.[1]

TABLE 3.1   **America's Largest Corporations**

Corporation	Location	Sales Revenue (in billions)
Walmart Stores	Bentonville, AR	$469.2
ExxonMobil	Irving, TX	449.9
Chevron	San Ramon, CA	233.9
Phillips 66	Houston, TX	169.6
Berkshire Hathaway	Omaha, NE	162.5

Source: *Fortune* 500 2013 Annual Ranking of America's Largest Corporations.

The extraordinary wealth of America's corporate institutions is such that they tower over most countries of the world by some measures of economic might. If we compare corporate revenue with gross national product, (a common approach, but one that somewhat overstates the size of corporations relative to countries) Walmart is the 25th largest economic entity in the world and 42 of the 100 largest economic entities are corporations.[2]

ExxonMobil, number two on the *Fortune* 500 list, is often cited as an example of threatening and sometimes abusive corporate power. Highly respected investigative journalist Steve Coll released *Private Empire: ExxonMobil and American Power*[3] his 2012 book detailing a company that operates much like a nation, as described by reviewer Adam Hochschild:

> [T]his book isn't so much a story of ExxonMobil's influence over the American government. Rather, it's a picture of a corporation so large and powerful—operating in some 200 nations and territories—that it really has its own foreign policy.

* * * * * *

... ExxonMobil has its own armies. ... In Chad, its 2,500 security men patrolled the countryside in white radio-equipped S.U.V.'s, watching for guerrillas as the company set up an intelligence operation bigger and better than the local C.I.A. station. In the war-[w]racked Niger Delta, it gave boats to the Nigerian Navy, deployed its own vessels at sea to scout for pirates and "recruited, paid, supplied and managed sections of the Nigerian military and police."[4]

Another reviewer reminds us, however, that Coll's book portrays ExxonMobil as possessing "an honorable if rigid culture that seeks to supply a product . . . that a functioning society actually must have."[5]

Predictably, we have a conflicted view of big corporations. Sixty-seven percent of Americans express a favorable opinion, according to a 2012 nationwide survey, but 76 percent say too much power is concentrated in a few large companies. In a bit of a surprise, younger Americans responding to the survey had a slightly more favorable attitude toward big business than did their elders.[6]

The Corporate State—Economics

Perhaps the most pressing and immediate fear about corporate power is that it threatens America's economy rather than strengthens it. Mounting evidence shows an ongoing shift in the distribution of national income from workers to owners, and economists are increasingly concerned that concentrated power is reducing America's legendary and crucial power to innovate and thereby improve life for all.[7]

We see most of America's 50 states fighting feverishly among themselves to attract new corporate investment. The states compete by improving their "business climates" with incentives such as reduced taxes, reduced regulations, and cash grants. According to *The New York Times,* those incentives total at least $80 billion per year.[8] Of course, that corporate investment brings new jobs, an expanded tax base, and better lives in many ways, but the critics are concerned about the point at which incentives become unjustified corporate welfare.

Sometimes communities have mixed feelings about their success in generating corporate investment. Quincy, Washington, for example, was able to attract a massive Microsoft data center with the help of substantial incentives only to find that the company allegedly polluted the local environment with exhaust from giant, backup diesel generators while disputing utility penalties, as reported by *The New York Times:*

> In an attempt to erase a $210,000 penalty the utility said the company owed for overestimating its power use, Microsoft proceeded to simply waste millions of watts of electricity, records show. Then it threatened to continue burning power in what it acknowledged was an "unnecessarily wasteful" way until the fine was substantially cut. . . ."[9]

Taxes

Ingeniously exploiting tax code loopholes, Apple reportedly shielded at least $74 billion in profits from U.S. taxation for the years 2009 to 2012 by setting up affiliates in Ireland that had no employees and no physical offices.[10] Those affiliates received most of Apple's European and Asian profits, but since they were incorporated in Ireland, they were exempt from immediate U.S. taxation. Then Apple reportedly demonstrated that the affiliates were managed from Apple's headquarters in California, thus exempting the profits from Irish taxes.[11]

Apple was not alone in its tax avoidance success. A 2011 study found that 78 of America's biggest publicly traded companies paid no federal income taxes in at least one of the three years studied. The corporate share of American taxes has fallen in recent years to about 1.3 percent of the gross domestic product, a decline from 6 percent during the 1950s (part of that decline is due to a reduction in the number of businesses filing taxes as corporations).[12] Nonetheless, many experts argue that we should lower or do away with corporate taxes. America's combined federal and state corporate tax rates are now considered the highest in the world at 39.2 percent.[13] "Loopholes," however, allow American corporations to pay an actual rate of about 29.2 percent, which is somewhat below average globally, according to a U.S. Treasury Department analysis.[14] Regardless of rates and loopholes, we should remember that many large corporations do pay very significant amounts of taxes. ExxonMobil paid about $31 billion in federal income taxes in 2012, ranking it first among American companies in payments, while Chevron ($20 billion) and Apple ($14.21 billion) ranked second and third.[15]

[See U.S. Senator Bernie Sanders's (Ind.-VT) brief speech criticizing corporate tax loopholes at **http://www.youtube.com/watch?v=Sknt-UBRhxo**]

Misconduct/Incompetence?

> When Fox News asked Americans in a recent poll to say whether a series of people and institutions were helping or hurting the economy, the lowest score went to corporate chief executives. By almost six to one, voters said corporate chiefs had done more to hurt than to help the economy—a worse rating than accorded the president, congressional Republicans or Democrats, labor unions or lawmakers affiliated with the tea party.[16]

Some polls[17] place more blame with politicians than with the business community, but the stunning scandals and financial failures of recent years (the subprime loan collapse, Bernard Madoff's $65 billion Ponzi scheme, Wall Street's meltdown, Enron, WorldCom, and so on) have strengthened doubts about corporate honor and competence. As we discussed in Chapter 2, the big banks in particular have been harshly criticized. *Rolling Stone* magazine said, "Financial crooks brought down the world's economy. . . ."[18] A *New York Times* headline ran, "On Wall Street, a Culture of Greed Won't Let Go."[19] *New York Times* columnist Eduardo Porter cites a recent Gallup Poll finding that only one in five Americans has much trust in banks and asks, "Have corporations lost whatever ethical compass they once had?"[20] Or perhaps, he says, we are simply paying closer attention in these troubled times.

Monopoly and More

To the critics, a big portion of the corporate power problem is attributable to the structure of our economy, a structure they believe to be so concentrated that many industries and companies are no longer fully responsive to market commands. Further, those industries and companies are so powerful that the government cannot meaningfully regulate them, the critics say. Barry C. Lynn's 2010 book, *Cornered: The New Monopoly Capitalism and the Economics of Destruction,* makes the claim that much of America's economy is dominated by shared monopolies allowing producers and retailers to charge inflated prices because of a lack of meaningful competition. He points to domination by two or three giants in a wide array of consumer product markets: beer, toothpaste, pet foods, milk, and so on. Walmart and other retail goliaths cooperate so closely with their suppliers in pricing, shelf space assignments, and other details, that, Lynn claims, real competition simply doesn't exist in many product lines.[21] (For much more detail about monopoly problems and antitrust law, see Chapters 10 and 11.)

Likewise, complaints about the corporate role in pollution, discrimination, white-collar crime, misleading advertising, and so on remain commonplace. But in a democratic, free-market society such as America's, presumably we all must share some of the blame for our problems. If we are not happy with, for example, Walmart's treatment of its employees, we are free to shop elsewhere. Arguably, then, the role of business in American life merely reflects the values of the American people.

Furthermore, as we continue to think about the corporate power theme, we should note the ongoing decline in the number of American public corporations (those whose securities are offered for sale to the general public). Public companies have driven capitalism since their invention in the mid-1800s, but their numbers have been shrinking in the United States. Scandals, increasing regulation, and alternative business forms, such as partnerships (see Chapter 9), are among the forces that have combined to reduce public corporation numbers. Increasingly, investment money is being raised privately rather than through open sales on stock markets. Whether we are seeing the twilight of public companies is highly debated, but we should not be surprised to see a continued reshaping of the business landscape in ways that may put a new slant on corporate power concerns.

Globalization

When the Rana Plaza eight-story garment factory collapsed outside Dhaka, Bangladesh, on April 24, 2013, at least 1,127 workers were killed, but perhaps a new global awareness of sweatshop working conditions and careless, if not abusive, international supply chains may have emerged. A Bangladeshi government report concluded that the building had been constructed with substandard materials and a disregard for building codes. Upper floors were illegally added to the building and large power generators installed on those floors shook the building when they were switched on. On the day of the collapse, factory owners apparently ordered workers to enter the building despite cracks in the walls and other evidence of safety hazards.[22] The collapse was one in a long line of accidents and fires in the Bangladeshi garment industry that provides desperately-need jobs but is caught in a *race to the bottom* to provide the globe's cheapest labor.

> A *race to the bottom* to provide the globe's cheapest labor.

Our tightly-interconnected, highly efficient global supply systems have brought millions of jobs, substantial capital, and vital first steps on a path toward prosperity for currently struggling nations such as Bangladesh. Only China exceeds Bangladesh's $20 billion annual apparel export business. But globalization of the garment industry and many others has also brought new challenges, particularly for the wealthy, powerful Western manufacturers who profit spectacularly from cheap labor in less developed nations. Major brands such as Gap, H&M, and Walmart are among the many that are supplied by garment factories in Bangladesh.

Who is responsible, and what should be done? At this writing, two apparel groups (a largely European collective including H&M and an American group headed by Walmart and The Gap) have reached a preliminary safety agreement with government and labor groups. Tentative requirements include factory inspections by experienced personnel, a limit to the number of machines per floor, and exits at intervals not to exceed 25 meters. The two apparel groups have committed to sharing the cost of the safety improvements. Meanwhile, the Bangladeshi government has taken initial steps toward raising the $38 per month minimum wage while many companies have quickly looked toward alternative supplier sites in countries such as Cambodia and Guatemala. Of course, other countries and other companies face similar problems. For example, Apple has been harshly criticized for abusive labor conditions in its Chinese supplier factories, including accusations of child labor, unlawful overtime, harsh discipline, and unsafe working conditions.

Question

Canada's Loblaw Companies Limited, owner of the Joe Fresh brand, was among the companies whose clothing was produced at the collapsed factory. (Loblaw quickly announced that it would pay compensation to the families of victims.) Ethics expert Chris MacDonald responded to the tragedy by saying, "I'm still shopping at Joe Fresh. . . and with a clear conscience."[23]

Can we all continue to shop for cheap clothing while maintaining a clear conscience? Explain.

Globalization Fears   The garment factory tragedy vividly illustrates the critics' worry that global free trade is merely an opportunity for America's giant corporations to exploit cheap, powerless labor abroad. Further, the *outsourcing* of good, high-paid factory jobs from the United States to less developed nations has fundamentally challenged and changed life in this country.

In general, we can see that concerns about corporate domination of American life are now being applied to the entire globe. With the triumph of capitalism, in its various permutations (see Chapter 1), the world has come to understand that free markets usually are more efficient decision makers than government rules. As a result, national boundaries are receding in importance, technology is shrinking the globe, multinational companies are treating the world as one big marketing opportunity, less developed countries are trying to improve their living standards by connecting to that market, financial assets are flowing freely and almost instantaneously from one edge of the globe to another, and the world is becoming one highly greased, interconnected mass market.

Clearly, the universal advance of American corporate interests has produced problems, but enormous gains have also been achieved. The interesting question for our purposes is whether globalization brings with it new responsibilities for American corporations such as those raised in the wake of the garment factory deaths in Bangladesh. As McDonald's, Apple, and American popular culture capture the attention of the global populace, does that increasing "Americanization" or "Westernization" bring new corporate duties? For example, does the corporate community bear any responsibility for the ongoing conflict between Western and Muslim values? For the most part, governments are expected to address questions of that nature, but as globalization has magnified corporate power, we must wonder whether corporations won't increasingly be expected to fulfill expanded, and, doubtless, uncomfortable new roles. Harvard Business School professor Christopher Bartlett explains:

> [T]hose leading today's multination corporations must become much more attuned to the ways in which their actions can and do impact the fragile social, political, and economic environments in which they operate worldwide. Yet far too often these powerful companies have been so focused on their core economic role that they have ignored the huge social and political impact they have.[24]

Corporations as Psychopaths?

The 2004 movie documentary *The Corporation* argues that the corporation has become the dominant institution in American life, exceeding the influence of both religion and government. One result is that corporations often demonstrate the "traits of the prototypical psychopath." The contemporary corporation is depicted as an "exploitative monster" driven not by the greater good but by its first responsibility to stockholders.

Questions

1. In your view are corporations more powerful than government, religion, our educational system, and all other American institutions? Explain.
2. According to some polls, nearly three-quarters of Americans think corporations have too much power. Do you agree that corporations are too powerful? Explain.

Source: Jim Keough, "Film Sees Evil in Corporations," *Worchester Telegram & Gazette,* September 29, 2004, p. C5.

[For *The Corporation* in 23 chapters, see **http://www.thecorporation.com/index.cfm? page_id=46**]

The Corporate State—Politics

We turn now to politics, where, critics argue, big money enables the business community to disproportionately influence the electoral and law-making processes.

In recent decades, the corporate community has taken an increasingly direct role in the political process. As a result, corporate critics have been concerned that the financial weight of big business will undermine our pluralist, democratic approach to governance.

Corporate funds cannot lawfully be given directly to candidates for federal office. However, corporations (as well as labor unions, special interest groups, and others) can lawfully establish political action committees (PACs) to solicit and disburse voluntary campaign contributions. That is, corporations can solicit contributions from employees, shareholders, and others. That money is then put in a fund, carefully segregated from general corporate accounts, and disbursed by the PAC in support of a political agenda preferred by officers, managers, or shareholders. Although PAC contributions are voluntary, corporate employees often feel pressured to participate. Unlike the federal rules, about one-half of the states allow corporations to lawfully donate corporate funds to parties and candidates for state elections.

The role of conventional PACs in the political process has receded in importance following a momentous U.S. Supreme Court decision in the 2010 *Citizens United* case[25] The Supreme Court's highly controversial 5–4 ruling held that federal laws limiting corporate campaign contributions violated corporate free speech rights. Essentially, the decision allows corporations, labor unions, and some other aggregations to spend unlimited organizational funds for candidates and causes so long as they do not coordinate that spending with parties and/or candidates.

> The Supreme Court's highly controversial 5–4 ruling.

The five "conservative" justices in the *Citizens United* majority, treating dollars as speech, saw political spending limits as a direct denial of liberty guaranteed by the First Amendment. Corporations and labor unions were viewed by the Court as associations of individuals that should possess the same constitutional rights as the individuals themselves. Previous high court rulings had frequently recognized that First Amendment rights extend to corporations and that corporations are persons for some legal purposes. The four dissenters, from the "liberal" wing of the Court, argued that corporations and unions, in many other ways, are not treated as people and doing so in the case of political contributions could allow those organizations to dominate and further corrupt the political process.

In practice, *Citizens United* and other court decisions have allowed rapid changes in the nature of the national political process by opening the door to gushers of personal and corporate money funneled through Independent Expenditure PACs (usually called Super PACs) and nonprofit 501(c)4 Social Welfare Organizations. The latter groups, such as volunteer fire departments, must be designed to serve the common good if they want to maintain their preferred Internal Revenue Service status which exempts them from paying federal income taxes on the money they raise. These organizations can make political contributions in support of their goals as long as political activity is not their primary purpose. Thus, 501(c)4 groups are created to receive giant sums of money in support of a social welfare cause such as reduced government spending and a portion of that money typically is then spent on political advertising. For some, the 501(c)4 groups are particularly attractive because contributors' names need not be disclosed while the names of Super PAC donors, on the other hand, must be revealed.

Corporate Influence

Independent groups, including various forms of Super PACs, spent more than $1 billion in trying to influence the 2012 national election in which President Obama secured his second term. Much of that money came from corporations and wealthy individuals. Were those big-money contributors able to "buy" the election? Did the broadly condemned *Citizens United* decision lead to corporate domination of the electoral process? The direct and immediate answer to those questions based upon results from the 2012 election was a resounding "no." The critics' worst fears simply were not realized. The U.S. Chamber of Commerce, for example, spent nearly $24 million backing conservative candidates in 15 U.S. Senate races, but only two of those candidates prevailed.[26] The Chamber spent more than $7 million in 22 U.S. House of Representatives races and enjoyed four wins.[27]

Despite those 2012 results, big money, of course, will continue to be a powerful force in electoral performance. Moreover, that money shapes the subsequent legislative process, as argued by Ezra Klein of *The Washington Post*:

> If you step back, then, two things are happening simultaneously among the key interest groups in American politics. Labor is getting weaker. And corporations, in part due to *Citizens United*, are getting much stronger. The electoral effect of that is obvious: It favors Republicans. But the legislative effect is, perhaps, more significant: It favors corporate interests in Congress, as Democrats will have to be that much more solicitous of business demands in order to keep from being spent into oblivion.[28]

Change the Law?   Many Americans are arguing that we should amend the U.S. Constitution to make it clear that money does not constitute speech and that corporations are not entitled to the inalienable rights of persons. Congress has considered but to this point rejected legislation requiring, in brief, the disclosure of all those giving more than $10,000 to political causes. The Securities and Exchange Commission (SEC) is considering a rule requiring all publicly held corporations to reveal their political spending. PACs already must do so, but the proposed SEC rule would reach the aforementioned "social welfare" groups and would include trade associations such as the Chamber of Commerce.

In considering these concerns about corporate political spending, we need to remember that labor unions and other groups also have a big monetary voice in the political process. Thus, as *The Wall Street Journal* argues, corporations need to be sure that their voices are heard in the political process:

> [P]oliticians have created a gargantuan state that is so intrusive that businesses have no alternative than to spend money to defend themselves and their shareholders. . . . Liberals want business to disarm unilaterally.[29]

Furthermore, a recent study found that "corporate political efforts generally have positive effects on a firm's market value and its shareholder returns."[30] Arguably, then, corporations, in looking out for shareholder welfare, need to be very active in the political process.

Boycott Target?

The *Citizens United* decision seems to have given a legal and psychological boost to corporate political contributions, but the risks can be significant. Minnesota-based Target's $150,000 contribution in 2010 to MN Forward, a group supporting a conservative candidate for Minnesota governor was angrily assailed by some company employees and many Minnesota progressives. The specific objection was that the candidate indirectly supported by Target was an outspoken opponent of gay marriage. Target said it supported the candidate's strong pro-business policies. Nonetheless, protesters rallied against the company and urged a boycott of Target stores. Target issued an apology, reaffirmed its commitment to diversity, and promised a review process for political donations. Then in 2012, Target upset those on the other side of the gay marriage debate by selling T-shirts to raise money for a group that supported lawful gay marriage.

Questions

1. Would you have boycotted Target under either of these circumstances? Explain.

2. Had you been Target's CEO, would you have issued an apology? Explain.

3. Should corporations be free under the law to donate corporate treasury funds as they see fit in federal elections? Explain.

Sources: Associated Press, "Target Sells Shirts to Help Pro-Gay Marriage Group," *Waterloo-Cedar Falls Courier,* June 3, 2012, p. A8; Tom Hamburger and Jennifer Martinez, "Target Stores Negotiate with Gay-Lesbian Group over Political Spending," *latimes.com,* August 13, 2010 [**http://www.latimes.com/**]; and Martiga Lohn, "Target's Gay Employees Are Angered by Political Donation," *The Des Moines Register,* July 28, 2010, p. 1A.

Lobbying

Lobbying is an essential ingredient in big business strategy. Lobbying also often serves the very useful role of efficiently educating busy politicians about the vast array of issues they must address but cannot possibly master without assistance. Of course, lobbying is not confined to the business community. Labor unions, consumer and environmental interest groups and myriad others battle to have their voices heard. So lobbying serves a valuable role in government. Unfortunately, that role is often thoroughly corrupt. The clubby, personal nature of the lobbying process with its revolving door of politicians becoming lobbyists and lobbyists taking important government roles often undermines the democratic process.

Part of the blame for the nation's disastrous subprime mortgage crisis, for example, doubtless rests with lenders' ability to exert influence over government decision making. *The Washington Post* recently reported about former mortgage giant Countrywide Financial Corp.'s practice of making discount loans to former and current members of Congress and to executives at the taxpayer-backed mortgage company, Fannie Mae. While extending those favors, Countrywide was lobbying to block legislation that would have decreased the sale of subprime mortgages. Indeed, when Countrywide employees resisted making loans to Jim Johnson, CEO of Fannie Mae from 1991 to 1998, because he reportedly had a low credit score, Countrywide CEO Angelo Mozillo rejected those concerns saying, "Jim Johnson continues to be a source of many loans for our company and this is just a small token of appreciation for the business that he sends to us."[31]

Lobbying by the Numbers

Total lobbying spending in Washington, D.C. for 2012 was about $3.3 billion and more than 12,000 individuals were registered as lobbyists.[32] Both numbers reflect a pattern of declines from previous years spurred, in part, by changes in federal lobbying rules. The Honest Leadership and Open Government Act of 2007 was part of the most comprehensive lobbying and ethics reform effort in the federal government in many years. Studies and expert opinion, however, indicate that some of those who influence government are able to avoid registering as lobbyists by turning from direct legislative contact to new influence-peddling tactics such as social media campaigns.[33] Furthermore, the "revolving door" between Congress and lobbying firms remains robust with more than 340 former members of Congress and nearly 3,700 former government staffers working in lobbying or in a related field, according to a 2011 report.[34] The biggest spenders among lobbyists continue to be business groups with the Chamber of Commerce at the top with nearly $17 million in expenditures in the first quarter of 2013.[35]

Buy Votes?

In the end, does all of the corporate money buy votes? In many cases, apparently not. A recent, highly respected study of lobbying results found that most lobbying simply maintains the status quo; that is, nothing happens. The study concluded that opposing lobbyists and interest groups hold each other in check about 60 percent of the time. Thus, lobbyists, over a four-year period are successful in influencing policy about 40 percent of the time. The study also concluded that money influenced outcomes only when heavily weighted to one side.[36]

On the other hand, when lobbying is successful the payoff can be enormous. Just two weeks after agreeing to pay $762 million in penalties for marketing fraud, Amgen, the world's largest biotechnology company, was able to celebrate, nonetheless, when Congress included language in a financing bill that gave Amgen and others two additional years to sell a particular class of drugs without government price controls.[37] The delay is expected to cost Medicare up to $500 million.[38] Amgen, with 74 Washington lobbyists, reportedly was the only company arguing aggressively for the delay.[39] *The New York Times* decried the deal: "This dreadful episode is a classic example of the power of special interests to shape legislation and shows how hard it may be to carry out the reforms needed to cut health care costs."[40]

A Sunlight Foundation study of 200 corporations found that those firms investing heavily in lobbying enjoyed lower federal tax rates.[41] Lobbying influence even extends to writing the law itself, as *The New York Times* reported in 2013 about a bill that is under consideration at this writing:

> Bank lobbyists are not leaving it to lawmakers to draft legislation that softens financial regulations. Instead, the lobbyists are helping to write it themselves. One bill that sailed through the House Financial Services Committee this month—over the objections of the Treasury Department—was essentially Citigroup's. . . . Citigroup's recommendations were reflected in more than 70 lines of the House committee's 85-line bill. Two crucial paragraphs, prepared by Citigroup in conjunction with other Wall Street banks, were copied nearly word for word. (Lawmakers changed two words to make them plural.)[42]

Of course, Congress benefits from lobbyists' expertise in drafting legislation dealing with highly technical dimensions of American life, including the financial services industry. [For the Center for Responsive Politics and its extensive database on money in politics, see **http://www.opensecrets.org/**]

The Corporate State—Social Issues and Institutions

Clearly, the business community's influence in America's economic and political life is enormous, but the critics' concerns do not end there. The corporate message, they say, pervades and shapes American life. Business products and services, business marketing, and business values saturate and dominate all corners of American life, the critics claim.[43]

Schools

Advertising and Promotion   Seeking quality education for their own needs and for the nation, corporations now prepare model curricula and lesson plans while donating money and other resources to improve school performance. Sometimes, however, those contributions can be unbalanced and self-serving while commercializing the classroom setting. Scholastic, the world's largest publisher of children's books, decided to revise its approach to corporate-sponsored projects after being criticized by the Boston advocacy group Campaign for a Commercial-Free Childhood. Scholastic had distributed learning materials from the coal industry, for example, that saluted the benefits of coal but failed to mention its environmental hazards. Brita, which sells water filters, had sponsored a Scholastic program featuring the environmental hazards of plastic water bottles. Those programs and some others sponsored by corporate interests reportedly have been removed from Scholastic's materials and a new vetting process is in place to review corporate contributions.[44]

Faced with public resistance to increased school funding, administrators in many school districts are selling ad space on school buses, websites, buildings, textbook covers, and even report cards. Critics worry that advertising in school settings encourages materialism, celebrates dubious values, and discourages critical thinking. Timothy Wysong, the transportation director at a Texas school district that sells bus advertising says, however, that students do not pay much attention to the ads and when they do notice they approve: "'They might refer to themselves as the Chick-fil-A bus, for example,' he said. 'It's a little identity for them.'"[45]

Channel One has supplied educational programming and television sets to schools that agree to show the programming and accompanying ads on a regular basis. About 5 million children watch Channel One. The 12-minute telecasts include two minutes of ads. Channel One says that advertisers do not influence the news content, and the programming has won awards for excellence.[46] A 2006 study of middle school students, however, demonstrates the commercial risks of Channel One. The students remembered more of the ads than they did the news programs, and the students reported buying or having their parents buy products advertised on Channel One.[47] (The study made no effort to separate the influence of Channel One ads from other ads that the students might have encountered.) [For the Channel One news, see **http://www.channelone.com**]

Manage Public Schools   Many K–12 school districts across the country (e.g., Philadelphia, Chicago, and Gary, Indiana) have contracted with private companies such as EdisonLearning to consult with or operate some of their struggling public schools. Furthermore, Edison and several other national, for-profit companies are competing from state to state to offer new, online schools. More than 30,000 Ohio students, for example, are enrolled in online schools.[48] The hope is that competition and for-profit efficiencies will improve educational quality while lowering costs, but the results to date have not been particularly encouraging,[49] and critics see these efforts as a dangerous expansion of corporate values and authority.

Higher Education   Big business is also accused of turning college campuses into marketing and development opportunities, as *The New York Times* vividly described:

> It's move-in day [Fall 2011] here at the University of North Carolina and Leila Ismail, stuffed animals in tow, is feeling some freshman angst. A few friendly upperclassmen

spring into action. But wait: there is something odd, or at least oddly corporate, about this welcome wagon. These U.N.C. students are all wearing identical T-shirts from American Eagle Outfitters. Turns out three of them are working for that youth clothing chain on this late August morning, as what are known in the trade as "brand ambassadors" or "campus Evangelists"—and they have recruited several dozen friends as a volunteer move-in crew.[50]

An estimated 10,000 students work on campus marketing Red Bull, Hewlett-Packard PCs, and much more, in unprecedented sales campaigns. As *The Times* observed, "Corporations have been pitching college students for decades on products from cars to credit cards. But what is happening on campuses today is without rival, in terms of commercializing everyday college life."[51]

From kindergarten through graduate school, education is increasingly viewed as a product to be marketed and consumed on the road to prosperity in the corporate state. Recently, Gene D. Block, chancellor of the University of California at Los Angeles, criticized those who encourage students to measure and evaluate the college experience as a financial equation:

> Universities, particularly those supported with public funds, exist to serve society. Asking students to choose a future based on a salary scale does not serve society and, often, does not serve the individual. Students need freedom and encouragement to find their passions and strengths. Framing decisions about college as a cost-benefit analysis will not encourage the creativity and risk-taking that has made this nation great.[52]

Questions

The Wall Street Journal recently talked with critics, including corporate recruiters who are increasingly skeptical about the value of an undergraduate business degree:

> [N]ow faculty members, school administrators and corporate recruiters are questioning the value of a business degree at the undergraduate level. The biggest complaint: The undergraduate degrees focus too much on the nuts and bolts of finance and accounting and don't develop enough critical thinking and problem-solving skills through long essays, in-class debates and other hallmarks of liberal-arts courses.[53]

1. Do you think business courses should have a stronger liberal arts flavor? Explain.

2. If you are a business major, do you think you chose the wrong field of study? Explain.

Religion

The ideas of management guru Peter Drucker have become the unexpected intellectual foundation of the megachurch movement in America. The giant churches with thousands of parishioners in cavernous halls have applied Drucker's business principles to their "businesses":

> Bill Hybels, the pastor of the 17,000-strong Willow Creek Community Church in South Barrington, Illinois, has a quotation from Mr. Drucker hanging outside his office: "What is our business? Who is our customer? What does the customer consider the value?"[54]

> Religion, in some sense, has become a product.

Churches now routinely employ standard business practices such as advertising, promotional giveaways, and marketing campaigns. Religion, in some sense, has become a product. Some pastors preach the "prosperity gospel" that material success is a mark of God's favor. The Reverend Troy Gramling, pastor of the Potential Church in Fort Lauderdale, Florida is building a global congregation. He says he has tried to copy the success of Starbucks' branding strategy, and he once attracted new members by giving away $10 Starbucks gift cards.[55]

Megachurch pastor David Platt questions the commercial direction of contemporary religion in his book, *Radical: Taking Back Your Faith from the American Dream.* Platt says the mega-churches have taken on corporate characteristics in competing for market share by serving as social centers while offering day care and comfortable entertainment. Platt asks his followers to put a cap on their consumer lives, believing that our pursuit of the materialist American Dream cannot be reconciled with an authentic spiritual life.[56]

> The megachurches have taken on corporate characteristics.

To many Christians, Jesus is a pop-culture icon and thus is the inspiration for a vast array of commercial expressions including T-shirts, license plates, dolls, video games, flip flops, perfume, golf balls, scripture chocolates, and much more. The marriage of religion and commerce has even reached the business of sports where "Faith Nights" have become popular promotional devices at professional ball games. Several major league baseball teams have sponsored Faith Nights, but that approach has been particularly successful in the minor leagues where Christian entertainers, player testimonies, faith trivia quizzes, and bobbleheads of Samson and other biblical characters draw big crowds. [For a review of *Christianity Incorporated: How Big Business Is Buying the Church,* see **http://www.directionjournal.org/article/?1301**]

Questions

1. Do you see any risks to religion in treating it as a product to be marketed and sold? Explain.
2. *a.* Why has religion increasingly become a product in the commercial world?

   b. Is everything a product in some sense?

Culture

Does America possess a cultural life? For decades, the concern was that so-called high culture—classical music, opera, ballet, and the like—would give way to rock and roll, television, and video games. Now that battle is over; Americans (and the world) have clearly voted for *The Voice* and *American Idol.*

> Americans (and the world) have clearly voted for *American Idol.*

Corporate America has been generous in its financial and organizational support for the traditional intellectual culture. At the same time, corporate bottom-line concerns appear to the critics to be steadily degrading America's cultural life.

For example, the world-famous art extravaganza Art Basel Miami Beach, a financial blessing to artists, is widely criticized for its celebration of money, consumer excess, and sometimes wretched taste. Much of that excess, according to the critics, is attributable to corporate sponsors, as *The New York Times* explained:

> In Miami Beach, at the main fair, the consumer-oriented glitter abounds this week: coffee carts with $20-a-glass Ruinart Champagne; Davidoff cigar rollers; BMW's artist-designed cars; and Takashi Murakami's $70,000-and-up commissioned portraits. One could almost imagine that the Barbara Kruger work on display at L & M gallery—a super-sized sign reading "Greedy" on

one line and an unprintable expletive on the next—had an invisible subtitle telling the wealthy V.I.P.'s who had come to shop, "I'm Talking to You—Yeah, You!"[57]

Even popular culture (rock, movies, television, hip hop, and so on), already considered a wasteland, has been further debased the critics say, not merely by a mindless market (that's us), but by limitless corporate greed, indifference to quality, and relentless consolidation.

> **Are the Corporate Suits Ruining TV?**

The *Los Angeles Times* asked: "Are the Corporate Suits Ruining TV?"[58] As the *Times* explained, "Your TV may receive 200 channels, but virtually every one of them is owned by one of six big companies— NBC Universal, Disney, Time Warner, Viacom/Paramount, Sony, and News Corp."[59] Similarly, one 850-station giant, Clear Channel, dominates and, critics say, debases the radio industry by its "McDonald's approach to programming" that makes one station virtually indistinguishable from another regardless of locale.[60] Syndicated shows and national DJs replace independent programming decisions and local personalities resulting in increasingly standardized playlists and programs.

Perhaps we should applaud corporate America and its acutely tuned marketing machine that efficiently provide us with precisely what we want, even if what we want is unlikely to meet the critics' approval. But what if we are mistaken? The consequences for the value of our lives might be devastating. Consider, for example, a recent study confirming what your parents have told you: "[M]usic has, indeed, become both more homogeneous and louder over the decades."[61] The 2012 study found that today's popular music relies largely on the same 10 most popular chords that were the foundation of music in the 1950s. The sound itself has changed, however, in that songs are about nine decibels louder on average; apparently part of a "loudness race" designed to catch our attention over the noise clutter of our lives.[62]

But does it matter that current popular music all sounds pretty much the same? Or that reality TV is a central feature of American daily life? Or that relentless violence seems to be the primary message of the video gaming industry? Does it matter that America's corporate powers quickly step back from the edgy hip hop message when it strays too far from the mainstream, as described in a 2013 *New York Times* commentary?

> Three times in recent weeks large companies have [severed] ties with rappers they had previously happily paid to endorse their products: Reebok dropped Rick Ross over objectionable lyrics, and PepsiCo's Mountain Dew did the same to Lil Wayne, just days after it had cut short an ad campaign it had worked on with Tyler, the Creator.[63]

Sports

Former National Collegiate Athletic Association (NCAA) president Myles Brand, speaking at an ethics conference, made the argument that "College sports is not a business. It's about educating young men and women in the field and in the classroom."[64] College men's basketball coaching legend Bob Knight did not agree:

> **College sports is not a business.**

> If it isn't a business then General Motors is a charity. College sports has turned into one of the biggest businesses in the whole sports industry. I use the word industry because that's what sport is. . . .[65]

Knight's point of view seems indisputable today as college sports programs at the highest level are in an increasingly desperate race for money. Most of that money, of course, is tied to and driven by another enormous industry: television. Louisiana State University chancellor Michael Martin wryly spoke to the power of the networks by saying, "I think we could end up with two enormous conferences, one called ESPN and one called FOX."[66] Sports commentator Eric Crawford concurred with Martin by saying, "We're not far away now. We even have a set of sub-conferences: Nike, Adidas, Reebok and Under Armour. College sports today are not about college and, increasingly, they are not about sports. It's all business."[67]

Of course, profit-seeking in collegiate sports is not without its benefits. Thousands of students complete college every year who might otherwise not have done so, funding is provided for many unprofitable sports including women's programs, and sports revenues often support academic programs. The market has spoken loudly and clearly for the excitement of college sports, but is the market mistaken?

What Have We Lost?   The conversion of athletics, both professional and collegiate, from sport to business is essentially an accomplished fact, but its significance remains unclear. What have we lost when the innocence and idealism of sports are forfeited in favor of profit? Or are innocence and idealism simply a myth? Perhaps we are better off when corporate and personal profit—the free market—drives sports. Or is the pursuit of profit the route to the slow but sure death of meaningful sports?

Marketing   Novelist Bill Morris recently bemoaned the "tsunami" of commercialism in college football.[68] In writing about the football bowl season, Morris pointed to the "dozens of brand names being spray-painted onto fields," ranging from the well-known—Allstate and Tostitos—to the largely unknown—Gildan and BBVA Compass.[69] This explosion of advertising caused Morris to argue that we should all pause to think about what the college bowl season says about the nation's soul.[70] Florida Atlantic University apparently was untroubled by metaphysical doubts when it accepted $6 million to name its new football facility GEO Group Stadium. GEO Group operates private prisons. David Ridpath, a sports administration professor and member of the Drake Group, a network of professors that lobbies for integrity in sports, said he felt "ambivalent" about that particular naming deal: "The short answer is, I understand to an extent. But it does appear we're prostituting ourselves to the highest bidder regardless of what they represent. Again—the sanctity of higher education matters little when the dollars are needed."[71]

High School Next?   Business values and practices having spread from professional sports to college athletics, we should not be surprised, although perhaps we should be dismayed, that the same influences are rapidly emerging in high school sports as well. Elite high school teams travel the country to play in special events, more and more games are televised, and high school sports facilities attempt to mimic the glow of college and professional experiences. In Texas, where football is particularly celebrated, the Allen High School Eagles play in a new stadium that cost about $60 million.[72]

Will high school football emerge as the next great sports marketing opportunity? Some business leaders think so:

> "I think high school sports is the next iteration where fans are going," said Ira Stahlberger, senior vice president of strategic partnerships for Intersport . . . "The market follows where the fans are. People are extremely passionate about the NFL. They are extremely passionate about college football. Next is high school football."[73]

PRACTICING ETHICS   The Sports Business and Compromised Values?

I. Beer.

At this writing, 22 of the 120 major college football stadiums sell beer at football games, a total that has more than doubled in the past 10 years. During the 2012 season, West Virginia University reported a net profit of $520,000 in its first year of stadiumwide beer sales. Bowling Green State University reportedly nets about $20,000 to $25,000 per season. For some schools, beer is sold largely to make the total experience more attractive to fans. The National Collegiate Athletic Association bans beer sales and alcohol-related signs at its championship events.[74]

Questions

1. Do you think universities that sell beer at football games are hypocritical in that those same schools energetically discourage binge drinking by students? Explain.

2. Do you think beer sales at collegiate football games is a good policy? Explain.

II. Nike.

Timothy Egan in *The New York Times* commented on Nike's relationship with Pittsburg Steelers quarterback Ben Roethlisberger, who was accused in 2010 of sexual assault on a 20-year-old woman:

> Is there anything creepier than a big, beer-breathed celebrity athlete exposing himself in a night club and hitting on underage girls, all the while protected by an entourage of off-duty cops? Well, yes. It's the big, corporate sponsor—Nike, in this case—that continues to sell product with the creep as their role model."[75]

No criminal charges were filed in the case, but Roethlisberger was suspended by the National Football League for four games, and the owner of the company that marketed "Big Ben's Beef Jerky" reportedly ended his company's endorsement relationship with the quarterback. Roethlisberger had been accused of similar misconduct in other episodes.

Questions

1. Was Nike wrong to retain its endorsement relationship with Roethlisberger? Explain.

2. Prior to Roethlisberger's appearance with the Steelers in the 2011 Super Bowl, Ward Headley, president of a Cincinnati-based sports marketing company, said the quarterback's endorsement future would be bright, despite past problems, if Pittsburg were to win the game:

> To me, winning cures everything. Not just to me, but the reality is to corporate America and to people, winning is the answer.[76]

> The Green Bay Packers won that game, but Headley's judgment that winning nullifies past transgressions seems to be accurate. Should we condemn corporate America or the American people for being so willing to forgive winners' past wrongdoing? Explain.

America's Soul?

Critics contend that the power of the business community has become so encompassing that virtually all dimensions of American life have absorbed elements of the business ethic. Values commonly associated with businesspeople (competition, profit-seeking, reliance on technology, faith in growth) have overwhelmed traditional humanist values (cooperation, individual dignity, human rights, meaningful service to society). In the name of wealth, efficiency, and productivity, the warmth, decency, and value of life have been debased. We engage in meaningless work. Objects dominate our existence. We operate as replaceable cogs in a vast, bureaucratic machine. Indeed, we lose ourselves, the critics argue. Charles

> Objects dominate our existence.

Reich, former Yale University law professor, addressed the loss of self in his influential book of the Vietnam War era, *The Greening of America*:

> Of all of the forms of impoverishment that can be seen or felt in America, loss of self, or death in life, is surely the most devastating. . . . Beginning with school, if not before, an individual is systematically stripped of his imagination, his creativity, his heritage, his dreams, and his personal uniqueness, in order to style him into a productive unit for a mass, technological society. Instinct, feeling, and spontaneity are repressed by over-whelming forces. As the individual is drawn into the meritocracy, his working life is split from his home life, and both suffer from a lack of wholeness. Eventually, people virtually become their professions, roles, or occupations, and are henceforth strangers to themselves.[77]

Some interesting empirical evidence supports Reich's view that we have become hollow men and women dominated by the demands of big institutions. The Harris Alienation Index measures feelings of economic inequity (the rich get richer, and the poor get poorer), feelings of powerlessness (being left out and not counting for much) and feelings that those running the country do not really care about the welfare of others. Those responses are combined into an alienation "score." That score stood at a low of 29 in its first year, 1966, and has generally been rising since with the 2011 score of 63 among the highest ever.[78]

> Actor Ben Stein lamented an increasingly divided America.

Actor and conservative commentator Ben Stein, speaking in 2006, lamented an increasingly divided America where the interests of corporations and the wealthy are dominant and the well-being of others is in danger of being forgotten:

> The Saturday before Memorial Day I spoke to a gathering of widows and widowers, parents and children of men and women in uniform who have lost their lives in Iraq and Afghanistan. The person who spoke before me was a beautiful woman named Joanna Wroblewski, whose husband of less than two years—after four years of dating at Rutgers—had been killed in Iraq. She cried as she spoke. . . . She spoke of her devotion to her country and her husband's pride in the flag. . . .
>
> Are we keeping the faith with Joanna Wroblewski? . . . Are we maintaining an America that is not just a financial neighborhood, but also a brotherhood and a sisterhood worth losing your husband for? Is this still a community of the heart, or a looting opportunity? Will there even be a free America for Mrs. Wroblewski's descendants, or will we be a colony of the people [foreign lenders] to whom we have sold our soul?[79]

Questions

1. A brief analysis of social media advertising techniques employed to promote Ford, Mello Yello, Grey Poupon, and Sephora emphasized the value and power of those ads on Facebook, Twitter, and other social media. The article, entitled "4 Examples of How Corporate America Is Crushing Social Media,"[80] argued that those four products were effectively marketed online by presenting interesting content that readers would be inclined to share with their social networks.

   a. Do those corporate advertising campaigns diminish the quality of your social media experience? Explain.

   b. Do we need a social media "zone" free of corporate advertising messages? Explain.

2. *a.* Do Americans trust the business community? Explain.

   b. Does it matter? Explain.

3. In 1980 Ted Peters, an associate professor of systematic theology at the Pacific Lutheran Seminary and the Graduate Theological Union, asked:

> How will the advancing postindustrial culture influence the course of religion? It is my forecast that religion will become increasingly treated as a consumer item. Because our economy produces so much wealth, we are free to consume and consume beyond the point of satisfaction. There is a limit to what we can consume in the way of material goods—new homes, new cars, new electronic gadgets, new brands of beer, new restaurants, and so on. So we go beyond material wants to consume new personal experiences—such as broader travel, exotic vacations, continuing education, exciting conventions, psychotherapy, and sky diving.
>
> What will come next and is already on the horizon is the consumption of spiritual experiences—personal growth cults, drug-induced ecstasy, world-traveling gurus, training in mystical meditation to make you feel better, etc. Once aware of this trend, religious entrepreneurs and mainline denominations alike will take to pandering their wares, advertising how much spiritual realities "can do to you." It will be subtle, and it will be cloaked in the noble language of personal growth, but nevertheless the pressure will be on to treat religious experience as a commodity for consumption.[81]

a. Is Peters's forecast coming true? Explain.
b. Is marketing necessary to the survival and growth of religion? Explain.
c. Is marketing a threat to the legitimacy and value of religion? Explain.

4. In your opinion, which of the following will be the biggest threat to America in the future: big government, big labor, or big business?

5. Do you think allegiance to the company will become more important than allegiance to the state? Is that a desirable direction? Raise the arguments on both sides of the latter question.

6. As expressed in *BusinessWeek,* "Increasingly, the corporation will take over the role of the mother, supplying day care facilities where children can be tended around the clock."[82] How do you feel about the corporation as mother? Explain.

Part Two—Corporate Social Responsibility

Introduction

We have seen that the business community is intensely criticized. Journalist Daniel Seligman put it this way:

> A standard view of the American corporation . . . is that it is an efficient deliverer of goods and services, yet also a wellspring of social injustice. Driven by a narrow calculus of profits, it is oblivious to the common good. And so, the litany goes, it degrades the environment, promotes unsafe products, skimps on workplace safety and . . . lays off workers who have given it years of service.[83]

That broadly shared perception of business misdeeds or indifference, in conjunction with the growing influence of business values throughout American life, has led in recent decades to the development of the doctrine of *corporate social responsibility* (CSR—sometimes also referred to as *corporate citizenship*). We can express the issue this way: Must business decision making include consideration not merely of the welfare of the firm but of society as a whole? For most contemporary readers, the answer is self-evident—of course business bears a social responsibility. Business has enjoyed a central and favored role in American life. As such, it must assume a measure of the burden for the welfare of the total society. Indeed, businesspeople themselves now generally endorse businesses' responsibility to help solve society's problems. The popular appeal and potential power of CSR is evident, for example, in a 2008 PricewaterhouseCoopers survey finding that 88 percent of millennials will choose employers based on strong social responsibility values and that 86 percent would think about leaving a company whose CSR values did not meet their expectations.[84] Similar philosophies such as the *triple bottom line* (giving close accounting attention to social and environmental performance as well as financial performance) and the *sustainable* corporation (operating the business with a focus on environmentally sensitive practices that will husband scarce resources and maintain a healthy community now and in the future) have powerful appeal to many students and managers.

Before turning to a more detailed analysis of corporate social responsibility practice, let's think about options you might employ to direct your forthcoming professional life toward socially responsible, ethically sustainable business practice. *Social enterprise or social entrepreneurship* is a movement in which people launch nonprofits and businesses or take jobs using entrepreneurial and managerial skills for the purpose, in part, of addressing social problems.

Social Enterprise/Social Entrepreneurship

Drew Chafetz, in his mid-twenties and a huge soccer fan, did not turn directly to the job market following college graduation. Rather, he cofounded love.futbol [see **http://www.lovefutbol .org**], an organization to help build safe soccer fields for children in impoverished nations who otherwise might be forced to play in the streets or other unsafe spaces. Since founding love.futbol in 2006, Chafetz and his cofounder, Alfredo Axtmayer, have encouraged about a dozen communities in Guatemala and Brazil to build durable, low-maintenance, concrete soccer pitches, and several other projects are in development. Chafetz says that love.futbol's core competency is not building fields but empowering and mobilizing communities to build their own. Love.futbol provides materials and direction, but communities must provide the land, project planning, and volunteer labor necessary for success.[85]

Others share Chafetz's social welfare goals but are pursuing them from a profit-seeking direction. T-shirt and hoodie maker Sevenly, for example, donates $7 to charitable causes for each item sold. Beer halls, pledged to donate their profits to charity, are springing up around America and in other nations. Some of those committed to social welfare simply seek jobs that allow them to apply their expertise and zeal directly to community causes. Dawn Carpenter gave up her high-paying job at JP Morgan to work for a small District of Columbia community bank whose customers include D.C. Habitat for Humanity and Bread for the City. Carpenter said she "needed to put over two decades of experience to work for my mission."[86] Still others believe they can make socially responsible contributions by taking mainstream, high-paying jobs that help build power stations in developing nations, improve financing opportunities for inner-city entrepreneurs, or enable medical care to more affordably reach poorer patients, for example. [For an introduction to B Corps—benefit corporations—a "new type of corporation that uses the power of business to solve social and environmental problems," see **http://www.bcorporation.net/about**]

Questions

1. *a.* Do you aspire to a social enterprise/social entrepreneurship role in your future professional life?

   b. Should you? Explain.

2. Have your business school courses given sufficient attention to social responsibility issues? Explain.

3. Do consumers care whether companies are socially responsible? Explain.

A New Ideology

The ascendance of the social responsibility doctrine represents a striking ideological shift. Historically, business was expected to concentrate on one goal—the production and distribution of the best products and services at the lowest possible prices. Business was largely exempt from any affirmative duty for the resolution of social problems until the 1950s when business scholars and critics began to encourage a broader conception of corporate duty. Now in the 21st century, expectations for business in society have been radically altered. Profit-seeking remains central and essential, but for most businesspeople, the sometimes awkward ingredient of social responsibility must be a consideration. [For the Business for Social Responsibility home page, see **www.bsr.org**]

What Is Social Responsibility?

The sweeping notion of corporate social responsibility is not readily reduced to a brief definition, but Davis and Blomstrom some years ago captured the core ingredients: "The idea of social responsibility is that decision makers are obligated to take actions which protect and improve the welfare of society as a whole along with their own interests."[87] More systematically, the social role of business can be thought of as an ideological continuum, corresponding roughly to the familiar American political spectrum of conservative/Republican views on the right, moderates in the middle, and liberal/Democrats on the left. Figure 3.1 depicts that continuum and is best understood by reading "backward" from right to left. On the right side of the spectrum lies the free-market view holding that *profit maximization* is the best measure of social responsibility. Across the middle

FIGURE 3.1
A Social Responsibility Continuum

Triple bottom-line/ sustainability (social + environmental + financial)	Long-term company interest (profit + good deeds)	Profit maximization (profit)

(*long-term company interest*) lies a hybrid, blended perspective where profits are the first consideration, but where satisfied workers, customers, and community members are also of importance, within some reasonable limits, to secure the firm's long-term survival. On the left side of the spectrum lies the *triple bottom-line/sustainability* movement that calls for a revolutionary re-visioning of corporate goals and practices such that profit maximization is only one of three key measures of success. Triple bottom-line advocates specifically call for managerial and accounting practices that respect and measure the firm's *social and environmental performance* just as the firm's *financial* performance is respected and measured. The goal is to ensure the long-term viability (sustainability) of the organization and the total society.

Now let's examine the continuum in a bit more detail. [For the "Global Reporting Initiative" on sustainability practices around the world, see **http://www.globalreporting.org**]

> The only responsible and moral course of behavior is to reap the highest return possible, within the law.

Profit Maximization   Here the dominant concern lies in maximizing shareholders' interests. Those shareholders, after all, are the owners of the firm. They are taking the financial risk. Hence, from a profit maximization point of view, the only responsible and moral course of behavior is to reap the highest return possible, within the law. Nobel prize–winning economist Milton Friedman was the most prominent advocate of the profit maximization view:

> [In a free economy] there is one and only one social responsibility of business—to use its resources and engage in activities designed to increase its profits, so long as it stays within the rules of the game, which is to say, engages in open and free competition, without deception or fraud.[88]

Friedman, employing free-market reasoning, believed the firm that maximizes its profits is necessarily maximizing its contribution to society. Furthermore, he argued that any dilution of the profit-maximizing mode—such as charitable contributions—is a misuse of the stockholders' resources. The individual stockholder, he contended, should dispose of assets according to her or his own wishes. Finally, he asked how managers could be expected to know what the public interest is.

Herbert Stein, former chair of the President's Council of Economic Advisers, shared Friedman's doubts about the idea of social responsibility, but Stein's concerns were of a more pragmatic nature. He argued that business is simply ill suited for solving social problems:

> Efficiency in maximizing the nation's product . . . is not the only objective of life. But it is the one that private corporations are best qualified to serve. I don't want to be a purist about this. I don't object to corporations contributing to the United Givers Fund. . . . But to rely on corporations' responsibility to solve major social problems—other than the problem of how to put our people and other resources to work most efficiently—would be a wasteful diversion from their most important function. Our other objectives can be better served in other ways, by individuals and other institutions.[89]

Long-Term Company Interest   Across the broad middle ground of our social responsibility continuum lie those firms, doubtless the great majority, who believe that a strong bottom line, in many cases, requires considerations beyond the immediate, short-run, profit-maximizing interests of the firm. In a sense, these managers are merely taking a longer term view of profit maximization. They recognize the imperative of a strong return on the shareholder's investment, but they also believe that achieving that return may require heightened sensitivity to the welfare of employees, consumers, and the community. Furthermore, they often embrace the view that socially responsible behavior, within reasonable bounds, is simply the "right thing" to do. [For the United Nations' initiative to encourage responsible corporate citizenship, see **http://www.unglobalcompact.org**]

Triple Bottom Line/Sustainability Managers are being pushed to adopt a bigger, broader conception of social responsibility, an approach that will produce a sustainable, enduring global community where our resources are not dangerously depleted or damaged. This expanded standard is explained by social responsibility expert Steve Rochlin:

> The new corporate citizenship challenges executives to find alternatives to zero-sum solutions that often emphasize shareholder value at the cost of social and environmental welfare. Instead, the new corporate citizenship challenges companies to deliver not just financial returns but also environmental and social value—together marking the pillars of what is called a "triple bottom line.". . .
>
> The new corporate citizenship requires business transparency and accountability regarding the ways in which business practices generate benefits and costs for issues ranging from employee diversity, community development, working conditions, clean air and water, human rights, poverty, and corruption.[90]

The triple bottom-line/sustainability approach employs free-market principles and recognizes the necessity for financial success but also argues that social and environmental responsibilities are of equal importance. According to sustainability advocates, corporations giving close attention to both social and economic duties have a powerful competitive advantage that will contribute to organizational and societal sustainability.

Building a just, healthy, sustainable future makes a lot of sense, but reasonable people continue to differ about the most effective path to that goal. For many companies, shorter term profit motives continue to dominate. Recent research findings show American firms lagging behind their European counterparts in sustainability performance with no American firms in the top 10 globally.[91] Nonetheless, progress is evident. Some big American corporations are appointing sustainability officers and committing themselves to global sustainability projects. For example, Muhtar Kent, Coca-Cola CEO, spoke recently of his company's close attention to improved practices in water, packaging, energy conservation, and climate. He went on to specifically cite one small but illustrative step forward:

> Preeti Gupti, for example, is a mother of three in rural India. In the town of Agra, about 125 miles south of Delhi, she has a small store in her home, which lacks reliable electrical service. With a solar-powered Coca-Cola cooler, she can now sell cold beverages, stay open later and help her children study after dark. Her income has also increased, creating still more opportunities for her children.[92]

[For a critique of triple bottom-line thinking, see **www.businessethics.ca/3bl**]

"Green" Jeans?

The ocean of apparel that Americans buy annually is the product of globe-spanning supply chains that consume enormous amounts of water, energy, chemicals, cotton, oil, and other resources while casting off equally enormous amounts of waste. Now the Sustainable Apparel Coalition, which represents more than one-third of the global apparel and footwear industries and includes such prominent companies as Adidas, Columbia Sportswear, Levi, and Walmart, is building a system to measure the environmental impact of the apparel production process. The Coalition is attempting to measure the apparel industry's environmental footprint, including water, energy, greenhouse gas, waste, chemicals, and toxicity. The Coalition hopes to build a database of scores assigned to all elements of every garment's life cycle—including cotton producers, dye suppliers, textile mill owners, shippers, retailers, and consumers—based on various social and environmental measures. The resulting scores could be used by apparel companies to choose materials and suppliers, and eventually the Coalition hopes a sustainability score can be calculated for all garments so consumers can make buying choices with those scores in mind.

Question

Think about shopping. Assume you are considering two pairs of jeans of equal style and quality, one with a favorable sustainability score, one without. Assume the jeans without the favorable score are priced at $50. How much more would you be willing to pay for the jeans with a favorable score?
  a. Nothing more.
  b. $1
  c. $5
  d. $10
  e. $25 Explain.

Sources: Textile News, "Sustainable Apparel Coalition Launches Higg Index," *Textile World,* July 31, 2012 [**http://www.textileworld.com/**]; and Tom Zeller, "Clothes Makers Join to Set 'Green Score,'" *The New York Times,* March 1, 2011 [**http://www.nytimes.com/2011/03/01/business/01apparel.html**].

Social Responsibility Pyramid

Professor Archie Carroll proposed another way of visualizing socially responsible business practice as depicted in Figure 3.2. Socially responsible business practice necessarily begins at the foundation of the pyramid with the duty to make a profit in a lawful fashion; but simultaneously the socially responsible firm moves (up the pyramid) beyond the fundamental demands of economics and law to pursue the ethical course of action—the behavior best suited to the demands of virtue and moral principle. In striving for profitable, lawful, ethical conduct, that company may also choose to engage in discretionary philanthropic (charitable) efforts (money, time, facilities, programs) to build a better community. While the social responsibility pyramid has been criticized and revised, it remains a useful way of thinking about corporations' expanding duties.[93] [ISO, the International Organization for Standardization, has developed a set of guidelines for socially responsible corporate behavior labeled ISO 26000. For an overview of ISO 26000, see **http://www.iso.org/iso /home/standards/iso26000.htm**]

FIGURE 3.2
The Social Responsibility (CSR) Pyramid

Source: Archie B. Carroll, "The Pyramid of Corporate Social Responsibility: Toward the Moral Management of Organizational Stakeholders." Reprinted from *Business Horizons* 34, no. 4 (July–August 1991), pp. 39, 42. Copyright 1991 by the Foundation for the School of Business at Indiana University. Used with permission.

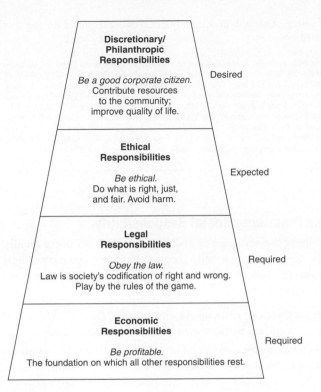

Discretionary/ Philanthropic Responsibilities

Be a good corporate citizen. Contribute resources to the community; improve quality of life.   Desired

Ethical Responsibilities

Be ethical. Do what is right, just, and fair. Avoid harm.   Expected

Legal Responsibilities

Obey the law. Law is society's codification of right and wrong. Play by the rules of the game.   Required

Economic Responsibilities

Be profitable. The foundation on which all other responsibilities rest.   Required

Toyota and the Social Responsibility Pyramid

As perhaps the most respected name in the automobile industry, Toyota's safety struggles of recent years have caused the powerful company to thoroughly review its practices and philosophies. Toyota has topped the U.S. auto industry in safety recalls in three of four recent years. Some 90 deaths have been associated with alleged Toyota problems. Toyota has agreed to pay well over $1 billion to settle claims that electronic malfunctions caused some of its cars to suddenly accelerate without warning. Toyota had previously paid nearly $50 million in fines for failing to inform regulators promptly about evidence of safety problems. Hundreds of personal injury and wrongful death lawsuits remain to be resolved. These problems led to a decline in market share, resale value, and quality ratings.

Thus, in applying Carroll's Social Responsibility Pyramid reasoning, we see that Toyota has struggled to fulfill its economic responsibilities, and has failed to meet at least some of its legal responsibilities. Furthermore, in its careful and doubtless painful self-examination, Toyota has raised doubts about its own ethical performance. President Akio Toyoda has acknowledged that quality had been sacrificed for faster growth and profits. Toyoda said, "[S]ome people just got too big-headed and focused too excessively on profit." Trying to restore its performance and ethical/reputational posture, Toyota has delegated more decision making authority to subsidiaries, overhauled its quality control methods, and expanded the power of executives in charge of safety. Although problems linger, Toyota regained the top spot in world auto sales in 2012.

Sources: Ken Bensinger and Ralph Vartabedian, "Toyota to Pay Record Fines for Disclosure Delay," *latimes .com,* December 20, 2010 [latimes.com/business/la-fi-toyota-fine-20101221,0,2995009.story]; Ken Bensinger, "Toyota Recalls 2.17 Million More Vehicles Over Sudden-Acceleration Problems," *latimes.com,* February 24, 2011 [latimes.com/business/la-fi-toyota-recall-20110225,0,6731783.story]; Chester Dawson and Yoshio Takahashi, "Toyota Makes New Push to Avoid Recalls," *The Wall Street Journal,* February 24, 2011, p. B1; Norihiko Shirouzu, "Toyoda Rues Excessive Profit Focus," *The Wall Street Journal,* March 2, 2010, p. B3; Norihiko Shirouzu, "Inside Toyota, Executives Trade Blame Over Debacle," *The Wall Street Journal,* April 13, 2010 [**http://online.wsj.com/**]; and Hiroko Tabuchi and Bill Vlasic, "Battered by Expensive Crises, Toyota Declares a Rebirth," *The New York Times,* January 2, 2013 [**http://www.nytimes.com/**].

Corporations Practicing Social Responsibility

Obviously we have no shortage of social problems both domestically and globally. In recent years the corporate community seems to have become increasingly convinced that it needs, for various reasons, to take a more active role in addressing those problems. Those efforts can take many forms.

- American corporations responded quickly to the January 2010 earthquake in Haiti by promising $43 million in aid within 72 hours after the quake struck.[94]
- Walt Disney Company announced in 2012 that it would be phasing out junk food ads on its child-focused television channels, websites, and radio stations.[95]
- McDonald's is requiring its pork suppliers to phase out sow gestation crates (metal stalls so small that pigs cannot turn) in favor of more humane arrangements.[96]
- The six-story Bullitt Center in Seattle opened in 2013 as an experiment in sustainability. The $30 million building—featuring composting toilets, an absence of on-site parking, a stairway designed to allow magnificent views of Puget Sound, and a slow elevator that requires a key card for use—is expected to achieve both water and energy self-sufficiency.[97]

Many social responsibility advocates, including Google, believe that an entrepreneurial, profit-seeking, capitalist approach is the best route to correcting social problems.

Google's Multiple CSR Strategies

Google hopes to use capitalism to make life better around the world. Google, through its $2 billion charitable arm, Google.org, makes many generous charitable contributions, but its version of CSR reaches beyond philanthropic efforts to attack some of the world's biggest problems (specifically, the environment, global poverty, and global health) by investing in businesses, lobbying for political causes, and directing portions of its employees' time to developing business and technology solutions for those problems. Google aids nonprofits by providing Google products free or at steep discounts and helps with disaster relief by making storm paths, emergency numbers, and donation opportunities readily accessible. Google.org has invested $45 million in recent years in an array of renewable energy projects hoping to back projects with breakthrough potential.

Google is only one of many companies that have expanded their CSR efforts from giving to building. Many of those companies view social responsibility as workable only if it contributes to the strategic mission of the business and ultimately to the bottom line. Nike, for example, turned aggressively to social responsibility measures as a way of restoring its brand image after criticism for its use of global sweatshop labor. Consumers are willing to pay higher prices at Whole Foods Market, the healthy food grocery chain, in part because of the company's reputation for good works. Goldman Sachs hopes to make money while doing good by investing in the nation's first "social impact bonds," innovative financing arrangements designed to leverage private money to underwrite social programs. One Goldman Sachs bond program of up to $7 million helps finance early childhood education for at-risk children in Salt Lake City, and a $9.6 million investment is using behavioral therapy intervention in an effort to reduce recidivism among male prisoners at Rikers Island, New York City's primary jail. Goldman will profit on these bond arrangements only if the projects' goals (improved educational results and reduced recidivism) are achieved. Savings from the performance improvements will be used to pay back Goldman Sachs and other investors.[98]

Questions

1. In general, we understand decisions to lay off employees when companies are losing money, but how should we feel about profitable companies that lay off employees? Powerful executive, Barry Diller, in 2009, condemned "preemptive" layoffs:

   The idea of a company that's earning money, not losing money, that's not, let's say, "industrially endangered," to have just cutbacks [sic] so they can earn another $12 million or $20 million or $40 million in a year where no one's counting is really a horrible act when you think about it on every level.[99]

   Do you think a socially responsible company that operates at a profit would engage in layoffs? Explain.

2. Some critics argue that Wall Street's financial collapse in 2008–2009 was, at least in part, a product of male "group think." They claim that men take excessive risks and women are more comprehensive thinkers. Hence, they say the financial community needs more women:

   Barnard College president Deborah Spar dubbed our predicament [the Wall Street crash] a "one gender crash," and *The New York Times*' Nicholas Kristof wonders if we might all have been better off had it been "Lehman Brothers and Sisters."[100]

   Do finance companies have a social responsibility to hire more women? Explain.

Finding an Employer with a Conscience

Surveys of young people in recent years suggest that employers trying to replace millions of retiring baby boomers may need to demonstrate a social commitment in order to be fully competitive in the hiring market. One of those surveys found that two-thirds of respondents 18 to 26 prefer jobs that would permit them to make a contribution to nonprofit groups.

Questions

1. *a.* Will you insist on a job with a "social purpose"?
   b. Do all jobs have a social purpose?
2. Would you expect money to replace social goals in the teen hierarchy as they age?
3. Given today's difficult job market, do you expect social goals to remain important to young people? Explain.

Sources: Lindsey Gerdes, "Get Ready for a Pickier Workforce," *BusinessWeek,* September 18, 2006, p. 82; and Ian Shapira, "For This Generation, Vocations of Service," *Washington Post,* October 14, 2008, p. B01.

CSR: Two Big Questions

I. Is CSR Good Business?

The evidence is at least mildly supportive of the idea that the market rewards socially responsible performance by business. A 2009 meta-analysis of 251 studies found a "positive but small" relationship between corporate social performance and corporate financial performance.[101] A 2012 study looked directly at the question of whether "high-sustainability" firms (committed to CSR) achieve better financial performance than otherwise comparable "low-sustainability" firms (committed to traditional profit seeking). The authors found that $1 invested in a high-sustainability portfolio in 1993 would have grown to $22.60 by 2010 but to only $15.40 for a low-sustainability portfolio.[102] Consumers themselves have mixed sentiments about CSR with 35 percent of North American respondents and 46 percent of all global responders to a 2012 survey indicating they would pay extra for products and services from socially responsible companies.[103]

II. Do We Have a Better Alternative? Creating Shared Value

Michael Porter, highly influential professor and corporate consultant, and others have recently been arguing for moving beyond CSR to a business model labeled *creating shared value* (CSV). They see creating shared value as a new form of capitalism that enhances economic competitiveness while simultaneously advancing social returns. They argue that CSR has often been treated merely as a necessary expense and a way to improve a firm's reputation. According to Porter and others, moving beyond philanthropy, good citizenship, and sustainability to integrating social value into the creation of economic value is the most effective way of achieving social progress.

Nestlé, for example, strives to create shared value by making nutritious, profitable products while protecting scarce water resources and helping coffee growers secure financing and improve production. Nestlé and other shared value advocates are identifying those opportunities where social and economic value creation align, thus enabling them to achieve favorable sustainability results for communities while also making money for shareholders. Low-cost cell phones, for example, can be profitable while serving poorer populations. Shared value advocates see businesses as the most powerful institutions for social change, but they also expect those businesses to recognize that their goal must be creating shared value rather than profit per se.[104]

Questions

1. Construct a list of the arguments for and against social responsibility for business.
2. In a recent commentary, ethicist Chris MacDonald explained the idea that businesses must earn and maintain an unwritten "social license" to operate. That is, businesses must secure the support and goodwill of the community. MacDonald then asked what steps a business can take to maintain its "social license" to operate. Answer MacDonald's question.

Part Three—Managing Social Responsibility

Stakeholder Approach

As the principle of social responsibility has become increasingly acceptable to the corporate community, the nature of the debate has shifted to identifying new duties and assessing whether the corporation is meeting those duties. Many corporations, particularly those of great size, are confronting the practical notion of how best to manage the firm's response to social issues. Corporations are increasingly considering what scholars have labeled the *stakeholder model* of social responsibility. Under that model, the corporation identifies all of the groups (stockholders, customers, employees, communities, governments, unions, schools, and the like) that may significantly affect the firm's performance or be affected by it. These are groups with a "stake" in the activities of the corporation. Of course, we have wide divisions of opinion about how expansive the list of stakeholders should be; and once identified, we have wide divisions of opinion about the extent of the corporation's duties toward those stakeholders. To stakeholder advocates, simply maximizing the interests of the primary stakeholders, that is, the shareholders, would not satisfy the corporation's social duties.

That more expansive view of social responsibility was emphasized in a 2010 discussion among corporate leaders who were thinking about how to restore the public's confidence in business after the financial collapse and scandals of recent years. First among the group's recommendations was "A New Stakeholder Approach":

> Companies should talk less about benefits to shareholders and short-term profits and instead focus on customer needs, investment in workers and sustainability (from ecology to education). We talk too much about benefits we provide to shareholders. We should be talking about benefits provided to our employees, customers and to the public. This will boost public confidence in business.[105]

Manage or Collaborate?   Whereas many companies now acknowledge the importance of their stakeholder relationships, their dominant goal often amounts to little more than controlling those relationships. An alternative and arguably more "progressive" approach to stakeholders involves a collaborative strategy in which stakeholder relationships are regarded as being mutually defined, cooperative, and reciprocal. The firm endeavors to understand and balance the interests and needs of all stakeholders with the view that this collaborative effort results in enhanced firm performance over the long term while building a healthier society.

A. G. Lafley, two-time Procter & Gamble CEO, has thoroughly and personally embraced stakeholder practice. Making money remains Lafley's first job, but he has led P&G on a broader mission, partly to ensure the company's continuing success. He came to think of consumers as citizens who often are concerned about P&G's approach to global warming or its animal-testing methods. Lafley, in fact, dealt directly with groups such as Greenpeace and People for the Ethical Treatment of Animals. Lafley also extended his stakeholder engagement to worldwide relief efforts on behalf of P&G. Those are citizenship responsibilities, he said, that go with P&G's big role in the changing global economy and global political environment. "At P&G, we believe part of our responsibility is to give back to the communities in which we work, whether it's the safe drinking water program that we've provided to the developing world or Pampers vaccinations for neonatal tetanus," Lafley said.[106]

As Lafley recognizes, profit now rests not merely in providing the best product or service at the lowest price, but in understanding and dealing with the complex interplay among the corporation, government, and society. Thus today's manager is likely to be increasingly involved in identifying and addressing social issues and stakeholder concerns.

Stakeholder Results   Assessing the success of social responsibility efforts is very difficult, but various measurement systems have emerged including, most prominently, Social Accountability 8000 (SA8000), the first global standard measuring companies' social and environmental records. Social Accountability Accreditation Services in New York City accredits companies that meet the SA8000 standards in the areas of child labor, forced labor, health and safety, freedom of association, discrimination, disciplinary practices, working hours, collective bargaining wages, and management systems. As of 2012, nearly 3,200 facilities employing nearly 2 million employees in 66 countries had been certified.[107] [For more, see **http://www.saasaccreditation.org**] [Also see the Global Reporting Initiative at **www.globalreporting.org**]

Bhopal: A Social Responsibility Failure?

One way of measuring the results of stakeholder activism is to review how the business community responds when wrongs occur. The devastating 1984 chemical spill at Bhopal, India, was one of the great tragedies in global industrial history. Water entered a methyl isocyanate storage tank at a Union Carbide plant producing an uncontrollable chemical reaction and a toxic cloud that spread across nearby slums. Up to 3,000 people were killed immediately and between 15,000 and 30,000 in total have perished. Nearly 600,000 people have qualified for compensation as a result of health problems attributed to the leak. Union Carbide reached a settlement in 1989 with the Indian government that absolved the company of liability and sent over $500 million to India, including $1,500 for each death and $550 for each contaminated person. Claims totaled $3 billion, and litigation continues over a quarter of a century later. Union Carbide maintained that the gas release resulted from sabotage.

Thousands of tons of toxic waste remain in the former factory and the nearby soil, and apparently it continues to pollute groundwater, kill crops and cause birth defects, cancer, and more. Both the governmental and corporate responses have been slow and frustrating to local residents. Indeed, Satinath Sarangi, a metallurgist and activist, argues that the fundamental problem is the close relationship between the two. *The New York Times* explained Sarangi's view:

> Union Carbide got off easy in the 1980s because pesticides were a cornerstone of [India's] "green revolution" policy to enhance agricultural productivity, [Sarangi] said. A quarter of a century later, multinationals continue to wield enormous influence over governments that measure progress solely in economic terms. "If you are an ordinary person, you can't depend on your government, judiciary or regulatory bodies to protect you from corporate crime." [Sarangi] said.[108]

Nonetheless, these cataclysmic events can produce a dramatic and positive corporate response as *The Wall Street Journal* reported about Bhopal:

> The chemical leak . . . spurred a revolution in approaches to safety, pollution, and community relations that have made chemical plants in the United States more accessible and more accountable to their neighbors. New laws forced plants to disclose safety and pollution data. And an army of community activists won new powers.[109] [A 2013 movie, *Bhopal: A Prayer for Rain,* is inspired by the Bhopal chemical disaster.]

Sources: "Asia: Bhopal's Deadly Legacy; India," *The Economist,* November 27, 2004, p. 76; Manjeet Kripalani, "Dow Chemical: Liable for Bhopal?" *BusinessWeek,* June 9, 2008, p. 061; Mark Magnier, "Anguish Lingers in Bhopal, 25 Years after Chemical Disaster," *latimes.com,* December 3, 2009 [latimes.com/news/nation-and-world/la-fg-india-bhopal3-2009dec03,0,3728767.story]; Susan Warren, "Chemical Companies Keep Lessons of Bhopal Spill Fresh," *The Wall Street Journal,* February 13, 2001, p. B4; and Julien Bouissou, "Why the Bhopal Disaster Site, 28 Years Later, Is Still a Toxic Killer," *Le Monde/Worldcrunch,* October 8, 2012 [**http://www.worldcrunch.com/**].

Shareholder Approach

Stakeholder theory and corporate social performance have gained great credibility with academics and many managers. Others, however, argue that profits and shareholders must remain the consuming concerns of management, and that a skilled focus on the bottom line will, incidentally but inevitably, result in the greatest good for society. That is, the company that maximizes its profits necessarily does not only what is best for its shareholders but also what is best for society generally. The shareholder/stakeholder debate is well illustrated by the heated competition between massive retailers Walmart and Costco. Each week Walmart saves money for millions of Americans by its relentless focus on the bottom line and hence on the interests of its shareholders. Costco, on the other hand, has drawn great praise from management scholars for its close attention to worker welfare. Costco workers average just under $21 per hour while Walmart pay averages about $13 per hour for full-time

Walmart pay averages about $13 per hour.

employees; over half of those workers earn less than $25,000 annually.[110] About 88 percent of Costco workers have company-sponsored health insurance, whereas Walmart reports "more than half" of its workers have company plans.[111] Costco's employee turnover is about 24 percent versus about 37 percent for Walmart.[112] Both companies have generally been performing well in the stock market during the recent economic uptick, and both are showing earnings gains, although Costco's recent sales growth has exceeded Walmart's.[113] Walmart has maintained a strong stock market position, in part, by relentless cost cutting, but some observers see problems in that approach. Although Walmart added 455 U.S. stores in the past five years, its total U.S. workforce declined by 1.4 percent, a boost in operating efficiency but one that may be hurting customer satisfaction. Walmart has ranked last or tied for last among department and discount stores in the American Customer Satisfaction Index for the past six years.[114] Nonetheless, Walmart's tough, bottom-line, shareholder focus continues to generate remarkable results for the world's largest corporation.

Critics

> Walmart is accused of widespread sex discrimination.

Walmart, the target of relentless criticism, is accused of widespread sex discrimination and failure to pay legally mandated overtime. (Costco has faced similar problems.) Entire communities have banished Walmart's big boxes. Walmart is dealing with a bribery scandal in Mexico (see Chapter 2). In response to these public relations shortcomings, Walmart has initiated new sustainable, green practices including slashing solid waste and greenhouse-gas emissions and significantly reducing energy consumption. Those efforts are part of a larger "good works" and public relations campaign that includes food donations and support for a universal health care policy in America. Walmart also points to its success in providing economic opportunities for its massive and often modestly educated workforce, 61 percent of whom are women and 32 percent minorities.[115] Walmart's big contribution, however, is in saving money for all Americans: an estimated $30 billion per year, or the equivalent of $270 per American family.[116]

Clearly, Walmart has felt harsh, market-based pressure to respond to social issues, but its shareholder orientation is intact and remains a strategic contrast to Costco's stakeholder approach.

[For a documentary critique of Walmart, see the trailer for *Wal-Mart: The High Cost of Low Price* at **http://www.walmartmovie.com**]

Questions

1. Retired Costco CEO James Sinegal says high employee pay makes for good business. How can that be so?

2. Professor William Beaver writes, "And what of the stakeholder model? Beyond generating some academic interest, perhaps the best that can be said is that although corporations will not be unmindful of their other stakeholders, the latter's concerns will remain a distant second to those holding the share."[117] Will shareholders or other stakeholders dominate corporate thought in the coming years? Explain.

3. In 1999, Bob Thompson sold his road-building firm for $422 million. Then he divided $128 million among his 550 workers, more than 80 of whom became millionaires. Thompson explained his generosity by saying, "I wanted to go out a winner, and I wanted to go out doing the right thing."[118]

   a. Which management strategy, Walmart's low wages or Thompson's bonuses, is the more socially responsible? Explain.

   b. Can Walmart, a publicly traded company owned by its shareholders, practice the same kind of generosity to employees that Thompson followed in distributing money that was literally his own? Explain.

   c. Stanford professor Jeffrey Pfeffer reflecting on the bonus strategy: "It's how you look at your workforce. . . . When I look at you, do I see a cost or do I see you as the only thing that separates me from my competition?"[119] Comment.

   d. Do you agree with Thompson that he did the "right thing"? Explain.

Part Four—Social Responsibility Cases
Case One: Guns

Does the gun industry bear any portion of the blame and responsibility for Adam Lanza's decision to murder 20 children and 6 adult staff members at Sandy Hook Elementary School in Newtown, Connecticut, on December 14, 2012? Lanza, who also killed his mother and himself, carried into the school a Bushmaster XM15 assault rifle along with two handguns. Efforts to pass new federal gun control legislation have, at this writing, been unsuccessful, but many scholars and journalists have suggested that the firearms industry should police itself as a means of reducing gun violence. They argue that the industry has been negligent in failing to take measures that would reduce the distribution of guns to criminals. Cornell University business ethics lecturer Dana Radcliffe commented on the industry's position:

> The U.S. rate of homicide by firearms is over thirty times that of Britain and Australia. Gun violence is a national plague. . . . However, this problem. . . is of no concern to the companies that make the weapons used in gun-related crimes. With regard to taking measures to keep their products out of the hands of criminals, their only responsibility is minimal compliance with the law. Beyond that, they have no obligation to try to prevent their dealers and distributors from engaging in illegal or suspicious sales.[120]

Reduce the number of guns diverted into criminal use.

When many guns used in crimes come from a particular source, law enforcement officials suspect possible gun trafficking. Police, lawmakers, and others have pressed the firearms industry to enforce policies voluntarily in their distribution chain that would reduce the number of guns diverted into criminal use. Radcliffe argues that the gun industry must do so:

> If the gun industry *could* act to reduce significantly the availability of their weapons to criminals, then it is reasonable to think it *should* do so. The commonsense assumption that gun makers have a special responsibility to help combat gun violence was expressed in an affidavit by Robert Hass, a former Smith & Wesson executive. As he put it, "[T]he nature of

the product demands that its distribution be handled in such a way as to minimize illegal and unintended use."[121]

Indeed, Smith & Wesson agreed in 2000 to take gun safety steps including forbidding its distributors from selling at gun shows unless background checks were conducted for all sales.[122] Smith & Wesson products were boycotted immediately, the safety plan was never enforced, and in 2012 Smith & Wesson was inducted into the National Rifle Association's "Golden Ring of Freedom," a group of donors who have given $1 million or more to the NRA.[123]

Congress and President George W. Bush substantially shielded the gun industry from liability in 2005 through the Protection of Lawful Commerce in Arms Act, which immunizes gun manufacturers and sellers from most civil claims (such as negligence and public nuisance) arising from the unlawful misuse of firearms. The gun industry argues that obeying the law, which does not impose a duty to police distributors and dealers, satisfies corporate responsibilities. Furthermore, they remind us that guns are not intrinsically evil, and those who fire guns must bear primary responsibility for the results. Expressing its frustration with new state gun-control legislation, gun manufacturer PTR Industries announced in 2013 that it was leaving Connecticut for the more gun-friendly climate of South Carolina. John McNamara, PTR's vice president of sales said, "One hundred percent of our product line is illegal in Connecticut. They just want to collect our tax dollars on a product that they don't think is safe to own."[124]

> Guns are not intrinsically evil.

Case One Questions

1. *a.* What did Robert Hass mean when he said "[T]he nature of the product demands that its distribution be handled in such a way as to minimize illegal and unintended use"?
   b. Do you agree with Hass? Explain.
   c. Do gun manufacturers have a social responsibility for their products beyond the demands of the market and the law? Explain.

2. Following the Newtown murders, Cerberus Capital Management, a very large investment firm, decided to seek a buyer for one of its companies, Freedom Group, which makes the Bushmaster rifle that was used in the school shootings. Apparently, the California State Teachers' Retirement System, which has $750 million invested with Cerberus, encouraged the sale. Cerberus said the sale was designed to meet its obligations to investors. Following Newtown, Dick's Sporting Goods suspended sales of what it called modern sporting rifles, and Walmart reportedly removed ads from its website for guns similar to the one used in Newtown.
   a. Do those decisions appear to represent a shareholder or stakeholder approach to management? Explain.
   b. As you develop your own financial portfolio, should you decline to hold investments in gun companies? Explain.

3. Law professors Lucinda M. Finley and John G. Culhane, writing in *The New York Times,* recently advocated imposing a new tax on gun manufacturers and importers.[125] The tax would be applied to each gun sold, and the proceeds would be used to create a compensation fund for innocent gun violence victims. What do you think of that idea? Explain.

Social Responsibility Cases Two to Four: Wages

Case Two: Fast-Food Pay Unfair/Unconscionable?

> Caroline Durocher joined co-workers in walking off the job.

Caroline Durocher, a fast-food server at a Taco Bell restaurant in Seattle, Washington, joined co-workers in walking off the job in late May 2013, thus shutting down the restaurant. Seattle became at least the seventh U.S. city facing strikes by fast-food workers. Durocher made $9.19 per hour and worked about 27 hours per week. She had been working on an associate of arts degree and had hopes of becoming a psychologist, but economic difficulties forced her to leave school. Durocher explained why she went on strike:

> My employer has pushed and pushed my co-workers and me and gotten everything they can out of us. This week we joined together and pushed back. I was one of the first fast-food workers to walk off the job . . . in Seattle, and . . . more workers are continuing to take a stand for a raise to $15 an hour and the right to organize without retaliation. We work in one of the fastest growing industries in the nation, and our companies are making huge—even record—profits, but we don't see enough of that money. We barely earn enough to pay for basics like rent, food and transportation to and from work. I have worked low-wage jobs since I was 16 years old, and now, at 21, am reluctantly sharing a studio apartment with my dad, working the late shift at Taco Bell.[126]

Seattle strikers also targeted Wendy's, McDonald's, Subway, and others. Chicago, New York City, St. Louis, and Detroit are among the other cities where fast-food workers went on strike, rallied, and demonstrated for $15 per hour wages and the right to organize without retaliation. The National Restaurant Association, responding to the strikes, said that the fast-food industry offers an entry to the American Dream and argued that margins are tight:

> It's important to remember that a typical restaurant operates on an average of 3–4 percent pretax profit margin, and more than 90 percent of restaurants are small businesses. Any additional labor cost can negatively impact a restaurant's ability to hire or maintain jobs.[127]

The U.S. Census Bureau's poverty threshold is about $23,000 for a family of four.[128] Fast-food workers nationally—median age 28, two-thirds of whom are women—when working 40 hours weekly, average about $8.76 per hour ($18,000 annually), a sum lower than all other reported occupations.[129] Big box retailers and fast-food chains are projected to provide 7 of 10 available jobs in the next decade as the U.S. economy is expected to continue reducing middle-class jobs while corporate wealth grows.[130]

Case Two Questions

1. *a.* Should the socially responsible company pay low-wage, fast-food workers more than the market requires? Explain.
   b. Is the free market the best measure of a "fair" wage for all? Explain.

2. Do you find anything morally amiss in an American economy that pays so poorly for hard-working, but low-skilled, fast-food labor? Explain.

3. Should we, as consumers, blame ourselves for the low wages of fast-food workers? Explain.

Case Three: Pay More Than the Law Requires?

In 2010, during very difficult economic times, the Hobby Lobby retail chain with 455 stores in 36 states raised its company minimum wage for full-time employees to $11 per hour, nearly $4 more than the $7.25 required under federal law. Why did the company raise its wages well beyond the law's requirements? David Green, the CEO of the privately owned corporation, said, "We have always tried to be a company that serves their employees."[131] Hobby Lobby had raised its minimum wage to $10 per hour in 2009, and the results were so positive that the company decided to provide another raise in 2010. Green explained the company's reasoning:

> Hobby Lobby raised its company minimum wage to $11 per hour.

We're 100 percent excited about what we've done. We have had single mothers who were able to quit their second jobs. We have had employees come up and cry. The math of it said it would have cost us millions of dollars. But the results from the employees showed us differently; it really didn't cost anything because retention is important.[132]

Case Three Questions

1. How can it make good business sense to pay employees more than the law and the market require?

2. Would you do as Hobby Lobby did? Explain.

Case Four: Making a Profit—Reduce Wages?

Three hundred workers at the Mott's apple juice plant (a Dr Pepper Snapple subsidiary) in Williamson, New York, waged a 16-week strike when the company demanded a $1.50 per hour pay cut even though Snapple had produced a $555 million profit in the previous year (2009)[133] and increased its dividend by 67 percent in May 2010.[134] Snapple claimed the wage cut was justifiable to increase competitiveness, because the workers were averaging $21 per hour while other similar workers were averaging $14.[135] The union, on the other hand, noted that the area suffers from nearly a 50 percent poverty level.[136] The strike ended in September 2010 with a three-year deal freezing rather than reducing wages. Snapple dropped a demand to freeze pensions for current employees, but new hires will join a 401(k) plan instead of receiving a pension. Snapple will save money on retirement plans. Both sides reportedly considered the result a victory.

Case Four Questions

1. Dr Pepper Snapple argued that it had a responsibility as a public company to seek concessions from its workers. Explain that argument.

2. Is it wrong in your judgment for a profitable company to seek wage concessions from its workers? Explain.

Internet Exercise

1. Many critics, activists, international scholars, and others are concerned that corporate/governmental interests threaten global human rights and the global natural environment. Using the Corporate Watch website [**http://www.corpwatch.org/**] and its Issues button, explain those concerns in more detail.

2. Using the website opensecrets.org, find the latest campaign finance data for your congressperson or one of your senators. While there, you can take a look at the personal financial condition of those same politicians. [See **http://www.opensecrets.org/pfds /overview.php**]

Chapter Questions

1. *a.* In general, do you think employers are more concerned with profits or with delivering quality goods and services? Explain.
   b. Which should they be more concerned about? Explain.
   c. Are you most concerned about receiving a quality education or earning a degree? Explain.

2. Scholar Denis Goulet argued that we will find no facile resolution to the conflict between the values of a just society and the sharply opposing values of successful corporations.[137]
   a. Do you agree that the values of a just society oppose those of successful corporations? Explain.
   b. Can a solution be found? Explain.

3. In 2010, the Center for Science in the Public Interest and a concerned parent sued McDonald's for deceptive advertising by using toys in Happy Meals to encourage children to consume unhealthy food.[138] San Francisco approved an ordinance, effective December 1, 2011, banning free toys with food that exceeds certain specified levels of fat, sugar, and calories.[139]
   a. Do you think McDonald's commits an ethical wrong by using toys in Happy Meals to attract children to unhealthy food? Explain.
   b. Should the legal system restrain McDonald's use of toys to encourage the consumption of unhealthy food? Explain.

4. In 2013, BizVizz introduced a free iPhone app that allows users to learn about major corporations by entering the corporate name or snapping a picture of the brand's logo on a store shelf. The information revealed includes taxes paid, government subsidies received, and political campaign donations.
   a. Are you trying to learn more about the social practices of companies with which you do business? Explain.
   b. Have you declined to do business with a company because of something you learned about its behavior? Explain.
   c. Have you shared information about a company's practices with friends or family? Explain.

5. A Pennsylvania Chick-fil-A franchise, on its own, provided food for a local marriage seminar, "The Art of Marriage: Getting to the Heart of God's Design." A group opposed to gay and lesbian marriage sponsored the seminar. Once news of Chick-fil-A's sponsorship became public, protests and calls for boycotts followed.

Chick-fil-A, a privately held company, is always closed on Sundays, has given millions to Christian causes, and includes the glorification of God among its corporate purposes.[140]

a. In your view, is the operation of a privately held business on Christian principles a moral wrong? Explain.

b. Would you consider it to be a moral wrong if Chick-fil-A actively opposed gay and lesbian marriage? Explain.

c. As a business matter, how should Chick-Fil-A handle the objections to its franchise's support of the seminar?

6. Worried about Junior misbehaving? Here's an answer:

> Call a board meeting. As crazy as it sounds, some Americans are trying to keep tabs on the kids by bringing business strategies into the traditional family meeting. They're hashing out everything from vacations to disputes over toys with techniques that seem right out of a management textbook: mission statements, rotating chairmanships, motivational seminars, even suggestion boxes. The most corporate of clans hire professional meeting facilitators, just to smooth over family squabbles.[141]

a. List some of the strengths and weaknesses of the business approach to raising children.

b. Do you regard the business approach in the home as a promising development or another encroachment of business values into life outside of work? Explain.

7. Sam Wong, speaking during his sophomore year at Iowa State University:

> Materialism, like patience, is a virtue. Ever since my parents bought me my first Transformer, almost everyone has tried to convince me that owning a lot of toys wouldn't make me happy. Oh, how wrong they were. Toys make me very, very happy. That's why today I have more of them than ever. I own every Nintendo. I own two CD-R burners. My drum set cost as much as a semester of school. I drive a Miata. What's more, I'm not ashamed to be a consumer. I consider it part of my American heritage, and I'm proud of it.[142]

Do you share Wong's values? Explain. Is materialism in America's best interests? Explain.

8. Knights Apparel, a privately held, Spartansburg, South Carolina, clothing company is the leading supplier of college logo apparel to American universities. Knights works closely with the Worker Rights Consortium, a group of 186 universities that lobbies for fair treatment for workers in the plants that produce college-logo goods. Knights contracts with 30 factories worldwide. One of those plants, Alta Gracia in the Dominican Republic, is a Knights experiment in social responsibility. Knights is paying Alta Gracia workers a "living wage" of about $2.83 per hour while the Dominican minimum wage is about 85 cents per hour. The factory was remodeled, including ergonomic chairs for workers and bright lighting. Unionization is permitted, and workers are treated with respect. T-shirts cost about $4.80 to produce, about 20 percent more than if Knights paid the minimum wage. Knights sells the shirts at $8 wholesale, and the normal retail price is about $18. Knights will achieve a lower than usual profit

margin on the Alta Gracia apparel.[143] The big question is whether customers will pay as much for the Knights clothing as for premium brands like Nike that are similarly priced. [For the Alta Gracia home page, see **http://altagraciaapparel.com**]

   a. Would you forgo the Nike clothing of similar price and quality to support the Alta Gracia brand? Explain.

   b. Do you, as a student, have a responsibility to protest if your college logo appears on sportswear made in low-wage sweatshops? Explain.

   c. Have you ever inquired about the manufacturing source of a product you were considering, or have you declined, as a matter of principle, to buy certain garments or other items because you believe the manufacturer engages in unfair labor practices? Explain.

9. Should American companies refuse to do business in countries that:

   a. Do not practice democracy?

   b. Routinely practice discrimination?

   c. Tolerate or even encourage the abuse of children? Explain.

10. In criticizing General Motors, Ralph Nader is reported to have said,

> Someday we'll have a legal system that will criminally indict the president of General Motors for these outrageous crimes. But not as long as this country is populated by people who fritter away their citizenship by watching TV, playing bridge and Mah-Jongg, and just generally being slobs.[144]

   a. Is the citizenry generally unconcerned about unethical corporate conduct? Explain.

   b. To the extent that corporations engage in misdeeds, does the fault really lie with the corporate community or with society at large?

11. The forepart of this chapter discusses the very substantial power exercised by America's giant corporations. One conglomerate, Samsung, accounts for approximately one-fifth of the South Korean economy. Samsung, well-known for electronics production, also builds roads, operates hotels, and sells insurance, among other activities. Critics say Samsung destroys smaller competitors, fixes prices, and avoids criminal punishment. "You can even say the Samsung chairman is more powerful than the South Korean President," said Woo Suk-hoon, host of a popular economics podcast. "Korean people have come to think of Samsung as invincible and above the law."[145] Of course, Samsung generates hundreds of thousands of jobs and makes the world's best-selling smartphone, the Galaxy.

   a. If not already the case, do you envision a future in which a relatively small number of corporations dominate world economics? Explain.

   b. Would we be better off if that domination were to transpire? Explain.

12. Abercrombie & Fitch, the clothing retailer, declines to offer women's clothing in plus sizes and continues to direct its business toward young, good-looking customers. A & F received harsh, widespread criticism in early 2013 when a 2006 *Salon* interview with its CEO Michael S. Jeffries surfaced and went viral:

> In every school there are the cool and popular kids, and then there are the not-so-cool kids. . . .Candidly, we go after the cool kids. We go after the attractive all-American kid with a great attitude and a lot of friends. A lot of people don't belong [in our clothes], and they can't belong. Are we exclusionary? Absolutely. . . ."[146]

    a. Do you think Abercrombie's business is harmed by its "exclusionary" policies? Explain.

    b. *Should* Abercrombie's business be hurt by its exclusionary policies? Explain.

    c. Do you decline to shop at Abercrombie? Explain.

13. Michael Vick, Kobe Bryant, Tiger Woods, and other high-profile athletes have been entangled in very serious legal problems. Disgraced cyclist, Lance Armstrong, has admitted to persistent cheating. Many major league baseball players have been linked to steroid use. Should you refuse to watch these tarnished athletes and refuse to buy products they endorse? Explain.

14. Make the argument that corporations are not well-suited to be stakeholder driven, "do-gooders" looking out for the general welfare of society.

15. You are the sole owner of a neighborhood drugstore that stocks various brands of toothpaste. Assume that scientific testing has established that one brand is clearly superior to all others in preventing tooth decay.

    a. Would you remove from the shelves all brands except the one judged best in decay prevention? Explain.

    b. What alternative measures could you take?

    c. Should the toothpaste manufacturers be required to reveal all available data regarding the effectiveness of their products? Explain.

16. The Santa Monica, California, City Council in 2013 approved a "Sustainability Bill of Rights" striving for a clearer environment and asserting that corporations do not have special privileges under the law that supersede community rights. The ordinance also requires a report every two years detailing the city's progress toward its Sustainable City Plan. According to councilmember Kevin McKeown, the ordinance shifts power away from the business community in a way that had not previously happened in the environmental movement. He blamed "unrestrained capitalism" for harming the environment.[147] In your view, should all communities adopt a "Sustainability Bill of Rights" confirming the importance of sustainability and asserting the supremacy of community rights over corporate authority? Explain.

17. Approximately $10 million is expended annually for alcohol ads in college newspapers. Many millions more are expended in other youth-oriented publications such as *National Lampoon* and *Rolling Stone*. The beer industry sponsors many campus athletic contests. Brewers have established promotional relationships with rock bands. Is beer and liquor advertising directed to the youth market unethical? Explain.

18. U.S. corporations routinely outsource programming, customer support, data entry, and various back-office jobs to lower-paid workers in countries as diverse as India, Romania, and Ghana. Now higher-paying, increasingly sophisticated jobs are also moving abroad. Some countries develop technical specialties, as is the case with Sri Lanka that has an abundance of well-trained accountants who do work for giants such as HSBC and Aviva. That work sometimes involves routine bookkeeping, but it also entails sophisticated derivatives pricing and risk management. In the United States, accounting salaries average just under $60,000 while $5,900 is the norm in Sri Lanka.[148]

   a. Is outsourcing good for America? Explain.
   b. Are you confident that you will be competitive in the American market of the future where outsourcing seems destined to strip away big pieces of the job market? Explain.

19. Former General Motors vice president John Z. DeLorean wrote in his book, *On a Clear Day You Can See General Motors:*

> It seemed to me then, and still does now, that the system of American business often produces wrong, immoral, and irresponsible decisions, even though the personal morality of the people running the business is often above reproach. The system has a different morality as a group than the people do as individuals, which permits it willfully to produce ineffective or dangerous products, deal dictatorially and often unfairly with suppliers, pay bribes for business, abrogate the rights of employment, or tamper with the democratic process of government through illegal political contributions.[149]

   a. How can the corporate "group" possess values at odds with those of the individual managers?
   b. Is DeLorean merely offering a convenient rationalization for corporate misdeeds? Explain.
   c. Realistically, can one expect to preserve individual values when employed in a corporate group? Explain.

20. Do you agree or disagree with the following statements? Explain.
   a. "Social responsibility is good business only if it is also good public relations and/or preempts government interference."
   b. "The social responsibility debate is the result of the attempt of liberal intellectuals to make a moral issue of business behavior."
   c. "'Profit' is really a somewhat ineffective measure of business's social effectiveness."
   d. "The social responsibility of business is to 'stick to business.'"[150]

Notes

1. "Walmart Corporate —Walmart Facts" [**news.walmart.com/walmart-facts**].
2. Global Trends, "Corporate Clout Distributed: The Influence of the World's Largest 100 Economic Entities," *SourceWire*, May 4, 2012 [**http://www.sourcewire.com**].
3. Steve Coll, *Private Empire: ExxonMobil and American Power* (New York: Penguin Press, 2012).
4. Adam Hochschild, "Well-Oiled Machine," *The New York Times,* June 8, 2012 [**http://www.nytimes.com**].
5. Dwight Garner, "Oil's Dark Heart Pumps Strong," *The New York Times,* April 26, 2012 [**http://www.nytimes.com**].
6. "Pinkham Discusses Pulse Survey on FOX Business," Public Affairs Council *Press Release,* 2012 [**pac.org/pinkham_fox_business**].
7. Thomas B. Edsall, "The Obama Coalition vs. Corporate America," *The New York Times,* January 9, 2013 [**http://opinionator.blogs.nytimes.com/**].
8. Louise Story, "Lines Blur as Texas Gives Industries a Bonanza," *The New York Times,* December 2, 2012 [**http://www.nytimes.com/**].
9. James Glanz, "Data Barns in a Farm Town, Gobbling Power and Flexing Muscle," *The New York Times,* September 23, 2012 [**http://www.nytimes.com/**].

10. Cecilia Kang, "Apple Avoids Taxes with 'Complex Web' of Offshore Entities, Senate Inquiry Finds," *The Washington Post,* May 20, 2013 [**http://www.washingtonpost.com/**].

11. Editorial, "It's Not Right When You Have to Pay but Giant, Profitable Companies Don't," *Des Moines Register,* November 13, 2011, p. 1 OP.

12. David Kocieniewski, "Biggest Public Firms Paid Little U.S. Tax, Study Says," *The New York Times,* November 3, 2011 [**http://www.nytimes.com/**].

13. Chris Isidore, "U.S. Corporate Tax Rate: No. 1 in the World," *CNNMoney,* March 27, 2012 [**http://money.cnn.com/**].

14. Ibid.

15. Douglas McIntyre, "Companies Paying the Most in Income Taxes," *USA Today*, March 17, 2013 [**http://www.usatoday.com/**].

16. Gerald F. Seib, "Populist Anger Over Economy Carries Risks for Big Business," *The Wall Street Journal,* October 11, 2011, p. A4.

17. Frank Newport, "Americans Blame Government More Than Wall Street for Economy," *Gallup Poll,* October 19, 2011 [**http://www.gallup.com/**].

18. Matt Taibbi, "Why Isn't Wall Street in Jail?" *Rolling Stone,* February 16, 2011 [**http://www.rollingstone.com/**].

19. Andrew Ross Sorkin, "On Wall Street, a Culture of Greed Won't Let Go," *The New York Times DealBook,* July 15, 2013 [**http://dealbook.nytimes.com/**].

20. Eduardo Porter, "The Spreading Scourge of Corporate Corruption," *The New York Times,* July 10, 2012 [**http://www.nytimes.com/**].

21. Barry C. Lynn, *Cornered: The New Monopoly Capitalism and the Economics of Destruction* (Hoboken, NJ: Wiley, 2010).

22. This paragraph relies heavily on Jim Yardley, "Report on Deadly Factory Collapse in Bangladesh Finds Widespread Blame," *The New York Times,* May 22, 2013 [**http://www.nytimes.com/**].

23. Chris MacDonald, "Bangladesh, Joe Fresh and the Burden of Responsibility," *Canadian Business,* April 26, 2013 [**http://www.canadianbusiness.com/**].

24. Christopher A. Bartlett, "Losing in the Court of Public Opinion," *Across the Board,* January–February 2002, p. 27.

25. *Citizens United v. Federal Election Commission,* 130 S.Ct. 876 (2010).

26. Jia Lynn Yang and Tom Hamburger, "For U.S. Chamber of Commerce, Election was a Money-Loser," *The Washington Post,* November 7, 2012 [**http://www.washingtonpost.com/**].

27. Ibid.

28. Ezra Klein, "Wonkbook: Wisconsin Recall Shows Labor Isn't Coming Back. So What's Next?" *The Washington Post,* June 6, 2012 [**http://www.washingtonpost.com/**].

29. "Political Spending Pays," *The Wall Street Journal,* June 20, 2012 [**http://online.wsj.com/**].

30. Ibid.

31. Clea Benson and Roxana Tiron, "Countrywide Used a Special VIP Loan Program to Influence Lawmakers, Report Says," *The Washington Post*, July 5, 2012 [**http://www.washingtonpost.com**].

32. "Lobbying Database," *OpenSecrets.org,* April 29, 2013 [**http://www.opensecrets.org/lobby/**].

33. Thomas B. Edsall, "The Shadow Lobbyist," *The New York Times,* April 25, 2013 [**http://opinionator.blogs.nytimes.com/**].

34. Dana Milbank, "Big Business Is Back," *The Washington Post,* January 12, 2011 [**http://www.washingtonpost.com/**].

35. Russ Choma, "Quarterly Lobbying Reports Show Yet Another Decline," *OpenSecrets Blog,* May 2, 2013 [**http://www.opensecrets.org/**].

36. Melinda Burns, "K Street and the Status Quo," *Miller-McCune,* September–October 2010, p. 62.

37. Eric Lipton and Kevin Sack, "Fiscal Footnote: Big Senate Gift to Drug Maker," *The New York Times,* January 19, 2013 [**http://www.nytimes.com/**].

38. Ibid.

39. Ibid.

40. Editorial, "Amgen Gets a Gift from Congress," *The New York Times,* January 22, 2013 [**http://www.nytimes.com/**].

41. Thomas B. Edsall, "Kill Bill," *The New York Times,* May 22, 2013 [**http://opinionator.blogs.nytimes.com/**].

42. Eric Lipton and Ben Protess, "Banks' Lobbyists Help in Drafting Financial Bills," *The New York Times Dealbook,* May 23, 2013 [**http://dealbook.nytimes.com/**].

43. See, e.g., Robert Bridge, *Midnight in the American Dream: How Corporations and Their Political Servants Are Destroying the American Dream* (CreateSpace Independent Publishing Platform, 2013).

44. Tamar Lewin, "Children's Publisher Backing Off Its Corporate Ties," *The New York Times,* August 1, 2011, p. A8.

45. Morgan Smith, "Seeking Money, Texas Schools Turn to Advertisements," *The New York Times,* February 16, 2012 [**http://www.nytimes.com/**].

46. Carla K. Johnson, "Ads More Memorable Than News, Study Says," *The Des Moines Register,* March 6, 2006, p. 8A.

47. Ibid.

48. Molly Bloom, "EdisonLearning, K12 Inc. among National Companies Looking to Open New Online Charter Schools in Ohio," *StateImpact Ohio,* May 15, 2013 [**http://stateimpact.npr.org/ohio/**].

49. Christin Nance Lazerus, "EdisonLearning Has Had Successes, Down Sides," *Post-Tribune,* November 4, 2011 [**http://posttrib.suntimes.com/**].

50. Natasha Singer, "On Campus, It's One Big Commercial," *The New York Times,* September 10, 2011 [**http://www.nytimes.com/**].

51. Ibid.

52. Gene D. Block, "College Is More Than a 'Return on Investment,'" *The Washington Post,* March 14, 2013 [**http://articles.washingtonpost.com/**].

53. Melissa Korn, "Wealth or Waste? Rethinking the Value of a Business Major," *WSJ.com,* April 5, 2012 [**http://online.wsj.com/**].

54. "Peter Drucker—Toward a More Gentle Marketplace," *Austrian Information* 59, (March/April 2006), p. 9.

55. Alexandra Alter, "Inspired by Starbucks," *The Wall Street Journal,* June 13, 2008, p. W1.

56. David Brooks, "The Gospel of Wealth," *The New York Times,* September 6, 2010 [**http://www.nytimes.com/**].

57. Patricia Cohen, "An Art World Gathering, Divided by Money," *The New York Times,* December 7, 2012 [**http://www.nytimes.com/**].

58. Marshall Herskovitz, "Are the Corporate Suits Ruining TV?" *latimes.com,* November 7, 2007 [**http://www.latimes.com/news/opinion/la-oe-herskovitz7nov07,0,5402981.story?coll=la-tot-opinion&track=ntothtml**].

59. Ibid.

60. Jacques Steinberg, "Radio Days," *The New York Times,* April 13, 2008 [**http://www.nytimes.com/**].

61. L. R., "Same Old Song," *The Economist,* July 26, 2012 [**http://www.economist.com/**].

62. Ibid.

63. Jon Caramanica, "Rap, Both Good and Bad for Business," *The New York Times,* May 7, 2013 [**http://www.nytimes.com/**].

64. "Knight, Big 12 Coaches Agree: College Sports Are Big Business," *USA TODAY,* February 16, 2004 [**http://www.usatoday.com/sports/college/2004-02-16-notes_x.htm**].

65. Ibid.

66. Eric Crawford, "It's Time for Leagues to Pay Up," *Louisville Courier-Journal.com,* October 27, 2011 [**http://www.courier-journal.com/**].

67. Ibid.

68. Bill Morris, "Explosion of Brands and Erosion of Soul," *The New York Times,* December 21, 2012 [**http://www.nytimes.com/**].

69. Ibid.

70. Ibid.

71. Greg Bishop, "A Company That Runs Prisons Will Have Its Name on a Stadium," *The New York Times,* February 19, 2013 [**http://www.nytimes.com/**].

72. Daniel Roberts, "Gridiron Green," *Fortune,* September 26, 2011, p. 21.

73. Josh Barr, "Business Embraces Prep Football," *The Washington Post,* September 2, 2007, p. D05.

74. David Briggs, "Trend Brewing to Sell Beer at Games," *Toledo Blade,* June 14, 2013 [**http://www.toledoblade.com/**].

75. Timothy Egan, "Nike's Women Problem," *The New York Times,* April 21, 2010 [**http://opinionator.blogs.nytimes.com/**].

76. "Analyst: Endorsements Will Come for Ben Roethlisberger with a Victory," *USA TODAY,* February 6, 2011 [**http://content.usatoday.com/**].

77. Charles Reich, *The Greening of America* (New York: Bantam Books, 1970), pp. 7–8.

78. "Harris Alienation Index Jumps Up Considerably to a Level Not Seen Since the Clinton Years," Harris Poll *Press Release,* September 13, 2011 [**http://www.harrisinteractive.com/**].

79. Ben Stein, "A City on a Hill, or a Looting Opportunity," *The New York Times,* July 9, 2006 [**http://www.nytimes.com/**].

80. Joseph Pickett, "4 Examples of How Corporate America Is Crushing Social Media," *Business 2 Community,* February 8, 2013 [**www.business2community.com/**].

81. Ted Peters, "The Future of Religion in a Post-Industrial Society," *The Futurist,* October 1980, pp. 20, 22.

82. "More Leisure in an Increasingly Electronic Society," *BusinessWeek,* September 3, 1979, pp. 208, 212.

83. Daniel Seligman, "Helping the Shareholder Helps the Society," *The Wall Street Journal,* June 21, 1996, p. A12.

84. "Managing Tomorrow's People—Millennials at Work: Perspectives from a New Generation," PricewaterhouseCoopers, 2008 [**www.pwc.com/gx/en/managing-tomorrows-people/future-of-work/pdf/mtp-millennials-at-work.pdf**]

85. This paragraph relies on materials from Ian Shapira, "For This Generation, Vocations of Service," *washingtonpost.com*, October 14, 2008, p. B01, Kristie Wang, "love.futbol: Engaging a Global Passion for Soccer and Youth," *Changemakers*, February 17, 2011 [**http://www.changemakers.com/node/101116/**]; and **lovefutbol.wordpress.com/page/2/**.

86. Thomas Heath, "Capital Buzz: Banker Switches Jobs in Order to Help Others Do Good," *The Washington Post*, June 23, 2013 [**http://www.washingtonpost.com/**].

87. Keith Davis and Robert L. Blomstrom, *Business and Society: Environment and Responsibility,* 3rd ed. (New York: McGraw-Hill, 1975), p. 6.

88. Milton Friedman, *Capitalism and Freedom* (Chicago: University of Chicago Press, 1962), p. 133.

89. Herbert Stein, "Corporate America, Mind Your Own Business," *The Wall Street Journal,* July 15, 1996, p. A10.

90. Steven A. Rochlin, "The New Corporate Citizenship," *BusinessWeek,* December 13, 2003, p. 66.

91. See E. Lynn Grayson, "Sustainability Remains a Challenge for U.S. Businesses," *LEXOLOGY,* May 10, 2012 [**http://www.lexology.com/**]; and David Leiter, Sarah Litke, and Daniel Phillips, "Corporate Sustainability Ratings," *LEXOLOGY,* May 6, 2012 [**http://www.lexology.com/**].

92. Muktar Kent, "Toward a Sustainable Future," *Raytheon Lectureship in Business Ethics of Bentley University,* April 5, 2012 [**www.bentley.edu/cbe**].

93. Archie Carroll and others have pointed to some descriptive and theoretical limitations associated with Carroll's social responsibility pyramid; and Carroll has proposed a three-domain approach of economic, legal, and ethical responsibilities arrayed in a Venn framework. The newer model appears to satisfy some of the concerns of Carroll and others about Carroll's pyramid, but for both teaching and research purposes, the pyramid remains a useful construct. For Carroll's newer construct, see Mark S. Schwartz and Archie B. Carroll, "Corporate Social Responsibility: A Three Domain Approach," *Business Ethics Quarterly* 13, no. 4 (October 2003), p. 503. For an example of research employing the Carroll pyramid and a discussion of some of the strengths and weaknesses of the pyramid, see Dane K. Peterson, "The Relationship between Perceptions of Corporate Citizenship and Organizational Commitment," *Business & Society* 43, no. 3 (September 2004), p. 296.

94. Chris Herring and Dana Mattioli, "Companies Send Aid to Haiti," *The Wall Street Journal,* January 19, 2010 [**http://online.wsj.com/**].

95. Bettina Elias Siegel, "Why Disney's Junk Food Ad Ban Marks the Future of Food Reform," *HuffPost Food,* June 6, 2012 [**http://www.huffingtonpost.com/**].

96. Mark Bittman, "OMG: McDonald's Does the Right Thing," *The New York Times Opinionator*, February 13, 2012 [**http://opinionator.blogs.nytimes.com/**].

97. Bryn Nelson, "A Building Not Just Green, but Practically Self-Sustaining," *The New York Times,* April 2, 2013 [**http://www.nytimes.com/**].

98. The Goldman Sachs discussion is drawn from Stephanie Strom, "Philanthropists Take on Big Problems by Enlisting Capitalists," *The New York Times,* December 12, 2012, p. F19; and "Social Impact Bond for Early Childhood Education" [**http://www.goldmansachs.com/**].

99. Aaron Task, "Mass Layoffs by Profitable Firms a 'Horrible Act,' Diller Says," *Yahoo! Finance,* December 10, 2008 [**http://finance.yahoo.com/**].

100. Linda Basch, "More Women in Finance, A More Sustainable Economy," *The Christian Science Monitor,* June 24, 2009 [**http://www.csmonitor.com/2009/0624/p09s02-coop .html**].

101. Joshua Margolis, Hillary Elfenbein, and James Walsh, "Does It Pay to Be Good . . . And Does It Matter? A Meta-Analysis of the Relationship between Corporate Social and Financial Performance," March 2009 [**http://ssrn.com/abstract=1866371**].

102. Robert Eccles, Loannis Loannou, and George Serafeim, "The Impact of a Corporate Culture of Sustainability on Corporate Behavior and Performance," No. w17950, National Bureau of Economic Research, 2012 [**http://www.nber.org/papers/w17950**].

103. Sheila Shayon, "Report: Nielsen Defines the Socially Conscious Consumer," *brandchannel,* April 3, 2012 [**http://www.brandchannel.com/**].

104. Michael E. Porter and Mark R. Kramer, "Creating Shared Value," *Harvard Business Review* 89, no. 1–2 (January–February 2011), p. 2.

105. John Bussey, "CEO Council (A Special Report)—Restoring Confidence in Business: Not Just about Shareholders," *The Wall Street Journal,* November 22, 2010, p. R3.

106. Cedric Rose, "Q&A: A. G. Lafley," *Cincinnati Magazine,* May 1, 2013 [**http://www .cincinnatimagazine.com/**].

107. Social Accountability Accreditation Services, "Certified Facilities List," September 30, 2010 [**http://www.saasaccreditation.org/certfacilieslist.htm**].

108. Mark Magnier, "Anguish Lingers in Bhopal, 25 Years after Chemical Disaster," *latimes.com,* December 3, 2009 [**latimes,com/news/nation-and-world/la-fg-india-bhopal3-2009dec03,0,3728767.story**].

109. Susan Warren, "Chemical Companies Keep Lessons of Bhopal Spill Fresh," *The Wall Street Journal,* February 13, 2001, p. B4.

110. Brad Stone, "Costco CEO Craig Jelinek Leads the Cheapest, Happiest Company in the World," *Bloomberg Businessweek,* June 6, 2013 [**http://www.businessweek.com/**]; and Susan Berfield, "More Than Half of Wal-Mart's Hourly Workers Make Less than $25,000, *Bloomberg Businessweek,* October 23, 2013 [**http://www.businessweek.com/**].

111. Stone, "Costco CEO Craig Jelinek Leads."

112. Claire Gordon, "Walmart vs. Costco: How Do They Really Compare?" *AOL Jobs,* June 16, 2013 [**http://jobs.aol.com/**].

113. Renee Dudley, "Customers Flee Wal-Mart Empty Shelves for Target, Costco," *Bloomberg,* March 26, 2013 [**http://www.bloomberg.com/**].

114. Ibid.

115. "Wal-Mart Releases Employment Data," *The Des Moines Register,* April 12, 2006, p. 6C.

116. David Vogel, "When Do 'Good' Firms Go 'Bad'?" *latimes.com,* February 13, 2007 [**http:// www.latimes.com/news/opinion/la-oe-vogel13feb13,0,4670297.story?track=tottext**].

117. William Beaver, "Is the Stakeholder Model Dead?" *Business Horizons* 42, no. 2 (March–April 1999), p. 8.

118. Associated Press, "Boss Rewards Workers' Loyalty—Shares $128 Million," *Waterloo/Cedar Falls Courier,* September 12, 1999, p. B1.

119. Greg Miller, "Extreme Generosity Shocks Firm's Employees, Analysts," *The Des Moines Register,* December 18, 1996, p. 1A.

120. Dana Radcliffe, "Gun Makers See No Problem Selling for Self-Defense and Allowing Sales to Criminals," *Huff Post Politics,* June 28, 2013 [**http://www.huffingtonpost.com/**].

121. Ibid.

122. Mike McIntire and Michael Luo, "Gun Makers Saw No Role in Curbing Improper Sales," *The New York Times,* May 27, 2013 [**http://www.nytimes.com/**].

123. Ibid.

124. Editorial Board, "A Gun Maker Moves On," *The New York Times,* June 29, 2013 [**http://www.nytimes.com/**].

125. Lucinda M. Finley and John G. Culhane, "Make Gun Companies Pay Blood Money," *The New York Times,* June 23, 2013 [**http://www.nytimes.com/**].

126. Caroline Durocher, "Fast Food Workers in Another City Strike: 'We've Been Pushed to the Edge,'" *AOL Jobs,* May 30, 2013 [**http://jobs.aol.com/**].

127. Ibid.

128. United States Census Bureau, "Poverty," September 17, 2013 [**www.census.gov/hhes/www/poverty/data/threshld/**].

129. Elizabeth Olson, "Could a Fast Food Strike Work?" *CNNMoney,* April 9, 2013 [**http://management.fortune.cnn.com/**].

130. Ibid.

131. Jim Offner, "Hobby Lobby Proactively Hikes Minimum Wage for Full-Timers," *Waterloo/Cedar Falls Courier,* May 30, 2010, p. D1.

132. Ibid.

133. Steven Greenhouse, "Ending Strike, Mott's Plant Union Accepts Deal," *The New York Times,* September 13, 2010 [**http://www.nytimes.com/**].

134. Steven Greenhouse, "In Mott's Strike, More Than Pay at Stake," *The New York Times,* August 17, 2010 [**http://www.nytimes.com/**].

135. Greenhouse, "Ending Strike . . .," September 13, 2010.

136. Dan Margolis, "Mott's Workers OK New Contract," *Peoplesworld,* September 14, 2010 [**http://peoplesworld.org/mott-s-workers-ok-new-contract/**].

137. For an overview of Denis Goulet and his work, see [**http://www.nd.edu/~krocinst/faculty_staff/fellows/goulet.html**]

138. Gael O'Brien, "McDonald's Happy Meal Challenge," *The Week in Ethics,* December 27, 2010 [**http://theweekinethics.wordpress.com/**].

139. Joshua Sabatini, "Happy Meal Toy Ban Official," *San Francisco Examiner,* November 23, 2010 [**http://www.sfexaminer.com/blogs/under-dome/2010/11/happy-meal-toy-ban-official**].

140. Kim Severson, "A Chicken Chain's Corporate Ethos Is Questioned by Gay Rights Advocates," *The New York Times,* January 29, 2011 [**http://www.nytimes.com**].

141. Nancy Jeffrey, "Kids, Come to Order," *The Wall Street Journal,* August 10, 2001, p. W1.

142. Sam Wong, "Materialism Makes Me Feel Happy, Not Guilty," *The Des Moines Register,* September 10, 2000, p. 11A.

143. Steven Greenhouse, "Factory Defies Sweatshop Label, but Can It Thrive?" *The New York Times,* July 16, 2010 [**http://www.nytimes.com**].

144. Charles McCarry, *Citizen Nader* (New York: Saturday Review Press, 1972), p. 301.

145. Chico Harlan, "In South Korea, the Republic of Samsung," *The Washington Post,* December 9, 2012 [**http://articles.washingtonpost.com**].

146. Benjamin O'Keefe, "Why I'm Optimistic That Abercrombie & Fitch Learned a Big Lesson," *theguardian,* May 25, 2013 [**http://www.theguardian.com/**].

147. Ashley Archibald, "City Council Passes Environmental Bill of Rights," *Santa Monica Daily Press,* March 14, 2013 [**http://smdp.com/**].

148. Heather Timmons, "Sri Lankan Accountants Lure Global Outsourcers," *The New York Times,* November 29, 2010 [**http://www.nytimes.com/**].

149. John Z. DeLorean with J. Patrick Wright, "Bottom-Line Fever at General Motors" (excerpted from *On a Clear Day You Can See General Motors*), *The Washington Monthly,* January 1980, pp. 26–27.

150. Steven N. Brenner and Earl A. Molander, "Is the Ethics of Business Changing?" *Harvard Business Review* 55, no. 1 (January–February 1977), p. 68.

Introduction to Law

CHAPTER FOUR

The American Legal System

After completing this chapter, students will be able to:

1. Describe the importance of law to private enterprise.

2. Compare and contrast the objectives of law in society.

3. Differentiate the elements of a case brief.

4. Distinguish between substantive and procedural law.

5. Differentiate constitutional law, case law, and statutory law.

6. Compare and contrast civil and criminal law.

7. Describe the elements of the basic court system structure.

8. Explain the purposes of subject matter and personal jurisdiction as requirements for a court's power to hear a dispute.

9. Describe the typical steps in the civil trial process.

10. Distinguish trials and appeals.

11. Identify dispute resolution alternatives to trials.

Introduction

Presumably we can agree that some business behavior is bad for society. This text examines what should be done to change that behavior. In the United States, four basic options exist: Let the market "regulate" the behavior; leave the choice to the individual decision maker's own ethical dictates; pass a law; or rely on some combination of the market, ethics, and law. Market regulation was discussed in Chapter 1. Self-regulation through ethics was explored in Chapters 2 and 3. This chapter begins the discussion of the legal regulation of business with a brief outline of the American legal system. We will also look at alternative conflict resolution processes such as negotiation, mediation, and arbitration that do not resort to the court system. We begin by reminding ourselves of the indispensable role of law in supporting business practice.

Law and the Market   Whatever we may think about lawyers, judges, and America's dispute resolution methods, the crucial role of a reliable legal system in fostering and maintaining capitalism is indisputable. The following law review excerpt explains.

READING

The Importance of Law to the Private Enterprise System

Deb Ballam

Nobel economist Frederich von Hayek describes the theoretical importance of law to private enterprise. According to Hayek, law that secures property rights in modern society is a prerequisite to private enterprise. Without the order of law enforcing private property ownership and facilitating the transfer of property rights, business enterprise in a complex, heterogeneous culture is simply infeasible.

The importance of law to the conduct of private enterprise is evident in economic developments in . . . the Republic of China. In moving from state-controlled to private enterprise, [China] faced substantial difficulties arising from the lack of a legal system that would secure property ownership and the contractual transfer of property rights.

. . . China's economy has grown steadily in recent years. Minxin Pei, a political scientist at Princeton University, explains law's contribution to that growth: "Legal reform has become one of the most important institutional changes in China since the late 1970s. . . . Within China, the changing legal institutions have begun to play an increasingly important role in governing economic activities, resolving civil disputes, enforcing law and order, and setting the boundaries between the power of the state and the autonomy of society. . . ."

Of course, the importance of law to private enterprise goes far beyond its initial support as an institutional framework guaranteeing ownership rights. As the market system grows more complex both nationally and internationally, the legal recognition of promise keeping becomes increasingly significant in facilitating business. A condition for emerging economies entering international trade is learning how to keep promises to strangers, and whether enforced through litigation or arbitration, promise keeping in business requires the ordering presence of contract law.

In a democracy, law is important to business for another reason quite separate from its function in establishing ownership rights and facilitating promise keeping necessary to their transfer: It provides the formal expression of democratic social will. That expression implicates private enterprise in a plethora of ways, including regulation of the environment, employment laws, securities regulation, consumer protection statutes, and product liability. As contemporary society becomes increasingly diverse, law grows, not diminishes, in its importance to private enterprise; and in spite of valid concerns about the impact of law on efficiency, future business managers will need to know more, not less, about how law affects business operations. No evidence suggests any other conclusion.

Source: Deb Ballam, quoting from "The Importance of Law to the Private Enterprise System," *The American Legal Studies in Business Task Force Report* by O. Lee Reed. *American Business Law Journal* 36, no. 1 (Fall 1998), p. ix. Reprinted by permission.

Question

As reported by *The Wall Street Journal* in 2011, a recent trend among the major oil companies is to shift investment of resources to economically developed countries. This strategy is reflected in Royal Dutch Shell's 2012 Annual Report, which noted Shell's investments in countries with the "necessary infrastructure," such as, among others, Australia, Canada, the United Kingdom, Norway, Germany, Denmark, and the United States. What role might the law play in creating a favorable environment for oil companies' investments?

Sources: Guy Chazan, "Big Oil Heads Back Home," *The Wall Street Journal*, December 5, 2011, p. R1; and Royal Dutch Shell, *2012 Annual Report: Business Overview* [http://reports.shell.com/annual-report/2012/businessreview/ourbusinesses/businessoverview.php].

Part One—Legal Foundations

Objectives of the Law

Americans differ dramatically in their views of the role the law should play in contemporary life. For some, the courts and the police primarily act as obstructions to personal freedom and to a fully efficient marketplace. Others seek much more law to ensure that everyone who is in need is cared for and everyone is sheltered from wrongdoers. Although we may argue about the law's precise path in our lives, most of us can agree on some foundational expectations for a fair, efficient legal system. Certainly we expect the law to *maintain order* in our diverse, rapidly changing society. Of course, we rely on law to peacefully, fairly, and intelligently *resolve conflict.* Perhaps less obvious, but no less important, the law serves to *preserve dominant values.* Americans differ about core values, but we have reached a workable accord about our most fundamental beliefs. Some of those, such as freedom of speech, press, and religion, are guaranteed by our Bill of Rights, thus setting a steady foundation for an enduring nation. We can see that the law is a vital force in *guaranteeing freedom.* (But freedom can be confusing: Are you free to smoke wherever you wish, or do I have a right to smoke-free air?)

Justice

Broadly, we count on the law to *achieve and preserve justice.* The pursuit of justice often relies on honorable, efficient government. The World Justice Project's 2013 "Rule of Law Index" ranks governmental quality by such measures as criminal and civil justice, order and security, open government, and limited corruption. Among the 97 countries studied, Sweden ranked particularly well. In most categories, the United States ranked in the bottom half of the 29 high-income nations studied.[1] Perhaps the study is correct in the sense that America still has abundant room for improvement. Nonetheless, Americans can properly be proud of a long struggle to build a more just society for all. Efforts, for example, to curb discrimination, guarantee due process, reduce violence, protect those in need, maintain order and security, build fair, efficient regulatory systems and respect the rights of all are central practices in an extraordinarily complex and rapidly evolving American culture. As you read this chapter, ask yourself repeatedly, "Does this rule (this procedure, this case) contribute to the search for justice?" In the end, all legal studies must involve the search for justice. [For a daily update of legal news, see **www.law.com**]

> All legal studies must involve the search for justice.

Question

In 2010, a New York City lower court judge ruled that a four-year-old girl can be sued for negligence. According to *The New York Times,* the young girl was riding her bicycle with training wheels on a Manhattan sidewalk. She joined in a race against a five-year-old boy during which the children struck an 87-year-old woman who suffered a hip injury requiring surgery. The woman died three months later of unrelated causes. Both children were under the supervision of their mothers.

The girl's attorney argued that she was too young to be responsible for negligent actions and that she was not engaging in an adult activity at the time of the injury. The judge cited cases dating back to 1928 in concluding that the girl could be sued. The judge noted that children under the age of four are conclusively presumed to be incapable of negligence, but he was unwilling to extend that presumption to the girl who was three months shy of her fifth birthday. (The other child and his mother did not seek dismissal of the negligence action against them.)

As a matter of justice, do you think a four-year-old child should be the subject of a negligence action? Explain. See Alan Feuer, "4-Year-Old Can Be Sued, Judge Rules in Bike Case," *The New York Times,* October 28, 2010 [**http://www.nytimes.com/**].

Cyberbullying

In the fall of 2010, 20-year-old Rutgers University student Dharun Ravi secretly activated the webcam in his dorm room so that he and a friend could watch his roommate, 18-year-old Tyler Clementi, engage in a romantic encounter with another male. Ravi used texts and Twitter to encourage friends to watch a second planned video that did not occur. Clementi subsequently committed suicide. In March 2012, Ravi was convicted of invasion of privacy and bias intimidation, among other crimes, and sentenced to 30 days in jail, 300 hours of community service, and a fine of $10,000 to be paid to hate crime victims.

The Tyler Clementi Higher Education Harassment Act, reintroduced in Congress in February 2013, would require colleges and universities receiving federal student aid funding to have and distribute a policy prohibiting harassment. Prohibited harassment would include cyberbullying of enrolled students by other students, faculty, and staff based on, among other things, actual or perceived, sexual orientation.

Questions

1. Do you think the Tyler Clementi Higher Education Act should be enacted? Explain.
2. Co-sponsors of the bill, New Jersey senator Frank Lautenberg and New Jersey representative Rush D. Holt, pointed to the actions and subsequent firing in 2013 of Mike Rice, head basketball coach at Rutgers University, as proof of the need for such antibullying legislation. Rice was videotaped making slurs regarding sexual orientation to players and engaging in other harassing conduct. Do you agree? Explain.
3. Although he was not charged with causing Clementi's death, Ravi was facing a possible 10 years in state prison. Do you think Ravi's actual sentence was fair or too light? Explain.

Sources: Mark Trumbull, "Why Dharun Ravi Got 30 Days in Jail in Rutgers Webcam Spying Case," *The Christian Science Monitor*, May 21, 2012 [**http://www.christiansciencemonitor.com**]; Niels Lesniewski and Emily Bazelon, "Make the Punishment Fit the Cyber-Crime," *The New York Times,* March 19, 2012 [**http://www.nytimes.com**]; "Rutgers Firing Prompts New Look at Anti-Bullying Bill," *Rollcall*, April 3, 2013 [**http://www.rollcall.com**]; and H.R.482 – Tyler Clementi Higher Education Anti-Harassment Act of 2013, 113th Congress (2013–2014) [**http://beta.congress.gov/bill/113th-congress/house-bill/482**].

Primary Sources of Law

U.S. law is a vast, constantly growing, and mutating body of rules and reason. That law is derived from four primary sources: constitutions, statutes, regulations, and cases (called the *common law* or judge-made law).

Constitutions

These are the supreme expressions of law at both the federal and state levels of government. All other law is subordinate to federal constitutional law. Among other things, constitutions prescribe the general structure of governments and provide protection for individual rights. Chapters 5 and 8 give extensive attention to the U.S. Constitution and the Bill of Rights.

Statutes

These are laws that are adopted by legislative bodies, particularly Congress and the state legislatures. City councils enact statutes that usually are called *ordinances*. Legislators and the statutes they enact shape the policy direction of U.S. law. Of course, legislators are not free of constraints. Federal legislation cannot conflict with the U.S. Constitution, and state legislation cannot violate either federal law or the constitutions of that state and the nation.

Regulations

Administrative agencies include such bodies as the Federal Trade Commission and the Securities and Exchange Commission at the federal level, and a Public Service Commission (to regulate utilities) and a Human Rights Commission (to address discrimination problems) at the state level. These agencies have the specialized expertise to carry out much of the day-to-day business of government. Among other duties, they produce and oversee regulations that add the details needed to implement the broader mandates provided by federal and state statutes. (For more detail, see Chapter 8.)

Common Law (Also Called Case Law or Judge-Made Law)

Our case law has its roots in the early English king's courts, where rules of law gradually developed out of a series of individual dispute resolutions. That body of law, the common law, was imported to America where it is has grown and evolved as the courts address the constantly changing legal requirements of our complex society.

The development of English common law and American judicial decisions into a just, ordered package is attributable in large measure to reliance on the doctrine of *stare decisis* (let the decision stand). That is, judges endeavor to follow the precedents established by previous decisions. Following precedent, however, is not mandatory. As societal beliefs and practices change, judges are called on to not only interpret precedent, but to create new law as cases reflecting these changes are brought. For example, a U.S. Supreme Court decision approving racially separate but equal education was eventually overruled by a Supreme Court decision mandating integrated schools. Nonetheless, the principle of stare decisis is generally adhered to because of its beneficial effect. It offers the wisdom of the past and enhances efficiency by eliminating the need for resolving every case as though it were the first of its kind. Stare decisis affords stability and predictability to the law.

The Case Law: Locating and Analyzing

To prepare for the *Nichols* case, which follows, a bit of practical guidance should be useful. The study of law is founded largely on the analysis of judicial opinions. Except for the federal level and a few states, trial court decisions are filed locally for public inspection rather than being published. Appellate (appeals court) opinions, on the other hand, are generally published in volumes called *reports*. State court opinions are found in the reports of that state, and in a regional reporter series published by West Publishing Company that divides the United States into units, such as South Eastern (S.E.) and Pacific (P.).

Within the appropriate reporter, the cases are cited by case name, volume, reporter name, and page number. For example, *Nichols v. Niesen*, 746 N.W.2d 220 (Wisc. S. Ct. 2008) means that the opinion will be found in volume 746 of the *North Western Reporter*, 2nd series, at page 220 and that the decision was reached in 2008 by the Wisconsin Supreme Court. Federal court decisions are found in several reporters, including the *Federal Reporter* and the *United States Supreme Court Reports*. In practice, of course, those cases can most readily be found via a standard search engine or in online databases such as LexisNexis and Westlaw. [For broad databases of law topics, see **http://www.findlaw. com, http://www.yahoo.com/government/law or www.justia.com**]

Briefing the Case

Most students find the preparation of *case briefs* (outlines or digests) to be helpful in mastering the law. A brief should evolve into the form that best suits the individual student's needs. The following approach should be a useful starting point:

1. Parties   Identify the plaintiff and the defendant at the trial level. At the appeals level, identify the appellant (the party bringing the appeal; Nichols, in this instance) and the appellee (the other party on appeal; Niesen, in this instance).

2. Facts   Summarize only those facts critical to the outcome of the case.

3. Procedure   How did the case reach this court? Who won in the lower court(s)?

4. Issue   Note the central question or questions on which the case turns.

5. Holding   How did the court resolve the issue(s)? Who won?

6. Reasoning   Explain the logic that supported the court's decision.

LEGAL BRIEFCASE

Nichols v. Niesen
746 N.W.2d 220 (Wisc. S. Ct. 2008)

Justice N. Patrick Crooks

The court of appeals allowed the claim of Shannon, Lee, Brooke, and Brittney Nichols (the Nichols) to proceed against the Niesens for common-law negligence. The Nichols claimed that the Niesens were social hosts, who did not provide any alcoholic beverages to underage guests, but allegedly were aware that minors were on their property consuming alcoholic beverages. After leaving the Niesens' premises, one of these guests allegedly caused injuries while driving intoxicated. The circuit court had granted the Niesens' . . . motion to dismiss the Nichols' complaint, after concluding that the complaint failed to state a claim in common-law negligence. The primary

issue upon review is whether a claim for common-law negligence should be permitted against social hosts under these circumstances.

I

On June 5, 2004, the Nichols were in a motor vehicle on County Trunk Highway J in Columbia County, Wisconsin, when that vehicle was struck by another motor vehicle, driven by Beth Carr (Carr), which had crossed the highway's center line. The Nichols alleged that the accident was caused by Carr's "failure to properly manage and control the vehicle she was operating, due in part to the voluntary ingestion by her of intoxicating beverages." As a result of the accident, Shannon

Nichols "suffered very severe personal injuries," and Brittney, Brooke, and Lee Nichols "suffered injuries requiring medical care and treatment."

On the night of June 4, 2004, and into the early morning of June 5, 2004, the Nichols alleged that "a large gathering of underage high school students" congregated and consumed alcohol at the premises controlled by the Niesens. . . . [T]he Nichols alleged that "the Niesens were aware that the minors on their property were consuming alcohol." The Nichols did not allege that the Niesens knew, in advance, that the students would be consuming alcohol. The Nichols contended that the Niesens "had a duty to supervise and monitor the activities on their property" and that they were negligent because they failed to do so.

The Nichols contended that the consumption of alcohol by Carr was a substantial factor in causing the accident. Defendant Michael Shumate (Shumate), "or one or more adult residents of his household[,]" not the Niesens, was alleged to have provided the alcohol that was consumed by Carr on the Niesens' property. There was no allegation that Shumate was at the Niesens' property.

II (OMITTED-ED.)

III

On review, the Nichols claim that the Niesens' conduct was negligent, and that it was reasonably foreseeable that someone drinking on the Niesens' property would cause an accident. . . .

[T]he Niesens argue that knowledge of someone drinking on one's premises does not create a foreseeable risk of harm to others, and that public policy issues preclude liability in cases such as this one. The Niesens argue that the court of appeals created a new basis of liability for social hosts in Wisconsin. They argue that social hosts have never been held liable in Wisconsin solely because they were aware that an underage person had been consuming alcohol. To allow the court of appeals' decision to stand would mean that liability would apply to any social hosts who knew of underage drinking, regardless of where the alcohol was possessed or consumed, which would lead to liability with no sensible stopping point. The Niesens argue that they had limited involvement with the party outside of their alleged knowledge of underage drinking at the party, and, as a result, they should not be held liable. To hold social hosts liable in such circumstances would place an unreasonable burden on social hosts. The Niesens argue that a reasonable person would not foresee that knowledge of some unidentified underage person drinking would create an unreasonable risk to others. Rather, a reasonable person would conclude that any such risk was created by the

provider of the alcohol and the underage drinker. The Niesens contend that, because they played no role in procuring or furnishing the alcohol, a negligence analysis should not be applied to their actions in this matter. Finally, the Niesens argue that the legislature, not the judiciary, is the branch of Wisconsin's government that should impose any new liability on social hosts who do not provide alcoholic beverages to underage guests.

Whether the Nichols' complaint states a claim for common-law negligence depends on whether they sufficiently pled facts, which if proven true, would establish all four required elements of an actionable negligence claim. First, the plaintiff must establish "the existence of a duty of care on the part of the defendant. . . ." Second, the plaintiff must establish that the defendant breached that duty of care. Third, the plaintiff must establish "a causal connection between the defendant's breach of the duty of care and the plaintiffs injury. . . ." Fourth, the plaintiff must establish that he or she suffered an actual loss or damage that resulted from the breach.

* * * * *

The court of appeals framed the issue for the first element of the test for common-law negligence as "whether the Niesens owed a duty to refrain from knowingly permitting minors to consume alcohol on their property, thus enabling them, including Carr, to drive away from their property while intoxicated." As a result, the court held that the first factor had been met because "it was reasonably foreseeable that permitting underage high school students to illegally drink alcohol on the Niesens' property would result in harm to some person or something," and because the Nichols had adequately "alleged the Niesens had a duty to refrain from knowingly permitting underage high school students from engaging in illegal alcohol consumption on their property."

[T]he court of appeals also determined that the Nichols had appropriately alleged the second factor of an actionable common-law negligence claim, which is that the Niesens had breached a duty of care that they owed to the Nichols. The court stated, "Because the Nichols' complaint alleges the Niesens knowingly permitted and failed to supervise underage alcohol consumption on their property, it alleges 'a breach of their duty to exercise ordinary care.'" . . .

The court also held that the Nichols had established the third factor of a common-law negligence claim by showing "a causal connection between the defendant's breach of the duty of care and the plaintiff's injury. . . ." That court stated, "The Nichols have sufficiently alleged that the Niesens' permitting underage alcohol consumption on their property was a substantial factor in causing the automobile accident that resulted in their injuries."

The court of appeals further held that the Nichols had appropriately alleged the fourth factor of a common-law negligence claim, that they had suffered an actual loss or damage that resulted from the Niesens' breach. . . .

For purposes of our public policy analysis, we will assume, without deciding, that the court of appeals was correct in holding that the Nichols had stated a common-law negligence claim. [E]ven if a plaintiff adequately establishes all four elements of a common-law negligence claim, Wisconsin courts have "reserved the right to deny the existence of a negligence claim based on public policy reasons. . . ." As a result, "even if all the elements for a claim of negligence are proved, or liability for negligent conduct is assumed by the court, the court nonetheless may preclude liability based on public policy factors." This is so because '"negligence and liability are distinct concepts.'"

In turning to our analysis of the public policy factors that bear on the Nichols' common-law negligence claim against the Niesens, it is instructive to note what is not alleged by the Nichols. The Nichols do not allege that the Niesens provided alcohol to Carr, that the Niesens were aware that Carr (specifically) was consuming alcoholic beverages, that the Niesens knew or should have known that Carr was intoxicated, or that the Niesens knew or should have known that Carr was not able to drive her motor vehicle safely at the time of the accident We note that there also is no allegation by the Nichols that the Niesens aided, agreed to assist, or attempted to aid Carr or any other person in the procurement or consumption of alcohol on premises under their control. There also are no allegations that the Niesens knew in advance that any underage individuals would be drinking.

*   *   *   *   *

If one or more of the public policy "factors so dictates, the court may refuse to impose liability in a case."

The first public policy factor upon which recovery against a negligent tortfeasor may be denied is when "the injury is too remote from the negligence. . . ."

The second public policy factor upon which recovery against a negligent tortfeasor may be denied is when "the injury is too wholly out of proportion to the tortfeasor's culpability. . . ."

The third public policy factor upon which recovery against a negligent tortfeasor may be denied is when "in retrospect it appears too highly extraordinary that the negligence should have brought about the harm. . . ."

The fourth public policy factor upon which recovery against a negligent tortfeasor may be denied is when "allowing recovery would place too unreasonable a burden upon the tortfeasor. . . ."

The fifth public policy factor upon which recovery against a negligent tortfeasor may be denied is when "allowing recovery would be too likely to open the way to fraudulent claims. . . ."

The sixth, and here perhaps the most significant, public policy factor upon which recovery against a negligent tortfeasor may be denied is when "allowing recovery would have no sensible or just stopping point. . . ."

*   *   *   *   *

Here, the Niesens and their insurer argue that there would be no sensible or just stopping point if the court of appeals' decision stands. They claim that the decision of the court of appeals would put tort law on the path of strict liability for anyone who owns property in Wisconsin, and who knows even scant details of an underage person consuming alcohol on the property under his or her control. They argue that the next step, beyond such a proposed expansion in common-law negligence liability, may be to include in the framework of liability not just social hosts but anyone who knows that an underage person was drinking on property that is not even under their control, or to include anyone, not just property owners, who knows that any underage individual has had too much to drink.

We note that there is no allegation by the Nichols here that the Niesens knew Carr was intoxicated, impaired, or unable to safely drive a vehicle. The Niesens argue that they could not have foreseen that people coming onto their property, who already had broken the law before they arrived, would break the law again after leaving. The Niesens could not reasonably have foreseen that an underage guest who they were not specifically aware was intoxicated, and who arrived at the premises under their control with alcohol purchased elsewhere, would cause foreseeable harm to others.

We agree with the Niesens . . . that allowing recovery here would have no sensible or just stopping point.

*   *   *   *   *

If the Nichols' claim were allowed to proceed, the expansion of liability might also include liability for parents who allegedly should have known that drinking would occur on their property while they were absent, based on the proclivities of teenagers in a given area to consume alcohol. Imposing such liability would be only a short step away from imposing strict liability upon property owners for any underage drinking that occurs on property under their control. As Judge David G. Deininger stated in his dissent in the court of appeals, "if liability is permitted to extend to parents and property owners who fail to 'supervise and monitor the activities on their property,'" as the Nichols contend of the Niesens, "then parents or other owners of property occupied by sixteen- to twenty-year-olds" would "be well-advised to never leave home, or if they must, to ensure that all underage persons go elsewhere as well...." As a result, even assuming that the Nichols had pled a viable claim for common-law negligence against the Niesens using the four-factor test, we are satisfied that the Nichols' claim should be barred on public policy considerations, since allowing recovery here would have no sensible or just stopping point.

* * * * *

Liability has never been applied to conduct like that of the Niesens, and liability has required active, direct and affirmative acts, such as the provision of alcohol. Neither the legislature nor this court has expanded liability to social hosts who have not provided alcohol to minors. The legislature is the appropriate governmental branch to expand liability if it desires to do so. As a result for the reasons stated herein, we reverse the court of appeals, and hold that such an expansion of liability should come from the legislature, if it is to occur at all.

* * * * *

Questions

1. Explain the Nichols' legal claim.

2. *a.* Who won this case and why?
   b. Do you agree with the Court's decision and its reasoning? Explain.

3. LaMarre rode with his wife and their neighbors, the Plummers, in the Plummers' modified golf cart to have dinner at the nearby Fort Mitchell Country Club. As per Mr. Plummer's request, country club staff retrieved and chilled two bottles of champagne from Plummer's locker. During dinner, the couples consumed one of the champagne bottles as well as a bottle of red wine that Plummer retrieved from his locker. The two couples opened the second bottle of champagne in the golf cart after dinner. After making a stop on the way home at another neighbor's house, Mr. Plummer accelerated the golf cart while Mr. LaMarre was trying to take his seat. LaMarre fell and sustained serious injuries. The LaMarres filed a lawsuit against the Plummers and the Fort Mitchell Country Club. Should the country club be liable for LaMarre's injuries? Explain. See *Fort Mitchell Country Club v. LaMarre,* 394 S.W.3d 897 (Ky. 2012).

4. Nichols, age 26, and Dobler, a minor, were guests at Maldonado's party. Dobler was served alcohol and, while intoxicated, repeatedly hit Nichols with a hammer. Nichols sued Maldanado for negligence in serving alcohol to a minor. The jury found for Nichols. Maldanado appealed. How would you rule on that appeal? Explain. See *Nichols v. Dobler,* 655 N.W.2d 787 (Mich. Ct. App. 2002).

5. Richard Paul Dube suffered serious injuries when the vehicle he was driving was struck head-on by a vehicle being driven in the wrong direction on a Massachusetts highway by Ravindra Bhoge. Bhoge had earlier in the evening consumed a number of drinks with three friends at a bar. Bhoge and his friends met regularly on Fridays after work to drink at local bars. Each person took turns paying the bill, or on some occasions, payment would be equally divided. On the night of the accident Bhoge drank enough that the trial judge inferred that Bhoge's intoxication would have been apparent. Bhoge's three friends said they saw nothing to indicate that Bhoge was impaired, although Bhoge had left his coat behind in the bar on a particularly cold evening, and he was outside the bar for 45 minutes prior to his departure. Bhoge indicated to his friends that he was "okay" as they all prepared to leave in their vehicles. Dube sued Bhoge's three friends claiming they were social hosts and were negligent in permitting Bhoge to continue drinking. How would you rule on Dube's claim? Explain. See *Dube v. Lanphear & Others,* 868 N.E.2d 619 (2007). [For the National Center for State Courts, see **http://www. ncsconline.org/**]

Classifications of Law

We can divide the law into some categories that will help us better understand the many legal domains and processes.

Substantive and Procedural Law

Substantive laws create, define, and regulate legal rights and obligations. Thus, for example, the federal Civil Rights Act of 1964 forbids discrimination in employment and other matters (see Chapter 13).

Procedural law embraces the systems and methods available to enforce the rights specified in the substantive law. So procedural law includes the judicial system and the rules by which it operates. Questions of where to hear a case, what evidence to admit, and which decisions can be appealed fall within the procedural domain. [For a "community built, freely available legal dictionary and encyclopedia," see **http://www.law.cornell.edu/wex**]

Law and Equity

Following the Norman conquest of England in 1066, a system of king's courts was established in which the king's representatives settled disputes. Those representatives were empowered to provide remedies of land, money, or personal property. The king's courts became known as *courts of law,* and the remedies were labeled *remedies of law.* Some litigants, however, sought compensation other than the three provided. They took their pleas to the king.

Typically the chancellor, an aide to the king, would hear these petitions and, guided by the standard of fairness, could grant a remedy (such as an injunction or specific performance—see the glossary of legal terms in the back of the book) specifically appropriate to the case. The chancellors' decisions accumulated over time such that a new body of remedies—and with it a new court system, known as *courts of equity*—evolved. Both court systems were adopted in the United States following the American Revolution, but today actions at law and equity are typically heard in the same court.

Public Law and Private Law

Public law deals with the relationship between government and the citizens. Constitutional, criminal, and administrative law (relating to such bodies as the Federal Trade Commission) fall in the public law category. *Private law* regulates the legal relationship among individuals. Contracts, agency, and commercial paper are traditional business law topics in the private category.

Civil Law and Criminal Law

The legislature or other lawmaking body normally specifies that new legislation is either *civil* or *criminal* or both. Broadly, all legislation not specifically labeled criminal law falls in the civil law category. *Civil law* addresses the legal rights and duties arising among individuals, organizations such as corporations, and governments. Thus, for example, a person might sue a company raising a civil law claim of breach of contract. *Criminal law,* on the other hand, involves wrongs against the general welfare as formulated in specific criminal statutes. Murder and theft are, of course, criminal wrongs because society has forbidden those acts in specific legislative enactments. (For a brief discussion of business and white-collar crime and the federal sentencing guidelines, see Chapter 2.)

Crimes   Crimes are of three kinds. In general, *felonies* are more serious crimes, such as murder, rape, and robbery. They are typically punishable by death or by imprisonment in a federal or state penitentiary for more than one year. In general, *misdemeanors* are less serious crimes, such as petty theft, disorderly conduct, and traffic offenses. They are typically punishable by fine or by imprisonment for no more than one year. *Treason* is the special situation in which one levies war against the United States or gives aid and comfort to its enemies.

Elements of a Crime   In a broad sense, crimes consist of two elements: (1) a wrongful act or omission (*actus reus*) and (2) evil intent (*mens rea*). Thus, an individual who pockets a pen and leaves the store without paying for it may be charged with petty theft. The accused may defend, however, by arguing that he or she merely absentmindedly and unintentionally slipped the pen in a pocket after picking it off the shelf to consider its merits. Intent is a state of mind, so the jury or judge must reach a determination from the objective facts as to what the accused's state of mind must have been.

Criminal Procedure   In general, criminal procedure following an arrest, and an initial appearance before a magistrate, (and in some cases a preliminary hearing) is structured as follows: For misdemeanor cases, prosecutors typically file what is called an *information,* a formal expression of the charges. The information may be reviewed by a magistrate before issuance. For felony cases, the process begins with the prosecuting officials either filing an information or seeking an *indictment* by bringing their charges before a grand jury of citizens to determine whether the charges have sufficient merit to justify a trial.

After an indictment or information, the individual is brought before the court for *arraignment,* where the charges are read and a plea is entered. If the individual pleads not guilty, he or she will go to trial, where guilt must be established *beyond a reasonable doubt.* In a criminal trial, the burden of proof is on the state. The defendant is, of course, presumed innocent and is entitled to a jury trial, but she or he may choose to have the case decided by the judge alone. If found guilty, the defendant can, among other possibilities, seek a new trial or appeal errors in the prosecution. If found innocent, the defendant may, if necessary, invoke the doctrine of *double jeopardy* under which a person cannot be prosecuted twice in the same tribunal for the same criminal offense. [For an extensive criminal justice database, see **https://www.ncjrs.gov/**]

Miranda **Warnings**

The 1966 *Miranda v. Arizona* U.S. Supreme Court decision provided that a suspect in police custody must be told:

> You have the right to remain silent. Anything you say can and will be used against you in a court of law. You have the right to an attorney. If you cannot afford an attorney, one will be appointed for you.

If warnings are not properly provided, any statements made by the suspect and any evidence derived from those statements cannot subsequently be used in court. The warnings are highly controversial, and the current Supreme Court appears to be inclined to relax the *Miranda* requirements.

Michigan police informed a suspect, Van Thompkins, of his Fifth Amendment rights against self-incrimination including the right to remain silent. Thompkins said he understood, but he did not say he wanted the questioning to stop or that he wanted a lawyer. Rather, he sat through two hours and 45 minutes of questioning without speaking until an officer asked: "Do you pray to God to forgive you for shooting that boy down?" Thompkins said, "Yes." He did not speak further, and he did not sign a confession. He was later convicted of murder, that verdict being based largely on his one-word reply. The U.S. 6th Circuit Court of Appeals overturned the conviction, ruling that the use of the incriminating answer violated Thompkins's Fifth Amendment rights, as defined and required by *Miranda.*

The case, *Berghuis v. Thompkins,* then reached the U.S. Supreme Court in 2010 where the Court chipped away at the *Miranda* requirements in a 5–4 reversal of the Court of Appeals ruling. The Court said, "A suspect who has received and understood the *Miranda* warnings and has not invoked his *Miranda* rights waives the right to remain silent by making an uncoerced statement to the police." The Court's decision requires a criminal suspect to explicitly and unambiguously tell the police he or she wants to remain silent. Merely remaining silent had previously been treated as an invocation of the right to remain silent, but the Court's *Thompkins* ruling changed that practice and, in the view of critics, ill advisedly diminished rights previously guaranteed to defendants.

The Supreme Court further relaxed the Miranda requirements in two other 2010 decisions (*Florida v. Powell* and *Maryland v. Shatzer*), but in 2011, the Court strengthened *Miranda* protection for young people when it ruled that the police must consider the age of a suspect in deciding whether *Miranda* warnings must be issued. In *J.D.B. v. North Carolina,* a 13-year-old Chapel Hill, North Carolina, student confessed to a pair of home break-ins during a half hour of questioning by police officers and school administrators in a middle school conference room. The warnings were not issued and J.D.B. was not permitted to call his grandmother, who was his guardian. The state, however, claimed J.D.B. was not in custody and therefore the warnings were not required. In general, a suspect is considered not to have been in custody if a "reasonable person" under the circumstances would have felt free to leave. The North Carolina courts ruled that J.D.B. was not in custody, but the U.S. Supreme Court held that the police must consider the suspect's age when deciding if custody has been achieved such that the warnings are required. The case was returned to North Carolina to determine whether J.D.B., given his age, was in custody during the questioning.

Questions

1. Do you think Thompkins's response of "yes" to the police inquiry should have been admissible in court against him? Explain.

2. In general, do you think the *Miranda* warnings offer too much protection for criminal suspects? Explain.

Sources: Berghuis v. Thompkins, 130 S. Ct. 2250 (2010), *Florida v. Powell,* 130 S. Ct. 1195 (2010), *J.D.B. v. North Carolina,* 2011 U.S. LEXIS 4557, *Maryland v. Shatzer,* 130 S. Ct. 1213 (2010), *Miranda v. Arizona,* 86 S. Ct. 1602 (1966); Jesse J. Holland, "Miranda Warning Rights Trimmed Bit by Bit by High Court," *Christian Science Monitor,* August 2, 2010 [**http://www.csmonitor.com/**]; and David Savage, "Supreme Court Backs Off Strict Enforcement of Miranda Rights," *latimes.com* [**latimes.com/news/la-na-court-miranda-20100602,0,2431552.story**].

PRACTICING ETHICS   "Stand Your Ground" on a Slippery Slope?

On February 26, 2012, Trayvon Martin, a 17-year-old African-American male, was shot and killed by 28-year-old George Zimmerman. In the early evening, Martin, wearing a hooded gray sweatshirt, had walked from his relative's town house to a nearby convenience store to buy candy and a soft drink; he was unarmed. On his way back, he called his girlfriend to tell her that he was being followed. Zimmerman called 911 from his car to report that he saw someone suspicious in his neighborhood. Although the 911 operator told Zimmerman that he should not follow Martin, Zimmerman apparently got out of his car when Martin began to run. Although it was dark, eyewitness accounts reported seeing two men fighting and then seeing one of them laying on the grass, apparently shot.[2] On July 13, 2013, a jury found Zimmerman not guilty of second-degree murder and manslaughter based on Florida's 205 stand-your-ground law.[3]

Under Florida's stand-your-ground law, those who "reasonably believe" that force—even deadly force—is necessary to protect against death or great bodily harm may use such force instead of retreating.[4] This expanded right to defend oneself now exists in more than 30 states. As *The Wall Street Journal* reported in 2012, justifiable homicide nearly doubled from 2000 to 2010, whereas overall U.S. homicide rates declined.[5] A 2012 study by an economics professor and PhD student at Texas A&M University concluded that stand-your-ground laws do not deter burglary, robbery, or aggravated assault.[6]

Questions

1. In your view, are stand-your-ground laws moral? Explain.

2. Under the castle doctrine, recognized in more than 20 states, generally homeowners may use force—including deadly force—to defend themselves in their own home.

    a. How might the castle doctrine be supported morally?

    b. In 2012, Fredenberg, an unarmed Montana resident, was shot and killed by Harper, a man who was romantically involved with Fredenberg's wife. Fredenberg had gone to Harper's home to confront him about the affair. Under Montana's castle doctrine, Harper did not face charges.[7] In your view, is this an appropriate application of the castle doctrine? Explain.

Questions—Part One

1. Jonathan Rauch argued that America is making a mistake in allowing what he calls Hidden Law to be replaced by what he calls Bureaucratic Legalism. Hidden Law refers to unwritten social codes, whereas Bureaucratic Legalism refers to state-provided due process for every problem. Thus, universities formerly expected insults and epithets among students to be resolved via informal modes such as apologies, while today many universities have written codes forbidding offensive or discriminatory verbal conduct. Similarly, four kindergarten students in New Jersey were suspended from school for three days because they were observed "shooting" each other with their fingers serving as guns.

    a. Should we leave campus insults and school-yard finger "shootings" to the Hidden Law? Explain.

    b. Can you think of other examples where we have gradually replaced Hidden Law with Bureaucratic Legalism?

    c. Rauch argued that the breakdown of one Hidden Law, the rule that a man must marry a woman whom he has impregnated, may be "the most far-reaching social change of our era." Do you agree? Explain. See George Will, "Penalizing These Kids Is Zero Tolerance at a Ridiculous Extreme," *The Des Moines Register*, December 27, 2000, p. 11A.

2. Should we remove criminal penalties from all of the so-called victimless crimes including vagrancy, pornography, and gambling? Should we regulate those practices in any way? Explain.

3. According to the National Conference of State Legislatures, as of 2013, at least 29 states had either enacted or introduced legislation prohibiting the practice of "sexting" (cell phone transmission of nude photos of themselves and other risqué material) by minors.[8]

   a. What objections would you raise to a criminal law forbidding sexting by minors?

   b. Is this an area where the government should simply refrain from intervention? Explain.

4. A Rhode Island man pleaded guilty to child molestation. As an alternative to imprisonment and as a condition of his probation, the judge ordered him to purchase a newspaper ad displaying his picture, identifying himself as a sex offender, and encouraging others to seek assistance. One Florida judge has sentenced hundreds of shoplifters to carrying in public a sign that reads: "I stole from this store." Constitutional law expert Jonathan Turley says "creative sentencing" is growing, a trend he disapproves of and regards as a strategy for entertaining the public more than deterring crime.[9]

   a. What objections would a defendant's lawyer raise to these public humiliation punishments?

   b. Would you impose a "humiliation sentence" if you were the judge? Explain.

Part Two—The Judicial Process

Most disputes are settled without resort to litigation, but when agreement cannot be reached, we can turn to the courts—a highly technical and sophisticated dispute resolution mechanism.

State Court Systems

While state court systems vary substantially, a general pattern can be summarized. As shown in Figure 4.1, at the base of the court pyramid in most states is a trial court of general jurisdiction, commonly labeled a *district court* or a *superior court*. Most trials—both civil and criminal—arising out of state law are heard here, but certain classes of cases are reserved to courts of limited subject-matter jurisdiction or to various state administrative agencies (such as the state public utilities commission and the workers' compensation board). Family, small claims, juvenile, and traffic courts are examples of trial courts with limited jurisdiction. At the top of the judicial pyramid in all states is a court of appeals, ordinarily labeled the *supreme court*. A number of states also provide for an intermediate court of appeals located in the hierarchy between the trial courts and the highest appeals court.

FIGURE 4.1   State and Federal Court Systems

Federal Court System

District Courts

The Constitution provides for a Supreme Court and such inferior courts as Congress shall authorize. Pursuant to that authority, Congress has established at least one district court for each state and territory. The 94 district courts serve as the foundation of the federal judicial system. These are trial courts where witnesses are heard and questions of law and fact are resolved. Most federal cases begin in the district courts or in a federal administrative agency (such as the Federal Communications Commission). Congress has also provided for several courts of limited jurisdiction, including the U.S. Tax Court and the U.S. Court of International Trade.

[For access to all federal court websites, see the Federal Judicial Center at **www .fjc.gov**]

Courts of Appeals

Congress has divided the United States geographically into 11 judicial circuits and the District of Columbia and has established a court of appeals for each. Those courts hear appeals from the district courts within their circuit and review decisions and enforce orders of the various federal administrative agencies. In addition, the U.S. Court of Appeals for the Federal Circuit hears, among others, all patent appeals and all appeals from the U.S. Court of Federal Claims (monetary claims against the United States).

Supreme Court

The Supreme Court consists of nine justices. Those justices (along with the federal district and appeals court judges) are appointed for life by the president and confirmed by the Senate. Almost all of the Supreme Court's work consists of reviewing lower court decisions, principally from the courts of appeal with a small number from state high courts. Virtually all parties seeking Supreme Court review must petition the Court for a *writ of certiorari,* which commands the lower court to forward the trial records to the Court.

Decisions regarding those petitions are entirely discretionary with the Court. Typically it will hear those cases that will assist in resolving conflicting courts of appeal decisions, as well as those that raise questions of special significance about the Constitution or the national welfare. Petitions to the Supreme Court in recent years typically total approximately 8,000 cases per year. Formal, written opinions, however, are issued in only about 70 to 90 cases, a decline from, for example, 175 in 1986. Thus, in terms of numbers alone, the Court has backed away from its more activist approach of the 1960s, 1970s, and 1980s.

Critics

Questions of "judicial activism," the liberal/conservative balance on the Supreme Court, the politics of the justices, and the justices' deference to big business interests have made the Court a target for criticism. Journalist E. J. Dionne, Jr. has written about the "Court's Defense of the Powerful:"

> The current Supreme Court is "the most conservative in decades."

> The United States Supreme Court now sees its central task as comforting the already comfortable and afflicting those already afflicted.[10]

More specifically, the current Court is accused of being particularly friendly to business interests and free market values. A 2013 scholarly study ranked the 36 justices who served on the U.S. Supreme Court from 1946 to 2011 by their pro-business vote rate; the five most conservative justices on the current Court were in the top 10.[11] On the other hand, several decisions in late 2010 and early 2011 supported fired workers, expanded antidiscrimination law, and ruled against the Chamber of Commerce position in four of the five cases the Chamber addressed.[12]

Ideological Rulings?

We want to believe that the Supreme Court reaches its decisions in a rational, objective fashion relying on the commands of the Constitution and precedent to maintain a consistent, fair, orderly judicial system free of political influence. A study by the Brookings Institution provided "striking evidence of a relationship between the political party of the appointing president and judicial voting patterns."[13] Critics say that those conservative ideological inclinations have led the Roberts Court to at times abandon traditional judicial restraint and decide issues that were broader than required by the case before it.[14]

In 2012, Justice Scalia drew criticism for reading aloud his dissenting opinion that criticized President Obama's immigration policy; both conservative and liberal observers voiced concerns that Scalia's political pronouncements undermined the integrity of his opinion.[15]

Of course, public respect for the fairness and the rationality of Supreme Court decisions could be undermined if they come to be viewed as the product of liberal or conservative political/ideological views, rather than dispassionate, lawyerly analysis. Shortly before Justice Scalia read his controversial dissenting opinion described above, a *New York Times* and *CBS News* poll showed that three-quarters of Americans believe the Supreme Court justices' decisions may be influenced by their political views.[16] Declining respect for Supreme Court rulings would undermine the rule of law in America and perhaps threaten democracy itself.[17] [For an overview of the Supreme Court, see **http://www.supremecourt.gov/**]

Jurisdiction

A plaintiff may not simply proceed to trial at the court of his or her preference. The plaintiff must go to a court with *jurisdiction*—that is, a court with the necessary power and authority to hear the dispute. The court must have jurisdiction over both the subject matter and the persons (or, in some instances, the property) involved in the case.

Subject-Matter Jurisdiction

Subject-matter jurisdiction imposes bounds on the classes of cases a court may hear. The legislation or constitution creating the court will normally specify that court's jurisdictional authority. State courts of general jurisdiction, for example, may hear most types of cases, but a criminal court or probate court is limited in the subject matter it may hear.

Whereas the outer bounds of federal jurisdiction are specified in the Constitution, Congress has further particularized that issue by statute. Essentially, the federal district courts may hear two types of cases: (1) those involving a federal question and (2) those involving diversity of citizenship and more than $75,000.

Federal question jurisdiction exists in any suit where the plaintiff's claim is based on the U.S. Constitution, a U.S. treaty, or a federal statute. Thus litigants can bring cases to the federal courts involving, for example, the federal antitrust statutes, federal criminal laws, constitutional issues such as freedom of the press, and federal tax questions. Federal question jurisdiction does not require an amount in controversy exceeding $75,000. Furthermore, federal and state courts have *concurrent jurisdiction* for some federal questions. Thus, some federal question cases are decided in state courts applying federal law. Federal courts can also hear cases involving state laws. Congress has accorded the federal courts exclusive jurisdiction over certain subjects, including federal criminal laws, bankruptcy, and copyrights.

Under *diversity jurisdiction,* federal district courts may hear cases involving more than $75,000 where the plaintiff(s) and the defendant(s) are citizens of different states. (Corporations are treated as citizens both of their state of incorporation and the state in which their principal place of business is located.) Diversity cases may also be heard in state courts, but plaintiffs frequently prefer to bring their actions in federal courts. The quality of the federal judiciary is generally believed to be superior to that of the states, and the federal courts are considered less likely to be influenced by local bias.

Personal Jurisdiction

Judicial authority over the person is known as *in personam jurisdiction.* In general, a state court's powers are limited to the bounds of the state. Broadly, we can say that state court jurisdiction can be established in three ways: (1) When the defendant is a resident of the state, a summons may be served at that residence. (2) When the defendant is not a resident, a summons may be personally served should he or she be physically present in the state. (3) Most states have legislated "long-arm" statutes that allow a state or federal court to secure jurisdiction against an out-of-state party where the defendant has committed a tort in the state or where the defendant is conducting business in the state. Hence, in an auto accident in Ohio involving both an Ohio resident and a Kentucky resident, the Ohio resident may sue in Ohio and use the long-arm statute to achieve service of process over the defendant living in Kentucky.

A state court may also acquire jurisdiction via an *in rem action.* In that instance the defendant may be a nonresident, but his or her property, which must be the subject of the suit, must be located within the state.

The following case involves a dispute about the commercial use of the name of celebrated actor and former California governor, Arnold Schwarzenegger.

LEGAL BRIEFCASE

Arnold Schwarzenegger v. Fred Martin Motor Company
374 F. 3d 797 (9th Cir. 2004)

Circuit Judge Fletcher

Arnold Schwarzenegger, an internationally known movie star and, currently, the governor of California, appeals the district court's dismissal of his suit against Fred Martin Motor Company ("Fred Martin"), an Ohio car dealership, for lack of personal jurisdiction. Fred Martin had run a series of five full-page color advertisements in the *Akron Beacon Journal,* a locally circulated Ohio newspaper. Each advertisement included a small photograph of Schwarzenegger, portrayed as the "Terminator," without his permission. Schwarzenegger brought suit in California, alleging that these unauthorized uses of his image infringed his right of publicity. We affirm the district court's dismissal for lack of personal jurisdiction.

I. BACKGROUND

Schwarzenegger is a resident of California. When Schwarzenegger brought this suit, he was a private citizen and movie star, best known for his roles as a muscle-bound hero of action films and distinctive Austrian accent. As explained in his complaint, Schwarzenegger was generally cast as the lead character in so-called star-driven films. One of Schwarzenegger's most popular and readily recognizable film roles is that of the title character in "The Terminator" (1984). . . .

Fred Martin is an automobile dealership incorporated under the laws of Ohio and located in Barberton, Ohio, a few miles southwest of Akron. There is no evidence in the record that Fred Martin has any operations or employees in California, has ever advertised in California, or has ever sold a car to anyone in California. Fred Martin maintains an Internet website that is available for viewing in California and, for that matter, from any Internet cafe in Istanbul, Bangkok, or anywhere else in the world.

In early 2002, Fred Martin engaged defendant Zimmerman & Partners Advertising, Inc. ("Zimmerman") to design and place a full-page color advertisement in the *Akron Beacon Journal,* a local Akron-based newspaper. The advertisement ran in the *Akron Beacon Journal* five times in April 2002. Most of the advertisement consists of small photographs and descriptions of various cars available for purchase or lease from Fred Martin. Just below a large-font promise that Fred Martin "WON'T BE BEAT," the advertisement includes a small, but clearly recognizable photograph of Schwarzenegger as the Terminator. A "bubble quotation," like those found in comic strips, is drawn next to Schwarzenegger's mouth, reading, "Arnold says: 'Terminate EARLY at Fred Martin!'" This part of the advertisement refers to a special offer from Fred Martin to customers, inviting them to close out their current leases before the expected termination date, and to buy or lease a new car from Fred Martin.

Neither Fred Martin nor Zimmerman ever sought or received Schwarzenegger's permission to use his photograph in the advertisement. Schwarzenegger states in his complaint that, had such a request been made, it would have been refused. The advertisement, as far as the record reveals, was never circulated outside of Ohio.

Schwarzenegger brought suit against Fred Martin and Zimmerman in Los Angeles County Superior Court alleging six state law causes of action arising out of the unauthorized use of his image in the advertisement. He claims that the defendants caused him financial harm in that the use of his photograph to endorse Fred Martin "diminishes his hard earned reputation as a major motion picture star, and risks the potential for overexposure of his image to the public, thereby potentially diminishing the compensation he would otherwise garner from his career as a major motion picture star." According to Schwarzenegger's complaint, his compensation as the lead actor in star-driven films was based on his ability to draw crowds to the box office, and his ability to do so depended in part on the scarcity of his image. According to his complaint, if Schwarzenegger's image were to become ubiquitous—in advertisements and on television, for example—the movie-going public would be less likely to spend their money to see his films, and his compensation would diminish accordingly. Therefore, Schwarzenegger maintains, it is vital for him to avoid "oversaturation of his image." According to his complaint, he has steadfastly refused to endorse any products in the United States, despite being offered substantial sums to do so.

Defendants removed the action to federal district court in California, and Fred Martin moved to dismiss the complaint for lack of personal jurisdiction. The district court granted Fred Martin's motion, and Schwarzenegger appealed.

II. PERSONAL JURISDICTION

For a court to exercise personal jurisdiction over a nonresident defendant, that defendant must have at least "minimum contacts" with the relevant forum such that the exercise of jurisdiction "does not offend traditional notions of fair play and substantial justice." *International Shoe Co. v. Washington,* 326 U.S. 310, 316. (1945)

A. General Jurisdiction

Schwarzenegger argues, quite implausibly, that California has general personal jurisdiction over Fred Martin. For general jurisdiction to exist over a nonresident defendant such as Fred Martin, the defendant must engage in "continuous and systematic general business contacts," *Helicopteros Nacionales de Colombia, S.A. v. Hall,* 466 U.S. 408 (1984) that "approximate physical presence" in the forum state. *Bancroft & Masters,* 223 F. 3d at 1086. This is an exacting standard, as it should be, because a finding of general jurisdiction permits a defendant to be haled into court in the forum state to answer for any of its activities anywhere in the world.

Schwarzenegger contends that Fred Martin's contacts with California are so extensive that it is subject to general jurisdiction. He points to the following contacts: Fred Martin regularly purchases Asian-made automobiles that are imported by California entities. However, in purchasing these automobiles, Fred Martin dealt directly with representatives in Illinois and New Jersey, but never dealt directly with the California-based importers. Some of Fred Martin's sales contracts with its automobile suppliers include a choice-of-law provision specifying California law. In addition, Fred Martin regularly retains the services of a California-based direct-mail marketing company; has hired a sales training company, incorporated in California, for consulting services; and maintains an Internet website accessible by anyone capable of using the Internet, including people living in California.

These contacts fall well short of the "continuous and systematic" contacts that the Supreme Court and this court have held to constitute sufficient "presence" to warrant general jurisdiction. Schwarzenegger has therefore failed to establish a prima facie case of general jurisdiction.

B. Specific Jurisdiction

Alternatively, Schwarzenegger argues that Fred Martin has sufficient "minimum contacts" with California arising from, or related to, its actions in creating and distributing the advertisement such that the forum may assert specific personal jurisdiction. We have established a three-prong test for analyzing a claim of specific personal jurisdiction:

(1) The nonresident defendant must purposefully direct his activities or consummate some transaction with the forum or resident thereof; or perform some act by which he purposefully avails himself of the privilege of conducting activities in the forum, thereby invoking the benefits and protections of its laws;

(2) the claim must be one which arises out of or relates to the defendant's forum-related activities; and

(3) the exercise of jurisdiction must comport with fair play and substantial justice, i.e., it must be reasonable.

The plaintiff bears the burden of satisfying the first two prongs of the test. If the plaintiff fails to satisfy either of these prongs, personal jurisdiction is not established in the forum state. If the plaintiff succeeds in satisfying both of the first two prongs, the burden then shifts to the defendant to "present a compelling case" that the exercise of jurisdiction would not be reasonable. For the reasons that follow, we hold that Schwarzenegger has failed to satisfy the first prong.

1. Purposeful Availment or Direction Generally

Under the first prong of our three-part specific jurisdiction test, Schwarzenegger must establish that Fred Martin either purposefully availed itself of the privilege of conducting activities in California, or purposefully directed its activities toward California.

* * * * *

A showing that a defendant purposefully availed himself of the privilege of doing business in a forum state typically consists of evidence of the defendant's actions in the forum, such as executing or performing a contract there. By taking such actions, a defendant "purposefully avails itself of the privilege of conducting activities within the forum State, thus invoking the benefits and protections of its laws." *Hanson v. Denckla,* 357 U.S. 235, 253 (1958). In return for these "benefits and protections," a defendant must—as a quid pro quo—"submit to the burdens of litigation in that forum." *Burger King,* 471 U.S. at 476.

A showing that a defendant purposefully directed his conduct toward a forum state, by contrast, usually consists of evidence of the defendant's actions outside the forum state that are directed at the forum, such as the distribution in the forum state of goods originating elsewhere.

2. Purposeful Direction

Schwarzenegger does not point to any conduct by Fred Martin in California related to the advertisement that would be readily susceptible to a purposeful availment analysis. Rather, the conduct of which Schwarzenegger complains—the unauthorized inclusion of the photograph in the advertisement and its distribution in the Akron Beacon Journal—took place in Ohio, not California. Fred Martin received no benefit, privilege, or protection from California in connection with the advertisement, and the traditional quid pro quo justification for finding purposeful availment thus does not apply. Therefore, to the extent that Fred Martin's conduct might justify the exercise of personal jurisdiction in California, that conduct must have been purposefully directed at California.

* * * * *

Here, Fred Martin's intentional act—the creation and publication of the advertisement—was expressly aimed at Ohio rather than California. The purpose of the advertisement was to entice Ohioans to buy or lease cars from Fred Martin and, in particular, to "terminate" their current car leases. The advertisement was never circulated in California, and Fred Martin had no reason to believe that any Californians would see it and pay a visit to the dealership. Fred Martin certainly had no reason to believe that a Californian had a current car lease with Fred Martin that could be "terminated" as recommended in the advertisement. It may be true that Fred Martin's intentional act eventually caused harm to Schwarzenegger in California and Fred Martin may have known that Schwarzenegger lived in California. But this does not confer jurisdiction, for Fred Martin's express aim was local. We therefore conclude that the advertisement was not expressly aimed at California.

CONCLUSION

We hold that Schwarzenegger has established neither general nor specific jurisdiction over Fred Martin in California. Schwarzenegger has not shown that Fred Martin has "continuous and systematic general business contacts," Helicopteros, 466 U.S. at 416, that "approximate physical presence" in California, Bancroft & Masters, 223 F. 3d at 1086, such that it can be sued there for any act it has committed anywhere in the world. Further, while Schwarzenegger has made out a prima facie case that Fred Martin committed intentional acts that may have caused harm to Schwarzenegger in California, he has not made out a prima facie case that Fred Martin expressly aimed its acts at California.

Affirmed.

AFTERWORD

Schwarzenegger's claim was settled out of court in 2004 when the Fred Martin Motor Company issued a written apology and agreed to pay a "substantial" sum to Arnold's All-Stars, an after-school program founded by Schwarzenegger.

Questions

1. Explain Schwarzenegger's complaint.

2. Why was Schwarzenegger unable to sue Fred Martin in California?

3. Nicastro injured his hand while using a metal-shearing machine in New Jersey manufactured by J. McIntyre Machinery, a company incorporated and operating in England. Nicastro filed a products liability lawsuit against J. McIntyre Machinery in a New Jersey state court, basing personal jurisdiction in New Jersey on three primary facts: A U.S. distributor agreed to sell the company's machines in the United States; J. McIntyre officials attended trade shows in several other states; and four of the company's machines were located in New Jersey. J. McIntyre Machinery had not advertised in or sent goods to New Jersey.

   a. Build an argument to support the claim of jurisdiction in the New Jersey court.

   b. Decide. See *J. McIntyre Machines Ltd. v. Nicastro,* 131 S. Ct. 2780 (2011).

4. Burger King conducted a franchise, fast-food operation from its Miami, Florida, headquarters. John Rudzewicz and a partner, both residents of Michigan, secured a Burger King franchise in Michigan. Subsequently, the franchisees allegedly fell behind in payments, and after negotiations failed, Burger King ordered the franchisees to vacate the premises. They declined to do so, and continued to operate the franchise. Burger King brought suit in a federal district court in Florida. The defendant franchisees argued that the Florida court did not have personal jurisdiction over them because they were Michigan residents and because the claim did not arise in Florida. However, the district court found the defendants to be subject to the Florida long-arm statute, which extends jurisdiction to "[a]ny person, whether or not a citizen or resident of this state" who, "[b]reach[es] a contract in this state by failing to perform acts required by the contract to be performed in this state." The franchise contract provided for governance of the relationship by Florida law. Policy was set in Miami, although day-to-day supervision was managed through various district offices. The case ultimately reached the U.S. Supreme Court.

   a. What constitutional argument would you raise on behalf of the defendant franchisees?

   b. Decide. See *Burger King Corp. v. Rudzewicz,* 471 U.S. 462 (1985).

Venue

Once jurisdictional authority—that is, the power to hear the case—is established, the proper *venue* (geographic location within the court system) comes into question. Ordinarily, a case will be heard by the court geographically closest to the incident or property in question or to where the parties reside. Sometimes one of the parties may seek a *change of venue* based on considerations such as unfavorable pretrial publicity or the pursuit of a more favorable legal climate. The importance of venue is evident in a 2010 decision forcing Los Angeles-based Occidental Petroleum to defend itself in an environmental dispute in California rather than in Peru where the conflict emerged. Members of the Achuar tribe, indigenous to the Amazon rain forest, brought a class action in Los Angeles against Occidental alleging the oil company dumped millions of gallons of waste water into their rivers and contaminated their land with waste.[18] A California federal district court dismissed the Achuar claim, but the 9th Circuit U.S. Court of Appeals reversed the district court. The appeals court ruled, among other things, that Occidental had failed to demonstrate that Peru was the more convenient forum for the lawsuit.[19] On April 22, 2013, the U.S. Supreme Court denied Occidental's petition for

> The Achuar tribe, indigenous to the Amazon rain forest, brought a class action in Los Angeles.

review.[20] The Achuar plaintiffs want the case tried in California, in part, because the Peruvian courts have a history of favoring corporate interests in conflicts with natives. At this writing, the case is expected to go forward in Los Angeles.

Standing to Sue

All who wish to bring a claim before a court will not be permitted to do so. To receive the court's attention, the litigant must demonstrate *standing to sue*. That is, the person must show that her or his interest in the outcome of the controversy is sufficiently direct and substantial as to justify the court's consideration. The litigant must show that she or he is personally suffering, or will be suffering, injury. Mere interest in the problem at hand is insufficient to grant standing to sue. We all suffer injustices. We all have complaints in life. But have we suffered an injury to a legally protected right or interest? That is the question in the *Mayer* case that arose out of "Spygate," an alleged National Football League cheating scandal.[21]

Mayer v. Bill Belichick; The New England Patriots; National Football League
605 F. 3d 223 (3d Cir. 2010); Cert. Den. 2011 U.S. LEXIS 2027

LEGAL BRIEFCASE

FACTS
In an episode popularly known as "Spygate," an employee of the New England Patriots National Football League team was caught videotaping New York Jets' sideline signals, in violation of NFL rules, during a 2007 game with the Jets. The taping was later discovered to have been part of an illicit taping program that reportedly had been ongoing since the 2000 season. The NFL penalized the Patriots and their coach, Bill Belichick. Mayer sued on behalf of himself and a class of Jets season ticketholders claiming the improper conduct violated the contractual expectations and rights of the ticketholders who had paid to observe an honest football game played in conformance with the rules. Mayer lost at trial where the federal district court ruled that he had failed to demonstrate an actionable injury; that is, he was unable to show the court that the facts he asserted

could support a right to relief under the law. Put another way, he did not have standing to sue. Mayer then appealed to the Third Circuit Federal Court of Appeals.

Circuit Judge Cowen

(I-III OMITTED-ED.)

IV
The District Court, while noting that Mayer alleged numerous theories of liability in this case, appropriately turned to the following dispositive question: namely, whether or not he stated an actionable injury (or, in other words, a legally protected right or interest) arising out of the alleged "dishonest" videotaping program undertaken by the Patriots and the NFL team's head coach.

* * * * *

Initially, we consider how tickets to sporting and other entertainment events have been treated in the past. New Jersey has generally followed a so-called "license" approach[#]. . . .

Although it did not use the specific term "license," the ticket stub provided by the Patriots nevertheless appears consistent with this traditional approach. For example, it unambiguously stated that "[t]his ticket only grants entry into the stadium and a spectator seat for the specified NFL game." The stub further made clear that the Jets and the owners of the stadium retain sole discretion to refuse admission or to eject a ticket-holder. . . . Given that Mayer was never barred or expelled from any game at Giants Stadium, much more is needed to establish a cognizable right, interest, or injury. . . .

Mayer possessed either a license or, at best, a contractual right to enter Giants Stadium and to have a seat from which to watch a professional football game. In the clear language of the ticket stub, "[t]his ticket only grants entry into the stadium and a spectator seat for the specified NFL game." Mayer actually was allowed to enter the stadium and witnessed the "specified NFL game[s]" between the Jets and Patriots. He thereby suffered no cognizable injury to a legally protected right or interest.

Accordingly, we need not, and do not decide, whether a ticket-holder possesses nothing more than a license to enter and view whatever event, if any, happens to transpire. Here, Mayer undeniably saw *football* games played by two *NFL* teams. This therefore is not a case where, for example, the game or games were canceled, strike replacement players were used, or the professional football teams themselves did something nonsensical or absurd, such as deciding to play basketball.

* * * * *

Furthermore, we do recognize that Mayer alleged that he was the victim, not of mere poor performance by a team or its players, but of a team's ongoing acts of dishonesty or cheating in violation of the express rules of the game. Nevertheless, there are any number of often complicated rules and standards applicable to a variety of sports, including professional football. It appears uncontested that players often commit intentional rule infractions in order to obtain an advantage over the course of the game. . . . Mayer further does not appear to contest the fact that a team is evidently permitted by the rules to engage in a wide variety of arguably "dishonest" conduct to uncover an opponent's signals. For example, a team is apparently free to take advantage of the knowledge that a newly hired player or coach takes with him after leaving his former team, and it may even have personnel on the sidelines who try to pick up the opposing team's signals with the assistance of lip-reading, binoculars, note-taking, and other devices. In addition, even Mayer acknowledged in his amended complaint that "[t]eams are allowed to have a limited number of their own videographers on the sideline during the game."

In fact, the NFL's own commissioner did ultimately take action here. He found that the Patriots and Belichick were guilty of violating the applicable NFL rules, imposed sanctions in the form of fines and the loss of draft picks, and rather harshly characterized the whole episode as a calculated attempt to avoid well-established rules designed to encourage fair play and honest competition. At least in this specific context, it is not the role of judges and juries to be second-guessing the decision taken by a professional sports league purportedly enforcing its *own* rules. . . .

This Court refuses to countenance a course of action that would only further burden already limited judicial resources and force professional sports organizations and related individuals to expend money, time, and resources to defend against such litigation. . . .

In conclusion, this Court will affirm the dismissal of Mayer's amended complaint. Again, it bears repeating that our reasoning here is limited to the unusual and even unique circumstances presented by this appeal. We do not condone the conduct on the part of the Patriots and the team's head coach, and we likewise refrain from assessing whether the NFL's sanctions (and its alleged destruction of the videotapes themselves) were otherwise appropriate. We further recognize that professional football, like other professional sports, is a multi-billion dollar business. In turn, ticket-holders and other fans may have legitimate issues with the manner in which they are treated. . . . Significantly, our ruling also does not leave Mayer and other ticket-holders without any recourse. Instead, fans could speak out against the Patriots, their coach, and the NFL itself. In fact, they could even go so far as to refuse to purchase tickets or NFL-related merchandise. However, the one thing they *cannot* do is bring a legal action in a court of law.

Affirmed.

[#]A license, for our purposes, is generally defined as "[a] permission . . . to commit some act that would otherwise be unlawful; esp., an agreement that it is lawful for the licensee to enter the licensor's land to do some act that would otherwise be illegal, such as hunting game." *Black's Law Dictionary* 1002 (9th ed. 2009).

Questions

1. *a.* Why did Mayer lose this case?
   b. Do you think he should have won?
2. According to the Court, under what circumstances might a plaintiff conceivably have an actionable claim involving a sports event gone wrong?
3. To some extent, the Court's decision was influenced by a decision to protect the judicial system from a flood of litigation. Explain what kinds of legal claims might have been filed if this Court had found that the plaintiff, Mayer, had stated an actionable injury.

Class Actions

In some instances, multiple plaintiffs may join together to represent themselves and all others who are similarly situated to file a single lawsuit alleging similar harm arising from the same, or substantially the same, wrong. The high cost of litigation, the great uncertainty of victory and the likelihood of small individual recoveries have made the class action a very useful tool for plaintiffs. Of course, the class action also enhances judicial efficiency by bringing many claims together in one case.

Several recent U.S. Supreme Court rulings have impacted the viability of the class action in business disputes. For example, a small group of Walmart employees sued the company for sex discrimination on behalf of a nationwide class of 1.5 million female employees; Walmart challenged the class action certification. The Court held that the claims against Walmart did not share enough common elements to tie together the millions of employment decisions affecting women at Walmart. As a matter of company policy, discretion over pay and promotions rested with local managers at the 4,000 or so company stores; without a specific employment practice that tied all of their claims together, the class lacked the necessary commonality.[22]

The Supreme Court's decision led to regional class-action suits by female Walmart workers; at this writing, Walmart has successfully challenged class certification in these cases.[23] In two 2013 decisions regarding antitrust class actions, the Supreme Court underscored its ruling in *Dukes.* In *Comcast v. Behrend,* the Court held that class certification requires courts to examine carefully whether classwide damages can be proved.[24] Further, in *American Express Co. v. Italian Colors Restaurant,* the Court held that a waiver of class arbitration was enforceable even when arbitrating a claim individually would cost far more than the potential recovery.[25]

The Civil Trial Process

Civil procedure varies by jurisdiction. The following generalizations merely typify the process. (See Figure 4.2.) [For a vast "catalog" of law on the Internet, see **catalaw .com**]

Pleadings

Pleadings are the documents by which each party sets his or her initial case before the court. A civil action begins when the plaintiff files his or her first pleading, which is labeled a

FIGURE 4.2 **Stages of a Lawsuit**

Pleading stage
- Complaint
- Answer
- Reply

Discovery stage
- Deposition
- Written interrogatories
- Request for admissions
- Production of documents
- Request for physical examination
- Request for mental examination

Trial stage
- Jury selection
- Opening statements
- Cases in chief
- Arguments
- Instruction to jury
- Verdict
- Judgment

Appellate stage
- Filing the appeal
- Submission of briefs
- Arguing the case
- Decision of the court

complaint. The complaint specifies (1) the parties to the suit, (2) evidence as to the court's jurisdiction in the case, (3) a statement of the facts, and (4) a prayer for relief (a remedy).

The complaint is filed with the clerk of court and a summons is issued, directing the defendant to appear in court to answer the claims alleged against him or her. A sheriff or some other official attempts to personally deliver the summons to the defendant. If personal delivery cannot be achieved, the summons may be left with a responsible party at the defendant's residence. Failing that, other modes of delivery are permissible, including a mailing. Publication of a notice in a newspaper will, in some instances, constitute good service of process. Ordinarily, a copy of the complaint accompanies the summons, so the defendant is apprised of the nature of the claim.

The defendant has several options. He or she may do nothing, but failure to respond may result in a *default judgment* in favor of the plaintiff. The defendant may choose to respond by filing a *demurrer* or a *motion to dismiss,* the essence of which is to argue that even if the plaintiff's recitation of the facts is accurate, a claim on which relief can be granted has not been stated.

Alternatively, the defendant may file with the court an initial pleading, called an *answer,* wherein the defendant enters a denial by setting out his or her version of the facts and law, or in which the defendant simply concedes the validity of the plaintiff's position. The answer may also contain an *affirmative defense,* such as the statute of limitations or the statute of frauds that would bar the plaintiff's claim. The defendant's answer might include a *counterclaim* or *cross-claim.* A counterclaim is the defendant's assertion of a claim of action against the plaintiff. A cross-claim is the defendant's assertion of a claim of action against a codefendant. In some states, these would be labeled *cross-complaints.* In the event of a counterclaim or the assertion of new facts in the answer, the plaintiff will respond with a *reply.* The complaint, answer, reply, and their components are the pleadings that serve to give notice, clarify the issues, and limit the dimensions of the litigation. [For a summary of "Famous Trials" in history, see **http://law2.umkc.edu/faculty/projects /ftrials/ftrials.htm**]

Served on Facebook?

After U.S. rapper Trammar Dillard, known as Flo Rida, allegedly failed to appear at a 2011 music festival in Newcastle, Australia, the festival organizer, Mothership Music, sued him in an Australian court for breach of contract. After apparent attempts to serve notice on the performer personally failed, the Australian judge gave Mothership Music permission to serve Flo Rida by Facebook. Flo Rida appealed the ruling, and the Australian appellate court agreed with the defendant that he had not been properly served. The appellate court noted that the Facebook page used may not have actually belonged to the defendant; further, the posting may not have come to Flo Rida's attention.

Source: Stephanie Francis Ward, "Flo Rida Rides Past Lawsuit Served via Facebook," *ABA Journal*, August 20, 2013 [**www.abajournal.com/**].

Motions

As necessary during and after the filing of the pleadings, either party may file motions with the court. For example, a party may move to clarify a pleading or to strike a portion deemed unnecessary. Of special importance is a *motion for a judgment on the pleadings* or a *motion for summary judgment.* In a motion for a judgment on the pleadings, either party simply asks the judge to reach a decision based on the information in the pleadings. The judge will do so only if the defendant's answer constitutes an admission of the accuracy of the plaintiff's claim, or if the plaintiff's claim clearly has no foundation in law.

In a motion for a summary judgment, the party filing the motion is claiming that no facts are in dispute. Therefore, the judge may make a ruling about the law without taking the case to trial. In a summary judgment hearing, the court can look beyond the pleadings to hear evidence from affidavits, depositions, and so on. These motions avoid the time and expense of trial.

Discovery

Discovery is the primary information-gathering stage in the pretrial process. That information clarifies the trial issues, promotes pretrial settlements, and helps prevent surprises at the trial, among other things. Discovery may consist of *depositions* (recorded, sworn testimony in preparation for trial), physical and mental examinations, answers to written questions (*interrogatories*), requests for access to documents and property to inspect them prior to trial, and *admissions* (agreement by the parties to stipulated issues of fact or law prior to trial).

The era of electronic communication and storage has added important new expectations and burdens to the discovery process by requiring that litigants exchange all relevant electronically stored information (ESI) during the discovery phase. Individuals and companies must be able to produce ESI from all sources, including e-mail, files, scanned handwritten notes, stored records, voice mail, fax data, instant messages, spreadsheets, videos, PowerPoint presentations, and so on.

Pretrial Conference

Either party may request, and many courts require, a pretrial meeting involving the attorneys, the judge, and occasionally the parties. Usually following discovery, the conference is designed to plan the course of the trial in the interests of efficiency and justice. The participants seek to define the issues and settle the dispute in advance of trial. If no settlement is reached, a trial date is set.

The Judge and Jury

The federal Constitution and most state constitutions provide for the right to a jury trial in a civil case (excepting equity actions). Some states place dollar minimums on that guarantee. At the federal level and in most states, unless one of the parties requests a jury, the judge alone will hear the case and decide all questions of law and fact. If the case is tried before a jury, that body will resolve questions of fact, but all questions of law will be resolved by the judge who will also instruct the jury as to the law governing the case.

Jurors are selected from a jury pool composed of a cross section of the community. A panel is drawn from that pool. The individuals in that panel are questioned by the judge, by the attorneys, or by all to determine if any individual is prejudiced about the case such that he or she could not reach an objective decision on the merits. The questioning process is called *voir dire*.

From an attorney's point of view, jury selection is often not so much a matter of finding jurors without bias as it is a matter of identifying those jurors who are most likely to reach a decision favorable to one's client. To that end, elaborate mechanisms and strategies have been employed—particularly in criminal trials—to identify desirable jurors. For example, sophisticated, computer-assisted surveys of the trial community have been conducted to develop objective evidence by which to identify jurors who would not admit to racial prejudice but whose "profile" suggests the likelihood of such prejudice.

After questioning, the attorneys may *challenge for cause,* arguing to the judge that the individual cannot exercise the necessary objectivity of judgment. Attorneys are also afforded a limited number of *peremptory challenges,* by which the attorney can have a potential juror dismissed without the judge's concurrence and without offering a reason. Peremptory challenges may not be used to reject jurors on the basis of race or gender.

Facebook the Jury Pool

Social media, such as Facebook, MySpace, and Twitter, can be a valuable source of information to attorneys as they try to shape the composition of juries. Information that might not be revealed in voir dire sometimes comes to light online. Jury consultant Amber Yearwood in San Francisco discovered online that a member of a jury pool was highly opinionated and often dispensed medical and sex advice, a personality not well suited to the client's cause. The prospective juror was dismissed.

Source: Ana Campoy and Ashby Jones, "Searching for Details Online, Lawyers Facebook the Jury," *The New York Times,* February 22, 2011, p. A2.

Misleading the Jury?

The case that follows examines allegations of trial misconduct by the plaintiff's attorney in an apparent effort to prejudice the jury.

Judges Buckley, Rosenberger, Lerner, Rubin, Marlow

[P]laintiff alleges that he was verbally and physically abused by defendants because of his sexual orientation and then wrongfully discharged when he refused to voluntarily relinquish his position at the Supper Club.

The Supper Club is a dining and dancing establishment operated by defendant, Edison Associates, L.P. (hereinafter Edison), a limited partnership. Defendant Martin Theising is a partner in Edison and defendant Andre Cortez is the general manager of The Supper Club and is responsible for its day-to-day operations. Defendant Oliver Hoffman was an independent consultant to The Supper Club.

In November 1992, plaintiff was hired as The Supper Club's late night manager initially responsible for its disco and later for its cabaret until he was discharged in July 1995. Plaintiff alleges in his complaint, that during the course of his employment, he was repeatedly subjected to humiliation and to discriminatory epithets regarding his sexual orientation and that, two weeks before he was discharged, he was physically held down by Hoffman and another individual while Cortez threatened to cut off his ponytail with a pair of scissors.

After a lengthy trial, the jury found that plaintiff had been subjected to a hostile work environment and had been discharged because of his sexual orientation and that Cortez had committed assault and battery. The jury awarded $160,000 in lost wages, finding that plaintiff could not have mitigated his damages. It further awarded $8,000,000 for past pain, suffering, and emotional distress and $2,000,000 for such future damages. The jury also awarded punitive damages of $1,000,000 against The Supper Club, $54,000 against Cortez and $2,200,000 against Theising with respect to the discrimination claims.

Defendants contend that the damages awarded were so grossly excessive as to be the result of passion and prejudice born of plaintiff's counsel's misconduct and judicial error, that a mere reduction of the awards would not be an adequate remedy.

"When misconduct of counsel in interrogation or summation so violates the rights of the other party to the litigation that extraneous matters beyond the proper scope of the trial may have substantially influenced or been determinative of the outcome, such breaches of the rules will not be condoned." (*Kohlmann v. City of New York,* 8 AD2d 598, 598.) Although evidence of hostility and harassment to other minorities may be relevant to a claim of a hostile work environment based on sexual orientation, the cumulative effect of the many irrelevant

and highly prejudicial comments made by plaintiff's counsel in the course of this trial only served to incite the jury's passion and sympathy and effectively prevented a fair and dispassionate consideration of the evidence. Plaintiff's counsel referred to Theising, a German national with an apparent accent, as someone who exhibited an "attitude of hatred" and made forced analogies to Nazi Germany and the Holocaust. While the issue of this case was sexual orientation discrimination, plaintiff's counsel presented to the jury inappropriate matters involving African Americans, Latinos, and Jews that went far beyond any permissible boundaries and served no other purpose than to incite the jury's passions. Similarly, plaintiff's counsel elicited testimony about an alleged physical attack by an assistant to Cortez on an employee dying of AIDS and extensive testimony from several witnesses regarding the consumption of alcoholic beverages by Cortez, Hoffman, and Theising which was highly prejudicial with little or no probative value.

We find that the aggregate effect of such comments and conduct of plaintiff's counsel, which cannot be characterized as inadvertent or harmless, inflamed the jury's passion and sympathy to such an extent as to render the resulting judgment meaningless

The trial court erred in refusing to allow defendants to introduce evidence that no other employees were treated abusively . . . and in denying defendants' requested jury charge on mitigation. Likewise, . . . the trial court made a number of demeaning comments in the presence of the jury demonstrating a marked antipathy toward defense counsel which, in light of the totality of circumstances at trial, warrant a new trial.

Were this Court not to reverse and remand for a new trial for the reasons stated above, we would have nevertheless reversed on the issue of damages. The jury's grossly excessive compensatory and punitive damages awards totaling approximately $20,000,000 have no rational basis. . . . [Reversed. Remanded to "a different justice."]

Questions

1. *a.* Why did this appeals court reverse the decision of the lower court?

   b. Why was the case remanded to "a different justice"?

2. Did this decision conclude that the plaintiff had not been a victim of sexual harassment, wrongful dismissal, or the like? Explain.

3. According to this appeals court, what errors were made by the judge at trial?

The Trial

The trial begins with opening statements by the attorneys. Each is expected to outline what he or she intends to prove. The plaintiff, bearing the burden of proof, then presents evidence, which may include both testimony and physical evidence, such as documents and photos. Those are called *exhibits.*

The plaintiff's attorney secures testimony from his or her own witnesses via questioning labeled *direct examination.* After the plaintiff's attorney completes direct examination of a witness, the defense attorney may question that witness in a process labeled *cross-examination. Redirect* and *recross* may then follow. After all of the plaintiff's witnesses have been questioned, the plaintiff rests his or her case.

At this stage, the defense may make a motion for a *directed verdict,* arguing, in essence, that the plaintiff has offered insufficient evidence to justify relief, so time and expense may be saved by terminating the trial. Understandably, the judge considers the motion in the light most favorable to the plaintiff. Such motions ordinarily fail, and the trial goes forward with the defendant's presentation of evidence.

At the completion of the defendant's case, both parties may be permitted to offer *rebuttal* evidence, and either party may move for a directed verdict. Barring a directed verdict, the case goes forward, with each party making a closing argument. When the trial is by jury, the judge must instruct the jurors as to the law to be applied to the case. The attorneys often submit their views of the proper instructions. In most civil cases, a verdict for the plaintiff must be supported by a *preponderance of the evidence* (more likely than not). After deliberation, the verdict of the jury is rendered, and a judgment is entered by the court. [For a company providing a virtual jury in advance of trial, see **http://www.virtualjury.com**]

Experts

In this highly technological and scientific era, one of the biggest dilemmas facing judges and juries is the weight to give to expert testimony. Very often, in cases such as medical malpractice and product liability (see Chapter 7), the testimony of experts is decisive to the outcome; but that testimony varies wildly in its reliability and credibility. The golfing case that follows investigates the theme of experience as a qualification for expert testimony.

LEGAL BRIEFCASE

Nickles v. Schild
617 N.W.2d 659 (S. D. S. Ct. 2000)

Justice Gilbertson

Larry Nickles, the guardian of Mark Nickles, appeals the trial court's admission of expert testimony.

FACTS

On May 5, 1996, Jay Schild (Schild), Mark Nickles and Schild's younger brother drove to the Human Services Golf Course in Yankton, South Dakota, to play golf. All three boys were minors. Both Nickles and Schild had previously received golf instructions and had been taught some golfing rules.

After playing five holes, Schild and Nickles proceeded to the next tee box. Schild's younger brother was still on the fifth hole green retrieving his ball, which Nickles had knocked a short distance from the green. Schild proceeded to tee up his ball at the front center of the tee box and was preparing to hit his next drive. In the meantime, Nickles moved off the tee box approximately 10 feet and was facing the previous green watching Schild's brother. Schild, who had seen Nickles walk off the tee box, stepped back from his ball and took three practice swings. On the third practice swing, Schild hit Nickles in the head, fracturing his skull and permanently injuring his left eye.

Guardian (*sic*) commenced a personal injury action against Schild for damages sustained as a result of Schild's negligence and failure to exercise reasonable care in swinging his golf club. Schild denied he was negligent and claimed that Nickles was contributory (*sic*) negligent and assumed the risk of his injuries. During trial, Schild called Robert Boldus as an expert witness. Boldus was a former member of the Professional Golfer's (*sic*) Association and golf professional at Fox Run Golf Course in Yankton, South Dakota. Boldus had often given golfing lessons to junior golfers while at Fox Run.

Schild asked Boldus whether "as a golf professional," he had "formed any opinions as to what had happened in this case?" Nickles immediately requested permission to briefly interrogate Boldus for purposes of objecting to his opinion. During this interrogation, the following discussion occurred:

Q: (Nickles's attorney): Mr. Boldus, as a professional golfer, a member of PGA or based upon your experience, have you had any training in evaluating liability or standards of care required in golf liability cases?

A: (Boldus): No, I haven't.

Nickles then objected to the opinion by Boldus regarding standards of care or the ultimate issue. The trial judge overruled Nickles's objection and allowed Boldus to give his opinion:

Q: (Schild's attorney): And could you tell the jury what opinions you have come to?

A: (Boldus): In my opinion it was an accident. But one of the players moved, and when you're in your preshot routine if you move, you back away from the ball six inches to a foot or one step, and then you take your practice swings. My opinion, somehow Mark Nickles had moved in the way of the swing and got hit.

Q: (Schild's attorney): In your opinion did [Schild] violate any standards of care?

A: (Boldus): No.

The jury returned a verdict in favor of Schild. Nickles appealed, raising the following issue:

> Whether the trial court abused its discretion by permitting expert testimony from Boldus.

* * * * *

DECISION

* * * * *

[A]n expert is not limited to testifying only upon those areas in which he or she has received formal training. Rather, when giving an opinion, an expert is allowed to draw upon all the knowledge, skill, or experience that he or she has accumulated.

[W]hile Boldus may not have had any formal classroom "training" in the applicable liability standards, it is clear Boldus was no novice at the game of golf. He was a former member of the PGA and a golf professional at Fox Run Golf Course in Yankton. While at Fox Run, he had often given golf lessons to junior golfers, which included golf etiquette and safety. He had even previously given golf lessons to Nickles. By any of these methods of acquiring the appropriate expertise or combination thereof, he could have qualified himself as an expert to testify as to "what happened."

It is quite clear from the testimony of Boldus and his vitae that he did have an opinion on the standards of care required in golf and the expertise to give such an opinion. The following testimony regarding the standard of care applicable to the game of golf was elicited from Boldus during direct testimony:

Q: When someone has addressed the ball and stepped back and they're doing their practice swings, what is the person's duty when they're doing those practice swings?

A: Well, basically there's nothing stated that says that you have to look around. You should be, when you begin your preshot routine, prior to taking your practice swings you should look and kind of [get] an idea where people are at so they are out of your way so you can take a swing. Once you begin your practice swings I think it's a duty of the other person to stay out of the way.

Q: So once, right before you start your preshot routine is when you have the duty to check what's going around?

A: Yes.

Q: And then as you start your preshot routine then it's the duty of those around you to become aware that that's what you're going to do, to watch?

A: Yes.

* * * * *

Boldus merely described, in his opinion, "what happened in this case" and that Schild's actions did not violate any standard of care concerning the game of golf. He did not invade the province of the jury as Nickles suggests. Boldus did not testify as to the ultimate issue of negligence. In fact, Boldus did not discuss the issue of liability at all until he was asked upon cross-examination, "but one party is liable, aren't they?" Boldus responded, "I wouldn't—yah—I don't know about liable, but somebody [is responsible for that]."

Nickles' objection as to the qualifications of Boldus goes in part to formal training concerning the issue of ultimate liability. The ultimate liability of one of the parties is not the same as standard of care. One can violate a standard of care and still not be held liable. There could be further potential questions of contributory negligence, assumption of the risk, financial responsibility of a minor and/or his parents, questions of duty to supervise a minor and the like, all of which can have a decisive effect on liability and which clearly are outside the expertise of a golf pro and his knowledge of golf standards of care. Boldus did not testify as to any of these issues; his testimony was limited to describing the standard of care for the game of golf.

Affirmed.

DISSENT

Justice Sabers

I dissent.

I write specially to point out that the majority opinion misses the point—not once, but several times.

Whether Boldus was qualified as an expert witness is immaterial. The point is that under the pretense of being an expert witness, Boldus cannot testify as a fact witness. He was not present at the scene. He does not know what happened. Only fact witnesses can testify "as to what happened?" Therefore, under these circumstances it was totally improper for Boldus to testify to his opinion "as to what happened in this case."

Questions

1. What were Nickles's objections to the expert, Boldus's, testimony?

2. What objection was raised by the dissenting Justice Sabers?

3. Do you agree with the expert, Boldus, that once a golfer has properly started the preshot routine the duty of care shifts to those around the golfer to be aware of what is happening and to keep themselves out of harm's way? Explain.

4. Dodge slipped leaving work and claimed that she suffered knee, ankle, and back injuries. Dodge sued the workplace cleaning service, but she provided no expert testimony to establish that the fall caused the injuries. Rather Dodge provided her own explanation of the fall and resulting injuries. Did the trial court err in admitting Dodge's lay person testimony? Explain, See *Dodge-Farrar v. American Cleaning Services Co.,* 54 P. 3d 954 (Ida. Ct. App. 2002).

Post-Trial Motions

The losing party may seek a *judgment notwithstanding the verdict (judgment n.o.v)* on the grounds that the jury's decision was clearly inconsistent with the law or the evidence. Such motions are rarely granted. The judge is also empowered to enter a judgment n.o.v on his or her own initiative.

Either party may also move for a new trial. The winning party might do so on the grounds that the remedy provided was inferior to that warranted by the evidence. The losing party commonly claims an error of law to support a motion for a new trial. Other possible grounds for a new trial include jury misconduct or new evidence.

Appeals

After the judgment is rendered, either party may appeal the decision to a higher court. The winner may do so if he or she feels the remedy is inadequate. Ordinarily, of course, the losing party brings the appeal. As noted, the appealing party is the *appellant* or the *petitioner,* while the other party is the *appellee* or *respondent.* The appeals court does not try the case again. In theory, at least, its consideration is limited to mistakes of law at the trial level. The appellant will argue, for example, that a jury instruction was erroneous or that the judge erred in failing to grant a motion to strike testimony alleged to have been prejudicial. The appeals court does not hear new evidence. Its decision is based on the trial record, materials filed by the opposing attorneys, and oral arguments.

The appellate court announces its judgment and ordinarily explains that decision in an accompanying document labeled an *opinion.* (Most of the cases in this text are appellate court opinions.) If no error is found, the lower court decision is *affirmed.* In finding prejudicial error, the appellate court may simply *reverse* (overrule) the lower court. Or the judgment may be to *reverse and remand,* wherein the lower court is overruled and the case must be tried again in accordance with the law as articulated in the appeals court opinion. After the decision of the intermediate appellate court, a further appeal may be sought at the highest court of the jurisdiction. Most of those petitions are denied.

Questions—Part Two

1. What are the purposes and uses of the concept of jurisdiction? Why do we limit the courts to which a claim can be taken?

2. Law cases often read like soap operas even as they reveal important truths. A woman and man, each married to others, had engaged in a long-term love affair. The woman's husband died, and she pleaded with her paramour to leave his New York home to visit her in Florida. She affirmed her love for the man. They made arrangements to meet in Miami, but on his arrival at the airport he was served a summons informing him that he was being sued. His Florida "lover" sought $500,000 for money allegedly loaned to him and for seduction inspired by a promise of marriage.
   a. Does the Florida court have proper jurisdiction over him?
   b. What if he had voluntarily come to Florida on vacation? See *Wyman v. Newhouse,* 93 F.2d 313 (2d Cir. 1937).

3. Sea Pines, a privately owned suburban community on Hilton Head Island, South Carolina, was designated a wildlife sanctuary by the state legislature. After study, the state Department of Natural Resources decided to issue permits to allow limited deer hunting on the land to reduce overpopulation. Various environmental groups challenged the issuance of the permits. What defense would you expect the state to offer in court? Explain. See *Sea Pines Ass'n for Protection of Wildlife v. South Carolina Dept. of Natural Resources,* 550 S.E. 2d 287 (S.C. S. Ct. 2001).

Part Three—Criticism and Alternatives

Criticism

To many Americans, our system of justice is neither systematic nor just. With more than 1.2 million lawyers in a population of over 312 million people, critics argue that excessive, unproductive litigation is inevitable.

Too Many Lawyers and Lawsuits?

Many lawsuits are less a search for justice and more a pursuit of big dollars for attorneys, the critics claim. A large law firm sued an energy industry executive for unpaid legal bills, resulting in a counterclaim asserting that the firm overbilled as a matter of practice. During discovery, e-mails between three attorneys at the firm surfaced that included such statements as "That bill shall know no limits." Even though the firm described the e-mail exchange as "unfortunate banter" between colleagues, the messages may reflect a larger problem with the approaches that law firms have to billing.[26] A confidential settlement ended the litigation.[27]

> "That bill shall know no limits"

Legal critic Philip K. Howard argues that we need fewer lawsuits, fewer rules, and greater personal responsibility. He thinks we feel powerless in the face of rules:

> Ordinary choices–by teachers, doctors, officials, managers, even volunteers—are paralyzed by legal self-consciousness. Did you check the rules? Who will be responsible if there is an accident? . . . We have become a culture of rule followers, trained to frame every solution in terms of existing law or possible legal risk. . . . [28]

Even Supreme Court Justice Antonin Scalia has argued that we have too many lawyers:

> Lawyers don't dig ditches or build buildings. When a society requires such a large number of its best minds to conduct the unproductive enterprise of the law, something is wrong with the legal system.[29]

Polling results suggest that Americans have deep reservations about our legal system, but they also recognize its indispensable role in maintaining a just society. A 2012 survey conducted by the American Tort Reform Association, for example, shows that nine of 10 American voters believe lawsuit abuse is a problem, and 60 percent believe that consumers and small businesses are hurt by it.[30] On the other hand, a 2007 national poll by the American Association for Justice (formerly the American Trial Lawyers Association) found more concern about corporate abuse than about lawyers and the legal system.[31]

> Nine of 10 American voters believe lawsuit abuse is a problem.

The Corporate Perspective

The legal system plays an invaluable role in facilitating and stabilizing commercial practice, but for corporate America the law is also a source of significant expense and abundant frustration. As one expert explained, dealing with legal responsibilities and problems has become a central ingredient in management practice:

> Only a few decades ago, the law was peripheral to the core activities of doing business. When I became a business lawyer in the late 1950s, for example, our involvement was generally limited to forming a corporation or partnership for a client, providing for the investment capital, doing a lease for an office or factory, and maybe handling a key contract with a CEO or a major supplier. . . . Today the law can affect almost every action a manager takes. It has moved closer to the core activities of conducting business and succeeding in a red-hot, competitive environment. More people now have "rights" they can assert against your company, so you face claims from employees, consumers, competitors, and the government.

Consequently, today's manager needs to know something about employment law, discrimination claims, sexual harassment rules, product safety issues, the rules of advertising and competition, antitrust rules, environmental law, the value of intellectual property, and more.[32]

[For a site dedicated to laughing at lawyers, see **http://www.power-of-attorneys.com/**]
[For a critique of the American legal system, see the U.S. Chamber Institute for Legal Reform (an affiliate of the U.S. Chamber of Commerce) at **http://www.facesoflawsuitabuse.com/**]
[For a critique of the U.S. Chamber Institute for Legal Reform, see the American Association for Justice's 2011 report, "Do as I Say, Not as I Sue" at **www.justice.org/cps/rde/xbcr /justice/Do_As_I_Say_Not_As_I_Sue_2011.pdf**]

Pants: Abusing the Legal System?

Washington, DC administrative law judge, Roy Pearson, attracted the attention of journalists from around the world by suing his neighborhood laundry for $54 million, down from an earlier claim of $67 million, over the alleged loss of the pants belonging to his $1,000 suit. Pearson thought he was entitled to $18,000 per day for each day the pants were missing over a period of nearly four years. Owners Soo and Jin Chung of Custom Cleaners attempted to give Pearson a pair of pants they said were the missing item, but he said the ones offered were not his. Pearson brought claims of mental suffering, inconvenience, discomfort, and fraud (based on the "Satisfaction Guaranteed" sign at Custom Cleaners). Along the way, Pearson had rejected settlement offers that reached $12,000. The Chungs won an easy trial victory with the court concluding that Pearson was unable to prove the pants offered to him were not his and that the "Satisfaction Guaranteed" sign did not require the Chungs to satisfy a customer's unreasonable demands. Pearson was ordered to pay the Chungs' court costs, and the legal fees for the Chungs' defense were covered by contributions. The Chung's dry cleaner went out of business. Pearson subsequently failed in his bid to be reappointed to his judge's position. He sued for wrongful discharge and lost at the federal district court and then appealed to the federal court of appeals where he also lost.

Sources: Henri E. Cauvin, "Court Rules for Cleaners in $54 Million Pants Suit," *The Washington Post,* June 26, 2007, p. A01; and "'Pants Judge' Roy Pearson Strikes Out in Court," *The Wall Street Journal,* May 27, 2010 [**http:// blogs.wsj.com/law/**].

Criticized in America; Embraced Abroad

The United States is not alone in its ongoing debate about whether more or fewer lawyers and lawsuits are needed.

Japan Historically in Japan, lawsuits have seldom been used to settle disputes, as reflected in its relatively small number of attorneys. In March 2011, there was approximately one attorney for every 4,000 persons in Japan. With the rise of international mergers, bankruptcy, patents, and other business disputes, in 2002 Japan became concerned with its lawyer shortage. Through its Ministry of Internal Affairs and Communications, Japan sought to expand the number of lawyers; with a new bar exam, the Japanese bar pass rates went from 2 to 3 percent to between 40 and 50 percent. A recent survey found that approximately 25 percent of the Japan Bar Association was admitted between 2007 and 2012.[33]

In 2012, the Ministry of Internal Affairs and Communications determined that there were now too many lawyers in Japan: The influx of new attorneys and the global economic crisis had hurt lawyers' employment prospects. It recommended to the Ministry of Justice and the Ministry of Education, Culture, Sports and Science to reduce the number of law schools and law school graduates.[34]

PRACTICING ETHICS) Private Law for Walmart?

A portion of Walmart's Ethical Standards Program demands employee welfare throughout its vast supply chain:

> We do not own, operate, or manage any factories. Instead, we purchase merchandise from suppliers located in more than 60 countries. Our Ethical Standards team is dedicated to verifying that these supplier factories are in compliance with our Standards for Suppliers. These standards cover compliance with local and national laws and regulations governing compensation, hours of labor, forced/prison labor, underage labor, discrimination, freedom of association and collective bargaining, health and safety, environment, and the right of audit by Walmart Stores, Inc.[35]

Law professor Larry Cata Backer argues that Walmart and other global giants are effectively legislating their own private law in the form of contract and business relationships and ethics standards governing product quality, working conditions and similar matters. Walmart's Standards for Suppliers are the core of its global governance system that, according to Backer, is "an important emerging phenomenon: the development of efficient systems of private law making by nongovernmental organizations that sometimes supplement, and sometimes displace traditional legal systems."[36] Working with the media, nongovernmental organizations (NGOs), consumers, and investors, Walmart and other multinationals, Backer argues, are beginning to build independent mechanisms for efficient regulation of economic behavior on a global scale that may lead to systems of law beyond governments and moderated largely by stakeholders.[37]

Question

Should we welcome and encourage the development of a private law system enforced through contractual and ethical standards by giant multinationals, or should we be concerned that strengthened, strictly enforced private law arrangements would place too much authority in the hands of already powerful organizations? Explain.

On the Other Hand—Litigation as a Last Resort

Almost everyone seems to be unhappy about lawyers and lawsuits, but at the same time Americans expect lawyers and the courts to settle disputes, preserve freedom and justice and correct problems not satisfactorily addressed by the market, legislatures, and regulators. Feeling threatened by abusive bosses, corporate fraud, dangerous drugs, defective products, environmental decline, and so on, Americans count on the justice system to protect our pecuniary interests as well as the personal freedom and democracy we prize. Lawyers and the courts often are the only available weapons to right what we believe to be a wrong. So the frustration many feel about exploding litigation may be attributable to us as much as to greedy lawyers. Furthermore, laws and lawyers are central to economic efficiency. Lawyers devise the rules, processes, and structures that permit capitalism to operate effectively. As we have read, the balance of the world is coming to recognize that law and lawyers are prerequisites to economic stability and progress.

Fewer Trials   A National Center for State Courts study of the state courts in 75 of the most populous counties revealed that from 1992 to 2005, the number of civil trials decreased by more than 50 percent.[38] In 2005, approximately 7.4 million civil cases were filed in state courts; approximately 27,000 were disposed of through a jury or bench trial.[39] Trials often are an inefficient way of resolving disputes so these numbers may be considered very good news. On the other hand, trials are visible affirmations of the indispensability of justice, and they provide the careful reasoning and precedents that identify impermissible behavior.

> Trials often are an inefficient way of resolving disputes.

PRACTICING ETHICS   Declining Access to Lawyers?

One of the reasons for the declining number of trials, despite increasing disputes, may be difficulty in affording a lawyer in civil suits. *The New York Times* and other publications have reported an increasing number of cases going forward with one of the parties serving as a "do-it-yourself" lawyer.[40] Pursuing a claim in a federal district court costs an average of $15,000 with more complicated cases involving scientific evidence often reaching $100,000.[41] The expense of bringing lawsuits has attracted litigation funders, who invest in business disputes in exchange for a portion of the proceeds received by the party to whom they have given capital.[42] Litigation funders assert that they are helping litigants seek justice from wealthier opponents and not supporting frivolous lawsuits, which would be risky investment.[43] One other possible result is that some litigants appear to be victimized by lawsuit lenders in a lightly regulated industry where interest rates " often exceed 100 percent per year."[44]

A 2012 San Francisco ordinance created a right to civil counsel, similar to what criminal defendants receive. Those living within 200 percent of the federal poverty line and who have a case regarding such key issues as housing, safety, or child custody would be eligible for free legal assistance.[45] Although critics may view such programs as being best left to private legal aid organizations, supporters believe that by providing legal assistance to civil litigants in need, the city will avoid the long-term costs arising from self-represented parties, such as court delays.[46]

Question

While indigent criminal defendants are assured the right to counsel under American law, the same is not assured in civil disputes. Do you think San Francisco's Civil Justice initiative should be followed throughout the United States? Explain.

Reform: Judicial Efficiency

Governments, businesses, lawyers, judges—all are frustrated with the expense and inefficiency of our overburdened judicial system. Some small businesses are now buying legal services insurance or prepaid legal services for a flat monthly fee.

Some cities have taken novel approaches to adjudication such as business courts that hear only commercial claims, thus allowing jurists to become very efficient in handling contract problems, shareholder claims, and the like. Those systems are variations on the small claims courts that have long proven effective in settling minor disputes.

Small Claims Courts

Suppose you move out of your apartment and your landlord refuses to return your $500 damage deposit even though the rooms are spotless. Hiring a lawyer doesn't make good financial sense and is beyond your means anyway, but a small claims court may provide an effective solution.

Small claims courts, for the most part, resolve relatively minor disputes, like your landlord–tenant problem. A wide range of problems, such as divorce or bankruptcy, cannot be litigated in small claims courts. Maximum recoveries vary from place to place but typically range from a few thousand dollars up to $7,500 or so. To prepare for a small claims case, the key is developing and presenting to the judge as much credible evidence as possible. If you can present witnesses on your behalf, do so, but if not, clearly written memos expressing what the witnesses would have said may be acceptable to the judge. You need not hire a lawyer, but in most states you may do so if you wish. Should the small claims litigation not work out well for you, an appeal is permitted in many states.[47]

Honda in Small Claims Court

After rejecting a class-action settlement that would have paid Honda Civic hybrid owners $100 to $200 each and offer some rebates on a new Honda purchase, in 2012 Heather Peters sued Honda in small claims court and won $9,867.19 in damages after the judge ruled that Honda misled her into thinking her hybrid could get 50 miles per gallon, when its fuel economy actually dropped from approximately 42 miles per gallon to 30 miles per gallon after a software update. Honda successfully appealed to the Los Angeles County Superior Court. Even though she lost on appeal, Peters prompted other customers to file lawsuits against Honda in small claims courts across the United States, including in New Bedford, Massachusetts; St. Louis, Missouri; and Arlington, Washington.

Sources: Jerry Hirsch, "Honda Loses Civic Hybrid Small Claims Court Lawsuit," *Los Angeles Times,* February 1, 2012 [**www.latimes.com**]; Jerry Hirsch, "Honda Wins Appeal in Civic Hybrid Mileage Lawsuit," *Los Angeles Times,* May 10, 2012 [**www.latimes.com**].

Alternative Dispute Resolution

Businesses, in particular, are increasingly looking outside the judicial system for dispute resolution strategies. Dot-com entrepreneurs are developing interesting new online mechanisms for conveniently addressing Internet-based disputes. Networks of human mediators, dispute resolution software, and PayPal dispute resolution are among the online methods of settling problems outside of court.

Cybersettle is an online system for resolving insurance disputes, often of the fender-bender or slip-and-fall variety. The parties log on to Cybersettle and type in their monetary demands or offers. The system works 24 hours a day, seven days a week. The computer compares the bids, round by round. When those numbers come within a predetermined range, the two sides are notified that a settlement has been achieved. If necessary, a telephone facilitator may join the process to help reach the final sum to be paid. Cybersettle has patented its system and says it has settled more than 200,000 transactions and has facilitated over $1.9 billion in settlements. [See **http://www.cybersettle .com/**] In 2011, New York City comptroller John Liu replaced the city's Cybersettle process to settle small personal injury and property damages claims with an in-house staff of claims adjusters as a more cost-effective alternative.[48] Critics say some Internet legal resources such as **http://www.whocanisue.com/**, a highly advertised website that matches potential clients with lawyers, may degrade the legal profession and serve primarily to generate litigation.[49]

What Is Alternative Dispute Resolution?

Of course, any form of negotiation and settlement would constitute an alternative to litigation, but mediation and arbitration are the most prominent of the substitutes. Given the expense, frustration, and risk of lawsuits, we are seeing increasing imagination in building other alternative dispute resolution (ADR) options including private trials and minitrials. [For many ADR links, see **www.hg.org/adr.html**]

Mediation

Mediation introduces a neutral third party into the resolution process. Ideally, the parties devise their own solution, with the mediator as a facilitator, not a decision maker. Even if the mediator proposes a solution, it will likely be in the nature of a compromise, not a determination of right and wrong. The bottom line is that only the disputing parties can adopt any particular outcome. The mediator may aid the parties in a number of ways, such as opening up communication between them.

Arbitration

In *arbitration* a neutral third party is given the power to determine a binding resolution of the dispute. Depending on the situation, the resolution may be either a compromise solution or a determination of the rights of the parties and a win–lose solution. Even in the latter case, however, arbitration may be quicker and less costly than a trial, and the arbitrator may be an expert in the subject area of the dispute instead of a generalist, as a judge would be. Arbitration is procedurally more formal than mediation, with the presentation of proofs and arguments by the parties, but less formal than court adjudication.

The arbitrator's decision ordinarily is legally binding and final, although an increasing but still small number of arbitration decisions are reaching court.[50]

Private Trials

A number of states now permit mutually-agreed-on private trials, sometimes labeled "rent-a-judge." Normally a third party such as a mediation firm makes the necessary arrangements, including hiring a retired judge and jurors. The proceedings are conducted much as in a courtroom. Because the

"Rent-a-Judge"

parties are paying, however, the process normally moves along more rapidly, and the proceeding may be conducted in private. Appeals to the formal judicial system are provided for in some states. Critics question the fairness of the private system and wonder if it will further erode faith in public trials, but the time and money saved can be quite substantial.

Mini-trials

In recent years, some corporations have agreed to settle their disputes by holding informal hearings that clarify the facts and the issues that would emerge if the dispute were litigated. In the mini-trial, each organization presents its version of the case to a panel of senior executives from each organization. The trial is presided over by a neutral third party who may be expected to issue a nonbinding opinion as to the likely result were the case to be litigated. The executives then meet to attempt to negotiate a settlement. The neutral third party sometimes facilitates that discussion. Mini-trials are voluntary and nonbinding, but if an agreement is reached, the parties can formalize it by entering a settlement contract.

ADR Assessed

ADR mechanisms generally have been sustained in the courts. ADR—particularly arbitration—is often the required dispute-resolution mechanism for employee complaints such as discrimination or harassment. Mandatory arbitration clauses are often included in consumer transactions involving loans, credit cards, cable service, auto warranties, brokerage accounts, insurance and more. Ordinarily, ADR costs less and is resolved more quickly than litigation. ADR is less formal and less adversarial than the judicial process. Furthermore, the parties have more control over the proceedings in that they can choose the facilitator, they can choose when and where the dispute will be heard, and they can keep the dispute private if they wish. Despite those strengths, alternative dispute resolution has some limitations when compared with litigation.

A recent study of nearly 4,000 employee arbitration cases found an employee win rate of only 21.4 percent, a lower result than in litigation. In arbitration cases won by employees, the median recovery was $36,500 and the mean was $109,858, both of which are substantially lower than awards reported from litigation. On the other hand, arbitration, on average, was both quicker and less expensive than litigation.[51]

A 2011 U.S. Supreme Court decision makes arbitration less functional for consumers by allowing businesses to continue their commonplace practice of requiring arbitration of disputes but forbidding class action arbitration (and litigation) thus compelling consumers to individually arbitrate alleged wrongdoing. In that case, Vincent and Liza Concepcion complained that AT&T Mobility charged them $30.22 in sales tax and other fees for what was advertised as a "free" phone. They sought class-action status for themselves and others, but the 5–4 Supreme Court ruling denied that possibility and left the Concepcions and others similarly aggrieved to file individual claims for very small amounts of money.[52] The case that follows examines whether a mandatory arbitration clause in a travel agency contract to climb Mount Kilimanjaro was unconscionable under California law.

> AT&T Mobility charged them $30.22 for a "free" phone.

Judge Siggins

Geographic Expeditions, Inc. (GeoEx), appeals from an order denying its motion to compel arbitration of a wrongful death action brought by the survivors of one of its clients who died on a Mount Kilimanjaro hiking expedition. . . .

BACKGROUND

Jason Lhotka was 37 years old when he died of an altitude-related illness while on a GeoEx expedition up Mount Kilimanjaro with his mother, plaintiff Sandra Menefee. GeoEx's limitation of liability and release form, which both Lhotka and Menefee signed as a requirement of participating in the expedition, provided that each of them released GeoEx from all liability in connection with the trek and waived any claims for liability "to the maximum extent permitted by law." The release also required that the parties would submit any disputes between themselves first to mediation and then to binding arbitration. It reads: "I understand that all Trip Applications are subject to acceptance by GeoEx in San Francisco, California, USA. I agree that in the unlikely event a dispute of any kind arises between me and GeoEx, the following conditions will apply: (a) the dispute will be submitted to a neutral third-party mediator in San Francisco, California, with both parties splitting equally the cost of such mediator. If the dispute cannot be resolved through mediation, then (b) the dispute will be submitted for binding arbitration to the American Arbitration Association in San Francisco, California; (c) the dispute will be governed by California law; and (d) the maximum amount of recovery to which I will be entitled under any and all circumstances will be the sum of the land and air cost of my trip with GeoEx. I agree that this is a fair and reasonable limitation on the damages, of any sort whatsoever, that I may suffer. I agree to fully indemnify GeoEx for all of its costs (including attorneys' fees) if I commence an action or claim against GeoEx based upon claims I have previously released or waived by signing this release." Menefee paid $16,831 for herself and Lhotka to go on the trip.

A letter from GeoEx president James Sano that accompanied the limitation of liability and release explained that the form was mandatory and that, on this point, "our lawyers, insurance carriers and medical consultants give us no discretion. A signed, unmodified release form is required before any traveler may join one of our trips. Ultimately, we believe that you should choose your travel company based on its track record, not what you are asked to sign. . . . My review of other travel companies' release forms suggests that our forms are not a whole lot different from theirs."

After her son's death, Menefee sued GeoEx for wrongful death and alleged various theories of liability including fraud, gross negligence and recklessness, and intentional infliction of emotional distress. GeoEx moved to compel arbitration.

The trial court found the arbitration provision was unconscionable and on that basis denied the motion.

* * * * *

This appeal timely followed.

DISCUSSION

The question . . . posed here[is] whether the agreement to arbitrate is unconscionable and, therefore, unenforceable.

* * * * *

II. Unconscionability (I omitted-Ed.)

(1) We turn first to GeoEx's contention that the court erred when it found the arbitration agreement unconscionable. . . .

"[U]nconscionability has generally been recognized to include an absence of meaningful choice on the part of one of the parties together with contract terms which are unreasonably favorable to the other party. Phrased another way, unconscionability has both a 'procedural' and a 'substantive' element." The procedural element requires oppression or surprise. Oppression occurs where a contract involves lack of negotiation and meaningful choice, surprise where the allegedly unconscionable provision is hidden within a prolix printed form. The substantive element concerns whether a contractual provision reallocates risks in an objectively unreasonable or unexpected manner. Under this approach, both the procedural and substantive elements must be met before a contract or term will be deemed unconscionable. Both, however, need not be present to the same degree. A sliding scale is applied so that 'the more substantively oppressive the contract term, the less evidence of procedural unconscionability is required to come to the conclusion that the term is unenforceable, and vice versa.'" . . .

A. Procedural Unconscionability

* * * * *

GeoEx led plaintiffs to understand not only that its terms and conditions were nonnegotiable, but that plaintiffs would encounter the same requirements with any other travel company. This is a sufficient basis for us to conclude plaintiffs lacked bargaining power.

GeoEx also contends its terms were not oppressive . . . because Menefee and Lhotka could have simply decided not to trek up Mount Kilimanjaro. It argues that contracts for recreational activities can *never* be unconscionably oppressive because, unlike agreements for necessities such as medical care or employment, a consumer of recreational activities *always* has the option of foregoing the activity. . . .

(2) While the nonessential nature of recreational activities is a factor to be taken into account in assessing whether a contract is oppressive, it is not necessarily the dispositive factor.

* * * * *

(3) Here, certainly, plaintiffs could have chosen not to sign on with the expedition. That option, like any availability of market alternatives, is relevant to the existence, and degree, of oppression. . . .

But we must also consider the other circumstances surrounding the execution of the agreement. . . .

GeoEx presented its terms as both nonnegotiable and *no different than what plaintiffs would find with any other provider* Under these circumstances, plaintiffs made a sufficient showing to establish at least a minimal level of oppression to justify a finding of procedural unconscionability.

B. Substantive Unconscionability

With the "sliding scale" rule firmly in mind, we address whether the substantive unconscionability of the GeoEx contract warrants the trial court's ruling.

The arbitration provision in GeoEx's release is . . . one-sided. . . . It guaranteed that plaintiffs could not possibly obtain anything approaching full recompense for their harm by limiting any recovery they could obtain to the amount they paid GeoEx for their trip. In addition to a limit on their recovery, plaintiffs, residents of Colorado, were required to mediate and arbitrate

in San Francisco—all but guaranteeing both that GeoEx would never be out more than the amount plaintiffs had paid for their trip, and that any recovery plaintiffs might obtain would be devoured by the expense they incur in pursing their remedy. The release also required plaintiffs to indemnify GeoEx for its costs and attorney fees for defending any claims covered by the release of liability form. Notably, there is no reciprocal limitation on damages or indemnification obligations imposed on GeoEx. Rather than providing a neutral forum for dispute resolution, GeoEx's arbitration scheme provides a potent disincentive for an aggrieved client to pursue any claim, in any forum—and may well guarantee that GeoEx wins even if it loses. Absent reasonable justification for this arrangement—and none is apparent—we agree with the trial court that the arbitration clause is so one-sided as to be substantively unconscionable.

Affirmed.

Questions

1. Why was the Lhotka/Geographic Expeditions agreement to arbitrate ruled unconscionable?

2. Differentiate procedural and substantive unconscionability.

3. Kalliope and David Valchine entered court-ordered mediation to try to resolve the problems that had led them to seek a divorce. Lawyers represented both Kalliope and David at mediation. The mediation led to a marital settlement agreement between Kalliope and David. One month later, Kalliope sought to set aside the agreement, arguing that she had been coerced by her husband, her husband's attorney, and the mediator. Kalliope testified that the mediator threatened to report her to the judge for being uncooperative in refusing to sign a reasonable settlement offer. She claimed that the mediator also told her that she could sign the agreement and then object to its provisions at the final hearing. See *Kalliope Vitakis-Valchine v. David L. Valchine*, 793 So.2d 1094 (Fla. App. 4th Dist. 2001); 34 So.3d 17 (Fla. App. 4th Dist. 2010).
   Should the settlement be set aside? Explain.

4. Is an arbitration clause as a condition of employment a fair method of alternate dispute resolution, if entered knowingly and voluntarily? Explain.

5. In an effort to reduce legal expenses, some major banks and other businesses follow policies providing that all customer complaints will be subject to arbitration. Is mandatory arbitration fair to consumers? Explain.

Internet Exercise

Go to the "2012 Lawsuit Climate Study" of the U.S. Chamber of Commerce Institute for Legal Reform (ILR) at [**http://www.instituteforlegalreform.com/states/**] and click on your state. Scroll down to "All Results" for your state and select articles to read opinions on legal issues facing your state. For a critique of the ILR's Lawsuit Climate Study, go to [**http://www.justice.org/cps/rde/xchg/justice/hs.xsl/11932.htm**].

Chapter Questions

1. Economist Stephen Magee argues that one way to strengthen the American economy would be to close the law schools:

   > Every time you turn out one law school graduate, you've got a 40-year problem on your hands, he says. These guys run around and generate a lot of spurious conflict. They're like heat-seeking missiles.[54]

   Comment.

2. The National Registry of Exonerations, a joint project of the University of Michigan Law School and Professor Samuel Gross of the University of Michigan Law School, shows that from January 1989 through January 2014, 1,304 convicted individuals were exonerated.[55] In 2013, 87 exonerations were recorded; of these, 15 had pleaded guilty, 40 had been convicted of murder, and 18 had been convicted of rape or sexual assault.[56]

   a. The U.S. prison population has been estimated at approximately 2 million, generally viewed as the highest number of incarcerations in the world. In your opinion, what may the number of exonerations recorded in the National Registry of Exonerations compared to the U.S. prison population show about the U.S. criminal justice system? Explain.

   b. Trends of the National Registry of Exonerations show both an increase in the number of those exonerated who had pleaded guilty, as well as an increase in the investigations by law enforcement into possible false convictions. What conclusions might be drawn from these trends? Explain.

3. Crowley, who became intoxicated at a postrace party on McRoberts's boat, was driving after the party and caused a multicar accident that resulted in serious injuries to Culver, who was driving one of the other vehicles. Culver's passenger was killed, and Crowley was later convicted of reckless homicide. Culver sued McRoberts for negligence. Crowley's drinking took place in the galley of McRoberts's 40-foot boat. McRoberts did not provide the liquor and McRoberts, who was busy with recording race results, was not aware of how much drinking Crowley had done. The Indiana Dram Shop statute provided that "it is unlawful for a person to sell, barter, deliver, or give away an alcoholic beverage to another person who is in a state of intoxication if the person knows that the other person is intoxicated." Expert testimony and a blood alcohol reading suggested that Crowley may have been visibly drunk, but several witnesses on the boat said they did not observe visible signs of intoxication. Did McRoberts violate the Indiana Dram Shop law, and was McRoberts negligent in failing to properly supervise Crowley? Explain. See *Culver v. McRoberts,* 192 F.3d 1095 (7th Cir. 1999).

4. Dubuque, Iowa's City Council and mayor in 2011 enacted a parental responsibility ordinance providing that: "A failure by a parent to exercise reasonable control over the parent's minor which causes the minor to commit an unlawful act is a violation . . ."

The ordinance is directed to derelict parents whose negligence or indifference facilitates criminal behavior by children and leads to big investments of police time in simply locating parents. A violation initially results in a warning with increasing fines (or parenting classes) for violations thereafter. The city's plan is to provide resources to aid parents who are in violation of the ordinance. The city has indicated that "reasonable control" means doing what the average person would do.[57]

   a. What objections would you raise to this ordinance?

   b. Do you think a parent would violate the reasonable control standard if his or her child failed to come home from the movies by the hour agreed on, but the parent then made an effort to find the child? Explain.

   c. Is the ordinance a good idea in your judgment? Explain.

5. In 2013, Megan Thode, a former graduate student, sought $1.3 million in damages from Lehigh University for receiving a C+ in a class in which a B or above was needed to enroll in the next required course toward her goal of becoming a licensed professional counselor. Thode's complaint was based on claims of breach of contract and sexual discrimination. The trial judge ruled for the defendant, Lehigh University.[58]

   a. If you were the trial judge, what information would you expect to be presented at trial? Explain.

   b. What could be the impact of Thode's lawsuit on student–professor relations and grading in college? Explain.

6. The California Medical Injury Compensation Reform Act (MICRA) of 1975 capped non-economic damages such as pain and suffering at $250,000; as of this writing, the cap has never been adjusted for inflation. Such award caps have been criticized as limiting those injured from seeking legal redress, as most attorneys representing plaintiffs in medical malpractice actions work on contingency. Further, plaintiffs with permanent injuries will be able to collect no more for their pain and suffering than those who will recover fully.[59]

   As of this writing, a campaign is underway in California to raise the MICRA cap to meet inflation, along with other measures to increase patient safety.[60]

   To learn more about the Troy and Alanna Pack Patient Safety Act, visit [**www .youtube.com/watch?feature=player_embedded&v=cSDqWx3r5o4**]

   What are the advantages and disadvantages of limiting damages in medical malpractice suits? Explain.

7. In your opinion are attractive criminal defendants likely to receive more favorable treatment in the courts than similarly situated but less attractive defendants? Explain.

8. According to Warren Avis, founder of Avis Rent-a-Car,

> We've reached a point in this country where, in many instances, power has become more important than justice—not a matter of who is right, but of who has the most money, time, and the largest battery of lawyers to drag a case through the courts.[61]

   a. Should the rich be entitled to better legal representation, just as they have access to better food, better medical care, better education, and so on? Explain.

   b. Should we employ a nationwide legal services program sufficient to guarantee competent legal aid to all? Explain.

9. Peremptory challenges may not constitutionally be used to exclude a potential juror from a trial on racial or gender grounds.
    a. Must a criminal jury reflect the ethnic or racial diversity of the community? Explain. See *Powers v. Ohio,* 111 S. Ct. 1364 (1991).
    b. Could potential jurors lawfully be rejected on the basis of their place of residence? Explain. See *U.S. v. Bishop,* 959 F.2d 820 (9th Cir. 1992).

10. French journalist Alain Clement offered a partial explanation for Americans' increasing reliance on lawsuits to resolve conflicts:

    > Diverse causes explain the growth of the contentious mood in America. One could be called the devaluing of the future. In 1911, the Russian political scientist Moise Ostrgorski wrote, "Confident of the future, Americans manifest a remarkable endurance to an unhappy present, a submissive patience that is willing to bargain about not only civic rights, but even the rights of man."[62]

    a. What does Clement mean?
    b. How do you explain our increased reliance on litigation?

11. In 1982, a security guard was murdered during a robbery of a south Chicago McDonald's. Alton Logan was sentenced to life in prison for that murder. At the same time, two Chicago public defenders, Dale Coventry and Jamie Kunz, were representing Andrew Wilson, who was accused of murdering two police officers. Based on a tip, Coventry and Kunz suspected that Wilson was the actual murderer in the McDonald's case. They questioned Wilson who admitted that he, not Logan, was the murderer. Because of their duties under the attorney–client privilege, Coventry and Kunz felt they could not reveal what they knew. Logan, therefore, went to prison an innocent man, they believed. The public defenders decided to write the story in a notarized affidavit and lock it in a box in case something should happen that would allow them to reveal what they knew. When Wilson died in prison of natural causes in 2008, Coventry and Kunz revealed their client's confession. After 26 years, Logan was released from prison. He was granted a certificate of innocence; in 2013, the city of Chicago agreed to pay Logan $10.25 million.[63]
    a. Why does the legal profession expect lawyers to keep secret their clients' confidential communications?
    b. Had you been Coventry and Kunz, would you have revealed what you knew in order to immediately secure justice for Logan? Explain.

12. On July 5, 1884, four sailors were cast away from their ship in a storm 1,600 miles from the Cape of Good Hope. Their lifeboat contained neither water nor much food. On the 20th day of their ordeal, Dudley and Stevens, without the assistance or agreement of Brooks, cut the throat of the fourth sailor, a 17- or 18-year-old boy. They had not eaten since day 12. Water had been available only occasionally. At the time of the death, the men were probably about 1,000 miles from land. Prior to his death, the boy was lying helplessly in the bottom of the boat. The three surviving sailors ate the boy's remains for four days, at which point they were rescued by a passing boat. They were in a seriously weakened condition.
    a. Were Dudley and Stevens guilty of murder? Explain.
    b. Should Brooks have been charged with a crime for eating the boy's flesh? Explain. See *The Queen v. Dudley and Stephens,* 14 Queen's Bench Division 273 (1884).

13. Tompkins was a citizen of Pennsylvania. While walking on a railroad footpath in that state, he was struck by an object protruding from a passing freight train owned by the Erie Railroad Company, a New York corporation. Tompkins, by virtue of diversity of citizenship, filed a negligence suit against Erie in a New York federal court. Erie argued for the application of Pennsylvania common law, in which case Tompkins would have been treated as a trespasser. Tompkins argued that the absence of a Pennsylvania statute addressing the topic meant that federal common law had to be applied to the case. Should the federal court apply the relevant Pennsylvania state law, or should the court be free to exercise its independent judgment about what the common law of the state is or should be? See *Erie Railroad v. Tompkins,* 304 U.S. 64 (1938).

14. In July 2011, two high-speed trains collided near Wenzhou, China. Shortly after, law offices in Wenzhou were notified by the local judicial bureau and lawyers' association to "immediately report" requests for legal assistance and told not to respond "without authorization."[64]

    In your view, would China benefit from a Western-style approach to litigation? Explain.

15. Boschetto, a California resident, bought a 1964 Ford Galaxie 500XL advertised on eBay from Hansing, a Wisconsin resident. Hansing said the car was in excellent condition, including an "R code" classification. After delivery to California, Boschetto discovered many problems including the fact that the car was not an "R code." The parties could not reach an out-of-court settlement so Boschetto sued. Hansing moved for dismissal of the claim on the grounds of lack of personal jurisdiction. Does the fact that the transaction was conducted via eBay satisfy the jurisdictional requirement? Explain. See *Boschetto v. Hansing,* 539 F.3d 1011 (9th Cir. 2008); cert. den. *Boschetto v. Hansing,* 129 S. Ct. 1318 (2009).

16. University of Chicago law professor Richard Epstein pointed out how quickly Americans turn to legal remedies rather than relying on informal social customs (negotiation, neighborhood groups, simply accepting small losses and disturbances rather than fighting about them) to resolve conflicts. In your view, why are social customs often ineffective in settling disputes in this country? Explain.

17. Judicial reform advocates often argue that the United States should adopt the English rule providing that the losing party in a lawsuit must pay the reasonable litigation expenses of the winner.
    a. In brief, what are the strengths and weaknesses of the English rule?
    b. Would you favor it? Explain. See "Loser Pays, Everyone Wins," *The Wall Street Journal,* December 15, 2010 [**http://online.wsj.com/**].

18. Plaintiff Jonathan Gold was hired to work at defendant Deutsche Bank after completing his MBA degree at New York University. Before beginning employment, Gold signed various documents, including Form U-4 that the National Association of Securities Dealers (NASD) required all registered representatives to sign. Form U-4 provided for arbitration for all employment disputes. Gold was fired after working about one year. He then filed suit claiming sexual harassment based on his sexual orientation. Deutsche Bank moved to compel arbitration. Gold resisted arbitration arguing, among other things, that Form U-4 was too difficult to understand and that it raised questions in his mind.

Gold also showed that Deutsche Bank had certified that it provided Gold with the relevant NASD rules when it had not. Was Gold required to submit his claim to arbitration? Explain. See *Gold v. Deutsche Aktiengesellschaft,* 365 F.3d 144 (2d Cir. 2004); cert. den. *Gold v. Deutsche Aktiengesellschaft,* 543 U.S. 874 (2004).

Notes

1. The World Justice Project, Rule of Law Index 2012–2013 [**http://worldjusticeproject.org/sites /default/files/WJP_Index_Report_2012.pdf**].

2. Tina Susman, "Last Phone Call May Provide Clues in Florida Teen's Shooting Death," *Los Angeles Times,* March 20, 2012 [**http://www.latimes.com**].

3. Lizette Alvarez and Cara Buckley, "Zimmerman Is Acquitted in Trayvon Martin Killing," *The New York Times,* July 13, 2013 [**http://www.nytimes.com**].

4. Robert Leider, "Understanding 'Stand Your Ground'," *The Wall Street Journal,* April 18, 2012, p. A17.

5. Joe Palazzolo and Rob Barry, "More Killings Called Self-Defense," *The Wall Street Journal,* March 31–April 1, 2012, p. A1.

6. Joe Palazzolo, "Study Says 'Stand Your Ground' Laws Increase Homicides," *The Wall Street Journal Law Blog,* June 11, 2012 [**http://blogs.wsj.com/law**].

7. Jack Healy, "Unarmed and Gunned Down by Homeowner in His Castle," *The New York Times,* October 23, 2012 [**http://www.nytimes.com**].

8. National Conference of State Legislatures, Sexting Legislation in 2013 [**http://www.ncsl.org**].

9. *Orlando Sentinel,* "More U.S. Judges Impose Creative Punishments," *The Des Moines Register,* October 29, 2010, p. 10A.

10. E. J. Dionne, Jr., "The Supreme Court's Defense of the Powerful," *The Washington Post,* June 29, 2011 [**http://www.washingtonpost.com/**].

11. Adam Liptak, "Corporations Find a Friend in the Supreme Court," *The New York Times* May 5, 2013 [**http://www/nytimes.com**].

12. David G. Savage, "Justices Have Been Siding with Workers, Underdogs," *latimes.com,* March 13, 2011 [**latimes.com/news/nationworld/nation/la-na-court-unanimous-20110313,0,4601488.story**].

13. John C. Henry, "Do You Know Who Works Here? They Can Change Your Life," *AARP.org /Bulletin,* November 2010, p. 26.

14. Editorial, "Our Constitutional Court," *The New York Times,* November 22, 2010 [**http://www. nytimes.com/**].

15. Ethan Bronner, ""A Dissent by Scalia is Criticized as Political," *The New York Times,* (June 27, 2012) [**http://www.nytimes.com**].

16. Adam Litpak and Allison Kopicki, "Approval Rating for Justices Hits Just 44% in New Poll," *The New York Times,* (June 7, 2012) [**http://www.nytimes.com**].

17. Lincoln Caplan, "A Judge's Warning about the Legitimacy of the Supreme Court," *The New York Times,* September 26, 2010 [**http://www.nytimes.com/**].

18. Editorial, "Case Against Oxy Hits Home," *latimes.com,* December 10, 2010 [**latimes.com /news/opinion/opinionla/la-ed-peru-20101210,0,2576676.story**].

19. *Carijano v. Occidental Petroleum,* 626 F.3d 1137(9th Cir. 2010).

20. *Occidental Petroleum v. Carijano,* 133 S. Ct. 1996 (2013).

21. For an archive of "Spygate" articles, see "Spygate," *The New York Times,* July 12, 2011 [**http:// topics.nytimes.com/**].

22. *Wal-Mart Stores v. Dukes,* 2011 U.S. LEXIS 4567.

23. Andrew W. Volin, "Wal-Mart Wins Again in a Regional Class Action," *Sherman & Howard Blog,* May 31, 2013 [**blog.shermanhoward.com/**].

24. *Comcast Corp. v. Behrend,* 133 S. Ct. 1426 (2013).

25. *American Express Co. v. Italian Colors Restaurant,* 133 S. Ct. 2304 (2013).

26. Steven J. Harper, "The Tyranny of the Billable Hour, *The New York Times* (March 28, 2013) [**http://www.newyorktimes.com**].

27. Peter Latiman, "Settling Fee Dispute, Law Firm Denounces 'Email Humor'," *DealBook* April 17, 2013 [**dealbook.nytimes.com/**].

28. Philip K. Howard, "How Modern Law Makes Us Powerless," *The Wall Street Journal,* January 26, 2009 [**http://online.wsj.com/**].

29. Lyric Wallwork Winik, "Are There Too Many Lawyers?" *Parade,* September 14, 2008, p. 9.

30. Luce Research, "Americans Speak on Lawsuit Abuse: Results of a National Survey," *American Tort Reform Association,* (August 2012) p. 2 [**http://atra.org/sites/default/files/documents/ATRA%20SOL%20Voter%20Survey%20Summary%20FINAL.pdf**]

31. John O'Brien, "Poll: Voters Not Worried about Tort Reform," *LegalNewsline.com,* July 12, 2007 [**http://www.legalnewsline.com/news/197868-poll-voters-not-worried-about-tort-reform**].

32. Milton Bordwin, "Your Company and the Law," *Management Review,* January 2000, p. 58.

33. Majirox News, "Too Many Lawyers in Japan, Says Ministry of Internal Affairs," *Majirroxnews.com* [**www.majirrox.news.com**].

34. Ibid.

35. "Learn How to Become a Walmart Supplier" [**http://corporate.walmart.com/suppliers/**].

36. Larry Cata Backer, "Economic Globalization and the Rise of Efficient Systems of Global Private Lawmaking: Wal-Mart as Global Legislator," 39 *Connecticut Law Review* 1741 (2007).

37. Ibid.

38. "Civil Bench and Jury Trials in State Courts, 2005," U.S. Department of Justice, Bureau of Justice Statistics [**www.bjs.gov**].

39. Ibid.

40. John T. Broderick Jr. and Ronald M. George, "A Nation of Do-It-Yourself Lawyers," *The New York Times,* January 2, 2010 [**http://www.nytimes.com/**].

41. Binyamin Appelbaum, "Investors Put Money on Lawsuits to Get Payouts," *The New York Times,* November 14, 2010 [**http://www.nytimes.com**].

42. Jennifer Smith, "Lawsuit Investors Gain in U.S.," *The Wall Street Journal,* January 13, 2014, p. B7.

43. Ibid.

44. Binyamin Appelbaum, "Lawsuit Loans Add New Risk for the Injured," *The New York Times,* January 16, 2011 [**http://www.nytimes.com/**].

45. Mike Rosen, "Testing Civil Gideon," *California Lawyer*, June 2012 [**www.callawyer.com**].

46. Ibid.

47. This paragraph is derived from "Small Claims Court FAQ," NOLO [**http://www.nolo.com**].

48. Vanessa O'Connell, "At GE, Robo-Lawyers," *The Wall Street Journal,* October 10, 2011 [**online.wsj.com**].

49. Missy Diaz, "Lawyers Are Divided over WhoCanISue.com," *latimes.com,* October 11, 2009 [**http://www.latimes.com/**].

50. "Arbitration: Increasingly, It's Not Over until the Vacatur Motion Fails," *The Wall Street Journal,* February 14, 2011 [**http://blogs.wsj.com/**].

51. Alexander J.S. Colvin, "An Empirical Study of Employment Arbitration: Case Outcomes and Processes," *Journal of Empirical Legal Studies* 8, Issue 1, (March 2011), p. 1.

52. *AT&T Mobility v. Vincent Concepcion,* 131 S. Ct. 1740 (2011).

53. See related proceedings *Geographic Expeditions, Inc. v. Lhotka,* 2010 U.S. LEXIS 6305.

54. "An Economist Out to Be Sued," *Los Angeles Times,* October 8, 1990, p. D1.

55. "Known Exonerations in the United States as of January 1, 2014," National Registry on Exonerations, University of Michigan Law School and Center on Wrongful Convictions, Northwestern University, February 4, 2014 [**https://www.law.umich.edu/special/exoneration /Documents/Exonerations_in_2013_Report.pdf**].

56. Ibid.

57. Dubuque, Iowa Ordinance No. 28-11, March 21, 2011, and Andy Piper, "Police: Ordinance Will ID Derelict Parents," *Dubuque Telegraph Herald,* March 23, 2011 [**http://www.thonline.com /article.cfm?id=315715**].

58. Carolyn Foster Segal, "The Curious Case of Megan Thode," *Inside Higher Ed,* February 19, 2013 [**www.insidehighered.com**].

59. Nora Freeman Engstrom and Robert L. Rabin, "Limiting Damages Limits Justice," *Los Angeles Times,* August 13, 2013, p. A11.

60. Marc Lifsher, "Watchdog Group, Father Begin Medical Malpractice Initiative Campaign," *Los Angeles Times,* July 25, 2013 [**www.latimes.com**].

61. Warren Avis, "Court before Justice," *The New York Times,* July 21, 1978, p. 25.

62. Alain Clement, "Judges, Lawyers Are the Ruling Class in U.S. Society," *The Washington Post,* August 22, 1980, p. A25.

63. Associated Press, "Illinois Man Imprisoned for 26 Years Declared Innocent," *Springfield State Journal-Register,* April 17, 2009 [**http://www.sj-r.com/**]; Fran Speilman, "Chicago to Pay $10.25 Million in Another Burge Case," *Chicago Sun-Times,* January 14, 2013 [**www.suntimes .com**]; and "26-Year Secret Kept Innocent Man in Prison," *60 Minutes,* March 8, 2008 [**http:// truthinjustice.org/alton-logan.htm**].

64. Yu Hua, "In China, the Grievances Keep Coming," *The New York Times,* January 1, 2012 [**www.nytimes.com**].

CHAPTER FIVE

Constitutional Law and the Bill of Rights

After completing this chapter, students will be able to:

1. Recognize the purposes of the U.S. Constitution.

2. Describe the separation of powers under the U.S. Constitution.

3. Identify the freedoms protected under the First Amendment.

4. Describe the powerful role the Bill of Rights plays in protecting personal freedoms.

5. Discuss the differences between First Amendment protections of commercial speech versus political speech.

6. Explain the "exclusionary rule."

7. Describe some of the issues arising under the Fourth Amendment "search and seizure" rules.

8. Describe the law of the Fifth Amendment "Takings Clause" and the property rights controversy associated with it.

9. Compare and contrast substantive due process and procedural due process.

10. Identify some examples of the impact of the Equal Protection Clause on business and society.

We the people of the United States, in order to form a more perfect union, establish justice, insure domestic tranquility, provide for the common defense, promote the general welfare, and secure the blessings of liberty to ourselves and our posterity, do ordain and establish this Constitution for the United States of America.

The Preamble to the United States Constitution is both inspiring and touching in its expression of the founders' idealistic goals for America. In reading the Preamble, we should reflect on the dream of America and the Constitution's role in molding and protecting an entirely new image of a nation. That we continue to be guided, more than 220 years later, by the Constitutions rather few words is testimony to the brilliance and wisdom of its creators and to Americans' determination to build a free, democratic, just society. The U.S. Constitution is a remarkable document, so powerful in its ideas and images that it has helped shape the entire world. (See the Constitution in Appendix A at the back of this text.)

Creating a Constitution—The United States

You may recall that the Constitution grew out of the 1778 Articles of Confederation. The Articles contemplated a "firm league of friendship," but each state was to maintain its "sovereignty, freedom, and independence." The Articles soon proved faulty. Seven years of war had basically bankrupted the colonies. Currency was largely worthless. The 13 new states fought over economic resources, interstate disputes were routine, and the federal union that emerged under the Articles of Confederation had little real authority. As a result of this turmoil, and in an effort to strengthen the Articles, the Constitutional Convention was called to order in Philadelphia on May 25, 1787.

The decision to convene the Convention may have been a first in world history in that the state leaders themselves acknowledged that the existing federal government was faulty, the citizenry calmly talked things over, violence was avoided, and the decision was made to go forward with the Convention. In the hot Philadelphia summer, with windows and curtains closed to assure secrecy (as a means of encouraging open debate), the often chubby and usually heavily clothed delegates sweated their way toward a new government. All 55 delegates, our Founding Fathers, were white males, and most of them were wealthy landowners, but they were also immensely talented with a wide range of interests and experiences.

> All 55 delegates, our Founding Fathers, were white males.

The delegates agreed that a stronger central government was needed, but they were split on just how far that notion should go. Virginia, led by the brilliant James Madison, favored a dominant central government with greatly diminished state authority. Alexander Hamilton wanted to go further yet by, among other things, instituting the presidency as a lifetime office. On the other hand, several states, led by New Jersey, wanted to retain strong states' rights. After weeks of debate, a middle ground began to emerge that led toward our current balance of power between big states and small states and between all of the states and the federal government. In the end, the delegates reached consensus on a Constitution that guaranteed the revolutionary notion of rule by the people.

On September 17, 1787, the great document, one of the most influential expressions in human history, was formally signed. Following bitter disputes in some states, the Constitution was ratified and the new government haltingly moved forward under the leadership of George Washington and John Adams.[1] [For links to national constitutions around the globe, see **http://confinder.richmond.edu**]

A Right to Bear Arms

Addressing one of the most contentious questions in American constitutional history, the U.S. Supreme Court in 2008 ruled 5–4 that the Second Amendment guarantees individual Americans a fundamental right to bear arms. The Supreme Court's four conservative justices, joined by the more moderate Justice Kennedy, ruled that individuals have a constitutional right to keep loaded arms for self-defense, at least in the home. The majority view was based on its reading of the historical record associated with the Second Amendment, while the four dissenting, liberal justices argued that the Second Amendment guaranteed only a collective right to bear arms in a militia.

The decision struck down a District of Columbia law that effectively banned handgun possession. Security guard Dick Heller applied for and was denied a permit for a handgun in his home located in a dangerous Washington, D.C. neighborhood. He sued the District arguing that the gun ban violated his individual rights under the Second Amendment. The Court did preserve the constitutionality of "reasonable" gun regulations and Justice Scalia, writing for the majority, said nothing in the ruling should "cast doubt on long-standing prohibitions on the possession of firearms by felons or the mentally ill, or laws forbidding the carrying of firearms in sensitive places such as schools and government buildings, or laws imposing conditions and qualifications on the commercial sale of arms." "Dangerous and unusual" weapons also could be banned.

In its 2010 *McDonald v. Chicago* decision,[2] the Supreme Court extended its *Heller* reasoning (applying only to federal jurisdictions) to the states and cities. Much more litigation remains. Lower court decisions are thus far split on the crucial question of whether states may lawfully bar or strictly limit carrying guns in public for self-defense. Recent mass murders in a Wisconsin Sikh temple, in an Aurora, Colorado, movie theater, and at Sandy Hook Elementary School in Newtown, Connecticut, have energized the national debate over gun control. But according to a 2012 Gallup Poll, a record 74 percent of Americans support the right to own a handgun,[3] and Congress rejected new gun control measures following the Sandy Hook shootings.

Questions

1. As you interpret the Second Amendment, did the Supreme Court reach a *correct* decision in the *Heller* case? Explain.

2. In Chicago, 32 public school students died of gunshot wounds in 2009.[4] In all of Australia in 2008, by contrast, 30 people died by gun homicide.[5] As a matter of public policy, did the Supreme Court reach a *wise* decision in the *Heller* case? Explain.

3. Six states specifically permit the concealed carrying of weapons on campus by students and others with the remaining states about evenly split between those that ban the concealed carrying of weapons on college campuses and those that leave the decision to the school. What are your thoughts about students and faculty members carrying guns on your campus?

Sources: District of Columbia v. Dick Anthony Heller, 2008 U.S. LEXIS 5268; and Dina Temple-Raston, "Supreme Court: Individuals Have Right to Bear Arms," National Public Radio, June 27, 2008 [**http://www.npr.org/ templates/story.php?storyId=91911807**].

Structure and Purpose

The Preamble identifies certain goals for our society, such as unity (among the various states), justice, domestic tranquility (peace), defense from outsiders, increasing general welfare, and liberty. Article I creates Congress and enumerates its powers. Article I, Section 8, Clause 3 is particularly important because it gives Congress the power to regulate commerce (the Commerce Clause). Article II sets up the executive branch, headed by the president, while Article III establishes the court system. Articles IV and VI, as well as the 14th Amendment, address the relationship between the federal government and the states. Article VI provides in Clause 2 (the Supremacy Clause) for the supremacy of federal law over state law. Article V provides for amendments to the Constitution. The first 10 amendments, known as the Bill of Rights, were ratified by the states and put into effect in 1791. The remaining 17 amendments (11 through 27) were adopted at various times from 1798 through 1992.

From this review we can see that the Constitution serves a number of broad roles:

1. It establishes a national government.
2. It controls the relationship between the national government and the government of the states.
3. It defines and preserves personal liberty.
4. It contains provisions to enable the government to perpetuate itself.[6]

The Founding Fathers—Should We Move On?

Author Mark Kurlansky argues that the Founding Fathers' great accomplishment is losing its luster:

> I am sick and tired of the founding fathers and all their intents. The real American question of our times is how our country in a little over 200 years sank from the great hope to the most backward democracy in the West. The U.S. offers the worst healthcare program, one of the worst public school systems and the worst benefits for workers. The margin between rich and poor has been growing precipitously while it has been decreasing in Europe. Among the great democracies, we use military might less cautiously, show less respect for international law and are the stumbling block in international environmental cooperation. Few informed people look to the United States anymore for progressive ideas. We ought to do something. Instead, we keep worrying about the vision of a bunch of sexist, slave-owning 18th century white men in wigs and breeches.

Question

As noted on the first page of this chapter, the United States Constitution has been one of the most influential documents in global history. In recent decades, however, critics such as Kurlansky have criticized our Constitution for being out of touch with the times. They criticize our distinguished system of checks and balances as a source of the current political gridlock in Washington, and they argue for a Constitution that can more easily be amended, among other complaints. They point to empirical evidence showing that constitutional similarities between other nations and the United States have plunged while emulation of the Canadian constitution, in particular, has soared. Canada's charter guarantees equal rights for women and people with disabilities, permits affirmative action, and requires notice of their rights to those who are arrested. Those rights are balanced against "such reasonable limits" as "can be demonstrably justified in a free and democratic society." Other national constitutions protect the right to food, education, and health care.

Do you think our Constitution is out of touch with contemporary times and should specifically be amended to guarantee the personal rights noted above? Explain.

Source: Mark Kurlansky, "WWFFD? Who Cares," *Los Angeles Times,* July 4, 2006 [**http://www.latimes. com /news/opinion/la-oe-kurlansky4jul04,0,2811373.story?track=totext**].

Government Power and Constitutional Restraints

Among other goals, the Constitution was designed to protect the citizenry from the government. The Constitution does not protect citizens from purely private concentrations of power, such as large corporations. In fact, corporations themselves are often entitled to the protections of the Constitution. (Remember the *Citizens United* discussion in Chapter 3.) The Constitution divides governmental power between the federal and state governments. Congressional authority is formally limited to certain *enumerated powers* (Article I, Section 8), such as the authority to regulate commerce. The 10th Amendment provides that all power not expressly accorded to the federal government in the Constitution resides in the states or the people. Certain constitutional checks or restraints, including the Bill of Rights, limit how far Congress can reach even within its enumerated powers. In practice, however, those enumerated powers have been expansively interpreted, giving Congress extensive authority in American life. Furthermore, in the landmark 1819 Supreme Court decision, *McCulloch v. Maryland,*[7] the U.S. Supreme Court interpreted the Necessary and Proper Clause (Article I, Section 8) to afford Congress those implied powers necessary to execute the enumerated powers, thus achieving a workable national government. The *McCulloch* court also ruled that the Constitution's Supremacy Clause (Article VI—"This Constitution and the Laws of the United States . . . shall be the Supreme Law of the Land.") nullifies state action that conflicts with federal law. Thus, in one sweeping decision, the Supreme Court dramatically expanded the power of Congress and certified the federal government's superior authority relative to the states.

Too Much Government?

Has that federal power and regulation gone too far? Massive federal intervention in health care, to combat the "Great Recession," to deal with the subprime mortgage crisis, and to reform banking practices (see Chapter 8) generated renewed pleas for restraints on an "overreaching" federal government. The Tea Party movement emerged in 2009, and a heated national debate has ensued about the appropriate balance between individual rights as expressed in the free market versus an interventionist federal government designed to correct market failures and protect those least able to care for themselves.

> The "Tea Party" movement emerged.

Separation of Powers

As a further means of controlling the power of government, the Constitution sets up the three federal branches and provides mechanisms for them to act as checks and balances on each other. The President, Congress, and the courts each have specialized areas of authority, as provided for by the Constitution. Congress has the sole power to legislate at the federal level, whereas the president, among other things, executes laws, makes treaties, and commands the armed forces; the Supreme Court and the inferior courts have judicial authority at the federal level. The result is a system of separation of powers designed to prevent too much authority from residing in any one branch. Thus, the president has the power to veto acts of Congress; those vetoes can be overridden by a two-thirds vote of each house, and the judiciary can find those acts unconstitutional.

The role of the judiciary has been a matter of particular controversy in recent years. The historic 1803 *Marbury v. Madison* decision[8] was the first time the Supreme Court had declared an act of Congress unconstitutional, and the decision also established the principle of judicial review; that is, the power of the courts to consider and, if necessary, invalidate congressional and executive branch decisions. Although neither of those powers was expressly provided for in the Constitution, the Court considered them to be implicit in the legal structure created by the Constitution. Critics today argue that the *Marbury* reasoning has been stretched too far and that, in effect, courts have been making law, rather than merely interpreting it. Those critics say that federal and state judicial decisions finding a "constitutional right" to, for example, abortion or same-sex marriage, have reduced the authority of our directly elected legislators and placed too much power in the hands of jurists who are necessarily somewhat removed from the weight of public opinion.[9] On the other hand, an aggressive judiciary has played a crucial role in the advance of justice and the protection of personal freedom. [For the National Constitution Center, see **http://www.constitutioncenter.org**]

Questions

1. As noted, the Constitution does not expressly authorize judicial review. Should we, therefore, assume that the framers of the Constitution did not intend to afford that power to the courts?
2. In your view, do the courts have too much power in our lives? Explain.

Federalism

The U.S. government is built on *federalism* principles; that is, the Constitution provides for shared power among national, state, and local governments. A primary role of the Constitution is to balance central federal authority with dispersed state power. The American Civil War was provoked in part because of differing conceptions of federalism. Southerners held the view, labeled *states rights*, that each state was entitled to make its own policy decisions about crucial matters such as slavery, while Northerners favored a strong central government. That constitutional divide over federalism persists today. Many "conservative" Americans distrust big government and favor bringing power closer to the people. They think the federal government has often exercised authority beyond its express constitutional powers. "Liberals," on the other hand, tend to fear local biases and favor a more unified national approach to issues such as regulation of business, educational policy, medical care, and civil rights.

The Constitution and the New Federalism

After decades of interpreting the Constitution in a flexible, expansive manner that accorded great power to the federal government, the Supreme Court in the mid-1990s revisited the federal–state balance of power with some decisions curbing federal authority. No major federal initiative was struck down, but the Court signaled legislators and lower courts to look more closely at the federal–state level.

The new federalism expressed itself in a landmark 2013 U.S. Supreme Court decision, *Shelby County v. Holder,*[10] that challenged the constitutionality of the federal Voting Rights Act of 1965 which, among other things, subjected nine mostly southern states to

Long history of discrimination in voting practices.

federal supervision of their election processes because of a long history of discrimination against minorities in voting practices. Those states often gerrymandered election districts and imposed "voter integrity" rules (e.g., literacy tests, character standards, and onerous identification requirements) that officially were designed to assure honesty in elections, but often had sought to exclude minorities from voting.

Under the 1965 act any change to voting rules in the covered states required "preclearance" from the federal government. Shelby County, Alabama, challenged the Voting Rights Act, claiming, in brief, that in reauthorizing the act in 2006, Congress exceeded its constitutional authority and in so doing violated state and local rights. By a 5–4 vote, divided on familiar conservative–liberal grounds, the Supreme Court ruled for Shelby County saying that Section 4(b) of the act, determining which jurisdictions' voting practices were tainted by discrimination and thus required pre-clearance, was based on 40-year-old discrimination data and thus did not necessarily speak to current conditions. The Supreme Court acknowledged the effectiveness of the act in reducing voting discrimination, but said that discriminatory practices and the states that use them have changed and Congress must keep the law up to date. The act and its supporting data can, of course, be revisited, but given Congress's current fractures, analysts do not expect quick action. A number of southern states rushed to enforce or enact new restrictions on voting following the *Shelby County* decision. In response, Attorney General Eric Holder in 2013 filed a federal suit asking that Texas get federal permission before making election law changes over the next 10 years.[11]

Like the voting rights struggle, we are in the midst of a furious immigration dispute pitting global federal control versus individual states that want to address their specific problems through their own legislation. On the other side of the coin, when a state like California, known for its aggressive rules on workplace safety, consumer protection, and environmental quality, imposes new restrictions, the business community may fight back in Washington, D.C. by seeking federal laws to make uniform rules for all the states, thus restraining or preempting California's protective measures.[12]

Question

California rules, for example, prohibit the sale of eggs laid by hens confined to very small cages. What issues would you cite if Congress were to respond to the California standards by considering new federal rules?

The Constitution, the Bill of Rights, and Business

The Constitution and, in particular, the Commerce Clause profoundly shape the practice of American business. Indeed, in some important ways, the Constitution is a commercial document reflecting the economic interests of the framers. We will defer further discussion of the Commerce Clause and the Supremacy Clause until Chapter 8. In this chapter, we will devote our attention primarily to the Bill of Rights, which serves to limit the powers of the federal government and the states. When we think of the Bill of Rights, corporations ordinarily do not come to mind. Extensive litigation in recent years, however, serves notice that the relationship between the corporate "person" and the fundamental freedoms is both important and unclear.

The Bill of Rights protects our personal freedoms (speech, religion, and more) from encroachment by the federal government. Furthermore, the Supreme Court has ruled that the Due Process Clause of the 14th Amendment, which is directed at the states, absorbs or incorporates those fundamental freedoms and protects them against intrusion by state governments. [For the "Guide to Law Online," prepared by the U.S. Law Library of Congress, see **http://www.loc.gov/law/help/guide.php**]

The First Amendment

> Congress shall make no law respecting an establishment of religion, or prohibiting the free exercise thereof; or abridging the freedom of speech, or the press; or the right of the people peaceably to assemble, and to petition the Government for a redress of grievances.

These few words constitute one of the most powerful and noble utterances in history. Much of the magnificence that we often associate with America is embodied in the protections of the First Amendment. Surely we must feel some sense of wonder that our more than 316 million independent citizens continue to rely on that sentence as a cornerstone of American life. [For the First Amendment Center, see **http://www. firstamendmentcenter.org/**]

1. Freedom of Religion

The First Amendment forbids (1) the establishment of an official state religion (the Establishment Clause) and (2) undue state interference with religious practice (the Free Exercise Clause). Government may neither encourage nor discourage the practice of religion generally, nor may it give preference to one religion over another. Broadly, the idea of the First Amendment is to maintain a separation between church and state. The precise boundary of that separation, however, has become one of the more contentious social issues in contemporary life. Prayer in the schools and Ten Commandment displays have received extensive publicity, but the debate is widespread. [For the Freedom Forum database on the First Amendment, see **http://www.freedomforum.org**]

Official State Religion?

North Carolina state legislators introduced a resolution in 2013 asserting the state has a right to declare an official state religion (presumably Christianity). The bill apparently was a response to an American Civil Liberties Union lawsuit saying that Rowan County was violating the First Amendment by opening most of its meetings with a prayer. (A federal court of appeals in 2011 had ruled that another North Carolina county's public prayers did violate the First Amendment.)[13] The bill was quickly withdrawn by the state Speaker of the House. The bill's sponsors employed reasoning that has gained some currency on the right, namely that the Establishment Clause applies only to the federal government, not to the states. A series of cases, however, seems to have established the First Amendment application to state governments.[14]

A 2013 national poll found that 34 percent of Americans would favor establishing Christianity as the official state religion in their own state, and 32 percent favor a constitutional amendment that would make Christianity the nation's official religion.

Source: Rick Ungar, North Carolina Religion Bill Killed—But One Third of Americans Want Christianity as Official Religion of USA," *Forbes,* April 7, 2013 [**http://www.forbes.com/**].

God, the Pledge, and Currency

Addressing two long-standing sources of constitutional ferment, three-judge panels of the Ninth U.S. Circuit Court of Appeals in 2010 ruled that the use of the words "Under God" in the Pledge of Allegiance and "In God We Trust" on U.S. currency do not violate the separation of church and state principles of the First Amendment.

An atheist, Michael Newdow, said those references amount to an endorsement of religion, thus violating the Establishment Clause of the First Amendment. Newdow argued that the phrase "Under God" was placed in the pledge for religious purposes. Indeed, the pledge was amended in 1954 to include the words "Under God," and some members of Congress, at the time, said it was needed to distinguish the United States from "Godless Communists."[15] The panel, however, saw the Pledge of Allegiance as an expression of American ideals rather than as a religious endorsement. Students are not required to recite the pledge.[16] As to currency, a separate panel said that the phrase "In God We Trust" is simply patriotic and ceremonial and has nothing to do with the establishment of religion.[17]

Godless Communists.

God and Student Organizations

The University of California Hastings College of the Law refused to recognize a student organization, the Christian Legal Society (CLS). Hastings said the group's faith-based rules discriminate against gays, lesbians, and others who do not share the group's religious beliefs. The organization's rules require members to pledge they will not engage in a "sexually immoral lifestyle" including "all acts of sexual conduct outside God's design for marriage between one man and one woman." Thus to Hastings officials, the Pledge represented discrimination based on religion and sexual orientation, whereas CLS members regarded it as an expression of faith. CLS challenged Hastings's policy as a violation of the member students' First Amendment rights to freedom of religion, speech, and association. The U.S. Supreme Court, by a 5–4 margin, ruled in 2010 that the students' constitutional rights were not violated in that the university policy was a reasonable, viewpoint-neutral condition on access to student recognition in a public university. The majority reasoned that Hastings was concerned about the group's exclusionary conduct rather than its religious beliefs. That is, all student groups must be open to all students. Dissenting justices said the decision supported suppression of unpopular and politically incorrect speech.[18]

According to *The Huffington Post,* 41 InterVarsity Christian Fellowship campus chapters say they were challenged following the CLS decision (many of those disputes were resolved). Critics point out that fraternities and sororities are allowed to discriminate based on gender, but overall, campus religious organizations seem to be adapting to the changing legal landscape.[19]

Veils and French Values

France, in 2011, began enforcing its new law forbidding, with some exceptions, the wearing of a garment in public that hides the wearer's face. The law was promoted as a matter of security and of cultural assimilation while it was assailed as an affront to the Muslim faith and a political move designed to appeal to voters worried about threats to traditional European values and culture. Only an estimated 2,000 women of the 5 million French Muslims are believed to wear burqas or niqabs covering the face.

Following a little more than one year of experience with the veil law, France reported that 425 women had been fined $188 each, and 66 others had received warnings. Police say they rarely enforce the law because they do not want to enflame existing tensions, but some Muslim women believe the law stigmatizes them and prevents them from moving about freely.

Sources: Robert Marquand, "Face Veil Ban: Will France Take a Hard Line?" *The Christian Science Monitor,* April 11, 2011 [**http://www.csmonitor.com/**]; and Steven Erlanger and Elvire Camus, "In a Ban, a Measure of European Tolerance," *The New York Times,* September 1, 2012 [**http://www.nytimes.com/**].

2. Freedom of Speech

Hustler Magazine publisher Larry Flynt: "If the First Amendment will protect a scumbag like me, then it will protect all of you. Because I am the worst."[20]

Freedom of speech is the primary guarantor of the American approach to life. Not only is it indispensable to democracy and personal dignity, but Americans believe that the free expression of ideas is the most likely path to the best ideas. We believe in a marketplace of ideas just as we believe in a marketplace of goods.

> We cannot freely yell "Fire" in a crowded theater.

Freedom of speech is not absolute. Clearly we cannot freely make slanderous statements about others, publicly utter obscenities at will, speak "fighting words" that are likely to produce a clear and present danger of violence, or yell "Fire" in a crowded theater.

At the same time, in general, the state cannot tell us what we can say; that is, the state cannot, for the most part, regulate the *content* of our speech. On the other hand, the state does have greater authority to regulate the *context* of that speech; that is, the state may be able to restrict where, when, and how we say certain things if that regulation is necessary to preserve compelling state interests. We have broad free speech rights in so-called *public forums* such as downtown business districts, parks, college campuses, and public plazas. Even in those places, however, the state may need to impose reasonable time and manner regulations. Thus, although the Ku Klux Klan can express hatred for black people (the content of the message), the state may restrict where and when and how those expressions are made (the context of the message) if necessary for the public safety. [For freedom of speech links, see **http://gjs.net/freetalk.htm**]

What Is Expression?

Expression is not limited to oral and written utterances. Freedom of speech clearly extends to messages not communicated with words. Disrobing, for example, might well constitute expression under some conditions. In *Tinker v. Des Moines School District,* one of the leading free speech cases in American history, the U.S. Supreme Court found First Amendment protection for the wearing of a black armband to a high school as a protest against the Vietnam War where no evidence of disruption was presented.[21]

Free Speech Analysis

How do we decide when the government has violated speech rights? The courts have taken numerous approaches to that question. We will look briefly at cases involving content and context issues. Another tool frequently employed by the courts is the *balancing test,* where the judges must try to weigh the interests of the state against the expressive rights of the individual.

Content: Vile Words   One of the most controversial Supreme Court cases of recent years involved the Topeka, Kansas, Westboro Baptist Church and its practice of protesting at the funerals of American soldiers killed in service. Pastor Fred W. Phelps and his small congregation, most of whom are family members, contend that battlefield deaths are God's punishment for

America's sins, including homosexuality. The funeral protests include signs displaying messages such as "Thank God for dead soldiers," and "God Hates Fags." Pastor Phelps and his family picketed the 2006 funeral of Matthew Snyder, a Marine who had been killed in Iraq.

God's punishment for America's sins.

Snyder's father sued Phelps and Westboro and won a $10.9 million damage award (reduced by the judge to $5 million) based on his claims of invasion of privacy and intentional infliction of emotional distress. That decision was reversed on appeal, and the case reached the U.S. Supreme Court in 2011 where the church's First Amendment freedom of expression argument prevailed by an 8–1 margin.[22] The majority ruled that the Westboro protests addressed matters of public importance on a public street at a distance from the funeral (approximately 1,000 feet) specified by authorities. The picketing was quiet and without violence.

Thus, the Court's unpopular decision affirmed the longstanding position that the government ordinarily cannot restrict speech based on its content, however tasteless or valueless. As lawyer and commentator Adam Cohen said about the Westboro speech, "We defend it not because these ideas are particularly worthy of being protected, but because all ideas, even the most loathsome, are."[23] Recent federal legislation requires demonstrators to be at least 300 feet from military funerals from two hours before to two hours after the ceremonies.

Context: Panhandling   Courts have consistently concluded that begging for money on the street constitutes expression. The context of the begging, that is, when, where, and how the begging is conducted may affect its constitutionality. Thus, for example, some restraints on panhandling *in the street at stop signs* or on *aggressive* panhandling might well be permissible. The content of the message (begging) is not restricted, but for compelling reasons, authorities might lawfully shift the time, place, or manner of the expression.

Balancing Interests: Speech at School   Joseph Frederick was across the street from his school with many other students watching, with school permission, an Olympic torch parade when Frederick, a Juneau, Alaska, high school senior, and some friends unfurled a large banner reading "Bong Hits 4 Jesus." The banner was a prank designed to attract attention from television cameras. The school principal, Deborah Morse, told Frederick to lower the banner. He refused, and he was suspended from school. Frederick sued, and the case reached the

"Bong Hits 4 Jesus."

U.S. Supreme Court. Does the First Amendment protect Frederick? [See *Deborah Morse v. Joseph Frederick,* 127 S.Ct. 2618 (2007); and Mark W. Cordes, "Making Sense of High School School Speech after *Morse v. Frederick,*" 17 *Wm. & Mary Bill Rts. J.* 657 (2009)]

Public Sector Workers Off the Job? On the Job?

Remember that the Constitution and Bill of Rights protect us from the government but not from, for example, our corporate employer. On the other hand, the First Amendment does generally shield *public-sector* workers' *off-the-job* expressions when speaking as citizens about matters of public concern. Nonetheless, employer restrictions necessary to effective operation of the government enterprise may sometimes be permissible, as illustrated by the 2008 dismissal of Crystal Dixon, an African-American woman and the University of Toledo's interim associate vice president for human resources. Dixon wrote, in response to another commentary and during off-work hours, an op-ed column in the *Toledo Free Press* newspaper in which she said, among other things, that homosexuals should not be considered civil rights victims because they choose their lifestyle whereas race is a matter of genetics. Dixon's comments did not mention her job. Soon thereafter Dixon was fired because her views were inconsistent with established university goals and values, including its diversity policies. Dixon sued, claiming, among other things, that her free speech rights were violated. In 2012, the Sixth Circuit Federal Court of Appeals ruled against Dixon, reasoning that the university's interest in efficient, effective operations outweighed Dixon's First Amendment rights since she was a university policy maker who spoke on a policy related to her position.[24]

> Homosexuals should not be considered civil rights victims.

Government employees' free speech rights are substantially limited *on the job.* Los Angeles Deputy District Attorney Richard Ceballos lost his job in a whistle-blowing episode. Ceballos sued; the U.S. Supreme Court in 2006 ruled that government employees who speak out "pursuant to their official duties" are speaking as employees, not citizens, and therefore are not protected by the First Amendment. From discipline, regardless of the content of their message. The Court pointed to the government's need for efficiency and order in its workplace.[25] In 2014, the United States Supreme Court clarified that public workers act as citizens when they testify under oath; therefore, the First Amendment protects them from retaliation based on their testimony.

Politically Correct Speech

We are largely free of government restraints on what we can say, but should it be so? Is free speech often too hurtful to be tolerated? In 2013, celebrity chef Paula Deen lost her Food Network job and business relationships with J. C. Penney, Sears, Target, and others when she acknowledged that she had, in the past, used the "N word" in remarks to others. New editions of the Mark Twain novels *Adventures of Huckleberry Finn* and *Tom Sawyer* have recently been published with the "N-word" being replaced by the word "slave" in an effort to avoid disturbing readers. Disputes about offensive language often arise in university life where the law requires policies to curb and punish civil rights violations, including racial and sexual harassment. As a result, many universities have "speech codes" of one form or another designed to stop hate speech, harassment, bullying, and other offensive conduct. In 2013, the federal Departments of Justice and Education issued a "blueprint" for colleges nationwide that, according to critics, redefines sexual harassment to include "unwelcome conduct of a sexual nature."[26] The breadth and vagueness of that phrase and other elements of the blueprint caused U.S. Senator John McCain (R-AZ) to write to U.S. Attorney General Eric Holder asking, among other things, if sexual harassment might arise from, for example, a professor showing a movie with sexual content, a student overhearing a joke with sexual content, or a student asking another student for a date.[27] The government has indicated that the blueprint is designed to help students feel comfortable in reporting harassment, and it is not intended to alter legal standards for establishing unlawful harassment (see Chapter 13). The federal blueprint and campus speech codes are designed to maintain safe, civil learning environments that embrace diverse cultures, but critics argue that the restraints are unconsti-

> Many universities have "speech codes."

tutional and that they amount to a demand for politically correct speech, that is, speech that avoids hurtful words.

Yale   Complaints of a hostile sexual environment and intimidation of female students caused Yale University in 2011 to impose a five-year ban on all campus activities for a prestigious fraternity that counts both Bush presidents among its alumni. One of the complaints involved the fraternity's pledges chanting, "No means yes! Yes means anal!" outside a women's dormitory area. Other, more individualized and more threatening concerns were also raised. Following a federal investigation, Yale agreed to changes in its harassment policy and reached a settlement that did not involve disciplinary action.[28] To what extent should university officials and the government be able to curb student speech, however infantile and offensive, in order to achieve a laudable goal?

> "The right to provoke, offend, and shock lies at the core of the First Amendment."

Maricopa CCC   A number of university speech codes have been invalidated as violations of First Amendment rights.[29] Recently, a Maricopa County Community College (Arizona) math instructor won a Ninth Circuit U.S. Court of Appeals decision involving his right to send racially charged e-mails over the school district–maintained server to all employees with an e-mail address. Professor Walter Kehowski sent three messages declaring, for example, that: "It's time to acknowledge and celebrate the superiority of Western Civilization." On his university-maintained website, he said, "[T]he only immigration reform imperative is preservation of White majority (*sic*)." A group of Hispanic employees then sued the school district claiming that it had failed to properly respond to Kehowski's remarks, thus allowing the creation of a hostile work environment. The Court of Appeals, however, ruled that the e-mails addressed matters of public concern and were protected by the First Amendment and thus could not constitute illegal harassment. The Court did note that some workplace harassment, such as racial insults or sexual advances toward particular individuals, may be prohibited because it lacks the expressive quality of speech directed toward a larger audience.[30]

"Be Happy, Not Gay"

Following a day designated to show support for gays and lesbians at her high school in Naperville, Illinois, student Heidi Zamecnik wore a T-shirt to school displaying the expression "Be Happy, Not Gay." The school's dean forbade the expression at the school. Another student, Alexander Nuxoll, unsuccessfully sought to wear a similar shirt. Both students objected to homosexuality on religious grounds. The two students subsequently sued the school for infringing their free speech rights. The Seventh Circuit U.S. Circuit Court of Appeals reasoned that the forbidden expression did not constitute "fighting words" or some other recognized First Amendment exception and ruled that the students had a right to wear the shirts and express their opinions.

Judge Richard Posner said:

> [A] school that permits advocacy of the rights of homosexual students cannot be allowed to stifle criticism of homosexuality. The school argued (and still argues) that

banning "Be Happy, Not Gay" was just a matter of protecting the "rights" of the students against whom derogatory comments are directed. But people in our society do not have a legal right to prevent criticism of their beliefs or even their way of life.

Source: *Zamecnik and Nuxoll v. Indian Prairie School District,* 636 F.3d 874 (7th Cir. 2011).

Ole Miss   Notwithstanding decisions such as *Maricopa CCC*, colleges and universities have sometimes been accorded considerable latitude in dealing with speech issues. The Fifth Circuit Court of Appeals, for example, upheld the right of the University of Mississippi to ban flags, including the Confederate flag, at campus events.[31] Specifically banning only the Confederate flag presumably would not have met with the Court's approval.

George Mason   Many First Amendment scholars believe the correct antidote to hate speech is simply more speech; that is, they place their faith in the marketplace of ideas rather than in rules, however well intended. The decision that follows demonstrates the First Amendment's role in resolving claims of racism, sexism, and general insensitivity springing from a George Mason University fraternity's "ugly woman contest." [For a vigorous critique of campus "political correctness," see the Foundation for Individual Rights in Education at **http://thefire.org/**]

LEGAL BRIEFCASE

IOTA XI Chapter v. George Mason University
993 F.2d 386 (4th Cir. 1993)

Senior Circuit Judge Sprouse

George Mason University appeals from a summary judgment granted by the district court to the IOTA XI Chapter of Sigma Chi Fraternity in its action for declaratory judgment and an injunction seeking to nullify sanctions imposed on it by the University because it conducted an "ugly woman contest" with racist and sexist overtones.

I

Sigma Chi has for two years held an annual "Derby Days" event, planned and conducted both as entertainment and as a source of funds for donations to charity. The "ugly woman contest," held on April 4, 1991, was one of the "Derby Days" events. The Fraternity staged the contest in the cafeteria of the student union. As part of the contest, eighteen Fraternity members were assigned to one of six sorority teams cooperating in

events. The involved Fraternity members appeared in the contest dressed as caricatures of different types of women, including one member dressed as an offensive caricature of a black woman. He was painted black and wore stringy, black hair decorated with curlers, and his outfit was stuffed with pillows to exaggerate a woman's breasts and buttocks. He spoke in slang to parody African-Americans.

There is no direct evidence in the record concerning the subjective intent of the Fraternity members who conducted the contest. The Fraternity, which later apologized to the University officials for the presentation, conceded during the litigation that the contest was sophomoric and offensive.

Following the contest, a number of students protested to the University that the skit had been objectionably sexist and racist. Two hundred forty-seven students, many of them members of the foreign or minority student body, executed a petition, which stated, "[W]e are condemning the racist and sexist implications of this event in which male members dressed as women. One man in particular wore a black face, portraying a negative stereotype of black women."

Dean for Student Services Kenneth Bumgarner discussed the situation with representatives of the objecting students [and] student representatives of Sigma Chi. [The University decided to impose sanctions on Sigma Chi including] suspension from [most] activities for the rest of the 1991 spring semester and a two-year prohibition. . . .

On June 5, 1991, Sigma Chi brought this action against the University and Dean Bumgarner. It requested declaratory judgment and injunctive relief to nullify the sanctions as violative of the First and Fourteenth Amendments. Sigma Chi moved for summary judgment on its First Amendment claims on June 28, 1991.

. . . University President George W. Johnson . . . presented the "mission statement" of the University:

*   *   *   *   *

(3) George Mason University is committed to promoting a culturally and racially diverse student body. . . . Education here is not limited to the classroom.

(4) We are committed to teaching the values of equal opportunity and equal treatment, respect for diversity, and individual dignity.

(5) Our mission also includes achieving the goals set forth in our affirmative action plan, a plan incorporating affirmative steps designed to attract and retain minorities to this campus.

*   *   *   *   *

(7) George Mason University is a state institution of higher education and a recipient of federal funds.

*   *   *   *   *

The district court granted summary judgment to Sigma Chi on its First Amendment claim, 773 F.Supp. 792 (E.D. Va. 1991).

II (OMITTED-ED.)

III

We initially face the task of deciding whether Sigma Chi's "ugly woman contest" is sufficiently expressive to entitle it to First Amendment protection.

*   *   *   *   *

A

First Amendment principles governing live entertainment are relatively clear: Short of obscenity, it is generally protected. As the Supreme Court announced in *Schad v. Borough of Mount Ephraim,* 452 U.S. 61 (1981), "[e]ntertainment, as well as political and ideological speech, is protected; motion pictures, programs broadcast by radio and television, and live entertainment . . . fall within the First Amendment guarantee." Expression devoid of "ideas" but with entertainment value may also be protected because "[t]he line between the informing and the entertaining is too elusive." *Winters v. New York,* 333 U.S. 507, 510 (1948).

*   *   *   *   *

Even crude street skits come within the First Amendment's reach. In . . . *Schacht v. United States,* 398 U.S. 58, 61–62 (1970), . . . Justice Black [declared] that an actor participating in even a crude performance enjoys the constitutional right to freedom of speech.

Bearing on this dichotomy between low- and high-grade entertainment are the Supreme Court's holdings relating to nude dancing. See *Barnes v. Glen Theatre, Inc.,* 111 S.Ct. 2456, 2460 (1991).

[I]n *Barnes,* the Supreme Court conceded that nude dancing is expressive conduct entitled to First Amendment protection.

*   *   *   *   *

. . . [I]t appears that the low quality of entertainment does not necessarily weigh in the First Amendment inquiry. It would seem, therefore, that the Fraternity's skit, even as low-grade entertainment, was inherently expressive and thus entitled to First Amendment protection.

B

The University nevertheless contends that discovery will demonstrate that the contest does not merit characterization as a skit but only as mindless fraternity fun, devoid of any artistic expression. It argues further that entitlement to First Amendment protection exists only if the production was intended to convey a message likely to be understood by a particular audience. . . .

As indicated, we feel that the First Amendment protects the Fraternity's skit because it is inherently expressive entertainment. Even if this were not true, however, the skit, in our view, qualifies as expressive conduct under the test articulated in *Texas v. Johnson,* 491 U.S. 397 (1989). It is true that the *Johnson* test for determining the expressiveness of conduct requires "'[a]n intent to convey a particularized message'" and a great likelihood "'that the message would be understood by those who viewed it.'"

*   *   *   *   *

[T]he affidavits establish that the punishment was meted out to the Fraternity because its boorish message had interfered with the described University mission. It is manifest from these circumstances that the University officials thought the Fraternity intended to convey a message. The Fraternity members' apology and post-conduct contriteness suggest that they held the same view.

* * * * *

As to the second prong of the *Johnson* test, there was a great likelihood that at least some of the audience viewing the skit would understand the Fraternity's message of satire and humor. Some students paid to attend the performance and were entertained. . . .

* * * * *

. . . [W]e are persuaded that the Fraternity's "ugly woman contest" satisfies the *Johnson* test for expressive conduct.

IV

If this were not a sufficient response to the University's argument, the principles relating to content and viewpoint discrimination recently emphasized in *R.A.V. v. City of St. Paul,* 112 S.Ct. 2538 (1992) provide a definitive answer. Although the Court in St. Paul reviewed the constitutional effect of a city "hate speech" ordinance, and we review the constitutionality of sanctions imposed for violating University policy, St. Paul's rationale applies here with equal force. Noting that St. Paul's city ordinance prohibited displays of symbols that "arouse[d] anger, alarm, or resentment in others on the basis of race, color, creed, religion, or gender," but did not prohibit displays of symbols which would advance ideas of racial or religious equality, Justice Scalia stated, "The First Amendment does not permit St. Paul to impose special prohibitions on those speakers who express views on disfavored subjects."

As evidenced by their affidavits, University officials sanctioned Sigma Chi for the message conveyed by the "ugly woman contest" because it ran counter to the views the University sought to communicate to its students and the community. The mischief was the University's punishment of those who scoffed at its goals of racial integration and gender neutrality, while permitting, even encouraging, conduct that would further the viewpoint expressed in the University's goals and probably be embraced by a majority of society as well. "The First Amendment generally prevents government from proscribing . . . expressive conduct because of disapproval of the ideas expressed."

The University, however, urges us to weigh Sigma Chi's conduct against the substantial interests inherent in educational endeavors. We agree wholeheartedly that it is the University officials' responsibility, even their obligation, to achieve the goals they have set. On the other hand, a public university has many constitutionally permissible means to protect female and minority students. We must emphasize, as have other courts, that "the manner of [its action] cannot consist of selective limitations upon speech." The University should have accomplished its goals in some fashion other than silencing speech on the basis of its viewpoint.

Affirmed.

Questions

1. Is speech that consists merely of entertainment without benefit of meaningful ideas protected by the First Amendment? Explain.

2. Explain the Court's conclusion that the fraternity skit met the *Texas v. Johnson* test of "an intent to convey a particularized message" and a great likelihood "that the message would be understood by those who viewed it."

3. *a.* Should racist/sexist remarks be forbidden in college classrooms?

    b. The Stanford University speech code was ruled unconstitutional and the Superior Court judge in that case said, among other things, that the code was "overbroad."[32] What did he mean?

    c. Do we give too much attention to freedom of speech at the expense of community civility? Explain.

4. T.W., a minor, was suspended from school for three days after he drew a picture of a Confederate flag on a piece of paper. The Kansas school, Derby Unified, suspended T.W. because it believed he had violated the district's "Racial Harassment or Intimidation" policy, which prohibits students from possessing at school "any written material, either printed or in their own handwriting, that is racially divisive or creates ill will or hatred." Confederate flags were included in a list of prohibited items. The Court found that Derby Unified had a history of racial harassment. Were T.W.'s First Amendment rights violated? Explain. See *West v. Derby Unified School District # 260,* 206 F.3d 1358 (10th Cir. 2000); cert. den. 531 U.S. 825 (2000).

5. The U.S. Supreme Court and lower federal courts have repeatedly ruled that burning the American flag is speech protected by the First Amendment. Congress often considers a flag protection amendment to the Constitution to make flag burning illegal. Would you favor that amendment? Explain.

Commercial Speech

Governments often want to regulate commercial expressions ranging from advertisements and billboards to real estate "for sale" signs and circulars placed on car windshields. Does the First Amendment protect those messages from government intervention in the same manner that it protects political speech? In 1942, the U.S. Supreme Court ruled that *commercial speech* was not entitled to First Amendment protection.[33] Subsequently the Court changed its stance and extended First Amendment rights to commercial speech, but those rights were much more limited than for political speech. In more recent years, the Court has been gradually expanding protection for commercial speech.

Corporate/Commercial Speech Should corporations enjoy full First Amendment rights? Can we properly think of corporate political expressions as commercial speech? Or is commercial speech limited to those expressions that propose a commercial transaction? Experts differ on these questions, but their importance is evident if we think for a moment about the controversial 2010 *Citizens United* decision allowing corporations to spend more freely on elections (discussed previously in Chapter 3).[34] In the late 1970s, Justices William Rehnquist and Byron White had described corporations as "creatures of the law" possessed of wealth-creation powers but not entitled to the rights possessed by voters. By contrast, the *Citizens United* majority described corporations as "associations of citizens" deserving of free speech rights in the manner of individuals.[35] Justice Scalia said: "To exclude or impede corporate speech is to muzzle the principal agents of the modern economy." "We should celebrate rather than condemn the addition of this speech to the public debate."[36] This shift in constitutional interpretation reflects, according to a *Los Angeles Times* analysis, the President Ronald Reagan-era efforts to reduce government regulation of business. All five justices in the *Citizens United* majority were either appointed to the Court by Reagan or worked as young lawyers in the Reagan administration.[37] Hence, shifting political views sometimes influence the course of judge-made law. Do you think a corporation should be regarded as a person for First Amendment purposes?

Cigarette Packs and Graphic Warnings

The federal Food and Drug Administration (FDA) recently issued rules requiring, among other things, graphic antismoking warnings covering the top half of the front and back of cigarette packs. The warnings, in color, included, for example, images of a man exhaling cigarette smoke through a tracheotomy hole in his throat and a cloud of cigarette smoke surrounding a mother kissing her baby. Tobacco companies challenged the warnings as violations of their freedom of expression rights. One federal court of appeals upheld the constitutionality of the rules, but another struck them down. The FDA decided to rewrite its rules in an effort to resolve the First Amendment issues.

1. In your view, are the tobacco companies' speech rights violated by the government's warning requirements? Explain.
2. Should the government require graphic smoking warnings? Explain.

Sources: *R.J. Reynolds Tobacco Co. v. Food & Drug Administration,* 696 F.3d 1205 (D.C. Cir. 2012); *Discount Tobacco City v. United States of America,* 674 F.3d 509 (2012); and cert. den. *Am. Snuff Co. v. United States,* 2013 U.S. LEXIS 3279.

Animal Cruelty Commercial speech disputes raise very difficult legal questions in a wide variety of venues. The Supreme Court in 2010 supported the First Amendment rights of a business selling videos depicting animal cruelty. Robert J. Stevens advertised and sold pit bull–related videos showing dog fights and dogs attacking wild boar. Stevens was criminally indicted for violating a federal statute forbidding knowingly creating, selling, or possessing "a depiction of animal cruelty" to be sold for commercial gain in interstate or foreign commerce. Stevens moved to dismiss the indictment saying that the statute violated his First Amendment right to free speech. The Supreme Court, in an 8–1 ruling, agreed with Stevens by finding the federal statute overbroad in that it could legitimately be applied to legal activities such as hunting or the inhumane treatment of livestock as well as to the dog fights Stevens filmed.[38]

> Selling videos depicting animal cruelty.

In an illustration of the balance of powers concept, Congress and President Obama quickly approved new federal legislation designed to attack certain animal cruelty videos while meeting constitutional requirements. The Animal Crush Video Prohibition Act of 2010 bans the creation and distribution of obscene animal torture videos. Those videos often depict women in high heels slowly crushing small animals, images that appeal to certain sexual fetishists. By limiting the law to obscene crush videos, Congress and the president believe the statute will address the overbreadth problem while fitting the statute into the well-settled obscenity exception to the First Amendment's speech protections.

The *Bad Frog* decision below examines the question of free speech protection for beer advertising.

LEGAL BRIEFCASE

Bad Frog Brewery v. New York State Liquor Authority
134 F.3d 87 (2d Cir. 1998)

Judge Newman

BACKGROUND

Bad Frog is a Michigan corporation that manufactures and markets several different types of alcoholic beverages under its "Bad Frog" trademark. This action concerns labels used by the company in the marketing of Bad Frog Beer, Bad Frog Lemon Lager, and Bad Frog Malt Liquor. Each label prominently features an artist's rendering of a frog holding up its four-"fingered" right "hand," with the back of the "hand" shown, the second "finger" extended, and the other three "fingers" slightly curled.

Bad Frog does not dispute that the frog depicted in the label artwork is making the gesture generally known as "giving the finger" and that the gesture is widely regarded as an offensive insult, conveying a message that the company has characterized as "traditionally . . . negative and nasty." Versions of the label feature slogans such as "He just don't care," "An amphibian with an attitude," "Turning bad into good," and "The beer so good . . . it's bad." Another slogan, originally used but now abandoned, was "He's mean, green and obscene."

Bad Frog's labels have been approved for use by the Federal Bureau of Alcohol, Tobacco, and Firearms, and by authorities in at least 15 states and the District of Columbia, but have been rejected by authorities in New Jersey, Ohio, and Pennsylvania.

In May 1996, Bad Frog's authorized New York distributor, Renaissance Beer Co., made an application to the New York State Liquor Authority (NYSLA) for brand label approval and registration. . . .

In September 1996, NYSLA denied Bad Frog's application. . . . Explaining its rationale for the rejection, the Authority found that the label "encourages combative behavior" and that the gesture and the slogan, "He just don't care," placed close to and in larger type than a warning concerning potential health problems,

> foster a defiance to the health warning on the label, entice underage drinkers, and invite the public not to heed conventional wisdom and to disobey standards of decorum.

In addition, the Authority said that it

> considered that approval of this label means that the label could appear in grocery and convenience stores, with obvious exposure on the shelf to children of tender age

and that it

> is sensitive to and has concern as to [the label's] adverse effects on such a youthful audience.

Finally, the Authority said that it

> has considered that within the state of New York, the gesture of "giving the finger" to someone has the insulting meaning of "**k You," or "Up Yours," . . . a confrontational, obscene gesture, known to lead to fights, shootings, and homicides . . . concludes that the encouraged use of this gesture in licensed premises is akin to yelling "fire" in a crowded theater, . . . [and] finds that to approve this admittedly obscene, provocative confrontational gesture would not be conducive to proper regulation and control and would tend to adversely affect the health, safety, and welfare of the People of the State of New York.

Bad Frog filed the present action in October 1996 and sought a preliminary injunction barring NYSLA from taking any steps to prohibit the sale of beer by Bad Frog under the controversial labels. The District Court denied the motion [and Bad Frog now appeals the District Court decision].

* * * * *

COMMERCIAL OR NONCOMMERCIAL SPEECH?

In Bad Frog's view, the commercial speech that receives reduced First Amendment protection is expression that conveys commercial information. The frog labels, it contends, do not purport to convey such information, but instead communicate only a "joke." As such, the argument continues, the labels enjoy full First Amendment protection, rather than the somewhat reduced protection accorded commercial speech.

* * * * *

NYSLA agrees with the District Court that the labels enjoy some First Amendment protection, but are to be assessed by the somewhat reduced standards applicable to commercial speech.

Bad Frog's label attempts to function, like a trademark, to identify the source of the product. The picture on a beer bottle of a frog behaving badly is reasonably to be understood as attempting to identify to consumers a product of the Bad Frog Brewery. In addition, the label serves to propose a commercial transaction. Though the label communicates no information beyond the source of the product, we think that minimal information, conveyed in the context of a proposal of a commercial transaction, suffices to invoke the protections for commercial speech. . . .

Bad Frog contends that its labels deserve full First Amendment protection because their proposal of a commercial transaction is combined with what is claimed to be political, or at least societal, commentary.

* * * * *

We are unpersuaded by Bad Frog's attempt to separate the purported social commentary in the labels from the hawking of beer. Bad Frog's labels meet the three criteria identified in *Bolger* [463 U.S. 60 (1983)]: the labels are a form of advertising, identify a specific product, and serve the economic interest of the speaker. Moreover, the purported noncommercial message is not so "inextricably intertwined" with the commercial speech as to require a finding that the entire label must be treated as "pure" speech.

* * * * *

We thus assess the prohibition of Bad Frog's labels under the commercial speech standards outlined in *Central Hudson* [447 U.S. 557 (1980)].

THE *CENTRAL HUDSON* TEST

Central Hudson sets forth the analytical framework for assessing governmental restrictions on commercial speech:

> At the outset, we must determine whether the expression is protected by the First Amendment. For commercial speech to come within that provision, it at least must concern lawful activity and not be misleading. Next, we ask whether the asserted government interest is substantial. If both inquiries yield positive answers, we must determine whether the regulation directly advances the government interest asserted, and whether it is not more extensive than is necessary to serve that interest.

* * * * *

A. Lawful Activity and Not Deceptive

We agree with the District Court that Bad Frog's labels pass *Central Hudson's* threshold requirement that the speech "must concern lawful activity and not be misleading." The consumption of beer (at least by adults) is legal in New York, and the labels cannot be said to be deceptive, even if they are offensive.

B. Substantial State Interests

NYSLA advances two interests to support its asserted power to ban Bad Frog's labels: (i) the State's interest in "protecting children from vulgar and profane advertising," and (ii) the State's interest "in acting consistently to promote temperance, i.e., the moderate and responsible use of alcohol among those above the legal drinking age and abstention among those below the legal drinking age."

Both of the asserted interests are "substantial" within the meaning of *Central Hudson.* States have "a compelling interest in protecting the physical and psychological well-being of minors," and "[t]his interest extends to shielding minors from the influence of literature that is not obscene by adult standards."

The Supreme Court also has recognized that states have a substantial interest in regulating alcohol consumption. We agree with the District Court that New York's asserted concern for "temperance" is also a substantial state interest.

C. Direct Advancement of the State Interest

To meet the "direct advancement" requirement, a state must demonstrate that "the harms it recites are real and that its restriction will in fact alleviate them *to a material degree*" [*Edenfield v. Fane,* 507 U.S. 761, 771 (1993)].

(1) *Advancing the interest in protecting children from vulgarity.*

* * * * *

NYSLA endeavors to advance the state interest in preventing exposure of children to vulgar displays by taking only the limited step of barring such displays from the labels of alcoholic beverages. In view of the wide currency of vulgar displays throughout contemporary society, including comic books targeted directly at children, barring such displays from labels for alcoholic beverages cannot realistically be expected to reduce children's exposure to such displays to any significant degree.

* * * * *

(2) *Advancing the state interest in temperance.* We agree with the District Court that NYSLA has not established that its rejection of Bad Frog's application directly advances the state's interest in "temperance."

NYSLA maintains that the raised finger gesture and the slogan "He just don't care" urge consumers generally to defy authority and particularly to disregard the Surgeon General's warning, which appears on the label next to the gesturing frog. NYSLA also contends that the frog appeals to youngsters and promotes underage drinking.

The truth of these propositions is not so self-evident as to relieve the state of the burden of marshalling some empirical evidence to support its assumptions. All that is clear is that the gesture of "giving the finger" is offensive. Whether viewing that gesture on a beer label will encourage disregard of health warnings or encourage underage drinking remain matters of speculation.

NYSLA has not shown that its denial of Bad Frog's application directly and materially advances either of its asserted state interests.

D. Narrow Tailoring

Central Hudson's fourth criterion, sometimes referred to as "narrow tailoring," requires consideration of whether the prohibition is more extensive than necessary to serve the asserted state interest. Since NYSLA's prohibition of Bad Frog's labels has not been shown to make even an arguable advancement of the state interest in temperance, we consider here only whether the prohibition is more extensive than necessary to serve the asserted interest in insulating children from vulgarity.

* * * * *

In this case, Bad Frog has suggested numerous less intrusive alternatives to advance the asserted state interest in protecting children from vulgarity, short of a complete statewide ban on its labels. Appellant suggests "the restriction of advertising to point-of-sale locations; limitations on billboard advertising; restrictions on over-the-air advertising; and segregation of the product in the store." Even if we were to assume that the state materially advances its asserted interest by shielding children from viewing the Bad Frog labels, it is plainly excessive to prohibit the labels from all use, including placement on bottles displayed in bars and taverns where parental supervision of children is to be expected. Moreover, to whatever extent NYSLA is concerned that children will be harmfully exposed to the Bad Frog labels when wandering without parental supervision around grocery and convenience stores where beer is sold, that concern could be less intrusively dealt with by placing restrictions on the permissible locations where the appellant's products may be displayed within such stores. Or, with the labels permitted, restrictions might be imposed on placement of the frog illustration on the outside of six-packs or cases sold in such stores.

NYSLA's complete statewide ban on the use of Bad Frog's labels lacks a "reasonable fit" with the state's asserted interest in shielding minors from vulgarity, and NYSLA gave inadequate consideration to alternatives to this blanket suppression of commercial speech.

* * * * *

[W]e conclude that NYSLA has unlawfully rejected Bad Frog's application for approval of its labels.

* * * * *

[Reversed and remanded.] [For an update on Bad Frog, see **http://badfrog.com**]

Questions

1. *a.* Why did the Court of Appeals conclude that the Bad Frog label constituted commercial speech?
   b. What is the significance of that decision?
2. Why did the Court of Appeals rule in Bad Frog's favor?
3. A letter to the *Buffalo News* objecting to the *Bad Frog* decision:

   . . . The U.S. Court of Appeals' reasoning was that "vulgar materials enjoy wide currency in society today—including comic books for children." Therefore, while offensive it is not illegal. I guess this means the sickies of the world can show us anything they want, even if we don't want to see it. They have the right to offend us, but we have no rights not to be offended.

   We all know what the extended middle finger means. I personally get offended when this gesture is directed at me, whether by humans or cartoon animals. I would like to show the Court of Appeals my opinion of their decision by extending my middle finger in their direction. I hope they enjoy this gesture. After all, it's not illegal. But maybe it should be.[39]

   a. Do you agree with the letter writer that *Bad Frog* is an unwise decision? Explain.
   b. Should "the finger" be an illegal gesture? Explain.
4. In online fantasy sports leagues, fans "draft" current professional players in baseball, football, etc. to create their own teams that then compete based on the actual performance of those players. A Missouri company, C.B.C. Distribution and Marketing, Inc., operated a for-profit online league. In 2005, Major League Baseball changed its licensing policies and declined to allow C.B.C. a license to continue using the names and statistics of major league baseball players. C.B.C. then sued claiming it had a First Amendment right to use the information while M.L.B. argued that the information was protected by the intellectual property/publicity rights of the players. Decide the case. Explain. See *C.B.C. Distribution and Marketing, Inc. v. Major League Baseball Advanced Media,* 505 F.3d 818 (8th Cir. 2007); cert. den. *Major League Baseball v. C.B.C. Distrib. & Mktg,* 2008 U.S. LEXIS 4574.
5. Two Rhode Island statutes prohibited all price advertising on liquor in the state, except for price tags and signs within a store itself which were not visible on the street. The state sought to reduce alcohol consumption. Two licensed liquor dealers challenged the statutes' constitutionality.
   a. How would you rule on that challenge? Explain.
   b. Why would the elimination of price advertising arguably contribute to reduced alcohol consumption? See *44 Liquormart, Inc. v. Rhode Island,* 116 S.Ct. 1495 (1996).

The Fourth Amendment

Antoine Jones, a nightclub owner, was suspected of being associated with an illegal narcotics operation. Police lacked a valid warrant but nonetheless put a GPS tracker on Jones's Jeep and followed his movements for four weeks. Jones was arrested in 2005 and in a 2008 trial a jury found him guilty of intent to distribute cocaine for which he was sentenced to life in prison. On appeal, Jones argued that his conviction should be overturned because the warrantless use of the GPS tracker violated his Fourth Amendment right to be protected from unreasonable search and seizure. His case reached the U.S. Supreme Court, which unanimously ruled that installing a GPS device is, indeed, a *search* in constitutional law terms.[40] The Court did not resolve the question of whether a search warrant is required in such situations. Future decisions will address that crucial question as the Court tries to achieve a coherent line of reasoning in applying the centuries-old Fourth Amendment to the complex new world of high technology.

The Fourth Amendment provides that:

> [T]he right of the people to be secure in their persons, houses, papers, and effects, against unreasonable searches and seizures, shall not be violated, and no Warrants shall issue, but upon probable cause.

Drug-Sniffing Dog

The Miami-Dade Police Department received a tip that the residence of Joelis Jardines was being used to grow marijuana. A drug-sniffing dog was taken to the door of the home. The dog signaled the presence of marijuana, a search warrant was obtained, and a search discovered marijuana growing in the house. Jardines was arrested. Did the use of the drug-sniffing dog constitute an unconstitutional search? Explain.

Source: Florida v. Jardines, 133 S.Ct. 1409 (2013).

The authorities are under great pressure to cope with America's crime and terrorism problems. They must do so, however, within the confines of the Constitution, which is designed to protect us all—including criminals and terrorists—from the power of an unfair, overreaching government. Two crucial inquiries in search and seizure cases are whether a search has, in fact, occurred (as in the *Jones* and *Jardines* cases) and whether the search violated the subject's reasonable expectation of privacy (which is much more likely in one's home than on the street, for example.)

Certainly, the most controversial dimension of Fourth Amendment interpretation is the *exclusionary rule,* which provides that, as a matter of due process, evidence secured in violation of the Fourth Amendment may not be used against a defendant at trial. As ultimately applied to all courts by the 1961 U.S. Supreme Court decision in *Mapp v. Ohio,*[41] we can see that the exclusionary rule, while a very effective device for discouraging illegal searches, seizures, and arrests, also from time to time has the effect of freeing guilty criminals.

The Supreme Court restricted the exclusionary rule in 2006 holding that the government need not forfeit evidence collected in constitutionally improper "no knock" searches.[42] For many years, police conducting a search have been required to knock and announce themselves then wait a reasonable time to enter. Michigan police, in executing a search warrant, announced themselves but did not wait a reasonable time before entering and finding crack cocaine in Booker T. Hudson's pockets. Hudson was convicted of drug violations, and his appeal eventually reached the U.S. Supreme Court where Justice Antonin Scalia, writing the 5–4 opinion upholding Hudson's conviction, expressed concern about guilty defendants who have been allowed to go free because of the exclusionary rule. He concluded that the social harm accompanying the knock and announce rule was too great as compared with the added privacy offered by the rule. Then in 2009, the Court, in another 5–4 decision, further limited the exclusionary rule by finding that unlawful police conduct does not require the suppression of evidence if the misconduct involved only "isolated negligence."[43]

Guilty defendants allowed to go free.

In general, a *search warrant* issued by a judge is necessary to comply with the Constitution in making a narcotics search. A warrantless search is permissible, however, where reasonable, as in association with an arrest or where probable cause exists to believe a drug-related crime has been committed but circumstances make securing a warrant impracticable. Incident to an arrest, a search may lawfully include the person, a car, and the immediate vicinity of the arrest. Furthermore, a police officer may lawfully secure drugs that have been abandoned or that are in plain view even though a warrant has not been obtained. Search/privacy problems pervade our lives:

1. **Vehicle Searches.** For nearly 30 years, police officers have commonly understood that lawfully arresting an occupant of a vehicle confers the right to search the passenger compartment of that vehicle. In a 2009 decision, *Gant v. Arizona,*[44] the U.S. Supreme Court significantly diminished that authority by ruling that such searches are permissible in only two circumstances:

   a. when the individual being arrested is close enough to the vehicle to reach in for a weapon or evidence and

   b. when the officer can reasonably believe that the vehicle contains evidence relevant to the crime of arrest.

   Thus, arrests for routine traffic stops ordinarily would not justify vehicle searches while such searches are more likely to be permissible incident to arrests for more serious crimes.[45]

2. **Cell Phones.** An Ohio woman, Wendy Thomas Northern, was hospitalized because of a drug overdose. During police questioning she agreed to call Antwaun Smith, whom she identified as the source of the drugs. Police arrested Smith, searched him and his cell phone, and discovered call records and numbers confirming that his phone had been used to talk with Northern. That evidence was used at trial against Smith, who argued that the cell phone search violated his Fourth Amendment rights. The Ohio Supreme Court agreed with Smith and ruled that the cell phone evidence should have been suppressed.[46] Court decisions supporting cell phone searches have relied on well-settled Supreme Court decisions allowing police to conduct searches incident to lawful arrest. The arrestee's person and immediate area of control including any closed containers in possession of the suspect may be examined by the police to ensure their safety and to prevent the destruction of evidence. The Ohio Supreme Court declined to treat Smith's cell phone as a container. The California Supreme Court, however, ruled that an arrestee had no reasonable expectation of privacy in his cell phone as long as it was with him at the time of arrest.[47] In 2014, the U.S. Supreme Court held that, unlike wallets or purses, cell phones could not be searched upon arrest without a warrant. Why?

   > Police searched him and his cell phone.

3. **Testing Students.** In 1998, the school board in rural Tecumseh, Oklahoma, instituted a mandatory random urinalysis drug-testing program for all students participating in competitive extracurricular activities. The tests checked for illegal drugs but not for alcohol. Test results were not turned over to the police. An honor student, Lindsay Earls, challenged the program as a violation of her Fourth Amendment rights. A U.S. Court of Appeals agreed with her, ruling that school officials needed

to provide evidence of an "identifiable drug abuse problem."[48] The U.S. Supreme Court, however, reversed that decision and held by a 5–4 margin that the school's interest in addressing drug problems outweighed students' privacy rights.[49] The Court reasoned that those participating in extracurricular activities are subjected to many rules and restrictions that diminish their expectation of privacy, and the Court said the program is a health and safety measure rather than an assault on personal privacy. Some state supreme courts, however, have ruled that school drug testing violates state constitutional law,[50] but even middle schools in at least eight states are now requiring drug testing for students participating in activities ranging from athletics to scrapbooking.[51]

> Drug problems outweighed students' privacy.

4. **Voyeurism and the Surveillance Society.** In Washington State, Richard Sorrells and Sean Glas were found guilty of violating a state voyeurism statute for taking pictures up the skirts of some women who were working and shopping in a public mall. Both men appealed their convictions and won a 2002 decision because the voyeurism law did not apply, the Washington State Supreme Court unanimously ruled, to actions in public places.[52] The women had no "reasonable expectation of privacy" in the shopping mall, so their privacy could not have been invaded. A federal law, the Video Voyeurism Prevention Act (limited to federal jurisdiction/property), and a number of state laws have expanded protection against photographic voyeurism, but those laws may not meet constitutional requirements.

5. **DNA Samples.** Alonzo King was arrested in 2009 on an assault charge and, without first obtaining a search warrant, police swabbed the inside of his cheek for a DNA sample. Several months later his DNA was matched with a 2003 rape case. He was then convicted of that rape. He appealed his conviction arguing that he was a victim of an unreasonable search in violation of his Fourth Amendment rights. Maryland law allowed the sampling in cases where the suspect had been arrested, but not yet convicted, of serious crimes including burglaries, rape, and murder. The U.S. Supreme Court, in a 2013 ruling, upheld the conviction by a 5–4 vote saying that DNA collection is simply a part of the booking process, much like fingerprinting, and thus was a minimal intrusion on privacy.[53] DNA testing is a valuable tool in prosecuting criminals and in exonerating the innocent, but DNA collection by the government of suspicionless persons who are presumed innocent at the time raises significant privacy issues. In the future, might DNA collection be extended to all arrests, or might the government misuse its vast DNA database, at least some of which will have been collected from people who are innocent? Over half of the states collect DNA upon arrest for serious crimes. [For an overview of privacy issues, see **http://epic.org/**]

Questions

1. More than 13 million people are admitted to American jails each year. Albert Florence was mistakenly arrested and subjected to two strip searches involving showering with a delousing agent, officers checking for gang tattoos and scars, lifting his genitals, officers looking in his body openings, and more. Does the Constitution allow authorities to strip

search those admitted to jail for minor violations? Explain. See *Florence v. Board of Chosen Freeholders,* 132 S.Ct. 1510 (2012).

2. Police stopped and arrested McFadden for riding a bicycle on a sidewalk in violation of New York City code. A search incident to the stop revealed a firearm. McFadden was later convicted of the crime of being in possession of a firearm as a previously convicted felon. McFadden appealed, claiming the search was unconstitutional. Was he correct? Explain. See *United States v. McFadden*, 238 F.3d 198 (2001); cert. den. 122 S.Ct. 223 (2001).

3. *a.* Can the police lawfully search an individual's garbage once it has been placed at the curb for disposal? A Connecticut resident, Paul DeFusco, was convicted of drug trafficking based on evidence found in his home. The police conducted the home search with a warrant secured on the basis of an informant's information as well as evidence (some short cut straws, glassine baggies, and prescription bottles) turned up in sifting through DeFusco's garbage.

   b. Explain the central issue in this case. See *State of Connecticut v. Paul DeFusco*, 620 A.2d 746 (Conn. S.Ct. 1993).

4. Tucson, Arizona, police, cruising in an area associated with the Crips street gang, stopped a car because its insurance coverage had been suspended. Johnson, a backseat passenger, was wearing the blue colors associated with the Crips and Officer Trevizo saw that Johnson had a police scanner in his pocket. Trevizo questioned Johnson learning that he was from a town frequented by the Crips gang, that he had recently been in prison and that he had no identification with him. Trevizo asked Johnson to exit the car. He did so. Trevizo conducted a pat-down search, and she felt a gun. Johnson struggled but he was arrested, and a further search revealed marijuana. Johnson was charged with unlawful possession of a gun, possession of marijuana, and resisting arrest. In court, Johnson challenged the legality of the search saying it had nothing to do with the traffic stop. Did the pat-down violate the Fourth Amendment's prohibition on unreasonable searches and seizures? Explain. See *Arizona v. Johnson,* 555 U.S. 323 (2009).

Business Searches

Government tries to protect us from business hazards including pollution, defective products, and unsafe workplaces as well as business crimes such as fraud and bribery. To do so, government agents often want to enter company buildings, observe working conditions, and examine company books. We know our homes are generally protected from searches in the absence of a warrant. Excepting urgent circumstances such as terrorism concerns, can the same be said for a place of business? The Supreme Court has answered that question:

> The Warrant Clause of the Fourth Amendment protects commercial buildings as well as private homes. To hold otherwise would belie the origin of that Amendment, and the American colonial experience. . . . "[T]he Fourth Amendment's commands grew in large measure out of the colonists' experience with the writs of assistance . . . [that] granted sweeping power to customs officials and other agents of the king to search at large for smuggled goods." Against this background, it is untenable that the ban on warrantless searches was not intended to shield places of business as well as of residence.[54]

The Fifth Amendment

Takings—Eminent Domain

The Fifth Amendment prohibits the taking of private property for public use without *just compensation* for the owner. In cases where owners do not want to sell, governments often use the power of *eminent domain* to take private property for public uses such as building highways, bike trails, and parks, while providing just compensation. But what about the situation where the condemned property is to be used for a *private* purpose? Communities across America, hungry for an improved tax base and more jobs, have made the practice routine, but are they violating the Fifth Amendment rights of the property owners? The following 5–4 Supreme Court decision involves a challenge to a New London, Connecticut, plan to clear a portion of the city to make way for a private-sector office/research park along with a waterfront hotel, conference center, residences, a marina, and a river walk. Small businesses and residences were to make room for bigger, more successful private ventures providing a stronger tax base for New London.

LEGAL BRIEFCASE

Kelo v. City of New London, Connecticut Supreme Court of the United States 545 U.S. 469 (2005)

Justice Stevens

In 2000 the city of New London approved a development plan that, in the words of the Supreme Court of Connecticut, was "projected to create in excess of 1,000 jobs, to increase tax and other revenues, and to revitalize an economically distressed city, including its downtown and waterfront areas" (843 A.2d 500, 507 [2004]). In assembling the land needed for this project, the city's development agent has purchased property from willing sellers and proposes to use the power of eminent domain to acquire the remainder of the property from unwilling owners in exchange for just compensation. The question presented is whether the city's proposed disposition of this property qualifies as a "public use" within the meaning of the Takings Clause of the Fifth Amendment to the Constitution.

I

The city of New London (hereinafter City) sits at the junction of the Thames River and the Long Island Sound in southeastern Connecticut. Decades of economic decline led a state agency in 1990 to designate the City a "distressed municipality." In 1996 the

Federal Government closed the Naval Undersea Warfare Center, which had been located in the Fort Trumbull area of the City and had employed over 1,500 people. In 1998 the City's unemployment rate was nearly double that of the State, and its population of just under 24,000 residents was at its lowest since 1920.

These conditions prompted state and local officials to target New London, and particularly its Fort Trumbull area, for economic revitalization. To this end, respondent New London Development Corporation (NLDC), a private nonprofit entity established some years earlier to assist the City in planning economic development, was reactivated. In January 1998 the State authorized a $5.35 million bond issue to support the NLDC's planning activities and a $10 million bond issue toward the creation of a Fort Trumbull State Park. In February the pharmaceutical company Pfizer Inc. announced that it would build a $300 million research facility on a site immediately adjacent to Fort Trumbull; local planners hoped that Pfizer would draw new business to the area. Upon obtaining state-level approval, the NLDC finalized an integrated development plan focused on 90 acres of the Fort Trumbull area.

The Fort Trumbull area is situated on a peninsula that juts into the Thames River. The area comprises approximately 115 privately owned properties, as well as the 32 acres of land formerly occupied by the naval facility (Trumbull State Park now occupies 18 of those 32 acres). The development plan encompasses seven parcels. Parcel 1 is designated for a waterfront conference hotel at the center of a "small urban village" that will include restaurants and shopping. . . . Parcel 2 will be the site of approximately 80 new residences organized into an urban neighborhood and linked by public walkway to the remainder of the development, including the state park. This parcel also includes space reserved for a new U.S. Coast Guard Museum. Parcel 3, which is located immediately north of the Pfizer facility, will contain at least 90,000 square feet of research and development office space. Parcel 4A is a 2.4-acre site that will be used either to support the adjacent state park, by providing parking or retail services for visitors, or to support the nearby marina. Parcel 4B will include a renovated marina, as well as the final stretch of the riverwalk. Parcels 5, 6, and 7 will provide land for office and retail space, parking, and water-dependent commercial uses.

* * * * *

The city council approved the plan in January 2000 and designated the NLDC as its development agent in charge of implementation. The city council also authorized the NLDC to purchase property or to acquire property by exercising eminent domain in the City's name. The NLDC successfully negotiated the purchase of most of the real estate in the 90-acre area, but its negotiations with petitioners failed. As a consequence, in November 2000 the NLDC initiated the condemnation proceedings that gave rise to this case.

II

Petitioner Susette Kelo has lived in the Fort Trumbull area since 1997. She has made extensive improvements to her house, which she prizes for its water view. Petitioner Wilhelmina Dery was born in her Fort Trumbull house in 1918 and has lived there her entire life. Her husband Charles has lived in the house since they married some 60 years ago. In all, the nine petitioners own 15 properties in Fort Trumbull. . . . There is no allegation that any of these properties is blighted or otherwise in poor condition; rather, they were condemned only because they happen to be located in the development area.

In December 2000 petitioners brought this action in the New London Superior Court. They claimed, among other things, that the taking of their properties would violate the "public use" restriction in the Fifth Amendment. After a seven-day bench trial, the Superior Court granted a permanent restraining order prohibiting the taking of the properties located in parcel 4A (park or marina support). It, however, denied petitioners relief as to the properties located in parcel 3 (office space).

After the Superior Court ruled, both sides took appeals to the Supreme Court of Connecticut. That court held that all of the City's proposed takings were valid.

* * * * *

III

Two polar propositions are perfectly clear. On the one hand, it has long been accepted that the sovereign may not take the property of A for the sole purpose of transferring it to another private party B, even though A is paid just compensation. On the other hand, it is equally clear that a State may transfer property from one private party to another if future "use by the public" is the purpose of the taking; the condemnation of land for a railroad is a familiar example. Neither of these propositions, however, determines the disposition of this case.

As for the first proposition, the City would no doubt be forbidden from taking petitioners' land for the purpose of conferring a private benefit on a particular party. Nor would the City be allowed to take property under the mere pretext of a public purpose, when its actual purpose was to bestow a private benefit. The takings before us, however, would be executed pursuant to a "carefully considered" development plan. The trial judge and all the members of the Supreme Court of Connecticut agreed that there was no evidence of an illegitimate purpose in this case.

* * * * *

On the other hand, this is not a case in which the City is planning to open the condemned land—at least not in its entirety—to use by the general public. Nor will the private lessees of the land in any sense be required to operate like common carriers, making their services available to all comers. But although such a projected use would be sufficient to satisfy the public use requirement, this "Court long ago rejected any literal requirement that condemned property be put into use for the general public." Indeed, while many state courts in the mid-19th century endorsed "use by the public" as the proper definition of public use, that narrow view steadily eroded over time. Not only was the "use by the public" test difficult to administer (e.g., what proportion of the public need have access to the property? at what price?), but it proved to be impractical given the diverse and always evolving needs of society. Accordingly, when this Court began applying the Fifth Amendment to the States at the close of the 19th century, it embraced the broader and more natural interpretation of public use as "public purpose."

* * * * *

The disposition of this case therefore turns on the question whether the City's development plan serves a "public purpose." Without exception, our cases have defined that concept broadly, reflecting our long-standing policy of deference to legislative judgments in this field.

In *Berman v. Parker,* this Court upheld a redevelopment plan targeting a blighted area of Washington, D.C., in which most of the housing for the area's 5,000 inhabitants was beyond repair. Under the plan, the area would be condemned and part of it utilized for the construction of streets, schools, and other public facilities. The remainder of the land would be leased or sold to private parties for the purpose of redevelopment, including the construction of low-cost housing.

* * * * *

IV

Those who govern the City were not confronted with the need to remove blight in the Fort Trumbull area, but their determination that the area was sufficiently distressed to justify a program of economic rejuvenation is entitled to our deference. The City has carefully formulated an economic development plan that it believes will provide appreciable benefits to the community, including—but by no means limited to—new jobs and increased tax revenue.... Given the comprehensive character of the plan, the thorough deliberation that preceded its adoption, and the limited scope of our review, it is appropriate for us to resolve the challenges of the individual owners, not on a piecemeal basis, but rather in light of the entire plan. Because that plan unquestionably serves a public purpose, the takings challenged here satisfy the public use requirement of the Fifth amendment.

To avoid this result, petitioners urge us to adopt a new bright-line rule that economic development does not qualify as a public use. Putting aside the unpersuasive suggestion that the City's plan will provide only purely economic benefits, neither precedent nor logic supports petitioners' proposal. Promoting economic development is a traditional and long accepted function of government.

* * * * *

In affirming the City's authority to take petitioners' properties, we do not minimize the hardship that condemnations may entail, notwithstanding the payment of just compensation. We emphasize that nothing in our opinion precludes any State from placing further restrictions on its exercise of the takings power. Indeed, many States already impose "public use" requirements that are stricter than the federal baseline.

* * * * *

Affirmed.

AFTERWORD—PROPERTY RIGHTS REVOLUTION?

The *Kelo* decision was an angry disappointment for property rights advocates. A government taking of Americans' long-time homes, even for just compensation, is a powerful and frightening image. Susette Kelo eventually settled with New London, vacated her home and received $442,000. Her "little pink house"

was disassembled and moved to another lot where it stands as something of a national symbol for property rights.

Clearly, however, governments need, and have long exercised, substantial authority to take property for economic development. Of course, government planning sometimes does not work out as expected, and the Pfizer development appears to be one of those failures. In 2009, Pfizer announced it was abandoning the Fort Trumbull office complex as a cost-saving measure. Fourteen hundred jobs were departing. The hotels, stores, and condominiums planned for the lots taken from Kelo and her neighbors have yet to materialize.

Kelo produced one of the angriest backlashes to any Supreme Court decision in history. At least 44 states have passed legislation or amended their constitutions to limit eminent domain, but the effectiveness of those measures is unclear. Some of them still allow takings involving "blighted" property, an exception readily subject to abuse, from the critics' point of view. [For property rights analysis and updates and more on the *Kelo* story, see **www.ij.org**]

Questions

1. What reasoning was offered by Justice Stevens to support the majority view that the New London development complied with due process requirements?

2. *a.* What was the issue, the central question, in this case and how did the majority answer that question?

   b. How would you expect the dissent to answer that question?

3. From the dissenting point of view, what harm is likely to emerge from this decision?

4. Marilyn and James Nollan applied for a permit to replace their beachfront home with a larger structure. The California Coastal Commission agreed on the condition that the Nollans grant an easement on their beach that would allow the public to cross that property and thus facilitate movement between the public beaches that lay on both sides of the Nollan beach. The Nollans sued, claiming a violation of the Takings Clause. Decide. Explain. See *Nollan v. California Coastal Commission,* 483 U.S. 825 (1987).

5. Tina Bennis sued when Wayne County (Detroit), Michigan, authorities took the car she jointly owned with her husband after police arrested him for receiving oral sex from a prostitute while parked in the car. A 1925 anti nuisance law permitted the seizure, but Tina Bennis claimed it amounted to an unconstitutional taking because she was an innocent half owner of the 1977 Pontiac for which the couple had paid $600. Bennis's claim eventually reached the U.S. Supreme Court. Decide the case. Explain. See *Bennis v. Michigan,* 116 S.Ct. 994 (1996).

Takings—Regulatory

We have seen how the law treats situations where the government uses its power of eminent domain to condemn property for either public or private use and pays just compensation. What happens when the government does not take the property but rather *regulates* it in a manner that deprives that property of some or all of its economic usefulness? For example, without providing just compensation, can a state lawfully limit the amount a landlord can charge for rent in an effort to preserve low-income housing? Can the state forbid billboards in order to enhance roadside beauty?

These *regulatory takings,* whether temporary or permanent, normally do not require government compensation because doing so would severely impair the state's ability to govern in an orderly manner. Nonetheless, in recent years the courts have been more aggressive about requiring just compensation for some regulatory takings. Three broad classes of such takings have emerged in court decisions.

1. **Total Takings.** If a governmental body acts in a way that permanently takes all of the economic value of a property or permanently physically invades the property, the taking requires just compensation unless the government is (1) preventing a nuisance or (2) the regulation was permissible under property law at the time of the purchase of the property. When the South Carolina Coastal Commission passed erosion rules having the effect of preventing David Lucas from building any permanent structure on his $975,000 beachfront lots, Lucas sued, claiming a Fifth Amendment violation. The U.S. Supreme Court agreed with Lucas and held that a taking requiring just compensation had occurred because the state had deprived Lucas of *all* economically beneficial use of the property, and the property did not fall in one of the two exceptions.[55]

> The South Carolina Coastal Commission passed erosion rules having the effect of preventing David Lucas from building any permanent structure on his $975,000 beachfront lots.

2. **Exaction/Mitigation.** A second class of regulatory takings involves situations where the government allows land development only if the owner dedicates some property interest (called an *exaction*) or money (called a *mitigation* or *impact fee*) to the government. Thus if you are developing land for housing, the city government might require that you devote a portion of that land to parks or pay a fee to help with community recreation needs. The Supreme Court dealt with just such a case in *Dolan v. Tigard.*[56] Florence Dolan, owner of a plumbing and electrical supply store in Tigard, Oregon, applied for a city permit to nearly double the size of her store and to pave her parking lot. Concerned with increased traffic and water runoff due to the proposed expansion, the city granted the permit, subject to a pair of conditions: (1) Dolan was to dedicate the portion of her property that lay within the 100-year floodplain to the city to improve drainage for the creek that ran along her property, and (2) she was to dedicate an additional 15-foot strip of her land adjacent to the floodplain for use as a bicycle path/walkway to relieve traffic congestion. Dolan sued and eventually the U.S. Supreme Court ruled that government can compel a dedication of private property to public use where it can establish two factors: (1) A nexus or relationship between the government's legitimate purpose (flood and traffic control in *Dolan*) and the condition imposed (the land Dolan was to dedicate to public purposes) and (2) a "rough proportionality" between the burden imposed (the land given over to public use) and the impact of the development (increased water

runoff and increased traffic).[57] The Supreme Court ruled that Tigard had failed to meet those standards, and Dolan won the case.

A 2013 U.S. Supreme Court decision stretched the *Dolan* reasoning and strengthened property rights. Coy Koontz, Sr., wanted to build on his wetlands property, but the local water management district, consistent with Florida law, denied permission. Koontz was unwilling to either turn over part of his property for public purposes or pay for improvements on other public land as a way of "offsetting" the environmental damage that would have accompanied the development. Koontz sued. The Court, by a 5–4 vote, said the water management district's requirements constituted a taking and were subject to *Dolan*.[58]

3. **Partial Takings.** Government may take part of a piece of property in order to expand a road, install a bike path, or establish a buffer zone, for example. These are neither total takings nor exactions, but rather fall into a case-by-case analysis that, very briefly, considers the importance of the government's goals and the extent of the burden on the property owner.

Zoning in the Sixth Century

Government restraints on property development are not merely a modern imposition, as we learn from the following description of a zoning law in the Byzantine Empire:

> Next came the first zoning law for the beach. Coastal vistas were so cherished, and the competition for them so keen, that by the sixth century the Emperor Justinian the Great was compelled to pass an ordinance barring construction within 100 feet of the shore to protect sea views.

Source: Lena Lencek and Gideon Bosker, *The Beach: The History of Paradise on Earth* (New York: Penguin Group, 1998), p. 31.

The 14th Amendment

Due Process

The Due Process Clauses of both the Fifth Amendment (applying to the federal government) and the 14th Amendment (applying to the states) forbid the government to deprive citizens of life, liberty, or property without due process of law.

Substantive Due Process

Laws that arbitrarily and unfairly infringe on fundamental personal rights and liberties such as privacy, voting, and the various freedoms specified in the Bill of Rights may be challenged on due process grounds. Basically, the purpose of the law must be so compelling as to outweigh the intrusion on personal liberty or the law will be struck down. For example, the U.S. Supreme Court ruled that a Connecticut statute forbidding the use of contraceptives violated the constitutional right to privacy (although the word *privacy* itself does not appear in the U.S. Constitution).[59] By judicial interpretation, the 14th Amendment Due Process Clause "absorbs" the fundamental liberties of the *federal*

Constitution and prohibits *state* laws (in this case, the Connecticut contraceptive ban) that abridge those fundamental liberties such as privacy.

Procedural Due Process

Basically, procedural due process means that the government must provide a fair procedure including *notice* and a *fair hearing* before taking an action affecting a citizen's life, liberty, or property. A fair hearing might require, among others, the right to present evidence, the right to a decision maker free of bias, and the right to appeal. The precise nature of procedural due process depends, however, on the situation. A murder trial requires meticulous attention to procedural fairness; an administrative hearing to appeal a housing officer's decision to banish a student from a dormitory, while required to meet minimal constitutional standards, can be more forgiving in its procedural niceties.

Due Process: Void for Vagueness

A statute may violate due process rights if it is so vaguely written that the ordinary person cannot understand it. The *Skilling* case that follows involves a *void for vagueness* claim arising from the infamous Enron fraud scandal that caused the former Houston, Texas, energy giant—then the seventh largest company in America—to collapse into bankruptcy in 2001. Enron founder Ken Lay (now deceased), chief executive officer Jeffrey Skilling, and chief accounting officer, Richard Causey, were among those indicted for various crimes in association with Enron's spectacular rise from its founding in 1985 to its collapse fewer than 20 years later. Among other alleged wrongs, Skilling was convicted of depriving the corporation and the public of his "honest services" by deceiving the investors about Enron's finances. Skilling allegedly pumped up Enron's share prices by failing to reveal the company's true financial condition. His appeal reached the Supreme Court in 2010 where he claimed that pretrial publicity and Enron's financial damage to Houston poisoned the jury pool and denied him his Sixth Amendment right to trial by an impartial jury. That claim was rejected by the Supreme Court, but Skilling also argued that the language of the "honest services" federal statute used to convict him was so vague that he was deprived of his due process rights.

> Skilling allegedly pumped up Enron's share prices.

LEGAL BRIEFCASE

Skilling v. United States
130 S.Ct. 2896 (2010)

Justice Ginsburg

(I AND II OMITTED-ED.)

III

We next consider whether Skilling's conspiracy conviction was premised on an improper theory of honest-services wire fraud. The honest-services statute, Section 1346, Skilling maintains, is unconstitutionally vague. . . .

A

To place Skilling's constitutional challenge in context, we first review the origin and subsequent application of the honest-services doctrine.

1

Enacted in 1872, the original mail-fraud provision, the predecessor of the modern-day mail- and wire-fraud laws, proscribed, without further elaboration, use of the mails to advance "any scheme or artifice to defraud." See *McNally v. United States,* 483 U.S. 350, 356, 107 S.Ct. 2875, 97 L.Ed.2d 292 (1987). In 1909, Congress amended the statute to prohibit, as it does today, "any scheme or artifice to defraud, *or for obtaining money or property by means of false or fraudulent pretenses, representations, or promises."* Section 1341 (emphasis added); Emphasizing Congress' disjunctive phrasing, the Courts of Appeals, one after the other, interpreted the term "scheme or artifice to defraud" to include deprivations not only of money or property, but also of intangible rights.

* * * * *

2

In 1987, this Court, in *McNally v. United States,* stopped the development of the intangible-rights doctrine in its tracks. *McNally* involved a state officer who, in selecting Kentucky's insurance agent, arranged to procure a share of the agent's commissions via kickbacks paid to companies the official partially controlled. The prosecutor did not charge that, "in the absence of the alleged scheme[,] the Commonwealth would have paid a lower premium or secured better insurance." Instead, the prosecutor maintained that the kickback scheme "defraud[ed] the citizens and government of Kentucky of their right to have the Commonwealth's affairs conducted honestly."

We held that the scheme did not qualify as mail fraud. "Rather than constru[ing] the statute in a manner that leaves its outer boundaries ambiguous and involves the Federal Government in setting standards of disclosure and good government for local and state officials," we read the statute "as limited in scope to the protection of property rights." "If Congress desires to go further," we stated, "it must speak more clearly."

3

Congress responded swiftly. The following year, it enacted a new statute "specifically to cover one of the 'intangible rights' that lower courts had protected . . . prior to *McNally:* 'the intangible right of honest services.'" In full, the honest-services statute stated:

> For the purposes of th[e] chapter [of the United States Code that prohibits, *inter alia,* mail fraud, Section 1341, and wire fraud, Section 1343], the term "scheme or artifice to defraud" includes a scheme or artifice to deprive another of the intangible right of honest services.

B

Congress, Skilling charges, reacted quickly but not clearly: He asserts that Section 1346 is unconstitutionally vague. To satisfy due process, "a penal statute [must] define the criminal offense [1] with sufficient definiteness that ordinary people can understand what conduct is prohibited and [2] in a manner that does not encourage arbitrary and discriminatory enforcement." *Kolender v. Lawson,* 461 U.S. 352, 357, 103 S.Ct. 1855, 75 L.Ed.2d 903 (1983). The void-for-vagueness doctrine embraces these requirements.

According to Skilling, Section 1346 meets neither of the two due process essentials. First, the phrase "the intangible right of honest services," he contends, does not adequately define what behavior it bars. Second, he alleges, Section 1346's "standardless sweep allows policemen, prosecutors, and juries to pursue their personal predilections," thereby "facilitat[ing] opportunistic and arbitrary prosecutions."

In urging invalidation of Section 1346, Skilling swims against our case law's current, which requires us, if we can, to construe, not condemn, Congress' enactments.

* * * * *

There is no doubt that Congress intended Section 1346 to refer to and incorporate the honest-services doctrine recognized in Court of Appeals' decisions before *McNally* derailed the intangible-rights theory of fraud. . . . Congress enacted Section 1346 on the heels *of McNally* and drafted the statute using that decision's terminology.

* * * * *

Satisfied that Congress, by enacting Section 1346, "meant to reinstate the body of *pre-McNally* honest-services law," we have surveyed that case law. In parsing the Courts of Appeals decisions, we acknowledge that Skilling's vagueness challenge has force, for honest-services decisions preceding *McNally* were not models of clarity or consistency.

* * * * *

Although some applications of the *pre-McNally* honest-services doctrine occasioned disagreement among the Courts of Appeals, these cases do not cloud the doctrine's solid core: The "vast majority" of the honest-services cases involved offenders who, in violation of a fiduciary duty, participated in bribery or kickback schemes.

* * * * *

In view of this history, there is no doubt that Congress intended Section 1346 to reach *at least* bribes and kickbacks. Reading the statute to proscribe a wider range of offensive conduct, we acknowledge, would raise the due process concerns underlying the vagueness doctrine. To preserve the statute without transgressing constitutional limitations, we now hold that Section 1346 criminalizes *only* the bribe-and-kickback core of the pre-*McNally* case law.

* * * * *

Interpreted to encompass only bribery and kickback schemes, Section 1346 is not unconstitutionally vague. Recall that the void-for-vagueness doctrine addresses concerns about (1) fair notice and (2) arbitrary and discriminatory prosecutions. . . .

As to fair notice, "whatever the school of thought concerning the scope and meaning of" Section 1346, it has always been "as plain as a pikestaff that" bribes and kickbacks constitute honest-services fraud, *Williams v. United States*, 341 U.S. 97, 101, 71 S.Ct. 576, 95 L.Ed. 774 (1951). . . .

As to arbitrary prosecutions, we perceive no significant risk that the honest-services statute, as we interpret it today, will be stretched out of shape. Its prohibition on bribes and kickbacks draws content not only from the *pre-McNally* case law, but also from federal statutes proscribing—and defining—similar crimes.

* * * * *

C

It remains to determine whether Skilling's conduct violated Section 1346. Skilling's honest-services prosecution, the Government concedes, was not "prototypical." The Government charged Skilling with conspiring to defraud Enron's shareholders by misrepresenting the company's fiscal health, thereby artificially inflating its stock price. It was the Government's theory at trial that Skilling "profited from the fraudulent scheme . . . through the receipt of salary and bonuses, . . . and through the sale of approximately $200 million in Enron stock, which netted him $89 million."

The Government did not, at any time, allege that Skilling solicited or accepted side payments from a third party in exchange for making these misrepresentations. ("[T]he indictment does not allege, and the government's evidence did not show, that [Skilling] engaged in bribery.") It is therefore clear that, as we read Section 1346, Skilling did not commit honest-services fraud.

* * * * *

Affirmed in part. Vacated in part. Remanded.

AFTERWORD

The Supreme Court returned Skilling's case to the federal Fifth Circuit Court of Appeals where, in 2011, the Skilling saga appeared to be nearing its conclusion. The Fifth Circuit upheld Skilling's conviction finding the honest services error was "harmless" in that ample evidence unrelated to the honest services charge supported Skilling's conviction on 19 counts of securities fraud, conspiracy, insider trading and making false representations.[60] At this writing, Skilling is serving his sentence in a Colorado prison, but an agreement was reached to reduce his 24-year sentence by 10 years because of a mistake in interpreting the federal sentencing guidelines. Skilling also agreed to give up about $42 million, all of which will go to Enron fraud victims. The case now seems to be at an end, and Skilling may depart prison as early as 2017.[61]

Questions

1. Why did the Court conclude that Skilling did not commit honest-services fraud?

2. Why did the Court conclude that the honest services statute was unconstitutional?

3. How did the Court correct the unconstitutional infirmity in the honest-services statute?

Equal Protection

The 14th Amendment provides that no state shall "deny to any person within its jurisdiction the equal protection of the laws." The Due Process Clause of the Fifth Amendment has been interpreted to provide that same protection against the power of the federal government. Fundamentally, these laws forbid a government from treating one person (including a corporation) differently from another without a rational basis for doing so. Most notably, the Equal Protection and Due Process Clauses have played an enormous role in attacking discrimination (see Chapter 13), but they can also significantly influence routine business practice in many ways. For example, can we lawfully impose higher taxes on a gambling casino than we impose on the sale of groceries? Or can we require the oil industry to follow more rigorous environmental standards than we expect of coal mines? In general, the answer to these questions is yes, but only if the legislation can pass the rational basis test. If not, such legislation would be unconstitutional and unenforceable.

[The U.S. Supreme Court, in *Loving v. Virginia,* 388 U.S. 1 (1967), employed due process and equal protection principles to declare unconstitutional Virginia's anti-miscegenation statute, thus ending race-based restrictions on marriage in the United States. [For a video of the Loving family and its legal battle, see **http://abcnews.go.com/video /playerIndex?id=3278653**]

How Many Renters?

Trying to reduce the flow of university students into certain portions of the community, Ames, Iowa, home of Iowa State University, passed a zoning ordinance that permitted only single-family residences in specified areas. Under the ordinance, "family" was defined as any number of related persons or no more than three unrelated persons. The Ames Rental Property Association challenged the constitutionality of the ordinance.

Questions

1. Describe the constitutional claim raised by the plaintiffs.
2. Criticize the Ames' standards for achieving its housing goals.
3. Decide the case. Explain.

Source: Ames Rental Property Association v. City of Ames, 736 N.W.2d 255 (Ia. S.Ct. 2007).

Same-Sex Marriage: Equal Rights?

> Edie Windsor struck an historic blow for gay and lesbian rights.

Edie Windsor, an 83-year-old lesbian, struck an historic but not yet definitive blow for gay and lesbian rights when she successfully sued the U.S. government to strike down Section 3 of the federal Defense of Marriage Act (DOMA). Windsor sued because the government, consistent with DOMA, did not recognize her 2007 marriage to Thea Spyer, her long-time partner, who died in 2009. The couple had lived together for 40 years in New York City prior to their marriage in Canada. New York accepted their marriage, but Section 3 of the 1996 DOMA forbids the federal government from recognizing same-sex marriage for the purposes of federal laws and programs. Consequently, the Internal Revenue Service required Windsor to pay $363,053 in taxes on the estate Spyer had left to her. Windsor claimed the federal estate tax exemption for surviving spouses, but because DOMA disallowed recognition of the marriage the federal exemption was not available to Windsor.

Windsor's challenge succeeded when the U.S. Supreme Court in 2013 ruled that Section 3 of DOMA was unconstitutional as a denial of equal protection and due process.[62] The Court's constitutional law reasoning in the case was somewhat undeveloped, but elements of federalism (the states' traditional role in regulating marriage versus broad federal authority—see Chapter 8 for more about federalism), equal protection (DOMA causes some state-sanctioned marriages to be treated differently from others) and substantive due process (the statute denies respect and dignity to same-sex married couples) were all noted.[63] Justice Kennedy, writing for the five-person majority, said that DOMA treated same-sex marriages as "second class," a denial of equal protection.

On the same day as the *Windsor* ruling, the Supreme Court in *Hollingsworth v. Perry* effectively allowed the resumption of same-sex marriages in California.[64] Voters in that state had approved Proposition 8, a ballot initiative prohibiting same-sex marriage that was subsequently ruled unconstitutional (on due process and equal protection grounds) in lower federal court decisions. Proposition 8 proponents took their case to the U.S. Supreme Court, which ruled that those proponents did not suffer direct injury from Proposition 8 and therefore did not have *standing* (see Chapter 4) to sue in federal court. The Supreme Court dismissed the case and same-sex marriage is expected to resume in California.

Responding to the two same-day decisions, superstar lawyer David Boies said, "Today the United States Supreme Court . . . brings us that much closer to true equality."[65] He went on to say, "Everything the Supreme Court said in the Defense of Marriage opinion (*Windsor*) . . . demonstrates that when that case finally does come to the Supreme Court on the merits, marriage equality will be the law throughout this land."[66]

> Marriage equality will be the law throughout this land.

Whether marriage equality is in the offing remains to be seen, but *Windsor* is having an immediate impact. At a practical level, federal marriage benefits under more than 1,000 federal laws will now be available to same-sex couples who were legally married in states recognizing same-sex marriage. Those benefits affect health care, Social Security, hospital visitation rights, taxes, immigration, and much more. Sixteen states and the District of Columbia permit same-sex marriages, but 33 states forbid them. Lawsuits will be filed and, at some point, the Supreme Court presumably will directly address the marriage equality question. Public support for same-sex marriage has shifted very rapidly with 50 percent of Americans favoring those marriages in 2013 whereas only 39 percent supported them just five years earlier in 2008.[67]

Although the *Windsor* decision struck down Section 3 of DOMA, it did not address Section 2, which allows states to refuse to recognize same-sex marriages performed in other states. What happens then to those same-sex couples who are lawfully married but who subsequently move to a state that does not recognize their union? Some federal benefits, such as student aid, are extended according to the law of the place of marriage whereas conferral of other benefits, such as Social Security, looks to the law of the state of residence.[68] Much remains to be litigated. At this writing, for example, three same-sex couples—two of whom are unmarried and were denied marriage licenses and one lawfully married in Iowa—are suing in Utah claiming that the state's constitutional amendment 3, defining marriage as a union exclusively between a man and a woman, is an unconstitutional denial of equal protection and due process of law. In response, Utah's lawyers said the state has a *sovereign* right to define and regulate marriage. Utah points out that state law does not prevent same-sex marriage, but it does prevent those unions from being recognized by the state.[69] Many cases of this kind are expected around the country as the legal system works its way toward addressing the larger question of whether same-sex marriage prohibitions are impermissible under the U.S. Constitution or whether that question resides with the states under federalism principles. That is, which level of government should decide if same-sex couples can be married? Traditionally, the states have done so, but is marriage such a fundamental institution that the federal Constitution's equal protection and due process provisions must be invoked?

PRACTICING ETHICS — Same-Sex Marriage: How Do You Feel?

At this writing in 2013, about 94 million Americans (nearly one-third of the population) live in states that allow same-sex marriage.[70] Worldwide about 585 million people (about 8 percent of the global population) live in countries where same-sex marriage is lawful.[71] Those numbers represent extraordinarily rapid changes in American and global views of gay and lesbian marriage, but the debate is far from settled.

Morally and ethically speaking, which side is "right" about same-sex marriage? How do we decide? Consider some questions that help us sort through this moral thicket:

1. What issues should one consider in deciding whether gay and lesbian marriages are morally defensible?

2. Is a civil union arrangement an acceptable "middle ground?

3. If the American people ultimately favor gay and lesbian marriage, could we then consider a morally defensible practice?

4. Are children at moral risk if raised by same-sex couples?

5. If scholarly studies ultimately demonstrate that homosexuality and lesbianism are substantially commanded by genetic characteristics, would we be morally required to permit same-sex marriage?

Stop-and-Frisk

The New York City police department practices a "stop-and-frisk" policy by which a police officer can stop and question those whom the officer reasonably believes to have committed, be committing, or be about to commit a felony or serious misdemeanor. Those stopped can be frisked for weapons if the officer reasonably believes he or she is in danger of physical injury.

The stop-and-frisk police practice is constitutionally permissible if conducted properly, but in a 2013 class-action lawsuit, *Floyd v. City of New York,* federal district court judge Shira Scheindlin ruled that stop-and-frisk, as practiced in recent years in New York City, is an impermissible violation of citizens' Fourth Amendment (search and seizure) and 14th Amendment (equal protection) rights. The judge ruled that police had routinely stopped innocent people without reasonable suspicion and that the police had been engaging in racial profiling. About 83 percent of the 4.4 million stops between 2004 and 2012 had involved blacks and Hispanics, two demographics that make up slightly more than 50 percent of the city population. The city argued that the racial pattern of the stops reflected the disproportionate share of crimes committed by young minority men, but the judge rejected that reasoning saying that comparison would be valid only if those stopped were criminals, but 88 percent of those stopped were released with no finding of a justification for the stops. Judge Scheindlin did not order a halt to stop-and-frisk, which is an important law enforcement tool if properly employed. She did appoint a monitor to ensure police compliance with remedies including the use of body-worn cameras by some officers. The case is on appeal at this writing.

Question

Judge Scheindlin said, "It is impermissible to subject all members of a racially defined group to heightened police enforcement because some members of that group are criminals." Do you agree? Explain.

Sources: Joseph Goldstein, "Judge Rejects New York's Stop-and-Frisk Policy, *The New York Times,* August 12, 2013 [**http://www.nytimes.com/**]; and *Floyd v. City of New York,* 2013 U.S. Dist. LEXIS 113271.

Internet Exercise

At the First Amendment Center, read "About the First Amendment" [**www.firstamendmentcenter.org/about-the-first-amendment**]. Explain the importance of the First Amendment and why Americans are divided about its application.

Chapter Questions

1. Members of the Jefferson County High School, T varsity football team circulated a petition that said: "I hate Coach Euvard [*sic*] and I don't want to play for him." Thereafter, all team members were asked if they were involved. Euverard dismissed four players who admitted they signed the petition and refused to apologize for doing so. The players who signed the petition but apologized were retained on the team. The four dismissed players filed suit. (*a*) Explain their primary legal claim. (*b*) Decide the case. Explain. See *Lowery v. Euverard,* 497 F.3d 584 (6th Cir. 2007).

2. Bradley Johnson, a high school mathematics teacher, posted on his classroom walls large banners with familiar phrases such as "In God We Trust," "One Nation Under God," and "God Shed His Grace on Thee." School officials told him he needed to put the phrases in context (e.g., put the entire Declaration of Independence on the wall) or remove them. He did the latter and sued the school district for violating his First Amendment free speech and religious expression rights. In part, he defended his banner by pointing to displays in other classrooms that included Tibetan prayer flags, a Dalai Lama poster, and others. Decide Johnson's lawsuit. See *Johnson v. Poway Unified School District,* 658 F.3d 954 (9th Cir. 2011); cert. den. *Johnson v. Poway Unified School District,* 132 S.Ct. 1807 (2012).

3. Several city ordinances in Arkansas made it illegal for "any person to place a hand-bill or advertisement on any other person's vehicle parked on public property within city limits." Church members contested the constitutionality of the ordinances, which prevented them from lawfully placing religious handbills on parked cars. Decide. Explain. See *Krantz v. City of Fort Smith,* 160 F.3d 1214 (8th Cir. 1998).

4. The Georgia Outdoor Advertising Control Act, in essence, prohibited any off-premises outdoor advertising of commercial establishments where nudity was exhibited. Cafe Erotica lawfully provided food and adult entertainment, including nude dancing, and advertised those services on billboards. Cafe Erotica challenged the constitutionality of the Advertising Control Act. Decide. Explain. See *Georgia v. Cafe Erotica,* 507 S.E.2d 732 (Ga. S.Ct. 1998).

5. Early in the morning hours, McNeeley was stopped by Missouri police for speeding and erratic driving. McNeeley was required to take a blood test after he had refused a breath test with a portable machine. His blood alcohol content was about twice the legal limit. He was charged with driving while intoxicated. Was the warrantless blood test an unreasonable search? Explain. See *Missouri v. McNeely*, 133 S.Ct. 1552 (2013).

6. Police officer Hughes, from Council Bluffs, Iowa, saw Sorick, 28 years of age, riding his bicycle at 12:35 a.m. without lights in violation of a city ordinance. Hughes stopped Sorick, asked if he was carrying a weapon, and then frisked him, at which time he felt what he believed to be a baggie containing a hard substance. Hughes asked Sorick what the substance was, and Sorick said it was marijuana. Hughes issued a citation for possession of marijuana. Sorick was found guilty at trial but appealed, claiming the frisk was an unreasonable search. Hughes testified that he searched Sorick because Hughes feared for

his safety. The episode was late at night, the street was not lit, Sorick was in close proximity to Hughes, and people in that neighborhood were known to have weapons. Was the search lawful? Explain. See *Iowa v. Sorick*, 810 N.W.2d 896 (Ia. Ct. App. 2012).

7. James D. Harmon, Jr., owns an apartment building on West 76th Street near Central Park in New York City. Three of his apartments are subject to rent control, a long-time city program designed to maintain affordable housing in the very expensive Manhattan market. The rent-stabilized tenants were paying rent at 59 percent below market rates, according to Harmon.
   a. Harmon called rent control "privatized welfare." Explain what he meant.
   b. Harmon challenged the rent restriction. What constitutional law claim(s) was(were) raised by Harmon?
   c. Who won the case? Explain. See *Harmon v. Markus*, 2011 U.S. App. LEXIS 4629; cert. den. *Harmon v. Kimmel*, 132 S.Ct. 1991 (2012).

8. An Erie, Pennsylvania, public indecency ordinance prohibited knowingly or intentionally appearing in public in a "state of nudity." Pap's, the owners of Kandyland, an Erie establishment featuring totally nude dancers, challenged the constitutionality of the ordinance.
   a. Explain the nature of that constitutional challenge.
   b. Decide the case. Explain. See *City of Erie v. Pap's A.M.*, 529 U.S. 277 (2000).

9. An individual and a group applied to the Chicago Park District for permits to hold rallies advocating the legalization of marijuana. The Park District, a municipal agency, required a permit to conduct a public assembly, parade, or other event involving more than 50 individuals. Applications for permits had to be processed within 28 days, and denials had to be clearly explained. Denials could be appealed to the general superintendent and then to the courts. The Park District denied some of the permits for pro-marijuana rallies. Those denied filed suit, claiming the Park District permit rules were unconstitutional.
   a. What constitutional challenge was raised by the plaintiffs?
   b. Decide the case. Explain. See *Thomas and Windy City Hemp Development Board v. Chicago Park District*, 534 U.S. 316 (2002).

10. U.S. Supreme Court Justice Antonin Scalia was asked if the judicial system had "gone off in error" by applying the equal protection requirements of the 14th Amendment to sex discrimination and sexual orientation discrimination. Scalia responded, "Yes, yes. . . . Certainly the Constitution does not require discrimination on the basis of sex. The only issue is whether it prohibits it. It doesn't. . . ."[72]
    a. Explain why Scalia believes the 14th Amendment does not forbid discrimination based on sex and sexual orientation.
    b. Do you agree with Scalia? Explain.

11. Lancaster, California, located about 45 miles from Los Angeles, was trying to build its local economy but was tripped up by the U.S. Constitution. Costco, a big-box retailer, wanted to expand into next-door space leased to 99 Cents Only Stores. Costco told the city it would move to Palmdale if it could not expand. Lancaster tried to buy 99 Cents' lease, but the company refused. Lancaster then used its power of eminent domain to condemn the 99 Cents property for the purpose of making it available to Costco. The city noted that blight might follow if Costco left, and the city contrasted 99 Cents' under $40,000 per year

in sales taxes generated with Costco's more than $400,000. 99 Cents then sued the city seeking an order blocking the effort to take the 99 Cents property.

a. How would you have ruled on the case when it was tried in 2001? Explain.

b. Would the result be any different today after the Supreme Court's 2005 decision in the *Kelo* (New London, Connecticut) case? Explain. See *99 Cents Only Stores v. Lancaster Redevelopment Agency,* 237 F.Supp.2d 1123 (C.D. Cal. 2001). Appeal dismissed, 2003 U.S. App. LEXIS 4197.

12. Long Island, New York, resident Stephanie Fuller was secretly videotaped by her landlord, who had installed a video camera in the smoke detector above her bed. Fuller's landlord was found guilty of trespassing and was fined $1,500 and sentenced to 280 hours of community service.

a. Why was the landlord not charged with a more serious felony offense?

b. After Fuller's experience, New York enacted a criminal unlawful surveillance statute; the statute includes language forbidding secret surveillance in places where the victim has "a reasonable expectation of privacy." What significance attaches to that language?

13. Former North Carolina State University basketball stars Tom Gugliotta and Chris Corchiani were ejected from North Carolina State's arena during a 2012 game with Florida State University. Referee Karl Hess asked a police officer to eject the two men who were seated immediately behind the scorer's table. Hess said he requested the ejections because of excessive demonstration by the two men that incited the crowd. Both men said they had not used inappropriate language. The Atlantic Coast Conference reprimanded Hess for not following conference protocol in the incident. Home game management officials rather than a security officer should have been involved in ejecting the fans. Does the First Amendment protect speech uttered at sporting events? Explain.

14. Milwaukee prostitutes, who had been arrested on multiple occasions, sued to block the city from enforcing a court-ordered injunction that permanently enjoined them from engaging in certain specified activities in certain specified areas of the city. They were prohibited from "engaging in beckoning to stop, or engaging male or female passersby in conversation, or stopping or attempting to stop motor vehicle operators by hailing, waving of arms or any other bodily gesture, or yelling in a loud voice" and other such activities. The women challenged the order on constitutional grounds.

a. Explain the nature of that constitutional challenge.

b. Decide the case. Explain. See *City of Milwaukee v. Burnette,* 637 N.W.2d 447 (Wis. App. 2001); 638 N.W.2d 590 (Wis. S.Ct. 2001).

15. Jennifer O'Brien, a tenured teacher in the Paterson, New Jersey, schools with an unblemished performance record, was assigned to teach first grade in a school populated primarily by minority students. After a time, O'Brien concluded that several students in the class had behavioral problems that were disturbing the learning environment. Some students were hitting each other, one struck O'Brien, and another stole money from O'Brien and other students. O'Brien felt administrators had not responded adequately to her complaints, and she posted on her own Facebook page after school hours: "I'm not a teacher—I'm a warden for future criminals." Parents and others were outraged. Protests followed. O'Brien said her remarks were not a commentary on race or ethnicity but were legitimate concerns about the behavior of some students. O'Brien was

dismissed from her teaching position. She sued, claiming, among other things, her actions were protected by the First Amendment. Decide the case. Explain. See *In the Matter of the Tenure Hearing of Jennifer O'Brien, State Operated School District of the City of Paterson, Passaic County,* 2013 N.J. Super. Unpub. LEXIS 28 (Sup. Ct. of N.J. App. Div. 2013).

16. Paul Palmer submitted three shirts to his Waxahachie, Texas, school for approval under the school's dress code. Two of the shirts said "John Edwards for President" and one said "Freedom of Speech" on the front and had the text of the First Amendment on the back. The shirts were rejected as violations of the school's dress code that did not allow shirts with printed messages except for those related to the school and those smaller than two inches by two inches. Political messages were permitted on pins, buttons, bumper stickers, and the like. The dress code was designed to curb gang problems, reduce distractions, encourage professional dress, and maintain a safer, more orderly learning environment. Palmer sued the school claiming a violation of his First Amendment freedom of speech rights. Decide that case. Explain. See *Palmer v. Waxahachie Independent School District,* 579 F.3d 502 (5th Cir. 2009); cert. den. *Palmer v. Waxahachie Independent School District,* 130 S.Ct. 1055 (2010).

17. The sons of a murder victim brought a wrongful death/negligence action against a magazine, *Soldier of Fortune,* alleging that it had published an ad creating an unreasonable risk of violent crime. A former police officer had placed the ad offering his services as a bodyguard under the heading "Gun for Hire." The ad resulted in the officer being hired to kill the plaintiffs' father. The ad included the phrases "professional mercenary," "very private," and a statement indicating that "all jobs" would be considered, but it also included a list of legitimate jobs that involved the use of a gun. The plaintiffs won the negligence action and were awarded a $4.3 million judgment. *Soldier of Fortune* appealed on First Amendment grounds. Decide. See *Braun v. Soldier of Fortune Magazine, Inc.,* 968 F.2d 1110 (11th Cir. 1992); cert. den. 113 S.Ct. 1028 (1993).

18. The Madisonian idea of the First Amendment was to protect serious political discourse. Now the First Amendment often protects hate speech and commercial babble. In a 1996 book review and commentary, lawyer Paul Reidinger raised the concern that we may have "too much" free speech. Reidinger said, "The question these days is not whether government threatens free speech, but whether free speech threatens us. . . . [T]here is a tidal wave of fetid speech washing over the American landscape." Has the marketplace of ideas failed? See Paul Reidinger, "Weighing Cost of Free Speech," *ABA Journal* 82 (January 1996), p. 88.

Notes

1. Portions of this history of the U.S. Constitution rely on Gordon Lloyd, "Introduction to the Constitutional Convention," [**http://teachingamericanhistory.org/convention/intro.html**].

2. *McDonald v. Chicago,* 130 S.Ct. 3020 (2010).

3. Aaron Blake, "Record Number of Americans Oppose Handgun Ban," *The Washington Post,* December 27, 2012 [**http://www.washingtonpost.com/**].

4. Editorial, "The Court: Ignoring the Reality of Guns," *The New York Times,* June 28, 2010 [**http://www.nytimes.com**].

5. Jeffrey Brumer, "Comparing Gun Homicides in U.S. vs. Other Countries," *The Des Moines Register,* January 23, 2011, p. 2A.

6. Jerre Williams, *Constitutional Analysis in a Nutshell* (St. Paul: West, 1979), p. 33.

7. *McCulloch v. Maryland,* 17 U.S. 316 (1819).

8. *Marbury v. Madison,* 5 U.S. (1 Cranch) 137 (1803).

9. For a discussion of judicial activism, see Kevin Baine, "Making Law on the Court," *The Washington Post,* June 9, 2009 [**http://www.washingtonpost.com/**].

10. *Shelby County v. Holder,* 133 S.Ct. 2612 (2013).

11. Charles Savage and Adam Liptak, "Holder Wants Texas to Clear Voting Changes with the U.S.," *The New York Times,* July 25, 2013 [**http://www.nytimes.com/**].

12. Evan Halper, "Landmark California Regulations Under Federal Fire," *latimes.com,* July 28, 2013 [**http://www.latimes.com/**].

13. *Joyner v. Forsyth County North Carolina,* 653 F.3d 341 (4th Cir. 2011).

14. See *Lemon v. Kurtzman,* 403 U.S. 602 (1971).

15. Terence Chea, "'Under God' in Pledge of Allegiance Upheld by Court," *Huffington Post,* March 12, 2010 [**http://www.huffingtonpost.com/**].

16. *Newdow v. Rio Linda Union School District,* 597 F.3d 1007 (9th Cir. 2010).

17. *Newdow v. Lefevre,* 598 F.3d 638 (9th Cir. 2010); cert. den., *Newdow v. Peter Lefevre,* 131 S.Ct. 1612 (2011).

18. *Christian Legal Society v. Leo P. Martinez,* 130 S.Ct. 2971 (2010).

19. Adelle M. Banks, "*Christian Legal Society v. Martinez* Decision Upends Campus Religious Groups," *HuffPost Religion,* May 11, 2012 [**http://www.huffingtonpost.com/**].

20. Cheryl Lavin, "The Redemption of Larry Flynt," *Chicago Tribune,* December 27, 1996 [**http://articles.chicagotribune.com/**].

21. 393 U.S. 503 (1969).

22. *Snyder v. Phelps,* 131 S.Ct. 1207 (2011).

23. Adam Cohen, "Why Spewing Hate at Funerals Is Still Free Speech," *Time,* September 29, 2010 [**http://www.time.com/**].

24. *Dixon v. University of Toledo,* 702 F.3d 269 (6th Cir. 2012).

25. *Garcetti v. Ceballos,* 126 S.Ct. 1951 (2006).

26. Alexandra Petri, "As Sexual Harassment 'Blueprint' Restricts Verbal Conduct: Things Not to Say on Campus," *The Washington Post,* June 6, 2013 [**http://www.washingtonpost.com/**].

27. "Senator John McCain Sends Letters to DOJ and EPA on Obama Administration Settlement Abuse," *Press Release,* June 26, 2013 [**http://www.mccain.senate.gov/**].

28. David Ariosto and Leigh Remizowski,"Yale Settles Sexual Harassment Complaint," *CNN.com,* [**http://www.cnn.com/**].

29. Erica Goldberg, "Universities' Compliance with Speech Code Decisions Leaves Much to Be Desired," September 24, 2009, *Foundation for Individual Rights in Education—The Torch* [**http://thefire.org/article/11121.html**].

30. *Rodriguez v. Maricopa County Community College,* 605 F.3d 703 (9th Cir. 2010).

31. *Barrett v. University of Mississippi,* 232 F.3d 208 (5th Cir. 2000); cert. den. 531 U.S. 1052 (2000).

32. *Corry v. Stanford University,* Superior Court, Santa Clara County (CA), #740309, February 27, 1995.

33. *Valentine v. Chrestensen,* 316 U.S. 52 (1942).

34. *Citizens United v. Federal Election Commission,* 130 S.Ct. 876 (2010).

35. David G. Savage, "Corporate Free-Speech Ruling Speaks of Shift in Supreme Court," *Los Angeles Times* February 9, 2010 [**http://www.latimes.com/**].

36. *Citizens United,* 2010.

37. David G. Savage, "Corporate Free-Speech," February 9, 2010.

38. *United States v. Stevens,* 130 S.Ct. 1577 (2010).

39. Norman M. Cheektowaga, "And a Rude Gesture to You, Too, Judges," *Buffalo News,* February 5, 1998, p. 3B.

40. *United States v. Jones,* 132 S.Ct. 945 (2012).

41. 367 U.S. 643.

42. *Hudson v. Michigan,* 126 S.Ct. 2159 (2006).

43. *Herring v. United States,* 555 U.S. 135 (2009).

44. *Arizona v. Gant,* 129 S.Ct. 1710 (2009).

45. This paragraph is derived in part from Adam Liptak, "Supreme Court Cuts Back Officers' Searches of Vehicles," *The New York Times,* April 22, 2009 [**http://www.nytimes.com/**].

46. *Ohio v. Smith,* 920 N.E.2d 949 (Ohio S.Ct. 2009).

47. *The People v. Gregory Diaz,* 244 P.3d 501 (Cal. S.Ct. 2011).

48. *Board of Education of Pottawatomie County v. Earls,* 122 S.Ct. 2559 (2002).

49. *Earls v. Board of Education,* 242 F.3d 1264 (10th Cir. 2001).

50. Floralynn Einesman, "Drug Testing Students in California—Does It Violate the State Constitution?" *San Diego Law Review* 47 (Summer 2010), p. 681.

51. Mary Pilon, "Middle Schools Add a Team Rule: Get a Drug Test," *New York Times,* September 22, 2012 [**http://www.nytimes.com**].

52. *State of Washington v. Glas,* 2002 Wash. LEXIS 596.

53. *Maryland v. King,* 133 S.Ct. 1958 (2013).

54. *Marshall v. Barlow's,* 436 U.S. 307 (1978).

55. *Lucas v. So. Carolina Coastal Commission,* 112 S.Ct. 2886 (1992).

56. *Dolan v. City of Tigard,* 114 S.Ct. 2309 (1994).

57. Frank A. Vickory and Barry A. Diskin, "Advances in Private Property Protection Rights: The States in the Vanguard," *American Business Law Journal* 34, no. 4 (Summer 1997), p. 561.

58. *Koontz v. St. Johns River Water,* 133 S.Ct. 2586 (2013).

59. *Griswold v. Connecticut,* 381 U.S. 479 (1965).

60. *United States v. Skilling,* 2011 U.S. App. LEXIS 7031.

61. Peter Lattman, "Ex-Enron Chief's Sentence Is Cut by 10 Years, to 14, *The New York Times Dealbook,* June 21, 2013 [**http://dealbook.nytimes.com/**].

62. *United States v. Windsor,* 133 S.Ct. 2675 (2013).

63. Linda Greenhouse, "Current Conditions," *The New York Times Opinionator,* June 26, 2013 [**http://opinionator.blogs.nytimes.com/**].

64. *Hollingsworth v. Perry,* 133 S.Ct. 2652 (2013).

65. Stephanie Condon, "Supreme Court Strikes Down Key Part of DOMA, Dismisses Prop. 8 Case," *CBS News,* June 26, 2013 [**http://www.cbsnews.com/**].

66. Ibid.

67. Geoffrey Fowler and Vauhini Vara, "Public Shifts Fast on Same-Sex Union Support," *The Wall Street Journal,* June 23, 2013 [**http://online.wsj.com/**].

68. Victoria Stilwell, Jeanna Smialek, and Meera Louis, "Gay Marriage Shows States Luring Discriminated Couples," *Bloomberg,* August 14, 2013 [**http://www.bloomberg.com/**].

69. Brooke Adams and Ray Parker, "Utah: State Has 'Sovereign' Right to Bar Same-Sex Marriages," *Salt Lake Tribune,* August 14, 2013 [**http://www.sltrib.com/**].

70. Nate Silver, "Same-Sex Marriage Availability Set to Double in One-Year Span," *The New York Times FiveThirtyEight,* June 26, 2013 [**http://fivethirtyeight.blogs.nytimes.com/**].

71. Ibid.

72. "The Originalist," *California Lawyer,* January 2011 [**http://www.callawyer.com/story.cfm?eid=913358&evid=1**].

CHAPTER SIX

Contracts

After completing this chapter, students will be able to:

1. Explain the importance of contracts to a capitalist, free-market system.

2. Determine whether the Uniform Commercial Code or common law governs a contract dispute.

3. Identify the elements of a legally enforceable contract.

4. Classify a contract as bilateral or unilateral; express or implied; executory or executed.

5. Distinguish between valid, unenforceable, void, and voidable contracts.

6. Describe the elements of a valid offer.

7. Describe the elements of a valid acceptance.

8. Explain the significance of consideration as an element of a legally enforceable contract.

9. Compare and contrast the rights and duties arising in contractual assignment and delegation.

10. Compare and contrast different types of third-party beneficiaries to a contract.

11. Explain how a contract may be discharged.

12. Describe the remedies available for breach of contract.

Preface: The Role of Contracts in a Complex Society

A capitalist, free-market system cannot operate effectively and fairly without a reliable foundation in contract law. At the practical level, all buyers and sellers must be confident that the deal they are about to make will be completed as specified, or that they will have a remedy available if it is not completed. Otherwise, the legal risk in making deals would act as a drag on the commercial process, reducing certainty and depreciating the extraordinary efficiency of the free market. At the philosophical level, the fundamental point of a contract is personal freedom. Contract law gives each of us a reliable mechanism for freely expressing our preferences in life. From buying a tube of toothpaste, a car, or a house, to paying tuition, to accepting an employment offer, to franchising a business, to borrowing millions of dollars, to adopting a child, and so on, the direction and value of our lives are shaped and protected to a significant degree by our contractual choices. To a considerable extent, we define ourselves by the contractual choices we make, and contract law protects those choices. The indispensable role of contract law is revealed in the remarkable Facebook story that follows.

Sharing Facebook?

Mark Zuckerberg, Facebook CEO, developed the fabulously successful social network while still a student at Harvard. However, prior to Facebook becoming a publicly traded company in 2012, Zuckerberg's ownership was challenged twice. In 2011, entrepreneur Paul Ceglia, for whom Zuckerberg apparently agreed to write computer code while at Harvard, claimed that he and Zuckerberg entered into a contract in 2003 that entitled Ceglia to a 50 percent share in the company. In 2013, Ceglia's lawsuit was dismissed based on a federal judge's conclusion that there was "clear and convincing evidence" that the contract on which Ceglia based his complaint was forged. In 2012, Ceglia pleaded not guilty to federal charges of mail and wire fraud for forging evidence in his lawsuit. [For the alleged Ceglia–Zuckerberg contract, see "Work for Hire Contract" at **http:// www.businessinsider.com/mark-zuckerbergs-facebook-contract-with-paul-ceglia**]

The battle between Zuckerberg and his college business partners, twins Cameron and Tyler Winklevoss, over the rights to the Facebook idea was the subject of the 2010 movie, *The Social Network.* The twins claim Zuckerberg stole their social networking idea. Zuckerberg denied that accusation, but the parties reached a settlement of about $65 million in 2008. The twins sued, however, to have the settlement overturned on the grounds that Facebook had not provided accurate valuation information during the settlement process. A court of appeals panel in 2011 rejected the twin's request; the Winkelvoss twins later dropped their U.S. Supreme Court appeal of that decision.

Also in 2011, Boston software developer Wayne Chang sued the Winklevoss twins for breach of contract, among other claims. Chang believes he is entitled to a share of the Winklevoss–Zuckerberg settlement (currently valued at around $160 million) based on a partnership and other understandings he claims to have entered with the twins during their Harvard years to create and operate a social networking site named ConnectU.

Sources: Jonathan Stempel and Nate Raymond, "Judge Recommends Ceglia Case vs. Facebook Be Dismissed," *Reuters.com,* March 26, 2013 [**www.reuters.com**]; Bob Van Voris, "Facebook Says Ceglia Fraud Is Proven by 'Authentic Contract' sent in 2004," *Bloomberg Technology,* August 18, 2011 [**www.bloomberg.com**]; Galen Moore, "Boston Entrepreneur Chang Seeks Half of Winklevoss' Facebook Settlement," *Boston Business Journal,* June 23, 2011 [**www.bizjournals.com**]; Bob Van Voris, "Facebook Claimant Says He Owns 50%, Has E-Mails as Proof," *Bloomberg Businessweek,* April 12, 2011 [**http://www.businessweek.com**]; "Boston Developer Wants Cut of Winklevoss Twins' $65-Million Facebook Settlement," *Los Angeles Times,* May 12, 2011 [**http://latimesblogs.latimes.com/technology/2011/05/boston-developer-wants-cut-of-winklevoss-twins-65-million-facebook-settlement.html**]; Alice Gomstyn and Ki Mae Heussner, "Paul Ceglia: Facebook Claim Stemmed from Arrest," ABC News, August 2, 2010 [**http://abcnews.go.com**]; and Henry Blodget, "Analyzing the Facebook Contract: Is Mark Zuckerberg Screwed?" *Business Insider,* July 23, 2010 [**http://www.businessinsider.com**].

Part One—Building a Binding Contract

Introduction

Have you breached a contract?

We make promises routinely in our lives. Some of those create binding contracts; some do not. You promise, for example, to meet a friend after class, but you break your promise. Could your friend sue you in court for breach of contract? Doubtless your answer is "no" and, barring unusual circumstances, you would be correct. But why? This raises the central question in this chapter: Under what circumstances do promises become enforceable contracts? For the most part, the answer to that question has been provided by court decisions (the common law) accumulating over the many centuries of evolving contract law stretching from the ancient Middle East to England and across the Atlantic to America. Those centuries of decisions have provided a substantially fair, consistent, and predictable body of contract law, particularly in a culture where the parties normally dealt with each other face-to-face, often as acquaintances. As business transactions became more complicated, the parties more and more distant from each other, and the comparative power between individuals and corporations evermore unbalanced, the need for government intervention increased. State legislatures began to impose new rules on what had been purely private transactions. Look, for example, at state and federal regulation of employment contracts/relationships governing working conditions such as hours of work, safety on the job, break time, and more (as explained in detail in Chapter 12). State laws and court decisions resulted, to some extent, in a confusing, inefficient patchwork of laws that didn't conform to the reality of complex, contemporary business practice. As a result, the Uniform Commercial Code, a body of rules on commercial law across the United States, was developed and then adopted by state legislatures.

The Uniform Commercial Code

The National Conference of Commissioners on Uniform State Laws (NCCUSL) and the American Law Institute (ALI) developed, for state-by-state approval, the Uniform Commercial Code (UCC), a body of rules designed to render commercial law consistent across the 50 states. The UCC has been adopted in 49 states, and Louisiana has adopted portions of it. With a set of uniform, predictable rules, business can be practiced with confidence and minimal legal confusion.

The UCC is divided into a series of articles addressing the multitude of potential issues that arise in complex commercial practice. For our purposes the most important of those articles is Number 2, Sales, which governs all transactions involving the *sale of goods*. Section 2-105 of the UCC defines goods as tangible, movable, things. Hence cars, clothing, appliances, and the like are covered. Real estate, stocks, bonds, money, and so forth are not covered. Nor are contracts for services governed by the UCC. Of course, many transactions involve both goods and services. Characteristically, in determining whether the UCC applies, the courts have asked whether the dominant purpose of the contract is to provide a service or to sell a good. Appendix B, at the back of the text, sets out the complete Article 2.

The first question, then, in contract disputes is whether the UCC or the common law governs the situation. Throughout this chapter, you should remember that the UCC is always controlling (1) if the transaction is addressed by the UCC—that is, it involves a contract for the sale of goods—and (2) if a UCC rule applies to the issue in question. On the other hand, the judge-made, common law of contracts continues to govern transactions (1) not involving the sale of goods or (2) involving the sale of goods but where no specific UCC provision applies. Increasingly, in non-UCC cases, the courts are analogizing to UCC reasoning to render their judgments; that is, the common law is borrowing or absorbing UCC principles. This chapter, while focusing primarily on the common law of contracts, will introduce the role of the sales article in the practice of business. Article 2A of the UCC governs *leases* of goods. In essence, Article 2A mimics the sales article except that it governs leases of goods rather than sales. Because of space constraints, Article 2A will not receive further attention in this text. In 2011, the NCCUSL/ALI withdrew the 2003 recommended revisions to Articles 2 and 2A; no state had yet adopted these revisions, and the prospect for adoption was dim.

What Is a Contract?

Legally enforceable contracts must exhibit all of the following features:

1. **Agreement.** A meeting of the minds of the parties based on an offer by one and an acceptance by the other. The determination as to whether the parties have actually reached agreement is based on the *objective* evidence (the parties' acts, words, and so on) as a "reasonable person" would interpret it rather than on an effort to ascertain the subjective or personal intent of the parties.

2. **Consideration.** The bargained-for legal value that one party agrees to pay or provide to secure the promise of another.

3. **Capacity.** The parties must have the legal ability to enter the contract; that is, they must be sane, sober, and of legal age.

4. **Genuineness of assent.** The parties must knowingly agree to the same thing. Their minds must meet as shown by the objective evidence. If that meeting does not occur because of, for example, mistake or fraud, or the like, a contract does not exist because the parties' assent was not real.

5. **Legality of purpose.** The object of the contract must not violate the law or public policy.

Contracts embracing these five features are enforceable by law; therefore, they are distinguishable from unenforceable promises. As explained later, some contracts must also be in writing to be enforceable.

Classification of Contracts

Contracts fall into a series of sometimes overlapping categories. These categories reveal the rather well-ordered logic of our contract system (see Figure 6.1).

Contract Formation

1. **Bilateral and unilateral contracts.** A *bilateral contract* emerges from a situation in which *both* parties make promises. A *unilateral contract* ordinarily involves a situation in which one party makes a promise and the other *acts* in response to that promise. For example, as you establish your new restaurant, you promise a college friend that if he completes his degree, you will hire him. He can accept your promise—or offer—by the act of completing college.

2. **Express and implied contracts.** When parties overtly and explicitly manifest their intention to enter an agreement, either in writing or orally, the result (if other requirements are fulfilled) is an express contract. For example, in managing the accounting department at an insurance firm, you sign a form contract with a local computer store ordering a new computer. In turn, the supplier's signature on the form creates an express, bilateral agreement.

FIGURE 6.1
Classification of Contracts

Contract Formation
1. Bilateral/unilateral
   a. Bilateral contract—a promise for a promise.
   b. Unilateral contract—a promise for an act.
2. Express/implied
   a. Express contract—explicitly stated in writing or orally.
   b. Implied-in-fact contract—inferred from the conduct of the parties.
   c. Quasi-contract—implied contract created by a court to prevent unjust enrichment.

Contract performance
1. Executory contract—not yet fully performed.
2. Executed contract—fully performed by all parties.

Contract enforceability
1. Valid contract—includes all of the necessary ingredients of a binding contract.
2. Unenforceable contract—contract exists, but a legal defense prevents enforcement.
3. Void contract—no enforceable contract at all.
4. Voidable contract—one party has the option of either enforcing or voiding the contract.

If, on the other hand, you ask your local computer service to repair a computer that is down and one of the service's technicians does so, you have probably entered an *implied-in-fact contract*. A court would infer a promise by you to pay a reasonable price in return for the service's promise to make a commercially reasonable effort to repair the computer. The contract is inferred on the basis of the facts—that is, by the behavior of the parties.

Suppose in managing the accounting department at the insurance firm, you receive a premium payment for a policy that was not issued by your company, but rather by your rival firm. In these circumstances, it would be unfair for you to be able to keep the unearned money; therefore, the courts construct an implied-in-law or quasi-contract permitting the actual insurer to collect the money. This unusual situation in which the court infers the existence of a contract is employed only when necessary to prevent *unjust enrichment* (as would have been the case if you were to collect an insurance premium without having issued a policy).

Contract Performance

1. **Executory contracts.** A contract is labeled *executory* until all parties fully perform.

2. **Executed contracts.** When all parties have completed their performances, the contract is *executed*.

Contract Enforceability

1. **Valid contracts.** A valid contract meets all of the established legal requirements and thus is enforceable in court.

2. **Unenforceable contracts.** An unenforceable contract meets the basic contractual requirements but remains faulty because it fails to fulfill some other legal rule. For example, an oral contract may be unenforceable if it falls in one of those categories of contracts, such as the sale of land, which must be in writing (see the Statute of Frauds later in this chapter).

3. **Void contracts.** A void contract is, in fact, no contract at all because a critical legal requirement is missing; usually it is either an agreement to accomplish an illegal purpose (such as to commit a crime) or an agreement involving an incompetent (such as an individual judged by a court to be insane). In either case what is otherwise an enforceable contract is in fact void.

4. **Voidable contracts.** A voidable contract is enforceable but can be canceled by one or more of the parties. The most common voidable contracts are those entered by minors who have the option, under the law, of either disaffirming or fulfilling most contracts (explained later).

Can I Change My Mind?

Australian Vin Thomas placed his 1946 World War II Wirraway plane for sale on eBay. The plane reportedly is one of only five in the world still flying. Peter Smythe, also of Australia, matched the $128,640 reserve price moments before the online auction ended in 2006. Thomas then declined to convey the airplane to Smythe apparently because Thomas had already agreed to sell the plane to another party for $85,800 more than Smythe's bid. The case involved, among others, a pair of issues frequently arising in contracts law disputes: (1) Did the facts (the eBay auction) create a contract? (2) Can Thomas change his mind about selling the plane to the highest bidder?

Answer those questions according to the U.S. contract law that follows.

The Agreement: Offer

Characteristically, an offer consists of a promise to do something or to refrain from doing something in the future. A valid offer must include all of these elements:

1. Present *intent* to enter a contract.
2. Reasonable *definiteness* in the terms of the offer.
3. *Communication* of the offer to the offeree.

Intent

Assume that you are the purchasing manager for a trucking firm, and you need a small used van to do some local light hauling. Because time is of the essence, you decide to bypass the normal bidding process and go directly to the local dealers to make a quick purchase. At the first lot you find a suitable van. In discussing it, the sales manager says, "Well, we don't usually do this, but since you've been such a good customer, I'll tell you, we paid $10,000 for this one so I guess we are gonna need about $11,000 to deal with you." You say, "Fine. That's reasonable. I'll take it." The manager then says, "Now wait a minute, I was just talking off the top of my head. I'll have to punch up the numbers to be sure."

Do you have a deal at that point? The core question is whether the sales manager made an *offer*. Normally, language of that kind has been treated by the courts as preliminary negotiation lacking the necessary *intent* to constitute an offer. Of course, if no offer exists, you cannot accept, and no contract can emerge absent further negotiation.

Gambling

In 2006, Troy Blackford, a Des Moines, Iowa, truck driver, won $9,387 gambling at Prairie Meadows casino. Blackford tried to collect the winnings, but his request was denied by the casino. Officials said that he had been banned from the casino since 1996, and the ban had not been lifted. (In the 1996 episode, Blackford had punched a slot machine and was belligerent with casino security.) Blackford sued the casino.

1. What was the central issue in the case? Explain.
2. Decide the case. Explain.

Source: Blackford v. Prairie Meadows Racetrack & Casino, 778 N.W.2d 184 (Ia. S.Ct. 2010).

> Suppose you were responding to an ad that said, "2010 full-size Ford cargo van, $20,000." Is that ad language an offer such that you can accept by promising to pay $20,000?

Advertisements   The question of intent sometimes arises with advertisements. In buying the van for your business, suppose you were responding to an ad that said, "2010 full-size Ford cargo van, $20,000." Is that ad language an offer such that you can accept by promising to pay $20,000? Ordinarily, ads do not constitute offers, but rather are treated by the courts as *invitations to deal.* Were an ad actually treated as an offer, it would put the seller in the commercially impracticable position of being required to provide the advertised product at the advertised price to everyone who sought one, regardless of available supply. Presumably, that open-ended duty was not the seller's intent when issuing the ad. It follows then that the buyer, in responding to an ad, is technically making an offer, with the seller free to accept or decline.

On the other hand, courts have held that some ads do manifest a present intent to make an offer. The critical terms in those ads must be highly specific and complete, leaving nothing open for negotiation.

A Jet Fighter from Pepsi?

A 1995 Pepsico promotion offered merchandise in exchange for points earned by buying Pepsi-Cola. The television ad showed a teenager modeling some of the available merchandise. A Pepsi T-shirt was displayed for 75 points and a leather jacket for 1450 points. At the end of the ad, a U.S. Marine Corps Harrier "jump jet" landed outside a school, and the boy said, "Sure beats the bus." The ad said the jet was redeemable for 7 million points. John D. R. Leonard, at the time a 21-year-old business student in Seattle, Washington, joined five investors in writing a check to Pepsi for $700,008.50 and demanded the 7 million Pepsi points. Pepsi returned the check and said it had no intention of giving Leonard the $24 million jet. Leonard sued. Who wins? Explain.

Source: John D.R. Leonard v. Pepsico, 210 F.3d 88 (2d Cir. Ct. App. 2000).

[For a video of the ad, see **https://www.youtube.com/watch?v=ZdackF2H7Qc.** Other versions of the ad can be found at pepsi2 and pepsi3]

Definiteness

Suppose you have completed a management training program for a "big box" retailer. In your first assignment as an assistant manager, your boss asks you to seek bids and make the other arrangements (subject to her approval) to resurface the store's large asphalt parking lot. You secure bids, and the lowest bidder offers to complete the work "later this summer" for $120,000. You briefly explain the offer to your boss, who tells you to take care of all the details. You are busy with other matters and you put off the parking lot project for a couple of weeks. When you get back to the contractor, he says, "Sorry, man, we hadn't heard from you, and we got another deal." Can you hold that contractor to his initial offer?

One of the requirements of a binding offer is that all of its critical terms must be sufficiently clear that a court can determine both the intentions of the parties and their duties. Clearly, in the asphalt case, many critical details—such as precisely when the work would be done, the quality of the surfacing material, its thickness, and the like—had not been established. Consequently, no offer existed. In a contract for the sale of goods, UCC 2-204 relaxes the definiteness standard by providing that "one or more terms" may be missing but the court can find a contract, nonetheless, where (1) "the parties have intended to make a contract" and (2) "there is a reasonably certain basis for giving an appropriate remedy." Under the UCC, the courts can actually fill in missing terms such as specifying a reasonable price where the contract had omitted a stipulation. The following case involving Mariah Carey, the pop music star, demonstrates some of the problems that can arise when an understanding is indefinite.

LEGAL BRIEFCASE

Vian v. Carey   1993 U.S. Dist. Lexis 5460 (U.S. Dist. Ct. S.D.N.Y. 1993)

Judge Mukasey

Defendant Mariah Carey is a famous, successful and apparently wealthy entertainer. Plaintiff Joseph Vian was her stepfather before she achieved stardom, but at the start of this litigation was in the process of becoming divorced from defendant's mother. He claims defendant agreed orally that he would have a license to market singing dolls in her likeness. . . . Plaintiff claims that he and Carey had an oral contract for him to receive a license to market "Mariah dolls." These dolls would be statuettes of the singer and would play her most popular songs. Plaintiff claims that the contract was in consideration of his financial and emotional support of defendant, including picking her up from late-night recording sessions, providing her with the use of a car, paying for dental care, allowing her to use his boat for business meetings and rehearsals, and giving her various items, including unused wedding gifts from his marriage to her mother, to help furnish her apartment.

The alleged basis of the oral contract is that on at least three occasions, twice in the family car and once on Vian's boat, Vian told Carey, "Don't forget the Mariah dolls," and "I get the Mariah dolls." According to Vian, on one occasion Carey responded "okay" and on other occasions she merely smiled and nodded. Although Carey admits Vian mentioned the dolls two or three times, she testified that she thought it was a joke. For 30 years plaintiff has been in the business of designing, producing, and marketing gift and novelty items. Although it is not clear from the evidence the parties have submitted, it will be assumed that the alleged contract was formed after defendant turned 18. Under New York law, an oral agreement can form a binding contract. . . . In determining whether a contract exists, what matters are the parties' expressed intentions, the words and deeds that constitute objective signs in a given set of circumstances.

Therefore, the issue is whether the objective circumstances indicate that the parties intended to form a contract. Without such an intent, neither a contract nor a preliminary agreement to negotiate in good faith can exist. In making such a determination, a court may look at "whether the terms of the contract have been finally resolved." In addition, a court may consider "the context of the negotiations." Plaintiff has adduced no evidence that defendant ever intended by a nod of her head or the expression "okay" to enter into a complex commercial licensing agreement involving dolls in her likeness playing her copyrighted songs. The context in which this contract between an 18-year-old girl and her stepfather allegedly was made was an informal family setting, either in the car or on plaintiff's boat, while others were present. Vian's own version of events leads to the conclusion that there was no reason for Carey to think Vian was entirely serious, let alone that he intended to bind her to an agreement at that time. He admits he never told her he was serious. The objective circumstances do not indicate that Carey intended to form a contract with plaintiff. Although plaintiff's five-page memorandum of law fails to raise the possibility, plaintiff also has not shown that Carey intended to be bound to negotiate with plaintiff at some later date over the licensing of "Mariah dolls."

There can be no meeting of the minds, required for the formation of a contract, where essential material terms are missing. Thus, even if the parties both believe themselves to be bound, there is no contract when "the terms of the agreement are so vague and indefinite that there is no basis or standard for deciding whether the agreement had been kept or broken, or to fashion a remedy, and no means by which such terms may be made certain."

. . . The word "license" was not even used. As defendant points out, no price or royalty term was mentioned, nor was the duration or geographic scope of the license, nor was Carey's right to approve the dolls. Plaintiff admits he would not have gone ahead without defendant's approval, thus conceding the materiality of that term.

* * * * *

In sum, plaintiff has not raised a triable issue of fact as to the existence of a contract. Defendant's motion for summary judgment is granted.

Questions

1. Why did the court find for Carey?

2. As noted in the text, in UCC cases judges fill in contract terms where the parties clearly intended a deal. Should the court here fill in the missing terms to provide the necessary definiteness? Explain.

3. Pilgrim Village Company had employed Petersen as a construction manager at a specified annual salary and "a share of the profits." Petersen worked at salary for several years and then asked for a 10 percent share of the profits. The company refused, and Petersen sued seeking "some share of the profits." How should the court rule on Petersen's claim? Explain. See *Petersen v. Pilgrim Village*, 42 N.W.2d 273 (Wis. S.Ct., 1950).

Communication

As explained, an effective offer must be the product of a present intent, it must be definite, and it must be communicated to the offeree. Communication of an offer expresses the offeror's intent to make that offer. Suppose a friend tells you that your neighbor has offered to sell his classic jukebox for $10,000. You call your neighbor and say, "I accept. I'll be right over with the $10,000." Do you have a deal? No. The owner did not communicate the offer to you. The fact that it was not communicated to you may suggest that your neighbor does not want to sell or does not want to sell to you.

Duration of an Offer   Communication of an offer affords the offeree the opportunity to create a contract by accepting that offer, but how long does that opportunity last? Here are some general rules:

1. The offeror may revoke the offer anytime prior to acceptance. (Some exceptions are explained later.) Normally, revocation is effective on receipt by the offeree. Under common law the offeror has the right to revoke at any time prior to acceptance, even if he or she expressly promised to keep the offer open for a specified period.

2. The offer may specify that it is open for an express period (such as 10 days).

3. Where a time limit is not specified in the offer it will be presumed to be open for a reasonable period.

4. An offer expires if rejected or on receipt of a counteroffer.

Irrevocable Offers

Some kinds of offers may not be revoked. We will note three of them.

1. **Option contracts.** When an offeror promises to keep an offer open for a specified period and, in return, the offeree pays consideration (usually money), the parties have created an option contract, which is a separate agreement and is enforceable by its terms. For example, a friend has offered to sell to you his customized car that you have long cherished, but you want to think about it for a few days. You might enter an option contract with your friend under which you pay $100 for the seller's promise to keep the offer open for seven days. You are under no obligation to buy the car, but the seller is under a binding obligation not to withdraw the offer or sell to another during the seven days.

2. **Firm offers.** Under the UCC, if the owner of that customized car is a dealer (a merchant) and he made a written, signed offer to sell that car (a good) to you, indicating that his offer would remain open for seven days, he is bound to that promise whether you paid consideration for it or not. That situation is labeled a firm offer as specified in UCC 2-205, which also provides that such offers will be kept open for a reasonable period if the agreement does not mention a time, but that period cannot exceed three months.

3. **Offers for unilateral contracts.** A problem sometimes arises when the offeror attempts to revoke a unilateral offer after the offeree has begun to perform. For example, your neighbor invites you to rake her leaves for $10, and then, when you are virtually done, she yells from the doorway, "Oh, sorry, I changed my mind. You go home now." Historically, the offeror (the neighbor, in this case) was free to revoke at any time, but the modern position holds that the offeror normally cannot revoke if the offeree (you) has commenced performance. If that performance is then completed (you ignore your neighbor's admonition to go home, and you finish the raking), the offeror (your neighbor) is bound to perform fully by paying the $10.

The Agreement: Acceptance

Suppose you are in training with a large real estate firm and your boss has authorized you to enter negotiations to buy a parcel of farmland that your company hopes to develop for housing. After preliminary discussions, you extend a written offer to the owner indicating, among other terms, that your company is willing to pay $10,000 per acre for a 10-acre parcel. Assume the owner responds by writing, "I accept your offer at $10,000 per acre, but I need to keep the two-acre homesite." The offeree has used the word *accept,* but does the response constitute a legally binding *acceptance?*

The general rule is that an effective acceptance must be a mirror image of the offer; that is, ordinarily its terms must be the same as those in the offer. Here the offeree has changed the terms of the offer and in so doing has issued a *counteroffer,* thus extinguishing the original offer.

Communication of Acceptance

An offer may be accepted only by the offeree—that is, the person to whom the offer was directed. Because unilateral offers are accepted by performance, no communication of acceptance beyond that performance ordinarily is necessary. In the case of a bilateral contract (a promise for a promise), acceptance is not effective until communicated.

Broadly, acceptance can be accomplished by a "yes" communicated face-to-face, by a nod of the head or some other appropriate signal, by phone, or by other unwritten means, unless the law of the state requires writing in that particular kind of transaction.

Mailbox   Confusion sometimes arises when the parties are not dealing face-to-face. In general, acceptance is effective upon dispatch by whatever mode of communication has been explicitly or implicitly authorized by the offeror. This well-settled position is labeled the *mailbox rule* and means, among other things, that an acceptance is effective when sent even if never received. [For one professor's review of the mailbox rule and related rules, see **http://www.tomwbell.com/teaching/KMailbox.pdf**]

Authorization   The offeror controls the acceptance process and may specify an exclusive manner in which an acceptance must be communicated. If so, a contract is not created if the acceptance is communicated in anything other than the stipulated fashion. Traditionally, if the offeror did not give an *express authorization* to a means of communication, an acceptance by the same or faster means than that used by the offeror was implied. *Implied authorization* might also arise from such factors as prior dealings between the parties and custom in their industry.

Modern View   Under the UCC the rules have relaxed a bit. If no specific instructions for acceptance are included in the offer, the offeree is free to accept in any reasonable manner within a reasonable period, and acceptance is effective upon dispatch. Even when the means chosen are "unreasonable," acceptance is effective on dispatch under the UCC 1-201(38) if it is actually received in a timely manner.

Consideration

Earlier we identified the five key ingredients in an enforceable contract: agreement, consideration, capacity, genuineness of assent, and legality of purpose. Having examined the agreement (offer/acceptance) process, we turn now to consideration. As noted earlier, consideration is the bargained-for legal value that one party agrees to pay or provide to secure the promise of another. It is what the promisor demands and receives in exchange for his or her promise. Consideration is used by the courts to distinguish a contract (enforceable) from a gratuitous promise (unenforceable). The *promisee* must suffer a *legal detriment;* that is, the promisee must give up something of value (an act or a promise) or must refrain from doing something that she or he has a legal right to do in order to enforce the promise offered by the *promisor.* Each party, then, must pay a "price" for a contract to be enforceable. In sum, consideration consists of a detriment to the promisee that is bargained for by the promisor.

The classic case that follows explores the idea of consideration and demonstrates that consideration can have legal value without involving monetary loss to the promisee.

Hamer v. Sidway
27 N.E. 256 (N.Y. 1891)

FACTS

In 1869 William E. Story Sr. promised his nephew, W.E. Story II, that he would pay the nephew $5,000 upon his 21st birthday if the nephew would refrain from drinking liquor, using tobacco, swearing, and playing cards or billiards for money until he reached that 21st birthday. The nephew agreed and performed his promise, but the uncle died in 1887 without paying the money, and the administrator of the estate, Sidway, declined to pay the $5,000 plus interest. The nephew had assigned (sold) his rights to the money to Louisa Hamer, who sued W.E. Story Sr.'s estate. Hamer, the plaintiff, won at the trial level, lost on appeal, and then appealed to the New York Court of Appeals.

* * * * *

Judge Parker

When the nephew arrived at the age of 21 years and on the 31st day of January 1875, he wrote to his uncle informing him that he had performed his part of the agreement and had thereby become entitled to the sum of $5,000. The uncle received the letter and a few days later and on the sixth of February, he wrote and mailed to his nephew the following letter:

> Buffalo, February 6, 1875
> W.E. Story, Jr.
> Dear Nephew:
> Your letter of the 31st came to hand all right, saying that you had lived up to the promise made to me several years ago. I have no doubt but you have, for which you shall have five thousand dollars as I promised you. I had the money in the bank the day you was 21 years old that I intend for you, and you shall have the money certain. Now, Willie I do not intend to interfere with this money in any way till I think you are capable of taking care of it and the sooner that time comes the better it will please me. I would hate very much to have you start out in some adventure that you thought all right and lose this money in one year. The first five thousand dollars that I got together cost me a heap of hard work. You would hardly believe me when I tell you that to obtain this I shoved a jackplane many a day, butchered three or four years, then came to this city, and after three months' perseverance I obtained a situation in a grocery store. I opened this store early, closed late, slept in the fourth story of the building in a room 30 by 40 feet and not a human being in the building but myself. All this I done to live as cheap as I could to save something. I don't want you to take

up with this kind of fare. I was here in the cholera season '49 and '52 and the deaths averaged 80 to 125 daily and plenty of smallpox. I wanted to go home, but Mr. Fisk, the gentleman I was working for, told me if I left then, after it got healthy he probably would not want me. I stayed. All the money I have saved I know just how I got it. It did not come to me in any mysterious way, and the reason I speak of this is that money got in this way stops longer with a fellow that gets it with hard knocks than it does when he finds it. Willie, you are 21 and you have many a thing to learn yet. This money you have earned much easier than I did besides acquiring good habits at the same time and you are quite welcome to the money; hope you will make good use of it. I was 10 long years getting this together after I was your age. Now, hoping this will be satisfactory, I stop . . .
> Truly Yours,
> W.E. STORY
> P.S.—You can consider this money on interest.

The nephew received the letter and thereafter consented that the money should remain with his uncle in accordance with the terms and conditions of the letter. The uncle died on the 29th day of January 1887, without having paid over to his nephew any portion of the said $5,000 and interest.

* * * * *

The defendant contends that the contract was without consideration to support it, and, therefore, invalid. He asserts that the promisee by refraining from the use of liquor and tobacco was not harmed but benefited; that that which he did was best for him to do independently of his uncle's promise, and insists that it follows that unless the promisor was benefited, the contract was without consideration. A contention, which if well founded, would seem to leave open for controversy in many cases whether that which the promisee did or omitted to do was, in fact, of such benefit to him as to leave no consideration to support the enforcement of the promisor's agreement. Such a rule could not be tolerated, and is without foundation in the law.

* * * * *

"In general a waiver of any legal right at the request of another party is a sufficient consideration for a promise" (Parsons on Contracts).

Pollock, in his work on contracts, says, "Consideration means not so much that one party is profiting as that the other abandons some legal right in the present or limits his legal freedom of action in the future as an inducement for the promise of the first."

Now, applying this rule to the facts before us, the promisee used tobacco, occasionally drank liquor, and had a legal right to do so. That right he abandoned for a period of years upon the strength of the promise of the testator that for such forbearance he would give him $5,000. We need not speculate on the effort which may have been required to give up the use of those stimulants. It is sufficient that he restricted his lawful freedom of action within certain prescribed limits upon the faith of his uncle's agreement, and now having fully performed the conditions imposed, it is of no moment whether such performance actually proved a benefit to the promisor, and the court will not inquire into it, but were it a proper subject of inquiry, we see nothing in this record that would permit a determination that the uncle was not benefited in a legal sense.

* * * * *

Reversed.

Questions

1. *a.* What detriment, if any, was sustained by the nephew?
   b. What benefit, if any, was secured by the uncle?
   c. As a matter of law, do we need to inquire into the uncle's benefit? Explain.
2. Lampley began work as an at-will (can be dismissed or can quit at any time) employee of Celebrity Homes in Denver, Colorado, in May 1975. On July 29, 1975, Celebrity announced a profit-sharing plan for all employees if the company reached its goals for the fiscal year, April 1, 1975, to March 31, 1976. Lampley was dismissed in January 1976. Celebrity distributed its profits in May 1976. Lampley sued when she did not receive a share of the profits. Celebrity argued that its promise to share its profits was a gratuity, unsupported by consideration. Decide. Explain. See *Lampley v. Celebrity Homes,* 594 P.2d 605 (Col. Ct. App. 1979).
3. An accident in the early 1960s rendered Hoffman paraplegic. At Hoffman's invitation, Thomas lived with and provided extensive physical care for Hoffman until Hoffman's death in 2004. Thomas did not pay rent and Hoffman paid for Thomas' food, provided her with a car and cell phone, and made occasional cash payments to Thomas. While never married, the couple exchanged rings in 2002 and Thomas testified that she felt they "lived as man and wife." Thomas filed suit seeking $44,625 for services rendered to Hoffman. According to the trial court, her claim was based on the theories of "express or implied contract of employment" or "unjust enrichment." Thomas lost at the trial level. How would you rule on appeal? Explain. See *In Re Estate of Hoffman,* 2006 Ia. App. LEXIS 473. [For a detailed analysis of *Hamer v. Sidway,* see **http://www.law.smu .edu/firstday/contracts/case.htm**]

Adequacy of Consideration

With certain exceptions, the courts do not, as Judge Parker indicated in the *Hamer* case, inquire into the economic value of the consideration in question. Legal sufficiency depends not on the value of the consideration but on whether the promisee suffered a detriment in some way. To hold otherwise would put the courts in the place of the market in deciding the value of transactions. We are all free to make both good and bad bargains.

On the other hand, the courts will rule that consideration is found wanting in situations of pretense or sham where the parties have clearly agreed on token or nominal consideration in an effort to present the transaction as a contract rather than a gift. Likewise, an extreme inadequacy of consideration will sometimes cause the court to question a contract on the grounds of *fraud, duress, or unconscionability* (all are discussed later in this chapter). In these instances, the agreements would be unenforceable because of a failure of consideration. These cases are uncommon, however, and the courts rarely inquire into the adequacy of consideration.

Appearance of Consideration

Some agreements appear to be accompanied by consideration, but in fact, that appearance turns out to be an illusion. Hence, if one agrees to perform a preexisting duty, consideration would be found wanting. For example, if you were to pay your neighbor $50 to keep his dog chained when outdoors and a city ordinance already requires dogs to be chained if outdoors, your promise would be unenforceable because your neighbor already had a preexisting duty under the law to keep his dog chained. So performance of a preexisting legal duty does not constitute consideration because no legal detriment or benefit has arisen.

Similarly, preexisting duties sometimes arise from contracts. Suppose you hire a contractor to resurface the parking lot at your real estate office. You agree on a price of $12,000. With a portion of the work completed, the contractor asks you to amend the agreement to add $2,000 because the project is requiring more time than anticipated. You agree. The work is completed. Could you then legally refuse to pay the additional $2,000? The answer is yes because the contractor failed to provide consideration for the modification of your contract. He was under a preexisting duty to finish the contract; hence, he did not sustain a legal detriment in the modified agreement. Note, however, that UCC section 2-209(1) provides that "an agreement modifying a contract within this Article needs no consideration to be binding."

Suppose you learn from your neighbor that your friend Ames wants to sell his house. You, as a realtor, find a buyer for the house and make all of the necessary arrangements for the sale out of regard for your friendship with Ames. Then when the transaction is complete, Ames says, "Well, this has been great of you, but I don't feel right about it. When I get my check for the sale, I'll pay you $2,000 for your hard work. I really appreciate it." What if Ames does not then pay the $2,000? Do you have recourse? No. This is a situation of *past consideration,* where the performance—arranging the sale of your friend's house—was not bargained for and was not given in exchange for the promise and thus cannot constitute consideration. In effect, the performance was a gift. Of course, past consideration is really not consideration at all. In some states, courts enforce promises to pay for benefits already received where doing so amounts to a moral obligation that must be enforced to prevent injustice.

Substitutes for Consideration

When necessary to achieve justice, the courts sometimes conclude that a contract exists even though consideration is clearly lacking. Moral obligation and quasi-contract (discussed earlier) are two such instances, but the most prominent of these substitutes for consideration is the doctrine of *promissory estoppel,* in which the promisor is "stopped" from denying the existence of a contract where the promisee has detrimentally relied on that promise. Promissory estoppel requires the following:

1. A promise on which the promisor should expect the promisee to rely.
2. The promisee did justifiably rely on the promise.
3. Injustice can be avoided only by enforcing the promise.

Consider the following. You have been a part-time employee of a small fast-food chain restaurant while attending college. Upon graduation, you tell the manager of the restaurant that you think you could handle your own franchise. He says you need to get more experience and advises you to take a full-time position with the company. You do so. Everything goes well, and when you next approach the manager, he says, "If you can come up with the $50,000 and a good location, we will get you in a franchise right away. But you've gotta move on this. Maybe you better quit your job with us and concentrate on this thing." You take his advice and quit your job. You raise the $50,000 and find a vacant building to rent in a good location for a franchise. You show the building to the manager, and he agrees that it looks like a favorable location and one that can easily be converted to the company's needs. He says, "Looks like you have everything in place. If you can come up with $50,000 more we will make this thing happen." You refuse and decide to bring suit against the fast-food chain for breach of contract. The chain defends by saying that you did not provide consideration for its promise. No formal financing arrangement was ever agreed to, and you had not committed yourself to any franchising obligations. Under these circumstances you may well prevail using a promissory estoppel claim. In brief, you would argue that you had changed your position in reliance on the franchisor's promises and that relief is necessary to prevent injustice. [For a similar case see *Hoffman v. Red Owl Stores,* 133 N.W.2d 267 (Wis. S.Ct. 1965).]

Capacity

Having examined two of the required ingredients in an enforceable contract, agreement and consideration, we turn now to a third, capacity to contract. To enter a binding agreement, one must have the legal ability to do so; that is, one's mental condition and maturity must be such that the agreement was entered with understanding and in recognition of one's own interests. The three primary areas of concern are intoxication, mental impairment, and minority (infancy/youthfulness), with minority being much the more common area of dispute.

> The three primary areas of concern are intoxication, mental impairment, and minority.

Intoxication

Assume you have been drinking to celebrate your 21st birthday. You enter a contract with a friend to sell him your autographed Michael Jordan basketball card for $200. You receive the money and turn over the card. Later, when sober, you regret the deal. Will a court nullify that contract on the grounds of your intoxication? That decision depends on whether you were sufficiently intoxicated that you did not understand the nature and purpose of the contract. If the objective evidence suggests that you did not understand the transaction, the contract would be considered voidable, in which case you could probably disaffirm the contract and demand the return of the card, although courts are often not sympathetic with people who attempt to escape contracts made while intoxicated. In most states, if you recovered the card, you would be required to return the $200 to your friend.

If on recovering your sobriety, your friend argued that the contract was invalid because of your intoxication, and he demanded the return of his $200 in exchange for the card, you could then *ratify* (affirm) the contract and hold him to it. If the contract had been for one of life's *necessaries* (food, shelter, clothing, medical care, tools of one's trade, or the like), you would have been liable for the reasonable value of that necessary.

Mental Incompetence

In most cases an agreement involving a mentally incompetent person is either *void or voidable.* The transaction would be void—that is, no contract would exist—where the impaired party had been *adjudged* insane. If the impaired party was unable to understand the purpose and effect of the contract but had not been legally adjudged insane, the contract would be voidable (void in some states) at the option of the impaired party. The competent party cannot void the contract, and the impaired party would have to pay the reasonable value of any necessaries received under the contract.

Minority

Minors may complete their contracts if they wish, but they also have an absolute right to rescind most of those contracts. They may rescind until they reach adulthood and for a reasonable time thereafter. (Many states have enacted statutes forbidding minors from disaffirming some classes of contracts such as those for marriage, student loans, and life insurance.) The minor has a right of recovery for everything given up in meeting the terms of the contract. Similarly, the minor must return everything that remains in her or his possession that was received from the contract. In many states, if nothing of the bargained-for consideration remains or if its value has been depreciated, the minor has no duty to replace it but can still recover whatever she or he put into the contract. If not disaffirmed in a reasonable time after the minor reaches the age of majority, the contract is considered to be ratified, and the minor is bound to its terms. The minor is also liable for the reasonable value (not necessarily the contract price) of necessaries purchased from an adult. That is, a minor must pay the adult the reasonable value of contracted-for items such as food, clothing, shelter, medical care, basic education, and tools of the minor's trade.

> Minors may complete their contracts if they wish, but they also have an absolute right to rescind most of those contracts.

Despite the flexibility accorded to minors entering contracts, the adults who are parties to those contracts are bound to them and do not have the power to disaffirm. Hence, adults put themselves at risk when they choose to bargain with minors. As noted, in many states a minor need not make restitution if the consideration is lost, destroyed, or depreciated. On the other hand, the case that follows illustrates the growing view that minors do have some monetary obligation after disaffirming a contract.

LEGAL BRIEFCASE

Dodson v. Shrader
824 S.W.2d 545 (Tenn. S.Ct. 1992)

Justice O'Brien

In early April of 1987, Joseph Eugene Dodson, then 16 years of age, purchased a used 1984 pickup truck from Burns and Mary Shrader. The Shraders owned and operated Shrader's Auto Sales in Columbia, Tennessee. Dodson paid $4,900 in cash for the truck, using money he borrowed from his girlfriend's grandmother. At the time of the purchase there was no inquiry by the Shraders, and no misrepresentation by Dodson, concerning his minority. However, Shrader did testify that at the time he believed Dodson to be 18 or 19 years of age.

In December 1987, nine months after the date of purchase, the truck began to develop mechanical problems. A mechanic diagnosed the problem as a burnt valve, but could not be certain without inspecting the valves inside the engine. Dodson did not want, or did not have the money, to effect these repairs. He continued to drive the truck despite the mechanical problems. One month later, in January, the truck's engine "blew up" and the truck became inoperable.

Dodson parked the vehicle in the front yard at his parents' home, where he lived. He contacted the Shraders to rescind the purchase of the truck and requested a full refund. The Shraders refused to accept the tender of the truck or to give Dodson the refund requested.

Dodson then [sued] to rescind the contract and recover the amount paid for the truck. Before the circuit court could hear the case, the truck, while parked in Dodson's front yard, was struck on the left front fender by a hit-and-run driver. At the time of the circuit court trial, according to Shrader, the truck was worth only $500 due to the damage to the engine and the left front fender.

The case was heard in the circuit court in November 1988. The trial judge, based on previous common-law decisions, and under the doctrine of stare decisis, reluctantly granted the re-scission. The Shraders were ordered, upon tender and delivery of the truck, to reimburse the $4,900 purchase price to Dodson. The Shraders appealed.

[T]he rule in Tennessee is in accord with the majority rule on the issue among our sister states. This rule is based on the underlying purpose of the "infancy doctrine," which is to pro-tect minors from their lack of judgment and "from squandering their wealth through improvident contracts with crafty adults who would take advantage of them in the marketplace."

There is, however, a modern trend among the states, either by judicial action or by statute, in the approach to the problem of balancing the rights of minors against those of innocent merchants. As a result, two minority rules have developed that allow the other party to a contract with a minor to refund less than the full consideration paid in the event of rescission.

The first of these minority rules is called the "Benefit Rule." The rule holds that, upon rescission, recovery of the full pur-chase price is subject to a deduction for the minor's use of the merchandise. This rule recognizes that the traditional rule in regard to necessaries has been extended so far as to hold an infant bound by his contracts, where he failed to restore what he has received under them to the extent of the benefit actu-ally derived by him from what he has received from the other party to the transaction.

The other minority rule holds that the minor's recovery of the full purchase price is subject to a deduction for the minor's "use" of the consideration he or she received under the con-tract, or for the "depreciation" or "deterioration" of the con-sideration in his or her possession.

We are impressed by the statement made by the Court of Appeals of Ohio:

> At a time when we see young persons between 18 and 21 years of age demanding and assuming more responsibilities in their daily lives, when we see such persons emancipated, married, and raising families; when we see such persons charged with the responsibility for committing crimes; when we see such persons being sued in tort claims for acts of negligence; when we see such persons subject to military service; when we see such persons engaged in business and acting in almost all other respects as an adult, it seems timely to reexamine the case law pertaining to contractual rights and responsibilities of infants to see if the law as pronounced and applied by the courts should be redefined.

* * * * *

We state the rule to be followed hereafter, in reference to a contract of a minor, to be where the minor has not been over-reached in any way, and there has been no undue influence, and the contract is a fair and reasonable one, and the minor has actually paid money on the purchase price, and taken and used the article purchased; that he ought not be permitted to recover the amount actually paid, without allowing the vendor of the goods reasonable compensation for the use of, depreciation, and willful or negligent damage to the article purchased, while in his hands. If there has been any fraud or imposition on the part of the seller or if the contract is unfair, or any unfair advan-tage has been taken of the minor inducing him to make the pur-chase, then the rule does not apply. Whether there has been such an overreaching on the part of the seller, and the fair market value of the property returned, would always, in any case, be a question for the trier of fact. . . .

This rule is best adapted to modern conditions under which minors are permitted to, and do in fact, transact a great deal of business for themselves, long before they have reached the age of legal majority. Many young people work and earn money and collect it and spend it oftentimes without any oversight or restric-tion. The law does not question their right to buy if they have the money to pay for their purchases. It seems intolerably burden-some for everyone concerned if merchants and businesspeople cannot deal with them safely, in a fair and reasonable way.

* * * * *

We note that in this case, some nine months after the date of purchase, the truck purchased by the plaintiff began to develop mechanical problems. Plaintiff was informed of the probable na-ture of the difficulty, which apparently involved internal problems in the engine. He continued to drive the vehicle until the engine "blew up" and the truck became inoperable. Whether or not this involved gross negligence or intentional conduct on his part is a matter for determination at the trial level. It is not possible to determine from this record whether a counterclaim for tortious damage to the vehicle was asserted. After the first tender of the vehicle was made by plaintiff, and refused by the defendant, the truck was damaged by a hit-and-run driver while parked on plain-tiff's property. The amount of that damage and the liability for that amount between the purchaser and the vendor, as well as the fair market value of the vehicle at the time of tender, are also an issue for the jury.

[Reversed and remanded.]

Questions

1. What was the issue in this case?

2. Distinguish the two minority rules that are summarized in this case.

3. To achieve justice in contract cases involving a minor and an adult, what would you want to know about the adult's behavior toward the minor?

4. White, a 17-year-old high school sophomore, operated a trucking business, including hiring drivers, securing jobs, and so forth. He lived with his parents and received his food, clothing, and shelter from them. Valencia operated a garage and repaired White's equipment until they had a disagreement over replacement of a motor. White then disaffirmed his contract with Valencia and refused to pay what he owed. At trial the jury found that White had caused the damage to the motor, but the court held that White could disaffirm the contract and required Valencia to refund any money paid to White under the contract. Valencia appealed.

   a. Is the fact that White was in business for himself in any way relevant to the outcome of this case? Explain.

   b. Decide the case. Explain. See *Valencia v. White*, 654 P.2d 287 (Ariz. Ct. App. 1982).

Genuineness of Assent

Sometimes parties appear to have concluded a binding contract, but the courts will allow them to escape that obligation because they had not, in fact, achieved an agreement. They had achieved the appearance of agreement, but not the reality. That situation arises when the contract is the product of misrepresentation, fraud, duress, undue influence, or mistake. Ordinarily, such agreements are voidable and may be rescinded by the innocent party because of the absence of genuine assent, the fourth of five ingredients in a binding contract.

Misrepresentation and Fraud

An innocent untruth is a misrepresentation. Intentional untruths constitute fraud. In either case, a party to a contract who has been deceived may rescind the deal, and restitution may be secured if benefits were extended to the party issuing the untruth. The test for fraud is as follows:

1. Misrepresentation of a material fact.

2. The misrepresentation was intentional.

3. The injured party justifiably relied on the misrepresentation.

4. Injury resulted.

Note that the test requires a misrepresented fact. In general, misrepresented opinions are not grounds for action, but many courts are now recognizing exceptions to that rule, especially when the innocent party has relied on opinion coming from an expert.

> **You are selling a house that allegedly is "haunted."**

If you are selling a house that allegedly is "haunted," does your failure to reveal the ghostly presence constitute a misrepresentation? The *Stambovsky* case that follows addresses that unusual question.

Justice Rubin

Plaintiff, to his horror, discovered that the house he had recently contracted to purchase was widely reputed to be possessed by poltergeists, reportedly seen by defendant seller and members of her family on numerous occasions over the last nine years. Plaintiff promptly commenced this action seeking rescission of the contract of sale.

The unusual facts of this case clearly warrant a grant of equitable relief to the buyer who, as a resident of New York City, cannot be expected to have any familiarity with the folklore of the Village of Nyack. Not being a "local," plaintiff could not readily learn that the home he had contracted to purchase is haunted. Whether the source of the spectral apparitions seen by defendant seller are parapsychic or psychogenic, having reported their presence in both a national publication (*Readers' Digest*) and the local press (in 1977 and 1982, respectively), defendant is estopped to deny their existence and, as a matter of law, the house is haunted. More to the point, however, no divination is required to conclude that it is defendant's promotional efforts in publicizing her close encounters with these spirits which fostered the home's reputation in the community. In 1989, the house was included in five-home walking tour of Nyack and described in a November 27th newspaper article as "a riverfront Victorian (with ghost)." The impact of the reputation thus created goes to the very essence of the bargain between the parties, greatly impairing both the value of the property and its potential for resale.

While I agree that the real estate broker, as agent for the seller, is under no duty to disclose to a potential buyer the phantasmal reputation of the premises and that, in his pursuit of a legal remedy for fraudulent misrepresentation against the seller, plaintiff hasn't a ghost of a chance, I am nevertheless moved by the spirit of equity to allow the buyer to seek rescission of the contract of sale and recovery of his down payment. New York law fails to recognize any remedy for damages incurred as a result of the seller's mere silence, applying instead the strict rule of caveat emptor. Therefore, the theoretical basis for granting relief, even under the extraordinary facts of this case, is elusive if not ephemeral.

From the perspective of a person in the position of plaintiff herein, a very practical problem arises with respect to the discovery of a paranormal phenomenon: "Who you gonna' call?" as a title song to the movie "Ghostbusters" asks. Applying the strict rule of caveat emptor to a contract involving a house possessed by poltergeists conjures up visions of a psychic or medium routinely accompanying the structural engineer and Terminix man on an inspection of every home subject to a contract of sale. It portends that the prudent attorney will establish an escrow account lest the subject of the transaction come back to haunt him and his client—or pray that his malpractice insurance coverage extends to supernatural disasters. In the interest of avoiding such untenable consequences, the notion that a haunting is a condition which can and should be ascertained upon reasonable inspection of the premises is a hobgoblin which should be exorcised from the body of legal precedent and laid quietly to rest.

It has been suggested by a leading authority that the ancient rule which holds that mere nondisclosure does not constitute actionable misrepresentation "finds proper application in cases where the fact undisclosed is patent, or the plaintiff has equal opportunities for obtaining information which he may be expected to utilize, or the defendant has no reason to think that he is acting under any misapprehension" (Prosser, Torts Section 106, at 696 [4th ed 1971]). However, with respect to transactions in real estate, New York adheres to the doctrine of caveat emptor and imposes no duty upon the vendor to disclose any information concerning the premises unless there is a confidential or fiduciary relationship between the parties or some conduct on the part of the seller which constitutes "active concealment." Normally, some affirmative misrepresentation or partial disclosure is required to impose upon the seller a duty to communicate undisclosed conditions affecting the premises.

Common law is not moribund. . . . Where fairness and common sense dictate that an exception should be created, the evolution of the law should not be stifled by rigid application of a legal maxim.

The doctrine of caveat emptor requires that a buyer act prudently to assess the fitness and value of his purchase and operates to bar the purchaser who fails to exercise due care from seeking the equitable remedy of rescission. For the purposes of the instant motion to dismiss the action . . . plaintiff is entitled to every favorable inference which may reasonably be drawn from the pleadings, specifically, in this instance, that he met his obligation to conduct an inspection of the premises and a search of available public records with respect to title. It should be apparent, however, that the most meticulous inspection and the search would not reveal the presence of poltergeists at the premises or unearth the property's ghoulish reputation in the community.

Therefore, there is no sound policy reason to deny plaintiff relief for failing to discover a state of affairs which the most prudent purchaser would not be expected to even contemplate.

* * * * *

Where a condition which has been created by the seller materially impairs the value of the contract and is peculiarly within the knowledge of the seller or unlikely to be discovered by a prudent purchaser exercising due care with respect to the subject transaction, nondisclosure constitutes a basis for rescission as a matter of equity. Any other outcome places upon the buyer not merely the obligation to exercise care in his purchase but rather to be omniscient with respect to any fact which may affect the bargain. No practical purpose is served by imposing such a burden upon a purchaser. To the contrary, it encourages predatory business practice. . . .

* * * * *

In the case at bar, defendant seller deliberately fostered the public belief that her home was possessed. Having undertaken to inform the public-at-large, to whom she has no legal relationship, about the supernatural occurrences on her property, she may be said to owe no less a duty to her contract vendee. . . . Where, as here, the seller not only takes unfair advantage of the buyer's ignorance but has created and perpetuated a condition about which he is unlikely to even inquire, enforcement of the contract (in whole or in part) is offensive to the court's sense of equity. Application of the remedy of rescission, within the bounds of the narrow exception to the doctrine of caveat emptor set forth herein, is entirely appropriate to relieve the unwitting purchaser from the consequences of a most unnatural bargain.

Accordingly, the judgment of the Supreme Court, New York County (Edward H. Lehner, J.), entered April 9, 1990, which dismissed the complaint should be modified and the first cause of action seeking rescission of the contract reinstated.

DISSENT

Justice Smith (dissenting).

I would affirm the dismissal of the complaint. . . .

* * * * *

"It is settled law in New York State that the seller of real property is under no duty to speak when the parties deal at arm's length. The mere silence of the seller, without some act or conduct which deceived the purchaser, does not amount to a concealment that is actionable as a fraud. . . ."

The parties herein were represented by counsel and dealt at arm's length. . . . There is no allegation that defendants, by some specific act, other than the failure to speak deceived the plaintiff. . . .

Finally, if the doctrine of caveat emptor is to be discarded, it should be for a reason more substantive than a poltergeist. The existence of a poltergeist is no more binding upon the defendants than it is upon this court.

Based upon the foregoing, the [lower] court properly dismissed the complaint.

Questions

1. *a.* According to the court, did the defendant seller engage in a fraudulent misrepresentation in failing to disclose the "ghostly" condition of her house?
   b. The plaintiff won this case on equitable/fairness grounds. Explain the court's reasoning.
   c. Do you agree with the court's equity/fairness reasoning? Explain.
   d. Did the real estate agent engage in fraud for failing to disclose the house's haunted reputation? Explain.

2. *a.* What did the court mean by the phrase "caveat emptor?"
   b. Why did the court find for the plaintiff buyer, even though "caveat emptor" seemed to be the controlling law in this situation?
   c. Would the buyer have been successful in a misrepresentation claim if the seller had said: "This house is so peaceful. We never have any disturbances."?
   d. The defendant seller had fostered the belief that her house was haunted. Did that promotional effort by the defendant influence the court's decision making? Explain.

3. Explain dissenting Justice Smith's objection to the majority's ruling.

4. In 2007, soon after moving from California into the home she had bought in Pennsylvania, Janet Milliken learned that previous occupants, Konstantinos Koumboulis and his wife, died in an apparent murder/suicide after Koumboulis allegedly shot his wife and himself in the house. The sellers, Kathleen and Joseph Jacono, had later bought the home in a real estate auction. Milliken filed a complaint against the Jaconos and the real estate firms involved in her purchase of the house, alleging fraud and misrepresentation for failure to disclose the murder/suicide. Milliken stated in her opening brief that after she and her family had moved into the home, various paranormal events had occurred. How should the court rule? Explain. See *Milliken v. Jacono*, 60 A.3d 133 (Pa. 2012).

Toy Yoda

Former Hooters waitress Jodee Berry sued Gulf Coast Wings for not awarding a new Toyota as a prize for her victory in an April 2001 sales contest. Berry alleged that her manager told the waitresses in their Florida Hooters that the server selling the most beer would be entered in a drawing (involving other Hooters locations) with the winner receiving a new Toyota. At one point during the contest, the manager allegedly said he did not know whether the winner would receive a Toyota car, truck, or van, but he did know that the winner would be required to pay registration fees. At the close of the contest, the manager told Berry that she had won. He blindfolded her and took her to the restaurant parking lot. He laughed when Berry found, not the car she expected, but a doll based on the character Yoda in the Star Wars movie (a toy Yoda). Berry did not laugh, but she did sue. The case was settled out of court. The terms of that settlement were not disclosed, but Berry's lawyer did say that she would be able to afford whatever Toyota she wanted.

Questions

1. What contract-based causes of action did Berry bring in this case?
2. Defend Hooters.
3. Make the argument that the Hooters manager never actually made an offer to the waitresses.
4. If an offer was made, how did Berry accept that offer?
5. Make the argument that the offer and acceptance, if they existed, were not supported by consideration.

Sources: Berry v. Gulf Coast Wings, Inc., Div. J (Fla. 14th Cir. Ct. July 24, 2001); and Keith A. Rowley, "You Asked for It, You Got It . . . Toy Yoda: Practical Jokes, Prizes, and Contract Law," 3 *Nevada Law Journal* 526 (2003).

Duress

Sometimes genuine assent is not secured and a contract may be rescinded because one of the parties is forced to agree. Fear lies at the heart of a duress claim. The party seeking to escape the contract must establish that a wrongful act was threatened or had occurred, causing the party to enter the contract out of fear of harm such that free will was precluded. Increasingly, courts are also setting aside contracts on the grounds of economic duress. For example, suppose you know that one of your regular customers depends on your timely delivery of steel to his factory and that he cannot expeditiously find an alternative supply. Therefore, you tell your customer that delivery will be delayed until he agrees to pay a higher price for the steel. If he agrees, the resulting contract probably could be rescinded on the grounds of economic duress.

Undue Influence

Under some circumstances, the first party to an apparent contract can escape its terms by demonstrating that the second party so dominated her will that she (the first party) did not act independently. These claims are most common in cases involving those who are old or infirm and who lose their independence of thought and action to the undue influence of a caregiver or adviser.

Mistake

Most of us, on taking a new job, operate at least for a time in fear that we will make a mistake. Assume you are new to your job and are preparing a bid that your company will submit in hopes of securing the general maintenance contract for a large office building. In preparing the bid, you inadvertently submit a final price of $50,000 rather than $500,000. What happens? Do you lose your job?

> You inadvertently submit a final price of $50,000 rather than $500,000. What happens?

In some cases, mistakes involving critical facts can be grounds for rescinding contracts. A *mutual mistake* is one in which both parties to the contract are in error about some critical fact. With exceptions, either party can rescind those contracts because genuine assent was not achieved. Your erroneous bid, however, is a *unilateral mistake;* that is, only one party to the contract made an error. The general rule is that those contracts cannot be rescinded. However, if you are able to show that the other party to the contract knew or should have known about your mistake, many courts would allow you to rescind. Certainly you would make that argument in this instance because the $50,000 bid presumably is dramatically out of line with the other bids and at odds with reasonable business expectations about the value of the contract. In cases where an error is made in drafting a contract, and both parties are unaware of the error (a mutual mistake), the courts will reform the contract rather than void it. That is, the contract will be rewritten to reflect what the parties actually intended.

$4,934 Discount on Alitalia?

The Italian national airline, Alitalia, was charging more than $5,000 for trans-Atlantic, round-trip, business class airfares in 2006, but by mistake a fare was briefly listed online at $66.00. About the same time, Marriott was offering rooms at a New York City hotel for $24.90 when the intended price was $249.00. Alitalia honored 509 reservations at an expected cost of about $2.6 million. Marriott, however, raised the $24.90 rate to the intended $249.00. Errors of this kind happen with some frequency in the travel industry.

Questions

1. As a matter of business practice, how would you have dealt with your company's error had you been in charge at Alitalia or Marriott?

2. As a matter of law, was Alitalia or Marriott obligated to honor the low prices?

Source: Scott McCartney, "When a Fare Is Too Good to Be True," *The Wall Street Journal,* April 25, 2006, p. D5.

Legality of Purpose

Having examined agreement, consideration, capacity, and genuineness of assent, we turn now to the final requirement for the creation of a binding contract: legality of purpose (see Figure 6.2). *Illegality* refers to bargains to commit a crime or a tort (such as a deal with a coworker to embezzle funds from one's employer); but more broadly, illegality involves bargains that are forbidden by statute or violate public policy. We can identify three general categories of illegal agreements: (1) contracts that violate statutes, (2) contracts that are unconscionable, and (3) contracts that violate public policy. In general, the effect of an illegal contract is that it cannot be enforced, and the courts will not provide a remedy if its terms are unfulfilled. With exceptions, the parties to illegal deals are left where the courts find them.

FIGURE 6.2
Five Requirements of a Binding Contract.

1. Agreement
2. Consideration
3. Capacity
4. Genuineness of assent
5. Legality of purpose

1. ***Contracts violating statutes.*** As noted, a contract to commit a crime or a tort is illegal and unenforceable. The states have also specified certain other agreements that are illegal. Those provisions vary from state to state, but they commonly include antigambling laws, laws forbidding the conduct of certain kinds of business on Sundays (*blue laws*), laws forbidding *usury,* and laws forbidding the practice of certain professions (law, real estate, hair care) without a license.

Modern Family Contract Feud

On July 24, 2012, cast members of the popular and Emmy Award–winning television comedy *Modern Family* filed a breach of contract lawsuit against producer 20th Century Fox, seeking to have their current contracts declared null and void under California law prohibiting enforcement of a personal service contract after seven years. Shortly after the lawsuit was filed, Fox agreed to enter into new agreements with the cast members, who then dropped the lawsuit. If the lawsuit had gone to trial, what issues would have to be decided? Who would have won? Explain.

Sources: California Labor Code Sec. 2855; and Joe Flint, "Cast of *Modern Family* Strikes New Deal," *Los Angeles Times,* July 27, 2012 [**www.latimes.com**].

---

2. ***Unconscionable contracts.*** Certain agreements are so thoroughly one-sided that fairness precludes enforcing them. Problems of unconscionability often arise in situations in which the bargaining power of one of the parties is much superior to the other—where one can, in effect, "twist the arm" or otherwise take advantage of the other. Both the common law of contracts and UCC 2-302 give the courts the power to modify or refuse to enforce such deals.

> Certain agreements are so thoroughly one-sided that fairness precludes enforcing them.

3. ***Public policy.*** The courts may decline to enforce certain otherwise binding contracts because to do so would not be in the best interest of the public. For example, an agreement between the local convenience stores to charge $5.00 for a gallon of gasoline would be a restraint of trade (price fixing) and as such would be contrary to public policy and to antitrust laws (see Chapter 10) and thus would be unenforceable. Similarly, suppose as a condition of being hired for a job you must sign an agreement providing that you will not

leave your employer to work for one of your employer's competitors. These *noncompete* clauses (see Chapter 12) are common and may be fully lawful depending largely on whether the time and geographic restrictions imposed are reasonable. If unreasonable, the courts will either not enforce the clause or will alter it to achieve a fair result.

Another commonplace public policy concern is the *exculpatory clause, limited liability clause, or release.* If you participate in any potentially hazardous activity such as attending a professional hockey game, whitewater rafting, joining a school field trip, or entering an amusement park you may be required to agree to release others of any liability for harm that might befall you. If you own or manage a potentially hazardous enterprise such as a water slide, bungee tower, or even a health spa, you may try to protect yourself from litigation should a customer be hurt by including a release in the customer agreement. Often, such agreements are enforceable in the manner of any other contractual provision, but sometimes they are not. Many factors can influence that decision, including how sweeping the exculpation is, whether it was knowingly entered, and the relative bargaining power of the parties. The case that follows examines an airline contract clause limiting liability for lost luggage.

LEGAL BRIEFCASE

Hanson v. America West Airlines 544 F.Supp.2d 1038 (U.S. Dist. Ct. Central Dist. Cal. 2008)

Judge Guilford

BACKGROUND

Plaintiff David Hanson ("Plaintiff") has lost his head. More specifically, Plaintiff has lost an artistically and scientifically valuable robotic head modeled after famous science fiction author Philip K. Dick ("Head"). Dick's well-known body of work has resulted in movies—such as *Total Recall, Blade Runner, Minority Report,* and *A Scanner Darkly,* and a large group of admirers has grown following his death in Orange County, California, in 1982. His stories have questioned whether robots can be human so it seems appropriate that Plaintiff reincarnated Dick as a robot which included the Head, valued at around $750,000.

Plaintiff lost his Head on one of Defendant's planes when flying from Texas to San Francisco with a connection in Las Vegas. Plaintiff brought the Head onto the plane in a carry-on duffel bag and stored it in the overhead bin. Plaintiff fell asleep during the flight from Texas to Las Vegas, and woke up when the plane arrived in Las Vegas. On waking, Plaintiff immediately left the plane to catch his connecting flight to San Francisco. Perhaps because he had just woken up, Plaintiff lacked the total recall to remember to retrieve the Head from the overhead bin.

According to Plaintiff, as soon as he got to San Francisco, he went to the baggage counter, spoke to Defendant's employee, Leanne Miller ("Miller"), and informed her of the problem. Miller told him that the airplane with his Head was in flight, and could not be checked until it landed in Southern California. Plaintiff offered to fly to Southern California to regain his Head, but Miller told him not to do that. According to Plaintiff, he informed Miller of the importance and value of the Head, and she replied that all efforts would be made to recover the Head and that it would receive "special treatment."

Plaintiff asserts that about 45 minutes later, Miller called him with the good news that the Head had been found in Orange County. Plaintiff "remained willing" to go retrieve his Head, but Miller replied that it would be sent to San Francisco. According to Plaintiff, Miller then informed him of the special security procedures that would be taken to protect and deliver the Head. Plaintiff told Miller that Plaintiff's friend Craig Grossman would be at the airport to pick up the Head. Grossman waited for the Head at the San Francisco airport, but it never arrived and has not been found since. While hearts may be left in San Francisco, heads apparently are left in Orange County, or are simply lost or stolen.

Plaintiff sued Defendant in California state court for conversion, negligence, and involuntary bailment. Defendant removed the case to federal court, and here moves for summary judgment.

ANALYSIS
1. Contractual Liability Limitations

Defendant argues that it contractually limited its liability for loss of Plaintiff's goods. . . .

Federal common law allows a carrier to limit its liability for lost or damaged goods if the contract limiting liability offers the shipper (1) reasonable notice of the limited liability, and (2) a fair opportunity to buy higher liability.

* * * * *

If the contract states the limited liability provision and a means to avoid it, the contract is considered prima facie valid. Defendant has satisfied the elements of an enforceable limited liability provision under federal common law. The Contract of Carriage provides that "liability of loss, delay, or damage to baggage is limited as follows unless a higher value is declared in advance and additional charges are paid." The contract later provides that the monetary limit is "USD 2,800.00 per ticketed passenger for checked baggage." More specifically for this case, the Contract of Carriage provides that Defendant "assumes no responsibility or liability for baggage, or other items, carried in the passenger compartment of the aircraft." Plaintiff admits that he was aware of the limited liability provision. Thus, Defendant provided Plaintiff with reasonable notice of limited liability and a fair opportunity to buy higher liability.

2. Plaintiff's Arguments

Plaintiff argues that Defendant is liable for the lost head because (1) there was a material deviation from the Contract of Carriage and (2) Plaintiff's discussion with Miller altered the terms of the original Contract of Carriage or created a new contract.

2.1 Material Deviation Doctrine

* * * * *

[T]he material deviation doctrine states that where a carrier effects a fundamental breach of a contract by materially deviating from the contract's terms, the carrier is liable for damage to or loss of the shipped goods. Cases have further defined the boundaries of this doctrine. For example, in *Nipponkoa Ins. Co., Ltd., v. Watkins Motor Lines, Inc.,* 431 F.Supp.2d 411 (S.D.N.Y. 2006), a carrier promised to take special measures to protect a shipment of laptop computers, including using high security locks and video surveillance. The court found that the carrier breached that promise by failing to use either high security locks or video surveillance. The court held that the carrier was responsible for the loss of the computers under the

material deviation doctrine. The court explained that the doctrine applies when a carrier breaches a "separate, risk-related promise" about the shipment of goods. The court emphasized that the agreement was specific and that the carrier deviated from the expressly agreed-upon security measures.

* * * * *

The Ninth Circuit has limited the material deviation doctrine. In *Vision Air,* for example, a carrier destroyed two trucks by using an inadequate pulley system to transport them. *Vision Air,* 155 F.3d at 1167–68. The Ninth Circuit held that even if that behavior constituted gross negligence or recklessness, it did not constitute a material deviation. "[W]e reject the notion that mere negligence may constitute an unreasonable deviation . . . we reject the notion that gross negligence or recklessness may constitute an unreasonable deviation." The court emphasized that only "more culpable misconduct" could be considered a deviation.

In the cases just discussed, the courts focused on the actual express terms of the agreement, showing that the material deviation doctrine applies only when the shipper makes a "separate, risk-related promise," and then breaches that promise.

With these boundaries, Plaintiff's argument that Defendant materially deviated from the original Contract of Carriage fails. There were no provisions in the original Contract of Carriage directly concerning transporting the Head. Indeed, the original Contract of Carriage disclaimed any responsibility for carry-on baggage. Further, nothing in the original Contract of Carriage made provisions for travelers leaving baggage on the airplane. Thus, Defendant did not breach a "separate, risk-related promise" in the original Contract of Carriage, and is not liable under this theory.

2.2 Altered or New Contractual Terms and Agency Law

Plaintiff also argues that Miller either altered the terms of the original Contract of Carriage or created a new contract with Plaintiff, and that Defendant is liable under the new or altered contract.

Agents can bind their principals only if they have actual or apparent authority to do so. Actual authority may be either express or implied. If a principal specifically authorizes an agent to act, the agent has express authority to take that action. If a principle "merely states the general nature of what the agent is to do, the agent is said to have implied authority to do acts consistent with the direction."

Miller did not have express authority to contract with Plaintiff. The original Contract of Carriage provided that:

> No employee of U.S. Airways has the authority to waive, modify, or alter any provisions of these terms of

transportation or any applicable fares/charges unless authorized by a corporate officer of U.S. Airways. U.S. Airways-appointed agents and representatives are only authorized to sell tickets for air transportation on U.S. Airways pursuant to the terms of transportation and applicable fares/charges of U.S. Airways.

There is no evidence that Miller was either a corporate officer of Defendant or that she was authorized by such an officer to modify the terms of transportation. Thus, under the Contract of Carriage, Miller had no express authority either to change the terms of the contract or to create a new contract. Indeed, Miller had express authority only to "sell tickets for air transportation." Likewise, there is no evidence that Miller had implied authority.

The Contract of Carriage also leads to the conclusion that Miller had no apparent authority to change the terms of the contract or to create a new contract. "Apparent authority results when the principal does something or permits the agent to do something which reasonably leads another to believe that the agent had the authority he purported to have." *Hawaiian Paradise Park Corp.,* 414 F.2d at 756 (9th Cir. 1969). Only the acts of the principal, not of the agent, give rise to apparent authority. Plaintiff argues that Miller's station behind a desk near the baggage claim area led Plaintiff to reasonably believe that Miller had the authority to make contracts for the delivery of lost baggage. The Court disagrees.

Plaintiff is a frequent flyer and was aware of the applicable tariffs. Thus, before he lost his Head and spoke with Miller, he was aware of the tariff limiting Miller's authority. Aware of that tariff, he could not reasonably conclude, based on Miller's position behind a desk, that she suddenly had authority to contract with him.

* * * * *

Plaintiff cannot rely on representations altering the contract or creating a new contract when those representations were made by someone whose authority had been expressly limited by contract. The Court must find that Miller had neither actual nor apparent authority to either alter the Contract of Carriage or create a new contract.

2.3 Even Under the New Terms Alleged, Liability Has Not Been Established

Even if Miller had authority to alter the Contract of Carriage or create a new contract, Defendant would still not be liable for the lost Head because there is no evidence that Defendant breached the contract even under the new terms alleged. Plaintiff alleges new terms that provided for tagging and boxing the Head, informing everyone of the value, and scheduling the Head on the next flight. But Plaintiff presents no evidence that such terms were breached. Instead, Plaintiff offers theories of

Defendant's potential conduct, such as, "potentially informing the wrong crew of the value of the HEAD" and "potentially informing the thief of the high value of the HEAD." These theories, while heady, are insufficient.

At best, Plaintiff's theory is that, since the Head did not arrive at its destination, Defendants must have done something wrong. This is not evidence of a breach or material deviation. Defendant may have done everything as promised, only to fall victim to a head hunting thief or other skullduggery. Alternatively, Defendant could have been negligent, and still not have committed a fundamental breach. The possibility of such negligence is "considered an inherent risk of shipping." *Information Control,* 73 Cal. App. 3d at 641. Thus, even if Plaintiff's discussion with Miller altered or created a new contract, there is no evidence establishing Defendant's liability based on breach or material deviation.

CONCLUSION

Philip K. Dick and other science fiction luminaries have often explored whether robots might eventually evolve to exercise freedom of choice. But there is no doubt that humans have the freedom of choice to bind themselves in mutually advantageous contractual relationships. When Plaintiff chose to enter the Contract of Carriage with Defendant he agreed, among other things, to limit Defendant's liability for lost baggage. Failing to show that he is entitled to relief from that agreement, Plaintiff is bound by the terms of that contract, which bars his state law claims.

The Court must GRANT Defendant's Motion. But it does so hoping that the android head of Mr. Dick is someday found, perhaps in an Elysian field of Orange County, Dick's homeland, choosing to dream of electric sheep.

Questions

1. As a matter of law, why did America West win this case?

2. Why was this Contract of Carriage not considered unfair and one-sided and thus unenforceable?

3. Why did America West's behavior not constitute a "material deviation" from the Contract of Carriage?

4. Ning Yan went to Gay's fitness center to use a one-week complimentary pass. On each visit he signed in on a sheet that contained a standard exculpatory clause including this language: "I also understand that Vital Power Fitness Center assumes no responsibility for any injuries and/or sicknesses incurred to me. . . ." On February 18, 1999, Yan fell from a treadmill and sustained a severe head injury. He later died from that injury. No one witnessed the fall. Yan's estate claims he struck his head against a window ledge because the treadmill was placed too close to the window. If he did strike the window ledge, who would likely win this case? Explain. See *Xu v. Gay,* 668 N.W.2d 166 (Ct. App. Mich. 2003).

PRACTICING ETHICS 2010 Gulf Oil Disaster: BP Contracts Unfair/Unconscionable?

In May 2010, British Petroleum (BP) oil company was in the midst of frantic efforts to stop the oil flowing into the Gulf of Mexico from its doomed Macondo 252 well while also trying to clean up the immense quantity that escaped after the explosion of the Deepwater Horizon drilling vessel. "Several hundred" shrimpers, oyster harvesters, and others making their living from the Gulf signed contracts with BP to work as paid volunteers in the cleanup process. Among the provisions in those contracts were promises by the volunteers not to file legal claims against the oil company should they sustain damages of any kind in the cleanup process. The provisions, which many of those signing may not have fully understood, included promises not to sue in case of accident or injury and not to talk to anyone about the disaster or cleanup without BP approval. Those provisions also required a 30-day notice before pursuing legal claims against BP, even in the event of an emergency. Reportedly, BP also expected workers to add the oil giant to their personal insurance policies so that worker injuries or damages would fall to each worker's insurance rather than to BP. Commercial fisherman and United Commercial Fisherman's Association president, George Barisich, filed suit to block enforcement of the restrictive promises and U.S. District Judge Helen Berrigan ruled the offending provisions were overbroad and "unconscionable" and declared them null and void. BP and the Fisherman's Association soon reached an agreement removing the waiver language and agreeing not to enforce those provisions in contracts already signed. BP officials said the provisions were a "mistake," and they ordered the provisions removed as soon as they learned about them.

Questions

1. *a.* Were BP's protective provisions "wrong" as a matter of ethical business practice? Explain.

   b. If you were a boss or lawyer at BP, would you have included those protective provisions? Explain.

2. *a.* If you were a boss and you knew you could compel an employee to accept a pay cut in order to enhance an already healthy bottom line, would you do so? Explain.

   b. In your personal life, do you think you have made agreements with friends that were "one-sided" and "unconscionable" because of your possession of superior leverage of some kind?

   c. If so, were you "wrong" to do so. Explain.

Sources: Sabrina Canfield, "Judge Enjoins BP's Unconscionable Contract with Fishermen-Volunteers," *Courthouse News Service*, May 4, 2010 [http://www.courthousenews.com] and Brendan Kirby, "Full Report: BP Backs Away from Controversial Oil Spill Settlement Language," May 5, 2010 [http://blog.al.com].

Part Two—Interpreting and Enforcing Contracts

We have examined the five ingredients in a binding contract: agreement, consideration, capacity, genuineness of assent, and legality of purpose. Having established those conditions, a contract may have been created, but the door to contract problems has not been closed. Contracts sometimes must fulfill writing formalities to be enforceable. Third parties may have claims against some contracts. And what happens when a party to a contract does not perform as called for by the agreement?

In Writing?

> In most cases, oral contracts are fully enforceable.

Certainly a common belief is that agreements must be in writing to be enforceable; but in most cases, oral contracts are fully enforceable. The exceptions, however, are important. Oral contracts are subject to misunderstanding or to being forgotten, and fraudulent claims can readily arise from oral understandings. Consequently, our states have drawn on the English *Statute of Frauds* in specifying that the following kinds of contracts, in most cases, must be in writing to be enforceable:

1. **Collateral contract.** Assume you have just graduated from college, and you want to get started in a small printing business. You secure a bank loan on the condition that you find a creditworthy third party as a guarantor for the loan. Jacobs, a family friend, agrees with the bank to pay the debt if you fail to do so. Jacobs' promise to pay the debt must be in writing to be enforceable.

2. **The sale of land.** Broadly, land is interpreted to include the surface itself, that which is in the soil (minerals) or permanently attached to it (buildings), and growing crops when accompanying the transfer of land. Thus, if a building was permanently attached to a lot you seek for the aforementioned printing business, that building would need to be included in the written contract, but if you contracted to have a building constructed on your lot, you would not need (at least for the purposes of the Statute of Frauds) to execute a written agreement with the building contractor because you would not be contracting for an interest in land. A long-term lease (normally more than one year) for that land and building would, in most states, need to be in writing. All of these principles simply reflect the special role of land in our view of wealth and freedom.

3. **Promises that cannot be performed within one year.** This requirement springs from a concern about faulty memories, deaths, and other impediments to the satisfactory conclusion of long-term contracts. The courts have interpreted this provision narrowly, in effect saying that such a contract need not be in writing if it is *possible,* according to its terms, to perform it within one year from the day of its creation. It follows then that a contract for an indefinite period (such as an employment contract "for the balance of the employee's life") need not be in writing to be enforceable. (It is possible that the employee will die within one year.)

4. **Contracts for the sale of goods at a price of $500 or more.** With exceptions, under both the English-derived Statute of Frauds and UCC 2-201, contracts for the sale of goods (having a value of $500 or more under the UCC) must be in writing to be enforceable. Under the UCC, informal writing will suffice so long as it indicates that a contract was made, it contains a quantity term, and it was signed "by the party against whom enforcement is sought." Section 2-201 provides exceptions for certain transactions of $500 or more in goods in which a contract will be enforceable even though not in writing.

5. **Contracts in consideration of marriage.** The mutual exchange of marriage promises need not be in writing, but any contract that uses marriage as the consideration to support the contract must be in writing to be enforceable. Such contracts would include, for example, prenuptial agreements that are entered prior to marriage and serve the purpose, among others, of specifying how the couple's property will be divided in the event of a divorce. Those contracts must be in writing to be enforceable.

6. **Executor/administrator's promise.** When an individual dies, a representative is appointed to oversee the estate. A promise by that executor/administrator to pay the estate's debts must be in writing if the payment will be made from the executor/administrator's personal funds. Thus, where the executor of an estate contracts with an

auctioneer to dispose of the decedent's personal property, the executor's promise to pay the auctioneer must be in writing if the funds are to come from the executor's personal resources; the promise need not be in writing if the payment is to come from the estate.

E-mail Exchanges and Statute of Frauds

The Uniform Electronic Transactions Act, widely adopted by state legislatures, gives electronic records and signatures the same legal power as paper documents and manually signed signatures. Under Tennessee's adoption of the Uniform Electronic Transactions Act, attorneys' exchange of e-mails setting forth proposed settlement terms to resolve a family dispute over the ownership of a parcel of land was determined to create a signed, binding agreement, satisfying the state's Statute of Frauds. See *Waddle v. Elrod*, 367 S.W.3d 217 (Tenn. 2012).

Questions

1. What are the advantages of allowing e-mail exchanges to satisfy the Statute of Frauds?
2. What are the disadvantages of allowing e-mail exchanges to satisfy the Statute of Frauds? Explain.

Sources: Waddle v. Elrod, 367 S.W.2d 217 (Tenn. 2012); and National Conference of Statute Legislatures, "Uniform Electronic Transactions Act" [**http://www.ncsl.org/research/telecommunications-and-information -technology/uniform-electronic-transactions-acts.aspx**].

Failure to Comply   A fully performed oral contract, even though not in compliance with the Statute of Frauds, will not be rescinded by the courts. However, incomplete oral contracts that fail to comply with the statute are unenforceable. If a party to an unenforceable oral contract has provided partial performance in reliance on the contract, the courts will ordinarily provide compensation under quasi-contract principles for the reasonable value of that performance. [For more on the Statute of Frauds, see **www.expertlaw.com/library/ business/statute_of_frauds.html**]

The Parol Evidence Rule

Suppose you are the purchasing manager for a large manufacturer. You entered a written contract for 50 new personal computers. During negotiations, the seller said they would "throw in" 10 new printers if they got the computer order, but you failed to include a provision for the printers in the contract. Is your boss about to have a fit? Perhaps, because you probably will not be able to introduce evidence of that oral understanding to alter the terms of the written contract. In general, whenever a contract has been reduced to writing with the intent that the writing represents a complete and final integration of the parties' intentions, none of the parties can introduce parol evidence (oral or written words outside the "four corners" of the agreement) to add to, change, or contradict that contract when that evidence was expressed/created at the time of or prior to the writing. The written agreement is presumed to be the best evidence of the parties' intentions at the time they entered the contract. (The parol evidence rule under UCC section 2-202 is essentially the same as the common-law provisions discussed here.)

Exceptions   Parol evidence may be admissible under the following exceptional circumstances:

1. To add missing terms to an incomplete written contract.
2. To explain ambiguities in a written contract.

3. To prove circumstances that would invalidate a written contract; that is, to establish one of the grounds of mistake, fraud, illegality, and so forth explained earlier in this chapter.

Contract's Terms: Paper versus Website?

Fadal Machining Centers, a machine and machine parts manufacturer, sued Compumachine, one of its distributors, for breach of contract. Under the distributorship agreement, a hard copy of which was attached to Fadal's complaint, any legal action arising out of the contract would be heard in a California federal district court. The agreement also stated that Fadal could establish the terms of sale on occasion. Each of the fifteen allegedly unpaid invoices referred to Fadal's website for the terms and conditions of sale. The terms found on the website under the label "Contract" in large bold type, included an arbitration clause and a statement that they would prevail over any other agreement. Should Fadal's claim be heard in the California federal district court, or be submitted to arbitration? Decide and explain.

Source: See *Fadal v. Compumachine*, 461 Fed. Appx. 630 (9th Cir. 2011).

Third Parties

We turn now to the rights and duties of those who are not parties to a contract but hold legally recognizable interests in that contract. Those interests arise when (1) contract rights are assigned to others, (2) contract duties are delegated to others, or (3) contracts have third-party beneficiary provisions.

Assignment of Rights

Ordinarily, a party to a contract is free to transfer her or his rights under the contract to a third party. Thus, if Ames owes Jones $500 for work performed, Jones can assign that right to Smith, who can now assert her right to collect against Ames. That transfer of rights is labeled an assignment (see Figure 6.3). Jones, the party making the transfer, is the assignor; Smith, the one receiving the right, is the assignee; and Ames, the party who must perform, is the obligor. Ames, the obligor, must now perform the contract for the benefit of the assignee; that is, Ames must pay the $500 to Smith. The completed assignment then extinguishes the assignor's rights under the contract.

FIGURE 6.3
Assignment of Rights.

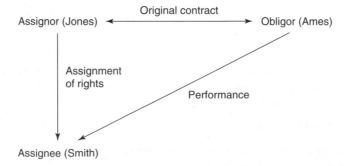

Some contracts are not assignable without consent of the obligor. That would be the case where the obligor's duties are materially altered by the assignment. For example, if you have a contract to serve as a personal fitness trainer for a busy chief executive officer, your contract could not be assigned without your consent to another CEO, or movie star, or the like because the highly personal and specific obligations under the contract would necessarily be materially altered with a different client.

Delegation of Duties

The parties to a contract may also delegate their duties under the contract to one or more third parties. Assume Allen has secured a contract to install windows in Boyd's new office building (see Figure 6.4). Allen could delegate that duty to another contractor, Harms (although Allen would more commonly simply enter a subcontracting arrangement without actually transferring the underlying contract). A delegation of duty leaves Harms, the delegatee (the one to whom the duty is delegated), primarily responsible for performance; but Allen, the obligor/delegator (the one who made the delegation), remains secondarily liable in case Harms, the delegatee, fails to fulfill the duty to Boyd, the obligee (the one to whom the duty is owed under both the original contract and the delegation). As with the assignment of rights, some contractual duties, particularly those of a personal service nature, cannot be delegated without consent.

FIGURE 6.4
Delegation of Duties.

Third-Party Beneficiary Contracts

Normally, those not a party to a contract have no rights under that contract. As we have seen, however, third parties may be assigned rights or delegated duties under a contract. A third party may also enforce a contract where that contract was expressly intended to benefit the third party. An agreement of that nature is a third-party beneficiary contract. Third-party beneficiaries are of three kinds: creditor, donee, and incidental. In general, creditor and donee beneficiaries can enforce contracts made by others for their benefit; incidental beneficiaries cannot do so.

Creditor Beneficiary   Assume you decide to expand your used-car business by advertising on television. Your ads appear on TV; therefore, you owe the local television station $2,000. Rather than paying the bill directly, you transfer a used car to your friend Gleason, with the understanding that he will pay off your bill with the television station. Thus, the station becomes the creditor beneficiary of the contract between you and Gleason, and the station can sue Gleason for that money if necessary while you remain secondarily responsible for the payment.

Donee Beneficiary When the promisee's primary purpose in entering a contract is to make a gift to another, that third party is a donee beneficiary of the contract. The most common of these situations involves an ordinary life insurance policy for which the owner (the promisee) pays premiums to the life insurance company (the promisor), which is obliged to pay benefits to the third party upon the death of the promisee/policy owner. If necessary, the third-party beneficiary can sue the insurance company for payment.

Incidental Beneficiary Often a third party receives benefit from a contract although conferring that benefit was not the contracting parties' primary purpose or intent. For example, assume a General Motors car dealer enters into a contract to buy land adjacent to your used-car lot for the purpose of opening a large dealership. You would benefit immensely from the spillover effect of the large, adjacent dealership. In such a situation, you would be an incidental beneficiary of the land sale contract because that contract was not intended for your benefit. If the landowner or the GM dealer failed to perform, you, as an incidental beneficiary, would have no legal rights against either of them.

The case that follows involves a third-party claim by Gill Plumbing against its subcontractor, Jimenez. The dispute arose out of a dormitory construction contract where the general contractor, Gilbane Building, had hired Gill to do the dormitory plumbing and Gill, in turn, had hired Jimenez to install some portion of that plumbing.

LEGAL BRIEFCASE

Jimenez v. Gilbane Building Company, et al.
693 S.E.2d 126 (Ga. Ct. App. 2010)

* * * * *

Judge Adams

The background facts are that Gilbane Building Company was the general contractor for the construction of a new dormitory at Georgia Southern University. Gilbane hired Gill Plumbing as the plumbing contractor, and Gill Plumbing, in turn, hired Jose Alfredo Jimenez to perform plumbing installation work. The building was completed in July 2005, but in October, after the dormitory was occupied by students, a pipe failed causing extensive water damage to the dormitory and to some students' personal belongings. Gilbane was forced to hire Belfor USA Group, Inc., to perform remediation and repair work. Belfor's $990,060.63 bill for the services has not been paid.

Belfor filed this action against Gilbane, Gilbane filed a third-party action against Gill Plumbing, and Gill Plumbing filed a fourth-party action against Jimenez. The parties have since been realigned. Currently, both Belfor and Gilbane have claims against Gill Plumbing, and Gill Plumbing has a third-party claim against Jimenez for the costs of the remediation and repair.

In its third-party claim, Gill Plumbing asserts that it had a written agreement with Jimenez that included an indemnity agreement, and that the damages to the dormitory resulted from negligent work performed by Jimenez. Jimenez denied that he entered into a valid and enforceable contract or an indemnity agreement with Gill Plumbing and denied the negligence. The trial court granted Gill's motion for partial summary judgment against Jimenez, finding that he was liable "for indemnification to Gill Plumbing" "in the amount, if any, of damages proven to have resulted from Mr. Jimenez's defective work." Jimenez appeals this ruling and contends that "no contract existed between Mr. Jimenez and the

Appellee as a matter of law" or, at least, that there are material issues of fact regarding the contract and the indemnity agreement.

Summary judgment is proper when there is no genuine issue of material fact and the movant is entitled to judgment as a matter of law. . . .

There is no question that the parties had an oral agreement. The issue before us is whether there was an enforceable written agreement and, if so, what were the terms of that agreement. The undisputed facts show that Jimenez was hired by Gill Plumbing to perform plumbing services in the "Eagle Village" construction project at Georgia Southern University, that he performed plumbing services, and that he has been paid for the work in the amount of $167,000.

Jimenez has never worked for any company other than Gill Plumbing and the two have worked together for at least 15 years. On September 15, 2004, Jimenez signed two documents, which, Gill Plumbing contends, constitute the parties' entire written agreement; Jimenez has signed other documents for Gill Plumbing in the past. The first document is contained on one page, it is dated September 15, 2004, and it has Jimenez's typewritten name and his signature. The main body of the document is as follows:

LABOR CONTRACT
Project: Eagle Village.

Item 1	Slab	50,100.00
Item 2	Rough	66,800.00
Item 3	Set Out	50,100.00

- Weekly billing to be submitted in draw format. All work must be approved by Larry Pollett.
- Weekly safety meetings must be attended. Sub required to attend all jobsite agenda and safety meetings.
- Subs required to comply with all general contractor regulations and jobsite regulations
- All Subs required to provide certificate of insurance with adequate coverages per limits set by general contractor.
- Subs are required to honor subcontractor Warranty for labor and installation free of all defects for a period of (1) year from date of substantial completion.
- *Subs agree & abide by all terms in the attached Exhibit 'A' for insurance & indemnity.*

Total Contract Amount $167,000.00

(Emphasis supplied.) Jimenez's signature appears below the following words, which are written on the side of the above chart:

Sub-Labor

Affidavit

I certify the work for which above payment is requested has been completed according to the plans and specifications and in compliance with the terms of our contract and all labor and material bills applicable to this job have been paid to date and that Federal income, social security, and unemployment taxes have been withheld and will be paid when due on all employees employed by me on this job.

_____ /s/ _____ CONTRACTOR

Notably, this first document does not name Gill Plumbing anywhere, and the "affidavit" is written in the past tense, as if the project had already been completed, but as of the date on the document, Jimenez's work at Eagle Village had not begun. The second document—"Exhibit A"—is two pages long, and it begins as follows:

INSURANCE AND INDEMNITY SUBCONTRACTOR AGREEMENT

The Work performed by the Subcontractor shall be at the risk of the Subcontractor exclusively. To the fullest extent permitted by law, Subcontractor shall indemnify, defend (at Subcontractor's sole expense) and hold harmless Contractor, the Owner (if different from Contractor), affiliated companies of Contractor, . . . from and against any and all claims for . . . damage to property . . . which arise or are in any way connected with the Work performed, Materials furnished, or Services provided under this Agreement by Subcontractor or its agents. . . .

The exhibit goes on to require the "Subcontractor" to obtain commercial general liability insurance in the amount of $1,000,000, and to meet other related requirements. The exhibit is signed by Jimenez on the second page over the word "Subcontractor," but it is not dated. Also, the document does not include Gill Plumbing's name anywhere. Finally, Jimenez never performed any work at Eagle Village that could be called "Set Out" as stated on page one of the document.

Jimenez contends the three-page document is not an enforceable agreement because it does not state who the other party is or mention Gill Plumbing's name; it does not include a promise by Gill Plumbing, or anyone else, to pay him; it does not specify the location or address where the work is to be performed; it leaves several terms undefined; it does not specify the time for performance; it does not direct Jimenez to perform any work at all; and although it mentions additional documents, none are attached or defined. He argues the "sub-labor affidavit" found on page one of the document is written in the past tense, suggesting that the work was already completed when, in fact, it had not begun as of the only date indicated on the document. He also complains that the indemnification provision fails to identify who should be indemnified and that it fails to define the terms "subcontractor," "contractor," or "owner." Finally, Jimenez contends he cannot read or communicate well in English and he did not know what he signed.

In Georgia,

> The first requirement of the law relative to contracts is that there must be a meeting of the minds of the parties, and mutuality, and in order for the contract to be valid the agreement must ordinarily be expressed plainly and explicitly enough to show what the parties agreed upon. A contract cannot be enforced in any form of action if its terms are incomplete or incomprehensible.

Bagwell-Hughes, Inc. v. McConnell, 224 Ga. 659, 661–662 (164 SE2d 229) (1968). But "[a]n objection of indefiniteness may be obviated by performance on the part of one party and the acceptance of the performance by the other." *Aukerman v. Witmer,* 256 Ga. App. 211, 216 (1) (568 SE2d 123) (2002). Nevertheless, performance as a cure has its limits:

> Performance does not cure the deficiencies in an agreement that is so vague, indefinite, and uncertain "as to make it impossible for courts to determine what, if anything, was agreed upon, therefore rendering it impossible to determine whether there had been performance."

Razavi v. Shackelford, 260 Ga. App. 603, 605 (1) (580 SE2d 253) (2003).

Here, the attendant and surrounding circumstances show that Jimenez entered into an agreement with Gill Plumbing, that he performed work, and that he was paid by Gill Plumbing. The three-page document shows that the work was to be performed on the "Eagle Village" project; it stated the amount to be paid for each phase of the work, and the total equaled the amount that Jimenez was paid for the work. And Jimenez attended weekly safety meetings. Thus, there is some evidence of performance consistent with the three-page document. But there is also evidence of performance that is inconsistent with the three-page document. Jimenez did not perform some of the work listed in the document, and the document suggests that the work had already been completed when the document was signed.

In addition, the document is ambiguous at best, and the rules of construction do not resolve the ambiguity. Jimenez is identified as the "subcontractor" in the indemnification agreement, which provides that he is to identify the "contractor" and others. Yet, the first page of the three page document identifies Jimenez as the "contractor," suggesting that he should indemnify himself. And there are two contractors who are parties to the lawsuit and other contractors on the entire project.

* * * * *

Here, among other problems, it is impossible to tell from the terms of the written document who Jimenez may have promised to indemnify, and that fact has not been made sufficiently clear by either the rules of construction or any performance under the agreement. The trial court erred by granting partial summary judgment in favor of Gill Plumbing on the purported indemnification agreement. Jury issues remain on the terms of the parties' agreement.

Judgment reversed.

Questions

1. Explain what the trial court meant in finding that Jimenez was liable "for indemnification to Gill Plumbing" "in the amount, if any, of damages proven to have resulted from Mr. Jimenez's defective work."

2. Why did the court conclude that Gill did not have an enforceable agreement with Jiminez?

3. Why did the appeals court overturn the trial court's summary judgment?

Discharge

At some point, obligations under a contract come to an end. When that moment arrives, we say the duties of the contracting parties have been discharged. In this section, we examine some of the methods of contract discharge. Discharge can occur in many ways, but the most important of these are (1) conditions, (2) performance or breach, (3) lawful excuses, (4) agreement, and (5) by operation of law.

Discharge by Conditions

Sometimes a contract is useful to one or more of the contracting parties only if some future event occurs or fails to occur. Under those circumstances, the parties may write into the contract a clause providing that performance is required only if the specified condition occurs or fails to occur. Otherwise, the duty to perform is discharged. Those conditions take three forms: conditions precedent, conditions subsequent, and conditions concurrent.

Conditions Precedent A conditions precedent clause specifies that an event must occur before the parties to the contract are obliged to perform. Assume you are attempting to establish a business booking rock-and-roll acts for performances. You sign a deal with the rock group Passion Pit, providing for a performance "contingent upon obtaining satisfactory lease arrangements for the university field house within 14 days." If you are unable to achieve an acceptable lease, both parties are discharged from performance requirements under the contract.

> You sign a deal with the rock group Passion Pit.

Conditions Subsequent A conditions subsequent clause excuses performance if a future event transpires. Thus, in the Passion Pit example, the band might include a clause providing that the agreement will be null and void if any member of the band is ill or otherwise unable to perform on the contracted evening. Hence in a contract with a condition subsequent the parties have bound themselves to perform unless a specified event occurs; whereas in a contract with a condition precedent the parties have no binding duties until the specified event occurs.

Conditions Concurrent Here the contract simply specifies that the parties are to perform their duties at the same time. Each performance is dependent on the other. So if Passion Pit performs as contracted, you have a simultaneous duty to pay for the band's performance. Your duty to pay is conditioned on Passion Pit's performance and vice versa.

Express or Implied Conditions Another way of classifying the aforementioned conditions is to treat them either as express or implied. Express conditions are those explicitly agreed to by the parties, as in the situation where you, a concert promoter, expressly conditioned performance on your ability to secure the university field house for the concert. Express conditions are often prefaced by words such as *when, if, provided,* and so forth.

Implied-in-fact conditions are not explicitly stated in the contract but are derived by the court from the conduct of the parties and the circumstances surrounding the bargain. Suppose you contract to remove snow from your neighbor's driveway during the winter. An implied-in-fact condition of your neighbor's duty to pay would be that you would complete the work within a reasonable period.

Implied-in-law conditions (also called *constructive conditions*) are those that, although not expressly provided for in the contract or not able to be reasonably inferred from the facts, the court imposes on the contract to avoid unfairness. Hence, if you contracted to put a new roof on your neighbor's house but your written contract did not include a date for payment, the court might imply a contract clause providing that your neighbor need not pay you until the job is complete.

Whose Ring?

Barry Meyer and Robyn Mitnick became engaged on August 9, 1996, at which time Barry gave Robyn a custom-designed, $19,500 engagement ring. On November 8, 1996, Barry asked Robyn to sign a prenuptial agreement, but Robyn refused. The parties agree the engagement ended at that point, but they each blame the other for the breakup. Robyn did not return the ring, and Barry sued for its return.

Questions

1. Explain each party's argument using contract principles.
2. Does it matter who was "at fault" in the breakup? Explain.
3. Who gets the ring? Explain.

Source: Meyer v. Mitnick, 625 N.W.2d 136 (Ct. App. Mich. 2001).

Discharge by Performance or by Breach of Contract

Complete performance is, of course, the normal way of discharging a contract. Failure to fully perform without a lawful excuse for that failure results in a breach of contract. The consequences of both full performance and breach of contract can be described in four parts.

Complete Performance—No Breach of Contract   Here we find the most common method of discharge—the situation in which the parties simply do precisely what the contract calls for: pay $500, provide a particular product, present the deed for a piece of land, and so on. When fully performed, a contract has been *executed.*

Substantial Performance—Nonmaterial Breach of Contract   In some cases complete performance is not achieved because of minor deviations from the agreed-on performance. Most notably in construction contracts and in many personal or professional service contracts, the courts have recognized the doctrine of substantial performance. For example, assume a contractor painted a house as agreed, except that he replaced the Benjamin Moore paint called for in the contract with a Sherwin-Williams paint of comparable quality. Assuming the variation has not materially altered the end product and assuming that the variation was not the result of bad faith, the court will enforce the contract as written, but require a deduction for any damages sustained as a consequence of the imperfect performance.

Unacceptable Performance—Material Breach of Contract   When a party falls beneath substantial performance and does not have a lawful excuse for that failure, a material breach of contract has occurred. No clear line separates substantial performance (a nonmaterial breach) from unacceptable performance (a material breach). Such decisions must be made case by case. We can say that material breaches are those that fall short of what the nonbreaching party should reasonably expect—that is, full performance in some cases and substantial performance in others. A material breach discharges the nonbreaching party's duties and permits that party to sue for damages or rescind the contract and seek restitution.

Duke University Breached Its Contract with a Student?

Andrew Giuliani (son of former New York mayor, Rudy Giuliani) was recruited by Coach Rod Myers to play golf at Duke University. Coach Myers allegedly said that Giuliani would be given "life-time access" to Duke's "state-of-the-art" training facilities when he became a Duke alum, and that he would be able to compete for the opportunity to play against the best golfers in the NCAA. Giuliani said those promises and others were instrumental in his decision to attend Duke. Giuliani alleged that Duke "promised to provide [Mr. Giuliani] with various educational services, lodging, and a right of access to the Athletic Department's Varsity program and facilities." Coach Myers unexpectedly passed away in the spring of 2007 and Coach O.D. Vincent took over. Vincent decided to cut the squad in half and announced that he was canceling Giuliani's golf eligibility. Vincent pointed to several incidents of alleged bad behavior by Giuliani. Vincent then presented Giuliani with a written agreement setting out the steps that would have allowed Giuliani to rejoin the team. Giuliani refused to sign the agreement. Giuliani then filed a breach of contract suit against Duke University and Vincent.

Questions

1. Giuliani claimed that his contractual right to play golf at Duke was based on (a) Coach Myers's oral statements and (b) Duke's Student-Athlete Handbook, the Duke Student Bulletin, the Duke Athletic Policy Manual, and the NCAA Division I Manual. Giuliani lost the case. Why did the Court reject Giuliani's contract claims?

2. Could you successfully sue your university for breach of contract if you were dismissed from school because of low grades? Explain. See, for example, *Bissessur v. The Indiana University Board of Trustees*, 581 F.3d 599 (7th Cir. 2009).

Source: Giuliani v. Duke University, 2010 U.S. Dist. LEXIS 32691 (M.D.N.C.).

Advance Refusal to Perform—Anticipatory Breach of Contract   Sometimes one of the parties, before performance is due, indicates by word or deed that she or he will not perform. Normally an anticipatory breach (also called anticipatory repudiation) is the equivalent of a material breach, discharging the nonbreaching party from any further obligations and allowing the nonbreaching party to sue for damages, if any.

When Has a Breach of Contract Occurred? When Should the Law Intervene in a Contract?

The brief case that follows raises many claims, including breach of contract, but it also serves as an interesting test of the role of law. Should sports fans be able to secure a remedy through contract law when an event merely does not meet their expectations? The idea seems preposterous and another instance of abuse of the legal system, but consider the facts.

> Tyson spit out his mouthpiece and bit both of Holyfield's ears.

The case deals with ex-convict and former heavyweight boxing champion Mike Tyson and his famous 1997 bout with then-champion Evander Holyfield, a fight ended by disqualification in the third round when Tyson bit both of Holyfield's ears. Incensed pay-per-view customers joined in a class action seeking their money back

($50–$60 each) claiming they were "ripped off" or "scammed" by Tyson. They sued Tyson, fight promoters, and fight telecasters. A lower court dismissed the complaint for failure to state a cause of action. The plaintiffs appealed.

LEGAL BRIEFCASE

Castillo v. Tyson   701 N.Y.S. 2D 423
(N.Y. S.Ct. App. Div. 2000)

Judge Ramos

Plaintiffs claim that they were entitled to view a "legitimate heavyweight title fight" fought "in accordance with the applicable rules and regulations" of the governing boxing commission—that is, a fight that was to end either in an actual or technical knockout or by decision of the judges after 12 rounds—and that they are entitled to their money back because the fight ended in a disqualification. Many legal theories are invoked in support of this claim—breach of contract, breach of implied covenant of good faith and fair dealing, unjust enrichment, breach of express and implied warranties, tortious interference with contractual relations, "wantonness," fraud, negligent representation—none of which have merit. Plaintiffs are not in contractual privity with any of the defendants, and their claim that they are third-party beneficiaries of one or more of the contracts that defendants entered into among themselves was aptly rejected by the motion court as "contrived." Nothing in these contracts can be understood as promising a fight that did not end in a disqualification. The rules of the governing commission provide for disqualification, and it is a possibility that a fight fan can reasonably expect. Plaintiffs could not reasonably rule out such a possibility by the boxer's and promoters' public statements predicting a "sensational victory" and "the biggest fight of all time," and assuming other representations were made promising or implying a "legitimate fight," there can be no breach of warranty claim absent privity of contract between plaintiffs and defendants and also because defendants provided only a service. Nor is a claim of fraud supported by plaintiffs' allegations that the boxer's former trainer predicted that the boxer would get himself disqualified if he failed to achieve an early knockout and that the boxer came out without his mouthpiece in the beginning of the round that he was disqualified. Plaintiffs' claim for unjust enrichment was properly dismissed by the motion court on the ground that plaintiffs received what they paid for, namely,

"the right to view whatever event transpired." We have considered plaintiffs' other arguments . . . and find them unpersuasive. Affirmed.

Questions

1. Why did the court reject the plaintiffs' breach of contract claim?

2. What is unjust enrichment, and why was that claim denied by the court?

3. Defects discovered in the Michelin tires to be used by 14 of the 20 teams in a Formula One race at the Indianapolis Speedway caused those teams to withdraw prior to the start, leaving only six cars running in the race. The race was completed, but fans sued for breach of contract claiming the race was not what they had purchased tickets to see and that the race advertising had indicated that 20 cars would be racing. Decide the case. Explain. See *Bowers v. Federation Internationale de L'Automobile,* 489 F.3d 316 (7th Cir. 2007).

4. Pelullo promoted boxers and boxing matches through his company, Banner Productions. In 1999 Echols signed an agreement with Banner giving Echols a $30,000 bonus and giving Banner "the sole and exclusive right to secure all professional boxing bouts" for Echols. Banner was to provide no fewer than three bouts per year, and Echols was to be paid not less than a specified minimum amount for each fight, but the payments could be lowered or the whole agreement canceled, at Banner's option, if Echols lost a fight. Echols lost a championship bout, and Banner said it would thereafter negotiate each purse on a bout-by-bout basis. Echols continued to fight for Banner, but various disputes over purses arose, and Echols sued. Among other claims, Echols argued that the agreement was unenforceable for indefiniteness. Decide that claim. Explain. See *Echols v. Pelullo,* 377 F.3d 272 (3d Cir. 2004).

Discharge by Lawful Excuses (for Nonperformance)

Sometimes contracts are discharged lawfully even in the event of nonperformance. This can occur when performance is either impossible or impractical.

Impossibility   After agreement is reached but performance is not yet due, circumstances may be so altered that performance is a *legal impossibility*. In such situations nonperformance is excused. Impossibility here refers not simply to extreme difficulty but to objective impossibility; that is, the contracted-for performance cannot be accomplished by anyone. Notable examples of such situations are a personal service contract where the promisor has died or is incapacitated by illness, a contract where the subject of the agreement was rendered illegal by a change in the law subsequent to the agreement but prior to its performance, or a contract where an ingredient essential to performance has been destroyed and no reasonable substitutes are available. [For more on impossibility of performance, see **www.west.net/~smith/imposbl.htm**]

Commercial Impracticability   Akin to the doctrine of impossibility is the situation in which duties are discharged because of unforeseen events that render performance exorbitantly expensive or thoroughly impractical. Commercial impracticability is specifically provided for in UCC 2-615, which reads, "Delay in delivery or nondelivery in whole or in part by a seller . . . is not a breach of his duty under a contract for sale if performance as agreed has been made impracticable by the occurrence of a contingency the nonoccurrence of which was a basic assumption on which the contract was made. . . ."

The UCC's commercial impracticability standard is more easily established than the impossibility doctrine of the common law, but note that only exceptional and unforeseeable events fall within the impracticability excuse for nonperformance. Mere changes in market conditions do not give rise to commercial impracticability. Historically, the commercial impracticability doctrine had been applied only to transactions involving the sale of goods, but now we see courts increasingly willing to apply it to other kinds of contracts as well.

Discharge by Agreement

A contractual discharge is sometimes achieved by a new agreement arrived at after entering the original contract. These agreements take a variety of forms, but one—*accord and satisfaction*—will serve here to illustrate the general category. Parties reach an accord when they agree to a performance different from the one provided for in their contract. Performance of the accord is called satisfaction, at which point the original contract is discharged. A binding accord and satisfaction must spring from a genuine dispute between the parties, and it must include consideration as well as all of the other ingredients in a binding contract.

Discharge by Operation of Law

Under some circumstances, contractual duties are discharged by the legal system itself. Among those possibilities: (1) The contractual responsibilities of a debtor may be discharged by a bankruptcy decree. (2) Each state has a *statute of limitations* that specifies the time within which a performing party can initiate a lawsuit against a nonperforming party. For the UCC statute of limitations, see 2-725.

Remedies

We have looked at the elements of a binding contract and at those circumstances that discharge a party's duties under a contract. Now our concern is with what happens when one of the parties does not fulfill his or her contractual duties—that is, when the contract is breached. Remedies are provided in both law and in equity (see Glossary and Chapter 4).

Remedies in Law

In general, a *breach of contract* allows the nonbreaching party to sue for money damages. The general goal of remedies law is to put the parties in the position they would have occupied had the contract been fulfilled. Normally, the best available substitute for actual performance is monetary damages.

Compensatory Damages   In brief, the plaintiff in a breach of contract action is entitled to recover a sum equal to the actual damages suffered. The plaintiff is compensated for her losses by receiving a sum designed to "make her whole," to put her where she would have been had the contract not been breached.

   Sale of Goods A breach involving a sale of goods is governed by the UCC. Typically the measure of *compensatory damages* would be the difference between the contract price and the market price of the goods at the time and place the goods were to be delivered (see UCC 2-708 and 2-713). Suppose you are working for a newly established computer manufacturer, and you have contracted with the Internal Revenue Service to deliver 1,000 laptop computers at $1,500 each, although the current market price is $1,600. If you fail to make that delivery, damages could be assessed in the amount of $100,000 ($100 $\times$ 1,000), which is the additional amount the IRS would need to pay to make the substitute purchase.

Consequential Damages   The victim of a breach may be able to recover not just the direct losses from the breach but also any indirect losses that were incurred as a consequence of that breach. Such consequential damages are recoverable only if they were foreseen or were reasonably foreseeable by the breaching party. For example, if you

> The grand opening of your new bar and the band fails to appear.

contract for a well-known local band to play for the grand opening of your new bar and dance club and the band fails to appear, you may be able to recover damages for any lost profits that you can attribute to the band's absence. Those lost profits are a reasonably foreseeable *consequence* of the breach. Of course, you will have some difficulty in specifying the profits lost and in proving that the loss was attributable to the band's failure to perform.

Not a Fan?

Construction worker Brent Loveland showed up at the home of Oklahoma State University football coach Mike Gundy to begin work on a trim installation—wearing a University of Oklahoma Sooners baseball T-shirt. He was fired from the job that day. Loveland sued Gundy and his wife, Kristen, alleging, among other things, breach of contract. Loveland's lawsuit sought the $80,600 that he was allegedly to be paid for the 13-week job, and the potential income of over $30,000 he lost because he turned down other jobs owing to his commitment to work on the Gundy home.

Questions

1. What are the issues in this case?
2. Decide.

Sources: Zac Ellis, "Report: Lawsuit Against Oklahoma State Coach Will Move Forward," *Sports Illustrated Campus Union,* June 5, 2013 [**college-football.si.com**]; and Gina Mizell, "Oklahoma State Football: Lawsuit Against Mike Gundy Dismissed," August 7, 2013 [**newsok.com**].

Incidental Damages   The costs incurred by the nonbreaching party in arranging a substitute performance or otherwise reducing the damages sustained because of the breach are recoverable as incidental damages. They would include such items as phone calls and transportation expenses.

Nominal Damages   In some cases of breach, the court will award only an insignificant sum, perhaps $1.00 (plus court costs), because the nonbreaching party has suffered no actual damages. The point of nominal damages is to illustrate the wrongfulness of the breach.

Punitive Damages   Sometimes when the breaching party's conduct is particularly reprehensible, the court will penalize that wrongful behavior by awarding punitive damages to the injured party. The idea is to deter such conduct in the future. Normally punitive damages cannot be awarded in breach of contract cases except when provided for by statute or when the breach is accompanied by a tort such as fraud (as where one buys a defective car having reasonably relied on the falsehoods of a salesperson).

Rescission and Restitution   In some instances, including a material breach, mistake, fraud, undue influence, and duress, the wronged party may rescind (undo) the contract. The effect of a contract rescission is to return the parties to the positions they occupied before they entered the agreement. Generally, both parties must then make restitution to each other by returning whatever goods, property, and so forth were transferred under the contract or an equivalent amount of money.

Mitigation   Obviously the law should penalize a breaching party, as we have discussed, but you may be surprised to learn that the law also imposes expectations on the victim (the non breaching party). Specifically, the nonbreaching party is required to take reasonable steps toward mitigation—that is, to minimize her or his damages. What happens, for example, if you are wrongfully dismissed in breach of contract from your first job after college? You are expected to mitigate your damages by seeking another job. You need not take an inferior job, nor must you disturb your life by moving to another state or community, but you must take reasonable measures to minimize your claim against your former employer.

Liquidated Damages   We have reviewed both the legal penalties for breach and the duty to mitigate damages. The law also offers the opportunity to provide some control over the penalty for breach by including in the contract a liquidated damages clause. Here you and the other party to the contract agree in advance about the measure of damages should either of you default on your duties. That clause is fully enforceable so long as it is not designed to be a penalty but rather a good faith effort to assess in advance an accurate measure of damages. A valid liquidated damages clause limits the nonbreaching party to recovery of the amount provided for in that clause.

Remedies in Equity

Where justice cannot be achieved via money damages alone, the courts will sometimes impose equitable remedies. The chief forms of equitable remedy in contract cases are specific performance, injunction, reformation, and quasi-contract.

Specific Performance   In unusual circumstances the court may order the breaching party to remedy its wrong by performing its obligations precisely as provided for in the contract. Normally that specific performance is required only where the subject matter of the contract is unique and thus cannot be adequately compensated with money. Examples of such subject matter might include a particular piece of land, an art work, or a family heirloom. By contrast, specific performance would not be available in contracts involving conventional personal property such as a television or a car unless those items were unique (such as a one-of-a-kind Rolls Royce).

   Normally the courts will not grant a specific performance remedy in personal service contracts (such as an agreement by a cosmetic surgeon to perform a face-lift). If the surgeon refused to perform, specific performance probably would not be ordered. The quality of the surgery likely would not be equal to what had been bargained for; courts do not want to be in the position of supervising the completion of contracts, and as a matter of public policy, we do not want to put parties, in this case, the surgeon, in a position that amounts to involuntary servitude.

Injunction   An injunction is a court order that may either require or forbid a party to perform a specified act. Injunctions are granted only under exceptional circumstances. Perhaps the most common of those are the noncompetition agreements. For example, you take a computer programming job that will afford you access to company secrets. To protect itself, the company expects you to sign an agreement specifying that you will not take employment with a competing firm for one year after departure from your employer. If you should quit and seek to work for a competitor within one year, your former employer might be able to secure an injunction preventing you from doing so until the year has passed.

Reformation   Reformation is an equitable remedy that permits the court to rewrite the contract where it imperfectly expressed the parties' true intentions. Typically such situations involve a mutual mistake or fraud. Thus, if the parties sign a contract to sell a lot in a housing development, but the contract is written with an incorrect street address for the lot, an equity court could simply correct the error in the contract.

Quasi-Contract   What happens if one party has conferred a benefit on another, but a contract has not been created because of a failure of consideration, the application of the statute of frauds, or something of the sort? To prevent unjust enrichment, the court might then imply a contract as a matter of law. For example, assume a lawn service mistakenly trims your shrubs and you watch them do so, knowing that they are supposed to be caring for your neighbor's lawn. You have not entered a contract with the lawn service, but a court might well require you to pay the reasonable value of trimming your shrubs. To do otherwise would unjustly enrich you.

PRACTICING ETHICS   Bloggers Work for Free?

Liberal journalism blog aggregator and opinion site *The Huffington Post* was sued in a class action in 2011 on the grounds that the blog had failed to pay the more than 9,000 bloggers who had provided content for the blog over a period of years. In submitting copy to *The Huffington Post,* bloggers knew they would not be paid, but presumably they valued the professional/political/personal exposure afforded by publication. The lawsuit, however, claimed the agreement to provide content without compensation had resulted in unjust enrichment for Huffington. AOL purchased *The Huffington Post* earlier in 2011 for $315 million; the bloggers sought approximately a third of the purchase price, asserting their contributions had made *The Huffington Post* that valuable an acquisition. In 2012, a federal judge dismissed the lawsuit, concluding that the bloggers had not expected money in return for their contributions to *The Huffington Post.*

Question

The law aside, does *The Huffington Post* have a moral duty to compensate the bloggers who knowingly gave away their content when that content subsequently proved to be instrumental in building Huffington into a valuable property? Explain. Do you feel a duty to pay others when you are the beneficiary of "unjust enrichment?" Explain.

Sources: Chad Bray, "*Huffington Post* Wins Dispute with Unpaid Bloggers," *Wall Street Journal Law Blog,* March 30, 2012 [http://blogs.wsj.com/law/2012/03/30/huffington-post-wins-dispute-with-unpaid-bloggers/]; and Stephanie Francis Ward, "*Huffington Post* Bloggers Sue, Seeking Payment for Writing," *ABA Journal,* April 12, 2011 [www.abajournal.com/news/article/huffpo_bloggers_sue_seeking_payment_for_writing/].

Internet Exercise

Go to the *ContractsProf Blog* [**http://lawprofessors.typepad.com/contractsprof_blog/**] for August 17, 2010. Read about and explain the breach of contract lawsuit filed against Paris Hilton. Do a broader Internet search to update the status of the Hilton lawsuit.

Chapter Questions

1. Wardle made a standard real estate offer to buy a house owned by Kessler. The offer contained a "time is of the essence" clause specifying that the deal had to be completed on or before 11 AM on September 26, 1997. Owen then submitted a backup purchase offer for the same price as offered by Wardle. Wardle's completed contract was not delivered to Kessler until approximately 11:20 AM on September 26, so Kessler sold to Owen. Wardle then sued Kessler. Decide. Explain. See *Owen v. Kessler,* 778 N.E.2d 953 (App. Ct. Mass. 2002).

2. In a 2013 televised interview with Oprah Winfrey, Lance Armstrong admitted to taking performance-enhancing drugs during his cycling career. Afterward, Armstrong faced several lawsuits, including one from SCA Promotions, seeking to recover approximately $12 million in bonuses it had paid Armstrong for several Tour de France victories. SCA, already suspecting Armstrong of taking performance-enhancing drugs in the 2004 Tour de France, had tried to withhold payment of his bonus for winning that race. Armstrong had sued, and the parties entered into a settlement agreement under which Armstrong received the bonus money. Under the terms of that agreement, an award that "no party may challenge, appeal or attempt to set aside." How should this case be decided? Explain.

3. Allen M. Campbell Co. sought a contract to build houses for the U.S. Navy. Approximately one half hour before the housing bids were due, Virginia Metal Industries quoted Campbell Co. a price of $193,121 to supply the necessary doors and frames. Campbell, using the Virginia Metal quote, entered a bid and won the contract. Virginia Metal refused to supply the necessary doors, and Campbell had to secure an alternative source of supply at a price $45,562 higher than Virginia Metal's quote. Campbell sued. Explain Campbell's claim. Defend Virginia Metal. Decide. See *Allen M. Campbell Co. Inc. v. Virginia Metal Industries,* 708 F.2d 930 (4th Cir. 1983).

4. Jesse Dimmick, trying to escape police questioning in a murder investigation, burst into Jared and Lindsay Rowley's Kansas home with a knife. After gaining his trust by feeding him and watching a movie with him, the Rowleys were able to escape when Dimmick fell asleep. Police entered the house and arrested Dimmick, who was accidentally shot in the process. The Rowleys sued Dimmick for damages; Dimmick countersued for breach of contract, seeking $160,000 to cover hospital bills and $75,000 for pain and suffering. Dimmick said the Rowleys had broken their promise to keep him hidden from authorities in return for cash. What defenses could the Rowleys raise to this claim? Explain. See http://cjonline.com/news/2011-11-28/dimmick-sues-couple-he-kidnapped.

5. Blette contracted with ANC in May 2008 for a one-year apartment lease at $605 per month. In February 2009, Blette complained to ANC about substandard maintenance and other problems. Blette tendered a $752.54 check and wrote an accompanying letter saying that the payment was to settle her forthcoming March, April, and May rent minus her alleged damages. She also wrote that if the check were cashed her terms were being accepted. ANC wrote back saying it would cash the check but that her demands were unacceptable. Was Blette in breach of contract when she failed to make full payment? Explain. See *THG/Apartments Near Campus v. Deeanna Blette,* 2010 Ia. App. LEXIS 571.

6. Sherwood agreed to purchase a cow, Rose 2d of Aberlone, from Walker at a price of 5 1/2 cents per pound (about $80). The parties believed the cow to be barren. Sherwood came to Walker's farm to collect the cow, but at that point it was obvious that Rose was pregnant. Walker refused to give over the cow, which was then worth $750 to $1,000. Sherwood sued. Should he get the cow? Explain. See *Sherwood v. Walker,* 33 N.W. 919 (Mich. S.Ct. 1887).

7. Weaver leased a service station from American Oil. The lease included a clause providing that Weaver would hold American Oil harmless for any negligence by American on the premises. Weaver and an employee were burned when an American Oil

employee accidentally sprayed gasoline while at Weaver's station. Weaver had one and one half years of high school education. The trial record provides no evidence that Weaver read the lease, that American's agent asked him to read it, or that Weaver's attention was drawn to the "hold harmless" clause. The clause was in fine print and contained no title heading. Is the contract enforceable against Weaver? Explain. See *Weaver v. American Oil Co.,* 276 N.E.2d 144 (Ind. S.Ct. 1971).

8. Republic Bank acquired medical equipment through a lease default and contracted Tetra Financial Services to facilitate sale of the equipment. Mark, a Tetra employee, was assigned to the task. West Penn, a large hospital system in the Pittsburgh, Pennsylvania, area, expressed an interest in purchasing the equipment and had one of its contract negotiators, Michele, handle it.

   Michele sent Mark an e-mail on February 26, stating:

   > We are interested in the 64-slice scanner, CT workstation, ultrasound, and ultrasound table.

   Our offer is as follows:

   Scanner: $600,000

   CT workstation: $50,000

   Ultrasound and ultrasound table: $26,500

   On March 13, Mark sent Michele an e-mail stating:

   > Michele: I met with the bank president this morning and he gave me approval to sell West Penn the 64-slice scanner, CT workstation, and ultrasound unit with table for the total amount offered below [referring to Michele's February 26 e-mail]. There is still some question regarding the cooler unit being moved to your location or left in place and a replacement provided for you. We can discuss that issue.

   > Please let me know if you work through a purchase order system or if we need to put together a sales agreement.

   Is there a contract between Republic Bank and West Penn for the purchase of the medical equipment? Decide. Explain. See *Republic Bank v. Allegheny Health,* 475 Fed. Appx. 692 (10th Cir. 2010).

9. A building was rented "for use as a saloon" under an eight-year lease. Five years thereafter the state passed a law making the sale of liquor illegal. The renter, a brewery, argued that it no longer had any duties under the contract. Was the brewery correct? Explain. See *Heart v. East Tennessee Brewing Co.,* 113 S.W. 364 (Tenn. S.Ct. 1908).

10. The Landes entered into a contract with Flynn, owner of Flynn Builders, to construct a new home for which Flynn had submitted a bid of $259,576. Construction began in May 2009. In early July, the Landes discovered that Flynn had not disclosed a $20,000 markup in a line item for "materials package." Although the markup did not increase the agreed-upon price, Landes refused to continue payments to Flynn, and construction halted. Flynn filed a mechanic's lien for approximately $28,000. Flynn testified that his job as general contractor were nearly completed at the time he left, with arrangements having been made with various subcontractors to complete the remaining

work such as plumbing and drywall. Flynn's employee testified that Flynn had completed approximately 80 to 85 percent of the work before leaving the project. Should Flynn be able to enforce the mechanic's lien? Decide. Explain. See *Flynn Builders v. Landes,* 814 N.W.2d 542 (La. 2012).

11. Preference Personnel, a North Dakota corporation, entered a contract with Peterson to help him find employment in the tax law field. The contract provided that the employer would pay the placement fee, unless Peterson voluntarily quit within 9 days, in which case he would be responsible for the fee, which was 20 percent of one year's salary. Peterson was placed in a job with an annual salary of $60,000, but he quit after one month. Peterson refused to pay the fee, and Preference sued for breach of contract. The lower court found that Peterson breached the contract, but at the time of the contract, Preference Personnel's state-required license to operate had been allowed to lapse. The court, therefore, dismissed the Preference claim ruling that the agreement was unenforceable as a matter of public policy. Preference appealed. Rule on that appeal. Explain. See *Preference Personnel, Inc. v. Peterson,* 710 N.W.2d 383 (N.D.S.Ct. 2006).

12. Panera, the bakery/café chain, had a clause in its lease that prevented the White City Shopping Center in Shrewsbury, Massachusetts, from renting space to another sandwich shop: "Landlord agrees not to enter into a lease, . . . for a bakery or restaurant reasonably expected to have annual sales of *sandwiches* (emphasis added) greater than ten percent (10%) of its total sales . . . " Panera asked a Massachusetts Superior Court to block the Shopping Center from leasing space to a Qdoba Mexican Grill on the grounds that a lease with the Grill would violate the terms of the Panera lease. How should the Court rule? Explain. See *White City Shopping Center, LP v. PR Restaurants, LLC,* 2006 Mass. Super. LEXIS 544.

CHAPTER SEVEN

Business Torts and Product Liability

After completing this chapter, students will be able to:

1. Compare and contrast the three fundamental kinds of torts: intentional, negligent, and strict liability.

2. Describe selected intentional torts against persons including battery, assault, fraud, invasion of privacy, intentional infliction of emotional distress, and defamation.

3. Describe selected intentional torts against property such as trespass and nuisance.

4. Identify selected intentional tort defenses.

5. Discuss the impact of product liability on business practice.

6. Identify the requirements of a successful negligence claim.

7. Differentiate between types of negligence claims emerging from defective products.

8. Analyze whether negligence defenses may be successfully asserted in a negligence claim.

9. Compare and contrast claims based on express warranties and implied warranties.

10. Identify the elements of the strict liability cause of action.

11. Identify the defenses available in strict liability cases.

12. Evaluate arguments for and against tort reform.

PRACTICING ETHICS   Trampled to Death

Despite his 6'5", 270-pound frame, Jdimytai Damour, 34, was no match for the unruly crowd of an estimated 2,000 Black Friday, 2008 shoppers at a Long Island, New York, Walmart. The crowd, some of whom had been waiting for many hours, pushed against the double glass doors. Damour, a worker of one week hired through a temporary agency, and 6 to 10 other Walmart employees pushed back from the inside, but at 4:55 AM the doors bowed in and the shoppers surged through crushing Damour to his death and injuring others. Damour had no experience with crowd control and reportedly had not been trained for that purpose. Crowd control barriers were not employed and security personnel reportedly were inside the store rather than being outside to monitor and manage the crowd. Police had been on the scene for 30 minutes at 3 AM, but the crowd of 400 at the time was orderly and the police left. Walmart argued that it had taken appropriate and sufficient safety measures, but authorities subsequently questioned those measures and compared them unfavorably with other retailers' approaches.

Without admitting guilt, Walmart avoided criminal charges by agreeing to pay $400,000 into a victims' compensation fund, along with $1.5 million to local social services causes. Walmart also agreed to build improved holiday crowd management plans for all of its New York stores. (Changes also were to be implemented nationwide on a store-by-store basis.) The federal Occupational Safety and Health Administration (OSHA; see Chapter 12) imposed a $7,000 fine for failing to maintain a safe workplace; Walmart lost its appeal of the OSHA fine. Damour's family sued Nassau County officials and Walmart. To avoid criminal prosecution in Nassau County, Walmart agreed to improve its Black Friday crowd control, donate approximately $1.2 million to local community programs, and create a $400,000 victims' compensation fund.

Sources: Steve Greenhouse, "Judge Upholds $7,000 Fine in Trampling at Walmart," *The New York Times,* March 25, 2011 [**www.nytimes.com**]; "Walmart Settles Trampling Case," *The New York Times,* May 6, 2009 [**www.nytimes.com**]; Associated Press, "Wal-Mart Worker Trampled to Death Lacked Training, Attorney Says," Fox News.com, December 1, 2008; Robert D. McFadden and Angela Macropoulos, "Wal-Mart Employee Trampled to Death," *The New York Times,* November 29, 2008; and Associated Press, "Wal-Mart Fights $7,000 Fine in Black Friday Death," *USA TODAY,* July 8, 2010.

Questions

1. *a.* Who bears the blame for Damour's death? Explain.
   b. How do we decide where blame lies?

2. *a.* Were the shoppers guilty of criminal behavior? Explain.
   b. Immoral behavior? Explain.

3. Did Walmart fail to fulfill its responsibilities to its employees and customers? Explain.

4. Do you think the OSHA fine and Walmart's donations to community programs, victims' compensation fund, and improved crowd control plans achieved justice? Explain.

Part One—Torts: An Introduction

We have looked at the Walmart Black Friday story as an ethics dilemma. Now we turn to the law that resolves personal injury claims like those asserted against Walmart. From the Damour family's point of view, Walmart's Black Friday promotion and the subsequent crowd stampede involved both torts and crimes. *Torts* are civil wrongs not arising from contracts. Torts involve breaches of duty to particular persons causing loss or injury, while *crimes* are regarded as public wrongs breaching duties to society as a whole (although, of course, they are most commonly directed at a specific person or persons). Crimes are prosecuted by the state; tort actions are initiated by individuals. Criminal law punishes wrongdoers, but the point of tort law is to make whole an injured party. At the same time, many acts can be treated either as a civil wrong (a tort) or as a crime, or both. For example, a physical attack on another can, of course, lead to criminal charges, but it can also produce civil tort claims, most commonly *assault* and *battery.*

The injured party in a tort litigation can seek *compensatory damages* to make up for the harm suffered. Those damages may consist of medical expenses, lost income, and pain and suffering, among other possibilities. In some cases, *punitive damages* may be awarded to punish the wrongdoer and to discourage others from similar behavior.

Tort Categories

Fundamentally, torts are of three kinds: (1) intentional, (2) negligent, and (3) strict liability. *Intentional torts* involve voluntary acts that harm a protected interest. Intent is established by showing the defendant meant to do the act that caused the harm. The plaintiff need not show that the harm itself was intended. The defendant would be liable for all reasonably foreseeable injuries from that intentional act.

To explain, if you run an advertisement defaming a fast-food competitor by saying its food processing does not meet government standards, but you cannot prove the truth of your allegations, you will probably be guilty of the intentional tort of *injurious falsehood* (product disparagement).

Negligence involves situations in which harm is caused accidentally. Intent is absent, but because of one party's carelessness, another has suffered injury. Thus, if one of your employees is making a delivery for the printing business you are managing, and carelessly runs a red light, striking another car, the employee appears to be guilty of negligent conduct for which both she and your firm may be subject to civil damages. Furthermore, you and/or your firm might bear responsibility if, for example, you hired her knowing that she had been a careless driver in the past.

A detailed discussion of negligence law follows in Part Two of this chapter, but for the moment we should notice that negligence concerns are ubiquitous in our lives, ranging from traffic accidents, to inadequate snow clearance from our sidewalks, to failure to keep dangerous kitchen utensils away from children, to ill-timed golf shots, and on and on. Negligence ordinarily is the core claim for those suffering a personal injury caused by the carelessness of another. Broadly, negligence litigation involves an analysis of when that alleged carelessness amounts to a breach of the "duty of due care." For example, can an injured party properly bring a negligence claim against homeowners when parts of their dismantled but not yet stowed away trampoline blow into the nearby road causing a passing driver to crash? The Iowa Supreme Court said "yes" because the homeowners had a duty to exercise reasonable care to see that obstructions did not reach the roadway and they breached that duty by creating a foreseeable risk in dismantling the trampoline but failing to secure the parts over the passage of several weeks time. [For the Court's complete negligence analysis, see *Thompson v. Kaczinski,* 774 N.W.2d 829 (Ia. S.Ct. 2009).]

Strict liability is, in essence, a no-fault concept where an individual or organization is responsible for harm without proof of carelessness. Strict liability expands the reach of the law beyond instances where carelessness (negligence) must be established to situations where actual proof of breach of the duty of due care; that is, proof of negligence, is not required because the risks inherent in that situation are so great. Strict liability is limited to "unreasonably dangerous" products and practices about which we have decided, as a matter of social policy, that responsibility for injury will automatically attach without establishing blame. Thus, if a product is (1) defective and (2) unreasonably dangerous and someone is hurt, strict (absolute) liability may attach even though fault is not established. Strict liability is explained in the *Gallagher* case below and in greater detail in Part Two of this chapter.

Tort Law

Selected Intentional Torts against Persons

Suppose you are warehouse manager for a plumbing supply business, and a subordinate does a poor job with some work, which in turn brings your boss down on you. In your frustration, you call the subordinate into your office where you chastise him and then light up a cigar and casually but pointedly blow smoke in his face. Could he file a tort claim against you for your insulting behavior? Let's look at the law in this area. (Of course, many states forbid workplace smoking.)

Battery

Intentionally touching another in a harmful or offensive way without legal justification or the consent of that person is a *battery*. Merely touching another's clothing or touching an occupied car may constitute a battery. Our concern here is with civil wrongs, but perhaps the most interesting recent battery allegation involves a criminal claim. Believing his student, Krista Bowman, was Web surfing in class, Professor Frank J. Rybicki of Valdosta State University (Georgia) reportedly asked her to be attentive. Rybicki apparently believed Bowman continued to surf. Bowman claims that Rybicki then closed the laptop on her fingers, injuring one or more of them. Bowman filed a criminal battery charge against Rybicki, who was arrested, but later found not guilty by a jury. [For more details, see Scott Jaschik, "Not Guilty, and Not Long Employed," *Inside Higher Education,* August 25, 2011, at **www.insidehighered.com/news/2011/08/25/ jury_rejects_charges_against_professor_in_case_of_student_laptop**]

> Krista Bowman was Web surfing in class. Bowman claims Professor Rybicki closed the laptop on her fingers.

Assault

Intentionally causing another to reasonably believe that he or she is about to be the victim of a battery is an *assault.* The battery need not occur and the victim need not be frightened, but an assault nonetheless transpires if the victim reasonably anticipated a substantially imminent battery. Thus, raising one's hand as if to strike another even though the blow never transpires constitutes the tort of assault if the victim reasonably thought herself to be in immediate danger.

False Imprisonment

If you have anticipated a career in retailing, you may have given thought to the problem of shoplifters and strategies for preserving your inventory without yourself violating customers' rights. The statutory and common (judge-made) law of most states now protects store managers and owners from *false imprisonment* claims if they justifiably detain a suspected shoplifter for a reasonable period and in a reasonable manner. Broadly, false imprisonment occurs when someone is intentionally confined against his or her will; that is, his or her freedom of movement is restricted. That restriction might include being shut in a room, being bound, being threatened, and so on. Even a moment could conceivably constitute imprisonment, although simply sending a customer, for example, through a more distant store exit ordinarily would not meet the test.

Nine Hours on Grounded Plane: False Imprisonment?

Catherine Ray and her husband were flying from Oakland, California, to Dallas, Texas, in 2006 when their American Airlines plane was rerouted to Austin, Texas, because of bad weather in Dallas. Their flight landed in Austin around noon, refueled, and began to depart, but the weather problems had then closed the Dallas airport. After an hour on the ground, a bus took some passengers to the terminal, but Ray and her husband chose not to deplane because, according to Ray's testimony, the pilot said the flight would likely resume in about an hour and anyone who left the plane "would be on their own," a remark Ray interpreted to mean that departing passengers would need to fund their further transportation, something the Rays could not afford. Two to three hours later another bus arrived and, according to Ray, passengers were told that bus offered their last chance for departure. The Rays decided to remain on the plane. Catherine Ray testified that deteriorating conditions on the plane included little food and drink, agitated passengers, and at least some nonfunctioning lavatories. About 6 PM, the pilot said he could no longer fly because he had reached his maximum duty hours. Lightning in Austin delayed ground crew work, but at about 9 PM, the plane was taken to a gate where Ray and all other passengers deplaned. Some time after deplaning, food and lodging vouchers were provided. Ray and her husband decided to spend the night in the terminal. They flew from Austin the following morning. Ray subsequently filed a civil action for false imprisonment, among other claims. How would you rule on that claim? Explain.

Source: Catherine Ray v. American Airlines, 2010 U.S. App. LEXIS 13582.

Fraud

Intentional misrepresentations of facts, sometimes identified by the formal title of *deceit,* can lead to tort claims. We discuss *fraud* in the contracts (Chapter 6) and consumer protection (Chapter 15) chapters. For now, simply note the general test for fraud:

1. A material fact was misrepresented.
2. The misrepresentation was intentional.
3. The injured party justifiably relied on the misrepresentation.
4. Injury resulted.

Father of the Child?

Peters told Dier that he was the father of her baby. Dier paid child support. Through paternity tests, however, he learned he was not the father. Can Dier sue Peters for fraud? What additional facts might you need to know before making a decision? Explain.

Source: See *Dier v. Peters,* 815 N.W.2d 1 (Ia. 2012).

Defamation

Uttering an untruth about another may constitute a tort. *Slander* is the spoken form of the tort of *defamation*. *Libel* is defamation in print or some other tangible form such as a picture, movie, or video. Most courts also treat defamatory radio and television statements as forms of libel. The basic test for establishing defamation includes:

1. A false statement.
2. Harm to the victim's reputation.
3. Publication of the statement. (The statement must reach someone other than the one being defamed.)

The law's interest here is in protecting reputations. Any living person or any organization can be the victim of defamation, although *public figures* such as politicians or actors face the additional burden of proving *malice* if they are to be successful in a defamation claim. Malice generally requires a showing of actual knowledge of the falsehood or reckless disregard for the truth. Libel or slander about a company's products or property often is treated as the tort of injurious falsehood, which is discussed below.

A one-star review on Yelp led to a lawsuit against the reviewer. In 2011, after contractor Christopher Dietz completed plumbing, painting, and other work on her Fairfax, Virginia, home, Jane Perez posted a scathing review of Dietz's contracting firm on the

> A one-star review on Yelp has led to a lawsuit against the reviewer.

online review site Yelp. Perez claimed that her house had been damaged, that she was billed for work not done, and that jewelry had disappeared from her home. Dietz rebutted online that Perez had stolen his goods and services by not paying him and did not allow him to pick up valuable items from her house. Claiming Perez's negative reviews on Yelp as well as on Angie's List (another online review site) caused him to lose business and suffer personally, Dietz filed a defamation lawsuit against Perez seeking $750,000 in damages. At trial, the jury decided that both Dietz and Perez had defamed each other, but neither was awarded damages.[1]

In general, a claim of slander requires a showing of actual harm, such as job loss. Some statements, however, are so inherently damaging that actual injury need not be shown. Those statements are labeled *slander per se* and include allegations of serious sexual misconduct, commission of a serious crime, professional incompetence, or having a loathsome disease. Similarly, libel, leaving a more permanent stain, generally does not require a showing of actual harm.

Truth acts as a complete defense to a defamation claim. Hence, if we tell the truth about others, we cannot be guilty of the tort of defamation, regardless of our evil intentions. Furthermore, many statements are protected because of the circumstances in which they are made. We label these protections either absolute or qualified privileges. An *absolute privilege* to defame includes, for example, remarks by government officials in the course of their duties or by participants in a trial. A *qualified privilege* to defame protects, most notably, former employers providing references for a job applicant. In that instance, the reference will not be treated as defamatory, even though false, unless it was motivated by malice. [For an overview of online defamation law for bloggers, see **www.eff.org/issues /bloggers/legal/liability/defamation**]

An Angry Dad

On September 24, 2008, Ed Doherty, a franchisee/owner of about 80 Applebee's restaurants in New Jersey, New York, and Pennsylvania said in a newspaper interview that he treats employees "with dignity and respect" and offers "a great opportunity for them to have a good job." Previously, Michael Murray had represented his daughter, Erin Duby, a former Applebee's employee, in an arbitration claim alleging that she was sexually harassed by managers and other employees. In December 2007, Murray rejected a settlement offer arising out of the arbitration process.

Murray then posted an online response to Doherty's interview by saying that "women . . . are routinely sexually harassed and that this behavior is condoned by high-level management at Doherty Enterprises right up to the top." He warned that "any reader who has a daughter, wife, etc. working for Doherty are [*sic*] more than likely being subjected to similar treatment." Doherty then sued Murray on defamation grounds.

Was Doherty a victim of defamation? Explain.

Source: Mary Pat Gallagher, "Applebee's Restaurateur . . . Over Internet Post Charging Harassment," *Corporate Counsel,* May 20, 2009.

Invasion of Privacy

A key ingredient in personal freedom is the right to be left alone. Our courts recognize a right of recovery in tort law when we are the victims of some kind of unconscionable exposure of our private lives. *Invasion of privacy* takes four forms:

1. **Misappropriation of a person's name or likeness.** When an individual's name or image is wrongfully used without permission for commercial purposes (called a *misappropriation*) that person probably has a cause of action for invasion of privacy. Typically, this tort involves a company's use of a celebrity's name or picture to imply that he or she has endorsed a product even though no such approval was secured. A celebrity's name or likeness may also be wrongfully used in the product itself, such as in a video game. In 2013, a federal appeals court ruled that Ryan Hart, former Rutgers University quarterback, could sue Electronic Arts (EA), maker of a college football video game, for allegedly misappropriating his likeness through animation.[2] EA soon settled with Hart and other college athletes with similar claims. Although the settlement's terms are confidential, EA announced it would not release that video game in 2014.[3]

   > College athletes claiming EA's college football video game featured their animated likenesses.

2. **Intrusion.** An intentional invasion of a person's solitude is labeled an intrusion if it would be highly offensive to a reasonable person. Physical intrusions such as opening an employee's mail or more subtle strategies such as an electronic probe of an employee's bank account are examples of tortious intrusion.

3. **Public disclosure of private facts.** We believe that certain elements of one's life, such as debt payment practices or sexual preferences, are, with rare exceptions, no one else's business. If the disclosure would be highly offensive to a reasonable person, and the

subject of the disclosure is not a matter of public importance, the tort of public disclosure of private facts might be invoked. In these cases, the truth may not constitute a complete defense.

4. **False light.** When claims are published about another that have the effect of casting the victim in a false light in the public mind, a tort claim may emerge. False light claims involve injury to one's mental or emotional well-being rather than one's reputation. Again, the claim would need to be highly offensive to the reasonable person. The courts have struggled to differentiate defamation and false light claims, and we will not pursue the distinction further here.

Intentional Infliction of Emotional Distress

Employment terminations (firings), drug tests, and sexual harassment cases have become particularly fertile grounds for emotional distress claims, although it should be understood that the courts have demanded compelling evidence of *outrageous conduct causing severe emotional pain.* Thus, Mahmoud Abdul-Malik, a ramp agent for AirTran at the Atlanta, Georgia, airport was unsuccessful in his intentional infliction of emotional distress claim against his employer after he was fired for allegedly threatening to blow up the house of another employee. Abdul-Malik claimed that his distress from being fired caused him to lose sleep and gain weight, but the Georgia Court of Appeals ruled, among other things, that those problems did not rise to the level of severity needed for a successful claim. [For the full case, see *Abdul-Malik v. Airtran Airways,* 678 S.E.2d 555 (2009); cert den. *Mahmoud Abdul-Malik v. Airtran Airways,* Inc., 2009 Ga. LEXIS 711 (Ga. S.Ct.).]

Selected Intentional Torts Against Property

We will briefly examine four prominent tort claims arising from wrongs to property.

Trespass to real property (land and immovable objects attached to it) occurs with the intentional entry on to the land of another without consent. *Trespass to personal property* (movable property; all property other than real property) involves an intentional interference with a person's right to enjoy his or her personal property—for example, the manager of a parking lot refuses for a day to return a car to its owner in the mistaken belief that the owner has not paid his monthly bill.

More serious and extensive interference with personal property may be labeled a *conversion.* For example, if the parking lot company kept the car for months, and it suffered damage during the impoundment, a conversion probably occurred.

Injurious falsehood, sometimes called *trade libel,* is a form of defamation that is directed against the property of a person. Thus, falsely claiming that a competitor's product is defective or harmful might constitute injurious falsehood. As with defamation, the statement must be false and it must be published. Damages must result. Often malice/intent must also be shown.

Nuisance is the situation in which enjoyment of one's land is impaired because of some tortious interference. That interference often takes the form of light, noise, smell, or vibration. Here, the owner is not deprived of the land and the land has not been physically invaded, but the full enjoyment of the land cannot be achieved because of the interference. The case that follows involves the owner of an historic Baltimore, Maryland, home who raises both strict liability and nuisance claims in a dispute over alleged damage to her home from nearby pile driving. [For the Jurist Torts Guide, see **http://jurist.law.pitt.edu/sg_torts.htm**]

Michela Gallagher v. H.V. Pierhomes, LLC et al.

957 A.2d 628 (Md. Ct. of Spec. App., 2008)

Judge Rubin

THE PROCEEDINGS BELOW

On June 14, 2005, Gallagher sued HV Pierhomes LLC and HV Development & Contracting Co. The initial complaint contained claims for negligence, strict liability, and public and private nuisance. On December 21, 2005, Gallagher filed an amended complaint, which abandoned the negligence claim. All of Gallagher's claims for relief arose out of the pile driving operations conducted by the defendants on the site of the former Key Highway Shipyard. Gallagher contended that vibrations from the pile driving damaged her home, located at 423 East Hamburg Street in Baltimore. Key Highway; a row of mixed use properties; Covington Street; a retaining wall; and a solid earthen wall, on which Gallagher's house rests, separate Gallagher's house from the pile driving site.

The Key Highway Shipyard, formerly owned by the Bethlehem Steel Corporation, was used to repair naval (sic) ships during World War II and through the Vietnam War. A shipyard of some sort has operated at this location from the beginning of the 20th century until 1982, when Bethlehem Steel closed the facility.

The defendants demolished the original shipyard piers, which were built 40 to 50 years ago and constructed new piers in the same location, by driving piles into the Baltimore Inner Harbor. The defendants built 58 townhomes on these new piers. Pile driving was the only method of constructing the new townhomes in this particular location because the U.S. Army Corps of Engineers would not allow the Inner Harbor to be "back filled." The pile driving of which Gallagher complained occurred periodically between September 2003 and October 2004.

The plaintiff's home was constructed shortly before the War of 1812. She testified that no pile driving was conducted in the area during the years she lived in the house, beginning in 1997, until the defendants' activities commenced in September 2003. Previously, pile driving was used to build the Seagirt Marine Terminal, the Dundalk Marine Terminal, as well as the Pratt and Light Street Pavilions, which are located across from the plaintiff's residence in the Inner Harbor.

Before the defendants began their project, permits were received from the U.S. Army Corps of Engineers, the Maryland Department of the Environment, and the City of Baltimore. The permitting process took approximately two years. Pile driving on the site began only after geotechnical studies were conducted by engineering firms. During the course of actual pile driving, two permanent seismic stations and five mobile geophones were placed in the surrounding neighborhood to ensure that vibrations were monitored and did not exceed the limits established by the engineers. During the course of the defendants' activities, there was only a single recorded vibration that exceeded the limits.

The case proceeded to trial on December 15, 2006. The plaintiff testified that she heard and felt vibrations from the pile driving in her home. She further testified that cracks began to develop in her plaster walls and in other portions of her home soon after the pile driving began and that no cracks occurred once the pile driving was completed. She was not aware of any other residents in the area who made claims or filed lawsuits for damage to their homes as a result of the vibrations caused by the defendants' pile driving. No evidence of any other claims or suits on account of pile driving vibrations was presented at trial.

*   *   *   *   *

On December 21, 2006, the jury returned a verdict in Gallagher's favor. The jury found that: (1) pile driving caused damage to Gallagher's home, and HV Pierpont and HV Development were responsible for the pile driving; (2) the pile driving created a public nuisance; (3) the pile driving created a private nuisance; and (4) Gallagher suffered damages in the amount of $ 55,189.14.

After the jury's verdict was announced, the defendants renewed their motions for judgment. . . . By Order entered on August 20, 2007, the circuit court granted the defendants' motion for judgment notwithstanding the verdict [The judge overruled the jury—Ed.] on all claims. Gallagher [appealed].

*   *   *   *   *

STRICT LIABILITY IN MARYLAND

*   *   *   *   *

[The Restatement of Torts,] Section 519, sets forth the general principle upon which courts have held defendants to be liable regardless of fault: "One who carries on an abnormally dangerous activity is subject to liability for harm to the person, land or chattels of another resulting from the activity, although he has exercised the utmost care to prevent the harm."

*   *   *   *   *

In summary, Maryland recognizes strict liability, [and] adopts the definition of abnormally dangerous activity as set forth in

Section 519 of the Restatement (Second) of Torts (1977). In many, but not all cases, the "thrust of the doctrine is that the activity be abnormally dangerous in relation to the area where it occurs."

STRICT LIABILITY IN PILE DRIVING CASES

The circuit court acknowledged that "whether pile driving is an abnormally dangerous activity has yet to be determined by the Maryland Court of Appeals." The circuit court nevertheless concluded, after applying sections 519 and 520 to the facts of the case, that the Court of Appeals would hold that the pile driving activity in this case would not warrant the application of strict liability.

In the 1984 revision of Dean Prosser's landmark treatise, Professor Page Keaton observed that varying formulations of strict liability have been applied by some courts to hold that pile driving is an abnormally or unreasonably dangerous activity warranting liability without fault. The reasoning of these decisions, as well as the results, is far from uniform. Some courts consider pile driving to be no different than blasting, and therefore dangerous enough to warrant strict liability regardless of the place in which it occurs. Others have taken a more fact-based approach, considering the activity in conjunction with the locale and the type of harm that resulted.

For example, in *Caporale v. C.W. Blakeslee & Sons, Inc.*, 149 Conn. 79, 175 A.2d 561 (1961), the Supreme Court of Connecticut held that pile driving activity during the construction of the Connecticut turnpike in 1958 and 1959, in close proximity to the plaintiff's business premises, warranted the application of strict liability. The Connecticut court analogized pile driving to blasting and aligned itself with those courts that imposed strict liability not only for flying debris but also for the vibrations caused by the explosive force of the blast. The Connecticut court noted, but declined to follow, a line of New York decisions, illustrated by *Fagan v. Pathe Industries, Inc.*, 274 A.D. 703, 86 N.Y.S.2d 859, 863-64 (App. Div., 1st Dept. 1949), that rejected strict liability for pile driving where the damage was caused only by vibrations.

* * * * *

STRICT LIABILITY IN THIS CASE

* * * * *

The appellant argues that pile driving should be considered abnormally dangerous simply because it produces uncontrollable vibrations, similar to blasting. She also asserts that pile driving created an abnormal risk to persons, such as Gallagher, who have historic homes, and that damage resulting from the inevitable emission of vibration cannot be eliminated through the exercise of due care. Although some courts have adopted this view, others have declined to impose strict liability for vibrations resulting from blasting (as opposed to flying debris).

The circuit court, after reviewing the evidence presented at trial, concluded that the defendants' pile driving in the Inner Harbor did not involve a high degree of risk of harm to the person, land or chattels of another, ... We agree. Comment g to section 520 states: "The harm threatened must be major in degree, and sufficiently serious in its possible consequence to justify holding the defendant strictly liable for subjecting others to an unusual risk." The risk of harm proven in this case, relatively minor damage to a 200-year-old home from the vibrations of the pile driving, simply is not a high degree of risk which requires the application of strict liability. . . .

[A] plaintiff must show that the defendants' pile driving was likely to produce significant harm, not simply that she suffered some harm as a result of the pile driving activity.

After considering the factors of section 520 of the Restatement, we agree with the circuit court's conclusion that the pile driving in this case was not an abnormally dangerous activity.

NUISANCE

Gallagher also contends that the defendants' conduct interfered with the use and enjoyment of her land, amounting to a public and private nuisance. The circuit court disagreed, concluding that Gallagher's evidence of a private or public nuisance was insufficient as a matter of law.

Under Maryland law, to sustain a private nuisance claim "there must be a substantial interference with the plaintiff's reasonable use and enjoyment of its property." *Exxon Corp. v. Yarema,* 69 Md. App. 124, 151, 516 A.2d 990 (1986), *cert. denied,* 309 Md. 47, 522 A.2d 392 (1987). In *Yarema,* we held that the defendants' "contamination of ground water imposed crippling restrictions not only on the contaminated land but on all the property adjacent to the land." A private nuisance requires the interference to be "substantial and unreasonable and such as would be offensive or inconvenient to the normal person."

Nothing of that order occurred in this case. The defendants' activity was reasonable in time, place, manner, and duration and did not substantially interfere with Gallagher's use and enjoyment of her land. . . . Residents of Baltimore City must accept the occasional annoyance and discomforts incidental to city life.

The elements of a public nuisance were discussed by the Court of Appeals in *Tadjer v. Montgomery County.* Quoting Dean Prosser, the Court of Appeals said: "To be considered public, the nuisance must affect an interest common to the general public, rather than peculiar to one individual, or several."

* * * * *

The circuit court concluded that the evidence produced at trial was insufficient to prove a public nuisance under these standards. We agree.

Affirmed.

Questions

1. *a.* The plaintiff, Gallagher, brought three causes of action in her amended complaint. List them.
   b. Why do you think the jury ruled in favor of Gallagher?
   c. Why did Gallagher lose at the trial level even though the jury had ruled in her favor?
   d. Explain why the appeals court upheld the judgment against Gallagher.
   e. Who do you think should have won this case? Explain.

2. Rattigan and Horvitz owned a house and prime oceanfront lot in Beverley Farms, Massachusetts. The house was rented during the summer months. Wile owned an adjacent undeveloped oceanfront lot. The only land access to Wile's lot was through the Rattigan/Horvitz lot. Rattigan and Horvitz successfully challenged Wile's application for a building permit and thereafter, Wile began a series of retaliatory acts, including putting several portable toilets on his lot immediately adjacent to the Horvitz swimming pool, landing his helicopter on his vacant lot, placing debris such as a rusted crane bucket, broken cement, and the bed of a pickup truck on his property, and holding parties (not attended by Wile) for 150 to 200 guests from the local youth shelter. Some of these tactics by Wile were sporadic rather than persistent. Were Rattigan and Horvitz the victims of a nuisance? Explain. See *Rattigan v. Wile*, 841 N.E.2d 680 (Mass. S. Judicial Ct. 2006).

Selected Intentional Tort Defenses

Let's take a brief look at a few of the more significant defenses to the intentional torts that we have been examining.

Consent

Clearly, if you consent to the use of your picture in an advertising campaign and you subsequently feel that your public image has been harmed, you will have difficulty in pursuing a tort claim. Of course, if you gave permission under mistake, fraud, or duress, your consent was not meaningful.

Mistake

As store security manager, you are radioed by a clerk to "stop the guy in the New York Yankees cap" on suspicion of shoplifting. After stopping someone fitting that description, you later discover that someone else, also wearing a Yankees cap, was the actual suspect. If the store is sued for false imprisonment, can it successfully raise a mistake defense? Unless protected under state law, probably not. Having acted intentionally, you and, by extension, your employer probably will bear responsibility. Of course, false imprisonment does not occur unless the detention was unreasonable.

On the other hand, mistake can be a good defense, particularly in instances in which events happen rapidly. Say, for example, a store's security personnel broke up what looked like an assault and battery in the mall parking lot, only to discover that the incident was merely horsing around by the parties. A mistake defense might be appropriate here.

Necessity

In what we would broadly label emergency situations, one may intentionally commit a tort and yet be excused. A case of public necessity might involve, for example, a person breaking into an unoccupied building late at night because he saw a fire burning inside. An example of a private necessity is when a defendant intrudes on the property of another to save himself only; he might thereafter raise a necessity defense against the tort claim of trespass.

Self-Defense

Suppose your career has taken you into retail management, and you have now decided to buy your own hardware store. You encounter the ups and downs that characterize entrepreneurial life, but you become particularly frustrated by the theft and vandalism that seem so much a part of small business. Finally, in an effort to stop the breaking, entering, and minor theft that has troubled your business, you build a trap in your store. You take up a few floorboards in a rear entryway where vandals have broken in, and you pound nails (points facing up) into those boards. Then you cover the nail points with some soft felt so they are not visible; but when stepped on, the nails will pierce the felt and stab the feet of any intruder. Suppose your trap works, and an intruder is injured. Suppose the intruder then sues you for his injury. Could you cite self-defense of your property as an excuse? What if a police officer stepped on a nail responding to an alarm at your business? The *Katko* case that follows looks at the self-defense theme.

LEGAL BRIEFCASE ▶ Katko v. Briney, 183 N.W.2d 657 (Ia. S.Ct. 1971)

FACTS

The Brineys, defendants/appellants in this case, owned an unoccupied farmhouse. During the period from 1957 to 1967, trespassers broke into the house, broke windows, and stole some items. The Brineys boarded windows and erected "no trespassing" signs on the land. On June 11, 1967, the Brineys attached a 20-gauge, loaded shotgun to a bed in the house, pointing the barrel toward the bedroom door. They attached a wire to the trigger and the bedroom doorknob so that the gun would fire if the door were opened. At first, Mr. Briney directed the gun so that it would hit an intruder in the stomach, but agreed with Mrs. Briney's suggestion to lower the barrel so that it would strike an intruder's legs. The gun could not be seen from the outside, and no warning about it was posted.

Katko, the plaintiff/appellee, worked in an Eddyville, Iowa, gas station. He and a friend, McDonough, had found antiques— old bottles and fruit jars—on their first trip to the Briney house, which Katko considered to be abandoned. On their second trip, they entered the house through a window. Katko opened the bedroom door and was shot in the right leg. Much of that leg, including part of the tibia, was blown away. Katko was hospitalized for 40 days. His leg was in a cast for approximately one year, and he was required to wear a brace for an additional year. His leg was permanently shortened by the trauma.

Katko sued the Brineys and secured a jury verdict of $30,000. The Brineys appealed to the Iowa Supreme Court.

* * * * *

Chief Justice Moore

The primary issue presented here is whether an owner may protect personal property in an unoccupied, boarded-up farmhouse against trespassers and thieves by a spring gun capable of inflicting death or serious injury.

We are not here concerned with a man's right to protect his home and members of his family. Defendant's home was several miles from the scene of the incident to which we refer.

* * * * *

Plaintiff testified he knew he had no right to break and enter the house with intent to steal bottles and fruit jars therefrom. He further testified he had entered a plea of guilty to larceny in the nighttime of property of less than $20 value from a private building. He stated he had been fined $50 and costs and paroled during good behavior from a 60-day jail sentence. Other than minor traffic charges this was plaintiff's first brush with the law. . . .

The main thrust of the defendants' defense in the trial court and on this appeal is that "the law permits use of a spring gun in a dwelling or warehouse for the purpose of preventing the unlawful entry of a burglar or thief." . . .

In the statement of issues the trial court stated plaintiff and his companion committed a felony when they broke and entered defendant's house. In instruction 2 the court referred to the early case history of the use of spring guns and stated under the law their use was prohibited except to prevent the commission of felonies of violence and where human life is in danger. The instruction included a statement that breaking and entering is not a felony of violence.

Instruction 5 stated, "You are hereby instructed that one may use reasonable force in the protection of his property, but such right is subject to the qualification that one may not use such means of force as will take human life or inflict great bodily injury. Such is the rule even though the injured party is a trespasser and is in violation of the law himself."

Instruction 6 stated, "An owner of premises is prohibited from willfully or intentionally injuring a trespasser by means of force that either takes life or inflicts great bodily injury; and therefore a person owning a premise is prohibited from setting out 'spring guns' and like dangerous devices which will likely take life or inflict great bodily injury, for the purpose of harming trespassers. The fact that the trespasser may be acting in violation of the law does not change the rule. The only time when such conduct of setting a 'spring gun' or a like dangerous device is justified would be when the trespasser was committing a felony of violence or a felony punishable by death, or where the trespasser was endangering human life by his act." . . .

The overwhelming weight of authority, both textbook and case law, supports the trial court's statement of the applicable principles of law.

Prosser on Torts, Third Edition, pages 116–18, states,

> [T]he law has always placed a higher value upon human safety than upon mere rights in property; it is the accepted rule that there is no privilege to use any force calculated to cause death or serious bodily injury to repel the threat to land or chattels, unless there is also such a threat to the defendant's personal safety as to justify a self-defense . . . spring guns and other man-killing devices are not justifiable against a mere trespasser, or even a petty thief. They are privileged only against those upon whom the landowner, if he were present in person, would be free to inflict injury of the same kind.

* * * * *

In *Hooker v. Miller,* 37 Iowa 613, we held defendant vineyard owner liable for damages resulting from a spring gun shot although plaintiff was a trespasser and there to steal grapes. At pages 614, 615, this statement is made: "This court has held that a mere trespass against property other than a dwelling is not a sufficient justification to authorize the use of a deadly weapon by the owner in its defense; and that if death results in such a case it will be murder, though the killing be actually necessary to prevent the trespass. . . ."

In Wisconsin, Oregon, and England the use of spring guns and similar devices is specifically made unlawful by statute.

* * * * *

Affirmed.

Questions

1. Why did the Iowa Supreme Court rule in favor of the criminal intruder, Katko?
2. What classes of people other than intruders are of concern to the courts in cases like *Katko?*
3. Did the Iowa Supreme Court reach a just verdict? Explain.
4. A businessman in Cordele, Georgia, troubled by small thefts from a cigarette machine in front of his store, allegedly booby-trapped the machine after hours with dynamite. A teenager then died when tampering with the machine. What legal action should be taken? Resolve.

Part Two—Product Liability

Introduction

We have examined intentional torts against both persons and property. Now we turn to tort and contract claims arising from products.

How does the law handle the situation where a wheel falls off a car, or a lighter explodes in a consumer's face? Product liability lawsuits deal with cases where buyers, users, and in some cases bystanders are injured or killed by defective products. Those harmed may have causes of action in torts (negligence or strict liability) or contracts (breach of warranty). If so, the manufacturers, distributors, and sellers of that product must then defend themselves against often enormously expensive claims. Part Two of this chapter explains product liability law and raises some of the public policy considerations that have caused critics to call for legal reforms to reduce the burden of product liability lawsuits. [For a product liability overview, see **http://topics.law.cornell.edu/wex/Products_liability**]

Product Liability and Business Practice   When Blitz USA, manufacturer of the familiar red plastic gasoline cans, filed for bankruptcy and shut its Oklahoma factory, *The Wall Street Journal* described Blitz and its employees as the "latest victims" of trial lawyers after spending millions on product liability lawsuits, which, in turn, increased its product liability insurance costs.[4] Plaintiffs in these lawsuits sought damages for serious burn injuries and deaths suffered when Blitz gas cans exploded after gasoline vapors outside the can were ignited. The claims alleged that these "flashback" explosions could have been prevented had "flame arrester" shields been installed in the cans.[5]

Why did Blitz not add the flame arrester to its plastic gasoline cans? Predictably, the answers to that question offered by trial lawyers and Blitz executives vary greatly. According to lawyers responding to *The Wall Street Journal* editorial, these shields were included in Blitz's metal gasoline cans but were removed from their plastic containers, and arguably cost less than $1.00 per can.[6] A lawyer representing plaintiffs against Blitz contended that the company dropped plans to add the arresters to their plastic cans as a money-saving maneuver shortly before being acquired by a private equity firm.[7] Blitz asserted that adding a flame arrester would not have been effective. This defense was successful in a Texas case involving a man who died in an explosion when he poured gasoline from a Blitz can onto a fire; however, a federal judge subsequently ruled that internal documents later uncovered might have eliminated that defense if it had been presented at trial.[8] For example, in 2005, Blitz's then-CEO, Rocky Flick, wrote a 2005 memo entitled "My Wish List," in which he indicates his desire that Blitz cans would soon include a "device to eliminate flashback from a flame source."[9] Blitz was ordered to pay sanctions and to give the court's opinion and order to each plaintiff who had sued Blitz in the previous two years.[10] Flick countered that Blitz executives believed the flame arresters, if installed, would cause other safety problems, such as creating a false sense of security when pouring gas on an open flame.[11]

Whether you believe that corporate greed or trial lawyers were to blame, Blitz's closure offers a cautionary tale on the importance of anticipating litigation expenses as a part of business strategy. [For a general database on defective products, see **http://consumerlawpage.com/resource/defect.shtml**]

Justice for Consumers and for Toyota

As we have seen, product liability law can sometimes be devastating to a company or industry. As harsh as the consequences may be, the law is often the only recourse for those wronged by defective products, and it is one of the most effective methods of curbing dangerous business practices. Toyota's massive product liability dispute has blemished the company's quality image while also apparently threatening the safety of many Toyota customers. Along with financial losses, Toyota has faced allegations of causing hundreds of injuries and deaths. Several safety problems have been raised, but the core allegation is that some Toyota vehicles accelerate suddenly and uncontrollably. The plaintiffs attribute the problem to defects in the electronic throttle control, but a federal study released in 2011, concluded that the likely culprits were mechanical defects in the accelerator system and floor mats that trapped the accelerator pedal. Plaintiffs also argue that Toyota failed to disclose what it knew about the acceleration problem, and that Toyota was negligent in failing to install a brake-override system that would automatically release the throttle if the brake is depressed. Toyota reportedly discussed the override system with the federal government in 2007 but did not begin installations until 2010. Toyota acknowledges some problems with floor mats, but argues that many of the incidents are attributable to operator error. In one case, a $10 million settlement was reached following the deaths of four in a California accident after the Lexus they were driving sped out of control in a sudden acceleration episode that apparently stemmed from an oversized floor mat trapping the accelerator.

In July 2013, Toyota settled a class-action lawsuit for financial losses for $1.6 billion. In October 2013, an Oklahoma jury found Toyota's electronic throttle system led to injury and death in a car crash. At this writing, Toyota is seeking to negotiate a settlement of hundreds of personal injury and wrongful death actions.

Question

Could the market alone protect us satisfactorily from dangerous products, or do you think the threat of very costly lawsuits is necessary to force American manufacturers to be fully responsible in monitoring the safety of the products they build? Explain.

Sources: Jacklyn Trop, "Toyota Seeks a Settlement for Sudden Acceleration Cases," *The New York Times,* December 13, 2013 [**www.nytimes.com**]; Ken Bensinger and Ralph Vartabedian, "Toyota Kept Sudden Acceleration Issue Silent, Lawsuit Says," *latimes.com,* October 29, 2010 [**latimes.com/business/la-fi-toyota-suit-20101029,0,5864831.story**], Ken Bensinger and Ralph Vartabedian, "Toyota Sudden-Acceleration Lawsuits Focus on Lack of Brake Override," *latimes.com,* January 3, 2011 [**latimes.com/business/la-fi-toyota-legal-20110104,0,867993.story**]; and Mike Ramsey, "U.S. Ends Toyota Probe," *The Wall Street Journal,* February 25, 2011, p. B2.

Negligence

The three major product liability causes of action are negligence, breach of warranty, and strict liability. In dangerously simplified terms, negligence is a breach of the duty of due care. A negligent act is the failure to do what a reasonable person would do or doing what a reasonable person would not do. Thus, a producer or distributor has a duty to exercise reasonable care in the entire stream of events associated with the development and sale of a product. In designing, manufacturing, testing, repairing, and warning of potential dangers, those in the chain of production and distribution must meet the standard of the reasonably prudent person. Failure to do so constitutes negligence. Some decisions also extend potential liability to situations in which a product is being put to an unintended but reasonably foreseeable *misuse*.

Historically, consumers dealt face-to-face with producers and could bring breach of contract claims if injured by a defective product. However, the development in the modern era of multilayered production and distribution systems eliminated that contractual relationship between producer and consumer, making it difficult for consumers to sue producers. Then in a famous 1916 decision (*McPherson v. Buick Motor Co.*),[12] the New York high court ruled that a consumer could bring a negligence claim against the manufacturer of a defective automobile even though the consumer did not purchase the car directly from that manufacturer. That view has since been broadly adopted, thus permitting victims of negligence to bring actions against all careless parties in the chain of production and distribution.

Donald Trump Owes a Duty?

In 1996, Mark Merrill entered a clinic for compulsive gamblers and wrote to Trump Indiana, a casino in Gary, Indiana, asking that he be evicted if he ever entered to gamble. Merrill's name appeared on Trump Indiana's eviction list. Nonetheless, Merrill later gambled at the casino suffering substantial losses. In December 1998 and January 1999, Merrill robbed banks, apparently to cover his gambling losses. He was convicted of bank robbery, but while in prison he filed suit claiming Trump Indiana was negligent in failing to keep him from gambling at the casino. Rule on Merrill's negligence claim. Explain. The four-part negligence test that follows will help you resolve Merrill's claim.

Source: Mark Merrill v. Trump Indiana, Inc., 320 F.3d 729 (7th Cir. 2003).

Negligence Test

To establish a successful negligence claim, the plaintiff must meet each of the following requirements:

1. **Duty.** The plaintiff must establish that the defendant owed a duty of due care to the plaintiff. In general, the standard applied is that of the fictitious reasonable man or woman. That *reasonable person* acts prudently, sensibly, and responsibly. The standard of reasonableness depends, of course, on the circumstances of the situation.

2. **Breach of duty.** The plaintiff must demonstrate that the defendant breached the duty of due care by engaging in conduct that did not conform to the reasonable person standard. Breach of the duty of due care may result from either the commission of a careless act or the omission of a reasonable, prudent act. Would a reasonable man or woman discharge a firearm in a public park? Would a reasonable person foresee that failure to illuminate one's front entry steps might lead to a broken bone? More formally, we might think of reasonable behavior as decision making that weighs the costs and benefits of acting or not acting. The reasonable person "takes precautions against harms when doing so costs less than the discounted value of the harms risked."[13]

3. **Causation**
   a. **Actual cause.** Did the defendant's breach of the duty of due care in fact cause the harm in question? Commonly, the "but for" test is applied to determine cause in fact. For example, but for the defendant's failure to stop at the red light, the plaintiff pedestrian would not have been struck down in the crosswalk.

b. **Proximate cause.** The plaintiff must establish that the defendant's actions were the proximate cause of the injury. As a matter of policy, is the defendant's conduct sufficiently connected to the plaintiff's injury as to justify imposing liability? Many injuries arise from a series of events—some of them wildly improbable. Did the defendant's negligence lead directly to the plaintiff's harm, or did some intervening act break the causal link between the defendant's negligence and the harm? For example, the community's allegedly negligent maintenance resulted in a blocked road, forcing the plaintiff to detour. While on the detour route, the plaintiff's vehicle was struck by a plane that fell from the sky when attempting to land at a nearby airport. Was the community's negligence the proximate cause of the plaintiff's injury?[14]

4. **Injury.** The plaintiff must have sustained injury, and, due to problems of proof, that injury often must be physical. [For a tort law library, see **www.findlaw.com/01topics/22tort**]

The case that follows asks whether a bowling alley is liable for a patron's injuries resulting from an altercation on its premises.

LEGAL BRIEFCASE

Hoyt v. Gutterz Bowl & Lounge 829 N.W.2d 772 (Ia. S.Ct. 2013)

Justice Hecht

Defendant—appellee Gutterz Bowl & Lounge (Gutterz) is a bowling alley and tavern located in Guthrie Center, Iowa. On March 20, 2009, Curtis Hoyt and several members of his construction crew finished work and went to Gutterz for refreshments. Curtis Knapp was also a customer at Gutterz that afternoon. Hoyt soon came to believe that Knapp was scowling at him. Hoyt and Knapp had formerly been friendly, but tension had arisen between them as a result of Hoyt's alleged mistreatment of the sister of Knapp's friend.

* * * * *

[T]he staff of Gutterz had [no] knowledge of this history between Hoyt and Knapp.

After consuming a few beers, Hoyt and coworker Chris Brittain approached and verbally confronted Knapp. Knapp did not respond and continued to scowl at Hoyt. The waitress serving Hoyt and Brittain observed their behavior with concern and threatened to discontinue serving them unless they calmed down. Hoyt and Brittain ignored the waitress's warning, and thus she requested and secured permission from Gutterz's owner, Rodney Atkinson, to discontinue serving them. Atkinson, who had been preparing food in the kitchen, went to the bar area to assess the situation. Hoyt and Brittain complained to Atkinson that they were no longer being served and continued to taunt Knapp.

Shortly thereafter, Atkinson grew concerned that an altercation might occur. He requested that Hoyt and Brittain leave.

* * * * *

Hoyt finished his beer and exited the tavern. As Hoyt walked through the parking lot toward his vehicle, [Knapp] . . . struck him in the back of the head, knocking him unconscious. Hoyt suffered several injuries including a compound fracture of his ankle. Knapp admitted to police who later arrived on the scene that he had struck Hoyt, but claimed he had done so in self-defense.

* * * * *

Hoyt filed this action alleging that Knapp and Gutterz were liable for the injuries he sustained when Knapp assaulted him. Gutterz moved for summary judgment, alleging Gutterz owed Hoyt no duty of reasonable care, there was no evidence of a breach of any duty, and the assault by Knapp and Hoyt's injury were not foreseeable. The district court granted Gutterz's motion for summary judgment and dismissed Gutterz from the lawsuit.

* * * * *

The court of appeals reversed the district court's summary judgment ruling.

* * * * *

III. DISCUSSION

Hoyt contends the district court erred in concluding as a matter of law that Gutterz did not breach a duty of reasonable care under these circumstances. Further, Hoyt contends, the district court erred in its consideration of foreseeability of injury to Hoyt in making its summary judgment ruling.

* * * * *

A. Duty

[T]he determination of whether a duty is owed under particular circumstances is a matter of law for the court's determination.

* * * * *

Traditionally . . . a property owner "is ordinarily under no duty to exercise any care until he knows or has reason to know that the acts of the third person are occurring, or are about to occur."

* * * * *

That general proposition was subject to the caveat that a duty would be imposed in scenarios where the property owner knew or had reason to know of a likelihood of third party conduct that could endanger visitors or where the place or character of the business was such that the property owner should reasonably anticipate careless or criminal conduct by third parties.

* * * * *

Recently . . . we examined a scenario in which the trampoline of a landowner had been blown by high winds into a nearby roadway, obstructing the travel of and causing injury to a driver. . . . We questioned and then rejected an assessment of foreseeability of risk in determining whether the landowner owed the driver a duty.

* * * * *

Instead . . . no-duty rulings should be limited to exceptional cases in which "an articulated countervailing principle or policy warrants denying or limiting liability in a particular class of cases."

* * * * *

Removing foreseeability from the duty analysis, we must consider whether some principle or strong policy consideration justifies exempting Gutterz, or the class of tavern owners in general, from the duty to exercise reasonable care. . . . [W]e cannot discern . . . any such considerations compelling exemption of tavern owners from the duty.

* * * * *

Accordingly, we conclude Gutterz owed Hoyt a duty of reasonable care under the circumstances presented here. We now turn to the question of whether Hoyt raised a genuine issue of material fact regarding the alleged breach of this duty.

B. Reasonable Care

* * * * *

While taverns are not insurers of patrons' safety against third-person criminal attacks, various jurisdictions have explained taverns must make reasonable efforts to maintain order and supervise and control patrons.

* * * * *

That a tavern may create a physical environment where instances of misconduct are likely to take place raises converging questions of reasonable care and the appropriate scope of liability for the defendant. . . . In a tavern, for example, the environment may foreseeably bring about the misconduct of a third party, resulting in injury to a plaintiff. While the foreseeability of misconduct raises an issue of the appropriate level of care, it also raises the issue of whether the harm suffered by the plaintiff is within the range of risks that may make the defendant's conduct negligent in failing to exercise that care.

* * * * *

Here, the district court found that Gutterz exercised reasonable care as a matter of law, based largely on the notion that the information available to Gutterz at the time failed to suggest any possibility of harm to Hoyt.

* * * * *

[W]e disagree that the record established as a matter of law that an injury to Hoyt was unforeseeable. Gutterz's duty of reasonable care applied . . . to risks arising from Hoyt's conduct, as well as those created by a third party's conduct, whether innocent, negligent, or intentional.

* * * * *

[B]ars are business venues in which alcohol-fueled disturbances causing injury and even death are known to occur.

* * * * *

Given the . . . general tenor of bar behavior, and Atkinson's own testimony regarding concern about a physical altercation, we conclude that a reasonable person might find the risk of harm to Hoyt foreseeable. Accordingly, that Hoyt may have initiated the conflict cannot serve as the basis for summary judgment that Gutterz acted reasonably under the circumstances.

* * * * *

Hoyt contends that Gutterz could have exercised reasonable care by any of the following: (1) calling the police when the conflict developed, (2) escorting Hoyt to his vehicle in the parking lot, or (3) verifying that Knapp was not lying in wait in the parking lot. Gutterz contends that it did escort Hoyt to his vehicle, and that its precautions here were reasonable as a matter of law. . . . [R]esolution of the factual dispute is best left to the fact finder. . . .

* * * * *

[Reversed]

DISSENT

WATERMAN, Justice joined by Cady, C. J., and Mansfield, J.

I respectfully dissent. . . . Uncontroverted facts establish the defendant acted reasonably as a matter of law.

There is no evidence or claim that prior fights or third-party criminal acts showed a need for a bouncer or other security at Gutterz. Bars are not insurers strictly liable for injuries on their premises inflicted by others.

* * * * *

Having kicked out the troublemakers—Hoyt and his companion—what else should Gutterz have done? How was the bar negligent? The majority concludes a jury could find Gutterz negligent for failing to call the police. But, no crime had (yet) been committed, and Hoyt exited the bar when told to leave. Knapp was not threatening anyone or misbehaving in any way. At that point, why call the police? From Gutterz's standpoint, the incident had been defused by Hoyt's departure. The majority also argues Atkinson should have done more to ensure Hoyt left the parking lot safely. This theory assumes Atkinson reasonably should have foreseen *Knapp*

would attack Hoyt. Knapp had not so much as even raised his voice.

* * * * *

I would affirm the district court's summary judgment in favor of Gutterz.

Questions

1. Why did the Iowa Supreme Court conclude that Gutterz owed a duty of reasonable care to Hoyt? According to the Court, when would a landowner not owe a duty of reasonable care to a plaintiff? Describe a scenario in which a landowner would not owe such a duty to an injured party.

2. Why should Hoyt, who initiated the conflict with Knapp in the Gutterz bar area, be able to recover from Gutterz for his resulting injuries? Explain.

3. Both the majority and dissenting opinions offer that taverns are not ensurers of safety of their patrons against injury caused by third parties. On what point does the dissenting opinion disagree with the majority? Do you agree with the majority or dissenting opinion? Explain.

4. Jerry Colaitis, 47, went with his family to a Benihana steakhouse in Munsey Park, New York. The Benihana chain is well-known for hibachi-style cooking with diners gathered around a rectangular wooden table with a hot grill in the middle from which the chef, as a form of entertainment, often casually tosses pieces of cooked food at the diners. Mrs. Colaitis claimed that the chef struck and burned some family members with pieces of tossed food. Mr. Colaitis asked the chef to stop, but as he was speaking a piece of shrimp was tossed his way, causing Mr. Colaitis to jerk away from it resulting in two wrenched vertebrae in his neck. Mr. Colaitis underwent a corrective operation then suffered a post-operative complication that resulted in a blood-borne infection that caused Mr. Colaitis' death. The Colaitis family sued Benihana for negligence causing the death. At trial, the head chef at the Munsey Park restaurant conceded that the food tossing practice could be dangerous. The restaurant discontinued the practice. During the last year of his life, Mr. Colaitis had suffered from fevers that were not associated with his surgery. How would you rule on the Colaitis' negligence claim? Explain. See *Estate of Colaitis v. Benihana, Inc.*, 015439-2002 (Nassau County Supreme Court, 2006) and Andrew Harris, "Jury: Flying Shrimp . . . Kill Diner," **www.law.com/jsp /article. jsp?id51139479516332.**

5. Johnny Burnett, described by his mother, Sheila Watters, as a devoted "Dungeons & Dragons" player, killed himself. (The record did not disclose his age at the time of death.) Watters blamed the death on her son's absorption in the game. She claimed that "he lost control of his own independent will and was driven to self-destruction."

   "Dungeons & Dragons" is an adventure game set in an imaginary ancient world; the players assume the roles of various characters as suggested by illustrated booklets. The play is orchestrated by a player labeled the "Dungeon Master." The outcome of the play is determined by using dice in conjunction with tables provided with the game. The game's materials do not mention suicide or guns. More than 1 million copies of the game have been sold, many to schools where it is used as a learning tool.

   In federal district court, Watters brought a wrongful death claim against TSR, the manufacturer of "Dungeons & Dragons." The plaintiff's complaint alleged that TSR violated its duty of care in two ways: It disseminated "Dungeons & Dragons" literature to "mentally fragile persons," and it failed to warn that the "possible consequences" of playing the game might include "loss of control of the mental processes." Decide. Explain. See *Watters v. TSR, Inc.,* 904 F.2d 378 (6th Cir. 1990).

6. Plaintiff was seven months pregnant and the mother of 17-month-old James. She was standing on the sidewalk, and James was in the street. A truck being negligently driven bore down on the boy, running him over. The shock caused the mother to miscarry and suffer actual physical and emotional injury. She brought suit against the driver for harm to herself and the infant child.
   a. What is the issue in this case?
   b. Decide the case. Explain. See *Amaya v. Home Ice, Fuel & Supply Co.,* 379 P.2d 513 (Cal. S.Ct. 1963). But also see *Dillon v. Legg,* 441 P.2d 912 (Cal. S.Ct. 1968).

7. Is a fireworks manufacturer liable for harm to children who ignited an explosive that had failed to detonate in the town public display the previous day? Explain.

8. An individual took his car to Quality Pontiac in Albuquerque, New Mexico, for repairs and was told to leave the car unlocked with the keys in the ignition. The lot was fenced, but the gate was unlocked. Billy Garcia entered the car lot at 9 PM, apparently looking in the cars for something to steal. Garcia stole the individual's car. The next day at approximately 11 AM, a deputy sheriff observed Garcia driving quickly through a school zone and pursued him, engaging his sirens and emergency lights. Garcia sped the car up to 90 miles an hour and collided with Herrera's car, killing one occupant and seriously injuring the other; Herrera and others sued Quality Pontiac. The complaint included an affidavit of a sociologist asserting that Albuquerque's car theft rate was the second highest in the United States, and that a significant portion of cars stolen had been left unlocked and with keys in the ignition. Further, stolen cars were highly likely to be involved in joy riding, and nearly 17 percent of stolen cars were involved in accidents shortly after the theft. Should Quality Pontiac be held liable? Explain. See *Herrera et al. v. Quality Pontiac,* 73 P.3d 181 (N.M. S.Ct. 2003).

Classes of Negligence Claims

Negligence claims emerging from defective products fall into three categories of analysis: (1) manufacturing defects, (2) design defects, and (3) inadequate warnings.

Manufacturing Defects

McDonald's sells a billion cups of coffee each year, in part because its coffee is extremely hot—180 to 190 degrees—which is exactly what its customers prefer and which, McDonald's believes, produces tastier coffee than the 140 to 145 degrees normally achieved at home. In 1992, then 79-year-old Stella Liebeck ordered coffee at an Albuquerque, New Mexico, McDonald's drive-through. Her grandson, who was driving, pulled forward and stopped so that Liebeck could add cream and sugar to her coffee. The dashboard of the car was slanted so that the coffee could not be set on it. Liebeck, therefore, placed the coffee between her legs, and while trying to get the top off the container, she spilled the coffee on her lap, resulting in third-degree burns. She was hospitalized, required skin grafts, and was disabled for two years. She sought a settlement with McDonald's, but according to her family, McDonald's offered only $800.[15] Liebeck sued, accusing McDonald's of gross negligence for selling coffee that was "unreasonably dangerous" and "defectively manufactured."[16]

Liebeck was awarded $200,000 in compensatory and $2.7 million in punitive damages. The jury found Liebeck 20 percent responsible for her own injury, thus reducing her compensatory award to $160,000. The judge subsequently reduced the punitive award to $480,000. The parties then settled out of court for an undisclosed amount. According to news reports, the jury awarded Liebeck $2.7 million in punitive damages because of what it perceived to be McDonald's callous attitude toward the accident and because of the more than 700 previous coffee-burn claims that had been filed against McDonald's. A McDonald's human factors engineer testified that the number of hot coffee burns was "statistically insignificant" when compared with the billions of cups sold by McDonald's annually.[17] [For the "actual facts" on the Liebeck/McDonald's episode, see **www.lectlaw.com/files/cur78.htm**]

> The number of hot coffee burns was "statistically insignificant."

[For the *Hot Coffee* trailer, see **http://hotcoffeethemovie.com**]

A British High Court justice, however, viewed the hot coffee situation quite differently:

> Persons generally expect tea or coffee purchased to be consumed on the premises to be hot. . . . They accordingly know that care must be taken to avoid such spills.[18]

[For a practical guide to the law of accidents and injuries, see **www.nolo.com /legal-encyclopedia/accident-law/**]

McDonald's "Exploding" Chicken Sandwich

Frank Sutton bought a McDonald's fried chicken sandwich at the Daniel Boone Truck Stop in Duffield, Virginia, on August 8, 2005. When he bit into the sandwich, Sutton said, "the grease from the inside of the chicken sandwich spread out all over my bottom lip, my top lip, down onto my chin." Sutton immediately dropped the sandwich. His wife dabbed his face with ice as blisters formed on his lips. Sutton reported the incident to a pair of McDonald's employees, one of whom reportedly said, "This is what happens to the sandwiches when they aren't drained completely." Sutton's lips continued to bother him. He went to a doctor who provided lip balm and told Sutton to avoid excessive exposure to sunlight. Sutton thereafter sued McDonald's and the local franchise owner, Roth, for negligence, among other claims. At trial in a Virginia federal district court, Sutton testified that he thought the sandwich was "negligently prepared" or "defective," but the judge rejected Sutton's negligence claim reasoning that Sutton failed to establish the standard of care that Virginia product liability law requires. (Using either federal standards, state standards, or reasonable consumer expectations, Sutton was required to demonstrate a standard of care that was breached leading to his injury.) The judge also ruled that

Sutton was contributorily negligent (contributed to his own harm) by failing to "exercise reasonable care to see that [he wasn't] eating something too hot." Sutton appealed to the Fourth Circuit Court of Appeals.

> *a.* In your judgment, was McDonald's negligent in this episode? Explain.
> *b.* Did Sutton contribute to his own injury? Explain.

Source: Sutton v. Roth, L.L.C.; John Doe; McDonald's Corporation, 361 Fed. Appx. 543 (4th Cir. 2010) (unpublished opinion).

Res Ipsa   As we see with the McDonald's cases, allegedly improper manufacturing of products often generates negligence claims. However, the extremely complex process of producing, distributing, and using a product sometimes so obscures the root of the injury in question that proof of fault is nearly impossible to establish. In those circumstances, many courts have adopted the doctrine of *res ipsa loquitur* (the thing speaks for itself), which in some cases permits the court to infer the defendant's negligence even though that negligence cannot be proved—that is, the facts suggest that the plaintiff's injury must have resulted from the defendant's negligence, but the circumstances are such that the plaintiff is unable to prove negligence. A showing of res ipsa loquitur requires that (1) the injury was caused by an instrumentality under the control of the defendant, (2) the accident ordinarily would not happen absent the defendant's negligence, and (3) there is no evidence of other causes for the accident.[19]

Design Defects

From Cessna's single-engine airplanes to five-gallon buckets (which may hold liquid sufficient to drown a child) to automobile seat belts and on across the spectrum of American products, manufacturers must think about designing products to anticipate and avoid consumer injury. Two principal lines of analysis have emerged in these cases: (1) The *risk–utility test* holds that a product is negligently designed if the benefits of a product's design are outweighed by the risks that accompany that design. (2) The *consumer expectations test* imposes on the manufacturer a duty to design its products so that they are safe not only for their intended use but also for any reasonably foreseeable use.

In 1997 members of the American Law Institute, a group of legal experts, approved the *Restatement of the Law Third, Torts: Products Liability,* which does not constitute law but represents those experts' best judgment about what the law should be. They have recommended to the courts a design defect standard that supports the balancing/risk–utility model and gives much less attention to consumer expectations. Furthermore, a product would be considered defective in design only if its foreseeable risks could have been reduced or avoided by a reasonable alternative design and if failure to include that design makes the product not reasonably safe. That is, plaintiffs would need to show that some better design was available and was not incorporated in the product in question. The case that follows involves, according to the California Supreme Court, a risk–benefit argument by the plaintiffs seeking civil damages after a mass murder.[20]

Marilyn Merrill v. Navegar, Inc. 28 P.3d 116 (Cal. S.Ct. 2001)

Justice Chin

On July 1, 1993, Gian Luigi Ferri killed eight people and wounded six—and then killed himself—during a shooting rampage at 101 California Street, a high-rise office building in San Francisco. Survivors and representatives of some of Ferri's victims (plaintiffs) sued defendant Navegar, Inc., which made two of the three weapons Ferri used.

We granted review to determine whether plaintiffs may hold Navegar liable on a common law negligence theory.

* * * * *

Navegar advertised the TEC-9/DC9 in a number of gun-related magazines and annuals. . . . A typical advertisement claimed that in light of the TEC-9/DC9's design features—including "32 rounds of firepower," a "'TEC-KOTE' finish," and "two-step disassembly for easy cleaning"—the weapon is "ideal for self-defense or recreation," "stands out among high-capacity assault-type pistols," and "delivers more gutsy performance and reliability than ANY other gun on the market." Navegar also distributed an advertising brochure or catalog describing its guns and accessories, which it mailed to anyone interested and, on at least one occasion, printed in special issue magazines. In a page describing the TEC-KOTE finish, Navegar claimed the finish provided "natural lubicity [sic] to increase bullet velocities, excellent resistance to fingerprints, sweat rust, petroleum distillates of all types, gun solvents, gun cleaners, and all powder residues. Salt spray corrosion resistance, expansion and contraction of the metal will not result in peeling of finish." A different brochure advertising to retailers used the slogan, "Intratec: Weapons that are as tough as your toughest customer."

Navegar included a manual with each TEC-9/DC9 it sold. The 1993 manual contained safety warnings, technical information, and operating instructions. It also claimed the gun was "a radically new type of semi automatic pistol," which was "designed to deliver a high volume of firepower" and, "thanks to its dimensions and designs," could "be used in modes of fire impossible with most handguns." Regarding the latter claim, the manual described and illustrated several recommended shooting positions, including "hipfire at shortest range," a two-handed hold with the nontrigger hand placed on the upper part of the magazine well.

In early 1993 Ferri, a Southern California resident, bought a [used] TEC-9 from the Pawn & Gun Shop in Henderson, Nevada. . . . According to the salesperson, Ferri looked at a wide variety of handguns, but seemed mainly interested in a "high-capacity type" gun, "something relatively compact that holds a lot of rounds." He gave no indication he had previously heard of the TEC-9 or the Intratec brand . . . Later that day, he returned the weapon, stating that he wanted a new gun instead.

On April 25, 1993, Ferri bought a new TEC-DC9 from Super Pawn, a gun store in Las Vegas, Nevada. . . . Ferri questioned [another] customer about the TEC-DC9. . . . The customer said that people at a shooting range would "probably laugh at" Ferri if he used a TEC-DC9 "because it wasn't really an accurate weapon" and that a .22-caliber gun was better for "plinking" than a gun because ammunition for the former was much cheaper. Ferri nevertheless chose the TEC-DC9.

Ferri purchased another TEC-DC9 on May 8, 1993, at a Las Vegas gun show. . . .

To purchase the new weapons, Ferri showed an apparently valid Nevada driver's license and answered required questions about his criminal history and residency. All of the distributors and retailers were licensed by the federal Bureau of Alcohol, Tobacco, and Firearms, and [s]o far as the record shows, all of the transactions were legal . . . other than Ferri's misrepresentations as to his state of residence.

On July 1, 1993, Ferri entered 101 California Street carrying the TEC-9/DC9s and a .45-caliber Norinco Model 1911A1 pistol in a large briefcase and another bag. He had added to the TEC-DC9's Hell-Fire brand trigger systems that made the weapons fire in rapid bursts, and he was equipped with hundreds of rounds of ammunition preloaded into 40- to 50-round magazines. He went to the 34th floor, to the office of a law firm he held a grudge against, and started shooting. During his rampage, he killed eight people and wounded six on three different floors, and then killed himself.

* * * * *

PROCEDURAL BACKGROUND

Plaintiffs' first amended complaint asserted a cause of action against Navegar for "common law negligence." In this claim, plaintiffs alleged that Navegar knew or should have known that (1) the TEC-9/DC9 is a "small, easily concealable military, assault weapon; (2) it has "no legitimate sporting . . . or self-defense purpose and is particularly well adapted to a military-style assault on large numbers of people"; (3) it is "disproportionately associated with criminal activity"; (4) it is "more attractive to criminals" because of its "firepower" and "other features"; (5) its "firepower was likely to be enhanced by the addition of products such as high-capacity magazines" and "the Hell-Fire trigger system"; and (6) it "would be used to kill or injure innocent persons in violent criminal acts such as the mass killing committed by Ferri." Plaintiffs also alleged that Navegar "acknowledges that publicity surrounding the [TEC-9/DC9s] reputation as a weapon favored by criminals increases its sales." Thus, plaintiffs alleged, Navegar "acted negligently by manufacturing, marketing, and making available for sale to the general public" the TEC-9/DC9.

* * * * *

Navegar moved for summary judgment. As to common law negligence, it argued it owed plaintiffs no duty not to advertise the TEC-9/DC9 and that plaintiffs had no evidence Ferri saw or was affected by a Navegar advertisement.

In opposing the motion, plaintiffs argued that Navegar had misconstrued the ordinary negligence claim. They explained that, contrary to Navegar's assertion, their negligence claim did "not depend on whether" Navegar had a "duty . . . not to advertise" or "whether there is a causal link between Navegar's advertising and plaintiffs' injuries." From the start, plaintiffs have made clear their ordinary negligence claim is not based on Navegar's negligent advertising but rather its decision to "'make available for sale to the general public guns . . . which [it] knew or should have known have "no legitimate sporting or self-defense purpose" and which are "particularly well-adapted to a military-style assault on large numbers of people."' Simply put, Navegar breached a duty of care by making the TEC-9 available to the general public, i.e., "by releasing the weapons for sale to the general public even though it knew or should have known that the TEC-9 was particularly attractive to criminals and particularly suited for mass killings." Plaintiffs concluded their argument regarding duty by asserting that "Navegar breached a legal duty to forebear [sic] distributing the TEC-9 to the general public given the likelihood that doing so would lead to the sort of violent criminal act that occurred at the 101 California Street Building."

As to causation, plaintiffs also argued that in light of their negligence theory, "whether Ferri actually saw or was influenced by any particular Navegar advertising is immaterial." They explained, "The ordinary negligence claim is directed to Navegar's conduct in making the TEC-9 available to the public. It is that unreasonable conduct that was a substantial factor in causing plaintiffs' injuries, not Navegar's marketing efforts." "Navegar's advertising is only material to the ordinary negligence claim in that it underscores that the criminal use of the weapon was foreseeable to Navegar. . . . Plaintiffs are not alleging that Ferri was induced to purchase the TEC-DC9s or to

commit the 101 massacre by any particular advertisements. The significance of the advertisements is what they say about [Navegar's] knowledge of [its] market."

* * * * *

DISCUSSION

* * * * *

[I]n the trial court, Navegar argued in effect that the Legislature, through section 1714.4, established an exception that applies in this case. Section 1714.4 provides; "(a) In a products liability action, no firearm or ammunition shall be deemed defective in design on the basis that the benefits of the product do not outweigh the risk of injury posed by its potential to cause serious injury, damage, or death when discharged. (b) For purposes of this section: (1) The potential of a firearm or ammunition to cause serious injury, damage, or death when discharged does not make the product defective in design. (2) Injuries or damages resulting from the discharge of a firearm or ammunition are not proximately caused by its potential to cause serious injury, damage, or death, but are proximately caused by the actual discharge of the product. (c) This section shall not affect a products liability cause of action based upon the improper selection of design alternatives." . . . Navegar argues that this statute, by establishing a state policy of exempting manufacturers of legal, nondefective firearms "from liability for their criminal use," bars plaintiffs' negligence claim.

Plaintiffs respond that section 1714.4 "has no application to this case because it is not a products liability action." Plaintiffs assert that they "seek to hold Navegar liable for its negligent conduct, not for making a defective product," and that they "make no assertion that Navegar should be liable because the risks posed by the TEC-9 outweigh its benefits." . . . [W]e reject plaintiffs' argument that section 1714.4 is inapplicable because this case "is not a products liability action.". . .

[C]ontrary to the assertion of plaintiffs, the record demonstrates that plaintiffs do, in fact, seek to hold Navegar liable precisely because, as the trial court stated, the TEC-9/DC9's "potential for harm substantially outweighs any possible benefit to be derived from [it]." In their brief, plaintiffs assert that Navegar is liable because it "designed and widely distributed a weapon uniquely suited for mass killing and lacking legitimate civilian uses."

Using the words of the risk–utility test for both products liability theories, plaintiffs essentially allege, argue, and hope to prove that the TEC-9/DC9 is defective in design. Thus this is a products liability action based on negligence, which asserts that the TEC-9/DC9 was defective in design because the risks of making it available to the general public outweighed the benefits of that conduct, and that defendants knew or should have known this fact.

* * * * *

Finally, we also conclude that the evidence in the record regarding Navegar's promotional activities and the literature it distributed with the TEC-9/DC9 does not save plaintiffs' negligence claim. As we have previously explained, in opposing Navegar's summary judgment motion, plaintiffs insisted that "their ordinary negligence claim" was not "directed to" or "based on Navegar's negligent advertising but rather its decision to make [the TEC-9/DC9] available for sale to the general public. . . ." Plaintiffs also insisted that it was Navegar's "unreasonable conduct" in "making the TEC-9 available to the public . . . that was a substantial factor in causing [their] injuries, not Navegar's marketing efforts." Thus, they maintained, "whether Ferri actually saw or was influenced by any particular Navegar advertising is immaterial.". . . . Plaintiffs are not alleging that Ferri was induced to purchase the TEC-DC9s or to commit the 101 massacre by any particular advertisements. The significance of the advertisements is what they say about [Navegar's] knowledge of [its] market."

* * * * *

In any event, the evidence in the record fails to raise a triable factual issue as to whether Navegar's advertising and literature were substantial factors in causing plaintiffs' injuries. Regarding this question, plaintiffs' counsel asserted at oral argument that "Navegar's liability does not depend on its telling the public, here's a great gun to commit a crime," but on its "communicating a message that people who want above all else in their weapons firepower, the capacity to shoot many, many rounds without the need to reload, and to use that gun in a combat fashion, this is the gun for you."

* * * * *

To the extent plaintiffs rely on allegedly more inflammatory aspects of Navegar's advertising, they fail to raise a triable factual issue regarding causation. For example, they offer no evidence, direct or circumstantial, that Ferri ever saw the promotional materials sent to dealers, which used the phrase "tough as your toughest customer," or the early version of the TEC-KOTE product brochure description, which promised "excellent resistance to fingerprints." Moreover, plaintiffs do not dispute that (1) San Francisco police inspectors did "not recall" finding "any TEC-DC9 magazine advertisement in Ferri's apartment" and found "no evidence" that any advertisement caused Ferri to travel to Nevada to purchase the TEC-DC9s;

(2) "there is otherwise no Navegar magazine advertisement in the possession of the City and County of San Francisco as evidence collected in the 101 California Street shootings"; (3) the salesman at the Pawn & Gun Shop in Henderson, Nevada, where Ferri bought the used TEC-9, "never" saw Ferri in possession of any advertisement or literature for the TEC-9 or TEC-DC9, and never heard Ferri mention he had seen any advertisement for the TEC-9 or TEC-DC9; (4) when Ferri bought the first new TEC-9/DC9, he had no firearms advertisement or other type of literature in his possession and did not ask for the TEC-9/DC9 by name; and (5) when Ferri bought the second new TEC-9/DC9, he indicated he already owned another TEC-9/DC9. Plaintiffs have failed to produce, or show that they will be able to produce at trial, substantial evidence "that Navegar's marketing style was 'a factor' in" Ferri's conduct. . . .

In arguing to the contrary, plaintiffs cite evidence that Ferri went to Nevada, where the TEC-9/DC9 was available, to buy guns for his planned attack and that the two stores where he bought TEC-9/DC9s had Las Vegas Yellow Pages advertisements picturing, among other guns, assault weapons. Although this evidence does tend to show Ferri sought to purchase high-firepower guns, it does not tend to show Ferri went to Nevada or the stores in search of a TEC-9/DC9 or other assault pistol in response to Navegar's marketing efforts. The existence of various high-firepower rifles and pistols would have been so widely known from other sources (especially to a reader of gun magazines as, apparently, Ferri was) as to render unjustified any inference that Navegar's marketing efforts were a substantial factor in motivating Ferri's decision to seek such a gun. Thus, we agree with the trial court that "the links plaintiffs seek to establish between advertisements and carnage amount to little more than guesswork." . . .

Accordingly, we conclude the trial court properly granted Navegar summary judgment. . . . In section 1714.4, the Legislature has set California's public policy regarding a gun manufacturer's liability under these circumstances. Given that public policy, plaintiffs may not proceed with their negligence claim.

Reversed.

DISSENTING OPINION BY JUSTICE WERDEGAR

I cannot accept the majority's conclusion that plaintiffs are statutorily barred from suing the maker of the semiautomatic assault weapon used to massacre the victims in this case.

* * * * *

Civil Code section 1714.4 bars product liability actions against gunmakers based on the risk–benefit theory of product defect. The legislative policy behind the statute might, at most, be deemed also to encompass negligence claims that are substantially identical to risk–benefit product defect claims. Plaintiffs' claim is neither. Plaintiffs' claim of negligence is, at bottom, that defendant Navegar, Inc., acted without due care in distributing the TEC-9/DC9 to the general civilian public rather than restricting its sales to police and military units that might have a legitimate call for such a military-style assault pistol. Plaintiffs do not claim that the TEC-9/DC9 is defective; nor do they even claim that defendant acted negligently simply by making the TEC-9/DC9. Plaintiffs allege negligence, rather, in Navegar's selling that firearm on the general civilian market knowing it would attract purchasers likely to misuse it, rather than restricting sales to buyers with a lawful use for the tools of assaultive violence. . . . This theory of negligence, resting on the allegation that particular marketing choices by Navegar were imprudent, is not substantially identical to a claim of product defect and thus is within neither the letter nor the spirit of Civil Code section 1714.4.

Navegar's conduct was allegedly negligent not because its gun was defective but because, in light of the gun's known attractiveness to violent users and the lack of a compelling need for its availability on the civilian market, a reasonably careful distributor would have restricted sales to groups unlikely to misuse the firearm. Civil Code section 1714.4 simply does not address such a negligent distribution claim.

*   *   *   *   *

AFTERWORD

Subsequent to the *Merrill v. Navegar* decision, Congress and President Bush enacted a 2005 law, the Protection of Lawful Commerce in Arms Act, to substantially shield firearms manufacturers and dealers from civil claims when guns are used in violent crimes.

Questions

1. *a.* Why did the California Supreme Court rule in favor of Navegar in this case?
   b. Explain the plaintiffs' cause of action.
   c. Explain the dissenting opinion.
   d. Argue that the plaintiffs' claim did not involve a risk–benefit analysis of the kind forbidden by the California statute.

2. In your opinion, should gun manufacturers be liable for the criminal use of their products? Explain.

3. Some observers argued that a decision for the plaintiffs in the *Merrill/Navegar* case would have led to a product liability "slippery slope." Explain that argument. Do you agree with it? Explain.

4. Hollister was badly burned when her shirt came into contact with a burner as she leaned over her electric stove. She sued the store where she bought the shirt, claiming that it was defectively designed. What proof will Hollister need to provide to win her defective design claim? See *Hollister v. Dayton-Hudson,* 188 F.3d 414 (6th Cir. 1999).

Warnings

Warnings seem to be everywhere in our lives. Some of them seem downright silly—so much so that the Foundation for Fair Civil Justice [**www.foundationforfairciviljustice .org/**] hosts a "Wacky Warning Labels" contest. Leading recent entries included these:

"Remove child before folding"—on a child car safety seat!
"Harmful if swallowed"—a warning on a brass fishing lure with a three-pronged hook.[21]

Even though the use of warnings can be abused, we should remember that they help protect us from foreseeable dangers. For example, in 2007, the federal Consumer Product Safety Commission (see Chapter 15) ordered warnings on all new generators and generator packaging after recording 94 deaths in 2005 from generator-related carbon monoxide poisoning with at least 83 more deaths in 2006 and 43 in 2007.[22]

A product may be considered defective because of inadequate warnings when reasonable warnings would have reduced or avoided the foreseeable risks and the failure to warn resulted in a product that was not reasonably safe. Courts might also consider the feasibility of an effective warning and the probable seriousness of the injury. The case that follows raises a failure to warn product liability claim.

White v. Victor Automotive Products   2010 Mich. App. LEXIS 914

LEGAL BRIEFCASE   (unpublished)

Per Curium (Judges Michael J. Kelly and Douglas B. Shapiro)

1. Summary of Facts and Proceedings

Plaintiff's decedent, Craig White, purchased a muffler repair kit manufactured and marketed by defendants. The kit included a metal patch to be placed over the hole in the muffler, a strip of "bandage" to be wrapped around the patch and the muffler to hold the patch in place, and mechanic's wire to wrap around and secure the bandage. The packaging described the product as a "Muffler and Tail Pipe Repair Kit" and stated, "Just wrap it on for instant repair." The instructions included with the kit, however, directed the user to "start the engine and run at idle for at least 10 minutes" after applying the "bandage." The instructions provided with the kit read in total:

INSTRUCTIONS:

1. Allow exhaust system and muffler to cool to a touch.
2. Clean surface of muffler or pipe to be repaired with sand paper, steel wool, or wire brush.
3. Cover holes with included metal heat shield, or by using metal or tin can.
4. Open foil packet containing bandage.
5. Wrap bandage completely around damaged area, overlapping each wrapping at least 3/4 inch. Note: Large repairs may require more than one bandage to adequately cover repair.
6. Secure bandage with mechanic's wire enclosed.
7. Start engine and run at idle for at least 10 minutes.
8. Bandage will cure with heat from exhaust system.

WARNING: Always wear safety classes and cloth or leather gloves when working on exhaust systems. Rust and debris can injure eyes and skin. Flush eyes thoroughly with water if contacted—for skin use soap and water. Never work on vehicle suspended in air NOT supported by adequate jack stands.

IF SWALLOWED, DRINK WATER AND GET IMMEDIATE MEDICAL ATTENTION. [Emphasis in original.]

White attempted to perform the muffler repair on April 29, 2005. According to the testimony of White's wife and son, when they left the house at about 11:00 A.M., White was in the driveway, working on the muffler. When they returned at about 2:15 P.M., they found White dead in the garage with the car up on a floor jack, the motor running and the garage door closed.[1] Tools were under the car and the bandage was found wrapped around the muffler. White was found near the exit to the garage. The police report stated in pertinent part:

> In the garage I observed the Buick to be elevated on a jack stand. Underneath the Buick I observed a small, rolling platform, that is used to enable a subject to crawl underneath a vehicle and assist with mobility while working on the vehicle. I further observed an activated utility light as well as several tools and accessories lying on the floor. On the rear trunk area of the Buick, I observed an empty package that contained a muffler repair kit. By looking at the picture on the muffler repair kit, and observing the muffler underneath the Buick, it was apparent that the victim had in fact used the kit as its contents were on the muffler.
>
> When Detective Steinaway arrived, I assisted in his investigation. During the investigation, I collected the empty package from the Buick to be placed as evidence at LCSD. While reading instructions listed on the back of the package, *it appeared as though the victim went step by step with the directions. The final instruction on these directions was to turn on the automobile and allow it to run for approximately ten minutes,* which would in turn allow the bonding agent applied to the muffler to heat up and activate properly. This could be a possible explanation for why the vehicle's ignition was activated and running. *While reading the warning label on the package listed directly below the instructions, it did not advise of the dangers of carbon monoxide.* [Emphasis added.]

An autopsy confirmed that White died of asphyxiation from carbon monoxide.

> Plaintiff's complaint alleged two violations of the duty to warn. First, plaintiff alleged that "Defendants breached their duty of care . . . in failing to include an instruction with the product that vehicles should not be run in an enclosed space or must be moved outside before starting the engine as directed [in the instructions]." Second, that "Defendant's breached their duty of care . . . in failing to warn of the dangers of carbon monoxide poisoning."

* * * * *

After a hearing, the trial court granted summary disposition to defendants, concluding:

> [I]t's clear that the material risk of death due to carbon monoxide poisoning as a result of running a car in an

---

[1] The reason why White moved from the driveway into his garage remains unknown.

enclosed garage would be obvious to the reasonably prudent user of a muffler repair kit. I don't think you can really argue that much about it. . . . I think it would be obvious and that would be to the general public, and it would be especially obvious to someone who used motors. Granted he may have been an . . . outboard engine mechanic, but nevertheless, it seems to me that he was in a position especially to know this even more than an average citizen. But nevertheless, to a reasonably prudent person it would be obvious this was a highly dangerous thing. I think it is common knowledge that it's a dangerous thing and—especially when you look at so many other options he would have had, like just open the garage door, might have been a lot better.

Plaintiff now appeals.

* * * * *

A. REASONABLY PRUDENT PRODUCT USER

[T]he first issue is whether a reasonable juror could find that the material risk of remaining in a closed garage with a running automobile while the muffler bandage cures is or should be "obvious to a reasonably prudent product user.". . .

* * * * *

Given the lack of an obvious risk of harm contained within the product's appearance or function, defendants argue that no reasonable person could fail to know that remaining present while running a car in a closed garage while the muffler bandage cured carried with it a risk of material harm. For reasonable minds not to differ on the issue, it would have to be obvious that the exhaust contained carbon monoxide or other injurious chemicals and that exposure for a period long enough for the muffler bandage to cure created a material risk of harm.

A fact finder may ultimately conclude that defendants are correct that a reasonably prudent person would be aware that automobile exhaust contains carbon monoxide or other injurious chemicals and that exposure for a period long enough for the muffler bandage to cure creates a material risk of harm. However, defendants have not provided any *evidence* from which such a conclusion may be drawn. . . .

At the time of the motion, plaintiff had proffered several articles and data that significant numbers of people, as many as 100 per year die, from accidental carbon monoxide poisoning in Michigan in a manner that supports plaintiff's claim that the danger of exposure to automobile exhaust is not necessarily "obvious to a reasonably prudent user." Plaintiff also presented an expert affidavit in this regard. Finally, plaintiff submitted warnings from devices that create carbon monoxide exhaust.

* * * * *

In contrast to plaintiff's presentation, the defense did not proffer *any* evidence supporting its contention that a reasonable person would know that carbon monoxide is present in automobile exhaust or that an exposure long enough for the muffler bandage to cure presents a material risk of harm.

* * * * *

Defendants provided no evidence in the present case that a reasonable person would know that an exposure to automobile exhaust in a garage for the time needed to cure the muffler repair presented a risk of material harm. Indeed, the only evidence in the record at this time is the data provided by plaintiff that significant numbers of people die from accidental carbon monoxide poisoning and the affidavit from plaintiff's expert supporting plaintiff's claim that the danger was not obvious. Under these circumstances, defendants were not entitled to summary disposition on the question of whether the risk of material harm from carbon monoxide inhalation from running an automobile long enough to cure this muffler product is or should be obvious to a reasonably prudent product user.

* * * * *

We take no position on whether a reasonably prudent user knows that automobile exhaust contains carbon monoxide nor that a exposure long enough to cure the muffler bandage can cause material harm. . . . Rather, we hold that there was insufficient evidence in the record as it presently exists to make that determination as a matter of law. . . .

Reversed and remanded.

Judge Kirsten F. Kelly Dissenting

I disagree with my colleagues' conclusion that the trial court's grant of summary disposition in this matter was premature. . . . [R]unning the engine of a car in a small, enclosed space, such as a garage, is an obvious material risk to a reasonably prudent product user and would be especially obvious to a person like decedent whose employment involved servicing and repairing engines. I would affirm the trial court.

* * * * *

Questions

1. Do you agree with the lower court that the risk of carbon monoxide poisoning from running a car in an enclosed garage would be obvious to the reasonably prudent user? Explain.

2. Why did the plaintiff win this case on appeal?

3. Michigan law bars liability in these situations if the risk "is or should be a matter of common knowledge to persons in the same or similar positions." Craig White had some, unspecified experience in servicing and repairing marine engines. He had also served as an "engine dynamo technician" and a "marine technician." Is that background, in and of itself, sufficient to establish that the carbon monoxide risk was a matter of "common knowledge" to White? Explain.

4. Bresnahan, age 50 and 5'8" tall, was driving her Chrysler LeBaron, equipped with a driver's side air bag, at between 25 and 30 miles per hour. She was seated less than one foot from the air bag cover. Bresnahan was distracted by police lights and rear-ended a Jaguar, triggering the LeBaron air bag, which broke Bresnahan's arm and caused various abrasions. The vehicle did not include a warning about the danger of sitting too close to the air bag. Was the vehicle defective because of the absence of a warning? Explain. See *Bresnahan v. Chrysler Corp.,* 65 Cal. App. 4th 1149 (1998).

5. Laaperi installed a smoke detector in his bedroom, properly connecting it to his home's electrical system. Six months later, Laaperi's house burned and three of his children were killed. A short circuit, which caused the fire, also deprived the A.C.-powered smoke detector of electricity. Thus, the detector did not sound a warning. Laaperi then claimed that Sears, Roebuck, where he purchased the detector, was guilty of negligence for failing to warn him that a fire might disable his smoke detector such that no warning would issue. How would you rule in this case? See *Laaperi v. Sears, Roebuck & Co.,* 787 F.2d 726 (1st Cir. 1986).

Negligence Defenses: Introduction

Even if the plaintiff has established all of the necessary ingredients in a negligence claim, the defendant may still prevail by asserting a good defense. The two most prominent legal defenses in these cases are (1) comparative or contributory negligence and (2) assumption of the risk.

A trampoline at the Beta Theta Pi fraternity house at the University of Denver led to a broken neck and paralysis when a 20-year-old fraternity member, Oscar Whitlock,

> Oscar Whitlock unsuccessfully attempted a flip at 10 PM in the dark.

unsuccessfully attempted a flip at 10 PM in the dark. Whitlock had extensive experience with trampolines. The day of the accident he had slept until 2 PM after drinking that morning until 2 AM. The trampoline was located in front of the house on university land that was leased by the fraternity. The trampoline had been used over a 10-year period by students and community members. A number of injuries had resulted. The university kept its own trampoline under lock and key because of safety concerns.

At trial the jury found the university 72 percent at fault, with the remainder of the blame lying with the plaintiff/student. He recovered 72 percent of $7,300,000 ($5,256,000). On appeal the judgment was upheld but the dissent argued that the university had no duty to warn against obvious risks, saying that "no reasonable person could conclude that the plaintiff was not at least as negligent as the defendant." Hence the dissent was saying, in effect, that the plaintiff had assumed the risk and, in any case, was himself arguably more negligent than the university.[23]

The Colorado State Supreme Court then reviewed the appeals court decision and reversed on the grounds that the university did not maintain a "special relationship" with the plaintiff that would have justified imposing a duty of due care on the university to ensure safe use of the trampoline.[24]

Questions

Assume you own an amusement park.

1. Would the dissent's reasoning in the *Whitlock* court of appeals decision apply to the trampoline in your amusement park business? Explain.
2. Would a warning and close supervision protect you from liability under the court of appeals decision? Explain.
3. Would you have the duty of due care for your customers that the Supreme Court said the University of Denver did not have for Whitlock? Explain.

Negligence Defenses: Rules

Let's look more closely at the central defenses in negligence cases.

Comparative Negligence

Most states have adopted comparative negligence as a defense; an approach that involves weighing the relative negligence of the parties. Though the formula varies from state to state, typically the plaintiff's recovery is reduced by a percentage equal to the percentage of the plaintiff's fault in the case. Assume a plaintiff sustained $10,000 in injuries in an accident. If the plaintiff's own negligence is found to be 20 percent responsible for the injuries, then the plaintiff's recovery will be reduced to $8,000. In many states, however, when the plaintiff is more than 50 percent at fault, she or he will be barred from recovery.

Contributory Negligence

Rather than employing the comparative negligence doctrine, a few states continue to follow the historic rule that any contribution by the plaintiff to his or her own harm constitutes a complete bar to recovery. This is called contributory negligence. If the plaintiff is found to have contributed in any way to his or her injury, even if that contribution is minuscule, he or she is unable to recover.

Assumption of Risk

A plaintiff who willingly enters a dangerous situation and is injured, in many states, will be barred from recovery. For example, if a driver sees that the road ahead is flooded, he probably will not be compensated for the injuries sustained when he loses control as he attempts to drive through the water. His recovery is barred even though the road was flooded owing to operator error in opening a floodgate. The requirements for use of the assumption of risk defense are (1) knowledge of the risk and (2) voluntary assumption of the risk. Assumption of the risk and contributory negligence are distinguishable in that the former is based on consent whereas the latter is rooted in carelessness. Increasingly, states that have adopted the comparative negligence doctrine do not treat assumption of the risk as a complete bar to recovery, but rather as a factor in negligence balancing.

Do Cheerleaders Assume the Risk of Injury?

Underlying the assumption of the risk doctrine is one of the central philosophical themes in this book: To what extent should the law/government shield us from life's risks? Departing for a moment from product liability considerations, how should the law resolve disputes arising from potentially hazardous recreational activities entered freely? Gabriella Ballou, then-9th grader and experienced cheerleader, allegedly improperly performed the "prep cradle twist" causing her head to miss the safety mat and strike the floor. An expert witness testified that the stunt was inadequately supervised, among other problems. Should Ballou be able to recover for injuries she sustained in high school cheerleading tryouts, or should she be deemed to have assumed the risks attendant to that activity?

Source: Ballou v. Ravena-Coeymans-Selkirk School District, 72 A.D.3d 1323 (N.Y. S.Ct. App. Div. 3d Dept. 2010).

Warranties

As explained previously, negligence claims often are difficult to prove. For that reason and others, a wronged consumer may wish to bring a breach of warranty claim in addition to or in place of a negligence action. A warranty is simply a contractually based guarantee. If the product does not conform to the standards of the warranty, the contract is violated (breached), and the wronged party is entitled to recovery. [For the text of the Uniform Commercial Code, Article II, Sales, see Appendix B at the back of this text. For the UCC, in total, see **www.law.cornell.edu/ucc**]

Express Warranties

An express warranty exists if a seller of goods states a fact or makes a promise regarding the character or quality of the goods. (Some lease arrangements are also covered by warranty law, but we will limit our discussion to the sale of goods.) Warranties are governed primarily by the Uniform Commercial Code. The UCC is designed to codify and standardize the law of commercial practice.

UCC 2–313. Express Warranties by Affirmation, Promise, Description, Sample

1. Express warranties by the seller are created as follows:
   a. Any affirmation of fact or promise made by the seller to the buyer which relates to the goods and becomes part of the basis of the bargain creates an express warranty that the goods shall conform to the affirmation or promise.
   b. Any description of the goods which is made part of the basis of the bargain creates an express warranty that the goods shall conform to the description.
   c. Any sample or model which is made part of the basis of the bargain creates an express warranty that the whole of the goods shall conform to the sample or model.

The UCC 2–313 standard is straightforward: The seller who seeks to enhance the attractiveness of her product by offering representations as to the nature or quality of the product must fulfill those representations or fall in breach of contract and pay damages. [At this writing, the various state legislatures are considering changes to the UCC.]

Puffing

Perhaps the area of greatest confusion in determining the existence and coverage of an express warranty is distinguishing a seller's promise from a mere expression of opinion. The latter, often referred to as sales talk or puffing, does not create an express warranty. The UCC requires an affirmation of fact or promise. Hence, a statement of opinion is not covered by the code. For example, the sales clerk who says, "This is the best TV around," would not be guaranteeing that the television in question is the best available. The salesperson is expressing a view. We, as consumers, seem to be quite patient with sellers' exaggerations. If, on the other hand, the clerk said, "This TV is rated at 1080 pixels," when in fact it offered only 768 pixels, a breach of warranty action might ultimately be in order. The reasonable expectations test is to be applied in such situations. An expression of opinion coming from an expert may well create an express warranty because the buyer should reasonably be able to rely on the expert's affirmations. That would particularly be the case if the buyer is not knowledgeable about the product.

Implied Warranties

When a seller enters a contract for the sale of goods an implied warranty arises by operation of law. That is, an implied warranty automatically attaches to the sale of goods unless the warranty is disclaimed (disavowed) by the seller.

Two types of implied warranties are provided:

UCC 2–314. Implied Warranty: Merchantability; Usage of Trade

(1) Unless excluded or modified (Section 2–316), a warranty that the goods shall be merchantable is implied in a contract for their sale if the seller is a merchant with respect to goods of that kind. Under this section the serving for value of food or drink to be consumed either on the premises or elsewhere is a sale.

UCC 2–315. Implied Warranty: Fitness for Particular Purpose

Where the seller at the time of contracting has reason to know any particular purpose for which the goods are required and that the buyer is relying on the seller's skill or judgment to select or furnish suitable goods, there is unless excluded or modified under the next section an implied warranty that the goods shall be fit for such purpose.

The implied warranty of merchantability is a powerful tool for the wronged consumer. If the seller is a merchant regularly selling goods of the kind in question, the warranty of merchantability automatically accompanies the sale unless the warranty is excluded via a disclaimer (explained below). The warranty arises even if the seller made no certification as to the nature or quality of the goods. UCC 2–314 enshrines the consumer's reasonable expectation that only safe goods of at least ordinary quality will appear on the market.

The implied warranty of fitness for a particular purpose likewise arises by operation of law, but only when the seller (merchant or not) knows (or has reason to know) that the goods are to be used for a specific purpose, and the seller further knows that the buyer is relying on the seller's judgment. If those conditions obtain, the warranty exists automatically unless disclaimed. For example, Chris Snapp engages an audio products clerk in a discussion regarding the proper sound system for Chris's classic Austin Healey 3000 sports car. Chris explains the joy he expects to receive in driving his car along the winding Kentucky roads with the convertible top down and his songs booming. Unfortunately, the audio system selected on the clerk's advice proves insufficiently powerful to be heard clearly above the rushing wind. Should Chris recover for breach of the implied warranty of fitness for a particular purpose? Merchantability?

Disclaimers

Express warranties may be disclaimed (excluded) or modified only with great difficulty. In any contract displaying both an express warranty and language disclaiming that warranty (for example, sold "as is" or "with all faults"), the warranty will remain effective unless the warranty and the disclaimer can reasonably be read as consistent.

Implied warranties may be excluded or modified by following either of the two patterns explained in UCC sections 2–316(2) and (3)(a).

2. Subject to subsection (3), to exclude or modify the implied warranty of merchantability or any part of it the language must mention merchantability and in case of a writing must be conspicuous, and to exclude or modify any implied warranty of fitness the exclusion must be by a writing and conspicuous.

3. Notwithstanding subsection (2)

   a. unless the circumstances indicate otherwise, all implied warranties are excluded by expressions like as is, with all faults, or other language which in common understanding calls the buyer's attention to the exclusion of warranties and makes plain that there is no implied warranty.

Finally, when a buyer, before entering a contract, inspects the goods (or a sample thereof) or declines to inspect, no implied warranty exists with regard to defects that should have been apparent on inspection. See UCC 2–316(3)(b).

Magnuson–Moss Warranty Act

The federal Magnuson–Moss Warranty Act extended and clarified UCC warranty rules. Congress found that warranties were often vague, deceptive, or simply incomprehensible to the average purchaser. The act, administered by the FTC, applies only to consumer products and only to written warranties. It does not require offering an express written warranty, but where such a warranty is offered and the cost of the goods is more than $10, the warranty must be labeled full or limited. A full warranty requires free repair of any defect. If repair is not achieved within a reasonable time, the buyer may elect either a refund or replacement without charge. If a limited warranty is offered, the limitation must be conspicuously displayed.

If a warranty is offered on goods costing more than $15, the warrantor must "fully and conspicuously disclose in simple and readily understandable language the terms and conditions of the warranty."

The effect of the Magnuson–Moss Act has not been entirely consistent with Congress's hopes. In practice, many sellers have either offered limited warranties or eliminated them entirely.

In many states, implied warranty law has been incorporated within broader product liability actions reflecting an emerging preference for treating personal injury and property damages as torts rather than contract-based (warranty) claims. The *Hodges* case that follows, however, finds the Kansas Supreme Court examining a breach of warranty claim under conventional contracts reasoning. Notice that the Kansas court struggles, as other courts have, in determining when the warranty of merchantability should apply to used goods.

LEGAL BRIEFCASE

Hodges v. Johnson
199 P.3d 1251 (Kansas S.Ct. 2009)

Justice Davis

FACTS

Jim Johnson owns a car dealership in Saline County that sells high-end, used vehicles. In January 2005, Johnson sold Dr. Merle Hodges and Melissa Hodges a 1995 Mercedes S320 with 135,945 miles for $17,020 (the sales price of $ 15,900 plus tax). Johnson had been driving the Mercedes as his personal vehicle for roughly 2 years before the sale. Johnson testified before the district court in this case that he told the Hodgeses when they purchased the Mercedes that it was a nice car in good condition. Dr. Hodges testified that Johnson said the car "was just pretty much a perfect car" and that Johnson "loved driving it."

At the time the Hodgeses bought the Mercedes from Johnson, there was no discussion about the operation of the air conditioning, heating, or other components of the vehicle. Both Dr. Hodges and Johnson testified that they had no reason to believe that the air conditioner did not work when the Mercedes was sold to the Hodgeses.

In February 2005, about a month after he had bought the car from Johnson, Dr. Hodges noticed that the vent in the Mercedes did not circulate cool air and that the car emitted a strange smell. In March of the same year, the Hodgeses noticed that the Mercedes' air conditioning did not work and contacted the Hodgeses' mechanic, Virgil Anderson. Anderson added Freon to the air conditioner. About a month later, the air conditioner again was not working; Anderson added more Freon. The Hodgeses contacted Johnson to notify him of the air conditioning problem, and Johnson told them that some older vehicles may need a yearly boost of Freon to work properly.

In May 2005, the air conditioner failed a third time. After checking the air conditioning system for leaks, Anderson informed the Hodgeses that the Mercedes' evaporator, condenser, and compressor needed to be replaced. Anderson explained that these repairs would cost approximately $3,000 to $ 4,000.

At some time around May 2005, a mechanic who worked for Anderson told the Hodgeses that Johnson had requested that the mechanic put a product called Super Seal into the Mercedes' air conditioner in May 2003 (when he was using the car as his personal vehicle). The mechanic explained that the use of Super Seal complicated the current repair of the air conditioner and that the mechanic personally would not recommend Super Seal or apply it unless requested.

Johnson testified that he did not recall any problems with the Mercedes' air conditioner after the mechanics added Super Seal in May 2003, though he could not recall whether additional Freon was added during that time. Johnson further testified that the air conditioning problem in 2003 only involved the car's evaporator.

Anderson identified the condenser as the main problem with the Mercedes' air conditioner in 2005. Anderson testified during the pendency of this case that he could not determine whether the problem with the Mercedes' air conditioner existed at the time that the Hodgeses bought the car from Johnson or occurred at some time later.

The Hodgeses asked Johnson to pay to repair the air conditioning unit in the Mercedes. Johnson refused.

Shortly thereafter, the Hodgeses filed an action in small claims court against Johnson, alleging he caused them damages of $3,474—Anderson's estimate of the repair costs. The small claims court found in favor of the Hodgeses and awarded them $3,474 damages, plus $56 in costs and interest.

Johnson appealed to the district court. [T]he district court also found in favor of the Hodgeses, noting that "while [Johnson] may not have known of the failure of the air conditioning unit[,] . . . there is an implied warranty of merchantability," and Johnson "is responsible to the plaintiffs to provide a car that is merchantable." The court therefore entered a judgment in favor of the Hodgeses for $3,474, together with costs of $56 plus interest. The court found that attorney fees were not warranted because Johnson's actions did not rise "to a level of misrepresentation."

[Both parties appealed] to the Court of Appeals. . . . The Court of Appeals reversed . . . and held as a matter of law that the implied warranty of merchantability on a used vehicle extends only to "the operation of major components that are necessary for the vehicle to operate, such as the engine and transmission." The court further held that "it is the responsibility of the buyer to ensure that the components incidental to operation are in working condition."

* * * * *

This court granted the Hodgeses' petition for review.

IMPLIED WARRANTY OF MERCHANTABILITY

Kansas' implied warranty of merchantability is contained in K.S.A. 84-2-314, which states that "a warranty that the goods shall be merchantable is implied in a contract for their sale if the seller is a merchant with respect to goods of that kind." K.S.A. 84-2-314(1). The statute further states that in order for goods to be "merchantable," they must be "at least such as . . . are fit for the ordinary purposes for which such goods are used." K.S.A. 84-2-314(2)(c).

* * * * *

ANALYSIS

The comments to K.S.A. 84-2-314 make clear that this implied warranty of merchantability applies by operation of law to "all sales by merchants" and "arises from the fact of the sale." K.S.A. 84-2-314, Kansas Comment 1. Applying this standard to the facts before us, it is clear that the transaction in this case—the sale of the Mercedes by Johnson to the Hodgeses—fits within the implied warranty. There is no dispute that Johnson is a merchant dealing in the sale of used vehicles or that the Mercedes is a "good" within the meaning of the statute. Thus, when Johnson sold the Mercedes to the Hodgeses, he implicitly warranted that the Mercedes would be "merchantable."

* * * * *

The Court of Appeals majority recognized that the sale of the Mercedes triggered the implied warranty but concluded as a matter of law under K.S.A. 84-2-314(2) that the vehicle's air conditioner was not covered by the warranty because the air conditioner did not affect the vehicle's merchantability. To reach this conclusion, the majority employed a three-part syllogism: First, for goods to be merchantable under the statute, they must be "fit for the ordinary purposes for which such goods are used." K.S.A. 84-2-314(2)(c). Second, the majority concluded that the primary purpose for which used vehicles are used is transportation; thus only the major components of a vehicle that bear upon its ability to effectively transport people from one location to another affect the vehicle's merchantability. Finally, the majority interpreted our past cases involving the warranty of merchantability in the sale of used vehicles to suggest that the warranty may not apply "unless a major component or several components are defective, causing the vehicle to become virtually inoperable." 39 Kan. App. 2d at 225.

Applying this syllogism, the Court of Appeals majority determined that the air conditioner was not a major component of the Mercedes and thus did not impair the primary purpose for which used cars vehicles are employed:

"An air conditioner is not a major component of a car that is 10 years old with over 135,000 miles on it, and does not fall within the implied warranty of merchantability. We find no implied warranty of merchantability, considering the age of the car, the high mileage, and the fact that the Hodges provided no proof that the air conditioner did not work when they purchased the vehicle." *Hodges,* 39 Kan. App. 2d at 225.

This conclusion is not supported by the case law. Although it may be that the implied warranty of merchantability does not extend to some components of a used vehicle in a particular transaction, this is a case-by-case determination in most cases—not a question of law. . . .

The Court of Appeals majority's approach is similarly unsupported by the statutes. K.S.A. 84-2-314(2)(c) defines merchantable goods as goods that are "fit for the ordinary *purposes* for which such goods are used." (Emphasis added.) The Court of Appeals interpreted this provision to mean that a used vehicle must be fit for the *primary* purpose of transportation. This interpretation is inconsistent with the plain language of K.S.A. 84-2-314(2)(c), which clearly contemplates goods that may be put to more than one use. Although there can be little doubt that the *primary* purpose of a vehicle is transportation, the Court of Appeals' opinion ignores the reality that a buyer may purchase a particular vehicle for a number of other purposes—among which may be safety, fuel economy, utility, or *comfort* in traveling to and from various destinations.

Contrary to the Court of Appeals' conclusion, the extent of a merchant's obligation under the implied warranty of merchantability depends on the circumstances of a transaction. . . . The determination as to whether the implied warranty has been breached turns on a number of factors, including "[t]he buyer's knowledge that the goods are used, the extent of their prior use, and whether the goods are significantly discounted." 230 Kan. at 457.

The broad range of used goods that may be covered by the implied warranty of merchantability underscores the wisdom of this court's previous recognition that a "late model, low mileage car, sold at a premium price, is expected to be in far better condition and to last longer than an old, high mileage, 'rough' car that is sold for little above its scrap value." *Dale,* 234 Kan. at 844. In this case, we have a 1995 Mercedes S320 with 135,945 miles selling for $17,020 in 2005. Johnson related to the buyer that it was a nice car in good condition; Dr. Hodges testified that he was told the car "was pretty much a perfect car." In short, this vehicle falls somewhere between the extremes of a "late model, low mileage car, sold at a premium price" and "an old, high mileage, 'rough' car . . . sold for little above its scrap value." 234 Kan. at 844.

The question remaining to be resolved is not the existence of this warranty, but rather the *extent of the seller's obligation* under the warranty. Because this case does not involve either extreme on the spectrum of used vehicles, the resolution of this question is not a question of law, but rather a factual determination. . . .

After hearing the evidence in this case, the district court determined that the Hodgeses were entitled to judgment against Johnson for the sum of $3,474, together with costs of $56 and interest, and thus affirmed the award of the small claims court.

To demonstrate a breach of the implied warranty of merchantability, a plaintiff must show that the purchased goods were defective, that the defect was present when the goods left the seller's control, and that the defect caused the injury sustained by the plaintiff. The circumstantial evidence in this case is sufficient to establish that the defect in the air conditioner existed at the time of sale. In 2003, 2 years before the Hodgeses purchased the vehicle, the Mercedes' air conditioner failed while Johnson was using it as his personal vehicle. Johnson insisted that his mechanic, against the mechanic's advice, use a product called Super Seal to fix the problem. The Hodgeses discovered that the air conditioner was again defective as soon as the weather became warm enough to require climate control. The use of the Super Seal, the strong odor emanating from the vehicle's ventilation system immediately after the sale, and the complete breakdown of the air conditioner when the buyer first attempted to use it all tend to establish that it was defective at the time of sale. While Johnson may not have known that the Mercedes' air conditioner was defective when he sold the vehicle to the Hodgeses, there is no requirement that a buyer establish that the seller knew of a defective component at the time of sale to trigger the implied warranty.

With regard to damages, there is no question that the complete failure of the air conditioner's operation led to the buyer replacing it. As this court has concluded:

> . . . As concerns used or secondhand goods it is generally understood that the measure of damages is the cost of repair when repair is possible." *International Petroleum Services,* 230 Kan. at 460.

* * * * *

We find that there is substantial competent evidence to support the district court's conclusion that the implied warranty of merchantability in this transaction was not limited to only the Mercedes' major components affecting transportation, but rather extended at a minimum to the vehicle's air conditioning unit. We also find that there was substantial competent evidence to demonstrate that the air conditioning unit was defective at the time of sale and that the required repairs would cost $3,474. Accordingly, we reverse the Court of Appeals' reversal of the district court's judgment in favor of the Hodgeses and affirm the district court's decision.

* * * * *

Questions

1. *a.* Why did the Court of Appeals rule for Johnson, the car dealer?
   b. Why did the Supreme Court reverse the Court of Appeals' judgment that the vehicle's air conditioner was not covered by a warranty?
   c. What test did the Kansas Supreme Court employ to determine whether the implied warranty of merchantability had been breached?
   d. How would the Kansas Supreme Court determine when a used car would be protected by the implied warranty of merchantability?

2. In buying a new motor home, Leavitt told the dealer that he wanted to have plenty of power and braking capacity for driving in the mountains. He was assured by the dealer on both counts. He brought the motor home and found it unsatisfactory for mountain use. After many warranty repairs, he sued for breach of warranty.
   a. What warranty was breached, according to Leavitt?
   b. Decide the case. Explain. See *Leavitt v. Monaco Coach,* 616 N.W.2d 175 (Mich. Ct. App. 2000).

3. Priebe bought a used car without a warranty (sold as is). The seller, Autobarn, told Priebe that the car had not been in any accidents. After driving the car more than 30,000 miles, Priebe crashed the car. Priebe sued Autobarn claiming the car was dangerous to drive because of a previous, undisclosed accident. Priebe did not show that Autobarn had knowledge of the previous accident; nor did Priebe show that the value of the car was reduced by the previous accident. Priebe sued for breach of warranty. Decide. Explain. See *Priebe v. Autobarn,* 240 F.3d 584 (7th Cir. 2001).

4. Douglas Kolarik alleged that he used several imported, pimento-stuffed green olives in a salad. In eating the salad, he bit down on an olive pit and fractured a tooth. The olive jar label included the words "minced pimento stuffed." The defendants are importers and wholesalers of Spanish olives that reach the defendants in barrels and are then inspected for general appearance, pH and acid level and then washed and placed in glass jars suitable for distribution for the purpose of retail sales.

   a. What legal claim would be expected from the plaintiff based on the "minced pimento stuffed" language?

   b. Decide that claim. Explain. See *Kolarik v. Cory International,* 721 N.W.2d 159 (Ia. S.Ct. 2006).

Skoal and Copenhagen and Death?

Bobby Hill of Canton, North Carolina, began chewing tobacco at age 13. He died in 2003 at age 42. U.S. Smokeless Tobacco Co., makers of Skoal and Copenhagen, agreed in 2010 to pay Hill's family $5 million to settle the relatives' wrongful death claim. Apparently, the settlement was the first of its kind involving smokeless tobacco.

Source: Associated Press, "First Lawsuit Won on Chewing Tobacco," *The Des Moines Register,* December 8, 2010, p. 7A.

Strict Liability

Sometimes things happen that businesses can neither prevent nor even explain and yet liability may attach. For example, imagine you are operating a clothing store. A customer enters and decides to try on a pair of slacks. You show her to the dressing room. Soon after, you hear a scream from the room. As it turns out, your customer has been bitten by a spider. Not surprisingly, she thinks the blame lies with your store. She sues, but her negligence and breach of warranty claims are rejected by the court. (Can you explain why she loses?) Finally, she raises a strict liability in tort argument, but the court denies that claim also. Read the overview of strict liability that follows and think about why the court denied her claim. See *Flippo v. Mode O'Day Frock Shops of Hollywood,* 449 S.W.2d 692 (Ark. S.Ct. 1970).

> Your customer has been bitten by a spider.

Strict Liability: Overview

Negligence and warranty claims are helpful to the harmed consumer. However, rapid changes in the nature of commercial practice, as well as an increasing societal concern for consumer protection, led the legal community to gradually embrace yet another cause of action. Strict liability in tort offers the prospect of holding all of those in the chain of distribution liable for damages from a defective product, rather than imposing the entire burden on the injured consumer. Manufacturers and sellers are best positioned to prevent the distribution of defective products, and they are best able to bear the cost of injury by spreading the loss via pricing policies and insurance coverage.

Strict liability as an independent tort emerged in 1963 in the famous California case of *Greenman v. Yuba Power Products, Inc.*[25] In the ensuing 40 years, most states have adopted strict liability in concept. The essence of the strict liability notion is expressed in Section 402A of the Restatement (Second) of Torts. In brief, 402A imposes liability where a product is sold in a defective condition, unreasonably dangerous to the user. Here is the 402A test:

1. One who sells any product in a defective condition, unreasonably dangerous to the user or consumer or to his property, is subject to liability for physical harm thereby caused to the ultimate user or consumer, or to his property, if
   a. the seller is engaged in the business of selling such a product, and,
   b. it is expected to and does reach the user or consumer without substantial change in the condition in which it is sold.
2. The rule stated in Subsection (1) applies although
   a. the seller has exercised all possible care in the preparation and sale of his product, and
   b. the user or consumer has not bought the product from or entered into any contractual relation with the seller.

Thus, we see that strict liability does not require proof of negligence on the part of the defendant. Strict liability law focuses on the condition of the product, rather than the conduct of the parties. Therefore, a seller who is free of actual fault may, nonetheless, be liable for injuries caused by a defective and unreasonably dangerous product. The Aim N Flame lighter case that follows considers the conditions under which a strict liability claim may be raised.

LEGAL BRIEFCASE

Calles v. Scripto-Tokai,
832 N.E.2d 409 (III. S.Ct. 2007)

Justice Burke

On March 31, 1998, plaintiff Susan Calles resided with her four daughters, Amanda, age 11, Victoria, age 5, and Jenna and Jillian, age 3. At some point that night, Calles left her home with Victoria to get videos for Amanda. When she left, the twins were in bed and Amanda was watching television. Calles returned to find fire trucks and emergency vehicles around her home. It was subsequently determined by a fire investigator, Robert Finn, that Jenna had started a fire using an Aim N Flame utility lighter Calles had purchased approximately one week earlier. The Aim N Flame was ignited by pulling a trigger after an "ON/OFF" switch was slid to the "on" position. As a

result of the fire, Jillian suffered smoke inhalation. She was hospitalized and died on April 21.

Calles filed suit against Tokai, designer and manufacturer of the Aim N Flame, and Scripto-Tokai, distributor (collectively Scripto), alleging that the Aim N Flame was defectively designed and unreasonably dangerous because it did not contain a child-resistant safety device. According to the complaint, a safety device was available, inexpensive, and would have reduced the risk that children could ignite the lighter. Calles' claims sounded in strict liability.

Thereafter, Scripto filed a motion for summary judgment. . . . In her deposition, Calles admitted she was aware of the risks and dangers presented by lighters in the hands of children, and, for this reason, she stored the Aim N Flames on the top shelf of her kitchen cabinet. Calles further admitted that the Aim N Flame operated as intended and expected.

In opposition to Scripto's motion for summary judgment, Calles offered affidavits from several experts. . . . All of [the] experts opined that the Aim N Flame was defective and unreasonably dangerous because it lacked a child-resistant design. They also opined that a technologically and economically feasible alternative design, which included a child-resistant safety device, existed at the time the Aim N Flame was manufactured. Several of the experts averred that Scripto was aware of the desirability of a child-safety device because it knew children could operate the Aim N Flame. Further, according to these experts, Scripto owned the technology to make the Aim N Flame child resistant in 1994 and 1995.

With respect to the cost of an alternative design, . . . the Consumer Product Safety Commission, the regulatory body for lighters, estimated the increased cost of adding a safety device to the lighter would be $ 0.40 per unit. However [one of Calles' experts estimated], the cost would have been negligible.

Calles also offered evidence of the dangerousness of lighters in the hands of children and Scripto's awareness of such dangers. . . . Scripto admitted they had been named as defendants in 25 lawsuits filed between 1996 and 2000 for injuries that occurred between 1992 and 1999 under circumstances similar to this case.

The trial court granted summary judgment in favor of Scripto. . . .

On appeal, the appellate court reversed [the trial court's summary judgment in favor of Scripto. . . .]

STRICT LIABILITY

This court adopted the strict liability doctrine set forth in section 402A of the Second Restatement of Torts. Under this doctrine, strict liability is imposed upon a seller of "any product in a defective condition unreasonably dangerous to the user or consumer or to his property." The test outlined in section 402A for determining whether a product is "unreasonably dangerous" is known as the consumer-expectation test. This test provides that a product is "unreasonably dangerous" when it is "dangerous to an extent beyond that which would be contemplated by the ordinary consumer who purchases it, with the ordinary knowledge common to the community as to its characteristics."

* * * * *

An ordinary consumer would expect that a child could obtain possession of the Aim N Flame and attempt to use it.

Thus, a child is a reasonably foreseeable user. Likewise, an ordinary consumer would appreciate the consequences that would naturally flow when a child obtains possession of a lighter.

Under the facts of this case, the Aim N Flame performed as an ordinary consumer would expect—it produced a flame when used in a reasonably foreseeable manner, i.e., by a child. This leads to the inescapable conclusion that the ordinary consumer's expectations were fulfilled. . . . Thus, as a matter of law, no fact finder could conclude that the Aim N Flame was unreasonably dangerous under the consumer-expectation test. Therefore, Calles cannot prevail under this theory.

This does not end our analysis, however. Though the Aim N Flame satisfies the consumer-expectation test, it may, nonetheless, be deemed unreasonably dangerous under the risk–utility test.

RISK–UTILITY TEST

Under the risk–utility test, a plaintiff may prevail in a strict liability design-defect case if he or she demonstrates that the magnitude of the danger outweighs the utility of the product, as designed.

* * * * *

Under the risk–utility test, a court may take into consideration numerous factors. In past decisions, this court has held that a plaintiff may prove a design defect by presenting evidence of "the availability and feasibility of alternate designs at the time of its manufacture, or that the design used did not conform with the design standards of the industry. . . ."

Calles presented specific and detailed evidence as to the likelihood of injury and the seriousness of injury from lighters which do not have child-safety devices.

Factors which would favor Scripto and a finding that the product is not unreasonably dangerous are the utility of the Aim N Flame and the user's awareness of the dangers. As to the utility of the Aim N Flame, it is both useful and desirable to society as a whole—it serves as an inexpensive alternative source of fire. . . . With respect to the user's awareness of the dangers, there is no question, based on Calles' deposition testimony, that it was obvious to her that the lighter could come into the hands of a child and the dangers and risks that situation would pose.

In connection with the remaining relevant factors, we find that these neither weigh for nor against a finding of unreasonably dangerous. Calles claims that a substitute product was available, but the only evidence she relies upon is the fact Bic introduced a child-resistant utility lighter in March 1998, the very same month of the incident here. This is insufficient to demonstrate that a substitute product was available at the time of the manufacture of the Aim N Flame.

Calles offered expert affidavits regarding the availability and feasibility of an alternative design, including product impairment and cost factors, along with industry standards. Each expert opined that a feasible alternative design existed.

* * * * *

There is nothing in our record showing Scripto provided any amount as to the increase in cost of incorporating a safety device. Apparently . . . an internal Scripto memorandum estimated the cost increase would be $0.03 per unit. In light of the foregoing, we conclude that the question of whether there was a feasible alternative design available cannot be determined on the basis of the record as it currently stands.

Lastly, with respect to the user's ability to avoid the danger, Calles testified she put the Aim N Flames on the top shelf of her kitchen cabinet. However, she also acknowledged she could have left them on the counter.

* * * * *

Based on a review of the foregoing factors, reasonable persons could differ on the weight to be given the relevant factors and thus could differ on whether the risks of the Aim N Flame outweigh its utility. Therefore, reasonable persons could differ as to whether the Aim N Flame is unreasonably dangerous, and we cannot say that Scripto was entitled to judgment as a matter of law. As such, we affirm the appellate court's decision reversing the trial court's decision granting summary judgment in favor of Scripto on the strict liability claims.

* * * * *

Questions

1. *a.* Explain the plaintiff Calles' claim that the Aim N Flame lighter was defective and unreasonably dangerous.

   b. Explain the court's resolution of Calles' claim.

2. What evidence must a plaintiff provide to maintain a successful defective design product liability claim?

3. Is the manufacturer excused from liability if the product's danger is obvious or if the product is used in an unintended but foreseeable fashion?

4. In a case similar to *Calles* [*Griggs v. Bic Corp.*, 981 F.2d 1429 (3rd Cir. 1992)] the court, employing a negligence analysis, found that the central question was whether the foreseeable risk was unreasonable. The court noted that residential fires started by children playing with lighters are estimated to take an average of 120 lives each year, and total damages amount to $300–$375 million or 60–75 cents per lighter sold.

   a. Is the foreseeable risk unreasonable, in your judgment?

   b. How did you reach your conclusion?

   c. In your view, are the parents the responsible parties in these episodes? Explain.

5. Alison Nowak, a 14-year-old girl, tried to spray her hair with Aqua Net. Because the spray valve on the recently purchased aerosol can would not work properly, she punctured the can with an opener. She was standing in her kitchen near a gas stove at the time, and the cloud of spray that gushed from the can ignited. She was severely burned. Nowak sued Faberge, the maker of the spray, on strict liability grounds. Although the back of the can contained the warnings, "Do not puncture," and "Do not use near fire or flame," the jury determined that Faberge had not adequately warned of the fire hazard and awarded her $1.5 million. Faberge appealed. Decide. Explain. See *Nowak v. Faberge USA Inc.*, 32 F.3d 755 (3d Cir. 1994).

Strict Liability: Coverage

All of those engaged in the preparation and distribution of a defective product may be liable for any harm caused by the defect, regardless of proof of actual fault. Furthermore, the courts have extended strict liability coverage to reach injured bystanders. Coverage generally extends to both personal injuries and property damage, but in some states the latter is excluded. Some states limit strict liability recovery to new goods, and some have limited liability to a designated period (for example, 15 years) after the manufacture or sale of the product.

Furthermore, the *Restatement of the Law Third, Torts* recommends applying strict liability claims to manufacturing defects but not to design and warning defect cases. Thus, in effect, the latest *Restatement* recommends applying the reasonableness, fault-based analysis explained earlier in the negligence material to all defective design and failure to warn cases. Of course, the courts may choose to stick with the current expansive use of the strict liability doctrine.

Strict Liability: Defenses

Assumption of risk and *product misuse* are both good defenses and, if factually supported, in many states can act as a complete bar to strict liability recovery. Assumption of the risk involves the plaintiff's decision to proceed to use the product despite obvious dangers associated with that use. Thus, if a pilot decided to fly knowing that the plane's wing flaps were not operating properly, she may well have assumed the risk if she subsequently crashed. When the product is used improperly, or its directions are ignored, or it is used in an unforeseeable way, the defendant would raise the misuse defense. Suppose you find yourself late for class and you decide to save time by drying your tennis shoes in your microwave or ironing your clothes after you have put them on your body. If the microwave blows

> Drying your tennis shoes in your microwave.

up or you burn yourself with the iron, not only have you had a very bad day, you probably would not be able to sue successfully for damages because you likely would be found to have misused the products. Some courts, however, hold those in the chain of distribution liable for foreseeable misuses. Because strict liability is a no-fault theory, contributory negligence ordinarily is not a recognized defense. [For the "evolution" of product liability laws, see **www .productliabilitylawyer.com/evolutionOfProductLiability.cfm**]

Video Games and *The Basketball Diaries*

Michael Carneal, a 14-year-old high school freshman in Paducah, Kentucky, brought a .22-caliber pistol and five shotguns to Heath High School on December 1, 1997, where he shot and killed three students and wounded a number of others. Carneal regularly played violent video games such as *Doom and Quake,* and viewed violent Internet sites. He also watched violent movies including *The Basketball Diaries,* in which a high school student dreams of killing his teacher and other students. The parents of the dead children sued several video game, movie production, and Internet content providers raising negligence and strict liability claims. Who should win that case? Explain.

Sources: James v. Meow Media, 300 F.3d 683 (6th Cir. 2002); cert. den. *James v. Meow Media,* 537 U.S. 1159 (2003).

Part Three—Product Liability and Public Policy

Giant tort awards involving products such as asbestos and breast implants have bankrupted businesses. When we hear about a $28 *billion* punitive damage award in 2002 for a 64-year-old smoker suffering from lung cancer, we may wonder if the justice system has lost its bearings.[26] We may not understand that those giant awards are almost always dramatically reduced.[27] Furthermore, awards in big class action cases often come in the form of product coupons or gifts to charity.[28] *The Wall Street Journal* reported, for example, that exploding tires on Ford Explorers resulted in a 2008 class action settlement for 1,647 eligible claimants of $500 toward the purchase of a new Explorer and $300 toward the purchase of any other Ford vehicle. Only 148 of the eligible claimants redeemed a coupon, while the attorneys who led the litigation received about $19 million in fees.[29] Nonetheless, the threat of tort litigation significantly affects business decision making and, in some instances, actually prevents products from reaching the market.

Because of those problems, many critics, particularly in the business community and among free market advocates, have argued for *tort reform.* They want to change the legal system in ways that would reduce the heavy costs of personal injury claims. The proposed reforms vary widely, but common prescriptions include: limiting class actions, reducing or eliminating punitive damages, curbing attorneys' fees, penalizing frivolous lawsuits, and imposing "loser pays" rules requiring the losing party in a civil lawsuit to pay the other party's legal fees and related costs.

Are big tort judgments harming the American economy and distorting justice, or are lawsuits Americans' only effective protection against callous corporations? Consider some of the evidence.

For Tort Reform   Consultants Towers Watson estimated that 2010 tort costs (not limited to product liability) for the United States totaled $264.6 billion: a sum amounting to a "tort tax" of $857 per year for every American.[30] As a result, critics say, American businesses must struggle with rising costs, innovation is reduced, and new jobs are less plentiful. Critics are particularly frustrated that much of the tort money goes to lawyers rather than to the injured plaintiffs. Although U.S. tort costs increased by 5.1 percent in 2010, the Towers Watson report attributed that rise to the *Deepwater Horizon* oil rig explosion and resulting oil spill in the Gulf of Mexico; not accounting for that event, tort costs actually decreased overall by 2.4 percent, extending the decrease seen in 2009. The Towers Watson report also noted that a weakened economy has offered less opportunity for tort actions, most notably in the commercial auto industry, despite the well-known products liability actions against Toyota discussed previously.[31] A number of states have imposed caps on punitive damages while, as noted in Chapter 5, the U.S. Supreme Court has handed down several decisions curbing punitives. [For further criticism of tort claims and our legal system generally, see **overlawyered.com or www.legalreform-now.org/.** For a critique of the 2009 Towers Watson (formerly Towers Perrin), see J. Robert Hunter and Joanne Doroshow, "Towers Perrin: 'Grade F' for Fantastically Inflated 'Tort Cost' Report," **www.consumerfed.org/elements/www.consumerfed.org/file/Insurance%20Report%20Towers%20Perrin%202010(1).pdf**]

> A "tort tax" of $857 per year for every American.

Against Tort Reform   Can we rely on the market and managerial ethics to protect us from dangerous products? Lawyers Mark Robinson and Kevin Calcagnie, writing in *The Wall Street Journal,* point to the long-running battle over Toyota's sudden acceleration problems as evidence that the market alone does not adequately protect consumers from dangerous products.[32] Robinson and Calcagnie argue that nearly a decade passed by before Toyota and the federal government began to aggressively examine the several thousand sudden acceleration claims.[33] Improvements in products such as air bags, seat belts, tires, tobacco products, antidepressants, and many more have been encouraged by product liability litigation, as Robinson and Calcagnie note.[34]

More broadly, those opposing tort reform say that the tort burden simply is not of the magnitude suggested by the critics. Lawsuits, consuming less than 2 percent of spending, constitute a modest part of the cost of doing business; product liability claims are a small fraction of the total legal landscape; and studies show that insurance costs do not decline appreciably when damages are capped.[35] Furthermore, only about 3 percent of tort cases ever make it to trial; those cases that are settled before judgment often involve reasonable sums of money[36] and punitive damages are awarded in only about 3.3 percent of tort cases won by plaintiffs.[37] Even ardent defenders of tort practice often agree, however, that the system needs to be improved so that lawyers do not gobble up so much of the money themselves and so that the system produces a more consistent, predictable form of justice.[38] [For a debate among prominent legal scholars about the value of product liability law, see A. Mitchell Polinsky and Steven Shavell, "The Uneasy Case for Product Liability," *123 Harvard Law Review* 1437 (2010); John C.P. Goldberg and Benjamin C. Zipursky, "The Easy Case for Products Liability Law: A Response to Professors Polinsky and Shavell," *123 Harvard Law Review* 1919 (2010); and A. Mitchell Polinsky and Steven Shavell, "A Skeptical Attitude about Product Liability Is Justified: A Reply to Professors Goldberg and Zipursky," *123 Harvard Law Review* 1949 (2010).]

Kids Need to Swing?

Aggressive public safety programs and the threat of lawsuits have made playground swings, particularly the tall 16-footers, a vanishing delight. Tall swings and slides along with sliding poles are rapidly being replaced by safer but less thrilling playground devices. U.S. playground safety standards, widely adopted in the 1990s, called for new safety surfaces to cushion falls with the result that the swings became very costly. A swing set once costing $800 now costs $4,000. Thus, government rules and the threat of lawsuits have made playgrounds safer while reshaping childhood fun and virtually eliminating the challenge of overcoming the terror of big swings and slides. Are we better off?

Source: Gregg Toppo, "The Great American Swing Set Is Teetering," *USA TODAY,* March 19, 2006 [**www.usatoday.com/news/nation/2006-03-19-swing-sets_x.htm**].

Big Case: Lead Paint?

A helpful way to look at tort reform is to consider one of the massive claims that have emerged periodically as plaintiffs attempt to prove themselves wronged by a defective product or wrongful conduct. Tobacco smokers, Ford Explorer drivers, Vioxx users, and victims of gun violence are among those who have made headlines pursuing alleged corporate wrongdoers. Lead paint, banned since 1978, often produces developmental difficulties, including IQ deficiencies, learning disabilities, hyperactivity, and impaired hearing, when ingested or inhaled by children. Ordinarily, lead paint is troublesome only when it is reduced to flakes or dust; commonly in buildings that have not been properly maintained. While the potential for exposure to lead has declined dramatically in recent years, an estimated several hundred thousand young children, often living in old, inner city housing have been victims:

> Crawling across the wooden floor of his mother's Brooklyn (New York) apartment, Jaylin paused to lick his chubby hand, swallowing flecks of toxic paint. The boy's mother had no idea the poison lurked within the cracks of the baseboard.[39]

Should paint manufacturers be responsible for the harm caused by paint applied decades back by willing consumers before anyone fully understood the long-term hazards? What about owners and landlords who failed to properly maintain painted surfaces? Even if we can establish responsibility, how do we apportion damages when we cannot identify the specific producers of the paint in question? Or should we expect the paint manufacturers to share the damages burden according to the percentage each holds in the market (a product liability claim labeled *market share liability*)?

Lead paint lawsuits have been pursued in a number of states. In most cases, the plaintiffs have been states and municipalities that have sued paint manufacturers or landlords/property owners for creating a *public nuisance* (a significant interference with a right common to the general public such as the public health, public safety, or public peace). Market share liability claims have also been raised in some instances, but most claims under both theories of recovery have been rejected in court. For example, a unanimous Rhode Island Supreme Court in 2008 overturned a jury verdict against three paint companies when the Court concluded that "however grave the problem of lead poisoning is in Rhode Island, public nuisance law simply does not provide a remedy for this harm."[40] Lawsuits continue, however, and in 2009, a Mississippi jury ruled that Sherwin-Williams paint company was liable for illnesses suffered by a young boy who had eaten paint chips. The jury awarded $7 million in damages, but Sherwin-Williams successfully appealed that verdict.[41] However, in 2014, the Mississippi Supreme Court reversed a trial court's grant of summary judgment to Sherwin-Williams in another case brought by five adults who as minor children, attended a local Head Start program to which Sherwin-Williams sold paint used on its playground equipment, causing injury to the plaintiffs.[42]

> A young boy who had eaten paint chips.

Fast Food = "Fat" Lawsuits?

Fortune magazine's February 2003 issue asked "Is Fat the Next Tobacco?" *Fortune* and many other publications suggested that fast-food companies might soon be buried in lawsuits like those attacking the tobacco industry. Although the prospect of blaming McDonald's, Wendy's, and others for obese people's health problems caused dismay, those lawsuits, for the most part, have not materialized. Most of the handful of cases filed have been unsuccessful, and those that did gain some traction were based in mislabeling and consumer fraud. Furthermore, at least 24 states have passed "cheese-burger bills" providing some protection for fast-food companies facing obesity lawsuits. However, in vetoing the Minnesota state legislature's Personal Responsibility in Food Consumption Act, Minnesota governor Mark Dayton observed that although he supported the bill's intent, he believed the bill would create too broad an exemption from liability for food manufacturers and sellers.

Sources: Jennifer Pomeranz and Lainie Rutkow, "Efforts to Immunize Food Manufacturers from Obesity-Related Lawsuits: A Challenge for Public Health," *Corporations and Health Watch,* August 17, 2011 [**http://corporationsandhealth .org/2011/08/17/efforts-to-immunize-food-manufacturers-from-obesity-related-lawsuits-a-challenge-for-public-health/**]; and Lianne S. Pinchuk, "Are Fast-Food Lawsuits Likely to Be the Next 'Big Tobacco'?" *The National Law Journal,* February 28, 2007.

Too Much Law?

Perhaps we rely too much on the law. Clearly, legal intervention often is necessary to achieve justice. At the same time, that intervention sometimes can be inefficient and unproductive. As we conclude this chapter, give some thought to the cases you have read. On balance, do you think legal intervention was necessary in those situations, or would our society be stronger if we resolved more of those problems through private arrangements such as arbitration, as we discussed in Chapter 4, or risk assignment provisions included in contracts when we buy a new product?

[For the American Tort Reform Association, see **www.atra.org**]

Internet Exercise

The Pacific Research Institute's 2010 U.S. Tort Liability Index ranks the 50 states according to their "tort climates."

1. Go to the report's state rankings [**http://special.pacificresearch.org/pub/sab/ entrep/2010/Tort-Index/state.html/**] and determine your state's rank, according to the PRI study. According to the study, is your state's tort system a "Saint," "Sinner," "Salvageable," or "Sucker," and why does it matter?

2. Read the press release for the study [**www.pacificresearch.org/press/2010-tort-liability-index-ranks-states-tort-climate**] and explain how U.S. tort costs compare with other nations and why high tort costs matter, according to the study.

Chapter Questions

1. Cotillo, a power lifter with 10 years experience, attempted to lift 530 pounds during an American Powerlifting Association–sponsored meet, organized by Duncan, the faculty sponsor of the local high school's weightlifting club and Taylor, the APA president. Lifters were allowed to use spotters of their own choice or those provided by the meet. Cotillo used those provided by the meet, who were high school students with weightlifting experience. As Cotillo attempted the lift, Duncan was positioned "in the middle," and a student was on each side of the bar. Cotillo dropped the weight shattering

his jaw and causing other injuries. The spotters were in the proper positions to provide assistance, but they could not do so quickly enough to prevent injury. Cotillo then sued Duncan, the APA, and the APA Board, claiming, among other things, that the spotters were improperly trained. The spotters had received some instruction prior to the meet, but the record was unclear as to whether the training was improper or inadequate.

    a. What was Cotillo's cause of action?

    b. Defend Duncan et al.

    c. Decide the case. Explain. See *American Powerlifting Association v. Cotillo,* 934 A.2d 27 (Ct. App. Md., 2007).

2. Stopczynski, age 17, had used her neighbor's pool "hundreds of times." Stopczynski and her neighbor's nephew, a 34-year-old male, went to the pool. Stopczynski was noticed floating face down in the pool. She had broken her neck, apparently from diving into the four-foot deep, above-ground pool. She died a few hours later. The pool originally had stickers around the edge that said "no diving," but that edge had been replaced and the stickers were gone. Stopczynski's mother sued the property owner, Woodcox, for negligence. Decide the case. Explain. See *Stopczynski v. Woodcox,* 258 Mich. App. 226 (2003).

3. Soon after Granny's Rocker Nite Club opened in the mid-1980s, it began having a weekly "fanny" contest, which involved male and female volunteer contestants competing for cash prizes by dancing. The audience judged the contest. While attending the fanny contest on April 4, 1990, plaintiff Jeffrey Loomis got into a fight with another patron. Loomis's right ear was bitten and torn.

    Loomis's claim against Granny's Rocker had two counts, one based on the Illinois Dramshop Act and one based on negligence. The jury found for the defendant on the dramshop count, but it found that Granny's Rocker was negligent in failing to have adequate security to stop a physical altercation on the nights of the fanny contests when it knew or should have known that such contests would result in a large and rowdy group of patrons. Granny's Rocker appealed. Decide the appeal. Explain, See *Loomis v. Granny's Rocker Nite Club,* 620 N.E.2d 664 (Ill. App. 1993).

4. Thomas Woeste died as a result of contracting a bacteria after eating about one dozen raw oysters at the Washington Platform Saloon & Restaurant. The bacteria, vibrio vulnificus, is naturally occurring in oysters harvested in warm waters. Most people are unaffected by the bacteria, but those with weakened immune systems like Woeste can be susceptible to illness or death. Washington Platform's menu contained the following warning:

> There may be risks associated when consuming shell fish. . . . If you suffer from chronic illness of the liver, stomach or blood. . . or if you have other immune disorders, you should eat these products fully cooked.

Woeste ordered and ate the oysters without opening the menu and reading the warning. A civil lawsuit was filed against Washington Platform alleging that the restaurant was both negligent and strictly liable for failure to adequately warn. Decide that case. Explain. See *Woeste v. Washington Platform Saloon & Restaurant,* 836 N.E.2d 52 (Ohio Ct. App., First App. Dist. 2005).

5. An 11-month-old child pushed on a window screen that gave way, allowing him to fall from the second story of his aunt's house. The child's parents sued the screen maker.
   a. What product liability claims could they legitimately raise?
   b. Decide. Explain. See *Brower v. Metal Industries, Inc.,* 719 A.2d 941 (Del. S.Ct. 1998).

6. Sandage loaded a car on a transport trailer. The car door could not be fully opened because of a support bar on the trailer. He suffered a back injury when he squeezed out of the car. The trailer had been modified to add several feet to its length, and support poles, including the one in question, had been added. Sandage sued the company that modified the trailer. Sandage sued in strict liability and negligence. Decide the case. Explain. See *Sandage v. Bankhead Enterprises, Inc.,* 177 F.3d 670 (8th Cir. 1999).

7. In 1995, a young Oklahoma couple shot and paralyzed a store clerk, Patsy Byers. The young couple had repeatedly viewed Oliver Stone's 1994 movie *Natural Born Killers,* which is about a young couple who go on a killing spree. The Byers family sued Stone and Warner Brothers movie studio, the film distributor. Should a filmmaker and studio be liable for the alleged copycat behavior of those viewing a movie? Explain.

8. A deputy sheriff drove his marked police cruiser through a Burger King drive-through in Vancouver, Washington. After ordering his hamburger, he decided to check his food. When he pulled into a nearby parking lot and lifted the bun, he found what looked like spit on the meat patty. DNA testing later confirmed that the substance was spit belonging to an employee at the Burger King. The deputy sheriff brought a product liability and negligence lawsuit against Burger King and its franchisee, alleging that he suffered emotional distress as a result of the incident, including vomiting and sleeplessness. Should contaminated food be the basis for such a lawsuit? Decide. Explain. See *Bylsma v. Burger King* (Wash. 293 P.3d 1168 2013).

9. Plaintiffs Dr. Arthur Weisz and David and Irene Schwartz bought two paintings at auctions conducted by Parke-Bernet Galleries, Inc. The paintings were listed in the auction catalog as those of Raoul Dufy. It was later discovered that the paintings were forgeries. The plaintiffs took legal action to recover their losses. Parke-Bernet defended itself by, among other arguments, asserting that the conditions of sale included a disclaimer providing that all properties were sold "as is." The conditions of sale were 15 numbered paragraphs embracing several pages in the auction catalog. The bulk of the auction catalog was devoted to descriptions of the works of art to be sold, including artists' names, dates of birth and death, and, in some instances, black-and-white reproductions of the paintings. It was established at trial that plaintiff Weisz had not previously entered bids at Parke-Bernet, and he had no awareness of the conditions of sale. Plaintiffs David and Irene Schwartz, however, were generally aware of the conditions of sale. Is the Parke-Bernet disclaimer legally binding on the plaintiffs? Explain. See *Weisz v. Parke-Bernet,* 325 N.Y.S.2d 576 (Civ. Ct. N.Y.C. 1971), but see *Schwartz v. Parke-Bernet,* 351 N.Y.S.2d 911 (1974).

10. After being told that Yonaty was gay or bisexual, Mincolla relayed the rumor to Koffman, longtime friend of Yonaty's girlfriend, hoping the girlfriend would learn of the rumor. The girlfriend was told; Yonaty believed that caused the termination of their romantic relationship. Yonaty, who is not gay, sued Mincolla and Koffman for slander

and intentional infliction of emotional distress. Decide the case. Explain. See *Yonaty v. Mincolla*, 97 A.D.3d 141 (N.Y. 2012).

11. A passenger ran after a train as it was leaving a station. Two railroad employees boosted the passenger aboard, but as they did so a package carried by the passenger fell beneath the wheels of the train and exploded. The package, unbeknownst to the employees, contained fireworks. The force of that explosion caused a scale many feet away to topple over, injuring the plaintiff, Palsgraf. Palsgraf sued the railroad on negligence grounds.

    a. Defend the railroad.

    b. Decide. Explain. See *Palsgraf v. Long Island R.R.,* 162 N.E. 99 (N.Y. 1928).

12. On September 8, 2009, Coomer went to the Kansas City Royals baseball game with his father. Instead of sitting in their ticketed seats, Coomer and his father sat in open seats six rows behind the third base dugout, to be closer to the game. Between the third and fourth innings, the Royals had a promotional event called the "Hotdog Launch," which it had held at home games for several years. The Royals mascot launched 20 to 30 hotdogs at the fans, either by throwing or fired through an air gun. The hotdogs shot out of the air gun were wrapped in bubble wrap and the ones thrown by hand were typically wrapped in foil. As the mascot prepared to throw hotdogs from behind his back in Coomer's direction, Coomer looked over at the scoreboard just before something hit him in the face. The impact caused a detached retina and other eye problems, leading to two surgeries. Coomer brought a personal injury lawsuit against the Kansas City Royals.

    a. How might the baseball team defend itself? Explain.

    b. Decide the case. Explain. See *Coomer v. Kansas City Royals*, 2013 Mo. App. LEXIS 46 (2013).

13. Diane Elsroth was visiting her boyfriend, Michael Notarnicola, in the home of his parents. Diane complained of a headache, and Michael provided a Tylenol that his mother had bought earlier that week. Michael noted nothing unusual about the Tylenol packaging. After consuming two Tylenol capsules, Diane went to bed. She died during the night. The medical examiner concluded that the Tylenol had been contaminated with potassium cyanide. The murder was not solved. The evidence established that the tampering with the Tylenol occurred after the product left the manufacturer's control. The packaging included a foil seal glued to the mouth of the container, a "shrink seal" around the neck and cap of the container, and a box with its ends glued shut. The manufacturer, McNeil, a wholly owned subsidiary of Johnson & Johnson, knew through its research that a determined, sophisticated tamperer could breach the packaging and reseal it in a manner that would not be visible to the average consumer. John Elsroth sued McNeil on behalf of Diane's estate. Was the Tylenol packaging defective in design? Explain. See *Elsroth v. Johnson & Johnson,* 700 F. Supp. 151 (S.D.N.Y. 1988).

14. Jennifer Strange, a 28-year-old mother of three living in Sacramento, California, entered a 2007 KDND-FM radio contest to drink as much water as possible without urinating. The prize was a Nintendo Wii game console. She drank nearly 2 gallons in three hours. She commented on her pain to the disc jockeys (DJs); one DJ commented she looked like she was pregnant. Listeners called in to warn of the dangers of water

intoxication. The DJs replied, "We are aware of that," and later said the contestants had signed a release so "we're not responsible." During the show, the DJs jokingly discussed the risks. "Maybe we should have researched this before," one DJ added.[43] Apparently, these warnings were not shared with the contestants.[44] Strange finished second in the contest, called in sick to work, and died a few hours later. The Strange family sued the radio station's owners and its parent company for wrongful death.[45] Did the radio station cause Strange's death? Explain.

15. Joseph Birdsong and Bruce Waggoner both purchased iPods manufactured by Apple, Inc. Their iPods came equipped with detachable earbuds. Birdsong and Waggoner sued Apple for, among other claims, breach of implied warranty of merchantability, alleging the iPod is defective because of an unreasonable risk of hearing loss created by the supplied earbuds, which are designed to be placed in consumers' ears. Birdsong and Waggoner did not allege they or other consumers had suffered hearing loss. Apple includes a warning with each iPod regarding the risk of permanent hearing loss. Decide. Explain. See *Birdsong v. Apple, Inc.* 590 F.3d 955 (9th Cir. 2009).

16. On July 5, 2005, Dr. Smriti Nalwa took her nine-year-old son and six-year-old daughter to Great America amusement park in California where they went on the park's Rue le Dodge bumper car ride. The ride consisted of small, two-seat, electrically powered vehicles that moved around a flat surface. Each car was ringed with a rubber bumper and had a padded interior and seatbelts for both driver and passenger. The driver of each car controlled its steering and acceleration. Nalwa rode as a passenger in a bumper car her son drove, while her daughter drove a car by herself. The bumper car in which Nalwa was riding was bumped from the front and then from behind. Feeling a need to brace herself, the plaintiff put her hand on the car's "dashboard." According to her son, "something like cracked" before his mother cried out; her wrist was fractured. The Rue le Dodge ride was inspected annually for safety by state safety regulators, and was inspected daily by the park's maintenance and ride operations staff. On the morning of Nalwa's injury, the ride was found to be working normally. Although other injuries had been reported in 2004 and 2005, Nalwa's was the only fracture reported. Nalwa brought a personal injury lawsuit against the owner/operator of the park.
    a. What defense might be raised in this case? Explain.
    b. Should that defense be successful? Explain. See *Nalwa v. Cedar Fair*, 55 Cal. 4th 1148.

Notes

1. Justin Jouvenal, "In Defamation Lawsuit over Yelp Reviews, Neither Side Wins Damages," *The Washington Post*, January 31, 2014 [**www.washingtonpost.com**].

2. *Hart v. Electronic Arts*, 717 F.3d 141 (3rd Cir. 2013).

3. Steve Berkowitz, "EA Drops Football in '14, Settles Cases as NCAA Fights," *USA TODAY*, September 26, 2013 [**www.usatoday.com**].

4. "The Tort Bar Burns On," *The Wall Street Journal*, July 23, 2012, p. A12.

5. Clifford Krauss, "A Factory's Closing Focuses Attention on Tort Reform," *The New York Times*, October 4, 2012 [**www.nytimes.com**].

6. "Letters to the Editor: Tort Suits Exist to Punish Bad Behavior, Help Victims," *The Wall Street Journal*, July 31, 2012, p. A12.

7. Clifford Krauss, "A Factory's Closing."

8. Ibid.

9. Ibid.

10. Ibid.; See *Green v. Blitz USA*, 2011 U.S. Dist. LEXIS 20353 (E.D.Tex. 2011).

11. Clifford Krauss, "A Factory's Closing Focuses Attention."

12. 111 N.E. 1050 (N.Y. 1916).

13. Heidi Hurd, "The Deontology of Negligence," *Boston University Law Review* 76 (April 1996), p. 249.

14. *Doss v. Town of Big Stone Gap,* 134 S.E. 563 (Va. S.Ct. 1926).

15. Aric Press, Ginny Carrol, and Steven Waldman, "Are Lawyers Burning America?" *Newsweek,* March 20, 1995, p. 30.

16. Ibid., p. 34.

17. Kevin Cane, "And Now the Rest of the Story . . . About the McDonald's Coffee Lawsuit," *45 Houston Lawyer* 24 (July/August 2007).

18. Anthony Ramirez, "Hot Coffee Justice," *National Post,* April 11, 2002, p. FP15.

19. *Pat Stalter v. Coca-Cola Bottling Company of Arkansas and Geyer Springs Food City, Inc.,* 669 S.W.2d 460 (Ark. S.Ct. 1984).

20. For another judicial examination of risk-utililty and the Restatement 3d, see *Mikolajczyk v. Ford Motor Co.,* 901 N.E.2d 329 (Ill. S.Ct. 2008).

21. Press Release, "13th Annual Wacky Warning Labels Contest Winners Selected on National Television," July 12, 2010, Foundation for Fair Civil Justice [**www.wackywarninglabel-stv.com/**].

22. "Generator Danger Warning," The Consumer Product Safety Commission January 2007 [**www.cpsc.gov/generator.html**].

23. *Whitlock v. University of Denver,* 712 P.2d 1072 (Col. Ct. App. 1985).

24. *University of Denver v. Whitlock,* 744 P.2d 54 (Col. S.Ct. 1987).

25. 27 Cal. Rptr. 697, 377 P.2d 897 (Cal. S.Ct. 1963).

26. Associated Press, "California Jury Awards Former Smoker $28 Billion," *Waterloo/Cedar Falls Courier,* October 6, 2002, p. A10.

27. Associated Press, "Huge Awards Aside, Few Companies Forced to Write Big Checks," *Waterloo/Cedar Falls Courier,* October 12, 1997, p. C5.

28. Dionne Searcey, "Toyota Owners May Reap Little," *The Wall Street Journal,* May 20, 2010, p. B1.

29. Ibid.

30. Towers Watson, "2011 Update on U.S. Tort Cost Trends," [**www.towerswatson.com/en-US/Insights/IC-Types/Survey-Research-Results/2012/01/2011-Update-on-US-Tort-Cost-Trends**].

31. Ibid.

32. Mark Robinson and Kevin Calcagnie, "Why We Need Trial Lawyers," *The Wall Street Journal,* February 24, 2010, p. A17.

33. Ibid.

34. Ibid.

35. Dan Zegart, "Tort Reform Advocates Play Fast and Loose with Facts," *The Seattle Post-Intelligencer,* November 21, 2004, p. F1.

36. Lou Dobbs, "Tort Reform Important to U.S. Future," CNN, January 6, 2005 [**http://articles.cnn.com/**].

37. Public Citizen, "Department of Justice Study Disproves Tort 'Reform' Myths," [**www.citizen.org**].

38. Zegart, "Tort Reform Advocates Play Fast and Loose with Facts," p. F1.

39. Tina Moore and Benjamin Lesser, "How City Is Poisoning Kids," *New York Daily News,* January 14, 2007, p. 5.

40. Jeremy Singer-Vine and Joseph Pereira, "Court Scraps Key Lead-Paint Verdict," *The Wall Street Journal,* July 2, 2008, p. B1.

41. *Sherwin-Williams v. Gaines,* 75 So.2s 41 (Miss. 2011).

42. *Banks v. Sherwin-Williams,* 2014 Miss. LEXIS 29 (Miss. 2014).

43. "Too Much of Water Hast Thou," *Harper's Magazine*, May 2007 [**http://harpers.org/ archive/2007/05/too-much-of-water-hast-thou/**].

44. Bruce Maiman, "Who to Blame in a Sacramento Mom's Death from Wii Water-Drinking Contest," *The Examiner.com*, November 1, 2009 [**www.examiner.com/article/who-to-blame-a-sacramento-mom-s-death-from-wii-water-drinking-contest**].

45. Martha Neil, "Jury Says Radio Station Must Pay $16.6 Million In Woman's Water Intoxication Death," *ABA Journal*, October 30, 2009 [**www.abajournal.com/mobile/article/jury_says_ radio_station_must_pay_16.6m_in_womans_water_intoxication_death**].

Trade Regulation and Antitrust

CHAPTER EIGHT

Government Regulation of Business

After completing this chapter, students will be able to:

1. Describe the concept of market failure.

2. Explain some of the considerations involved in deciding to impose government regulations on business practice.

3. Explain the roles of the police power, the Supremacy Clause, the preemption doctrine, and the Commerce Clause in regulating business practice.

4. Explain when the federal government has exceeded its authority in regulating commerce.

5. Describe some of the ways in which state and local regulation affects business practice.

6. List some of the federal agencies that regulate business practice.

7. Identify the three broad categories of federal regulatory agencies' authority.

8. Compare and contrast the federal agencies' executive, legislative, and judicial roles.

9. Describe the executive, congressional, and judicial controls placed on agency conduct to maintain appropriate "checks and balances."

10. Analyze the Federal Communications Commission (FCC) role in regulating indecency in broadcasting.

11. Evaluate criticisms of the federal regulatory process.

Part One—An Introduction

PRACTICING ETHICS   Regulate Video Games?

Americans were shocked and searching for answers when Adam Lanza, 20, shot and killed 20 children, six Sandy Hook Elementary School staff members, his mother, and himself in Newtown, Connecticut on December 14, 2012. One of the initial areas of concern was the video game industry. Lanza reportedly was "enthralled" by violent video games, including one called *School Shooting*, although the state's official investigation of the shooting was unable to establish a motive for his behavior.[1]

Even though video games are subject to an industry-wide rating system, a number of states have also legislated restrictions on minors' access to violent video games. California, for example, approved a 2005 law forbidding the sale or rental of violent video games to minors.[2] The video game industry sued to block the law; that challenge reached the U.S. Supreme Court in 2011 where the California law was struck down as a violation of free speech rights.[3] The Court ruled that the statute was a content-based restraint on speech requiring California to establish a compelling reason for the law; a standard the state could not satisfy. Studies linking violent video games and harm to children have not established a clear causal relationship between the two. The majority further reasoned that video games are like books, plays and other forms of protected expression. Video games, they said, communicate ideas and even social messages. While the state has the power to protect children, that power does not extend to restricting the ideas children can receive. Some justices pointed specifically to the vagueness of the law that left uncertainty about which games would have been restricted by the law.[4]

Video Game Addiction?
Notwithstanding the Supreme Court's conclusion that California was unable to show a sufficient link between violent video games and damage to children, some of the evidence about video game use generally is disquieting. For example, a 2009 Iowa State University study found that almost one in ten American children, ages 8 to 18 are addicted to video games (the study was not limited to

games) in much the way some people are addicted to drugs or gambling.[5] And a 2013 Iowa State University study of 227 juvenile offenders in Pennsylvania found a strong association between violent video game use and juvenile violence and delinquency, even when controlling for a history of violence and for psychopathic traits among those studied.[6] [For the Entertainment Software Rating Board, see **www.esrb.org/index-js.jsp**]

Questions

1. In your judgment, are violent and sexually explicit videos harmful to children?

2. Ethics expert Chris MacDonald said that the video game industry should not be proud of selling "gory games" to kids. He has argued that video games are "fertile terrain for industry self-regulation. . . ." "Such a move toward social responsibility might go some distance toward proving that the video game industry is worthy of the constitutional protections it enjoys." See Chris McDonald, "In Praise of Self-Regulation," *Canadian Business*, July 14, 2011 [**www.canadianbusiness.com/**].

   a. In your judgment, has the video game industry breached its social responsibility to American consumers? Explain.

   b. Would an ethical, socially responsible video store owner decline to sell violent or sexually explicit videos if evidence revealed that those videos often reach children? Explain.

3. a. Will the free market and industry ethics satisfactorily protect society from any harm that may emerge from video game playing or is legal intervention necessary? Explain.

   b. Should the First Amendment protect video games from government oversight? Explain.

4. a. Do we need to protect children from video games, whether violent or not? Explain.

   b. If so, would government intervention be the most effective way of offering that protection? Explain.

5. Daniel Akst asks, "Part of the fun of video games is the chance to inhabit an exciting fictional world. So do people who play these games feel free to behave immorally toward the characters on screen?" Answer Akst's question. See Daniel Akst, "In Playing Video Games, Morality Rules," *The Wall Street Journal*, October 9, 2012 [**http://blogs.wsj.com/**].

How Much Government?

In this chapter and all those that follow our central question will be: How much government do we need? In the first three chapters we looked at the role of the free market and ethics as "regulators" of business behavior. In Chapters 4 through 7 we introduced the foundations of the American legal system. Now we turn to the role the law plays in supplementing the market and ethics/self-regulation. The alleged link between video game use and social problems, including violence, is one relatively small example of an enormous array of disputes about the optimal balance between unconstrained business practice and government intervention in the market. America's ongoing financial struggles, health care reform, the near-death of giants such as General Motors, the Gulf Oil spill, accommodating immigration, climate change—these are several of the most visible areas of public policy concern. Do we need more rules to address these problems or does the market in combination with corporate ethics/social responsibility provide the most efficient, effective response? How do we decide when a new rule is needed?

Why Regulation?

Market Failure

In theory, government intervention in a free enterprise economy would be justified only when the market is unable to serve the public interest—that is, in instances of market failure. Market failure is attributed to certain inherent imperfections in the market itself.

Imperfect Information

Can the consumer choose the best pain reliever in the absence of complete information about the characteristics of the competing products? An efficient free market presumes reasoned decisions about production and consumption. Reasoned decisions require adequate information. Because we cannot have perfect information and often will not have adequate information, the government, it is argued, may impose regulations either to improve the available information or to diminish the unfavorable effect of inadequate information. Hence, we have, for example, labeling mandates for consumer goods, licensure requirements for many occupations, and health standards for the processing and sale of goods.

The 2001 Nobel Prize for economics was awarded to three Americans whose research indicates that markets cannot behave as theorized—that is, rationally and efficiently—in part because buyers and sellers often do not have the information they need to make the best decisions. Put another way, their research demonstrates that we often face situations of *asymmetric information* where some parties to a transaction simply know more than the other parties to that transaction, with the result that optimal efficiency cannot be achieved. Furthermore, recent research in behavioral economics suggests that we often pursue social goals and act in other altruistic ways that are contrary to our direct, personal economic interests. More alarmingly, a new line of research suggests that decision making among male financial traders is significantly influenced by testosterone levels, thus supporting the revisionist view that financial decisions may prove to be less a product of rational calculus than we have long believed.[7] Thus, while our free market system assumes rational decision making, we might more accurately recognize that we operate with limited or *bounded rationality*. Hence, government intervention might be appropriate.

Monopoly

Of course, the government intervenes to thwart anticompetitive behaviors throughout the marketplace. (That process is addressed in Chapters 10 and 11.) Historically, the primary concern in this area was how to deal with the so-called *natural monopoly* where a single large firm, such as a utility, was more efficient (a natural monopoly) than several small ones. Today, attention in the monopoly area is largely directed to anticompetitive conduct such as price fixing and abuse of market dominance that results in a reduction of open, efficient competition.

Externalities

When all the costs and benefits of a good or service are not fully internalized or absorbed by producers or consumers, those costs or benefits fall elsewhere as what economists have labeled *externalities, neighborhood effects, or spillovers*. Pollution is a characteristic example of a *negative externality*. The environment is used without charge as an ingredient in the production process (commonly as a receptacle for waste). Consequently, the product is underpriced. The producer and consumer do not pay the full social cost of the product, so those remaining costs are thrust on parties external to the transaction. Government regulation is sometimes considered necessary to place the full cost on those who generated it, which in turn is expected to result in less wasteful use of resources. *Positive externalities* are those in which a decision maker does not receive the full benefit of a decision because a portion of those benefits "spill over" on to third parties (often society at large) who were not direct participants in the decision. An example of such a positive externality is a business firm that landscapes its grounds and develops a sculpture garden that benefits the firm but also benefits the neighborhood. Positive externalities ordinarily are not the subject of regulation. [See the work of Nobel Prize-winning economist Ronald Coase for the view that, under certain conditions, solutions for negative externalities and other market failures could be more efficiently and effectively resolved through private negotiations than through government intervention.]

Public Goods

Some goods and services cannot be provided through the pricing system because we have no method for excluding those who choose not to pay. For such public goods, the added cost of benefiting one person is zero or nearly so, and, in any case, no one can effectively be denied the benefits of the activity. National defense, insect eradication, street lighting, and pollution control are examples of this phenomenon. Presumably most individuals would refuse to voluntarily pay for what others would receive free. Thus, in the absence of government regulations, public goods would not be produced in adequate quantities.

Regulatory Life Cycle?

These market failures and other forces, to be explained later, sometimes lead to government intervention such as the Clean Air Act (see Chapter 17) or the Occupational Safety and Health Act (see Chapter 12). Looking at the historical record, law school dean Joseph Tomain argued that a rather predictable pattern or life cycle typically emerges when the government decides to regulate an industry. Stage One in Tomain's life cycle is the free market itself, the period when government regulation is absent from the market in question. In Stage Two, a market failure is identified, suggesting the need for government intervention. In Stage Three, government regulation is imposed in the form of a rule (such as a minimum drinking age). In Stage Four, regulatory failure occurs because, in brief, we believe the benefits of the rule in question no longer exceed its costs. In Stage Five, the government may respond with regulatory reform to correct the failure, or it may move to Stage Six, where the regulation in question is simply eliminated. The market, thus fully deregulated, has returned to Stage One (the free market) and the regulatory life cycle is complete.[8]

Wall Street's financial collapse and our ongoing recession seem to support Tomain's regulatory cycle hypothesis. Ben Bernanke, former Federal Reserve chair, attributed our recent housing bubble and the subsequent financial collapse to regulatory failure.[9] Rather than deregulation as a solution, however, Bernanke called for (and, generally, received) greater financial oversight authority for the Federal Reserve; that is, he called for greater supervision by the government as the best way to prevent a future financial calamity. Of course, Bernanke's many critics believe excessive government intervention was the root cause of the housing collapse and that reduced, rather than increased, regulation is the better remediation. [To read about and submit comments on proposed rules affecting small businesses, see **www.sba.gov/advo/laws/law_regalerts.html**]

Steroids

The steroid scandal in baseball allegedly involving Roger Clemens, Barry Bonds, Jason Giambi, and other major league stars led the *The Des Moines Register* to argue for the value of regulation:

> Businesses forever complain about being regulated, but the truth is that reasonable regulation is good for business. It's easier to sell insurance to people who know regulators are helping keep the insurance companies solvent. It's easier to sell stocks to investors who think the SEC is on the job and easier to sell food to shoppers who trust the labels the FDA requires. Name an industry, and a case can be made that regulation helps it.
>
> Unfortunately, the barons of baseball never figured that out. The owners and players in big-league baseball resisted any regulation of performance-enhancing chemicals in their business.
>
> *   *   *   *   *
>
> Baseball had slipped in the affections of many Americans even before the scandal. Now, it's doubtful the sport can ever reclaim its good name.

Question

In your view, should the government regulate performance-enhancing drug use in sports, or will self-regulation by the sports be sufficient?

Source: "Baseball Barons Betrayed Game," *The Des Moines Register,* December 14, 2004, p. 8A.

Philosophy and Politics

Correction of market failure arguably explains the full range of government regulation of business, but an alternative or perhaps supplemental explanation lies in the political process. Three general arguments have emerged.

1. One view is that regulation is necessary for the protection and general welfare of the public. We find the government engaging in regulatory efforts designed to achieve a more equitable distribution of income and wealth (such as Social Security and the minimum wage). Many believe government intervention in the market is necessary to stabilize the economy, thus curbing the problems of recession, inflation, and unemployment. Affirmative action programs seek to compensate for racism and sexism. We even find the government protecting us from ourselves, both for our benefit and for the well-being of the larger society (consider seat belt requirements).

2. Another view is that regulation is developed at the request of industry and is operated primarily for the benefit of industry. Here the various subsidies and tax advantages afforded to business might be cited. In numerous instances, government regulation has been effective in reducing or entirely eliminating the entry of competitors. Government regulation has also permitted legalized price-fixing in some industries. Of course, it may be that regulation is often initiated primarily for the public welfare, but industry eventually "captures" the regulatory process and ensures its continuation for the benefit of the industry. On the other hand, some corporations seek government standards so they can do what is best for society without being undercut by their less socially responsible competitors.

3. Finally, bureaucrats who perform government regulation are themselves a powerful force in maintaining and expanding that regulation.

Bring Back Danger?

We often count on government rules to shelter us from dangers with which the market seems ill-suited to deal. Hence, we created the federal Food and Drug Administration (FDA) to protect us from dangerous food, drugs, and medical devices (see Chapter 15). But sometimes rules do harm. Indeed, safety may not always be in our best interest. Some critics argue that boys, in particular, need a certain amount of danger in their lives. Brothers Conn and Hal Iggulden wrote *The Dangerous Book for Boys* as a manual of activities for boys. Their book describes how to make a bow and arrow, hunt and cook a rabbit, build a tree house, set a trip wire, and so on. They believe our "safety culture" has gone a bit too far. They point to that bygone era when every boy had a jackknife. They believe that taking risks is important to a boy's joy and maturation.

Questions

1. Do you agree with the Iggulden brothers that we should allow boys to experience a certain amount of danger in their lives?

2. How about girls? [See Andrea Buchanan and Miriam Peskowitz, *The Daring Book for Girls*. For an online discussion about giving children greater freedom, see **http:// freerangekids.workpress.com**]

The Constitutional Foundation of Business Regulation

The Commerce Clause of the U.S. Constitution broadly specifies the power accorded to the federal government to regulate business activity. Article I, Section 8 of the Constitution provides that: "The Congress shall have the power . . . to regulate Commerce with foreign Nations, and among the several States, and with the Indian Tribes." State authority to regulate commerce resides in the *police power* specified by the Constitution. Police power refers to the right of the state governments to promote the public health, safety, morals, and general welfare by regulating persons and property within each state's jurisdiction. The states have, in turn, delegated portions of the police power to local government units.

Commerce Clause Examined

The Commerce Clause, as interpreted by the judiciary, affords Congress exclusive jurisdiction over foreign commerce. States and localities, nevertheless, sometimes seek in various ways to regulate foreign commerce. For example, a state may seek, directly or indirectly, to impose a tax on foreign goods that compete with those locally grown or manufactured. Such efforts are unconstitutional violations of the Commerce Clause and thus are unenforceable.

Federal authority over "commerce among the several states," that is, *interstate commerce,* affords the federal government very broad power to regulate commercial activities across the United States and was designed to create an open, effectively borderless market throughout the nation, wherein goods would move freely among the states, unimpeded by state and local tariffs and duties. The Constitution does not, however, expressly forbid state regulation of interstate commerce. As with foreign commerce, the states and localities pass laws to influence interstate commerce, often to favor local economic interests. The judiciary has aggressively curbed those efforts, and in the process, the reach of the federal government has been dramatically expanded. Even purely *intrastate* activities can be regulated by the federal government if they have a substantial effect on interstate commerce. In the 1942 case *Wickard v. Filburn,*[10] the U.S. Supreme Court, in interpreting a federal statute regulating the production and sale of wheat, found that one farmer's production of 23 acres of homegrown and largely home-consumed wheat, in combination with other similarly situated farmers growing and consuming wheat locally, could substantially affect the interstate wheat market by reducing demand for that wheat among those such as Wickard, who grew it locally. Thus, a local product could be subject to federal regulation. In 2005, the Supreme Court affirmed the *Wickard* reasoning in an interesting California case, *Gonzalez v. Raich,*[11] involving the federal government's constitutional authority to regulate the use of medical marijuana.

In 1996, California decriminalized the doctor-approved medical use of marijuana. The federal Controlled Substances Act (CSA), on the other hand, forbids the use, cultivation, or possession of marijuana for any purpose. A Californian, Angel Raich, who, under a doctor's prescription, used marijuana for pain control, challenged the application of the CSA against California medical marijuana users. The heart of her claim was

> Angel Raich used marijuana for pain control.

that the Commerce Clause does not give the federal government the authority to regulate the noncommercial cultivation and personal, medical use of marijuana that does not cross state lines. She won at the U.S. Court of Appeals for the Ninth Circuit, but the U.S. Supreme Court, by a 6–3 vote, ruled against Raich. Addressing the central question, the Court reasoned that the wholly *intrastate* use of marijuana had a substantial effect on *interstate* commerce in marijuana and thus was subject to federal regulation, as the Court had ruled decades earlier in *Wickard.* Personal consumption of marijuana, even for medical purposes, has the potential to displace demand for marijuana in the illegal interstate market, thus substantially affecting interstate commerce.

Nearly half of the states have reduced their restraints on marijuana use, and in two states, Washington and Colorado, voters have "legalized" adult, recreational consumption of the drug. The result is a conflicting patchwork of laws and enforcement practices that includes a recent federal government decision to shut down hundreds of California medical marijuana dispensaries believed not to be restricting their operations to lawful medical marijuana sales. At this writing, the federal Justice Department has announced that it will not sue to challenge the Colorado and Washington marijuana laws, but it still expects the states to impose careful regulations restricting sales to minors, among other considerations.

Too Much Federal Power?

Dissenting in *Raich,* Supreme Court Justice Thomas warned:

> If Congress can regulate this under the Commerce Clause, then it can regulate virtually anything—and the federal government is no longer one of limited and enumerated powers.[12]

Perhaps seeking to demonstrate that the Constitution does not accord unlimited power to the federal government, the Supreme Court in recent years has issued two particularly noteworthy Commerce Clause decisions. In the 1995 *United States v. Lopez* case,[13] the Supreme Court clearly spoke for states' rights. In 1990 the federal government approved the Gun-Free School Zones Act, which forbade "any individual knowingly to possess a firearm at a place that [he] knows . . . is a school zone."[14] Congress claimed that gun possession in school zones would increase violence, retard learning, and discourage travel, thus affecting commerce. Lopez, a 12th-grade San Antonio, Texas, student carried an unloaded, concealed gun into his high school and was charged with violating the act. His case reached the Supreme Court, where he claimed and the Court agreed that Congress did not have the constitutional authority to regulate the matter. By a 5–4 vote, the Court held that the possession of a gun at a school is not an economic activity that could, even if repeated elsewhere, have a substantial effect on interstate commerce.

> A 12th-grade San Antonio, Texas, student carried an unloaded, concealed gun into his high school.

Strengthening its *Lopez* reasoning, the U.S. Supreme Court in the 2000 *Brzonkala* case[15] ruled by a 5–4 vote that Congress exceeded its Commerce Clause authority in approving some portions of the federal Violence Against Women Act (VAWA). The law allowed women who had been victims of gender-based violence to sue in federal court even though the crimes did not directly involve more than one state. In debating VAWA,

Congress held hearings and developed a record on the aggregate economic impact of violence against women, including driving up medical costs and discouraging women from traveling and from holding jobs, but the Supreme Court said Congress did not have the power to regulate noneconomic violent crime because it does not have a substantial effect on interstate commerce. To rule otherwise, the Court said, might "obliterate" the constitutional distinction between federal and state/local authority.

The case involved a woman, Brzonkala, who claimed she was raped by two football players, Morrison and Crawford, when all three were students at Virginia Polytechnic Institute:

> Brzonkala alleges that soon after she met Morrison and Crawford, the two defendants pinned her down on a bed in her dormitory and forcibly raped her. Afterward, Morrison told Brzonkala, "You better not have any f* *ing diseases." And, subsequently, Morrison announced publicly in the dormitory's dining hall, "I like to get girls drunk and f* * * the s* * * out of them."[16]

> **Brzonkala claimed she was raped by two football players.**

After Brzonkala complained to the university, Morrison was found guilty of abusive conduct by the VPI judicial committee and was suspended for one year, but that punishment was subsequently lifted. Brzonkala then sued for civil damages in federal court under the VAWA. As explained above, Brzonkala eventually lost, however, when the Supreme Court invalidated the portions of the VAWA that she was relying on by ruling that the acts of violence the VAWA was aimed at did not have a substantial effect on interstate commerce. [For the federal Violence Against Women Office and for discussion of the 2013 congressional reauthorization and strengthening of VAWA, see **www.ovw.usdoj.gov/**]

Obamacare

In June 2012, the U.S. Supreme Court, by a 5–4 vote, upheld the constitutionality of the Affordable Care Act (Obamacare), but the decision raised further doubts about the federal government's Commerce Clause power.[17] The core of the Supreme Court review involved what is called the "individual mandate:" a requirement in the bill forcing most Americans to maintain "minimum essential" health insurance. The mandate was challenged on the grounds that it violated the Commerce Clause by attempting to regulate *in* activity (commanding action from those who are not buying health insurance) rather than regulating already existing interstate activity. The Court, by a 5–4 margin, ruled that the individual mandate was, indeed, a violation of the Commerce Clause. The Court reasoned that construing the Commerce Clause to allow Congress to regulate in-activity would open up potentially expansive new territory to congressional intervention. Nonetheless, the case turned out to be a victory for Obamacare. The Court, once again by a 5–4 margin, ultimately upheld the constitutionality of the individual mandate on the grounds that it constituted a *tax* on those who do not have health insurance. In as much as Congress clearly has the constitutional authority to "lay and collect Taxes" (Article I, Section 8, Clause 1—See the Constitution in Appendix A at the back of this text), the Court ruled that Obamacare's individual mandate is constitutionally permissible.

Our Guns: Feds Must Stay Out?

Gary Marbut of Missoula, Montana, hopes to manufacture .22-caliber rifles he calls Montana Buckaroos. He wants to produce and sell the guns exclusively in Montana from materials originating in Montana." He has also drafted and promoted the Montana Firearms Freedom Act, which has been adopted in Montana and which provides, generally, that Montana guns cannot be subject to federal regulation if made and sold only on an intrastate basis. Other states have approved similar legislation. Marbut (and others) recently brought suit seeking a court order affirming the right in Montana to manufacture and sell guns free of federal regulation. Marbut lost at the federal district court and the Ninth Circuit Court of Appeals, but he hopes to reach the Supreme Court to challenge *Wickard v. Filburn* and federal regulatory authority.

Sources: Tim Murphy, "Gun Enthusiasts' Hot New Idea: You Can't Regulate Guns We Make In-State," *Mother Jones,* February 1, 2013 [**www.motherjones.com/**]; and *Montana Shooting Sports Association v. Holder,* 2013 U.S. App. LEXIS 17662 (9th Cir.).

The classic decision that follows illustrates the importance of Commerce Clause reasoning. In this case Congress used its economic authority under the Commerce Clause to open public accommodations (hotels, restaurants, and the like) to all persons, thus reshaping American social and racial practices.

LEGAL BRIEFCASE

Heart of Atlanta Motel v. United States, 379 U.S. 241 (1964)

Justice Clark

This is a declaratory judgment action, attacking the constitutionality of Title II of the Civil Rights Act of 1964. [The lower court found for the United States.]

1. THE FACTUAL BACKGROUND AND CONTENTIONS OF THE PARTIES

. . . Appellant owns and operates the Heart of Atlanta Motel, which has 216 rooms available to transient guests. The motel is located on Courtland Street, two blocks from downtown Peachtree Street. It is readily accessible to interstate highways 75 and 85 and state highways 23 and 41. Appellant solicits patronage from outside the State of Georgia through various national advertising media, including magazines of national circulation; it maintains over 50 billboards and

highway signs within the state, soliciting patronage for the motel; it accepts convention trade from outside Georgia, and approximately 75 percent of its registered guests are from out of state. Prior to passage of the act the motel had followed a practice of refusing to rent rooms to Negroes, and it alleged that it intended to continue to do so. In an effort to perpetuate that policy this suit was filed.

The appellant contends that Congress in passing this act exceeded its power to regulate commerce under [Article I] of the Constitution of the United States. . . .

The appellees counter that the unavailability to Negroes of adequate accommodations interferes significantly with interstate travel, and that Congress, under the Commerce Clause, has power to remove such obstructions and restraints. . . .

[A]ppellees proved the refusal of the motel to accept Negro transients after the passage of the act. The district court sustained the constitutionality of the sections of the act under attack and issued a permanent injunction. . . . It restrained the appellant from "[r]efusing to accept Negroes as guests in the motel by reason of their race or color" and from "[m]aking any distinction whatever upon the basis of race or color in the availability of the goods, services, facilities, privileges, advantages, or accommodations offered or made available to the guests of the motel, or to the general public, within or upon any of the premises of the Heart of Atlanta Motel, Inc."

2. THE HISTORY OF THE ACT

. . . The act as finally adopted was most comprehensive, undertaking to prevent through peaceful and voluntary settlement discrimination in voting, as well as in places of accommodation and public facilities, federally secured programs, and in employment. Since Title II is the only portion under attack here, we confine our consideration to those public accommodation provisions.

3. TITLE II OF THE ACT

This Title is divided into seven sections beginning with Section 201(a), which provides,

> All persons shall be entitled to the full and equal enjoyment of the goods, services, facilities, privileges, advantages, and accommodations of any place of public accommodation, as defined in this section, without discrimination or segregation on the ground of race, color, religion, or national origin.

4. APPLICATION OF TITLE II TO HEART OF ATLANTA MOTEL

It is admitted that the operation of the motel brings it within the provisions of Section 201(a) of the act and that appellant refused to provide lodging for transient Negroes because of their race or color and that it intends to continue that policy unless restrained.

The sole question posed is, therefore, the constitutionality of the Civil Rights Act of 1964 as applied to these facts. . . .

[Part 5 omitted.]

6. THE BASIS OF CONGRESSIONAL ACTION

While the act as adopted carried no congressional findings, the record of its passage through each house is replete with evidence of the burdens that discrimination by race or color places upon interstate commerce. . . . This testimony included the fact that our people have become increasingly mobile with millions of people of all races traveling from state to state; that Negroes in particular have been the subject of discrimination in transient accommodations, having to travel great distances to secure the same; that often they have been unable to obtain accommodations and have had to call upon friends to put

them up overnight; and that these conditions have become so acute as to require the listing of available lodging for Negroes in a special guidebook which was itself "dramatic testimony to the difficulties" Negroes encounter in travel. These exclusionary practices were found to be nationwide, the Under Secretary of Commerce testifying that there is "no question that this discrimination in the North still exists to a large degree" and in the West and Midwest as well. This testimony indicated a qualitative as well as quantitative effect on interstate travel by Negroes. The former was the obvious impairment of the Negro traveler's pleasure and convenience that resulted when he continually was uncertain of finding lodging. As for the latter, there was evidence that this uncertainty stemming from racial discrimination had the effect of discouraging travel on the part of a substantial portion of the Negro community. This was the conclusion not only of the Under Secretary of Commerce but also of the Administrator of the Federal Aviation Agency, who wrote the Chairman of the Senate Commerce Committee that it was his "belief that air commerce is adversely affected by the denial to a substantial segment of the traveling public of adequate and desegregated public accommodations." We shall not burden this opinion with further details since the voluminous testimony presents overwhelming evidence that discrimination by hotels and motels impedes interstate travel.

7. THE POWER OF CONGRESS OVER INTERSTATE TRAVEL

The power of Congress to deal with these obstructions depends on the meaning of the Commerce Clause.

* * * * *

In short, the determinative test of the exercise of power by the Congress under the Commerce Clause is simply whether the activity sought to be regulated is "commerce which concerns more States than one" and has a real and substantial relation to the national interest. Let us now turn to this facet of the problem.

* * * * *

The same interest in protecting interstate commerce which led Congress to deal with segregation in interstate carriers and the white-slave traffic has prompted it to extend the exercise of its power to gambling, to criminal enterprises, to deceptive practices in the sale of products, to fraudulent security transactions, and to racial discrimination by owners and managers of terminal restaurants. . . .

That Congress was legislating against moral wrongs in many of these areas rendered its enactments no less valid. In framing Title II of this act Congress was also dealing with what it considered a moral problem. But that fact does not detract from the overwhelming evidence of the disruptive effect the racial discrimination has had on commercial intercourse. It was this burden which empowered Congress to enact appropriate legislation, and, given this basis for the exercise of its power, Congress was not restricted by the fact that the particular obstruction to interstate commerce with which it was dealing was also deemed a moral and social wrong.

It is said that the operation of the motel here is of a purely local character. But, assuming this to be true, "[i]f it is interstate commerce that feels the pinch, it does not matter how local the operation which applies the squeeze."

* * * * *

Thus the power of Congress to promote interstate commerce also includes the power to regulate the local incidents thereof, including local activities in both the states of origin and destination, which might have a substantial and harmful effect upon that commerce. One need only examine the evidence which we have discussed above to see that Congress may—as it has—prohibit racial discrimination by motels serving travelers, however "local" their operations may appear.

* * * * *

The only questions are (1) whether Congress had a rational basis for finding that racial discrimination by motels affected commerce, and (2) if it had such a basis, whether the means it selected to eliminate that evil are reasonable and appropriate. If they are, appellant has no "right" to select its guests as it sees fit, free from governmental regulation.

* * * * *

It is doubtful if in the long run appellant will suffer economic loss as a result of the act. Experience is to the contrary where discrimination is completely obliterated as to all public accommodations. But whether this be true or not is of no consequence since this Court has specifically held that the fact that a "member of the class which is regulated may suffer economic losses not shared by others . . . has never been a barrier" to such legislation. . . .

We, therefore, conclude that the action of the Congress in the adoption of the act as applied here to a motel which concededly serves interstate travelers is within the power granted it by the Commerce Clause of the Constitution, as interpreted by this Court for 140 years. . . .

Affirmed.

Questions

1. In your judgment, does the Commerce Clause afford the federal government the authority to regulate a local business like the Heart of Atlanta motel? Explain.

2. Should the federal government regulate local business to further the cause of racial equity? Explain.

3. What arguments were offered by the government to establish that the Heart of Atlanta racial policy affected interstate commerce? Are you persuaded by those arguments? Explain.

4. What test did the Court articulate to determine when Congress has the power to pass legislation based on the Commerce Clause?

5. Ollie's Barbecue, a neighborhood restaurant in Birmingham, Alabama, discriminated against black customers. McClung brought suit to test the application of the public accommodations section of the Civil Rights Act of 1964 to his restaurant. In the suit, the government offered no evidence to show that the restaurant ever had served interstate customers or that it was likely to do so. Decide the case. See *Katzenbach v. McClung,* 379 U.S. 294 (1964).

6. Juan Paul Robertson was charged with various narcotics offenses and with violating the federal Racketeer Influenced and Corrupt Organizations Act (RICO) by investing the proceeds from his unlawful activities in an Alaskan gold mine. He paid for some mining equipment in Los Angeles and had it shipped to Alaska. He hired seven out-of-state employees to work in the Alaskan mine. Most of the resulting gold was sold in Alaska, although Robertson transported $30,000 in gold out of the state. He was convicted on the RICO charge, but appealed claiming that the gold mine was not engaged in or affecting interstate commerce. Was Robertson's gold mine engaged in or affecting interstate commerce? Explain. See *United States v. Juan Paul Robertson,* 115 S.Ct. 1732 (1995).

Supremacy Clause

Sometimes state or local law conflicts with federal law. As we discussed in Chapter 5, such situations are resolved by the Supremacy Clause of the Constitution (Article VI, paragraph 2), which provides that: "This Constitution and the Laws of the United States . . . shall be the Supreme Law of the Land." As explained in Chapter 5, ours is a federalist form of government wherein we divide authority among federal, state, and local units of government. Conflicts are inevitable, but each level of government brings strengths to the process. State rules benefit from being enacted by bodies very close to the people themselves. On the other hand, optimal efficiency, especially for the business community, often demands one uniform federal rule rather than a patchwork of 50 state rules.[18]

In the event of an irreconcilable conflict between federal and state law, the Supremacy Clause, as interpreted by the courts, provides that federal law will preempt (supersede) state or local law rendering it unconstitutional. In general, Supreme Court decisions have affirmed the federal government's regulatory authority even when faced with conflicting state rules. Were it not so, we would have great difficulty in achieving a unified national policy on any issue. Recent Supreme Court preemption decisions have been split, some allowing state law to stand despite conflicts with federal law, others being struck down.[19]

Regardless, the federalism doctrine has become a major source of conflict between states' rights activists and those favoring more unified, federal doctrine. Tea Party supporters and others are making the case for a renewal of attention to the Tenth Amendment command: "The powers not delegated to the United States by the Constitution, nor prohibited by it to the States, are reserved to the States, respectively, or to the people." The challengers believe the federal government often reaches beyond its constitutional authority.

> The challengers believe the federal government often reaches beyond its constitutional authority.

Nullification

A number of states have passed or are considering laws to at least partially *nullify* (render void and inoperative) federal laws they believe to be unconstitutional extensions of federal power. State laws "legalizing" recreational marijuana use are an example of attempts to at least partially nullify federal laws. Other *nullification* efforts address, for example, the federal Affordable Care Act (Obamacare), gun control laws, and federal abortion laws. Although states do have some power to resist federal laws, most constitutional law authorities and the relevant Supreme Court decisions [see, e.g., *Ableman v. Booth*, 62 U.S. 506 (1859)] hold that state governments do not have general nullification power.

Question

When confronting federal laws they believe to be unconstitutional, should states have the right to pass their own laws that would nullify those federal laws? Explain. For some advice on that question as well as a brief history of nullification, see Robert A. Levy, "The Limits of Nullification," *The New York Times*, September 3, 2013 [**www.nytimes.com/**].

Part Two—State and Local Regulation of Interstate Commerce

As noted, the states via their constitutional police power have the authority to regulate commerce within their jurisdictions for the purpose of maintaining public health, safety, and morals. We have seen, however, that the Commerce Clause accords the federal government broad authority over commerce. As explained, the federal government has exclusive authority over foreign commerce. Purely intrastate commerce, having no significant effect on interstate commerce, is within the exclusive regulatory jurisdiction of the states and localities. Of course, purely intrastate commerce is uncommon. The confusion arises in the middle ground of interstate commerce where regulation by the federal government or state governments or both may be permissible. Although federal government regulation of interstate commerce is pervasive, it is not exclusive, especially in matters involving the states' police powers.

Our concern in this section is with commerce that is clearly interstate in nature but is, nonetheless, subjected to state and/or local regulation. The issue is whether that regulation is unconstitutional because it (1) *discriminates* against interstate commerce or (2) *unduly burdens* interstate commerce such that the burden imposed clearly exceeds the local benefits.

In the *Granholm* case that follows, we see elements of the continuing conflict between federal and state control of interstate commerce, especially in matters of health and safety (police power). At the commercial level, the case is about another classic conflict: free trade versus protectionism. Can states lawfully protect their local wineries from out-of-state competition? The lower courts were divided on the question of whether the Commerce Clause of the federal constitution is violated when a state permits in-state wineries to ship directly to in-state customers while not permitting out-of-state wineries to do the same. Historically, only a few states had allowed wineries to ship directly to customers, but gradually about half of the states allowed direct shipments, resulting in a confusing situation where some states allowed all shipments, some permitted in-state shipments only, and some forbade all shipments. In the 5–4 decision that follows, the U.S. Supreme Court narrowly resolved the split in the lower courts. The central question facing the Court was the conflict between the requirements of the Commerce Clause versus the requirements of the Twenty-First Amendment to the U.S. Constitution. That amendment ended Prohibition in 1933 and gave the states broad authority to regulate the sale of alcohol.

> **Can states lawfully protect their local wineries from out-of-state competition?**

LEGAL BRIEFCASE

Granholm v. Heald
544 U.S. 460 (2005)

Justice Kennedy

These consolidated cases present challenges to state laws regulating the sale of wine from out-of-state wineries to consumers in Michigan and New York. The details and mechanics of the two regulatory schemes differ, but the object and effect of the laws are the same: to allow in-state wineries to sell wine directly to consumers in that state but to prohibit out-of-state wineries from doing so, or, at the least, to make direct sales impractical from an economic standpoint. It is evident that the object and design of the Michigan and New York statutes is to grant in-state wineries a competitive advantage over wineries located beyond the states' borders.

* * * * *

I

Like many other states, Michigan and New York regulate the sale and importation of alcoholic beverages, including wine, through a three-tier distribution system. Separate licenses are required for producers, wholesalers, and retailers. . . . We have held previously that states can mandate a three-tier distribution scheme in the exercise of their authority under the Twenty-First Amendment. As relevant to today's cases, though, the three-tier system is, in broad terms and with refinements to be discussed, mandated by Michigan and New York only for sales from out-of-state wineries. In-state wineries, by contrast, can obtain a license for direct sales to consumers. The differential treatment between in-state and out-of-state wineries constitutes explicit discrimination against interstate commerce.

This discrimination substantially limits the direct sale of wine to consumers. . . . From 1994 to 1999, consumer spending on direct wine shipments doubled, reaching $500 million per year, or 3 percent of all wine sales. . . . [T]he number of small wineries in the United States has significantly increased. At the same time, the wholesale market has consolidated. . . . The increasing winery-to-wholesaler ratio means that many small wineries do not produce enough wine or have sufficient consumer demand for their wine to make it economical for wholesalers to carry their products. This has led many small wineries to rely on direct shipping to reach new markets. Technological improvements, in particular the ability of wineries to sell wine over the Internet, have helped make direct shipments an attractive sales channel.

Approximately 26 states allow some direct shipping of wine, with various restrictions. Thirteen of these states have reciprocity laws, which allow direct shipment from wineries outside the state, provided the state of origin affords similar nondiscriminatory treatment. In many parts of the country, however, state laws that prohibit or severely restrict direct shipments deprive consumers of access to the direct market.

The wine producers in the cases before us are small wineries that rely on direct consumer sales as an important part of their businesses. Domaine Alfred, one of the plaintiffs in the Michigan suit, is a small winery located in San Luis Obispo, California. . . . Domaine Alfred has received requests for its wine from Michigan consumers but cannot fill the orders because of the state's direct shipment ban. . . .

Similarly, Juanita Swedenburg and David Lucas, two of the plaintiffs in the New York suit, operate small wineries in Virginia (the Swedenburg Estate Vineyard) and California (the Lucas Winery). Some of their customers are tourists from other states, who purchase wine while visiting the wineries. If these customers wish to obtain Swedenburg or Lucas wines after they return home, they will be unable to do so if they reside in a state with restrictive direct shipment laws. . . .

A

We first address the background of the suit challenging the Michigan direct shipment law. Most alcoholic beverages in Michigan are distributed through the state's three-tier system. Producers or distillers of alcoholic beverages, whether located in state or out of state, generally may sell only to licensed in-state wholesalers. Wholesalers, in turn, may sell only to in-state retailers. Licensed retailers are the final link in the chain, selling alcoholic beverages to consumers at retail locations and, subject to certain restrictions, through home delivery.

Under Michigan law, wine producers, as a general matter, must distribute their wine through wholesalers. There is,

however, an exception for Michigan's approximately 40 in-state wineries, which are eligible for "wine maker" licenses that allow direct shipment to in-state consumers. The cost of the license varies with the size of the winery. For a small winery, the license is $25. Out-of-state wineries can apply for a $300 "outside seller of wine" license, but this license only allows them to sell to in-state wholesalers.

*　*　*　*　*

B

New York's licensing scheme is somewhat different. It channels most wine sales through the three-tier system, but it too makes exceptions for in-state wineries. As in Michigan, the result is to allow local wineries to make direct sales to consumers in New York on terms not available to out-of-state wineries. Wineries that produce only from New York grapes can apply for a license that allows direct shipment to in-state consumers. These licensees are authorized to deliver the wines of other wineries as well, but only if the wine is made from grapes "at least seventy-five percent the volume of which were grown in New York state." An out-of-state winery may ship directly to New York consumers only if it becomes a licensed New York winery, which requires the establishment of "a branch factory, office, or storeroom within the state of New York."

*　*　*　*　*

C

We consolidated these cases and granted certiorari on the following question: "Does a state's regulatory scheme that permits in-state wineries directly to ship alcohol to consumers but restricts the ability of out-of-state wineries to do so violate the Commerce Clause in light of Section 2 of the Twenty-First Amendment?"

II

A

Time and again this Court has held that, in all but the narrowest circumstances, state laws violate the Commerce Clause if they mandate "differential treatment of in-state and out-of-state economic interests that benefits the former and burdens the latter." This rule is essential to the foundations of the Union. The mere fact of nonresidence should not foreclose a producer in one state from access to markets in other States. States may not enact laws that burden out-of-state producers or shippers simply to give a competitive advantage to in-state businesses. This mandate "reflects a central concern of the Framers that was an immediate reason for calling the Constitutional Convention: the conviction that in order to succeed, the new Union would have to avoid the tendencies toward economic Balkanization that had plagued relations among the Colonies and later among the States under the Articles of Confederation."

* * * * *

B

The discriminatory character of the Michigan system is obvious. Michigan allows in-state wineries to ship directly to consumers, subject only to a licensing requirement. Out-of-state wineries, whether licensed or not, face a complete ban on direct shipment. The differential treatment requires all out-of-state wine, but not all in-state wine, to pass through an in-state wholesaler and retailer before reaching consumers. These two extra layers of overhead increase the cost of out-of-state wines to Michigan consumers. The cost differential, and in some cases the inability to secure a wholesaler for small shipments, can effectively bar small wineries from the Michigan market.

* * * * *

The New York scheme grants in-state wineries access to the state's consumers on preferential terms. . . . In-state producers, with the applicable licenses, can ship directly to consumers from their wineries. Out-of-state wineries must open a branch office and warehouse in New York, additional steps that drive up the cost of their wine.

* * * * *

We have no difficulty concluding that New York, like Michigan, discriminates against interstate commerce through its direct shipping laws.

III

State laws that discriminate against interstate commerce face "a virtually per se rule of invalidity." The Michigan and New York laws by their own terms violate this proscription. The two states, however, contend their statutes are saved by Section 2 of the Twenty-First Amendment, which provides,

> The Transportation or importation into any State, Territory, or possession of the United States for delivery or use therein of intoxicating liquors, in violation of the laws thereof, is hereby prohibited.

* * * * *

State policies are protected under the Twenty-First Amendment when they treat liquor produced out of state the same as its domestic equivalent. The instant cases, in contrast, involve straightforward attempts to discriminate in favor of local producers. The discrimination is contrary to the Commerce Clause and is not saved by the Twenty-First Amendment.

IV

We still must consider whether either state regime "advances a legitimate local purpose that cannot be adequately served by reasonable nondiscriminatory alternatives." The states offer two primary justifications for restricting direct shipments from out-of-state wineries: keeping alcohol out of the hands of minors and facilitating tax collection.

The states claim that allowing direct shipment from out-of-state wineries undermines their ability to police underage drinking. Minors, the states argue, have easy access to credit cards and the Internet and are likely to take advantage of direct wine shipments as a means of obtaining alcohol illegally.

The states provide little evidence that the purchase of wine over the Internet by minors is a problem. Indeed, there is some evidence to the contrary. A recent study by the staff of the FTC found that the 26 states currently allowing direct shipments report no problems with minors' increased access to wine.

* * * * *

Even were we to credit the states' largely unsupported claim that direct shipping of wine increases the risk of underage drinking, this would not justify regulations limiting only out-of-state direct shipments. As the wineries point out, minors are just as likely to order wine from in-state producers as from out-of-state ones. Michigan, for example, already allows its licensed retailers (over 7,000 of them) to deliver alcohol directly to consumers. . . .

The states' tax collection justification is also insufficient.

* * * * *

Michigan and New York benefit from provisions of federal law that supply incentives for wineries to comply with state regulations. The Tax and Trade Bureau has authority to revoke a winery's federal license if it violates state law. Without a federal license, a winery cannot operate in any state. . . .

These federal remedies, when combined with state licensing regimes, adequately protect states from lost tax revenue.

* * * * *

V

If a state chooses to allow direct shipment of wine, it must do so on evenhanded terms. Without demonstrating the need for discrimination, New York and Michigan have enacted regulations that disadvantage out-of-state wine producers. Under our Commerce Clause jurisprudence, these regulations [are unconstitutional].

* * * * *

Afterword

Approximately 40 states and the District of Columbia now allow wineries to ship directly to residents, although those shipments are often limited to just a few cases or to small wineries, and the *Granholm* decision applied to wineries only so retailers, in most states, still cannot ship directly to consumers.[20] The alcohol industry continues to resist an open market preferring instead the three-tier producer, wholesaler, retailer distribution system that has been in place for decades, in part, to restrict access by minors and to encourage a broader selection of products while affirming states rights. Despite *Granholm*, a maze of state rules continues to discourage online wine sales. Only about 5 percent of U.S. retail wine sales are achieved by direct shipment to consumers.[21]

Questions

1. *a.* Why did the *Granholm* court strike down the New York and Michigan laws?

   b. What legal and practical justifications were presented by New York and Michigan in defense of their laws?

2. *a.* What choice faced the states affected by this decision?

   b. What practical effect has this decision likely had on the wine industry?

3. In 1988, Oneida and Herkimer counties in upstate New York created a Solid Waste Management Authority and enacted a "flow control ordinance" requiring that all waste generated within their borders was to be delivered to the Authority's newly created waste processing facilities. In 1995, six waste haulers and a trade association sued the Authority and the counties claiming that the flow control ordinance and associated regulations violated the Commerce Clause by discriminating against interstate commerce. The plaintiffs provided evidence that they could dispose of the waste much less expensively at out-of-state facilities. How would you rule in this case? Explain. See *United Haulers Assn., Inc. v. Oneida-Herkimer Solid Waste Management Authority,* 127 S.Ct 1786 (2007).

4. North Dakota rules required those bringing liquor into the state to file a monthly report, and out-of-state distillers selling to federal enclaves (military bases, in this instance) were required to label each item indicating that it was for consumption only within the enclave. The United States challenged those rules after sellers said they would discontinue dealing with the military bases or they would raise their prices to meet the cost of dealing with the two rules.

   a. What were the constitutional foundations of the federal government's challenge?

   b. What were the state's reasons for adopting the rules?

   c. Decide. Explain. See *North Dakota v. United States,* 495 U.S. 423 (1990).

5. Premium Standard Farms, a large Missouri hog-raising operation, was pumping manure through a two-mile-long pipe into Iowa to be spread on a farm whose operator sought the manure for fertilizer. Iowa citizens objected and asked Attorney General Tom Miller to act. Could the Iowa attorney general stop the pumping? Explain.

Summary of State and Local Regulation

The federal government receives greater attention, but state and local rules have an enormous impact on business practice. The states are primarily responsible for regulating the insurance industry and are heavily involved in regulating banking, securities, and liquor sales. Many businesses and professions—from psychology to funeral preparation to barbering to the practice of medicine—require a license from the state. Public utilities (gas, electricity, sewage disposal) are the subject of extensive regulation governing entry, rates, customer service, and virtually all of the companies' activities. All states have some form of public service commission charged with regulating utilities in the public interest. Many states seek to directly enhance competition via antitrust legislation. Many states have passed laws forbidding usury, false advertising, stock fraud, and other practices harmful to the consumer. [For the "largest Internet compilation" of state government materials, see **www.hg.org/index.html**]

Big Soda Ban

Inspired by then-mayor Michael Bloomberg, the New York City Board of Health in 2012 approved a ban on the sale of sugary drinks in containers over 16 ounces in restaurants, stadiums, theaters, and other establishments regulated by the city health department. The rule did not forbid refills. According to the city, a switch from 20- to 16-ounce drinks by New Yorkers would "save" 2.3 million pounds per year.[22] Americans drink much more soda than residents of other nations, and the U.S. bill for diabetes is about $245 billion annually.[23] Opponents see the rule as more government overreach by a "nanny state" determined to diminish personal freedom. A *New York Times* poll found about 6 in 10 New Yorkers opposed the ban.[24] Some critics even consider the ban a discriminatory and paternalistic attack on minority populations who tend to suffer most from obesity-related problems. *The New York Times* has pointed out, however, that many of the minority groups opposing the ban are the beneficiaries of tens of millions of dollars in beverage industry scholarships, conferences, and financial literacy classes.[25]

The contentious soda ban was struck down by a local state court judge in 2013, determining the rule wasn't founded in fact and was riddled with loopholes and exceptions, making it unlawfully "arbitrary and capricious." The judge also found that the board of health "trespassed" on the legislative powers of the New York City Council, thus "eviscerating" the constitutional separation of powers doctrine.[26]

Questions

1. In 2014, New York state's highest court declined to reinstate the soda ban. Would you approve of a nationwide soda ban? Explain. See Michael Grynbaum, "New York's Ban on Big Sodas is Rejected by Final Court," *The New York Times,* June 27, 2014 [**www .nytimes.com/2014/06/27/nyregion/city-loses-final-appeal-on-limiting-sales-of -large-sodas.html?_r=0**]

2. *a. New Republic* senior editor Timothy Noah: "[E]ven as liberals and conservatives profess to hate the idea of government paternalism, both practice it." Provide some examples of government restrictions on individual choices as favored by liberals and as favored by conservatives.

   b. Do you support these restraints? Explain. See Timothy Noah, "Nanny Dearest," *The New Republic*, June 8, 2012 [**www.tnr.com/article/politics/magazine/103938/ bloomberg-nanny-soda-limit**].

3. Professor David B. Agus asks: "[W]hen does regulating a person's habits in the name of good health become our moral and social duty?" Answer his question. See David B. Agus, "The 2,000-Year-Old Wonder Drug," *The New York Times*, December 11, 2012 [**www.nytimes.com/**].

Licensure   Local regulation is much less economically significant than state regulation. Local government intervention in business typically involves various licensure requirements. For example, businesses like bars and theaters are often required to obtain a local permit to operate. More broadly, more than 1,000 of America's occupations (medicine, law, building construction, electrical work, and so on) can be practiced only by those who have secured licensure from federal, state, and/or local authorities. Licensure is to protect the public from unsafe, unhealthful, and substandard goods and services, but critics contend that licensure is often designed to block the entry of competitors and that the benefits of licensure are exceeded by its costs in increased prices, decreased services, and administrative overhead.

Benedictine monks at St. Joseph Abbey outside New Orleans recently challenged a state licensure rule when they were ordered by the Louisiana State Board of Embalmers and Funeral Directors to close their business of building and selling caskets. The funeral industry cited a Louisiana regulation making it a crime for anyone other than state-licensed funeral directors to sell coffins in Louisiana. The monks sued and won when the Fifth U.S. Circuit Court of Appeals held that the funeral directors did not provide a rational basis for the challenged rule. Judge Patrick Higginbotham wrote that the rule "adds nothing to protect consumers and puts them at a greater risk of abuse including exploitative prices."[27] Other courts have upheld state regulatory policy in similar cases, but the state funeral directors' petition for review to the U.S. Supreme Court was rejected, and the monks can continue their work.

Cabs Need Rules?

New Orleans recently imposed new rules on all taxi cabs used to pick up passengers at Louis Armstrong International Airport. The rules require, among other things, credit card machines in the cabs, GPS devices, security cameras, working air conditioners, working meters, and drivers who speak English. In 2014, cabs cannot be older than seven years, regardless of condition. New Orleans has capped its "certificates of public necessity and convenience" (cab licenses) at 1,600. New Orleans also decided to treat the Certificates of Public Necessity (or CPNCs) as a "privilege" rather than as property. The average price for a CPNC in the secondary market reportedly is about $26,000. Legal challenges to the new rules have been unsuccessful, as of this writing.

Questions

1. Explain the significance of treating a CPNC as a "privilege" rather than as a property right.

2. Why do most cities closely regulate the cab industry?

 Sources: Nick Sibilla, "The Big Easy Needlessly Burdens Taxi Cab Drivers," *The Institute for Justice* [**www.ij.org**]; and *Dennis Melancom, Inc. v. City of New Orleans*, 703 F.3d 263 (5th Cir. 2012). For a brief free-market, libertarian view of taxi regulation, see the video "IJ's Jeanette Petersen Explains Three Reasons You Can't Get a Cab," at [**www.youtube.com/watch?v=Oq-hPuESJng**].

Rules and Community Welfare   Most of us would say, in the abstract, that we need less government in our lives, but when we are the victims of problems that the market is ill-suited to resolve, those rules become much more attractive. The case that follows shows how Tampa, Florida, tried to apply its rules to the age-old problem of adult entertainment businesses but with a new twist—product distribution by the Internet rather than by face-to-face commerce.

Circuit Judge Dubina

This appeal arises from Voyeur Dorm L.C.'s alleged violation of Tampa's City Code based on the district court's characterization of Voyeur Dorm as an adult entertainment facility.

BACKGROUND

Voyeur Dorm operates an Internet-based Web site that provides a 24-hour-a-day Internet transmission portraying the lives of the residents of 2312 West Farwell Drive, Tampa, Florida. Throughout its existence, Voyeur Dorm has employed 25 to 30 different women, most of whom entered into a contract that specifies, among other things, that they are "employees," on a "stage and filming location," with "no reasonable expectation of privacy," for "entertainment purposes." Subscribers to "voyeurdorm.com" pay a subscription fee of $34.95 a month to watch the women employed at the premises and pay an added fee of $16.00 per month to "chat" with the women. From August 1998 to June 2000, Voyeur Dorm generated subscriptions and sales totaling $3,166,551.35.

In 1998 Voyeur Dorm learned that local law enforcement agencies had initiated an investigation into its business. In response, counsel for Voyeur Dorm sent a letter to Tampa's zoning coordinator requesting her interpretation of the city code as it applied to the activities occurring at 2312 West Farwell Drive. In February of 1999, Tampa's zoning coordinator, Gloria Moreda, replied to counsel's request and issued her interpretation of the city code:

* * * * *

It is my determination that the use occurring at 2312 W. Farwell Dr., is an adult use. Section 27-523 defines adult entertainment as "Any premises, except those businesses otherwise defined in this chapter, on which is offered to members of the public or any person, for a consideration, entertainment featuring or in any way including specified sexual activities, as defined in this section, or entertainment featuring the displaying or depicting of specified anatomical areas, as defined in this section; 'entertainment' as used in this definition shall include, but not be limited to, books, magazines, films, newspapers, photographs, paintings, drawings, sketches or other publications or graphic media, filmed or live plays, dances or other performances distinguished by their display or depiction of specified anatomical areas or specified anatomical activities, as defined in this section."

Please be aware that the property is zoned RS-60 Residential Single Family, and an adult use business is not permitted use. You should advise your client to cease operation at that location.

Thereafter, in April of 1999, Dan and Sharon Gold Marshlack [owners of the property located at 2312 W. Farwell] appealed the zoning coordinator's decision to Tampa's Variance Review Board. On or about July 13, 1999, the Variance Review Board conducted a hearing. At the hearing, Voyeur Dorm's counsel conceded the following: that five women live in the house; that there are cameras in the corners of all the rooms of the house; that for a fee a person can join a membership to a Web site wherein a member can view the women 24 hours a day, seven days a week; that a member, at times, can see someone disrobed; that the women receive free room and board; that the women are part of a business enterprise; and that the women are paid. At the conclusion of the hearing, the Variance Review Board unanimously upheld the zoning coordinator's determination that the use occurring at 2312 West Farwell Drive was an adult use. Subsequently, Mr. and Mrs. Marshlack filed an appeal from the decision of the Variance Review Board to the City Council. The Tampa City Council . . . unanimously affirmed the decision of the Variance Review Board.

Voyeur Dorm filed this action in the middle district of Florida. The City of Tampa and Voyeur Dorm then filed cross-motions for summary judgment. The district court granted Tampa's motion for summary judgment, from which Voyeur Dorm now appeals.

ISSUE

1. Whether the district court properly determined that the alleged activities occurring at 2312 West Farwell Drive constitute a public offering of adult entertainment as contemplated by Tampa's zoning restrictions.

[Issues 2. and 3. are omitted.—Ed.]

DISCUSSION

The threshold inquiry is whether section 27-523 of Tampa's city code applies to the alleged activities occurring at 2312 West Farwell Drive. Because of the way we answer that inquiry, it will not be necessary for us to analyze the thorny constitutional issues presented in this case.

* * * * *

Tampa argues that Voyeur Dorm is an adult use business pursuant to the express and unambiguous language of

Section 27-523 and, as such, cannot operate in a residential neighborhood. In that regard, Tampa points out that members of the public pay to watch women employed on the premises; that the employment agreement refers to the premises as "a stage and filming location;" that certain anatomical areas and sexual activities are displayed for entertainment; and that the entertainers are paid accordingly. Most importantly, Tampa asserts that nothing in the city code limits its applicability to premises where the adult entertainment is actually consumed.

In accord with Tampa's arguments, the district court specifically determined that the "plain and unambiguous language of the city code . . . does not expressly state a requirement that the members of the public paying consideration be on the premises viewing the adult entertainment." While the public does not congregate to a specific edifice or location in order to enjoy the entertainment provided by Voyeur Dorm, the district court found 2312 West Farwell Drive to be "a premises on which is offered to members of the public for consideration entertainment featuring specified sexual activities within the plain meaning of the city code."

Moreover, the district court relied on Supreme Court and Eleventh Circuit precedent that trumpets a city's entitlement to protect and improve the quality of residential neighborhoods. *Sammy's of Mobile, Ltd. v. City of Mobile* (noting that it is well established that the regulation of public health, safety, and morals is a valid and substantial state interest); *Corn v. City of Lauderdale Lakes* (noting that the "Supreme Court has held [that] restrictions may be imposed to protect 'family values, youth values, and the blessings of quiet seclusion'").

In opposition, Voyeur Dorm argues that it is not an adult use business. Specifically, Voyeur Dorm contends that section 27-523 applies to locations or premises wherein adult entertainment is actually offered to the public. Because the public does not, indeed cannot, physically attend 2312 West Farwell Drive to enjoy the adult entertainment, 2312 West Farwell Drive does not fall within the purview of Tampa's zoning ordinance.

The residence of 2312 West Farwell Drive provides no "offering [of adult entertainment] to members of the public." The offering occurs when the videotaped images are dispersed over the Internet and into the public eye for consumption. The city code cannot be applied to a location that does not, itself, offer adult entertainment to the public.

* * * * *

It does not follow, then, that a zoning ordinance designed to restrict facilities that offer adult entertainment can be applied to a particular location that does not, at that location, offer adult entertainment. Moreover, the case law relied upon by Tampa and the district court concerns adult entertainment in which customers physically attend the premises wherein the entertainment is performed. Here, the audience or consumers of the adult entertainment do not go to 2312 West Farwell Drive or congregate anywhere else in Tampa to enjoy the entertainment. Indeed, the public offering occurs over the Internet in "virtual space." While the district court read Section 27-523 in a literal sense, finding no requirement that the paying public be on the premises, we hold that section 27-523 does not apply to a residence at which there is no public offering of adult entertainment.

* * * * *

Reversed.

Questions

1. *a.* Why did the court rule against Tampa?
    b. Make the argument, as the lower court did, that the Tampa statute does apply to Voyeur Dorm.
    c. Why was Tampa concerned about Voyeur Dorm operating in a residential neighborhood?
    d. Does Tampa have any additional legal grounds for challenging Voyeur Dorm? Explain.

2. The city government in Cedar Falls, Iowa, home of the University of Northern Iowa, declined to renew the liquor license of a local bar after 58 of 100 "bar checks" over a period of nearly two years found minors drinking illegally. One hundred and seventy four alcohol-related tickets were issued over that period.[28]
    a. Could the free market satisfactorily protect the public from the various risks associated with excessive drinking by college-age students, or are rules necessary?
    b. Would you vote to renew this bar's liquor license? Explain.

3. Two Dallas, Texas, ordinances were challenged in court. One gave the police very broad authority to deny licenses to "adult" businesses such as bookstores. The other, which was directed at prostitution, barred motel owners from renting rooms for fewer than 10 hours.
    a. What challenges would you raise against these ordinances?
    b. How would you rule? Explain. See *FW/PBS Inc v. City of Dallas,* 493 U.S. 215 (1990).

4. The Los Angeles municipal code prohibits some types of new billboards and restricts the size, placement, and illumination of others. The Los Angeles code seeks to "promote public safety and welfare" by "providing reasonable protection to the visual environment" and by ensuring that

billboards do not "interfere with traffic safety or otherwise endanger public safety." One provision of the code specifically forbids new "Freeway Facing Signs" located within 2,000 feet of and "viewed primarily from" a freeway or an on-ramp/off-ramp. Another forbids, with exceptions, new "supergraphics," large format signs projected onto or hung from building walls. The Los Angeles rules allow new signs in some portions of the city while banning them in others.

a. The billboard rules were challenged on constitutional grounds. Explain those grounds and rule on the constitutionality of the rules. See *World Wide Rush v. City of Los Angeles,* 606 F.3d 676 (9th Cir. 2010).

b. Should Los Angeles simply allow the market to determine where billboards are placed? Explain.

5. Tattoo and body piercing statutes sometimes require liability insurance, licensing, training, and health inspections, and parents are to accompany minors. Does each of those requirements seem appropriate to you? Explain.

6. a. Can we rely on the market to protect teens from excessive tanning? Explain.

b. Has the market failed? Explain.

Questions—Parts One and Two

1. Matthew Hale, a law school graduate, was denied a license to practice law in Illinois because Hale was an avowed racist and the leader of a white supremacist group. A state panel assessed the character and general fitness of all those who had passed the bar exam and graduated from law school and decided that Hale's active racism disqualified him. Illinois is one of 32 states with character and fitness standards. Hale appealed on First Amendment grounds, among others. Should Hale be excluded from the practice of law, or should we let the market decide his fitness? Explain.

2. City officials in Machesney Park, Illinois required nine-year-old Gregory Webb to tear down his makeshift tree house on the grounds that it was a nuisance. Webb had built the structure from lawn chairs, leftover carpet, and a pet carrier, among other objects. The city was criticized for its decision.

   a. Why would a city choose to exercise its police power over nuisances in this seemingly trivial case?

   b. What would you do if you were the city planning and zoning director and thus responsible for the situation?

3. Notwithstanding the successful deregulation efforts in recent decades, the larger trend in the United States over the past 50 years, and particularly since the financial crisis of recent years, has been increased government regulation of business. How do you explain that trend?

4. As a safety measure, Arizona enacted a statute that limited the length of passenger trains to 14 cars and freight trains to 70 cars. Trains of those lengths and greater were common throughout the United States. The Southern Pacific Railroad challenged the Arizona statute.

   a. What was the legal foundation of the Southern Pacific claim?

   b. Decide the case. Explain. See *Southern Pacific Railroad v. Arizona,* 325 U.S. 761 (1945).

5. At this writing in 2013, a Florida state senate committee has passed new rules for parasailing, a largely unregulated commercial recreational activity. The new rules, if fully approved, would require insurance for operators, an onboard observer, and allow operation only when winds do not exceed 20 miles per hour.

In 2012, a Connecticut woman dropped from her harness to her death while parasailing near Pompano Beach, Florida. Such deaths are unusual with several dozen having been estimated worldwide in the past 30 years, but Florida has seen four in the past two years.

a. How would you argue that parasailing deaths often constitute a market failure?

b. Would you vote for a parasailing rule, or would you leave parasailing safety to the market? Explain.

Part Three—Administrative Agencies and the Regulatory Process

Introduction to Administrative Agencies[29]

Suppose you start a business: a small, relatively simple business, perhaps a restaurant. You quickly come to realize that the government is going to be your partner in that business. Taxes, wages, hours, sanitation, safety, advertising, zoning—at every turn a government rule shapes the conduct of your business. In many cases those rules are created and enforced by administrative agencies, a powerful subset of government little understood by the public but immensely influential in every corner of American life.

The Federal Agencies

Federal law defines an *agency* as any government unit other than the legislature and the courts. Thus, the *administrative law* governing those agencies technically addresses the entire executive branch of government. Our attention, however, will be directed to the prominent regulatory agencies (Federal Trade Commission, Federal Communications Commission, Securities and Exchange Commission, and the like) rather than the various executive departments (Agriculture, Defense, and so on) and nonregulatory welfare agencies (Social Security Administration and Veterans Administration). We will focus on the federal level, but administrative law principles are generally applicable to the conduct of state and local governments. At the state level, public utility commissions and the various state licensure boards for law, medicine, architecture, and the like are examples of administrative agencies. At the local level, one might cite planning and zoning boards and property tax assessment appeals boards. [To search for federal government information on the World Wide Web, see **www.gpoaccess.gov/index.html** or **www.fedworld.gov**]

History

Congress established the Interstate Commerce Commission (ICC), the first federal regulatory agency, in 1887 for the purpose of regulating railroad routes and rates. The Food and Drug Administration (FDA—1907) and the Federal Trade Commission (FTC—1914) followed, but federal regulation became pervasive only in response to the Great Depression of the 1930s. Congress created the Securities and Exchange Commission (SEC—1934), the Federal

Communications Commission (FCC—1934), the Civil Aeronautics Board (CAB—1940; abolished 1985), and the National Labor Relations Board (NLRB—1935), among others, as a response to the widely shared belief that the stock market crash and the Depression were evidence of the failure of the free market.

The next major burst of regulatory activity arrived in the 1960s and 1970s when Congress created such agencies as the Equal Employment Opportunity Commission (EEOC—1965), the Environmental Protection Agency (EPA—1970), the Occupational Safety and Health Administration (OSHA—1970), and the Consumer Product Safety Commission (CPSC—1972).

Note that the work of most of the early agencies was directed to controlling entire industries such as transportation or communications and that the primary purpose of most of those agencies was to address economic concerns. Then with the arrival of the prosperity and social turbulence of the 1960s and 1970s, Congress built a rather massive array of new agencies directed not to economic issues but to social reform in such areas as discrimination, the environment, job safety, and product safety.

The free market enthusiasm of the 1980s resulted in strenuous efforts to deregulate the economy and reduce the influence of the federal agencies and the government generally. Now, in the early 21st century we have been in a period of general respect for the free market, but current problems in the finance industry, particularly in home mortgages, have resulted in aggressive new rules, as explained below.

Creating the Agencies

Federal agencies are of two kinds: executive and independent. Executive agencies usually are located within the departments of the executive branch of the government. The Federal Aviation Administration, for example, is a part of the Department of Transportation. Our primary interest is in the independent agencies (FTC, FCC, and SEC). Congress created those agencies via statutes labeled *enabling legislation* and accorded them substantial authority to regulate a specified segment of American life. The FTC, for example, is empowered by its enabling legislation to pursue unfair trade practices. The president has direct authority over the executive agencies while the independent agencies are intended to operate with less fear of interference. In practice, of course, the president and Congress have substantial influence on all the agencies.

In creating an agency, Congress delegates a portion of its authority to that body. Congress acknowledges the existence of a problem and recognizes that it is not the appropriate body to address the specific elements of that problem—hence the agency. The president, ordinarily with the advice and consent of the Senate, appoints the administrator or the several commissioners who direct each agency's affairs. Commissioners are appointed in staggered terms, typically of seven years' duration. The appointment of commissioners for most of the independent agencies must reflect an approximate political balance between the two major parties.

In effect, Congress has created a fourth branch of government. Possessing neither the time nor the expertise to handle issues arising from nuclear power, product safety, racial discrimination, labor unions, and much more, Congress wisely established "mini governments" supported by the necessary technical resources and day-to-day authority to address those complicated problems.

Agency Duties

The authority of the federal regulatory agencies falls broadly into three categories.

1. **Control of supply.** Some agencies control entry into certain economic activities. The Federal Communications Commission grants radio and television licenses. The Food and Drug Administration (see Chapter 15) decides which drugs may enter the American market. The Securities and Exchange Commission (see Chapter 9) acts as a gatekeeper, preventing the entry of new securities into the marketplace until certain standards are met. The general concern is that the market alone cannot adequately protect the public interest.

2. **Control of rates.** Historically, those federal agencies charged with regulating utilities and carriers (Federal Energy Regulatory Commission, ICC, and CAB) set the prices to be charged for the services offered within their jurisdictions, but the deregulation movement resulted in the elimination of the CAB and the ICC and a general decline in agency rate-setting. The federal government decided to reduce or eliminate its authority in decisions such as the price of airline tickets, cable TV rates, and long-distance telephone rates.

3. **Control of conduct.**

a. Information. Agencies commonly compel companies to disclose consumer information that would otherwise remain private. Warning labels, for example, may be mandated.

b. Standards. Where simply requiring information is deemed inadequate for the public needs, the government may establish minimum standards that the private sector must meet. A ladder might be required to safely hold at least a specified weight, or workers might lawfully be exposed to only a specified maximum level of radiation.

c. Product banishments. In rare circumstances, products can be banned from the market. The Consumer Product Safety Commission banned the flame retardant Tris (used in children's sleepwear) because of evidence of the product's cancer-causing properties.

Questions

1. The phrase "government regulation" embraces many functions. Define it.
2. Is the federal regulatory process limited in its goals to the correction of market failures? Should it be so limited? Explain.

Operating the Agencies

As we have noted, the administrative agencies act as mini governments, performing quasi-executive, quasi-legislative (rule-making), and quasi-judicial (adjudicatory) roles broadly involving control of supply, rates, and conduct in large segments of American life. Agency action is guided generally by the 1946 Administrative Procedure Act (APA), which Congress enacted to provide a framework for agency rule-making and to detail broad standards for judicial review of agency decisions. Let's look at how those agencies practice their business.

Executive Functions

The basic executive duty of the various agencies is to implement the policy provided for in the enabling legislation and in the agencies' own rules and regulations. A large part of agency activity consists of performing mundane, repetitive tasks. Agencies enter into contracts, lease federal lands, register securities offerings, award grants, resolve tax disputes, settle workers' compensation claims, administer government benefits to the citizenry, and so on. Of course, a big part of the agencies' executive duties is the protection of the public by ensuring compliance with laws and regulations. Therefore, most agencies spend a great deal of time conducting inspections and investigations and collecting information.

Most agencies offer informal advice, both in response to requests and on their own initiative, to explain agency policy and positions. Each year the Federal Trade Commission, for example, receives many complaints about alleged fraud in advertising, telemarketing, identity theft, Internet commerce, and so on. Supervisory duties, including most notably the active and close attention given to the banking industry, are a further illustration of agency executive duties.

Legislative Functions

The agencies create *rules* that, in effect, are laws. These rules provide the details necessary to carry out the intentions of the enabling legislation. In day-to-day business practice, the rules are likely to be much more important than the original congressional legislation. The Occupational Safety and Health Act calls for a safe and healthful workplace, but the rules necessary for interpreting and enforcing that general mandate come, not from Congress, but from OSHA.

Rules

Agencies enact three types of rules: (1) procedural, (2) interpretive, and (3) legislative. Procedural rules delineate the agency's internal operating structure and methods. Interpretive rules offer the agency's view of the meaning of those statutes for which the agency has administrative responsibility. Internal Revenue Service regulations are an example of interpretive rules. Legislative rules are policy expressions having the effect of law. The agency is exercising the law-making function delegated to it by the legislature. Federal Trade Commission rules providing for a cooling-off period of three business days within which the buyer may cancel door-to-door sales contracts are an example of agency lawmaking that significantly affects business behavior.

The Rule-Making Process

The Administrative Procedure Act provides for both *informal* (often called "notice and comment") and *formal* rule-making processes for legislative rules. Under both approaches, the process begins with the publication of a Notice of Proposed Rule Making in the *Federal Register* (a daily publication of all federal rules, regulations, and orders). Thereafter, in the case of informal rule making, the agency must permit written comments on the proposal and may hold open hearings. To enhance participation in the rule-making process, the federal government provides an online portal where the public can comment on proposed rules [**see www.regulations.gov**]. Having received public comments, the agency either discontinues the process or prepares the final rule.

In the case of formal rule-making, after providing notice, the agency must hold a public hearing conducted with most of the procedural safeguards of a trial, where all interested parties may call witnesses, challenge the agency evidence, and so on.

Hybrid Rule-Making Although not specifically provided for in the APA, agency rule-making now is often achieved by a compromise (hybrid) process that combines elements of formal and informal rule-making. Hybrid rule-making is informal rule making with additions in the form of some trial elements (more oral testimony and hearings) that have the effect of providing a more detailed record without all of the procedural requirements of formal rule-making.

Whether by formal, informal, or hybrid procedures, final agency rules are published in the *Federal Register* and later compiled in the *Code of Federal Regulations*. [To search the Federal Register, see **www.gpoaccess.gov/fr/index.html**]

Challenging an Agency Rule

At this writing the Federal Communications Commission (FCC) is in the midst of a long-running dispute with Congress and the courts about the Commission's interest in continued relaxation of rules limiting a single company's ownership (called cross-ownership) of radio stations, television stations, and newspapers in the same market.[30] The rules were designed to protect communities from media monopolies and to increase diversity in the marketplace of ideas.[31] The FCC, however, points to the Internet and other technological advances that reduce the threat of media monopoly, thus providing some space for increased cross-ownership. On the other hand, the critics, including many in Congress, maintain a firm stance against most further consolidation. They note the FCC's 1996 decision to lift its limit on how many radio stations one company could own nationally. The result was the development of the Clear Channel network (currently about 850 stations) that has been broadly criticized for "homogenizing" radio and sharply reducing local programming. Notwithstanding the continuing struggle over media ownership, we should remember that the FCC and other agencies often successfully achieve voluntary arrangements with those being regulated.[32]

> Clear Channel has been criticized for "homogenizing" radio.

The cross-ownership debate illustrates a pair of economic policy questions at the core of this text: Will the market and corporate social responsibility provide for the nation's best interests? Or are legal restraints necessary to prevent too much concentration of power and authority in too few hands? [For a "source of regulatory news, analysis, and opinion," see *RegBlog* at **www.law.upenn.edu/blogs/regblog/**]

Judicial Functions

Although informal procedures such as settlements are preferred, agencies commonly must turn to judicial proceedings to enforce agency rules. The National Labor Relations Board may hold a hearing to determine if an employee was wrongfully dismissed for engaging in protected union activities. The Federal Communications Commission may decide whether to remove a radio license because of a failure to serve the public interest. The Federal Trade Commission may judge whether a particular ad is misleading.

Rule-Making or Adjudication?

Many issues facing agencies could properly be resolved either by rule-making or by adjudication. Characteristically, however, an adjudication addresses specific parties involved in a specific present or past dispute. Rule-making ordinarily involves standards to be applied to the future conduct of a class of unspecified parties. The rule-making/adjudication decision is discretionary with the agency (subject to judicial review) and is based on the nature of the issue and fairness to the parties. Regardless, the agencies are, in effect, "making law" either by setting a judiciallike precedent in the case of an adjudication or by passing a rule that has authority much like a law.

Administrative Hearing

Typically, after an investigation, a violation of a statute and/or rule may be alleged. Affected parties are notified. An effort is made to reach a settlement via a *consent order,* in which the party being investigated agrees to steps suitable to the agency but under which the respondent makes no admission of guilt (thus, retarding the likelihood of subsequent civil liability).

Administrative Law Judge

Failing a settlement, the parties proceed much as in a civil trial. Ordinarily the case is heard by an *administrative law judge (ALJ)*. The respondent may be represented by counsel. Parties have the right to present their cases, cross-examine, file motions, raise objections, and so on. They do not have the right to a jury trial, however. The ALJ decides all questions of law and fact and then issues a decision (*order*). In general, that decision is final unless appealed to the agency/commission. After exhausting opportunities for review within the agency, appeal may be taken to the federal court system.

PRACTICING ETHICS   Agency Capture, Iron Triangles, and Revolving Doors?

The Minerals Management Service (MMS) was a federal agency charged with collecting oil and gas royalties from companies drilling on federal lands. A 2008 Interior Department internal investigation concluded that several MMS officials "frequently consumed alcohol at industry functions, had used cocaine and marijuana, and had sexual relationships with oil and gas company representatives."[33] Reportedly, MMS staffers took gifts from oil and gas officials with "prodigious frequency."[34] Some MMS decisions, while less vivid than the sex, drugs, and payoffs, were of much more far reaching consequence. The MMS reportedly gave British Petroleum's Gulf of Mexico oil lease a "categorical exclusion" that exempted the lease from a detailed environmental impact analysis in 2009.[35] BP's *Deepwater Horizon* drilling rig exploded in 2010, leading to the calamitous oil spill that polluted much of the Gulf of Mexico. MMS, now disbanded, has been replaced by two new federal agencies, but its misconduct

is a particularly lurid and frustrating example of the risk that agencies will be improperly influenced (captured) by the industries they are intended to regulate.

Scholars argue that *agency capture* is a form of government failure that can occur when regulators are too cozy with the industry being regulated or when industry representatives have the interest and resources to offer detailed advice on agency business while the public voice, being much less focused, is seldom or never heard by the agency. Political scientists argue that regulatory capture of both agencies and congressional committees sometimes produces a stable, nearly impregnable, *iron triangle.* Powerful interest groups (often businesses), occupy one corner of the triangle, congressional committees are at another corner, and agency bureaucrats occupy the third. In the resulting alliance, each group cultivates its own welfare by providing political support (from interest groups to members of Congress) writing favorable laws (from Congress to interest groups) and by agency enforcement of those laws in ways favorable to the interest groups and Congress. The likely result is diminished attention to the public good.

Regulatory capture is facilitated by a revolving door wherein agency officials often come from the very industry they are hired to regulate and agency regulators often leave government to work for the industry formerly regulated. A 2011 study found that nearly 5,400 congressional employees left government work to become federal lobbyists during the previous 10 years.[36] Troublesome as these government/industry ties may seem, we should remember that we want and need close associations between government agencies and the industries being regulated. Each benefits from the expertise of the other. Further, federal conflict of interest laws do impose some restrictions on private-sector work following government service.[37]

Controlling the Agencies

Although agency influence in business practice and in American life generally is enormous, none of these agencies and their thousands of employees is directly accountable to the people, and all of them operate under necessarily broad grants of power. What is to keep them from abusing their discretion or from being "captured" by special interests? Just as with our constitutional system generally, certain checks and balances constrain agency conduct while allowing the latitude necessary to achieve effectiveness.

Executive Constraints

As noted, the president appoints the top administrators for the various agencies, thus significantly influencing the conservative or liberal slant of the agency. Furthermore, the president obviously has great influence in the budget process.

Recent presidents have strengthened executive oversight of agency action by requiring *cost-benefit analyses* for new rules (President Clinton) and commanding agencies to cite a specific *market failure* before issuing a new rule (President George W. Bush). President Obama has maintained the cost-benefit expectation and he has introduced a new initiative to get rid of what he has labeled "dumb" rules. Recently, President Obama ordered all federal agencies to eliminate outdated rules that "stifle job creation and make our economy less competitive," and he has asked Congress for authority to consolidate a number of federal agencies.[38] [For an OMB "watchdog" see **www.ombwatch.org/**]

Congressional Constraints

Congress creates and can dissolve the agencies. Congress controls agency budgets and thus can encourage or discourage particular agency action. Broadly, Congress oversees agency action, and agencies often check with Congress before undertaking major initiatives. Congress can directly intervene by amending the enabling legislation or by passing laws that require agencies to take specific directions. The difficulty in balancing congressional and agency authority is well illustrated by an important 2001 Supreme Court decision involving the federal Clean Air Act (CAA). The case, *Whitman v. American Trucking Associations, Inc.*[39] raised the question of whether Congress had improperly delegated its authority to the Environmental Protection Agency and whether the EPA must take the cost of implementing clean air regulations into consideration when developing new rules. A unanimous Supreme Court ruled that

Congress had built into the CAA constitutionally sufficient limitations on agency action, and the Court ruled that Congress clearly did not require the EPA to conduct cost–benefit analyses before establishing new rules. Thus the Court concluded that Congress can constitutionally offer agencies broad authority in carrying out Congress's general intentions.

Judicial Review

Agency rules and orders may be challenged in court. Historically, however, the courts have taken a rather narrow approach to judicial review. The jurists, being generalists in the field of law, have been reluctant to overrule the judgment of specialists, and very crowded judicial calendars act as a natural brake on activist judicial review. For those reasons, judges readily sustain the judgment of the agency where reasonable. Of course, the courts overrule the agencies when appropriate, and review of controversial, high visibility rules such as many of those issued by the Environmental Protection Agency is common.

Not surprisingly, judicial review of agency decisions raises a variety of technical issues of law. Cases turn on questions like these:

1. Does the legislature's delegation of authority meet constitutional requirements?
2. Has the agency exceeded the authority granted by the enabling legislation?
3. Are the agency's findings of fact supported by substantial evidence in the record as a whole?
4. Was the agency's decision "arbitrary and capricious" (a standard provided for in the Administrative Procedure Act and discussed in the *FCC v. Fox* case below)?

While these issues are technically important, their detailed exploration is not necessary for our purposes. The case that follows will be our only consideration of the formalities of judicial review. This 8–0 U.S. Supreme Court ruling examines the question of when the government should regulate distasteful expression over the regulated airways.

LEGAL BRIEFCASE

Federal Communications Commission v. Fox Television Stations and Federal Communications Commission v. ABC   132 S. Ct. 2307 (2012)

Facts

Three episodes of alleged indecency on network television are at issue in this case. First, at the 2002 Billboard Music Awards, televised by Fox, Cher made the following unscripted remark: "I've also had my critics for the last 40 years saying that I was on my way out every year. So f*** 'em." Second, during the Fox telecast of the 2003 Billboard Music Awards, Nicole Richie made the following unscripted remark: "Have you ever tried to get cow s*** out of a Prada purse? It's not so f***ing simple." Third, ABC's February 25, 2003, telecast of *NYPD Blue* displayed the nude buttocks of an adult female character for about seven seconds and the side of her breast for a moment, as she was preparing for a shower. A child portraying her boyfriend's son entered the bathroom during the scene.

Then in 2004 the Federal Communications Commission sanctioned NBC for the following remark by Bono, who won an award at the 2003 Golden Globe Awards show: "This is really, really, f***ing brilliant. Really, really great." The FCC found use of the F-word actionably indecent. Reversing prior rulings, the Commission ruled that even fleeting expletives, like the single use of the F-word by Bono, were actionable. The isolated and apparently impromptu nature of the remark did not excuse its indecency.

Applying its new policy to the Cher, Richie, and *NYPD Blue* cases, the FCC then ruled that Fox and ABC had violated the Commission's indecency standards by televising fleeting expletives and fleeting nudity. Fox was not punished, but ABC and its affiliates were fined $1.24 million. The Fox case *(Fox I)* then went to the United States Court of Appeals for the Second Circuit, which overturned the Commission ruling saying it was "arbitrary and capricious" in that the FCC made a 180-degree turn regarding fleeting expletives without providing a reasoned explanation. *Fox I* then went to the Supreme Court in 2009 where the Court of Appeals ruling was reversed with the Court saying that a change in FCC policy must be announced, but detailed justifications are not required as a matter of law. *Fox I* then returned to the Second Circuit Court of Appeals which struck down the Commission's entire indecency policy finding it unconstitutionally vague because it failed to give broadcasters sufficient notice of what would be considered indecent. In light of that decision, the Second Circuit vacated the forfeiture order against ABC. The federal government sought review of both decisions, which was granted by the Supreme Court leading to the opinion *(Fox II)* that follows.

Justice Kennedy

* * * * *

I

A

Title 18 U.S.C. § 1464 provides that "[w]hoever utters any obscene, indecent, or profane language by means of radio communication shall be fined . . . or imprisoned not more than two years, or both." The Federal Communications Commission (Commission) has been instructed by Congress to enforce § 1464 between the hours of 6 am and 10 pm.

This Court first reviewed the Commission's indecency policy in *FCC v. Pacifica Foundation*, 438 U.S. 726 (1978). In *Pacifica*, the Commission determined that George Carlin's "Filthy Words" monologue was indecent. It contained "language that describes, in terms patently offensive as measured by contemporary community standards for the broadcast medium, sexual or excretory activities and organs, at times of the day when there is a reasonable risk that children may be in the audience." *Id.*, at 732. This Court upheld the Commission's ruling.

* * * * *

In 2001, the Commission . . . [in describing] what it considered patently offensive, . . . explained that three factors had proved significant:

"(1) [T]he explicitness or graphic nature of the description or depiction of sexual or excretory organs or activities; (2) whether the material dwells on or repeats at length descriptions of sexual or excretory organs or activities; (3) whether the material appears to pander or is used to titillate, or whether the material appears to have been presented for its shock value."

As regards the second of these factors, the Commission explained that "[r]epetition of and persistent focus on sexual or excretory material have been cited consistently as factors that exacerbate the potential offensiveness of broadcasts. In contrast, where sexual or excretory references have been made once or have been passing or fleeting in nature, this characteristic has tended to weigh against a finding of indecency."

* * * * *

B

It was against this regulatory background that the three incidents of alleged indecency at issue here took place.

* * * * *

II

A fundamental principle in our legal system is that laws which regulate persons or entities must give fair notice of conduct that is forbidden or required. . . . This requirement of clarity in regulation is essential to the protections provided by the Due Process Clause of the Fifth Amendment. . . . It requires the invalidation of laws that are impermissibly vague. . . .

Even when speech is not at issue, the void for vagueness doctrine addresses at least two connected but discrete due process concerns: first, that regulated parties should know what is required of them so they may act accordingly; second, precision and guidance are necessary so that those enforcing the law do not act in an arbitrary or discriminatory way. When speech is involved, rigorous adherence to those requirements is necessary to ensure that ambiguity does not chill protected speech.

These concerns are implicated here because . . . the broadcasters claim they did not have, and do not have, sufficient notice of what is proscribed. . . . Under the 2001 Guidelines in force when the broadcasts occurred, a key consideration was "'whether the material dwell[ed] on or repeat[ed] at length'" the offending description or depiction. 613 F.3d, at 322. In the 2004 *Golden Globes* Order, issued after the broadcasts, the Commission changed course and held that fleeting expletives could be a statutory violation. *Fox I,* 556 U.S., at 512. In the challenged orders now under review the Commission applied the new principle promulgated in the *Golden Globes* Order and determined fleeting expletives and a brief moment of indecency were actionably indecent. This regulatory history, however, makes it apparent that the Commission policy in place at the time of the broadcasts gave no notice to Fox or ABC that a fleeting expletive or a brief shot of nudity could be actionably indecent; yet Fox and ABC were found to be in violation. The Commission's lack of notice to Fox and ABC that its interpretation had changed so the fleeting moments of indecency contained in their broadcasts were a violation of § 1464 as interpreted and enforced by the agency "fail[ed] to provide a person of ordinary intelligence fair notice of what is prohibited." *Williams, supra,* at 304.

* * * * *

The Commission failed to give Fox or ABC fair notice prior to the broadcasts in question that fleeting expletives and momentary nudity could be found actionably indecent.

Therefore, the Commission's standards as applied to these broadcasts were vague, and the Commission's orders must be set aside.

* * * * *

The judgments of the United States Court of Appeals for the Second Circuit are vacated, and the cases are remanded.

Questions

1. Following the *Fox I* Supreme Court decision in 2009, the case went back down to the Second Circuit Court of Appeals, which ruled that the entire FCC indecency policy was unconstitutional. What constitutional infirmity did the Second Circuit cite in striking down the indecency policy? Explain.

   Did the Supreme Court in *Fox II* agree with the Second Circuit Court of Appeals that the FCC indecency policy was unconstitutional in its entirety? Explain.

2. When would an agency ruling be considered "arbitrary or capricious?"

3. Balancing First Amendment considerations (not addressed by the Supreme Court in the *Fox II* case) with concerns about the social effects of indecent language and behavior, what policy do you personally think the FCC should follow in regulating "fleeting expletives" like those uttered on television by Cher and Nicole Richie? Explain.

4. In commenting on the ongoing indecency debate, *The New York Times* argued: "The Supreme Court . . . should end all government regulations on the content of broadcasts. Technological change has undermined any justification for limiting the First Amendment rights of broadcast media outlets but not others."[40]

   Explain what the *Times* meant about technology eliminating the need for government oversight of broadcasting content.

The FCC and Indecency Today

We seem to be in the midst of a cultural war over social values, none of which is more hotly contested than the public role of sex in American life. Most famously, perhaps, Janet Jackson's "wardrobe malfunction" (when her right breast was momentarily bared during the halftime show of the 2004 Super Bowl) led to a $550,000 FCC fine levied against CBS television. In 2011, the Third Circuit Court of Appeals threw out the fine, calling the FCC action was "arbitrary and capricious" in that it was an unexplained departure from the agency's longtime tolerance of fleeting indecency.[41] The Supreme Court declined to review that decision[42] and the eight-year exposed breast saga came to an end. Supreme Court Chief Justice Roberts, however, reminded us that the courts' detailed examination of the FCC indecency policy has clarified some aspects of the law such that similar episodes may be subject to future penalties:

> It is now clear that the brevity of an indecent broadcast—be it word or image—cannot immunize it from FCC censure. Any future "wardrobe malfunctions" will not be protected on the ground relied on by the court below.[43]

As noted in *Fox II,* FCC rules forbid indecent materials on conventional broadcast services between 6 AM and 10 PM—hours when children are likely to be in the audience. The

10 PM to 6 AM slot, on the other hand, offers a "safe harbor" for indecent programming. The rules do not reach subscription services such as programming delivered via satellite and cable services.

The safe harbor hours are straightforward. *Fox II* and other cases have brought deeper understanding to the notice and due process elements of FCC practice. The Supreme Court, however, will likely need to revisit the First Amendment issues that were avoided in *Fox I* and *Fox II*. Parents and other critics favor sterner broadcast oversight as exemplified in the fleeting expletives/nudity situations whereas the broadcast industry and civil liberties advocates prefer generous room for expression in the media along with aggressive defense of First Amendment free speech standards.

> **Fines for indecency can reach as high as $325,000.**

Fines for indecency can reach as high as $325,000 per violation. That stiff penalty along with the FCC's broadly drawn indecency standards have caused some stations to refrain from broadcasting shows with profanity, such as the acclaimed movie, *Saving Private Ryan*. Critics worry that FCC rules, designed to protect viewers—particularly children—may have a "chilling effect" on the free flow of ideas that is so vital to the nation's political, cultural, and economic health.

At this writing in 2013, the FCC is reviewing its indecency policies and enforcement to ensure compliance with First Amendment principles. During the period of the review, the commission is pursuing only "egregious" indecency cases. The FCC solicited comments from the public about its indecency policy, specifically including whether fleeting expletives and brief, nonsexual nudity should be actionable. [For continuing analysis of broadcast law, see **www.broadcastlawblog.com**]

Parents' Duty?

Caroline Fredrickson explained the American Civil Liberties Union's objections to close government oversight of broadcasting:

> Congress should reject any proposals that would allow the FCC to regulate what the public sees on television. Members of the American Civil Liberties Union (ACLU) strongly believe that the government should not replace parents as decision makers in America's living rooms. There are some things the government does well, but deciding what is aired on television, and when, is not one of them. Parents already have many tools to protect their children, including blocking programs and channels, changing the channel, or (my personal favorite) turning off the television. . . . Our concern is that imposing standards for television programming would be unconstitutional and damage important values that define America: the right to free speech, and the right of parents to decide the upbringing of their children.

Questions

1. Can we realistically expect parents to be able to fully shield their children from indecent broadcasting?
2. Should parents do so? Explain.

Source: Caroline Fredrickson, "Why Government Should Not Police TV Violence and Indecency," *The Christian Science Monitor*, September 6, 2007 [**www.csmonitor.com/2007/0906/p09s01-coop.html**].

Questions—Part Three

1. The Parents Television Council filed 36 indecency complaints with the FCC alleging that popular television shows, including *Friends* and *The Simpsons,* contained indecent scenes that were either sexually explicit or used indecent or profane language. How would you vote on the following scenes?

   a. In the *Gilmore Girls,* one character says to another, "You're a dick."

   b. In *The Simpsons,* students carry picket signs with the phrases "What would Jesus glue?" and "Don't cut off my pianissimo."

2. The Parents Television Council contacted sponsors of the April 6, 2005, episode of the television program *The Shield* to complain about a "graphic" scene in which a police captain was forced to perform fellatio on a gang member at gunpoint. Kia and Castrol were among those sponsors. What would you do if you were in charge of advertising for Kia or Castrol, and you received that complaint?

3. Cable television operators use signal scrambling to ensure that only paying customers have access to some programming. Congress was concerned that some sexually explicit cable programming, even though scrambled, might reach children via signal "bleeding." Section 505 of the Telecommunications Act of 1996 required cable operators to fully block sexually oriented channels or to "time channel"—that is, transmit only in hours when children are unlikely to be viewing. Most cable operators adopted the latter approach, with the result that for two-thirds of the day no viewers in the operators' service areas could receive the sexually explicit programming. Section 504 of the Telecommunications Act required cable operators to block undesired channels at individual households on request. A supplier of sexually oriented programming challenged Section 505 on First Amendment grounds. Decide the case. Explain. See *United States v. Playboy Entertainment Group,* 529 U.S. 803 (2000).

Part Four—The Federal Regulatory Process Evaluated

Free market advocates want to sharply reduce government, while free market skeptics favor an activist government engaged in preventing and correcting market failure. At this writing, President Obama and the Democratic Party have elevated the role of the federal government in American life in an effort to correct problems they believe the market cannot successfully address. Republicans and Tea Party activists, on the other hand, have angrily resisted what they see as an overreaching government intruding in matters such as education and energy policy better left to local communities and the market. They believe the federal government spent so much money stimulating the failing economy and bailing out big banks, car manufacturers, and others that the fiscal health of the nation is at risk.

> Republicans and Tea Party activists have angrily resisted what they see as an overreaching government.

The resulting political war has been powerfully projected to the populace through the debate over the 2010 national health care reform law, the Patient Protection and Affordable Care Act (Obamacare). As noted, the Affordable Care Act cleared a big hurdle in withstanding constitutional challenges, but its likely effectiveness is unclear at this writing.

The government projects Obamacare to reduce the total number of uninsured American residents from 53 million to 30 million and to significantly contain costs. Critics, on the other hand, forecast big increases in insurance premiums, doctors retiring early or reducing their hours, and employers dropping health care coverage. Certainly Obamacare raises new financial questions for employers. The Affordable Care Act requires companies with 50 or more full-time employees to pay a penalty if they do not provide health care coverage for their full-time employees (defined as those working at least 30 hours per week). Some organizations reportedly are cutting employees' hours to avoid the law's requirements, but a 2013 survey found nearly 90 percent of employers do not intend to shift workers from full-time to part-time and most companies intend to maintain coverage for their full-time workers.[44]

TARP

Fearing the collapse of the American economy, the Bush administration in 2008 and the Obama administration thereafter loaned over $400 billion in government money to giant banks such as Citigroup and Goldman Sachs, insurance colossus AIG, General Motors, Chrysler, and many others, large and small. Although much of the Troubled Asset Relief Program (TARP) money has been repaid, taxpayers are still expected to lose as much $25 billion when the program is eventually concluded. Many financial leaders continue to believe the intervention was necessary to save those companies, though free-market advocates are unconvinced. They think TARP subjected the marketplace to a dangerous *moral hazard;* an economics argument claiming that an individual or business that is protected from risk (by government intervention, in this case) will increase its risk-taking behavior in the future in the belief that a bailout will follow, if needed. That is, if these giant firms are *"too big to fail"* as federal decision makers apparently believed, they will in the future be able to operate in less disciplined ways because they can assume, based on the TARP experience, that they will be rescued if necessary for the country's welfare.

> "Too big to fail."

Financial Reform

Concluding that the financial markets needed more effective and thorough oversight in light of the nation's near crash, Congress and President Obama in 2010 approved the Dodd–Frank Wall Street Reform and Consumer Protection Act to improve America's financial regulatory structure. Dodd–Frank is primarily directed to large financial institutions whereas smaller, community banks are exempt from many of its provisions. As perhaps its chief goal, the new law is designed to prevent "systemic risks," financial collapses that would threaten the entire economy. Toward that objective, a 15-member Financial Stability Oversight Council headed by the Secretary of the Treasury monitors the health of the entire U.S. financial system. Banks are required to maintain larger capital holdings in order to reduce risky lending, provide funds for emergencies, and make becoming dangerously large a less attractive direction. Big financial companies must create and update "funeral plans" to provide for their own quick and orderly shutdown in the event of financial failure. Those changes and others seek to prevent a recurrence of the recent collapse that arguably left taxpayers with little choice but to bail out failing financial giants. The act also reforms mortgage lending practices in an effort to ensure that borrowers actually have the wherewithal to repay. The enormous bill (more than 2,300 pages) has many more provisions, including the creation of the Consumer Financial Protection Bureau (see Chapter 15), other mortgage reforms, increased oversight of derivatives and hedge funds, new rules for credit rating agencies, a larger shareholder voice in executive pay decisions, and limits (under the so-called Volcker Rule) on the amount of a bank's own assets that can be used for some risky forms of proprietary trading (investing the firm's own money rather than that of its clients).

At this writing, more than three years after the enactment of Dodd–Frank, many of its provisions have yet to be implemented. Federal regulators are slowly creating new rules, and lobbyists for the banking industry and philosophical opposition from free-market politicians are challenging those rules and restraining funding. Critics believe Dodd–Frank threatens small business and consumers by raising borrowing costs and limiting services while giving too much power to government.

Notwithstanding those complaints about excessive government, many political leaders and economists believe Dodd–Frank does not do enough to address its central concern: the stability of the American banking system. Six giant firms—Bank of America, Citigroup, Goldman Sachs, JPMorgan Chase, Morgan Stanley, and Wells Fargo—hold about $9.6 trillion in assets, equal to over 62 percent of the American gross domestic product (up from about 14 percent for the six biggest banks in 1994).[45] Liberals see the big banks as the product of unrestrained capitalism and excessive lobbying power whereas many conservatives also oppose the big banks because they see them as the product of big government cronyism and government safety nets (see the aforementioned moral hazard discussion). Of course, the banking industry and many experts believe big banks are necessary to achieve big deals in a global economy, and they fear that China might well replace the United States as the world's financial leader if the big banks are downsized.

Bigger Government?

Until the recent subprime mortgage crisis and our ongoing recession, the United States had been in a period, since the late 1970s, of *deregulation,* during which great efforts were made to reduce the role of government in big portions of American life. Once tightly controlled industries, energy, transportation, and telecommunications were substantially returned to market forces. The results often included lower prices and increased innovation. Republicans and Democrats alike generally embraced the idea that greater efficiency, competitiveness, and freedom would accompany reduced government oversight. Of course, government authority remained enormous, and "sensible regulations" in workplace safety, the environment, equal opportunity, and consumer protection persisted and often grew. Broadly, in the 40 years or so prior to the 2008 economic crisis, there was a decline in government efforts to manage some sectors of the economy, accompanied by an increase in government efforts to manage social issues such as discrimination and clean air— problems the market didn't seem to be satisfactorily addressing.

Now, as we have seen, the threat of a banking collapse and economic chaos for America and the world has generated a resurgence in federal economic intervention. Obamacare, Dodd–Frank, and very aggressive Federal Reserve and Treasury Department policies have brought squarely to the attention of the American people the crucial but divisive question of just how much government we need in our lives. Are our lives excessively regulated or insufficiently regulated? Or are government regulations too often ineffective? Consider the evidence that follows.

I. Excessive Regulation

In brief, the excessive regulation argument is that government rules reduce business efficiency, curb freedom, and unjustly redistribute resources while expanding the government bureaucracy and the taxes/borrowing that fund it.

The Federal Register, the daily journal of federal rules (both final and proposed) along with presidential orders, totaled more than 82,000 pages, near records, in 2010 and 2011, before falling back to just over 77,000 pages in 2012.[46] The conservative American Action Forum estimated that about 87 million worker hours (a year's work for about 43,000 full-time employees) were required to complete the 2012 paperwork burdens associated with the federal government's rules.[47]

Federal government civilian employees total about 1.9 million, and a new study suggests those people are paid about $8,000 more annually in salary and about $30,000 more annually in benefits than their private sector equivalents.[48] (Critics say the study failed to properly match job categories and that federal employees are generally better educated and older than those in the private sector.)

[For a Cato Institute video, "There Are Too Many Bureaucrats and They Are Paid Too Much," see **www.youtube.com/watch?v=5xzd3puYmiM**]

Perhaps the biggest risk from excessive government is slower economic growth and fewer jobs. The U.S. Chamber of Commerce argues that the threat of ever-growing regulations brings such uncertainty to the economy that businesses simply decline to invest out of fear that government might impose costly, new rules at any time. The Chamber pointed to the $1.8 trillion in cash reserves held by American businesses in 2010 and said: "Businesses are reacting by sitting on capital, afraid to invest or hire."[49] [For an array of conservative analyses of tax issues, see **www.atr.org.** For more detailed criticisms of the federal regulatory process, see **www.heritage.org or http://cei.org or www.cato.org /pubs/regulation**]

Shrink Big Government?

Given the enormous costs involved and the long-term threat of too much government, Americans routinely plead for lower taxes and smaller government, but when it comes to actually cutting specific programs that benefit them, sentiments change dramatically. A 2010 poll found 57 percent of respondents uncomfortable with raising the Social Security retirement age to 69 over the next 60 years. About 70 percent resisted cuts to Medicare, Social Security, and defense. Peter Hart, a codirector of the poll said: "Everybody wants to cut the deficit and cut the spending. But at the end of the day, everybody wants a choice that doesn't affect their well-being."

Source: Peter Wallsten, "Deficit Proposal Draws Mixed Review," *The Wall Street Journal,* November 18, 2010 [**http://online.wsj.com/**].

II. Insufficient Regulation

Relentless change and our continuing search for justice mean that new rules are inevitable. Responding, for example, to consumer anxiety over food hazards, Congress and President Obama in late 2010 approved the Food Safety Modernization Act, the first big upgrade in federal food safety requirements in 70 years (for more, see Chapter 15). Advocates of increased regulation point to the many successes of government intervention: a vast highway network, legal equality for minorities and women, cleaner air, safer workplaces, greatly diminished child labor, enhanced auto safety, and so on.

> Does government intervention pay off?

Does government intervention pay off? Free market advocates say "no" in many instances, but some powerful numbers and respected opinions say "yes." The federal Office of Management and Budget's 2013 draft "Report to Congress on the Benefits and Costs of Federal Regulations" found that the estimated annual benefits of major federal rules reviewed by the OMB for which data were available from 2002 to 2012 totaled between $193 billion and $800 billion whereas the estimated costs were between $57 billion and $84 billion.[50] Legendary investor Warren Buffet weighed in enthusiastically in a 2010 *New York Times* letter to "Uncle Sam" applauding what he viewed as a necessary and highly successful federal government intervention to save the financial markets in 2008 and thereafter. Buffet reminded readers of the economic meltdown the nation faced, the giant banks that were teetering, the major industrial companies that were running out of money and the millions of Americans whose prosperity was at risk. The threat was enormous, as Buffet saw it, and he judged the government to have provided the proper remedy:

> So, again, Uncle Sam, thanks to you and your aides. Often you are wasteful, and sometimes you are bullying. On occasion, you are downright maddening. But in this extraordinary emergency, you came through—and the world would look far different now if you had not.[51]

Does regulation actually harm economic growth in America? Considerable evidence suggests that fear is not convincing. For example, the federal Bureau of Labor Statistics asks employers why they have laid off workers. In 2010, only 0.3 percent of those laid off lost their jobs because of government regulation or intervention.[52] A *Washington Post* overview of economists' judgments as to the effect of regulations on job loss found generally that those effects were "minimal."[53] More broadly, the World Bank's 2013 "Doing Business" report placed the United States fourth highest in the world in the ease of doing business, ranking behind only Singapore, Hong Kong, and New Zealand.[54]

III. Ineffective Regulation

Just as the market can fail, so can the regulatory system. The sources of that regulatory failure are multiple, but one problem is highlighted in a recent Government Accountability Office (GAO) report detailing duplication of tasks in the federal government. According to the report, 15 different agencies oversee food safety, 80 programs address economic development, 82 programs improve teacher quality, 56 help people understand finances, and so on.[55] Critics further charge that the regulatory process is corrupted by familiar bureaucratic problems including inefficiency, incompetence, low productivity, and inconsistent policy enforcement. Of course, the problem of regulatory capture, explained earlier in this chapter, can play a powerful role in ineffectual regulation as Jacob Laksin explains in reviewing Timothy Carney's book *The Big Ripoff:*

> Another myth—debunked by Mr. Carney—holds that regulations are the scourge of the business world. In fact, as he argues, many top companies welcome these rules. The airline industry sees burdensome federal oversight as a means of discouraging upstart competition. Tobacco giant Philip Morris is only too happy to submit to government curbs on advertising, confident that the effect is to keep smaller, lesser-known manufacturers on the margins, to the benefit of its already famous Marlboro, Merit, and other brands.[56]

Your Life: $7 Million?

How much is a life worth? That question is probably the crucial cost–benefit inquiry. When imposing new environmental or car safety rules, for example, we are forced to think about how much money we should spend to save an additional life. Recently, leading scholar Kip Viscusi and colleagues put a $7 to $8 million value on human life based on what we are willing to pay to save an average American life. (In 2010, the FDA valued a life at $7.9 million, while the EPA put the figure at $9.1 million.)

The National Highway Traffic Safety Administration (NHTSA) has announced that it will recommend the inclusion of rear-view video systems in new cars. New rules were called for by Congress in the 2008 Cameron Gulbransen Kids Transportation Safety Act. The law was named after a two-year-old boy who was killed in the family driveway when his father accidentally backed over him. According to NHTSA, backover accidents cause an average of 229 deaths and more than 18,000 injuries per year, most involving those under 5 or over 70. NHTSA estimates the rule would save 95 to 112 lives per year and prevent 7,000 to 8,000 injuries at a cost of about $11.8 million per life saved. The cost would range from $159 to $203 per vehicle or somewhat less if the vehicle is already equipped with a display screen, but often the safety features are available only as part of more expensive option packages.

Questions

1. Would you favor the camera requirement? Explain your reasoning, including the issues and evidence you evaluated in reaching your conclusion.
2. *a.* How much is your life worth?
   b. Should the value of lives be a consideration in federal rules and spending decisions? Explain.

Sources: Binyamin Appelbaum, "As U.S. Agencies Put More Value on a Life, Businesses Fret," *The New York Times,* February 16, 2011 [**www.nytimes.com**]; Thomas J. Kniesner, W. Kip Viscusi, and James P. Ziliak, "Policy Relevant Heterogeneity in the Value of Statistical Life: New Evidence from Panel Data Quantile Regression," *Journal of Risk and Uncertainty* 40 (2010), p. 15; and Peter Vales-Dapena, "Autos May Be Required to Have Back-Up Cameras," CNNMoney.com, December 3, 2010 [**http://money.cnn.com/2010/12/03/autos/backup_cameras_nhtsa/index.htm**].

Further Deregulation or Reregulation?

Financial Services

The near collapse of America's banking system in 2008 offers a superb "test case" to examine the "What Went Wrong?" question posed by *The Washington Post:*

> How did the world's markets come to the brink of collapse? Some say regulators failed. Other claim deregulation left them handcuffed. Who's right? Both are. . . .[57]

The federal government's Financial Crisis Inquiry Commission's study of the financial collapse pointed to an array of problems including ineffective government oversight; corporate governance failures; reckless borrowing; lending and investment practices; ethical failures, an unregulated financial derivatives market, and failures in the credit rating agencies (e.g., Fitch Ratings, Moody's and Standard & Poor's). [For the Commission's report, see **http://fcic.law.stanford.edu/**]

Doubtless many factors contributed to the meltdown, but our primary concern is the issue of market and ethical failure and the resulting need for government intervention. Did the market and self-regulation (ethics and social responsibility) fail? Unsurprisingly, free-market advocates say the market performed well. They blame the subprime problems on government intervention, especially easy credit policies designed to extend home ownership to as many as possible, with reduced attention to ability to pay.[58] Critics of the free market on the other hand say that deregulation was a big factor in the collapse. For 30 years prior to the meltdown, the government gradually diminished its oversight of the banking industry in an effort to allow the market a greater voice and to render American banks more competitive in the global market. Most prominently perhaps, the 1933 Glass–Steagall Act was partially repealed in 1999, thus allowing a mingling of commercial and investment banks. In total, the regulatory walls separating commercial banks, investment banks, brokerage firms, insurance, and commodities trading came down, giant "financial supermarkets" emerged, and risky investing arguably grew.[59]

> Did the market fail?

> Alan Greenspan acknowledged a "breakdown" in self-regulation.

The financial crisis shattered the confidence of some staunch free market advocates including former Federal Reserve chair, Alan Greenspan, who acknowledged, in 2009, a "breakdown" in self-regulation.[60] Testifying before Congress, he said:

> I made a mistake in presuming that the self-interests of organizations, specifically banks and others, were such as that they were best capable of protecting their own shareholders and their equity in the firms.[61]

Whether the market failed or not, we should note general agreement that the government failed in its oversight responsibilities. As former Securities and Exchange Commission chair, Republican Chris Cox, said: "The last six months (of the financial crisis) have made it abundantly clear that voluntary regulation does not work."[62]

Regulatory Virtue

Historian John Steele Gordon argues that capitalism needs regulation and that regulation has made the country more stable and richer:

> Capitalism without regulation and regulators is inherently unstable, Gordon claims, "as people will usually put their short-term interests ahead of the interests of the system as a whole, and either chaos or plutocracy will result. . . . The country since the New Deal has been a far richer, far more economically secure, far more just society."[63]

God Up; Government Down

How much government do we need in our lives? Our answers to this important question apparently depend, in part, on our view of God. The Baylor (University) Religion Survey, conducted by the Gallup Poll in 2011, found that people who strongly believe "God has a plan for me" were much more likely to also believe that "the government does too much." Those people, according to the survey, tend to earn less and to be less educated than those who do not believe God has a plan for them. Sociologist Paul Froese, coauthor of the study, says the strong believers see the invisible hand of the free market as God at work. Those who do not believe in God or who believe God to be more removed from daily affairs tend to be more supportive of government.

Sources: Cathy Lynn Grossman, "Baylor Religion Survey Reveals Many See God Steering Economy," *USA TODAY*, September 20, 2011 [**http://usatoday.com**]; and G. Jeffrey MacDonald, "Does Government Do Too Much? That Could Depend on Your View of God," *The Christian Science Monitor*, September 23, 2011 [**www.csmonitor.com/**].

The Winner: The Mixed Economy?

Economist and columnist Sebastian Mallaby argues that we should acknowledge a role for both the market and government in our mixed economy and recognize that the American people will continue to demand more and more from the government (security from criminals and terrorists, clean air, safe food, good schools, and so on).[64] Indeed, he argues that those public goods in our prosperous society probably matter more than private pleasures such as DVDs and fancy vacations. As a result, government will likely be under great pressure to spend more, but we should also "be ruthless about making government and markets more efficient."[65]

Young People?

What does the future hold for big government in America? Is Mallaby right that the market and government working together are necessary for success in tomorrow's America? *The New York Times* in 2013 took an interesting look at those questions by interviewing young people in the Montana college town of Missoula, a majority of whom see government as a constructive force:

> Young people absolutely believe that there's a role for government," said Matt Singer, a founder of Forward Montana. "At the same time, this is not a generation of socialists. They are highly entrepreneurial, and know that some of what it takes to create an environment where they can do their own exciting, creative things is having basic systems that work.[66]

According to a Pew Research Center survey, under-30 voters are "the only age group in which a majority said the government should do more to fix problems."[67] What role do you see for government in your life? Do you think big government is an impediment to your happy, prosperous future? Or do you view government as a natural, necessary ally of the market?

Global Regulation

We should remember that regulation in the United States remains modest relative to the balance of the globe. Even though the cost of regulation in the United States is great, government rules are, in fact, less burdensome in America than in most nations. *The Washington Post* in 2013 reported the critics' view that France is "drowning in rules and regulations,"[68] and *The New York Times* in 2012 applied the word *abysmal* to Greece's climate for doing business while citing a McKinsey & Company study that found start-ups in Greece facing "immense amounts of red tape, complex administrative and tax systems and procedural disincentives."[69] The global trend, however, seems to be toward more sensible rules. The 2013 World Bank *Doing Business 2013* report found that significant progress has been made in the last 10 years in improving business regulatory practices around the globe. Since 2005, the average time to start a business has fallen from 50 to 30 days.[70]

We should also understand that regulation, particularly in the banking sector, is an increasingly cooperative, international process recognizing the value of cutting global red tape while also acknowledging the necessity of firm rules to maintain a healthy global economy and prevent future financial crises. The big industrial nations, at this writing, are phasing in new measures (labeled Basel III) to promote global financial stability. At the center of those rules are increased capital adequacy standards that basically require banks to hold 7 percent of certain core assets in reserve with the biggest, most deeply interconnected banks being required to hold up to 10.5 percent. Those reserve funds are meant to both discourage risk taking and to be available for use if a crisis occurs. At this writing in 2013, the United States is still writing its rules to comply with Basel III. Big banks around the world have made progress in building their capital reserves, but objections to Basel III have mounted, implementation has been slow, and the "too big to fail" problem clearly remains unsolved.

Basel III

Two Concluding Cases

Let's close this chapter about government rules by asking if we should have more of them.

Case I. FDA Ban on Menthol Cigarettes?

At this writing, the federal Food and Drug Administration (see Chapter 15) is considering whether it should forbid the use of menthol as a flavoring in cigarette products. All other flavored cigarettes were previously banned by the FDA. Antismoking groups say about 80 percent of black smokers prefer the menthol variety. In general, black smokers have the highest rates of smoking-related diseases. Critics also say that menthol cigarettes are particularly appealing to young people because the flavoring causes a cooling sensation in the mouth and hides the harsh cigarette taste. One study found that 45 percent of smokers aged 12 to 17 used menthol brands. The FDA in 2013 concluded that menthol cigarettes probably pose a greater health risk than standard brands because their flavoring facilitates addiction and makes quitting harder.

Lorillard, maker of Newport, is leading the fight against a ban. Lorillard wants to protect the growing popularity of Newport, which accounts for 13 percent of cigarette sales. Lorillard has pointed to the thousands of jobs that are at stake, and the company argues that a ban would result in a large unregulated black market for the cigarettes. Lorillard also disputes the claim that menthol cigarettes pose greater medical risks than other varieties.

Question

1. The website "Hot Air" thinks the government should not intervene in the menthol cigarette market:

> Once again, we have the federal government acting as nanny rather than allowing adults to make their own decisions. No one forces people to use tobacco products, after all, and we have literally spent decades educating people about the dangers. . . .[71]

What do you think the government should do? Explain.

Sources: Michaela L. Duckett, "The Push to Ban Menthol Cigarettes," *The Charlotte Post,* April 25, 2013 [**www.thecharlottepost.com**]; and David Kesmodel, "Lorillard Fights to Snuff Menthol Ban," *The Wall Street Journal,* January 5, 2011, p. A1.

Case II. Cell Phones: A Deadly Distraction?

Nearly 70 percent of young drivers text behind the wheel and 48 percent admit to accessing the Web while driving.[72] The federal Department of Transportation reported that 3,331 people died in distraction-related crashes in 2011.[73] Research at the University of Utah found that cell phone conversation is a much more dangerous distraction than passenger conversation.[74] A *Houston Chronicle* editorial argued for measures to curb driving while using a cell phone:

> Even a cursory glance at the statistics is evidence enough that swift, comprehensive action must be taken on a national level to curb this reckless, potentially deadly, behavior: Driving while using a cell phone incurs a fourfold greater risk of crashing, equivalent to driving while drunk (with a 0.08 blood-alcohol level). For texters, the risk is eight times greater. A recent study by the Virginia Tech Transportation Institute, which videotaped truck drivers over 18 months, showed that texting made them 23 times more likely to crash or narrowly avoid a crash.[75]

No state forbids all cell phone use while driving, but 39 ban text messaging for all drivers, and 10 states forbid all drivers from using handheld cell phones while driving.[76] Are these restraints effective? The evidence shows little, if any, reduction in cell phone use while driving, despite mounting evidence of the dangers. Of course, the real problem may be distractions of all kinds, but survey results find 96 percent of Americans agreeing that cell phone use should not be permitted while driving.[77]

Questions

1. Mike Hashimoto, assistant editorial page editor at the *Dallas Morning News:*

> I get as mad as the next person at the minivan driver cruising along 5 mph below the speed limit in the left lane, basically causing everyone else with someplace to be to dodge around him/her in a slightly dangerous way. That doesn't mean we need another annoying law in the long-running series of laws intended to remove all risk from our daily lives. . . . A cell phone

ban might make us feel better, but at best, it would have the same practical effect as banning Big Macs while driving, shaving while driving, reading a map while driving or reaching into the back seat for your kid while driving. . . .[78]

a. Would you favor government rules forbidding cell phone use while driving? Explain.

b. What about text messaging, grooming, eating, and so on? Explain.

2. Technology companies are rapidly bringing powerful information technology to car dashboards. Government regulators argue that those products are slowing their efforts to reduce hazards from distracted driving. According to National Transportation Safety Board chair, Deborah Hersman:

> If the technology producers focused more on what is safe than what sells, we'd see highway fatalities go down.[79]

Do you agree that technology companies are irresponsibly putting profit before safety in developing ever more advanced, and doubtless distracting, technology in cars? Explain.

3. Distinguished economist Herbert Stein, perhaps best known as father of celebrity Ben Stein, said that we are desperate for cell phone conversations to ward off our loneliness:

> It is the way of keeping contact with someone, anyone who will reassure you that you are not alone. You may think you are checking on your portfolio but deep down you are checking on your own existence.[80]

a. Are you dependent on your cell phone?

b. If so, should the government discourage that use by, for example, imposing higher taxes on cell phone purchases? Explain.

Guy Davenport: "The telephone is God's gift to the bore."

Source: Interview by John Jeremiah Sullivan. *The Paris Review.* Fall 2002.

Internet Exercise

Should the U.S. government impose new rules requiring all bicyclists to wear helmets? New Zealand has enforced a national mandatory all-age bicycle helmet law since 1994. To help with your recommendation for the United States, consider the evidence from the New Zealand experience at **http://en.wikipedia.org/wiki/Bicycle_helmets_in_New_Zealand**.

Chapter Questions

1. Colorado and Washington have legalized marijuana use with both states instituting regulatory systems somewhat like those for alcohol. Marijuana use remains illegal under federal law, but as previously noted, the Obama administration has announced that it will not aggressively enforce federal standards as long as the states establish satisfactory regulatory oversight. Should the federal government enforce its criminal laws in those states? Should the federal government attempt to preempt the state laws, asserting that those laws are in unconstitutional conflict with federal law? Explain.

2. *The Des Moines Register* advocated a free-market approach to cable television, labeling it a "nonessential activity."

a. Should the government be involved in regulating only those products and services that we cannot do without? Explain.

b. Do you trust the free market? The government? Both? Neither? Explain.

c. Do you think the Consumer Financial Protection Bureau is necessary to reduce the risk of a future banking crisis such as the one we have faced in recent years? Explain.

3. Nevada in 2013 became the first state to legalize and offer online gambling. Nevada limits its online gaming to poker, but other states, including New Jersey, are expected to follow with a full array of lawful, online offerings. The federal government is considering legislation to achieve a uniform, national policy that is expected to allow poker but forbid, under federal law, other forms of online gambling. Currently, the unauthorized online gambling market in the United States is estimated at about $4 billion.

a. List some of the pros and cons of allowing and regulating Internet gambling.

b. Would you favor that direction? Explain.

4. The Heritage Foundation's 2013 global Index of Economic Freedom generally demonstrates that the nations most successful in increasing their economic freedom (by reducing taxes and so forth) enjoy, according to the editors of the study, higher per capita incomes, and higher overall well-being.[81] When the Index was first published in 1995, the United States ranked fifth in the world, but it fell to tenth in the 2013 study. Hong Kong ranked first in 2013, with Canada sixth and the United Kingdom fourteenth.[82]

a. What is economic freedom?

b. The Heritage Foundation lists 10 factors including, for example, business freedom, in its list of ingredients in measuring economic freedom. In addition to business freedom, what other factors would you include in a list designed to measure a nation's level of overall economic freedom?

c. How does economic freedom help an economy grow?

5. Former Secretary of Labor Robert Reich: "The era of big government may be over, but the era of regulation through litigation has just begun.[83] Explain what Reich meant.

6. At this writing in 2013, the National Collegiate Athletic Association (NCAA), the primary governing body for college athletics, is in the midst of a heated debate about proposals for deregulating NCAA oversight practices. A primary area of concern involves the detailed set of rules currently governing the recruiting of high school athletes. The NCAA proposes reducing those rules by, for example, allowing schools to make an unrestricted number of phone calls and texts to recruits, allowing any staff member (not just coaches) to contact recruits and permitting schools to send unlimited print material to recruits.

Many coaches oppose the changes. Northwestern University head football coach Pat Fitzgerald actually favored greater regulation:

> The term that makes the hair stand up on the back of my neck is "deregulate." The question we should be asking is how can we re-regulate, get up to the 21st century and make best practices in recruiting for all those involved.[84]

a. How do you think college football programs' recruiting practices would change in response to the proposed changes noted above?

b. Broadly, do you think NCAA rules governing sports recruiting should be deregulated or "re-regulated" toward best practices, as suggested by Coach Fitzgerald?

c. In raising children of high school age, would you favor a parental approach involving heavy reliance on rules, or would you prefer a more deregulated, free-market approach? Explain.

7. Although frustrating and imperfect, government regulation often leads to better lives. We notice, for example, that seat belt use in 2012 reached a record high with 86 percent of motorists buckled up as compared with 58 percent in 1994[85], and we know that smoking bans have directly and quickly led to reductions in heart attacks and other ailments.[86] "Fracking" technology necessary to our current natural gas drilling boom was significantly propelled by more than $100 million in government subsidies and much more in tax breaks.[87] Given those successes and many others, do we need more aggressive government intervention in America's endangered family life? At first glance, most Americans would probably say "no," but a 2012 University of Virginia (UVA) study argued that government intervention is needed to restore the institution of marriage among the 60 percent of our population that does not have a college education. In the 1980s, about 13 percent of American children were born outside of marriage; now that number is about 44 percent. The UVA study estimates the cost to taxpayers at over $100 billion annually when stable families do not develop.[88] The study suggests, among other things, various tax and welfare policy changes to encourage marriage.

Is marriage a private and personal affair that should be left free of further government intervention? Explain. [For more information, see **statcofourunions.org**]

8. The expense of government regulation is not limited to the direct cost of administering the various agencies. Explain and offer examples of the other expenses produced by regulation.

9. To the extent the federal government achieves deregulation, what substitutes will citizens find for protection?

10. Pulitzer Prize–winning author and presidential adviser Arthur Schlesinger:

> The assault on the national government is represented as a disinterested movement to "return" power to the people. But the withdrawal of the national government does not transfer power to the people. It transfers power to the historical rival of the national government and the prime cause of its enlargement—the great corporate interests.[89]

a. Using 19th- and 20th-century American economic history, explain Schlesinger's claim that corporate interests are the primary cause of big government.

b. Do you agree with Schlesinger that we continue to need big government to counteract corporate interests and achieve fairness for all in American life? Explain.

11. Make the argument that increasing government rules and jobs leads to decreasing private-sector businesses and jobs.

12. One authority estimates that obesity contributes to the deaths of 100,000 Americans annually.[90] A strategy for reducing the health risks of obesity is to impose a tax on high calorie junk foods such as soda, donuts, and potato chips. Maine, for example, imposed a 5.5 percent snack tax as a means of closing a budget gap, but that state's adult obesity rate

doubled during the 10 years the tax was in place.[91] Two-thirds of the states already impose a tax (averaging 5.2 percent) on soft drinks, but for a 5-foot-10, 279-pound person, the average weight loss associated with the tax has been about 3 ounces.[92]

a. What objections would you raise to increased taxes on junk food.

b. Would you support a significant tax, say, 25 percent, on junk food? Explain.

c. Would subsidies to lower the price of healthy food be a more effective strategy than taxes on unhealthy food? Explain.

13. The British government spends about $340 per year per Briton on drug costs whereas the United States spends about $800 per year per American. As *The Wall Street Journal* reported, Great Britain is struggling to find ways to curb rocketing health care costs:

> Millions of patients around the world have taken drugs introduced over the past decade to delay the worsening of Alzheimer's disease. While the drugs offer no cure, studies suggest they work in some patients at least for a while. But this year, an arm of Britain's government health-care system, relying on some economists' number-crunching, said the benefit isn't worth the cost. It issued a preliminary ruling calling on doctors to stop prescribing the drugs. The ruling highlighted one of the most disputed issues in medicine today. If a treatment helps people, should governments and private insurers pay for it without question? Or should they first measure the benefit against the cost, and only pay if the cost-benefit ratio exceeds some preset standard?[93]

Should the U.S. government and insurers employ cost-benefit calculations in deciding which illnesses and patients receive coverage? Explain.

14. Joseph Stiglitz, the chief White House economist at the time, argued in 1996 that "a huge economic literature" supports his view that "appropriately circumscribed government programs can lead to a higher-growth economy."[94] How can government programs stimulate the economy rather than act as a drag on it?

15. A major issue facing the Federal Aviation Administration is congestion in the airways caused by too many planes seeking to take off or land at peak times at high-demand airports. How might we solve that problem while maintaining reasonable service?

16. In calculating the costs and benefits of a new rule, make the argument that added regulation normally slows the economy and leads to increased deaths.

17. Eighty-three percent of teens had at least one sunburn in 1999, whereas the comparable figure in 1986 was 30 percent.[95] "Right now, we're at the apex of the 'bronze goddess era,'" said Atoosa Rubenstein, editor-in-chief of *CosmoGIRL* magazine.[96] More than a third of the 17-year-old girls in a recent survey reported going to a tanning salon in the previous year.[97] In 2009 the International Agency for Research on Cancer classified tanning beds as Group 1 carcinogens, meaning the evidence is sufficient for experts to conclude that the beds cause cancer.[98] A scientific review of the tanning data found that the risk of melanoma increases by 75 percent if tanning beds and lamps are used prior to age 30.[99] The American Academy of Dermatology Association (AADA) has urged the FDA to ban the sale and use of indoor tanning equipment for non-medical purposes and has called for state or federal laws to, among other things, forbid minors from using tanning devices. Do you support limits on teen tanning? Explain?

18. A bipartisan coalition labeled "Mayors Against Illegal Guns" released a 2010 study finding that 43,000 of the guns confiscated at crimes scenes in 2009 came from out-of-state gun dealers. Georgia, Virginia, West Virginia, Alabama, Mississippi, and Alaska were among the largest gun exporters. States with strong restrictions export guns at only about one seventh the rate of those with lax rules. About 12,000 Americans annually are murdered by guns.[100] Commenting in *The New York Times,* columnist Nicholas Kristof said:

> To protect the public, we regulate cars and toys, medicines and mutual funds. So, simply as a public health matter, shouldn't we take steps to reduce the toll from our domestic arms industry?[101]

Adam Lanza, 20, fatally shot 20 children and 6 school personnel at Sandy Hook Elementary School in Newtown, Connecticut, on December 14, 2012. He also murdered his mother and shot himself. Once again we ask ourselves what can be done to reduce gun violence. Do you think firmer gun regulations are needed? Explain.

Notes

1. Joseph Berger and Marc Santora, "Chilling Look at Newtown Killer, but No 'Why,'" *The New York Times,* November 25, 2013 [**www.nytimes.com/**].

2. California Civil Code sections 1746-1746.5.

3. *Brown v. Entertainment Merchants Association,* 2011 U.S. LEXIS 4802.

4. Ibid.

5. Staci Hupp, "Nearly 1 in 10 U.S. Kids Addicted to Video Games, ISU Study Finds," *The Des Moines Register,* April 20, 2009, p. 1A.

6. Matt DeLisi, et al., "Violent Video Games, Delinquency, and Youth Violence," *Youth Violence and Juvenile Justice* 11 (2, April 2013), p. 132.

7. Rob Stein, "Born to Be a Trader? Fingers Point to Yes." *The Washington Post,* January 13, 2009, p. A02.

8. Joseph P. Tomain, "American Regulatory Policy: Have We Found the 'Third Way'?" *Kansas Law Review* 48 (May 2000), p. 829.

9. Catherine Rampell, "Lax Oversight Caused Crisis, Bernanke Says," *The New York Times,* January 4, 2010 [**www.nytimes.com/2010**].

10. 317 U.S. 111 (1942).

11. 545 U.S. 1 (2005).

12. *Gonzalez v. Raich,* 545 U.S. 1, 57-8 (2005).

13. 115 S.Ct. 1624 (1995).

14. 18 U.S.C. 922 (q) (1) (A).

15. *Brzonkala v. Morrison and United States v. Morrison,* 529 U.S. 598 (2000).

16. *Brzonkala v. Virginia Polytechnic Institute,* 169 F.3d 820, 827 (4th Cir. 1999).

17. 132 S.Ct. 2566 (2012).

18. John F. Cooney, "Federalism Spring: Evolution of the Federal-State Balance of Power," *Bloomberg Law Reports-Administrative Law,* No. 4 (2009).

19. See, e.g., *Williamson v. Mazda Motor of Am., Inc.,* 131 S.Ct. 1131 (2011) [state tort suit not preempted], *Bruesewitz v. Wyeth LLC,* 131 S.Ct. 1068 (2011) [state tort suit preempted], and *Kurns v. Railroad Friction Products Corp.,* 132 S.Ct. 1261 (2012) [state tort suit preempted].

20. Greg Bensinger, "Wine: The Web's Final Frontier," *The Wall Street Journal,* October 27, 2012, p. B3.

21. Ibid.

22. Alice G. Walton, "Large-Size Sugary Drink Ban Passes in NYC, Opponents Vow a Fight," *Forbes,* September 14, 2012 [**www.forbes.com/**].

23. "Soda Consumption, Obesity Both Sky-High in U.S.," *HUFFPOST HEALTHY LIVING,* March 13, 2013 [**www.huffingtonpost.com/**].

24. Walton, "Large Size Sugary Drink Ban."

25. Nicholas Confessore, "Minority Groups and Bottlers Team Up in Battles over Soda," *The New York Times,* March 12, 2013 [**www.nyt.com/**].

26. Bianca Nunes, "NYC 'Soda Ban' Overturned: An Analysis of the Opinion," *Reg Blog,* April 2, 2013 [**www.law.upenn.edu/blogs/regblog/2013/04/02-nunes-nyc-soda-ban-overturned .html**].

27. See *St. Joseph Abbey v. Castille,* 2013 U.S. App. LEXIS 5701.

28. Jennifer Jacobs, "Judge Backs City's Refusal to Renew Bar's License," *Waterloo/Cedar Falls Courier,* November 22, 1998, p. C3.

29. The organizational structure of the introductory administrative law materials owes a great deal to the suggestions of Professor Cynthia Srstka, Augustana College (South Dakota).

30. For a recent federal court rejection of FCC cross-ownership policies, see *Prometheus Radio Project v. Federal Communications Commission,* 652 F.3d 431 (3d Cir. 2011).

31. Matt Schafer, "FCC Defends Discredited Media Ownership Rules," *Free Press,* July 22, 2010 [**www.stopbigmedia.com/blog/2010/**].

32. David Rauf, "FCC Tries Voluntary Approach," *Politico,* May 20, 2012 [**http://dyn.politico .com/**].

33. Charlie Savage, "Sex, Drug Use and Graft Cited in Interior Department," *The New York Times,* September 11, 2008 [**www.nytimes.com/2008/09/11/**].

34. Ibid.

35. Juliet Eilperin, "U.S. Exempted BP's Gulf of Mexico Drilling from Environmental Impact Study," *The Washington Post,* May 5, 2010, p. A04.

36. T.W. Farnam, "Revolving Door of Employment between Congress, Lobbying Firms, Study Shows," *The Washington Post,* September 13, 2011 [**articles.washingtonpost.com/2011-09 -13/politics/35274736_1_lobbyists-podesta-group-hill-workers**].

37. See Jack Maskell, "Post-Employment, 'Revolving Door,' Laws for Federal Personnel," *Congressional Research Service,* May 12, 2010 [**www.fas.org/sgp/crs/misc/97-875.pdf**].

38. Lori Montgomery, "Obama Orders All Fed Agencies to Review Regulations," *The Washington Post,* January 18, 2011 [**www.washingtonpost.com/**].

39. 531 U.S. 457 (2001).

40. Editorial, "Free Speech for Broadcasters," *The New York Times,* July 16, 2010 [**www.nytimes .com**].

41. *CBS v. FCC,* 663 F.3d 122 (2011).

42. *Federal Communications Commission v. CBS Corporation,* 132 S.Ct. 2677 (2012).

43. Ibid.

44. "Most Employers Won't Drop Health Care Coverage Because of Obamacare: Survey," *HuffPost Business*, April 13, 2013 [**www.huffingtonpost.com**].

45. "Six Largest Banks Getting Bigger, Brown Said," *PolitiFact,* April 25, 2010 [**www.politifact .com/**].

46. "Federal Register Pages Published Annually," [**www.llsdc.org/attachments/wysiwyg/544 /fed-reg-pages.pdf**].

47. "Piling On: The Year in Regulation," *American Action Forum,* January 14, 2013 [**americanactionforum.org/topic/piling-year-regulation**].

48. Dennis Cauchon, "Federal Pay Ahead of Private Industry," *USA TODAY,* March 8, 2010 [**www.usatoday.com**].

49. U.S. Chamber of Commerce, "Regulations Pile Up," *Free Enterprise Magazine,* September 2010 [**www.uschambermagazine.com**].

50. Office of Management and Budget, "2013 Draft Report to Congress on the Benefits and Costs of Federal Regulations and Unfunded Mandates on State, Local, and Tribal Entities," [**www .whitehouse.gov/sites/default/files/omb/inforeg/2013/_cb/draft_2013_cost_benefit_report .pdf**].

51. Warren E. Buffett, "Pretty Good for Government Work," *The New York Times,* November 16, 2010 [**www.nytimes.com/**].

52. Jia Lynn Yang, "Does Government Regulation Really Kill Jobs? Economists Say Overall Effect Minimal," *The Washington Post,* November 13, 2011 [**www.washingtonpost.com/**].

53. Ibid.

54. The World Bank and the International Finance Corporation, "Doing Business 2013" [**www .doingbusiness.org**].

55. Damian Paletta, "Billions in Bloat Uncovered in Beltway," *The Wall Street Journal,* March 1, 2011, p. A1.

56. Jacob Laksin, "Why Corporate America Needs Welfare Reform," *The Wall Street Journal,* July 29–30, 2006, p. P9.

57. Anthony Faiola, Ellen Nakashima and Jill Drew, "What Went Wrong?" *The Washington Post,* October 15, 2008, p. A01.

58. John H. Makin, "A Government Failure, Not a Market Failure," *Commentary,* July/August 2009 [**www.commentarymagazine.com/viewarticle.cfm/a-government-failure -not-a-market-failure-15191**].

59. Jake Ackman,"Economist Richard Parker Discusses Past and Future of Financial Deregulation," *Harvard Kennedy School News & Events,* March 18, 2009 [**www.hks.harvard.edu /news-events/news/articles/parker-economy-talk**].

60. Alan Greenspan, "We Need a Better Cushion Against Risk," *Financial Times,* March 26, 2009 [**www.ft.com/**].

61. Neil Irwin and Amit R. Paley, "Greenspan Says He Was Wrong on Regulation," *The Washington Post,* October 24, 2008, p. A01.

62. Stephen Labaton, "S.E.C. Concedes Oversight Flaws Fueled Collapse," *The New York Times,* September 27, 2008, Section A, p. 1.

63. John Steele Gordon, *An Empire of Wealth: The Epic History of American Economic Power* (New York: Harper Collins, 2004). Quoted by Wayne E. Yang, "The Wealth of America Is Wealth," *Christian Science Monitor,* December 7, 2004 [**www.csmonitor.com/2004/ 1207 /p15s02-bogn.html**].

64. Sebastian Mallaby, "Capitalism: The Remix," *Washingtonpost.com,* December 4, 2008, p. A21.

65. Ibid.

66. Sheryl Gay Stolberg, "Young, Liberal and Open to Big Government," *The New York Times,* February 11, 2013 [**www.nytimes.com/**].

67. Ibid.

68. Edward Cody, "France Drowning in Rules and Regulations, Critics Say," *The Washington Post*, April 16, 2013 [**www.washingtonpost.com/**].

69. Suzanne Daley, "A Tale of Greek Enterprise and Olive Oil, Smothered in Red Tape," *The New York Times*, March 18, 2012 [**www.nytimes.com/**].

70. "World Bank & IFC Report Finds Developing Countries Made Significant Progress in Improving Business Regulations," World Bank Press Release, October 23, 2012 [**www.worldbank.org/**].

71. Ed Morrissey, "Should the FDA Ban Menthol Cigarettes?" *Hot Air,* September 10, 2010 [**http://hotair.com/archives/2010/09/10/should-the-fda-ban-menthol-cigarettes/**].

72. Larry Copeland, "Young Drivers Still Texting, Surfing the Web," *USA TODAY*, November 16, 2012, p. 3A.

73. "Half of Adults Text While Driving," *Des Moines Register*, March 28, 2013, p. 1A.

74. "Chatty Driving: Phones vs. Passengers," Well Blog, *The New York Times,* December 1, 2008 [**http://well.blogs.nytimes.com/2008/**].

75. Editorial, "Deadly Distraction," *Houston Chronicle,* September 22, 2009 [**www.chron.com/**].

76. National Highway Traffic Safety Administration, "Motorists Are Urged to Put Down Their Electronic Devices and Focus on Driving during National Distracted Driving Awareness Month," Press Release, April 5, 2013 [**www.nhtsa.gov/**].

77. Jenny Guarino, "Survey Reveals Public Open to Ban on Hand-Held Cell Phone Use and Texting," *Special Report, Bureau of Transportation Statistics*, January 2013 [**www.rita.dot.gov/bts/sites/rita.dot.gov.bts/files/bts_sr_distracted_driving.pdf**].

78. Nicole Stockdale, "Time to Ban Cell Phones while Driving? (Ed Board Sounds Off)," *Dallas Morning Star,* July 22, 2009 [**http://dallasmorningviewblog.dallasnews.com/**].

79. Angela Greiling Keane, "Gadgets Share Blame for Distracted Driving, NTSB Chief Says," *The Washington Post,* March 27, 2012 [**www.washingtonpost.com**].

80. James Gleick, *The Acceleration of Just about Everything* (New York: Vintage Books, 1999), p. 89.

81. The Heritage Foundation, "2013 Index of Economic Freedom" [**www.heritage.org/index**].

82. Ibid.

83. Robert Reich, "Regulation Is Out, Litigation Is In," *USA TODAY,* February 11, 1999, p. 15A.

84. Stewart Mandel, "Recruiting Deregulation Fiasco Underscores Deeper NCAA Disconnect," *SI.com,* April 30, 2013 [**www.si.com**].

85. John Bacon, "Seat Belt Use Reaches Record: 86% of All Motorists in USA," *USA TODAY*, November 15, 2012, p. 2A.

86. Liz Szabo, "Smoking Bans Cut Number of Heart Attacks, Strokes," *USA TODAY*, October 30, 2012, p. 4A.

87. Associated Press, "Shale Gas Supporters Give Credit to Government-Backed Research," *Waterloo/Cedar Falls Courier*, September 24, 2012, p. A6.

88. Kathleen Parker, "Un-Hitched Middle Class a Problem," *Waterloo/Cedar Falls Courier*, December 18, 2012, p. A5.

89. Arthur Schlesinger, Jr., "In Defense of Government," *The Wall Street Journal,* June 7, 1995, p. A14.

90. Karen Kaplan, "Calls to Tax Junk Food Gain Ground," *latimes.com,* August 23, 2009 [**www .latimes.com/**].

91. Ibid.

92. Ibid.

93. Jeanne Wilson, "Britain Stirs Outcry by Weighing Benefits of Drugs Versus Price," *The Wall Street Journal,* November 22, 2006, p. A1.

94. Bob Davis, "In Presidential Race, the Key Question Is, 'What Causes Growth?'" *The Wall Street Journal,* September 27, 1996, p. A1.

95. Julie Sevrens Lyons, "Doctors See Growing Cancer Risk with Trendy Tans," *Milwaukee Journal,* July 29, 2002, p. 3A.

96. Ibid.

97. Ibid.

98. "Tanning Beds Classified as 'Carcinogenic to Humans,'" *Daily Cancer News,* July 29, 2009 [**http://patient.cancerconsultants.com/**].

99. Steve Reinberg, "Tanning Beds Get Highest Carcinogen Rating," *U.S. News & World Report,* July 28, 2009 [**http://health.usnews.com/health-news/family-health/cancer /articles/2009/07/28/tanning-beds-get-highest-carcinogen-rating**].

100. Editorial, "Lax and Lethal," *The New York Times,* October 3, 2010 [**www.nytimes.com/**].

101. Nicholas D. Kristof, "Why Not Regulate Guns as Seriously as Toys?" *The New York Times,* January 12, 2011 [**www.nytimes.com**].

CHAPTER NINE

Business Organizations and Securities Regulation

After completing this chapter, students will be able to:

1. Describe the advantages and disadvantages of corporations, partnerships, and limited liability companies.

2. Identify and explain the business judgment rule.

3. Explain the relationship between limited liability and the doctrine of "piercing the corporate veil."

4. Compare and contrast C corporations and S corporations.

5. Define and describe common stock, preferred stock, and debt.

6. Identify the main concerns of corporate governance.

7. Identify some of the goals of the shareholder rights movement.

8. Define the term *initial public offering* (IPO).

9. Describe the securities registration process.

10. Compare and contrast the regulatory roles of the 1933 and 1934 federal securities acts.

11. Explain the due diligence defense.

12. Describe the fraud-on-the-market theory of reliance and explain its importance.

13. Define insider trading.

14. Contrast the classical fiduciary theory of insider trading with the misappropriation theory.

15. Describe the tender offer process and some defenses against it.

Introduction

Against a backdrop of the worst financial crisis since the Great Depression of the 1930s, this chapter provides a brief introduction to some of the fundamental laws governing business—the types and characteristics of available business entities, key corporate governance issues, and business access to capital.

From the outset we need to recognize the overlapping coverage of state and federal regulation of business. Historically, state law governed most issues—such as the creation of business entities, the powers and duties of management, and capital structure. Still today, the laws that regulate a partnership, both among the partners and with outside parties, are state laws; as are the laws that permit the creation of corporations, those under which limited liability companies (LLCs) have been allowed to form and those permitting numerous other business forms. The owners of a corporation are called *stockholders* or *shareholders* because the ownership interests are called shares of stock. The fundamental legal duties that corporations, corporate boards, and officers owe to their shareholders are defined by the state of incorporation. Over half of all publicly traded companies and more than 200,000 private firms are incorporated in Delaware.[1] Thus, when state corporate law issues are discussed, the corporate law of Delaware often drives the discussion. Part One of this chapter will discuss the key characteristics under state law of the most common business entity forms.

Delaware Seeks Exclusive Jurisdiction

Delaware generates over a third of its total state revenue from taxes and fees related to corporate domicile, each corporation paying up to $180,000 annually. In 2013, over 80 percent of all IPOs were by entities incorporated in that state.[2] Whether Delaware's primacy is related to its success in a race to the bottom or a race to the top, corporate management appreciates the state's business-friendly Court of Chancery. In June 2013, that body upheld a bylaw restricting shareholder lawsuits to the Delaware courts. Many believe such bylaws are adopted to give management the "home-field advantage" in that states more sympathetic to shareholders are deprived of jurisdiction. Approximately 300 corporations now have this bylaw, with many more expected if the ruling stands on appeal.[3]

The first decade of the 21st century has been scarred by two systemic failures involving corporate actors and the capital markets. The first is commonly referenced by the 2001 collapse of Enron (although that was not the largest of the corporate failures characterizing that era). The second was the financial crisis that struck in the fall of 2008 (which is often referenced by the collapse of Lehman Brothers). Contributing to both events were failures of corporate management. In each case, Congress responded with significant legislation that, in part, imposes additional requirements on the management of *publicly held corporations* (corporations with publicly traded shares). These federal laws are the Sarbanes–Oxley Act of 2002 (SOX) and the Dodd–Frank Act of 2010 (see Chapter 8 also). Part Two of this chapter will discuss corporate governance issues specific to public corporations, including the relevant provisions of these two federal laws.

Part Three will take a closer look at how businesses are financed—particularly their access to capital beyond the resources of the initial founders. Although state law plays a role here, federal regulation dominates. Triggered by the 1929 stock market crash and the continuing failure of the capital markets and banking system in the Great Depression of the 1930s, the federal government, largely under its powers to regulate interstate commerce, created the Securities and Exchange Commission (SEC) to regulate the securities markets.

Part Three of this chapter will focus on federal regulation of the securities markets, including relevant changes following the two financial crises of the last decade.

Part One—Business Entities and Their Defining Characteristics

One of the most significant decisions facing the founders of a business is the choice of a legal entity to house the business. Among other things, this decision will affect the legal relationships among the founders, the relationship between them, and the entity and between them and various third parties. It will also affect their access to outside capital and the tax treatment accorded business profits and losses. Thus, Part One outlines each of the principal choices available. It will conclude with a brief discussion of circumstances that might favor the use of one form over another, as well as a look at a few lesser-used forms and newly emerging forms.

The three traditional business forms are *corporations, partnerships,* and *sole proprietorships*. Partnerships and sole proprietorships are default forms. For example, if an individual starts a business and takes no active steps to house that business within an entity structure, the business will, by default, be classed as a sole proprietorship. Strictly speaking, a sole proprietorship is not a business entity at all—the law treats the business and the individual as the same legal person. If, on the other hand, two or more persons join together to start the business and take no active steps to create an entity structure, the law will, again by default, classify the business as a partnership. The only way to establish a business as a corporation, or indeed as any of the other entities discussed in this part, is for its founders to take deliberate steps, specified by state law, to create the entity.

One such other entity is the LLC or *limited liability company*. An LLC is often referred to as a *hybrid* because it was specifically designed to combine various desired characteristics of corporations with others of partnerships. Another hybrid form is known as a *subchapter S corporation,* (also called sub-S or S corporations). For state corporate law purposes, it is a corporation like any other, but for federal (and most state) income tax purposes the legal entity is largely ignored and all of the business tax consequences instead flow through to the tax returns of the individual shareholders. This is similar, but not identical, to the way the tax consequences of a partnership flow through to the tax returns of individual partners.

If we set aside businesses run as sole proprietorships, today more businesses are housed in these two hybrid entities, LLCs and S corporations, than in the traditional corporate and partnership forms. Based on IRS data for 2010 (the latest data available), LLC returns increased 250 percent from 2001 to 2.1 million, showing about $3 trillion in receipts. S corporations filed 4.1 million returns reporting $6 trillion in revenue. "Traditional" corporations (also known as C corporations) filed only 1.7 million returns but were responsible for $20 trillion in receipts.[4]

Each of these forms will be evaluated below according to the following considerations:

Formation and nontax costs. The method of and costs related to bringing a business form into existence.

Management structure. The degree to which control is centralized in a hierarchical structure or is dispersed among owners.

Limited liability. The extent to which business owners are personally liable for business obligations.

Transferability of ownership interests. Whether the business owners can transfer their interests without state law restrictions.

Duration of existence. The events, including those impacting the business owners, which will end the business entity's existence.

Taxes. The way each business form affects the income tax treatment of the business and its owners.

Capital structure. The impact of the business form on the organization's ability to access additional capital.

[For a table summarizing the key characteristics of each business form, see **www.bizfilings.com/learning/comparison.htm**]

Corporations

Although only 19 percent of all business entities are C corporations, they account for 67 percent of all business revenue. Together, C and S corporations represent 64 percent of all business entities and account for 87 percent of all business revenue.[5] There are good reasons for their financial success, which will become evident in the discussion to follow.

Throughout this discussion, we must keep in mind two very different corporate realities: the public corporation and the *closely held corporation* (a corporation with relatively few shareholders, the stock of which has no readily available market).

Corporate Constitutional Rights?

Under state law, corporations are legal persons.[6] This raises the question of whether corporations have constitutionally protected rights. Over the years, the Supreme Court has held that corporations are sometimes entitled to constitutional protections[7] and at other times not so entitled.[8] As discussed in Chapter 1, the issue arose again in *Citizens United v. Federal Election Com'n,* 130 S.Ct. 876 (2010), in which the Court, over a strong dissent, enunciated a wide-reaching principle that "the Government may not suppress political speech on the basis of the speaker's corporate identity." Justice Stevens, with three others, dissented:

> The real issue in this case concerns how, not if, [Citizens United] may finance its electioneering. Citizens United is a wealthy nonprofit corporation that runs a political action committee (PAC) with millions of dollars in assets. Under [the disputed law], it could have used those assets to televise and promote *Hillary: The Movie* wherever and whenever it wanted to. It also could have spent unrestricted sums to broadcast *Hillary* at any time other than the 30 days before the last primary election. Neither Citizens United's nor any other corporation's speech has been "banned." . . . In the context of election to public office, the distinction between corporate and human speakers is significant. Although they make enormous contributions to our society, corporations are not actually members of

it. They cannot vote or run for office. . . . The financial resources, legal structure, and instrumental orientation of corporations raise legitimate concerns about their role in the electoral process.

Question

When a corporation funds political speech, for whom is it speaking? Consider these possibilities from the *Citizens United* majority and dissenting opinions:

> [W]ealthy individuals and unincorporated associations can spend unlimited amounts on independent expenditures. Yet certain disfavored associations of citizens—those that have taken on the corporate form—are penalized for engaging in the same political speech. *Citizens United*, supra at 908 (majority opinion).
>
> It is an interesting question "who" is even speaking when a business corporation places an advertisement that endorses or attacks a particular candidate. Presumably it is not the customers or employees, who typically have no say in such matters. It cannot realistically be said to be the shareholders, who tend to be far removed from the day-to-day decisions of the firm and whose political preferences may be opaque to management. Perhaps the officers or directors of the corporation have the best claim to be the ones speaking, except their fiduciary duties generally prohibit them from using corporate funds for personal ends. *Citizens United,* supra at 972 (dissent).

Formation and Nontax Costs

To create a corporation, a *promoter* or *incorporator* files *articles of incorporation* with the state government. A modest fee is typically charged. The articles have mandatory elements, such as the corporation's name, the person designated to receive certain communications from the state (legal documents such as subpoenas), and a description of the stock the corporation is permitted to issue. Discretionary content like voting rules may also appear in the articles.

Once the articles are filed the corporation comes into existence. An *organizational meeting* will then be held at which the initial members of the *board of directors* will be appointed by the incorporators (unless they were already designated in the articles). The board will then meet to undertake the corporation's initial business. Among other things, it will appoint officers and adopt *bylaws*. Bylaws contain key policies and procedures, such as how meeting quorums will be determined and the percentage of shareholders that must approve major corporate actions like mergers. The issuance of stock will be authorized in exchange for contributions of capital, property, or services. [For a large library of business forms, see **www.lectlaw.com/formb.htm**]

At least annually the board of directors and shareholders must hold meetings and the corporation will have to make brief filings with the state to keep its records up-to-date, usually accompanied by a small fee. [To see how Delaware computes this fee, see **www .corp.delaware.gov/fee.shtml**]

Corporations are separate accounting entities and need to establish books of account. The cost of their accounting systems, however, generally reflects their scale of operation, rather than the decision to operate in corporate form.

Selection and Protection of the Corporate Name

Articles of incorporation are filed in the name of the soon-to-be corporation. States require corporate names to be distinguishable from names already registered, so it is a good thing to check the state's database in advance for the desired name and reserve it prior to filing the articles. Other steps an entrepreneur should consider include:

Trademark issues—Will someone sue to stop the use of the chosen name? Check with the U.S. Patent & Trademark Office database to see if the name has been trademarked. If it has, select a different name. It may be wise to protect the final name selected by registering it as a trademark [**www.uspto.gov/trademarks/process/index.jsp**].

Domain name—Do an Internet search on the selected corporate name. Is the name still available as a domain name? If yes, register it. If not, what name is available that will be effective for customers and others trying to find you? Will customers be confused by the website with your preferred domain name?

Fictitious name—If the domain name differs from the corporate name and will be used separately, it may be prudent to register it with the state as a fictitious name.

Doing business in other states   If business will be conducted in other states, the business name database of those states should also be checked and the corporation registered as a foreign corporation in those states.

Source: Kermit Pattison, "How to Register a Start-Up," *The New York Times,* March 31, 2010.

Management Structure

One strength of the corporate form, an attribute that has allowed it to become a very effective engine of economic growth, is its ability to separate ownership from management. Shareholders contribute the capital that allows the business to be established. In exchange shareholders receive stock, each share of which represents an ownership unit. Annually, the shareholders meet to elect a board of directors. All corporate powers are exercised by or under the authority of the board for and on behalf of the shareholders. Typically, boards do not operate the business on a day-to-day basis. Rather, they are policy and oversight bodies. To actually run the company, boards appoint *officers,* often a CEO (chief executive officer) or president, secretary, CFO (chief financial officer) or treasurer, and several vice presidents. Officers are employees of the corporation and they hire the other employees needed to run the business. This hierarchy is referred to as a centralized management structure. Keep in mind that a small corporation will likely have this same formal structure, but its operational dynamics may be quite different if, as is common, many of the same people who are shareholders are also directors and officers.

Both directors and officers have *fiduciary duties* to the corporation. A *fiduciary* is a person who acts on behalf of another (*beneficiary*) and is required to do so with great integrity. (Another fiduciary relationship is parent-to-minor child.) The *duty of loyalty* requires a fiduciary to act in the best interests of the beneficiary. This prohibits, for example, directors from authorizing the corporation to lease real estate from the board chairman unless the rental terms are consistent with the market. Directors and officers also owe the corporation a *duty of due care,* which requires that they act in good faith toward the corporation and in the manner a reasonably prudent person would employ under the same circumstances. [For an inside look at issues confronting board members today, see **http://boardmember.com**]

Business Judgment Rule

What happens if the board or CEO makes a decision that causes the stock value to decline by 30 percent? Has the duty of due care been violated? The judicial system has developed the *business judgment rule* to help make that determination. A good statement of the rule, which is explored in the *Wrigley* case below, is:

> The rule posits a powerful presumption . . . that a decision made by a loyal and informed board will not be overturned . . . unless it cannot be "attributed to any rational business purpose." [The] shareholder . . . challenging a board decision [must] rebut the . . . presumption [by] providing evidence that directors . . . breached any one of the triads of their fiduciary duty—good faith, loyalty or due care. . . . If a shareholder . . . fails to meet this . . . burden, the . . . rule attaches to protect . . . officers and directors and the decisions they make, and our courts will not second-guess these business judgments.[9]

LEGAL BRIEFCASE

Shlensky v. Wrigley
237 N.E.2d 776 (Ill. App. Ct. 1968)

FACTS

Shlensky, a minority stockholder in the Chicago Cubs, sued the directors on the grounds of mismanagement and negligence because of their refusal to install lights at Wrigley Field, then the only major league stadium without lights. One of the directors, Wrigley (80 percent owner), objected to lights because of his personal opinion that "baseball is a 'daytime sport' and that the installation of lights and night baseball games would have a deteriorating effect upon the surrounding neighborhood." The other directors deferred to Wrigley.

The Cubs were losing money. Shlensky attributed those losses to poor attendance and argued that without lights the losses would continue. His evidence was that the Chicago White Sox night games drew better than the Cubs' day games. Shlensky sought damages and an order requiring lights and night games. He lost at trial and appealed.

Justice Sullivan

* * * * *

. . . [D]efendants argue that the courts will not step in and interfere with the honest business judgment of the directors unless there is a showing of fraud, illegality, or conflict of interest.

The court in *Wheeler v. The Pullman Iron & Steel Co,.* said:

It is . . . fundamental in the law of corporations that the majority of its stockholders shall control the policy of the corporation. . . . Everyone purchasing [stock] impliedly agrees that he will be bound by the [lawful acts of] a majority of the shareholders, or [of their corporate agents duly chosen,] and courts . . . will not undertake to control the policy or business methods of a corporation, although it may be seen that a wiser policy might be adopted and the business more successful if other methods were pursued.

* * * * *

Plaintiff . . . argues that the directors are acting for reasons unrelated to the . . . welfare of the Cubs. However, we are not satisfied that the motives assigned to . . . Wrigley [and] the other directors . . . are contrary to the best interests of the corporation . . . . For example[,] the effect on the surrounding neighborhood might well be considered by a director who was considering the patrons who would or would not attend the games if the park were in a poor neighborhood. Furthermore, the long-run interest [in the] property value at Wrigley Field might demand all efforts to keep the neighborhood from deteriorating. [W]e do not mean to say . . . that the decision of the directors was a correct one. That is beyond our jurisdiction and ability. We are merely saying that the decision is one properly before the directors and the motives alleged . . . showed no fraud, illegality, or conflict of interest in their making of that decision.

While all . . . courts do not insist that one or more of [these] three elements must be present for a stockholder's derivative action to lie, nevertheless we feel that unless the conduct of the defendants at least borders on one of [them], the courts should not interfere. . . .

* * * * *

Finally, we do not agree . . . that failure to follow . . . the other major league clubs in scheduling night games constituted negligence. [It] cannot be said that directors, even those of corporations that are losing money, must follow the lead of [others] in the field. Directors are elected for their business . . . judgment and the courts cannot require them to forgo their judgment because of the decisions of directors of other companies.

Affirmed.

AFTERWORD—DUTY OF CARE

Some states now require proof of *intentional misconduct* or *recklessness* to establish a breach of the duty of care.

Questions

1. What was the issue in this case?
2. The Cubs added lights in 1988. How could the board be meeting its duty of due care both in the 1960s by not erecting lights and in the 1980s by doing so?

Director, Officer, Employee Liability

Wrigley involved a *shareholder derivative suit*. That action is initiated when the corporation is being harmed or defrauded and neither the board nor the senior executives will take action to protect it. This often involves self-dealing by these parties. The suit is brought by a minority shareholder, but any recovery inures to the corporation.

These cases are extremely difficult to win in light of the business judgment rule, which may apply to the board's decision not to pursue litigation, as well as to the underlying action that, it is argued, harmed the company. Nevertheless, many such suits are filed in the wake of any public corporate disaster. By one count, the Gulf of Mexico oil spill has "triggered more than 70 civil lawsuits."[10] With regard to the *Deepwater Horizon* rig, shareholders argue that the board and executives of British Petroleum "recklessly disregarded accidents and safety warnings for years" in violation of their fiduciary duties. Many such lawsuits have also been filed by shareholders against directors and officers of companies in the mortgage and financial services industry that played key roles in the 2008 financial crisis.

When an employee or director commits a tort or crime while conducting corporate business, both that person and the corporation are liable for the consequences. The legal doctrine that makes the employer liable for an employee's acts is *respondeat superior*. (For more, see Chapter 12.)

Because officers and directors are ultimately responsible for corporate acts and because corporations are frequently sued, these persons face a high risk of becoming involved in costly litigation. Most corporations, therefore, *indemnify* (pay for or reimburse) these individuals for the costs incurred to defend such suits. Many states permit indemnification even in some cases involving the breach of a fiduciary duty. Delaware, for example, permits indemnification for breaches of the duty of care, although not for breaches of the duty of loyalty or for intentional misconduct or knowing violations of the law.[11] When the SEC resolved its civil suit for securities fraud against Angelo Mozilo, CEO of Countrywide Financial, the nation's largest mortgage lender before the housing market collapse, Countrywide and Bank of America (which bought Countrywide in 2008) paid $45 million of Mozilo's $67.5 settlement.[12]

Limited Liability

To a lawyer there are two types of persons: natural and artificial. Natural persons are people. Artificial persons, like corporations, are entities created under the law of a state (or nation), which are considered to have separate legal existence. Corporations can own property, be sued, take on debts, and otherwise act as separate entities. As discussed, they even have limited constitutional rights. One of the great advantages of this status is that the owners of the corporation are generally not responsible for the corporation's obligations. Should the corporation find that its liabilities overwhelm its assets, its creditors cannot reach the personal assets of the shareholders. That is, the liability of shareholders is limited to the loss of their investment in the corporation, which is the essence of *limited liability* and perhaps the most cherished characteristic of the corporate form. However, for closely held corporations, this feature can be severely restricted because lenders are well aware of limited liability and usually require the principal shareholders to guarantee the corporation's debts. Still, limited liability will exist for other obligations, such as tort claims.

Closely held corporations also face the loss of limited liability through application of the doctrine known as *piercing the corporate veil*. This doctrine, explored in the *Wolfe* case that follows, usually has two elements: (1) misuse of the corporate form and (2) an unjust result if limited liability is allowed to stand.

LEGAL BRIEFCASE

Charles E. Wolfe v. United States   612 F.Supp. 605 (D Mont 1985); aff'd 798 F.2d 1241 (9th Cir. 1986)

Judge Battin

* * * * *

Charles E. Wolfe was the sole shareholder and president of [the corporation,] which leased tractor-trailers. [Mr.] Wolfe also operated a business as a proprietorship . . . which was an "over-the-road" trucking business.

[T]he corporation incurred a $114,472.91 federal tax bill. . . . [Mr.] Wolfe paid the taxes . . . after the Internal Revenue Service (Service) [levied against him]. The Service contends . . . the corporation was the alter ego of Mr. Wolfe, thus justifying the piercing of the corporate veil.

* * * * *

As a general rule, a corporation is treated as a legal entity, separate and distinct from its shareholders[, who] enjoy limited liability.

When the corporate entity is abused, however, the protection of limited liability may be lost. In such cases, courts may exercise their equitable powers to pierce the corporate veil. . . .

* * * * *

The facts . . . present the classic case of a shareholder so pervasively dominating corporate affairs that the shareholder and the corporation no longer have separate identities. . . . Mr. Wolfe was the sole shareholder[,] a director and the president of the corporation. Mr. Wolfe made all the corporate decisions without consulting the other directors. The corporation did not even have a bank account. All the corporation's banking transactions were done through the proprietorship's bank account. . . . The corporation and the proprietorship were housed in the same office. The corporation's employee was paid by the proprietorship. Some of the corporation's equipment was purchased on the proprietorship's credit. All of the corporation's purchases were paid for on a proprietorship bank account. When the corporation received payment from third parties, the money was deposited into the proprietorship's bank account. Even Mr. Wolfe could not distinguish between the corporation and the proprietorship. . . .

It is clear that the corporation and the proprietorship were operated as a single instrumentality under the sole control of Mr. Wolfe. Therefore, it was proper for the Service to look to Wolfe's personal assets to satisfy the taxes of his alter ego corporation.

[Held for the Internal Revenue Service.]

Questions

1. Who owed the taxes?
2. How was the corporate form misused?
3. What injustice would have resulted if Wolfe had not been required to pay?

Transferability of Ownership Interests

Federal securities laws impose broad restrictions on the transfer of stock, as will be seen in Part Three of this chapter. Beyond these (and analogous state) laws, no statutory restrictions are generally imposed on stock transfers. It is not uncommon, however, for dispositions to be restricted by contract. For example, an employment contract might require that corporate stock granted to an employee be held until the employee leaves the company.

A common contractual restriction in closely held corporations is a *buy-sell agreement* which, at a minimum, forces a shareholder to offer his or her stock to the corporation or other shareholders before selling it to a third party. [For more on buy-sell agreements, see **http://smallbusiness.findlaw.com/incorporation-and-legal-structures/faq-regarding-buy-sell-agreements.html**]

Duration of Existence

In general a corporation has indefinite duration. Nothing that transpires in the lives of the stockholders automatically affects the corporation's existence.

The termination of a corporation, however, can occur—either voluntarily or involuntarily. Voluntary termination requires a vote by the shareholders, who might do so if business prospects are no longer favorable. On termination the corporation is *liquidated,* which involves first satisfying all creditors and then distributing any remaining assets to the shareholders. *Articles of dissolution* are then filed, officially ending the corporation's existence.

Involuntary terminations are caused by the action of a court or of the state corporation regulator. A court might end a closely held corporation's existence if, for example, there is an irreconcilable deadlock among the shareholders. A common reason for the state to terminate a corporation is for failure to pay annual fees or make required annual filings.

Taxes

> "Taxes are what we pay for civilized society."

As Justice Oliver Wendell Holmes said, "Taxes are what we pay for civilized society."[13] But Justice Learned Hand also said, "[T]here is nothing sinister in so arranging one's affairs as to keep taxes as low as possible."[14]

Taxation transfers about one-quarter of the United States' economic output to the government. Virtually everyone wants to minimize tax payments, hopefully by legal *tax avoidance* (careful planning within the law), not by illegal *tax evasion* (committing fraud to lower taxes).

Because the corporation is a separate legal entity, it is subject to taxation in its own right. This leads to what many would say is the corporation's greatest disadvantage, *double taxation.* In the United States, a corporation pays tax on its income. When it later distributes its after-tax income to its shareholders as *dividends,* the shareholders are taxed on that amount as well, hence, "double taxation." Note, however, that dividends are not mandatory. They are paid only after the board declares them, which it is generally not required to do and which it legally cannot do if the corporation's solvency (cash flow and net worth) is insufficient.

To illustrate, assume a corporation is subject to income taxes at the rate of 35 percent[15] and its shareholders all face a marginal rate of 33 percent, but a lower rate on corporate dividends of 15 percent. On an income of $10 million, the corporation would pay $3.5 million in taxes, leaving only $6.5 million for distribution as dividends. If that entire amount were distributed, the shareholders would pay $975,000 in taxes. Thus, of the $10 million corporate income, only $5.525 million can actually be spent by the owners—an effective tax rate of about 45 percent. Had it been possible to own the business in a form that was not subject to taxation in its own right, the total income taxes would have been $3.3 million, leaving $6.7 million available for the owners to spend—21 percent more.[16]

The argument that corporations are necessarily disadvantageous because of double taxation can be misleading, however. There are a variety of circumstances in which employing the corporate form yields clear tax advantages, especially for smaller closely held corporations. For example, if such a corporation wants to inject much of its net income back into the business rather than distributing it as dividends, the corporate form may permit a lower tax rate on those reinvested funds. Another example results from corporations being the only form of business that comprehensively permits tax-deductible fringe benefits. [For more on fringe benefits, see **www.irs.ustreas.gov/pub/irs-pdf/p15b.pdf**]

The Hybrid S Corporation: Limited Liability Without Double Taxation

As previously discussed, many argue that the principal disadvantage of the corporate form is double taxation. In response in 1958, Congress amended the Internal Revenue Code to establish a separate tax status for some corporations, now known as *S corporations.* An S corporation's income is taxed only once—to the shareholders on their personal returns—much like partnerships, which will be discussed below. Also like partnerships, an S corporation is limited in the deductibility of some fringe benefits. However, unlike partnerships, to the extent the S corporation's income is allocated to its owners as dividends, no self-employment tax is imposed, which is a tax separate from the income tax with an effective tax rate of approximately 13 percent on the first $117,000 of earned income in 2014. The Internal Revenue Service, however, routinely challenges attempts to distribute an excessive amount as dividends where inadequate wages have been paid to S corporation owners.

Not all corporations can elect to be taxed as an S corporation. It is intended for use by smaller companies. Thus, S corporations may issue only one class of stock and may have no more than 100 shareholders, which in general may be individuals only. Interestingly, an entire family is treated as "one" individual for these purposes. Despite these restrictions, one can find S corporations with multi-billion-dollar revenues.

Keep in mind that "S" status is relevant only for federal (and some state) tax purposes. In all other respects the legal characteristics of S corporations are like all other corporations.

Capital Structure

Businesses often need access to *capital* to finance their activities. Capital is of two types: debt and equity—two ends of the spectrum with a boundary that can be challenging to identify. The providers of both debt and equity capital hold claims against the corporation's assets. However, creditors' claims are always satisfied before equity holders' claims.

Equity capital (stock) has a long-term horizon. Although any given shareholder may intend to hold the stock for only a short period, the stock itself is generally expected to exist for the full life of the corporation. Three *property rights* are associated with stock ownership: the right to participate in earnings (that is, dividends), the right to participate in assets upon liquidation, and the right to participate in control. There are two principal classes of stock: preferred and common. Where only one class exists, it is *common stock*. Common stockholders share all three property rights in proportion to their holdings.

> Institutional investors hold 73 percent of the largest 1000 US corporations' stock.

Preferred stock was created, largely for institutional investors (in 2009 institutional investors owned 73 percent of the largest 1000 US companies[17]) like pension funds, to fill the gap on the risk-return spectrum between long-term debt and common stock. Finance professionals find it advantageous to have many different ways to combine risk and return. Preferred stock is associated with "preferences," which relate to distributions. Preferred stockholders are paid their required annual dividend in full before any dividends are distributed to the common stockholders. In addition, preferred stockholders have a preference upon the corporation's liquidation. After the creditors are satisfied, the preferred stockholders receive the next round of distributions up to their stock's *liquidation value* (also called *redemption value*) —typically a few percent over the stock's par value.

The cost of these two preferences is the loss of the right to participate in control. Having no vote, preferred stockholders cannot elect directors to protect their interests. To help ensure that its holders regularly receive dividends, nearly all preferred stock is *cumulative*. This means that if a preferred stock dividend is missed, then before the common stockholders get any dividends, the preferred stock *arrearage* (all dividends not paid in any prior year) must be made up. Another protection occasionally granted to preferred stockholders is a contingent right to vote if, for example, a dividend is missed twice. This voting power would continue until all arrearages have been satisfied.

Because preferred stockholders never get more than their required dividends and, upon liquidation, little more than the purchase price, all corporate growth inures to the common stockholders. If both you and Bill Gates had invested $1 million in Microsoft at the outset, you taking preferred stock and Gates taking common stock, your stock would still be worth about $1 million, whereas Gates's stock would be worth tens of billions.

Debt capital may be short- or long-term. Companies that provide motherboards to Dell are a source of short-term debt capital. They expect to be paid fairly quickly, although not at the moment of delivery. They have extended to Dell a very short-term form of debt. The long-term debt of a closely held corporation is likely to come from a commercial lender who takes a security interest in specified property of the corporation. This is much like an individual who takes out a mortgage from a bank secured by the home the individual purchases with the borrowed funds. Large corporations have another alternative for obtaining long-term debt capital. Just as a public corporation may sell its stock to the public, large corporations may sell units of debt, called *bonds,* to the public. A pension plan that holds Dell's 20-year bonds is providing long-term debt capital to Dell.

Most debt capital specifies an interest rate (or a formula for computing the interest rate) to be paid on the principal borrowed, both of which (principal and interest) are required to be paid in set amounts, usually over a defined term.

Corporations carefully manage their *capital structures* (the balance between debt and equity). If the debt/equity ratio is too high, the corporation may be exposed to severe risk because debt obligations must be timely paid without regard to how profitable the business operations are. Further, the capital structure must be managed to ensure that *debt covenants* are not breached. A debt covenant is a term in the lending contract that makes the debt immediately payable should the condition specified not be satisfied (such as exceeding a specified debt/equity ratio). On the other hand, if the ratio is too low, opportunities for positive *financial leverage* (employing funds at a rate of return that exceeds the interest rate on the borrowed funds) may be forfeited. Executives also recognize that *interest* paid on debt is tax deductible, whereas dividends paid to shareholders are not. This places a strong emphasis on the use of debt capital.

If you compare the characteristics of debt capital with preferred and common stock, you can readily see that preferred stock indeed does bridge the gap between common stock and debt. Increasingly, preferred stock is being issued with more debtlike characteristics. This poses serious classification problems for accountants, tax authorities, and bankruptcy courts.

Questions

1. *a.* What characteristics of the corporate form make it particularly desirable as a business entity?
   b. Particularly undesirable?
   c. Do S corporations share those characteristics?
2. What are the two ends of the capital spectrum?
3. *a.* What property rights are associated with common stock?
   b. Does preferred stock have all of these rights?

Partnerships

This section discusses traditional, *general partnerships*. A partnership is two or more persons (*partners*) who carry on a business as co-owners. Recall that this is the default entity form for any business with two or more owners that does not specifically act to create a separate entity. About 7 percent of all businesses are general partnerships, generating less than 1 percent of all revenue. Whereas corporate ownership interests are called stock or shares, the equity interest of a partner is called a *partnership interest.*

> A general partnership is the default entity form for any business with two or more owners.

Partnerships are *mutual agencies*. Every partner is an agent of the partnership with the capacity to bind the partnership when acting within the scope of the partnership's business.

Knowledge held by any partner is deemed held by the partnership. As an agent, each partner is entitled to reimbursement for costs personally incurred in furtherance of the partnership's business. Each partner has the right to examine all partnership records and to demand a formal determination by a court of the value of the partner's interest (an *accounting*).

Although the law of partnerships originated in the common law, all states except Louisiana adopted the Uniform Partnership Act (UPA), originally developed by the National Conference of Commissioners on Uniform State Laws (NCCUSL) in 1914. The UCCUSL adopted a revised form of the UPA in 1994 (RUPA), which to date has been adopted by 37 states, the District of Columbia, and the Virgin Islands. Except as noted, the discussion below is based on the provisions of RUPA.

What Is the Law in Your State?

There are significant differences between UPA and RUPA. Which is the law in your state? You can find out at **www.uniformlaws.org/Act.aspx?title=Partnership%20Act.**

Formation and Nontax Costs

Under RUPA a partnership is a separate legal entity, distinct from its partners. However, no filing with the state is required to create it. If persons intend to go into business together and take no steps to establish a different form, they will automatically be a partnership. Mere co-ownership of property, however, does not create a partnership. The co-owners must intend to join in the sharing of risks and rewards via the active conduct of business.

As will be seen below, the partnership relationship carries substantial risks for the individual partners. One might expect the contract that creates and governs the partnership, the *partnership agreement*, to very precisely specify the terms of that relationship. This may be true if the partnership agreement is written. However, the vast majority are oral agreements. If disagreements arise over an oral agreement, the partners may find it very difficult to establish conclusively what the original agreement was. This will not be helped by the fact that when important disagreements arise, the partners often discover that their interests have become adverse and that the hopeful emotions shared at formation have been displaced by anger and a sense of betrayal.

So if the problems associated with a lack of clarity can be substantial, why are partnership agreements often oral and, even if written, often vague? The answer relates in part to the fact that to draft a quality partnership agreement a host of touchy, even unpleasant issues must be concretely addressed. The drafter must ask, "How should the profit-sharing arrangement change if a partner becomes ill or fails to meet expectations?" And, "If the partnership does not work out, how will the relationship be unwound?" Soon-to-be partners often shy away from tough questions like these; there may be a sense that asking them will sour the high spirits in which so many partnerships are born.

Partnership agreements also tend to be expensive to draft because of the many opportunities for customization, because state law provides only a general framework, and because the personal risks of being a partner are so significant. Similarly, partnership accounting systems can be among the most expensive of all the business forms because of the need to track the customized economic arrangements. However, the partnership form generally requires few, if any, annually recurring events such as state filings or statutorily mandated meetings of owners.

Management Structure

By default, management in a partnership is not centralized. Absent an agreement to the contrary, each partner has an equal right to participate in control on a one-partner, one-vote basis regardless of the size of the partner's ownership interest. As the number of partners grows this can make partnerships unwieldy. In response some partnerships create a central management structure by adding provisions to the partnership agreement in which the partners yield many of their management rights to a subset of partners (perhaps only one— a *managing partner*).

Partners owe each other the fiduciary duties of loyalty, confidentiality, sharing information, and exercising due care. The *Veale* case below explores some of these duties.

LEGAL BRIEFCASE

Veale v. Rose
657 S.W.2d 834 (Texas Ct. of App. 1983)

FACTS
Veal Sr., Beale Jr., Gibson, Parker, and Rose were partners in an accounting firm. The partnership agreement permitted partners to pursue other business interests so long as doing so did not conflict with the partnership practice. Rose performed accounting work for Right Away Foods and Payne, receiving the compensation personally. Rose's partners claimed that he owed them a share in that he had competed with the firm in violation of the partnership agreement. The jury held for Rose. The partners appealed.

Chief Justice Nye

* * * * *

The partnership agreement between Rose and the appellants provided in part:

> Except with the expressed approval of the other partners as to each specific instance, no partner shall perform any public accounting services . . . other than . . . on behalf of this partnership.

> Partners . . . occupy a fiduciary relationship towards one another which requires of them the utmost degree of good faith and honesty in dealing with one another. . . .

It is undisputed that while a partner . . . Rose rendered accounting services for Right Away Foods for which he billed and received payment personally. [The] partnership did not share in the proceeds. . . . There was some testimony from which the jury could have inferred that the work which Rose did for Right Away Foods . . . was of the type which did not require the services of a CPA. However, Rose . . . admitted that there was no reason why he could not have rendered [those services] as a partner in the accounting firm. . . . In fact in regard to services in connection with mergers and acquisitions, [Parker testified] that he was unaware of any [such work that was not] prepared by public accounting firms. The preponderance of all the evidence clearly establishes that Rose . . . performed accounting services for Right Away Foods . . . in competition with the partnership. The [jury] was in error.

. . . Rose also admitted that he performed accounting services for [Payne] for which he billed and received payment personally. There is no question that those services were public accounting services. His later testimony that he performed the services, in effect, after hours, or in addition to his duties to the partnership, is of no value in light of the obligations imposed by the partnership agreement and by the common understanding of the term "competition."

[Reversed and remanded.]

Questions
1. *a.* Why was Rose's work for Right Away Foods considered a violation of the partnership agreement?
   b. Why did Rose's "after-hours" argument fail?
2. Could Rose operate a gas station without violating the partnership agreement?

Limited Liability

Partners are personally liable
for all the partnership's
obligations should it default.

A partnership does not offer limited liability to its owners. The partners are personally liable for all of the partnership's obligations should it default. This is clearly the greatest disadvantage of the partnership form.

Under RUPA partners are *jointly and severally liable* for both contract obligations and torts.[18] If a partnership is found liable, the victorious claimant must first exhaust the partnership's assets, but then can proceed to collect the remainder from any or all of the partners.[19] If a wealthy partner pays the debt, that partner is entitled to recoup an appropriate share from the other partners under the *right of contribution*.

Under the doctrine of respondeat superior mentioned previously, the partnership, and therefore the partners, are liable for the torts of the partnership's employees and for the unintentional torts of the partners. For example, an individual injured by the negligent driving of an employee can sue and recover from the partnership and then from individual partners.

Under some circumstances, partners may be jointly and severally liable for crimes committed by partnership employees, but they ordinarily will not be liable for crimes committed by partners (unless they themselves participated in or authorized the crime).

Transferability of Ownership Interests

Because partnerships are mutual agencies, involve fiduciary relationships, and do not have limited liability, without an express agreement to the contrary, the law does not allow a partner to transfer a partnership interest to a third person without the unanimous consent of the other partners. A partnership interest can be assigned, but the *assignment* entitles the *assignee* only to the distribution rights of the assigning partner (*assignor*). The assignee has no right to participate in control and does not have the status of partner.

Duration of Existence

Under UPA, a partnership is automatically dissolved, or terminated, upon the death, incapacity, bankruptcy, expulsion, or withdrawal of any partner. Thus, events in the private lives of the partners can seriously impact the business venture. To minimize the harm from such an automatic dissolution, it is common practice to include a provision in the partnership agreement allowing a partnership to be immediately reformed by the remaining partners. The ex-partner's partnership interest would then be valued and paid out.

Under RUPA the only event listed above that will automatically dissolve a partnership is a partner's express withdrawal. The remaining events will result in the disassociation of the affected partner, but will not dissolve the partnership nor require the formation of a new partnership by the remaining partners. The power of any partner to withdraw cannot be removed by the partnership agreement, but the right to exercise that power can be circumscribed and a wrongfully withdrawing partner can be required to compensate the partnership for any resulting damages. The remaining partners have a statutory right to resume the business as if no dissolution had occurred.[20]

Taxes

The greatest advantage of the partnership form is the extraordinary range of economic relationships that can be crafted. Whereas a 10 percent shareholder is simply entitled to 10 percent of whatever distributions are made by the corporation, a partnership agreement can detach percentage ownership from the stream of distributions and tax consequences. For example, assume L contributes land to a real estate development partnership, K contributes knowledge as the general contractor, and C contributes the cash necessary to undertake the venture. It would be acceptable to allocate the partnership cash flow as follows: C gets all of the net cash flow until C's initial cash contribution is recouped, then L gets all of the net cash flow until the value of L's contributed land has been distributed, then all three share the remaining net cash flow equally.

Double taxation does not apply to partnerships because the Internal Revenue Code does not treat them as separate taxable entities, whether or not the state has adopted RUPA. The partnership's income is taxed only once—on the personal tax returns of the partners as allocated under the terms of the partnership agreement. There is a downside risk, however. Partners must pay tax annually on their share of the partnership income whether or not any cash or property has actually been distributed to them.

There are two important negative tax consequences of a partnership. First, fringe benefits provided to partners are generally not business deductions (although fringes provided to employees are). Second, all of a partner's allocable share of ordinary income is subject to the self-employment tax (at an effective rate of about 13 percent), as was previously discussed in the context of S corporations.

Capital Structure

The sole source of equity is the partners themselves, although new partners can be brought into the partnership to infuse new equity capital into the business. Debt capital can be raised based on the creditworthiness of the individual partners, as well as by offering assets to lenders as collateral for loans.

Question

What characteristics of the partnership form make it particularly desirable as a business entity? Particularly undesirable?

Limited Liability Companies

Today, a very popular business form is the *limited liability company* (LLC). After 1958, an S corporation could be elected that combined limited liability for owners with avoidance of double taxation. That form was not attractive to many businesses, however, because of the one class of stock limitation, the ceiling on the number of shareholders, and the requirement that all economic and tax benefits and burdens of the enterprise be shared pro rata according to stock ownership. Wide displeasure with the lack of a limited liability business form that had the flexible tax characteristics of partnerships led the Wyoming legislature to create the limited liability company in 1977. By 1997, LLCs were available nationally and are now the fastest-growing business form in the United States.

Although a uniform act for LLCs was first established by the NCCUSL in 1994, only nine states ultimately adopted it. In 2006, a revised act was adopted by the NCCUSL, which, as of this writing, has been adopted by nine jurisdictions (including the District of Columbia). Thus, there is still considerable variation in governing provisions from state to state. The general outlines of LLCs are discussed below.

To create an LLC, the owners (although some states allow one-member LLCs), called *members,* file *articles of organization* with the state, much as a corporation files articles of incorporation. The equity interests are called *members' interests*. An *operating agreement,* which can be oral or written but is most likely to be written, will be prepared which sets forth information similar to that often found in partnership agreements. Minor annual filings and fees are generally required, but statutes do not impose annual meetings on the members. The cost of setting up an accounting system for an LLC will be essentially the same as for a partnership because LLCs have the same flexibility over economic and tax matters as does the partnership form.

The management structure of LLCs is extremely flexible: the operating agreement generally specifies whether it will be centrally managed by managers (manager-managed: often one or two of the members) or member-managed (similar to a partnership). Many states require this choice to be set out in the articles of organization. Similarly, a multimember LLC can elect upon its creation whether to be taxed like a corporation or like a partnership. (A single-member LLC will elect between treatment as a corporation or as a sole proprietorship.)

LLCs are hybrids because, with regard to limited liability of the owners and the duration of existence, they more closely resemble corporations. With regard to transferability of ownership interests and access to equity capital, however, they more closely resemble partnerships. In many states it is still an open question whether the limited liability of LLC members can be "pierced" as is possible with corporate shareholders. Minnesota's LLC statute expressly provides for piercing the veil of LLCs.[21] In 2002, the Wyoming Supreme Court held, "We can discern no reason, in either law or policy, to treat LLCs differently than we treat corporations. If the members and officers of an LLC fail to treat it as a separate entity, they should not enjoy immunity from individual liability for the LLC's acts that cause damage to third parties."[22]

Sole Proprietorships

Sole proprietorships, business ventures undertaken by a single individual, are not entities—they have no legal existence apart from the owner. However, the same characteristics used to evaluate other business forms can be applied to them. A sole proprietorship comes into existence by the mere decision of the proprietor to pursue a venture. Thus, it is the default business form for single owners. This largely explains why the majority of all business endeavors are sole proprietorships, although they generate only 4 percent of all business revenue—averaging a little over $50,000. No legal filings or fees are required to establish a sole proprietorship, but a business license, sales tax license, fictitious name filing, or other permits may be required by the state, county, and/or city where the business is located. Since there is only one owner, centralization of management automatically exists. Like a partnership, the owner is personally liable for all obligations of the business.

A proprietor may dispose of the proprietorship freely, but such a transfer can be accomplished only through the transfer of the assets which underlie the business, not by a transfer of the "business" in its own right. Further, the lack of a separate legal entity generally results in the termination of a sole proprietorship if the owner becomes incapacitated or dies. Only a holder of a durable power of attorney, custodian or executor has the legal power to continue operations, but either of the latter two would be forced continually to seek court approval to perform the activities required to operate the business. This impractical arrangement would likely destroy the business's value in short order.

A sole proprietorship is not a taxable entity. All of its revenues and expenses will be incorporated into the personal tax return of the proprietor. Like partnerships, most fringe benefits are not deductible as business expenses and all business income is subject to self-employment tax. The capital structure issues for a sole proprietorship are similar to those of a partnership—without a change in business form, new equity can only come from the sole proprietor. Any debt will be based on the creditworthiness of the proprietor and the property the proprietor can offer as security.

Other Hybrid Forms

Limited Liability Partnerships

At the same time LLCs were being conceived, the great multinational accounting firms were reeling from an episode in which the quality of their audits proved less than advertised—the savings and loan collapse of the 1980s. Over $1.6 billion in settlements (a staggering sum for that era) was paid out and these firms feared extinction if professional liability damages could not be brought under control. Efforts to obtain tort reform that would limit such liability failed, so a new approach was sought—the *limited liability partnership* (LLP). These were first enacted in Texas in 1991 at the instigation of a number of its major law firms, who also sought relief from professional liability. Within a year, 1,200 law firms became LLPs.[23]

Most states now have some form of an LLP. In spite of the similarity of name and its creation in the shadow of LLCs, its closest analogue is a general partnership, not an LLC. For example, its governing law is included as Article 10 of RUPA. To bring an LLP into existence, a document, called a *statement of qualification* in RUPA, is filed with the state. Minor annual filings and fees are required. LLPs (and their partners) are taxed like a general partnership and in all other characteristics most closely resemble partnerships.

As originally conceived and as is still true in some states, an LLP partner's limited liability extended only to the negligence or malpractice of other partners, while retaining full liability for all other partnership obligations. RUPA, and many states, now provide full limited liability "whether arising in contract, tort, or otherwise" to all partners "solely by reason of being" a partner.[24] In those states the only individuals who would continue to use the general partnership form would likely be those without competent legal advice or who are unwilling to pay the modest filing fee.

Professional Limited Liability Companies (PLLCs) and Professional Limited Liability Partnerships (PLLPs)

Some states that have established LLPs that confer full limited liability for partners have chosen to prohibit their use by licensed professionals such as accountants, lawyers, and doctors. As an alternative, they have created entities (variously named depending on the state) that closely resemble the original Texas LLP concept. They delegate regulation relating to malpractice to an appropriate state-licensing body and/or set malpractice insurance standards for the protection of the public.

Limited Partnerships

Limited partnerships have existed for a considerable time in the United States and were extremely popular until the advent of limited liability companies. They are entities with two classes of owners: general partners and limited partners. *General partners* have the same legal benefits and burdens as the partners of a general partnership. They (often only one) are the sole managers of the entity. *Limited partners* invest in the entity by contributing capital but do not participate in control (except to a limited extent analogous to shareholders). In exchange for limited control, they receive limited liability. The principal disadvantage of general partner status is unlimited liability. In practice, however, most general partners are corporations with minimal capital investment, so unlimited liability is little threat unless grounds for piercing the corporate veil exist.

Forty-nine states have adopted the Uniform Limited Partnership Act (ULPA) in one of its three versions. The latest, ULPA (2001), has been adopted in 18 states and the District of Columbia. Limited partnerships come into existence only upon filing a *certificate of limited partnership*. Minor annual filings and fees are required. The law of limited partnerships provides that those events that would terminate a general partnership have minimal impact on a limited partnership's existence. In general, a limited partnership is taxed like a partnership. However, like an S corporation shareholder, the ordinary income of the limited partners is not subject to self-employment tax.

Limited Liability Limited Partnerships

State legislation establishing limited liability limited partnerships (LLLPs) is generally directed at facilitating the acquisition of limited liability for the general partners of preexisting limited partnerships. In some cases, reorganization of an existing limited partnership would have entailed expensive or impassable hurdles. Under ULPA (2001), an LLLP is created simply by stating that the limited partnership is an LLLP in the certificate of limited partnership.[25]

Series Limited Liability Companies

A handful of states, including Delaware, have enacted legislation enabling a new species of LLC. The concept is to create a related set of entities (referred to as "series" or "cells") through which the liability risks of different real estate investments or businesses are kept separate even though only one entity, the series LLC, is created under state law. This separation of liability for different activities is somewhat akin to an S corporation and its relationship to its wholly owned "qualified subchapter S subsidiaries," the tax consequences for all of which are reported on one federal income tax return. State series LLC statutes permit each cell to have different managers and different members.

International Hybrids

Dozens of other business forms exist throughout the world. For the most part, these forms are intended to achieve various combinations of the characteristics just discussed. Using these criteria, managers operating in a multinational environment should be able to evaluate form-of-business decisions under a variety of regimes.

Social Businesses on the Horizon?

The concept of a "social business" has been promoted by Dr. Muhammad Yunus, an economist and winner of the 2006 Nobel Peace Prize. The concept occupies a unique place on the continuum that runs from for-profit businesses to not-for-profit organizations. A social business is distinguished from a for-profit business in that it is formed to further a specific positive social objective, rather than primarily seeking profit-maximization for its owners. Profits are applied to the furtherance of its stated social objective; regular reporting would include both financial reporting and identification of concrete progress toward its social goals. A social business is distinct from a nonprofit enterprise in at least two key respects: it is intended to be an economically self-sustaining enterprise, which means it must adhere to commercially reasonable business practices, and its start-up capital is to be returned to its founding investors, although without interest. For such businesses to become a reality, another new form is required. Twenty states have adopted "benefit corporation" statutes, and another 17 are considering doing so. In such corporations, the directors' fiduciary duties require consideration of nonfinancial interests. [For more information see **http://benefit-corp.net/state-by-state-legislative-status**] In addition, 10 states have enacted "low-profit LLC statutes." Such LLCs require the entity's social mission to take priority over its profit objective. [For more information see **www.intersectorl3c.com/l3c_tally.html**]

Circumstances Favoring a Specific Business Form

Before the rise in the availability of the various hybrid forms discussed, some states required certain activities to be carried on in the partnership form, most notably the licensed professions. The primary concern was that these professionals should not be able to escape personal liability for malpractice by incorporating their practices. As noted above, all states now offer an alternative to a general partnership for these professions.

Today selection of a particular form is driven by market realities, as well as the founders' desires for certain characteristics that were previously discussed. Some of those market realities will now be addressed.

One consideration in the selection of an appropriate form is the total capital needed by the enterprise. Large businesses need billions of dollars. Only access to global capital markets (like the New York Stock Exchange) can fulfill this need. With only fairly recent exceptions (see the text box below), the only form of business that has met with success in these markets is the C corporation. In contrast, because partnerships do not offer limited liability, freely transferable interests, or indefinite life, they are (with few exceptions) not appropriate for ventures requiring large amounts of capital accessed via the financial markets.

The Rise of the Distorporation

Even as "regular" corporations continue to dominate the public capital markets, a new trend is under way. Noncorporate business forms, such as real estate investment trusts (REITs), regulated investment companies (RICs), and master limited partnerships (MLPs) are increasingly attracting capital. As of 2012, these entities (sometimes described as "distorporations") represented 9 percent of all listed companies but absorbed 28 percent of all new equity. Among the advantages, management is left firmly in control, double-taxation is avoided, and all investors enjoy limited liability. On the downside, because these entities generally must distribute all of their earnings annually, they are unable to fund growth internally. They therefore must return to the capital markets year after year to pursue expansion. Many believe distorporations will continue to erode corporate primacy in the securities markets.[26]

It is not rare to find someone with a great idea but insufficient resources to take the idea to market. Some investors, such as *venture capitalists*, seek out such persons. They will usually insist that the venture have limited liability, as would be true with a corporation or an LLC. [For more on venture capitalists, see **www.nvca.org**]

Similarly, *franchisors* normally demand that *franchisees* operate their *franchises* in a business form with limited liability. A franchise is the right to exploit the franchisor's intangible assets (trade name and business systems) and to partake of the franchisor's marketing, purchasing, and other services. The key advantages to the franchisee are a proven product or service, turn-key implementation, and access to support. The franchisor gains by earning fees and by achieving accelerated market penetration using the capital of others (franchisees). Unfortunately, franchisor fraud and oppression are not unusual, so careful investigation is essential. Furthermore, premium franchises can be expensive. [For an extensive listing of franchise opportunities and their minimum cash requirements, see **www.franchisedirect.com**]

With the development of such business forms as LLCs, LLPs, and S corporations, under most circumstances the disadvantages of the general partnership form are so severe that a person is usually well advised to avoid it.

Questions—Part One

1. *a.* Why are corporations the dominant form of business based on revenues in the United States?
   b. What is meant by a "distorporation"?
   c. Why are distorporations gaining ground against "regular" corporations in the public capital markets?
2. *a.* Why are sole proprietorships problematic if a proprietor dies or is disabled?
   b. Do partnerships experience similar problems? Explain.
3. *a.* What characteristics of an LLC cause it to be the fastest-growing business form in the United States?
   b. What are its advantages over a corporation?

Part Two—Corporate Governance in Public Corporations

Public corporations have thousands of shareholders. The vast majority of these shareholders do not plan to spend their time intimately involved in the company's business. They wish to entrust their resources to the stewardship of the company's management and return to their personal affairs. To ensure the corporation is acting to further their interests, the shareholders elect a board of directors. Public corporation boards generally have both inside and outside directors. *Inside directors* are senior executives. *Outside directors* are not employed by the company. These boards meet at regular intervals to monitor the corporation's activities, establish corporate policies, hire and replace corporate executives, and make major decisions.

> The accounting scandals of the Enron era and the 2008 collapse of the financial markets.

That at least is the textbook description of corporate governance. What has become painfully evident from both the accounting scandals of the Enron era and the 2008 collapse of the financial system is that reality can be quite different. Enron called the world's attention to extraordinary failings in corporate governance, but its demise was not an isolated event. Numerous predecessors failed to alert the markets and many more followed, at least three of which were actually larger (WorldCom, Parmalat, and Fannie Mae). The 2008 financial crisis made clear the ongoing corporate governance problems. The report of the Financial Crisis Inquiry Commission (the body charged by Congress to determine the causes of the financial crisis) identified serious issues As the majority report states, "We conclude dramatic failures of corporate governance and risk management at many systemically important financial institutions were a key cause of this crisis."[27] In the words of Carl Icahn, "The entirely preventable financial catastrophe . . . has many culprits: reckless executives who gambled with their company's futures, feckless regulators and somnambulant boards of directors."[28]

This part of the chapter will consider corporate governance issues, including reforms adopted in the wake of both Enron and the 2008 financial crisis, as well as reforms driven by the shareholder rights movement.

The Management Pyramid

Corporations have centralized management. At the apex of the management pyramid is the board of directors. Immediately below is the CEO. In the next layer are the vice presidents and other top officers and executives. This classic management pyramid further expands through layers of middle management, finally coming to the base comprised of rank-and-file employees. The light shed on the boardroom by various government investigations and shareholder lawsuits in the Enron era revealed that the pyramid had become inverted at the top. Far too frequently, boards simply abdicated responsibility to their CEOs who often held the ultimate power because of their strong influence over the board nomination process and their control over the information provided to the board. Directorships can be very lucrative—tens or hundreds of thousands of dollars annually for attendance at a modest number of meetings. Far too few directors were willing to challenge CEO actions out of fear of forfeiting their substantial compensation. In addition many conflicts of interest were discovered. At Enron, for example, some directors were personal friends of senior managers, others were academics whose institutions were receiving substantial contributions from the company or its officers, and still another was a former senior government official who had exempted Enron from the regulation of its principal line of business (dealing with energy derivatives).

The federal legislation passed in the wake of Enron, the Sarbanes–Oxley Act of 2002 (SOX), attempted to address some of these governance issues. To limit the CEO's control of audit information reaching the board, it requires a board audit committee consisting exclusively of independent directors—outside directors without conflicts of interest—one of whom is required to be a financial expert. SOX gives the audit committee direct responsibility for hiring the outside auditing firm and setting its compensation. It further prohibits that firm from also rendering most types of consulting services to audit clients. To limit the CEO's control over board membership SOX requires a nominating committee also composed solely of independent directors.

Even after SOX, there are still serious concerns about who truly sits at the top of the pyramid. The CEO still controls much of the information that reaches the board. Shortly before the financial crisis *The Wall Street Journal* published a special report on corporate governance, headlined "Why CEOs Need to Be Honest with Their Boards: Too Often Chief Executives Sugarcoat the Truth. That's More Dangerous Than Ever."[29] Many still wonder whether boards are active in setting policies and making major decisions or are simply following the CEO's lead. Such concerns seem plausible where, for example, immediately after Lehman Brothers' CEO announced a $3.9 billion third quarter loss in 2008 en route to an implosion not long after, he stated, "I must say the board's been wonderfully supportive."[30]

A logical response to this problem would be to require that the positions of board chair and CEO be held by different individuals. "No one can reasonably expect a person to oversee himself or herself.... The CEO works for the board, not the other way around; the continuation of combined roles inhibits the board in exercising its responsibilities because it creates an insurmountable imbalance of power."[31] At the time the "Great Recession" unfolded in 2008, both positions were more often than not held by a single person in *Fortune* 500 companies.[32] The Dodd-Frank Act, enacted in response to the financial crisis, now requires that corporations disclose the reasons for choosing the same person for both positions, but does not prohibit the practice.

Question

What should the board's role be? Consider the following two opinions:

> [B]oards [are] supposed to monitor risks, provide judgment and supervise managers on behalf of shareholders.[33]
>
> Most boards meet one or two days a month and are composed of individuals who also hold demanding full-time jobs. Given those circumstances, it's absurd to believe that board members, even the most experienced and best-intentioned of them, will uncover systemic flaws or acts of malfeasance. . . . That's what regulators, outside accountants, and internal controls are for—to help boards ferret out excessive risk and wrongdoing.[34]

The Shareholder Rights Movement

Although shareholders own the corporation, control rests with the board. As noted in the discussion of the business judgment rule, state law significantly restricts the shareholders' ability to control management, other than indirectly through the annual election of the board.

> The notion that shareholders can exercise control is doubtful.

The notion that shareholders can actually exercise control through the board election process is doubtful. As stated above, shareholders do not select the candidates for board positions; a committee of the existing board does. Could a dissatisfied shareholder offer a different slate of directors for the shareholders to vote on? In theory yes; in practice *proxy fights* are difficult, and expensive.

Management annually solicits proxies from its shareholders. A *proxy* is written permission to vote a shareholder's stock on an issue such as the election of directors. Management's solicitation is done in conjunction with its required notification to shareholders of the annual meeting and the cost is thus borne by the corporation. Shareholders wanting to propose alternative candidates have to be prepared to bear the entire cost themselves. State law gives shareholders the right of access to shareholder lists maintained by the company, but often a shareholder will have to sue, at a substantial cost in time and money, to force the corporation to comply. If successful, the shareholders involved must incur substantial costs to develop for SEC review the solicitation materials.

Not surprisingly, proxy fights are rare. Most shareholders who disagree with management's decisions simply sell their shares and invest elsewhere. From society's and the shareholders' points of view, the management of publicly held corporations proceeds largely unchecked, unless securities law violations (discussed in Part Three) are involved. Stephen Davis, the executive director of the Center for Corporate Governance at Yale, refers to this as "the myth that boards [are] accountable to shareholders."[35]

In recent years various proposals to give shareholders more input have been gaining ground, largely through the efforts of institutional investors and independent activists. Institutional investors, such as pension funds and mutual funds, have significant influence in the capital markets. When the largest U.S. public pension, the California Public Employees' Retirement System (CALPERS), contacts the C-suite at a company in which it holds substantial stock, management is likely to listen.

Majority Rules

One shareholder reform that has gained significant ground involves the number of votes required to elect a director. Many state laws, including Delaware, allow directors to be elected by just a plurality of the votes cast in person or by proxy. If the only names before the shareholders are management's slate of directors, management nominees will win even if a substantial number of shareholders withhold their votes in protest. In 2006, only 16 percent of firms in the S&P 500 had any form of majority vote requirement. Within 18 months the number was 60 percent.[36] Unfortunately, the impact is not as great as it might first appear. In most cases where management has agreed to a majority vote rule, it has not agreed to reject automatically a candidate who has commanded only a plurality, but only to review whether or not to seat such a candidate.

Broker Voting

Another area of movement concerns broker voting. Many individual shareholders do not hold their shares but leave them on account with their broker. Past practice was that, unless the account owner specifically directed otherwise, the broker could vote the shares, which typically occurred in a promanagement fashion. That practice has been reversed by the

Dodd–Frank Act, which prohibits broker voting unless specific instructions are received from the shareholder. The likely consequence is that fewer shares will be voted, shifting even greater influence to the large institutional shareholders who do vote.

Proxy Access

One of the most controversial issues of recent years has been proxy access. As previously discussed, though it is possible for dissatisfied shareholders to wage a proxy fight, it is usually not feasible to do so. A cost-effective solution would be to require management to include shareholder nominees on the company's ballot sent to shareholders in advance of the annual meeting. Although state law does not give shareholders that right, a corporation's bylaws could. To propose such a change would require a shareholder to submit the bylaw proposal to the corporation for inclusion in the annual meeting materials. If management wants to reject the request for inclusion of the proposal, it becomes a matter subject to regulation by the SEC. The SEC under the Bush administration took the position that management was not required to include such proposals in the company's proxy materials, but in 2006 a Federal Circuit Court ruled against the SEC's interpretation of the relevant regulation.[37] In response, the SEC opened a rule making proceeding on proxy access. In August 2010, after a change in both the administration and the composition of the SEC, the commission issued a new rule permitting shareholder groups (owning at least 3 percent of a company's stock for at least three years) to submit nominees for inclusion in the company's ballot, with the caveat that no more than 25 percent of the board can be elected in this fashion.

Executive Compensation

Executive compensation has long been an issue for shareholders. The 20th-century American economist John Kenneth Galbraith observed that "[t]he salary of the chief executive of a large corporation is not a market award for achievement. It is frequently in the nature of a warm personal gesture by the individual to himself." It is also an issue that is likely not to go away soon. In the late 1970s CEOs earned 30 to 40 times the income of average workers; by 2007, CEOs of large public corporations earned 344 times the income of average workers.[38] The Dodd–Frank Act now requires that the ratio be disclosed annually. It also requires disclosure of the relationship between executive compensation and the financial performance of the company, giving consideration to both stock price and dividends.

> By 2007, CEOs of large public corporations earned 344 times the income of average workers.

Efforts to control executive compensation appear to have borne little fruit. In 2012, the compensation of the top 200 CEOs of publicly traded companies increased 16 percent to a median of $15 million.[39] The highest paid was John Hammergren of McKesson, who received $131 million.[40] In addition, the average perquisites for the 100 highest-paid CEOs rose 19 percent to $321,000.[41]

Dodd–Frank also includes a *say on pay* provision requiring companies to put a separate, but nonbinding, resolution before the shareholders to approve the compensation paid to senior executives. This seems to have had little practical impact. During 2012, shareholders upheld about 98 percent of pay proposals.[42] Interestingly, the Swiss enacted a law providing for a binding shareholder say on pay for its executives.[43]

PRACTICING ETHICS | Excessive Executive Compensation?

An interesting shareholder derivative case alleging a violation of the duty of care arose out of CEO Michael Eisner's hiring, and subsequent firing, of Michael Ovitz from his position as president of Walt Disney Co. The suit alleged that Eisner and the Disney board had violated their duty of care by hiring Ovitz (who had no previous experience as an executive of a public company in the entertainment industry), as well as when Ovitz was granted a no-fault termination. The consequence of invoking the no-fault clause in Ovitz's employment contract was that, after barely one year of employment, Ovitz received more than $38 million in cash, as well as 3 million stock options. Notably, the maximum salary Ovitz could have earned actually working was $11 million annually. Following a three-month trial, the Delaware judge wrote, "For the future, many lessons of what not to do can be learned from defendants' conduct here. Nevertheless, I conclude that . . . the defendants did not act in bad faith, and were at most ordinarily negligent, in connection with the hiring of Ovitz. . . . In accordance with the business judgment rule, . . . ordinary negligence is insufficient to constitute a violation of the fiduciary duty of care." The court also found that Ovitz could not have been fired for cause because he did not commit gross negligence or malfeasance while serving as Disney's president. Thus, Eisner did not breach his duty of care by agreeing to the no-fault termination. In 2006, ten years after Ovitz was terminated, this decision was affirmed on appeal by the Delaware Supreme Court. [*In re Walt Disney Co. Derivative Litigation*, 907 A.2d 693 (Del. Ch. 2005), aff'd 906 A.2d 27 (Del. 2006).]

Since 2007, as a result of a change in SEC disclosure rules, shareholders have been receiving more information on executive compensation packages. According to one source, executive severance packages typically "include a payment of three times salary and bonus, immediate vesting of options and restricted stock awards, and, in many cases, payment of taxes owed. . . . [D]ozens of executives could have payouts of $100 million or more."

Questions

1. Apart from the legality, is it ethical for a board to agree to an executive severance package when an executive is terminated for poor performance?

2. Such packages are negotiated as part of the hiring process. Would it chill the negotiations for a board to state a corporate policy against severance payments under such circumstances?

Source: Jane Sasseen, "A Better Look at the Boss's Pay," *BusinessWeek*, February 26, 2007, p. 44.

Questions—Part Two

1. Why have corporate governance concerns arisen in the past decade with respect to the relationship between the board and the CEO? Do you believe there are still grounds for continuing concern?

2. Evaluate the opinion that board accountability to shareholders is a myth.

3. Why might it make sense to have only outside directors determine the compensation of senior executives?

4. Select one of the shareholder rights proposals discussed in Part Two and present arguments both for and against its adoption.

5. How is the "war" on excessive executive compensation faring?

Part Three—Regulation of the Securities Markets

Introduction

As the recent financial crisis has shown, the capital markets are much broader than the market for securities, which in turn is far broader than the market for corporate securities. Nevertheless, the focus of this part of the chapter is on business access to capital.

> Vast sums (have been) lost in companies with incompetent or corrupt management.

To amass the capital needed to pursue sizeable business opportunities, particularly global opportunities, a large number of investors must be convinced to entrust their wealth to third parties. History shows that this trust has often been misplaced, with vast sums lost in companies with incompetent or corrupt management. As a result the federal government has undertaken to promote the reliability of the U.S. securities markets through regulation. The backbone of this regulation grew out of the stock market crash of 1929 and the Great Depression that followed. As previously mentioned, significant additional regulation has followed the corporate failures of the Enron era and the Great Recession of 2008 regulation to which this chapter now turns.

Initial Public Offerings

When a corporation wants to sell a new security through the public capital markets (whether debt or equity), if the corporation (*issuer*) and any of the persons to whom the security is offered for sale (*offerees*) are domiciled in different states (*interstate offering*), federal law governs the sale. If the corporation and all offerees are domiciled in the same state (*intrastate offering*), state law (considered later) applies. If a company has not previously offered equity securities to the public, the offering is referred to as an *initial public offering* (IPO) or, more colloquially, *going public*. For example, on Thursday, November 7, 2013, Twitter went public at $26 a share. It immediately jumped to $45.[44] Conversely, if a private investor seeks to purchase all of the publicly held equity securities of a corporation, that company is said to be *going private*.

In this context, the term *security* embraces both the instruments commonly understood to be securities, like stocks and bonds, as well as a much broader class called investment contracts. The *Howey* case that follows defines the term.

LEGAL BRIEFCASE

SEC v. W. J. Howey Co.
328 U.S. 293 (1946)

FACTS

The Howey Company owned large tracts of citrus acreage in Florida. Each prospective customer was offered both a land sales contract and a service contract by which Howey maintained the groves and marketed the produce. Purchases usually were narrow strips that were arranged so that an acre consisted of a row of 48 trees. These tracts were not separately fenced and the purchaser had no right of entry and no right to specific fruit. All the produce was pooled. The purchasers were mostly non-residents of Florida and were predominantly professional people who lacked the knowledge and equipment necessary for the citrus business. They were attracted by the expectation of substantial profits.

Justice Murphy

* * * * *

It is admitted that the mails and instrumentalities of interstate commerce are used in the sale of the land and service contracts and that no registration statement . . . has ever been filed with the [Securities Exchange Commission.]

[The Securities Act of 1933] defines the term "security" to include the commonly known [instruments like stocks and bonds.] The definition also includes [the term] "investment contract". . . . The legal issue turns upon the legal determination of whether the land sales contract, the warranty deed and the service contract together constitute an "investment contract" within the meaning of [the Act]. An affirmative answer brings into operation the registration requirements. . . .

By including an investment contract within the scope of . . . the Securities Act, Congress was using a term the meaning of which had been crystallized by this prior judicial interpretation. It is therefore reasonable to attach that meaning to the term as used by Congress, especially since such a definition is consistent with the statutory aims. In other words, an investment contract for purposes of the Securities Act means a contract, transaction or scheme whereby a person invests his money in a common enterprise and is led to expect profits solely from the efforts of the promoter or a third party. . . .

The transactions in this case clearly involve investment contracts as so defined. The respondent [is] offering an opportunity to contribute money and to share in the profits of a large citrus fruit enterprise managed [by respondent. It is] offering this opportunity to persons who reside in distant localities and who lack the equipment and experience requisite to the cultivation, harvesting and marketing of the citrus products. . . .

[Respondent's] failure to abide by the statutory and administrative rules in making such offerings cannot be sanctioned under the Act. . . .

Questions

1. Would an investment in Microsoft stock satisfy the definition of "investment contract"?

2. Why do you think Congress added the term "investment contract" to the definition of "security"?

AFTERWORD

Following the *Howey* case, courts have looked more closely at the final criterion, that the investor "is led to expect profits *primarily* from the efforts" of others [emphasis added], and have generally taken a practical view of the requirement. The goal has been to distinguish circumstances in which investors will be primarily passive from those in which there is a reasonable expectation of significant investor control.[45] Thus, membership units in an LLC may or may not qualify as investment contracts, depending on the surrounding facts.[46]

1933 Act

The federal law governing initial securities offerings is the *Securities Act of 1933* (1933 Act), which is administered by the *Securities and Exchange Commission* (SEC). The 1933 Act does not guarantee the economic merits of any investment opportunity. Rather, it seeks (1) to ensure full disclosure of all material facts about the investment opportunity to offerees (potential investors) before they invest and (2) to eliminate fraudulent conduct in the markets. Thus, a securities offering that passes muster under the federal securities law has not been approved by the government as a good investment. [For more on the SEC, see **www.sec.gov**]

To promote full disclosure the 1933 Act forbids any interstate offering of a new security until a *registration statement* has been filed with and approved by the SEC. The *registration statement* has two parts: the prospectus and the supplemental information. The *prospectus* is the major component and is delivered to offerees to satisfy the requirement for preinvestment disclosure. There are three main sections in a prospectus. One contains general information about the company: the industry in which it operates, the quality of its products and services and of its management, its business plan, and so on. Another section contains a risk assessment of the business model, local operating conditions (such as political instability), and the like. For example, although companies have long been required to disclose possible impacts on the business from various environmental factors, in 2010 the SEC began requiring companies to disclose the risks that global climate change might pose to their business, such as whether any new law or treaty limiting carbon dioxide emissions might increase operating costs.[47]

The third portion of the prospectus is the *audited financial statements*. An investor's goal is to make money. Investors want to know how well the corporation under consideration has accomplished this in the past so they can estimate its future economic potential. A corporation's ability to make a profit is shown on its *income statement,* one of the three audited financial statements. The income statement shows the company's revenue and expenses on an annual basis.

Because the income statement seeks to measure economic income, it employs accrual accounting, which recognizes revenue when earned (not when cash is received) and which recognizes expenses in the period in which the related income is reported (regardless of when those expenses are paid). Since the income statement focuses only on economic income, a *statement of cash flows* reconciling the beginning and ending cash balances is also presented.

The third financial statement, the *balance sheet,* presents the company's assets, liabilities, and equity. Although balance sheets have numerous deficiencies (such as the use of historical cost rather than current value to measure assets), they attempt to describe the corporation's financial position as of a particular date, such as the end of the year presented in the income statement.

Technically, the financial statements are prepared by the corporation's management. To give comfort to investors that management has prepared these statements properly and honestly, independent *certified public accountants* (CPAs) are engaged to audit them. Audits must be performed in accordance with *generally accepted auditing standards* (GAAS). GAAS are intended to ensure that the procedures used to investigate the financial statements are thorough. The objective of the investigation is to determine whether the financial statements are *not materially misleading,* in accordance with *generally accepted accounting principles* (GAAP). GAAP provides the rules for how revenues, expenses, assets, liabilities, and equity are measured and disclosed. One might paraphrase an audit: independent experts (CPAs) are supposed to "look hard" (GAAS) and decide whether the financial statements accurately measure the income, cash flow, and financial position of the corporation (GAAP).

The *supplemental information* portion (the second part) of the registration statement, which is not distributed to offerees, describes such matters as how much it is costing to "float" the offering and what major contracts exist with unions, suppliers, or customers.

The SEC vigorously enforces the 1933 Act's prescribed relationship between solicitation or sales of a security and the registration process. There are three critical stages. During the *prefiling period* (before the registration statement has been filed with the SEC), no solicitation or sales are permitted. During the *waiting period* (after the registration statement has been filed, but before it has been approved by the SEC), no sales are permitted but a limited amount of solicitation is allowed. Specifically, a *tombstone* ad (so called because of its shape) may be published in forums like *The Wall Street Journal* to make the market aware of the upcoming issuance. In addition, a *red herring* prospectus (name taken from the prominent red ink cautionary statement required on its first page) may be distributed. This is the draft prospectus included with the filed registration statement. Once the SEC approves the registration statement, the *posteffective period* begins. Solicitations are permitted and sales may be made, but only if the offerees have first received the final prospectus.

Some companies do *shelf registrations* that allow them to issue securities in portions over a two-year period under a single registration statement. This allows issuers to float the securities when market conditions are most favorable, without having to place the entire issue shortly after the registration statement becomes effective.

Typically not wanting to sell the securities themselves, issuers employ one of two kinds of *underwriters*. A best-efforts underwriter acts as the issuer's sales agent, does not take title to the securities, and earns its profit from sales commissions. A *firm-commitment underwriter* purchases the securities at a discount, intending to profit by reselling them. Institutional investors and *dealers* typically purchase new offerings—the former for investment, the latter for resale to retail investors.

Private Placement General Solicitation Ban Lifted

In July 2013 the SEC reversed an 80-year-old prohibition on the general solicitation of unregistered securities. Private placements, which comprise over 40 percent of all securities issuances, can now be advertised to anyone, although only accredited investors (discussed below) can make purchases. Any means of solicitation, including the internet, is permitted. Advocates assert that the new rule promotes the ability of start-ups and small businesses to raise capital without going through the onerous registration process. Critics counter that allowing speculative start-ups and high-risk hedge funds to solicit investments through mass marketing will undermine the integrity of the market.[48]

PRACTICING ETHICS   Credit Rating Agencies—Another Cause for Concern?

Corporations may use the securities markets to obtain debt capital by selling corporate bonds. Bonds are "securities" and thus are governed by the federal securities laws. To issue new bonds, a corporation will usually seek to have the bond rated by a credit rating agency such as Moody's, Standard & Poor's, or Fitch. Without such a rating it may be hard for the corporation to sell a sufficient number of, or to obtain the maximum price for, its bonds. Most of the revenues of these agencies come from the fees paid by issuers seeking to have their debt rated. These facts raise potential conflicts of interest for the agencies—on the one hand they are in business to produce credible, independent evaluations of issuers and bonds, but on the other hand they have to compete with other agencies for issuers' business.

It seems clear that such conflicts played a role in the recent financial crisis—not from their rating of corporate bonds, but from their rating of mortgage-backed securities (investment vehicles based on the performance of a pool of mortgages). According to the Financial Crisis Inquiry Report, "Failures in credit rating and securitization transformed bad mortgages into toxic financial assets."[49] Congressional hearings uncovered internal e-mails containing such statements as "sold our soul to the devil for revenue" (Moody's) and "let's hope we are all wealthy and retired by the time this house of cards falters" (Standard & Poor's).[50]

So far the government has accomplished nothing in terms of new regulation.[51] Nonetheless, the agencies are facing a federal suit for fraud[52] and have become the subject of several lawsuits, including one for over $1 billion, all related to their top-tier ratings of various mortgage-backed securities and other credit derivatives.[53]

Question

A bondholder would be concerned about whether a corporation has purchased a favorable bond rating. Should a shareholder also be worried? Explain.

Exemptions

Exempt securities and *exempt transactions* do not require registration with the SEC. The most common exempt securities are those issued by governments, charities, educational institutions, and financial institutions such as banks and insurance companies. Thus, they have little application to most businesses.

Certain transactions, however, are also exempt from at least some of the registration requirements. Depending on the exemption, the presale disclosures and filings with the SEC range from none to something only slightly less than a full registration statement. Most exemptions do not permit general advertising or solicitation.

Five long standing categories of exempt transactions were created at least in part as an accommodation to small issuers, such as private and closely held businesses, to lessen the financial burdens of raising capital. (See the text box to follow for a discussion of the new crowdfunding exemption.) For example, all intrastate offerings are exempt transactions. There is a statutory exemption for purely private offerings, but it can sometimes be problematic to determine whether a particular offering will be considered private or public. Thus, small issuers are more likely to rely on one of the regulatory exemptions created by the SEC. Rules 504 (which exempts transactions with an aggregate offering amount of $1 million or less) and 505 (which exempts certain transactions with an aggregate offering amount of up to $5 million) are little used. The workforce is Rule S06, for which there is no amount limitation, but which can involve only *accredited investors* and up to 35 *sophisticated investors*. Accredited investors are individuals with a net worth over $1 million or with an income in excess of $200,000 (or married with a combined income of $300,000) for at least two years with the expectation of similar income in the current year. A sophisticated investor is one who has sufficient knowledge and experience in financial matters to be able to evaluate the merits and risks of an investment (or a person advised by a party with such expertise). Institutional investors are also deemed accredited.

Note that even when exemptions apply to registration under the 1933 Act, the act's sweeping antifraud provisions (discussed later) still apply.

Retail Securities Crowdfunding Emerges

Securities crowdfunding is the use of the Internet to raise capital, with each contributor investing a comparatively small amount. Until recently it has been limited to no-interest loans and donations because, if a return is provided (e.g., dividends or interest), the securities laws require the investment's registration with the SEC.[54]

Retail Securities crowdfunding was authorized by the 2012 JOBS Act through a new registration exemption. Companies will be allowed to raise up to $1 million annually by selling stock via the Internet using "intermediaries" (SEC-regulated third parties, which will manage the process). Individuals will be limited in the amount they can invest each year. For example, those whose annual income and net worth are both less than $100,000 will be permitted to invest 5 percent of the greater of those amounts (but not more than $2,000). Companies must disclose information about their business, their officers and directors, and how they will use the money. Audited financial statements are required if the amount to be raised exceeds $500,000. Nonetheless, the disclosure requirements are substantially less than those applicable to conventional initial public offerings (IPOs).[55]

The retail securities crowdfunding rules are controversial. Many are concerned about hucksters defrauding the naïve and financially unsophisticated investor. Others complain of the burdensome transaction and compliance costs. For example, simply raising $100,000 could cost $18,000, and over five years, $1 million of funding could cost $300,000.[56]

The SEC has not yet finalized the rules that will allow retail securities crowdfunding to begin. In frustration, Michigan, Georgia, and Kansas enacted their own versions, and other states are considering doing so.[57]

It remains to be seen whether retail securities crowdfunding can become a viable option for "democratizing" the capital markets.

The Secondary Securities Markets

Once a security is issued, it can be sold repeatedly. Such sales may be accomplished on a *physical exchange,* such as the New York Stock Exchange (NYSE), where agents of buyers and sellers deal directly with each other. Others may be made on an *over-the-counter market,* where trades occur electronically over a computer network linking dealers across the nation. An example is NASDAQ, the National Association of Securities Dealers Automatic Quotation system. [To learn more about these exchanges, see **https://nyse.nyx.com/** and **www.nasdaq.com**]

The federal law that governs these trades is the *Securities Exchange Act of 1934* (1934 Act), which also created the SEC. Its purposes are the same as those of its 1933 counterpart: (1) to ensure full disclosure of all material information so the market can make informed investment decisions and (2) to prevent fraudulent conduct in the markets. A company is generally subject to the 1934 Act's reporting requirements if it has publicly traded securities and it has both more than $10 million in assets and more than 500 nonaccredited shareholders.[58]

To promote full disclosure, the SEC requires registered corporations to file a variety of reports. Annually, each must file a *Form 10-K,* which includes information very similar to that found in a 1933 Act registration statement, including audited financial statements. Recall, as discussed in Part Two, that the Dodd–Frank Act added new disclosure requirements, such as the ratio of the CEO's compensation to that of the median compensation for all other employees. To increase the timeliness of information disclosures, the SEC requires additional reports, such as the quarterly *Form 10-Q* and *Form 8-K*. The latter is required whenever a material event occurs, such as a change in control, a major asset acquisition or disposition, bankruptcy, a change in auditor, and the resignation of the director.[59] [To retrieve filings for specific corporations, see **www.sec.gov /edgar.shtml**]

Not only are certain disclosures mandated, but all corporate communications are subject to regulatory standards. The SEC's Regulation FD requires companies to disseminate material information in a way that rapidly reaches the general public and gives no one an advantage. In April 2013, the SEC approved the use of social media such as Twitter and Facebook for such dissemination, as long as the company has previously advised the public what social media outlets it will use.[60]

Under the 1934 Act, the SEC has the power to *suspend trading* in any security "when it serves the public interest and will protect investors." Thus, the SEC may suspend trading if it suspects price manipulation or has serious questions about a company's assets or operations.[61] Typically, the market price of a security is devastated by a suspension, which provides a strong incentive for corporations to avoid misconduct.

Brokers and Online Trading

When individuals want to buy or sell securities listed on an exchange, they may do so through an intermediary—a broker. In addition to facilitating trades, brokers may provide advisory services and assess the suitability of investments for a particular investor. That is, they make recommendations and trades taking into account the investor's needs, financial situation, investment objectives, and risk tolerance.

> An 80-year-old woman with Alzheimer's disease entrusted $500,000 to a broker.

Occasionally, a broker has faced charges of *churning*—repeatedly and unnecessarily engaging in trades to generate commissions. In one case, an 80-year-old woman with Alzheimer's disease entrusted $500,000 to a broker. Fourteen months later, the account was worth only $15,000. The broker had engaged in over 300 trades and charged the account $94,000 in fees, purchasing only high-tech stocks (versus a balanced, conservative portfolio more appropriate to her situation).[62]

One impact of the Internet was the bypassing of full-service securities brokers through *online trading*. In response, most major full-service brokers added online trading services, which can be less expensive, but which also tend to leave investors without professional guidance.

Matters get worse when it comes to *day trading*. Day traders rarely hold any security more than a few hours, earning profits by exploiting volatility, not inherent value. It has been reported that only about 10 percent of day traders are successful.[63] The SEC has expressed great concern about advertising that suggests day trading is easy and certain to be profitable. It cautions that tips and analyses are frequently false.[64] Nonetheless, the market has moved inexorably toward global, 24-hour-a-day, electronic trading.

Violating Federal Securities Laws

The consequences for noncompliance with the securities laws are potentially staggering, including damages and civil and criminal penalties. Some of the provisions most commonly violated by corporations and their directors and executives are discussed below.

False or Misleading Statements in Required Filings—1933 Act

Perhaps the greatest deterrent to misconduct in the securities laws is the civil liability that can be imposed on wrongdoers by harmed investors. The 1933 Act's Section 11 establishes this liability with respect to false or misleading registration statements.

Virtually anyone with a significant role in preparing the registration statement can be sued (the issuer, its directors, its underwriters, and its accountants and other experts). The liability can be vast—essentially all damages sustained by investors while the misleading registration statements were outstanding. No proof of plaintiff reliance on the content of the registration statement is required. Accounting firms and investment bankers, because of their "deep pockets," are often at the top of the list of defendants. Accounting firms have paid hundreds of millions of dollars to settle securities fraud suits.

The principal defense against a Section 11 claim is *due diligence*. Every defendant, other than the issuer, can raise this defense. The defendant must show that, based on a reasonable investigation, he or she reasonably believed that the registration statement was not misleading. What constitutes "reasonable" is determined by reference to the conduct expected of a prudent person in the management of his or her own property.

The due diligence standard for experts (like accountants and lawyers) is much higher. Their inquiries must rise to the standards expected of professionals, not merely of prudent businesspersons. Thus, at an absolute minimum, an accounting firm that has audited the financial statements included in the registration statement must design its audit process to comport with GAAS and must evaluate the financial statement content in accordance with GAAP. Lawyers, actuaries, appraisers, and other experts whose work has a material impact on the registration statement must follow analogous rules established by their professional associations and regulators. The *BarChris* case, below, explores the due diligence defense.

LEGAL BRIEFCASE

Escott v. BarChris Construction Corporation
283 F.Supp. 643 (S.D.N.Y. 1968)

FACTS

Bowling as a leisure activity and sport grew rapidly in the 1950s. BarChris built alleys. Its revenues grew from $800,000 in 1956 to $9,165,000 in 1960. By 1962 overbuilding caused construction to halt. BarChris ran into serious financial problems. It filed a registration statement (effective May 1961) for new bonds to raise cash and the bonds were issued. Circumstances were grave when the registration statement became effective. BarChris filed for bankruptcy in October 1962.

BarChris's financial statements dated December 31, 1960, were included in the prospectus. They were audited by Peat, Marwick (predecessor to KPMG) and contained material errors. Revenues and current assets were overstated and contingent liabilities were understated.

The prospectus overstated the demand for alley construction. It misrepresented how the proceeds would be used (a large portion of which would actually go to pay overdue debts and retire loans from officers). It failed to note that, because of defaults, BarChris was now operating several alleys. Escott and other bondholders sued under Section 11 of the 1933 Act, alleging the prospectus was materially misleading. All defendants but BarChris raised the due diligence defense.

Judge Mclean

I turn now to the question of whether defendants have proved their due diligence defenses. The position of each defendant will be separately considered.

Russo

Russo was, to all intents and purposes, the chief executive officer of BarChris. He was a member of the executive committee. He was familiar with all aspects of the business. . . . [He] knew all the relevant facts. He could not have believed that there were no untrue statements or material omissions in the prospectus. Russo has no due diligence defenses.

Vitolo and Pugliese

They were the founders. . . . Vitolo was president and Pugliese was vice president. Despite their titles, their [control] over BarChris's affairs [was far less] than Russo's. [They are] each men of limited education. It is not hard to believe that for them the prospectus was difficult reading, if indeed they read it at all. But [the] liability of a director who signs a registration statement does not depend upon whether or not he read it or, if he did, whether or not he understood what he was reading.

And in any case, Vitolo and Pugliese were not as naive as they claim to be. They were members of BarChris's executive committee. . . . They must have known what was going on. Certainly they knew of the inadequacy of cash. . . . They knew of their own large advances to the company which remained unpaid. They knew that they had agreed not to deposit their checks until the financing proceeds were received. They knew and intended that part of the proceeds were to be used to pay their own loans.

All in all, [their situation] is not significantly different . . . from Russo's. They could not have believed that the registration statement was wholly true and that no material facts had been omitted. . . . They have not proved their due diligence defenses.

Trilling

[Trilling was . . . a CPA and former member of Peat, Marwick. He was BarChris'] controller. He signed the registration statement in that capacity, although he was not a director. . . .

Trilling may well have been unaware of several of the inaccuracies in the prospectus. But he must have known of some of them. . . . I cannot find that Trilling believed the entire prospectus to be true.

But even if he did, he still did not establish his due diligence defenses. He . . . failed to prove, as to the [nonaudited] parts of the prospectus . . ., that he made a reasonable investigation which afforded him a reasonable ground to believe that it was true. As far as appears, he made no investigation. . . . This would have been well enough but for the fact that he signed the registration statement. As a signer, he could not avoid responsibility. . . . [He has not proved] his due diligence defenses.

Birnbaum

Birnbaum was a young lawyer [employed as in-house counsel. He was] secretary and a director. . . . He signed the later amendments [to the registration statement], thereby becoming responsible for the accuracy of the prospectus. . . .

. . . He did not participate in the management of the company. As house counsel, he attended to legal matters of a routine nature. . . .

One of Birnbaum's more important duties . . . was to keep the corporate minutes. . . . This necessarily informed him to a considerable extent about the company's affairs. . . .

It seems probable that Birnbaum did not know of many of the inaccuracies in the prospectus. He must, however, have appreciated some of them. In any case, he made no investigation. . . . [He] was entitled to rely upon Peat, Marwick for the 1960 figures. . . . But he was not entitled to rely upon [anyone else] for the other portions of the prospectus. As a lawyer, he should have known his obligations. . . . Having failed to make such an investigation, he did not have reasonable ground to believe that all these statements were true. Birnbaum has not established his due diligence defenses except as to the audited 1960 figures.

Auslander

Auslander was an "outside" director. . . . He was chairman . . . of Valley Stream National Bank. [He became a director shortly before the sale of the bonds. He signed the registration statement.]

. . . As to the [financial statements], Auslander knew that Peat, Marwick had audited [them, so he] believed them to be correct. . . . He had no reasonable ground to believe otherwise.

As to the [non-audited portions of the prospectus], however, Auslander is in a different position. . . . [He] made no investigation of the accuracy of the prospectus. He relied on the assurance of Vitolo and Russo. . . .

It is true that Auslander became a director on the eve of the financing. He had little opportunity to familiarize himself with the company's affairs. . . .

Section 11 imposes liability . . . upon a director, no matter how new he is. He is presumed to know his responsibility when he becomes a director. He can escape liability only by using that reasonable care to investigate the facts which a prudent man would employ in the management of his own property. In my opinion, a prudent man would not act in an important matter . . . in sole reliance upon representations of persons who are comparative strangers. . . . To say that such minimal conduct measures up to the statutory standard would, to all intents and purposes, absolve new directors from responsibility merely because they are new. This is not a sensible construction of Section 11. . . .

Auslander has not established his due diligence defense [except as to the financial statements].

Grant

. . . [Grant's] law firm was counsel to BarChris in matters pertaining to the registration of securities. Grant drafted the registration statement. . . . As the director most directly concerned with writing [it] and assuring its accuracy, more was required of him in the way of reasonable investigation than could fairly be expected of a director who had no connection with this work. . . .

. . . I find that Grant honestly believed that the registration statement was true and that no material facts had been omitted from it.

In this belief he was mistaken, and the fact is that for all his work, he never discovered any of the errors or omissions which . . . could have been detected without an audit. The question is whether, despite his failure to detect them, Grant made a reasonable effort to that end.

. . . BarChris's affairs had changed for the worse. . . . Grant never discovered this. He accepted the assurances of [others] that any change which might have occurred had been for the better. . . .

It is claimed that a lawyer is entitled to rely on the statements of his client. . . . This is too broad a generalization. It is all a matter of degree. To require an audit would obviously be unreasonable. On the other hand, to require a check of matters easily verifiable is not unreasonable. Even honest clients can make mistakes. The statute imposes liability for untrue statements regardless of whether they are intentionally untrue. . . .

. . . Grant knew that minutes of certain meetings of the BarChris executive committee held in 1961 had not been

written up. . . . Grant did not insist that the minutes be written up, nor did he look at Kircher's notes. . . .

. . . He knew that BarChris was short of cash, but he had no idea how short. He did not know that BarChris was withholding delivery of checks already drawn and signed because there was not enough money in the bank to pay them. He did not know that the officers of the company intended to use immediately approximately one-third of the financing proceeds in a manner not disclosed in the prospectus, including approximately $1,000,000 in paying old debts. . . .

Grant was entitled to rely on Peat Marwick for the 1960 figures. [But as to the rest of the prospectus, Grant] was obliged to make a reasonable investigation. I am forced to find that he did not make one. . . . Grant has not established his due diligence defenses except as to the audited 1960 figures.

Peat, Marwick

. . . The part of the registration statement . . . made upon the authority of Peat, Marwick as an expert was . . . the 1960 [audited financial statements]. But because the statute requires the court to determine Peat, Marwick's belief, and the grounds thereof, "at the time . . . the registration statement became effective," . . . the matter must be viewed as of May 16, 1961. . . .

The 1960 Audit

[The audit] was in general charge of a member of the firm, Cummings. . . . Most of the actual work was performed by a senior accountant, Berardi, [who was about thirty]. He was not yet a C.P.A. He had no previous experience with the bowling industry. This was his first job as a senior accountant. . . .

The S-1 Review

The purpose of reviewing events subsequent to the date of a certified balance sheet, [an S-1 review,] is to ascertain whether any material change has occurred in the company's financial position which should be disclosed in order to prevent the . . . figures from being misleading. The scope of such a review [is not] a complete audit.

Peat, Marwick prepared a written program [which] conformed to generally accepted auditing standards. . . .

Berardi made the S-1 review in May 1961. He devoted a little over two days to it. . . . He did not discover any of the errors or omissions. . . . The question is whether, despite his failure to find out anything, his investigation was reasonable within the meaning of the statute.

What Berardi did was not look at a . . . trial balance as of March 31, 1961[,] compare it with the audited December 31, 1960 figures, discuss with Trilling certain unfavorable developments[,] and read certain minutes. He did not examine any [other] "important financial records." . . .

In substance, what Berardi did is . . . [he] asked questions, he got answers which he considered satisfactory, and he did nothing to verify them. . . .

Berardi had no conception of how tight the cash position was. He did not discover that BarChris was holding up checks in substantial amounts because there was no money in the bank to cover them. He did not know of . . . the officers' loans. Since he never read the prospectus, he was not even aware that there had ever been any problem about loans from officers. . . .

There had been a material change for the worse in BarChris's financial position. That change was sufficiently serious so that the failure to disclose it made the 1960 figures misleading. Berardi did not discover it. As far as results were concerned, his S-1 review was useless.

Accountants should not be held to a standard higher than that recognized in their profession. I do not do so here. Berardi's review did not come up to that standard. He did not take some of the steps which Peat, Marwick's written program prescribed. He did not spend an adequate amount of time on a task of this magnitude. Most important of all, he was too easily satisfied with glib answers to his inquiries.

. . . [T]here were enough danger signals in the materials which he did examine to require some further investigation on his part. Generally accepted accounting standards required such further investigation under these circumstances. It is not always sufficient merely to ask questions.

Here again, the burden of proof is on Peat, Marwick. I find that that burden has not been satisfied. I conclude that Peat, Marwick has not established its due diligence defense.

Questions

1. *a.* Why were so many defendants not held responsible for the misleading audited financial statements?

   b. Which defendants were not successful in claiming the due diligence defense with respect to these financial statements? Why were they denied the defense?

2. Does being "new" make any difference in terms of directorial liability for a signed registration statement?

3. What would you do differently in the future if you were Peat, Marwick?

False or Misleading Statements in Required Filings—1934 Act

Section 18 of the 1934 Act, relating to false or misleading statements in any filing required to maintain the registration of a security, is similar to the 1933 Act's Section 11. However, the only defense offered by Section 18 is that the defendant acted in good faith, without knowledge of the false or misleading nature of the statement. Furthermore, unlike the 1933 Act's Section 11 where reliance by the plaintiff on the false or misleading statements is presumed, under the 1934 Act's Section 18 the plaintiff must prove that he or she relied on the statements.

Fraud

Under the 1933 Act's Section 17(a) and the 1934 Act's Section 10(b) and its related Rule 10b-5, it is illegal, in connection with the sale or purchase of any security, to employ any

> Bernard Madoff was sentenced to 150 years in prison.

scheme or to engage in any practice that defrauds another person participating in the financial markets. These provisions intentionally cast a "broad net" and can reach such Ponzi schemes as the one run by Bernard Madoff, who in 2009 was sentenced to 150 years in prison for perpetrating a $50 billion fraud. In essence he promised very lucrative rates of return to investors, which returns were paid out of funds collected from an ever-increasing pool of new investors. When the economy turns down, such schemes collapse, revealing just how widespread the phenomenon is. More than 150 imploded in 2009, compared with about 40 in 2008.[65]

Fraudulent acts can be committed by corporate wrongdoers as well. For example, making misleading statements about material facts or failing to state material facts in required SEC disclosure documents or in other company communications can be fraudulent, providing powerful grounds for damage suits by harmed investors. Large companies have

> In 2009 Merrill Lynch settled a suit for $475 million.

paid substantial settlements in lawsuits arising from the recent financial collapse. For example, in 2009 Merrill Lynch settled a suit for $475 million with investors who alleged that it had understated its subprime debt exposure. Wells Fargo agreed in 2011 to pay $85 million to settle Federal Reserve claims that the firm pushed borrowers toward unnecessarily costly mortgage loans and falsified data in mortgage applications. In late 2013, J. P. Morgan agreed to pay $4.5 billion to settle charges that it misled investors in a complicated deal involving pooled mortgages.[66]

Bringing forward direct evidence of reliance on fraudulent statements can be difficult, so the *fraud-on-the-market* theory has evolved. It is the subject of the *Basic, Inc.* case below.

LEGAL BRIEFCASE

Basic Inc. v. Levinson et al.
485 U.S. 224 (1988)

FACTS

Prior to December 20, 1978, Basic Inc., was a publicly traded company primarily engaged in the business of manufacturing chemical refractories for the steel industry. As early as 1965 or 1966, Combustion Engineering, Inc., a company producing mostly alumina-based refractories, expressed some interest in acquiring Basic, but was deterred from pursuing this inclination seriously because of antitrust concerns. Beginning in 1976, Combustion had meetings with Basic concerning the possibility of a merger. During 1977 and 1978, Basic made three public statements denying merger negotiations. On December 19, 1978, Basic's board endorsed the merger.

Respondents were former Basic shareholders who sold their stock after Basic's first public denial but before the December 1978 announcement. They asserted that the defendants issued three false or misleading public statements in violation of Section 10(b) of the 1934 Act and of Rule 10b-5 and, further, that they were injured by selling Basic shares at artificially depressed prices in a market affected by petitioners' misleading statements and in reliance thereon.

Rule 10b-5 provides that it "shall be unlawful [t]o make any untrue statement of a material fact or to omit to state a material fact necessary . . . to make the statements made . . . not misleading . . . in connection with the purchase or sale of any security."

Justice Blackmun

* * * * *

. . . [T]o fulfill the materiality requirement "there must be a substantial likelihood that the disclosure of the omitted fact would have been viewed by the reasonable investor as having significantly altered the 'total mix' of information made available." . . .

* * * * *

We turn to the question of reliance and the fraud-on-the-market theory. Succinctly put:

> The fraud on the market theory is based on the hypothesis that, in an open and developed securities market, the price of a company's stock is determined by the available material information regarding the company and its business. . . . Misleading statements will therefore defraud purchasers . . . even if [they] do not directly rely on the misstatements. . . . The causal connection between the defendants' fraud and the plaintiffs' purchase . . . is no less significant than in a case of direct reliance on misrepresentations.

* * * * *

. . . Requiring proof of individualized reliance from each member of the proposed plaintiff class . . . would have prevented . . . a class action, since individual issues . . . would have overwhelmed the common ones. The District Court found that the presumption of reliance created by the fraud-on-the-market theory provided "a practical resolution to the problem of balancing the [need for] proof of reliance [against] the procedural [obstacles]." . . .

. . . Reliance provides the requisite causal connection between a defendant's misrepresentation and a plaintiff's injury. There is, however, more than one way to demonstrate the causal connection. . . .

The modern securities markets, literally involving millions of shares changing hands daily, differ from the face-to-face transactions contemplated by early fraud cases, and our understanding of Rule 10b-5's reliance requirement must encompass these differences.

With the presence of a market, the market is interposed between seller and buyer and, ideally, transmits information to the investor in the processed form of a market price. Thus the market is performing a substantial part of the valuation process performed by the investor in a face-to-face transaction. The market is acting as the unpaid agent of the investor, informing him that given all the information available to it, the value of the stock is worth the market price.

* * * * *

Presumptions typically serve to assist courts in managing circumstances in which direct proof, for one reason or another, is rendered difficult. The courts below accepted a presumption, created by the fraud-on-the-market theory and subject to rebuttal by petitioners, that persons who had traded Basic shares had done so in reliance on the integrity of the price set by the market, but because of petitioners' material misrepresentations that price had been fraudulently depressed. Requiring a plaintiff to show . . . how he would have acted if omitted material information had been disclosed . . . or if the misrepresentation had not been made, . . . would place an unnecessarily unrealistic evidentiary burden on the Rule 10b-5 plaintiff who has traded on an impersonal market.

. . . The presumption of reliance employed in this case is consistent with . . . congressional policy embodied in the 1934 Act. In drafting that Act, Congress expressly relied on the premise that securities markets are affected by information, and enacted legislation to facilitate an investor's reliance on the integrity of those markets. . . .

. . . Recent empirical studies . . . confirm Congress' premise that the market price . . . on well-developed markets reflects all publicly available information, and, hence, any material misrepresentations. . . . Because most publicly available information is reflected in market price, an investor's reliance on any public material misrepresentations, therefore, may be presumed for purposes of a Rule 10b-5 action.

* * * * *

Any showing that severs the link between the alleged misrepresentation and [the] decision to trade fair market price will be sufficient to rebut the presumption of reliance. For example, . . . if, despite petitioners' allegedly fraudulent attempt to manipulate market price, news of the merger discussions credibly entered the market and dissipated the effects of the misstatements, those who traded Basic shares after the corrective statements would have no direct or indirect connection with the fraud. . . .

In summary: . . . It is not inappropriate to apply a presumption of reliance supported by the fraud-on-the-market theory. That presumption, however, is rebuttable.

[Remanded for further proceedings consistent with the opinion.]

Questions

1. When is an item of undisclosed information about a company "material" for Rule 10b-5 purposes?

2. Is reliance on a misrepresentation essential in a Rule 10b-5 action?

3. *a.* Why would it be difficult for a plaintiff to demonstrate reliance in fact on a material omission?

   b. What solution did the courts create to deal with this problem?

AFTERWORD

As noted by the Court in *Basic, Inc.* and confirmed by the Seventh Circuit, investors who trade with knowledge of alleged misrepresentations will not be allowed to use the fraud-on-the-market theory. Those investors have not relied on the market price as an accurate reflection of material information.[67] In its 2014 decision in *Halliburton v. Erica P. John Fund*, the Supreme Court rejected the defendant's argument that the efficient markets hypothesis on which Basics, Inc. is grounded had been discredited by the financial crisis and various studies. In response, the court noted that Basic, Inc. recognized that markets are only imperfectly efficient and "based the presumption on the fairly modest premise that 'market professionals generally consider most publicly announced material statements about companies, [which] affect [s] stock . . . prices.'"[68]

Insider Trading

Classical illegal insider trading occurs when an "insider" breaches a fiduciary duty to shareholders by buying or selling a security while in possession of material, nonpublic information about the security. An insider is often a director, officer, or an employee of an issuer, but could also be someone who only temporarily has a confidential relationship with an issuer, such as an attorney, accountant, or consultant. The prohibition against trading on undisclosed inside information is based on Section 10(b) of the 1934 Act, which prohibits the use of any manipulative or deceptive device in connection with the purchase or sale of securities.

In recent years, prosecution of insider trading violations has increased substantially and headlines have often followed. Publicized incidents have run from sports to sex and from intricate and clandestine to sad to ridiculous and nearly everything else along the way:

- In the most high-profile insider-trading case in many years, billionaire Galleon Group hedge fund manager, Raj Rajaratnam, was convicted in 2011 on 14 counts of fraud and conspiracy that allegedly netted some $65 million in profits and losses averted. Rajaratnam allegedly tapped into a web of contacts in top-tier American businesses to secure information not publicly known.[69]

- In a related case, former Goldman Sachs director Rajat Gupta was sentenced in October 2012 to two years in prison for leaking inside information to Rajaratnam.[70]

- In November 2013, hedge fund SAC Capital Advisors pleaded guilty to criminal insider trading and agreed to pay a record $1.8 billion penalty.[71]

- A partner at Ernst & Young (EY) developed a relationship with a woman he found through a website for those in search of extramarital affairs. She testified against him in the trial in which he was convicted of insider trading. She had pled guilty to trading on information he passed to her, and she had agreed to cooperate with the government.[72]

- A respected, retired business school professor from St. John's University, who was a popular lecturer at a number of Wall Street firms, was accused by the SEC of passing inside information to another business professor at Pace University.[73]

- An executive secretary at Walt Disney and her boyfriend were charged with insider trading after sending 33 letters to investment firms offering to sell Disney's quarterly earnings reports before they were publicly released. A follow-up e-mail stated, "I was thinking $20,000 is a fair compensation but you are free to make an offer." Multiple hedge funds receiving the offer reported it to the SEC.[74]

The *Texas Gulf Sulphur* case below expresses the rule for those possessing inside information—either disclose the information or refrain from trading until the information is public.

LEGAL BRIEFCASE

SEC v. Texas Gulf Sulphur Co.
401 F.2d 833 (2d Cir. 1968)

FACTS

On November 12, 1963, TGS drilled a "discovery hole," K-55-1, in Canada which revealed possibly one of the largest ore strikes in history. Insiders (geologists at the drill site, certain company officers, and so on) began buying TGS stock at around $18. Lab testing and further test-hole drilling fully confirmed the magnitude of the strike. Rumors began to circulate.

On April 12, 1964, when the stock had passed $30 and when the best estimate was 8 million recoverable tons, TGS issued a press release naysaying the rumors. On April 16, a Canadian mining journal story, based on an April 13 site visit and interview, put the tonnage at 10 million. On the same day a Canadian government official, based on information current through April 15, put the tonnage at 25 million in a public announcement.

On this day the stock passed $36. By May 15, it exceeded $58. The SEC brought an insider-trading suit.

Judge Waterman

* * * * *

[Rule 10b-5] is based . . . on the justifiable expectation . . . that all investors trading on impersonal exchanges have relatively equal access to material information. . . . The essence of the Rule is that anyone who, trading for his own account [has access] to information intended to be available only for a corporate purpose . . . may not take "advantage of such . . . knowing it is unavailable to those with whom he is dealing," i.e., the investing public. Insiders . . . are, of course[,] precluded from so unfairly dealing, but the Rule is also applicable to one possessing the information who may not be strictly termed an "insider." . . . [A]nyone in possession of material inside information must either disclose it to the investing public [or] abstain from trading in or recommending the securities [while it] remains undisclosed. . . .

. . . An insider's duty to disclose [or] abstain . . . arises only in "those situations . . . which are reasonably certain to have a substantial effect on the market price [if] disclosed." . . .

* * * * *

. . . [W]hether facts are material [will depend] upon a balancing of both the indicated probability that the event will occur and the anticipated magnitude of the event. . . . [Here,] knowledge of the possibility, which surely was more than marginal, of the existence of a mine of the vast magnitude indicated by the remarkably rich drill core . . . would certainly have been an important fact to a reasonable . . . investor in deciding whether he should buy, sell, or hold. . . .

* * * * *

Finally, a major factor in determining whether the K-55-1 discovery was a material fact is the importance attached to the drilling results by those who knew about it. [T]he timing . . .

of their stock purchases . . . virtually compels the inference that the insiders were influenced by the drilling results. . . .

* * * * *

We hold, therefore, that all transactions in TGS stock . . . by individuals apprised of the drilling results of K-55-1 were made in violation of Rule 10b-5. . . .

* * * * *

. . . Coates, who placed orders . . . immediately after the official announcement . . . , [contends that his] purchases were not proscribed purchases for the news had already been . . . disclosed. We disagree.

. . . The reading of [the announcement] . . . is merely the first step in the process of dissemination required for compliance with the regulatory objective of providing all investors with an equal opportunity to make informed investment judgments. . . . [A]t the minimum Coates should have waited until the news could reasonably have been expected to appear over the media of widest circulation, the Dow Jones broad tape, rather than hastening to insure an advantage to himself. . . .

Questions

1. If you possess undisclosed inside information, what are your options for trading in the company's stock?

2. How soon after disclosure can an insider trade in the stock?

AFTERWORD

As stated by the *Texas Gulf Sulphur* court, the rule prohibits one who has access to information that was available to them only for a corporate purpose from trading in corporate securities with those who do not have that knowledge. This is the *classical* theory of insider trading. Officers and employees, for example, have a fiduciary duty not to use their principal's—that is, their employer's—information for personal gain.

[For a view of insider trading in China, see *Insider Trading Rats* at **www.youtube.com/ watch?v=IT3FAr0eIEo**].

Tippees

The insider concept has been extended to include *tippees*. In some cases, the *tipper* (the insider or an "upstream" tippee) intends to improperly convey the inside information to a third party and hopes to derive personal benefit therefrom. In such a case both the tipper and tippee are fully liable. In other cases, the tippee is deemed to "misappropriate" the inside information from the inadvertent tipper, knowing that it was confidential. This would occur, for example, if a psychiatrist learned material inside information during a session with a senior corporate executive and traded on that information. Here, the tippee, but not the tipper, would be liable. In the *O'Hagan* case, below, the U.S. Supreme Court approved this second theory, the *misappropriation* theory, that extends insider trading to outsiders.

LEGAL BRIEFCASE

United States v. O'Hagan
521 U.S. 642 (1997)

FACTS

O'Hagan was a partner in the law firm of Dorsey & Whitney. In July 1988, Grand Metropolitan retained the firm to represent it in a tender offer for Pillsbury stock. O'Hagan did no work on this matter. In August, O'Hagan began purchasing Pillsbury stock options. He also purchased Pillsbury stock at $39. When the tender offer was announced, the price rose to $60. O'Hagan sold his options and stock, making a profit of $4.3 million. He used the profits to conceal his previous embezzlement of unrelated client trust funds.

The SEC investigated. O'Hagan was convicted on securities fraud. The Eighth Circuit reversed, rejecting liability under Rule 10b-5 under the "misappropriation theory." The Supreme Court granted certiorari.

Section 10(b) proscribes (1) using any deceptive device (2) in connection with the purchase or sale of securities. It does not confine its coverage to deception of a purchaser or seller; rather, it reaches any deceptive device used "in connection with the purchase or sale of any security."

Justice Ginsburg

* * * * *

Under the "traditional" or "classical theory" of insider trading liability, Section 10(b) and Rule 10b-5 are violated when [an] insider trades in the securities of his corporation on the basis of material, nonpublic information. Trading on such information qualifies as a "deceptive device" . . . because "a relationship of trust [exists] between the shareholders [and the] insiders who have obtained confidential information by reason of their position with [the] corporation." That relationship . . . "gives rise to a duty to disclose [or to abstain from trading]". . . .The classical theory applies not only to officers, directors, and other permanent insiders . . ., but also to attorneys, accountants, consultants, and others who temporarily become fiduciaries of a corporation.

The "misappropriation theory" holds that a person commits fraud "in connection with" a securities transaction . . .

when he misappropriates confidential information for securities trading purposes, in breach of a duty owed to the source of the information. Under this theory, a fiduciary's undisclosed, self-serving use of a principal's information to purchase or sell securities, in breach of a duty of loyalty and confidentiality, defrauds the principal of the exclusive use of that information. In lieu of premising liability on a fiduciary relationship between company insider and purchaser or seller of the company's stock, the misappropriation theory premises liability on a fiduciary-turned-trader's deception of those who entrusted him with access to confidential information.

The two theories are complementary, each addressing efforts to capitalize on nonpublic information through the purchase or sale of securities. . . .

In this case, the indictment alleged that O'Hagan, in breach of a duty of trust . . . he owed to his law firm . . . and to its client . . . , traded on the basis of nonpublic information regarding the client's tender offer . . . . This conduct, the Government charged, constituted a fraudulent device in connection with the purchase and sale of securities. . . .

We agree . . . . We observe, first, that misappropriators . . . deal in deception. A fiduciary who "[pretends] loyalty to the principal while secretly converting the principal's information for personal gain" . . . defrauds the principal.

* * * * *

We turn next to the Section 10(b) requirement that the misappropriator's deceptive use of information be "in connection with the purchase or sale of [a] security." This element is satisfied because the fiduciary's fraud is consummated, not when the fiduciary gains the confidential information, but when, without disclosure to his principal, he uses the information to purchase or sell securities. . . .

* * * * *

The misappropriation theory . . . is also well-tuned to an animating purpose of the [1934] Act: to insure honest securities markets and thereby promote investor confidence. Although informational disparity is inevitable in the securities markets, . . . [an] investor's informational disadvantage vis-a-vis a misappropriator . . . stems from contrivance, not luck; it is a disadvantage that cannot be overcome with research or skill. . . .

[Reversed and remanded.]

Questions

1. Are both insider trading theories needed to fulfill the 1934 Act's desire to keep the markets "honest"?

2. Both insider trading theories depend heavily on fiduciary relationships. Contrast the parties in the fiduciary relationships under the "classical" and "misappropriation" theories.

3. Would it have made any difference if O'Hagan had established with his broker, long before this trading, a portfolio diversification plan such that, pursuant to the plan, the identical trading would have occurred?

Short-Swing Profits

Closely related to insider trading is liability for short-swing profits. An insider trading case requires proof that the insider had material inside information and traded to exploit it. A short-swing profit case conclusively presumes that the insider had such information and did unlawfully trade on it any time the insider engages in any purchase and sale, or sale and purchase, of an equity security issued by the insider's corporation if both transactions occur within a six-month period. The insider's actual motive is irrelevant. The goal is to prevent insiders from taking advantage of company information to secure short-term profits.

Securities Law Enforcement Actions

Most of the securities laws violations just discussed can be enforced against the violators by harmed private parties seeking damages and by the government seeking civil and/or criminal penalties. The SEC brings civil enforcement actions; the Justice Department brings criminal enforcement actions. In fact, all three types of suits can be brought against the same defendant for the same violation.

Private Enforcement

In civil damage cases harmed plaintiffs typically join together in a class-action lawsuit (see Chapter 4). Since the 1990s, actions taken by Congress and, more recently, decisions of the Supreme Court have combined to make the bringing of and prevailing in such suits much more difficult for injured plaintiffs. Some history may be illuminating.

As a consequence of the savings and loan debacle of the 1980s, major accounting firms paid out over $1.6 billion in class-action damages. Responding to these payouts, accounting firms and others began intense lobbying to curtail such suits. Among other things, they argued that law firms specializing in plaintiffs' securities actions selected and groomed "professional plaintiffs" to bring damage suits in which the allegations of wrongdoing were primarily supported by a significant drop in the market price of the securities. Then after filing a complaint, it was argued, plaintiffs could proceed to discovery and undertake "fishing expeditions" until sufficient facts were accumulated to motivate defendants to settle rather than endure litigation.

Some evidence of long-standing systemic abuse by plaintiffs' lawyers was revealed in September 2007 when William Lerach, a former partner of the law firm of Milberg Weiss, pleaded guilty to conspiracy. The allegations were that he and other lawyers in the firm had paid illegal kickbacks to individuals to serve as named plaintiffs in securities actions. This often allowed the firm to be the first to file suit, which in turn resulted in Milberg Weiss more frequently representing the lead plaintiff in many class action cases. The firm's payoff was a larger share of any legal fees.[75] On April 2, 2008, Melyvn Weiss, the senior securities law partner at Milberg Weiss, pleaded guilty to similar charges pursuant to a plea bargain. He was sentenced to 30 months in prison and fined $10 million.

The lobbying against runaway securities class-action suits paid off. In December 1995, Congress enacted the Private Securities Litigation Reform Act (1995 Act). The 1995 Act eliminates joint and several liability for accountants and underwriters whose deep pockets have historically attracted plaintiffs' lawyers. It also increased plaintiffs' procedural hurdles in bringing suit. No fraudulent conduct can be presumed from the simple fact that a security's price dropped precipitously. Plaintiffs in their complaints must state with particularity both the facts that constitute the alleged violation, as well as facts evidencing defendant's intention "to deceive, manipulate, or defraud."[76]

In early 2008, the Supreme Court reduced the exposure of some noncorporate defendants to claims of *aiding and abetting* securities fraud. In instances in which plaintiffs allege damage based on fraudulent representations by the corporation, third parties who may have aided the fraudulent conduct but whose deceptive acts were not communicated to the public are not liable to private plaintiffs.[77] As discussed below, only the government can bring such lawsuits. [For more on securities class-action lawsuits, see **http://securities.stanford.edu**]

Government Enforcement

The government can bring suits for aiding and abetting securities fraud against third parties. The Dodd–Frank Act expanded the government's reach in such cases to any third party who, knowingly or recklessly, substantially assists the primary wrongdoer.

Whereas private parties sue to recover damages suffered from the wrongdoing, the SEC enforces the law by imposing civil penalties up to $750,000 for individuals and $15 million for corporations, as well as forcing defendants to give up ill-gotten gains, called *disgorgement*. The SEC may impose a penalty of up to 300 percent of the profit gained or loss avoided by insider trading. In addition to imposing monetary penalties, the SEC can issue *cease-and-desist orders,* obtain injunctions against persons committing securities fraud, and prohibit violators in the future from serving as officers or directors of publicly traded companies.

In contrast, the Department of Justice seeks criminal sanctions for *willful* (knowing and deliberate) violations of the 1933 and 1934 Acts, including fines of up to $25 million and imprisonment for up to 20 years. As with criminal statutes in general, the principal problem for prosecutors is convincing a jury of the defendants' guilt beyond a reasonable doubt. As a result, civil penalties are often substituted for criminal prosecutions.

For decades the SEC has permitted parties to settle charges and claims without admitting guilt. In June 2013, Chair Mary Jo White announced that those committing serious securities law violations would now be required to admit culpability as a prerequisite to settlement. J. P. Morgan was among the first to confront this policy when, in September 2013, it was forced to admit that it had violated the securities laws by permitting an "'egregious' breakdown" in control and governance.[78]

Other Regulatory Oversight

Tender Offers

There are several ways to acquire control of a corporation. Where mergers or direct acquisitions fail, a *tender offer* (also called a *takeover*) can be attempted. Alternatively, the person seeking to acquire control can mount a *proxy fight,* as discussed in Part Two, by nominating an alternative slate of directors and then soliciting shareholders for their annual proxies in preference to returning proxies to current management.

In a tender offer, the offeror announces that it wishes to acquire a specific number of shares (often the number needed to gain control). It identifies where stockholders who want to participate must tender (that is, deliver) their shares. (Shares are returned if the tender offer fails.) It also specifies the opening bid price. If less than the desired number of shares is tendered, the tender offeror can either walk away or increase the offering price. Every tendering shareholder will receive the highest price offered by the tender offeror.

When faced with a tender offer, the target corporation's management realizes that a successful offer will likely result in its dismissal since the offeror will want to put its own management in place. Often the target's management will not be eager to leave. It will resist, which accounts for the term *hostile takeover.* Management has a problem, however, because it is supposed to act exclusively in the best interests of the shareholders and the tender offer may well be in their best interests. To avoid liability, management will generally try to style its resistance as "looking out for the stockholders."

Management can resist in various ways. It could launch its own tender offer (*go private*). Or it could start using corporate cash to buy back shares in the market, driving up the price to discourage the tender offeror. Here management has to worry that it could be sanctioned for violating Section 9 of the 1934 Act, which prohibits price manipulation. There is a safe harbor: Each day management is permitted to purchase up to 25 percent of the security's average daily trading volume.

Another resistance tactic is *greenmail,* in which the target's management uses corporate cash to buy back the tender offeror's current stake, with a significant premium to "go away." Changes in the federal tax law have discouraged this technique.

Management sometimes puts takeover defenses in place by arranging "disasters" if a tender offer is attempted. Two notorious tactics are the *crown jewel* and *poison pill* defenses. In general, the crown jewel defense involves the target company selling off its most attractive assets (its crown jewels). For example, the target company management might arrange for a friendly third party to purchase the target's critical assets at a reasonable price should a tender offer be launched, thus making the target company less appealing to the hostile bidder. At the same time, the target company's management is protected because the third party will continue to make these assets available to the company on "friendly" terms should the tender offer fail and management remains in place. Poison pill tactics take a variety of forms but one notable strategy gives current shareholders a tender offer-triggered right to buy additional stock at a discount, thus diluting the hostile bidder's shares.

If all else fails, the target's officers may find comfort in the *golden parachutes* (severance pay packages) they may have negotiated to protect themselves in the event of a takeover. The Dodd–Frank Act now requires a shareholder vote on such pay packages.

State Securities Regulation

After the enactment of the 1933 Act, the United States operated under a dual regulatory environment for securities. Both the state and federal governments were entitled to regulate the issuance of new securities and their subsequent purchases and sales. Eventually the lack of regulatory uniformity among the states led Congress in 1996 to enact the *National Securities Markets Improvement Act,* preempting state registration requirements for securities traded on national markets. Then in 1998, Congress mandated that securities fraud claims related to national market securities be litigated only in federal court under federal law. State securities regulations, known as *blue sky laws*, are now only a shadow of their former significance and are primarily applicable to solely intrastate offerings. [For more on state securities regulation, see **www.nasaa.org/about-us/our-role/**]

International Securities Regulation

Critics claim the United States is losing its place as the world's leading financial center, citing such evidence as the percentage of large IPOs being listed outside of the United States. Aggressive regulation in America is often blamed for driving those IPOs abroad.

American securities regulation is the world's strongest, but whether that will continue to be true and whether it is responsible for the growth in foreign securities markets is not clear. Other factors undoubtedly contribute to the shift, such as the natural maturation of international markets, the speed of overall economic growth elsewhere in the world, and the concomitant rise in wealth, especially in Europe and Asia.[79] "Because companies want to list in the fastest-rising markets, many are staying in their home countries, which have often outperformed the United States in recent years."[80] Further, stringent regulation in the United States is not necessarily a net disincentive for securities registration here. Foreign securities with dual listings in the United States and elsewhere appear to enjoy an advantage in the price they command.[81] Finally, as the securities markets in other countries mature, national regulation seems to be increasing in ways that model U.S. policies.

Nothing equivalent to the SEC exists in Europe. In the wake of the recent financial crisis, however, the European Union may be moving closer to such a body. In 2010, the EU finance ministers endorsed the creation of a supervisory structure for European securities markets, the European Securities and Markets Authority (ESMA). It began its work on January 1, 2011. One role it may eventually be called to play is the regulation of audit firms.[82] [For more on ESMA, see **www.esma.europa.eu**; for more on international securities regulation generally, see **www.iosco.org/about**]

Questions—Part Three

1. What is an IPO? What is meant by *going public?* By *going private?*
2. *a.* What information is contained in a registration statement under the 1933 Act?
   b. What role in the registration process is played by the prospectus?
   c. What are audited financial statements? Describe the three primary financial statements.
3. Explain the general purposes of the Securities Act of 1933 and the Securities Exchange Act of 1934.
4. Assume a midlevel manager learns that his corporation is about to go bankrupt because of about-to-be-disclosed improprieties. He calls his lawyer to ask about his personal exposure. After advising him, the lawyer immediately sells all of her holdings in that stock. Later that day the news breaks and the stock price tumbles 60 percent.
   a. Does anyone have insider trading liability?
   b. If so, in what amount?
5. If a corporate officer knowingly omits material adverse information from a corporate communication, by whom might he or she be sued?

Internet Exercise

Using the Frequently Asked Questions segment of **www.securitieslaw.com** answer the following questions:

1. What duties are owed by stockbrokers and brokerage firms to customers?
2. How does a customer know when he or she has been defrauded?

Chapter Questions

1. From initiating the process through the election of directors, describe the steps generally followed to bring a corporation into existence.
2. Modell owned 80 percent of the Cleveland Stadium Corporation (Stadium) and 53 percent of the Cleveland Browns Football Company (Browns). Gries owned 43 percent of Browns. The Browns' board consisted of Modell, the outside lawyer for both corporations, three individuals employed by both corporations, and Gries. Modell proposed that the Browns buy the Stadium for $6 million. Gries objected, saying that the Stadium appraised for only $2 million. The Browns' board, nonetheless, approved the purchase. (All directors other than Gries voted in favor of the purchase.) Gries commenced a shareholders derivative suit seeking to rescind the purchase. Who should win? See *Gries Sports Enterprises v. Cleveland Browns Football Company,* 496 N.E.2d 959 (Ohio S.Ct. 1986).
3. The Patels owned the CC Motel. They formed a partnership with their son, Raj, to own and operate the motel. Title to the motel was not transferred to the partnership. The partnership agreement required Raj to approve the motel's sale. The Patels sold the motel without telling Raj and without telling the buyers of Raj's right. He learned of the pending sale and refused to agree. The buyers asked the court to compel the sale. Who should win? See *Patel v. Patel,* 260 Cal. Rptr. 255 (Cal. Ct. App. 1989).
4. Each year many shareholder proposals are offered for inclusion in the annual meeting materials so as to be submitted to a vote of the shareholders. Assume you have a

significant investment in Corporation X and the following proposals are included in the proxy materials. Which would you vote for and why?

a. A recommendation that any bonus and performance compensation awarded to executives be paid out evenly over the four years following the grant of the bonus and only if the performance goals continue to be met.

b. A recommendation that the standards for all bonus and performance compensation be benchmarked against the performance of the company's market competitors, requiring superior performance for the award of any bonus.

c. A recommendation that shareholders be permitted to vote on the selection of the state in which to reincorporate the company.

d. A recommendation to the nominating committee that each year it include one "public director" selected in consultation with one or more nonprofit organizations whose missions encompass one or more significant activities of the corporation.

5. Ivan Landreth and his sons owned all of the stock in a lumber business they operated in Tonasket, Washington. The owners offered the stock for sale. During that time a fire severely damaged the business, but the owners made assurances of rebuilding and modernization. The stock was sold to Dennis and Bolten, and a new organization, Landreth Timber Company, was formed with the senior Landreth remaining as a consultant on the side. The new firm was unsuccessful and was sold at a loss. The Landreth Timber Company then filed suit against Ivan Landreth and his sons seeking rescission of the first sale, alleging, among other arguments, that Landreth and sons had widely offered and then sold their stock without registering it as required by the Securities Act of 1933. The district court acknowledged that stocks fit within the definition of a security, and that the stock in question "possessed all of the characteristics of conventional stock." However, it held that the federal securities laws do not apply to the sale of 100 percent of the stock of a closely held corporation. Here the district court found that the purchasers had not entered into the sale with the expectation of earnings secured via the labor of others. Managerial control resided with the purchasers. Thus, the sale was a commercial venture rather than a typical investment. The Court of Appeals affirmed, and the case reached the Supreme Court. Decide. See *Landreth Timber Co. v. Landreth,* 471 U.S. 681 (1985).

6. A *Fortune* 500 CFO admits to having deliberately treated $4 billion in operating expenses as assets, thereby allowing the corporation to show profits instead of losses. The auditor never detects this. The corporation's stock drops 95 percent and bond covenants related to billions in debt are breached. At its peak price last year, the CFO sold stock (acquired through options) for $15 million, generating a $10 million gain.

a. Why might the corporation have to file for bankruptcy protection?

b. What provisions of the securities law could be the basis for a class-action lawsuit by the stockholders?

c. Why will the 1995 Act probably not stop a class-action lawsuit from proceeding to the discovery phase?

d. Why will the CFO be subject to criminal (as well as civil) securities sanctions?

e. Will the SEC likely ever allow the CFO to be an officer or director of a publicly traded corporation in the future?

f. Will the SEC allow the CFO to keep the $10 million gain on the stock?

g. What kind of civil penalties could the SEC impose on the CFO?

Notes

1. "Corporate Courts: A New Judicial Boss," *The Economist*, November 23, 2013.

2. Ibid.

3. Peg Brickley, "Allowing Firms to Restrict Suits to Delaware to Change Legal Landscape," *The Wall Street Journal*, July 7, 2013.

4. Data was taken from **www.irs.gov/uac/Tax-Stats-2**.

5. Ibid.

6. See, for example, Section 1.40(9) and (16) of the Model Business Corporation Act.

7. *Grosjean v. American Press Co.*, 297 U.S. 233 (1936).

8. *Western & Southern Life Ins. Co. v. State Bd. of Equalization*, 451 U.S. 648 (1981).

9. *Cede & Co. v. Technicolor, Inc.*, 634 A.2d 345 (Del. 1993).

10. Tresa Baldas, "BP Shareholders Head to Court Over Oil Spill's Damage to Company," May 11, 2010 at *law.com*.

11. Del. Gen. Corp. Law Section 102(b)(7).

12. Gretchen Morgenson, "Case on Mortgage Official Is Said to Be Dropped," *The New York Times*, February 19, 2011.

13. *Compania General de Tabacos de Filipinas v. Collector of Internal Revenue*, 275 U.S. 87, 100 (1927) (J. Holmes, dissenting).

14. *Commissioner v. Newman*, 159 F.2d 848, 850 (2d Cir 1947).

15. The largest corporations pay a flat rate federal income tax of 35 percent. Small corporations with a taxable income of less than $75,000 face a marginal tax rate of up to 25 percent, still meaningful.

16. Noncorporate businesses (e.g., sole proprietorships and partnerships) would also have to contend with the substantial self-employment tax, which is discussed in the next text box.

17. **www.sec.gov/News/Speech/Detail/Speech/1365171515808#.UwpfeONdVD0.**

18. RUPA Section 306(a).

19. RUPA Section 307(d)(1).

20. RUPA Sections 103(b)(6); 601(3), (4), (6), (7); 602(c); 801(1); 802(b).

21. Minn. Stat. Section 322B.303, subd. 2 (1996).

22. *Kaycee Land and Livestock v. Flahive*, 46 P.2d 323 (Wyo. 2002).

23. Robert W. Hamilton, "Registered Limited Liability Partnerships: Present at the Birth (Nearly)," 66 *University of Colorado Law Review*, 1065 (1995).

24. RUPA Section 306(c).

25. ULPA (2001) Sections 102(9), 201(a)(4).

26. "The New American Capitalism: Rise of the Distorporation," *The Economist*, October 26, 2013.

27. Financial Crisis Inquiry Commission, *The Financial Crisis Inquiry Report*, January 2011 [**http://fcic.law.stanford.edu/report**].

28. Carl C. Icahn, "Corporate Boards That Do Their Job," *The Washington Post*, February 16, 2009.

29. Kaja Whitehouse, "Why CEOs Need to Be Honest with Their Boards," *The Wall Street Journal*, January 14, 2008.

30. Harry Hurt III, "Taking Away Directors' Rubber Stamps," *The New York Times*, January 17, 2010.

31. Ibid.

32. Icahn, "Corporate Boards That Do Their Job."

33. Hurt, "Taking Away Directors' Rubber Stamps."

34. Jack Welch and Suzy Welch, "How Much Blame Do Boards Deserve?" *BusinessWeek*, January 14, 2009.

35. Tara Siegel Bernard, "Voting Your Shares May Start to Matter," *The New York Times*, March 5, 2010.

36. Judith Burns, "Where the Action Is," *The Wall Street Journal*, January 14, 2008.

37. *American Federation of State, County & Municipal Employees, Employees Pension Plan v. American International Group, Inc.*, 462 F.3d 121 (2d Cir. 2006).

38. Nicholas D. Kristof, "Need a Job? $17,000 an Hour. No Success Required," *The New York Times*, September 18, 2008.

39. Gretchen Morgenson, "An Unstoppable Climb in CEO Pay," *The New York Times*, June 29, 2013.

40. **www.forbes.com/sites/scottdecarlo/2012/04/04/americas-highest-paid-ceos/.**

41. Nelson Schwartz, "The Infinity Pool of Executive Pay," *The New York Times*, April 6, 2013.

42. "Bargain Bosses," *The Economist*, September 8, 2012.

43. Rafael Minder, "Swiss Voters Approve a Plan to Severely Limit Executive Compensation," *The New York Times*, March 3, 2013.

44. Telis Demos, Chris Dietrich, and Yoree Koh, "Twitter IPO: Relief, Riches and a $25 Billion Finish," *The Wall Street Journal*, November 7, 2013.

45. *SEC v. Aqua-Sonic Prods. Corp.*, 687 F.2d 577 (2d Cir. 1982).

46. *U.S. v. Leonard*, 529 F.3d 83 (2d Cir. 2008).

47. John M. Broder, "SEC Adds Climate Risk to Disclosure List," *The New York Times*, January 28, 2010.

48. Peter Lattman, "SEC Lifts Advertising Ban on Private Investments," *The New York Times*, July 11, 2013.

49. Financial Crisis Inquiry Commission, "The Financial Crisis Inquiry Report," p. 418. This quote is from the minority report, but the majority came to a similar conclusion. Id. P. xxv.

50. Lorraine Woellert and Dawn Kopecki, "Credit-Rating Companies 'Sold Soul,' Employees Said," October 22, 2008 [**www.bloomberg.com**].

51. Jeannette Neumann, "Rating Firms Steer Clear of an Overhaul," *The Wall Street Journal*, May 12, 2013.

52. "America's Justice Department Charges Standard and Poor's with Fraud," *The Economist*, February 9, 2013.

53. Jeannette Neumann, "Bear Stearns Fund Liquidators Sue Credit-Rating Firms," *The Wall Street Journal*, July 10, 2013.

54. Amy Cortese, "Pennies from Many," *The New York Times*, September 25, 2011.

55. Patrick Clark, "State Lawmakers Are Getting on the Crowdfunding Bandwagon," *Bloomberg Businessweek*, January 7, 2014 [**www.businessweek.com/articles/2014-01-07/state-lawmakers-are-getting-on-the-crowdfunding-bandwagon**].

56. Yin Wilczek, "High Costs of SEC Approach Would Stymie Successive Crowdfunding, Commentators Warn," *Bloomberg Law* [**http://about.bloomberglaw.com/law-reports/high-costs-of-sec-approach-would-stymie-success-of-crowdfunding-commenters-warn/**].

57. Clark, "State Lawmakers Are Getting on the Crowdfunding Bandwagon."

58. **www.sec.gov/info/smallbus/qasbsec.htm**.

59. **www.sec.gov/about/forms/form8-k.pdf**.

60. Jessica Holzer and Greg Bensinger, "SEC Embraces Social Media," *The Wall Street Journal,* April 2, 2013.

61. **www.sec.gov/answers/tradingsuspension.htm**.

62. Ibid.

63. "The Return of the Day Trader," [**www.cbsnews.com/stories/2002/09/30/eveningnews /main523766.shtml**].

64. **www.sec.gov/investor/pubs/daytips.htm**.

65. Associated Press, "Meltdown Left Ponzi Schemes in Ashes," *The Des Moines Register,* December 29, 2009.

66. Dan Campbell, "Well Fargo to Pay $85M Fine," *Star Tribune,* July 20, 2011 [**www .startribunecom/business/125906238.html**]; Dan Fitzpatrick and Julie Steinberg, "J.P. Morgan Reaches $4.5 Billion Settlement with Investors," *The Wall Street Journal,* November 15, 2013.

67. *Stark Trading v. Falconbridge Ltd.,* 552 F.3d 358 (7th Cir. 2009).

68. *Halliburton v. Erica P. John Fund,* 573 U.S. _ (2014).

69. Michael Rothfeld and Chad Bray, "Galleon Founder Convicted on All Counts in Insider-Trading Trial," *The Wall Street Journal,* May 11, 2011 [**http://online.wsj.com/**].

70. Peter Lattman, "Ex-Goldman Director to Serve Two Years in Prison on Insider Trading Case," *The New York Times,* October 24, 2012.

71. Michael Rothfeld, "SAC Agrees to Plead Guilty in Insider-Trading Settlement," *The Wall Street Journal*, November 4, 2013.

72. "Insider Affair: An SEC Trial of the Heart," *The Wall Street Journal,* July 29, 2009.

73. Louise Story, "Charges of Insider Trading for a Wall Street Luminary," *The New York Times,* May 30, 2008.

74. Ethan Smith, "Disney Drama a Stock Plot Is Foiled," *The Wall Street Journal,* May 27, 2010.

75. Barry Meier, "Lawyer Pleads Guilty in Kickback Case," *The New York Times,* September 19, 2007.

76. *Tellabs, Inc. v. Makor Issues & Rights, Ltd.,* 127 S.Ct. 2499 (2007).

77. *Stoneridge Investment Partners LLC v. Scientific-Atlanta, Inc.,* 128 S.Ct. 761 (2008).

78. Jean Eaglesham, "A Historic Admission from J. P. Morgan," *The Wall Street Journal*, September 19, 2013.

79. Edgar Ortega and Elizabeth Hester, "IPO Fees in Europe Catch Wall Street for First Time Since WWII," May 29, 2007 [**www.bloomberg.com**].

80. Walter Hamilton, "Stock Rules Irk NYC as Wall Street Parties on," *The Log Angeles Times,* April 23, 2007.

81. John C. Coffee, "Law and the Market: The Impact of Enforcement," *Columbia Law and Economics Working Paper No. 304,* March 7, 2007 [**http://ssrn.com/abstract=967482**].

82. Stephen Fidler, "Plans Grow for European Audit Cop," *The Wall Street Journal,* October 12, 2010.

CHAPTER TEN

Antitrust Law— Restraints of Trade

After completing this chapter, students will be able to:

1. Recognize the changing goals of antitrust law.

2. Describe the key antitrust statutes.

3. Explain the meaning of "horizontal restraints of trade."

4. Analyze when an unlawful price-fixing arrangement has been created.

5. Identify a group boycott.

6. Define resale price maintenance.

7. Explain the requirements for establishing an unlawful tying arrangement.

8. Describe the commercial advantages and disadvantages of exclusive dealing.

9. Contrast price discrimination and predatory pricing.

10. Explain how predatory pricing may be proved.

Antitrust is a word that is only dimly recognizable to most of us, but antitrust law touches all corners of our lives and significantly shapes our economic and social practices reaching even amateur athletics, as described below.

PRACTICING ETHICS   More "Pay" for College Athletes?

Four former college athletes representing a class of more than 20,000 former college athletes sued the National Collegiate Athletic Association (NCAA) seeking to change NCAA limits on the amount of aid that student athletes can be granted. Under long-time NCAA rules, so-called full-ride scholarships were limited to tuition, books, room, and board. The athletes claimed they were denied approximately $2,500 annually because their universities were not allowed, under NCAA rules, to pay the "full cost of attendance," a package that would include money for insurance, laundry, school supplies, telephone, travel, and so on, in addition to the "full ride."

The class action involved all those playing "major college football" (what was Division I-A and is now the Football Bowl Subdivision) and "major college basketball" (16 top conferences) since 2002. Total damages were estimated at several hundred million dollars. The lawsuit claimed that the NCAA rules constituted a "contract, combination, and conspiracy to fix the amount of financial assistance available to student athletes," thus restraining trade in violation of section 1 of the Sherman Antitrust Act (explained below).

The case was settled in 2008 when the NCAA agreed, among other things, to set aside $10 million over three years to be paid to qualified class members (estimated at 12,000) to reimburse them for bona fide, future educational expenses. Athletes could apply for up to $2,500 per year for three years. The settlement also offers athletes easier access to an existing NCAA pool of $218 million over the years 2008 to 2013 for legitimate educational expenses beyond the "full ride."

As you read this chapter, think about whether the NCAA limit on scholarship funds was, in fact, a violation of antitrust law, but for our immediate purposes, think about the athletes' complaint as a matter of right and wrong; of fairness. [For more on this case, see **www.studentathleteclassaction.com**]

Questions

1. Was it unfair to deny athletes the additional $2,500 or so that they could "earn" in the market for their services (playing "major college" football or basketball)? Detail the fairness argument for both the athletes and the NCAA.

2. Should college athletes be free to "sell" their services to the highest bidder among America's colleges and universities? Explain.

3. Joseph Agnew and Patrick Courtney earned college football scholarships but were injured early in their college careers. Consistent with NCAA rules, both players were accorded one-year scholarships with the possibility of renewal. Neither Agnew nor Courtney received scholarship renewals following their injuries. Both players sued the NCAA claiming its rules forbidding multiyear scholarships and imposing caps on the number of scholarships given per team prevented them from securing scholarships that would have covered their full college experience.

    a. Explain why the two plaintiffs thought they had been wronged by the NCAA rules.

    b. Do you agree with the two plaintiffs? Explain. See *Agnew v. National Collegiate Athletic Ass'n.,* 683 F.3d 328 (7th Cir. 2012).

4. Ed O'Bannon, former UCLA basketball star, has been leading a group of athletes suing the NCAA on antitrust grounds seeking a 50 percent share of NCAA television royalties from collegiate athletic contests along with a share of licensing fees from football and basketball video games. Do you think players should receive a share of those two income streams? Explain. [EA Sports, creator of the video games, and Collegiate Licensing Company have settled claims that were raised against them in the O'Bannon lawsuit for a reported $40 million, which is expected to result in payments to players of a few hundred dollars each.]

Sources: *White, Polak, Harris and Craig v. National Collegiate Athletic Association,* Case No. CV 06-0999 RGK (MANx), (U.S. District Court Central District of California, Western Division). Second Amended Complaint for Violation of Section 1 of the Sherman Act, 15 U.S.C. Section 1, p. 25, lines 3-5; and "Settlement Raises Questions for NCAA, *Inside Higher Ed,* February 4, 2008 [**www.insidehighered.com/news/2008/02/04/ncaa**].

Part One—The Foundations of Antitrust Law

Antitrust—Early Goals

Antitrust, perhaps more than any other branch of the law, is a product of changing political and economic tides. Historically, antitrust law sought to allow every American, at least in theory, the opportunity to reach the top. More specifically, antitrust advocates were concerned about the following issues:

1. **The preservation of competition.** Antitrust law was designed to provide free, open markets resulting in enhanced efficiency and increased consumer welfare. The belief

was (and generally continues to be) that competition would generate the best products and services at the lowest possible prices.

2. **The preservation of democracy.** Many businesses in competition meant that none of them could corner economic, political, or social power.

3. **The preservation of small businesses, or more generally, the preservation of the American Dream.** Antitrust was designed to preserve the opportunity for ordinary Americans to compete with the giants.

4. **An expression of political radicalism.** At least for a segment of society, antitrust laws were meant to be tools for reshaping America to meet the needs of all people, thus counteracting, to some degree, the power of big business. [For professors' analyses of recent antitrust developments, see **http://lawprofessors.typepad.com/antitrustprof_blog**]

Antitrust: Balanced Enforcement?

Campaigning in 2008 for his first term, Barack Obama promised to "reinvigorate antitrust enforcement," following what critics took to be a rather passive antitrust policy during the George W. Bush years. The first-term Obama antitrust authorities did increase enforcement actions including challenges to several high-profile mergers. In particular, the Justice Department's Antitrust Division sued to block AT&T's proposed acquisition of T-Mobile, a deal the two companies subsequently abandoned. Likewise, in 2013, the Justice Department challenged Anheuser-Busch In Bev's proposed $20 billion takeover of competitor Grupo Modelo SAB and the $11 billion US Air and American Airlines merger. (For the results of those challenges, see Chapter 11.) Overall, the Justice Department had a record seven antitrust cases in litigation in early 2013.

On the other hand, critics were incensed by the Federal Trade Commission's 2013 closure of its 19-month inquiry into various Google business practices by deciding not to pursue charges stemming from the computer giant's market power. (For details, see Chapter 11.) And only one monopolization case was pursued during Obama's first term. On balance, the Obama administration can certainly make the case that antitrust has achieved renewed visibility and importance, although the Obama approach might best be labeled "balanced," with a preference for settlement over litigation.

Antitrust Enforcement and Statutes

The Justice Department and the Federal Trade Commission bring relatively few antitrust actions, but a government victory sends a powerful message to the business community about the risks of anticompetitive behavior. The government prefers to avoid litigation, and most cases are settled before going to court.

> A government victory sends a powerful message to the business community.

Furthermore, the Justice Department practices a leniency policy sometimes allowing cooperating defendants to avoid criminal prosecution. Private parties may also sue under the antitrust laws. Segments of the economy, such as the securities industry, that are already closely regulated by the government can sometimes successfully claim that they are immune from the antitrust laws. [For the Justice Department Antitrust Division, see **www.usdoj.gov/atr**]

Sherman Antitrust Act, 1890

Section 1 of the Sherman Antitrust Act forbids restraints of trade, and Section 2 forbids monopolization, attempts to monopolize, and conspiracies to monopolize. Two types of enforcement options are available to the federal government:

1. **Violation of the Sherman Act opens participants to criminal penalties.** The maximum corporate fine is $100 million per violation, whereas individuals may be fined as much as $1 million and/or imprisoned for up to 10 years.
2. **Injunctive relief is provided under civil law.** The government or a private party may secure a court order preventing continuing violations of the act and affording appropriate relief (such as dissolution or divestiture). Those harmed by a violation of the act also may bring a civil action seeking three times the actual damages (treble damages) sustained.

Clayton Act, 1914

The Clayton Act forbids price discrimination, exclusive dealing, tying arrangements, requirements contracts, mergers restraining commerce or tending to create a monopoly, and interlocking directorates. Civil enforcement of the Clayton Act is similar to the Sherman Act in that injured parties may sue for injunctive relief and treble damages. In general, criminal law remedies are not available under the Clayton Act. [For links to antitrust sites worldwide, see **www.justice.gov/atr/contact/otheratr.html**]

Federal Trade Commission Act

The Federal Trade Commission Act created a powerful, independent agency designed to devote its full attention to the elimination of anticompetitive practices in American commerce. The FTC proceeds under the Sherman Act, the Clayton Act, and Section 5 of the FTC Act itself, which declares unlawful "unfair methods of competition" and "unfair or deceptive acts or practices in or affecting commerce." The commission's primary enforcement device is the cease and desist order, but fines may be imposed. [For the FTC Guide to Antitrust Laws, see **www.ftc.gov/bc/antitrust/index.shtm**]

Federal Antitrust Law and Other Regulatory Systems

State Law

Most states, through legislation and judicial decisions, have developed their own antitrust laws. Some states have recently become more aggressive in antitrust enforcement, as illustrated by their resistance to the U.S. Supreme Court's controversial *Leegin* decision set out later in this chapter.

Patents, Copyrights, and Trademarks

Each of these devices offers limited, government-granted, government-shielded market strength, thus serving to protect and encourage commercial creativity and product development. The resulting antitrust problem essentially amounts to limiting the patent, copyright, or trademark holder to the terms of its government-granted privilege, rather than allowing that privilege to grow into an unlawful monopoly.

Law of Other Nations

Chapter 11 addresses the practical and ideological significance of international antitrust issues in this era of globalization. [For a guide to antitrust resources on the Internet, see **www.antitrustinstitute.org/content/antitrust-resources**]

Part Two—Horizontal Restraints

When competitors collude, conspire, or agree among themselves, they are engaging in *horizontal restraints of trade*. Instead of competing to drive prices down and quality up, they may be fixing prices, restricting output, dividing territories, and the like. The various horizontal restraints are governed by Section 1 of the Sherman Act, which forbids contracts, combinations, or conspiracies in *restraint of trade*. What is a restraint of trade? In the *Standard Oil*[1] decision of 1911, the U.S. Supreme Court articulated what has come to be known as the *rule of reason*. In essence, the Court said that the Sherman Act forbids only *unreasonable* restraints of trade. The reasonableness of a restraint of trade is largely determined by a detailed balancing of the pro- and anticompetitive effects of the situation. Thus, the plaintiff must prove the existence of an anticompetitive agreement or conduct and also prove that, on balance, the agreement or conduct harms competition. [For an antitrust overview, see **http://topics.law.cornell.edu/wex/antitrust**]

Some antitrust violations, such as horizontal price fixing, are so injurious to competition that their mere existence ordinarily constitutes unlawful conduct. Plaintiffs must prove that the violation in question occurred, but they need not prove that the violation caused, or is likely to cause, competitive harm. These *per se* violations are simply unlawful on their face.

Antitrust Enforcement Produces Lower Prices?

Antitrust law is often of direct value to consumers as illustrated by a 2008 settlement between the U.S. Justice Department and the National Association of Realtors in which the NAR guaranteed that realtors participating in the NAR-affiliated multiple listing services (MLS—local cooperative arrangements in which realtors list all of their properties for sale in a single database) will allow online real estate agents to have full access to those MLS listings. The newer Internet-based agents claimed they had often been blocked by local MLS associations from access to listings of houses for sale, thus restricting their ability to fully compete with the traditional brokers. The online brokers, often achieving productivity efficiencies, are able to charge fees about one percentage point beneath the traditional industry standard of 5 to 6 percent of the purchase price, thus generating substantial consumer savings.

Sources: "Justice Department Announces Settlement with the National Association of Realtors," Department of Justice Press Release, May 27, 2008 [**www.usdoj.gov/opa/pr/2008/May/08-at-467.html**]; Eric Lichtblau, "Realtors Agree to Stop Blocking Web Listings," *The New York Times,* May 28, 2008 [**nytimes.com**]; and Department of Justice Antitrust Division, "Enforcing Antitrust Laws in the Real Estate Industry," [**www.justice.gov/atr/public/real_estate/enforce.htm**].

Horizontal Territorial and Customer Restraints

Principal legislation—Sherman Act, Section 1.

> Every contract, combination in the form of trust or otherwise, or conspiracy, in restraint of trade or commerce, among the several states, or with foreign nations, is declared to be illegal . . .

Assume two big companies dominate the wholesale food market in their small state. Could they lawfully agree between themselves to divide their state geographically with one supplying the eastern half while the other supplies only the western half? Or could they lawfully allocate their customers such that one, for example, supplies all small town grocers while the other restricts itself to grocers in the few major cities? Suppliers might want to eliminate that competition among themselves, but such arrangements ordinarily are *per se* violations of the Sherman Act since they attempt to nullify the powerful benefits of competition.

Horizontal Price Fixing

Principal legislation—Sherman Act, Section 1.

Competitors may not lawfully agree on prices. That principle is simple and fundamental to an efficient, fair marketplace. Establishing the presence of an unlawful price-fixing arrangement, on the other hand, ordinarily is anything but simple.

Proof

The major dilemma in price fixing and all other Sherman Act Section 1 violations is the measure of proof that satisfies the requirement of a contract, combination, or conspiracy. Evidence of collusion arises in a variety of ways. For example, LaQuinta Inns entered an agreement in 2010 with the Connecticut Attorney General to stop its "call around" practice. Reportedly, motel managers identified their primary local competition and called them frequently to give and receive information about occupancy rates and room charges, a practice that is widespread in the motel industry. The fear is that the frequent exchange of information, in effect, constitutes collusion to fix prices among the competitors. LaQuinta agreed to desist from its call around practices throughout the United States.[2] Broadly, a showing of cooperative action amounting to an agreement may be developed by any of the following four methods of proof:

1. **Agreement with direct evidence.** In the easiest case, the government/plaintiff can produce direct evidence such as writings or testimony from participants proving the existence of collusion.

2. **Agreement without direct evidence.** Here the defendants directly but covertly agree, and circumstantial evidence such as company behavior must be employed to draw an inference of collusion.

3. **Agreement based on a tacit understanding.** In this situation no direct exchange of assurances occurs, but the parties employ tactics that act as surrogates for direct assurances and thus "tell" each other that they are, in fact, in agreement.

4. **Agreement based on mutual observation.** These defendants have simply observed each others' pricing behavior over time, and they are able therefore to anticipate each others' future conduct and act accordingly without any direct collusion but with results akin to those that would have resulted from a direct agreement.[3]

Poaching Employees

Seven of America's most prominent high-tech companies, including Apple and Google, recently settled a Justice Department complaint alleging that those companies agreed, among other things, not to "cold call" each other's employees for the purpose of hiring those employees (a practice sometimes labeled *employee poaching*). The companies agreed to cancel any such agreements. Then in 2013, a civil class action was filed by a group of employees claiming those high-tech companies damaged the employees by violating antitrust laws. News accounts also allege that deceased Apple cofounder Steve Jobs threatened to file a patent lawsuit against tech firm Palm if it did not agree to refrain from poaching Apple employees.

Questions

1. Why might high-tech companies be particularly concerned about employee poaching?
2. What antitrust claims would the plaintiffs raise?
3. What damages would the plaintiffs allege?

Sources: In Re High-Tech Employee Antitrust Litigation, No. 11-CV-02509-LHK (N.D.Cal. April 18, 2012); Daniel Antalics, "Federal Court Allows Silicon Valley Employee 'Poaching' Suit to Proceed," Weil, Gotshal & Manges LLP, *Antitrust Update*, Spring 2012; and Reuters, "Jobs Threatened Suit to Prevent Apple Poaching," *CNBC.COM*, January 23, 2013 [**www.cnbc.com**].

Parallel Conduct

An unlawful conspiracy is to be distinguished from independent but parallel business behavior by competitors. So-called *conscious parallelism* is fully lawful because the competitors have not agreed either explicitly or by implication to follow the same course of action. Rather, their business judgment has led each to independently follow parallel paths. On the other hand, a conspiracy can sometimes be established by proof that the parallel behavior in question was not arrived at independently, but rather was the product of a preceding agreement.[4]

Aggressive Enforcement

Both government intervention advocates and free-market champions agree that price fixing cripples the market. So government intervention, at the federal and state levels, and damage claims by wronged consumers are sometimes essential to maintain effective competition. Antitrust law, including price-fixing prohibitions, is designed to protect the consumer from a variety of commercial arrangements—some well-intentioned, some overt cheating—that nullify the favorable effects of competition. Consider some prominent examples.

- At this writing in 2013, a federal judge has given preliminary approval to a $7.2 billion settlement of an eight-year antitrust war between the plaintiffs, a coalition of large and small merchants, and the defendants, Visa Inc., MasterCard, and their associated banks (including, e.g., Bank of America and JPMorgan Chase). The defendants are accused of engaging in a price-fixing cartel to set arbitrarily high interchange or "swipe" fees that merchants pay to card-issuing banks and credit card companies for processing card transactions. (American Express and Discover were not involved in this lawsuit.) The settlement provides cash and temporary reductions in swipe fees for some 8 million merchants, and it allows small merchants to join together in future bargaining with Visa and MasterCard over swipe fees. Merchants will also be able for the first time to charge consumers extra for using credit cards. (Some states forbid such surcharges, and competitive pressure may prevent most merchants from assessing them.) The agreement does not apply to debit card transaction fees, which were capped by Congress through the Dodd–Frank bill (see Chapter 15). Many merchants, including Walmart and Target, oppose the settlement arguing the giant card companies and banks will retain the power to fix prices. The agreement also limits merchants' rights to file similar lawsuits in the future.

- At this writing, eight companies, including LG Display Co., Sharp Corp., and Chunghwa Picture Tubes, Ltd., have pleaded guilty or have agreed to plead guilty to federal criminal charges of conspiring to fix prices for about $75 billion in LCD panels and will pay fines totaling about $1.4 billion. Twelve executives have been sentenced to a total of more than 13 years in prison. Additional criminal and civil lawsuits around the world are likely to produce billions in further payouts. The panels were used in computer monitors, notebooks, televisions, and other electronic devices by Apple, Dell, and others. Reportedly, the LCD industry was facing an oversupply problem between October 2000 and August 2001, but despite that market condition, prices began to rise after August 2001, allegedly as a result of the companies working in concert to fix prices. The Justice Department described some of the conspiratorial behavior among three of the companies:

  > The three companies . . . allegedly held "crystal" meetings and engaged in communications about setting prices on the TFT-LCD displays. They agreed to charge predetermined prices for the displays, issued price quotes based on those agreements, and exchanged sales information on the display panels, in order to monitor and enforce the agreement, the Justice Department said.[5]

- According to a federal Justice Department investigation, executives at several major Japanese auto parts suppliers met in secret for over 10 years, sometimes speaking in code, to fix prices on a variety of parts. Hundreds of millions in fines and prison sentences for several executives have been imposed by U.S. authorities.[6]

- Ending nine years of litigation over alleged conspiracies to fix corn syrup prices, Archer Daniels Midland, A. E. Staley, and others agreed in 2004 to pay $531 million to settle a class action against them.[7] [For a movie account of former ADM executive Mark Whitacre's decision to blow the whistle on the alleged conspiracy, see *The Informant!* starring Matt Damon. The trailer is available at: **www.traileraddict.com/trailer/the -informant/trailer**]

These are only a few of the many examples in recent years of price-fixing conspiracies in America and around the world. The effect of these unlawful arrangements is to harm competition and raise prices. Antitrust expert John M. Connor has estimated that cartels "typically push prices up at least 20 percent and sometimes much more."[8]

PRACTICING ETHICS   Antitrust Law and the Price of Beer

We know that college students drink astonishing amounts of alcohol. Each year college students spend about $5.5 billion on alcohol, most of that on beer. That total exceeds what students spend on books, soda, coffee, juice, and milk combined. Could antitrust law affect the consumption, or at least the price, of beer? Perhaps. A group of consumers in Madison, Wisconsin, home of the University of Wisconsin, sued some local bars and the Madison-Dane County Tavern League, Inc., for price fixing. The plaintiffs claimed that the defendant bars had agreed to fix prices by adopting a "voluntary ban on drink specials." The plaintiffs pointed to a September 2002 press release from the "Downtown Tavern Working Group" announcing that drink specials would not be offered after 8 PM on Friday and Saturday nights for "at least a year."

The defendants said the new policy was a self-imposed effort to curb binge drinking, especially by students, and that the policy was a response to pressure from the city and the University of Wisconsin. Further, the defendants said that the press release did not reflect an agreement of any kind and thus could not violate the law because all bar owners remained free to do as they wished. Eventually, the Wisconsin Supreme Court held that the policy was immune from the antitrust laws because the city effectively compelled the arrangement. Given the state legislature's broad grant of regulatory authority over alcohol to municipalities, the Court concluded that the legislature must have intended the defendant taverns' actions to be exempt (immune from scrutiny) from the antitrust laws.

Questions

1. The legality of this arrangement aside, *should* bar owners be free to reach an agreement eliminating drink specials?

2. Is the Madison dispute too trivial and frivolous to justify court time? Explain.

3. Will the market satisfactorily protect youthful drinkers and society? Explain.

4. *a.* How would you expect the Supreme Court decision to affect the consumption of beer in Madison?

   b. Explain how a "voluntary ban on drink specials" might constitute price fixing.

Sources: Eichenseer v. Madison-Dane County Tavern League, 748 N.W.2d 154 (Wis. S.Ct. 2008); and "Frequently Asked Questions about College Binge Drinking," AlcoholPolicyMD.com [**www .alcoholpolicymd.com/alcohol_and_health/faqs.htm**].

Cigarette Pricing

The case that follows examines alleged horizontal price fixing in the oligopolistic cigarette industry.

LEGAL BRIEFCASE

Romero and Ferree v. Philip Morris, et al.   2010 N.M. LEXIS 370
(N.M. S.Ct.)

Justice Chavez

BACKGROUND

The following facts are undisputed. Plaintiffs are "[p]ersons in the State of New Mexico . . . who purchased cigarettes indirectly from Defendants, or any parent, subsidiary or affiliate thereof, at any time from November 1, 1993 to the date of the filing of this action [April 10, 2000]." The original Defendants were Philip Morris, R.J. Reynolds ("RJR"), Brown & Williamson ("B&W"), Lorillard, and Liggett. The events leading up to this lawsuit were set in motion in response to a Philip Morris strategy beginning with an event known as "Marlboro Friday." Prior to Marlboro Friday, Philip Morris, the market leader, had been steadily losing market share to discount and deep discount cigarettes since 1980, when Liggett pioneered the development of generic cigarettes. In an attempt to regain market share, Philip Morris announced Marlboro Friday on April 2, 1993, "a nationwide promotion on Marlboro that reduced prices at retail by approximately 20 percent, an average of 40[cents] per pack." In response, RJR and B&W instituted similar promotions. As part of its strategy, Philip Morris announced on July 20, 1993, that there would be a similar reduction on all premium brands, discount brands, and deep discount brands starting on August 9, 1993. Defendants RJR and B&W also followed these price reductions. After these decreases, Defendants began to increase their wholesale list prices on premium and discount cigarettes in near lock-step fashion. Some increases were due to settlements with the 50 states, some because of increases in federal excise taxes, and others were simply planned. Even with these increases, wholesale list prices did not exceed pre-Marlboro Friday levels until August 3, 1998, or when adjusted for inflation, ongoing settlement costs, and federal excise taxes, the list prices did not surpass pre-Marlboro Friday amounts until August 1999. During the time period of the alleged agreement to fix prices, 1993 to 2000, Defendants were engaged in competition with one another regarding promotions at the retail level, resulting in a direct reduction of the retail prices of cigarettes.

Plaintiffs filed this class action lawsuit on April 10, 2000, alleging violations of New Mexico antitrust and consumer protection laws. Defendants filed motions for summary judgment. In granting the motion for summary judgment, the district court held that Plaintiffs had met their initial burden of showing a pattern of parallel behavior, but failed to meet their second burden of showing the existence of plus factors that would tend to exclude the possibility that the alleged conspirators acted independently.

* * * * *

On appeal, the Court of Appeals acknowledged that "Marlboro Friday and the industry-wide price reductions that occurred afterward represented the triumph of competition over oligopolistic price coordination." Although the Court affirmed summary judgment in favor of Lorillard and Liggett because the evidence showed that they had merely acted "consistent with conscious parallelism," the Court reversed summary judgment in favor of Philip Morris, RJR, and B&W because "we think that a reasonable factfinder could view conscious parallelism as a relatively implausible explanation for the anticompetitive scenario that played out following Marlboro Friday."

* * * * *

FEDERAL SUBSTANTIVE ANTITRUST LAW: PROVING THE CONSPIRACY

* * * * *

There is no doubt that the tobacco industry, in which five companies manufacture more than 97% of the cigarettes sold in the United States, is a classic oligopoly. Because the cigarette industry is an oligopoly, it is likely that when one tobacco company (*i.e.,* Philip Morris) acts in a certain manner (*i.e.,* Marlboro Friday and subsequent price increases), the other firms (RJR, B&W, Lorillard, and Liggett) will determine whether it is in their best interest to follow the leader's actions. As we will discuss below, when Philip Morris began raising prices after Marlboro Friday, RJR's and B&Ws conduct in following subsequent price increases was just as likely due to their own independent analysis of what was in their best interests as it was the result of an illegal price-fixing agreement. Therefore, Plaintiffs must present evidence that tends to exclude the possibility that Defendants acted independently or they cannot meet their burden of establishing a genuine issue of material fact. . . .

The United States Supreme Court has explicitly stated that "when allegations of parallel conduct are set out in order to make a Section 1 claim, they must be placed in a context that raises a suggestion of a preceding agreement, not merely parallel conduct that could just as well be independent action." *Bell Atl. Corp.,* 550 U.S. at 557.

* * * * *

[W]e must determine whether Plaintiffs' proffered evidence of plus factors tends to exclude the possibility that Defendants acted independently. Plaintiffs cite to the following plus factors, in addition to parallel pricing, as tending to exclude the possibility that Defendants acted independently: (1) the economies of the marketplace, such as a highly concentrated market, cigarette fungibility, high barriers to entry in the industry, absence of close substitutes, and a history of collusion; (2) a strong motivation to conspire, resulting from the desperate times facing the cigarette industry, including "a dramatic decline in its sales as a result of . . . increased public awareness of the detrimental health effects of smoking"; (3) the condensation of price tiers to facilitate the conspiracy; (4) actions contrary to self-interest, including Philip Morris's pre-announcing its price reductions and Defendants' failure to attempt to re-widen the price gap by reducing discount prices; (5) conspiratorial meetings in other markets; (6) a smoking and health conspiracy; (7) the manner in which Defendants monitored the conspiracy through Management Science Associates ("MSA"); (8) opportunities to conspire; and (9) pricing decisions made at high levels.

We reject Plaintiffs' plus factors . . . because Defendants' conduct is just as consistent with lawful, independent action as it is with price fixing, and therefore it does not tend to exclude independent conduct. We briefly discuss Plaintiffs' plus factors to address why they do not tend to exclude the possibility of independent conduct by

Defendants. (1) The majority of the economies of the marketplace to which Plaintiffs cite are nothing more than inherent characteristics of an oligopoly and cannot tend to exclude independent action.

* * * * *

(2) The motivation to conspire cited by Plaintiffs cannot serve as tending to exclude independent conduct because "[p]rofit is a legitimate motive in pricing decisions, and something more is required before a court can conclude that competitors conspired to fix pricing in violation of the Sherman Act." *In re Baby Food Antitrust Litig.,* 166 F.3d at 134–35. (3) When Philip Morris took action to condense the price tiers, it is just as likely that they did so to reduce the price gap and maximize profits as to facilitate a price-fixing agreement, and thus this does not tend to exclude independent conduct. (4) Plaintiffs argue that Defendants took actions contrary to self-interest by preannouncing price decisions and failing to re-widen the price gap. Philip Morris argues that the June 20, 1993 preannouncement of a price decrease to take effect twenty days later was not a signal to the other cigarette manufacturers, but was made to allow wholesalers and retailers to avoid an immediate reduction in the value of their inventory and to accommodate the burden of implementing a price reduction.

* * * * *

(5) The alleged conspiratorial meetings in other markets cannot serve as tending to exclude independent conduct because Plaintiffs offered no support to connect the actions in foreign markets with the actions in the United States. . . . (6) Similarly, concluding that an alleged smoking and health conspiracy facilitated coordination of a conspiracy in this case would require the jury to engage in speculation. . . . (7) The manner in which Defendants monitored the conspiracy through MSA is not evidence tending to exclude independent conduct because there is an equally rational legal explanation for this such as to "devise competitive strategies, gauge the success of their promotions, monitor the impact of new styles or packing on the market, and determine whether increased promotional spending was needed in certain geographic areas to compete with competitors' programs." . . .

Defendants made a prima facie case supporting summary judgment by providing evidence of fierce retail competition that undermined the plausibility of a price-fixing agreement [and by] demonstrating that wholesale prices remained lower than pre-Marlboro Friday levels and did not exceed pre-Marlboro Friday levels until almost five years later. . . . This evidence showed that Defendants '"had no rational economic motive to conspire, and . . . their conduct is consistent with other, equally plausible explanations.'" *Clough,* 108 N.M. at 804, 780 P.2d at 630 (quoting *Matsushita Elec. Indus. Co.,* 475 U.S. at 596-97). In reviewing Plaintiffs' plus factors, we find that the district court properly granted summary judgment.

Reversed.

Questions

1. *a.* Who are the alleged conspirators in this price-fixing dispute, and how did they allegedly fix prices?

   b. Who won this case at the New Mexico Court of Appeals, and why did that court rule as it did?

   c. In general, is parallel pricing a lawful behavior? Explain.

2. *a.* Why did the New Mexico Supreme Court require a showing of "plus factors" to demonstrate that the cigarette companies had engaged in price fixing?

   b. Why did the Court reject the plus factors offered by the plaintiffs as evidence of a price-fixing conspiracy?

3. Why did the tobacco companies win this case?

4. Assume two drugstores, located across the street from each other and each involved in interstate commerce, agree to exchange a monthly list of prices charged for all nonprescription medications. Is that arrangement lawful in the absence of any further cooperation? Explain.

5. The "Three Tenors," Luciano Pavarotti, Placido Domingo, and Jose Carreras, recorded a 1990 World Cup concert, distributed by Polygram, and a 1994 World Cup concert, distributed by Warner. Polygram and Warner subsequently agreed to jointly distribute and share profits from the 1998 World Cup Three Tenors concert. The 1998 recording apparently was less "new and exciting" than had been hoped. Concerned that sales of the earlier recordings would drain interest from the 1998 recording, Polygram and Warner agreed to cease all discounting and advertising of the two earlier recordings for several weeks surrounding the release of the 1998 album. In 2001, the Federal Trade Commission issued complaints against Polygram and Warner. Those complaints eventually reached the District of Columbia Federal Circuit Court of Appeals where Polygram and Warner defended themselves by arguing that the agreement was good for competition in that it increased the joint venture's profitability from new recordings, and it eliminated free riding by each company (for the 1990 and 1994 recordings) on the joint venture's 1998 marketing.

   a. What antitrust violation was alleged by the Federal Trade Commission?

   b. What is free riding, and why is it a problem?

   c. Decide the case. Explain. See *Polygram v. Federal Trade Commission,* 416 F.3d 29 (D.C. Cir. 2005).

6. Assume that 10 real estate firms operate in the city of Gotham. Further assume that each charges a 7 percent commission on all residential sales.

   a. Does that uniformity of prices in and of itself constitute price fixing? Explain.

   b. Assume we have evidence that the firms agreed to set the 7 percent level. What defense would be raised against a price-fixing charge?

   c. Would that defense succeed? Explain. See *McLain v. Real Estate Board of New Orleans, Inc.,* 444 U.S. 232 (1980).

Refusal to Deal/Group Boycotts

Principal legislation—Sherman Act, Section 1.

In America we are free to do business with whomever we prefer, correct? Generally, yes; but antitrust problems sometimes emerge. When does a *refusal to deal* with another raise antitrust issues? The clearest problem is a *horizontal group boycott* where competitors agree not to deal with a supplier, customer, or another competitor. Ford and GM, for example, presumably could not jointly refuse to buy tires from Bridgestone/Firestone. Such arrangements so thoroughly subvert the market that they ordinarily are *per se* violations of Sherman I and thus do not require a detailed evaluation of competitive harm and benefits, although a showing of market power by those in the group may be required. A unilateral (individual) refusal to deal by a buyer or a seller sometimes raises antitrust concerns if the firm refusing to deal is a monopolist and harm to competition can be proven,[9] but the Supreme Court has severely restricted the use of the doctrine.[10]

A recent battle among the big bank card companies illustrates refusal to deal reasoning (although for technical reasons the case was not tried under the refusal to deal/boycott label). In 1996, American Express decided to open its own credit card network to compete with Visa and MasterCard. No bank, however, was willing to deal with American Express. Why would the banks turn down the potential to make more money by working with the respected American Express brand? They did so because Visa and MasterCard had rules forbidding their members from issuing American Express and Discover cards. Visa and MasterCard operate as nonprofit joint venture associations owned by the member banks that issue their credit cards. As long as those banks wanted to do business with Visa and MasterCard, the two giants, they could not deal with American Express and Discover. Were the Visa and MasterCard refusal to deal rules lawful? No, as it turns out. The antitrust division of the federal Department of Justice sued the two giants for their alleged exclusionary practices and won in the federal courts.[11] The six-year struggle turned largely on the finding that continued exclusion of Discover, American Express, and others from the market was a horizontal restraint that would likely harm future competition. A key finding was the conclusion that Visa and Master-Card, with their collective market share exceeding 70 percent, had market power. American

> MasterCard agreed to pay $1.8 billion to American Express.

Express subsequently sued Visa for damages inflicted by the alleged exclusionary practices. In 2007, Visa agreed to pay $2.1 billion to settle that lawsuit and in 2008 MasterCard Worldwide agreed to pay $1.8 billion to American Express. [For a trade regulation blog, see **http://traderegulation.blogspot.com/**]

Clarett Boycotted by NFL?

Antitrust shapes all dimensions of our lives, as football running back Maurice Clarett learned when he tried to enter the 2004 National Football League draft. Clarett, as a freshman, led Ohio State University to an undefeated season in 2002. Clarett was ineligible for college football in his sophomore year because of allegations that he accepted improper benefits and lied about doing so. Clarett then tried to enter the NFL draft but was barred by a league rule providing that players must have been out of high school for three seasons. Clarett sued the NFL, claiming its eligibility rules violated federal antitrust laws by, in effect, allowing competing teams to agree among themselves to boycott certain players (including Clarett). Clarett won at the federal district court level, but he lost on appeal when the court ruled that the eligibility rule is exempt from the antitrust laws. The NFL eligibility rule is the product of a collective bargaining agreement between the league and the players' union, the National Football League Players Association. Antitrust promotes competition while unions restrict it in various ways, but in balancing those competing interests, Congress and the courts have long granted unions certain exemptions from antitrust laws. The Supreme Court subsequently declined to review Clarett's case.

In 2010, Clarett was released from prison where he had served a three-and-one-half year sentence for aggravated robbery and carrying a concealed weapon. Following his release, Clarett played football with the Omaha Nighthawks and published a book about his life.

Questions

1. Should Clarett and future football players be free to sell their services on the open market?

2. Or is the NFL correct to encourage players to stay in college and mature before seeking to become professionals? Explain.

3. Congressman Steve Cohen, Democrat of Tennessee, wrote a letter in 2009 to the National Basketball Association and the NBA players union asking them to repeal the rule requiring players to be 19 years old and one year removed from high school before they are eligible for the NBA. The rule is part of the collective-bargaining agreement between the league and the players. Cohen labeled the law "a vestige of slavery."
   a. What did Cohen mean by his "vestige of slavery" remark?
   b. Does the rule constitute an unlawful restraint of trade? Explain.
   c. Do you agree that the rule should be repealed? Explain.

Sources: Clarett v. National Football League, 369 F.3d 124 (2d Cir. 2004); and Pete Thamel, "Congressman Asks N.B.A. and Union to Rescind Age Minimum for Players," *The New York Times,* June 4, 2009 [**www.nytimes.com**].

Questions

1. Baptist Eye Institute (BEI), a group of nonspecialized ophthalmologists in Jacksonville, Florida, controlling approximately 15 percent of the referral market, sent nearly all of its retina cases to the Florida Retina Institute. Is BEI engaging in an unlawful group boycott against plaintiff Retina Associates, a retina care provider in competition with the Florida Retina Institute? Explain. See *Retina Associates P.A. v. Southern Baptist Hospital of Florida Inc.,* 105 F.3d 1376 (11th Cir. 1997).

2. Discon, a telephone salvage company, sold services to MECo, a subsidiary of NYNEX, a phone company for the New York/New England area. MECo switched from Discon to AT&T Technologies, a Discon competitor, and paid a higher price to AT&T than it had paid to Discon. Discon claimed that the buyer and NYNEX then received a rebate from AT&T at the end of the year. Discon argued that NYNEX was able to pass on its higher costs to its customers because NYNEX was a part of a regulated phone market. Discon claimed that NYNEX, its subsidiaries, and AT&T were engaging in a group boycott in violation of the Sherman Act in order to drive Discon out of the market. Decide. Explain. See *NYNEX Corp. v. Discon, Inc.,* 119 S.Ct. 493 (1998).

Part Three—Vertical Restraints

We have been studying unfair trade practices by competitors—that is, horizontal restraints of trade. Now we turn to antitrust violations on the vertical axis—that is, restraints involving two or more members of a supply chain (such as a manufacturer and a retailer of that manufacturer's products). *Horizontal restraints* are those arising from an agreement among the *competitors* themselves, while *vertical restraints* ordinarily are those imposed by *suppliers* on their *buyers.* Horizontal restraints, in general, are *per se* unlawful while vertical restraints, in general, are to be resolved under the rule of reason. Horizontal restraints eliminate competition thereby undermining the power of the market while vertical restraints sometimes are harmful and sometimes are beneficial to competition and thus ordinarily should be evaluated on a case-by-case basis.

E-Books: Apple Fixing Prices?

[An ongoing price-fixing case involving Apple's e-book marketing practices illustrates some of the principles of horizontal price fixing, as discussed above, along with elements of vertical price fixing (resale price maintenance) discussed below.]

The Kindle e-book reader was introduced by Amazon in 2007, followed by Barnes & Noble's Nook reader (2009) and Apple's iPad (2010). Amazon priced many of its e-book best sellers at a very attractive $9.99 (often below its cost) to increase demand for the Kindle, to solidify its market position, and to encourage broader shopping at Amazon. By some measures, Amazon's share of digital book sales peaked as high as 90 percent of the market. Book publishers, including HarperCollins and Penguin, apparently fearing Amazon's power in the e-book market, allegedly entered negotiations among themselves and with Apple to change e-book pricing from Amazon's "wholesale" model (where Amazon itself set e-book retail prices) to an "agency" model (where the publishers set the retail price of books [e.g., $14.99] and the retailers, including Apple and Barnes & Noble, kept a 30 percent share). Having achieved an agreement with Apple, the publishers allegedly were able to compel Amazon to accept the same terms. Thereafter, Amazon's e-book market share reportedly fell to about 60 percent.

In April 2012, the Justice Department filed a civil complaint against Apple and five book publishers claiming that the defendant publishers had conspired among themselves and with Apple to fix prices in violation of the Sherman Act. The publishers denied misconduct but reached a settlement with the government. In their defense, the publishers and Apple claimed they acted independently in implementing agency pricing.

Relying principally on horizontal price-fixing reasoning, a federal judge in 2013 found Apple guilty of colluding with the publishers to fix prices. The judge ordered Apple to modify its contracts and submit to oversight. Apple is appealing. Critics fear the government victory over Apple may restore Amazon to its former position of complete e-book dominance. On the other hand, e-book prices fell after the publishers began settling with the government. Another likely result may be a reduction in the number of physical bookstores.

Sources: Thomas Catan, Jeffrey A. Trachtenberg, and Chad Bray, "U.S. Alleges E-Book Scheme," *The Wall Street Journal,* April 12, 2012, p. A1; Daniel Crane, "DOJ E-Book Price Fixing Lawsuit Is Superficial," *Jurist – Forum,* April 23, 2012 [**http://jurist.org/forum/2012/04/daniel-crane-ebook-pricing.php**]; Gilbert and Tobin, "Apple, Penguin and Macmillan File Response to US DOJ Lawsuit," *Lexology,* July 31, 2012 [**www.lexology.com/library/**]; and Hayley Tsukayama, "Judge Rule Apple Conspired with Publishers to Raise E-Book Prices," *The Washington Post,* July 10, 2013 [**www.washingtonpost.com/**].

Resale Price Maintenance

Principal legislation: Sherman Act, Section 1; Federal Trade Commission Act, Section 5.

Manufacturers and distributors often seek to specify the price at which their customers may resell their products, a policy we might think of as vertical price fixing but that is formally called *resale price maintenance*. Having sold its product, why should a manufacturer or distributor seek to influence the price at which the product is resold? The primary reasons are fourfold: (1) establishing a minimum price to enhance the product's reputation, (2) helping retailers make a profit sufficient to provide customer service, (3) preventing discount stores from pricing beneath full-price retail outlets, and (4) preventing *free riders*.

A *unilateral* specification of a resale price, with nothing more involved, has long been permissible. Under the Supreme Court's 1919 *Colgate*[12] decision, sellers can lawfully engage in resale price maintenance if they do nothing more than announce prices at which their products are to be resold and unilaterally refuse to deal with anyone who does not adhere to those prices. On the other hand, an *agreement* between a seller and a buyer dictating the price at which the buyer may resell the product was, for decades, a *per se* violation of the law. Then in 1997, the Supreme Court ruled that *agreements* specifying *maximum* resale prices would no longer be considered *per se* violations and must be evaluated under the rule of reason.[13] In the 2007 *Leegin* case that follows, the Supreme Court overturned a nearly 100-year-old precedent in the Dr. Miles case[14] to rule that *agreements* specifying *minimum* resale prices must also be analyzed under the rule of reason; that is, those agreements are no longer *per se* violations of the law. Rather, they must be considered on a case-by-case basis weighing their pro- and anticompetitive effects.

LEGAL BRIEFCASE

Leegin Creative Leather Products, Inc. v. PSKS, dba Kay's Kloset 127 S.Ct. 2705 (2007)

Justice Kennedy

I

Petitioner, Leegin Creative Leather Products, Inc. (Leegin), designs, manufactures, and distributes leather goods and accessories. In 1991, Leegin began to sell belts under the brand name "Brighton." The Brighton brand has now expanded into a variety of women's fashion accessories. It is sold across the United States in over 5,000 retail establishments, for the most part independent, small boutiques and specialty stores. . . . Leegin asserts that, at least for its products, small retailers treat customers better, provide customers more services, and make their shopping experience more satisfactory than do larger, often impersonal retailers. [Leegin's president, Jerry] Kohl explained: "[W]e want the consumers to get a different experience than they get in Sam's Club or in Wal-Mart. And you can't get that kind of experience or support or customer service from a store like Wal-Mart."

Respondent PSKS, Inc., operates Kay's Kloset, a women's apparel store in Lewisville, Texas. Kay's Kloset buys from about 75 different manufacturers and at one time sold the Brighton brand. It first started purchasing Brighton goods from Leegin in 1995. Once it began selling the brand, the store promoted Brighton. For example, it ran Brighton advertisements and had Brighton days in the store. Kay's Kloset became the destination retailer in the area to buy Brighton products. Brighton was the store's most important brand and once accounted for 40 to 50 percent of its profits.

In 1997, Leegin instituted the "Brighton retail pricing and Promotion Policy." Following the policy, Leegin refused to sell to retailers that discounted Brighton goods below suggested prices. . . . In the letter to retailers establishing the policy, Leegin stated:

> In this age of mega stores like Macy's, Bloomingdales, May Co. and others, consumers are perplexed by promises of

product quality and support of product which we believe is lacking in these large stores. Consumers are further confused by the ever popular sale, sale, sale, etc.

We, at Leegin, choose to break away from the pack by selling [at] specialty stores; specialty stores that can offer the customer great quality merchandise, superb service, and support the Brighton product 365 days a year on a consistent basis. . . .

Leegin adopted the policy to give its retailers sufficient margins to provide customers the service central to its distribution strategy. It also expressed concern that discounting harmed Brighton's brand image and reputation.

* * * * *

In December 2002, Leegin discovered Kay's Kloset had been marking down Brighton's entire line by 20 percent. Kay's Kloset contended it placed Brighton products on sale to compete with nearby retailers who also were undercutting Leegin's suggested prices. Leegin, nonetheless, requested that Kay's Kloset cease discounting. Its request refused, Leegin stopped selling to the store. The loss of the Brighton brand had a considerable negative impact on the store's revenue from sales.

PSKS sued Leegin in the United States District Court for the Eastern District of Texas. It alleged, among other claims, that Leegin had violated the antitrust laws by "enter[ing] into agreements with retailers to charge only those prices fixed by Leegin."

* * * * *

The jury agreed with PSKS and awarded it $1.2 million.

* * * * *

The Court of Appeals for the Fifth Circuit affirmed. We granted certiorari to determine whether vertical minimum resale price maintenance agreements should continue to be treated as *per se* unlawful.

* * * * *

II

Resort to *per se* rules is confined to restraints . . . "that would always or almost always tend to restrict competition and decrease output." *Business Electronics,* 485 U.S. at 723 . . .

As a consequence, the *per se* rule is appropriate only after courts have had considerable experience with the type of restraint at issue, and only if courts can predict with confidence that it would be invalidated in all or almost all instances under the rule of reason. . . .

III

The Court has interpreted *Dr. Miles Medical Co. v. John D. Park & Sons Co.,* 220 U.S. 373 (1911), as establishing a *per se* rule against a vertical agreement between a manufacturer and its distributor to set minimum resale prices. . . .

The reasons upon which *Dr. Miles* relied do not justify a *per se* rule. As a consequence, it is necessary to examine . . . the economic effects of vertical agreements to fix minimum resale prices, and to determine whether the *per se* rule is nonetheless appropriate.

A

Though each side of the debate can find sources to support its position, it suffices to say here that economics literature is replete with procompetitive justifications for a manufacturer's use of resale price maintenance.

* * * * *

The justifications for vertical price restraints are similar to those for other vertical restraints. Minimum resale price maintenance can stimulate interbrand competition—the competition among manufacturers selling different brands of the same type of product—by reducing intrabrand competition—the competition among retailers selling the same brand. The promotion of interbrand competition is important because "the primary purpose of the antitrust laws is to protect [this type of] competition." *Khan,* 522 U.S. at 15. . . .

Absent vertical price restraints, the retail services that enhance interbrand competition might be under provided. This is because discounting retailers can free ride on retailers who furnish services and then capture some of the increased demand those services generate.

Resale price maintenance, in addition, can increase interbrand competition by facilitating market entry for new firms and brands. "[N]ew manufacturers and manufacturers entering new markets can use the restrictions in order to induce competent and aggressive retailers to make the kind of investment of capital and labor that is often required in the distribution of products unknown to the consumer." *GTE Sylvania,* 433 U.S. at 55; . . .

Resale price maintenance can also increase interbrand competition by encouraging retailer services that would not be provided even absent free riding. It may be difficult and inefficient for a manufacturer to make and enforce a contract with a retailer specifying the different services the retailer must perform. Offering the retailer a guaranteed margin and threatening termination if it does not live up to expectations may be the most efficient way to expand the manufacturer's market share by inducing the retailer's performance and allowing it to use its own initiative and experience in providing valuable services.

* * * * *

B

While vertical agreements setting minimum resale prices can have procompetitive justifications, they may have anticompetitive effects in other cases; and unlawful price fixing, designed solely to obtain monopoly profits, is an ever-present temptation. Resale price maintenance may, for example, facilitate a manufacturer cartel. An unlawful cartel will seek to discover if some manufacturers are undercutting the cartel's fixed prices. Resale price maintenance could assist the cartel in identifying price-cutting manufacturers who benefit from the lower prices they offer. Resale price maintenance, furthermore, could discourage a manufacturer from cutting prices to retailers with the concomitant benefit of cheaper prices to consumers.

Vertical price restraints also "might be used to organize cartels at the retailer level." *Business Electronics,* at 725–726. A group of retailers might collude to fix prices to consumers and then compel a manufacturer to aid the unlawful arrangement with resale price maintenance.

A horizontal cartel among competing manufacturers or competing retailers that decreases output or reduces competition in order to increase price is, and ought to be, *per se* unlawful. To the extent a vertical agreement setting minimum resale prices is entered upon to facilitate either type of cartel, it, too, would need to be held unlawful under the rule of reason.

* * * * *

A manufacturer with market power . . . might use resale price maintenance to give retailers an incentive not to sell the products of smaller rivals or new entrants. As should be evident, the potential anticompetitive consequences of vertical price restraints must not be ignored or underestimated.

C

Notwithstanding the risk of unlawful conduct, it cannot be stated with any degree of confidence that resale price maintenance "always or almost always tend[s] to restrict competition and decrease output." Vertical agreements establishing minimum resale prices can have either procompetitive or anticompetitive effects, depending upon the circumstances in which they are formed.

Respondent contends, nonetheless, that . . . the *per se* rule is justified because a vertical price restraint can lead to

higher prices for the manufacturer's goods. . . . Respondent is mistaken in relying on pricing effects absent a further showing of anticompetitive conduct. . . . For, as has been indicated already, the antitrust laws are designed primarily to protect interbrand competition, from which lower prices can later result. . . .

Respondent's argument, furthermore, overlooks that, in general, the interests of manufacturers and consumers are aligned with respect to retailer profit margins. . . . A manufacturer has no incentive to overcompensate retailers with unjustified margins. The retailers, not the manufacturer, gain from higher retail prices. The manufacturer often loses; interbrand competition reduces its competitiveness and market share because consumers will "substitute a different brand of the same product." see *Business Electronics,* at 725. . . .

Resale price maintenance, it is true, does have economic dangers. If the rule of reason were to apply to vertical price restraints, courts would have to be diligent in eliminating their anticompetitive uses from the market. This is a realistic objective. . . .

As a final matter, that a dominant manufacturer or retailer can abuse resale price maintenance for anticompetitive purposes may not be a serious concern unless the relevant entity has market power. If a retailer lacks market power, manufacturers likely can sell their goods through rival retailers.

* * * * *

For all of the foregoing reasons, we think that were the Court considering the issue as an original matter, the rule of reason, not a *per se* rule of unlawfulness, would be the appropriate standard to judge vertical price restraints.

* * * * *

Reversed.

Questions

1. *a.* What potential procompetitive considerations were cited by the court in supporting a rule of reason approach to resale price maintenance?
   b. What potential anticompetitive considerations were cited by the court?
2. Could we fairly conclude from the *Leegin* decision that resale price maintenance agreements are now "*per se* legal"? Explain.
3. Explain why the court said the seller's market power is an important consideration in assessing the legality of a resale price-maintenance agreement.

Leegin in Practice (the Law) The *Leegin* ruling seems to affirm the Supreme Court's current preference for free-market principles and reduced judicial intervention in business practice. Accordingly, more competition and better service should follow, but critics think the decision simply allows manufacturers to pressure and cut out discounters with the result that consumers will pay higher prices. Of course, if anticompetitive behavior emerges, it still can be attacked under the rule of reason, but several states including California, Kansas, and New York continue to treat resale price maintenance as a *per se* violation of law. Similarly, the European Union generally forbids resale price maintenance, unless clear efficiencies are identified. France, for example, in 2012 fined Nestlé, Mars, and Colgate-Palmolive nearly $50 million for allegedly applying pressure to their distributors to maintain high pet food prices.

Leegin in Practice (the Business Response) Some product suppliers are using the *Leegin* decision to impose strict pricing policies throughout their chains of distribution. Thus in 2012, Sony and Samsung required all their U.S. retailers to charge full price for the two manufacturers' televisions. Of course, Sony and Samsung hope to boost their profits by reducing discounting, but manufacturers also use resale price maintenance to neutralize a series of competitive problems.

Commonly, manufacturers are worried that price discounts will diminish the image of their products, but they also want to discourage "free riders," and they are concerned about the new problem of "showrooming" in the age of the smartphone. That is, manufacturers want to protect themselves and their chains of distribution both from discounters who free ride on the advertising and promotion of full-service retailers and from consumers (showroomers) who educate themselves about products in brick-and-mortar stores, such as specialty shops or Target, and then often buy from an online competitor after making instant price comparisons.

Question

Is the *Leegin* decision good or bad for consumers? Explain.

Vertical Territorial and Customer Restraints

Principal legislation: Sherman Act, Section 1; Federal Trade Commission Act, Section 5.

In addition to price restraints, manufacturers commonly impose nonprice restraints including where and to whom their product may be resold. Those restrictions typically afford an exclusive sales territory to a distributor. Similarly, manufacturers may prevent distributors from selling to some classes of customers (for example, a distributor might be forbidden to sell to an unfranchised retailer). Of course, such arrangements, necessarily retard or eliminate *intrabrand* competition. Because price and service competition among dealers in the same brand ordinarily benefits the consumer, the courts have frequently struck down such arrangements. Still, those territorial and customer allocations also have merits. The *GTE Sylvania* case[15] enunciated those virtues and established the position that vertical restrictions are to be judged case-by-case, balancing interbrand and intrabrand competitive effects while recognizing that interbrand competition is the primary concern of antitrust law. Thus, the rule of reason is to be applied to vertical territorial and customer restraints.

Tying Arrangements

Principal legislation: Clayton Act, Section 3; Sherman Act, Sections 1 and 2; Federal Trade Commission Act, Section 5.

> Clayton act, section 3. That it shall be unlawful for any person engaged in commerce, in the course of such commerce, to lease or make a sale or contract for sale of goods . . . or other commodities . . . or fix a price charged therefore, or discount from or rebate upon, such price, on the condition, agreement, or understanding that the lessee or purchaser thereof shall not use or deal in the goods . . . or other commodities of a competitor or competitors of the lessor or seller, where the effect of such lease, sale, or contract for sale or such condition, agreement, or understanding may be to substantially lessen competition or tend to create a monopoly in any line of commerce.

Tying arrangements (sometimes called "bundling") are another form of nonprice vertical restraint. Typically, tying arrangements permit a customer to buy or lease a desired product (the tying product) only if the customer also buys or leases another, less desirable product (the tied product). In a battle between commercial titans, a large class of merchants led by Walmart, Sears, and others sued Visa and MasterCard, alleging that the bank card associations engaged in unlawful tying arrangements by requiring the merchants to accept the associations' debit cards (the tied product) if they wanted to retain the right to accept the very popular Visa and MasterCard charge cards (the tying product). The result, the merchant/plaintiffs said, was billions in losses because they were forced to pay higher fees for Visa and MasterCard debit cards rather than the lower fees of the competing debit cards they would have preferred to accept. The parties reached a $3 billion out-of-court settlement in 2003.[16] [See Chapter 11 for a discussion of Microsoft's alleged practice of tying its Internet Explorer browser (the tied product) to its dominant Windows operating system (the tying product).]

The Law Tying arrangements raise two primary antitrust concerns: (1) A party who already enjoys market power over the tying product is able to extend that power into the tied product market and (2) competitors in the tied product market are foreclosed from equal access to that market.

The basic tying violation test is as follows:

1. The existence of separate products. (That is, two products are present rather than one product consisting of two or more components, or two entirely separate products that happen to be elements in a single transaction.)
2. A requirement that the purchase of one of the products (the tying product) is conditioned on the purchase of another product (the tied product).
3. Market power in the tying product.
4. Substantial impact on commerce in the tied product market. (Some courts require a substantial anticompetitive effect in the tied product market.)

Proof of all four of those ingredients establishes *per se* illegality. When all four ingredients cannot be satisfied, the analysis may proceed on a rule of reason basis, weighing pro- and anticompetitive considerations. Critics argue that tying arrangements often enhance consumer welfare and, as such, the *per se* approach should be overturned, as in the *Leegin* case.

Cable/Satellite TV Bundling

Consumers often are frustrated because their cable and satellite television services ordinarily come in packages of channels rather than in an "a la carte" menu where the subscriber can choose and pay for only the subscriber's preferred individual channels. In a recent California case, a group of consumers sued several television networks and cable and satellite distributors, including NBC, Fox, and Time Warner Cable claiming, among other things, that the defendants engaged in Sherman Act violations. The defendant television networks sold television programming to the defendant cable distribution companies in bundles rather than on a per channel basis. The distributors, in turn, sold to consumers in those prepackaged bundles or on a "tier" basis. The plaintiff consumers claimed the practice of offering subscriptions only in bundles was unlawful under the Sherman Act.

Questions

1. Explain the nature of the alleged Sherman Act violation.
2. Who won the case? Explain.

Source: Brantley et al. v. NBC Universal, Inc. et al., 675 F.3d 1192 (2012); cert. den. 133 S.Ct. 573 (2012).

Franchise Tying?

The following case examines tying allegations in the context of Shell and Texaco gas station franchises. The case turns in part on market definition, a topic that we address more thoroughly in Chapter 11. In brief, in order to establish market power in the tying product, the market itself must be defined. In doing so we consider the geographic market (where the product is sold in commercially significant quantities) and the product market (those products that are interchangeable and thus compete, one with the other).

LEGAL BRIEFCASE

Rick-Mik Enterprises, Inc. v. Equilon Enterprises, LLC
532 F.3d 963 (9th Cir. 2008)

Judge King

Equilon Enterprises, LLC ("Equilon") does business as Shell Oil Products. Equilon's standard franchise agreement requires its franchisees, Shell and Texaco gasoline stations, to use Equilon to process credit-card transactions. In addition to payment for sales of petroleum products, Equilon allegedly gets (1) transaction fees associated with the processing, or (2) some kind of unspecified "kickback" from unidentified banks that process the transactions, or both. Rick-Mik Enterprises, Inc., Mike M. Madani, and Alfred Buczkowski (collectively "Rick-Mik") are Equilon franchisees who—on behalf of themselves and other, similarly situated Equilon franchisees—allege that Equilon violated antitrust laws by illegally tying two distinct products (the franchises and the credit-card processing services). Rick-Mik contends franchisees could pay lower transaction fees from others for credit-card processing. . . .

The district court dismissed the antitrust and related state-law counts. . . .

DISCUSSION
Tying Claim
a. The market power allegations are flawed.
The alleged tying product here is gasoline franchises. Rick-Mik has a contract for an Equilon franchise to sell Shell branded gasoline and diesel. The alleged tied-product is credit-card processing services. Rick-Mik alleges it cannot get a franchise without the "tied" credit-card processing services.

Rick-Mik's complaint does not allege that Equilon has market power in the relevant market, which is the market for the tying product—gasoline franchises. Indeed, other than stating that "[Equilon] rank[s] number one in the industry in branded gasoline stations," there are no specific allegations at all as to the franchise market. The complaint alleges nothing about, for example, what percentage of gasoline franchises are Equilon's (Shell/Texaco) as compared to other franchises like Chevron, Mobil, Marathon Oil, or Union 76. There are no factual allegations as to the percentage of gasoline retail sales that are made through *non-franchise* outlets. There are no factual allegations regarding the amount of power or control that Equilon has over prospective franchisees. There are no factual allegations regarding the relative difficulty of a franchisee to switch franchise brands.

If Equilon lacks market power in the gasoline-franchise market, there can be no cognizable tying claim. For, in that case, Equilon has no power to force, exploit, or coerce a franchisee to purchase a tied-product such as credit card processing (if the processing is a distinct product for tying purposes) or to affect competition in the tied-product market. Such an arrangement would not raise antitrust concerns.

* * * * *

Rick-Mik argues that it alleged sufficient facts to *infer* that Equilon has sufficient economic power in the gasoline-franchise market, which has significant barriers to entry. It points to statistics indicating Equilon is an important player in the petroleum industry. According to . . . the complaint: (1) Equilon sells petroleum products to approximately 9,000 Shell and Texaco-branded retail outlets; (2) it ranks first in the industry in branded gasoline stations; (3) at 13 percent of the market, it ranks first in total gallons of gasoline sold in the United States; (4) it has annual gross revenues of approxi-

mately $24 billion; (5) it is number one or two in gasoline market share in 17 states; (6) it has four refineries, refining approximately 753,000 barrels of petroleum products per day and owns a 50 percent interest in Motiva's three refineries, refining approximately 865,000 barrels of petroleum products per day; (7) it owns an interest in approximately 10,000 miles of pipeline used to transport its petroleum products throughout the United States; and (8) it serves, on average, more than six million customers per day and sells approximately 19 billion gallons of gasoline per year, most of which is purchased by customers' credit or debit cards issued by thousands of banks, banking associations and financial institutions throughout the United States.

All of those allegations, however, relate to the *retail* gasoline market—a market where Rick-Mik is a seller—not the relevant market for franchises where it is a buyer. Further, the statistics alleged in the complaint do not distinguish between franchise-based sales and other potential types of sales (e.g., sales by directly owned outlets or sales to other distributors). Thus, the complaint fails to allege market power in the relevant market.

Nor is Rick-Mik's complaint saved by the allegation that "Shell and Texaco-branded gasolines are protected by various trademarks, copyrights and patents providing Equilon sufficient economic power over Plaintiffs in connection with its tying products to appreciably restrain competition in the tied-product market." . . . Because intellectual property rights are no longer presumed to confer market power, *see Illinois Toolworks Inc.,* 547 U.S. at 42–43, Rick-Mik's conclusory allegation that Equilon's intellectual property rights nonetheless do confer market power, unaccompanied by supporting facts, is insufficient.

Finally, the complaint's allegation of a contractual franchise relationship also fails to plead market power. A tying claim generally requires that the defendant's economic power be derived from the market, not from a contractual relationship that the plaintiff has entered into voluntarily. *See, e.g., Queen City Pizza, Inc.,* 124 F.3d at 443 ("where the defendant's 'power' to 'force' plaintiffs to purchase the alleged tying product stems not from the market, but from plaintiffs' contractual agreement to purchase the tying product, no claim will lie.")

* * * * *

b. Credit-card processing is not a distinct product.
There is another fatal flaw in Rick-Mik's complaint. Equilon's franchises are not a separate and distinct product from the credit-card processing services that are part of the franchise.

Franchises, almost by definition, necessarily consist of "bundled" and related products or services—not separate products.

* * * * *

With franchises, "the proper inquiry is . . . whether [the allegedly tied-products] are integral components of the business method being franchised. Where the challenged aggregation is an essential ingredient of the franchised system's formula for success, there is but a single product and no tie in exists as a matter of law." *Principe v. McDonald's Corp.,* 631 F.2d 303, 309 (4th Cir. 1980).

Here, Equilon's credit card services are an essential part of its franchise. Its agreement authorizes Equilon to use credit card proceeds to pay off a franchisee's account (i.e., money the franchisee owes Equilon for the gasoline Equilon delivers to the franchisee). The agreement also authorizes Equilon to charge or refund unauthorized transactions to the franchisee, helping secure the integrity of point-of-sale transactions.

* * * * *

Equilon points to the many areas which are part and parcel of a franchise: signs, advertising, marketing, appearance, as well as methods of delivery and payment. Similarly, the method of receiving and processing credit transactions is an integral part of the franchise's operation. The franchise and the method of processing credit transactions are not separate products, but part of a single product (the franchise).

* * * * *

With franchises, the franchisee knows the contractual limitations and duties before entering into the contract. A complaint about such contractual obligations is not an antitrust matter.

* * * * *

Affirmed.

Questions

1. *a.* Identify the tying and tied products in the *Rik-Mik* case.
   b. Explain how Rik-Mik attempted to establish that Equilon had market power in the tying product.

2. How does Rik-Mik claim to have been harmed by the alleged tying arrangement?

3. Why did the Court reason that a franchising contract ordinarily cannot, by itself, be the basis for an antitrust claim?

4. Who won this case and why?

5. In recent years, Apple has been accused of tying violations both in the United States and in Europe. In brief, the plaintiffs are claiming that Apple's software prevents music bought from Apple's iTunes from being played on a player other than Apple's iPod. The plaintiffs argue that Apple has monopoly power in the portable digital player market and the online music market and that it uses that power to force consumers to bundle the iPod and iTunes music. The result, the plaintiffs' claim, is fewer options and higher prices. Do you share these concerns about Apple's iPod/iTunes strategy? Explain. For one decision in this ongoing litigation, see *Somers. v. Apple,* 2011 U.S. Dist. LEXIS 77165. For the class action website, see **https://ipodlawsuit.com.**

6. When *Late Night with David Letterman* was an NBC show, the network, for some time, reportedly required those wanting to advertise on *Late Night* (then generally favored by a younger audience) to also buy spots on another talk show, the *Tonight Show with Johnny Carson* (then generally favored by an older audience).
   a. Does that packaging constitute a tying arrangement?
   b. Was it lawful? Explain.

7. Chrysler included the price of a sound system in the base price of its cars. Chrysler's share of the auto market was 10 to 12 percent. Chrysler did not reveal the "subprice" for the sound systems. Independent audio dealers objected on antitrust grounds. Explain their claim. Decide. See *Town Sound and Custom Tops, Inc. v. Chrysler Motor Corp.* 959 F.2d 468 (3d Cir. 1992); cert. den., 113 S.Ct. 196 (1992).

Exclusive Dealing and Requirements Contracts

Principal Legislation: Clayton Act, Section 3; Sherman Act, Section 1.

An *exclusive dealing contract* is an agreement in which a buyer commits itself to deal only with a specific seller, thereby cutting competing sellers out of that share of the market. A *requirements contract* is one in which a seller agrees to supply all of a buyer's needs, or a buyer agrees to purchase all of a seller's output, or both. Exclusive dealing and requirements contracts typically are lawful, but antitrust problems can arise depending on harm to competition. By its nature an exclusive deal results in *market foreclosure;* that is, competitors are denied a source of supply or a market for sale. Thus, antitrust issues can emerge depending ordinarily on the market share controlled by the parties. In general, however, manufacturers, distributors, and retailers have broad latitude in negotiating exclusive deals. We want businesses to produce and distribute their products in the manner they consider most efficient.

Gore-Tex

The top of the line in waterproof, breathable fabric seems to be Gore-Tex, but its rivals, including Columbia Sportswear-owned OutDry, say they have better products but have difficulty marketing them because of Gore-Tex's exclusive dealing arrangements with outdoor clothing and sportswear brands. Gore-Tex allegedly requires those wanting to use its products to agree not to use competing brands. The result is an alleged market foreclosure that allows Gore to control an estimated 70 to 90 percent of the relevant market. Gore apparently is being investigated by both the FTC and European Commission antitrust authorities. *The Wall Street Journal* reported that the two Italian brothers who invented OutDry have received enthusiastic responses to their product. Nonetheless, brands say "almost universally" they cannot use OutDry without endangering their relationships with Gore. [For more details on the Gore-Tex antitrust story, see Thomas Catan, "Gore-Tex Runs into Antitrust Probes," *The Wall Street Journal,* June 22, 2011, p. B1.]

American Needle

> The National Football League was accused of restraint of trade.

In 2010, exclusive dealing concerns reached the U.S. Supreme Court when the National Football League was accused of restraint of trade for giving Reebok in 2000 an exclusive 10-year right to produce and market nearly all NFL-trademarked headware. The plaintiff, American Needle, a Downer's Grove, Illinois, apparel manufacturer, was cut out of the premium cap market by the NFL decision. The NFL won at both the trial and federal court of appeals level with both courts ruling that the NFL is a single entity (one business rather than a collection of competing teams/businesses) and thus could not have conspired as the Sherman Act requires. The U.S. Supreme Court, however, reversed the lower courts in 2010 by a 9–0 margin saying that each of the teams is independently owned and managed and each proceeds as a separate, competing economic enterprise pursuing separate economic interests.[17]

A nationwide class action was filed in 2012 on behalf of consumers claiming they have been overcharged for NFL gear. The plaintiffs argue that granting the exclusive license to Rebuke created a monopoly in licensing and manufacturing NFL team apparel, thereby harming competition and raising prices.[18]

Condoms

Church & Dwight Co. (C & D) manufactures and distributes Trojan and other brand-name latex condoms. C & D controls about 75 percent of the U.S. retail condom market. The number-two seller has about 14 percent and number three sells just under 10 percent.

Mayer Labs, with less than 1 percent of the market, raised antitrust claims against C & D. Mayer alleged that C & D had unlawful exclusive dealing arrangements with some retail chains, including 7-Eleven, and Mayer also argued that a C & D program granting kickbacks/rebates to retailers based on the amount of shelf space devoted to C & D products constituted a form of semi-exclusive dealing in that it put a ceiling or quota on the amount of shelf space competitors could secure.

The U.S. District Court for the Northern District of California ruled for C & D in 2012 finding, broadly, that Mayer had failed to show that C & D's marketing strategies had foreclosed competition. Despite C & D's large market share, the court reasoned that Mayer failed to show that C & D had market power because no evidence was presented of restricted output, supra-competitive prices, or barriers to entry. Further, the alleged exclusive dealing arrangements were of short duration, and they were voluntary. Finally, other channels of distribution were available to competitors. Thus, competition was not impaired.

Source: *Church & Dwight v. Mayer Laboratories,* No. C-10-4429 EMC, U.S. District Court, Northern District of California (2012).

Price Discrimination

Principal Legislation: Clayton Act, Section 2, as amended by the Robinson–Patman Act. [For the statutory language, see **http://assembler.law.cornell.edu/uscode/15/13.html**]

Price discrimination involves selling substantially identical goods (not services) at reasonably contemporaneous times to different purchasers at different prices, where the effect is to harm competition. A seller may resist a Robinson–Patman charge by establishing one of the following defenses: (1) The price differential is attributable to cost savings. (In practice, the cost savings defense has been difficult to establish.) (2) The price differential is attributable to a good faith effort to meet the equally low price of a competitor. (3) Certain transactions are exempt from the act. Of special note is a price change made in response to a changing market. Thus, prices might lawfully be altered for seasonal goods or perishables.

> A coalition of independent video stores sued Blockbuster.

In recent years, a coalition of independent video stores sued Blockbuster claiming that the rental chain and the movie studios conspired to drive the small stores out of business. That litigation failed, as perhaps it should have since the market itself seems to have resolved the dispute. Blockbuster declared bankruptcy in 2010. Apparently, its business model did not keep pace with current consumer demand which now favors newer, perhaps more technologically astute competitors, Redbox, Netflix, and others. Dish Network then acquired Blockbuster in 2011 for $320 million.

The video store cases are among a number in recent years pitting independent operators (such as neighborhood bookstores and local pharmacies) against chains (such as Barnes & Noble and big hospitals) where the independents claim that suppliers charge their giant rivals lower prices than those charged to the small stores. These complaints reflect the philosophical battle over the role of antitrust law in a rapidly changing global market.

Should we use antitrust to protect small businesses, thus protecting small towns and an historic way of life in America? Or should we accept the dictates of the market, where the efficiency of giants like Walmart brings low prices and high quality to all?

Free-market advocates condemn price discrimination law as an attack on common, consumer-friendly pricing practices that often result in reduced prices. Why, the critics ask, would we assault those who engage in vigorous price competition? Indeed, *The Wall Street Journal* recently labeled the Robinson-Patman Act "a powerful law" that is "losing a lot of its punch."[19] From 2006 through 2010, plaintiffs (often small businesses) won just 4 percent of the Robinson-Patman cases brought in the federal courts; down from 35 percent in the years 1982 to 1993.[20] Furthermore, the federal government seldom brings a Robinson-Patman action. Nonetheless, as the following case illustrates, smaller businesses often do turn to Robinson–Patman in their ongoing struggle against what they believe to be the unfair competition of "giants."

Drug Mart Pharmacy Corp. v. American Home Products

U.S. District Court for the Eastern District of New York, 2012 U.S. Dist. LEXIS 115882

LEGAL BRIEFCASE

United States Magistrate Judge Gold

This complex, long-pending antitrust litigation has been the subject of numerous written decisions by various courts. . . .

In short, plaintiffs are a number of individually-owned retail pharmacies. Plaintiffs allege that defendants, five manufacturers of brand name prescription drugs ("BNPDs"), offered discounts and rebates to plaintiffs' competitors but not to plaintiffs, and that this constitutes price discrimination in violation of the Robinson-Patman Act.

BACKGROUND

In 2007, Senior United States District Judge I. Leo Glasser granted defendants' motion for summary judgment ". . . on the ground that plaintiffs have failed to show they are entitled to damages."

* * * * *

After Judge Glasser dismissed the claims of the designated parties, approximately 3,700 individual retail pharmacy plaintiffs remained. Confronted with Judge Glasser's decision,

these remaining plaintiffs devised a plan to gather evidence in discovery that might show "that specific plaintiff pharmacies lost sales of BNPDs manufactured by defendants to any specific favored purchaser." Pursuant to this plan, which came to be known as the "matching process," plaintiffs compiled lists of specific BNPD customers who no longer purchased drugs from them, and then searched the databases of non-party favored purchasers (and one favored purchaser who is a party) to see whether those same individuals were obtaining the same BNPDs from those favored purchasers.

* * * * *

[O]nly approximately 3% (5,147 of 164,501) of the potential lost customers plaintiffs culled from their own records could be "matched" to a customer who subsequently filled the same prescriptions with one or more favored purchasers.

* * * * *

The de minimis nature of these results is further illustrated when they are broken down and analyzed by defendant.

According to defendants, when examined in this manner, the results are that approximately 88% of plaintiffs' claims against particular defendants are based on five or fewer lost customers per year. . . . This amounts to only slightly more than 1% of the total BNPD transactions conducted by an average retail pharmacy during any one year (252/22,000).

In short, no matter how analyzed, the matching process identified only a de minimis number of lost customers and transactions.

* * * * *

DISCUSSION

. . . I now consider whether plaintiffs' evidence, revealing as it does that plaintiffs lost only a trivial number of customers and sales to favored purchasers, is nevertheless sufficient to support a Robinson-Patman Act claim. . . .

The Robinson-Patman Act

* * * * *

In enacting Robinson-Patman, "Congress sought to target the perceived harm to competition occasioned by powerful buyers, rather than sellers; specifically, Congress responded to the advent of large chainstores, enterprises with the clout to obtain lower prices for goods than smaller buyers could demand." *Volvo*, 546 U.S. at 175. The purpose of the Act is to prohibit "price discrimination only to the extent that it threatens to injure competition." *Brooke Grp. Ltd. v. Brown & Williamson Tobacco Corp.*, 509 U.S. 209, 220, 113 S.Ct. 2578, 125 L. Ed. 2d 168 (1993).

* * * * *

1. Competitive Injury

The Robinson-Patman Act prohibits price discrimination only "where the effect of such discrimination may be substantially to lessen competition." 15 U.S.C. § 13(a).

* * * * *

[A]fter reviewing all of the pertinent authorities, . . . I conclude that a Robinson-Patman claim requires a showing of substantial competitive injury and that the de minimis sales identified by the matching process are insufficient to establish such an injury. . . .

2. Antitrust Injury

. . . A plaintiff seeking to recover damages on a Robinson-Patman claim must establish an antitrust injury.

* * * * *

Price discrimination does not entitle a disfavored purchaser to "automatic damages." *J. Truett Payne Co. v. Chrysler Motors*

Corp., 451 U.S. 557, 561, 101 S.Ct. 1923, 68 L. Ed. 2d 442 (1981). Rather,

* * * * *

Because they are essentially unable to match up a significant number of the customers they lost with those the favored purchasers gained, plaintiffs have failed to demonstrate antitrust injury. . . .

CONCLUSION

For all these reasons, defendants' motion for summary judgment is granted.

Questions

1. Why did the retail pharmacies lose this case?

2. *a.* In your opinion, have small pharmacies and small businesses generally lost significant revenue over the years to retail giants such as Walmart and Custom? Explain.

   b. If so, does that loss constitute an antitrust wrong that should be remedied by law? Explain.

3. In what sense does the Robinson–Patman Act arguably reduce efficiency, thus harming consumer welfare?

4. Texaco sold gasoline at its retail tank wagon prices to Hasbrouck, an independent Texaco retailer, but granted discounts to distributors Gull and Dompier. Dompier also sold at the retail level. Gull and Dompier both delivered their gas directly to retailers and did not maintain substantial storage facilities. During the period in question, sales at the stations supplied by the two distributors grew dramatically, while Hasbrouck's sales declined. Hasbrouck filed suit against Texaco, claiming that the distributor discount constituted a Robinson–Patman violation. Texaco defended, saying the discount reflected the services the distributors performed for Texaco, and that the arrangement did not harm competition. Decide. Explain. See *Texaco v. Ricky Hasbrouck*, 496 U.S. 543 (1990).

5. Utah Pie produced frozen pies in its Salt Lake City plant. Utah's competitors, Carnation, Pet, and Continental, sometimes sold pies in Salt Lake City at prices beneath those charged in other markets. Indeed, Continental's prices in Salt Lake City were beneath its direct costs plus overhead. Pet sold to Safeway using Safeway's private label at a price lower than that at which the same pies were sold under the Pet label. Pet employed an industrial spy to infiltrate Utah Pie and gather information. Utah Pie claimed that Carnation, Pet, and Continental were in violation of Robinson–Patman. Decide. Explain. See *Utah Pie Co. v. Continental Baking Co.*, 386 U.S. 685 (1967).

Predatory Pricing

Principal legislation—Sherman Act, Section 2.

Can a giant legally reduce its prices below operating costs until a competing discounter drops out of the market and then raise those prices to supracompetitive levels? In 2009, the European Commission fined Intel $1.45 billion for *predatory pricing* and other alleged misconduct. Essentially, Intel was accused of reducing prices for its chips by unlawfully paying rebates/discounts to computer manufacturers and retailers to persuade them not to use rival chips. Among other arguments, Intel claims the rebates had the desirable effect of saving money for consumers, but critics say consumer choice was reduced by discouraging deals with Intel rivals, resulting in higher prices and potentially reduced quality in the long term. Intel also agreed in 2009 to pay Advanced Micro Devices (AMD), a smaller, rival chipmaker, $1.25 billion to settle AMD's allegations of predatory pricing (among other claims).[21]

Predatory pricing charges under European precedents have some reasonable probability of success, but in the United States they are very difficult to win. The U.S. Justice Department claimed that American Airlines engaged in predatory pricing in attempting to monopolize air travel at the Dallas–Fort Worth Airport from 1995 to 1997. Justice argued that American Airlines lowered its prices to drive out seven discount carriers in the expectation that it could then recover its losses by charging monopoly prices. A federal court of appeals, however, ruled for American Airlines, holding that the government was unable to prove that American had priced its flights below cost (as measured by some appropriate formulation, such as average variable cost).[22] Thus, the government had failed to satisfy the standard U.S. two-part test for establishing predatory pricing:

- Pricing below cost.
- A "dangerous probability" of recouping the losses suffered from the below-cost pricing.[23]

The *American Airlines* decision could be seen as a great victory for consumers in that it supports the right to cut prices as low as possible. But consider *BusinessWeek*'s description of American's pricing practices:

> . . . Between Dallas and Kansas City, for instance, American's average one-way ticket was $108 before low-cost start-up Vanguard Airlines Inc. entered the market in early 1995. That prompted American to cut fares to $80 and almost double the number of daily flights to 14. When Vanguard gave up in December 1995, American jacked up prices to $147 and scaled back the number of flights. Justice lawyers even had memos from American execs plotting the upstart's demise.[24]

Antitrust Confronts Intellectual Property

When Google, Pfizer, Monsanto, Adobe, or any other technology innovator, big or small, introduces a new product we probably take for granted the resulting boost in the quality of our lifestyle, the jobs created, and the promise of additional advances in the future. More and more, however, our social and economic welfare is dependent on those technological breakthroughs. In order to encourage and protect *intellectual property* innovations, the law provides *patents* and *copyrights* as shields to preserve the innovator's rights. (For additional patent and copyright materials, refer to the index in the back of this text.) Preserving those rights, however, can lead to antitrust abuse since a patent or copyright often confers market power. In recent years, therefore, the federal government and legal experts have given attention to the increasing conflicts between antitrust law and intellectual property rights. Antitrust law, designed for smokestack industries, is struggling to adjust to our contemporary, knowledge-based economy.

We believe patent and copyright laws encourage innovation and protect creators' legitimate property interests, but we also believe in free access to knowledge as something of a personal right and as a necessary precondition to continued progress and prosperity. We need the stimulus of antitrust-protected competition to lower prices and maximize consumer welfare, but we also need the shelter of intellectual property rights to encourage innovation and investment. If we do not use patents and copyrights (and sometimes trademarks) to protect intellectual property, will creative efforts be diminished? In providing intellectual property protection, however, do we open the door to monopoly behaviors? As one high-tech blog put it, "Can Antitrust Law Stop Abuses of Intellectual Property and Free Access to Knowledge?"[25] [For more about open global access to knowledge (a2k), see **http://a2knetwork.org**]

The U.S. Supreme Court has ruled that patents should not automatically be treated as monopolies.[26] Abuse of the market power conferred by a patent, therefore, must be proven rather than presumed. And even if market power is established, an antitrust violation does not occur unless some competitive wrong is identified. As the Supreme Court said: "To safeguard the incentive to innovate, the possession of monopoly power will not be found unlawful unless it is accompanied by an element of anticompetitve *conduct*."[27] Generally, intellectual property disputes are analyzed by the same antitrust reasoning—monopoly, exclusive dealing, tying arrangements, etc.—as is applied elsewhere in the economy.

The most notable current struggle features Apple versus Samsung with each basically accusing the other of patent theft involving the iPad2, the Galaxy Tab, and other handheld products. Apple won an initial skirmish in a California district court,[28] but that decision is on appeal at this writing. The jury in that case found that Samsung had unlawfully copied certain essential patents (so-called standard essential patents or SEPs) controlled by Apple. Similar lawsuits are playing out in at least eight other nations. But should the Apple and Samsung essential patents be protected by law if doing so accords market power to the patent holder? Indeed, the Antitrust Division of the federal Justice Department has warned patent holders to avoid harming competition by charging unjustified royalties or simply denying access to essential patents.[29] To critics, some patent holders may be using their patent rights (sometimes bought in the open market by "patent trolls" seeking high license fees) to harm competition.

The Federal Trade Commission addressed these patent/antitrust conflicts in its 2013 settlement with Google, which agreed to license, under reasonable terms, essential patents to its competitors, such as Apple. The settlement came after a lengthy FTC investigation of Google's patent practices and its alleged dominance, particularly in the search engine market. (For more on Google as an alleged monopolist, see Chapter 11.)

Internet Exercise

Using the "Frequently Asked Questions" on the "Small Business Notes" Web page [**www.smallbusinessnotes.com/managing-your-business/frequently-asked-questions.html**], answer these questions:

1. Shopping for a stereo loudspeaker made by Sound Corporation, I couldn't find a dealer who would sell it for less than the manufacturer's suggested retail price. Isn't that price fixing?

2. I own a retail clothing store and the Brand Company refuses to sell me any of its line of clothes. These clothes are very popular in my area, so this policy is hurting my business. Isn't it illegal for Brand to refuse to sell to me?

3. I operate two stores that sell recorded music. My business is being ruined by giant discount store chains that sell their products for less than my wholesale cost. I thought there were laws against price discrimination, but I can't afford the legal fees to fight the big corporations. Can you help?

Chapter Questions

1. After reading this chapter, what is your judgment about the antitrust system?
   a. Does it work? Explain.
   b. How might it be altered?
   c. Could we place more reliance on the market? Explain.
   d. Do the statutes and case law, as a body, seem to form a rational package? Explain.
   e. Should antitrust policy focus exclusively on economic considerations or should social welfare goals (such as maintenance of full employment and the dispersal of political power) assume greater importance? Explain.

2. In recent years, Amazon, Walmart, Target, and others have been dramatically discounting some bestselling books; sometimes selling popular hardcover titles at under $10. In Europe's major publishing markets other than the United Kingdom, most new books, both print and online, must be sold at the price specified by the publisher; that is, discount pricing is forbidden by law.
   a. Why would Europeans accept antidiscounting laws that keep new book prices high?
   b. How would you expect the antidiscounting laws to affect the prices of used books?
   c. Germany, with a population of about 82 million, has about 7,000 bookstores while the United States, with a population of over 310 million, has about 11,000 bookstores. Is America's literary culture threatened by allowing giant retailers to aggressively discount? Explain.

3. Subway sandwich shops required all franchisees to employ a computerized point-of-sale (POS) system. The only approved system was provided by an unrelated company, RBS. Vendors of a competing POS system sued Subway's parent, Doctor's Associates, alleging, among other things, an unlawful tying arrangement.
   a. Describe the alleged tie.
   b. Defend Doctor's Associates (Subway).
   c. Explain what the plaintiffs would need to demonstrate in order to prevail. See *Subsolutions, Inc. v. Doctor's Associates, Inc.*, 62 F.Supp.2d 616 (D. Conn. 1999).

4. In *Continental T.V., Inc. v. GTE Sylvania, Inc.*, 433 U.S. 36 (1977), the U.S. Supreme Court took the position that interbrand, rather than intrabrand, agreements must be the primary concern of antitrust law.
   a. Why did the Court take that view?

     b. In your opinion, is the Court correct? Explain.

     c. Explain the "free-rider" problem that frequently concerns the courts in cases involving vertical territorial restraints, among others.

5. Could Whirlpool, the appliance manufacturer, lawfully refuse to deal with any purchaser that sells the products of a competitor such as General Electric? Explain.

6. Pool Corporation, as the largest wholesale distributor of swimming pool supplies in the United States and the only distributor with a nationwide distribution system, was accused in 2011 by the Federal Trade Commission of abusing its market power by pressuring its product manufacturers to refrain from selling to those seeking to enter the market as pool supply distributors (and thus competitors of Pool Corporation). The FTC found that manufacturers representing about 70 percent of all pool product sales declined to sell to new entrants. The FTC calculated that Pool Corporation accounted for 30 to 50 percent of most pool supply manufacturers' sales, making it by a wide margin the largest customer of those manufacturers.

     a. What antitrust violation(s) were alleged by the FTC?

     b. How would you rule on those alleged violations? Explain.

7. Tanaka played soccer at the University of Southern California, a member of the PAC 10 Conference. She became unhappy, asked if she could transfer, and was told that she could. She decided to go to another PAC 10 school, UCLA. USC, unhappy with that choice, invoked an NCAA rule limiting transfers within a conference. The rule required her to sit out one year and to lose one year of eligibility. She sued USC and the NCAA on restraint of trade grounds.

     a. Explain her claim.

     b. Decide the case. Explain your decision. See *Tanaka v. University of Southern California,* 252 F.3d 1059 (9th Cir. 2001).

8. Assume two fertilizer dealerships, Grow Quick and Fertile Fields, hold 70 percent and 30 percent, respectively, of the fertilizer business in the farm community of What Cheer, Iowa. Assume the owner of Fertile Fields learns via inquiry, hearsay, and the like of Grow Quick's price quotes. Then, each growing season the Fertile Fields owner sets her prices exactly equal to those of her competitor. Is that practice unlawful? Explain.

9. Given functionally identical competing products, why is identical pricing virtually inevitable—at least over the long run?

10. In 1968, Business Electronics Corporation (BEC) became the exclusive retailer in the Houston, Texas, area of electronic calculators manufactured by Sharp Electronics Corporation. In 1972, Sharp appointed Hartwell as a second retailer in the Houston area. Sharp published a list of suggested minimum retail prices, but its written dealership agreements with BEC and Hartwell did not obligate either to observe them or to charge any other specific price. BEC's retail prices were often below Sharp's suggested retail prices and generally below Hartwell's retail prices, even though Hartwell too sometimes priced below Sharp's suggested retail prices. Hartwell complained to Sharp on a number of occasions about BEC's prices. In 1973, Hartwell gave Sharp the ultimatum that Hartwell would terminate his dealership unless Sharp ended its relationship with BEC within 30 days. Sharp terminated BEC's dealership. BEC filed suit alleging that Sharp and Hartwell had unlawfully conspired to terminate BEC and that the conspiracy was

illegal *per se* under the Sherman Act, Section 1. Decide the case. Explain. See *Business Electronics Corporation v. Sharp Electronics Corporation,* 485 U.S. 717 (1988).

11. Some antitrust experts argue that a firm possessing market power should be challenged by the government with the goal of eradicating the power as quickly as possible. Others maintain that the government should be patient with short-term market power. Explain those two points of view.

12. Adidas contracts with NCAA schools and their coaches to promote its products. An NCAA rule limits the amount of advertising that may appear on uniforms and equipment. Adidas complained that those restrictions on promotional rights "artificially limit the price and quality options available to apparel manufacturers as consumers of promotional space, force manufacturers to pay additional amounts for billboard space or other advertising, decrease the selection of apparel offered to the end consumer, increase the price of the apparel for end consumers, and financially benefit the NCAA." Adidas sued the NCAA on antitrust grounds.

    a. What antitrust violations were cited by Adidas?

    b. Decide the case. Explain. See *Adidas v. NCAA,* 64 F.Supp.2d 1097 (1999).

13. A board-certified anesthesiologist was denied admission to the Jefferson Parish Hospital staff because the hospital had an exclusive services contract with a firm of anesthesiologists. The contract required all surgery patients at the hospital to use that firm for their anesthesiology work. Seventy percent of the patients in the parish were served by hospitals other than Jefferson. The anesthesiologist who was denied admission sued the hospital, claiming the contract was unlawful.

    a. What antitrust violation was raised by the plaintiff?

    b. Decide. Explain. See *Jefferson Parish Hospital District No. 2 v. Hyde,* 466 U.S. 2 (1984).

14. In 1990, the American Institute of Certified Public Accountants agreed to enforce a change in its ethics rules that allowed its members to accept contingent fees and commissions from nonaudit clients. The agreement was the result of a consent order between the AICPA and the Federal Trade Commission. Likewise, in 1990, the American Institute of Architects signed a consent order with the Justice Department that forbade the Institute from adopting policies that would restrain architects from bidding competitively for jobs, offering discounts, or doing work without compensation.

    a. What antitrust violation was the government seeking to stem in both of these cases?

    b. What defenses were offered by the professions for their policies?

15. Starter Sportswear had a license to manufacture and sell satin professional team jackets marketed as "authentic" because they were styled in the manner of jackets actually worn by the members of the various teams. A Starter policy statement provided that it would sell only to retailers that carry a representative amount of Starter's full line of jackets. Starter also had a minimum order policy specifying that it wouldn't deal with retailers who sought quantities beneath that minimum order. Trans Sport, a retailer, began selling Starter jackets to other retailers who did not meet Starter's requirements. At that point, Starter declined to deal further with Trans Sport. Trans Sport then sued Starter.

    a. List Trans Sport's claims against Starter.

    b. Resolve those claims, raising all the relevant issues. See *Trans Sport, Inc. v. Starter Sportswear, Inc.,* 964 F.2d 186 (2d Cir. 1992).

Notes

1. *Standard Oil Co. of New Jersey v. United States,* 221 U.S. 1 (1911).

2. Alexander McIntyre, Jr., "Halt to 'Call-Arounds' Puts La Quinta in Spotlight," *LEXOLOGY,* May 27, 2010 [**www.lexology.com/**].

3. This analysis is drawn from William Kovacic, "The Identification and Proof of Horizontal Agreements under the Antitrust Laws," *Antitrust Bulletin* 38, no. 1 (Spring 1993), p. 5.

4. *Bell Atlantic Corp. v. Twombly,* 127 S.Ct. 1955 (2007).

5. Dawn Kawamoto, "LG, Sharp, Chunghwa Admit to LCD Price Fixing," *Business Tech,* November 12, 2008 [**http://news.cnet.com/8301-1001_3-10095219-92.html**].

6. Jerry Hirsch and Ken Bensinger, "Two More Japanese Auto Parts Makers Admit to Price-Fixing Scheme," *latimes.com,* January 31, 2012 [**articles.latimes.com/2012/**].

7. Bill Myers, "$100 Million Accord in Price-Fix Lawsuit," *Chicago Daily Law Bulletin,* July 29, 2004.

8. Michael Orey, "Price Fixing, the Perpetual Sequel," *BloombergBusinessweek,* September 28, 2009 [**www.businessweek.com/**].

9. The analysis in this paragraph relies considerably on Donald M. Falk, "Antitrust and Refusals to Deal after *Nynex v. Discon,*" *Practical Lawyer* 46, no. 3 (2000), p. 25.

10. See, e.g., Herbert J. Hovenkamp, "Unilateral Refusals to Deal, Vertical Integration, and the Essential Facility Doctrine," July 1, 2008, *U. of Iowa Legal Studies Research Paper* No. 08-31. Available at SSRN: **http://ssrn.com/abstract=1144675**

11. *United States v. Visa and MasterCard,* 344 F.3d 229 (2d. Cir. 2003); cert. den. *Visa v. United States,* 125 S.Ct. 45 (2004).

12. *United States v. Colgate & Co.,* 250 U.S. 300 (1919).

13. *State Oil Co. v. Khan,* 118 S.Ct. 275 (1997).

14. *Dr. Miles Medical Co. v. John D. Park & Sons Co.,* 220 U.S. 373 (1911).

15. *Continental T.V., Inc. v. GTE Sylvania, Inc.,* 433 U.S. 36 (1977).

16. *Wal-Mart v. Visa and MasterCard,* 396 F.3d 96 (2005).

17. *American Needle v. National Football League,* 130 S.Ct. 2201 (2010).

18. *Dang v. San Francisco Forty Niners,* 12-5481, U.S. District Court, Northern District of California (San Francisco).

19. Robert J. Toth, "A Powerful Law Has Been Losing A Lot of Its Punch," *The Wall Street Journal,* May 21, 2012, p. R2.

20. Ibid.

21. Steve Lohr and James Kanter, "A.M.D.-Intel Settlement Won't End Their Woes," *The New York Times,* November 13, 2009 [**www.nytimes.com**].

22. *United States v. AMR Corp,* 335 F.3d 1109 (10th Cir. 2003).

23. *Brooke Group Ltd. v. Brown & Williamson Tobacco Corp.,* 509 U.S. 209 (1993).

24. Dan Carney, "Predatory Pricing: Cleared for Takeoff," *BusinessWeek,* May 14, 2001, p. 50.

25. Mike Masnick, "Can Antitrust Law Stop Abuses of Intellectual Property and Free Access to Knowledge?" *techdirt,* August 19, 2010. [**www.techdirt.com/articles/20100812/03235710603.shtml**].

26. *Illinois Tool Works v. Independent Ink,* 547 U.S. 28 (2006).

27. *Verizon Communications Inc. v. Law Offices of Curtis V. Trinko, LLP,* 540 U.S. 398, 407 (2004).

28. *Apple Inc. v. Samsung Electronics Co.,* 11-cv-01846, U.S. District Court, Northern District of California (San Jose).

29. Frank Caprio, Michael Denniston, and Jay Levine, "DOJ to Standard Essential Patent Holders– 'We Have Our Eye on You,'" *Lexology,* February 22, 2012 [**www.lexology.com/**].

Antitrust Law—Monopolies and Mergers

After completing this chapter, students will be able to:

1. Explain how Microsoft violated U.S. antitrust laws.

2. Analyze when a monopoly has been created.

3. Identify the potential benefits and hazards of mergers.

4. Distinguish between horizontal and vertical mergers.

5. Explain premerger notification requirements.

6. Describe remedies for mergers determined to be anticompetitive.

7. Analyze when a horizontal merger is anticompetitive.

8. Analyze when a vertical merger creates anticompetitive "market foreclosure."

9. Contrast antitrust enforcement in the United States and the European Union (EU).

Introduction—Google, Microsoft, and Monopoly

Google Too Big?

Jeffrey Katz, Nextag CEO and Google competitor, thinks so:

> Google . . . is the most popular search engine in the world, controlling 82 percent of the global search market and 98 percent of the mobile search market. Its annual revenue is larger than the economies of the world's 28 poorest countries combined. And its closest competitor, Bing, is so far behind . . . that Google has become, effectively, a monopoly.

In the United States, Google handles about two-thirds of all web searches, and it reportedly controls about 75 percent of the search advertising market. Nonetheless, the Federal Trade Commission (FTC) ended a 19-month investigation of Google by announcing in early 2013 that it would not pursue litigation against the giant. Rather, Google issued a pair of promises: (1) Google agreed to desist from scraping. Reportedly, Google, without permission or compensation, was taking ("scraping") reviews and other data from rival websites for use on its own websites; and (2) Google agreed to ease practices that had discouraged advertisers using Google's AdWords platform from simultaneously using rival platforms. As noted in Chapter 10, Google also agreed to a legally binding Consent Order with the FTC to allow competitors fair, reasonable access to essential patents held by Google. No action was taken, however, regarding the critics' biggest concern: Google's alleged "search bias," in which critics contend that Google's search results are "rigged" to favor its own commercial interests. Nevertheless, the FTC unanimously concluded that Google's search practices were not anticompetitive in that they were designed primarily to improve the quality of the product delivered to consumers.

The FTC's resolution of the Google investigation has been harshly criticized, but supporters note that dissatisfied consumers have a number of choices in the search market. Investigations of Google continue in a number of states. Further, the European Union is expected to reach a settlement with Google that may include more sweeping concessions than those required by the United States.

Sources: Jeffrey Katz, "Google's Monopoly and Internet Freedom," *The Wall Street Journal,* June 8, 2012, p. A15; Glenn Shewan and Penny Pasley, "Searching Questions—the FTC's Google Investigation," *LEXOLOGY,* February 11, 2013 **[www.lexology.com/]**; and Reuters, "Google's EU Antitrust Case May Soon Be Resolved," *MSN.COM,* February 1, 2013 **[http://news.msn.com/]**.

Microsoft a Monopolist? Is Microsoft an outsized, predatory lawbreaker, an amazing force for technological progress, or both? The U.S. Justice Department, 18 states, and the District of Columbia went to trial against Microsoft in 1998, claiming not that the software giant was too big, but that it had violated various antitrust laws in gaining and maintaining its market dominance. An epic legal struggle followed with major elements of the American justice system challenging one of the world's richest men, Bill Gates.

> An epic legal struggle followed with major elements of the American justice system challenging one of the world's richest men, Bill Gates.

A federal district court in 2000 and later a federal court of appeals ruled that Microsoft had violated federal antitrust laws by maintaining its 95 percent share of the Intel-compatible PC operating systems market through anticompetitive means (basically using its monopoly power to coerce customers to buy other Microsoft products such as its browser, Internet Explorer).[1] The district court judge ordered Microsoft split into two companies as a remedy for its antitrust wrongs, but the court of appeals threw out that order. Thereafter, the case was settled out of court with Microsoft agreeing, among other things, to not retaliate unfairly against other software and computer makers, to disclose some software code, and to be temporarily monitored by a federal judge.

The settlement, though somewhat of a victory for Microsoft, might also be regarded as a victory for common sense in allowing Microsoft to go forward with its remarkable work. The decision places considerable faith in the market, as it probably should in America; but the case also represents a powerful affirmation of the government's authority to attack monopoly behavior no matter how prominent the wrongdoer.

Settlements   As it turns out, the federal antitrust charges were only the beginning of Microsoft's battles. Settlements with Novell, Sun Microsystems, AOL, RealNetworks, and others cost Microsoft billions. European Union antitrust enforcers pursued Microsoft for a decade before settling their claims in 2009. The EU argument, much like the concerns in the United States, was that Microsoft's market dominance allowed it to effectively force its Windows operating system users to also use its Internet Explorer browser. The settlement required Microsoft to provide a pop-up screen that would allow European customers to choose among several browsers other than Explorer, thus likely building the market share of rival browsers. Just as the 2009 settlement appeared to have resolved Microsoft's European problems, the European Commission announced in 2013 that it had fined Microsoft over $730 million for breaking the terms of that settlement. Microsoft apologized for what it said was a technical problem that had temporarily denied about 15 million users the promised choice of browsers. The Microsoft struggles underline the aggressive stance of EU antitrust regulators. Since 25 percent of the global market for many products resides in the European Union, all big companies must now think more carefully about how their practices will be received by EU regulators even if those practices are not of concern to United States regulators.

> The Microsoft saga serves as a reminder of an important truth: Capitalists, for the most part, don't care much for capitalism. Their goal is to make money. And if they can do it without messy competition, so much the better. As long as it keeps its monopoly, Microsoft can afford to share the wealth with its onetime rivals. For Microsoft, those fines and payments add up to less than a year's profit from the operating system. For the others, it's easier to take Microsoft's money than fight.[2]

> ### Whether a giant bullied its rivals.

The Microsoft battle was about whether a giant bullied its rivals, but it was also about the very nature of capitalism—that is, the role of managerial ethics, the market, and government in American life. The case obliges us to think about what we want America to be and what role the law should play in securing that ideal. Most crucially, we should ask ourselves whether the market and ethics are sufficient to preserve genuine democracy and social justice, or whether we must employ antitrust law to attack those great concentrations of power that sometimes threaten our core values.

Questions

1. *a.* Do you see increasing concentrations of wealth and power as threats to America's long-term welfare? Explain.
   b. If that concentration is a concern, is antitrust law the best remedy?
2. Does the *Microsoft* case stand simply for the view that bigness is bad? Explain.
3. Critics have argued that technology is eliminating the imperfections of the market, making antitrust law enforcement obsolete in this high-tech era.
   a. Explain that argument.
   b. Now build the argument that high-tech industries may actually be especially susceptible to antitrust problems because of the need to maintain equipment compatibility.

Part One—Monopoly

Both the federal district court and the court of appeals in the *Microsoft* case concluded that the computer giant held monopoly power in the Intel-compatible PC operating systems market. How did those courts reach that conclusion? How do we know when an organization is an unlawful monopolist? An extensive, sophisticated, evolving system of analysis has emerged. [For the American Bar Association Antitrust section, see **www.americanbar.org/ groups/antitrust_law.html**]

Principal Monopoly Legislation: Sherman Act, Section 2

> Every person who shall monopolize, or attempt to monopolize, or combine or conspire with any other person or persons, to monopolize any part of the trade or commerce among the several States, or with foreign nations, shall be deemed guilty of a felony punishable by a fine.

Section 5 of the Federal Trade Commission Act applies to antitrust cases although the wisdom of that use is disputed.

Monopoly Defined From an economic viewpoint, a monopoly is a situation in which one firm holds the power to control prices and/or exclude competition in a particular market. The general legal test for monopolization is:

1. The possession of monopoly power in the relevant market, and
2. The willful acquisition or maintenance of that power, as distinguished from growth or development as a consequence of a superior product, business acumen, or historic accident.[3]

Thus, the critical inquiries are the percentage of the market held by the alleged monopolist and the behavior that produced and maintained that market share. Antitrust law does not punish efficient companies who legitimately earn and maintain large market shares.

Indeed, high market concentration often promotes competition, whereas a fragmented market of many small firms may produce higher prices. (Imagine a retail food market of many corner grocery stores and no supermarkets.) Nonetheless, the federal government continues to rely strongly on market concentration data (structure) in combination with evidence of actual behavior (conduct) to identify anticompetitive situations. Market share alone is highly unlikely to lead to antitrust action, but a high market share acquired and/or maintained via abusive conduct (as alleged in *Microsoft*) may be challenged.

Oligopoly A few firms sharing monopoly power constitute an oligopoly. Oligopolistic markets are common in American life, and they have emerged in some increasingly concentrated global markets as well. A recent *New York Times* headline read: "Rising Beer Prices Hint at Oligopoly."[4]

As *The New York Times* noted, we fear that oligopoly conditions will lead to higher prices (along with reduced quality and innovation). In industries such as telecom, food processing, credit ratings, and book publishing, we find enormous American and international markets dominated by a handful of companies. Of course, oligopolies often produce significant efficiencies, and they may leave market space for smaller competitors, including startups. But in many cases, we worry that oligopolies threaten consumer welfare. We see, for example, that only four railroads (Burlington Northern Santa Fe, CSX, Norfolk Southern, and Union Pacific) control approximately 90 percent of the rail freight market. Rail freight rates have been advancing, according to a *Fortune* inquiry, by about 6 percent per year while shipping rates by truck and air have increased about 1 to 2 percent per year.[5] And for the nation's many "captive" companies (served by one railroad), "rates are skyrocketing."[6] Not coincidentally, railroads enjoy government-granted exemptions from many antitrust rules. At the same time, a rather obscure federal agency, the Surface Transportation Board, is tasked with oversight of the rail industry. Furthermore, the railroads note that they enjoy only modest returns on capital, and they point to the huge investments they have made in upgrading their equipment and tracks. The railroads also argue that they are in direct competition with truck and air transport, although critics say those options are not feasible for many customers.

Apple a Monopoly?

In late April 2012, *Business Insider,* citing Apple's dominance in the mobile phone and tablet markets, argued that the "decline of Android signals the rise of Apple's monopoly." In recent years, other critics have pointed to Apple's nearly 70 percent share of the online music market.

Then, in mid-November 2012, Michael Wolff wrote in *USA Today* that "the age of Apple may be over." As Wolff explained, Apple became America's most valuable company in 2012 with its shares selling as high as $700, but then Apple's share price fell back dramatically in part because Samsung became a powerful competitor in the smartphone market. At the same time, Samsung tripled its tablet share to 18.4 percent while Apple's tablet share fell from 60 to 50 percent in one year .

In 2013, the Ninth Circuit Federal Court of Appeals dismissed a class action by iPod and iTunes buyers claiming that Apple is a monopolist. Analyst Tim Worstall, writing in *Forbes,* says that we should worry less about monopolies in the tech area because of their fleeting nature: "No one actually gets a monopoly for long enough to be able to fleece consumers through having that monopoly."

Questions

1. In your view, does the government, through antitrust law, have a useful, meaningful role to play in regulating high-tech companies such as Apple, Samsung, and Google? Explain.
2. Will the market automatically correct, in rather rapid fashion, any monopolistic conditions that may develop in the high-tech arena? Explain.

Sources: Roger Kay, "Apple, A Monopoly? It Could Happen," *Forbes,* August 28, 2012 [**www.forbes.com**]; Heather Leonard, "The Rise of Apple's Monopoly," *Business Insider,* April 27, 2012 [**www.articles.businessinsider.com**]; *Stacie Somers v. Apple, Inc.,* 2013 U.S. App. LEXIS 18246 (U.S. Court of Appeals for the Ninth Circuit); and Michael Wolff, "The Age of Apple May Be Over," *USA Today,* November 12, 2012 [**www.usatoday.com**].

Monopolization Analysis

Although the case law is not a model of clarity, a rather straightforward framework for monopoly analysis has emerged:

1. Define the relevant *product market*.
2. Define the relevant *geographic market*.
3. Compute the defendant's *market power*.
4. Assess the defendant's *intent* (predatory or coercive conduct).
5. Raise any available *defenses*.

1. Product Market

Here the court seeks, effectively, to draw a circle that encompasses categories of goods in which the defendant's products or services compete and that excludes those not in the same competitive arena. The fundamental test is *interchangeability* as determined primarily by the price, use, and quality of the product in question.

An analysis of cross-elasticity of demand is a key ingredient in defining the product market. Assume that two products, X and Y, appear to be competitors. Assume that the price of X doubled and Y's sales volume was unchanged. What does that tell us about whether X and Y are, in fact, in the same product market?

Defining the product market is really the process we all go through in routine purchasing decisions. Assume you feel a rather undefined hunger for salty snack food. You go to the nearby convenience store. Many options confront you, but for simplicity, let's confine them to chips, nuts, and popcorn. Of course, each of those food types is composed of variations. As you sort through the choices—corn chips, cheese curls, peanuts, potato chips, and so on—you employ the criteria of price, use, and quality in focusing your decision. In so doing, you are defining the product market for "salty snack food." Products closely matched in price, use, and quality are interchangeable, and thus are competitors in the same product market. But, for example, an imported salty cheese at $10 per quarter pound presumably is not in the same product market as salted sunflower seeds.

Expressed as a matter of elasticity, the critical question becomes something like the following: If the price of potato chips, for example, falls by 10 percent, does the sales volume of salted nuts likewise fall? If so, we have a strong indication that potato chips and salted nuts lie in the same product market and thus are competitors.

2. Geographic Market

Once the product market has been defined, we still must determine where the product can be purchased. The judicial decisions to date offer no definitive explanation of the geographic market concept. A working definition might be "any section of the country where the product is sold in commercially significant quantities." From an economic perspective, the geographic market is defined by elasticity. If prices rise or supplies are reduced within the geographic area in question (New England, for example) and demand remains steady, will products from other areas enter the market in a quantity sufficient to affect price and/or supply? If so, the geographic market must be broadened to embrace those new sources of supply. If not, the geographic market is not larger than the area in question (New England). Perhaps a better approach is to read the cases and recognize that each geographic market must simply be identified in terms of its unique economic properties.

3. Market Power (Market Share)

Does the market share held by the defendant threaten competition? How large that share must be to raise monopoly concerns depends on a variety of considerations including how fragmented or concentrated the market is. *The Harvard Law Review,* however, notes some approximate boundaries:

> Market share above 70 percent typically suffices to support an inference of monopoly power. Conversely, courts have rarely found monopoly power when a firm's market share is below 50 percent, leaving some uncertainty as to market shares between 50 and 70 percent.[7]

Market share alone, however, does not establish monopoly power. Barriers to entry, economics of scale, the strength of the competition, trends in the market, and pricing patterns all help to determine whether the market remains competitive despite a single firm's large share. (Why are the courts interested in barriers to entry?)

4. Intent (Predatory or Coercive Conduct)

Assuming a threatening market share is established, the next requirement is proof of an intent to monopolize. Remember that a monopoly finding requires a showing of both market power (*structure*) and willful acquisition or maintenance of that power (*conduct*). Antitrust law is not designed to attack legitimately earned market power. Rather, the concern lies with those holding monopoly power that was acquired or maintained wrongfully. Thus, a showing of deliberate, predatory, coercive, or unfair conduct (such as collusion leading to price fixing) will normally suffice to establish the requisite intent.

Intel, the dominant microchip maker with 80 to 90 percent of the microprocessor market, reached a 2010 settlement of Federal Trade Commission charges that it used unfair tactics to earn and maintain that market share. Basically, Intel was accused of providing discriminatory rebates to Dell, IBM, HP, and others in return for those purchasers' agreement not to buy central processing unit chips from Intel's rival, Advanced Micro Devices (AMD). Intel was also accused of designing its chips so that competing processors could not run efficiently with them. Among other terms, the FTC settlement prohibits those practices. In 2009, Intel agreed to pay $1.25 billion to settle claims AMD brought in a patent and antitrust lawsuit, and the European Union fined Intel a record $1.45 billion for antitrust offenses. [Explain why giving discounts could constitute an antitrust violation and defend Intel against those charges. See Edward Wyatt and Ashlee Vance, "Intel Settles with F.T.C. on Antitrust," *The New York Times,* August 4, 2010 (**www.nytimes.com/**); and Stephen Labaton, "Intel Facing Antitrust Investigation," *The New York Times,* June 7, 2008 (**www.nytimes.com**)].

5. Defenses

The defendant may yet prevail if the evidence demonstrates that the monopoly was innocently acquired via "superior skill, foresight, or industry;" that is, the monopoly was earned. Sometimes a monopoly may be "thrust upon" the monopolist because the competition failed or because of "natural monopoly" conditions where the market will support only one firm or where large economies of scale exist (such as for electricity suppliers).

Attempted Monopolization

The Sherman Act forbids attempts to monopolize as well as monopoly itself. In the 1993 *Spectrum Sports* decision,[8] the Supreme Court set out a three-part test for attempted monopolization: (1) that the defendant has engaged in predatory or anticompetitive conduct with (2) a specific intent to monopolize and (3) a dangerous probability of achieving monopoly power (by which the court was insisting on evidence of some "realistic" likelihood that monopoly would actually follow).

Is Bob Marley a Product Market?

Music producer Rock River released remixed Bob Marley and the Wailers recordings in 2006. Universal Music Group claimed exclusive rights to those recordings and sent "cease and desist" orders to music distributors (Amazon, iTunes, etc.) who immediately discontinued sale of the Rock River remix. Rock River then sued Universal alleging attempted monopoly of the reggae genre of sound recordings in the United States, among other claims. Rock River alleged that Universal "accounted for 81 percent of the reggae sound recordings sold, and Bob Marley recordings accounted for 76 percent of the total reggae recordings sold."

Questions

1. Is reggae music, in your judgment, an identifiable product market? Explain.
2. Universal claimed there were no significant barriers to entry in the alleged reggae music market. Explain why the absence of barriers to entry would be a significant consideration in resolving the case.
3. Assuming Universal's share of the alleged product market was correctly calculated by Rock River, who will win this lawsuit? Explain.

Source: Rock River Communications v. Universal Music Group, 2011 U.S. Dist. LEXIS 46023 (C.D. Cal., Western Div.).

Monopoly Case I

The case that follows is a private antitrust action involving a claim by Christy Sports, a Utah ski rental company, that Deer Valley Resort Company (DVRC), a ski resort developer/operator, had monopoly power over Deer Valley Resort's ski rental business and that DVRC abused that power to harm Christy Sports.

Christy Sports v. Deer Valley Resort Company
555 F.3d 1188 (10th Cir. 2009)

Circuit Judge McConnell

When the Deer Valley Resort Company ("DVRC") was developing its world-renowned ski resort in the Wasatch Mountains, it sold parcels of land within the resort village to third parties, while reserving the right of approval over the conduct of certain ancillary businesses on the property, including ski rentals. For about years, DVRC granted permission to Cole Sports and plaintiff-appellant Christy Sports to rent skis in competition with its own ski rental outlet. More recently, however, DVRC revoked that permission, presumably in order to gain more business for its own newly opened mid-mountain ski rental store. The question is whether this revocation violated the antitrust laws.

I. BACKGROUND

Deer Valley is one of three resorts in the vicinity of Park City, Utah. Many—indeed, "the vast majority," according to the Complaint of Deer Valley's patrons are destination skiers who fly into Salt Lake City and then take a forty-five minute bus or shuttle ride to the resort. The resort itself is divided into two areas: the base area, located at the bottom of the mountain, and the ritzier mid-mountain village, located halfway up the slope. DVRC has always been the sole provider of ski rentals at the base area, but at the mid-mountain village, Christy and Cole Sports have operated rental facilities; DVRC itself opened a mid-mountain ski rental facility in 2005.

Originally, DVRC owned all the property at the mid-mountain village, but over the years it has sold parcels to third parties. In 1990, DVRC sold one such parcel to S.Y. and Betty Kimball, subject to a restrictive covenant that prohibited use of the property for either ski rental or real estate sales office purposes without DVRC's express written consent. The Kimballs built a commercial building and leased space in it to Christy's corporate predecessor, Bulrich Corporation. The lease expressly prohibited both the rental of skis and the operation of a real estate office. The next year, though, DVRC gave Bulrich permission to rent skis in return for 15% of the rental revenue. When Bulrich merged with another company in 1994 and formed Christy Sports, LLC, Christy continued to operate the rental business. According to the complaint, Christy stopped paying DVRC 15% of its rental revenue in 1995, though the reason for this change is unknown. Christy rented skis at the Deer Valley mid-mountain village with no objection from DVRC until 2005. During that time, DVRC was the sole purveyor of rental skis at the base area but did not have a ski rental operation at mid-mountain.

DVRC opened a mid-mountain ski rental outlet in 2005. In August of that year, the resort notified Christy that, beginning the following year's ski season, the restrictive covenant would be enforced and Christy would no longer be allowed to rent skis. Christy believes that DVRC issued the same message to Cole's, leaving DVRC as the only rental ski provider at Deer Valley, with the exception of a small operation at the Stein Eriksen Lodge, which serves its own lodgers. This leaves that majority of skiers who fly into Salt Lake City and then shuttle to Deer Valley with few choices: they can carry unwieldy ski equipment onto the plane, take a shuttle into Park City and hunt for cheaper ski rentals in town, or rent from the more conveniently located DVRC location. Christy predicts, not improbably, that most consumers will choose the third option.

Christy argues that DVRC's decision to begin enforcing its restrictive covenant is an attempt to monopolize the market of ski rentals available to destination skiers in Deer Valley, or, alternatively, to the destination skiers in the mid-mountain village itself. It alleges that by eliminating its competitors, DVRC will be able to increase prices and reduce output, thus harming consumers. The complaint states that the number of skis available for rental mid-mountain will decline by 620 pairs, and the price will increase by at least twenty-two to thirty-two percent.

The district court dismissed Christy's antitrust complaints.

II. ANALYSIS

* * * * *

Christy has alleged that DVRC violated Section 2 of the Sherman Act by either actual or attempted monopolization. . . . Under both types of Section 2 claims Christy must plead both power in a relevant market and anticompetitive conduct. The relevant market, according to Christy's complaint, is the market for ski rentals to destination skiers in Deer Valley in general or, even more narrowly, the market for ski rentals in the mid-mountain village. The alleged anticompetitive conduct is the enforcement of the restrictive covenant.

A great many pages in the briefs are devoted to whether the defined market set forth in the complaint—destination skiers at Deer Valley, or alternatively at Deer Valley's mid-mountain village—is too small to constitute a market for antitrust purposes, in light of the proximity of a number of ski rental outlets in Park City, just down the road. For purposes of analyzing the complaint, however, we find it not implausible that destination skiers who arrive at the resort by bus or shuttle will find it sufficiently inconvenient to travel into town to rent skis that a successful monopolist over ski rental at Deer Valley could charge supracompetitive prices. The question, we believe, is not whether DVRC might be able to raise prices and reduce output by becoming the only purveyor of rental skis at the resort, but whether such a market is legally cognizable under the antitrust laws and whether the decision of a resort owner to reserve to itself the right to provide ancillary services counts as anticompetitive conduct.

* * * * *

We begin our analysis with DVRC's original decision to impose the restrictive covenant.

A. IMPOSITION OF THE RESTRICTIVE COVENANT

We agree with the defendant that the creator of a resort has no obligation under the antitrust laws to allow competitive suppliers of ancillary services on its property. A theme park, for example, does not have to permit third parties to open restaurants, hotels, gift shops, or other facilities within the park; it can reserve to itself the right to conduct such businesses and receive revenues from them. Accordingly, if it sells land within the resort to third parties, the antitrust laws do not bar the resort owner from imposing a covenant against use of the property for competitive businesses. This is so even if food, rooms, gifts, or other ancillary goods and services would be cheaper and more plentiful if the resort owner allowed competition in these businesses.

This conclusion can be reached either by reference to the proper definition of a market or by reference to the absence of anticompetitive conduct. Some courts, faced with cases of this sort, have found the market definition implausible. The Seventh Circuit took this approach in *Elliott* v. *United Center,* 126 F.3d 1003 (7th Cir. 1997), when a peanut vendor challenged a sports arena's decision to ban outside food and thereby monopolize the market for food concessions within the arena. The court rejected that market definition as implausible, saying:

> The logic of [the] argument would mean that exclusive restaurants could no longer require customers to purchase their wines only at the establishment, because the restaurant would be "monopolizing" the sale of wine within its interior. Movie theaters, which traditionally (and notoriously) earn a substantial portion of their revenue from the sale of candies, popcorn, and soda, would be required by the antitrust laws to allow patrons to bring their own food.

* * * * *

Although discussion of sports arenas . . . seems to suggest that Christy's shortcomings lie with its alleged geographic

market, the actual problem lies with its product market. In these cases the two are difficult to disentangle because the product (rental skis . . .) is intimately related to the location. Consumers do not travel to Deer Valley for rental skis. . . . The true product in these cases is the overall experience. Deer Valley offers a cluster of products that combine to create a destination ski experience; rental skis are only one small component. . . .

The complaint alleges nothing to suggest that destination skiers are choosing their ski resort based on the price of rental skis, separate and apart from the cluster of services associated with the destination-ski experience. To define one small component of the overall product as the relevant product market is simply implausible.

Alternatively, one could say that the monopolization claim would fail because the alleged conduct is not anticompetitive. Even if a firm has monopoly power in a relevant market, a plaintiff must also show "the willful acquisition or maintenance of that power as distinguished from growth or development as a consequence of a superior product, business acumen, or historic accident." *Grinnell Corp.,* 384 U.S. at 570-71. Deer Valley is not required to invite competitors onto its property to rent skis to its patrons, even if a failure to do so would mean it is the sole supplier of rental skis at the ski area.

The Supreme Court has recognized the economic value of allowing businesses to decide with whom they will deal, as it recently re-emphasized: "[A]s a general matter, the Sherman Act 'does not restrict the long recognized right of [a] trader or manufacturer engaged in an entirely private business, freely to exercise his own independent discretion as to parties with whom he will deal.'" *Verizon Commc'ns, Inc.* v. *Law Offices of Curtis V. Trinko, LLP,* 540 U.S. 398, 408 (2004). In *Trinko,* the Court acknowledged that in rare circumstances a refusal to cooperate with competitors might constitute a Section 2 violation, but that "such exceptions, because of the uncertain virtue of forced sharing and the difficulty of identifying and remedying anticompetitive conduct by a single firm," should be few.

Having invested time and money in developing a premier ski resort that attracts skiers from across the nation, DVRC could recoup its investment in a number of ways. It could increase the price of lift tickets, raise room rates, serve only high-priced food, or, as it seems to have chosen, delve more deeply into the rental ski market. . . . This does not mean consumers have no protection. The ski resort industry is competitive (and Christy does not allege otherwise). Families contemplating ski vacations have many options, and they presumably compare quality and price. If they are rational, the price they are concerned about is the sum of all of their prospective vacation costs, including not just lift ticket prices and resort lodging, but air fare, food and drink, apres-ski entertainment, ski rentals, and the like. A resort that facilitates lower ski rental prices by allowing competition is able to price other aspects of the ski vacation experience more aggressively. The competitive discipline comes not from introducing competition with respect to each component of the experience, but from competition with other ski resorts with respect to the entire package. Christy has not alleged, and it would not likely be plausible to allege, that DVRC's decision to foreclose competition in the ski rental business at the mid-mountain village will have any effect on the market for ski resort vacations as a whole.

Indeed, allowing resorts to decide for themselves what blend of vertical integration and third-party competition will produce the highest return may well increase competition in the ski resort business as a whole, and thus benefit consumers. This flexibility about business strategies induces entrants into the ski resort business by allowing them to reserve the benefits of their investments to themselves. . . .

Either line of reasoning—whether based on market definition or lack of anticompetitive conduct—leads to the same conclusion. Indeed, they are two sides of the same coin: having created a resort destination, antitrust will not force a resort developer to share its internal profit-making opportunities with competitors. The relevant market requirement reaches this result by finding implausible a market definition that singles out a small component of the cluster of services that constitutes the actual product; the anticompetitive conduct requirement reaches it by saying that it is not anticompetitive to refuse to grant access to competitors.

* * * * *

Although Christy insists that it has shown anticompetitive effects by its allegations of a decline in quantity and increase in price of rental skis at the mid-mountain village, this is just a repackaging of the argument rejected above. A resort operator's ability to reserve to itself the operation of ancillary businesses within the resort is not dependent on the quantity of output being as high or the price being as low as they would be if there were competition from third parties within the resort. It depends, instead, on either the proposition that a market that involves only one component of an interrelated package of services is not a relevant market for purposes of the Sherman Act or that it is not anticompetitive conduct for a resort owner to refuse to invite competitors to supply ancillary services within its resort. The fact . . . that fewer skis will be available for rental and that prices for rental skis will be higher, does not refute either of these legal propositions.

* * * * *

Affirmed.

Questions

1. *a.* Explain why the court concluded that "destination skiers at Deer Valley" or at "Deer Valley's mid-mountain village" constitute a market separate from ski rental outlets in nearby Park City.
   b. How did the Court define the "true product" market?

2. *a.* The plaintiff failed to establish the two core elements of its proof as required by the court. Explain those elements and describe why the court ruled against the plaintiff.
   b. How will consumers be protected from monopoly behavior by the defendant Deer Valley?

3. Why should Deer Valley be allowed to restrict output and raise prices by denying the plaintiff the continuing opportunity to rent skis at Deer Valley?

4. The U.S. government sued DuPont, claiming monopolization of the cellophane market. DuPont produced almost 75 percent of the cellophane sold in the United States. Cellophane constituted less than 20 percent of the "flexible packaging materials" market. The lower court found "[g]reat sensitivity of customers in the flexible packaging markets to price or quality changes."
   a. What is the relevant product market?
   b. Who wins the case? Explain. See *United States v. E.I. DuPont de Nemours & Co.*, 351 U.S. 377 (1956).

Monopoly Case II

The *Syufy* case that follows reflects what may be the dominant "ideological" view of monopoly among federal court judges. The decision embodies the free-market philosophy of the Reagan and Bush administrations and their judicial appointees, and it suggests an increasing judicial acceptance of the position that dominant market shares may be earned and maintained legitimately—particularly where competition can easily enter the market. Remember,

> Judge Kozinski managed to insert nearly 200 movie titles.

however, the Microsoft lesson that a dominant share gained and/or maintained by anticompetitive practices is impermissible.

The *Syufy* case is also notable because Judge Kozinski, in the spirit of the facts, managed to insert nearly 200 movie titles in his 25-page opinion (only a small portion of which is reprinted here).

LEGAL BRIEFCASE

U.S. v. Syufy Enterprises
903 F.2d 659 (9th Cir. 1990)

Circuit Judge Kozinski

Suspect that giant film distributors like Columbia, Paramount, and Twentieth Century Fox had fallen prey to Raymond Syufy, the canny operator of a chain of Las Vegas, Nevada, movie theaters, the U.S. Department of Justice brought this civil antitrust action to force Syufy to disgorge the theaters he had purchased in 1982–84 from his former competitors. The case is unusual in a number of respects: The Department of Justice concedes that moviegoers in Las Vegas suffered no direct injury as a result of the allegedly illegal transactions; nor does the record reflect complaints from Syufy's bought-out competitors, as the sales were made at fair prices and not precipitated by any monkey business; and the supposedly oppressed movie companies have weighed in on Syufy's side. The Justice Department nevertheless remains intent on rescuing this platoon of Goliaths from a single David.

After extensive discovery and an eight-and-a-half day trial, the learned district judge entered comprehensive findings of fact and conclusions of law, holding for Syufy. He found, inter alia, that Syufy's actions did not injure competition because there are no barriers to entry—others could and did enter the market—and that Syufy therefore did not have the power to control prices or exclude the competition. . . .

FACTS

Gone are the days when a movie ticket cost a dime, popcorn a nickel, and theaters had a single screen: This is the age of the multiplex. With more than 300 new films released every year—each potentially the next Batman or E.T.—many successful theaters today run a different film on each of their 6, 12, or 18 screens. . . .

Raymond Syufy understood the formula well. In 1981 he entered the Las Vegas market with a splash by opening a six-screen theater. Newly constructed and luxuriously furnished, it put existing facilities to shame. Syufy's entry into the Las Vegas market caused a stir, precipitating a titanic bidding war.

Soon theaters in Las Vegas were paying some of the highest license fees in the nation, while distributors sat back and watched the easy money roll in.

It is the nature of free enterprise that fierce, no-holds-barred competition will drive out the least effective participants in the market, providing the most efficient allocation of productive resources. And so it was in the Las Vegas movie market in 1982. After a hard-fought battle among several contenders, Syufy gained the upper hand. Two of his rivals, Mann Theatres and Plitt Theatres, saw their future as rocky and decided to sell out to Syufy. While Mann and Plitt are major exhibitors nationwide, neither had a large presence in Las Vegas. Mann operated two indoor theaters with a total of three screens; Plitt operated a single theater with three screens. Things were relatively quiet until September 1984; in September Syufy entered into earnest negotiations with Cragin Industries, his largest remaining competitor. Cragin sold out to Syufy midway through October, leaving Roberts Company, a small exhibitor of mostly second-run films, as Syufy's only competitor for first-run films in Las Vegas.

It is these three transactions—Syufy's purchases of the Mann, Plitt, and Cragin theaters—that the Justice Department claims amount to antitrust violations. As government counsel explained at oral argument, the thrust of its case is that "you may not get monopoly power by buying out your competitors.". . .

DISCUSSION

* * * * *

[O]f significance is the government's concession that Syufy was only a monopsonist, not a monopolist. Thus the government argues that Syufy had market power, but that he exercised this power only against suppliers (film distributors), not against consumers (moviegoers). This is consistent with the record, which demonstrates that Syufy always treated moviegoers fairly: The movie tickets, popcorn, nuts, and the Seven-Ups cost about the same in Las Vegas as in other, comparable markets. While it is theoretically possible to have a middleman who is a monopolist upstream but not downstream, this is a somewhat counterintuitive scenario. Why, if he truly had significant market power, would Raymond Syufy have chosen to take advantage of the big movie distributors while giving a fair shake to ordinary people? And why do the distributors, the alleged victims of the monopolization scheme, think that Raymond Syufy is the best thing that ever happened to the Las Vegas movie market?

* * * * *

There is universal agreement that monopoly power is the power to exclude competition or control prices. . . .

1. Power to Exclude Competition

It is true, of course, that when Syufy acquired Mann's, Plitt's, and Cragin's theaters he temporarily diminished the number of competitors in the Las Vegas first-run film market. But this does not necessarily indicate foul play; many legitimate market arrangements diminish the number of competitors. . . . If there are no significant barriers to entry, however, eliminating competitors will not enable the survivors to reap a monopoly profit; any attempt to raise prices above the competitive level will lure into the market new competitors able and willing to offer their commercial goods or personal services for less. . . .

* * * * *

The district court. . . . found that there were no barriers to entry in the Las Vegas movie market. . . . Our review of the record discloses that the district court's finding is amply supported by the record.

* * * * *

Immediately after Syufy bought out the last of his three competitors in October 1984, he was riding high, having captured 100 percent of the first-run film market in Las Vegas. But this utopia proved to be only a mirage. That same month, a major movie distributor, Orion, stopped doing business with Syufy, sending all of its first-run films to Roberts Company, a dark-horse competitor previously relegated to the second-run market. Roberts Company took this as an invitation to step into the major league and, against all odds, began giving Syufy serious competition in the first-run market. Fighting fire with fire, Roberts opened three multiplexes within a 13-month period, each having six or more screens. By December 1986, Roberts was operating 28 screens, trading places with Syufy, who had only 23. At the same time, Roberts was displaying a healthy portion of all first-run films. In fact, Roberts got exclusive exhibition rights to many of its films, meaning that Syufy could not show them at all.

By the end of 1987, Roberts was showing a larger percentage of first-run films than was the Redrock multiplex at the time Syufy bought it. Roberts then sold its theaters to United

Artists, the largest theater chain in the country, and Syufy continued losing ground. It all boils down to this: Syufy's acquisitions did not short-circuit the operation of the natural market forces; Las Vegas's first-run film market was more competitive when this case came to trial than before Syufy bought out Mann, Plitt, and Cragin.

The Justice Department correctly points out that Syufy still has a large market share, but attributes far too much importance to this fact. In evaluating monopoly power, it is not market share that counts, but the ability to maintain market share. . . . Syufy seems unable to do this. In 1985 Syufy managed to lock up exclusive exhibition rights to 91 percent of all the first-run films in Las Vegas. By the first quarter of 1988, that percentage had fallen to 39 percent; United Artists had exclusive rights to another 25 percent, with the remaining 36 percent being played on both Syufy and UA screens.

Syufy's share of box office receipts also dropped off, albeit less precipitously. In 1985 Syufy raked in 93 percent of the gross box office from first-run films in Las Vegas. By the first quarter of 1988, that figure had fallen to 75 percent. The government insists that 75 percent is still a large number, and we are hard-pressed to disagree, but that's not the point.

* * * * *

The numbers reveal that Roberts/UA has steadily been eating away at Syufy's market share: In two and a half years, Syufy's percentage of exclusive exhibition rights dropped 52 percent and its percentage of box office receipts dropped 18 percent. During the same period, Roberts/UA's newly opened theaters evolved from absolute beginners, barely staying alive, into a big business.

* * * * *

2. Power to Control Prices

The crux of the Justice Department's case is that Syufy, top gun in the Las Vegas movie market, had the power to push around Hollywood's biggest players, dictating to them what prices they could charge for their movies. The district court found otherwise. This finding too has substantial support in the record.

Perhaps the most telling evidence of Syufy's inability to set prices came from movie distributors, Syufy's supposed victims. At the trial, distributors uniformly proclaimed their satisfaction with the way the Las Vegas first-run film market operates; none complained about the license fees paid by Syufy. . . . Particularly damaging to the government's case was the testimony of the former head of distribution for MGM/UA that his company "never had any difficulty . . . in acquiring the terms that we thought were reasonable,". . . explaining that the license fees Syufy paid "were comparable or better than any place in the United States. And in most cases better.". . .

The documentary evidence bears out this testimony. Syufy has at all times paid license fees far in excess of the national average, even higher than those paid by exhibitors in Los Angeles, the Mecca of Moviedom. In fact, Syufy paid a higher percentage of his gross receipts to distributors in 1987 and 1988 than he did during the intensely competitive period just before he acquired Cragin's Redrock.

While successful, Syufy is in no position to put the squeeze on distributors. . . .

* * * * *

It is a tribute to the state of competition in America that the Antitrust Division of the Department of Justice has found no worthier target than this paper tiger on which to expend limited taxpayer resources. Yet we cannot help but wonder whether bringing a lawsuit like this, and pursuing it doggedly through 27 months of pretrial proceedings, about two weeks of trial, and now the full distance on appeal, really serves the interests of free competition.

Affirmed.

Questions

1. At one point, Syufy held 100 percent of the first-run market. Why was Syufy not a monopolist?

2. Is this decision rooted more in structural (market share) or conduct (e.g., predatory pricing) considerations? Explain.

3. What role did the issue of Syufy's intent to monopolize play in this case? Explain.

4. Assume we have historical data showing that when the price of rolled steel has increased, the sales volume of rolled aluminum has remained constant. What, if anything, does that fact tell us about the product market for rolled steel?

5. Define the product market for championship boxing matches. See *United States v. International Boxing Club of New York, Inc.*, 358 U.S. 242 (1959).

6. Adidas provides cash, sporting goods, and the like to universities in exchange for various promotional rights, including the team's or coach's agreement to wear Adidas clothing in athletic activities. National Collegiate Athletic Association (NCAA) rules limit the amount of advertising that may appear on a uniform being used in competition. Adidas sued the NCAA claiming, among other things, that the advertising restrictions constitute an attempted monopoly by the NCAA. In pursuing its monopoly claim, Adidas defined the relevant market as "the market for the sale of NCAA Promotional Rights." The NCAA responded by saying that a market consisting solely of the sale of promotional rights by NCAA member institutions (colleges and universities) on athletic apparel used in intercollegiate activity is not a plausible relevant market.

   a. Define the relevant product market from the NCAA point of view.

   b. How would the court decide where the product market actually lies? See *Adidas America, Inc v. NCAA*, 64 F.Supp.2d 1097 (1999).

PRACTICING ETHICS   Break Up the Biggest Banks?

Sanford Weill, one of the most famous names in banking history and the architect of one of the biggest financial mergers, the 1998 combination of Citicorp and Travelers Group, spoke to America's ongoing financial crisis in 2012:

> What we should probably do is go split up investment baking from banking, have banks be deposit-takers, have banks make commercial loans and real estate loans, have banks do something that's not going to risk the taxpayer dollars, that's not too big to fail."

By 2006 Weill had relinquished his Citicorp duties, and his colossal bank was reduced to taking huge government bailout funds during the recent financial crisis. His strategy had failed his bank and arguably threatened the welfare of the nation. Weill was reduced, basically, to calling for a return to the 1933 Glass–Steagall Act (separating commercial and investment banking), which Congress repealed in 1999, much to the delight of Wall Street bosses.

Questions

1. Do you believe the Wall Street banking industry operates by different ethical rules from those practiced by your hometown bankers? Explain.

2. Does the extraordinary size of the big banks (the five biggest: Bank of America, Citigroup, Goldman Sachs, JPMorgan Chase, Wells Fargo), of itself, lead to wrongful practices in those banks? Put another way, is bigness bad?

Source: Roben Farzad, "Sandy Weill's Untimely Second Thoughts," *Bloomberg Businessweek*, July 25, 2012 [**www.businessweek.com**/].

Questions—Part One

1. *a.* *The Harvard Law Review* argued, "In the New Economy (information technology) . . . there will inevitably be an increasing number of markets with only a few dominant players."[9] Why would that be so?

   b. Are we mistaken in pursuing Microsoft and other "new economy" giants with "old economy" antitrust principles? Explain.

2. Worldwide Basketball Sports Tours promoted early-season, NCAA-certified basketball tournaments. The National Collegiate Athletic Association's Two in Four Rule limited college basketball teams to "not more than one certified basketball event in one academic year, and not more than two certified basketball events every four years." The promoters sued the NCAA on antitrust grounds, claiming the Two in Four rule hampered their ability to make money. The NCAA argued that the limit on games was academically motivated.

   a. Does antitrust law apply to Division I collegiate basketball? Explain.

   b. Define the product market in this case. See *Worldwide Basketball & Sports Tours, Inc. v. NCAA*, 388 F.3d 955 (6th Cir. 2004).

3. *a.* A traditional concern about monopolies is that a lack of competition discourages efficiency and innovation. Argue that monopolies may actually encourage innovation.

   b. Even if monopolies do not discourage invention, we have firm economic grounds for opposing monopolies. Explain.

4. Real estate developer Ernest Coleman built an apartment complex in Stilwell, Oklahoma (population 2,700), and ordered electric service from an out-of-town utility, Ozark Electric. Stilwell officials said they would deny him city water and sewer service if he did not buy his electricity from the city-owned utility service. Because he could not buy water or sewer service elsewhere, Coleman decided to switch to Stilwell's utility. In 1996, the federal Justice Department sued Stilwell. Explain the federal government's complaint and decide the case. See Bryan Gruley, "Little Town Becomes First Municipality Sued by U.S. for Antitrust," *The Wall Street Journal,* June 3, 1996, p. A1.

5. Historically, perhaps the most important interpretation of the Sherman Act's proscription of monopolization was Judge Learned Hand's opinion in the *Alcoa* case. After finding that Alcoa controlled 90 percent of the aluminum ingot market, Hand had to determine whether Alcoa possessed a general intent to monopolize. Hand concluded that Alcoa's market dominance could have resulted only from a "persistent determination" to maintain control:

   > It was not inevitable that it should always anticipate increases in the demand for ingots and be prepared to supply them. Nothing compelled it to keep doubling and redoubling its capacity before others entered the field. It insists that it never excluded competitors; but we can think of no more effective exclusion than progressively to embrace each new opportunity as it opened, and to face every newcomer with new capacity already geared into a great organization.[10]

   Comment on Judge Hand's remarks.

6. Several smaller airlines sued two giants, United and American, claiming that the two violated the Sherman Act through their computerized reservation systems (CRSs). The heart of the plaintiffs' position was that United and American were monopolists who violated the law by denying other airlines reasonable access to their CRSs. American

and United had the largest CRSs, but other airlines also maintained CRSs. Neither had blocked any other airline's access to its CRS, but they had charged fees (in American's case, $1.75 per booking to the airline that secured a passenger through American's CRS). United and American each controlled about 12 to 14 percent of the total air transportation market. According to the court, the plaintiffs were "unhappy" about United and American's ability to extract booking fees from them for the use of the CRSs. The U.S. Ninth Circuit Court of Appeals ruled for the defendants, and the Supreme Court declined to review this case.

a. Explain why the plaintiffs felt wronged by American and United.

b. Explain the defendants's argument that they could not successfully charge "excessive" prices for the use of the CRSs. See *Alaska Airlines v. United Airlines,* 948 F.2d 536 (9th Cir. 1991), cert. den. 112 S.Ct. 1603 (1992).

Part Two—Mergers

At this writing in 2013, merger activity remains generally flat following the recession, but corporations are holding vast pools of cash so a new merger boom is not out of the question. The two most notable recent mergers are the $23 billion takeover of Pittsburgh ketchup maker, H.J. Heinz, by 3G Capital and Berkshire Hathaway, and the $11 billion merger of American Airlines and US Airways, creating the world's largest airline. The American Airlines and US Airways merger had been challenged by the federal Justice Department, but a settlement was reached requiring the combined airline (to be called American Airlines Group) to sell dozens of take-off and landing slots at key airports to discount competitors. At the same time, a private antitrust action has been filed claiming the merger may result in higher fares, reduced capacity, and other problems. American and US Airways say the merger will lower costs and allow American Airlines Group to better compete with entrenched giants Delta Air Lines and United Airlines. The government believes the settlement, giving low-cost airlines a bigger foothold at key airports, will produce more competitive pricing.

In general, the Obama Justice Department and the FTC have kept a close eye on potentially threatening mergers. Indeed, government resistance in 2011 caused AT&T, the nation's second-largest cell phone company, to give up its 2011 plan to acquire T-Mobile (fourth largest) for some $39 billion. Had the deal gone through, AT&T and Verizon would have controlled two-thirds of all wireless subscribers and about 80 percent of wireless revenue.[11] Regulators said the merger would have led to higher prices and lower-quality products in a less-competitive mobile wireless market. Nonetheless, *The Wall Street Journal* criticized the government's market intervention:

> Never mind that the FCC [recently] said that wireless competition was thriving and that most consumers have the choice of five or more providers. Or that market leader Verizon and third-largest player Sprint weren't about to roll over. . . . Or that new competitors are entering the market. . . .[12]

Sometimes mergers and the risk of rising consumer prices may be necessary to save failing companies, as was claimed by supporters of the US Airways and American Airlines deal. Sterne Agee analyst Jeff Kauffman advised that the bankrupt American could not stand alone:

> We believe that the stand-alone plan would have left [American] with a disadvantaged infrastructure, too small to compete effectively with carriers 40 percent larger for business travel, and too large to be a niche carrier and compete with carriers smaller and more nimble.[13]

Thus, some mergers may be considered a business necessity, but not infrequently they are much better for shareholders than for consumers. *The New York Times* in 2010 cited a study finding higher prices in oil after Pennzoil acquired Quaker State, in tampons after Procter & Gamble bought Tambrands, in cereal after General Mills acquired Chex brands, and in scotch whiskey after the merger of Guinness and Grand Metropolitan.[14] Nonetheless, in a global economy where oligopolies increasingly mark the landscape, mergers can make a great deal of economic sense.

Why? Technological change, efficiency enhancement, and piles of available cash are often important motivators for merger activity; but the big drivers often are growth opportunities and cost cutting. Many companies have extracted maximum value from their own products, making growth possible only by purchasing new lines, and cost savings have become essential in fierce global competition.

Merger Virtues

Mergers often have clearly beneficial effects. Some of the potential virtues of mergers include:

1. Mergers permit the replacement of inefficient management, and the threat of replacement disciplines managers to be more productive.
2. Mergers may permit stronger competition with previously larger rivals.
3. Mergers may improve credit access.
4. Mergers may produce efficiencies including economies of scale.
5. Mergers frequently offer a pool of liquid assets for use in expansion and in innovation.
6. Very often, mergers offer tax advantages.
7. Growth by merger is often less expensive than internal growth.
8. Mergers help satisfy the personal ambitions and needs of management.[15]

PRACTICING ETHICS Mergers That Abuse Customers?

In 2011, the federal government approved, with restrictions, a merger giving Comcast, the cable TV giant, a controlling interest in the NBC television network. Among other concerns, critics feared the merger would allow Comcast to arbitrarily favor NBC channels over those of competitors. Then in 2013, Comcast announced it was buying the remaining 49 percent of NBCUniversal. From the inception of the merger discussions, one of the parties most concerned was the Santa Monica, California-based Tennis Channel, which feared Comcast would favor its own sports channels (Golf Channel and NBC Sports Network) over the Tennis Channel and other independents.

The Tennis Channel filed a complaint with the Federal Communications Commission alleging that Comcast is violating the law and the terms of the merger agreement by favorable placement for the Golf Channel and NBC Sports Network while leaving the Tennis Channel on a little-watched sports tier. Comcast says the channel placements reflect market realities and a long-term contract signed when the Tennis Channel was a start-up. In 2012, the FCC ruled for the Tennis Channel finding that Comcast was violating federal antidiscrimination carriage rules. At this writing, the case is on appeal at the U.S. Court of Appeals for the D.C. Circuit (Case No. 12-1337) where the primary questions appear to be the statute of limitations for such complaints and whether restrictions on Comcast's treatment of the Tennis Channel would violate Comcast's freedom of speech.

Questions

1. Do you think Comcast has a responsibility to treat the independent Tennis Channel the same as its own affiliate sports networks, including the Golf Channel and NBC Sports Network? Explain.

2. If you were running a business would you treat all of your customers the same, regardless of their contributions to your bottom line? Explain.

3. In your view, should the government require Comcast to treat the Tennis Channel as well as it treats its own sports channels? Explain.

Sources: Michael Hiltzik, "Tennis Channel Gets No Love from Comcast," *latimes.com,* November 9, 2011 **[latimes.com/sports/la-fi-hiltzik-20111109,0,2769562.column]**; and Alina Selyukh, "Court Grills FCC, Tennis Channel in Comcast Discrimination Suit," *Reuters,* February 25, 2013 **[www.reuters.com/]**.

Merger Problems

Many studies show that mergers often fail in the sense that they do not add value to the merging companies. Experts generally estimate the merger failure rate, measured in

> "Mergers Fail More Often than Marriages."

various ways, at between 50 and 80 percent. As *CNN.com* described it, "Mergers Fail More Often than Marriages."[16] In addition to those frequent financial failures, other merger hazards should be noted:

1. Too much power is being concentrated in too few hands.
2. A particular merger, although not threatening in and of itself, may trigger a merger movement among industry competitors.
3. Higher market concentration may lead to higher prices.
4. Innovation may be harmed.
5. Some companies are so large that they can significantly shape political affairs.
6. Some companies may have become so large that we cannot allow them to fail.[17]

When Should the Government Intervene?   The U.S. Justice Department faced that question in reviewing Anheuser-Busch InBev's (ABI) proposed $20.1 billion acquisition of the 50 percent of Mexican brewer Grupo Modelo not already owned by ABI.[18] In early 2013, the Justice Department filed civil antitrust charges to block that deal; later that year the case was settled when ABI agreed to sell all of Grupo Modelo's U.S. assets (including beers such as Corona and Pacifico) and some other holdings to Constellation Brands, one of the world's largest wine companies.

Justice's core concern was that the acquisition would eliminate Modelo as a restraint on ABI's capacity to raise prices, increase its market share, and coordinate pricing policies with the remaining brewers. Justice noted that ABI had been raising prices with regularity and that even small price increases could lead to billions in total increased costs for consumers.[19] The

Justice Department also feared that the absorption of Modelo could result in reduced innovation. The settlement apparently diminished those Justice Department reservations.

ABI, SABMiller, and Grupo Modelo jointly control 72 percent of the $80 billion U.S. beer market.[20] ABI, the world's largest brewer, is the product of a 2008 merger between Anheuser-Busch and InBev, a Belgian-Brazilian goliath. The international brewing market has been consolidating rapidly such that a few companies are now dominant. ABI itself reportedly has announced a total of 15 takeovers since the middle of 2008.[21] Of course, small craft breweries have been an exploding market, although they still account for only about 6 percent of sales.[22]

On the other hand, the acquisition likely will help ABI reduce costs, a matter of particular concern for Budweiser whose sales have slumped for 25 consecutive years.[23] Further, the acquisition will strengthen ABI for what *The New York Times* has referred to as "the big beer fight of the 21st century;" the competition for lucrative new markets in China, India, Latin America, and the wealthier nations in Africa.[24] International competition is already fierce with ABI challenged by Denmark's Carlsberg, Britain's SABMiller, and Japan's Asahi. Thus, ABI and many experts argue that the merger is simply part of a much larger global pattern of consolidation necessary to operate efficiently. Indeed, since InBev acquired Anheuser-Busch, the new organization cut costs by several billion dollars and instituted tighter organizational controls.

Merger Law: Overview

Mergers are addressed by the Sherman Act, Section 1; but the Clayton Act, Section 7, offers the primary legislative oversight:

> That no person engaged in commerce shall acquire the whole or any part of the stock or the assets of another person engaged also in commerce where the effect of such acquisition may be substantially to lessen competition, or to tend to create a monopoly.

Technically, a merger involves the union of two or more enterprises wherein the property of all is transferred to the one remaining firm. However, antitrust law embraces all those situations in which previously independent business entities are united—whether by acquisition of stock, purchase of physical assets, creation of holding companies, consolidation, or merger.

Mergers fall, somewhat awkwardly, into three categories:

1. A horizontal merger involves firms that are in direct competition and occupy the same product and geographic markets. A merger of two vodka producers in the same geographic market would clearly fall in the horizontal category. Would the merger of a vodka producer and a gin producer constitute a horizontal merger?

2. A vertical merger involves two or more firms at different levels of the same channel of distribution, such as a furniture manufacturer and a fabric supplier.

3. A conglomerate merger involves firms dealing in unrelated products. Thus, the conglomerate category embraces all mergers that are neither horizontal nor vertical. An example of such a merger would be the acquisition of a pet food manufacturer by a book publisher. (Conglomerate mergers currently receive little attention from the government, and we will not examine them further.)

Premerger Notification   Under the Hart–Scott–Rodino Antitrust Improvements Act (HSR), mergers and acquisitions must be reported to the Federal Trade Commission and the Justice Department if those deals exceed certain dollar thresholds that change annually in accord with the gross national product. [For more HSR threshold details, see **www.ftc.gov/bc/hsr/index .shtm**] The parties are barred from closing the merger until 30 days after they have made the required HSR filing unless the waiting period is shortened (as it often is) or lengthened by the FTC or the Justice Department. The merging firms are required to provide documentation about the merger's impact on competition. The waiting period gives the government time and information by which to determine whether the merger should be challenged.

Remedies   After the HSR review, the government may decide that the merger is not threatening, and it will be allowed to proceed. The government may, on the other hand, conclude that the merger is anticompetitive. If the parties persist with a disfavored merger, the government can file suit. The preferred action, however, is to work out an agreeable settlement. A settlement might involve one of the parties selling some of its assets as we saw in the US Airways and American Airlines settlement explained above, or agreeing to forgo business in some geographic segment of the market for a time. Rental car stalwart Hertz, in 2012, secured FTC approval for its $2.3 billion acquisition of Dollar Thrifty (parent of the Dollar and Thrifty car rental brands) only after agreeing to sell both its Advantage car rental business and 29 existing Dollar Thrifty on-airport locations. The FTC feared reduced competition at 72 airports nationwide. Hertz has a 26 percent share of the U.S. airport car rental market and Thrifty holds a 12 percent share. Enterprise is the largest car rental company, trailed by Hertz and Dollar Thrifty, while fourth-place Advantage is now expected to become an effective competitor in the market.[25]

In cases where negotiation fails and the government decides to sue, it can ask the court for a remedy, such as an order stopping the merger or an order requiring divestiture of certain assets. Government litigation is infrequent, but the resulting message to the business community is powerful. Furthermore, private parties commonly use the antitrust laws to sue for treble damages when they believe a merger has harmed them unlawfully. The threat of those private actions as well as government oversight helps maintain a marketplace where consumers are offered the benefits of vigorous competition including lower prices, improved quality, and innovation. [To read summaries of recent developments in antitrust law, see *Antitrust Today* at **www.antitrusttoday.com/**]

[For a humorous treatment of mergers, see Stephen Colbert's 2007 video segment, "Mega-Mergers," at **www.businessinsider.com/stephen-colbert-att-2011-3**]

Horizontal Analysis

Horizontal mergers raise anticompetitive risks because direct rivals seek to join together. Horizontal merger analysis ordinarily follows the FTC/Justice Department merger guidelines, which focus on a pair of concerns:

1. **Coordinated effects/collusion.** Will the merger facilitate cooperation so that the parties might fix prices, reduce output, reduce quality, or otherwise coordinate their activities

rather than competing against each other? Broadly, the government takes the position that fewer firms and thus greater market concentration increases the likelihood of collusion—a position the courts often, but not always, embrace.

2. **Unilateral effects.** Will the merger allow a firm to unilaterally raise prices, restrict output, or control innovation? Normally, unilateral effects arise with products that significantly restrain each other prior to the merger. A merger's removal of a rival could allow the newly merged entity to exercise market power.

Market Power

Broadly, the guidelines are designed to identify mergers that may result in market power, defined as the ability of a seller "profitably to maintain prices above competitive levels for a significant period of time." The guidelines set out a five-step methodology for analyzing horizontal mergers:

1. Market definition.
2. Measurement of market concentration.
3. Identification of likely anticompetitive effects.
4. Likelihood of future entrants to the market.
5. Appraisal of efficiencies and other possible defenses.

Market

The market will be defined as the smallest product and geographic market in which a hypothetical monopolist could raise prices a small but significant and nontransitory amount (usually set at 5 percent above current prices).

Market Concentration

The Herfindahl–Hirschman Index (HHI) is employed to measure market concentration. Notwithstanding the formidable title, the index is computed quite easily. The market share of each firm is squared and the results are summed. Thus, if five companies each had 20 percent of a market, the index for that market would be 2,000. The HHI is useful because it measures both concentration and dispersion of market share between big and small firms. If 10 firms each have 10 percent of the market, the resulting HHI is 1,000. The larger the HHI, the more concentrated the market. In general, a postmerger HHI below 1,500 would reflect an unconcentrated market while a postmerger concentration of between 1,500 and 2,500 would be considered mildly concentrated and more than 2,500 a highly concentrated market. The greater the HHI and the greater the increase in the HHI, the more likely the government will be concerned about the merger. Thus, the aforementioned American Airlines and U.S. Airways merger with an HHI of 1,269 among the top four carriers in the national market (American after the merger—20 percent, Southwest—18 percent, United Continental—17 percent, and Delta—16 percent) would be classified as "unconcentrated."[26]

The guidelines provide that the potential for competitive concern also depends on the analysis of additional factors, such as a change in the number of competitors along with adverse effects and ease of entry, as explained below. Broadly, the government's guidelines reject the older notion of market size *alone* as a threat to the welfare of the economy.

Adverse Effects

The basic point here is the government's worry that the merger may permit monopoly behavior in the merged firm's market.

Ease of Entry

If new competitors can readily enter the postmerger market, the existing firms will be forced to charge competitive prices and otherwise conform to the discipline of the market.

Defenses

An otherwise unacceptable merger may be saved by certain defenses. The *failing company doctrine* permits a merger to preserve the assets of a firm that would otherwise be lost to the market. *Efficiencies* include such desirable economic results as economies of scale or reduced transportation costs as a result of the merger.

Guideline Changes

In 2010, the Justice Department and the Federal Trade Commission announced revisions to the Horizontal Merger Guidelines that bring the Guidelines more in line with actual government practice. Much of the analysis will continue as outlined above, but a key revision involves a reduced role for market definition/market share and increased attention to likely adverse competitive effects. The new reasoning is that the analysis will begin in identifying practical, real-world competitive harm (such as customer injury, reduced innovation, or reduced product variety) at which point market definition and the balance of the analysis outlined above would be influential. This approach may, therefore, allow the government greater flexibility in proving competition problems even if high market shares cannot be established. Future antitrust decisions will indicate how closely the courts actually follow the new guidance.

Horizontal Merger Blocked

The Justice Department's successful 2011 challenge to a proposed horizontal merger between tax preparers H&R Block and TaxACT illustrates many of the aforementioned considerations described to evaluate the legality of a horizontal merger. Judge Beryl Howell at the District Court for the District of Columbia agreed with the Justice Department that the relevant product market was digital do-it-yourself (DDIY) tax preparation products (thus excluding assisted and manual tax preparation) with the three largest firms controlling 90 percent of the market (Intuit—62.2 percent, HRB—15.6 percent, and TaxACT—12.8 percent) and the remaining 10 percent split among a number of smaller firms. The merger would have increased the HHI in the DDIY market by 400 points to 4,691. The court concluded that H&R Block had failed to show that collusion would not result in what would have become a highly concentrated postmerger market.

Judge Howell also considered various company documents; in one H&R Block allegedly said the merger would allow it to "regain control of industry pricing and avoid further price erosion." When looking at anticompetitive effects from the proposed merger, the court reasoned that TaxACT's "impressive history of innovation and competition in the DDIY market," had been important in constraining prices, a role that would have disappeared had the merger been consummated. Given these considerations and insufficient evidence that dramatic efficiencies would accompany the merger, Judge Howell ruled for the government.

H&R Block announced that it would not appeal. For the government, the victory was important evidence of its commitment to vigorous antitrust oversight.

Sources: King & Spaulding, "DOJ Antitrust Division Wins Major Victory in H&R Block Case," *Client Alert,* November 17, 2011 **[www.kslaw.com/]**; Michael H. Pryor, "What the H&R Block Merger Opinion Can Tell Us about the AT&T/T-Mobile Merger Case," *LEXOLOGY,* November 16, 2011 **[www.lexology.com/]**; and *United States of America v. H&R Block, Inc.,* 833 F. Supp.2d 36 (U.S. Dist. Ct. DC 2011).

Vertical Analysis

A vertical merger typically involves an alliance between a supplier and a purchaser. The primary resulting threat to competition is labeled *market foreclosure*. As illustrated in Figure 11.1, a vertical merger may deny a source of supply to a purchaser or an outlet for sale to a seller, thus potentially threatening competition in violation of the Clayton Act. The government would then look closely at that foreclosure to determine whether it actually has an anticompetitive effect. In addition to foreclosing sources of supply or outlets for sale, the government may be concerned about other anticompetitive effects such as raising rivals' costs, facilitating collusion, and raising barriers to entry.

FIGURE 11.1
Vertical Merger.

A supplies B. A and B merge. X (A's competitor) had traditionally sold to B, and Y (B's competitor) had traditionally purchased from A. Is the merger lawful? How do we decide?

Vertical Merger Challenge   The government has practiced a generally lenient approach to vertical mergers, but under some conditions they will be challenged. That was the case with

Ticketmaster–Live Nation merger.

the Ticketmaster–Live Nation merger that was largely vertical in character although it included some horizontal features. Ticketmaster, the nation's largest ticketing company, also owns a controlling share in Front Line Management whose 200-plus clients include the Eagles and Miley Cyrus.[27] Live Nation, the country's largest concert promoter, was a recent entrant to the ticketing business.[28] Live Nation also owns or manages 135 major concert venues around the world, is the world's largest artist-management company, and operates related businesses including online fan clubs and T-shirts.[29] Obama administration antitrust officials made it clear that the government would resist the merger.[30] Litigation was not necessary, however, because the merger partners and the Justice Department in 2010 agreed to a settlement allowing the creation of the new company—to be called Live Nation Entertainment. Ticketmaster agreed to divest itself of one of its ticketing divisions while licensing its ticketing software to a competitor, thus effectively allowing the creation of two new competitors for Ticketmaster. The newly merged firm also agreed to Justice Department monitoring to enforce "tough anti-retaliation provisions" so Live Nation Entertainment will not be able to abuse its power in ticketing, concert venues, artist management, and concert touring.[31]

Horizontal Merger Case

The Staples–Office Depot litigation that follows illustrates the standard horizontal merger analysis.

LEGAL BRIEFCASE

Federal Trade Commission v. Staples, Inc. and Office Depot, Inc. 970 F.Supp. 1066 (D.D.C. 1997)

Judge Hogan

BACKGROUND

* * * * *

Staples is the second largest office superstore chain in the United States with approximately 550 retail stores located in 28 states and the District of Columbia, primarily in the Northeast and California. In 1996, Staples' revenues from those stores were approximately $4 billion through all operations. Office Depot, the largest office superstore chain, operates over 500 retail office supply superstores that are located in 38 states and the District of Columbia, primarily in the South and Midwest. Office Depot's 1996 sales were approximately $6.1 billion. OfficeMax, Inc., is the only other office supply superstore firm in the United States.

On September 4, 1996, defendants Staples and Office Depot . . . entered into an "Agreement and Plan of Merger" whereby . . . Office Depot would become a wholly owned subsidiary of Staples. . . . The FTC filed this suit on April 9, 1997, seeking a temporary restraining order and preliminary injunction against the merger. . . .

I. Discussion

Analysis of the likely competitive effects of a merger requires determinations of (1) the "line of commerce" or product market in which to assess the transaction, (2) the "section of the

country" or geographic market in which to assess the transaction, and (3) the transaction's probable effect on competition in the product and geographic markets.

II. The Geographic Market

One of the few issues about which the parties to this case do not disagree is that metropolitan areas are the appropriate geographic markets for analyzing the competitive effects of the proposed merger. In its first amended complaint, the FTC identified 42 such metropolitan areas as well as future areas which could suffer anticompetitive effects from the proposed merger. . . .

III. The Relevant Product Market

* * * * *

The Commission defines the relevant product market as "the sale of consumable office supplies through office superstores," with "consumable" meaning products that consumers buy recurrently, i.e., items which "get used up" or discarded. For example, under the Commission's definition, "consumable office supplies" would not include capital goods such as computers, fax machines, and other business machines or office furniture, but does include such products as paper, pens, file folders, self-stick notes, computer disks, and toner cartridges. The defendants characterize the FTC's product market definition as "contrived" with no basis in law or fact, and counter that the appropriate product market within which to assess the likely competitive consequences of a Staples–Office Depot combination is simply the overall sale of office products, of which a combined Staples–Office Depot accounted for 5.5 percent of total sales in North America in 1996.

* * * * *

The general rule when determining a relevant product market is that "[t]he outer boundaries of a product market are determined by the reasonable interchangeability of use [by consumers] or the cross-elasticity of demand between the product itself and substitutes for it." Interchangeability of use and cross-elasticity of demand look to the availability of substitute commodities, i.e., whether there are other products offered to consumers which are similar in character or use to the product or products in question. . . .

[T]he Commission has argued that a slight but significant increase in Staples–Office Depot's prices will not cause a considerable number of Staples–Office Depot's customers to purchase consumable office supplies from other nonsuperstore alternatives such as Wal-Mart, Best Buy, Quill, or Viking. On the other hand, the Commission has argued that an increase in price by Staples would result in consumers turning to another office superstore, especially Office Depot, if the consumers had that option. Therefore, the Commission concludes that the sale of consumable office supplies by office supply superstores is the appropriate relevant product market in this case, and products sold by competitors such as Wal-Mart, Best Buy, Viking, Quill, and others should be excluded. . . .

The Court acknowledges that there is, in fact, a broad market encompassing the sale of consumable office supplies by all sellers of such supplies, and that those sellers must, at some level, compete with one another. However, the mere fact that a firm may be termed a competitor in the overall marketplace does not necessarily require that it be included in the relevant product market for antitrust purposes. The Supreme Court has recognized that within a broad market, "well-defined submarkets may exist which, in themselves, constitute product markets for antitrust purposes."

* * * * *

[In defining the submarket] the FTC focused on what it termed the "pricing evidence." . . . First, the FTC presented evidence comparing Staples' prices in geographic markets where Staples is the only office superstore, to markets where Staples competes with Office Depot or OfficeMax, or both. Based on the FTC's calculations, in markets where Staples faces no office superstore competition at all, something which was termed a one-firm market during the hearing, prices are 13 percent higher than in three-firm markets where it competes with both Office Depot and OfficeMax.

* * * * *

This evidence suggests that office superstore prices are affected primarily by other office superstores and not by nonsuperstore competitors such as mass merchandisers like Wal-Mart, Kmart, or Target, wholesale clubs such as BJ's, Sam's, and Price Costco, computer or electronic stores such as Computer City and Best Buy, independent retail office supply stores, mail-order firms like Quill and Viking, and contract stationers.

* * * * *

In addition, Staples' own pricing information shows that warehouse clubs have very little effect on Staples' prices.

* * * * *

There is similar evidence with respect to the defendants' behavior when faced with entry of another competitor. The evidence shows that the defendants change their price zones when faced with entry of another superstore, but do not do so for other retailers.

* * * * *

Despite the high degree of functional interchangeability between consumable office supplies sold by the office superstores and other retailers of office supplies, the evidence presented by the Commission shows that even where Staples and Office Depot charge higher prices, certain consumers do not go elsewhere for their supplies. This further demonstrates that the sale of office supplies by non-superstore retailers is not responsive to the higher prices charged by Staples and Office Depot in the one-firm markets. This indicates a low cross-elasticity of demand between the consumable office supplies sold by superstores and those sold by other sellers.

* * * * *

The Court has observed that office supply superstores look far different from other sellers of office supplies. Office supply superstores are high-volume, discount office supply chain stores averaging in excess of 20,000 square feet, with over 11,000 of those square feet devoted to traditional office supplies, and carrying over 5,000 SKUs of consumable office supplies in addition to computers, office furniture, and other nonconsumables. In contrast, stores such as Kmart devote approximately 210 square feet to the sale of approximately 250 SKUs of consumable office supplies. Kinko's devotes approximately 50 square feet to the sale of 150 SKUs. Both Sam's Club and Computer City each sell approximately 200 SKUs.

In addition to the differences in SKU numbers and variety, the superstores are different from many other sellers of office supplies due to the type of customer they target and attract. The superstores' customer base overwhelmingly consists of small businesses with fewer than 20 employees and consumers with home offices. In contrast, mail-order customers are typically midsized companies with more than 20 employees. . . .

* * * * *

[T]he Court finds that the unique combination of size, selection, depth, and breadth of inventory offered by the superstores distinguishes them from other retailers.

* * * * *

While it is clear to the Court that Staples and Office Depot do not ignore sellers such as warehouse clubs, Best Buy, or Wal-Mart, the evidence clearly shows that Staples and Office Depot each consider the other superstores as the primary competition.

* * * * *

[T]he Court finds that the sale of consumable office supplies through office supply superstores is the appropriate relevant product market for purposes of considering the possible anticompetitive effects of the proposed merger between Staples and Office Depot.

* * * * *

IV. Probable Effect on Competition

[T]he Court next must consider the probable effect of a merger between Staples and Office Depot in the geographic markets previously identified. One way to do this is to examine the concentration statistics and HHIs within the geographic markets. If the relevant product market is defined as the sale of consumable office supplies through office supply superstores, the HHIs in many of the geographic markets are at problematic levels even before the merger. Currently, the least concentrated market is that of Grand Rapids–Muskegon–Holland, Michigan, with an HHI of 3,597, while the most concentrated is Washington, D.C., with an HHI of 6,944. In contrast, after a merger of Staples and Office Depot, the least concentrated area would be Kalamazoo–Battle Creek, Michigan, with an HHI of 5,003, and many areas would have HHIs of 10,000. The average increase in HHI caused by the merger would be 2,715 points. The concentration statistics show that a merged Staples–Office Depot would have a dominant market share in 42 geographic markets across the country. The combined shares of Staples and Office Depot in the office superstore market would be 100 percent in 15 metropolitan areas. It is in these markets the postmerger HHI would be 10,000. In 27 other metropolitan areas, where the number of office superstore competitors would drop from three to two, the postmerger market shares would range from 45 percent to 94 percent, with postmerger HHIs ranging from 5,003 to 9,049. Even the lowest of these HHIs indicates a "highly concentrated" market.

* * * * *

The HHI calculations and market concentration evidence, however, are not the only indications that a merger between Staples and Office Depot may substantially lessen competition. Much of the evidence already discussed with respect to defining the relevant product market also indicates that the merger would likely have an anticompetitive effect. The evidence of the defendants' own current pricing practices, for example, shows that an office superstore chain facing no competition from other superstores has the ability to profitably raise prices for consumable office supplies above competitive levels. The fact that Staples and Office Depot both charge higher prices where they face no superstore competition demonstrates that an office superstore can raise prices above competitive levels. The evidence also shows that defendants also change their price zones when faced with entry of another office superstore, but do not do so for other retailers.

* * * * *

V. Entry into the Market

"The existence and significance of barriers to entry are frequently, of course, crucial considerations in a rebuttal analysis. . . ."

* * * * *

The Commission offered Office 1 as a specific example of the difficulty of entering the office superstore arena. Office 1 opened its first two stores in 1991. By the end of 1994, Office 1 had 17 stores, and grew to 35 stores operating in 11 Midwestern states as of October 11, 1996. As of that date, Office 1 was the fourth largest office supply superstore chain in the United States. Unfortunately, also as of that date, Office 1 filed for Chapter 11 bankruptcy protection. Brad Zenner, president of Office 1, testified through declaration that Office 1 failed because it was severely undercapitalized in comparison with the industry leaders, Staples, Office Depot, and Office-Max. In addition, Zenner testified that when the three leaders ultimately expanded into the smaller markets where Office 1 stores were located, they seriously undercut Office 1's retail prices and profit margins. Because Office 1 lacked the capitalization of the three leaders and lacked the economies of scale enjoyed by those competitors, Office 1 could not remain profitable.

For the reasons discussed above, the Court finds it extremely unlikely that a new office superstore will enter the market and thereby avert the anticompetitive effects from Staples' acquisition of Office Depot.

* * * * *

VI. Efficiencies

* * * * *

First, the Court notes that the cost savings estimate of $4.947 billion over five years which was submitted to the Court exceeds by almost 500 percent the figures presented to the two Boards of Directors in September 1996, when the Boards approved the transaction. The cost savings claims submitted to the Court are also substantially greater than those represented in the defendants' Joint Proxy Statement/Prospectus "reflecting the best currently available estimate of management," and filed with the Securities and Exchange Commission on January 23, 1997. . . .

* * * * *

[T]he Court cannot find that the defendants have rebutted the presumption that the merger will substantially lessen competition . . .

CONCLUSION

* * * * *

[T]he Court finds that the Commission has shown a likelihood that it will succeed in proving, after a full administrative trial on the merits, that the effect of the proposed merger between Staples and Office Depot "may be substantially to lessen competition" in violation of Section 7 of the Clayton Act. . . . The FTC's motion for a preliminary injunction shall be granted.

AFTERWORD

Citing the time and money involved in battling the federal government, Staples and Office Depot officially called off their proposed merger days after Judge Hogan's decision.

In 2013, 16 years after the rejection of the Staples and Office Depot merger, the Federal Trade Commission allowed after careful investigation the merger of Office Depot and Office Max (the nation's second- and third-largest office supply superstores). The FTC concluded that the competitive dynamics in the market had changed in those years. Online sales have seen explosive growth and the big box retailers (Walmart, Target, etc.) have significantly expanded their supply of office products, thus producing a broader product market than the configuration on which the *Staples* court settled. The two decisions show that a close look at the specifics of the market is required on a case-by-case basis.

Questions

1. *a.* What "general rule" did the *Staples* court employ in determining the relevant product market?

    b. What evidence supported the use of the "office supply superstore submarket" as the relevant product market?

2. *a.* What evidence supported the FTC's claim that the merger would lead to anticompetitive effects?

    b. In weighing the "public and private equities," why did the court come down on the side of the government?

3. Analysts have argued that in the *Staples* case the government was less worried about market shares than about the price impact of the merger were it to be approved. Explain what those analysts meant.

4. Three firms controlled the $1 billion U.S. baby food market (Gerber—65 percent, Heinz—17.4 percent, and Beech-Nut—15.4 percent). Gerber was sold in over 90 percent of American supermarkets, and it had greater brand loyalty than any other product sold in the United States. Heinz was sold in 40 percent of the supermarkets and Beech-Nut in 45 percent. The baby food HHI was 4775, which would increase by 510 HHI points if Heinz and Beech-Nut were to merge. Heinz and Beech-Nut agreed to merge. The Federal Trade Commission opposed the merger.

    a. What other facts would you want to know to decide the legality of this proposed merger?

    b. Defend the merger.

    c. Decide. Explain. See *Federal Trade Commission v. H. J. Heinz Co.*, 246 F.3d 708 (D.C. Cir. 2001).

5. In 1958, Pabst Brewing Company acquired Blatz Brewing Company. Pabst was America's 10th largest brewer, while Blatz was the 18th largest. After the merger, Pabst had 4.49 percent of the nationwide beer market and was the fifth-largest brewer. In the regional market of Wisconsin, Michigan, and Illinois, the merger gave Pabst 11.32 percent of the sales. After the merger, Pabst led beer sales in Wisconsin with 23.95 percent of that statewide market. The beer market was becoming increasingly concentrated, with the total number of brewers declining from 206 to 162 during the years 1957 to 1961. In *United States v. Pabst Brewing Co.*, 384 U.S. 546 (1966), the Supreme Court found the merger violated the Clayton Act, Section 7. The Court did not choose among the three geographic market configurations, saying that the crucial inquiry is whether a merger may substantially lessen competition anywhere in the United States. Thus the Court held that, under these facts, a 4.49 percent share of the market was too large.

    Respected scholar and jurist Richard Posner labeled the Pabst decision an "atrocity" and the product of a "fit of nonsense" on the part of the Supreme Court.[32] What economic arguments would support Posner's colorful complaint?.

Part Three—American Antitrust Laws and the International Market

America's commercial market embraces the entire globe. Antitrust questions can become extremely complex in transactions involving multiple companies in multiple nations, where those transactions are potentially governed by both U.S. and foreign antitrust laws. United States antitrust laws are, of course, applicable to foreign firms doing business here. The Sherman, Clayton, and FTC acts, among others, are all potentially applicable to American business abroad.

Sherman Act

The Sherman Act applies to the conduct of American business abroad when that business has a direct effect on American commerce. That the business was conducted entirely abroad or that the agreement was entered into another nation does not excuse an American firm from the reach of the Sherman Act (assuming American courts can achieve the necessary jurisdiction).

Clayton Act

Section 7 of the Clayton Act is clearly applicable to acquisitions combining domestic and foreign firms and is potentially applicable to acquisitions not involving American firms if the effect would harm competition in the American market.

Federal Trade Commission Act

As noted earlier, the FTC shares antitrust enforcement authority with the Justice Department, and Section 5 of the act strengthens Clayton 7.

Extraterritoriality

Since 1992, the U.S. Justice Department has claimed national authority to apply American antitrust law abroad. The general idea is to sue foreign firms that violate U.S. antitrust laws even when the anticompetitive actions take place entirely overseas (extraterritorial application). In practice, the Justice Department files suit in U.S. courts against foreign companies operating in the United States if those foreign companies are taking action abroad that (1) harms competition in the United States or (2) limits American access to markets in other nations. Those lawsuits are permissible under U.S. law only where the conduct abroad has a "direct, substantial, and reasonably foreseeable" effect on the United States' domestic market. Extraterritoriality does not mean, however, that the United States will become the world's antitrust police department. Indeed, the European Union and China likewise have claimed extraterritorial antitrust power. [For a brief assessment of China's Anti-Monopoly law, see **www.insidecounsel.com/ Exclusive/2010/6/Pages/Chinas-AntiMonopoly-LawCause-for-Hope-and-Concern.aspx**]

International Antitrust Enforcement

Markets increasingly extend around the globe, thus encouraging international antitrust enforcement. Most antitrust enforcement occurs in the United States and the European Union, but other nations are taking a more aggressive stance, usually by employing laws that largely mimic those of the United States or the European Union.

European Union Antitrust Enforcement   In general, American and European Union antitrust policies are compatible and are the product of constant consultation. Nonetheless, EU regulators have demonstrated that they are willing to part ways with America if market conditions require. We have seen in this chapter that the European Union arguably has taken a more aggressive stance toward Microsoft's alleged anticompetitive behaviors than has been the case in the United States. Certainly the EU regulators are not timid about blocking American business activities in Europe. UPS, for example, announced in 2013 that it would drop its bid to acquire competing Dutch delivery company TNT Express when it became clear that the European Commission would raise antitrust concerns. Given the European Union's powerful economic role, the antitrust decisions of EU regulators necessarily influence business practices worldwide. [For access to EU antitrust law, see **http://ec.europa.eu/competiton/index_en.html**]

Other Nations   The number of nations with competition laws soared from 40 in 1995 to more than 125 in 2009,[33] and we are seeing the beginning of a worldwide convergence of those laws led by the United States, the European Union, and China.[34] Indeed, in 2012, the European Union and China signed a memorandum of understanding affirming antitrust cooperation, much as the United States and China had done in 2011.[35] Despite borrowing extensively from the United States and the European Union, China has shown a willingness to chart its own antitrust course when deemed necessary, as was the case in its 2012 approval of Google's $12.5 billion acquisition of Motorola Mobility Holdings. Although the United States and the European Union approved the deal without conditions, China imposed a number of expectations on Google, including, for example, a requirement that Google continue to license Android on a free and open basis.[36] Reflecting the broadened importance of antitrust in our complex global markets, regulators in 2012 began to assert themselves more aggressively in India where Apple and Google reportedly are both under investigation and where a wide range of industries, including cement and tire manufacturing, are being scrutinized for alleged price fixing.[37] [For periodic overviews of global antitrust policies and practices, see *Antitrust Review* produced and published by the British law firm, Clifford Chance (**www.cliffordchance.com/**)].

[For an update of China's new Anti-Monopoly Law, see Michael Han and Jenny Connolly, "China's Anti-Monopoly Law Celebrates Fifth Anniversary," *LEXOLOGY,* August 16, 2013 (**www.lexology.com/**)].

Internet Exercise	"What Do the Antitrust Laws Do for the Consumer?" For an answer, see the U.S. Department of Justice, Antitrust Division, brochure, "Antitrust Enforcement and the Consumer." [**www.justice.gov/atr/public/div_stats/antitrust-enfor-consumer.pdf**].
Chapter Questions	1. The Chicago Skyway, a toll bridge connecting Chicago and Indiana, was owned and operated by the City of Chicago. Chicago earned $52 million in tolls beyond the amount needed to meet bond payments and to maintain the Skyway. The excess was used to pay for other transportation expenses. Skyway tolls were higher than those of other area highways. Endsley, a bridge user, joined others in a class action against Chicago claiming that the city's control of the Skyway provided monopoly power in high-speed limited access

travel between Indiana and Chicago and that the city was abusing that power by collecting excessive fees. Chicago demonstrated that at least two alternative, if less desirable, routes were in competition with the Skyway. Is Chicago a monopolist? Explain. See *Endsley v. City of Chicago,* 230 F.3d 276 (7th Cir. 2000); cert. den. 532 U.S. 972 (2001).

2. Major League Soccer (MLS) was the exclusive Division I professional soccer league in the United States, as recognized by the U.S. Soccer Federation (USSF), the national soccer governing body. MLS owned all of the league's 12 teams, set all schedules, negotiated all stadium leases, controlled all intellectual property rights, and controlled all player contracts. Partial control over some teams was transferred by MLS to certain investors. The investors did not hire their own players. Each employment contract was between the player and the league. MLS assigned the players in a manner designed to maintain competitive balance. MLS had been preceded in U.S. professional soccer by the North American Soccer League, which had failed financially. A group of players sued the MLS on antitrust grounds.
   a. What were the players' antitrust claims?
   b. Decide those claims. Explain. See *Fraser v. Major League Soccer,* 284 F.3d 47 (1st Cir. 2002).

3. Poplar Bluff is a city of 17,000 people in southeastern Missouri. Sikeston and Cape Girardeau, Missouri, both towns with populations of over 40,000, are 40 and 60 miles away from Poplar Bluff. Tenet Healthcare owns Lucy Lee Hospital in Poplar Bluff and proposed to buy Doctors' Regional Medical Center, also in Poplar Bluff. Both hospitals are profitable, but both are underutilized and have had trouble attracting specialists. The Federal Trade Commission filed suit to block the acquisition. The key question involved definition of the geographic market. The FTC proposed a relevant geographic market that essentially matched the service area: a 50-mile radius of downtown Poplar Bluff. Ninety percent of the two hospitals' patients come from that area. Four other hospitals are in that area. The merged hospital would have 84 percent of the patients in that geographic market. Tenet argues that the geographic market should encompass a 65-mile radius from downtown Poplar Bluff. That area includes 16 hospitals. How should the Court of Appeals decide where the geographic market lies? See *FTC v. Tenet Health Care Corp.,* 186 F.3d 1045 (8th Cir. 1999).

4. In 2011, the U.S. Justice Department sent a letter to the National Collegiate Athletic Association raising antitrust questions about the Bowl Championship Series (BCS) which is used to determine a national college football champion. The letter asked why the BCS schools had not established a playoff system. Then pressure from critics and the promise of huge payouts pushed the BCS to establish a four-team playoff system to commence in 2014. In your judgment, should federal antitrust law be applied to the Bowl Championship Series? Explain.

5. A major concern with horizontal mergers is the increased potential for collusion. List the structural conditions that would encourage coordinated interaction between competitors.

6. Critics are concerned that increasing mergers, especially those involving media firms, threaten democracy.
   a. Explain that argument.
   b. Do you agree? Explain.

7. In 1986 distinguished economist William Shepherd argued,

    > It may not be too late to turn back from this road to serfdom by reviving the case for antitrust, but the odds aren't favorable. More probably, antitrust will continue to sink.[38]

    a. What did Shepherd mean about "this road to serfdom?"

    b. In reading this chapter, do you think antitrust has been revived? Explain.

    c. Is bigness bad, or is it necessary in today's global economy? Explain.

8. Whole Foods, the natural foods chain, in 2007 acquired its chief competitor, Wild Oats Market. Whole Foods had about 12 percent of the natural foods market, and Wild Oats held about 3 percent. Whole Foods had 197 stores and added 110 by purchasing Wild Oats. About 72 percent of Wild Oats' sales were in markets where the two overlapped. Whole Foods argued that the merger was necessary to allow it to compete effectively with big chains such as Safeway and Walmart.

    Prior to the purchase, Whole Foods cofounder and CEO John Mackey allegedly said that the proposed merger would end "forever or almost forever" the possibility of a big grocery chain buying an existing natural foods chain to compete with Whole Foods. Mackey also allegedly said that buying Wild Oats would prevent "nasty price wars."

    The Federal Trade Commission challenged the Whole Foods purchase of Wild Oats.

    a. What was the primary issue facing the federal courts that reviewed the FTC challenge?

    b. Decide the case. Explain. See *Federal Trade Commission v. Whole Foods Market,* 502 F. Supp.2d 1 (2007), *Federal Trade Commission v. Whole Foods Market,* 533 F.3d 869 (D.C. Cir. 2008), and David Kesmodel and Jonathan Eig, "A Grocer's Brash Style Takes Unhealthy Turn," *The Wall Street Journal,* July 20, 2007, p. A1.

9. Is the influence of big business so persuasive that it nullifies the effective enforcement of the antitrust laws? Explain.

10. Antitrust authorities must address a critical and empirically difficult policy problem: Does seller concentration in a market ordinarily result in increased prices? That is, in a particular market, are fewer firms with larger shares likely to produce higher prices than would be the case with a more fragmented market? Free-market theorists are generally untroubled by concentration. What do you think? Explain.

11. Is a monopolist required to deal with its competitors? That question was the core of a 2004 Supreme Court decision in *Verizon Communications v. Law Offices of Curtis V. Trinko.*[39] The Trinko law firm bought its local phone service from AT&T. Trinko brought a class action claiming Verizon maintained a monopoly by exclusionary practices. Trinko contended that local phone services had difficulty connecting with the giant regional Bell operating companies' (Verizon, Qwest, BellSouth, and SBC) local exchange facilities, thus harming competition and consumers. The Telecommunications Act of 1996 specifically requires the regional Bell companies to provide the local phone services with fair, reasonable access. The Supreme Court, however, ruled in favor of Verizon and concluded that antitrust liability in these telephone situations would apply only where a telephone monopolist discontinues a voluntary business

relationship with a competitor for the purpose of destroying that competitor. Explain why the Supreme Court decided that Verizon, a telephone monopolist, had no duty to deal with those telephone competitors with whom it had not previously dealt. See Matthew Cantor, "Is Trinko the Last Word on a Telephone Monopolist's Duty to Deal?" *New York Law Journal* 96 (May 19, 2004), p. 4.

12. In the period 1917 to 1919, DuPont acquired 23 percent of the stock in the then-fledgling General Motors Corporation. By 1947, DuPont supplied 68 percent of GM's automotive finish needs and 38 percent of its fabric needs. In 1955, General Motors ranked first in sales and second in assets among all U.S. industrial corporations, while accounting for approximately two-fifths of the nation's annual automobile sales. In 1949, the Justice Department challenged Dupont's 1917–19 acquisitions of GM stock.

    a. Why did the government challenge DuPont's acquisition?

    b. May an acquisition be properly challenged 30 years after the fact, as in DuPont? Explain.

    c. Given your general understanding of finishes and fabrics, how would you defend DuPont?

    d. Decide. Explain. See *United States v. E.I. DuPont de Nemours & Co.,* 353 U.S. 586 (1957).

13. How can a merger benefit society?

14. Which economic considerations support the view that unilateral growth is preferable to growth by merger?

15. Excel, a division of Cargill, was the second-largest firm in the beef-packing market. It sought to acquire Spencer Pack, a division of Land-O-Lakes and the third-largest beef packer. After the acquisition, Excel would have remained second ranked in the business, but its market share would have been only slightly smaller than that of the leader, IBP. Monfort, the nation's fifth-largest beef packer, sought an injunction to block the acquisition, claiming a violation of Clayton Section 7. In effect, Monfort claimed the merger would result in a dangerous concentration of economic power in the beef-packing market, with the result that Excel would pay more for cattle and charge less for its processed beef, thus placing its competitors in a destructive and illegal price–cost squeeze. Monfort claimed Excel's initial losses in this arrangement would be covered by its wealthy parent, Cargill. Then, when the competition was driven from the market, Monfort claimed, Excel would raise its processed beef prices to supracompetitive levels. Among other defenses, Excel averred that the heavy losses Monfort claimed were merely the product of intense competition, a condition that would not constitute a violation of the antitrust laws. The district court found for Monfort, and the appeals court, considering the cost–price squeeze a form of predatory pricing, affirmed. Excel appealed to the Supreme Court. Decide. Explain. See *Cargill, Inc. v. Monfort of Colorado, Inc.,* 479 U.S. 104 (1986).

Notes

1. See *United States v. Microsoft Corporation,* 87 F.Supp.2d 30 (D.D.C. 2000), and *Microsoft v. United States,* 253 F.3d 34 (D.C. Cir. 2001); cert. den. 122 S.Ct. 350 (2001).

2. Alan Murray, "Microsoft Foe Quits Antitrust Crusade—with Check in Hand," *The Wall Street Journal,* December 7, 2004, p. A4.

3. *United States v. Grinnell*, 384 U.S. 563, 570-1 (1966).

4. BreakingViews.COM, "Rising Beer Prices Hint at Oligopoly," *The New York Times*, August 27, 2009 [**www.nytimes.com**].

5. Mina Kimes, "Showdown on the Railroad," *Fortune*, September 26, 2011, p. 161.

6. Ibid.

7. Note, "Antitrust and the Information Age: Section 2 Monopolization Analyses in the New Economy," *Harvard Law Review* 114 (March 2001), p. 1623.

8. *Spectrum Sports, Inc. v. Shirley McQuillan*, 506 U.S. 447 (1993).

9. Note, "Antitrust and the Information Age," pp. 1623, 1645.

10. *United States v. Aluminum Co. of America*, 148 F.2d 416 (2d Cir. 1945).

11. David Lazarus, "Surrender by AT&T Is Victory for Consumers and Regulators," *latimes.com*, December 19, 2011 [**latimes.com/business/la-fi-att-lazarus-20111220,0,448316.column**].

12. Editorial, "No Justice for Cellphone Users," *The Wall Street Journal*," December 20, 2011, p. A18.

13. Justin Bachman, "The American–US Airways Deal: You're Going to Pay More," *Bloomberg Businessweek*, February 12, 2013 [**www.businessweek.com/**].

14. Editorial, "Big Food," *The New York Times*, January 25, 2010 [**http://nytimes.com**].

15. How do mergers affect consumer prices? See Orley Ashenfelter and Daniel Hosken, "The Effect of Mergers on Consumers Prices: Evidence from Five Selected Case Studies," *Economist's View*, April 23, 2008 [**economistsview.typepad.com/economistsview/2008/04/the-effect-of-m.html**].

16. "Kevin Voigt, "Mergers Fail More Often than Marriages," *CNN.com/world business*, May 22, 2009 [**http://edition.cnn.com/2009/BUSINESS/05/21/merger.marriage/index.html**].

17. See Michael J. Mandel, "All These Mergers Are Great, But . . ." *BusinessWeek*, October 18, 1999, p. 48; and Jeffrey Garten, "Megamergers Are a Clear and Present Danger," *BusinessWeek*, January 25, 1999, p. 28.

18. Bruce D. Sokler, et al., "DOJ Assistant Attorney General William Baer's First Merger Challenge Confirms Continued Aggressive Merger Enforcement by Antitrust Division," *LEXOLOGY*, February 4, 2013 [**www.lexology.com/**].

19. Ibid.

20. Michael J. De La Merced, "Justice Dept. Seeks to Block Anheuser's Deal for Modelo," *Deal Book, The New York Times*, January 31, 2013 [**http://dealbook.nytimes.com/**].

21. Ibid.

22. Ibid.

23. Adam Davidson, "Are We in Danger of a Beer Monopoly?" *The New York Times*, February 26, 2013 [**www.nytimes.com/**].

24. Ibid.

25. "FTC Requires Divestitures for Hertz's Proposed $2.3 Billion Acquisition of Dollar Thrifty to Preserve Competition in Airport Car Rental Markets," *FTC Press Release*, November 15, 2012 [**http://ftc.gov/opa/2012/11/hertz.shtm**].

26. Scott D. Thompson, "Clear Skies Seen Ahead for the American Airlines/U.S. Airways Merger," *LEXOLOGY*, February 22, 2013 [**www.lexology.com**].

27. Ben Sisario, "Justice Dept. Clears Ticketmaster Deal," *The New York Times*, January 26, 2010 [**www.nytimes.com**].

28. Press Release, "Justice Department Requires Ticketmaster Entertainment Inc. to Make Significant Changes to Its Merger with Live Nation, Inc., United States Department of Justice, January 25, 2010 [**www.justice.gov/atr/public/press_releases/2010/254540.htm**].

29. Ethan Smith, "High-Decibel Criticism Greets Completion of Live Nation Merger," *The Wall Street Journal,* January 27, 2010 [**http/online.wsj.com/**].

30. Sisario, "Justice Dept. Clears Ticketmaster Deal, *New York Times,* January 25, 2010 [**www.nytimes.com**]."

31. Ibid.

32. Richard Posner, *Antitrust Law* (Chicago: The University of Chicago Press, 1976), p. 130.

33. Howard W. Fogt, Jr., Alan D. Rutenberg, Max Lin and Wen (Jo) Xu, "Evolving Convergence: Antitrust/Competition Law and Policy/Procedure in the United States, European Union, and China, *LEXOLOGY,* December 9, 2009 [**www.lexology.com/**].

34. Ibid.

35. Adrian Emch, "EU and China Sign Agreement to Deepen Antitrust Cooperation," *LEXOLOGY,* October 31, 2012 [**www.lexology.com/**]; and Orrick, Herrington & Sutcliffe LLP, "China Anti-Monopoly and U.S. Antitrust Agencies Sign Memorandum of Understanding," *LEXOLOGY,* December 1, 2011 [**www.lexology.com/**].

36. Amber Liu, "China's Merger Control Regime," *LEXOLOGY,* December 10, 2012 [**www.lexology.com/**].

37. Amol Sharma and R. Jai Krishna, "India Trust Buster Turns Up the Heat," *The Wall Street Journal,* May 11, 2012, p. B4.

38. William G. Shepherd, "Bust the Reagan Trustbusters," *Fortune,* August 4, 1986, pp. 225, 227.

39. 540 U.S. 398 (2004).

Employer–Employee Relations

CHAPTER TWELVE

Employment Law I: Employee Rights

After completing this chapter, students will be able to:

1. Distinguish between an employee and an independent contractor.

2. Identify potential legal challenges an employer faces in the hiring process.

3. Describe employers' liability under the doctrine of "respondeat superior."

4. Analyze claims of negligent hiring, supervision, and retention.

5. Explain employees' rights under the Fair Labor Standards Act.

6. Describe the role of the Occupational Safety and Health Administration (OSHA) in protecting employees' health and safety at work.

7. Describe the benefits, coverage, and requirements for bringing a successful claim under workers' compensation law.

8. Discuss workplace drug testing and the legal challenges it faces.

9. Describe the Family and Medical Leave Act (FMLA).

10. Distinguish between defined benefit and defined contribution pension plans.

11. Analyze whether a dismissed at-will employee may bring a claim of wrongful discharge.

12. Recognize the purpose and requirements of the employment eligibility verification form (I-9).

Introduction

Scott Rodrigues was fired in 2006 by The Scotts Company, the lawn care giant, because a required drug test revealed nicotine in his urine. Company policy forbade employee smoking both on and off the job. Scotts announced in 2005 that it would no longer hire smokers, and it gave its employees one year to comply with the new policy, a policy designed to improve employee wellness and reduce company health care costs. Rodrigues was a pack-a-day smoker when he was hired. He was aware of the no-smoking policy, and he had been warned to quit when a supervisor saw a pack of cigarettes on the dashboard of his car. Rodrigues acknowledged his smoking habit, but said he was trying to quit smoking when he was fired. Rodrigues complained that the company had not offered to help him quit smoking. The Scotts' plan does, however, pay for smoking cessation programs for its employees. Scotts said they were not interested in influencing workers' behavior in their free time, except in the case of smoking.[1] Rodrigues decided to file suit against Scotts because:

> What's to make them stop at just cigarettes? If they're a Republican company, can they try and figure out who you vote for and if you vote for the Democrats, they'll fire you? . . .[2]

According to the American Lung Association's Tobacco Policy Project/State Legislated Actions on Tobacco Issues (SLATI), as of 2013, 29 states and the District of Columbia have laws protecting smokers from adverse employment action based on smoking tobacco.[3] While Massachusetts law does not provide explicit shelter for smokers, it offers statutory protection from "unreasonable, substantial, or serious interference" with an individual's privacy.[4] Rodrigues brought suit against the Scotts Company claiming, among other things, invasion of privacy.

Questions

1. How would you rule on Rodrigues's right to privacy claim?
2. Should employers be able to fire employees who smoke off the job? Explain. See *Rodrigues v. the Scotts Company,* 639 F.Supp.2d 131 (D. Mass 2009).

Managing Lawsuits Managers traditionally have balanced multiple responsibilities, but in recent years the law has added complex, sometimes daunting expectations. Addressing and mitigating the risk of employment-related lawsuits, like Rodrigues's, has become an important consideration in management decision making. As union strength has declined (see Chapter 14), government regulations and court decisions have arguably broadened employee rights. These increased legal protections, a volatile economy, downsizing, weakened employer–employee loyalty, and other forces have contributed to higher levels of employee litigation.[5]

Part One—The Employment Relationship

Job Classification Employment-related legal rights and responsibilities depend on the type of relationship the employer decides to build with the worker. The traditional, stable model of long-term direct employer–employee relationships now is often replaced with new, flexible, nontraditional staffing arrangements including outsourcing and employee leasing, along with the use of freelancers and temporary agencies. These *contingent workers,* along with *independent contractors,* who are increasingly relied on to perform specific, shorter-term, nonrecurring jobs, permit employers to rapidly and inexpensively inflate or shrink their workforces as competitive and regulatory conditions change. Employers who choose to provide health and retirement benefits for their traditional employees need not do so for their contingent workers. Nor must they withhold income, Social Security, Medicare, and unemployment taxes. With fringe benefit costs skyrocketing, benefits reduction has become an important consideration for most firms. A firm might contract with professional employer organizations (PEOs) to take responsibility for and administer its payroll and human resources operation. [For an overview of PEOs and their functions, see **www.napeo.org/**]

Employee or Independent Contractor?   A key question underlying the legal issues discussed in this chapter is whether the worker in question is an employee or an independent contractor: one who enters a contractual rather than employment relationship with an organization in order to perform a specific task. Degree of control is the dominant test in determining whether a worker is an employee or independent contractor. Where an employer controls or has the right or ability to control the worker's performance, the worker is likely to be considered an employee. CBS used the distinction between "independent contractor" and "employee" to successfully appeal the FCC's fine after Justin Timberlake and Janet Jackson appeared to cooperatively expose Ms. Jackson's breast at the end of their performance during the 2004 Super Bowl half-time show that CBS broadcast. CBS argued that the performers were independent contractors, not employees, and, therefore, CBS could not be held liable for actions taken outside their control.[6] In 2012, the U.S. Supreme Court declined to review the federal appellate court's decision to throw out the FCC's fine.[7]

What other advantages might a business gain from hiring an independent contractor rather than an employee? A business that hires an independent contractor generally is not required to comply with a wide range of employment and labor law standards that would apply were the worker an employee. Thus a business must provide, for example, unemployment insurance to its employees, but generally would not need to do so for independent contractors. Furthermore, employers generally are not liable for employment discrimination claims by independent contractors or for most torts committed by independent contractors in the course of work. While employers are responsible for payroll taxes such as FICA and federal and state unemployment insurance, as well as for withholding income tax from their employees, these tax obligations of a business do not extend to its independent contractors. [For a sample of independent contractor agreement from the Society of Human Resource Management, see **www.shrm.org/TemplatesTools/Samples/HRForms /Articles/Pages/1CMS_006447.aspx**]

Classification Problems   Employers anxious to reduce financial and legal burdens sometimes improperly classify workers as independent contractors rather than employees. In 2007, a California federal district court ordered a house cleaning service to pay $4.5 million to provide minimum wages and overtime pay for workers who had been misclassified as independent contractors. Employees, unlike independent contractors, are protected by the Fair Labor Standards Act (detailed later in this chapter), which requires, among other things, the payment of the federal minimum wage and overtime pay. The employer claimed that the workers were independent contractors and thus not covered by the FLSA, but the court pointed to a variety of considerations, including control and supervision, that confirmed the workers' correct status as employees.[8] The Internal Revenue Service (IRS) has created a Voluntary Classification Settlement Program under which employers who meet certain criteria are able to reclassify workers as employees for employment tax purposes with partial relief from federal employment taxes.[9] [For IRS guidance on determining whether a worker is an employee or independent contractor, see **www.irs.gov /Businesses/Small-Businesses-&-Self-Employed/Independent-Contractor-Self -Employed-or-Employee**]

Selection and Hiring   An array of potential legal problems have arisen from the increasingly complex process of choosing and employing new workers.

- ***Résumé Fraud.*** Scott Thompson, former Yahoo CEO, left the company after revelations that he had falsely claimed to hold a computer science degree; he graduated with an accounting degree from a college that apparently did not have a computer science program at the time.[10] Along with Thompson, David J. Edmonson, former chief executive of Radio Shack, also left his post after his exaggerated academic credentials were discovered.[11] Misstated qualifications of corporate executives at Herbalife Ltd. and Usana Health Sciences have also been uncovered. A 2008 online poll of 3,000 hiring managers revealed that 49 percent had uncovered a lie on a résumé, including exaggeration of job responsibilities and skills, false claims regarding education, and inflated job titles. One of the more unusual lies involved an applicant who pretended to be related to the Kennedy clan.[12]

- ***Background Checks.*** Although concerns ranging from résumé fraud to employee theft and workplace violence may have led to background checks becoming an expected part of the hiring process, a 2012 survey conducted by the Society for Human Resource Management (SHRM) showed a decrease in the number of employers who check applicants' credit history and criminal backgrounds compared to 2010. Less than half of employers run credit checks on applicants for at least some positions, compared to 60 percent in 2010, while the percentage of employers *not* checking criminal backgrounds doubled from 7 percent to 14 percent.[13] Using credit checks in hiring arguably helps protect an employer against fraud and employee theft, since applicants who have not handled their personal finances responsibly might be more likely to engage in such misconduct. However, questions about the validity and unintended impact of this practice have been raised in recent years. Not only has the connection between a bad credit report and poor job performance been disputed, but studies showing that African Americans and Latinos tend to have lower credit scores cause concern that credit checks can create a discriminatory impact on these groups' ability to gain employment.[14] Several states have passed legislation limiting the use of credit checks. The Illinois Employee Credit Privacy Act, for example, generally prohibits employers from using an employee's or applicant's credit history in making employment decisions such as hiring.[15]

  In 2012, the U.S. Equal Employment Opportunity Commission (EEOC) issued an enforcement guidance on the use of criminal background checks. Although employers' use of criminal background checks is not banned, employers cannot use this tool to screen applicants or current employees unless the conviction is relevant to the position for which they are being considered. The EEOC noted that an arrest does not establish criminal conduct and therefore cannot be used in hiring; however, the conduct underlying the arrest could be considered by an employer in making an employment decision. [For the full text of the EEOC Enforcement Guidance on the Consideration of Arrest and Conviction Records in Employment Decisions, see **www.eeoc.gov/laws/guidance/arrest_conviction.cfm**]

> Employers using social media in the hiring process want to see whether candidates present themselves professionally.

At the same time, employers are increasingly searching the online reputation of job applicants. In a 2012 survey, 37 percent of hiring managers polled revealed that they browse applicants' social media profiles; approximately two-thirds of employers using social media in the hiring process want to see whether candidates present themselves professionally.[16] As discussed further in this chapter, concern for privacy over this practice has led to state legislation preventing employers from requiring social media passwords as part of the application process.

- ***Inappropriate Questions.*** According to a recent survey, 22 percent of job seekers cited interviewers "asking inappropriate questions" as a "top turn-off" in the interview process.[17] Furthermore, such questions as "How old are you?" and "Are you married?" also expose employers to potential liability for discrimination (see Chapter 13). But what about the enormous array of awkward, intrusive, but nondiscriminatory interview questions that might leave the candidate feeling uncomfortable if not wronged? For example: "What would you do if I gave you an elephant?" has questionable relevance in a job interview.[18]

- ***Restrictive Covenants.*** Chris Botticella, a former executive with Bimbo Bakeries, which operates under popular brand names such as Thomas' and Entenmann's, was unable to start work for Hostess, Inc. because of the confidentiality agreement and other restrictive covenants he had signed with Bimbo. Information such as recipes and business strategies to which Botticella had access would likely be shared with Hostess.[19] To address problems like these, employers sometimes require employees to sign agreements providing they will not compete with their employer, solicit its customers or employees, pass trade secrets to others, and so on, for a specified period of time. Such agreements are not limited to upper management,[20] and generally are fully enforceable if reasonable in their requirements. California law, however, prohibits noncompetition agreements in employment, with narrow statutory exceptions.[21] Even if such an agreement is enforceable, employers who take such actions as hiring a private investigator to determine whether a former employee is in breach could face liability for intrusion (see Chapter 7).[22]

- ***Arbitration.*** New employees are often expected to sign agreements specifying that disputes with the employer will be settled by arbitration (see Chapter 4) rather than by litigation. A recent study of 21 major corporations' employment contracts found that 93 percent contained mandatory arbitration clauses.[23] Employers like arbitration because it can be cheaper, faster, and less adversarial than a trial. Employees, on the other hand, argue that arbitration is stacked in favor of corporate interests and amounts to a denial of the fundamental right of access to the legal system. Employment arbitration agreements have been supported by recent U.S. Supreme Court decisions, such as *Circuit City Stores, Inc. v. Adams* upholding the enforceability of legitimate, equitable employment arbitration agreement.[24] In *Nitro-Lift Technologies v. Howard,* the Court vacated a state supreme court ruling that the arbitration clause in a restrictive covenant not to sue in court was void under state policy limiting the enforceability of noncompetition agreements in employment; the U.S Supreme Court held that whether the restrictive covenant was enforceable was for the arbitrator to decide.[25] However, the U.S. Equal Employment Opportunity Commission (see Chapter 13) still retains authority to file discrimination lawsuits on behalf of employees despite an arbitration agreement.[26]

> You decide to fire an employee.

• **References.** As a manager, you decide to fire an employee, Brown, because of what you believe to be convincing evidence that he had sexually harassed a coworker. Brown applies for a new job, and that employer seeks your evaluation of Brown's work. What should you do? If you tell what you know, you and your employer fear Brown might sue you for *defamation* (*slander* when spoken; *libel* when written). If you fail to say what you know, you fear you might be sued for *misrepresentation* or *negligent referral* if Brown is hired and commits further harassment on his new job. Because of those risks, employers often limit their references to purely factual details such as the date of hire, date of departure, and job title.

Broadly, a successful defamation suit requires the following conditions:

1. A false statement.
2. The statement must be "published" to a third party.
3. The employer must be responsible for the publication.
4. The plaintiff's reputation must be harmed.

Truth is a complete defense in defamation cases, and managers who offer factual, honest professional judgments are unlikely to face such claims. Further, many state courts provide the protection of a *qualified privilege*. Under this privilege, legitimate business communications, with some exceptions, are shielded from liability. Similarly, a number of states have enacted legislation providing employers with immunity from liability for good faith employment references.

Part Two—Liability

Once hired, what happens when employees make mistakes or engage in misconduct on the job that hurts others? Must the employer bear the loss in these situations? Job classification is an important first question in determining company liability for workers' job-related injuries, harm to others, and crimes. An enterprise ordinarily will not be liable for the acts of its independent contractors. Employers, on the other hand, often bear legal responsibility for employees' accidents or wrongs. That liability may spring from the doctrine of *respondeat superior* (let the master answer), a form of *vicarious liability* (sometimes called *imputed liability*).

Scope of Employment Employer liability for employee injuries, accidents, or wrongs is largely dependent on whether the employee was on the job at the time of the incident in question. Employers will be held liable under respondeat superior/vicarious liability reasoning for harm to third parties caused by the intentional or negligent acts of their employees when those acts occur within the *scope of employment* (on the job). A finding of employer liability, of course, does not excuse the employee from her personal liability, but the respondeat superior reasoning does have the potential effect of opening the employer's deeper pockets to the plaintiff. The following questions ordinarily determine whether the harm occurred in the scope of employment:

1. Was the employee subject to the employer's supervision?
2. Was the employee motivated, at least in part, by a desire to serve the employer's business interests?
3. Did the problem arise substantially within normal working hours and in a work location?
4. Was the act in question of the general kind the employee had been hired to perform?

> The City was held liable for a sexual assault committed by a police officer.

In *Mary M. v. City of Los Angeles,*[27] the city was held liable under the doctrine of respondeat superior for a sexual assault committed by a police officer. At 2:30 AM on October 3, 1981, Sergeant Leigh Schroyer was on duty, in uniform, carrying a gun, and patrolling in his marked police car. He stopped Mary M. for erratic driving. She pleaded not to be arrested. He ordered her to enter his patrol car and took her to her home. He entered her home and said that he expected "payment" for not arresting her. He raped her and was subsequently sentenced to a term in state prison.

Mary M. sued the City of Los Angeles. The general inquiry was whether Schroyer was acting within the scope of his employment during the rape episode. The jury found for Mary M. and awarded $150,000 in damages. The Court of Appeals reversed, saying that Schroyer was not acting within the scope of his employment. The case went to the California Supreme Court. The city argued that Schroyer was acting on behalf of his own interests rather than those of the city, and that the city had not authorized his conduct. Therefore, Schroyer could not have been acting within the scope of employment. However, the court said that the correct question was not whether the rape was authorized but whether it happened in the course of a series of acts that were authorized. The court reversed, saying that a jury could find the city vicariously liable (imputed to the principal from the agent) given the unique authority of police officers in our society.

Questions

1. Jean was carrying groceries out of the grocery store Hy-Vee when she was struck and injured by a bicycle driven by Lewis, a 16-year-old Hy-Vee employee. Lewis was hurrying home to get a belt to complete his required Hy-Vee work uniform. He had received permission from his supervisor to return home for that purpose; Lewis had neither clocked in nor started his shift. Jean sued Hy-Vee for her resulting injuries.
   a. What is Jean's claim?
   b. Decide the case. Explain. See *Jean v. Hy Vee, Inc.* 825 N.W.2d 327 (Ct. App. Iowa 2012).

2. Ahern, a chef at the Heathwood Nursing and Rehabilitation Center in Chestnut Hill, Massachusetts, left work and went to the South Pacific Chinese Restaurant where he met his supervisor, Pacitti, to socialize and discuss work-related matters. Ahern purchased two drinks and consumed at least one drink and one-half of the other before leaving to go home. On his way home, Ahern's vehicle struck Lev as he was crossing a street, causing severe and debilitating injuries. Ahern was arrested and eventually convicted of operating a motor vehicle while under the influence of intoxicating liquor. Lev sued Heathwood's owner and operator, Beverly Enterprises, alleging that Beverly was vicariously liable for Ahern's negligence based on their employment relationship.

   a. What was the central issue in this case?

   b. Decide the case. Explain. See *Lev v. Beverly Enterprises,* 457 Mass. 234 (Sup. Jud. Ct. Mass. 2010)

3. What policy justifications support the imposition of liability on an employer for the wrongs of an employee operating within the scope of employment?

A Side Order of Pistol-Whipping?

Harris placed his order with a cashier at a Kentucky Fried Chicken (KFC) restaurant in Philadelphia, Pennsylvania, but hesitated in selecting his side orders that were part of the meal he had selected. Another KFC employee, Henry, told Harris to "hurry up." Harris replied, "I am not dealing with you." Henry then asked Harris: "Do you want the [expletive] chicken or not?" Taken aback, Harris further hesitated; Henry pulled out a gun. Harris put up his hands and asked if Henry was "going to shoot [him] over a bucket of chicken?" While another employee yelled at Henry, Harris tried to escape, but Henry followed and pistol-whipped Harris before he could leave the restaurant, causing him injuries. Harris sued KFC for negligently failing to conduct a criminal background check. In rejecting the claim, the federal district court noted that KFC was not legally required to conduct a criminal background check, and that Henry's criminal history only would have revealed two prior convictions for nonviolent crimes over 5 years old.

Questions

1. Do you agree with the court's ruling? Explain.

2. How else might KFC have prevented this situation? Explain. See *Harris v. KFC,* 2012 U.S. Dist. LEXIS 84668 (E.D. Pa. 2012).

Hiring/Retention/Training/Supervision

Negligence

In addition to vicarious liability for employees' actions, employers may be directly liable for negligence in hiring an employee or retaining an employee who subsequently causes harm to a third party, or for careless training or supervision. Typically, the employer is liable on negligence grounds for hiring or retaining an employee whom the employer knew or should have known to be dangerous, incompetent, dishonest, or the like where that information was directly related to the injury suffered by the plaintiff. Note that under negligence liability an employer may be liable for acts *outside* the scope of employment. The case that follows examines the law of negligent hiring, supervision, and retention.

LEGAL BRIEFCASE

Yunker v. Honeywell, Inc.
496 N.W.2d 419 (Minn.App. 1993)

Judge Lansing

FACTS

Honeywell employed Randy Landin from 1977 to 1979 and from 1984 to 1988. From 1979 to 1984 Landin was imprisoned for the strangulation death of Nancy Miller, a Honeywell coemployee. On his release from prison, Landin reapplied at Honeywell. Honeywell rehired Landin as a custodian in Honeywell's General Offices facility in South Minneapolis in August 1984. Because of workplace confrontations Landin was twice transferred, first to the Golden Valley facility in August 1986, and then to the St. Louis Park facility in August 1987.

Kathleen Nesser was assigned to Landin's maintenance crew in April 1988. Landin and Nesser became friends and spent time together away from work. When Landin expressed a romantic interest, Nesser stopped spending time with Landin. Landin began to harass and threaten Nesser both at work and at home. At the end of June, Landin's behavior prompted Nesser to seek help from her supervisor and to request a transfer out of the St. Louis Park facility.

On July 1, 1988, Nesser found a death threat scratched on her locker door. Landin did not come to work on or after July 1, and Honeywell accepted his formal resignation on July 11, 1988. On July 19, approximately six hours after her Honeywell shift ended, Landin killed Nesser in her driveway with a close-range shotgun blast. Landin was convicted of first-degree murder and sentenced to life imprisonment.

Jean Yunker, as trustee for the heirs and next-of-kin of Kathleen Nesser, brought this wrongful death action based on theories of negligent hiring, retention, and supervision of a dangerous employee. Honeywell moved for summary judgment and, for purposes of the motion, stipulated that it failed to exercise reasonable care in the hiring and supervision of Landin. The trial court concluded that Honeywell owed no legal duty to Nesser and granted summary judgment for Honeywell.

ISSUE

Did Honeywell have a duty to Kathleen Nesser to exercise reasonable care in hiring, retaining, or supervising Randy Landin?

ANALYSIS

In determining that Honeywell did not have a legal duty to Kathleen Nesser arising from its employment of Randy Landin, the district court analyzed Honeywell's duty as limited by its ability to control and protect its employees while they are involved in the employer's business or at the employer's place of business. Additionally, the court concluded that Honeywell could not have reasonably foreseen Landin's killing Nesser.

Incorporating a "scope of employment" limitation into an employer's duty borrows from the doctrine of *respondeat superior*. However, of the three theories advanced for recovery, only negligent supervision derives from the *respondeat superior* doctrine, which relies on connection to the employer's premises or chattels. We agree that negligent supervision is not a viable theory of recovery because Landin was neither on Honeywell's premises nor using Honeywell's chattels when he shot Nesser.

The remaining theories, negligent hiring and negligent retention, are based on direct, not vicarious, liability. Negligent hiring and negligent retention do not rely on the scope of employment but address risks created by exposing members of the public to a potentially dangerous individual. These theories of recovery impose liability for an employee's intentional tort, an action almost invariably outside the scope of employment, when the employer knew or should have known that the employee was violent or aggressive and might engage in injurious conduct.

I

Minnesota first explicitly recognized a cause of action based on negligent hiring in *Ponticas* in 1983. *Ponticas* involved the employment of an apartment manager who sexually assaulted a tenant. The Supreme Court upheld a jury verdict finding the apartment operators negligent in failing to make a reasonable investigation into the resident manager's background before providing him with a passkey. The court defined negligent hiring as

> predicated on the negligence of an employer in placing a person with known propensities, or propensities which should have been discovered by reasonable investigation, in an employment position in which, *because of the circumstances of the employment,* it should have been foreseeable that the hired individual posed a threat of injury to others.

Honeywell argues that under *Ponticas* it is not liable for negligent hiring because, unlike providing a dangerous resident manager with a passkey, Landin's employment did not enable him to commit the act of violence against Nesser. This argument has merit, and we note that a number of jurisdictions have expressly defined the scope of an employer's duty of reasonable care in hiring as largely dependent on the type of responsibilities associated with the particular job. See *Connes,* 831 P.2d at 1321 (employer's duty in hiring is dependent on anticipated degree of contact between employee and other persons in performing employment duties).

Ponticas rejected the view that employers are required to investigate a prospective employee's criminal background in every job in which the individual has regular contact with the public. Instead, liability is determined by the totality of the circumstances surrounding the hiring and whether the employer exercised reasonable care. The court instructed that

> [t]he scope of the investigation is directly related to the severity of the risk third parties are subjected to by an incompetent employee. Although only slight care might suffice in the hiring of a yardman, a worker on a production line, or other types of employment where the employee would not constitute a high risk of injury to third persons, when the prospective employee is to be furnished a passkey permitting admittance to living quarters of tenants, the employer has the duty to use reasonable care to investigate his competency and reliability prior to employment.

Applying these principles, we conclude that Honeywell did not owe a duty to Nesser at the time of Landin's hire. Landin was employed as a maintenance worker whose job responsibilities entailed no exposure to the general public and required only limited contact with coemployees. Unlike the caretaker in *Ponticas,* Landin's duties did not involve inherent dangers to others, and unlike the tenant in *Ponticas,* Nesser was not a reasonably foreseeable victim at the time Landin was hired.

To reverse the district court's determination on duty as it relates to hiring would extend *Ponticas* and essentially hold that ex-felons are inherently dangerous and that any harmful acts they commit against persons encountered through employment will automatically be considered foreseeable. Such a rule would deter employers from hiring workers with a criminal record and "offend our civilized concept that society must make a reasonable effort to rehabilitate those who have erred so they can be assimilated into the community."

Honeywell did not breach a legal duty to Nesser by hiring Landin because the specific nature of his employment did not create a foreseeable risk of harm, and public policy supports a limitation on this cause of action. The district court correctly determined that Honeywell is not liable to Nesser under a theory of negligent hiring.

II

In recognizing the tort of negligent hiring, *Ponticas* extended established Minnesota case law permitting recovery under theories of negligent retention.

* * * * *

The difference between negligent hiring and negligent retention focuses on when the employer was on notice that an employee posed a threat and failed to take steps to ensure the safety of third parties. The Florida appellate court has provided a useful definition:

> Negligent hiring occurs when, prior to the time the employee is actually hired, the employer knew or should have known of the employee's unfitness, and the issue of liability primarily focuses upon the adequacy of the employer's pre-employment investigation into the employee's background. Negligent retention, on the other hand, occurs when, during the course of employment, the employer becomes aware or should have become aware of problems with an employee that indicated his unfitness, and the employer fails to take further action such as investigating, discharge, or reassignment.

. . . The record contains evidence of a number of episodes in Landin's postimprisonment employment at Honeywell that demonstrate a propensity for abuse and violence toward coemployees.

While at the Golden Valley facility, Landin sexually harassed female employees and challenged a male coworker to fight. After his transfer to St. Louis Park, Landin threatened to kill a coworker during an angry confrontation following a minor car accident. In another employment incident, Landin was hostile and abusive toward a female coworker after problems developed in their friendship. Landin's specific focus on Nesser was demonstrated by several workplace outbursts occurring at the end of June, and on July 1 the words "one more day and you're dead" were scratched on her locker door.

Landin's troubled work history and the escalation of abusive behavior during the summer of 1988 relate directly to the foreseeability prong of duty. The facts . . . show that it was foreseeable that Landin could act violently against a coemployee and against Nesser in particular.

This foreseeability gives rise to a duty of care to Nesser that is not outweighed by policy considerations of employment opportunity. An ex-felon's "opportunity for gainful employment may spell the difference between recidivism and rehabilitation," but it cannot predominate over the need to maintain a safe workplace when specific actions point to future violence.

Our holding is narrow and limited only to the recognition of a legal duty owed to Nesser arising out of Honeywell's continued employment of Landin. It is important to emphasize that in reversing the summary judgment on negligent retention, we do not reach the remaining significant questions of whether Honeywell breached that duty by failing to terminate or discipline Landin, or whether such a breach was a proximate cause of Nesser's death. These are issues generally decided by a jury after a full presentation of facts . . .

DECISION

We affirm the entry of summary judgment on the theories of negligent hiring and supervision, but reverse the summary judgment on the issue of negligent retention.

AFTERWORD

Published reports indicate the *Yunker* case was settled out of court soon after this decision was handed down.

Questions

1. What did the court mean when it said that "negligent hiring and negligent retention are based on direct, not vicarious, liability?"

2. Why did the court reject the negligent supervision claim?

3. Why did the court reject the negligent hiring claim?

4. Why did the court allow the negligent retention issue to go to trial?

5. Gary Weimerskirch, assistant manager at Main Lanes Bowling Alley, walked in on David Coakley, a mechanic at the bowling alley, and Coakley's girlfriend as they were getting dressed, apparently having just engaged in sexual relations. Coakley then told Weimerskirch that he quit and he began to collect his belongings from the work area. Suddenly, Coakley then grabbed a two-by-four plank, ran toward Weimerskirch, and struck him on the head with it. Coakley's criminal record included drug and alcohol-related offenses, along with one misdemeanor assault. However, his employer did not have any knowledge of this criminal record. Furthermore, Coakley had not acted violently at work previously.

   a. What causes of action might Weimerskirch bring against the bowling alley?

   b. Decide the case. Explain. See *Weimerskirch v. Coakley et al.,* 2008 Ohio 1681 (10th App. Dist. 2008).

Part Three—Fair Labor Standards Act

A note was passed to President Franklin D. Roosevelt in 1936 from a young girl:

> I wish you could do something to help us girls. We have been working in a sewing factory . . . getting our minimum pay of $11 a week. Today, the 200 of us girls have been cut down to $4 and $5 and $6 a week.[28]

Roosevelt reportedly remarked that something needed to be done about child labor. The Depression and its tragic suffering, even of those working hard, shattered many Americans' faith in the free market and led to government intervention including, in 1938, the Fair Labor Standards Act (FLSA), which is directed toward these major objectives:

1. The establishment of a minimum wage that provides at least the foundation for a modest standard of living for employees.

2. A flexible ceiling on hours worked weekly, the purpose of which is to increase the number of employed Americans.

3. Child labor protection.

4. Equal pay for equal work regardless of gender. (See Chapter 13.)

[For the U.S. Department of Labor home page, see **www.dol.gov**]

Minimum Wage   In 2009, the federal minimum wage was increased to $7.25 per hour. Critics of a federally mandated minimum wage argue that the government should not interfere in the marketplace, and that increases in minimum wages threaten not only job growth but the livelihoods of many small business owners. Supporters of minimum wage increases point to recent studies concluding that raising the minimum wage does not lead to the loss of low-paying jobs.[29] More than 130 municipalities, many where living costs are particularly high, have adopted their own "living wage" requirements.[30] For example, San Francisco, known for its high cost of living, at this writing has a minimum wage of $10.74.[31] However, as a 2014 study by the National Low Income Housing Coalition shows, minimum-wage workers across the United States cannot afford a one- or two-bedroom apartment at fair market rent.[32] [For state minimum wage laws, see **www.dol.gov/whd/minwage/america.htm**]

Overtime   Most workers covered under FLSA must receive overtime pay of at least 1½ times their regular pay rate for hours worked over 40 hours per week. However, FLSA also recognizes exemptions for certain occupations, such as managers, outside salespersons, administrators, and professionals with advanced degrees; these workers are referred to as "exempt" employees. *Misclassification* of "nonexempt" employees who have overtime rights under FLSA is a common basis for wage-and-hour claims against employers, which have led to high-profile settlements. In 2013, Walmart vision center managers and asset-protection coordinators who were once considered exempt but then reclassified as nonexempt received $4.8 million in back wages and damages.[33] In 2011, Levi-Strauss was ordered to pay over $1 million in overtime back wages to misclassified workers, including employees who held the title of assistant store manager but were incorrectly treated as exempt, given the actual nature of their work.[34] However, the U.S. Supreme Court in 2012 ruled in *Christopher v. Smith-Kline Beecham Corp.* that pharmaceutical sales representatives were not entitled to overtime pay.[35]

Overtime claims often involve disputes over whether the employee was actually working, rather than being engaged in a noncompensable activity. These *off-the-clock* claims in which employers are accused of not giving employees recorded credit for all of the time they have worked sometimes spring from advancing technology. A 2013 poll showed that more than half of employed adults check work messages at least once a day over the weekend, before or after work during the week, and even when they are home sick.[36] An overtime class action suit filed by Jeffrey Allen, a Chicago police sergeant, highlights the impact of technology on time spent working: he says he received a nearly constant barrage of e-mails, text messages, and calls on his government-issued BlackBerry into the late evening, each requiring a response.[37]

In March 2014, President Obama directed the U.S. Department of Labor to address the changing nature of the workplace by updating overtime protections consistent with FLSA's intent. [For President Obama's Memorandum for the Secretary of Labor, see **www .whitehouse.gov/the-press-office/2014/03/13/presidential-memorandum-updating -and-modernizing-overtime-regulations**]

Student Interns   In a tough job market, unpaid internships become more attractive to job seekers and employers alike. To address potentially abusive situations in which employers seek "free labor," the U.S. Department of Labor in 2010 issued a test for unpaid internships to determine whether the interns are employees with wage rights or trainees who are receiving an educational opportunity for their sole benefit and are thus excluded from FLSA protection. Generally, the more an internship focuses on an academic or classroom experience rather than the host's operations, the more likely it need not be a paid position. If interns, on the other hand, are assisting with the employer's daily operations such as clerical work, then they have a right to minimum wage and overtime. [For the six criteria of the U.S. Department of Labor's test for unpaid internships, see **www.dol.gov/whd/regs/compliance /whdfs71.pdf**]

Questions

1. Answer this person's question: "I work as a pharmacist in a large discount retail store. My employer classifies me as exempt under FLSA. Like other pharmacists, I agree to work a specific number of base hours per week which determines my specific rate of pay. However, the employer has changed my base hours so frequently lately that I am effectively being treated as an hourly employee. There have been weeks I have worked more than 40 hours a week. Do I have a right to overtime?"[38]

2. Answer this person's question: "Before I resigned as a sewing manager for a small manufacturing company, where I supervised several employees and received an hourly wage, I regularly arrived at the factory 15 to 45 minutes before the start of my 5:00 AM shift, spending most of that time doing such tasks as reviewing employee schedules, gathering and distributing fabric to my subordinates' workstations, cleaning work area, etc.—but without pay. Does my former employer owe me overtime pay?"[39]

Part Four—Health and Safety at Work

Gordon Jones   "I am here to describe the profound impact my brother's death, while working on a rig engaged in deepwater drilling, has had on our family," Chris Jones told the U.S. House Committee on Natural Resources in March 2011. He was testifying as the surviving brother of Gordon Jones, one of 11 workers killed in the 2010 oil well explosion in the Gulf of Mexico. "[Gordon] was tragically killed aboard the Deepwater Horizon while earning his living as a mud engineer for MI SWACO, a contractor for BP [British Petroleum]. Gordon had nothing to do with this disaster. He was simply doing his job and making his way through his shift so he could get back home to his family. Instead, he never saw his family again. We can thank poor, and likely grossly negligent, decisions by many people and companies for that."[40] In 2012, BP agreed to plead guilty

> He was simply doing his job and making his way through his shift so he could get back home to his family.

and pay $4.5 billion to settle criminal charges. As of this writing, individual managers face manslaughter charges stemming from the fatal 2010 explosion.[41]

Fifteen Die in 2005 Refinery Blast   The 2010 Gulf of Mexico oil well explosion echoed the 2005 disaster at the BP oil refinery in Texas City, Texas. Workers were doing their day's work by restarting a unit that had been down for repair when a gasoline overflow exploded, injuring 170 and killing 15. BP attributed the 2005 disaster primarily to operator error and six employees were fired, but government investigators concluded that management authorized the restart knowing that three key pieces of equipment were not working properly:

> These things do not have to happen. They are preventable. They are predictable, and people do not have to die because they're earning a living.[42]

In August 2010, BP agreed to pay $50.6 million in fines for failing to fix safety hazards at the Texas City refinery after the 2005 explosion.[43]

Deaths, Illnesses, and Injuries   Some workplaces are unacceptably risky, but America has achieved considerable progress in building safety on the job. Workplace fatalities that totaled 6,632 in 1995 fell to 4,383 in 2012, continuing a decreasing trend over the previous several years.[44]

Nonfatal injuries and illnesses have also declined from 3.9 per 100 workers in 2008 to 3.3 in 2012.[45] The overall job safety improvement should be viewed in the context of the U.S. labor shift away from such industries as manufacturing to service roles.

OSHA

A federal agency, the Occupational Safety and Health Administration (OSHA), is responsible for ensuring safe workplaces. The 1970 Occupational Safety and Health Act imposes a *general duty* on most employers to provide a workplace free of "recognized hazards causing or likely to cause death or serious physical harm to employees." Employers have an absolute duty to remove any serious and preventable workplace hazards that are generally recognized in the industry and are known to the employer or should be known to the employer. That general duty is then supplemented with numerous specific *standards*. [For the OSHA home page, see **www.osha.gov**]

Standards

OSHA, under the U.S. Department of Labor, promulgates and enforces health and safety standards that identify and seek to correct specific workplace hazards and problems. These can range from exposure to cancer-causing agents (such as the chemical benzene) to the surprisingly commonplace problem of one worker restarting a machine while another is servicing it. For example, under a long-fought-for OSHA standard made effective in 2008, employers must pay for all OSHA-mandated personal protective equipment (safety-specific eyewear, skin creams, clothing, etc.).[46] In 2012, culminating a rule-making process that began in 2006, OSHA issued a revised the Hazard Communication Standards to align with an international system adopted by the United Nations in 2002.[47]

More New Standards?

The protracted development of OSHA regulations typifies the ongoing ideological and practical conflict over imposing additional safety rules in American workplaces. Some of the competing considerations are illustrated by recent disputes over ergonomics and workplace violence.

Ergonomics   Repetitive motion and overexertion injuries, such as carpal tunnel syndrome and back strains, account for about one-third of workplace injuries.[48] Employers often try to address these problems with ergonomics, "the science of fitting the job to the worker"[49] (for example, changing the height of a workstation). After years of work, OSHA issued ergonomics standards in 2000, but Congress repealed those rules in 2001 after business complaints about the costs of implementation. OSHA now employs a system of voluntary ergonomics guidelines, but critics consider them weak and vague. OSHA also can apply its general duty authority to address repetitive motion and over exertion. Experts now believe the carpal tunnel fears about keyboarding may have been exaggerated, although many blue-collar, assembly-line workers certainly are at risk. [For advice on measures to reduce repetitive stress problems for students, see **http://ergo.human.cornell.edu/**]

Violence

"Going postal."   "Going postal" became an unfortunate but recognizable shorthand expression for violence in the workplace. Workplace shootings have made for sadly familiar headlines, with no particular job site immune from such tragedy.

Should OSHA create specific duties for employers regarding workplace violence? Would those rules be effective? Or will the market and naturally evolving workplace conditions provide the most effective and efficient protection?

Responses to these questions might be informed by legislation enacted in more than 20 states prohibiting employers from banning firearms in parking areas, and employers' reactions to these laws. Concerned with maintaining workplace safety, employers have focused on spotting and protecting against employees' aggression through trainings and increased security when, for example, terminating an employee.[50]

Variances

Employers may seek both permanent and temporary *variances* (exceptions) from OSHA standards. A permanent variance may be granted only if the workplace will be as safe as if the standard were enforced. A temporary variance permits additional time to put in place the necessary compliance measures. Employees have a right to a hearing to contest variances.

Mine Safety

On Monday, April 5, 2010, an explosion at the Upper Big Branch Mine-South in Montcoal, West Virginia, owned by a subsidiary of Massey Energy, Inc., killed 29 miners. In 2009, the Upper Branch Mine suffered a "significant spike in safety violations" leading the U.S. Department of Labor's Mine Safety and Health Administration (MSHA) to issue 515 citations and orders at that mine, and another 124 by April 2010. In November 2010, MSHA took the toughest enforcement measure ever against a mine, seeking a court order to temporarily close a Massey-owned mine in Kentucky which MSHA believed to be engaged in a pattern of failing to inspect and maintain critical areas.

In January 2011, MSHA announced a court order requiring Massey to comply with a plan to ensure the miners' health and safety.

Sources: Briefing by Department of Labor Mine Health and Safety Administration on Disaster at Massey Energy's Upper Big Branch Mine-South [**www.msha.gov/performancecoal/DOL-MSHA_president_report.pdf**] (April 26, 2010); and **www.dol.gov/opa/media/press/MSHA/MSHA20101533.htm**] [**www.msha.gov/media/PRESS/201 1/NR110105.asp**].

OSHA Information Requirements

Right to Know

OSHA has adopted an employee *hazard communication standard* to protect employees from the dangers associated with chemicals and other toxins in the workplace. Chemical manufacturers and importers must develop *material safety data sheets* (MSDS) for all chemicals. Employers must then label all chemical containers so that employees will know about the chemical and its dangers, and employers must educate employees about chemical hazards and how to deal with them.

Records

As a general rule, businesses must maintain records listing and summarizing work-related injuries, illnesses, and deaths. A summary of those records must be posted at the job. Notice of any OSHA citations of imminent dangers on the job must also be posted at the job site. OSHA recently reformed and simplified the record-keeping process. Some smaller companies, especially those engaging in nonhazardous activities, do not need to meet the record-keeping requirements.

Does an employee's injury suffered in a go-cart race held as part of an off-site team building event need to be reported? According to a 2009 letter from OSHA responding to this inquiry, an injury in those circumstances is work-related, and therefore reportable, even if the employee had the option to return to work or take a half-day vacation instead of participating in the go-cart race that followed a mandatory off-site meeting.[51] A recent federal appellate decision suggested that requiring record keeping of all workplace injuries may be more efficient than analyzing whether such an injury is work-related.[52]

Enforcement

OSHA's most publicized enforcement mechanism is the unannounced on-site inspection. Inspections arise at the initiative of the agency itself or at the request of employees or their representatives. The inspections must be conducted in a reasonable manner during working hours or other reasonable times, and ordinarily they must not be announced in advance. Employers can demand a warrant prior to inspection. With proper justification, warrants can easily be secured from a federal magistrate. Employer and employee representatives may accompany the inspector.

To enhance efficiency, OSHA practices a targeted, site-specific inspection plan designed to identify and monitor the workplaces most likely to have safety and health problems. A 2012 academic study found a nearly 10 percent drop in injuries in the four years following a randomized governmental safety inspection.[53] However, an employer can become exempt from such inspections under OSHA's Voluntary Protection Program (VPP), a program that has drawn criticism.[54]

Citations

Citations may be issued if violations are discovered during the inspection process. Immediate, serious threats can be restrained with a court order. Following a citation, the employer may ask to meet with an area OSHA official to discuss the problem. Often a settlement emerges from these meetings. Failing a settlement, the employer can appeal to the independent OSHA Review Commission and thereafter to the federal court of appeals. Violations may lead to fines and/or imprisonment. In 2012, for example, OSHA cited and fined Excel, a company packing Hershey's chocolates, $283,000 for failing to report dozens of serious injuries to its workers, including students on an international exchange program.[55]

Firmer Enforcement?   The business community criticizes OSHA for unfairly increasing the cost of production by imposing inflexible and overzealous expectations. Labor organizations and job safety advocates, on the other hand, have criticized OSHA as a timid, faltering safety shield.

As part of the Obama administration's efforts to increase enforcement and become more aggressive in protecting workers' safety, OSHA, in 2010, announced its Severe Violator Enforcement Program (SVEP). SVEP concentrates on employers who have demonstrated indifference to their safety obligations by engaging in willful, repeated, or "failure to abate" violations. SVEP uses mandatory follow-up inspections, press releases, and increased fines, among other tools, to send a clear message that such conduct will be rigorously addressed by OSHA.[56] OSHA makes public its list of severe violators. [For the current SVEP logs, see **https://www.osha.gov/dep/**]

But the critics' question remains: Is the market the best vehicle for achieving job safety?

Workers' Compensation

Korey Stringer, a 27-year-old Pro Bowl tackle, died of heatstroke complications.

Korey Stringer, a 27-year-old Pro Bowl tackle, died of heatstroke complications on August 1, 2001, after going through a preseason Minnesota Vikings workout.[57] Normally, when an employee is injured or dies on the job, the employee or the estate may not sue for damages. Rather, recovery is limited to the fixed sum provided for by the workers' compensation statute, regardless of fault. Stringer's family, however, filed a wrongful death suit seeking to hold the Vikings and various individuals responsible for gross negligence and other wrongs in responding to Stringer's heatstroke. The Vikings argued that the Stringer suit was barred by the state workers' compensation law. Minnesota is one of a number of states, however, that recognize an exception to workers' compensation exclusivity provisions in cases of *gross negligence* by the defendants.[58] The Stringers' case reached the Minnesota Supreme Court in 2005 where the 4–2 majority ruled on technical grounds against the family's gross negligence claim, thus limiting their remedy to workers' compensation, a sum much beneath Stringer's projected commercial worth.[59]

Early in the 20th century, the states began enacting workers' compensation laws to provide an administrative remedy for those, like Stringer, who are injured or killed on the job. Previously, employers' superior financial resources and various technical legal defenses meant that employees often could not successfully sue to recover damages for their on-the-job injuries. All states now provide some form of workers' compensation not requiring a lawsuit. Instead, workers or their families apply for compensation based on illness, injury, or death. Typically, the system is governed by a state board or commission. Most decisions are routine and based on the completed application. Often a claims examiner will verify the nature and severity of the injury. Although workers' compensation is generally the exclusive remedy for workplace injury or death caused by employers' negligence, many states recognize an exception for intentional torts. An exception based on gross negligence, however, is rare.

In most states, employers are compelled to participate in workers' compensation, depending on state law, either by purchasing insurance privately, by contributing to a state-managed fund, or by being self-insured (paying claims directly from their own funds). Firms with good safety records are rewarded with lower premium payments.

No Joke?

Matthew Simms worked as a server in the Manassas, Virginia, location of a national chain restaurant. During his work shift, Simms walked into the kitchen to enter an order into a computer and to print a check for a customer. Three other employees in the kitchen who were Simms's friends started throwing ice at him, apparently as a joke. As Simms lifted his hand in an attempt to block the ice, he felt his left shoulder dislocate. Simms was taken to a hospital for treatment of his injury. As a result of the injury, Simms alleged he was unable to use his shoulder in daily activities and was unable to work for a period of time. Should Simms receive workers' compensation for his injuries? Explain.

Source: Simms v. Ruby Tuesdays, Inc., 281 Va. 114, 704 S.E.2d 359 (Va. 2011).

Benefits

Medical and rehabilitation expenses along with partial income replacement are provided according to state law. The amount of the income award is normally a percentage of the worker's salary either for a specified period or indefinitely, depending on the severity of the injury. Injury benefits normally amount to one-half to two-thirds of regular wages. Death benefits ordinarily are tied to the wages of the deceased.

Coverage

Certain employment classifications such as agriculture may be excluded from workers' compensation, but about 90 percent of the labor force is covered. Most on-the-job injuries are covered, but those that are self-inflicted (including starting a fight) and others such as those springing from alcohol or drug use may not be.

Legal Requirements

In general, injuries, illnesses, and deaths are compensable where the harm (1) *arose out of the employment* and (2) *occurred in the course of employment* (explained next in *Wait*). Proof of employer negligence is not required, and the traditional defenses such as contributory negligence are not available to the employer. Thus, workers' compensation provides a form of no-fault protection in the workplace. Workers give up the right to sue, and employers participate in an insurance system that recognizes the inevitability of workplace harm.

Although workers' compensation recovery is the exclusive remedy for workplace injury, illness, or death, some jurisdictions allow litigation in cases of intentional torts and/or gross negligence, as noted earlier. [For the Workers' Compensation Research Institute, see **www.wcrinet.org**]

Litigation

Notwithstanding its no-fault character, workers' compensation has generated many lawsuits. Consider the example of David Gross, a 16-year-old employee at KFC, who was injured when he placed water in a pressurized deep fryer to clean it. KFC's employee handbook explicitly instructed against such an action, as did a warning label on the fryer. Furthermore, immediately preceding the incident, Gross's supervisor and two coworkers admonished him to not do it. The employer fired Gross for violating an important workplace safety rule. The Ohio Supreme Court initially terminated his workers' compensation benefits using the "voluntary abandonment" doctrine under which workers' compensation benefits may be terminated because the loss of income is not due to the injury itself. However, the Court then reconsidered and ordered reinstatement of Gross's benefits.[60] The *Wait* case that follows raises some current issues regarding workers' compensation for the telecommuting employee.

LEGAL BRIEFCASE

Wait v. Travelers Indemnity Company of Illinois
240 S.W.3d 220 (Tenn. S.Ct. 2007)

Chief Justice Barker

I. FACTUAL BACKGROUND

From October 1998 until September 3, 2004, the plaintiff, Kristina Wait, worked as Senior Director of Health Initiative and Strategic Planning for the American Cancer Society ("ACS"). Because of the lack of office space at its Nashville, Tennessee facilities, the ACS allowed the plaintiff to work from her East Nashville home. The plaintiff converted a spare bedroom of her home into an office, and the ACS furnished the necessary office equipment, including a printer, a facsimile machine, a dedicated business telephone line, and a budget to purchase office supplies. In all respects, the plaintiff's home office functioned as her work place. Not only did the plaintiff perform her daily work for the ACS at her home office, the plaintiff's supervisor and co-workers attended meetings at the office in her house. There is no evidence in the record with respect to any designated hours or conditions of the plaintiff's employment, nature of her work space, or other work rules. Significantly, the plaintiff's work for the ACS did not require her to open her house to the public. In fact, during working hours the plaintiff locked the outside doors of her home and activated an alarm system for her protection. Unfortunately, however, on September 3, 2004, the plaintiff opened her door to a neighbor, Nathaniel Sawyers ("Sawyers"), who brutally assaulted and severely injured the plaintiff.

The plaintiff met Sawyers in May or early June of 2004 at a neighborhood cookout she attended with her husband. Thereafter, Sawyers, who lived approximately one block from the plaintiff's home, came to the plaintiff's home for a short social visit on a *weekend* day in late June. The plaintiff and her husband spoke with Sawyers for approximately five minutes, and then Sawyers left. In August, Sawyers came to the plaintiff's home on a weekday for a social visit; however, the plaintiff was preparing to leave her home office for a job-related television interview. The plaintiff told Sawyers that she was going to a business meeting. When Sawyers replied that he was on his way to a job interview in Nashville, the plaintiff allowed Sawyers to ride with her to his job interview.

On September 3, 2004, the plaintiff was working alone at her home office. Around noon, the plaintiff was in her kitchen preparing her lunch when Sawyers knocked on her door. The plaintiff answered and invited Sawyers into the house, and he stayed for a short time and then left. However, a moment later, Sawyers returned, telling the plaintiff that he had left his keys in her kitchen. When the plaintiff turned away from the door, Sawyers followed her inside and brutally assaulted the plaintiff without provocation or explanation, beating the plaintiff until she lost consciousness. As a result of this assault, the plaintiff suffered severe injuries, including head trauma, a severed ear, several broken bones, stab wounds, strangulation injuries, and permanent nerve damage to the left side of her body.

On December 12, 2005, the plaintiff filed a complaint seeking workers' compensation benefits from Travelers Indemnity Company of Illinois, the insurer of the ACS. (The plaintiff did not name the ACS as a defendant.) The plaintiff alleged that the she was entitled to workers' compensation benefits for the injuries she sustained in the assault because the assault arose out of and occurred in the course of her employment with the

ACS. The defendant . . . [denied] that the injuries arose out of or occurred in the course of the plaintiff's employment.

Following discovery, the defendant filed a motion for summary judgment, which the chancery court granted. The chancery court concluded that the plaintiff's injuries did not arise out of or occur in the course of her employment with the ACS. Additionally, the chancery court noted that Sawyers "was not [at the plaintiff's home office] on any kind of business with the [ACS], nor was he really there on any kind of business with the [p]laintiff."

The plaintiff appealed. We accepted review.

* * * * *

(II OMITTED-ED.)

III. ANALYSIS

A. The Workers' Compensation Act and Telecommuting

The Workers' Compensation Act ("Act"), codified at Tennessee Code Annotated sections 50-6-101 to -801 (2005), is a legislatively created quid pro quo system where an injured worker forfeits any potential common law rights for recovery against his or her employer in return for a system that provides compensation completely independent of any fault on the part of the employer. The Act should be liberally construed in favor of compensation and any doubts should be resolved in the employee's favor. However, this liberal construction requirement does not authorize courts to amend, alter, or extend its provisions beyond its obvious meaning.

* * * * *

This case requires us to apply the Act to a new and growing trend in the labor and employment market: telecommuting. An employee telecommutes when he or she takes advantage of electronic mail, internet, facsimile machines and other technological advancements to work from home or a place other than the traditional work site. In 2006, approximately thirty-four million American workers telecommuted to some degree.

* * * * *

Not surprisingly, however, this innovative working arrangement has resulted in an issue of first impression: whether the injuries a telecommuter sustains as a result of an assault at her home arise out of and occur in the course of her employment.

B. Did the plaintiff's injuries occur in the course of her employment?

It is well settled in Tennessee, and in many other jurisdictions, that for an injury to be compensable under the Act, it must both "arise out of" and occur "in the course of" employment. Although both of these statutory requirements seek to ensure a connection between the employment and the injuries for which benefits are being sought, they are not synonymous. As such, the "arising out of" requirement refers to cause or origin; whereas, "in the course of" denotes the time, place, and circumstances of the injury. Furthermore, we have consistently abstained from adopting any particular judicial test, doctrine, formula, or label that purports to "clearly define the line between accidents and injuries which arise out of and in the course of employment [and] those which do not[.]"

* * * * *

In this case, we will consider the second requirement first. An injury occurs in the course of employment "when it takes place within the period of the employment, at a place where the employee reasonably may be, and while the employee is fulfilling work duties or engaged in doing something incidental thereto."

Generally, injuries sustained during personal breaks are compensable.

* * * * *

[T]he defendant here argues that the plaintiff's injuries are not compensable because the plaintiff was not "fulfilling a work duty" in admitting Sawyers into her kitchen. It is true that the plaintiff suffered her injuries while preparing her lunch in the kitchen of her home; however, the plaintiff's work site was located within her home. Under these circumstances, the plaintiff's kitchen was comparable to the kitchens and break rooms that employers routinely provide at traditional work sites. Moreover, the ACS was aware of and implicitly approved of the plaintiff's work site. Her supervisor and co-workers had attended meetings at the plaintiff's home office. It is reasonable to conclude that the ACS realized that the plaintiff would take personal breaks during the course of her working day. . . .

Thus, after careful review, we conclude that the injuries the plaintiff sustained while on her lunch break, occurred during the course of the plaintiff's employment. The plaintiff was assaulted at a place where her employer could reasonably expect her to be. The ACS permitted the plaintiff to work from home for approximately four years. The plaintiff's supervisor and co-workers regularly came to her home office for meetings. The record does not suggest that the ACS restricted the plaintiff's activities during working hours or prohibited her from taking personal breaks. The facts do not show that the plaintiff was engaging in any prohibited conduct or was

violating any company policy by preparing lunch in her kitchen. It is reasonable to conclude that the ACS would have anticipated that the plaintiff would take a lunch break at her home just as employees do at traditional work sites. Importantly, Sawyer's initial visit was very brief and spontaneous. Unless instructed otherwise by the employer, an employee working from a home office who answers a knock at her door and briefly admits an acquaintance into her home does not necessarily depart so far from her work duties so as to remove her from the course of her employment. This is not to say, however, that situations may never arise where more prolonged or planned social visits might well remove the employee from the course of the employment.

In arguing that the plaintiff's injury did not occur "in the course of" her employment, the defendant maintains that the plaintiff's decision to admit Sawyers into her home was not a work duty. However, this argument misses the mark on this requirement because the Act does not explicitly state that the employee's actions must benefit the employer; it only requires that the injuries occur in "the course of" the employment. Because the plaintiff was engaged in a permissible personal break incidental to her employment, we reject the defendant's narrow interpretation of the Act. The question is not whether the plaintiff's injuries occurred while she was performing a duty owed to the ACS, but rather whether the time, place, and circumstances demonstrate that the injuries occurred while the plaintiff was engaged in an activity incidental to her employment. Accordingly, we hold that the plaintiff suffered her injuries during the course of her employment and disagree with the chancery court's conclusion on this important point.

C. Did the plaintiff's injuries arise out of her employment?

Even though the plaintiff's injuries occurred "in the course of" her employment, we nevertheless hold that they did not "arise out of" her job duties with the ACS. The phrase "arising out of" requires that a causal connection exist between the employment conditions and the resulting injury. With respect to whether an assault arises out of employment, we have previously delineated assaults into three general classifications:

(1) assaults with an "inherent connection" to employment such as disputes over performance, pay or termination; (2) assaults stemming from "inherently private" disputes imported into the employment setting from the claimant's domestic or private life and not exacerbated by the employment; and (3) assaults resulting from a "neutral force" such as random assaults on employees by individuals outside the employment relationship.

When an assault has an "inherent connection" to the employment it is compensable. On the other hand, assaults originating from "inherently private" disputes and imported into the work place are not compensable. However, whether "neutral assaults" are compensable turns on the "facts and circumstances of the employment."

The assault in this case is best described as a "neutral assault." In granting the defendant's motion for summary judgment, the chancery court commented: "[T]here's certainly not any evidence that this person who committed the assault was part of the working employment relationship and was not there on any kind of business related to the [ACS] or really any business with the employee." We agree with the chancery court's conclusions. A "neutral force" assault is one that is "neither personal to the claimant nor distinctly associated with the employment."

The categories focus on what catalyst spurred the assault, i.e., was it a dispute arising from a work-related duty, was it a dispute arising from a personal matter, or was it unexplained or irrational? An assault that is spurred by neither a catalyst inherently connected to the employment nor stemming from an inherently private dispute is most aptly labeled as a "neutral force" assault. Here, the undisputed facts clearly show that the assault had neither an inherent connection with the employment, nor did it stem from a personal dispute between Sawyers and the plaintiff. Therefore, we must focus our attention on the facts and circumstances of the plaintiff's employment and its relationship to the injuries sustained by the plaintiff.

Generally, for an injury to "arise out of" employment, it must emanate from a peculiar danger or risk inherent to the nature of the employment. However, in limited circumstances, where the employment involves "indiscriminate exposure to the general public," the "street risk" doctrine may supply the required causal connection between the employment and the injury.

* * * * *

[T]his Court held that the "street risk" doctrine satisfied the causal connection requirement where the employee was assaulted by unknown assailants as he removed paperwork from his employer's van while it was parked at his residence. We carefully limited application of the street risk doctrine to "workers whose employment exposes them to the hazards of the street, or who are assaulted under circumstances that fairly suggest they were singled out for attack because of their association with their employer. . . ."

Unlike our previous cases in which the facts supported application of the "street risk" doctrine to provide the necessary causal connection, the facts here do not establish that the plaintiff's employment exposed her to a street hazard or that she was singled out for her association with her employer. There is nothing to indicate that she was targeted because of her association with her employer or that she was charged with safeguarding her employer's property. Additionally, the plaintiff was not advancing the interests of the ACS when she allowed Sawyers into her kitchen, and her employment with the ACS did not impose any duty upon the plaintiff to admit Sawyers to her home.

The plaintiff argues that had it not been for her employment arrangement, she would not have been at home to suffer these attacks. However, we have never held that any and every assault which occurs at the work site arises out of employment. Additionally, although Sawyers knew from a previous visit that the plaintiff was home during the day, there is nothing in the record which indicates that there was a causal connection between the plaintiff's employment and the assault.

* * * * *

Affirmed.

Questions

1. The Tennessee Supreme Court in *Wait* (and most courts in workers' compensation cases) required a two-part showing that the injury must "arise out of" and "in the course of" employment.
   a. Explain those two standards.
   b. Must an employee be engaged in an activity that benefits the employer in order to be "in the course of employment?" Explain.
   c. Why did the court conclude that Wait's injuries did not arise out of her employment?

2. Why did the court conclude that the "street risk" doctrine did not apply to Wait's injuries?

3. Fernandez, an exotic dancer, left her job drunk and was seriously injured in a crash while riding as a passenger in a car driven by another dancer. The crash came within one hour of leaving work. Her intoxication led to her decision to ride with her intoxicated coworker. Fernandez sought workers' compensation. She claimed that her employer, Bottoms Up Lounge in Council Bluffs, Iowa, required her to socialize with male customers when not dancing and to generate at least two drinks per hour from customers. Dancers were not required to drink, but most dancers consumed six to eight drinks per night or more. Did Fernandez's injury arise out of and in the course of

employment so that she can recover workers' compensation? Explain. See *2800 Corp. v. Fernandez*, 528 N.W.2d 124 (Ia. S.Ct. 1995).

4. Joseph Smyth, a college mathematics instructor, was killed while driving his personal auto home from work. At the time, Smyth had student papers with him, which he intended to grade that evening. He often worked at home. Many faculty members took work home in the evenings. However, the college did not require that practice. Indeed, the college neither encouraged nor discouraged working at home.

The widely adopted "going and coming rule" provides that employees injured while commuting to and from work, in general, are not covered by workers' compensation.

a. Should Smyth (and other teachers) be exempted from the going and coming rule, thus permitting recovery by Smyth's family? Explain. See *Santa Rosa Junior College v. Workers' Compensation Appeals Board and Joann Smyth,* 708 P.2d 673 (Cal. S.Ct. 1985).

b. Would you reach a different conclusion had a student been accompanying Smyth? Explain.

5. Casimer Gacioch worked at a Stroh Brewery. The company provided free beer at work. When he began work in 1947 he drank only three to four beers on the weekend. He was fired in 1974, by which time he was drinking 12 bottles of beer daily. After Gacioch's death, his wife sought workers' compensation benefits. The evidence indicated that Gacioch had a predisposition to alcoholism but was not an alcoholic at the time he was hired. How would you rule on the widow's workers' compensation claim? Explain. See *Gacioch v. Stroh Brewery,* 466 N.W.2d 303 (Mich Ct. of Appeals, 1991).

Part Five—Employee Privacy

Privacy on the Job? More than half of Americans between 18 and 25 have done at least one of the following: gotten a tattoo, dyed their hair an untraditional color, or had a body piercing other than on their ear lobe. Fewer than a quarter of those between 40 and 64 have done any of these.[61] Will you have to give up that butterfly tattoo on your ankle when you move on to the "real world" of professional employment? Typically, employers have dress codes requiring a neat, clean appearance. Other employers might have specific requirements, such as covering tattoos during work hours.[62]

> Will you have to give up that butterfly tattoo?

Employer oversight extends well beyond appearance policies. Drug tests, integrity tests, personality tests, surveillance, and as seen earlier in this chapter, searches for applicants' online reputations are routine personnel practices in many firms. Employers have an interest in these strategies not only to hire better employees and improve productivity but to protect coworkers, reduce insurance claims, and shield consumers from poor products and service. On the other hand, job applicants and employees resist parking their personal identity and privacy at the office door.

Privacy off the Job? A growing number of employers offer incentives such as financial rewards or prizes to employees who try to get healthier. These wellness programs may reward employees for taking part in a fitness assessment or weight-loss program, or attaining certain health metrics such as an ideal blood pressure or cholesterol level. Penalties can also be exacted in the form of higher health care premiums or an actual payment.[63] Although supporters praise such programs as benefitting employees who otherwise might not have the incentive or opportunity to improve their health, critics observe that such programs overstep boundaries in the employment relationship, intruding into employees' rights to make their own health-related choices. As Randall Wilson, general counsel of the Iowa Civil Liberties Union, explained:

> The concern is that with the rise of corporate power, we're beginning to feel at the mercy of a government operating outside a government.[64]

Robert Barbee was fired for dating Melanie Tomita.

And what about office romance? Robert Barbee, former national sales manager for Household Automotive Finance, sued HAF after he was fired for dating Melanie Tomita, an HAF salesperson. They worked in different locations, and he did not directly supervise her. He claimed that the dismissal violated his right to privacy, but a California appeals court ruled for HAF in part on the grounds that the company needed to prevent conflicts of interest, sexual harassment claims, and the appearance of favoritism.[65] Although relatively few office romance cases have reached the courts, most employers appear comfortable in restricting office romance to some degree, such as prohibiting relationships between a supervisor and subordinate or requiring employees who are dating to inform their supervisor.[66]

Monitoring

The City of Ontario, California, Police Department issued pagers to its police officers for business purposes. The city paid for a text messaging plan, but officers who exceeded the allotted messaging quota were required to pay overage charges. While at work, Sargeant Jeff Quon sent personal, sometimes sexually explicit, text messages on his police department-issued pager to both his then-wife and a coworker with whom he was romantically involved. Noticing a frequency in overage charges, the police department audited the content of police officers' texts to determine whether the overage charges were the result of work-related messages that might show the need to upgrade the text-messaging plan. Although a workplace policy stated that employees had no expectation of privacy in using Internet or e-mail provided them at work, it did not address the pagers given to the police officers. As a result of the audit, Quon was disciplined for misusing the pager.

The question facing the Supreme Court in 2010 was whether the police department's review of Sargeant Quon's text messages violated his Fourth Amendment right to privacy. Acknowledging that "workplace norms" regarding technology are evolving, in 2010 the U.S. Supreme Court held in *City of Ontario v. Quon* that even assuming Quon had a reasonable expectation of privacy in his text messages, the police department's review of the text messages did not violate Quon's Fourth Amendment rights. Ontario had a legitimate reason for the search, and the search was not excessive in scope.[67]

Employers' rights to monitor electronic messages may be defined on a case-by-case basis. A former employee had sent e-mails to her attorney regarding a possible workplace discrimination claim using a company laptop computer and her personal, password-protected e-mail account rather than her business e-mail address. After she resigned and sued, her former employer hired a computer expert who retrieved the e-mails between her and her attorney, which were then reviewed by the company's attorney. Holding that the employee had a reasonable expectation of privacy in those e-mails, the New Jersey Supreme Court also acknowledged that although employers can establish rules regarding use of workplace computers and discipline employees accordingly, this power did not include the right to read privileged communications between an employee and her attorney.[68]

The Law

In general, employers can lawfully monitor workers' attendance, performance, e-mail, use of the Internet, and so on, but uncertainty remains. Having a clear, written workplace policy regarding the use and monitoring of workplace technology is a good employment practice. [For a sample policy regarding technology in the workplace, see **www.shrm.org /TemplatesTools/Samples/Policies/Pages/CMS_000558.aspx**]

The primary federal legislation, the 1986 Electronic Communications Privacy Act, prohibits private individuals and organizations from intercepting wire, oral, or electronic communications. The act provides for two exceptions, however: (1) prior consent by one of the parties to the communication, and (2) employer monitoring in the "ordinary course of business" by telephone or other device furnished by a provider of wire or electronic communication service. Thus, workplace monitoring of phone calls (except for purely private conversations), workplace computers, voice mail, e-mail, and Internet use are all likely to be considered lawful at this point if approached in a reasonable manner.

As discussed previously in this chapter, job applicants face the possibility that their prospective employers might be researching their online reputations. Should the employer be allowed to require job applicants to disclose their passwords to their Facebook and other social media accounts? In 2012, six states—California, Delaware, Illinois, Maryland, Michigan, and New Jersey—enacted legislation prohibiting an employer from requesting or requiring an employee or applicant to disclose a user name or password for a personal social media account.[69]

Requesting access to employees' social media accounts, even in the absence of legislation, still creates potential liability for the employer, as illustrated in a 2009 case involving a restaurant employee's invitation-only group on MySpace.com for coworkers to "vent" about work. Posts included sexual comments about the employer's managers and customers as well as references to illegal drug use. When one member showed the MySpace profile to a manager, she was later asked by another manager to share the password to access the profile. The employer terminated the profile's creator as well as another one of the invited coworkers, who sued for, among other claims, invasion of privacy. Given that a jury could reasonably find that the invited member of the MySpace group was coerced into providing the password, making the employer's access unauthorized, a federal district court upheld the jury's verdict against the employer.[70]

"BYOD" to Work

While some employers provide employees with a cell phone or tablet for work use, others may encourage use of employees' own personal devices, known as "bring your own device (BYOD)." According to a 2013 survey, approximately one-fifth of employers may perform "remote wipes" of employees' devices such as cell phones during or after employment as a means of securing data. This practice results in employees losing photos, contact lists, and other personal data. Employees who are asked to BYOD face the dilemma of either risking the loss of personal information when a cell phone is erased, or appearing to be not committed to their jobs for refusing to use a personal device to stay electronically connected to work.

Question

How may an employer limit liability for invasion of privacy claims arising from remote wipes of employees' personal cell phones? Explain.

Source: Lauren Weber, "BYOD? Leaving a Job Can Mean Losing Pictures of Grandma," *The Wall Street Journal*, January 21, 2014 [**http://online.wsj.com/news/articles/SB10001424052702304027204579335033824665964**].

LEGAL BRIEFCASE

Koeppel v. Speirs   2010 Iowa
App. LEXIS 25 (Ct.App. Iowa 2010) (unpubd op.)

EISENHAUER, P. J.

I. BACKGROUND FACTS AND PROCEEDINGS

[Sara] Koeppel and Deanna Miller were the only employees of Speirs, an insurance agent. A small (4' x 7') bathroom with a sink and toilet is located in the office. On December 27, 2005, Koeppel discovered a digital surveillance camera hidden inside the office bathroom. After contacting the Waterloo Police Department, a search warrant was obtained and officers located the camera in the bathroom. The camera was positioned to view the toilet and surrounding area. When confronted by police, Speirs produced the receiver and monitor for the camera from a locked drawer in his desk.

When questioned about the presence of the camera, Speirs admitted he had placed it in the bathroom on December 26, 2005, and stated he did so because he suspected one of his employees was abusing drugs while at work and was concerned she would embezzle money. Speirs claimed he was unable to get a signal from the camera when it was in the bathroom. At the time the officers arrived, the surveillance system was not set up to receive images from the camera. However, setup could be completed by plugging the equipment found in Speirs's desk drawer into an electrical outlet.

After connecting the equipment, the officers tested it and found it did not work. Speirs told the officers the camera battery was likely dead. After changing the battery at Speirs's

suggestion, a fuzzy picture of the toilet seat and bathroom wall was visible. The image would cut in and out every few seconds. Videotapes located in Speirs's office were blank.

Speirs purchased the camera on November 20, 2005. Miller told the police, when interviewed on December 28, she saw the camera in the bathroom on November 28, 2005. Speirs, in another proceeding, testified he used the camera to monitor Miller at her desk on December 10, 2005, and in seven or ten viewings, he observed no wrongdoing.

* * * * *

Koeppel [sued] Speirs, alleging . . . invasion of privacy. . . . Speirs then filed a motion for summary judgment . . . claiming there was no actual intrusion upon Koeppel's privacy because there is no evidence he viewed her in the restroom. Koeppel [argued] Speirs's act of placing the camera in the bathroom with the intent to view her was an invasion of her privacy. She also argued there was sufficient evidence for the jury to find the camera was operational. . . . The district court entered its ruling, granting Speirs's motion. The court agreed Speirs intended to view Koeppel while she was in the bathroom, but concluded Koeppel could only be liable for an actual intrusion on her privacy, not an attempted intrusion. Finding no evidence Speirs viewed Koeppel in the bathroom, the court dismissed the claim.

On November 25, 2008, Koeppel appealed. . . .

* * * * *

III. INVASION OF PRIVACY

Koeppel first contends the court erred in granting summary judgment on her invasion of privacy claim. She contends Speirs's act of placing a camera in the bathroom with the intent to view her is sufficient to support a cause of action for invasion of privacy. In the alternative, she contends there is a question of fact as to whether there was an actual intrusion into her privacy.

. . . Iowa has adopted the tort of invasion of privacy, as set forth in the Restatement (Second) of Torts (1977), which provides the right to privacy can be invaded by "unreasonable intrusion upon the seclusion of another." . . . Under this theory,

> [o]ne who *intentionally intrudes,* physically or otherwise, upon the solitude or seclusion of another or his private affairs or concerns, is subject to liability to the other for invasion of privacy, if the intrusion would be *highly offensive to a reasonable person.*

. . . To recover under this theory, Koeppel must show Speirs intentionally intruded upon her seclusion, and that a reasonable person would find the intrusion "highly offensive." . . . .

There is no question viewing or recording Koeppel while in the bathroom would be considered "highly offensive" by any reasonable person. There also can be no dispute a bathroom is a place where one enjoys seclusion. Nor is it debatable that Speirs acted intentionally in placing a recording device in the bathroom. The question presented in this case is whether there is enough evidence to create a question of fact as to whether there was an intrusion on Koeppel's privacy.

The district court concluded an actual invasion of privacy must occur for the cause of action to stand and found no facts supported an actual invasion. Koeppel argues intent to intrude on privacy is enough to maintain a cause of action. She cites *In re Marriage of Tigges* and two cases outside this jurisdiction in support of her argument.

In the case of *Tigges,* our supreme court addressed the question of unreasonable intrusion upon the seclusion of another where a husband secretly videotaped his wife in their bedroom. *Tigges,* 758 N.W.2d at 825. The husband argued there was no invasion of privacy because the video captured nothing "private" or "sexual" in nature. *Id.* at 829. In rejecting this claim, our supreme court stated:

> The wrongfulness of the conduct springs not from the specific nature of the recorded activities, but instead from the fact that Cathy's activities were recorded without her knowledge and consent at a time and place and under circumstances in which she had a reasonable expectation of privacy.

Id. at 830. We disagree with Koeppel's assertion that *Tigges* supports the proposition that the focus of invasion of privacy claims are on the intent of the perpetrator; as our supreme court states, it's the fact the victim was *recorded* without her knowledge and consent that results in the intrusion. *See id.*

* * * * *

Koeppel cites *Harkey v. Abate,* . . . . In that case, the plaintiffs brought an invasion of privacy suit after using a roller-skating rink restroom with see-through panels installed in the ceiling, which permitted surreptitious observation from above. The Michigan Court of Appeals stated:

> In our opinion, the installation of the hidden viewing devices alone constitutes an interference with that privacy which a reasonable person would find highly offensive. And though the absence of proof that the devices were utilized is relevant to the question of damages, it is not fatal to plaintiff's case.

. . . Although this case does not support Koeppel's argument that mere intent to intrude on privacy is enough, it provides guidance in establishing the proof necessary to survive summary judgment on an invasion-of-privacy claim.

* * * * *

In its summary judgment ruling, the trial court . . . cites *Brazinski v. Amoco Petroleum Additives Co.,* . . . , where a female business invitee brought an invasion-of-privacy claim after learning the defendant had a television camera trained on the entrance of a locker room for its female employees. The court . . . concluded the plaintiff's claim could not stand because she was unable to show she had been in the locker room during the period the surveillance was being conducted. . . . . The case is distinguishable from Koeppel's case, however, because as a business invitee, the plaintiff in *Brazinski* was not presumed to have used the locker room as the defendant's female employees did. . . . Unlike *Brazinski,* there is no doubt in the present case that Koeppel used the office bathroom.

* * * * *

From the foregoing cases, we conclude to succeed on her claim, Koeppel must show the surveillance camera was capable of functioning while in the bathroom. Speirs claims it was not, that he was unable to receive any signal from the camera in the bathroom. Other evidence shows when a new battery was in the camera, a picture of the bathroom was visible on the monitor in Speirs's office, albeit not a clear and consistent one. The images obtained from the bathroom need not have been of high quality to establish an invasion of privacy, nor did the camera need to be pointed at the toilet—it is sufficient that the seclusion of the bathroom, a private area, was intruded upon. There is also evidence the camera was in the bathroom earlier in November.

* * * * *

Accordingly, we reverse the district court ruling granting summary judgment in favor of Speirs on this claim.

* * * * *

Questions

1. At trial, how could Speirs be found liable for invasion of privacy if the bathroom camera was not operating? Explain.

2. The court in *Koeppel* cited an additional case involving the following facts: The director of a nonprofit residential facility for neglected and abused children learned that someone was accessing pornographic websites late at night from a facility office computer located in an enclosed office. The two employees stationed in that office performed clerical work during normal business hours and were not suspected. Without telling them, the director installed a hidden camera in the office, trained on the computer in question. The camera did not operate during the day. After discovering the camera, the employees sued for invasion of privacy.

   a. How might this case support the court's decision in *Koeppel*?

   b. Decide. Explain. See *Hernandez v. Hillsides*, 47 Cal. 4th 272 (Cal. 2010).

3. Young was the pastor of Ft. Caroline United Methodist Church in Florida. Young was provided with a private office and a computer in that office. The computer was not networked to any other computers. Young and the church administrator had keys to the office. No one was permitted in the office without Young's permission, and the church administrator was not permitted to log on to the computer unless Young was present.

   The church administrator received notice from the church's Internet service provider that spam was linked to the church's Internet address. The administrator ran a "spybot" program on the church computers and found questionable Web addresses. The church's district supervisor and bishop were contacted and permission was given to involve police officials. Officers came to the church, the administrator unlocked Young's office and signed "consent to search" forms for the office and the computer. Officers searched the office and computer and found proscribed images and websites.

   Young subsequently filed a trial court motion to suppress the evidence gained from the office and computer search. The trial judge granted that motion ruling that the search violated Young's Fourth Amendment right to be free of unreasonable searches and seizures. The state appealed. Rule on that appeal. See *State v. Young*, 974 So.2d 601 (Fla. App. 1 Dist. 2008).

Drug Testing

Mary Wheeler decided that she had to institute an employee drug-testing program for her Chagrin Falls, Ohio, landscaping company. One job applicant at Wheeler's company told the interviewer that he would have no problem with the drug test. Then according to Wheeler: "While filling out his paperwork, the interviewer asked the applicant for a driver's license. The applicant reached into his pocket, and by accident pulled out a small bag of cocaine."[71] That episode certainly confirmed Wheeler's judgment that workplace drug tests were necessary for her company, and the data support Wheeler's fears. According to a federal government study, nearly one out of five workers between the ages of 18 and 25 used illicit drugs in the past month, along with one out of ten between the ages of 26 and 34.[72] One employee high on marijuana dropped his forklift five feet off a loading dock and employees at another job built a meth lab in the back of a truck.[73]

In an effort to address those workplace drug problems, employers provide information about illicit drug abuse, have written policies regarding drug use in the workplace, and offer employee assistance programs (EAPs).[74] Furthermore, as a 2010 Society for Human

Resource Management (SHRM) poll revealed, 55 percent of employers use drug testing in hiring employees, whereas 80 percent of employers conduct "reasonable suspicion" workplace drug testing.[75]

Drug-Free Workplace

The Drug-Free Workplace Act of 1988 applies to employers who have contracts of $100,000 or more with the federal government or who receive aid from the government. Those employers are required to develop an antidrug policy. for employees. They must provide drug-free awareness programs for employees, and they must acquaint employees with available assistance for those with drug problems, while also warning them of the penalties that accompany violation of the policy. The act requires employees to adhere to the company policy and to inform the company within five days if they are convicted of or plead no contest to a drug-related offense in the workplace. [For more information on the Federal Drug-Free Workplace Program, see **www.workplace.samhsa.gov/**]

Drug Testing in Law and Practice

Drug testing is regulated primarily by state law so generalizations are difficult. Broadly, we can say, however, that private-sector drug testing, properly conducted, ordinarily is lawful in the following five situations:

1. *Preemployment testing.* State and local law may impose some restrictions.
2. *In association with periodic physical examinations.* Advance notice is often required.
3. *For cause.* An employer has probable cause or reasonable suspicion.
4. *Postaccident testing* where drug use is suspected.
5. *Follow-up testing* for those returning from drug (or alcohol) rehabilitation.

Random testing, on the other hand, sometimes produces significant legal issues. A number of states forbid random drug testing or limit it to safety-sensitive situations. The U.S. Supreme Court has upheld such testing for public-sector employees where public safety is involved and for those having access to particularly sensitive information.[76] The legality of drug testing often reduces to a balancing test where the employee's right to privacy is balanced against the employer's business needs. Where safety and security are involved and when notice is provided, the courts are more supportive of testing. Particularly intrusive or careless testing often tilts that balance toward employees. Beyond the balancing test, a number of other legal considerations influence employer drug-testing practices, particularly in public-sector jobs:

1. **U.S. Constitution.** As explained in Chapter 5, the Fourth Amendment to the U.S. Constitution forbids unreasonable searches and seizures. Thus, government employers ordinarily cannot conduct a search without individualized suspicion—that is, without probable cause. Certain exceptions, however, have been recognized in cases involving such issues as safety, national security, and athletic participation. Remember that the U.S. Constitution protects citizens from the government, not from private-sector employers (with limited exceptions).

2. **State constitutions.** Many state constitutions offer privacy protection, but court decisions, to date, have generally not extended those protections to private-sector employers. On the other hand, certain states, such as California and Massachusetts, explicitly offer constitutional protection to private-sector employees.

3. **Federal statutes.** Drug testing could violate Title VII of the Civil Rights Act of 1964 or the Americans with Disabilities Act (see Chapter 13) if the testing fails to treat all individuals equally. The ADA protects *recovering* drug addicts and those erroneously believed to be drug abusers, but not employees or applicants who are currently abusing drugs.

4. **State and local statutes.** Historically, most state and local drug-testing legislation placed limits on that testing, but in recent years, fears about drug use in the workplace and often intense business community lobbying have, in some cases, relaxed those testing restraints.

5. **Common law claims.** Some of the more prominent judge-made (common law) claims that might provide a challenge to drug testing include invasion of privacy, defamation (dissemination of erroneous information about an employee), negligence (in testing or in selecting a test provider), intentional infliction of emotional distress, and wrongful discharge (discussed later in this chapter).

Legalizing Marijuana . . . in the Workplace?

Colorado and Washington have legalized the possession of up to one ounce of marijuana for personal use. Although marijuana is considered an illegal drug under the federal Controlled Substance Act, the U.S. Department of Justice announced in August 2013 that "at this time," the federal government was, "deferring its right to challenge" the laws passed by Colorado and Washington, given that both states had promised to create a "strict regulatory system."

Question

What impact might these laws have on Colorado and Washington employers' drug-testing policies and practices? Explain.

Sources: Niraj Chokshi, "Marijuana Sales Commence in Colorado for Recreational Use," *The Washington Post,* January 1, 2014 [**www.washingtonpost.com/politics/marijuana-sales-commence-in-colorado-for-recreational -use/2014/01/01/977040d0-7320-11e3-8b3f-b1666705ca3b_story.html**]; National Conference of State Legislatures, "Medical Marijuana Laws," March 27, 2014 [**www.ncsl.org/research/health/state-medical-marijuana -laws.aspx**]; and U.S. Department of Justice, "Justice Department Announces Update to Marijuana Policy," August 29, 2013 [**www.justice.gov/opa/pr/2013/August/13-opa-974.html**].

Part Six—Employee Benefits and Income Maintenance

In recent years, employee benefits have been the subject of political debate and legislative action, and the object of employers' reactions to an uncertain economy.[77] For example, in the last five years as health insurance costs rose, the number of workplace wellness initiatives—discussed previously in this chapter—also increased. During the economic downturn, one-third of employers reported reducing the scope of health care benefits or increasing cost-sharing, although the number of employers offering health care benefits actually increased.[78] The 2010 Patient Protection and Affordable Care Act (ACA; colloquially labeled Obamacare), which became effective in 2014, has raised concerns that employers' decisions to provide health insurance coverage will be negatively impacted. However, as discussed below, surveys throw into question the actual impact of the ACA on employers' practices.

Notably, the number of Americans without health insurance dropped in recent years. This increase in coverage has been attributed to government programs.[79]

Under the ACA, which became effective in 2014, employers with 50 or more employees that do not provide affordable health insurance coverage for their employees will face penalties. Those with fewer than 50 employees that do not provide health insurance will not face a penalty, but are eligible for tax credits. Critics argue that this amounts to a mandate for larger employers to provide health insurance for their employees in order to avoid paying penalties, or contrarily, to provide an incentive for employers for whom health care costs outweigh the penalties. A 2013 survey by the International Foundation of Employee Benefit Plans found that 69 percent of employers planned to continue their health care coverage after ACA became effective in 2014; an increase from the 46 percent of employers in 2012 that intended to do so.[80] A 3 to 4 percent increase in costs are typically anticipated.[81] These numbers could be viewed either as a sign that some employers will opt out of health insurance, or as evidence that most employers will still offer health care plans under the ACA. In 2012, the U.S. Supreme Court rejected a constitutional challenge to the ACA, holding that the individual penalties under ACA could be deemed as a tax, which Congress has the power to levy.[82] [For more information on ACA, see **https://www .healthcare.gov/**]

The federal Consolidated Budget Reconciliation Act (COBRA) requires employers with 20 or more employees to permit departing employees to retain group health coverage at their own expense for up to 18 months as long as they are not terminated for gross misconduct.

Unfortunately, COBRA policies are often too expensive for workers who have lost their jobs. The American Recovery and Reinvestment Act of 2009 provides health benefit premium reductions for those who were involuntarily unemployed within a particular time frame.[83]

Along with health care, another pressing social issue affecting the workplace is the care of children and elderly parents: 29 percent of adults in the United States are caregivers to an elderly parent or child with special needs. They provide care an average of 20 hours per week. Approximately three-fourths of these caregivers work outside the home while caregiving, and an increasing number of them report having to make workplace accommodations.[84]

Family Leave

The Family and Medical Leave Act (FMLA) entitles eligible employees of covered employers to take job-protected, *unpaid* leave for certain family-related or medical reasons. Eligible employees are entitled to 12 weeks of FMLA leave in a 12-month period for the birth, adoption, or foster care placement of a child, to care for a child, spouse, or parent who has a serious medical condition, or for the employee's own serious medical condition. Employees taking leave are entitled to reinstatement to the same or equivalent job. Employers with 50 or more employees are covered by FMLA. The 2008 National Defense Authorization Act (NDAA) amended FMLA to provide military family leave to eligible employees to care for their spouse, child, or parent who is undergoing medical treatment for a serious injury or illness incurred in the line of duty, or for "qualifying exigencies" including child care and counseling arising from their spouse's, child's, or parent's call to active duty status from the military reserves.[85] However, under a 2012 U.S. Supreme Court decision, state workers who are denied sick leave cannot sue the states that employ them under the FMLA.[86]

Although most worksites are not covered by the FMLA, over half of American employees are eligible for its protections, reflecting the FMLA's coverage of larger workplaces.[87] Lost wages often make FMLA leave unattractive; however, approximately two-thirds of employees taking FMLA leave receive either full or partial pay, typically by using paid vacation leave, sick leave, or other forms of paid time off.[88] Employers in California, New Jersey, and Rhode Island must provide paid family and medical leave; all three states fund these programs through employee-paid payroll taxes.[89] The State of Washington passed such legislation but, at this writing, has indefinitely postponed its implementation.[90] [For more on the FMLA, see **www.dol.gov/whd/fmla/**]

Work Abroad?

Of the 38 countries represented in a 2013 study, the United States stood alone as a nation not mandating paid leave for new mothers. In comparison, Estonia offers about 2 years of paid leave, and Hungary and Lithuania offer 1½ years or more of fully paid leave. The median amount of fully paid time off available to a mother for the birth of a child is about 5 to 6 months. In most countries providing paid leave, the government pays the bill.

Source: Gretchen Livingston, "Among 38 Nations, the U.S. Is the Outlier When It Comes to Paid Parental Leave," Pew Research Center, December 12, 2013 [**www.pewresearch.org/fact-tank/2013/12/12/among-38-nations-u-s-is-the-holdout-when-it-comes-to-offering-paid-parental-leave/**].

Unemployment Compensation

The tragedy of the Great Depression, when up to 25 percent of the workforce was unemployed, led in 1935 to the passage of the Social Security Act, one portion of which provided for an unemployment insurance program. Today, all 50 states and the federal government are engaged in a cooperative system that helps protect the temporarily jobless. The system is financed through a payroll tax paid by employers.

The actual state tax rate for each employer varies, depending on the employer's *experience ratings*—the number of layoffs in its workforce. Thus, employers have an incentive to retain employees.

Rules vary by state, but in general, employees qualify for unemployment benefits by reaching a specified total of annual wages. Those losing their jobs must apply to a state agency for unemployment compensation, which varies by state. Benefits may be collected up to a specified maximum period, usually 26 weeks. During that time, those collecting compensation must be ready to work and must make an effort to find suitable work. Workers who quit or who are fired for *misconduct* are ineligible for unemployment compensation. The episodes that follow illustrate the improbable cases where compensation has been denied:

- The Swiss Valley Farms dairy worker who led her coworkers in an after-hours swim in the cheese vat (filled with water at the time).[91]
- The on-patrol police officer who was charged with having sex with a woman multiple times, sometimes in parking lots.[92]
- The 25-year-old Sheraton hotel worker who used her employer's computer to write a 300-page manuscript describing her successful efforts to avoid doing any work.[93]

On a sobering note, 1.8 million adults and 620,000 children would have fallen below the poverty line in 2012 without unemployment insurance.[94]

WARN

The Worker Adjustment and Retraining Notification Act (WARN) requires firms with 100 or more employees to provide 60 days notice if they lay off one-third or more of their workers at any site employing at least 150 workers, drop 500 employees at any site, or close a plant employing at least 50 workers. A General Accounting Office study concluded, however, that the law had been ineffectual, with half of plant closings not covered by the law.

Pensions

> Nearly a quarter of American workers are not at all confident in their ability to retire.

A 2014 survey revealed that although Americans have recovered some of their confidence about retirement that were at record lows in recent years, nearly a quarter of American workers are not at all confident in their ability to retire.[95] Confidence was strongly correlated with participation in retirement plans.[96]

Broadly, pensions take two forms: *defined benefit plans* and *defined contribution plans*. Defined benefit pensions are of the traditional form providing specified monthly payments upon retirement. Although many workers have lost those pensions in recent years, some 40 million Americans remain protected by defined benefit plans.[97] Defined contribution plans, such as the popular 401(k), specify in advance the "match" the employer will provide to go with the employee's own contributions. The employee is offered a menu of investment options for that retirement money, but no promises are made about the amount that will be paid upon retirement. Defined contribution plans are now much more common than defined benefit plans. Defined contribution plans can be attractive to employees because the money *vests* (the point at which the employee has a nonforfeitable right to the funds) quickly and follows the employee who changes jobs. From the employer's point of view, the defined contribution plans are less expensive to manage, and they shift the risk from employer to employee.

Various hybrid pension plans have also been developed. A particularly prominent hybrid, a *cash balance plan,* is a defined benefit plan that acts somewhat like a defined contribution plan.The employer makes regular, defined contributions and guarantees a benefit amount to employees based on an established formula, but the benefits are maintained in individual accounts and are expressed in terms of an accumulated lump sum, a cash balance, rather than as a periodic payment during retirement. All of the investment risk in cash balance plans remains with the employer.[98] [See **www.401khelpcenter.com** and **www.ebri.org** for large databases on 401(k) and other retirement topics.]

Pension Law   The federal Employee Retirement Income Security Act (ERISA) regulates pension funds to help ensure their long-term financial security by reducing fraud and mismanagement. ERISA requires that fund managers keep detailed records, engage in prudent investments, and provide an annual report that has been certified by qualified, impartial third parties. ERISA also establishes strict vesting rights to ensure that employees actually receive the pensions to which they are entitled. Employer contributions typically vest after three years or in a six-year, graduated system. The Pension Benefit Guaranty Corporation (PBGC), funded by company contributions, was created as an element of ERISA to insure defined benefit plans so that vested persons will be paid up to a specified maximum if their plan cannot meet its obligations. Defined contribution arrangements are not covered by the PBGC.

Fears that companies were not sufficiently funding their traditional pension plans led to provisions in the federal Pension Protection Act of 2006 requiring companies to more adequately fund those plans. However, recent studies found pension funds are seriously underfunded, with less than three-quarters of the money needed to meet their obligations.[99]

Now millions of Americans depend on their own investment wisdom and the reliability of their 40l(k) plan for their retirement security. In 2012, the Department of Labor issued disclosure guidelines designed to assist employees in managing and investing their 401(k) plans.[100] In 2008, the U.S. Supreme Court strengthened that oversight a bit by finding that retirement account holders can sue if the administrator of their plan fails to follow their investment instructions. On the other hand, in 2010 the Court extended the deference given to plan administrators' discretion to include a plan administrator whose first attempt at interpreting the plan had already been ruled unreasonable.[101]

In 2011, the Court reviewed a district court's ruling in a class action brought by Cigna employees alleging their employer deceived them in statements made about its pension plan. The lower court had determined the employer had modified the plan's terms under which benefits should be calculated through affirmative misstatements to employees. In a decision hailed by both federal regulators and employers, the Court vacated the district court's ruling, finding that plan participants can sue to enforce but not modify a plan's terms, but also sending the case back to the lower court to determine whether a remedy could be found under another ERISA provision. On remand, the district court ordered enforcement of a reformed plan.[102]

The Future? Employer-provided pension and health care benefits for retirees increasingly are at risk. As expenses, including pensions and health care, continue to rise, can American companies compete successfully with lower-cost foreign competition? Will the social constructions of "the good life" and the "golden years" be altered, and how? Will you need to work years longer than your parents?

> Will you need to work longer than your parents?

Part Seven—Termination: Protection from Wrongful Discharge

Catherine Wagenseller, an Arizona nurse, her boss, Kay Smith, and some coworkers joined a Colorado River rafting trip where Wagenseller declined to participate in a "Moon River" skit in which the group allegedly "mooned" the audience. Likewise, Wagenseller did not join Smith in the heavy drinking, "grouping up," public urination, and similar behaviors that allegedly marked the trip. Despite favorable job evaluations preceding the trip, Wagenseller's relationship with Smith deteriorated following the trip, and eventually

> Wagenseller declined to participate in a "Moon River" skit.

she was terminated. Wagenseller, an at-will employee, sued, claiming that she was wrongfully discharged. An *at-will employee,* by definition, is not under contract for a definite period of time, and as such can be fired at any time. Wagenseller, however, argued that Arizona should adopt the *public policy exception* to the at-will doctrine. She claimed that she was fired because she refused to engage in behaviors that might have violated the Arizona indecent exposure statute. The state Supreme Court agreed with Wagenseller by finding in the statute a public policy favoring privacy and decency. The case was returned to the trial level, giving Wagenseller the opportunity to prove that her refusal to violate state public policy by engaging in public indecency led to her dismissal.[103]

The *Wagenseller* decision is an exception to the long-standing American rule that at-will employees can be fired for good reasons, bad reasons, or no reason at all. Of course, the employee is likewise free to quit at any time. Furthermore, both employer and employee freely entered the bargain understanding its terms, and thus the court should, in general, enforce those terms. Critics, however, argue that the doctrine ignores the historic inequality of bargaining power between employers and employees. In recent decades the at-will rule has been softened in most states by legislative and judicially imposed limitations. Statutory exceptions to the at-will rule include our labor laws protecting union workers (see Chapter 14) and the equal employment opportunity laws that forbid the dismissal of an employee for discriminatory reasons (see Chapter 13).

Judicial Limitations on At-Will Principles

An increasing number of court decisions provide grounds for dismissed at-will employees to claim that they have been *wrongfully discharged.* Those judicial decisions were often provoked by transparently unjust dismissals including, for example, whistle-blowers who exposed their employers' misdeeds and employees who declined to commit perjury on behalf of their employers. Those judicial limitations to the at-will doctrine fall into three categories: (1) express or implied contracts, (2) an implied covenant of good faith and fair dealing, and (3) the tort of violating an established public policy, as in *Wagenseller*. Additional tort claims may substitute for or supplement wrongful discharge claims.

1. **Express or implied employment contracts.** A number of states have adopted a contractual protection for at-will employees arising, typically, either from the employee handbook or from the employer's conduct and oral representations. For example, an employee handbook might contain a policy expecting employees to arrive on time to start their shift, and describing the progressive discipline tardy employees will face— such as an oral warning the first time they are late, a written warning for a second late arrival, and other discipline up to dismissal for continued incidents. This policy creates a contract that employees will not be terminated the first, or even second, time they arrive late to work. Similarly, oral assurances of continued employment, or an employer's practice of providing mentorship to rehabilitate employees' poor performance rather than firing them may create contracts that protect at-will employees from termination.

2. **Implied covenant of good faith and fair dealing.** A few state courts have held that neither party to a contract may act in bad faith to deprive the other of the benefits of the contract. For example, Bruce Rubenstein gave up his job with Arbor Mortgage to take an at-will position with Huntington Mortgage with the understanding that he would be manager of a new branch office to be opened in central New Jersey. After a few weeks, however, Huntington decided on a downsizing strategy under which the new branch would not be opened. Rubenstein was offered a job as a Huntington loan originator, but he declined. He sued Huntington asserting, among other things, that Huntington had breached the covenant of good faith and fair dealing. Reubenstein believed that Huntington knew of the possibility of downsizing before hiring him. The court agreed that Rubenstein may have had a viable claim for breach of the implied covenant of good faith and fair dealing if the facts, at trial, proved to be as Rubenstein alleged.[104]

3. **Public policy.** Most states have now adopted some form of "public policy" exception to at-will employment, under which a dismissal is wrongful if it results from employee conduct that is consistent with a public good or the public interest as expressed in legislation, constitutional protections, and the like. These exceptions are established case by case, and may differ from state to state. In addition to reporting an employer's illegal activity, commonly known as "whistle-blowing," or refusing to commit an illegal act such as perjury, the exception often protects, for example, employees fired for pursuing a lawful claim against their employer (e.g., workers' compensation or wage claims) as well as those fired for fulfilling a civic responsibility such as jury duty.

Only Funny until Someone Quits: The Firing Contest

The owner of a chain of QC Mart convenience stores in Bettendorf, Iowa, offered a $10 cash prize to workers who could predict which of them would be the next to be fired. A memo distributed to all employees asked them to write down and seal in an envelope the name of the coworker they thought would be fired next. The owner explained that secret shoppers would visit the store to see which cashiers were committing such offenses as wearing a hat, talking on a cell phone, and not wearing a QC Mart shirt. Once a firing occurred, the contest would begin again. After receiving the memo, QC Mart cashier Misty Shelsky, along with her store manager and a few other employees, quit. When Shelsky applied for unemployment benefits, the owner challenged the claim, asserting that she had left the job voluntarily. As defined by the Department of Labor, a constructive discharge (treated as a termination) occurs when a worker's resignation may be found not to be voluntary because the employer has created a hostile or intolerable work environment or has applied other forms of pressure or coercion which forced the employee to quit or resign. Should Shelsky be viewed as a terminated employee? Decide. Explain.

Sources: Clark Kauffman, "Firing Contest by Boss Leads Employees to Quit," *Des Moines Register*, October 2, 2011, p. 1B; and U.S. Department of Labor, "WARN Advisor Glossary: Constructive Discharge" [**www.dol.gov/elaws/eta/warn/glossaryall.asp#Constructive_Discharge**].

Additional Torts Dismissed employees are increasingly turning to a variety of tort actions often labeled "tag-along torts"—seeking compensatory and punitive damages to enhance their potential financial recovery. Potential tort claims arising from termination include, among others, defamation, intentional infliction of emotional distress, interference with contract, and invasion of privacy. The following case raises public policy issues in an employment termination.

LEGAL BRIEFCASE

Lloyd v. Drake University
686 N.W.2d 225 (Iowa S.Ct. 2004)

JUSTICE STREIT

* * * * *

FACTS

Nicholas Lloyd was a Drake University security guard on duty at the annual Drake Relays street-painting event on April 20, 2002. A student told Lloyd about an apparent altercation between Philippe Joseph, a Drake football player, and Erin Kane. Lloyd and Kane were white; Joseph was black. Joseph was holding Kane in the air with her feet kicking. Lloyd and another security guard, Steven Smith, thought Joseph was holding Kane in a headlock. Although Kane later claimed she and Joseph were just friends engaged in horseplay, Lloyd alleges Joseph's girlfriend called Lloyd and said Joseph had admitted

to her that he and Kane were fighting. Lloyd ordered Joseph to release Kane. After Lloyd's second command, Joseph did so. Joseph suddenly made a 180-degree turn and lunged toward Lloyd with his fists raised to his chest and "an angry look on his face." Lloyd feared for his own safety and pepper sprayed Joseph. Smith reached for his pepper spray at the same time and would have sprayed Joseph if Lloyd had not done so first. Another Drake security guard, Sergeant Risvold, attempted to handcuff Joseph, but was unable to do so—Joseph was still writhing from the pepper spray. Lloyd hit Joseph on the thigh with his baton, forcing him to the ground.

Des Moines police officers took Joseph to the police station, where he was charged with disorderly conduct. Meanwhile, witnesses began screaming "racist, racist" at Lloyd. Students immediately discussed the incident with Drake's president, David Maxwell. Maxwell obtained Joseph's release and took him for medical treatment, even though he had not previously complained about any injuries resulting from the arrest. Joseph later pled guilty to disturbing the peace. He also received a settlement from Drake.

As local media reported on the street-painting episode, Lloyd's actions became the subject of a heated controversy. After the NAACP and Black Student Coalition demanded an investigation, Drake organized a panel to study the incident and related topics. The panel concluded Lloyd had overreacted and used unnecessary force. Although the panel determined Lloyd's actions at the street-painting event were not overtly racially motivated, the panel discovered some prior complaints against Lloyd involving minority students. (Lloyd, however, points out he was never reprimanded on any of those occasions.) The panel also criticized Drake for insufficiently training its security guards and its "ambiguous philosophy for security." During the investigation, Drake assigned Lloyd to a desk job. Maxwell assured Lloyd he would not lose his job. One of Lloyd's supervisors told Lloyd he was still in line for a promotion. Nonetheless, Drake fired Lloyd from his security position on June 16, 2002. . . .

WRONGFUL DISCHARGE

Lloyd does not dispute he was an at-will employee. As a consequence, Drake could fire him for any lawful reason, or for no reason at all. A discharge is not lawful, however, when it violates public policy. Lloyd claims Drake violated public policy and thereby committed the tort of wrongful discharge when it fired him simply for upholding the criminal laws, i.e., attempting to arrest Joseph, a man he thought was assaulting a student.

The district court dismissed Lloyd's wrongful-discharge claim. . . . ruling Drake had fired Lloyd for a variety of other lawful reasons, including (1) a desire to capitulate to outside pressures in the hopes of forestalling a lack of public confidence in Drake's security system; and (2) a determination—based upon newly rediscovered prior complaints and the panel's conclusion Lloyd used premature and excessive force in subduing Joseph—that Lloyd lacked the appropriate demeanor of a security guard. (On appeal, Drake also points out Lloyd's conduct affected its relationships with a variety of constituencies, and his retention could have cost it essential financial support.) . . . We take a different route than the district court, but reach the same conclusion. . . . Even assuming Lloyd was fired simply for upholding the law, we think his claim still fails because the public policy against discharge that Lloyd asserts is neither clearly defined nor well recognized.

. . . [I]n order to prevail on his wrongful-discharge claim Lloyd must first identify a clearly defined and well-recognized public policy that would be undermined by his dismissal. . . . Only such policies are weighty enough "to overcome the employer's interest in operating its business in the manner it sees fit," which we have long and vigorously protected. Over the years we have recognized a number of clearly defined public policies. . . . To date, however, we have not held that a private security guard's actions in "enforcing the criminal laws of the state" to be a well-recognized and clearly defined public policy.

. . . [Lloyd's] argument mostly consists of vague generalizations about the social desirability of upholding the criminal laws of the state. . . . Lloyd also points out that there need not be an express statutory prohibition against discharge to underpin the public policy. In a number of cases, we have "found an implied prohibition against retaliatory discharge based on an employee's exercise of a right conferred by a clearly articulated legislative enactment." The gist of Lloyd's argument is that because upholding the criminal laws is important and socially desirable conduct, this court should find a public-policy exception to the at-will employment doctrine for a private security guard who tried to effectuate an arrest of a suspected criminal.

Lloyd's argument is not well taken. We have little quarrel, however, with one of the basic premises of Lloyd's argument: namely, that the criminal laws of the state reflect a general public policy against crime, and in favor of the protection of the public. That said, the public policy asserted here is far too generalized to support an argument for an exception to the at-will doctrine. In short, the public policy is not clearly defined. Apart from a vague reference to the whole of the criminal law, Lloyd cites no statutory or constitutional provision to buttress his claim. Divorced from any such provision or equivalent expression of public policy, we cannot find a well-recognized and clearly defined public policy in such vague generalizations. "Any effort to evaluate the public policy exception with generalized concepts of fairness and justice will result in an elimination of the at-will doctrine itself."

* * * * *

[W]e can find no origin for the well-recognized and clearly defined public policy essential to carve out an exception to the at-will employment doctrine. There is nothing, then, to sustain the tort of wrongful discharge on these facts—however encouraged or frequently beneficial it may be to have private citizens take it upon themselves to enforce the criminal laws. . . . The point is simply this: while we might be persuaded that society would be better off if private security personnel investigated and attempted to stop crimes in progress, we are not convinced it is a clear and well-recognized public policy of this state "that we all become citizen crime fighters."

Affirmed.

Questions

1. *a.* Why did Lloyd lose this lawsuit?
   b. Why did the Iowa Supreme Court decide that Lloyd had failed to establish the public policy exception?
   c. Are you more convinced by the Iowa Supreme Court's reasoning, or the rationale offered by Drake to the District Court and on appeal? Explain.

2. Was Drake's decision to terminate Lloyd an appropriate response to this difficult situation? Explain.

3. Schuster worked, in an at-will relationship, for Derocili for 15 months, during which time she claims he touched her inappropriately and made numerous sexual comments despite her repeated rejections of those behaviors. Schuster received bonuses and good evaluations, but in a meeting between Schuster, Derocili, and Schuster's direct supervisor, Goff, she was fired for poor performance. Schuster's sexual harassment complaint with the Delaware Department of Labor was rejected as unsubstantiated. She sued Derocili for breach of contract, but the trial court dismissed that complaint. She appealed.
   a. Does Schuster have a legitimate wrongful discharge claim? Explain.
   b. Does she have any other plausible causes of action? Explain. See *Schuster v. Derocili*, 775 A.2d 1029 (Del. S.Ct. 2000).

4. In 2004, Touchstone Television Productions hired Nicollette Sheridan to play Edie Britt in the television series *Desperate Housewives*. Touchstone's agreement with Sheridan gave it the exclusive option to renew her services on an annual basis for up to an additional six seasons; Touchstone exercised this option for seasons 2 through 5. In February 2009, Touchstone informed the actress that it would not exercise its option for season 6, and that Edie Britt would be killed in a car accident during season 5. Sheridan alleged that Touchstone's decision was motivated by her complaint regarding a September 2008 incident in which Marc Cherry, the show's creator, allegedly

hit her, amounting to a wrongful termination in breach of public policy. Decide. Explain. *Touchstone Television Prod. v. Sheridan,* 208 Cal. App. 4th 676 (Cal.Ct.App. 2012).

5. IBP operated a large hog-processing plant in Storm Lake, Iowa. IBP prohibited possession of "look-alike drugs" on company property. An employee, Michael Huegerich, was randomly and lawfully inspected as he was entering the plant. The inspection revealed an asthma medication, Maxalert, which was identical in appearance to an illegal street drug, "speed." Maxalert contained the stimulant ephedrine. The pills actually belonged to his girlfriend and were in his possession by accident. Huegerich was terminated for possessing a look-alike drug in violation of company policy. Huegerich admitted that he was generally aware of IBP drug policies, but since he was a transfer from another IBP division, he had not gone through the company orientation program where new employees were advised of the policy against look-alike drugs. About six months after his dismissal, two IBP employees told Huegerich that they had heard he was fired for possessing speed. Huegerich then sued IBP for, among other claims, wrongful discharge and defamation.

   At trial, Huegerich provided no evidence as to how, when, and from whom the IBP employees had heard that he was terminated for possession of speed. The district court found for Huegerich in the amount of $24,000 on the wrongful discharge claim and $20,000 on the defamation claim. The court said that IBP was guilty of negligent discharge in failing to inform Huegerich about its drug policy. IBP appealed to the Iowa Supreme Court. Iowa law recognizes the doctrine of at-will employment with "narrow" exceptions for public policy violations and where a contract is created by an employer's handbook. Decide. Explain. See *Huegerich v. IBP*, 547 N.W.2d 216 (Iowa S.Ct. 1996).

6. Freeman, a television anchorperson employed by KSN, gave birth to her second child. On the day she returned from the hospital, she was notified that she had been dismissed. Six weeks later, she became unable to lactate. She sued KSN for wrongful discharge, tortious interference with contract, and negligent infliction of emotional distress. Decide. Explain. See *Freeman v. Medevac Midamerica of Kansas, Inc.*, 719 F.Supp. 995 (D Kan. 1989).

PRACTICING ETHICS   Hearing the Whistle Blow?

Kevin Lamson was a sales manager for an Oregon car dealership, Crater Lake Motors. Crater Lake hired Real Performance Marketing Company (RPM), to conduct a five-day sales promotion at the dealership. During the first few days of the sales event, Lamson observed or was informed of a number of activities that he considered to be unethical and possibly unlawful, such as misrepresenting the event as a bank sale, and including various insurance and service agreements in the sales contract without the knowledge of the customer. Lamson complained to the Crater Lake Motors General Manager, Shevlin, who told him to "just go home." The next week, Lamson again expressed his concerns at a Crater Lake Motors meeting.

About a month later, Shevlin criticized Lamson's attitude and recent performance, stating that Lamson "wasn't getting the job done." Shevlin also told Lamson of another planned RPM sales event, and asked if Lamson intended to quit. Lamson replied that he did not intend to quit but that it seemed like Shevlin did not want him to work at Crater Lake Motors anymore. Shevlin replied that he did not want the Lamson he had seen recently.

Lamson later complained to the Crater Lake Motors owner, Coleman, about RPM. Coleman told Lamson that working at the second RPM event was mandatory and that failure to attend could result in dismissal. Lamson told Coleman that he could not participate because doing so would condone unethical behavior. Coleman said the agreement with RPM had been amended to explicitly forbid misrepresentations. Lamson did not attend the second RPM event, and was fired. Lamson then sued Crater Lake Motors for wrongful discharge.

Questions

1. Was Crater Lake Motors wrong to hire RPM?
2. Was Lamson wrong to refuse to work at the second RPM event?
3. Did Lamson have a duty to complain about the conduct he had observed during the first RPM event?
4. Was Crater Lake wrong to terminate Lamson?
5. Who won the wrongful termination lawsuit?

Source: *Lamson v. Crater Lake Motors,* 346 Ore. 628 (Ore. 2009).

Part Eight—Immigration

Immigration is a vital fuel for America's economic and cultural growth, but immigration is also a source of deep political and public policy divisions. In 2010, Arizona became the focus of this debate when it passed an aggressive piece of legislation requiring police officers to make a reasonable attempt to determine the immigration status of anyone lawfully stopped, detained, or arrested whom they suspect might be in the United States illegally.[105] While striking down other provisions of the law, including one making it a crime for immigrants without work permits to seek employment, the U.S. Supreme Court allowed the controversial section regarding immigration status checks by police to stand.[106]

In 2011, Alabama enacted a law that encompassed many of the 2010 Arizona provisions but was more broadly restrictive in that it, for example, required public schools to check the immigration status of their students, and made it a crime for landlords to knowingly rent to, harbor, or transport a known unauthorized ("illegal") immigrant. After the U.S. Supreme Court's ruling on the Arizona legislation, a federal appellate court blocked the Alabama law; the Court declined to hear Alabama's appeal.[107] The outcomes of these cases underscore that federal immigration policy trumps state efforts on this issue under the U.S. Constitution's Supremacy Clause. (see Chapters 5 and 8).

Illegal immigrants total about 11.7 million.

One in eight people living in the United States is an immigrant (about 40 million), and immigration has steadily grown over the last decade. From 2007 to 2012, the number of immigrants living in the United States increased by 2.4 million.[108] In 2012, illegal immigrants in the United States totaled about 11.7 million.[109]

Immigration policy is one of the most divisive issues in American public life. A Pew poll showed that 59 percent of Americans approved of the 2010 Arizona measure.[110] The support for directing police to stop and ask for documentation from those reasonably suspected of being in the United States illegally might reflect resistance to immigration generally, and the perception that illegal immigrants create an economic burden. Furthermore, concerns about the negative impact of large legal and illegal immigrant populations on low-income Americans have been raised.[111] However, immigrants to California appear to drive wages up.[112] A group of 500 economists wrote to Congress in 2006 arguing that immigration yields a "modest" net gain for the American economy.[113] In a more subjective sense, advocates claim that we must benefit from immigration's steady pipeline of new talent and energy which includes thousands of unaccompanied young children, many of whom literally walk to the United States from Central America.[114] The *Los Angeles Times* asked if America's "sheltered and chaperoned children" could manage that feat on their own.[115]

American Immigration Law   Businesses in the United States have used the H-1B visa program to bring foreign workers to the United States to fill positions requiring special theoretical or technical expertise in specialized fields such as science, engineering, or computer programming. In seeking an H-1B visa, an employer must affirm to the U.S. Department of Labor that the hiring will not harm wages and working conditions of employees in similar jobs. The number of H-1B visas available annually is limited, and after a decline in 2009 in which it took eight months for the H-1B cap to be met, in 2012 it took just over two months for the 2013 slots to be filled.[116]

In hiring those already in the United States, federal immigration law, including the 1986 Immigration Reform and Control Act, requires employers to verify that each new hire is a U.S. citizen, a permanent resident, or a foreign national with permission to work in this country. To meet this requirement, employers must complete an employment eligibility verification form (I–9) for each new employee. New employees must present documents establishing the employee's identity and eligibility to work in the United States. The employer must examine the documents and complete the I–9 if the documents appear legitimate. Of course, employers cannot knowingly hire illegal immigrants, but neither can they discriminate against legal immigrants because of national origin and similar factors. [For links to the I–9 form and other immigration information, see **www.uscis.gov/portal/site/uscis**]

Enforcement   Enforcement of immigration laws focuses on two issues: hiring of illegal immigrants, and employers' illegal discrimination against applicants based on citizenship status or national origin. Critics charge that these policies create a conflict for employers: on the one hand, employers must be sure to verify applicants' ability to work in the United States, but on the other hand, they must take care not to place extra burdens on applicants because they are of a particular national origin, or are U.S. permanent residents as opposed to U.S. citizens.[117] For example, under a settlement reached with the U.S. Department of Justice, a California company, American Education and Travel Services Inc., agreed to pay $10,000 in back pay and compensatory damages to a lawful permanent resident who was denied a residential counselor position because he was not a U.S. citizen or native English speaker.[118] At the same time, the Obama administration's use of immigration audits, rather than Bush-era workplace raids, has led to illegal immigrants being fired. In 2011, for example, fast-food chain Chipotle fired hundreds of illegal immigrants as a result of an audit by U.S. Immigration and Customs Enforcement.[119]

E-Verify is a free online system run by the federal government that determines an employee's eligibility to work in the United States, comparing information reported on an employee's Form I-9 with federal records. Since 2009, the federal government mandates certain federal contractors to use the program. Approximately 20 states required the use of E-Verify for at least some employers.[120] In 2013, over 480,000 employers were enrolled in E-Verify, with over 23 million queries.[121] However, critics note that E-Verify does not address whether the identity provided is authentic, which could encourage identity theft to help illegal workers clear this employment hurdle.[122] [For overviews of many of the employment law topics in this chapter, see **http://topics.law.cornell.edu/wex/category /employment_law**]

Internet Exercise	Using the Frequently Asked Questions portion of the Occupational Safety and Health Administration (OSHA) website [**www.osha.gov/as/opa/osha-faq.html**], answer the following: 1. What is OSHA's budget, and how many inspectors does the agency have? 2. How can I get help from OSHA to fix hazards in my workplace? 3. What cooperative programs does OSHA offer?

Chapter Questions	1. In general, employers are forced to bear (or at least share) the legal burden for their employees' negligent conduct on the job.
	   a. Why do we force employers to bear that responsibility?
	   b. Should we do so? Explain.
	2. Abplanalp, a five-year employee of Com-Co Insurance, signed an employment agreement including a restrictive covenant providing that, should he leave Com-Co, he would not use Com-Co customer lists or solicit business from Com-Co clients for three years. Abplanalp moved to Service Insurance, where he sold insurance to some friends and relatives. He did not sell to any other persons whom he came to know while working for Com-Co. Abplanalp was sued by Com-Co for violating the restrictive covenant. Decide. Explain. See *Com-Co Insurance Agency v. Service Insurance Agency,* 748 N.E.2d 298 (Ill. App. Ct. 2001).

3. Many companies refer to credit reports when investigating job applicants. The Fair Credit Reporting Act requires employers to notify and receive authorization from applicants to use their credit reports in making hiring decisions, and to give them notice if they are rejected because of information in a credit report. (For more information on employers' responsibilities under The Fair Credit Reporting Act, see **http://business.ftc. gov/documents/bus08-using-consumer-reports-what-employers-need-know**).

   a. In your judgment, does evidence of failure to pay debts constitute useful information in the job selection process? Explain.

   b. Is the use of that information an "invasion of privacy" as you understand it? Explain.

4. A group of Fargo, North Dakota, nurses were paid a subminimum wage for their "on-call" time. When on call, the nurses were required to be able to report to their hospital within 20 minutes, they were required to provide a phone number where they could be reached, and they were not to consume alcohol or drugs. After being called, nurses returned to regular pay. In three years, 36 of the 135 nurses who sued had been called in more than once. The nurses sued the hospital for violating the Fair Labor Standards Act's minimum wage provision. Decide. Explain. See *Reimer v. Champion Healthcare Corp.,* 258 F.3d 720 (8th Cir. 2001).

5. Simons, an engineer at the CIA, downloaded child pornography on his workplace computer. The computer was to be used only for work. The pornography was discovered by a search of employee computers. Simons was then convicted of receiving and possessing child pornography. Simons appealed on Fourth Amendment grounds. Decide. Explain. See *United States v. Simons,* 206 F.3d 392 (4th Cir. 2000); cert. den. 122 S.Ct. 292 (2001).

6. Guz, a longtime Bechtel employee, was dismissed during what Bechtel said was a business slump. Bechtel's personnel policy included a provision saying employees "may be terminated at the option of Bechtel." Guz sued for wrongful dismissal claiming, among other things, that Bechtel breached an implied contract to be terminated only for good cause, and that Bechtel breached the implied covenant of good faith and fair dealing. A lower court concluded that Guz's promotions, raises, favorable performance reviews, together with Bechtel's progressive discipline policy and Bechtel officials' statements of company practices supported Guz's position. Bechtel appealed. Decide. Explain. See *Guz v. Bechtel National Inc.,* 8 P.3d 1089 (Cal. S.Ct. 2000).

7. Hershey Company Retail Sales Representatives (RSRs) were classified as exempt under the Fair Labor Standards Act (FLSA), and Hershey never paid hourly compensation to RSRs for any overtime they worked. While the RSRs received bonuses based on performance, they were not eligible to receive sales commissions. RSRs are part of teams that help sell Hershey products to retail outlets of various sizes from Walmart to independently owned shops. In a wage and hour claim seeking overtime compensation, RSRs contended that they are primarily responsible for merchandising tasks such as delivering and setting up product displays, tagging products, and stocking shelves. Hershey defended that RSRs' job duties include selling products directly to retailers, meeting with their key decision makers to increase sales, and only occasionally assisting with merchandising at their stores. Are the RSRs nonexempt employees with rights

to overtime compensation under FLSA? Decide. Explain. See *Campanelli v. Hershey Co.,* 2011 U.S. Dist. LEXIS 17483 (N.D. Cal. 2011).

8. As discussed in this chapter, April 2010 U.S. Department of Labor guidelines require employers to provide educational benefits to interns who participate in unpaid internships. If the interns are completing tasks that further the organization's interests rather than their own, they should be compensated with wages.
   a. What benefit might a college student derive from an unpaid internship, apart from academic credit or an educational experience?
   b. What effect might these guidelines have on the availability of internships?
   c. Why do you think the U.S. Department of Labor addressed unpaid internships in 2010?

9. Safeway in Denver hosted a picnic for its employees. Safeway bought a 40-pound gas tank to use with a grill that was designed for a 20-pound tank. A label on the grill warned against that use. The grill failed to operate properly and a manager asked Lewis to try to fix it. When Lewis did so a "ball of fire" erupted and Lewis was badly burned. The Occupational Safety and Health Administration then issued a citation against Safeway. Safeway appealed to the courts.
   a. Defend Safeway.
   b. Decide the case. Explain. See *Safeway, Inc. v. Occupational Safety & Health Rev. Comm.,* 382 F.3d 1189 (10th Cir. 2004).

10. In most drug-testing cases, courts have balanced the employee's privacy interests against the employer's need for information. What business justifications are likely to be most persuasive to a court reviewing the legality of employee drug testing?

11. In 2009, Mitchell was employed at-will as an anesthesia technician at the University of Kentucky (UK) Chandler Medical Center, while also attending the university as a graduate student. He had a valid license to carry a concealed deadly weapon under Kentucky law. On April 22, 2009, several of Mitchell's coworkers were under the impression that he had a firearm in his employee locker, and they reported this to hospital administration. Hospital administrators contacted the UK police department. When questioned, Mitchell denied having a firearm in his locker. Police and hospital administrators searched Mitchell's locker with his permission but found no weapons. Mitchell informed the police officers that he had a concealed carry license and admitted that he kept a firearm in his vehicle, which was parked on campus. Campus police escorted Mitchell to his car, where he showed them the semiautomatic pistol he had stored in his vehicle. On April 29, 2009, the university terminated Mitchell's employment for violation of its policy prohibiting possession of a deadly weapon on university property or while conducting university business. Mitchell filed suit, alleging termination in violation of public policy. Decide. Explain. See *Mitchell v. University of Kentucky,* 366 S.W.3d 895 (Ky. 2012).

12. A reader sent the following story to a newspaper question and answer forum:

> I was fired recently by my employer, an architecture firm, immediately after serving for one month on a federal grand jury. From the moment I informed my boss . . . I was harassed . . . and told I was not putting the company first. I was told to get out of my jury service, "or else." . . . I was fired exactly one week after my service ended.[123]

Was the dismissal of this at-will employee lawful? Explain.

13. Katherine Born and Rick Gillispie were employed by a Blockbuster Video store in Iowa. Blockbuster maintained a policy that forbade dating between supervisors and their subordinates. Born and Gillispie were dismissed for violating the policy. They denied that they were romantically involved and filed suit for wrongful dismissal. Under Iowa law, an at-will employee can be discharged at any time for any reason, but Iowa law does recognize the public policy exception. To prevail in this lawsuit, what must the plaintiffs show about Iowa law? See *Katherine Born and Rick Gillispie v. Blockbuster Videos, Inc.,* 941 F.Supp. 868 (S.D. Ia. 1996).

14. Dancers at Club Orleans in Topeka, Kansas, who earned only tips without a regular wage, were subject to house rules that prohibited illicit or illegal conduct and regulated interaction among the dancers and between the dancers and customers. Violations of the rules could result in the dancer being fined or terminated. The rules also set minimum tips for various types of dances, which were enforced. The dancers were allowed to schedule their own shifts. One of the dancers filed an unemployment benefits claim against Milano's, the company that owned Club Orleans. Is the dancer an employee or an independent contractor? Decide. Explain. See *Milano's v. Kansas Department of Labor,* 296 Kan. 497 (KS 2013).

15. Diana Vail, who received medical treatment for migraine headaches, worked at Raybestos, a car parts manufacturer. Raybestos had been giving Vail intermittent leave under FMLA for her migrane headaches since April 2004. From May to September 2005, Vail's requests for FMLA leave due to migraine headaches became more frequent, often falling on weekdays when her husband's mowing company was busiest. Growing suspicious that Vail's requests were not genuine, Raybestos monitored Vail's activities by hiring an off-duty police officer to conduct video surveillance. The officer reported that Vail mowed the lawns of a cemetery, her husband's client, on a day when Vail called prior to her shift to request leave. Vail was subsequently terminated based on her performance of physical labor while on FMLA.

    a. Did Vail's termination violate FMLA? Explain.

    b. Did the employer's surveillance of Vail interfere with her rights under FMLA? Explain. See *Vail v. Raybestos,* 533 F.3d 904 (7th Cir. 2008).

    c. An employee who had been on FMLA leave for incapacitating back pain posted photos to her Facebook page (as did her friend) showing her drinking and dancing over a period of at least eight hours at a local festival. Several of the employees' coworkers who were her Facebook friends told management what they had seen on the employee's page; the employee was fired as a result. The employee sued the employer for retaliation and interference with her FMLA rights. Decide. Explain. See *Jaszczyszyn v. Advantage Health Physician Network,* 2012 U.S. App. LEXIS 23162 (6th Cir. 2012), unpubd. op.

16. An employee of Triple B Cleaning in Texas requested personal protective equipment while performing dry cleaning duties. Triple B denied the request. The employee notified the media, and after a reporter contacted the employee's supervisor, the employee

was demoted and assigned menial tasks. Following the airing of the employee's complaint by local news, the employee was terminated.

After being terminated, the employee filed a whistle-blower complaint alleging that Triple B acted in retaliation for contacting the media about unsafe working conditions. OSHA investigated the complaint and determined that Triple B Cleaning's decision to terminate the employee was in violation of the whistle-blower provisions of the Occupational Safety and Health Act.

The company entered into a consent judgment under which it paid the employee $30,000 for lost wages, agreed to an injunction prohibiting future discrimination, and posted a notice advising its employees of their rights under OSHA's whistle-blower protection provision.

a. What public policy—or policies—are at issue in this situation?

b. Did Triple B act ethically? Did the employee act ethically? Explain.

c. In OSHA's press release regarding the settlement, OSHA Regional Administrator Dean McDaniel stated: "Employees should be free to exercise their rights under the law without fear of retaliation by their employers . . ." What consequences might be expected to accompany the fear of retaliation employees often feel when exercising their rights?

See OSHA Regional News Release, "U.S. Department of Labor Settles Whistleblower Case Against Commercial and Industrial Steam Cleaning Company in Houston" April 6, 2009 [**www.osha.gov/pls/oshaweb/owadisp.show_document?p_table=NEWS _RELEASES&p_id=17720**].

Notes

1. Sacha Pfeiffer, "Off-the-Job Smoker Sues over Firing," *The Boston Globe,* November 30, 2006 [**www.boston.com**].

2. Ibid.

3. American Lung Association's Tobacco Policy Project/State Legislated Actions on Tobacco Issues (SLATI) State "Smoker Protection" Laws [**www.lungusa2.org/slati/appendixf.php**].

4. Annotated Laws of Massachusetts, ALM GL ch. 214, Section 1B (2010).

5. Johnathan D. Glater, "Layoffs Herald a Heyday for Employee Lawsuits, *The New York Times,* January 30, 2009 [**www.nytimes.com/2009/01/31/business/economy/31employ.html**].

6. *CBS v. FCC,* 535 F.3d 167 (3rd Cir. 2008).

7. *FCC v. CBS,* 132 S.Ct. 2677 (U.S. S.Ct. 2012).

8. *Chao v. Southern California Maid Services & Carpet Cleaning, Inc.,* 2007 U.S. Dist. LEXIS 96143 (C.D. Cal. 2007).

9. "Voluntary Classification Settlement Program," *Internal Revenue Service,* December 3, 2013 [**www.irs.gov/Businesses/Small-Businesses-&-Self-Employed/Voluntary-Classification -Settlement-Program**].

10. James B. Stewart, "In the Undoing of a CEO, a Puzzle," *New York Times,* May 18, 2012 [**www .nytimes.com**].

11. Floyd Norris, "RadioShack Chief Resigns after Lying," *The New York Times,* February 21, 2006, sec. C, p. 1.

12. Dan Mascai, "And I Invented Velcro," *BusinessWeek,* June 9, 2008, p. 15.

13. Society for Human Resource Management, "SHRM Finds Fewer Employers Using Background Checks in Hiring," Society for Human Resource Management Press Releases, July 19, 2012 [**www.shrm.org/about/pressroom/PressReleases/Pages/BackgroundChecks.aspx**].

14. Sara Murray, "Credit Checks on Job Seekers by Employers Attract Scrutiny," *The Wall Street Journal,* October 21, 2010, p. A5.

15. Chris Dettro, "New Law Bars Most Credit Checks in Hiring," *The State Journal-Register,* January 1, 2011 [**www.sj-r.com/top-stories/x1733657992/New-law-bars-most-credit-checks-in-hiring**].

16. Jacquelyn Smith, "How Social Media Can Help (or Hurt) You in Your Job Search," Forbes, April 16, 2013 [**www.forbes.com/sites/jacquelynsmith/2013/04/16/how-social-media-can-help-or-hurt-your-job-search/**].

17. Scott Erker and Kelli Buczynski, "Are You Failing the Interview?: 2009 Survey of Global Interviewing Practices and Perceptions," p. 14 [**www.ddiworld.com/DDIWorld/media/trend-research/are-you-failing-the-interview_tr_ddi.pdf**].

18. Ann Howard, Johanna Johnson, White Paper: "If You Were a Tree, What Kind Would You Be?" Development Dimensions International [**www.ddiworld.com/DDIWorld/media/white-papers/interviewing_wp_ddi.pdf?ext=.pdf**].

19. *Bimbo Bakeries v. Botticella,* 613 F.3d 102 (3rd Cir. 2010).

20. Kris Maher, "The Jungle," *The Wall Street Journal,* June 8, 2004, p. B4.

21. *Edwards v. Arthur Andersen,* 44 Cal. 4th 937 (Cal. 2008).

22. *Lawlor v. North American Corp. of Illinois,* 983 N.E.2d 414 (Ill. S.Ct. 2012).

23. Amalia D. Kessler, "Stuck in Arbitration," *The New York Times,* March 6, 2012 [**www.nytimes.com**].

24. *Circuit City Stores, Inc. v. Adams,* 532 U.S. 105 (2001).

25. *Nitro-Lift Technologies v. Howard,* 133 S.Ct. 500 (2012).

26. *Equal Employment Opportunity Commission v. Waffle House,* 534 U.S. 279 (2002).

27. 54 Cal. 3d 202; 814 P.2d 1341 (Cal. S.Ct. 1991).

28. Jenny B. Davis, "Still Working after All These Years," *ABA Journal,* October 2001, p. 67.

29. Arindrajit Dube, T. William Lester, and Michael Reich, "Minimum Wage Effects Across State Borders: Estimates Using Contiguous Counties," *The Review of Economics and Statistics,* September 25, 2010.

30. National Employment Law Project, "Living Wage and Minimum Wage," [**http://www.nelp.org/index.php/content/content_issues/category/living_wage_and_minimum_wage/**].

31. City and County of San Francisco General Services Agency, "Minimum Wage Ordinance," [**http://sfgsa.org/index.aspx?page=411**].

32. Andrew Khouri, "Low-Wage Workers Can't Afford Rent," *The Los Angeles Times,* March 25, 2014, p. B2.

33. Ylan Q. Mui, "Wal-Mart to Pay $4.8 Million in Back Wages," *The Washington Post,* May 1, 2012 [**www.washington.post.com**].

34. U.S. Department of Labor Wage and Hour Division Press Release, "Levi Strauss Agrees to Pay More than $1 Million in Overtime Back Wages to Nearly 600 Employees Following US Labor Department Investigation," March 29, 2011 [**www.dol.gov/opa/media/press/whd/WHD20110379.htm**].

35. *Christopher v. SmithKline Beecham Corp.,* 132 S.Ct. 2156 (2012).

36. American Psychological Association, "Americans Stay Connected to Work on Weekends, Vacation and Even When Out Sick," American Psychological Association Press Releases, September 4, 2013 [**www.apa.org/news/press/releases/2013/09/connected-work.aspx**].

37. Paul Davidson, "Overworked and Underpaid?" *USA Today,* April 16, 2012, p. 1A.

38. *Archuleta v. Wal-Mart Stores,* 543 F. 3d 1226 (10th Cir. 2008).

39. *Kellar v. Summit Seating Inc.,* 664 F.3d 169 (7th Cir. 2011).

40. Testimony before the House Committee on Natural Resources, U.S. House of Representatives, March 16, 2011, The Effect Of—A Brother's Statement. Testimony of Christopher K. Jones [**http://naturalresources.house.gov/UploadedFiles/C.JonesTestimony03.16.11.pdf** at p. 2].

41. Julia Werdiger, "BP to Admit Crimes and Pay $4.5 Billion in Gulf Settlement," *The New York Times,* November 15, 2012 [**www.nytimes.com**].

42. Associated Press, "Federal Probe of Fatal Texas Plant Explosion Cites Oversight," *Waterloo/Cedar Falls Courier,* March 21, 2007, p. B4.

43. Melanie Trottman, "BP to Pay $50.6 Million Fine in Texas Refinery Case," *The Wall Street Journal,* August 12, 2010 [**www.wsj.com**].

44. U.S. Department of Labor Bureau of Labor Statistics Economic News Release, "Census of Fatal Occupational Injuries Summary, 2012," August 22, 2013 [**www.bls.gov/news.release/cfoi.nr0.htm**].

45. U.S. Department of Labor Bureau of Labor Statistics News Release, "Workplace Injury and Illness Summary. 2012," November 7, 2013 [**www.bls.gov/news.release/osh.nr0.htm**].

46. Employer Payment for Personal Protective Equipment, Final Rule, 29 CFR Parts 1910, 1915, 1917 et al.

47. U.S. Department of Labor, "US Department of Labor's OSHA Revises Hazard Communication Standard," March 20, 2012 [**https://www.osha.gov/pls/oshaweb/owadisp.show_document?p_table=NEWS_RELEASES&p_id=22038**].

48. OSHA, "Prevention of Musculoskeletal Disorders in the Workplace," [**https://www.osha.gov/SLTC/ergonomics/index.html**].

49. Robert J. Grossman, "Making Ergonomics," *HR Magazine,* April 2000, p. 36.

50. Sara Murray, "Guns in the Parking Lot: A Delicate Workplace Issue," *The Wall Street Journal,* October 15, 2013 [**http://online.wsj.com/news/articles/SB10001424052702303983904579095532026750354**].

51. OSHA Letter of Interpretation on Standard 1904, 1904.5(b) (1), February 24, 2009 [**www.osha.gov/pls/oshaweb/owadisp.show_document?p_table=INTERPRETATIONS&p_id=27415**].

52. *Caterpillar Logistics v. Solis,* 674 F.3d 705 (7th Cir. 2012).

53. "New Study Finds That OSHA Inspections Reduce Worker Injuries While Saving Employers Money," *OSHA QuickTakes,* May 29, 2012 [**https://www.osha.gov/as/opa/quicktakes/qt-05292012sis.html**].

54. Roy Maurer, "OSHA's Oversight of Model-Workplace Program Criticized," *Society for Human Resource Management,* December 30, 2013 [**https://www.shrm.org/hrdisciplines/safetysecurity/articles/Pages/OSHA-Oversight-VPP-Criticized.aspx**].

55. Julia Preston, "Hershey's Packer Is Fined Over Its Safety Violations," *The New York Times,* February 21, 2012 [**www.nytimes.com**].

56. OSHA Instruction, Severe Violators Enforcement Program (SVEP) [**www.osha.gov/dep/svep-directive.pdf**].

57. Associated Press, "Stringer's Widow Settles Lawsuit with NFL," *The New York Times,* January 26, 2009 [**www.nytimes.com/2009/01/27/sports/football/27stringerbox .html?ref=koreystringer**]. Kelci Stringer settled her claim against the NFL. Before her lawsuit against football equipment maker Riddell for her husband's death was settled, the federal district court ruled that Riddell had a duty to warn a football player of the risk of heat exhaustion. *Stringer v. NFL,* 2010 U.S. Dist. LEXIS 98874 (S. Ohio 2010) ; Associated Press, "Lawsuit Over Stringer's Death Settled," June 2, 2014 [**http://www.foxsports.com/nfl/story/Lawsuit-in-Minnesota -Vikings-Korey-Stringer-death-settled-080811**].

58. *Stringer v. Minnesota Vikings,* 705 N.W. 2d 746 (Minn. S.Ct. 2005).

59. Ibid.

60. *State ex. Rel. Gross v. Industrial Commission of Ohio,* 115 Ohio St. 3d 249 (Ohio 2007).

61. The Pew Research Center for The People and The Press, "A Portrait of 'Generation Next'," January 9, 2007, p. 21 [**http://people-press.org/files/legacy-pdf/300.pdf**].

62. See, e.g., Crisis Collection Management's dress code [**www.crisiscollections.com/about /eh/cpa/**].

63. Jen Wieczner, "Your Company Wants to Make You Healthy," *The Wall Street Journal,* April 8, 2013 [**http://online.wsj.com/news/articles/SB100014241278873233933045783602522841 51378**].

64. S. P. Dinnen, "Employers Slap Fees on Workers Who Smoke," *The Des Moines Register,* November 20, 2005, p. 1A.

65. *Robert Barbee v. Household Automotive Finance,* 113 Cal. App. 4th 525 (2003).

66. Sue Shellenbarger, "For Office Romance, the Secret's Out," *The Wall Street Journal,* February 10, 2010, p. D1.

67. *City of Ontario v. Quon,* 130 S.Ct. 2619; 177 L. Ed. 2d 216, 227 (2010).

68. *Stengart v. Loving Care Agency,* Inc., 201 N.J. 300, 308; 990 A.2d 650 (N.J. 2010).

69. National Conference of State Legislatures, "Employer Access to Social Media Usernames and Passwords," January 17, 2013 [**www.ncsl.org/research/telecommunications-and -information-technology/employer-access-to-social-media-passwords.aspx**].

70. *Pietrylo v. Hillstone Rest. Group,* 2009 U.S. Dist. LEXIS 88702 (D. N.J. 2009); unpubd. op.

71. Dalia Fahmy, "Aiming for a Drug-Free Workplace," *The New York Times,* May 10, 2007, Sec. C, p. 6.

72. Worker Substance Abuse and Workplace Policies and Programs (2007): Substance Abuse and Mental Health Services Administration (SAMHSA), U.S. Department of Health and Human Services, [**http://oas.samhsa.gov/work2k7/toc**].

73. George Lenard, "Employers Falling Off Drug Testing Bandwagon," February 28, 2005 [**www .employmentblawg.com/2005**].

74. Worker Substance Abuse and Workplace Policies and Programs (2007): Substance Abuse and Mental Health Services Administration (SAMHSA), U.S. Department of Health and Human Services [**http://oas.samhsa.gov/work2k7/toc**].

75. "Background Checking: Drug Testing," SHRM Poll, January 22, 2010 [**www.shrm .org/Research/SurveyFindings/Articles/Pages/BackgroundCheckDrugTesting.aspx**].

76. *National Treasury Employees Union v. Von Raab,* 109 S.Ct 1384 (1989).

77. Society for Human Resource Management, "2013 Employee Benefits: An Overview of Employee Benefits Offerings in the U.S." [**www.shrm.org/research/surveyfindings/articles/ documents/13-0245%202013_empbenefits_fnl.pdf**].

78. Gary Claxton, et al., "Heath Benefits in 2010: Premiums Rise Modestly, Workers Pay More Toward Coverage" [**http://content.healthaffairs.org/content/early/2010/09/02/hlthaff.2010.0725.abstract**].

79. Robert Pear, "Percentage of Americans Lacking Health Coverage Falls Again," *The New York Times,* September 17, 2013 [**http://www.nytimes.com/2013/09/18/us/percentage-of-americans-lacking-health-coverage-falls-again.html?_r=0**].

80. International Foundation of Employee Benefit Plans, "2013 Employer-Sponsored Health Care: ACA's Impact," May 16, 2013 [2013 Employer-Sponsored Health Care: ACA's Impact].

81. Ibid.

82. *National Federation of Independent Business v. Sebelius,* 132 S.Ct. 2566 (2012).

83. U.S. Department of Labor Fact Sheet, "COBRA Premium Reduction," April 26, 2010 [**www.dol.gov/ebsa/newsroom/fscobrapremiumreduction.html**].

84. National Alliance of Caregiving and AARP, "Caregiving in the U.S. 2009" [**www.aarp.org/relationships/caregiving/info-12-2009/caregiving_09.html**].

85. U.S. Department of Labor, "Military Family Leave Provisions of the FMLA: Frequently Asked Questions and Answers," [**www.dol.gov/whd/fmla/finalrule/MilitaryFAQs.pdf**].

86. *Coleman v. Court of Appeals of Md.,* 132 S.Ct. 1327 (2012).

87. Abt Associates, "Family and Medical Leave in 2012: Technical Report," September 7, 2012 [**www.dol.gov/asp/evaluation/fmla/FMLA-2012-Technical-Report.pdf**].

88. Ibid.

89. National Conference of State Legislatures, "State Family Medical Leave and Parental Leave Laws," December 2013 [**www.ncsl.org/research/labor-and-employment/state-family-and-medical-leave-laws.aspx**].

90. Ibid.

91. Patt Johnson, "Getting the Boot," *The Des Moines Register,* May 4, 2003, p. 1D.

92. W. Zachary Malinowski, "Unemployment Benefits Denied for Fired Cranston Cop," *The Providence Journal* blog, www.projo.com, July 26, 2010 [**http://newsblog.projo.com/2010/07/unemployment-benefits-denied-f.html**].

93. Clark Kauffman, "Diary of a Goof-Off: No Work, No Pay," *The Des Moines Register,* January 19, 2007, p. 1A.

94. Joint Economic Committee, U.S. Congress, "The Economic Case for Continuing Federal Unemployment Insurance," January 2014 [**www.jec.senate.gov/public/?a=Files.Serve&File_id=cf231ec5-d46e-471e-bac7-63c8bb79fb9c**].

95. Employee Benefit Research Institute, "EBRI's 2014 Retirement Confidence Survey: Confidence Rebounds—for Those with Retirement Plans," March 18, 2014 [**www.ebri.org/pdf/surveys/rcs/2014/PR1066.RCS.18Mar14.pdf**].

96. Ibid.

97. Mark Trumbull, "Reform Erodes the Future of US Pensions," *The Christian Science Monitor,* August 18, 2006 [**www.csmonitor.com/2006/0818/p02s02-usec.html**].

98. U.S. Department of Labor, "Fact Sheet: Cash Balance Pension Plans," May 2003, [**www.dol.gov/ebsa/newsroom/fscashbalanceplans.html**].

99. Marc Lifsher, "Pension Funds Seriously Underfunded," *Los Angeles Times,* July 17, 2012 [**http://articles.latimes.com/2012/jul/17/business/la-fi-pension-shortfalls-20120718**].

100. U.S. Department of Labor, "Final Rule to Improve Transparency of Fees and Expenses to Workers in 401(k)-Type Retirement Plans," February 2012 [**www.dol.gov/ebsa/newsroom/fsparticipantfeerule.html**].

101. *LaRue v. DeWolff, Boberg& Associates, Inc.,* 128 S.Ct. 1020 (2008) and *Conkright v. Frommert,* 130 S.Ct. 1640 (2010).

102. *Cigna Corp. v. Amara,* 131 S.Ct. 1866 (2011); and *Amara v. Cigna Corp.,* 925 F. Supp. 2d 242 (D.Conn. 2012).

103. *Wagenseller v. Scottsdale Memorial Hospital,* 710 P.2d 1025 (Az. S.Ct. 1985).

104. *Rubenstein v. Huntington Mortgage Company,* N.J. Sup. Ct., App. Div., 1997. For a journalistic account of the case, see Pitney, Hardin, Kipp, and Szuch, "Employers Must Be Cautious about Failing to Disclose Business Plans that Will Affect the Jobs of New Hires," *New Jersey Employment Law Letter,* September 1997.

105. Arizona State Senate Fact Sheet for SB 1070 [**www.azleg.gov/legtext/49leg/2r/summary/s.1070pshs.doc.htm**].

106. *Arizona v. U.S.,* 132 S.Ct. 2492 (2012).

107. David G. Savage, "Supreme Court Won't Revive Alabama Immigration Law," April 29, 2013 [**http://articles.latimes.com/2013/apr/29/nation/la-na-court-immigration-20130430**].

108. Pew Research "A Nation of Immigrants," *Pew Research Hispanic Trends Project,* January 29, 2013 [**www.pewhispanic.org/2013/01/29/a-nation-of-immigrants/**].

109. Jeffrey S. Passel et al., "Immigrants Stalls, May Have Reversed," *Pew Research Hispanic Trends Project,* September 23, 2013 [**www.pewhispanic.org/2013/09/23/population-decline-of-unauthorized-immigrants-stalls-may-have-reversed/**].

110. Pew Research Center for the People and the Press, "Public Supports Arizona Immigration Law," May 12, 2010 [**http://pewresearch.org/pubs/1591/public-support-arizona-immigration-law-poll**].

111. Lawrence Harrison, "The US Should Think Long and Hard about the High Numbers of Latino Immigrants," *The Christian Science Monitor.com,* May 28, 2009 [**www.csmonitor.com**].

112. Teresa Watanabe, "Immigrants Boost Pay, Not Prison Populations, New Studies Show," *Los Angeles Times,* February 28, 2007 [**www.latimes.com/news/local/la-me-immigstudy-28feb28,0,7851813.story?track=ntottext**].

113. David Streitfeld, "Illegal—but Essential," *Los Angeles Times,* October 1, 2006 [**www.latimes.com/business/la-fi-immigecon1oct01,0,2945710.story?track=tottext**].

114. Rosa Brooks, "How Immigrants Improve the Curve," *Los Angeles Times,* June 29, 2007 [**www.latimes.com/news/opinion/la-oe-brooks29jun29,0,1106152.column?coll=la-tot-opinion&track=ntottext**].

115. Ibid.

116. Elizabeth Dwoskin, "H-1B Visas Hit the Cap, Sending Companies to Plan B," *Bloomberg Businessweek,* June 13, 2012 [**www.businessweek.com/articles/2012-06-13/h1-b-visas-hit-the-cap-companies-go-to-plan-b**].

117. Miriam Jordan, "Policing Illegal Hires Puts Some Employers in a Bind," *The Wall Street Journal,* July 15, 2010, p. A5.

118. "Justice Department Resolves Citizenship Status Discrimination Charge against California Employer." March 8, 2011 [**www.justice.gov/opa/pr/2011/March/11-crt-294.html**].

119. Lisa Baertlein and Mary Milliken, "Fired Workers Say Chipotle Was Soft on Immigration," *Reuters.com,* April 13, 2011 [**www.reuters.com/article/2011/04/13/us-chipotle-idUSTRE73C0P220110413**].

120. National Conference of State Legislatures, "E-Verify," December 18, 2012 [**www.ncsl.org /research/immigration/everify-faq.aspx**].

121. U.S. Citizenship and Immigration Services, "E-Verify History and Milestones" [**www.uscis .gov/e-verify/about-program/history-and-milestones**].

122. Bruce A. Morrison and Paul Donnelly, "A Simple Way to Keep Illegal Immigrants from Getting Jobs," *The Washington Post,* May 1, 2010, A 15.

123. *Washington Post*, "The Boss Can't Fire You for Doing Your Civic Duty," *Waterloo/Cedar Falls Courier,* May 26, 1999, p. C8.

CHAPTER THIRTEEN

Employment Law II: Discrimination

After completing this chapter, students will be able to:

1. Discuss the purpose and history of legal protections against employment discrimination.

2. Compare and contrast the protections offered under the federal statutes prohibiting employment discrimination: Title VII of the Civil Rights Act of 1964; the Equal Pay Act; the Americans with Disabilities Act; and the Age Discrimination in Employment Act.

3. Explain the role of the Equal Employment Opportunity Commission (EEOC) in enforcing federal statutes prohibiting employment discrimination.

4. Identify remedies available to victims of unlawful employment discrimination.

5. Distinguish the primary forms of employment discrimination analysis: disparate treatment and disparate impact.

6. Identify when unlawful sexual harassment has occurred.

7. Identify when employers are liable for unlawful sexual harassment.

8. Describe protections against retaliation offered under the federal statutes prohibiting employment discrimination.

9. Discuss the purposes and development of affirmative action.

10. Describe the concept of reasonable accommodation as applied to religious- and disability-based discrimination claims.

11. Discuss the current status of protections against sexual orientation discrimination in the workplace.

Introduction

PRACTICING ETHICS) A "Look" at A & F

Abercrombie & Fitch (A & F or Abercrombie), the clothing retailer, was accused in 2003 of maintaining a virtually all-white image by discriminating in recruiting, hiring, and promoting women and minorities. A nationwide class-action lawsuit was filed claiming that Abercrombie disproportionately assigned minority employees to stockrooms and other jobs out of the public eye, while white employees were conspicuously on display as a means of projecting the company's "clean-cut, classic" image.

Abercrombie denied the charges, but it decided to settle in 2005 by agreeing to pay $40 million along with $10 million in attorney fees and other expenses. The settlement also required the company to promote diversity in its workforce.[1] In addition, Abercrombie agreed to manifest a more diverse image in its marketing materials, including its catalogs, shopping bags, and store posters.[2]

In September 2013, Abercrombie settled two religious discrimination lawsuits filed by the federal government's Equal Employment Opportunity Commission, both involving Muslim teens who wore headscarves (hijabs). One teen had been terminated from her stockroom job at Hollister for refusing to remove her hijab in violation of the store's "Look Policy," and another who was denied employment at an Abercrombie outlet had been asked about her hijab and religion during her interview. Two federal judges had ruled against A & F prior to the settlement, under which the store paid $71,000 and promised to change its policies.[3] However, the next month, a federal appellate court judge reversed a trial court's ruling against Abercrombie in a third religious discrimination lawsuit involving a refusal to hire based on the applicant's hijab. The Court agreed with A & F that its "Look Policy" was necessary to maintain its "classic East Coast collegiate style of clothing."[4]

Questions

1. A & F defenders have argued that the clothier has the right to promote an image of its choice as a means of making a profit.
   a. The law aside, is Abercrombie simply wrong to project an image that, however it is labeled, may be described as a "white image" if, indeed, it does so? Explain.
   b. Would it be wrong for a store promoting a "hip hop" image to refuse to hire an applicant because she wears a hijab? How about if that store refused to hire a white applicant based on race? Explain.
   c. What if a store selling hunting and fishing gear refused to hire African-American applicants for cashier and sales associate positions—would that be wrong? Explain.

2. A college student decided not to apply for a job at Abercrombie because she didn't feel "appropriate" for the job after she observed all of the store's "tall, skinny white girls." The college student stated that, in the long run, hiring only employees with that particular look will "hurt Abercrombie."[5]
   a. Would the market punish Abercrombie, even if the law had not intervened? Explain.
   b. Should the market punish Abercrombie? Put another way, should you as a consumer decline to shop at Abercrombie stores based on its apparent employment practices? Explain.

3. a. In your opinion, should an employer be able to specify a reasonable dress code?
   b. Do you think a "no-head coverings" policy is reasonable and enforceable even if it excludes some religious groups from employment? Explain.
   c. Under the settlement reached with the EEOC, Abercrombie now allows employees to request exceptions to its dress code. Do you think this is a fair result? Explain.

Continuing Discrimination   The ethical issues raised by Abercrombie & Fitch's hiring and staffing practices highlight the challenges of enforcing legal protections against employment discrimination, often referred to as Equal Employment Opportunity (EEO) laws.

Employers compare, distinguish, and choose among applicants and employees based on many factors. However, EEO laws forbid those considerations that would undermine equal employment opportunity. Prohibited factors, also called "protected categories," or "protected classes" include an applicant's or employee's race, color, and gender, among other characteristics. Generally, EEO laws protect all employees and are not restricted to certain groups such as women or racial minorities.

Do we still need EEO laws in the United States? Consider a recent study in which black and white men applied for the same entry-level jobs with nearly identical résumés. Some of the white men were instructed to tell the employer that they had felony drug convictions. Who would receive the employer's call—the white ex-convict or the black with no criminal record? Most likely, the study found, the white applicant with the criminal record would be preferred over the black applicant with no criminal record.[6] As diversity grows in the United States, EEO laws may serve to support and sustain a more inclusive, and, ultimately, more productive workplace.[7]

> **Most likely, the white applicant would be preferred.**

2060: Plurality Nation

The 2012 U.S. Census revealed that over one-third of Americans reported their race and ethnicity as "minority;" that is, something other than non-Hispanic white. By 2060, the U.S. Census Bureau projects that although overall population growth will slow down, this figure will increase to 57 percent. Although non-Hispanic whites will remain the largest part of the U.S. population, no one group will hold a majority, making the United States a "plurality nation."

Source: U.S. Census Bureau, U.S. Census Bureau, "U.S. Census Bureau Projects Show a Slower Growing, Older, More Diverse Population a Half Century from Now," December 12, 2012 **[http://www.census.gov/newsroom /releases/archives/population/cb12-243.html]**.

Part One—Employment Discrimination: The Foundation in Law

History

In the Reconstruction Era following the Civil War, Congress passed the Civil Rights Act of 1866 to provide the newly freed black slaves with the same right to make and enforce contracts as was enjoyed by white citizens. This law still exists today, with updated language emphasizing its protection against racial discrimination. The Civil Rights Act of 1866 has been interpreted to forbid discrimination on the basis of race in employment, which is essentially a contractual relationship.

However, this legal protection did not prevent discriminatory practices in housing, education, business, and employment. In 1941, A. Philip Randolph, president of the predominantly black Brotherhood of Sleeping Car Porters, organized black leaders who threatened a massive march in Washington, DC, protesting employment discrimination. In response, President Franklin Roosevelt issued Executive Order 8802, which created a Fair Employment Practice Committee. Congress limited the committee's budget, but Roosevelt's action was a striking step for the federal government in addressing racial discrimination.

The next big step toward racial equality was the landmark *Brown v. Board of Education*[8] decision in 1954, in which the Supreme Court forbade "separate but equal" schools. Following *Brown,* citizens engaged in sit-ins, freedom rides, boycotts, and the like to press claims for racial equality. It was a turbulent, sometimes violent, era, but those activities were critical ingredients in subsequent advances for the black population. With the passage of the 1964 Civil Rights Act, the campaign against discrimination solidified as one of the most energetic and influential social movements in American history.[9] The Civil Rights Act of 1964 changed American life by forbidding discrimination in education, housing, public accommodation, and, perhaps most importantly, employment. [For the National Civil Rights Museum, see **www.civilrightsmuseum.org**]

Civil Rights Act of 1964

Reflecting the increased diversity of the U.S. workforce, in which women had gone beyond traditional roles and where immigrants from around the world could be found, Title VII of the Civil Rights Act of 1964 ("Title VII") marked a new era in employment practices. Title VII forbids discrimination in employment on the basis of race, color, religion, sex, or national origin. Relying on its authority to regulate commerce, Congress applied Title VII to private-sector employers with 15 or more employees, employment agencies, labor unions with 15 or more members as well as those operating a hiring hall, state and local governments, and most of the federal government. Private clubs are exempt from Title VII, and religious organizations may discriminate in employment on the basis of religion. Broadly, Title VII forbids discrimination in hiring, firing, and all aspects of the employment relationship.

Other Legislation and Orders

Title VII is the core of EEO laws in the United States. Other federal statutes, such as the Americans with Disabilities Act of 1990 (ADA) and its 2008 amendments (ADAAA), and the Age Discrimination in Employment Act of 1967 (ADEA), have established additional protected categories. The Equal Pay Act of 1963 and the Civil Rights Act of 1991 address particular issues in employment discrimination. For example, the Civil Rights Act of 1991 provides that U.S. citizens working abroad for American-owned or American-controlled companies are protected from discrimination under Title VII and the ADA unless such protection would require the employer to violate the laws of its host nation. Later in this chapter, these federal laws will be discussed further.

The Constitution

As explained in Chapter 5, the federal constitution, among other purposes, protects us from wrongful government action. The Fourteenth Amendment to the Constitution provides that no state shall deny to any person life, liberty, or property without *due process of law* or deny him or her the *equal protection of the laws*. Thus, citizens are protected from discrimination via state government action. Similarly, the Supreme Court has interpreted the Due Process Clause of the Fifth Amendment ("nor shall any person . . . be deprived of life, liberty, or property, without due process of law") to forbid discrimination by the federal government.

Stopping Discrimination through Corporate Pledges

In his 2014 State of the Union Address, President Obama announced that he had secured voluntary pledges from a number of major U.S. companies to not discriminate against applicants who are currently unemployed. In seeking employment, those who are jobless, particularly those who have been unemployed for a significant period of time, often face discrimination based on their employment status. Legislative attempts to ban such discriminatory practices have met with limited success and offer narrow protections against express exclusions of the unemployed in help-wanted ads.

Questions

1. What are the advantages of the corporate pledge approach to protecting against emerging areas of discrimination? Explain.

2. Assume that a job applicant at one of the U.S. companies that had pledged not to discriminate against the unemployed was rejected because she has been jobless for over two years. Would the applicant have any recourse? Explain.

Source: Ben Leubsdorf, "Obama Tries New Tack for Long-Term Jobless," *The Wall Street Journal,* January 28, 2014 [**http://online.wsj.com/news/articles/SB10001424052702303277704579347082417660564**].

Employment Discrimination Enforcement

EEOC and State Fair Employment Practice Agencies

The Equal Employment Opportunity Commission (EEOC), an independent federal agency, has the authority to issue regulations and guidelines as well as to receive, initiate, and investigate charges of discrimination against employers covered by federal antidiscrimination statutes such as Title VII. [See the Equal Employment Opportunity Commission's website at **www/eeoc.gov**]

State fair employment practices legislation often mirrors or expands the antidiscrimination protections found in federal statutes such as Title VII. State fair employment practice agencies may serve the same function as the EEOC in enforcing these laws. [For an example, see California Department of Fair Employment and Housing's website at **www.dfeh.ca.gov**] Municipal ordinances may also address employment discrimination, enforced by a particular branch of the city's government. [For the San Francisco Human Rights Commission, see **www.sfgov.org/site/sfhumanrights_index.asp**]

Litigation

The first step in lawsuits claiming employment discrimination is not taken in a courthouse. A victim of employment discrimination, usually referred to as the "charging party," will file a complaint within a limited period of time with either the EEOC or, where applicable, the local or state fair employment practices agency.

What if the allegedly discriminatory act is ongoing rather than an incident occurring on a certain date—at what moment does the clock start ticking on the victim's time to file an

EEOC complaint? After 19 years as a Goodyear employee, Lily Ledbetter discovered that her wages were much lower than her male coworkers. She filed an EEOC complaint alleging gender discrimination and later won a jury verdict for back pay and punitive damages. In 2007, the U.S. Supreme Court held in *Ledbetter v. Goodyear Tire & Rubber Co.* that Ledbetter's claim should have been brought within 180 days of the first paycheck at issue.[10] Congress reacted to *Ledbetter* by passing The Lily Ledbetter Fair Pay Act of 2009, signed into law by President Obama in the first days of his administration. Under this statute, each paycheck issued by an employer engaged in pay discrimination is a discriminatory act, meaning that the clock resets on potential discrimination claim each time the affected employee is paid, with a two-year cap on back pay damages.[11]

Typically, the EEOC will refer the charging party and employer to its free mediation program. If mediation does not resolve the complaint, then the EEOC will investigate. If the investigation reveals that there is reasonable cause to believe that discrimination has occurred, the EEOC will invite the parties to engage in conciliation to resolve the matter. If conciliation fails, the EEOC either files a civil suit on behalf of the charging party or issues a "right to sue" letter. The "right to sue" letter allows the party who filed the EEOC complaint to file a lawsuit, but also removes the EEOC from the matter.

Many potential employment discrimination lawsuits no longer reach the judicial system because they are resolved in arbitration. Many businesses are now including binding arbitration agreements in job offers, requiring job seekers, as a condition of employment, to waive the right to trial and turn any grievance over to arbitration. A series of U.S. Supreme Court decisions has firmly established the enforceability of those agreements when the arbitration process provided for is legitimate and fair. The Court has also ruled, however, that the EEOC retains its right to sue on behalf of an employee even if the worker has signed away his or her own rights.[12]

Despite headline-grabbing settlements in discrimination cases, a 2010 American Bar Foundation (ABF) study found that discrimination lawsuits rarely make it to trial and usually end with a modest settlement. If these cases go to court, the plaintiffs have only a one-in-three chance of winning.[13]

Another ABF study found that although plaintiffs begin the process optimistically, they rarely get a final ruling based on the substantive merits of a case, causing them to view employment litigation as favoring defendant-employers. On the other hand, defendant employers view the process as unfair because the employee has the power to initiate what they view as a "meritless" suit requiring their response.[14]

Remedies

Recognizing the gravity and nature of injuries caused by intentional discrimination in the workplace, Congress expanded the remedies available for such injury under Title VII and the Americans with Disabilities Act (ADA) to include compensatory damages as well as punitive damages in some cases. Compensatory damages may be sought to redress, for example, emotional pain and suffering, but combined compensatory and punitive damages are capped at $50,000 to $300,000, depending on the size of the employer's workforce. Damages are not capped for front pay (awarded for future earnings) or in cases of intentional discrimination based on race. The EEOC often negotiates consent decrees that may require new procedures to correct wrongful practices. [For the Civil Rights Division of the U.S. Justice Department, see **www.justice.gov/crt/**]

EEOC's Strategic Plan

Under the EEOC's Strategic Plan for FY 2012–2016, the EEOC has made "systemic enforcement" a priority. In 2013, the EEOC obtained $372.1 million in monetary relief for victims of private-sector workplace discrimination, the EEOC's highest level of recovery in its history. At the same time, a federal appellate court restricted the EEOC's systemic enforcement efforts by ruling that the EEOC would have to determine the individuals in a class action against an employer before litigation, not during discovery (see Chapter 4). The employer should then have the opportunity to resolve the matter through the EEOC's conciliation process. However, in denying an employer's motion for summary judgment, a federal district judge allowed an EEOC action to proceed without the names of the discrimination victims being identified before the lawsuit was filed.

Questions

1. Why might the EEOC have decided to focus on "systemic enforcement" as part of its strategic plan? What are the advantages and disadvantages of such a focus? Explain.

2. Should the EEOC be able to investigate and bring an enforcement action against an employer suspected of a systemic pattern of discrimination without a specific individual complaint? Explain.

3. If the EEOC is required to always identify individual victims of a potentially discriminatory employment practice prior to bringing a class-action lawsuit against the employer, how might this impact its systemic enforcement efforts? Explain.

Sources: U.S. Equal Employment Opportunity Commission, "EEOC Issues FY 2013 Performance Report," December 16, 2013 [**www.eeoc.gov/eeoc/newsroom/release/12-16-13.cfm**]; Court Affirms EEOC'S Authority to Proceed on Behalf of Discrimination Victims Even If Not Yet Identified Individually [**http://www.eeoc.gov/eeoc/newsroom/release/5-15-12.cfm**]; and *EOC v. CRST Van Expedited,* 670 F.3d 897 (8th Cir. 2012).

Part Two—"Types of Discrimination"

There are three basic types of illegal employment discrimination: disparate treatment, disparate impact, and harassment. In addition, Title VII and other antiemployment discrimination statutes prohibit *retaliation* for opposing an employment practice reasonably believed to be discriminatory, or for participating in a claim of employment discrimination. Plaintiffs may raise claims of more than one type of employment discrimination, as well as retaliation, against an employer.

Disparate Treatment and Disparate Impact

Title VII of the 1964 Civil Rights Act provides two primary theories of recovery for individuals—disparate treatment and disparate impact (sometimes labeled *adverse impact*). A disparate treatment claim addresses *intentional* discrimination by an employer who has purposefully treated an employee or applicant less favorably because of his or her race, color, religion, national origin, gender, or membership in a group under another protected category. Disparate impact claims arise from "unintentional" discrimination where an employment practice appearing to be neutral has the effect of adversely impacting a particular group under a protected category more than it impacts other groups.

As we turn now to a close look at disparate treatment and disparate impact analysis, keep in mind the various constitutional, statutory, and executive order protections just outlined.

Disparate Treatment

Employees or applicants making claims of disparate treatment must prove their employers' intent to discriminate with either direct or indirect evidence. For example, a company president's remarks that "women were simply 'not tough enough' to supervise collections and that it was a 'man's job,'" (even if tempered by his statement that "I felt that a woman was not competent enough to do this job, but I think maybe you're showing me that you can do it,") may constitute *direct evidence* of intentional sex discrimination, as a federal court of appeals found.[15] A warehouse company seeking truck loaders might send a letter to an employment agency stating: "Women would not be welcome as applicants for this physically taxing job." That letter could be used as direct evidence of the employer's intent to treat female applicants adversely compared with male applicants. More often, however, disparate treatment claims rely on *indirect evidence* in accord with the following test:

1. **Plaintiff's (employee's) *prima facie case*** (sufficient to be presumed true unless proven otherwise) is confirmed by proving each of the following ingredients:

   a. Plaintiff belongs to a protected class.
   b. Plaintiff applied for a job for which the defendant was seeking applicants.
   c. Plaintiff was qualified for the job.
   d. Plaintiff was denied the job.
   e. The position remained open, and the employer continued to seek applicants.

2. **Defendant's (employer's) case.** If the plaintiff builds a successful prima facie case, the defendant must "articulate some *legitimate, nondiscriminatory reason* for the employee's rejection" (e.g., greater work experience). However, the defendant need not prove that its decision not to hire the plaintiff was, in fact, based on that legitimate, nondiscriminatory reason. The defendant simply must raise a legitimate issue of fact disputing the plaintiff's discrimination claim.

3. **Plaintiff's response.** Assuming the defendant was successful in presenting a legitimate, nondiscriminatory reason for its action, the plaintiff must show that the reason offered by the defendant was false and thus was merely a *pretext* to hide discrimination. [For an overview of disparate treatment analysis, see **www.hr-guide.com/data/G701.htm**]

Questions

Kim Ondricko, a white female, was discharged from her job as floor supervisor at the MGM Grand Detroit casino for violating procedures regarding card shuffling, which breached the employer's policy: "What in the business judgment of MGM Grand Detroit jeopardizes the efficiency or integrity of the gaming operation is prohibited." As Ondricko supervised a dealer at a blackjack table, the automatic card shuffler malfunctioned, causing a bad shuffle. Ondricko informed her supervisor, the pit boss. Prior to this incident, at least six other supervisors had engaged in shuffle-related misconduct, but only two had been terminated. One of the terminated supervisors, a black female who had assisted a dealer having trouble removing cards from the shuffler by retrieving and giving the dealer the unshuffled cards to deal , had retained attorneys. A black male supervisor had been given a three-day suspension for approving a bad shuffle. When an assistant shift manager asked Mike O'Connor, vice president of operations, why Ondricko was being terminated, O'Connor stated, "Do you think I wanted to fire Kim, I didn't want to fire Kim, how could I keep the white girl?" Ondricko sued her former employer, claiming race and gender discrimination.

1. How would you resolve this case? Explain.
2. Would Ondricko still be able to bring Title VII discrimination claims if O'Connor had not made the statement about why he believed he had to fire her? Explain.
3. Stalter, an African American, was fired for theft after working at a Walmart loading dock for four months. While eating a handful of taco chips from an open bag on the countertop in the break room, a coworker entered the room, took the bag from Stalter, and placed it in her locker. Stalter later apologized to her and offered to buy a new bag. She said the incident was "no big deal" and told him to "forget about it." Management then investigated, concluded Stalter had stolen the chips, and fired him. Stalter sued, claiming his termination was race based. What questions would you have if you were on the jury? Explain. See *Stalter v. Wal-Mart Stores*, 195 F.3d 285 (7th Cir. 1999).

Disparate Impact

Disparate impact analysis involves situations in which employers use legitimate employment standards that, despite their apparent neutrality, impose a heavier burden on a protected class than on other employees. For example, a preemployment test, offered with the best of intentions and constructed to be a fair measurement device, may disproportionately exclude members of a protected class and thus be unacceptable (barring an effective defense). Alternatively, an employer surreptitiously seeking to discriminate may establish an apparently neutral, superficially valid employment test that has the effect of achieving the employer's discrimination goal. For example, a tavern might require its bouncer to be at least 6 feet 2 inches tall and weigh at least 200 pounds. Generally, height and weight are not protected classes. However, the tavern's requirement will disproportionately exclude women, and perhaps members of certain ethnic groups as well. Was this the tavern's intent? Most likely it was not, but remember that whereas disparate treatment requires proof of intent, disparate impact does not.

The Test

Disparate impact analysis requires the following:

1. The plaintiff/employee must identify the *specific employment practice or policy* (such as test score, skill, or height) that caused the alleged disparate impact on the protected class.
2. The plaintiff must prove (often with statistical evidence) that the protected class is suffering an *adverse or disproportionate impact* caused by the employment practice or policy in question. The statistical analysis to establish a disparate impact (against black job applicants, for example) must be based on a comparison of the racial composition of

the group of persons actually holding the jobs in question versus the racial composition of the *job-qualified* population in the relevant labor market.

3. Assuming a prima facie case is established in steps 1 and 2, the plaintiff/employee wins unless the defendant/employer demonstrates that the employment practice/policy is (a) *job related* and (b) *consistent with business necessity*. In the bouncer example above, the tavern would have to demonstrate that the height and weight requirements were related to the job in accordance with the needs of taverns.

4. If the defendant/employer succeeds in demonstrating job relatedness and business necessity, the employer wins unless the plaintiff/employee demonstrates that *an alternative, less discriminatory business practice is available and that the employer refuses to adopt it.*

The following classic case examines disparate impact analysis.

LEGAL BRIEFCASE

Griggs v. Duke Power Co.
401 U.S. 424 (1971)

Chief Justice Burger

We granted the writ in this case to resolve the question whether an employer is prohibited by the Civil Rights Act of 1964, Title VII, from requiring a high school education or passing of a standardized general intelligence test as a condition of employment in or transfer to jobs when (a) neither standard is shown to be significantly related to successful job performance, (b) both requirements operate to disqualify Negroes at a substantially higher rate than white applicants, and (c) the jobs in question formerly had been filled only by white employees as part of a longstanding practice of giving preference to whites.

Congress provided, in Title VII of the Civil Rights Act of 1964, for class actions for enforcement of provisions of the Act and this proceeding was brought by a group of incumbent Negro employees against Duke Power Company. . . .

The district court found that prior to July 2, 1965, the effective date of the Civil Rights Act of 1964, the company openly discriminated on the basis of race in the hiring and assigning of employees at its Dan River plant. The plant was organized into five operating departments: (1) Labor, (2) Coal Handling, (3) Operations, (4) Maintenance, and (5) Laboratory and Test. Negroes were employed only in the Labor Department where the highest-paying jobs paid less than the lowest-paying jobs in the other four "operating" departments in which only whites were employed. Promotions were normally made within each department on the basis of job seniority. Transferees into a department usually began in the lowest position.

In 1955 the company instituted a policy of requiring a high school education for initial assignment to any department except Labor, and for transfer from the Coal Handling to any "inside" department (Operations, Maintenance, or Laboratory). When the company abandoned its policy of restricting Negroes to the Labor Department in 1965, completion of high school also was made a prerequisite to transfer from Labor to any other department. From the time the high school requirement was instituted to the time of trial, however, white employees hired before the time of the high school education requirement continued to perform satisfactorily and achieve promotions in the "operating" departments. Findings on this score are not challenged.

The company added a further requirement for new employees on July 2, 1965, the date on which Title VII became effective. To qualify for placement in any but the Labor Department it became necessary to register satisfactory scores on two professionally prepared aptitude tests, as well as to have a high school education. Completion of high school alone continued to render employees eligible for transfer to the four desirable departments from which Negroes had been excluded if the incumbent had been employed prior to the time of the new requirement. In September 1965 the company began to permit incumbent employees who lacked a high school education to qualify for transfer from Labor or Coal Handling to an "inside" job by passing two tests—the Wonderlic Personnel Test, which purports to measure general intelligence, and the Bennett Mechanical Comprehension Test. Neither was directed or intended to measure the ability to learn to perform a particular job or category of jobs. The requisite scores used for both initial hiring and transfer approximated the national median for high school graduates.

The District Court had found that while the company previously followed a policy of overt racial discrimination in a period prior to the Act, such conduct had ceased. The District Court also concluded that Title VII was intended to be prospective only and, consequently, the impact of prior inequities was beyond the reach of corrective action authorized by the Act.

. . . The Court of Appeals concluded there was no violation of the Act.

* * * * *

The objective of Congress in the enactment of Title VII is plain from the language of the statute. It was to achieve equality of employment opportunities and remove barriers that have operated in the past to favor an identifiable group of white employees over other employees. Under the Act, practices, procedures, or tests neutral on their face, and even neutral in terms of intent, cannot be maintained if they operate to "freeze" the status quo of prior discriminatory employment practices.

The Court of Appeals' opinion, and the partial dissent, agreed that, on the record in the present case, "whites register far better on the company's alternative requirements" than Negroes. This consequence would appear to be directly traceable to race. Basic intelligence must have the means of articulation to manifest itself fairly in a testing process. Because they are Negroes, petitioners have long received inferior education in segregated schools.

. . . Congress did not intend by Title VII, however, to guarantee a job to every person regardless of qualifications. In short, the Act does not command that any person be hired simply because he was formerly the subject of discrimination, or because he is a member of a minority group. Discriminatory preference for any group, minority or majority, is precisely and only what Congress has proscribed. . . .

. . . The Act proscribes not only overt discrimination but also practices that are fair in form, but discriminatory in operation. The touchstone is business necessity. If an employment practice which operates to exclude Negroes cannot be shown to be related to job performance, the practice is prohibited.

On the record before us, neither the high school completion requirement nor the general intelligence test is shown to bear a demonstrable relationship to successful performance of the jobs for which it was used. Both were adopted, as the Court of Appeals noted, without meaningful study of their relationship to job-performance ability. Rather, a vice president of

the company testified, the requirements were instituted on the company's judgment that they generally would improve the overall quality of the workforce.

The evidence, however, shows that employees who have not completed high school or taken the tests have continued to perform satisfactorily and make progress in departments for which the high school and test criteria are not used. . . .

The Court of Appeals held that the company had adopted the diploma and test requirements without any "intention to discriminate against Negro employees." We do not suggest that either the District Court or the Court of Appeals erred in examining the employer's intent; but good intent or absence of discriminatory intent does not redeem employment procedures or testing mechanisms that operate as "built-in headwinds" for minority groups and are unrelated to measuring job capability.

* * * * *

The facts of this case demonstrate the inadequacy of broad and general testing devices as well as the infirmity of using diplomas or degrees as fixed measures of capability. . . .

The company contends that its general intelligence tests are specifically permitted by Section 703(h) of the Act. That section authorizes the use of "any professionally developed ability test" that is not "designed, intended *or used* to discriminate because of race. . . ." (Emphasis added.)

The Equal Employment Opportunity Commission, having enforcement responsibility, has issued guidelines interpreting Section 703(h) to permit only the use of job-related tests. The administrative interpretation of the Act by the enforcing agency is entitled to great deference. Since the Act and its legislative history support the commission's construction, this affords good reason to treat the guidelines as expressing the will of Congress.

. . . From the sum of the legislative history relevant in this case, the conclusion is inescapable that the EEOC's construction of Section 703(h) to require that employment tests be job related comports with congressional intent.

Nothing in the Act precludes the use of testing or measuring procedures; obviously they are useful. What Congress has forbidden is giving these devices and mechanisms controlling force unless they are demonstrably a reasonable measure of job performance. Congress has not commanded that the less qualified be preferred over the better qualified simply because of minority origins. Far from disparaging job qualifications as such, Congress has made such qualifications the controlling factor, so that race, religion, nationality, and sex become irrelevant. What Congress has commanded is that any tests used must measure the person for the job and not the person in the abstract.

The judgment of the Court of Appeals is . . . reversed.

Questions

1. According to the Supreme Court, what was Congress's objective in enacting Title VII?

2. Had Duke Power been able to establish that its reasons for adopting the diploma and test standards were entirely without discriminatory intent, would the Supreme Court have ruled differently? Explain.

3. What is the central issue in this case?

4. Why was North Carolina's social and educational history relevant to the outcome of the case?

5. Statistical evidence showed that 35 percent of new hires in grocery and produce at Lucky Stores, a retail grocery chain, were women, while 84 percent of new hires in deli, bakery, and general merchandise were women. Statistical evidence also showed that 31 percent of those promoted into apprentice jobs in grocery and produce were women, while women comprised 75 percent of those promoted into apprentice jobs in deli, bakery, and general merchandise. Grocery and produce jobs generally were higher-paying jobs than those in deli, bakery, and general merchandise. Women received significantly fewer overtime hours than men.

   Do these facts regarding Lucky Stores suggest discrimination? Explain. See *Stender v. Lucky Stores,* Inc., 803 F.Supp. 259 (DC Cal. 1992).

6. To determine whether police officers were using illegal drugs, the Boston Police Department used hair tests. The police department took adverse employment actions against several African-American police officers who had failed the test. The officers brought a Title VII action claiming the test created a disparate impact based on race. African-American officers had passed the test at rates between 97 and 99 percent, while white officers' pass rate was 99 and 100 percent. However, the officers' expert offered evidence that fail rates of African-American police officers were "statistically significant"—between two and four standard deviations. The Boston Police Department asked for summary judgment. Should the disparate impact claim be allowed to proceed? Explain. *See Jones v. City of Boston,* 2012 U.S. Dist. LEXIS 141440 (D. Mass. 2012).

7. Eighty-one percent of the hires at Consolidated Service Systems, a small Chicago janitorial company, were of Korean origin. The EEOC brought a disparate treatment claim, saying the firm discriminated in favor of Koreans by relying primarily on word-of-mouth recruiting. Hwang, the owner, is Korean. Seventy-three percent of the job applicants were Korean. One percent of the Chicago-area workforce is Korean, and not more than 3 percent of the janitorial workforce for the area is Korean. The court found no persuasive evidence of intentional discrimination, although the government claimed that 99 applicants were denied jobs because they were not Koreans.

   a. Does restricting hiring to members of one ethnic group constitute discrimination where hiring is accomplished by word of mouth? Explain.

   b. What if a firm, using the word-of-mouth approach, hired only white applicants? Explain.

   c. In this case, the EEOC brought but dropped a disparate impact claim. Analyze the case using the disparate impact test. See *Equal Employment Opportunity Commission v. Consolidated Service Systems,* 989 F.2d 233 (7th Cir. 1993).

Statutory Defenses

In addition to the aforementioned defenses against disparate treatment and disparate impact claims, Title VII also affords specific exemptions or defenses, three of which are of particular note: (1) seniority, (2) employee testing, and (3) bona fide occupational qualification. Bona fide occupational qualifications are addressed in the next section as part of the sex discrimination discussion.

Seniority

Differences in wages and conditions of employment are permissible under the Civil Rights Act of 1964 where those differences are the result of a bona fide (good faith) seniority system, as long as the system was not intended to hide or facilitate discrimination. Seniority is important because it often determines who is laid off first and who gets promotions, vacations, and so forth. Because white people often have greater seniority than blacks, the result is that seniority may perpetuate the effects of historical discrimination. The Supreme Court has made it clear, however, that a bona fide seniority system that perpetuates past wrongs is illegal only if discriminatory intent is proven.[16]

Job-Related Employee Testing

Many employers use testing in making hiring and promotion decisions. The availability of online applications has contributed to an increase in this practice.[17] To avoid a disparate impact created by employee testing, an employer must be able to show that the test in question is job-related and consistent with business necessity; that is, the test must evaluate an individual's skills as they relate to the relevant employment opportunity. To prevent unlawful disparate treatment, an employer's test must be uniformly applied regardless of an applicant's or employee's race, sex, or other protected categories. For example, Title VII prohibits an employer from testing the reading ability of African-American applicants or employees while not requiring the same test of their white counterparts.[18]

Spousal Discrimination?

Craig Holcomb, a white male and assistant coach for the Iona College men's basketball team, married an African-American woman. While the team enjoyed a successful record for several years, its lackluster performance and player misconduct between 2001 and 2004 led to changes in the Iona basketball program including the dismissal of Holcomb and an African-American assistant coach. Another white assistant coach, who was not engaged in an inter-racial relationship, was not fired. Holcomb brought a Title VII claim asserting that he had been discharged because his wife is African American. Holcomb alleged that Iona College's athletic director had made several racist and derogatory remarks about African Americans on the basketball team and had derided Holcomb's decision to marry his wife, whom he referred to as "Aunt Jemima." How would you rule on this case? Explain.

Source: *Holcomb v. Iona College*, 521 F.3d 130 (2nd Cir. 2008).

The Four-Fifths Rule and Disparate Impact

If the selection rate (such as the percentage passing a test, being hired, or being promoted) for any protected class is less than 80 percent of the selection rate for the group with the highest selection rate, then the employment practice in question will be presumed to create a disparate impact. An employer falling below that standard must prove the job relatedness of the employment practice in question and demonstrate that a good-faith effort was made to find a selection procedure that lessened the disparate impact on protected classes. [For an extensive employment discrimination database, see **http://topics.law.cornell.edu/wex /Employment_discrimination**]

Question

David Dunlap, a 52-year-old African-American man, had 20 years' experience as a boiler-maker, including 15 years as a foreman. Most of Dunlap's work experience had involved contract or temporary jobs in Tennessee Valley Authority facilities, but he had never been directly employed by the TVA. Dunlap asserted that he had been applying for a position with TVA since the 1970s but had not been successful. When he was one of 21 applicants interviewed for 10 available boilermaker positions, he was rejected. The selection commit-tee, made up of five whites and one African American, individually scored the interviews before engaging in "score balancing" where they discussed their individual opinions to even out the scores, which changed considerably through that process. Dunlap's technical exper-tise equaled that of five of the selected applicants, but his interview score was lower. Dunlap showed that he received lower scores on attendance than white applicants with similar records, as well as on safety compared with white applicants who had inferior records, as disclosed in the interview process. Dunlap was ranked 14th out of the 21 candidates. One African-American applicant was hired after he filed a discrimination complaint with the EEOC based on his similar failed attempts to secure employment with TVA. What claim or claims under Title VII might Dunlap have against the TVA? How would you rule? Explain. See *Dunlap v. Tennessee Valley Authority,* 519 F.3d 626 (6th Cir. 2008).

National Origin

Employment discrimination often reflects larger social issues that come to influence work-place relations. A dramatic example is found in the aftermath of the September 11, 2001, terrorist attacks on the United States: Between September 11, 2001, and September 11, 2004, the EEOC processed more than 900 claims of national origin discrimination associated with the September 11 attacks, resulting in approximately $3.2 million in monetary relief.[19]

In 2005, the EEOC settled a claim it brought against Pesce, an upscale Houston-based restaurant on behalf of Karim El-Raheb, former Pesce general manager. In his August 2001 review, El-Raheb had been told he was doing very well. After business declined following the September 11 terrorist attacks, Pesce's co-owners speculated that customers may be frightened by El-Raheb's appearance and name, suggesting that he could "pass for Hispanic" and should change his name to "something Latin." In November 2001, El-Raheb was fired because "things weren't working out." El-Raheb received $150,000 in monetary relief.[20]

Such harassment has been the subject of more recent national origin discrimination com-plaints. In 2013, an aeronautical services company resolved an EEOC complaint for $50,000 brought by a Turkish-Palestinian former employee who had quit his job because of the com-pany's failure to stop workplace derogatory jokes about "terrorists and Arabs" and comments such as "I don't know why we don't just kill all them towelheads."[21]

Speak English Only?

Reflecting a national debate over whether English should be the official language of the United States, "Speak English Only" rules in the workplace have generated controversy as well as national origin discrimination claims based on the disparate impact these rules may have on members of ethnic groups whose primary language is not English.

Employers argue that the rules are necessary when dealing with customers, to maintain job safety, and to encourage congenial worker relations. EEOC guidelines prohibit employers from imposing a blanket ban on employees speaking their primary language in the workplace, but an English-only rule at certain times is permissible if justified by business necessity and if ade-quately explained to the employees. However, in its 2011 report, "English Only Policies in the Workplace," the U.S. Commission on Civil Rights (USCCR) recommended that the EEOC instead advise employers that English-only policies in the workplace are lawful unless intended to harass, embarrass, or exclude employees and applicants based on their national origin.[22]

In *Garcia v. Spun Steak Co.,* the employer, a producer of meat products, instituted an English-only rule for its bilingual employees to enhance safety and product quality and to address allegations that some employees were making rude comments in Spanish to English-speaking employees. The English-only rule applied to work but not to lunch, breaks, or employees' own time. The employer's rule was upheld by a federal appellate court on the grounds that it was narrowly defined and did not create a discriminatory atmosphere.[23]

Question

Rodriguez, a FedEx employee of Hispanic origin, informed FedEx's regional human resources manager Adkinson that he wanted to obtain a promotion to a supervisory position. After applying and interviewing for an available supervisory position, Rodriguez was rejected. The manager who interviewed Rodriguez found him to be qualified, but did not hire him because of Adkinson's expressed concerns that Rodriguez's "accent and speech pattern" would undermine his ability to rise through the corporate ranks. Another FedEx manager stated that when he asked Adkinson why Rodriguez had not received the promotion, Adkinson made derogatory comments about Rodriguez's "language" and "how he speaks." Is FedEx liable for national origin discrimination based on its failure to promote Rodriguez? Decide. Explain. See *Rodriguez v. FedEx Freight East, Inc.,* 487 F.3d 1001 (6th Cir. 2007).

Racial Harassment

The hangman's noose.

The hangman's noose, perhaps the most hurtful and disgraceful expression of racism, has sadly appeared in recent racial harassment cases. In 2008, the EEOC announced the $465,000 settlement of a racial harassment lawsuit on behalf of African-American employees of Henredon Furniture Industries, who had been subjected to a persistent racially hostile work environment that included the display of hangman's nooses.[24] In 2013, a federal jury awarded $200,000 in compensatory and punitive damages against a North Carolina trucking company on behalf of two former African-American truck drivers who were subjected to racial slurs and threats involving nooses. One of the drivers was approached by a white coworker with a noose who said, "This is for you. Do you want to hang from the family tree?" The other driver had been told by a supervisor: "Don't find a noose with your name on it."[25] In 2012, an Atlanta manufacturer settled an EEOC lawsuit that alleged that racially charged graffiti and comments were directed at African-American employees, one of whom found a hangman's noose at his workstation.[26]

As startling as these claims may seem, whether racially charged workplace conduct rises to the level of unlawful harassment appears to be a subject of conflict among federal courts. In October 2012, a federal judge granted the EEOC a partial summary judgment in a racial harassment case, holding that conduct that included racial slurs and "jokes" about lynching was "constitutionally offensive in any setting."[27] However, the next month, an Arkansas federal court found that the use of a racial slur in the workplace was not derogatory but at "most coarse jesting."[28]

In addition to overt forms of workplace harassment such as racial slurs and threats, the use of more subtle "code words" may constitute racial and/or national origin harassment. In 2006 the U.S. Supreme Court unanimously held that calling African-American male employees "boy" could have racial overtones, even if not modified with a reference to African Americans.[29] In *Aman v. Cort Furniture Rental Corporation,*[30] two black employees claimed that they were subjected to a racially hostile work environment in part because black employees were labeled by coworkers and managers with racist "code words" such as "all of you," "one of them," and "poor people." The court, in finding for the employees, ruled that certain phrases in the employment setting cannot be excused as mere rudeness and may, in the totality of the circumstances, add up to discrimination so severe that it creates an abusive work environment.

Legal requirements and the evolving standards for analyzing harassment claims will be explored later in the context of sexual harassment—perhaps the most familiar form of workplace harassment.

Black History Month

In February 2010, the "Compton Cookout," an off-campus party near the University of California, San Diego (UC San Diego) was organized in apparent mockery of Black History Month. The invitation detailed a dress code based on racial stereotypes. The university responded with a teach-in to explore how such incidents arise and the importance of "mutual respect and civility" on its campus. The Office of the Chancellor issued a statement: "We strongly condemn [the party] and the blatant disregard of our campus values. Although the party was not a UC San Diego student-organization sponsored event, participants did include UC San Diego students and that causes us great concern."

Source: UC San Diego Office of the Chancellor, "Condemnation of Off-Campus Party and Affirmation of Principles of Community," *Diversity Matters,* February 16, 2010 [**http://diversity.ucsd.edu/statement.html**].

Part Three—Sex Discrimination

Gender Equality

A discussion of gender inequality in the workplace typically begins with the gender-wage gap, which persists through the 50-year anniversary of the 1963 Equal Pay Act: In 2013, the U.S. Bureau of Labor Statistics (BLS) reported that American women working full-time earn on average about 81 cents for every dollar earned by men.[31] However, supported by other statistics, a rise in women's power in the workplace has been observed. For example, childless women in their 20s earn more than their male counterparts.[32] Yet women's perception of gender bias—such as lower pay and other forms of discrimination—have remained high.[33]

The power and limits of statutory protections against sex discrimination are evident in recent Title VII class-action lawsuits brought by female employees alleging disparity in pay, work assignments, and promotion. In 2007, a federal judge approved a $46 million settlement of a class-action lawsuit brought against Morgan Stanley representing 3,000 female financial advisers and trainees claiming discrimination in compensation, promotion, and work assignments.[34] But the class-action approach to discrimination litigation suffered a significant setback in 2011 when the U.S. Supreme Court denied class-action status in a sex discrimination case against Walmart. The plaintiffs argued, among other things, that women have occupied 70 percent of Walmart's hourly jobs but only 33 percent of management positions.

The Supreme Court decision did not reach the substantive merits of the discrimination complaint. Rather, the Supreme Court ruled that the case could not go forward as a class action because the plaintiffs did not point to specific, consistent, nationwide employment policies or practices that harmed the class members. (See Chapter 4 for more on the *Walmart* case and its impact on class actions.)[35]

Glass Ceiling?   Does a "glass ceiling" of prejudice hold women back from roles of power and career advancement? A 2011 study found a 40 percent disparity between male and female MBAs 10 years after graduation.[36]

Lean In

In her 2013 book entitled *Lean In*, Facebook chief operating officer Sheryl Sandberg observes that too few women are reaching leadership positions in business because, among other factors, of women's choices to curtail their own career ambitions. To support women's professional success and leadership, Sandberg advises women to "lean in" to their careers and make themselves more visible and heard at the workplace.

Questions

1. Do you agree with Sandberg's observations? Explain.
2. What choices might women make that interfere with their career advancement? What other factors may blunt women's career growth? Explain.
3. A recent study involving fictitious chief executive officers (CEOs) revealed that women who are seen as "chatty" or talkative are viewed as less competent, whereas men who dominate workplace conversations are more likely to succeed. A quiet female is viewed far more favorably than her chatty female counterpart: Her competence is assumed to be about equal to that of a talkative male. What might this mean for women who "lean in" at the workplace? Explain.

Sources: David Wessel, "The Positive Economics of 'Leaning In,'" *The Wall Street Journal*, April 3, 2013 [**http://online.wsj.com/news/articles/SB10001424127887323916304578400192414995044?mg=reno64-wsj**]; and Leslie Kwoh, "Talkative Women Lose at Work, Study Says," *Wall Street Journal*, May 16, 2012, p. B8. [For a video of Sheryl Sandberg discussing "Lean In," visit: **http://leanin.org/book/**]

Analysis of Sex Discrimination: Current Issues

Sex discrimination claims brought under Title VII include disparate treatment and disparate impact, as well as sexual harassment. Employee training and policies targeting sex discrimination have become common in the American workplace. However, sex discrimination claims remained the basis for approximately 30 percent of the charges filed with the EEOC from 1997 to 2013.[37] Thus, sex discrimination claims remain a critical area of Title VII analysis.

Sex Discrimination and Disparate Impact

The following case illustrates the analysis of a sex discrimination claim alleging disparate impact.

Circuit Judge Calabresi

The district court found that Farmingville's physical agility test ("PAT"), which all probationary volunteer firefighters were required to pass in order to become full-fledged volunteer firefighters, had a disparate impact on women.

* * * * *

BACKGROUND

Farmingville is the governing body of a volunteer fire department that has approximately 100 members. Pietras was a probationary (i.e., trainee) firefighter in the Farmingville Department. Even as a probationary volunteer, Pietras was entitled to numerous firefighter benefits under state law and the by-laws of the department. These included (1) a retirement pension, (2) life insurance, (3) death benefits, (4) disability insurance, and (5) some medical benefits.

Before Pietras could become a full member of the department, however, she and all other probationary volunteers were required to pass a newly instituted PAT.* The PAT consisted of a series of physical tasks that the applicants had to complete within a specified time limit. The most difficult of these nine labors was the "charged hose drag," which involved dragging a water-filled hose—weighing approximately 280 pounds—over a distance of 150 feet.

To determine the appropriate time limit for the PAT, Farmingville officials asked various members of the department to take the test. Forty-four firefighters participated in these trials. Of the 44 test-takers, 33 were males who served as full firefighters, 6 were male probationary members, 3 were male junior members, one was Jeanine Serpe, a female full firefighter, and one was Pietras. The average times of these subgroups were:

Sample Pool	Average Time
Full males (33)	3:12
Probationary males (6)	2:47
Junior males (3)	2:52
Full female (Serpe)	5:30
Probationary female (Pietras)	5:21

From these results, Farmingville set four minutes as the time within which the labors had to be completed. The

four-minute threshold was determined by taking the average of all the (mostly male) test runs (approximately 3:30) and then adding an extra half-minute "to have some leeway." There was some concern expressed at a 1993 Farmingville Board meeting that neither Serpe nor Pietras had been able to finish the PAT in anything close to four minutes, but Farmingville nevertheless instituted the four-minute cutoff.

Following the implementation of the PAT, Pietras tried and failed the test twice. During this same period, six other female probationary firefighters took the test. Four of these women completed the PAT in under four minutes and therefore passed. One woman failed to complete the test for an unknown reason. And one woman did not complete the test despite repeated efforts to drag the water-filled hose over the required distance. All of the 24 male probationary volunteers who took the test at about this time passed.

Following her second failure to pass the PAT, Pietras was fired from her volunteer position at Farmingville.

* * * * *

Pietras filed suit in district court, alleging that Farmingville had violated Title VII of the Civil Rights Act of 1964.

* * * * *

At trial . . . , Pietras presented testimony from Dr. Robert Otto, an expert exercise physiologist. Dr. Otto conducted an extensive review of the physical agility tests administered by various volunteer and paid fire departments and concluded (a) that the four-minute limit in the Farmingville test had a disparate impact on women, and (b) that it was not job related.

After reviewing the evidence, the district court ruled for Pietras.

* * * * *

[T]he court concluded that "the record is bereft of any evidence" that a four-minute time limit to finish the PAT was job related.[†]

In support of its finding of disparate impact, the court noted that the male pass rate on the PAT was 95 percent (63 out of 66) while the female pass rate was only 57 percent (4 out of 7). Relying on the "four-fifths" rule set forth in the EEOC Guidelines, the court reasoned that "a pass rate for women which is

---

*Pietras passed both a medical exam and a written exam that were also preconditions to becoming a full firefighter.

†[T]here is no evidence at all to indicate that the time chosen for the test reflected the needs of the job. In fact, the record makes clear that Farmingville selected the four-minute figure simply by taking the average of all the test scores and then arbitrarily adding some extra time.

less [than] four-fifths (or 80 percent) of the pass rate for men typically signifies disparate impact sufficient to establish a prima facie case. . . . Therefore, the gender imbalance [in this case] more than satisfies the 80 percent standard." This statistical evidence (which was corroborated by Dr. Otto's testimony concerning the effect of the PAT on women) was deemed by the district court to be enough to establish disparate impact.

Farmingville appeals.

DISCUSSION

*   *   *   *   *

Disparate Impact

*   *   *   *   *

Farmingville asserts that, even if the statistical figures before the district court were correct, a sample of seven female test takers is simply too small to support a disparate impact finding.

*   *   *   *   *

In the case before us, however, Pietras presented more than just statistics. After conducting an exhaustive analysis of the practices of other fire departments, Dr. Otto provided expert testimony on the disparate impact of Farmingville's PAT. This expert testimony, combined with the statistics Pietras did present, comfortably tips the scales in favor of the district court's finding of disparate impact.

Affirmed.

Questions

1. *a.* Why did the court conclude that the Farmingville Fire Department had discriminated against Pietras?

   b. Did the court conclude that Farmingville intended to discriminate? Explain.

   c. What, if anything, could Farmingville have done differently to win this case?

2. *a.* Shouldn't we always choose the strongest, fastest fire-fighters as long as they are otherwise well qualified? Explain.

   b. After being rejected for employment as police officers with the Southeastern Pennsylvania Transportation Authority (SEPTA), several women sued SEPTA for sex discrimination based on disparate impact. The women were unable to run 1½ miles in 12 minutes, a job requirement. Fifty-six percent of the men applying for the position passed the related test, but 93 percent of the female applicants could not pass. Resolve the case. Explain. See *Lanning v. SEPTA,* 308 F.3d 286 (3d Cir. 2002).

3. *a.* How would you argue that Women's Workout World, a health and exercise club, should be able to lawfully decline to accept men as customers and/or employees?

   b. Decide the case. Explain. See *U.S. EEOC v. Sedita,* 816 F.Supp. 1291 (N.D. Ill. 1993).

4. Dianne Rawlinson sought employment as a prison guard in Alabama. She was a 22-year-old college graduate with a degree in correctional psychology. She was denied employment because she failed to meet the 120-pound weight requirement for the job. The state also required such employees to be at least 5 feet 2 inches tall. Alabama operated four all-male, maximum-security prisons. The district court characterized the Alabama prison system as one of "rampant violence." Rawlinson sued, claiming employment discrimination. Decide. Explain. See *Dothard v. Rawlinson,* 97 S.Ct. 2720 (1977).

Bona Fide Occupational Qualification

Often in intentional sex discrimination cases, the key inquiry involves the *bona fide occupational qualification (BFOQ)* defense provided by Title VII. Discrimination is lawful where sex, religion, or national origin is a BFOQ reasonably necessary to the normal operation of that business. The exclusion of race and color from the list suggests Congress thought those categories always unacceptable as bona fide occupational qualifications. The BFOQ was meant to be a very limited exception applicable to situations where specific inherent characteristics are necessary to the job (for example, wet nurse) or where authenticity (actors), privacy (nurses), or safety (guards) is required. Broadly, the BFOQ defense rests on this question: Is being a female, for example, necessary to perform the *essence* of the job?

Essence

An employer can lawfully insist on a woman to fill a woman's modeling role because being female goes to the essence of the job. Airlines, on the other hand, cannot hire only women as flight attendants even if customers prefer females and even if females perform the supplementary elements of the job (like charming passengers) better than most men. Those duties "are tangential to the essence of the business involved"[38] (the essence being the maintenance of safe, orderly conditions, providing service as needed, etc). Presumably, gender has little to do with the ability to perform those essential ingredients of the job.

Many employers have simply assumed that women could not perform certain tasks. For example, women were thought to be insufficiently aggressive for sales roles, and women were denied employment because they were assumed to have a higher turnover rate because of the desire to marry and have children. Those stereotypes are at the heart of sex discrimination litigation generally and do not support a BFOQ defense.

What about Hooters?

Can the Hooters restaurant chain lawfully decline to hire men to be food servers? Scantily clad "Hooters girls" serve food and beverages to Hooters restaurant customers. In the 1990s, several class-action lawsuits were brought against Hooters on behalf of rejected male applicants. Under the 1997 settlement reached in the consolidated class action, Hooters was allowed to maintain its policy of hiring females only as food servers, but it agreed to create other restaurant positions such as bartenders for which men would have equal hiring opportunities. A 2009 gender discrimination claim brought by a Texas man who was allegedly told by a manager at the Corpus Christi Hooters restaurant that he would not be hired as a waiter because of his gender resulted in a confidential settlement with Hooters.

Questions

1. If the lawsuits against Hooters had not settled, do you think Hooters would have been able to raise a successful BFOQ defense? Explain.

2. Is Hooters' hiring policy better left to the market and ethics than to the courts? Explain.

Sources: "Hooters Agrees to Hire Men in Support Roles . . . ," *Baltimore Sun,* October 1, 1997, p. 3C; Matthew Heller, "Texas Man Aims to Bust Open Hooters Girl Hiring," On Point.com (January 13, 2009) [**www.onpointnews .com/NEWS/texas-man-aims-to-bust-open-hooters-girl-hiring.html**]; and *Grushevski v. Hooters,* "Plaintiff's Original Complaint," (S.D. Tex. 2009) [**www.eeoc.net/CM/Custom/Hooters.pdf**] "Notice of Joint Settlement," April 13, 2009 [**www.onpointnews.com/docs/Hooters1.pdf**].

Looks Discrimination

Harrah's Reno, Nevada, casino instituted a "Personal Best" appearance policy requiring its female bartenders to wear makeup while prohibiting their male counterparts from wearing any. After a successful 20-year career as a Harrah's bartender, Darlene Jespersen was fired for refusing to wear makeup under the policy.

Brenna Lewis staffed the front desks of Heartland Inn motels near Des Moines, Iowa, including its Ankeny, Iowa, location. Her performance was excellent, earning her compliments from customers and merit raises. Heartland's new corporate director of operations, Barbara Cullinan, had approved hiring Lewis for a full-time position staffing the Ankeny motel's front desk during the day, but Cullinan became dissatisfied after seeing Lewis in person. Cullinan was heard saying that Heartland staff should be "pretty," especially those working at the front desk. Lewis was self-described as "slightly more masculine." She avoided makeup and often wore her hair short. The front desk job description in Heartland's personnel manual did not mention appearance, stating only that a guest service representative must create "a warm, inviting atmosphere" and perform tasks such as relaying information and receiving reservations. Cullinan instituted a policy requiring videotaping of interviews for front desk hires. Over protests of her direct manager, Lewis was eventually fired.

Both Jespersen and Lewis brought Title VII claims against their former employers.

Questions

1. What do these cases have in common? How do they differ? Explain. Decide each case.
2. Should the law recognize a separate cause of action for "looks discrimination?" Explain.

Sources: *Jespersen v. Harrah's,* 444 F.3d 1104 (9th Cir. 2006); and *Lewis v. Heartland Inns,* 591 F.3d 1033 (8th Cir. 2010).

Work-Life Balance and Sex Discrimination

Antidiscrimination law has been critical in allowing women to pursue careers and in providing some refuge from the professional disadvantages of pregnancy experienced at some workplaces. The Pregnancy Discrimination Act (PDA) amended Title VII of the Civil Rights Act of 1964 so that discrimination with regard to pregnancy is treated as a form of sex discrimination. Broadly, the PDA requires that pregnant employees be treated the same as all other employees with temporary disabilities. In general, an employer should not ask job applicants about pregnancy, and applicants have no duty to reveal that pregnancy. Nor can a pregnant employee be forced to take time off or be forced to quit due to pregnancy.

FRD

"Family Responsibilities Discrimination" has achieved increased recognition in recent years. While no express antidiscrimination statutory protection is afforded to parents or caregivers, FRD claims may be based on existing statutes such as Title VII. For example, in *Chadwick v. Wellpoint, Inc.,* a federal appeals court allowed the mother of 6-year-old triplets and an older child to proceed with a Title VII claim alleging that she was rejected for a promotion in favor of a less-qualified woman as a result of a sex-based stereotype that

> Stereotype that mothers with young children neglect their careers.

mothers with young children neglect their careers because of child care responsibilities.[39] [For the EEOC Enforcement Guidance on FRD, see "EEOC Enforcement Guidance: Unlawful Disparate Treatment of Workers with Caregiving Responsibilities" at **www.eeoc.gov/policy/docs/caregiving.html**]

CEOs on Maternity Leave

When Marissa Mayer was named chief executive officer (CEO) of Yahoo in July 2012, she was six months pregnant, a fact well noted in media reports of Yahoo's announcement. In 2014, after several months in her new position as WEX CEO, Melissa Smith announced in a companywide memo the impending birth of her first child. During her leave, the former WEX CEO and current chairman, Michael Dubyack, was prepared to help with the executive leadership functions. However, Ms. Smith indicated that, like Ms. Mayer, she planned a brief maternity leave during which she would stay involved with work.

Question

How might these high-profile maternity leaves affect perceptions of maternity leave and working women? Explain.

Sources: Jenna Goudreau, "New Yahoo CEO Marissa Mayer Is Pregnant. Does it Matter?" *Forbes,* July 17, 2012 [**www.forbes.com/sites/jennagoudreau/2012/07/17/new-yahoo-ceo-marissa-mayer-is-pregnant-does-it-matter/**]; and Sara Murray, "A Maternity Leave Memo from the Boss," *The Wall Street Journal,* April 1, 2014, p. D4.

Questions

1. Waitresses at the Rustic Inn were prohibited under a written policy from waiting tables past their fifth month of pregnancy and required either to suspend working or to switch to working as cashiers or hostesses, who are paid less since they do not receive gratuities. The EEOC filed a lawsuit against the employer on behalf of a class of three aggrieved employees, alleging that the policy violated the PDA. Decide. See *EEOC v. W&O Inc.,* 213 F.3d 600 (11th Cir. 2000).

2. Besides avoiding FRD liability, how might an employer benefit from effectively supporting employees' balancing of work and life responsibilities? Should parents and other caregivers be given express statutory protection against employment discrimination? Explain.

Equal Pay

Title VII affords broad protection from discrimination in pay because of sex. The Equal Pay Act of 1963 directly forbids discrimination on the basis of sex by paying wages to employees of one sex at a rate less than the rate paid to employees of the opposite sex for equal work on jobs requiring equal skill, effort, and responsibility and performed under similar working conditions (equal has been interpreted to mean "substantially equal"). The act provides for certain exceptions. Unequal wage payments are lawful if paid pursuant to (1) a seniority system, (2) a merit system, (3) a system that measures earnings by quantity or quality of production, or (4) a differential based on "any . . . factor other than sex." The employer seeking to avoid a violation of the Equal Pay Act can adjust its wage structure by raising the pay of the disfavored sex performing equal work. Lowering the pay of the favored sex violates the act.

If a male employee has a greater skill set—such as computer skills—than his female coworker doing "equal work," the employer may pay the man at a higher rate, as long as the male employee's superior skills are actually considered in making the pay decision.[40]

Salary Negotiating Skills

Dreves was terminated from her $48,500 job as a general manager of Hudson's retail operation at Burlington International Airport, and replaced Dixon, a male, at a salary of $52,500. Dreves filed an Equal Pay Act lawsuit and moved for summary judgment. In defending against the motion for summary judgment, Hudson argued that the salary difference was based on "factors other than sex:" Dixon had to relocate his family from another state, and had strong negotiating skills. Did the employer violate the Equal Pay Act? Decide. Explain. *Dreves v. Hudson Group*, 2013 U.S. Dist. LEXIS 82636 (D. Vt. 2013).

Sexual Harassment

If asked, "what is an example of sexual harassment?" a typical and reasonable response might be "a male boss making unwanted sexual advances on a female employee, telling her that such conduct is a job requirement," or "a male employee touching his female coworker in a sexual and unwanted manner." Although these examples offer solid bases for sexual harassment claims, they do not provide a complete picture. As a form of sex discrimination actionable under Title VII, sexual harassment protection covers both men and women and strives to maintain equal opportunity in the workplace.

According to a recent Society for Human Resource Management (SHRM) poll, nearly two-thirds of organizations received sexual harassment complaints from employees in the previous 24 months, and a quarter of organizations noted an increase in such claims during that time. Nearly one-fifth of organizations reported that the sexual harassment complaints were brought by male and female employees equally.[41]

Women in authority seem to be particularly susceptible to sexual harassment. A 2012 study showed that female supervisors were more likely to be harassed than women in subordinate positions.[42] Why might women in powerful positions be more likely to experience sexual harassment? How might an employer address this issue? (See Eve Tahmincioglu, "Female Managers Face More Sexual Harassment," *Careers on msnbc.com,* August 24, 2009 [**www.msnbc.msn.com/id/32476564/ns/business-careers/**])

The Customer Is Not Always Right

According to a lawsuit filed by the EEOC, two female cashiers at Love's truck stop in Buckeye, Arizona, ages 18 and 20, were allegedly subjected to unwanted sexual touching and pressing, crude and obscene remarks, sexual demands and innuendos, and demands for personal information—by customers, sometimes in front of other customers. The EEOC asserted that Love's management knew about and tolerated this sexually hostile work environment caused by its customers. Further, at least one manager allegedly laughed about it, and another manager said the harassment was to be expected because it is a truck stop. Managers also told the two cashiers to "deal with it," especially the misconduct of one repeat customer because "he's always like that." Should the employer be held liable for workplace harassment by its customers? Explain.

Source: The U.S. Equal Employment Opportunity Commission, "Arizona Truck Stop to Pay $70,000 to Settle EEOC Suit Charging Sex Harassment by Customers," press release, August 3, 2010 [**www.eeoc.gov/eeoc/newsroom/release/8-3-10a.cfm**].

The Law of Sexual Harassment

Sexual harassment, as a form of discrimination, consists of unwelcome sexual advances, requests for sexual favors, and other verbal or physical conduct of a sexual nature that (1) becomes a condition of employment, (2) becomes a basis for employment decisions, or (3) unreasonably interferes with work performance or creates a hostile working environment.

There are two types of sexual harassment: *quid pro quo* ("this for that," such as a sexual favor in exchange for keeping one's job) and *hostile work environment* (a workplace rendered offensive and abusive by such conduct as sexual comments, pictures, jokes, sexual aggression, and the like where no employment benefit is gained or lost). As discussed earlier in this chapter, hostile work environments may be created by offensive or abusive conduct involving protected categories other than sex, including race, religion, national origin, and disability. The law of sexual harassment, particularly in regard to hostile work environments, may apply to these cases.

The Test

Once we have some idea of behavior that constitutes sexual harassment, our concern turns to which remedies are available for the victims. Although the question is not settled, most federal courts to date have ruled that victims of sexual harassment seeking recovery under Title VII cannot sue the person who actually committed the harassment. The victim might be able to sue the wrongdoer under a state statute or by using a tort claim such as assault, but under Title VII, *personal liability* appears not to be available. This result, if the current judicial pattern continues, is not as unfair as might at first appear because well-settled principles of justice hold the employer and not the employer's agents or employees, generally responsible for workplace wrongdoing. The victim, therefore, can seek damages from the employer as the responsible party. A pair of 1998 U.S. Supreme Court decisions in the *Burlington Industries* and *Faragher*[43] cases considerably clarified the circumstances under which an employer is liable for sexual harassment in the workplace. The analysis proceeds as follows:

1. **Proof of sexual harassment**—The plaintiff/employee/victim must prove items a to c:

   a. The harassing conduct is unwelcome.
   b. The harassing conduct is because of sex.
   c. The harassing conduct resulted in a tangible employment action, or was sufficiently severe or pervasive as to unreasonably alter the conditions of employment and create a hostile, abusive work environment.

If the plaintiff is unable to prove items a to c, the claim fails. If the plaintiff proves items a to c, the inquiry then turns to the question of whether the employer bears responsibility for the harassment, as analyzed in Part 2.

2. **Employer liability and the affirmative defense**

   a. If the wrongdoer is a coworker, the plaintiff/employee can bring a negligence claim seeking to prove that the employer unreasonably failed to prevent or remedy the discriminatory harassment of the plaintiff/employee where management knew or should have known about the harassment.

b. If the wrongdoer is a supervisor with authority over the plaintiff/employee, and if the employee suffered a *tangible employment action* (job loss, demotion) because of the harassment, the employer is vicariously liable (indirect liability—see Chapter 12) for the employee's losses. That is, the employer is strictly liable for the employee's wrong and cannot offer a defense regardless of lack of knowledge, absence of negligence, or any other factor.

c. If the wrongdoer is a supervisor with authority over the plaintiff/employee, but the employee suffered no tangible employment action, the employer can avoid liability by proving both elements of the following affirmative defense:

(1) The employer exercised reasonable care to prevent and correct the harassment promptly (by instituting antiharassment training programs, having a policy for reporting harassment, and so on) and (2) the employee unreasonably failed to take advantage of those opportunities.

In its 2012 decision in a Title VII sexual harassment claim, *Vance v. Ball State,* the U.S. Supreme Court restricted the definition of *supervisor* to one who could take a tangible employment action against the allegedly harassed employee.[44] The impact of that decision is illustrated in the case that follows.

LEGAL BRIEFCASE

McCormack v. Safeway
2014 U.S. Dist. LEXIS 17805 (D. Ariz. 2014)

David G. Campbell

I. BACKGROUND

Plaintiffs are two women, Mary McCormack and Samantha Stabenchek, who worked as cashiers for a Safeway store in Scottsdale, Arizona. McCormack is the mother of Stabenchek. Stabenchek was 17 years old when she started work at Safeway and appears to have been a minor during the events at issue in this case.

On March 3, 2011, Jose Lopez, a general clerk at the store, cornered Ms. Stabenchek, grabbed her buttocks, and kissed her. Plaintiffs allege that the assault was the culmination of months of sexual harassment in which Lopez made inappropriate comments to Stabenchek in the workplace and sent her sexually explicit text messages. After the assault, McCormack re-ported Lopez's conduct. Stabenchek participated in Safeway's internal investigation of the assault, which led to Lopez's termination on March 26, 2011.

Less than a month after reporting the sexual assault, Plaintiffs were both interviewed about McCormack's alleged violation of Safeway's coupon policy. Safeway alleges that in late December 2010, a Safeway security analyst reported that it appeared as though McCormack was violating the company's coupon policies. The analyst allegedly discovered more evidence of coupon abuse, which she reported to a loss prevention investigator in April 2011. The investigator confronted Stabenchek and McCormack in connection with his investigation. McCormack was suspended pending further investigation. Feeling that their honesty was impugned "on the heels" of their reports about Lopez's misconduct, Plaintiffs resigned on April 13, 2011.

Stabenchek has asserted [a] sexual harassment . . . [claim] against Safeway under Title VII of the Civil Rights Act of 1964 . . . ("Title VII").

* * * * *

III. HARASSMENT CLAIMS

Title VII provides that an employer may not "discriminate against an individual with respect to [her] compensation, terms, conditions, or privileges of employment because of [her] . . . sex[.]" . . . Sexual harassment constitutes unlawful discrimination under Title VII. *Meritor Sav. Bank v. Vinson.* . . . If the harassing employee is the victim's coworker, the employer may be held liable only if it was negligent in controlling working conditions. *Vance v. Ball State Univ. . . .* " In cases in which the harasser is a 'supervisor,' however, different rules apply, "and the employer may be held vicariously liable." . . .

A. Vicarious Liability

Safeway asserts that it cannot be held vicariously liable for Lopez's harassment because Lopez was not Stabenchek's supervisor. "[A]n employee is a 'supervisor' for purposes of vicarious liability under Title VII if he or she is empowered by the employer to take tangible employment actions against the victim." *Vance* . . . "The ability to direct another employee's tasks is simply not sufficient" to give rise to "supervisor" status. Instead, supervisors are a "*distinct class* of agent [empowered] to make economic decisions affecting other employees under his or her control. . . . Tangible employment actions are the means by which the supervisor brings the official power of the enterprise to bear on subordinates." . . . [internal quotation marks and citation omitted] [emphasis in original].

Lopez was a front end manager when Stabenchek became an employee at Defendant's Scottsdale location, but he had been demoted to general clerk by the time much of the alleged harassment took place, including the sexual assault. The distinction is not important, however, because neither front end managers nor general clerks qualify as supervisors under *Vance*. Front end managers and general clerks lack authority to make economic decisions affecting other employees under their control. Front end managers and general clerks are not empowered by Safeway to hire, promote, demote, fire, increase pay, decrease pay, or impose any economic change on any employees.

Plaintiffs assert that Lopez was Stabenchek's supervisor under *Vance* because he was in charge of the store during some of Stabenchek's shifts and because he sat in on Stabenchek's initial job interview and assured her that she would get her hired. Plaintiffs have presented evidence that front end managers occasionally directed other employees to sign documents that Safeway "uses to bind their employees."

In addition, Plaintiffs assert that front end managers are supervisors because they have significant decision-making power, including telling employees when to clock out and when to take breaks. But Plaintiffs have provided no evidence that Lopez had any ability to influence Stabenchek's employment beyond determining the timing of her breaks and the manner in which she performed her job, and *Vance* states that "the ability to direct employee's tasks is simply not sufficient" to justify a finding that a manager is a supervisor for purposes of Title VII vicarious liability. . . . *Vance* requires Plaintiffs to show that Lopez had power to make economic decisions affecting Stabenchek's employment at Safeway such as the ability to fire, hire, promote, or change Stabenchek's compensation. Plaintiffs have presented no evidence that Lopez possessed such authority.

Plaintiffs' reliance on *Lindquist v. Tanner* . . . is misplaced. . . . [I]n *Tanner* . . . the harasser was able to impact the plaintiff's employment status. The harasser actively recruited the plaintiff . . . [appeared] that he had the ability to determine whether or not plaintiff would become a full-time employee, and the harasser was the most senior employee on-site. . . .

* * * * *

Lopez participated in Stabenchek's hiring process. Safeway has shown, however, that while Lopez sat in on Stabenchek's initial 5-minute screening interview, . . . , the hiring decision was made by a different Safeway employee after an hour-long interview. . . . In addition, the fact that Lopez was occasionally the person in charge at Safeway's Scottsdale store is a far cry from the authority required by *Vance*.

Undisputed facts show that Lopez was not Stabenchek's supervisor as a matter of law. As a result, Safeway cannot be held vicariously liable for Lopez's harassment.

B. Liability in Negligence

Where harassment by a coworker is alleged, the employer can be held liable only if "its own negligence is a cause of the harassment." . . . Thus, an employer is responsible for its own actions or omissions and not for a coworker's harassment. "If the employer fails to take corrective action after learning of an employee's sexually harassing conduct, or takes inadequate action that emboldens the harasser to continue his misconduct, the employer can be deemed to have 'adopt[ed] the offending conduct and its results, quite as if they have been authorized affirmatively as the employer's policy.'"

An employer cannot be held liable for misconduct of which it is unaware. . . . Safeway asserts that it cannot be held liable under a negligence theory because, although Stabenchek claims that Lopez had been making hundreds of sexual comments and sending thousands of sexual messages to her for months before the March 3 incident, Stabenchek never told anyone about any alleged harassment until March 5, the day before McCormack reported it to Safeway. Plaintiffs rejoin that Safeway can be liable because one of Safeway's managers observed Lopez harassing Stabenchek and did nothing to stop it.

* * * * *

Stabenchek testified that about one month before the sexual assault, Megan Oxford, a second assistant manager, approached Stabenchek about an incident Oxford had witnessed. Oxford told Stabenchek that she saw an exchange between Lopez and Stabenchek after which Stabenchek looked at Lopez like she was disgusted. Oxford had not heard what Lopez said, but she urged Stabenchek to share anything that Stabenchek thought Oxford needed to know. Stabenchek declined to share any specific information with Oxford because she was uncomfortable and embarrassed. Oxford again asked Stabenchek if she wanted to report anything, but Stabenchek responded that Lopez was just being a "creep" and that she did not want to report anything.

Oxford's observations, and Stabenchek's subsequent responses to Oxford's questions, did not put Safeway on notice of Lopez's sexually harassing conduct toward Stabenchek.... Although Stabenchek told Oxford that Lopez was being a "creep," that uninformative comment was not enough to communicate that Lopez was sexually harassing Stabenchek.

* * * * *

Once Safeway actually learned of Lopez's sexually harassing conduct, it took prompt corrective action. Stabenchek told her mother about the Lopez's harassment on Saturday, March 5. McCormack told second assistant manager Ryan on Sunday, March 6. By Monday, March 7, the store manager, Anthony Duran, and a human resources advisor, Joyce Cameron, initiated an investigation of the incident. Lopez was interviewed later that day and was immediately suspended pending the results of the investigation. Lopez never returned to work at Safeway and was fired....

* * * * *

IT IS ORDERED that Defendant's motion for summary judgment is granted.

Questions

1. According to the court, under *Vance,* Lopez was not Stabenchek's supervisor for purposes of Title VII sexual harassment liability. Why?
   a. What was the basis for the plaintiffs' assertion that Lopez was Stabenchek's supervisor? Explain.

   b. Do you think Lopez and others who are, for example, placed in charge of a store during shifts, should be considered a supervisor for purposes of Title VII sexual harassment liability? Explain.

2. Truck driver Lesley Parkins claimed she was a victim of hostile environment sexual harassment while employed by Civil Constructors beginning in 1994. Parkins alleged that coworkers subjected her to foul language, sexual stories, and touching. Parkins complained to her dispatcher, Tim Spellman, and to one of her purported harassers, Robert Strong. She saw the job superintendent and the company EEO officer almost daily, but she did not complain to either. In 1996 Parkins filed a grievance with her union—Teamsters Local 325. The union contacted the company EEO officer, who immediately launched an investigation that led to punishment for the employees. Parkins conceded that she was not harassed following the company punishment. Parkins filed suit charging Civil Constructors with sexual harassment. Parkins claimed that two of her harassers, Strong and Charles Boeke, were foremen who supervised her work. Assuming Parkins can prove that she was, in fact, sexually harassed, what must she prove in order to hold Civil Constructors liable? See *Parkins v. Civil Constructors of Illinois,* 163 F.3d 1027 (7th Cir. 1998).

3. Eileen Craig worked for the Mahoney Group as the branch manager in Tucson and reported to Leon Byrd, the interim president. Over the course of several months, Byrd made repeated inappropriate comments to Craig about her legs and how she should wear shorter skirts. Although Craig thought the comments were obnoxious, she was not particularly offended. At Byrd's invitation, Craig met him for drinks after work at a restaurant, as they had done previously to discuss work-related matters. After Byrd made a sexual proposition, Craig laughed and shook her head but did not leave the restaurant. Byrd later followed Craig into the restaurant's restroom, grabbed her and kissed her. Craig did not report this incident. Byrd made further advances to Craig which she rejected. At some point Byrd told Craig that he didn't think he could work with her anymore. Craig finally reported Byrd's conduct under the company's sexual harassment policy. The company took immediate action: Byrd was instructed to stay away from Craig and to stop making sexual comments to her, and Craig began reporting to another company executive. The investigator retained by the employer recommended, among other things, that Byrd receive a reprimand and training. At the end of the investigation, Craig began reporting again to Byrd.

Eventually, Craig resigned and filed complaint asserting a Title VII sexual harassment claim.

a. Is Mahoney liable for quid pro quo sexual harassment? What questions would you have if you were on the jury? Explain.

b. Is Mahoney liable for hostile work environment sexual harassment? What other facts might you need to know before deciding? Explain.

4. A female employed as an Installation and Repairs Technician claimed a hostile work environment was created in the garage in which she worked by the routine use of profanity, crude humor, vulgar graffiti depicting sexual acts, and especially by sexually demeaning conversations conveying a profound disrespect for women. While the comments and graffiti demeaned some male employees, the conduct was directed at all the women working in the garage.

a. In deciding whether the conduct constituted hostile environment sexual harassment, should the court evaluate the facts from the point of view of a "reasonable person" or a "reasonable woman"? Explain.

b. Why does it matter? See *Petrosino v. Bell Atlantic,* 385 F.3d 210 (2d Cir. 2004); see also *Ellison v. Brady,* 924 F.2d 872 (9th Cir. 1991).

Consider the Source: Sexual Harassment at the Casino

While she was a bartender at Gold Strike Casino Resort in Tunica County, Mississippi, Debra Brockington allegedly was subjected to sexual harassment by her female supervisor, Wanda Haley, as well as her former boyfriend and coworker, Ed Ogden. The alleged harassment included Haley grabbing Brockington's breasts, making sexually suggestive remarks to others about Brockington, and snapping a towel against her buttocks. Brockington admitted to engaging in off-color conversations and conduct with her female coworkers. In her subsequent Title VII claim, a federal trial court, addressing Haley's behavior, held that "within the context of the plaintiff's work environment the alleged harassment in this case was neither severe nor pervasive."

Questions

1. Do you agree with the court's reasoning about the importance of workplace context in determining whether unlawful harassment has occurred? Explain.

2. In its ruling, the court said, "[C]asino bartenders have the same right as other employees to expect that they will not be subjected to unlawful harassment. . . ." What impact might the court's ruling on workplace context have on the sexual harassment protections of casino bartenders and others working in similar environments?

Source: Brockington v. Circus Circus Mississippi, 2008 U.S. Dist. LEXIS 39482 (N.D. Miss 2008).

Same Sex?

Joseph Oncale, a heterosexual who worked on an offshore oil rig, charged a supervisor and two male coworkers with sexually harassing him, including repeated taunts and several sexual assaults, one with a bar of soap while Oncale was showering. Oncale complained to superiors, but to no avail. He then quit his job and sued his employer for sexual harassment. The case went to the U.S. Supreme Court, which unanimously ruled that same-sex harassment is actionable under Title VII.[45] Oncale then settled out of court for an undisclosed amount of money. Justice Scalia, who wrote the Supreme Court opinion, explained that the harassment must be "because of sex" (that is, gender); that harassment can be motivated by hostility as well as by desire; and that common sense and social context count. Thus, smacking a football teammate on the rear end, horseplay, roughhousing, or occasional gender-related jokes, teasing, and abusive language normally would not constitute harassment. Ordinarily, plaintiffs in same-sex harassment cases must show that the behavior was motivated by (a) sexual desire, (b) general hostility to one or other gender, or (c) the victim's failure to conform to sexual stereotypes (such as effeminate behavior by a male). [For an analysis of the significance of the *Oncale* case, see **http://reason.com /archives/2003/01/01/man-trouble**]

> What if the harasser bothers both genders equally?

Oncale settles the big question of protection against same-sex harassment, but it raises other puzzles. For example, what if the harasser bothers both genders equally?

After *Oncale,* a husband and wife, who were also coworkers, brought a Title VII claim against their employer alleging that their supervisor had harassed both of them by soliciting sex from each of them on separate occasions. The federal appeals court affirmed the district court's dismissal, concluding that the "equal opportunity harasser" does not give rise to a Title VII sex discrimination complaint.[46]

Sexual Harassment in Other Nations

American managers working abroad must deal with international differences in attitudes toward sexual behavior in the workplace, although a general shift in harassment law in the direction of the American model is evident. This shift is significant for the American manager working abroad for a U.S.-based company, or a foreign employer controlled by an American company. The Civil Rights Act of 1991 extends Title VII's protection to American employees working abroad for such employers, but offers a "foreign law defense" under which the employer would not be required to comply with Title VII if doing so would violate the host country's law.[47] The European Union has adopted laws requiring harassment-free workplaces.[48] In Japan, sexual harassment law resembles the U.S. model.[49] In China, a woman who is sexually harassed in her workplace may file a complaint with the police under China's Protection of Rights and Interests of Women law.[50]

Retaliation

The power in an employment relationship often is unbalanced in favor of the employer. In bringing a discrimination claim, an employee is vulnerable to the employer's retaliatory action. In order to protect against an employer's abuse of power and to encourage exercise of employees' rights, Title VII's antiretaliation provision prohibits an employer from discriminating against an employee for engaging in a protected activity. Protected activities include opposing an employment practice that is reasonably believed to violate Title VII, or participating in a complaint made under Title VII, such as filing a charge of workplace discrimination. Other civil rights laws, including the Americans with Disabilities Act

(ADA), the Age Discrimination in Employment Act (ADEA), and the Civil Rights Act of 1866, offer similar protections against retaliation.

A prima facie case of retaliation requires:

1. Participation in a protected activity.
2. An employment action disadvantaging the plaintiff.
3. A causal connection between the protected activity and the adverse employment action.

In several recent cases, the U.S. Supreme Court has addressed Title VII's antiretaliation protection. In *Crawford v. Metropolitan Gov't of Nashville & Davidson County*,[51] Court held that employees who respond to questions about workplace discrimination during the employer's informal investigation are engaged in protected activity under Title VII's antiretaliation provision, even if they did not make the complaint being investigated. In *Burlington Northern & Santa Fe Railway v. White*,[52] the U.S. Supreme Court, recognizing that a broad range of employer conduct could discourage the reasonable employee from exercising Title VII rights, held that assigning a complainant to less desirable duties is an adverse employment action on which a Title VII retaliation claim may be based. In 2011, the U.S. Supreme Court held in *Thompson v. North American Stainless*[53] that an employee is protected against retaliation resulting when his fiancée and coworker file a Title VII claim, noting that it was "obvious" that a reasonable worker might hesitate to exercise Title VII rights if it would cause the person who he or she intended to marry to be fired.

After these employee-friendly rulings, the U.S. Supreme Court's 2013 decision in *University of Texas Southwestern Medical Center v. Nassar* created a higher standard for retaliation claims than applied to "status discrimination" claims such as, for example, gender or national origin.[54] Dr. Naiel Nassar, a physician of Middle Eastern descent who was both a medical school faculty member and a staff physician at the school's affiliated hospital, complained to his department chair, Dr. Fitz, that one of Dr. Nassar's other supervisors, Dr. Levine, was biased against him based on national origin and religion. Dr. Nassar arranged to continue working as a hospital staff physician without being a member of the medical school's faculty, and sent a resignation letter to Dr. Fitz and several others explaining that he was resigning owing to Dr. Levine's harassment. Upset at the letter's statements regarding Dr. Levine, Dr. Fitz objected to the hospital's arrangement with Dr. Nassar, asserting that it violated the hospital's affiliation agreement with the medical school under which its staff physicians were exclusively the school's faculty members; the offer was withdrawn. Dr. Nassar's resulting Title VII lawsuit included a retaliation claim based on Dr. Fitz's actions to stop his hospital employment because he had complained. A federal appellate court affirmed the trial court's finding of retaliation, as the evidence supported the conclusion that Dr. Fitz was, at least in part, motivated to retaliate against Dr. Nassar for his complaints. The U.S. Supreme Court reversed, interpreting Title VII's antiretaliation provision as requiring "but for" causation. Here, Dr. Nassar's continued employment with the hospital would have violated the hospital's affiliation agreement with the medical school, which arguably would have caused the medical school's objection to and ultimate withdrawal of Nassar's offer.

Part Four—Affirmative Action

Some viewed the 2008 election of Barack Obama, the first African-American president of the United States, as evidence that the racism staining the country's history was no longer an urgent concern. Therefore, it was argued, *affirmative action* efforts on behalf of minorities and women could be reduced or eliminated. However, a 2009 *Washington Post/ABC News* poll revealed that nearly half of African Americans and almost a quarter of white Americans continued to see racism as a significant social problem.[55] In the wake of a 2013 U.S. Supreme Court opinion that did not offer a definitive answer on whether race-based preferential treatment in college admissions are constitutional, a Pew Research Center poll found Americans deeply divided on affirmative action.[56]

In following an affirmative action plan, employers consciously take positive steps to seek out minorities and women for hiring and promotion opportunities, and they often employ goals and timetables to measure progress toward a workforce that is representative of the qualified labor pool. Affirmative action is a means of remedying past and present discriminatory wrongs in a more expeditious and thorough manner than the market might achieve on its own.

Affirmative action efforts arise in four ways: (1) Courts may order the implementation of affirmative action after a finding of wrongful discrimination, (2) employers may voluntarily adopt affirmative action plans, (3) some statutes require affirmative action, and (4) employers may adopt affirmative action in order to do business with government agencies. Federal contractors must meet the affirmative action standards of the Office of Federal Contract Compliance Programs. [For criticisms of affirmative action, see the Center for Equal Opportunity at **www.ceousa.org**]

Early Affirmative Action Law

For nearly 20 years, judicial decisions were firmly supportive of affirmative action. A massive system of remedies emerged at all levels of government and in the private sector. In a 1979 case, *United Steelworkers of America v. Weber,*[57] the U.S. Supreme Court set out perhaps its most detailed "recipe" for those qualities that would allow a voluntary affirmative action plan in the private sector to withstand scrutiny. Weber, a white male, challenged the legality of an affirmative action plan that set aside for black employees 50 percent of the openings in a training program until the percentage of black craft workers in the plant equaled the percentage of blacks in the local labor market. The plan was the product of a collective bargaining agreement between the Steelworkers and Kaiser Aluminum and Chemical. In Kaiser's Grammercy, Louisiana, plant, only 5 of 273 skilled craft workers were black, whereas the local workforce was approximately 39 percent black. In the first year of the affirmative action plan, seven blacks and six whites were admitted to the craft training program. The most junior black employee accepted for the program had less seniority than several white employees who were not accepted. Weber was among the white males denied entry to the training program.

Weber filed suit, claiming Title VII forbade an affirmative action plan that granted a racial preference to blacks where whites dramatically exceeded blacks in skilled craft positions but where there was no proof of discrimination. The federal district court and the federal court of appeals held for Weber, but the U.S. Supreme Court reversed. Several qualities of the Steelworkers' plan were instrumental in the Court's favorable ruling:

1. The affirmative action was part of a plan.
2. The plan was designed to "open employment opportunities for Negroes in occupations which have been traditionally closed to them."
3. The plan was temporary.
4. The plan did not unnecessarily harm the rights of white employees. That is,
   a. The plan did not require the discharge of white employees.
   b. The plan did not create an absolute bar to the advancement of white employees.

Then, in an important 1987 public-sector decision, *Johnson v. Transportation Agency,*[58] the Supreme Court approved the extension of affirmative action to women. The political tides were turning, however. The 1980s were politically conservative years. Appointments to the Supreme Court and to the lower federal courts, by President Reagan in particular, reflected that mood. Affirmative action was under attack.

Rethinking Affirmative Action

From the late 1980s to the present, a series of judicial decisions and increasing public and political skepticism have challenged the legality and the wisdom of affirmative action, at least where the government is involved. The 1989 *City of Richmond v. J. A. Croson Co.*[59] case struck down Richmond, Virginia's, minority "set-aside" program that required prime contractors who were doing business with the city to subcontract at least 30 percent of the work to minority businesses. The Court said such race-conscious remedial plans were constitutional only if (1) the city or state could provide specific evidence of discrimination against a particular protected class in the past (rather than relying on proof of general societywide discrimination) and (2) its remedy was "narrowly tailored" to the needs of the situation.

Then in *Adarand Constructors v. Pena,* a landmark 1995 decision, the Supreme Court struck down a federal highway program that extended bidding preferences to "disadvantaged" contractors.[60] The suit was brought by Randy Pech, a white contractor whose low bid on a Colorado guardrail project was rejected in favor of the bid of a minority firm. The Supreme Court ruled that the government's preference program denied Pech his right to equal protection under the law as guaranteed by the Fifth Amendment to the federal Constitution. [For a "Timeline of Affirmative Action Milestones," see **www.infoplease.com /spot/affirmativetimeline1.html**]

In the 2009 *Ricci v. DeStefano* decision that follows, the U.S. Supreme Court addressed the dilemma employers sometimes face in using hiring and promotion tests that may have a disparate impact on some groups of employees.

Ricci v. DeStefano
129 S.Ct. 2658 (2009)

Justice Kennedy

* * * * *

In 2003, 118 New Haven [Connecticut] firefighters took examinations to qualify for promotion to the rank of lieutenant or captain.... The results would determine which firefighters would be considered for promotions during the next two years, and the order in which they would be considered. Many firefighters studied for months, at considerable personal and financial cost.

When the examination results showed that white candidates had outperformed minority candidates, the mayor and other local politicians opened a public debate that turned rancorous. Some firefighters argued the tests should be discarded because the results showed the tests to be discriminatory. They threatened a discrimination lawsuit if the City made promotions based on the tests. Other firefighters said the exams were neutral and fair. And they, in turn, threatened a discrimination lawsuit if the City, relying on the statistical racial disparity, ignored the test results and denied promotions to the candidates who had performed well. In the end the City took the side of those who protested the test results. It threw out the examinations.

Certain white and Hispanic firefighters who likely would have been promoted based on their good test performance sued the City and some of its officials. Theirs is the suit now before us. The suit alleges that, by discarding the test results, the City and the named officials discriminated against the plaintiffs based on their race, in violation of.... Title VII of the Civil Rights Act of 1964.... The City and the officials defended their actions, arguing that if they had certified the results, they could have faced liability under Title VII for adopting a practice that had a disparate impact on the minority firefighters.

I

* * * * *

A

The [City] charter establishes a merit system. That system requires the City to fill vacancies in the classified civil-service ranks with the most qualified individuals, as determined by job-related examinations. After each examination, the New Haven Civil Service Board (CSB) certifies a ranked list of applicants who passed the test. Under the charter's "rule of three," the relevant hiring authority must fill each vacancy by choosing one candidate from the top three scorers on the list.

* * * * *

Under the [union] contract, applicants for lieutenant and captain positions were to be screened using written and oral examinations, with the written exam accounting for 60 percent and the oral exam 40 percent of an applicant's total score. To sit for the examinations, candidates for lieutenant needed 30 months' experience in the Department, a high-school diploma, and certain vocational training courses. Candidates for captain needed one year's service as a lieutenant in the Department, a high-school diploma, and certain vocational training courses.

* * * * *

The City hired Industrial/Organizational Solutions, Inc. (IOS) to develop and administer the examinations, at a cost to the City of $100,000. IOS is an Illinois company that specializes in designing entry-level and promotional examinations for fire and police departments. In order to fit the examinations to the New Haven Department, IOS began the test-design process by performing job analyses to identify the tasks, knowledge, skills, and abilities that are essential for the lieutenant and captain positions.

* * * * *

At every stage of the job analyses, IOS, by deliberate choice, oversampled minority firefighters to ensure that the results-which IOS would use to develop the examinations-would not unintentionally favor white candidates. With the job-analysis information in hand, IOS developed the written examinations to measure the candidates' job-related knowledge.

* * * * *

After IOS prepared the tests, the City opened a 3-month study period. It gave candidates a list that identified the source material for the questions, including the specific chapters from which the questions were taken. IOS developed the oral examinations as well. These concentrated on job skills and abilities.

* * * * *

Candidates took the examinations in November and December 2003. Seventy-seven candidates completed the lieutenant examination—43 whites, 19 blacks, and 15 Hispanics. Of those, 34 candidates passed—25 whites, 6 blacks, and 3 Hispanics. Eight lieutenant positions were vacant at the time of the examination. Under the rule of three, this meant that the top 10 candidates were eligible for an immediate promotion to lieutenant. All 10 were white.

* * * * *

Forty-one candidates completed the captain examination—25 whites, 8 blacks, and 8 Hispanics. Of those, 22 candidates passed—16 whites, 3 blacks, and 3 Hispanics. Seven captain positions were vacant at the time of the examination. Under the rule of three, 9 candidates were eligible for an immediate promotion to captain—7 whites and 2 Hispanics.

B

Based on the test results, the City officials expressed concern that the tests had discriminated against minority candidates.

* * * * *

[The City decided] not to certify the results.

C

The [City's] decision not to certify the examination results led to this lawsuit. The plaintiffs—who are the petitioners here—are 17 white firefighters and 1 Hispanic firefighter who passed the examinations but were denied a chance at promotions when the [City] refused to certify the test results. They include the named plaintiff, Frank Ricci. . . .

Petitioners . . . filed timely charges of discrimination with the Equal Employment Opportunity Commission (EEOC); . . . asserting that the City violated the disparate-treatment prohibition contained in Title VII of the Civil Rights Act of 1964. . . . Respondents [the defendants] asserted they had a good-faith belief that they would have violated the disparate impact prohibition in Title VII . . . had they certified the examination results. It follows, they maintained, that they cannot be held liable under Title VII's disparate-treatment provision for attempting to comply with Title VII's disparate-impact bar. Petitioners countered that respondents' good-faith belief was not a valid defense to allegations of disparate treatment. . . .

The District Court granted summary judgment for respondents. . . . The Court of Appeals affirmed. . . .

II

B (A OMITTED-ED.)

Petitioners allege that when the [City] refused to certify the captain and lieutenant exam results based on the race of the successful candidates, it discriminated against them in violation of Title VII's disparate-treatment provision. The City counters that its decision was permissible because the tests "appear[ed] to violate Title VII's disparate-impact provisions."

Our analysis begins with this premise: The City's actions would violate the disparate-treatment prohibition of Title VII absent some valid defense. All the evidence demonstrates that the City chose not to certify the examination results because of the statistical disparity based on race—i.e., how minority candidates had performed when compared to white candidates. . . .

We consider, therefore, whether the purpose to avoid disparate-impact liability excuses what otherwise would be prohibited disparate-treatment discrimination.

* * * * *

If an employer cannot rescore a test based on the candidates' race, then it follows . . . . that it may not take the greater step of discarding the test altogether to achieve a more desirable racial distribution of promotion-eligible candidates-absent a strong basis in evidence that the test was deficient and that discarding the results is necessary to avoid violating the disparate-impact provision. . . .

For the foregoing reasons, we adopt the strong-basis-in-evidence standard as a matter of statutory construction to resolve any conflict between the disparate-treatment and disparate-impact provisions of Title VII.

* * * * *

Title VII does not prohibit an employer from considering, before administering a test or practice, how to design that test or practice in order to provide a fair opportunity for all individuals, regardless of their race. . . . We hold only that, under Title VII, before an employer can engage in intentional discrimination for the asserted purpose of avoiding or remedying an unintentional disparate impact, the employer must have a strong basis in evidence to believe it will be subject to disparate-impact liability if it fails to take the race-conscious, discriminatory action.

* * * * *

C

The City argues that, even under the strong-basis-in-evidence standard, its decision to discard the examination results was permissible under Title VII. That is incorrect.

* * * * *

. . . .[T]here is no evidence—let alone the required strong basis in evidence—the tests were flawed because they were not job-related or because other, equally valid and less discriminatory tests were available to the City. Fear of litigation alone cannot justify an employer's reliance on race to the detriment of individuals who passed the examination and qualified for promotions. The City's discarding the test results was impermissible under Title VII. . . .

Our holding today clarifies how Title VII applies to resolve competing expectations under the disparate-treatment and disparate-impact provisions. If, after it certifies the test results, the City faces a disparate-impact suit, then in light of our holding today it should be clear that the City would avoid disparate-impact liability based on the strong basis in evidence that, had it not certified the results, it would have been subject to disparate-treatment liability.

[Reversed and remanded.]

Questions

1. *a.* Why did the city of New Haven reject the results of the promotion examination?

   b. Why did the court rule that the city had violated Title VII?

   c. Do you agree with the judgment of the court?

2. What could an employer do to avoid the situation New Haven faced in this case?

3. Frederick Claus, a white man with a degree in electrical engineering and 29 years of experience with Duquesne Light Company, was denied a promotion in favor of a black man who had not earned a bachelor's degree and did not have the required seven years of experience. Only 2 of 82 managers in that division of Duquesne Light were black. Claus sued, claiming in effect that he was a victim of "reverse discrimination." At trial, both sides conceded that the black candidate was an outstanding employee and that he was qualified to be a manager. Decide the case. Explain. See *Claus v. Duquesne Light Co.,* 46 F.3d 1115 (1994); cert. den. 115 S.Ct. 1700 (1995).

4. In 1974, Birmingham, Alabama, was accused of unlawfully excluding blacks from management roles in its fire department. After several years of litigation, Birmingham adopted an affirmative action plan that guaranteed black firefighters one of every two available promotions. The city, the Justice Department, and others applauded the arrangement, but a group of 14 white firefighters claimed they were victims of reverse discrimination. After years of wrangling, the white firefighters' claim reached the 11th Circuit Federal Court of Appeals. Was the affirmative action plan lawful? Explain. See *In re Birmingham Reverse Discrimination Employment Litig.,* 20 F.3d 1525 (11th Cir. 1994) cert. den. sub nom.; *Martin v. Wilks,* 115 S.Ct. 1695 (1995).

5. In a later case involving the same promotional examinations at issue in *Ricci,* Michael Briscoe, an African-American firefighter for the city of New Haven who applied to be promoted to lieutenant but was rejected brought a Title VII claim asserting that the city had created a disparate impact against African-Americans by weighing the written test more heavily than the oral examination. The city of New Haven brought a motion to dismiss in federal trial court. Decide. See *Briscoe v. New Haven,* 654 F.3d 200 (2nd Cir. 2011) cert. den. 132 S.Ct. 2741 (2012).

Affirmative Action: Where Are We?

Some confusion remains after *Ricci,* given differences in analysis between cases based on the Constitution and those brought under Title VII,[61] and whether those cases address employers' screening, set-asides, or other practices. What has been made clear is that both quotas and affirmative action justified broadly by "societal discrimination" are unconstitutional.

> Quotas are unconstitutional.

A lawful affirmative action remedy in employment cases apparently will be evaluated, in most cases, by the following considerations:

- The plan addresses a compelling interest such as remedying past or present discrimination or correcting the underutilization of women and minorities.

- The plan is temporary.

- The plan is narrowly tailored to minimize layoffs and other burdens.

In *Ricci,* the U.S. Supreme Court noted that employers could still make "affirmative efforts" to encourage equal opportunity in promotions.[62] While ensuring that screening procedures are not discriminatory or irrelevant,[63] employers may undertake diversity initiatives designed to create an inclusive workplace environment that supports fairness, respect, and equal opportunity. [For information on diversity programs at U.S. companies, see Diversity Inc. at **http://diversityinc.com/**]

Part Five—Additional Discrimination Topics

Religious Discrimination

Kimberly Cloutier was employed as a cashier at Costco in West Springfield, Massachusetts. The store revised its dress code in 2001 to prohibit all facial jewelry other than earrings.

> A member of the "Church of Body Modification."

Cloutier, a member of the "Church of Body Modification," was advised to remove her facial piercings. She declined to do so saying that her piercings were part of her religion. The church's approximately 1,000 members engaged in such practices as piercing, tattooing, branding, and cutting. Eventually, Cloutier was fired. She sued Costco claiming she was a victim of religious discrimination in violation of Title VII of the Civil Rights Act of 1964. Costco, however, prevailed when the federal First Circuit Court of Appeals ruled in 2004 that excusing Cloutier from the dress code would be an undue hardship for Costco because the company had a legitimate interest in presenting to the public a workforce that was reasonably professional in appearance.[64]

The Law

Title VII's protections against religious discrimination and harassment in the workplace include the employer's duty to reasonably accommodate employees' religious beliefs and practices. As was evident in Cloutier's conflict with Costco, reasonably accommodating religious practices often poses challenges for employers. Consider, for example, the employer who must balance an employee's religious practice of proselytizing or discussing religion in the workplace against other employees' right to be free from religious harassment.

Employers need not accommodate an employee's religious practice or belief if it creates an "undue hardship"—an unreasonable burden—on the workplace. The leading religious discrimination case is *Trans World Airlines, Inc. v. Hardison,* in which the plaintiff, who celebrated his religion on Saturdays, was unable to take that day off from his work in a parts warehouse.[65] Efforts to swap shifts or change jobs were unsuccessful. The company rejected Hardison's request for a four-day week because it would have required the use of another employee at premium pay. The Supreme Court's ruling in the case reduced the employer's duty to a very modest standard: "To require TWA to bear more than a *de minimis* cost in order to give Hardison Saturdays off is an *undue hardship*." Saturdays off for Hardison would have imposed extra costs on TWA and would have constituted religious discrimination against other employees who would have sought Saturday off for reasons not grounded in religion. So any accommodation imposing more than a *de minimis* cost on the employer represents an undue hardship and is not required by Title VII. Of course, the lower courts have differed considerably on what constitutes a *de minimis* cost and an undue hardship. For example, an Ohio court ruled that an employee, a Seventh Day Adventist, was discriminated against when he was fired for refusing to work from sundown Friday to sundown Saturday. The employee could have been moved to an earlier shift at no cost.[66]

An employer might be unsure whether employees who request accommodation are sincere in their religious beliefs or merely seeking an advantage such as a longer break or trying to avoid workplace requirements under attendance or grooming policies. The EEOC defines religion broadly as "moral and ethical beliefs of what is right and wrong which are sincerely held with the strength of religious views."[67] This broad view of religious beliefs arguably indicates that employers should err in favor of moving forward to the central issue: Is an accommodation reasonable or would it create an undue hardship?

Questions

1. Resolving job-related religious conflicts can be among the most emotionally demanding management dilemmas. For example, what challenges would you face as a manager if one of your subordinates, as an expression of her religious beliefs, wore to work an antiabortion button displaying a picture of a fetus? How would you address these challenges? See *Wilson v. U.S. West Communications,* 58 F.3d 1337 (8th Cir. 1995).

2. Yisrael worked as a dump truck driver for a North Carolina company providing paving, grading, and utility services for transportation projects. As a member of the Hebrew Israelite faith, Yisrael observed Sabbath on Saturday. After refusing to work three different Saturdays, he was terminated. The EEOC filed a lawsuit on behalf of Yisrael. What further information would you need to decide this case? Explain. See *EEOC v. Thompson Contracting, Grading, Paving, & Utilities, Inc.* 499 Fed. Appx. 275 (4th Cir. 2012) (unpub'd op.).

3. An Oklahoma lighting company, Voss, advertised a vacancy for an "operations supervisor" position at its Tulsa location through the website of a Tulsa-area church attended by a Voss supervisor. Wolfe, who had prior operations management experience, learned about the vacancy and applied for the position although he did not himself attend the church. Most of the job interview concerned Wolfe's religious activities and beliefs and whether he "would have a problem" coming into work early to attend Bible study before clocking in. The branch manager seemed hesitant to accept Wolf's answers as truthful. At the time Wolfe was interviewed, Voss had no viable candidates for the position being filled. Wolfe was not offered the job, and after continuing its search, the company hired an individual whose religious ideology matched that of the company's leadership. Wolfe filed an EEOC religious discrimination complaint.[68] Decide. Explain.

The Americans with Disabilities Act (ADA)

As a child, Edward Carmona was diagnosed with psoriasis, a skin disease causing intermittent but treatable inflammations. As an adult working as a flight attendant for Southwest Airlines, Carmona was diagnosed with psoriatic arthritis, which causes painful joint swelling and stiffness during attacks of psoriasis. Although medication eased some of his discomfort, these attacks left Carmona unable to walk without great pain for one-half to one-third of each month. After his intermittent leave under Family and Medical Leave Act (FMLA—see Chapter 12) expired, he was fired for excessive absenteeism. Carmona brought a disability discrimination claim against Southwest Airlines under the Americans with Disabilities Act (ADA), winning a jury verdict that was vacated by the federal trial court. A federal appeals court overturned the federal trial court's decision to vacate the jury's award, concluding that Southwest Airlines attendance policy was extremely lenient, and the jury could have reasonably found other nondisabled flight attendants with similar absenteeism not being fired, and that Carmona's supervisors were annoyed by his disability-related absences.[69]

This situation illustrates the general purpose of the ADA, which seeks to remove barriers to a full, productive life for individuals with disabilities. The ADA forbids discrimination in employment, public accommodations, public services, transportation, and telecommunications. Small businesses with fewer than 15 employees are exempted from the employment portions of the ADA. The Rehabilitation Act of 1973 protects public sector workers with disabilities from employment discrimination.

Under the ADA, a qualified individual who (1) has a physical or mental impairment that substantially limits one or more *major life activities,* (2) has a record of such an impairment, or (3) is regarded as having such an impairment may not be discriminated against in employment.

In a series of decisions, the U.S. Supreme Court narrowed the scope of the ADA, prompting a leading disabilities rights advocate to call the ADA "the incredible shrinking law."[70] In response, the Americans with Disabilities Amendments Act (ADAAA) was passed by Congress and signed into law by President George W. Bush in 2008 to overturn those decisions and establish broader definitional guidelines under the ADA.

Defining Disabilities

As amended by the ADAAA, the ADA emphasizes that "disability" should be defined broadly in offering protection from employment discrimination. Examples of such disabilities include epilepsy, hypertension, asthma, diabetes, major depressive disorder, bipolar disorder, and schizophrenia. A nonexhaustive list of major life activities specified by the ADAAA includes eating, sleeping, standing, lifting, bending, concentrating, thinking, communicating, and all major bodily functions, including reproduction.

Alcoholism, drug addiction, and AIDS are disabilities under the ADA. However, the ADA excludes from its protection job applicants and employees who *currently* use illegal drugs. Employees with past drug or alcohol problems are protected by the ADA, as are employees with current alcohol problems who are able to perform the essential functions of the job. An employer may lawfully take an adverse employment action on the basis of, for example, a drug test showing use of illegal controlled substances or alcohol-induced unprofessional conduct at work. Those who are rehabilitated or are currently in rehabilitation are protected from disabilities discrimination. In sum, the ADA treats alcoholism and drug addiction as medical conditions and protects those who are overcoming these impairments.

Taking medication or using a prosthetic device to overcome an impairment does not exclude an individual from the ADA's protection. Episodic conditions such as epilepsy, if creating a "substantial limitation" on an individual's major life activities, ordinarily would be covered by the ADA. In addition, an impairment in remission, such as cancer, is covered if it would substantially limit a major life activity when active.[71]

"Regarded as Having" a Disability

An individual who does not have a disability may still be protected under the ADA. If an employer incorrectly assumes that an applicant or employee has a disability, and then takes discriminatory action on that basis, the employer has violated the ADA. For example, an employer who denies an employee a promotion to a managerial position requiring extensive client contact is likely to have violated the ADA if the promotion was denied because of the employer's mistaken belief that the employee is a recovering alcoholic who would not be able to manage client meetings where alcohol is frequently served.

Accommodating Individuals with Disabilities

An employer may not discriminate in hiring or employment against a *qualified person with a disability*. A qualified person is one who can perform the *essential job functions* with or without *reasonable accommodation*. The ADA requires employers to make reasonable accommodations for disabled employees and applicants. Reasonable accommodations might include structural changes in the workplace, job reassignment, job restructuring, or new equipment. Employers are not required to provide an accommodation that would create an *undue hardship*. For example, the employer need not create a new position to reassign an employee who can no longer perform the essential job functions, but rather should place the employee in an appropriate vacant job. The employer should engage in an interactive dialogue with the employee to explore possible reasonable accommodations. [For EEOC advice about small employers and reasonable accommodation, see **www.eeoc.gov/facts/accommodation.html**]

"Getting to Work" with Reasonable Accommodation

Jeanette Colwell was hired as a part-time retail clerk at a Rite Aid store in Old Forge, Pennsylvania. She worked various shifts, including 5 PM to 9 PM, and she earned supervisors' recognition for good performance. A few months after being hired, Colwell was diagnosed with "retinal vein occlusion and glaucoma in her left eye," and eventually she became blind in that eye. Colwell informed her supervisor, Susan Chapman, that her partial blindness made it dangerous and difficult for her to drive to work at night. She asked to be assigned to day shifts only so that she would be able to get to work. (Bus service stopped at 6 PM, and there were no taxis serving the area where the store was located.) Chapman refused the request because it "wouldn't be fair" to other workers, and she continued to schedule Colwell for a mix of day and evening shifts. Colwell later sent Chapman a doctor's note recommending that Colwell not drive at night, but Chapman was still unwilling to assign Colwell to day shifts only. Colwell resigned and brought an ADA claim against Rite Aid. The federal trial court ruled that Rite Aid had no duty to accommodate Colwell because she was able to perform all her work duties at the store; Colwell appealed.

Questions

1. Is Colwell an "individual with a disability" under the ADA? Explain.
2. How should Chapman have responded to Colwell's request? Explain.
3. A part-time retail clerk who is unable to drive because he is "legally blind" requests a late arrival to his shift due to a long bus commute. The store manager refuses his request, and subsequently terminates him for being late to work on a number of occasions. The clerk brings an ADA claim against his former employer. Decide. Explain.

Source: Colwell v. Rite Aid, 602 F.3d 495 (3rd. Cir. 2010).

The ADA in Practice

In early 2014, the unemployment rate for individuals with a disability was 14.3 percent compared with 6.8 percent for those without a disability.[72] A greater disparity exists in the level of participation in the labor force, defined by those employed and those who are unemployed but looking for work. Although over two-thirds of working-age Americans with no disability participate in the labor force, the labor participation rate for those with a disability is less than 20 percent.[73] Some employers may hesitate to hire workers with disabilities out of misconceptions and fear of added costs for accommodations.[74] However, in recent years companies have made efforts to increase the presence of individuals with disabilities in the professional workforce. For example, the National Business & Disability Council runs "Emerging Leaders," a summer internship program offering business placements for college and graduate students with disabilities.[75] [For more information, see Emerging Leaders at **www.emerging-leaders.com/**]

Tax credits to hire and provide access to individuals with disabilities, as well as tax deductions to remove architectural barriers to make its facilities more accessible, also provide incentives for employers to hire and retain employees with disabilities.[76]

On the other hand, under federal regulations that became effective in 2014, federal contractors that have a workforce with less than 7 percent disabled workers or that do not take steps to achieve that goal could face penalties, including losing their contracts.[77]

Rosa's Law: Changing the Words

Rosa's Law, named after Rosa Marcellino, a 9-year-old with Down Syndrome, changes the language in all federal health, education, and labor laws to remove the phrase "mentally retarded" and replace it with "intellectual disability." President Obama has quoted Rosa's brother Nick as saying: "What you call people is how you treat them. If we change the words, maybe it will be the start of a new attitude towards people with disabilities."

Sources: S. 2781(2010) [**www.govtrack.us/congress/bill.xpd?bill=s111-2781**]; and The White House Office of the Press Secretary, "Remarks by the President at the Signing of the 21st Century Communications and Video Accessibility Act of 2010," The White House Press Office, October 8, 2010 [**www.whitehouse.gov/the-press-office/2010/10/08/remarks-president-signing-21st-century-communications-and-video-accessib**].

ADA Questions

1. Core, a social services worker, had difficulty breathing at work when she was exposed to the perfume Japanese Cherry Blossom, worn by coworkers; on one occasion, she sought emergency medical treatment. Core's coworkers allegedly mocked her condition on their Facebook pages. Her employer rejected several of her accommodation requests, including a proposed fragrance-free workplace policy. The employer sent an e-mail message to employees asking that they not enter into Core's cubicle but to communicate with her instead by telephone and e-mail only, and asked Core to hold office discussions in better ventilated areas. After exhausting her FMLA leave entitlements (see Chapter 12), Core was placed on inactive pay status. The employer offered to permit Core to return to work and make such accommodations as instructing staff to refrain from wearing Japanese Cherry Blossom, and allowing her to take breaks to get fresh air. Core rejected these offers and was effectively terminated. Core brought an ADA claim against her former employer. Decide. Explain. *Core v. Champaign County Bd. of Commrs*, 2012 U.S. Dist. LEXIS 149120 (S.D. Ohio 2012).

2. Foley was terminated from his job as a financial advisor with Morgan Stanley after he removed and took away the central processing unit (CPU)—including the hard drive—from his office computer without authorization, and was not truthful about his actions for several days after doing so. Morgan Stanley's employment policies and procedures forbid the removal of its "trade secrets," defined as including computer software or hardware used in computers or word processors. Foley admitted he was terminated because of his misconduct but argued that his actions in taking the computer and being untruthful were caused by a manic episode of bipolar disorder. Therefore, in bringing an ADA claim against Morgan Stanley, Foley argued that the resulting termination was "because of" his disability. Decide. Explain. See *Foley v. Morgan Stanley Smith Barney*, 2013 U.S. Dist. LEXIS 28873 (S.D. Fla. 2013).

Genetic Testing

Genetic testing in the workplace and its discriminatory effects have been addressed by the EEOC. In 2002, the Burlington Northern & Santa Fe Railway Co. agreed to pay 36 workers $2.2 million for the railway's use of a genetic testing program, which, without the workers' knowledge, identified predispositions to carpal tunnel syndrome. In 2008, Congress and the president approved the Genetic Information Nondiscrimination Act (GINA) that prohibits employers from discriminating because of genetic information. With few exceptions, employers are not allowed to gather genetic information regarding an employee or the employee's family members.[78]

For example, as the EEOC notes in its enforcement guidance on GINA, using "family medical history" as a basis for an employment decision because of an increased risk of heart disease in the future would be unlawful because it is not relevant to the individual's "current ability to work."[79]

Age Discrimination

Can a clothing store featuring styles designed for the college market lawfully prefer youthful salespersons? May a marketing firm reject older applicants in an effort to bring "new blood" into its workforce? While these questions are not definitively resolved, employers taking such actions might face liability for age discrimination.

ADEA Claims   The Age Discrimination in Employment Act (ADEA) protects those 40 years and older from employment discrimination based on their age. Disparate treatment and harassment claims may be brought under the ADEA, and a 2005 Supreme Court decision extended ADEA protection to disparate impact claims also.[80] In its 2009 *Gross v. FBL* decision, the U.S. Supreme Court made it more difficult to win an ADEA disparate treatment claim.[81] Jack Gross had worked for FBL for over 30 years when at age 54 he was reassigned from Claims Administration Director to Coordinator, while his former duties were transferred to a younger worker whom he had supervised. Gross filed an ADEA claim against FBL claiming the demotion violated the ADEA, and he won a jury verdict after showing that his age played a role in FBL's decision. FBL appealed. The U.S.

Supreme Court held that an ADEA disparate treatment claim requires the plaintiff to show that age was not just one factor, but the deciding or "but-for" factor in the employer's decision.[82] The proposed Protecting Older Workers Against Discrimination Act, which would have reversed *Gross,* was introduced in Congress but was not enacted.

Defenses The employer may defend against an age discrimination claim by showing that the termination was based on a *legitimate, nondiscriminatory reason* (such as poor performance) or that age is a bona fide occupational qualification (BFOQ). For example, if there is no test available to predict when a commercial airline pilot over 60 years of age might experience a medical emergency that could jeopardize aviation safety, then being under 60 years of age is arguably a BFOQ for that job.[83] The ADEA also provides that an employer can defeat an age discrimination claim by demonstrating that a "reasonable factor other than age" (like poor attendance) was the actual reason for terminating or otherwise disfavoring an older worker. In 2008, the U.S. Supreme Court held that an employer using this defense in a disparate impact case carries the burden of proving a "reasonable factor other than age."[84]

Reverse Age Discrimination?

Being young is cool, but younger workers may get cold treatment in the workplace. Younger workers often seem to take the brunt of layoffs. Recently, the unemployment rate for those between the ages of 25 and 34 was 9.6 percent as compared with 6.5 percent for those 55 or older. Fear of ADEA lawsuits may be one reason companies use seniority to determine who will be retained in a reduction in force.

Question

Should the ADEA protect against age discrimination, regardless of age? Explain.

Source: Dana Mattioli, "With Jobs Scarce, Age Becomes an Issue," *The Wall Street Journal,* May 19, 2009 [www/wsj.com].

Questions

1. Mary, 61 years old, worked as a leasing consultant for a realty company for over two years before she was fired. The primary duty of a leasing consultant is to rent apartments. The company used phone and video evaluations to assess employees' performance. During her employment, Mary's scores allegedly were, with one exception, consistently below expectations. Allegedly, she violated company policies by showing an apartment without getting the prospective tenant's proof of identification, holding an apartment without a deposit, and showing an apartment not to be shown. Mary, who allegedly had been warned and placed on probation, claimed that during the termination meeting, her supervisor made age-related comments, as she had on several prior occasions. Mary sued her former employer for discrimination under the ADEA. Decide. Explain. See *Marsh v. Associated Estates Realty Corp.* 521 Fed. Appx. 460 (6th Cir. 2013) (unpub'd. op.).

2. The Insurance Company of North America (ICNA) sought to hire a "loss control representative." The ad called for a B.S. degree, two years of experience, and other qualities.

The plaintiff, who had 30 years of loss control experience, applied for the job but was not interviewed. ICNA hired a 28-year-old woman with no loss control experience. The plaintiff sued claiming age discrimination. ICNA said the plaintiff was overqualified.

a. Explain both the plaintiff's and defendant's arguments.

b. Decide the case. Explain. See *EEOC v. Insurance Co. of N. Am.,* 49 F.3d 1418 (9th Cir. 1995).

Sexual Orientation Discrimination

In April 2014, just days after his appointment as CEO, Brendan Eich resigned from Mozilla after employees complained about his opposition to same-sex marriage as shown by his 2008 political donation to support a ban on gay marriage that had surfaced on the Internet. Mozilla's executive chair, Mitchell Baker, apologized for the appointment, saying that Mozilla had failed "to listen, to engage, and to be guided by our community."[85] While this situation has raised concerns over the political rights of corporate executives, it also underscores how the debate over sexual orientation discrimination in the workplace has shifted.

At this writing, federal law does not offer protection against discrimination on the basis of an employee's sexual orientation. The courts have consistently ruled that Title VII's prohibition of discrimination based on sex refers to gender only, and not sexual orientation. In 2013, the Employment Non-Discrimination Act (ENDA), which would prohibit employers from discriminating on the basis of an employee's actual or perceived sexual orientation was reintroduced and passed the Senate, after having been proposed but not enacted over the years.[86] At this writing, political support for ENDA appears to be stronger than in the past. A 2013 poll showed that a majority of Americans support legal protection against employment discrimination based on sexual orientation.[87] As of January 2014, 21 states and the District of Columbia prohibit employment discrimination based on sexual orientation.[88]

Sexual Orientation Discrimination or Sex Stereotyping?

Henderson began working for a staffing company that gave preference to employees with transportation. Although Henderson had transportation, he was assigned to projects when it was difficult to find someone else. Henderson filed a lawsuit alleging that he was routinely subjected to derogatory remarks by and in the presence of his supervisors, including that he "looked just like a woman," was not a "real man," and that he was a "woman pretending to be something else. . . ." In denying the company's motion for summary judgment on the Title VII claims, the court noted that Henderson's claim demonstrates the tension between two legal principles. On the one hand, Title VII does not protect against discrimination based on sexual orientation. On the other hand, an employer cannot discriminate against an employee who does not meet gender stereotypes or norms. See *Henderson v. Labor Finders of Va.*, 2013 U.S. Dist. LEXIS 47753 (E.D. Va. 2013).

Gender Identity Discrimination

Several states and the District of Columbia prohibit employment discrimination based on gender identity or expression.[89] The 2013 version of ENDA includes protection against gender identity discrimination.

In the 2012 case of *Macy v. Holder* the EEOC decided that it would treat transgender discrimination complaints as sex discrimination claims. Federal courts have also recognized such claims as sex discrimination based on stereotyping men and women.[90] In 2008, for example, a federal trial court ruled that discrimination against transsexuals based on sex stereotyping is prohibited under Title VII.[91] Diane Schroer is a male-to-female transsexual. In 2004, before she changed her legal name from David to Diane and began presenting as a woman, Schroer was offered a job by the Library of Congress as a specialist on terrorism and international crime. Schroer's military career that included serving as a Special Operations Colonel made her well qualified for the Library job, and she received the highest interview score of all the candidates. The offer was rescinded, however, and given to a less qualified male, when Schroer revealed to the supervisor that she would be transitioning from male to female. The supervisor expressed difficulty in understanding why a man with a military background would undergo gender transition. In viewing pho-

> The supervisor saw only a man in a woman's clothing.

tographs of Schroer dressed in female attire, the supervisor said she saw only a man in a woman's clothing. The court held that Schroer had been discriminated against "because of sex" and that she was a victim of sex stereotyping.[92]

[For an American Civil Liberties Union video advocating a transgender-inclusive Employment Non-Discrimination Act, see "New Video Shows the Need for a Transgender-Inclusive ENDA" at **www.aclu.org/lgbt-rights_hiv-aids/new-aclu-video-shows-need-transgender-inclusive-enda**]; for an EEOC training seminar on the *Macy* Decision, see EEOC Federal Training and Outreach Division, "What Does the *Macy* Decision Mean for Title VII?," June 15, 2012 [**www.eeoc.gov/federal/training/brown_bag_macy.cfm**].

Internet Exercise

At this writing, the Healthy Workplace bill addressing workplace bullying has been introduced in a number of state legislatures. Using the Healthy Workplace Campaign's Web page [**www.healthyworkplacebill.org/faq.php**] answer the following questions:

1. How is workplace bullying defined?
2. What is the argument supporting legislation addressing workplace bullying?
3. How is the Healthy Workplace bill different from antidiscrimination protections?
4. What arguments might be raised against the Healthy Workplace bill?

Chapter Questions

1. Blockbuster established a grooming policy forbidding long hair for men but allowing it for women. Four men, who were fired for refusing to cut their long hair, sued Blockbuster for sex discrimination. Has Blockbuster violated Title VII? Explain. See *Kenneth Harper, et al. v. Blockbuster,* 139 F.3d 1385 (11th Cir. 1998; cert. den. 525 U.S. 1000 (1998).

2. In 2006, the EEOC filed a class action against Lawry's Restaurants including Lawry's The Prime Rib, Five Crowns, and The Tam O'Shanter Inn, on behalf of all male applicants for server positions who were systematically rejected because of their gender. Since 1938, Lawry's hired only females as servers and did not update their policy after the passage of Title VII. Servers' uniforms are antiquated women's costumes. What might Lawry's defense be? Will this defense be successful? Explain. See EEOC Press Release, "Lawry's to Pay $1 Billion for Sex Bias Against Men in Hiring," November 2, 2009 [**www.eeoc.gov/eeoc/newsroom/release/11-2-09.cfm**].

3. Emma, a Chinese American, applies for an available server position in a Mexican restaurant and is rejected. She suspects it is because of her national origin. What might the Mexican restaurant say in defense of a national origin discrimination complaint made by Emma? Will this defense be successful? Explain. See EEOC Compliance Manual (2002) at 13-II-C [**www.eeoc.gov/policy/docs/national-origin.html**].

4. Reeves worked as a transportation sales representative at a shipping company. Reeves was the only woman working on the sales floor, an open area structured into a "pod" of cubicles. Six males worked with Reeves. Reeves could often hear the language of her male coworkers as they spoke over the phone or with each other. Reeves could also hear the central office radio located in the "pod" that was used by her coworkers to listen to a crude morning show. On a daily basis at work, Reeves heard vulgar language and discussions of sexual topics, including such derogatory terms as "bitch" and "whore," which her male coworkers used to describe customers. The male branch manager once asked Reeves to speak to "that stupid bitch on line 4." Reeves brings a Title VII. sexual harassment claim against her employer. Decide the case. Explain. See *Reeves v. Robinson Worldwide, Inc.,* 594 F.3d 798 (11th Cir. 2010).

5. In *McCormack v. Safeway,* included as a "Legal Briefcase" in this chapter, the plaintiffs brought a retaliation claim along with their sexual harassment claims. Less than a month after reporting the sexual assault, the plaintiffs were both interviewed about McCormack's alleged violation of Safeway's coupon policy. A Safeway loss prevention investigator confronted Stabenchek and McCormack in connection with his investigation. McCormack was suspended pending further investigation. Feeling their honesty was being questioned because of their complaint, plaintiffs resigned. Decide the retaliation claim. Explain. See *McCormack v. Safeway,* 2014 U.S. Dist. LEXIS 17805 (D. Ariz. 2014).

6. Rodriguez managed a Walmart store at Fajardo, Puerto Rico. Following an evaluation, his performance was considered unsatisfactory, and he was demoted to assistant manager at another store. Rodriguez filed suit claiming race and national origin discrimination. Rodriguez pointed to two favorable previous performance evaluations, and he argued that he was evaluated in a different manner than non-Puerto Rican managers. Rodriguez was evaluated with the use of an opinion survey given to all of his subordinates. Rodriguez claimed that non-Puerto Rican managers at other stores were not subject to opinion surveys. Assuming that claim is true, would Rodriguez be able to prevail on a disparate treatment cause of action? Explain. See *Rodriguez-Cuervos v. Wal-Mart Stores,* 181 F.3d 15 (1st Cir. 1999).

7. Assume a company located near your college has asked you to create an outreach program to increase diversity in its workforce. What challenges would you face? What steps would you take? Explain.

8. Diane Piantanida went on maternity leave. While absent, her employer discovered tasks that she had not completed. Before her return, Piantanida was informed that she was being reassigned to a lesser job because of her inability to keep up in her former job. Upon objecting to the change, Piantanida claims she was told that she was being given a position "for a new mom to handle." Piantanida admits that her demotion was not based on her pregnancy or her maternity leave. Piantanida declined the offer and sued, claiming a violation of the Pregnancy Discrimination Act stemming from her status as a new mother. Decide. Explain. See *Piantanida v. Wyman Center,* 116 F.3d 340 (8th Cir. 1997).

9. Thornton worked as a manager at a Connecticut retail store. In accordance with his religious beliefs, Thornton notified his manager that he could no longer work on Sundays as required by company (Caldor, Inc.) policy. A Connecticut statute provided that: "No person who states that a particular day of the week is observed as his Sabbath may be required by his employer to work on such day. An employee's refusal to work on his Sabbath shall not constitute grounds for his dismissal." Management offered Thornton the options of transferring to a Massachusetts store where Sunday work was not required or transferring to a lower-paying supervisory job in the Connecticut store. Thornton refused both, and he was transferred to a lower-paying clerical job in the Connecticut store. Thornton claimed a violation of the Connecticut statute. The store argued that the statute violated the Establishment Clause (see Chapter 5) of the First Amendment, which forbids establishing an official state religion and giving preference to one religion over another or over none at all. Ultimately the case reached the U.S. Supreme Court.
   a. Decide. Explain.
   b. Do the religious accommodation provisions of Title VII of the Civil Rights Act violate the Establishment Clause? See *Estate of Thornton v. Caldor, Inc.,* 472 U.S. 703 (1985).

10. Sanchez worked as a host and food server at a pair of Azteca restaurants. Throughout his work experience, male coworkers and a supervisor referred to him as "she" and "her." He was mocked for walking and carrying his serving tray "like a woman." He was called a "faggot" and a "female whore." This abuse occurred repeatedly.
   a. Make the argument that Sanchez was not a victim of sexual harassment.
   b. Decide the case. Explain. See *Nichols v. Azteca Restaurant Enterprises,* 256 F.3d 864 (9th Cir. 2001).

11. Jane Doe was employed by C.A.R.S. Protection Plus for nearly a year when she learned she was pregnant. After amniocentesis revealed severe defects, Doe decided to terminate her pregnancy. Doe then took one week of vacation to recuperate from the procedure. The following week, she was fired for unexcused absences and job abandonment. Doe filed a claim under the Pregnancy Discrimination Act (PDA), alleging she was fired because of her choice to undergo a surgical abortion. Decide the case. Explain. See *Doe v. C.A.R.S. Protection Plus,* 527 F.3d 358 (3d Cir. 2008).

12. A new Texas airline, flying out of Dallas's Love Field, was in a precarious financial posture. A campaign was mounted to sell itself as "the airline personification of feminine youth and vitality." In commercials, its customers, who were primarily businessmen, were promised "in-flight love," including "love potions" (cocktails), "love bites" (toasted almonds), and a ticketing process (labeled a "quickie machine") that delivered "instant gratification." A male was denied a job with the airline because of his sex. He filed a Title VII action. The airline argued that attractive females were necessary to maintain its public image under the "love campaign," a marketing approach that the company claimed had been responsible for its improved financial condition. Decide. Explain. See *Wilson v. Southwest Airlines Co.,* 517 F.Supp. 292 (ND Tex. 1981).

13. Michael Cooke, an African-American male, worked at Novellus Systems in Silicon Valley where he had to listen on a regular basis to a Vietnamese-American coworker playing and rapping aloud to music lyrics that included racial epithets such as the "N-word." Although Cooke complained several times to his supervisors and made it clear that the language was offensive to him, the coworker continued to sing along to offensive lyrics within Cooke's earshot, and to use slang including racial epithets. The EEOC, on behalf of Cooke, brought a Title VII claim against Novelle Systems for racial harassment. Decide. See U.S. Equal Employment Opportunity Commission, "Silicon Valley Manufacturer Novellus . . . Racial Harassment," press release, June 24, 2008 [**www.eeoc.gov/eeoc/newsroom/release/6-24-08.cfm**].

14. Should employment discrimination based on physical attractiveness be prohibited? Explain.

15. Should American firms abroad adhere to American antidiscrimination policies even if those policies might put the American firms at a competitive disadvantage or offend the values and mores of the host country? Explain.

16. John D. Archbold Memorial Hospital excluded all job applicants whose weight exceeded the maximum desirable weight (based on Metropolitan Life's actuarial survey) for large-framed men and women plus 30 percent of that weight. Sandra Murray claimed she was denied a job as a respiratory therapist because her height-to-weight ratio did not meet the guidelines. Murray did not claim to be morbidly obese.
    a. Explain the plaintiff's argument.
    b. Did the hospital violate the ADA? Explain. See *Murray v. John D. Archbold Memorial Hospital,* 50 F.Supp.2d 1368 (M.D. Ga. 1999).

Notes

1. AFjustice.com. Website of Lieff Cabraser Heimann & Bernstein, LLP [**www.afjustice.com**].
2. See Jenny Strasburg, "Abercrombie to Pay $50 Million in Bias Suits," *San Francisco Chronicle,* November 10, 2004, p. C1; and Julie Tamaki, "Judge Accepts Abercrombie Plan to Settle Hiring Lawsuits," *Los Angeles Times,* November 17, 2004, p. C2.
3. Equal Employment Opportunity Commission, "Abercrombie & Fitch Settles Two Pending Religious Discrimination Suits," press release, September 23, 2013 [**www.eeoc.gov/eeoc/newsroom/release/9-23-13c.cfm**].
4. *EEOC v. Abercrombie & Fitch,* 731 F.3d 1106 (10th Cir. 2013).
5. Michael Lopardi, "Minority Groups Sue Abercrombie for $40 M," *University Wire,* January 27, 2005.

6. Devah Pager, "The Mark of a Criminal Record," *American Journal of Sociology* 105, no. 5 (March 2003), pp. 937–975 [**www.northwestern.edu/ipr/publications/papers/2003/pagerajs .pdf**].

7. General Accounting Office, "Diversity Management: Expert-Identified Leading Practices and Agency Examples," GAO-05-90 (Washington, DC, January 14, 2005) [**www.gao.gov/htext /d0590.html**].

8. 347 U.S. 483 (1954).

9. A portion of this paragraph is drawn from William P. Murphy, Julius G. Getman, and James E. Jones Jr., *Discrimination in Employment,* 4th ed. (Washington, DC: Bureau of National Affairs, 1979), pp. 1–4.

10. 127 S.Ct. 2162 (2007).

11. S. 181 (2009–2010).

12. *EEOC v. Waffle House Inc.,* 534 U.S. 279 (2002).

13. Martha Neil, "Most Job Discrimination Suits Win, at Best, Small Settlements, Study Says," *ABA Journal,* June 9, 2010 [**www.abajournal.com/news/article/most_job_discrimination_suits _win_small_settlements_at_best_study_says/**].

14. American Bar Foundation, "ABF Study of Unfairness in Employment Discrimination Lawsuits Published in *Law & Society Review,*" press release, May 8, 2012 [**www.americanbarfoundation .org/news/331**].

15. *Haynes v. W.C. Caye & Co.,* 52 F.3d 926 (11th Cir. 1995).

16. See *International Brotherhood of Teamsters v. United States,* 97 S.Ct. 1843 (1977); *American Tobacco v. Patterson,* 456 U.S. 63 (1982); and *Firefighters Local Union No. 1784 v. Stotts,* 467 U.S.561 (1984).

17. Tresa Baldas, "Employment Tests May Fail Legal Exam," *National Law Journal,* February 18, 2008, p. 4.

18. Equal Employment Opportunity Commission Fact Sheet on Employment Tests and Selection Procedures [**www.eeoc.gov/policy/docs/factemployment_procedures.html**].

19. EEOC Receives Award for Post-9/11 Efforts," *HR.BLR.com,* October 4, 2004 [**http://hr.blr .com/news.aspx?id=10396**].

20. EEOC Litigation Settlements March 2005 [**www.eeoc.gov/litigation/settlements/settlement03-05 .html**].

21. EEOC, "Selected List of Pending and Resolved Cases Alleging Religious and National Origin Discrimination Involving the Muslim, Sikh, Arab, Middle Eastern and South Asian Communities," as of September 10, 2013 [**www.eeoc.gov/eeoc/litigation/selected/religion_nationalorigin .cfm**].

22. U.S. Commission on Civil Rights, "English Only Policies in the Workplace," October 3, 2011 [**www.usccr.gov/pubs/Re_EOPWORK_10-03-11.pdf**].

23. *Garcia v. Spun Steak Co.,* 998 F.2d 1480, cert. den. 114 S.Ct. 2726 (1994).

24. The U.S. Equal Employment Opportunity Commission, "Henredon Furniture Industries to Pay $465,000 for Racial Harassment, Hangman's Nooses," January 24, 2008 [**www.eeoc.gov /press/1-24-08.html**].

25. EEOC, "Jury Awards $200,000 in Damages Against A.C. Widenhouse in EEOC Race Harassment Suit," February 1, 2013 [**http://www.eeoc.gov/eeoc/newsroom/release/2-1-13.cfm**].

26. EEOC, "RockTenn Services Pays $500,000 to Settle EEOC Race Harassment Suit," December 3, 2012 [**www.eeoc.gov/eeoc/newsroom/release/12-3-12b.cfm**].

27. EEOC, "EEOC Wins Rare Partial Summary Judgment Ruling in Racial Harassment Case," October 16, 2012 [**www.eeoc.gov/eeoc/newsroom/release/10-16-12.cfm**].

28. *Tyrrell v. Oaklawn Jockey Club,* 2012 U.S. Dist. LEXIS 157482 (W.D. Ark. 2012).

29. *Ash v. Tyson,* 546 U.S. 454 (2006).

30. *Aman v. Cort Furniture Rental Corp.,* 85 F.3d 1074 (3d Cir. 1996).

31. U.S. Bureau of Labor Statistics, "Highlights of Women's Earnings in 2012," *BLS Reports*, October 2013 [**www.bls.gov/cps/cpswom2012.pdf**].

32. Kay Hymnowitz, "Why Women Make Less Than Men," *The Wall Street Journal*, April 26, 2012, p. A15.

33. Colleen McCain Nelson, "Most Women See Bias in the Workplace," *The Wall Street Journal*, April 11, 2013 [**http://online.wsj.com/news/articles/SB100014241278873246951045784170 20376740796**].

34. Associated Press, "Judge Approves $46 Million Settlement of Gender Discrimination Claims Against Morgan Stanley," *San Jose Mercury News,* October 11, 2007 [**www.mercurynews .com/portlet/article/html/fragments**].

35. *Wal-Mart Stores v. Dukes,* 2011 U.S. LEXIS 4567.

36. Stacy Blackman, "Study Examines Male–Female Wage Gap, Post, MBA," *US News: Education*, August 26, 2011 [**www.usnews.com/education/blogs/mba-admissions-strictly -business/2011/08/26/study-examines-male-female-wage-gap-post-mba**].

37. U.S. EEOC, "Charges FY 1997–2013" [**www.eeoc.gov/eeoc/statistics/enforcement/charges .cfm**].

38. See, generally, *Diaz v. Pan American World Airways Inc.,* 442 F.2d 385 (5th Cir.), cert. den. 404 U.S. 950 (1971).

39. *Chadwick v. Wellpoint Inc.,* 561 F.3d 38 (1st Cir. 2009).

40. *Warren v. Solo Cup,* 516 F.3d 627 (7th Cir. 2008).

41. Society for Human Resource Management, "Is Workplace Harassment on the Rise?" SHRM Poll, April 16, 2010 [**www.shrm.org/Research/SurveyFindings/Articles/Pages /SexualHarassmentontheRise.aspx**].

42. "Study Finds Link between Women in Power, Sexual Harassment" *Phys.org* [**http://phys.org /news/2012-08-link-women-power-sexual.html**].

43. *Burlington Industries v. Ellerth,* 524 U.S. 742 (1998); and *Faragher v. Boca Raton,* 524 U.S.775 (1998).

44. *Vance v. Ball State University*, 133 S.Ct. 2434 (2013).

45. *Oncale v. Sundowner Offshore Services,* 523 U.S. 75 (1998).

46. *Holman v. State of Indiana,* 211 F.3d 299 (7th Cir. 2000).

47. Kiren Dosanjh, "Crossing Boundaries: Sexual Harassment Liability of U.S.-Based Multi-National Corporations in Developing Countries," [**www.sba.muohio.edu/abas/2001/brussels /Dosanjh_Crossing_Boundaries.pdf**].

48. Stephen Miller, "Sexual Jokes No Laughing Matter," *Glasgow Herald,* June 7, 2002, p. 4.

49. Gerald L. Maatman Jr. "A Global View of Sexual Harassment," *HR Magazine,* July 2000, p. 151.

50. "Government Laws on Sexual Harassment in Various Countries," *The Economic Times*, August 22, 2010 [**http://articles.economictimes.indiatimes.com/2010-08-22/news/28445217_1 _sexual-harassment-title-vii-equal-employment-opportunity-commission**].

51. 555 U.S. 271 (2009).

52. 548 U.S. 53 (2006).

53. 131 S.Ct. 863 (2011).

54. 133 S.Ct. 2517 (2013).

55. Michael A. Fletcher and Jon Cohen, "Far Fewer Consider Racism Big Problem," *The Washington Post,* January 19, 2009 [**www.washingtonpost.com/wp-dyn/content /article/2009/01/18/AR2009011802538.html**].

56. Drew Desilver, "Supreme Court Defers Affirmative Action Ruling, Deep Divides Persist," *Pew Research Center Fact Tank,* June 24, 2013 [**www.pewresearch.org/fact-tank/2013/06/24 /as-supreme-court-defers-affirmative-action-ruling-deep-divides-persist/**].

57. 443 U.S. 193 (1979).

58. 480 U.S. 616 (1987).

59. 488 U.S. 469 (1989).

60. 115 S.Ct. 2097 (1995).

61. Charles A. Sullivan, "Circling Back to the Obvious: The Convergence of Traditional and Reverse Discrimination in Title VII Proof," *William and Mary Law Review* 46 (December 2004), p. 1031.

62. *Ricci v. DeStefano,* 129 S.Ct. 2658 at 2677 (2009).

63. Steven Greenhouse, "Supreme Court Ruling Offers Little Guidance on Hiring," *The New York Times,* June 30, 2009 [**www/nytimes.com**].

64. *Cloutier v. Costco,* 390 F.3d 126 (1st Cir. 2004); cert. den., 545 U.S. 1131 (2005).

65. 423 U.S. 63 (1977).

66. *Franks v. National Lime & Stone Co.,* 740 N.E. 2d 694 (Ohio Ct. App. 2000).

67. EEOC Compliance Manual Section 12, Religious Discrimination, July 22, 2008 [**www.eeoc .gov/policy/docs/religion.htm**].

68. U.S. Equal Employment Opportunity Commission, "Voss Lighting to Pay $82,500 to Settle Religious Discrimination Lawsuit," press release, March 19, 2013 [**www.eeoc.gov/eeoc /newsroom/release/3-19-13a.cfm**].

69. 604 F.3d 848 (5th Cir. 2010).

70. Joan Biskupic, "High Court Raises Bar for ADA," *USA TODAY,* January 9, 2002, p. 3A.

71. *Hoffman v. Carefirst of Fort Wayne Inc.,* 2010 U.S. Dist. LEXIS 107493 (N.D. Ind. 2010).

72. Lauren Weber, "Are You Disabled? Now Your Boss Wants to Know," *The Wall Street Journal,* March 19, 2014, p. B1.

73. Ibid.

74. Sara Murray, "Disabled Face Sharply Higher Jobless Rate," *The Wall Street Journal,* August 26, 2010, p. A5.

75. Suzanne Robitalle, "Support Grows for Disabled Job Seekers," *The Wall Street Journal,* July 22, 2008, p. D4.

76. Equal Employment Opportunity Commission, "Facts About Disability-Related Tax Provisions," [**www.eeoc.gov/facts/fs-disab.html**].

77. Weber, "Are You Disabled? Now your Boss Wants to Know," *The Wall Street Journal,* March 19, 2014, p. B1.

78. Pub. L. 110–233 (2008).

79. Equal Employment Opportunity Commission, "Genetic Information Discrimination," *Laws, Regulations, & Guidance, Types of Discrimination* [**www.eeoc.gov/laws/types/genetic.cfm**].

80. *Smith v. City of Jackson,* 2005 U.S. LEXIS 2931.

81. 129 S.Ct. 2343 (2009).

82. Ibid.

83. S. 2189 (112th): Protecting Older Workers Against Discrimination Act [**https://www.govtrack .us/congress/bills/112/s2189**].

84. *Meacham v. Knolls Atomic Power Laboratory,* 554 U.S. 84 (2008).

85. Alistair Barr, "CEO Quits Under Fire for Stance on Gay Marriage," *The Wall Street Journal,* April 4, 2014, p. A1.

86. S. 815 (113th): Employment Non-Discrimination Act [**https://www.govtrack.us/congress /bills/113/s815**].

87. Andrew Gelman, "Poll Says ENDA Has Majority Support in Every Congressional District," *The Washington Post,* November 20, 2013 [**www.washingtonpost.com/blogs/monkey-cage /wp/2013/11/20/polls-say-enda-has-majority-support-in-every-congressional-district/**].

88. National Conference of State Legislatures, "Employment Discrimination Based on Sexual Orientation," February 6, 2014 [**www.ncsl.org/research/labor-and-employment/employment -discrimination-sexual-orientation.aspx**].

89. Ibid.

90. U.S. Equal Employment Opportunity Commission, "Processing Complaints by LGBT Federal Employees," [**www.eeoc.gov/federal/directives/lgbt_complaint_processing.cfm**].

91. *Schroer v. Billington,* 577 F.Supp.2d 293 (D.D.C. 2008).

92. Ibid.

CHAPTER FOURTEEN

Employment Law III: Labor–Management Relations

After completing this chapter, students will be able to:

1. Describe both the decline of labor unions and their hopes for renewal.

2. Describe the goals of the National Labor Relations Act (NLRA).

3. Identify unfair labor practices by management and unions.

4. Describe the role of the National Labor Relations Board (NLRB) in enforcing the NLRA.

5. Describe the process of union organizing and the related legal issues.

6. Describe "bargaining in good faith."

7. Distinguish between "unfair labor practice strikes" and "economic strikes."

8. Compare and contrast "primary picketing" and "secondary picketing/boycotts."

9. Describe employees' rights within or against unions.

10. Explain the impact of "right-to-work" laws on union security agreements.

Introduction

Working behind the counter of a fast-food restaurant has been commonly thought of as the domain of teenagers looking for a temporary job to make "pocket money." However, the economic downturn found many older workers seeking employment in the fast-food industry. In 2013, protests in New York City and Los Angeles by fast-food workers demanding higher wages highlighted this shift and its impact. At a Los Angeles protest, one 26-year-old worker said she earned $7.25 an hour and worked 19 hours "on a good week."[1] A 36-year-old mother of four working at a hamburger fast-food restaurant said she was grateful to have a job, but uses her wages to pay rent, with no money left over to pay for school clothes for her children.[2]

Critics viewed the protests, which were supported by a labor union, as evidence that unions are focused on recruiting new groups of workers to bolster their declining membership.[3] Global economic shifts have split America's private-sector unions in two pieces: one, the old-line manufacturing organizations represented by the United Auto Workers (UAW), for example; the other, the emerging service sector organized most notably by the Service Employees International Union (SEIU), which represents approximately 2 million nurses, security guards, janitors, and others. Traditional union power in manufacturing has been deeply undercut by the outsourcing of jobs abroad to take advantage of cheaper wages. Substantial decreases in private consumption and investment in recent years, leading to declines in manufacturing and construction, have also significantly impacted union membership. In 2013, the union membership rate remained at 11.3 percent as in 2012; since 1983, union membership has fallen nearly 50 percent.[4] The union membership rate in the private sector is roughly 6 percent, whereas over two-thirds of public-sector workers are unionized.[5]

Auto Industry and Unions Union problems in the manufacturing sector were vividly illustrated by the 2007 settlements of new labor agreements between the UAW and the Big Three American automobile manufacturers: General Motors (GM), Ford, and Chrysler. In return for automakers' promises of investments to maintain manufacturing jobs in the United States, UAW members agreed to dramatic contract changes, allowing the Big Three to compete more effectively with their nonunion competitors, Toyota, Honda, and others.[6] The UAW's efforts to unionize auto workers in foreign-owned auto plants such as Nissan and Volkswagen in Mississippi have, at this writing, been generally unsuccessful. Workers at these plants who are opposed to unionizing point to high wages in a relatively poor state, while pro-union workers at Nissan are concerned about job security, as temporary help can cut Nissan's labor costs. With approximately half of U.S.-manufactured autos being made by nonunionized workers, GM, Ford, and Chrysler may be able to pressure UAW to allow the lowering of labor costs to the level of nonunion plants.[7]

Union Support According to a 2013 Pew poll, over half of Americans have a favorable view of labor unions, having rebounded nearly 10 percent from 2011.[8] However, laws curtailing the power of unions have been passed in state legislatures. For example, in 2011, Wisconsin passed a law restricting public-sector employees' collective-bargaining rights. In 2012, Michigan, known as the home of the unionized auto worker, became a "right to work" state, discussed later in this chapter.[9] A shift away from traditional unionized industries along with union corruption have certainly played big roles in union struggles, but union supporters say corporate resistance has made organizing very difficult. Working America, an organization allied with the AFL-CIO, seeks to engage nonunion members in unions' political causes, which may help increase workplace activism.[10] [For more on Working America, see **www .workingamerica.org/**]

Questions

1. Do we need labor unions to counterbalance the power of big corporations? Explain.
2. In the 2013 protests described at the beginning of the chapter, fast-food workers asked for higher wages; protesters in Los Angeles asked for a $15 an hour minimum wage. Supporters of a wage increase for fast-food workers point to the fast-food industry's large profits and generous executive salaries. What are the arguments both for and against a wage increase for fast-food workers? Explain.

Does the Union Have a Fight Song?

In 2014, Peter Ohr, a regional director of the National Labor Relations Board (NLRB), ruled that Northwestern University football players are university employees and are therefore able to form the first college athletes' union. The NCAA has treated college athletes as students first, and as athletes second; therefore, the NCAA believes these players should not be treated as employees. In ruling that these players are actually athletes first, Ohr noted that the athletes' duties to the university's team require 40 to 50 hours per week during the football season, which is not only more than what many other full-time employees spend on their jobs, but is more than the players spent on their studies. At this writing, Northwestern University plans to appeal this ruling.

Questions

1. Do you support the unionization of college athletes? Explain.
2. What obstacles might a college athletes' union face in negotiating with a university? Explain.

Source: Douglas Belkin, Melanie Trottman, and Rachel Bachman, "College's Football Team Can Unionize," *The Wall Street Journal,* March 27, 2014, p. A2.

Part One—History

As the United States moved from an agrarian to an industrial society in the late 1880s, business competition was fierce. Costs had to be cut. By paying workers as little as possible and making them work 14- to 18-hour days, employers could prosper. Farmers began moving to the city to be near their jobs and thus left their safety net of gardens, chickens, and cows. Similarly, immigrants streamed into the big cities, and competition for jobs became heated. Wages fell, and deplorable working conditions were the norm.[11] Some of those immigrants brought with them ideas and experiences in labor conflict and class struggle that would soon contribute to dramatic changes in the American workplace.

A Grim Picture

To say that working conditions for many people at this time were unpleasant or even dismal would be a vast understatement. The term *desperate* better describes the problem. Children were impressed into service as soon as they were big enough to do a job and then made to work 12- and 14-hour days.[12] In fact, small children were employed in coal mines for 10 to 12 hours each day, and at a rate of $1 to $3 per week, because they were small enough to fit in the confined spaces.[13] Textile companies sent men called *slavers* to New England and southern farm communities to gather young women to work in the mills.[14]

> Children were employed in coal mines because they were small enough to fit in the confined spaces.

The following firsthand report from the early 20th century reveals the grim picture:

> When I moved from the North to the South in my search for work, I entered a mill village to work in a cotton mill as a spinner. There I worked 11 hours a day, five and a half days a week, for $7 a week. In a northern mill I had done the same kind of work for $22 a week, and less hours. I worked terribly hard. . . .
>
> The sanitary conditions were ghastly. When I desired a drink of water, I had to dip my cup into a pail of water that had been brought into the mill from a spring in the fields. It tasted horrible to me. Often I saw lint from the cotton in the room floating on top of the lukewarm water. All of the men chewed tobacco, and most of the women used snuff. Little imagination is needed to judge the condition of the water which I had to drink, for working in that close, hot spinning room made me thirsty. Toilet facilities were provided three stories down in the basement of the mill in a room without any ventilation. Nowhere was there any running water. . . .
>
> Everything in the village is company owned. The houses look like barns on stilts, and appear to have been thrown together. When I would go inside one of them, I could see outside through the cracks in the walls. The workers do all of their trading at the company store and bank, and use the company school and library for they have no means of leaving the village.[15]

Compare those working-class conditions with the lifestyle of John D. Rockefeller, the great tycoon of the same era. Although Rockefeller was notoriously frugal, his estate at Pocantico Hills, New York, contained:

> . . . more than 75 buildings. . . . Within his estate were 75 miles of private roads on which he could take his afternoon drive; private golf links on which he could play his morning game; and anywhere from 1,000 to 1,500 employees, depending on the season.
>
> . . . Rockefeller also owned an estate at Lakewood, [New Jersey] which he occupied in the spring; an estate at Ormond Beach in Florida for his winter use; a townhouse . . . in New York; an estate at Forest Hill, Cleveland which he did not visit; and a house on Euclid Avenue in Cleveland, likewise unused by him.[16]

These circumstances enable us to better understand the sense of injustice felt by many workers and the belief that a redistribution of wealth might provide the only solution to class conflict. [For a timeline of the labor movement, see **http://75.afscme.org/history**]

Organizing Labor

The Knights of Labor, the first major labor organization in the United States, had a large following during the 1870s and 1880s.[17] The order admitted any workers to its ranks, regardless of occupation, gender, or nationality; in fact, the only people excluded from the group were gamblers, bankers, stockbrokers, and liquor dealers.[18] The Knights of Labor dedicated itself to principles of social reform, including the protection of wage and hour laws, improved health care systems, and mandatory education.[19] However, the goals of the Knights of Labor were perhaps too broad and far-reaching to bring workers any relief from their immediate problems. Great philosophical divisions within the Knights of Labor brought about its rapid decline.[20]

Skilled Workers

Samuel Gompers, who built and developed the American Federation of Labor (AFL), had more practical, attainable goals in mind for his organization. Gompers, a worker in the cigar industry, saw the need to organize workers along craft lines (such as plumbers, electricians, and machinists) so that each craft group could seek higher wages and better working conditions for its own workers, all of whom had the same type of skills and, presumably, shared the same occupational goals.[21] This approach, a national association of local unions directed to workers' pragmatic needs rather than the more politically motivated activities of the Knights of Labor, proved to be a successful formula for union organization.

Laborers

The Congress of Industrial Organizations (CIO) was organized in response to the needs of ordinary laborers not working in the skilled trades to which the AFL was devoted. The CIO was organized in 1935 and served assembly-line workers and others who often performed repetitive, physically demanding tasks. The AFL and CIO were fierce competitors, but after years of bitter conflict, the two groups united forces in 1955. They function together today as the AFL–CIO. [For the AFL–CIO home page, see **www.aflcio.org**]

Unions and the Developing Law

Labor Protection

Responding to mounting public pressure, Congress passed the Norris-LaGuardia Act in 1932 making clear that the terminology "restraint of trade," which was the heart of the 1890 Sherman Antitrust Act (see Chapter 10), was not meant to include labor organizations or activities.

From 1932 to 1935, labor tensions continued to mount. The nation was still caught in the Great Depression. Believing that one element essential to economic recovery was stability in the workforce, Congress addressed the labor question with the Wagner Act of 1935. This legislation gave workers for the first time the unequivocal right to organize and engage in concerted activities for their mutual aid and benefit. To protect this right, Congress identified and made illegal a number of unfair labor practices. Through the Wagner Act, Congress also established the National Labor Relations Board (see below).

Management Protection

Unions grew rapidly with the passage of the Wagner Act, and by 1947 Congress decided management might need a little help in coping with ever-growing labor organizations.[22] Congress enacted the Taft–Hartley Act, identifying as unfair labor practices certain activities unions used to exercise economic leverage over employers as part of the collective bargaining process. The Taft–Hartley Act also ensured employers' right to speak out in opposition to union organizing—in effect, protecting their First Amendment right to freedom of speech. Thus, the Taft–Hartley Act signaled a move by the government away from unconditional support for labor toward a balance of rights between labor and management.[23]

Corrupt Union Leaders

In response to the growing evidence that union leaders were benefiting at the expense of the membership, Congress in 1959 enacted the Landrum–Griffin Act, requiring unions to keep records of their funds. It also prohibits unions from lending money except under specified circumstances and procedures, all of which must be reported annually to the government.

Members' Rights

The Landrum–Griffin Act also contains a set of provisions often referred to as the "Bill of Rights" for individual union members. These provisions are designed to protect union members by requiring that union meetings be held, that members be permitted to speak and vote at these meetings, that every employee covered by a collective-bargaining agreement has the right to see a copy of that agreement, and that a union member be informed of the reasons and given a chance for a hearing if the union wishes to suspend or take disciplinary action against that member, unless he or she is being suspended for nonpayment of dues.[24]

The law has also regulated the manner in which unions represent employees in the collective-bargaining process. Because a union serves as employees' exclusive bargaining representative, the courts have devised a *duty of fair representation*.[25] To fulfill this duty, a union must represent employees, both in negotiating and enforcing the collective-bargaining agreement, "without hostility or discrimination . . . [and] . . . with complete good faith and honesty [so as to] avoid arbitrary conduct."[26]

Part Two—Labor Legislation Today

Today labor–management relations are governed by the National Labor Relations Act (NLRA), as enforced by the National Labor Relations Board (NLRB).[27] This act includes within it the Wagner Act, the Taft–Hartley Act, and portions of the Landrum–Griffin Act. The remaining provisions of the Landrum–Griffin Act make up the Labor–Management Reporting and Disclosure Act and the Bill of Rights of Members of Labor Organizations.

PRACTICING ETHICS   Reading Your Rights at Work

Posters by the U.S. Department of Labor (see Chapter 12) and the Equal Employment Opportunity Commission (EEOC—see Chapter 13) informing workers of their rights are familiar sights in the workplace. In 2012, the NLRB issued a Notice Posting Rule requiring most private-sector employers—regardless of whether their workers were unionized—to post a notice advising employees of their rights under the NLRA. Two federal appellate decisions invalidated this rule; the NLRB announced in 2014 that it would not seek review by the U.S. Supreme Court. Therefore, employers may choose not to post such a message. The workplace poster remains available on the NLRB website [see www.nlrb.gov/poster]. In addition, the NLRB has established a free NLRB mobile app for iPhone and Android users to provide the public with information about the National Labor Relations Act.

Questions

1. Legal requirements aside, are employers ethically obligated to inform their workers of NLRA rights? Explain.

2. From an ethical standpoint, should NLRA posting requirements be different for a nonunionized workplace versus a unionized workplace? Explain.

Source: NLRB Office of Public Affairs, "The NLRB's Notice Posting Rule," January 6, 2014 [**www.nlrb.gov/news-outreach/news-story/nlrbs-notice-posting-rule**].

Right to Organize

The NLRA gives employees the right to engage in concerted activity, including strikes and collective bargaining. Section 7 of the NLRA states:

> Employees shall have the right to self-organization, to form, join, or assist labor organizations, to bargain collectively through representatives of their own choosing, and to engage in other concerted activities for the purpose of collective bargaining or other mutual aid or protection, and shall also have the right to refrain from any and all of such activities except to the extent that such right may be affected by an agreement requiring membership in a labor organization as a condition of employment.

When political issues such as immigration become heated, employees' political advocacy efforts may affect the workplace. Political advocacy may in some circumstances be considered a *concerted activity* for "mutual aid or protection" under Section 7. Under 2008 NLRB guidelines, the first question to consider is whether there is a direct connection between the political issue at stake and a "specifically identified employment concern of the participating employees." Even if that direct connection is established, however, the employer may discipline the employees if the political activity, such as attending a rally, violates "neutrally applied" work rules, such as those forbidding stopping or leaving work without permission.[28] [For a vast database of federal and state labor law statutes and regulations, see **http://topics.law.cornell.edu/wex/labor**]

Bleeping Protected Activity?

During ongoing union negotiations, Bill Barker, a company vice president at the *Tampa Tribune,* sent employees a series of letters, which were legal and accurate, describing the negotiation process from his perspective. In talking to supervisors about the letters one night after he arrived for his third shift, an employee, Greg McMillen, said: "I hope that f**king idiot [Barker] doesn't send me another letter. I'm pretty stressed, and if there is another letter you might not see me. I might be out on stress." McMillen was fired for violating a company policy against using threatening and abusive language in the company building. McMillen complained to the NLRB. Did McMillen's firing violate Section 7 of the NLRA? Explain.

Source: Media General Operations v. NLRB, 560 F.3d 181 (4th Cir. 2009).

Unfair Labor Practices by Management

The NLRA describes and outlaws certain activities by employers that would hamper or discourage employees from exercising the rights granted to them in Section 7. Thus Section 8(a) of the act makes it an *unfair labor practice* for an employer to:

1. Interfere with, restrain, or coerce employees in the exercise of the rights given to them by Section 7;
2. Dominate, interfere, or assist with the formation of any labor organization, including contributing financial support to it;
3. Encourage or discourage membership in any labor organization by discrimination in regard to hiring, tenure of employment, promotion, salary, or any other term of employment;
4. Discharge or take any other action against an employee because he or she has filed charges or given testimony under the act; and
5. Refuse to bargain collectively with a duly certified representative of the employees.

These five provisions are designed to allow employees to organize in an atmosphere free from intimidation by the employer. In addition, if employees have chosen a union as their exclusive collective bargaining representative, Section 8(a) regulates the bargaining between the employer and the union. The provisions also ensure that the employer will not be able to interfere with union activities by either seizing control of the union or rendering it impotent by refusing to bargain collectively.

At-Will Disclaimers

Recently, the employee handbook has been the source of complaints that employers are violating their employees' NLRA rights. For example, the at-will provision, typically signed by new employees, may state: "I agree that the at-will employment relationship cannot be amended, modified, or altered in any way." This provision may be unlawful, because it waives the employee's right to act with other employees to change the nature of their employment relationship.[29] However, an at-will provision declaring that managers and supervisors have no authority to alter the employment relationship's at-will status, without restricting the employee's ability to engage in concerted activity to do so, has been considered valid by the NLRB.[30]

Dress Codes

Pro-union hats, T-shirts, and the like are commonly used in union campaigns. However, under recent federal court decisions, employers may limit such attire for a legitimate business interest. For example, Starbucks employees often wear buttons offering information on Starbucks products. During a campaign to unionize Starbucks, pro-union buttons were worn by some employees. Starbucks began prohibiting employees from wearing more than one pro-union button at work, which the NLRB determined to be an unfair labor practice. In rejecting the NLRB's ruling, a federal appellate court held that Starbucks had a legitimate interest in ensuring that its business-related messages did not get lost in an array of other buttons worn by its employees.[31] Similarly, a federal appellate court determined that an employer lawfully requested that its employee remove his T-shirt printed with a negative comment about the employer's performance recognition program. Medco, a pharmacy benefits program, started a "WOW awards" program to recognize employees' performance. The T-shirt in question had a union logo on the front, and the message, "I don't need a WOW to do my job" on the back. Because the WOW program was used to entice prospective and current clients, Medco's demand to remove the T-shirt was justified under its policy prohibiting clothing printed with "degrading . . . insulting or provocative" statements.[32]

All Because of a Bad Haircut?

Embarrassed over a bad haircut, Nichole Wright-Gore, a supply clerk for White Oak Manor, started wearing a hat to work. After several days, supervisors told her to remove the hat as it violated a company dress code prohibiting hats; she refused and was disciplined. Wright-Gore subsequently began to take photos of her coworkers, some with and without consent, showing them wearing hats and violating the dress code in other ways, which she shared with coworkers while discussing with them the unequal enforcement of the dress code. After employees complained about having their photos taken and shared with others without their consent, Wright-Gore was terminated for violating White Oak's policy prohibiting photos being taken in the facility. Did Wright-Gore's termination violate the NLRA? Explain.

Source: NLRB v. White Oak Manor, 452 Fed. Appx. 374 (4th Cir. 2011) (unpub'd. op.).

Social Media Policies

Can a Facebook posting or comment be protected activity under the NLRA? Coworkers who are "Facebook friends" or otherwise connected on social media may communicate about workplace issues through these venues. Employers, seeking to protect their online reputation and lessen their risk of employment-related liability for, as an example, harassment (see Chapter 13), may have a "social media policy" prohibiting certain conduct on Facebook and similar sites. In 2011 and 2012, the NLRB issued three Advice Memos to help employers avoid violating employees' NLRA Section 7's right to communicate about their terms and conditions of employment through social media policies. If employees would reasonably read the policy to mean, for example, they are not allowed to discuss wages or ask each other about perceptions of unfair treatment, then the policy would likely violate the NLRA.[33] In its 2012 decision in *Costco Wholesale Corporation,* the NLRB found that Costco's social media policy violated the NLRA in prohibiting employees from electronically posting statements that would, for example, "defame the Company" or "damage any person's reputation." Employees may have interpreted this broad policy as preventing them from engaging in such concerted activity as discussing possible mistreatment of employees.[34] In a 2013 case, the NLRB found that a clothing store wrongfully terminated several employees for posting negative comments on Facebook relating to a dispute with the store manager about closing time, given concerns with the store's location.[35] However, derogatory comments about customers or disrespectful statements about customers may not be protected.[36]

Unfair Labor Practices by Unions

Section 8(b) lists activities constituting unfair labor practices by a labor organization. Some of these provisions mirror some of the activities prohibited to employers. Moreover, at least since the enactment of the Taft–Hartley Act, the law is not sympathetic to labor organizations that try to use certain coercive tactics, threats of the loss of livelihood, or any other strong-arm methods. Finally, Section 8(b) also regulates the union's collective bargaining practices, including economic action. Thus, a labor organization is not permitted to:

1. Restrain or coerce any employee in the exercise of his or her rights as granted by Section 7.
2. Cause or attempt to cause an employer to discriminate against an employee who has chosen not to join a particular labor organization or has been denied membership in such an organization.
3. Refuse to bargain collectively with an employer on behalf of the bargaining unit it is certified to represent.
4. Induce or attempt to induce an employer to engage in secondary boycott activities.
5. Require employees to become union members and then charge them excessive or discriminatory dues.
6. Try to make an employer compensate workers for services not performed.
7. Picket or threaten to picket an employer in an attempt to force the employer to recognize or bargain with a labor organization that is not the duly certified representative of a bargaining unit.

Representation Procedures

Section 9 of the NLRA specifies the election procedures by which employees may choose whether to be represented by a particular union or no union at all.

National Labor Relations Board (NLRB)

The NLRB is a federal administrative agency responsible for regulating labor–management relations. Its primary tasks are designating appropriate bargaining units of workers (deciding which workers have a sufficient community of interest so that their needs can best be acknowledged and so that collective bargaining is efficient for the employer and the union); conducting elections for union representation within the chosen bargaining unit; certifying the results of such elections; and investigating, prosecuting, and adjudicating charges of unfair labor practices.[37]

Although the congressional mandate by which the NLRB was formed gives the agency jurisdiction theoretically to the full extent of the interstate commerce powers vested in Congress, the agency has neither the funding nor the staff to administer its duties to all of American industry. Some smaller businesses, government employees, railroad, and airline workers covered by the Railway Labor Act, agricultural workers, domestic workers, independent contractors, and supervisors and other managerial employees are not protected by the board.[38]

Over the years, the five-member NLRB has been criticized for sometimes reaching decisions based on political/philosophical considerations rather than legal reasoning and Board precedent. As successive presidential administrations appoint NLRB members, the Board's decisions often "seesaw" according to the changes in Washington political power. [For more on the NLRB, see **www.nlrb.gov**]

Part Three—Elections

Choosing a Bargaining Representative

Representation elections are the process by which the NLRB achieves the first of the two statutory goals under the act—employee freedom of choice. That goal, however, is sometimes in conflict with the other statutory goal—stable collective bargaining. The NLRB has devised rules to resolve such conflicts. [For the AFL–CIO view of why workers should join unions, see **www.workingamerica.org/issues**]

Election Petition

A union, employee, or employer initiates the formal organizing process by filing an election petition with the NLRB. The petition is sent to the employer, thus providing notice of union activity. Also, the employer must post notices supplied by the NLRB so that employees are aware of the petition. The NLRB then assumes its authority to closely oversee the conduct of employer and union. Of course at that point, the employer is free to simply acknowledge its employees' interest in joining a particular union and to engage in bargaining with that union, a decision normally called *voluntary recognition.*

Sometimes an employer enters an agreement with a union specifying that the employer will voluntarily recognize the union if the union can demonstrate that it has majority support among the employees. Majority support is often established by a *card check* method where employees signify their interest in the union simply by signing authorization cards. The card check approach thus bypasses the secret ballot election and can greatly ease union organizing. One of the controversial NLRB decisions of 2007, however, overturned 40 years of precedent and made the card check method less useful for union organizing. In *Dana Corporation/Metaldyne,*[39] the NLRB ruled that where an employer voluntarily recognizes a union based on a card check majority, antiunion employees now have 45 days to petition the board for a federally supervised, secret ballot election to *decertify* the newly recognized union or to support a petition by a rival union. Under previous rulings, that election ordinarily would not have been permitted until at least 12 months had passed. The NLRB majority believed that elections are more accurate representations of employee preferences than the more open, and easily influenced, card check.

Failing voluntary recognition, the process proceeds according to NLRB rules. The NLRB will accept only those election petitions supported by a substantial showing of interest, which, at a minimum, must include the signatures of at least 30 percent of the employees in the bargaining unit. (In practice today, most unions will not proceed toward an election without 50 to 65 percent of the employees' signatures.) Those signatures accompany the petition, or they may appear on the authorization cards.

Procedure

Prior to an election, the NLRB ordinarily will first attempt to settle certain issues such as whether a union contract already covers the employees or whether the election should be delayed. In determining the timing of the election, the two statutory goals of employee free choice and stable collective-bargaining may conflict. For example, if the employees are already covered by a collective-bargaining agreement, should they be able to choose again during the term of the agreement? Similarly, if the employees have rejected a union in an election, can they be prohibited from voting again in the name of stable collective bargaining? Alternatively, what if the employees choose to unionize in an election, but reconsider before a collective-bargaining agreement is reached? Can they have another election?

The crucial issue to be addressed at this point, however, is normally whether the proposed bargaining unit (the designated employee group—for example, all hourly workers, all welders, or all craftspersons) is appropriate for the election.

Appropriate Bargaining Unit

The key consideration in establishing an appropriate employee bargaining unit is the community of interest among the employees. The NLRB searches for an appropriate bargaining unit because collective bargaining will not be stable and efficient if it involves employees with diverse interests. Therefore, the bargaining unit may range from a portion of a plant to multiple employers in multiple plants. Plants may have more than one appropriate bargaining unit, depending on the composition of the workforce. The NLRB makes the decision regarding the appropriate bargaining unit on the basis of such considerations as physical location of the plants; physical contact among employees; similarity of wages, benefits, and working conditions; differences in skill requirements among job categories; and common supervision.

Certain classes of employees, such as supervisors, are excluded from the bargaining unit. Obviously supervisors are excluded because they act on behalf of the employer and, through their power to direct and assign work and to discipline and discharge employees, exert control over their subordinates who are or may be in the bargaining unit. Often labor and management do not agree about the classification of workers as supervisors. In a 2006 decision outraging union activists, the NLRB substantially expanded the range of employees who might lawfully be considered supervisors (and thus ineligible for union membership) to include those assigned supervisory duties just 10 or 15 percent of the time.[40]

Independent contractors are not protected under the NLRA. In 2009, a federal appeals court set aside the NLRB's decision that FedEx had unlawfully failed to bargain with a union which had been certified to represent drivers at two FedEx home terminals. The appeals court concluded that the drivers were independent contractors who had been *misclassified* as employees by the NLRB.[41]

Solicitation

A 1992 Supreme Court decision in the *Lechmere* case[42] made union organizing much more difficult by ruling that employers do not have to allow on their property union organizers who are not employees. One of the results of that decision has been an increase in *salting,* the practice of union organizers applying for jobs with the intent of unionizing the other employees from the inside. The Supreme Court's 1995 *Town & Country* decision[43] held that salts are employees, thus affording them NLRA protection that forbids discrimination based on union affiliation, but a 2007 NLRB decision limited protection under the NLRA to those salts who are "genuinely interested" in obtaining employment.[44] Many employers saw the *Town & Country* decision as an unfair intrusion on their property rights and on their preference to remain union-free. The case that follows involves a Walmart employee's efforts to interest coworkers in joining a union.

LEGAL RIEFCASE

Wal-Mart Stores, Inc. v. National Labor Relations Board 400 F.3d 1093 (8th Cir. 2005)

Circuit Judge Melloy

Petitioner appeals the National Labor Relations Board's order finding that it violated the National Labor Relations Act by punishing employee Brian Shieldnight for union solicitation.

I

This case arises from efforts to unionize employees at the Wal-Mart store in Tahlequah, Oklahoma. The store, like all Wal-Mart stores, maintains and enforces a policy that prohibits solicitation during employees' work time, regardless of the cause or organization.

Brian Shieldnight, an employee of the Tahlequah Wal-Mart, contacted the United Food and Commercial Workers Union, Local 1000 ("Union") about possible union representation. He obtained authorization cards from the union to organize employees at the Tahlequah store.

On January 29, 2001, Shieldnight entered the store while off-duty. He wore a T-shirt that read "Union Teamsters" on the front and "Sign a card . . . Ask me how!" on the back. Assistant Store Manager John Lamont and Assistant Night Manager Tammy Flute saw Shieldnight's T-shirt and saw him speak to an associate. Flute told the associate to return to work, and Lamont ordered Shieldnight to leave associates alone. Lamont then consulted a Wal-Mart "union hotline." The hotline representative told Lamont that Shieldnight's shirt constituted solicitation and that Shieldnight should be removed from the store. Lamont and Flute sought out Shieldnight. They found him in the jewelry department talking to two friends who were not associates. Lamont informed

Shieldnight that his shirt constituted a form of solicitation and that he would have to leave the store immediately. Lamont escorted Shieldnight to the front door of the store and instructed him to leave the store and Wal-Mart property.

The next incident occurred on January 30, 2001. While on duty at the store, Shieldnight invited Department Manager Debra Starr and associates Patricia Scott and James Parsons, all of whom were also on duty, to a union meeting. Shieldnight asked Starr to come to the meeting and stated that he would like her to consider signing a union authorization card. Shieldnight separately asked Scott and Parsons to attend the meeting to hear "the other side of the story."

Based on these two incidents, Co-Manager Rick Hawkins and Assistant Manager John Lamont held a written "coaching session" with Shieldnight for violating the no-solicitation rule. A "coaching session" is part of Wal-Mart's progressive discipline process. Verbal coaching and written coaching are the first two steps in a four-step process. Hawkins and Lamont explained to Shieldnight that he had violated the solicitation policy on January 29 by soliciting on the sales floor with his T-shirt and on January 30 by verbally soliciting employees while on-duty and on the sales floor. Lamont told Shieldnight that it was wrong to have sent Shieldnight off Wal-Mart property completely. Lamont clarified that while Shieldnight could not solicit on the sales floor, he could do so in the parking lot while not on duty. Hawkins, Lamont, and Shieldnight also discussed Shieldnight's questions and concerns regarding Wal-Mart employment policies, such as health insurance for associates. Lamont suggested Shieldnight should raise the matter in "grassroots" meetings that all Wal-Mart stores hold to identify the top three companywide issues. The three men arranged a time to meet in the future. That meeting never occurred.

The union subsequently filed an unfair labor practice charge against Wal-Mart. . . .

[A] divided Board panel found that Shieldnight had not engaged in solicitation when he (1) wore the T-shirt during his shift; (2) asked on-duty employees to attend a union meeting; or (3) asked a coworker to sign a union card. . . . Wal-Mart appeals. . . .

II

* * * * *

A. The T-Shirt

The union contends that Shieldnight's T-shirt did not constitute solicitation, but rather was a "union insignia." Wal-Mart argues that by encouraging people to approach him, Shieldnight's T-shirt was a form of solicitation. In *NLRB v. W.W. Grainger, Inc.,* the board held,

> "Solicitation" for a union usually means asking someone to join the union by signing his name to an authorization card in the same way that solicitation for a charity would mean asking an employee to contribute to a charitable organization . . . or in the commercial context asking an employee to buy a product or exhibiting the product for him. . . .

Ordinarily, employees may wear union insignia while on their employer's premises. . . .

The board stated that the T-shirt should be treated as union insignia because "it did not 'speak' directly to any specific individual . . . and it did not call for an immediate response, as would an oral person-to-person invitation to accept or sign an authorization card." The board found that there was "no claim or evidence that Shieldnight did anything in furtherance of the T-shirt message. . . . He merely walked around and socialized. . . about nonunion matters." Anyone, including any Wal-Mart employee who saw Shieldnight was free to ignore both Shieldnight and the message on the T-shirt. In contrast, a solicitation to sign an authorization card requires more interaction, likely a direct yes or no answer. Absent further evidence of direct inquiry by Shieldnight, the board's conclusion was supported by substantial evidence.

Wal-Mart alleges that the panel's conclusion is not reasonable because it ignores both Shieldnight's purpose and the long-held rule that an employer may implement rules against solicitation during work time to prevent interference with work productivity.

* * * * *

Wal-Mart failed to demonstrate how the T-shirt interfered in any manner with the operation of the store. Accordingly, substantial evidence supports the board's conclusion that Shieldnight's T-shirt did not constitute solicitation.

B. The Coworker Conversations

* * * * *

Shieldnight invited three coworkers to a union meeting. . . . Shieldnight's statements did not require an immediate response from the three coworkers. Instead of a solicitation that required a response, the record shows that Shieldnight's statements were more akin to a statement of fact that put his coworkers on notice that there was to be a union meeting that night and that they were welcome to attend. Nothing in the record suggests that the environment at Wal-Mart made Shieldnight's actions uniquely disruptive. Accordingly, the panel's conclusion regarding Shieldnight's conversations was supported by substantial evidence. Furthermore, the panel acted reasonably when it concluded that "simply informing another employee of an upcoming meeting or asking a brief, union-related question does not occupy enough time to be treated as a work interruption in most settings."

C. Asking Coworker to Sign a Card

The board concluded that it was not solicitation when Shieldnight asked a coworker to sign a union authorization card. . . .

In light of the totality of the circumstances, Shieldnight's actions constituted solicitation even though he did not actually offer Starr a card at the time he asked her to sign. Shieldnight had contacted the union about obtaining union representation and had obtained cards from the union for the purpose of organizing employees at the Tahlequah store. There is little doubt as to Shieldnight's intent in the words he spoke to Starr. The record indicates that Shieldnight did not have a card in his hand at the time he spoke to Starr. It is silent as to whether he had a card on his person. The fact that he did not place a card directly in front of Starr at the time of his statement makes little difference in regard to the nature of his conversation. Further, Shieldnight's actions in this instance are more analogous to a direct solicitation than when he asked his coworkers to attend the union meeting. Asking someone to sign a union card offers that individual person the choice to be represented by a union. Informing coworkers about a union meeting merely puts fellow employees on notice that a meeting is going to take place.

Accordingly, there is insufficient evidence to support the board's conclusion that Shieldnight's actions were not solicitation, and thus we reverse the board regarding the authorization card issue.

* * * * *

Questions

1. Why was the T-shirt not a form of solicitation?
2. Why was Shieldnight's invitation to three coworkers to attend a union meeting not a form of solicitation, whereas asking a coworker to sign a card was considered impermissible solicitation?

The Election for Union Representation

The union may be selected only by a majority of the votes cast by the employees. The NLRB oversees the election to ensure the process is carried on under "laboratory conditions."[45] In other words, elections must be held under circumstances that, to the extent possible, are free from undue or unfair influence by either the employer or by unions vying for the right to represent the bargaining unit.

In 2011, the NLRB passed rules that would have compressed the time between a call for a vote and the election to determine union representation. In 2012, a federal court held that these were invalid, because less than three of the five NLRB members had voted on the rules.[46]

Employers have the right to speak out against unions in the form of ads, speeches, and the like. Section 8(c) of the Taft–Hartley Act is designed to ensure employers' and labor organizations' traditional First Amendment rights as long as they do not overstep certain bounds:

> The expressing of any views, argument, or opinion, or the dissemination thereof, whether in written, printed, graphic, or visual form, shall not constitute or be evidence of an unfair labor practice . . . if such expression contains no threat of reprisal or force or promise of benefit.

Gooseplay?

During a union organizing campaign, a goose wandered from a company pond into the work area where a worker "talked" to the goose and determined that it favored the union. Workers then put a "Vote Yes" card around the goose's neck and drove the goose around the plant on a forklift. The workers were fired for disrupting work and creating a safety hazard. The union claimed the company illegally fired the workers for engaging in union organizing. An administrative law judge agreed with the union, but the NLRB reversed, saying, "Placing a 'Vote Yes' sign on a wild animal does not transform otherwise unprotected 'gooseplay' into activity protected by the National Labor Relations Act."

Source: NACCO Materials Handling Group, Inc., 331 NLRB No. 164 (August 25, 2000).

Threats of Reprisal or Force

Employers cannot discriminate in employment to encourage or discourage union membership. Clearly, an employer who tells employees, for example, that they will all be discharged if they engage in union activity, has interfered with their rights. Similarly, an employer who interrogates employees about their activities or spies on them while they attend union meetings has engaged in unlawful interference. Problems often arise, however, in determining whether antiunion arguments by an employer are legitimate or whether they contain veiled threats. Suppose, for instance, that a company owner tells her employees that in a unionized workplace, they would have to go through the union representative to make their complaints, who would decide whether to bring these to the company's attention. The NLRB has determined that such a statement is not a threat, but rather an accurate reflection of the nature of unionized workplaces.[47]

Promise of Benefit

Although threats of force or reprisal are clearly unlawful in union campaigns, the rationale behind the prohibition against promises of benefit is not as intuitively obvious.

In a dispute that reached the U.S. Supreme Court, Exchange Parts sent its employees a letter shortly before a representation election that spoke of "the empty promises of the union" and "the fact that it is the company that puts things in your envelope." After mentioning a number of benefits, the letter said, "The union can't put any of those things in your envelope—only the company can do that." Further on, the letter stated, "It didn't take a union to get any of those things and . . . it won't take a union to get additional improvements in the future." Accompanying the letter was a detailed statement of the benefits granted by the company and an estimate of the monetary value of such benefits to the employees.

> The union can't put any of those things in your envelope.

In the representation election two weeks later, the union lost, but the outcome was challenged in court. Eventually the Supreme Court ruled that the employer's actions constituted an unfair labor practice reasoning that "well-timed increases in benefits" provide a clear message that those who provide advantages are the same people who can withdraw those benefits should their wishes not be followed.[48]

Buying Votes?

An Atlantic City, New Jersey, limousine service held a union election-day raffle for a TV/VCR. The NLRB ruled, 3–2, that the raffle was an unfair labor practice that might reasonably be interpreted to be a reward that would influence voting. A new election was ordered. The NLRB order banned election-day raffles, but minor "gifts" such as food, drinks, and buttons would be considered case-by-case if an objection were lodged.

Source: Atlantic Limousine, 331 NLRB No. 134 (2000).

The case that follows involves allegations that a company illegally interfered with union organizing activity.

Judge Ripple

This petition asks us to review whether Multi-Ad Services, Incorporated ("Multi-Ad") violated the National Labor Relations Act ("Act") by interfering with its employees' efforts to form a union. The National Labor Relations Board ("Board") concluded that Multi-Ad violated the Act. . . .

BACKGROUND

Multi-Ad employs 450 workers at its full-service advertising art production facility in Peoria, Illinois. Multi-Ad hired Steele in 1989 to work in the bindery department. Fifteen employees work in the department, which manufactures loose-leaf, three-ring binders. The bindery department is a small operation, accounting for a limited percentage of the company's sales and profits. Steele's performance evaluations were above average throughout his tenure at the company.

* * * * *

On July 29, 1996, Multi-Ad held a quarterly meeting for employees of the bindery, press, and finishing departments. After discussing the company's financial performance, plant production manager Jerry Ireland announced the company's plan to implement a new drug testing policy. Following this announcement, Steele spoke up and openly criticized the policy, contending in a loud and persistent manner that such testing violated employees' right to privacy. Other employees also voiced their displeasure with the policy. Steele and Larry Clore, Multi-Ad's president, then began to argue about the policy's legality. At the end of this exchange, Steele requested a copy of Multi-Ad's laws and bylaws. Clore told Steele that he could have these materials after the meeting.

Later that day, the quarterly meeting split into separate departmental meetings. The bindery department meeting commenced around 3:00 p.m., the normal quitting time for day-shift employees. At this meeting, Clore gave Steele a summary plan description of Multi-Ad's corporate structure. After Steele pointed out that he wanted the complete bylaws and not a summary, Clore responded, "Have your lawyer get them." Clore then told Steele that if he did not like the company's drug policy, "Why don't you think about leaving the company?" Steele responded that he would not give Clore the pleasure of quitting. After Clore departed, Ireland tried to continue with the meeting, but Steele announced that he was leaving because "he was on his own time now." Steele testified that Ireland said, "Okay." Ireland, however, testified that Steele's remark had shocked him and that he had said nothing in

response. Ireland also testified that he had apologized to the group for Steele's behavior. Steele, however, was not ordered to remain for the rest of the meeting, which ended shortly after his exit.

Two days later, Steele and Ireland met at Steele's request. Steele apologized for his conduct at the department meeting and then told Ireland that hourly shop workers were dissatisfied with company policies. Steele told Ireland that "management needed to just sit down with the hourly employees and work some things out." Ireland replied, "That could not be done." Steele then told Ireland that, if they could not sit down and discuss these problems, he would organize a union. Ireland asked Steele to wait until Ireland returned from his vacation to discuss the issue further. Steele agreed and made no effort to contact a union while Ireland was away.

On August 16, 1996, Steele met with Ireland and bindery department manager Marty Heathcoat in Heathcoat's office. During this meeting, the two managers asked Steele why he would want to bring a union into the company. Steele told them that it would be nice to have seniority rights, better working conditions, and raises when possible. Ireland then asked what Steele could do to improve Steele's own situation at the company and pointed out that Multi-Ad posted job openings. After Steele expressed interest in a maintenance position, Ireland told him that he would set up an interview, even though the company did not have an opening for a maintenance position. At the end of the meeting, Ireland asked Steele "what it would take to satisfy him." Steele replied that it would satisfy him if management "would sit down with the hourly employees and work something out." After Ireland responded that he could not do that, Steele informed the two managers that he was leaving the meeting and was going to attempt to organize a union. Ireland asked Steele to come back and talk some more, but Steele responded that there was nothing left to talk about. Steele left at 3:30 p.m., 30 minutes after his shift had ended. No one told Steele to stay, nor was he reprimanded for having left the meeting. The next day, Steele interviewed for a maintenance position, but the interview revealed that he lacked the necessary qualifications. In any event, Steele said that he did not want the job.

Steele twice met with union officials in late August. During this time, employees began to talk about Steele's efforts at organizing a union. At a meeting of bindery department employees in late August, Heathcoat addressed rumors about a union and asked employees why they wanted a union. In response, Steele stated that everyone knew that Heathcoat was referring to Steele's desire to look into unionization. Ted DeRossett, Steele's supervisor, then warned that the bindery department would be the "first to go" if the company unionized. Steele immediately challenged the legality of closing the bindery department in such a fashion. After Steele and DeRossett began to argue heatedly, Heathcoat ended the meeting.

At another bindery department meeting in late August, management informed employees that they would be working mandatory 10-hour shifts. Steele protested that it was unfair to require employees to work overtime when in the past they had been able to decline overtime. Steele also stated that it was decisions like this that caused him to explore bringing in a union.

Shortly after the meeting, Multi-Ad announced that it was adding a second shift in the bindery department and that Steele would be the lead man. On August 29, 1996, Heathcoat and DeRossett asked Steele if he would work the second shift with a positive attitude. The two assured Steele that he could still take his scheduled vacation days from August 30 through September 3. Steele told them that he would go to the second shift, do the job, and represent the company as was expected of him.

The next day, while Steele was on vacation, Multi-Ad received a letter from Steele requesting copies of the company's policies and bylaws. When Steele returned from his vacation on September 4, Heathcoat and DeRossett were waiting for him at the plant's garage door. The two asked Steele if he still wanted to see the materials that he had requested in the letter. Steele said yes, and the two told him that he could pick up the materials in the office of Bruce Taylor, Multi-Ad's vice president of finance. Steele punched the time clock and, as he started to walk toward Taylor's office, noticed DeRossett and Heathcoat accompanying him. Steele told them that he did not need them to pick up the papers. The two replied that they were tagging along in case he had any questions. Steele told them that he could not possibly have any questions because he had not yet read the materials. Nevertheless, both managers followed Steele into Taylor's office. Ireland entered the office shortly thereafter. Steele first asked Taylor for the documents. Taylor replied that Steele already had been given the summary statement at the quarterly meeting. Steele responded that he was not asking for a summary but for complete documents. After again requesting the documents and receiving no response, Steele announced that he would no longer participate in the meeting and walked out. Heathcoat ordered him to remain or be fired. Steele ignored this command and walked back to the plant, pursued by Heathcoat and Ireland. Heathcoat repeated his order that Steele return to the office or be fired. Steele, again, refused.

Ireland then told Steele that "this is the third meeting you have walked out of, you are gone." Steele immediately demanded a termination letter.

Even though Ireland had made the decision to fire Steele, Heathcoat prepared the letter. The letter spells out the purported reasons for Steele's termination:

> He [Steele] said that he didn't come for a meeting, [sic] and then walked out of the room. I told him to get back in Bruce's [Taylor's] office to discuss this with us. He repeated himself again saying that he didn't want a meeting. Jerry Ireland then Fired [sic] him.
>
> Ted Steele has walked out of three meetings within a month because he didn't feel like hearing what was being said to him. He has said that he does not agree with corporate policies set for all the employees of Multi[-]Ad. He has interrupted the work flow of the Bindery Department by persuading it's [sic] employees that this is not a good place to work. Ted will never see eye to eye with Multi[-]Ad's policies and goals for it's [sic] employees and will not even conduct himself in a professional manner when talking to management about his concerns. Ted is terminated on 9-4-96 because of his unwillingness to abide to [sic] corporate policies.

Ireland testified that he fired Steele because he was totally disrespectful to management. Ireland also testified that Steele's exit from the meeting on September 4 was an act of insubordination, particularly after he ignored Heathcoat's order to return.

THE ADMINISTRATIVE PROCEEDINGS

On September 26, 1996, Graphic Communications Union, Local 68C, and Graphic Communications International Union, AFL–CIO, filed an unfair labor charge against Multi-Ad on behalf of its employees, including Steele. Soon thereafter, the Board's General Counsel issued a complaint and a notice of hearing. The complaint alleged that Multi-Ad violated the Act by (1) coercively interrogating Steele about his interest in forming a union during the August 16 meeting with Heathcoat and Ireland; (2) impliedly promising at the August 16 meeting to help Steele improve his employment situation without the need for representation; and (3) threatening to close the bindery department if its employees unionized. The complaint also alleges that Multi-Ad violated the Act by discharging Steele because it believed that he might contact a union to organize employees.

On May 29, 1997, the Administrative Law Judge (ALJ) conducted a hearing on the board's complaint. Based on the evidence presented at the hearing, the ALJ issued his decision on December 2, 1997, and found that Multi-Ad had committed the charged unfair labor practices. On August 25,

2000, the board issued a decision and order affirming the ALJ's conclusions.

On October 10, 2000, Multi-Ad filed this petition for review.

Substantial Evidence

Multi-Ad first challenges the Board's determination that Multi-Ad coercively interrogated Steele on August 16 in violation of the Act.

* * * * *

Substantial evidence supports the Board's conclusion that management coercively interrogated Steele on August 16. The closed-door meeting was conducted in a manager's office by Heathcoat and Ireland, two people who had authority to fire Steele. The two managers questioned Steele regarding why he would want to bring a union into the company. . . . Moreover, Ireland immediately thereafter asked Steele about his own career advancement and arranged an interview for a maintenance position, even though no such opening existed. The managers did not assure Steele that reprisals would not be taken against him for his answers, adding to the potentially coercive nature of the inquiry. Further, this meeting was conducted after company managers had expressed uneasiness over union activity. These circumstances are more than enough evidence to sustain the Board's findings.

Multi-Ad next challenges the Board's finding that it made an implied promise of benefits by asking Steele how he could help his own situation and by arranging the job interview. . . . Here, Ireland asked Steele why he wanted to form a union and then asked Steele how Steele could improve his own situation. Steele expressed an interest in a maintenance position, and Ireland arranged for an interview immediately, even though there were no such openings. The context in which this occurred is significant. Because the managers made this overture during a conversation about the need for a union, the Board reasonably could have concluded that the company was willing to confer a benefit to deter Steele from contacting a union. . . .

Next, Multi-Ad argues that substantial evidence does not support the Board's conclusion that Multi-Ad threatened to close the bindery department. Unlike an interrogation, which is coercive only if reasonable employees would perceive it as such, a threat of plant closure is per se a violation of Section 8(a)(1). In this case, three employees testified unequivocally that DeRossett said that the bindery department would be the "first to go" if they brought in a union, and this evidence is more than sufficient to establish a violation.

Finally, Multi-Ad disputes the Board's conclusion that Steele's discharge violates Sections 8(a)(1) and (3). An employer violates Sections 8(a)(1) or (3) of the Act by firing employees because of their union activities. To prove a violation, the Board must prove that antiunion animus was a substantial or motivating factor in the employer's decision to make the adverse employment decision. If the Board proves such a motivation by a preponderance of the evidence, the employer can avoid a finding of an unfair labor practice by showing that it would have taken the action regardless of the employee's union activities.

[S]ubstantial evidence supports a finding that the company harbored animus, including (1) the timing of Steele's firing, which coincided with his increased efforts to organize a union; (2) the coercive interrogation of Steele regarding his interest in forming a union; (3) management's questioning of other employees about their interest in forming a union; and (4) DeRossett's warning that the bindery department would close if employees unionized. Thus, the Board met its burden of establishing antiunion animus.

Multi-Ad claims as an affirmative defense that it fired Steele for leaving three meetings without permission. The Board concluded, however, that Multi-Ad's proffered reason was pretextual and that the company fired Steele because of his efforts to unionize. That conclusion is supported by substantial evidence, including (1) Multi-Ad's written explanation of termination stating a different reason—that he was discharged because he refused to abide by corporate policies; (2) the September 4 encounter was not a "meeting"— Steele entered the office to pick up materials to which he was legally entitled and twice denied access; and (3) no manager instructed Steele to remain at the previous two meetings, both of which occurred after shift hours. . . .

Order enforced.

Questions

1. *a.* List the four unfair labor practices identified by the court.
   b. What test did the court employ in determining whether the employer coercively interrogated Steele?
   c. What evidence supported the court's conclusion that Steele's firing was motivated by antiunion animus?
   d. Why did the court conclude that the employer's stated reason for dismissing Steele was pretextual?

2. Jose Ybarra was a labor consultant for Met West. A union election was pending at the company. An employee allegedly told Ybarra that his promised raise had not been delivered. Ybarra later allegedly told the employee that management had decided that wages could not be adjusted with an election pending. The union lost the election and filed suit claiming that Ybarra's statement was an

unfair labor practice. Decide. Explain. See *Met West Agri-business, Inc.,* 334 NLRB No. 14 (May 23, 2001).

3. During an election campaign, the general manager's office was used to interview employees in small groups of five or six. The employees had previously visited that office to discuss grievances and obtain loans. That office was the only space available for the conversations. The general manager's remarks were temperate and noncoercive. The union lost the election. Should that result be set aside for unlawful campaigning? Explain. See *NVF Company, Hartwell Division,* 210 NLRB 663 (1974).

Union Persuasion

Unions, like employers, are restricted in the type of preelection persuasion they employ. In cases involving promises of benefits made by the union, the NLRB has been more reluctant to set aside elections than it has when such promises have been made by management. The Board's reasoning is that employees realize that union preelection promises are merely expressions of a union platform, so to speak. Employees recognize that these are benefits for which the union intends to fight. Employers, on the other hand, really do hold the power to confer or withdraw benefits. Nonetheless, a union promise to employees to provide "the biggest party in the history of Texas" if the union won the next day's election was an unfair labor practice.[49]

> "The biggest party in the history of Texas."

Remedies for Election Misconduct

Unfair labor practices during a representation election can result in the imposition of penalties and remedies. If the union loses the election and the employer engaged in wrongful behavior, a new election or other remedies may be ordered.

Decertification

After a union has been certified or recognized, an employee or group of employees may continue to resist the union or may lose confidence in it. If so, they can file a decertification petition with the NLRB. The employees must be able to demonstrate at least 30 percent support for their petition. Once a decertification petition is properly filed with the board the usual election rules are followed to determine whether the union enjoys continuing majority support. If not, the union is decertified, and ordinarily at least one year must pass before a new representation election can be conducted. [For management advice about decertification, see **www.nrtw.org/d/decert.htm**]

Withdrawal of Recognition

An employer may unilaterally withdraw recognition of a union that has lost the support of a majority of its members. Objective evidence such as a petition signed by a majority of unit employer is required. The NLRB will review the petition and its specific language, however, to make sure that it shows employees' desire to decline union representation. For example, a petition entitled: "showing of interest for decertification" was found to be insufficient evidence, while a petition's statement of "wish for a vote to remove the Union" is more likely to show whether employees no longer desire the union's representation.[50]

Escape the Union?

If a union clearly is about to win a representation election or already has done so, thus establishing its right to collective bargaining, management sometimes continues to resist. One strategy is to declare bankruptcy. That tactic may be lawful but only after bargaining sincerely with the union and only after convincing the bankruptcy court that fairness requires modification or rejection of the collective-bargaining agreement. Similarly, a company may simply choose to shut down its business rather than engage in collective bargaining. Going out of business is fully lawful unless the reason for doing so was to

> Companies sometimes employ the *runaway shop* strategy.

discourage union efforts at plants in other locations. Likewise, companies sometimes employ the *runaway shop* strategy in which the about-to-be-unionized plant is simply shut down and replaced by another in a location less responsive to union interests. If that move was made for the purpose of thwarting union interests, it is an unfair labor practice, but if the move reflected legitimate economic goals such as reduced wages or taxes, the move is probably lawful.

The Union as Exclusive Bargaining Agent

Once a union has been elected and certified as the representative of a bargaining unit, it becomes the exclusive agent for all of the employees within that bargaining unit, whether they voted for the union or not. The exclusivity of the union's authority has a number of implications, but one is particularly relevant in determining whether an employer has failed to demonstrate good faith at the bargaining table. Specifically, the employer must deal with the certified representative who acts on behalf of all employees in the bargaining unit. The employer commits an unfair labor practice if she or he attempts to deal directly with the employees or recognizes someone other than the workers' chosen representative. In both instances, the issue is fairly straightforward. The employer is undermining the position of the representative by ignoring him or her.

Part Four—Collective Bargaining

Section 8(a)(5) of the NLRA requires an employer to engage in *good-faith* collective bargaining with a representative of the employees, and Section 8(b)(3) imposes the same duty on labor organizations. Failure to bargain by either an employer or representative of the employees constitutes an unfair labor practice.

What is collective bargaining? What must one do to discharge the duty imposed? According to Section 8(d) of the NRLA,

> To bargain collectively is the performance of the mutual obligation of the employer and the representatives of the employees to meet at reasonable times and confer in good faith with respect to wages, hours, and other terms and conditions of employment . . . but such obligation does not compel either party to agree to a proposal or require the making of a concession.

Note what is *not* included: The parties are not required to reach an agreement. Thus, the NLRA governs only the process, not the result, of collective bargaining.

Bargaining in Good Faith

The duty to bargain in *good faith* obligates the union and employer to participate actively in the deliberations, showing a sincere and honest effort to reach common ground. Whether a party is bargaining in good faith is determined by the totality of the circumstances. Some of the objective criteria used by the NLRB in reviewing complaints asserting that this duty has been violated include whether the party is willing to meet at reasonable times and intervals, and whether the party is represented by someone who has the authority to make decisions at the table.[51]

Mandatory Bargaining Subjects   Although employers and labor representatives are free to discuss whatever lawful subjects they mutually choose, Section 8(d) of the NLRA clearly sets out some mandatory subjects over which the parties must bargain. These are wages, hours, and "other terms and conditions of employment." Although these topics for mandatory bargaining seem simple enough, questions still arise frequently. For example, suppose the union and employer bargain over wages and agree to institute merit increases for employees. Must the employer also bargain over which employees are entitled to receive these increases or who will make the decision at the time they are to be given? What about a decision to close a plant?

Generally, the board and the courts will balance three factors. First, they look at the effect of a particular decision on the workers—how direct is it and to what extent is the effect felt? Second, they consider the degree to which bargaining would constitute an intrusion into entrepreneurial interest or, from the opposite side, an intrusion into union affairs. Third, they examine the practice historically in the industry or the company itself.[52]

Permissive and Prohibited Bargaining Subjects   Those matters not directly related to wages, hours, and terms and conditions of employment and not falling within the category of prohibited subjects are considered permissive. Either party may raise permissive subjects during the bargaining process, but neither may pursue them to the point of a bargaining impasse. Refusal to bargain over a permissive subject does not constitute an NLRA violation, and permissive subjects must simply be dropped if the parties do not reach agreement.

> Whether a union has a right to bargain over management's placement of hidden surveillance cameras in the workplace.

Permissive subjects ordinarily would include such items as alteration of a defined bargaining unit, internal union affairs, and strike settlement agreements. Prohibited bargaining subjects are those that are illegal under the NLRA or other laws. In the case that follows the NLRB had to decide whether a union has a right to bargain over management's placement of hidden surveillance cameras in the workplace.

FACTS

Colgate–Palmolive's Jeffersonville, Indiana, plant employed approximately 750 workers. Colgate and the employees had a collective bargaining arrangement for over 20 years. In 1994 an employee discovered a surveillance camera in a restroom air vent. The union president later discussed the matter with Colgate's human resources officer, who indicated that the camera had been placed in the vent because of theft concerns and that the camera had been removed after employees objected to it. The Union filed a grievance over the matter, and the parties met for discussion where Colgate argued that it had the absolute right to install internal surveillance cameras. Later, the Union sent a letter to Colgate demanding to bargain over the subject of cameras within the plant. Colgate did not respond, and the Union filed an unfair labor practice charge. The case was heard by an administrative law judge. Evidence indicated that Colgate had installed 11 secret cameras over four years to address problems of theft and misconduct, including sleeping on the job. The cameras were placed in several offices, a fitness center, a restroom, and as a monitor for an overhead door that was not a proper exit from the building. The Union and some employees were aware of various "unhidden" cameras in the workplace and in some instances fortuitously discovered some of the hidden cameras.

The Administrative Law Judge (ALJ) concluded that the use of hidden surveillance cameras is a mandatory subject of bargaining and by failing to do so, Colgate–Palmolive violated the National Labor Relations Act. The ALJ's ruling was then appealed to the National Labor Relations Board. The *NLRB* decision follows.

CHAIRMAN GOULD AND MEMBERS FOX AND HIGGINS

In *Ford Motor Co. v. NLRB,* the Supreme Court described mandatory subjects of bargaining as such matters that are "plainly germane to the 'working environment'" and "not among those 'managerial decisions, which lie at the core of entrepreneurial control.'" As the judge found, the installation of surveillance cameras is both germane to the working environment, and outside the scope of managerial decisions lying at the core of entrepreneurial control.

As to the first factor—germane to the working environment—the installation of surveillance cameras is analogous to physical examinations, drug/alcohol testing requirements, and polygraph testing, all of which the Board has found to be mandatory subjects of bargaining. They are all investigatory tools or methods used by an employer to ascertain whether any of its employees has engaged in misconduct.

The Respondent [Colgate–Palmolive] acknowledges that employees caught involved in theft and/or other misconduct are subject to discipline, including discharge. Accordingly, the installation and use of surveillance cameras has the potential to affect the continued employment of employees whose actions are being monitored.

Further, as the judge finds, the use of surveillance cameras in the restroom and fitness center raises privacy concerns which add to the potential effect upon employees. We agree that these areas are part of the work environment and that the use of hidden cameras in these areas raises privacy concerns which impinged upon the employees' working conditions. The use of cameras in these or similar circumstances is unquestionably germane to the working environment.

With regard to the second criterion, we agree with the judge that the decision is not a managerial decision that lies at the core of entrepreneurial control.

* * * * *

The use of surveillance cameras is not entrepreneurial in character, is not fundamental to the basic direction of the enterprise, and impinges directly upon employment security. It is a change in the Respondent's methods used to reduce workplace theft or detect other suspected employee misconduct with serious implications for its employees' job security, which in no way touches on the discretionary "core of entrepreneurial control."

The Respondent urges that bargaining before a hidden camera is actually installed would defeat the very purpose of the camera. The very existence of secret cameras, however, is a term and condition of employment, and is thus a legitimate concern for the employees' bargaining representative. Thus, the placing of cameras, and the extent to which they will be secret or hidden, if at all, is a proper subject of negotiations between the Respondent and the union. Concededly, the Respondent also has a legitimate concern. However, bargaining about hidden cameras can embrace a host of matters other than mere location. And, even as to location, mutual accommodations can and should be negotiated. The vice in the instant case was the respondent's refusal to bargain.

* * * * *

Accordingly, we affirm the judge's finding that the union has the statutory right to engage in collective bargaining over the installation and continued use of surveillance cameras, including the circumstances under which the cameras will be activated, the general areas in which they may be placed, and how affected employees will be disciplined if improper conduct is observed.

ORDER

The National Labor Relations Board adopts the recommended Order of the administrative law judge as modified and set forth in full below and orders that the Respondent, its officers, agents, successors, and assigns, shall

1. Cease and desist from

    a. Failing and refusing to bargain with Local 15, International Chemical Workers Union, AFL–CIO with respect to the installation and use of surveillance cameras and other mandatory subjects of bargaining.

2. Take the following affirmative action necessary to effectuate the policies of the Act.

    a. On request, bargain collectively with the Union as the exclusive bargaining representative of the Respondent's employees with respect to the installation and use of surveillance cameras and other mandatory subjects of bargaining.

    b. Within 14 days after the service by the Region, post at its facility in Jeffersonville, Indiana, copies of the attached notice:

Notice to Employees
Posted by Order of the
National Labor Relations Board
An Agency of the United States Government

The National Labor Relations Board has found that we violated the National Labor Relations Act and has ordered us to post and abide by this notice. Section 7 of the Act gives employees these rights.

To organize
To form, join, or assist any union
To bargain collectively through representatives of their own choice
To act together for other mutual aid or protection

To choose not to engage in any of these protected concerted activities.

We will not fail and refuse to bargain with Local 15, International Chemical Workers Union, AFL–CIO over the installation and use of surveillance cameras within our facility and other mandatory subjects of bargaining.

We will not in any like or related manner interfere with, restrain, or coerce you in the exercise of the rights guaranteed you by Section 7 of the Act.

We will, on request, bargain collectively with the Union as the exclusive bargaining representative of our employees with respect to the installation and use of surveillance cameras within our facility and other mandatory subjects of bargaining.

Colgate–Palmolive Company.

Questions

1. What test did the ALJ and the NLRB employ to determine whether the placement of hidden surveillance cameras was a mandatory subject of bargaining?

2. Why did the union win this case?

3. If you were managing a workplace where theft, sleeping on the job, and other misconduct were at a worrisome level, would you employ hidden, secret cameras to monitor restrooms, fitness areas, and the like? Explain.

4. At an Anheuser-Busch brewing facility, a supervisor discovered a table, four chairs, a number of foam mattress pads, and cardboard in a room where only authorized personnel were to be, but which was next to a break area. Suspecting illicit activities including illegal drug use, the company installed two surveillance cameras pointed at the entrance and stairs leading to the room. The cameras led to the company identifying 16 employees who engaged in misconduct. The company took down the cameras on June 30, 1998, and then informed the union of their existence. The company fired and otherwise disciplined the employees in question. Did Anheuser-Busch violate the NLRA? Explain. *Brewers & Maltsters v. NLRB,* 414 F.3d (D.C. Circuit 2005).

Administering the Agreement

Union–management bargaining does not end with the negotiation of a labor agreement. Rather, bargaining continues daily as the parties work out the disputes and confusions and conflicting interpretations that are bound to arise and that cannot be entirely provided for in the labor agreement. Often this process of contract maintenance takes the form of resolving *grievances,* as in the *Colgate–Palmolive* case. Those problems are addressed through the grievance procedure that is included in collective-bargaining agreements. Often the grievance procedure involves a series of steps beginning with informal discussion mechanisms. Failing there, the dissatisfied employee typically files a written complaint (the grievance). Normally, grievances are presented to management by a union representative, often with the worker also present.

Arbitration

If, after negotiation, the parties cannot resolve their dispute, the collective-bargaining agreement ordinarily provides for *final and binding arbitration.* Many court decisions have vigorously supported the arbitration process as the means of settling labor–management contract maintenance disputes and tend to find disputes arbitrable unless the labor agreement explicitly and unambiguously exempts the subject at issue from the arbitration process. Furthermore, but for rare exceptions, neither the company nor the union can turn to the courts to set aside arbitration decisions. However, in 2010 the U.S. Supreme Court held that a dispute between a union and employer over the ratification date of a collective-bargaining agreement containing an arbitration clause should be resolved by a court rather than an arbitrator.[53]

Fair Representation

Because grievance processing is part of a union's bargaining responsibility, the union might breach its duty if it declined to represent an employer's grievance. An employee who feels wronged when a union does not process his or her grievance has the option of appealing to the NLRB or to the courts. Nevertheless, as the U.S. Supreme Court ruled in *14 Penn Plaza LLC v. Pyett,* a union may collectively bargain for an agreement providing that individual members' employment discrimination claims must be submitted to arbitration.[54]

Part Five—Labor Conflict

PRACTICING ETHICS) Union Loyalty, Employee Loyalty, or Money?

The Writers Guild of America, the union for show business writers, struck the television and movie industries in 2007 to 2008 pushing for a bigger share of revenues, particularly revenues from movies and television shows distributed over the new media, such as the Internet. The late-night talk shows then featuring David Letterman, Jay Leno, Conan O'Brien, Jimmy Kimmel, and others respected the union for weeks by confining their telecasts to reruns. After six weeks, Letterman's production company, Worldwide Pants, was able to reach its own agreement with the striking union, thus allowing Letterman to return to the air with his full staff, including writers. The other talk shows decided to return to the air without their writers, although their network and studio owners had not reached agreements with the Writers' Guild. Many stars, however, declined to appear as talk show guests since they would have been forced to cross the striking writers' picket lines (explained below) to appear on the shows.

Leno and others argued that they needed to return to the air even without a strike settlement because they wanted to avoid laying off their many staff members who would have been without work if the shows stayed off the air. Indeed, some of those shows and hosts had paid their staffs while not working during the rerun period, but that financial burden reportedly could not be sustained. O'Brien, a strong union supporter, said he had to decide whether to "go back to work and keep my staff employed or stay dark and allow 80 people, many of whom have worked for me for 14 years, to lose their jobs."[55]

The 100-day strike was settled in February 2008.

Questions

1. Was it wrong of Leno, Kimmel, and the others to return to the air rather than continuing to honor the writers' strike? Explain.

2. Assume you are a Jimmy Kimmel fan, and you received tickets to the show during the strike. Would you support the writers by refusing to attend the Kimmel show? Explain.

Strikes

For many, the initial image of labor conflict is one of employees on strike, picketing a store or factory. Striking is, however, an extremely drastic measure under which employees must bear an immediate loss of wages and, in many instances, risk job loss. Similarly, employers bear the loss of a disruption to continued operations. Work stoppages have declined dramatically since World War II. However, the six-day sit-in of 240 workers at Chicago's Republic Windows and Doors in 2008—sparked by management's announcement that the plant would be closing in three days—became a national symbol of workers' frustration at the wave of layoffs around the United States. The sit-in succeeded in gaining bank loans for the company to meet the workers' demands for 60 days' severance pay and earned vacation time under the WARN Act (see Chapter 12).[56]

> The six-day sit-in became a national symbol of workers' frustration.

On the other hand, a strike's potential toll was seen in the 2012 strike at the Caterpillar factory in Joliet, Illinois, which lasted over three months. After workers rejected the company's demand for a six-year wage freeze for most of the factory's workers, at a time when the company was reporting record profits, more than 700 union members went on strike. Caterpillar had argued that wages for the higher-paid workers at the plant exceeded market levels. Faced with continuing a grueling strike, the workers ratified a deal with Caterpillar that included the wage freeze.[57]

We will examine two kinds of strikes:

1. *Unfair labor practice strikes* are those instituted by workers in response to the employer's commission of an unfair labor practice such as interfering with legitimate union activities or failure to bargain in good faith. These strikers can be temporarily, but not permanently, replaced.

2. *Economic strikes* are those used purely as economic weapons to persuade employers to provide more favorable benefits or better working conditions. All strikes not involving unfair labor practices fall into this category. With some exceptions, economic strikers cannot be fired, but they can be permanently replaced. In what has been labeled "the most significant change in collective bargaining to occur since the passage of the Wagner Act in 1934," employers are now increasingly willing to permanently replace economic strikers.[58] Employers had enjoyed that right where necessary "in an effort to carry on the business" since a 1938 Supreme Court decision, but for practical reasons they had rarely exercised it.[59] Later decisions imposed some limitations on that right. For example, any striker who is permanently replaced is put on a preferential hiring list and will have priority to be selected to fill subsequent vacancies. However, President Reagan's 1981 dismissal of 11,300 striking air traffic controllers effectively crushed their union (PATCO) and caused private-sector employers to reassess their long-standing reluctance to use replacements during and after strikes.[60] Thus, the use or threat to use permanent replacements has become a powerful tool for employers facing economic strikes.

The following case examines when employers can legitimately decline to reinstate strikers.

LEGAL BRIEFCASE

Diamond Walnut Growers, Inc. v. NLRB   113 F.3d 1259 (D.C. Cir. 1997); cert. den. 118 S.Ct.1299 (1998)

Circuit Judge Silberman

I

Diamond Walnut processes and packages walnuts for national and international distribution. . . . Diamond's employees have for years been represented by Cannery Workers, Processors, Warehousemen, and Helpers Local 601 of the International Brotherhood of Teamsters, AFL–CIO (the union). In September of 1991, following expiration of the most recent collective-bargaining agreement between Diamond and the union, nearly 500 of Diamond's permanent and seasonal employees went on strike. Diamond hired replacement workers to allow it to continue operations.

By all accounts, the strike was, and remains, a bitter affair. The strikers are alleged to have engaged in various acts of violence against the replacement workers. . . . In addition, as part of its effort to exert economic pressure on Diamond, the union undertook an international boycott of its product. The

boycott included a well-publicized national bus tour during which union members distributed to the public leaflets which described Diamond's workforce as composed of "scabs" who packaged walnuts contaminated with "mold, dirt, oil, worms, and debris."

Approximately one year into the strike, the Board held a representation election. The union lost the election, but its objections prompted the Board to order a rerun to be held in October of 1993. Just over two weeks prior to the new election, a group of four striking employees, represented by a union official, approached Diamond with an unconditional offer to return to work. According to the letter presented to the company at that time by their representative, the employees were convinced that "a fair election [was] simply impossible." Nonetheless, the employees "fe[lt] that it [was] important that the replacement workers . . . have an opportunity to hear from Union sympathizers." Thus, the group of strikers was "available and willing to return to immediate active employment." The following day, the union notified Diamond that pursuant to the above-quoted letter, two additional strikers were willing to return to work.

It is undisputed that for three of the returning strikers, neither the permanent jobs they held before the strike, nor substantially equivalent ones, were available at the time of their return. Diamond placed these three in various seasonal jobs. Prior to the strike, Willa Miller was a quality control supervisor; she was placed in a seasonal packing position even though a seasonal inspection job was available. Alfonsina Munoz had been employed as a lift truck operator and, despite the availability of a seasonal forklift job, was given a seasonal job cracking and inspecting nuts in the growers' inspection department at the front end of the production process. Mohammed Kussair, formerly an air separator machine operator, was, like Munoz, placed in a seasonal cracking and inspecting position in the growers' inspection department. . . .

The rerun election took place as scheduled, and the union lost. Following that election, the General Counsel filed a complaint alleging that Diamond had violated the National Labor Relations Act by unlawfully discriminating against Miller, Munoz, and Kussair. The General Counsel alleged that because of their protected activity, Diamond declined to put them in certain available seasonal positions for which they were qualified and that were preferable to the positions in which they were actually placed. After a hearing, an administrative law judge recommended that the charges be dismissed. He found that Diamond had "discriminated" insofar as it had placed the employees at least in part because of their protected activity, but he did not think that discrimination "unlawful."

* * * * *

[The NLRB reversed saying] "although [Diamond] was under no legal obligation . . . to reinstate the strikers . . ., once it voluntarily decided to reinstate them, it was required to act in a nondiscriminatory fashion toward the strikers." Diamond had discriminated against Miller, Munoz, and Kussair, in the Board's view, by declining "to place them in the [seasonal] positions of quality control assistant, lift truck operator, and loader, respectively, because of their union status and/or because of certain protected union activity they engaged in while on strike.". . . The Board rejected the contention that the placements were warranted by the employer's concern that the replacement workers might instigate violence against the three and thus justified placement in well-supervised jobs, since "there [was] no evidence that Miller, Munoz, or Kussair were involved" in the strike-related violence allegedly causing Diamond's concern. The Board also dismissed the notion that the placements of Miller and Munoz were justified by their participation in the boycott and the circulation of disparaging

leaflets: "[T]he strikers' conduct constituted protected . . . activity and there is no evidence indicating that such protection was lost because of threats made by Miller and Munoz to damage or sabotage [Diamond's] equipment or products." Since Diamond had failed to justify its discrimination, the Board found unfair labor practices.

* * * * *

[Diamond sought judicial review of the NLRB ruling.]

II

Diamond Walnut challenges the Board's determination that it lacked substantial business justification for refusing to place the three employees in the specific jobs they sought—quality control assistant, lift truck operator, and loader. It is undisputed that the *Fleetwood* framework governs this case. The General Counsel under *Fleetwood* must make out a *prima facie* case that the employer discriminated within the meaning of the Act, which means the employer's decision as to how to treat the three returning strikers was attributable to their protected activity. *Rose Printing* establishes that a struck employer faced with an unconditional offer to return to work is obliged to treat the returning employee like any other applicant for work (unless the employee's former job or its substantial equivalent is available, in which case the employee is preferred to any other applicant). But Miller and Munoz were not treated like any other applicant for work. Miller was qualified for a seasonal position in quality control that paid 32 cents per hour more than the packing job to which she was assigned. And Munoz was qualified to fill a forklift operating job, a position that paid between $2.75 and $5.00 per hour more than the walnut cracking and inspecting job she received. Diamond admits that it took into account Miller's and Munoz's protected activity in choosing to place them in jobs that were objectively less desirable than those for which they were qualified. Petitioner [Diamond], although it contended that the discrimination was comparatively slight, does not dispute that its action discriminated against Munoz and Miller within the meaning of the Act.

* * * * *

Under *Fleetwood,* after discrimination is shown, the burden shifts to the employer to establish that its treatment of the employees has a legitimate and substantial business justification. Petitioner declined to give Munoz the forklift driver job because of its concern that driving that piece of equipment throughout the plant would be unduly risky in two respects. First, because of the bad feeling between strikers and replacements, Munoz would be endangered if confronted by hostile replacement workers in an isolated area. Second, since Munoz had participated in the bus tour during which the union had accused the company of producing tainted walnuts, Munoz would be tempted to engage in sabotage by using the 11,000 pound vehicle to cause unspecified damage. As for Miller, who was also on the bus tour, the company declined to put her in the "sensitive position of quality control assistant" where "the final visual inspection of walnuts is made prior to leaving the plant." In that position, she would have "an easy opportunity to let defective nuts go by undetected . . . or to place a foreign object into the final product, thereby legitimizing the Union's claim of tainted walnuts."

* * * * *

A. Munoz

The Board rejected petitioner's proffered justifications for its placement of Munoz on the same ground as did the ALJ. As to Diamond's purported fear for her safety, no evidence had been produced that Munoz was thought to be responsible for any violence, so there was no reason to believe she would have been a special target. The Board said, "[T]here is no specific evidence that any replacements harbored hostility toward these three strikers, and, if such evidence did exist as [Diamond] claims, we fail to see how placing them in the positions to which they were assigned would lessen the perceived danger of retaliatory acts being committed against them." The Board discounted Diamond Walnut's contention that Munoz would be under greater protection if closely supervised, noting that petitioner had admitted that "Munoz freely roamed the plant unsupervised during her breaks."

* * * * *

As for the possibility that Munoz would engage in forklift sabotage, the Board was more terse, stating only that "the strikers' conduct [referring to the bus tour] constituted protected . . . activity," and there was no evidence indicating that such protection was lost because of threats made by Miller and Munoz. If Munoz had uttered specific threats of sabotage, however, she would have lost her protected status. . . . [T]he Board necessarily concluded that the possibility of Munoz engaging in future sabotage by misuse of her forklift was simply not a sufficient risk to constitute a substantial business justification for her treatment.

* * * * *

Similarly, the Board was reasonable in its determination that the risk of Munoz engaging in sabotage while riding

around on her 11,000 pound forklift—the petitioner seems to most fear her crashing the forklift into machinery—is not a substantial business justification for her disadvantageous placement in another job. Strikes tend to be hard struggles, and although this one may have been more bitter than most, there is always a potential danger of returning strikers engaging in some form of sabotage. There is therefore undeniably some risk in employing returning strikers during a strike. But it could not be seriously argued that an employer cannot be forced to assume *any* risk of sabotage, because that would be equivalent to holding that an employer need not take back strikers during an ongoing strike at all. . . .

* * * * *

B. Miller

The Miller case is another matter. It will be recalled that petitioner declined to assign her to the post of quality control assistant, the job responsible for the final inspection of walnuts leaving the plant (she received a job paying 32 cents an hour less). The Board rejected the employer's justification, which was based on Miller's participation in the product boycott and bus tour leafleting, saying only "the strikers' conduct constituted protected . . . activity and there is no evidence indicating that such protection was lost because of threats made by Miller and Munoz to damage or sabotage . . . equipment or products." With respect to Miller, we think the Board's determination that petitioner's business justification is insubstantial is flatly unreasonable.

All strikes are a form of economic warfare, but when a union claims that a food product produced by a struck company is actually tainted it can be thought to be using the strike equivalent of a nuclear bomb; the unpleasant effects will long survive the battle. . . . The company's ability to sell the product . . . could well be destroyed.

* * * * *

The Board's counsel argues that it is unfair to assume that an employee would behave in a disloyal and improper fashion. It is unnecessary, however, for us to make that assumption to decide the Board was unreasonable. The Board accepted petitioner's contention that Miller would have been placed "in the sensitive position . . . where final visual inspection of walnuts is made prior to leaving the plant." Miller would therefore have been put in a rather acute and unusual conflict of interest in which her job for her employer could be thought to have as a function the rebutting of her union's claim. A similar conflict would be raised if she wished a bargaining unit job in the company's public relations department. This conflict makes all too likely the possibility that Miller would be *at least* inattentive to her product quality duties. . . . To make matters worse, any "mistake" by Miller on the product quality control line would not be easily attributable to her unless petitioner paid someone to stand all day looking over Miller's shoulder. . . . If Munoz ran her forklift into valuable machinery, she would run a risk of being discovered and would therefore be deterred. But Miller, as a quality control assistant, could simply avert her eye and cause the damage with apparently little risk of discovery. . . .

In short, she would have had a special motive, a unique opportunity, and little risk of detection to cause severe harm. Both the risk Diamond faced in its placement of Miller was qualitatively different than a normal risk of sabotage, and the deterrence to Miller's possible misbehavior was peculiarly inadequate.

* * * * *

[W]e are obliged to ask in the last analysis whether the Board's decision, as to whether the employer's action was substantially justified by business reasons, falls within the broad stretch of reasonableness. In this case, at least with respect to one part of the Board's decision, we conclude the Board exceeded the reasonableness limits.

So ordered.

AFTERWORD

After nearly 14 years of bitter struggle, the Diamond Walnut strike was settled in March 2005. The settlement allowed strikers to return to work with full seniority and benefits, although many of them had already returned to Diamond Walnut or had moved to other jobs. [For a time line of the Diamond Walnut strike, see **www.teamster.org/divisions/foodprocessing/diamondwalnut/dwtimeline.htm**]

Questions

1. Set out the two-part test the court employed to determine whether Diamond Walnut violated the National Labor Relations Act by discriminating against its employees because of their participation in protected union activities.

2. Explain why the court found that Munoz had been wronged by Diamond but Miller had not.

3. *a.* How would you vote on federal legislation banning the practice of permanently replacing economic strikers? Explain.

   b. Is there any reason to distinguish between economic strikers and unfair labor practice strikers? Any reason not to do so? Explain.

4. A pilots' union, Airline Professionals Association, had a collective-bargaining agreement (CBA) with freight carrier Airborne Express (ABX). The union and ABX had a dispute about time-off provisions in the CBA. The union applied pressure to ABX by asking all pilots not to bid on open flying time not covered in the regular monthly schedule. ABX says it lost jobs due to the lack of pilots and filed a complaint saying the union was engaging in an illegal strike. A district court agreed with ABX, and the union appealed. Decide the case. Explain. See *ABX Air, Inc. v. Airline Professionals Assn.*, 266 F.3d 392 (2001); cert. den. 122 S.Ct. 1459 (2002).

Picketing and Boycotts

Primary Picketing In addition to striking, unions often picket or boycott to publicize their concerns and pressure employers during the negotiating process. Picketing is the familiar process of union members gathering and sometimes marching, placards in hand, at a place of business. Peaceful, informational picketing for a lawful purpose is protected by the NLRA. Some kinds of picketing, however, are forbidden, and all picketing can be regulated by the government to ensure public safety. Primary picketing is expressed directly to the employer with whom the picketers have a dispute. Primary picketing enjoys broad constitutional and statutory protection, but it may be unlawful if violent or coercive.

Secondary Picketing/Boycotts Secondary picketing or boycotting is directed to a business other than the primary employer, and ordinarily it is unlawful. That is, unions are engaging in an unfair labor practice if they threaten or coerce a third party with whom they are not engaged in a dispute in order to cause that third party to put pressure on the firm that is the real target of the union's concern. Consider, however, the mock funeral case summarized below.

Mock Funeral

The Sheet Metal Workers' union staged a mock funeral outside a Florida hospital in 2004. One person dressed in a "Grim Reaper" costume carrying a plastic sickle, and four "pall-bearers" carried a prop coffin and handed out leaflets. Various somber tunes played in the background on a portable audio system. The leaflets detailed several malpractice lawsuits against the hospital with the implication that the malpractice was linked to the hospital's decision to contract with nonunion labor. The demonstration was designed to pressure the hospital, a neutral entity, to stop doing business with the picketers' actual target, the non-union contractors. The "funeral" was conducted about 100 feet from the entrance and was separated from it by a street, a strip of grass, a hedge, and a parking lot. The hospital filed an unfair labor practice charge against the union claiming the funeral constituted illegal secondary picketing in violation of the NLRA. The NLRB issued an order commanding the union to cease and desist. That decision was reviewed by the federal District of Columbia Court of Appeals.

Questions

1. What constitutional law defense would you offer on behalf of the Sheet Metal Workers' union?

2. Decide the case. Explain.

Source: Sheet Metal Workers' International Association, Local 15, AFL-CIO v. National Labor Relations Board, 2007 U.S. App. LEXIS 14361.

Lockouts

Sometimes management takes the initiative in labor disputes by locking its doors to some or all of its employees. Both the NLRB and the courts allow lockouts as defensive acts to protect businesses against sudden strikes and to prevent sabotage or violence. Some court decisions have also expanded lawful lockouts to include those of an offensive nature designed to improve management's bargaining position. Lockouts, however, are clearly not lawful if designed to interfere with bargaining rights and other legitimate union activity.

> **Sports fans have learned some labor law.**

Sports fans have learned some labor law in recent years. National Hockey League owners locked out players and eventually canceled the entire 2004 to 2005 season. Major league baseball has survived several lockouts and player strikes in the last four decades.

Question

George A. Hormel & Co. and the United Food and Commercial Workers Union settled a long labor dispute. Thereafter, an unhappy, long-term employee, Robert Langemeier, drove his car in a parade and attended a rally, both of which were designed to encourage a nationwide boycott of Hormel Products. The employee did nothing to signal his feelings beyond his presence at the two events.

Employees may lawfully be dismissed for disloyalty to their employer. Supporting a boycott of an employer's products ordinarily constitutes disloyalty except where (1) the boycott is related to an ongoing labor dispute and (2) the support does not amount to disparagement of the employer's product.

Was this Hormel employee, Langemeier, engaged in protected activity such that his dismissal was unlawful? Explain. See *George A. Hormel and Company v. National Labor Relations Board,* 962 F.2d 1061 (D.C. Cir. 1992).

Part Six—Employees' Rights within or Against the Union

The Union's Duty of Fair Representation

As you have seen in previous sections of this chapter, the union is given statutory authority to be the exclusive bargaining agent for the employees in the designated bargaining unit. This means that even if an individual employee in the bargaining unit does not agree with union policies or is not a member of the union, he or she cannot bargain individually with the employer. Such an employee is bound by the terms of the collective-bargaining agreement, and the union has a duty to fairly represent that employee and all members of the bargaining unit, whether or not they become members of the union.

The Bill of Rights of Labor Organization Members

The Bill of Rights for members of labor organizations is contained in Title 1, Section 101 of the Labor–Management Reporting and Disclosure Act (LMRDA or Landrum–Griffin Act). The Bill of Rights was designed to ensure equal voting rights, the right to sue the union, and the rights of free speech and assembly. These rights of union members are tempered by the union's right to enact and enforce "reasonable rules governing the responsibilities of its members."[61]

Union Security Agreements and Right-to-Work Laws

To maintain their membership, unions typically seek a collective-bargaining clause requiring all employees to become union members after they have been employed for some period—generally 30 days (*union shop agreements*)—or, at the least, requiring them to pay union dues and fees (*agency shop agreements*). These "union security arrangements" are lawful under the NLRA.

Under the 1988 Supreme Court decision in *Communications Workers of America v. Beck*[62] nonunion employees can be compelled to pay union dues and fees only for core collective bargaining activities. Thus, nonunion employees' agency shop dues and fees must be reduced by an amount equal to that applied to such noncore purposes as lobbying and political campaigning. Similarly, public-sector unions with agency shop agreements can bill nonmembers for nonpolitical expenses related to collective bargaining but cannot require these members to fund political projects. In its 2012 decision in *Knox v. SEIU,* the U.S. Supreme Court reviewed whether a union's special assessment for a "political fight-back fund," aimed at two ballot initiatives the union opposed, required the union to provide nonunion employees with notice to allow them to opt out of paying into the fund. The court held that the union must gain the affirmative consent of the nonunion employees before imposing such an assessment on them.[63]

Right to Work   At this writing, twenty-four states including traditionally union strongholds, Indiana and Michigan, have enacted right-to-work laws that prohibit union security arrangements in collective-bargaining agreements. In these states, nonmembers do not pay dues or fees, but as members of the bargaining unit, they must be represented by the union. Unions regard those employees as *free riders,* but right-to-work supporters see the matter as one of personal freedom. [For questions and answers on right-to-work laws, see **www .nrtw.org/a/a_prime.htm**]

Closed Shop   At one time, powerful unions insisted on *closed-shop* arrangements wherein employers could hire only individuals who already belonged to unions, but those arrangements are now forbidden by the NLRA.

The Labor War and Dreamliner

Airplane manufacturer Boeing announced in 2009 its intention to open a second assembly line in a nonunion South Carolina facility to supplement its production of the company's wide-body "787 Dreamliner" at its union-organized Seattle-area plants. The expansion was not viewed by the company as a dilution of work in Washington, since it has been adding jobs in that state. Union officials, however, saw the decision as a transfer of jobs. Boeing's plan would create about 1,000 new jobs in South Carolina, a right-to-work state. Boeing expected to produce seven Dreamliners per month in Washington and three in South Carolina.

In March 2010, the International Association of Machinists and Aerospace Workers filed unfair labor practice charges against Boeing claiming that the decision to open the second production line in South Carolina was made in retaliation for its workers' past strikes in the state of Washington and to discourage them from striking in the future. If the union claims are accurate, that strategy would violate the National Labor Relations Act. In internal documents and statements to media, Boeing officials had cited strike activity and the threat of future such activity as motivations for the South Carolina decision. One Boeing executive, for example, said "We cannot afford to have a work stoppage, you know, every three years."

In April 2011, the NLRB issued a complaint against Boeing alleging a violation of federal labor law for coercing employees and, in effect, discriminating against the union by being motivated to place the new work in a right-to-work state in order to avoid the union presence. Section 8(a) of the NLRA provides that it is an unfair labor practice to "interfere with, restrain, or coerce employees in the exercise of the rights guaranteed" under the act. Similarly, employers may not encourage or discourage union membership "by discrimination in regard to hire or tenure of employment or any term or condition of employment." The NLRB complaint seeks a court order requiring Boeing to operate the second production line in Washington. In December 2011, the NLRB withdrew its complaint against Boeing, after the company and the union entered a contract that included building another jet in the Seattle area. The union leaders dropped their opposition to having some 787 Dreamliners built in South Carolina.

Questions

1. *a.* In your judgment, should the NLRB compel Boeing to keep the second production line in Washington State? Explain.
   b. In your judgment, should the NLRB have the authority to countermand Boeing's business decision?

2. In your judgment, would the nation be healthier, economically and otherwise, if all states enacted right-to-work laws? Explain.

Sources: Susanna Ray and Holly Rosenkrantz, "Boeing NLRB Complaint Withdrawn as Political Fallout Persists," *Bloomberg Businessweek,* December 15, 2011 [**www.businessweek.com/news/2011-12-15/boeing-nlrb -complaint-withdrawn-as-political-fallout-persists.html**]; "Boeing Complaint Fact Sheet," National Labor Relations Board [**www.nlrb.gov**]; and Hans A. von Spakovsky and James Sherk, "National Labor Relations Board Overreach Against Boeing Imperils Jobs and Investment," *Legal Memorandum* 66, May 11, 2011.

Part Seven—Other Unions

Public-Sector Unions

The public sector is a growth area for union membership. In 2013, 7.2 million public-sector employees belonged to a union, compared with 7.3 million union workers in the private sector.[64] However, the union membership rate for public-sector workers is more than five times higher than the rate for private-sector workers.[65] In 2011, the states of Wisconsin and Ohio approved legislation dramatically limiting public-sector workers' collective-bargaining rights (both prohibit bargaining over health coverage and pensions), and many other states are considering similar measures. The cutbacks in union authority are defended as necessary to curb workers' wages and benefits, but critics view the movement as a general assault on unions.

Legal regulation of public-sector labor–management relations begins with state law. Although the specific provisions of those laws vary, many NLRA concepts have been adopted. Some fundamental policies and doctrines are quite different, however. A particular distinction lies in the ability of public-sector employees to strike.

Some states prohibit those strikes and others permit them only under restricted conditions. In either case, the rationale for treating public employees differently than private-sector employees is the role of public employees as servants of the voters. Public servants arguably have a higher duty than private employees. In addition, certain public employees, including police officers and firefighters, work in positions that clearly involve public safety, and to permit them to strike might endanger the citizenry.

Internet Exercise

Go to National Labor Relations Board's frequently asked questions [**www.nlrb.gov/faq/nlrb**].

1. Explain what an employee at an unionized workplace who is "unhappy" with the union can do.

2. Explain how to file an unfair labor practice (ULP) claim.

Chapter Questions

1. As an employee of a BMW car dealership, Becker complained on his Facebook page about his employer serving hot dogs and potato chips at the launch of the BMW 5 Series. On the day of the event, at the adjacent Land Rover dealership also owned by Becker's employer, a 13-year-old drove a Land Rover into a pond. Becker took photos of the accident, which he also posted on his Facebook page along with some sarcastic comments. After a meeting with the general manager and other supervisors, in which Becker was confronted about his Facebook postings, Becker was fired. Did his termination violate the NLRA? Explain. See *Karl Knaus Motors, Inc.,* NLRB Case 13–CA–046452 (2012) [[**http://www.nlrb.gov/case/13-CA-046452**].

2. The Eugene, Oregon *Register-Guard* newspaper maintained a company policy prohibiting employees from using company communications systems such as e-mail to "solicit or proselytize for commercial ventures, religious or political causes, outside organizations, or other nonjob-related solicitations." Employees, however, had not been disciplined for using the e-mail system to invite coworkers to parties, sell sports tickets, etc. Suzi Prozanski, an employee and union president, used the employer's e-mail system to send three union-related messages to other employees at their work addresses. She was disciplined under the company policy. Did the *Register-Guard* violate the NLRA in disciplining Prozanski? Explain. See *Register-Guard v. NLRB*, 571 F.3d 53 (D.C. Cir. 2009).

3. You are the human resources manager for a manufacturing firm that is presently the subject of an organizing campaign by a union that has filed an election petition with the NLRB just 30 days ago. Your plant manager has come to you and said that she wishes to discharge one of her employees. She further explains that the employee in question has worked for the company for three years and throughout that time has had a terrible attendance record. She adds that up to this point the employee has not received any discipline for his attendance. Upon inquiry, the plant manager tells you that the employee has been seen on the plant floor wearing a button that says: "Union Yes!" In addition, the plant manager tells you that she knows that the employee is an outspoken union activist. How would you advise the plant manager? Explain.

4. ACE/CO, a Milwaukee automobile parts manufacturer, was accused of a series of unfair labor practices springing from company conduct both before and after a disputed union representation election. Among the charges were the following:

   • ACE/CO declined to grant its usual across-the-board wage increases and told employees that the union was responsible for the failure to grant a raise.

   • ACE/CO distributed a memorandum asking employees to inform supervisors whenever they felt pressured to sign a union authorization card. One employee testified that union representatives had visited his home 13 times and that he did feel "pressured" to support the union.

- ACE/CO included in its employee handbook a statement indicating the company's "intention to do everything possible to maintain our company's union-free status for the benefit of both our employees and [the company]."

  a. Why might ACE/CO legitimately decline to offer a wage increase during an organizing campaign?

  b. Do any of these company behaviors constitute unfair labor practices? See *NLRB v. Aluminum Casting & Engineering Co.,* 230 F.3d 286 (7th Cir. 2000).

5. When assistant manager Diane Gorrell was fired from a Bob Evans restaurant in East Peoria, Illinois, most of the employees walked off the job in protest. They stood outside the restaurant for a time and discouraged customers from entering. The restaurant was left in some disarray and problems persisted for a number of days, clearly harming business. Later all but one of the employees asked to return to their jobs, but were refused. The employees filed an unfair labor practices charge with the NLRB.

   a. Justify, as a matter of law, management's decision not to allow the employees to return to work.

   b. Explain the employees' unfair labor practices charge.

   c. Decide the case. Explain. See *Bob Evans Farms, Inc. v. NLRB*, 163 F.3d 1012 (7th Cir. 1998).

6. The Yuwei Plastics and Hardware Product Company Ltd. in Dongguan, China, manufactures and exports auto parts to Ford. The Institute for Global Labour and Human Rights reported that Yuwei workers earn 80¢ an hour, work 14-hour shifts seven days a week, and are docked three days' wages if they miss one day's work. Managers' instructions to turn off safety mechanisms to increase workers' speed have resulted in serious injuries. Managers and workers stated that Ford accounts for approximately four-fifths of Yuwei's total production. Should American corporations be held responsible for their global suppliers' oppressive working conditions? Explain.[66]

7. Midwestern Personnel Services provided truck drivers to employers in Indiana, Kentucky, and other locations. Midwestern wanted the drivers to join a union so they would be allowed to enter a unionized workplace, AK Steel, where they were to deliver cement. Midwestern management favored Teamsters Local 836 in Middletown, Ohio, for their drivers, but a majority of the drivers voted to join Teamsters Local 215 in Evansville, Indiana. Midwestern refused to recognize Local 215; management and the drivers could not reach agreement about pension rights and contract length; and the drivers went on strike. The drivers later made an unconditional offer to return to work, but Midwestern would not allow them to return because, in its view, the drivers were economic strikers. The NLRB concluded that the drivers were motivated in part by unfair labor practices, and thus should be reinstated to their jobs. Were the drivers entitled to reinstatement? Explain. See *NLRB v. Midwestern Personnel Services,* 322 F.3d 969 (7th Cir. 2003).

8. Local 582 engaged in an economic strike against Broadview Dairy of Spokane, Washington. Local 582 tried to distribute handbills at several Albertson's groceries in the Spokane area. The handbills urged customers to refrain from buying Broadview products, which Albertson's sold. Albertson's formal policy forbade all solicitations, but some groups, such as Boy Scouts and area schools, were allowed on company

property to make solicitations. Albertson's ordered the union members off its property. Later, Albertson's ordered union organizers off its property where they were trying to encourage Albertson's employees to join their union. Local 582 filed an unfair labor practices charge against Albertson's. Does Albertson's have the right to exclude from its property nonemployee union representatives who engage in either nonorganizing or organizing activities? Explain. See *Albertson's Inc. v. National Labor Relations Board,* 301 F.3d 441 (6th Cir. 2002).

9. The Sacred Heart Medical Center, an acute-care hospital, issued a memorandum prohibiting nurses' union members from wearing buttons which read "RNs Demand Safe Staffing" in any areas "on our campus where they may encounter patients or family members." Did the hospital's ban on these buttons constitute an unfair labor practice under the NLRA? Explain. See *Washington State Nurses Ass'n v. NLRB,* 526 F.3d 577 (9th Cir. 2008).

10. An employer, Ashley Furniture of Arcadia, Wisconsin, instructed its employees not to discuss such workplace issues as disciplinary infractions, the expiration of an employee's work permit, or the receipt of a "no-match" letter from the Social Security Administration. Did the employer violate the NLRA? Explain. See *Ashley Furniture Industries,* 353 NLRB 071 (2008).

11. Dick's Sporting Goods used a nonunion contractor to prepare for its opening in a Watertown, New York, shopping mall. The local carpenters' union requested permission of the shopping mall's operator to distribute literature in the mall protesting the use of a nonunion contractor. While the mall had previously allowed such charitable organizations as the American Cancer Society and the Boy Scouts to distribute materials on its property, it rejected the union's request. Did the shopping mall violate the NLRA? Explain. See *Salmon Run Shopping Center v. NLRB,* 534 F.3d 108 (2nd Cir. 2008).

12. Jerry Kirby was discharged from his job at Ford Motor Company, allegedly because of "being under the influence of alcohol, absenteeism, and threatening management." The United Auto Workers union (UAW) immediately filed a grievance on Kirby's behalf. Kirby lost through the first three steps of the grievance process, and the UAW declined to appeal to arbitration on Kirby's behalf. The UAW said that Kirby had no right to appeal because he had allowed his union membership to lapse. Kirby then filed an unfair labor practice charge against the union. Decide. Explain. See *International Union v. NLRB,* 168 F.3d 509 (D.C. Cir. 1999).

13. *a.* Can an employer lawfully discharge a group of employees who walk out in protest of working conditions?
    b. Would it matter if the collective-bargaining agreement contains a no-strike clause? Explain.

14. What steps can an employer lawfully take to provide the labor necessary to keep a plant operative during a strike?

15. During a strike resulting from failure to reach a collective-bargaining agreement, Pan American Grain laid off 15 striking workers, citing changing labor needs "due to economic reasons and as a result of a substantial decrease in production and sales." Where labor costs are one of the multiple motives for a layoff, does the employer have

a duty to bargain with the union over the decision to impose a layoff? Explain. See *Pan American Grain v. NLRB,* 558 F.3d 22 (1st Cir. 2009).

16. Should a union be able to access Department of Motor Vehicles records to find employees' residential addresses so union organizers can visit employees at home for organizing purposes? Explain. See *Pichler v. UNITE,* 585 F.3d 741 (3rd Cir. 2009).

Notes

1. Tiffany Hsu and Alana Semuels, "Fast-Food Workers Demand Higher Wages," *Los Angeles Times,* August 30, 2013, pp. B1–B5.

2. Ibid.

3. Ibid.

4. "Union Members Summary," *Bureau of Labor Statistics News,* January 24, 2014 [**www.bls.gov /news.release/union2.nr0.htm**].

5. Ibid.

6. Joseph Szczesny, "Big Three-UAW Contracts Even the Playing Field—Eventually," *Auto Observer,* November 18, 2007 [**www.autoobserver.com/2007/11/big-three-uaw-c.html**].

7. Damian Paletta, "UAW's Southern Push Faces Another Defeat," *The Wall Street Journal,* March 15, 2014, p. B3.

8. Pew Research Center for the People and the Press, "Favorable Views of Business, Labor Rebound," June 27, 2013 [**www.people-press.org/2013/06/27/favorable-views-of-business -labor-rebound/**].

9. Opinion, "Unions' Woes Are Largely of Their Own Making," *USA TODAY,* December 13, 2012, p. 8A.

10. Harold Meyerson, "Labor Wrestles with Its Future," *The Washington Post,* May 8, 2013 [**www .washingtonpost.com/opinions/harold-meyerson-labor-wrestles-with-its-future/2013/05/08 /852192d6-b74f-11e2-b94c-b684dda07add_story.html**].

11. Isaac A. Hourwich, *Immigration and Labor* (New York: Arno Press, 1969), pp. 125–45.

12. John J. Flagler, *The Labor Movement in the United States* (Minneapolis: Lerner Publications, 1972), pp. 26–28.

13. Alan Glassman, Naomi Berger Davidson, and Thomas Cummings, *Labor Relations: Reports from the Firing Line* (New York: Business Publications, 1988), pp. 5–6.

14. Flagler, *Labor Movement,* pp. 26–28.

15. Eli Ginzberg and Hyman Berman, *The American Worker in the Twentieth Century: A History Through Autobiographies* (New York: Free Press, 1963), pp. 193–95, in *I Am a Woman Worker,* ed. Andria Taylor Hourwich and Gladys L. Palmer (Affiliated Schools for Workers, 1936), pp. 17 ff.

16. Flagler, *Labor Movement,* pp. 33, 36, quoting Frederick Lewis Allen, *The Big Change: America Transforms Itself, 1900–1950* (New York: Harper, 1952).

17. Flagler, *Labor Movement,* p. 47.

18. J. David Greenstone, *Labor in American Politics* (New York: Alfred A. Knopf, 1969), p. 21.

19. Archibald Cox, with Derek Bok and Robert A. Gorman, *Cases and Materials on Labor Law,* 8th ed. (Mineola, NY: Foundation Press, 1977), pp. 7–8.

20. Greenstone, *Labor in American Politics,* p. 22.

21. Ibid., p. 23.

22. Patrick Hardin, *The Developing Labor Law* (Washington, DC: Bureau of National Affairs, 1992), pp. 31–32.

23. Ibid., p. 94.

24. Ibid., pp. 1, 108.

25. *Steele v. Louisville and Nashville Railroad,* 323 U.S. 192 (1944).

26. *Vaca v. Sipes,* 386 U.S. 171 (1967); *Miranda Fuel Co.,* 140 NLRB 181 (1962).

27. The National Labor Relations Act is found in Title 29 U.S.C. Section 151 et seq.

28. National Labor Relations Board, "Guideline Memorandum Concerning Unfair Labor Practice Charges Involving Political Advocacy," July 22, 2008 [**www.nlrb.gov/**].

29. *Red Cross Arizona Blood Services Region,* 2012 NLRB LEXIS 43 (2012).

30. Barry J. Kearney, Associate General Counsel, NLRB Advice Memorandum, *SWH Corporation d/b/a Mimi's Café*, October 31, 2012 [**www.minnesotalaboremploymentlawblog.com /uploads/file/Mimi%27s%20cafe%20NLRB.pdf**].

31. *Starbucks v. NLRB,* 679 F.3d 70 (2nd Cir. 2012).

32. *Medco Health Solutions v. NLRB,* 701 F.3d 710 (D.C. 2012).

33. National Labor Relations Board, "The NLRB and Social Media," *NLRB Fact Sheets,* [**www .nlrb.gov/news-outreach/fact-sheets/nlrb-and-social-media**].

34. *Costco Wholesale Corporation,* Case 34–CA–012421 (2012) [**http://www.nlrb.gov/case/34-CA-012421**].

35. *Design Technology Group, d/b/a Bettie Page Clothing,* Case 20–CA–035511 (2013) [**http:// www.nlrb.gov/case/20-CA-035511**].

36. Melanie Trottman, "For Angry Employees, Legal Cover for Rants," *The Wall Street Journal,* December 2, 2011, p. B1.

37. Cox, *Labor Law,* pp. 113–22.

38. Ibid., pp. 99–101.

39. 351 NLRB No. 28 (2007).

40. *Oakwood Healthcare, Inc.,* 348 NLRB No. 37 (2006).

41. *FedEx Home Delivery v. NLRB,* 563 F.3d 492 (D.C. Cir. 2009).

42. *Lechmere, Inc. v. NLRB,* 502 U.S. 527 (1992).

43. *NLRB v. Town & Country Electric, Inc.,* 516 U.S. 85 (1998).

44. *Toering Electric Company,* 351 NLRB No. 18 (2007).

45. See *Sewell Mfg. Co.,* 138 NLRB 66 (1962), which states that the board's goal is to conduct elections "in a laboratory under conditions as nearly ideal as possible to determine the uninhibited desires of employees" and "to provide an atmosphere conducive to the sober and informed exercise of the franchise free from . . . elements which prevent or impede reasonable choice."

46. Melanie Trottman, "Union-Organizing Rule Easing Votes Is Rejected," *The Wall Street Journal,* May 15, 2012, p. A3.

47. *Dish Network Corp.,* Cases 16–CA–027316, citing Tri-Cast, Inc., 274 NLRB 377 (1985), (2012) [**http://www.nlrb.gov/case/16-CA-027316**].

48. *NLRB v. Exchange Parts Co.,* 375 U.S. 405 (1964).

49. *Trencor, Inc. v. National Labor Relations Board,* 110 F.3d 268 (5th Cir. 1997).

50. Ronald Meisburg, NLRB Office of the General Counsel, Memorandum GC 09-04, Guideline Memorandum Concerning Withdrawal of Recognition Based on Loss of Majority Support, November 26, 2008, p. 4 citing *Highland Regional Medical Center,* 347 NLRB 1404, 1406 (2006), and *Wurtland Nursing,* 351 NLRB No. 50, slip op. at 2.

51. National Labor Relations Board, "Employer/Union Rights and Obligations" [**www.nlrb.gov /rights-we-protect/employerunion-rights-and-obligations**].

52. See *First National Maintenance Corporation v. NLRB,* 101 S.Ct . 2573 (1981).

53. *Granite Rock v. International Brotherhood of Teamsters,* 130 S.Ct. 2847 (2010).

54. *14 Penn Plaza LLC. v. Pyett,* 129 S.Ct. 1456 (2009).

55. Matea Gold, Maria Elena Fernandez, and Richard Verrier, "Jay Leno, Conan O'Brien to Return to the Air Jan. 2," *Los Angeles Times,* December 18, 2007 [**www.latimes.com/news/la-fi -strike18dec18,0,3643358.story?coll=la-tot-topstories&track=ntothtml**].

56. Michael Luo and Karen Ann Cullotta, "Even Workers Surprised by Success of Factory Sit-in," *The New York Times,* December 13, 2008 [**www.nytimes.com**].

57. Steven Greenhouse, "Caterpillar Workers Ratify Deal They Dislike," *The New York Times,* August 17, 2012 [**www.nytimes.com/2012/08/18/business/striking-caterpillar-workers -ratify-contract-offer.html?_r=0**].

58. Littler, Mendelson Fastiff, and Tichy, *The 1990 Employer* (San Francisco: Littler Mendelson, Fastiff and Tichy, P.C., 1990), p. V6.

59. *NLRB v. Mackay Radio & Tel. Co.,* 304 U.S. 333 (1938).

60. Littler et al., *The 1990 Employer,* p. V6.

61. *United Steelworkers of America v. Sadlowski,* 457 U.S. 102 (1982).

62. 487 U.S. 735 (1988).

63. 132 S.Ct. 2277 (2012).

64. "Union Members Summary," *Bureau of Labor Statistics News,* January 24, 2014 [**www.bls.gov /news.release/union2.nr0.htm**].

65. Ibid.

66. Charles Kernaghan, "Dirty Parts: Where Lost Fingers Come Cheap: Ford in China," International Institute for Global Labour and Human Rights, March 2011, pp. 1, 11 [**www .globallabourrights.org/admin/reports/files/110304-Dirty-Parts.pdf**].

Selected Topics in Government–Business Relations

CHAPTER FIFTEEN

Consumer Protection

After completing this chapter, students will be able to:

1. Identify some consumer protections offered under common law.

2. Describe "lemon laws" as an example of state consumer regulation.

3. Explain the purpose, roles, and power of the federal consumer protection agencies including the Consumer Financial Protection Bureau (CFPB), the Federal Trade Commission (FTC), the Consumer Product Safety Commission (CPSC), and the Food and Drug Administration (FDA).

4. Identify the circumstances in which the Truth in Lending Act (TILA) applies to a consumer loan.

5. Identify protections offered under the Fair Credit Reporting Act (FCRA).

6. Describe the protections offered by the Fair Credit Billing Act (FCBA).

7. Recognize the purpose of the Electronic Fund Transfer Act (EFTA).

8. Explain the purpose of the Equal Credit Opportunity Act (ECOA).

9. Identify debt collection practices forbidden by the Fair Debt Collection Practices Act (FDCPA).

10. Explain the purpose and effect of filing a Chapter 7 liquidation or "straight" bankruptcy.

Introduction

Doubtless the government and lawsuits should not always protect us from our own foolishness, but costly consumer fraud and other forms of consumer abuse (invasion of privacy, dangerous products, identity theft, false advertising, and so on) are not unusual in our consumption-driven lives. Historically, we relied on the market to address those problems; but in recent decades legislatures, courts, and administrative agencies have developed laws and rulings to protect us where the market arguably has failed. This chapter surveys some of those legal interventions.

For-profit schools like the University of Phoenix and Kaplan enroll nearly 2 million students, but the government is concerned that deceptive marketing practices, fraudulent claims about job placement, and huge student loan burdens are denying many of those students the better future they are seeking.

Chelsi Miller was managing a burger joint when she saw an ad for Everest University promising a better life. The single mother in a small town near Salt Lake City wanted an associate's degree as a first step toward medical school. She said she chose Everest, a for-profit college, after a recruiter guaranteed that she could apply her credits toward a higher degree at the University of Utah.[1]

Once Miller graduated in 2008, she learned that her credits would not transfer. After two years of school and $30,000 in student loans, Miller says she was sold "a lemon." Miller's experience was not unusual. Although public and private nonprofit colleges typically achieve graduation rates around 65 percent, the comparable number at the for-profits often falls below 30 percent, and those students are more likely to default on their student loans and have greater difficulty securing jobs than their nonprofit counterparts.[2] Indeed, government figures show that for-profits have twice the federal student loan default rate of public colleges.[3] Further, the for-profits are routinely accused of using high-pressure sales tactics and false promises to lure students. In response, the federal government imposed "gainful employment" regulations designed to cut off aid to colleges with poor job placement rates. After a federal court held in 2012 that the government had failed to provide a clear rationale for its new rules, new regulations were released in 2014, based in part on the mortgage industry's standard for sustainable levels of debt.[4] Meanwhile, the market seems to be asserting itself as for-profit enrollment has been falling and the industry leader, the University of Phoenix, has closed many of its locations. The schools defend themselves, in part, by saying that the students have more "risk factors" than traditional college students. Do you think higher education admissions practices are best left to the market, or is more aggressive government oversight needed?

Part One—Common-Law Consumer Protection

Later in this chapter we will explore government efforts to protect consumers from dangerous products, unfair lending practices, and the like. Before turning to that legislation, we need to appreciate the common law (judge-made law) that preceded and, in some respects, provided the foundation for the many federal, state, and local initiatives of recent years. In addition to the product liability protection (negligence, warranties, and strict liability) discussed in Chapter 7, injured consumers can look to several common-law protections, including actions for fraud, misrepresentation, and unconscionability. [For an extensive menu of consumer law sites, see **www.lectlaw.com/tcos.html**]

Fraud and Innocent Misrepresentation

If the market is to operate efficiently, the buyer must be able to rely on the truth of the seller's product claims. Regrettably, willful untruths appear to be common in American commerce. A victim of *fraud* is entitled to rescind the contract in question and to seek damages, including, in cases of malice, a punitive recovery. Although fraud arises in countless situations and is difficult to define, the legal community has generally adopted the following elements, each of which must be proved:

1. Misrepresentation of a material fact.
2. The misrepresentation was intentional.
3. The injured party justifiably relied on the misrepresentation.
4. Injury resulted.

PRACTICING ETHICS — Watery Beer?

Several class-action lawsuits were filed against Anheuser-Busch (AB) in 2013 claiming the brewing giant had intentionally watered down some of its beer products during the brewing process. The plaintiffs allege that AB intentionally deceived buyers by selling beer such as Budweiser, Bud Ice, and Michelob with less alcohol than was indicated on product labels.

Questions

1. Evidence indicates that many buyers do not read beer labels and perhaps do not care about precise alcohol content. Given that evidence, if AB did, in fact, dilute its beer, would that dilution constitute an ethical wrong? Explain.

2. Have you noticed other instances of arguable consumer fraud in your daily life? Explain.

Source: David Kouba, "Still Thirsty? Class Actions Claim Anheuser-Busch Watered-Down Beers," *LEXOLOGY*, March 6, 2013 [**www.lexology.com**/].

In identifying a fraudulent expression, the law distinguishes between statements of objective, verifiable facts and simple expressions of opinion. The latter ordinarily are not fraudulent even if erroneous. Thus normal sales *puffing* ("This baby is the greatest little car you're ever gonna drive") is fully lawful, and consumers are expected to exercise good judgment in responding to such claims. If a misleading expression of opinion comes from an *expert,* however, and the other party does not share that expertise (such as in the sale of a diamond engagement ring), a court probably would offer a remedy.

Did Apple Deceive Laptop Buyers?

Vitt, an Apple iBook G4 laptop purchaser, sued Apple, claiming that advertising words including "mobile," "durable," "rugged," "reliable," and "high value" allegedly constituted a misrepresentation of the durability, portability, and quality of the laptop. Vitt's laptop failed soon after the expiration of its one-year warranty. Vitt argued that it should be expected to last for "at least a couple of years." In Vitt's view, Apple's ads caused buyers to believe the computer was of better quality than it turned out to be. Was Vitt a victim of a misrepresentation? Explain.

Sources: See *Vitt v. Apple Computer, Inc.,* 2012 U.S. App. LEXIS 4419.

Of course, fraud can involve false conduct as well as false expression. A familiar example is the car seller who rolls back an odometer with the result that the buyer is misled.

A variation on the general theme of fraud is *innocent misrepresentation,* which differs from fraud only in that the falsehood was *unintentional.* The wrongdoer believed the statement or conduct in question to be true, but he or she was mistaken. In such cases, the wronged party may secure rescission of the contract, but ordinarily damages are not awarded. The following case involves a fraud claim against Harley-Davidson.

Justice Diane S. Sykes

The circuit court dismissed the entire action for failure to state a claim. [T]he court of appeals reinstated [the claims.]

* * * * *

FACTS AND PROCEDURAL HISTORY

Plaintiff Steven C. Tietsworth and the members of the proposed class own or lease 1999 or early-2000 model year Harley motorcycles equipped with Twin Cam 88 or Twin Cam 88B engines. Harley's marketing and advertising literature contained the following statement about the TC-88 engines:

> Developing [the TC-88s] was a six-year process. . . . The result is a masterpiece. We studied everything from the way oil moves through the inside, to the way a rocker cover does its job of staying oil-tight. Only 21 functional parts carry over into the new design. What does carry over is the power of a Harley-Davidson™ engine, only more so.

Harley also stated that the motorcycles were "premium" quality, and described the TC-88 engine as "eighty-eight cubic inches filled to the brim with torque and ready to take you thundering down the road."

On January 22, 2001, Harley sent a letter to Tietsworth and other owners of Harley motorcycles informing them that "the rear cam bearing in a small number of Harley-Davidson's Twin Cam 88 engines has failed. While it is unlikely that you will ever have to worry about this situation, you have our assurance that Harley-Davidson is committed to your satisfaction." The letter went on to explain that the company was extending the warranty on the cam bearing from the standard one-year/unlimited mileage warranty to a five-year/50,000 mile warranty. Separately, Harley developed a $495 "cam bearing repair kit" and made the kit available to its dealers and service departments "to expedite rear cam bearing repair."

* * * * *

The amended complaint alleges that the cam bearing mechanism in the 1999 and early-2000 model year TC-88 engines is inherently defective, causing an unreasonably dangerous propensity for premature engine failure. [T]he amended complaint alleged that Harley's failure to disclose the cam bearing defect induced the plaintiffs to purchase their motorcycles by causing them to reasonably rely upon Harley's representations regarding the "premium" quality of the motorcycles.

The amended complaint further alleges that if the plaintiffs had known of the engine defect, they either would not have purchased the product or would have paid less for it. The amended complaint does not allege that the plaintiffs' motorcycles have actually suffered engine failure, have malfunctioned in any way, or are reasonably certain to fail or malfunction. Nor does the amended complaint allege any property damage or personal injury arising out of the engine defect. Rather, the amended complaint alleges that the plaintiffs' motorcycles have diminished value, including diminished resale value, because Harley motorcycles equipped with TC-88 engines have demonstrated a "propensity" for premature engine failure and/or fail prematurely.

* * * * *

DISCUSSION
Common-Law Fraud Claim

The plaintiffs' common-law fraud claim is premised on the allegation that Harley failed to disclose or concealed the existence of the cam bearing defect prior to the plaintiffs' purchases of their motorcycles. It is well established that a nondisclosure is not actionable as a misrepresentation tort unless there is a duty to disclose. *Ullerman v. O'Rourke Co., Inc.,* 94 Wis.2d 17, 26, 288 N.W.2d 95 (1980). Our decision in *Ollerman* outlined the three categories of misrepresentation in Wisconsin law— intentional misrepresentation, negligent misrepresentation, and strict responsibility misrepresentation—and described the common and distinct elements of the three torts.

All misrepresentation claims share the following required elements: (1) the defendant must have made a representation of fact to the plaintiff; (2) the representation of fact must be false; and (3) the plaintiff must have believed and relied on the misrepresentation to his detriment or damage. The plaintiffs here allege intentional misrepresentation, which carries the following additional elements: (4) the defendant must have made the misrepresentation with knowledge that it was false or recklessly without caring whether it was true or false; and (5) the defendant must have made the misrepresentation with intent to deceive and to induce the plaintiff to act on it to his detriment or damage.

Ollerman reiterated the general rule that in a sales or business transaction, "silence, a failure to disclose a fact, is not an intentional misrepresentation unless the seller has a duty to disclose." The existence and scope of a duty to disclose are questions of law for the court. *Ollerman* held that "a subdivider-vendor of a residential lot has a duty to a 'noncommercial' purchaser to disclose facts which are known to the vendor, which are material to the transaction, and which are not readily discernible to the purchaser." We specified that this was a "narrow holding," premised on certain policy considerations present in noncommercial real estate transactions.

The transactions at issue here, however, are motorcycle purchases, not residential real estate purchases, and it is an open question whether the duty to disclose recognized in *Ollerman* extends more broadly to sales of consumer goods. . . .

No Legally Cognizable Injury

Ollerman also held that damages in intentional misrepresentation cases are measured according to the "benefit of the bargain" rule, "typically stated as the difference between the value of the property as represented and its actual value as purchased.". . .

[W]e have generally held that a tort claim is not capable of present enforcement (and therefore does not accrue) unless the plaintiff has suffered actual damage. . . . Actual damage is harm that has already occurred or is "reasonably certain" to occur in the future. . . . Actual damage is not the mere possibility of future harm. . . . [T]he amended complaint must adequately plead an actual injury—a loss or damage that has already occurred or is reasonably certain to occur—in order to state an actionable fraud claim. . . .

The injury complained of here is diminution in value only—the plaintiffs allege that their motorcycles are worth less than they paid for them. However, the amended complaint does not allege that the plaintiffs' motorcycles have diminished value because their engines have failed, will fail, or are reasonably certain to fail as a result of the TC-88 cam bearing defect. The amended complaint does not allege that the plaintiffs have sold their motorcycles at a loss because of the alleged engine defect. The amended complaint alleges only that the motorcycles have diminished value—primarily diminished potential resale value—because Harley motorcycles equipped with TC-88 engines have demonstrated a "propensity" for premature engine failure and/or will fail as a result of the cam bearing defect. This is insufficient to state a legally cognizable injury for purposes of a fraud claim.

Diminished value premised upon a mere possibility of future product failure is too speculative and uncertain to support a fraud claim. The plaintiffs do not specifically allege that their particular motorcycles will fail prematurely, only that the

Harley product line that consists of motorcycles with TC-88 engines has demonstrated a propensity for premature engine failure. An allegation that a particular product line fails prematurely does not constitute an allegation that the plaintiffs' particular motorcycles will do so, only that there is a possibility that they will do so.

We certainly agree with the court of appeals that the damage allegations in a fraud complaint are not evaluated against a standard of "absolute certainty" for purposes of a motion to dismiss for failure to state a claim. But an allegation that a product is diminished in value because of an event or circumstance that might—or might not—occur in the future is inherently conjectural and does not allege actual benefit-of-the-bargain damages with the "reasonable certainty" required to state a fraud claim.

* * * * *

[Reversed.] [The plaintiffs' additional claims are omitted.—Ed.]

Questions

1. *a.* According to the Wisconsin Supreme Court, under what circumstances might the nondisclosure by a seller of a defect constitute misrepresentation?

   b. Did the court find that Harley-Davidson had a duty to disclose in this case? Explain.

2. *a.* What injury, if any, do the plaintiffs claim they suffered in this episode?

   b. According to the Wisconsin Supreme Court, must a plaintiff in a fraud action prove that he or she has suffered actual damages prior to bringing a claim? Explain.

   c. What is the "benefit of the bargain" rule?

3. Why did the Wisconsin Supreme Court rule for the defendant Harley-Davidson in this case?

4. Robert McGlothlin, an employee of Thomson Consumer Electronics in Bloomington, Indiana, was injured while loading televisions into a semitrailer when the trailer's "landing gear" (retractable legs that support the front of the trailer when it is not attached to the semitractor) collapsed. McGlothlin sued the owner of the trailer, among others, claiming that the defendants' repair and inspection procedures for *latent* (hidden) defects were inadequate. Should the court treat latent defects differently than *patent* (observable) defects in determining when a legal duty exists? Explain. See *McGlothlin v. M & U Trucking,* 688 N.E.2d 1243 (Ind. S.Ct. 1997).

Unconscionable Contracts

The doctrine of unconscionability emerged from court decisions where jurists concluded that some contracts are so unfair or oppressive as to demand intervention. (Unconscionability is also included in state statutory laws via the Uniform Commercial Code 2—302.) The legal system intrudes on contracts only with the greatest reluctance. Mere foolishness or want of knowledge does not constitute grounds for unconscionability, nor is a contract unconscionable and hence unenforceable merely because one party is spectacularly clever and the other is not. Unconscionability can take either or both of two forms:

1. *Procedural unconscionability.* The bargaining power of the parties was so unequal that the agreement, as a practical matter, was not freely entered. Procedural unconscionability usually arises from lack of knowledge (e.g., fine print) or lack of choice (e.g., urgent circumstances).

2. *Substantive unconscionability.* The clause or contract in question was so manifestly one-sided, oppressive, or unfair as to "shock the conscience of the court." A contract that does not provide a remedy for a breach, or contract terms completely out of line with the relative risks assumed by the parties are among the conditions that might lead to a finding of substantive unconscionability.

Part Two—The Consumer and Government Regulation of Business

State Laws

Having looked at the common-law foundation of consumer protection, we turn to some of the many governmental measures that provide shelter in the marketplace. Many states have enacted comprehensive consumer protection statutes. States also have specific statutes addressing such problems as door-to-door sales, debtor protection, and telemarketing fraud. We will look at a pair of high-interest consumer loan situations as well as state "lemon laws," which address the particularly frustrating problem of a hopelessly defective vehicle.

Payday Loans

When Jeffrey Smith of Phoenix needed money quickly to pay a medical bill, he took out a string of payday loans (short-term, high-interest loans to be paid back with the borrower's next pay check) and fell into a downward spiral that found him calling in sick to work to give himself time to drive all over the city taking out new loans to cover those coming due. The result was bankruptcy along with thoughts of suicide by his despondent wife. Annual interest rates on those loans were as high as 459 percent.

At least 15 states now ban these loans and others cap interest rates. Loan volume is down considerably, but customers are estimated to number about 12 million annually. Looking for new profit centers, a few of the most mainstream of big banks, such as Wells Fargo and U.S. Bancorp, have begun offering a payday loan variant labeled direct deposit advance loans. The banks lend to current customers and repay themselves by deducting the amount due from the customer's account after the next paycheck has been deposited. Other big banks have established new payday profit lines by joining with smaller online lending operations sometimes operated by offshore entities or Native Americans. Payday lenders make the online loans and the big banks provide service for those loans. Interest to the online lenders and service fees to the big banks mount up and borrowers are quickly buried in debt.

Federal rules, proposed at this writing in 2013, would require big banks, among other things, to consider ability to pay before making payday-style, short-term loans. Whether more federal rules and existing state laws advance fairness, or simply reduce the availability of loans and increase interest rates is the subject of debate.

Sources: Associated Press, "States Increasingly Target Payday Lenders," *The Des Moines Register,* April 9, 2010, p. 8A; Jessica Silver-Greenberg, "Major Banks in Payday Loans Banned by States," *The New York Times,* February 23, 2013 [**www.nytimes.com/**]; and Alan Zibel and Robin Sidel, "U.S. Regulators to Warn Against Payday-Style Loans," *The Wall Street Journal,* April 23, 2013 [**online.wsj.com/**]

Lemon Laws   New car purchases are covered by warranty laws (see Chapter 7 for a discussion of UCC warranty provisions and the federal Magnuson–Moss Warranty Act); in addition, all 50 states have some form of law designed to provide recourse for consumers whose new vehicles turn out to be defective such that they cannot be repaired after a reasonable effort. The quarrel, of course, is about when a car is truly a lemon. Lemon laws differ significantly from state to state, but they often cover new cars for one to two years or up to 24,000 miles after purchase. Typically, state laws provide that the vehicle must have been returned to the manufacturer or dealer three or four times to repair the same defect and that defect must substantially impair the value or safety of the vehicle, or the vehicle must have been unavailable to the consumer for a total of at least 30 days in a 12-month period. A vehicle meeting either or both of those tests often would be a lemon, and the purchaser would be entitled to a replacement vehicle or full refund of the purchase price. In some states, used cars may also be treated as lemons. In almost all states, the determination about whether a car is a lemon is handled by an arbitration panel. If dissatisfied with the ruling, the consumer may then file suit.

> The quarrel, of course, is about when a car is truly a lemon.

The case that follows examines Minnesota's lemon law requirements. [For lemon laws in all 50 states, see **www.lemonlawusa.com**]

LEGAL BRIEFCASE

Paul Sipe v. Workhorse Custom Chassis
572 F.3d 525 (8th Cir. 2009)

Circuit Judge GRUENDER

I. BACKGROUND

On September 18, 2004, Paul Sipe purchased a motor home manufactured by Fleetwood Motor Homes of Pennsylvania, Inc. ("Fleetwood"), from Brambillas, Inc. ("Brambillas"), an authorized Fleetwood motor home dealer and repair facility located in Minnesota. Workhorse manufactured the motor home's chassis, which included the motor home's supporting frame, engine, transmission, and certain electrical components. Sipe purchased the motor home for $105,616.75, and Brambillas delivered it to Sipe on October 21, 2004. Sipe received an owner's manual with the motor home that contained Workhorse's limited warranty for the chassis.

Sipe began experiencing problems with the motor home's engine shortly after he bought it. The engine stalled on three occasions while being driven by Sipe, once in October 2004, once in May 2005, and once in June 2005. Sipe brought the motor home to Brambillas for repairs after each stalling incident. After the first incident, Brambillas conducted diagnostic tests but made no repairs because it found no defect in the engine. Sipe testified in his deposition that after the second and third incidents, Brambillas claimed it performed diagnostic tests and found no defect but that the work order he received contained no indication that Brambillas performed any such tests. Sipe further testified that the last time the engine stalled was in June 2005 and that the engine problem has not prevented him from taking trips in the motor home.

In February 2006, Sipe listed the motor home for sale for the price of $94,900. After receiving only two offers at lower prices, Sipe reduced the listing price to $84,900, the Kelley Blue Book value of the motor home. Sipe testified that he ultimately decided to reduce the price because of a crack in the kitchen counter and that he did not recall any other defects that contributed to his decision to reduce the asking price. Sipe did not sell the motor home.

In January 2007 and December 2007, Sipe experienced problems with the motor home's transmission when he discovered that transmission fluid had leaked. Sipe testified that Brambillas refused to diagnose or repair the transmission after both incidents of fluid leakage.

Sipe brought this action against Workhorse and Fleetwood in the District Court for Hennepin County, Minnesota, alleging violations of Minnesota's lemon law. . . . The court dismissed Sipe's lemon law claims, finding that Sipe presented no evidence that the alleged engine defect required repair or that the defect substantially impaired the motor home and concluding that Sipe's claim regarding the transmission was time-barred.

* * * * *

II. DISCUSSION
A. Lemon Law

Sipe contends that the district court erred in granting summary judgment to Workhorse on his lemon law claim because Workhorse failed to repair his motor home's engine and transmission. Minnesota's lemon law provides:

> If the manufacturer, its agents, or its authorized dealers are unable to conform the new motor vehicle to any applicable express warranty by repairing or correcting any defect or condition which substantially impairs the use or market value of the motor vehicle to the consumer after a reasonable number of attempts, the manufacturer shall either replace the new motor vehicle with a comparable motor vehicle or accept return of the vehicle from the consumer and refund to the consumer the full purchase price. . . .

The manufacturer must make the required repairs if "the consumer reports the nonconformity to the manufacturer, its

agents, or its authorized dealer during the term of the applicable express warranties or during the period of two years following the date of original delivery of the new motor vehicle to a consumer, whichever is the earlier date."

1. Engine Stalls

After thoroughly reviewing the record, we conclude that Sipe failed to present evidence showing a genuine issue of material fact about whether the engine stalls "substantially impair[ed] the use or market value of the motor [home]," as required by Minnesota's lemon law. In response to being asked if the engine defect "ever prevented [him] from going somewhere [or] taking a trip with [his] motor home," Sipe replied "no." In fact, Sipe traveled over 11,000 miles in the motor home since the first time the engine stalled. As Sipe explained, "I don't know if [the engine problem] affect[s] my use now because I know how to deal with it." Sipe also stated that he had not experienced an engine stall since June 2005. Thus, Sipe's own testimony shows that the engine defect has not impaired his use of the motor home; it follows that the defect has not substantially impaired his use.

With respect to the effect of the engine defect on the market value of the motor home, Sipe argues that the low number of offers he received for the motor home shows that its market value was substantially impaired. However, Sipe cannot avoid summary judgment by merely relying on his conclusory allegation that the engine defect caused the low number of offers. Sipe presented no evidence to suggest that his receipt of only two offers was in any way caused by the engine stalls and not some other factor, such as market conditions for used motor homes. He offered no evidence that potential buyers were even aware of the engine stalls, given that he described the motor home as being in "excellent condition" when he originally listed it for sale in February 2006. Sipe testified that he only reduced the original asking price to the Kelley Blue Book value because of a crack in the kitchen counter and that he did not recall any other defects "that played a role in reducing the price." Further, Sipe submitted no other evidence suggesting that the value of the motor home was impaired, such as expert testimony or an appraisal of the motor home. As with his testimony regarding his use of the motor home, Sipe's own testimony shows that the engine defect has not impaired, substantially or otherwise, the motor home's market value.

* * * * *

2. Transmission Fluid Leaks

When he received the motor home in October 2004, Sipe received a three-year limited warranty from Workhorse. Thus, to bring an actionable lemon law claim, Sipe must have reported any nonconformities within two years of the date of the original delivery of the motor home. *See* Minn. Stat. Section 325 F. 665, subdiv. 2 (requiring consumers to report a nonconformity "during the term of the applicable express warranties or during the period of two years following the date of original delivery of the new motor vehicle . . . , whichever is the earlier date"). Sipe first reported the transmission fluid leak to Brambillas in January 2007, which was more than two years after the delivery of the motor home. As such, we agree with the district court that Sipe's lemon law claim with respect to the transmission leaks is barred by statute.

* * * * *

[Affirmed.]

Questions

1. *a.* According to Minnesota's lemon law, what was Sipe required to show in order to win his engine defect claim?

   b. Why did Sipe lose his engine defect claim?

2. Why did Sipe lose his defective transmission claim?

3. Dieter and Hermes agreed to buy a new 1996 Dodge Ram pickup truck from Fascona Chrysler-Plymouth-Dodge Trucks on December 12, 1995. They requested the installation of some after-market accessories—a tonneau cover, a bug shield, and rust proofing. When Dieter and Hermes returned to take delivery of the truck, they noticed it had been scratched during the installation of the accessories. The salesperson told them the scratches would be repaired. Four months later the dealership sent the truck to a body shop for repairs. After repair, Dieter and Hermes noticed swirl marks in the truck's finish. Dieter then demanded that Frascona repurchase the truck. Eight months later Dieter and Hermes sued Chrysler Corporation under Wisconsin's lemon law.

   a. Make the argument that the lemon law does not apply to the facts of this case.

   b. Decide the case. Explain. See *Dieter and Hermes v. Chrysler Corporation,* 610 N.W.2d 832 (Wis. S.Ct. 2000).

Federal Laws and Consumer Protection Agencies

Much of the federal government's authority to protect consumers rests with some powerful agencies including a new one approved in 2010 when Congress and President Obama concluded that our financial markets had failed in some important respects.

Consumer Financial Protection Bureau

Placing a bold bet on the capacity of the federal government to protect consumers, Congress and President Obama approved the creation of the Consumer Financial Protection Bureau (CFPB) as a direct response to the financial calamity of recent years. The new agency, authorized by the 2010 Dodd–Frank Wall Street Reform and Consumer Protection Act, is charged with writing and enforcing rules covering consumer financial products and services including mortgages, credit cards, payday loans, loan servicing, check cashing, debt collection, and others. Another important element of the Bureau's charge is to provide financial education, thereby promoting Americans' financial literacy. [For the Consumer Financial Protection Bureau home page, see **www.consumerfinance.gov/**]

[For a CFPB video explaining the Bureau's mission, see **www.consumerfinance.gov /the-bureau/**]

Rather than counting on market forces to ensure financial transparency and fair treatment for consumers, new rules are being created in an effort to mandate those results. Broadly, the Bureau will be expected to prohibit and prevent the commission of "an unfair, deceptive, or abusive act or practice" in conjunction with a consumer financial product or service. The expectation is that the Bureau will protect us from a wide array of dishonest practices such as hidden credit card fees and misleading "teaser" rates for mortgages.

The Act generally accords the Bureau authority over financial service firms, including banks, thrifts, and credit unions, though it specifically excludes real estate brokerages, accountants, lawyers, and those selling nonfinancial goods and services, among others. The Bureau's new rules must be subjected to cost–benefit reviews, and those rules can be set aside by a two-thirds vote of the new Financial Stability Oversight Council (created as part of the Dodd–Frank bill) if the rule would threaten the nation's financial system.

Having broad authority over federal consumer finance law, the Bureau is consolidating consumer finance programs currently residing in other agencies, and it is responsible for enforcing the finance laws outlined later in this chapter, including the Electronic Fund Transfer Act, the Equal Credit Opportunity Act, the Fair Credit Billing Act, and many more. The CFPB quickly asserted its regulatory authority. In 2013, the Bureau began addressing the mortgage problems that led to the recent financial meltdown. For example, one new rule spells out standards for ensuring that borrowers will be able to afford their mortgages, and another new rule requires lenders to provide borrowers with direct and ongoing access to loan servicing personnel. And in 2012, the CFPB set up an online portal where consumers can file complaints about credit cards, mortgages, banking, student loans, and more (see **consumerfinance.gov/complaint**). Those complaints are easily accessible to the public, thus imposing pressure on financial institutions to improve customer service.

Of course, the Bureau has many doubters and outright enemies. A primary fear is that increased government regulation is likely to reduce the availability of credit or raise the cost of that credit, thereby potentially damaging consumers and the economy. Some of the critics simply want the government to leave the finance market alone while others suggest, for example, that government resources should be limited to consumer education and counseling rather than more rules. [For a "one-stop shop for the American people to learn how to protect themselves from fraud and to report it wherever—and however—it occurs," see the Federal Financial Fraud Task Force's website: **www.stopfraud.gov**]

> The Bureau has many doubters and outright enemies.

The Federal Trade Commission

The Federal Trade Commission (FTC) was created in 1914 to prevent "unfair methods of competition and unfair or deceptive acts or practices in and affecting commerce." The FTC operates as a miniature government with powerful quasi-legislative (rule-making) and quasi-judicial (adjudication) roles. [For the FTC's Bureau of Consumer Protection home page, see **www.ftc.gov/bcp/index.shtml**]

Rule Making

The FTC's primary legislative direction is in issuing trade regulation rules to enforce the intent of broadly drawn congressional legislation. That is, the rules specify particular acts or practices that the commission deems deceptive.

The FTC's quasi-legislative (rule-making) power is extensive, as evidenced by the following examples:

- The Federal Trade Commission's Do Not Call Registry forbids telemarketers, with certain exceptions, from placing calls to the more than 200 million Americans who have added their phone numbers to the Federal Trade Commission's list. Although some violations continue, the rule has clearly been a success for annoyed consumers. The FTC also issued a 2009 rule banning many types of so-called robocalls (prerecorded telemarketing solicitations). Under the rule, sellers and telemarketers who transmit prerecorded messages to consumers who have not agreed in writing to accept those messages will face penalties of up to $16,000 per call. [Those wanting to be added to the Do Not Call list and those wanting to file complaints can visit **www.donotcall.gov**]

> "Does a moment pass when Kim Kardashian isn't selling?"

- In 2009, the *Los Angeles Times* asked: "Does a moment pass when Kim Kardashian isn't selling? If she's not hyping her workout video, she's touting her online shoe club, her new book or her sisters' 'reality' TV spin-off, a gripping look inside their high-end Miami boutique."[5]

Kardashian and all others hyping products and services on the Internet are now subject to penalties for false or misleading advertising if they fail to comply with the FTC's "Guides Concerning Use of Endorsements and Testimonials in Advertising." The rules, among other things, require those offering endorsements on new media sites (blogs, Twitter, Facebook, etc.) to disclose any connection they have (including in most cases, receiving cash or gifts) in exchange for their testimonials.

Adjudication

On its own initiative or as a result of a citizen complaint, the FTC may investigate suspect trade practices. At that point the FTC may drop the proceeding, settle the matter, or issue a formal complaint.

Where a formal complaint is issued, the matter proceeds essentially as a trial conducted before an administrative law judge. The FTC has no authority to impose criminal sanctions.

Federal Trade Commission—Fraud and Deception

Unfair and deceptive trade practices, including those in advertising, are forbidden under Section 5 of the Federal Trade Commission Act. The FTC test for deception requires that the claim is (1) false or likely to mislead the reasonable consumer and (2) material to the consumer's decision making. Deception can take many forms, including, for example, testimonials by celebrities who do not use the endorsed product or do not have meaningful expertise. Product quality claims are an area of particular dispute.

Quality Claims

Under the FTC's ad substantiation program, advertisers are engaging in unfair and deceptive practices if they make product claims without some reasonable foundation for those claims. Skechers, for example, agreed to pay $50 million in 2012 to settle FTC and state charges that it misled the public by making unsupported claims that its toning sneakers allow buyers to, among other things, "Shape Up While You Walk" and "Get in Shape without Setting Foot in a Gym." According to the FTC, a Skechers' ad said that its fitness claims were backed by a chiropractor study. The study, however, did not produce the claimed results, and Skechers failed to disclose that the chiropractor was married to a Skechers executive and that the chiropractor was paid for doing the study.[6] Skechers denied the FTC allegations. Shoe purchasers are eligible for refunds ranging from $20 to $84 per product purchased. An FTC survey found that nearly 11 percent of American adults were victims of fraud in 2011.[7] Weight-loss products and prize promotions were the most common types of fraudulent products.

Federal Trade Commission—Consumer Privacy

Kellie Droste, a Maricopa, Arizona, resident was shocked in March 2013 when she learned that an identity thief had stolen her personal information and filed a tax return in her name to claim her tax refund.[8] According to the federal Justice Department, credit card data theft grew 50 percent from 2005 to 2010.[9] Millions of stolen card numbers are for sale at a price of perhaps $10 to $50 each, and a no-limit American Express card issued to a consumer with a high credit rating might sell for hundreds of dollars.[10] When businesses are hacked, millions of credit records may be compromised at a cost of an estimated $150 to $250 for each number stolen.[11] Of course, those costs are passed on to consumers. Despite these staggering numbers and the prospect for even greater losses in the future, identity theft expert Adam Levin reminds us that we don't seem to pay much attention:

> Despite considerable coverage and legislative initiatives, identity theft, cyber warfare, and the death of privacy at the hands of hackers and hyper-marketers are barely on the public radar. People say they care about identity theft but they don't really understand it.[12]

A 2013 federal government study found that 1 in 14 Americans age 16 and older were either targets of identity theft or actually experienced identity theft. The resulting financial losses for 2012 totaled nearly $25 billion.[13] [For a privacy database and links, see **www .privacyrights.org**].

Privacy Law

The Federal Trade Commission's authority to stop unfair methods of competition along with unfair and deceptive acts and practices gives the agency considerable power in policing consumer privacy breaches. The FTC also enforces the privacy provisions in a number of other federal laws, including those addressing the use of consumer credit reports, children's online privacy, identity theft, personal health information, personal financial information, and others. In 2011, the FTC began enforcing its "Red Flags Rule" that is designed to slow identity theft. Under the rule, all "financial institutions" and "creditors" must establish a written program to prevent identity theft in their organizations and then mitigate whatever losses may come from identity theft. The FTC identifies "Red Flags" as, for example, suspicious documents, financial account activities, or IDs .

As needed, the FTC has been aggressive in privacy enforcement, having recently reached agreements with both Google and Facebook to settle Commission charges of privacy violations. Furthermore, the FTC in 2012 called for Congress to enact additional general privacy legislation along with several other new laws to address expanding threats in our technology-driven culture. In addition, the Obama administration in 2012 issued a Consumer Privacy Bill of Rights, which addresses how businesses collect and use consumers' personal information and outlines core principles such as the expectation that consumers should control how their information will be used in the market. The administration expects to work with the various stakeholders in developing voluntary, but legally enforceable, codes of conduct that implement the Consumer Privacy Bill of Rights. Of course, rule-enhanced privacy comes with significant costs because constricted information flow risks reduced efficiency and increased costs.

The Federal Trade Commission recognizes the need for active engagement, especially in hot-button areas, such as a global "Do Not Track" standard that would strengthen users' ability to control when and how their online information is collected. In 2013, FTC Chair Edith Ramirez made it very clear, however, that the Commission should use its authority "very judiciously."[14] Speaking of the FTC's power to police unfairness in the market, Ramirez said, "I want to just emphasize that that's not a blank check for the FTC in going after privacy violations."[15] The market and self-regulation, from the FTC point of view, must remain the core methods for assuring consumer privacy.

The Consumer Product Safety Commission

Another reason to avoid sleeping with an ex: fear of contracting lead poisoning. Just ask Barbie, who got it from Ken. That's according to "Toxic Toys: A Poisonous Affair," a YouTube attack on the Consumer Product Safety Commission produced by the nonprofit Campaign for America's Future.[16]

The Consumer Product Safety Commission (CPSC) is the federal agency charged with protecting us from "unreasonable risks of injury and death" from consumer products. The YouTube attack was a product of frustration with the CPSC's response to a 2007 wave of toy recalls, largely because of dangerous levels of lead. Tens of millions of toys and children's items, most of them made in China, have been recalled in recent years. Widespread outrage over the lead risk led to the Consumer Product Safety Improvement Act that, among other things, lowered permissible levels of lead in children's (up to age 12) products. Critics, however, argued that the bill created excessive, unnecessary, and unintended costs, especially for small businesses. Responding to those concerns, Congress and President Obama in 2011 approved new legislation giving the CPSC greatly expanded latitude to grant exceptions to the Consumer Product Safety Improvement Act in situations where risk to human health does not exist.

> More than 30 infant and toddler deaths.

Cribs   After more than 30 infant and toddler deaths and millions of recalls in the past decade, the CPSC unanimously voted to ban, effective June 28, 2011, the manufacture, sale, and resale (including yard sales) of the traditional drop-side baby crib that has cradled millions. The new standard requires fixed sides.[17]

[For an ABC News visit to the Consumer Product Safety Commission Testing Lab, see **http://abcnews.go.com/GMA/video/consumer-product-safety-commission-test-lab-13827984**]

Reducing Risk   The CPSC, created in 1972, is responsible for reducing the risks in using consumer products such as toys, lawn mowers, washing machines, bicycles, fireworks, pools, portable heaters, and household chemicals. The CPSC pursues product safety, initially, by collecting data and issuing rules. The commission conducts research and collects information as a foundation for regulating product safety. Via its rule-making authority, the CPSC promulgates mandatory consumer product safety, performance, and labeling standards.

To enforce its policies and decisions, the CPSC holds both compliance and enforcement powers. In seeking compliance with safety expectations, the commission can exert a number of expectations. Manufacturers must certify before distribution that products meet federal safety standards. Manufacturing sites may be inspected, and specific product safety testing procedures can be mandated. Businesses other than retailers are required to keep product safety records. In cases of severe and imminent hazards, the CPSC has the power to enforce its decisions by seeking a court order to remove a product from the market. In less-urgent circumstances, the commission may proceed with its own administrative remedy. Preferring voluntary compliance, the commission may negotiate with companies to recall dangerous products. Product recalls issued in 2011 by the CPSC, the Food and Drug Administration, and the Department of Agriculture totaled 2,363 (up from 1,460 in 2007).[18] The result presumably is improved consumer safety, but we have some evidence of "recall fatigue." A 2009 study found 40 percent of Americans indicating they have never looked for recalled products in their home.[19] [For the federal government recall site, see **www.recalls.gov/**]

Where voluntary negotiations fail, the commission may proceed with an adjudicative hearing before an administrative law judge or members of the commission. That decision may be appealed to the full commission and thereafter to the federal court of appeals. Civil or criminal penalties may result. Only a few products, such as the drop-side cribs, have actually been banned from the market by the Commission. The CPSC launched a public database in 2011 that allows all of us to report dangerous products and to search complaints entered by others. [See **http://saferproducts.gov/**]

The Food and Drug Administration

Tobacco   The Food and Drug Administration announced in 2013 that it had begun exercising its authority over tobacco; power conferred by Congress and President Obama in 2009. For the first time, the FDA can keep tobacco products off the market if they pose public health risks beyond comparable products already on the market. Prior to the 2009 legislation, the FDA could not regulate tobacco, a process that was left to the limited authority of the states. The FDA can also regulate tobacco ingredients, including nicotine, but the agency is not yet exercising that power.

Drug Safety   The FDA monitors much of America's health landscape with responsibility for assuring the safety, effectiveness, and security of food, drugs (prescription and over-the-counter), medical devices, cosmetics, tobacco products, and more. Perhaps the biggest FDA duty is to decide when drugs should be approved for marketing. Companies must subject a new drug to laboratory, animal, and eventually human testing before the FDA will consider approval. FDA physicians and scientists review the scientific evidence, and thereafter the FDA approves a drug for marketing only if it is safe and effective. The FDA is empowered to impose fines and remove dangerous drugs from the market. Thus, arthritis

> A nearly-doubled risk of heart attack.

drug Vioxx, approved by the FDA in 1999, was pulled from the market in 2004 because the estimated 25 million Americans who took the drug faced a nearly-doubled risk of heart attack and stroke. An FDA study linked Vioxx to as many as 140,000 injuries and 56,000 deaths in the United States.[20] Merck, the drug's manufacturer, has paid billions of dollars to settle many civil lawsuits and, in 2011, Merck agreed to pay $950 million and pleaded guilty to a criminal charge over Vioxx marketing and sales practices.[21] Lawsuits continue, but at this writing no person has been penalized for the Vioxx wrongs.

> A series of massive food poisoning scares.

Food Safety   At this writing in 2013, the FDA has announced a preliminary determination that artificial trans fats are not safe in foods. After public comment and further review, the FDA may effectively banish trans fats from processed foods by allowing them only with scientific proof of safety. In recent years, food safety has climbed the list of FDA worries following a series of massive food poisoning scares. Vegetables, peanut products, eggs, and other foodstuffs have been contaminated by *salmonella* and *E. coli*. The 2010 salmonella outbreak in eggs (primarily regulated by the FDA, but assisted by the Agriculture Department and other agencies) sickened more than 1,600 people and led to the recall of 550 million eggs.[22] A 2012 salmonella outbreak in peanut butter prompted the FDA to force the closure of Sunland Inc.'s New Mexico production facility. FDA data show that one in six Americans suffers from a food-borne illness annually resulting in 3,000 deaths and 130,000 hospitalizations.[23]

The 2011 Food Safety and Modernization Act gave the FDA greatly expanded food safety power. With about one in six Americans suffering from eating contaminated food each year, the FDA has proposed new rules to implement the 2011 Act. The rules would require farmers to make sure, for example, that irrigation water is clean and that animals are kept out of fields. Food manufacturers will be expected to submit food safety plans to the government. Imported food would be subjected to the same standards as domestic production with importers being required to prove that their foreign suppliers have careful safety measures in place. Since the FDA is able to inspect only 1 to 2 percent of all imported food, the food safety burden will lie primarily with suppliers. The food industry has responded by, among other things, improving worker training and employing technological advances, including high-tech labels, which allow monitoring of food from the fields to the supermarket checkout.

Trust the Market or Strengthen the FDA?   Perhaps because of its crucial safety role in American life, the FDA is one of the most criticized divisions of the federal government. As noted, food safety worries, or at least publicity about them, seem to have spiraled in recent years. The drug approval process has been the subject of particularly fierce criticism. New drug approvals (39) in 2012 reached their highest level in 15 years despite tightened safety standards following several drug scandals—Vioxx in particular.[24] Nevertheless, critics argue that lifesaving new products could reach consumers much more quickly if we relied less on government rules and more on market forces. Reduced regulation, of course, carries its own risks. For example, during a recent five-year study period, more than 70 percent of 113 recalled medical devices (such as defibrillators and insulin pumps) had been approved by the FDA under an expedited system.[25] The devices were approved for sale more quickly because they were deemed sufficiently similar to products already on the market. Beyond safety concerns, experts Tomas Philipson and Andrew von Eschenbach argue that reduced and more efficient regulation could double medical innovation and sharply boost the American GDP.[26] Thus, to some critics, the FDA imposes too many rules; to others, too few.

Plan B

At this writing in 2013, the FDA is considering several new consumer rules including protection for children and adolescents from added caffeine in products such as Cracker Jack and a warning against tanning bed use for those under 18. The most controversial decision, however, has to do with the morning-after birth control pill, popularly known as Plan B. In early 2013, a federal judge ordered the FDA to make Plan B available without prescription to girls and women of all ages. The Obama administration announced that it would appeal the federal judge's order, but soon thereafter the appeal was dropped and the FDA was expected to approve Plan B for sale over the counter without restrictions.

Question

In your judgment, should the FDA make Plan B available to girls and women of all ages, to those 15 and above, to those 17 and over, as had been the case, to some other age, or not at all? Explain.

Part Three—Debtor/Creditor Law

Credit Regulations

> Angelique Trammel decided to buy a laptop on a "low weekly payment plan."

According to *The New York Times,* Angelique Trammel, a single mother and telephone operator, decided to buy a laptop for her son on a "low weekly payment plan." She paid $99 down and agreed to have $41 per week withdrawn from her bank account. After six months, a broken computer arrived. Having spent well over $1,000 and after having received two nonworking computers, she demanded a refund from the retailer, BlueHippo. Under her agreement, Ms. Trammel allegedly would have paid more than $2,000 for a computer worth much less. Describing sales schemes directed to the poor, Better Business Bureau spokesman Steve Cox said: "The way these companies operate is simply another form of predatory lending."[27] BlueHippo, on the other hand, said that, "before, during and after the sales transaction we fully disclose the total price and all shipping guidelines" to customers.[28]

Situations like Trammel's and broad fears of abuse in credit and lending led Congress and the state legislatures to supplement the market's powerful messages with a substantial array of protective legislation. We will turn now to a look at several particularly important pieces of federal lending practices law. [For a debtor/creditor law database, see **www.law .cornell.edu/topics/debtor_creditor.html**]

Dodd–Frank Wall Street Reform and Consumer Protection Act

In addition to creating the Consumer Finance Protection Bureau (CFPB), the 2010 Dodd–Frank bill provides increased legislative oversight of the nation's financial processes. (See Chapter 8 for the bill's provisions designed to stabilize and protect the banking system.) Broadly, the bill's consumer protection provisions move away from the old system that mandated disclosure to consumers of critical financial information (e.g., interest rates) to a more prescriptive regime that requires lenders to affirmatively protect borrowers.

Truth in Lending Act (TILA)

Consumers often do not understand the full cost of buying on credit. The TILA is designed primarily to assure full disclosure of credit terms. Having been designed for consumer protection, the TILA does not cover all loans. The following standards determine the TILA's applicability:

1. The debtor must be a "natural person" rather than an organization.
2. The creditor must be regularly engaged in extending credit and must be the person to whom the debt is initially payable. Dodd–Frank expressly amends the definition of creditor to include mortgage originators.
3. The purpose of the credit must be "primarily for personal, family, or household purposes" not in excess of $25,000, but "consumer real property transactions" are covered by the act. Hence home purchases fall within TILA provisions.
4. The credit must be subject to a finance charge or payable in more than four installments.

The TILA and Regulation Z interpreting the act were designed both to protect consumers from credit abuse and to assist them in becoming more informed about credit terms and costs so they could engage in comparison shopping. Congress presumed the increased information would stimulate competition in the finance industry. The heart of the act is the required conspicuous disclosure of the amount financed, the finance charge (the actual dollar sum to be paid for credit), the annual percentage rate (APR—the total cost of the credit expressed at an annual rate), and the number of payments. The finance charge includes not just interest but service charges, points, loan fees, carrying charges, and other costs. The TILA covers consumer loans generally, including credit cards and auto purchases. [For consumer information on "abusive lending," see **www.ftc.gov/bcp/menu-lending.htm**]

TILA amendments in the Dodd–Frank bill give extensive, new attention to residential mortgages, a recognition of our ongoing subprime mortgage crisis and its destructive impact on the entire American economy. Creditors, for example, are prohibited from making a residential mortgage loan without a good faith determination that the consumer has a reasonable "ability to repay" the loan. Likewise mortgage service providers must, for example, respond to error notices within a specified period of time.

The case that follows examines the application of TILA to a credit card interest rate dispute.

Circuit Judge O'Scannlain

We must decide whether a credit card company violates the Truth in Lending Act when it fails to disclose potential risk factors that allow it to raise a cardholder's Annual Percentage Rate.

I

A

Walter and Cheryl Barrer held a credit card account with Chase. The Barrers received and accepted the Cardmember Agreement ("the Agreement") governing their relationship at the relevant time in late 2004. In February 2005, Chase mailed to the Barrers a Change in Terms Notice ("the Notice"), which purported to amend the terms of the Agreement, in particular to increase the Annual Percentage Rate ("APR") significantly. It also allowed the Barrers to reject the amendments in writing by a certain date. They did not do so, and continued to use the credit card. Within two months, the new, higher, APR became effective.

According to the Barrers' First Amended Complaint, they enjoyed a preferred APR of 8.99% under the Agreement. In a section entitled "Finance Charges," the Agreement provided a mathematical formula for calculating preferred and non-preferred APRs and variable rates. In the event of default, the Agreement stated that Chase might increase the APR on the balance up to a stated default rate. The Agreement specified the following events of default: failure to pay at least a minimum payment by the due date; a credit card balance in excess of the credit limit on the account; failure to pay another creditor when required; the return, unpaid, of a payment to Chase by the customer's bank; or, should Chase close the account, the consumer's failure to pay the outstanding balance at the time Chase has appointed.

Another section entirely, entitled "Changes to the Agreement," provided that Chase "can change this agreement at any time, . . . by adding, deleting, or modifying any provision. [The] right to add, delete, or modify provisions includes financial terms, such as APRs and fees." The next section, entitled "Credit Information," stated that Chase "may periodically review your credit history by obtaining information from credit bureaus and others." These sections appeared five and six pages, respectively, after the "Finance Charge" section.

Around April 2005, the Barrers' noticed that their APR had "skyrocketed" from 8.99% to 24.24%, the latter a rate close to a non-preferred or default rate. None of the events of default specified in the Agreement, however, had occurred. When the Barrers contacted Chase to find out why their APR had increased, Chase responded in a letter citing judgments it had made on the basis of information obtained from a consumer credit reporting agency. In particular, Chase wrote that: "outstanding credit loan(s) on revolving accounts . . . [were] too high" and there were "too many recently opened installment/revolving accounts." The Barrers do not dispute the facts underlying Chase's judgments.

Despite the Barrers' surprise, the Notice they had received in February contained some indication of what would be forthcoming. Specifically, it disclosed that Chase would shortly increase the APR to 24.24%, a decision "based in whole or in part on the information obtained in a report from the consumer reporting agency."

The Barrers paid the interest on the credit account at the new rate for three months before they were able to pay off the balance. Then they sued Chase in federal district court.

B

The Barrers filed a class action lawsuit on their own behalf and on behalf of all Chase credit card customers similarly harmed and similarly situated. The complaint asserted one cause of action under the Truth in Lending Act ("the Act"), and Regulation Z. The Barrers claim to have been the victims of a practice they now call "adverse action repricing," which apparently means "raising . . . a preferred rate to an essentially non-preferred rate based upon information in a customer's credit report." Though the Barrers do not claim that the practice itself is illegal, they do claim that it was illegal for Chase not to disclose it fully to them or to the other members of the putative class.

[The federal district court dismissed the Barrers' cause of action. The Barrers appealed.]

II

The Truth in Lending Act is designed "to assure a meaningful disclosure of credit terms so that the consumer will be able to compare more readily the various credit terms available to him and avoid the uninformed use of credit." Rather than substantively regulate the terms creditors can offer or include in their financial products, the Act primarily requires disclosure.

* * * * *

In general, the Act regulates credit card disclosures at numerous points in the commercial arrangement between creditor and consumer: at the point of solicitation and application, at the point the consumer and the creditor consummate the deal, at each billing cycle, and at the point the parties renew their arrangement. Specifically, creditors must disclose "[t]he conditions under which a finance charge may be imposed," "[t]he method of determining the amount of the finance charge," and, "[w]here one or more periodic rates may be used to compute the finance charge, each such rate . . . and the corresponding nominal annual percentage rate."

Regulation Z, 12 C.F.R. Section 226, provides the precise regulations that the Barrers claim Chase violated. In general, these regulations establish two conditions a creditor must meet. "First, it must have disclosed all of the information required by the statute." That is, disclosures must be complete. "And second, [they] must have been true—i.e., . . . accurate representation[s] of the legal obligations of the parties at [the] time [the agreement was made]."

Section 226.6 lists the initial disclosures required of a creditor under a new credit agreement. The list includes "each periodic rate that may be used to compute the finance charge . . . and the corresponding annual percentage rate."

* * * * *

Just as section 226.6 states what must be disclosed, so section 226 describes how to disclose it. Among other things, creditors must make the required disclosures "clearly and conspicuously in writing." . . .

The Board has also recognized that creditors may reserve the general right to change the credit agreement, as Chase did in this case. Should the creditor make changes in these ways, it may have to disclose anew under Section 226.9(c).

III

The Barrers argue that . . . Chase failed to disclose completely under the Act why it would change the APRs of its cardholders, in violation of subsection 226.6(a)(2) of Regulation Z.

The Barrers do not argue that either the Agreement or the Notice failed to disclose the APR, which their complaint puts at 8.99% under the Agreement and 24.24% under the Notice. Rather, . . . the gravamen of the Barrers' complaint is that Chase did not disclose that if a cardholder's credit report revealed certain information, what Chase calls "risk factors," the APR might go up.

* * * * *

Regulation Z requires that creditors disclose any APR "that *may* be used to compute the finance charge," and that they do so "clearly and conspicuously."

* * * * *

We are persuaded that Chase adequately disclosed the APRs that the Agreement permitted it to use simply by means of the change-in-terms provision. That provision reserved Chase's right to change APRs, among other terms, without any limitation on why Chase could make such a change. The provision thus disclosed that, by changing the Agreement, Chase could use any APR, a class of APRs that logically includes APRs adjusted on the basis of adverse credit information. Apart from the gloss of Comment 11, neither the Act nor Regulation Z require Chase to disclose the basis on which it would change or use APRs. Therefore the failure to disclose the reason for the change to the Barrers' APR—adverse credit information—and that Chase would look up their credit history to acquire that information does not undermine the adequacy of Chase's disclosure.

Even so, such disclosure must be clear and conspicuous. Neither the Act nor Regulation Z define clarity and conspicuousness in this context. The Staff Commentary explains only that "[t]he clear and conspicuous standard requires that disclosures be in a reasonably understandable form." . . .

Clear and conspicuous disclosures, therefore, are disclosures that a reasonable cardholder would notice and understand. No particular kind of formatting is magical, but, in this case, the document must have made it clear to a reasonable cardholder that Chase was permitted under the agreement to raise the APR not only for the events of default specified in the "Finance Terms" section, but for any reason at all.

. . . [T]he change-in-terms provision appears on page 10–11 of the Agreement, five dense pages after the disclosure of the APR. It is neither referenced in nor clearly related to the "Finance Terms" section. This provision, as part of the APRs allowed under the contract, is buried too deeply in the fine print for a reasonable cardholder to realize that, in addition to the specific grounds for increasing the APR listed in the "Finance Charges" section, Chase could raise the APR for other reasons.

Therefore, the Barrers have stated a claim because Chase cannot show that, as a matter of law, the Agreement made clear and conspicuous disclosure of the APRs that Chase was permitted to use.

REVERSED and REMANDED.

Questions

1. *a.* How did Chase violate Regulation Z and the TILA?
   b. According to this decision, what is a "clear and conspicuous" disclosure?

2. Green Tree Financial financed Randolph's mobile home purchase. Randolph sued, claiming that Green Tree's financing

document contained an arbitration clause that violated TILA because it did not provide the same level of protection as TILA accords. If the arbitration clause provided lesser protection than that provided for by TILA, as Randolph claimed, should the arbitration go forward? Explain. See *Randolph v. Green Tree Financial Corp.,* 531 U.S. 79 (2000).

3. Sarah Hamm sued Ameriquest Mortgage Company claiming a violation of the Truth in Lending Act (TILA). Hamm borrowed money secured by a 30-year mortgage from Ameriquest. She signed a "Disclosure Statement" specifying, among other things, that she was responsible for 359 payments at a specified amount and one payment for the last month of a slightly smaller amount. The Statement did not, however, explicitly specify, as required by the TILA, the total payments due (360). Was the TILA violated? Explain. See *Hamm v. Ameriquest Mortgage,* 506 F.3d 525 (7th Cir. 2007).

Credit and Charge Cards

> College students are burying themselves in debt.

College students are burying themselves in debt. As of 2013, student loan debt (about $1 trillion) exceeded the total amount owed by all Americans on their credit cards.[29] Student credit card use, on the other hand, declined to 35 percent in 2012 from 42 percent in 2010.[30] That decline apparently was partially attributable to the 2009 federal Credit Card Accountability, Responsibility, and Disclosure Act (CARD Act). Among other things, CARD forbids lenders from issuing credit cards to those under age 21 without a parent as cosigner or without proof the applicant can make payments. Many colleges and universities that have allowed credit marketing on campus have profited handsomely from deals with card companies. While federal rules have significantly curbed campus credit card marketing, about 900 colleges maintain card partnerships with banks, and other commercial relationships are common.[31] For example, Ohio State University, while not allowing credit card marketing to students, reportedly receives $25 million from Huntington Bank in return for allowing branches and ATMs on campus. The deal allows Huntington the exclusive opportunity to directly tailor products and services to more than 600,000 students, faculty, staff, and alumni.[32]

Question

How would you argue that government intervention in the credit card market is not in the best interest of consumers generally and college students in particular?

TILA Protections

The law offers substantial protections for credit card users. The TILA provides that credit cards cannot be issued to a consumer unless requested. Cardholder liability for unauthorized use (lost or stolen card) cannot exceed $50, and the cardholder bears no liability after notifying the issuer of the missing card. In general, issuers must disclose key cost features, including APR, annual membership fees, minimum finance charges, late payment fees, and so on.

CARD

The aforementioned CARD Act of 2009 provides extensive additional protection for credit card holders. Some of the key provisions:

- Credit card companies are barred from increasing the annual percentage rate on existing account balances except when the cardholder's minimum payment is 60 days overdue.

- Issuers cannot charge interest on bills paid on time.
- Without specific agreement by the consumer, banks cannot accept charges where doing so puts creditors over their limits.
- Interest rates, with some exceptions, cannot be raised in the first year.

Beyond the CARD Act, other recent federal credit card rule changes have provided additional consumer shelter. Those rules cap fees for late payments, banish penalties for inactive accounts (although those accounts can still simply be closed), and allow merchants to set a $10 minimum for credit card purchases.

Success?

Skepticism is often the response to new rules, but the early evidence suggests that the federal government's credit card measures have been good for consumers. A 2011 Pew study found that penalty fees have dropped, overlimit fees (for charges beyond the credit limit) are now rare, and annual fees have not proliferated as some critics expected.[33] Furthermore, government officials have praised the industry itself for going even further than the law requires, although some banking officials believe the law has increased credit costs while decreasing credit availability.[34]

A Win for Consumers?

Debit card interchange fees (the charges paid by merchants to banks for providing debit processing services) had reached an average of 44¢ per transaction prior to the passage of the 2010 Dodd–Frank Act. By contrast, the median variable cost of each transaction was estimated at 7¢. Retailers and consumers argued that the two primary debit card processing services, Visa and MasterCard, were operating what amounted to a shared monopoly that permitted supracompetitive pricing.

Following a battle by armies of lobbyists, Congress approved new rules allowing the Federal Reserve (The Fed) to cap the interchange fees. The Fed in 2011 settled on a maximum charge of 21¢ per transaction with some additional small fees and a cap exemption for smaller banks. Following six months of transactions under the new rules, the Fed found that banks subject to the cap saw a 45 percent drop in their average fees—down to 24¢—whereas fees at smaller banks with an exemption stayed steady at about 43¢. The big banks say the fee cap merely shifts revenue to the big box retailers who are failing to pass on the fee savings to consumers. The banks also say the rule will force them to cut back on perks for customers while requiring new or increased fees on various services. At this writing, a federal district court judge has ruled that the 21¢ fee is higher than Congress intended in enacting Dodd–Frank. That decision has been appealed. [See *NACS v. Board of Governors of the Federal Reserve System,* 2013 U.S. Dist. LEXIS 107581]

Sources: Moe Bedard, "Fed's Rule on 'Swipe Fee' Cap Awaited," *Tulsa World,* April 25, 2011 [**www.tulsaworld.com/**]; Jim Puzzanghera, "Debit Card Fee Limits Hit a Snag," *latimes.com,* February 17, 2011 [**www.latimes.com/business/la-fi-debit-fees-20110218,0,3057034.story**]; Victoria McGrane and Robin Sidel, "Fed Softens 'Swipe' Fees," *The Wall Street Journal,* June 30, 2011, p. C2; and Peter Schroeder, "Federal Reserve: Debit Card Swipe Fees Falling Thanks to Durbin Amendment," *The Hill,* May 1, 2012.

Credit Cards Good for the World?

By 2025 or so, Chinese residents are expected to expand their credit card holdings from 331 million at the end of 2012 million to 1.1 billion and thereby pass the United States (536 million cards) as the world's biggest credit card market by number of cards. Credit cards are becoming a commonplace shopping tool in the developing world. As a result, those consumers are joining Americans and other Westerners in struggling to repay their credit card debt. For example, consumers in Turkey in recent years have embraced credit cards with enthusiasm, but having done so, they increasingly find themselves in a "debt trap" built by high interest rates (nearly 29 percent in 2011). Turkey has imposed some regulatory restraints, but consumer rights advocate, Turhan Cakar, foresees continuing problems: "Banks hand out cards too freely and then push a culture of consumption." Critics are concerned that consumers around the globe will be caught up in a debt cycle they often do not understand and that they cannot escape.

Question

Is the consumer credit path embraced by Americans a wise course for consumers in developing nations around the world? List some of the competing arguments.

Sources: Bloomberg News, "Credit-Card Companies Battle in China," *Bloomberg Businessweek,* May 2, 2013 [**www.businessweek.com/**]; and Carol Matlack and Steve Bryant, "Turkey's Credit-Card Crunch," *Bloomberg Businessweek,* October 27, 2011 [**www.businessweek.com**].

Consumer Credit Reports

Do you want to borrow money for a new car or a house? Want to get a better job? Success in each of those efforts may depend to a considerable extent on your credit score. A favorable credit rating is a vital feature of consumer life, and having reliable credit information is essential to efficient business practice. Thus, the three national credit information giants, Equifax, Experian, and TransUnion, as well as local credit bureaus, provide retailers, employers, insurance companies, and others with consumers' detailed credit histories. From those credit histories, a credit score is computed and sold to lenders. The federal Fair Credit Reporting Act (FCRA) affords consumers the following credit reporting protections, among others:

- Anyone using information from a credit reporting agency (CRA), such as Equifax, to take "adverse action" against you (denying you credit, a job, insurance) must notify you and tell you where it secured the information.

- At your request, a CRA must give you the information in your file and a list of all those who have recently sought information about you.

- If you claim that your credit file contains inaccurate information, the CRA must investigate your complaint and give you a written report. If you remain unsatisfied, you can include a brief statement in your credit file. Notice of the dispute and a summary of your statement normally must accompany future reports.

- All inaccurate information must be corrected or removed from the file, usually within 30 days.

- In most cases, negative information more than seven years old must not be reported.

- You must provide written consent before a CRA can provide information to your employer or prospective employer.
- You can sue for damages if your rights under the act have been violated.
- Lenders are required to provide a consumer's credit score as well as any factors that affected that score if the lender took any adverse action based on that score.[35]

The FCRA provides useful consumer protection, but serious weaknesses remain. The Federal Trade Commission released a 2013 study showing that 20 percent of consumers have a material error on at least one of their credit reports. At least 5 percent of consumers suffer errors serious enough that they may pay more than they should for products.[36] Thus, millions of Americans have been injured, including some who may have been denied jobs because of inaccurate credit reports. (Several states have limited the use of credit histories in making employment decisions.) When consumers try to correct their credit reports by filing complaints with the ratings agencies, the FTC found that the files are modified in about 80 percent of the cases.[37] In an effort to bring increased fairness to consumers, the Consumer Financial Protection Bureau now has supervisory authority over 30 of the largest credit bureaus, including the three biggest. Consumers can file credit report complaints with the CFPB.

[For an extensive set of practical questions and answers about consumer rights under the Fair Credit Reporting Act, see **www.ftc.gov/os/statutes/fcrajump.shtm**]

Fair Credit Billing Act

The Fair Credit Billing Act (FCBA) provides a mechanism to deal with the billing errors that accompany credit card and certain other "open-end" credit transactions. A cardholder who receives an erroneous bill must complain in writing to the creditor within 60 days of the time the bill was mailed. The creditor must acknowledge receipt of the complaint within 30 days. Then, within two billing cycles but not more than 90 days, the creditor must issue a response either by correcting the account or by forwarding a written statement to the consumer explaining why the bill is accurate. The creditor cannot threaten the consumer's credit rating or report the consumer as delinquent while the bill is in dispute, although the creditor can report that the bill is being challenged. Where a "reasonable investigation" determines the bill was correct but the consumer continues to contest it, the consumer may refuse to pay, and the creditor will then be free to commence collection procedures after giving the consumer 10 days to pay the disputed amount. If the bill is reported to a credit bureau as delinquent, that report must also indicate the consumer's belief that the money is not owed, and the consumer must be told who received the report. Wronged consumers may complain to the FTC and sue for damages.

Electronic Fund Transfers

The Electronic Fund Transfer Act (EFTA) provides remedies for lost or stolen cards, billing errors, and other such problems involving ATMs, point-of-sale machines, electronic deposits, and the like. Under the EFTA, liability for misuse of missing cards is capped at $50 if the consumer provides notice within two business days after learning of the loss. The loss could reach $500 if notice is provided within 60 days and could be unlimited thereafter. The Dodd–Frank Act amended the EFT to impose limits on debit card interchange fees. [For consumer information on electronic banking, see **www.ftc.gov/bcp/edu/pubs/consumer/credit/cre14.shtm**]

Equal Credit Opportunity

The Equal Credit Opportunity Act is designed to combat bias in lending. ECOA was in large part a response to anger over differing treatment of women and men in the financial marketplace. Credit must be extended to all creditworthy applicants regardless of sex, marital status, age, race, color, religion, national origin, good-faith exercise of rights under the Consumer Credit Protection Act, and receipt of public assistance (like food stamps). ECOA was in large part a response to anger over differing treatment of women and men in the financial marketplace. Creditors often would not lend money to married women in the women's own names, and single, divorced, and widowed women were similarly disadvantaged in securing credit. [For more details about ECOA, see **www.ftc.gov/bcp/pubs/consumer/credit/cre15.shtm**] The case that follows applies the ECOA to a "cross-dressing" male.

Lucas Rosa v. Park West Bank & Trust Co.

LEGAL   BRIEFCASE   214 F.3d 213 (1st Cir. 2000)

Judge Lynch

I

[O]n July 21, 1998, [Lucas] Rosa came to the [Park West] Bank to apply for a loan. A biological male, he was dressed in traditionally feminine attire. He requested a loan application from Norma Brunelle, a bank employee. Brunelle asked Rosa for identification. Rosa produced three forms of photo identification: (1) a Massachusetts Department of Public Welfare Card; (2) a Massachusetts Identification Card; and (3) a Money Stop Check Cashing ID Card. Brunelle looked at the identification cards and told Rosa that she would not provide him with a loan application until he "went home and changed." She said that he had to be dressed like one of the identification cards in which he appeared in more traditionally male attire before she would provide him with a loan application and process his loan request.

II

Rosa sued the Bank. Rosa charged that "by requiring [him] to conform to sex stereotypes before proceeding with the credit transaction, [the Bank] unlawfully discriminated against [him] with respect to an aspect of a credit transaction on the basis of sex." He claims to have suffered emotional distress.

Without filing an answer to the complaint, the Bank moved to dismiss. . . . The district court granted the Bank's motion. The court stated,

The issue in this case is not [Rosa's] sex, but rather how he chose to dress when applying for a loan. Because the Act does not prohibit discrimination based on the manner in which someone dresses, Park West's requirement that Rosa change his clothes does not give rise to claims of illegal discrimination. Further, even if Park West's statement or action were based upon Rosa's sexual orientation or perceived sexual orientation, the Act does not prohibit such discrimination.

PriceWaterhouse v. Hopkins, which Rosa relied on, was not to the contrary, according to the district court, because that case "neither holds, nor even suggests, that discrimination based merely on a person's attire is impermissible."

On appeal, Rosa says that the district court "fundamentally misconceived the law as applicable to the Plaintiff's claim by concluding that there may be no relationship, as a matter of law, between telling a bank customer what to wear and sex discrimination."

The Bank says that Rosa loses for two reasons. First, citing cases pertaining to gays and transsexuals, it says that the ECOA does not apply to cross-dressers. Second, the Bank says that its employee genuinely could not identify Rosa, which is why she asked him to go home and change.

III

The ECOA prohibits discrimination, "with respect to any aspect of a credit transaction[,] on the basis of race, color, religion, national origin, sex or marital status, or age." Thus to prevail, the alleged discrimination against Rosa must have been "on the basis of . . . sex."

While the district court was correct in saying that the prohibited bases of discrimination under the ECOA do not include style of dress or sexual orientation, that is not the discrimination alleged. It is alleged that the Bank's actions were taken, in whole or in part, "on the basis of . . . [the appellant's] sex." . . . Whatever facts emerge, and they may turn out to have nothing to do with sex-based discrimination, we cannot say at this point that the plaintiff has no viable theory of sex discrimination consistent with the facts alleged.

The evidence is not yet developed, and thus it is not yet clear why Brunelle told Rosa to go home and change. It may be that this case involves an instance of disparate treatment based on sex in the denial of credit. . . . It is reasonable to infer that Brunelle told Rosa to go home and change because she thought that Rosa's attire did not accord with his male gender: in other words, that Rosa did not receive the loan application because he was a man, whereas a similarly situated woman would have received the loan application. That is, the Bank may treat, for credit purposes, a woman who dresses like a man differently than a man who dresses like a woman. If so, the Bank concedes, Rosa may have a claim. Indeed, under *PriceWaterhouse,* "stereotyped remarks [including statements about dressing more 'femininely'] can certainly be evidence that gender played a part." It is also reasonable to infer, though, that

Brunelle refused to give Rosa the loan application because she thought he was gay, confusing sexual orientation with cross-dressing. If so, Rosa concedes, our precedents dictate that he would have no recourse under the federal Act. It is reasonable to infer, as well, that Brunelle simply could not ascertain whether the person shown in the identification card photographs was the same person that appeared before her that day. If this were the case, Rosa again would be out of luck. It is reasonable to infer, finally, that Brunelle may have had mixed motives, some of which fall into the prohibited category.

It is too early to say what the facts will show; it is apparent, however, that, under some set of facts within the bounds of the allegations and nonconclusory facts in the complaint, Rosa may be able to prove a claim under the ECOA.

We reverse and remand.

Questions

1. *a.* Did the court of appeals find that Park West Bank had violated the ECOA? Explain.
   b. If at trial, the facts reveal that the bank employee thought Rosa was gay and demanded that he change clothes for that reason, who will win this case? Explain.
   c. According to the court of appeals, how did the lower court misunderstand this case?
2. *a.* Does federal law protect bank customers based on their style of dress? Explain.
   b. Should it offer that protection? Explain.

PRACTICING ETHICS   Government-Mandated Diversity?

The 2010 Dodd–Frank Act includes a provision creating Offices of Minority and Women Inclusion at various government agencies (Treasury Department, Securities and Exchange Commission, the Consumer Financial Protection Bureau, and so on) charged with regulating the banking industry. Those offices are monitoring racial and gender diversity at the government agencies themselves as well as private law firms, accounting firms, investment banks, and others contracting and subcontracting with the agencies. If an agency compliance director determines that a contractor has not made a good faith

effort to achieve a diverse workforce, the contract may be canceled, among other possible remedies. One managing director at a minority-owned investment firm said the law may give firms like his "a chance to compete."

Question

Should the government intervene to improve opportunities for women and minorities in the investment banking industry?

Source: Kevin Roose, "Seeking Guidance on Dodd-Frank's Diversity Clause," *The New York Times,* November 11, 2010 [http://dealbook.nytimes.com].

Debtor Protection

> The debt collection process continues the nightmare.

Our ongoing financial crisis, one of the most destructive of modern times, has thrown millions of Americans deeply in debt. Wages can be *garnished*. Debts pile up on one another. Then the debt collection process continues the nightmare. *The New York Times* in 2010 recounted the story of Ruth M. Owens, a disabled Cleveland woman who was sued by Discover Bank in 2004 for an unpaid credit card bill. In six years, Ms. Owens had paid nearly $3,500 on her original balance of $1,900, but Discover sued her for $5,564 that had accumulated from late fees, compound interest, penalties, and charges even though she had not used the card to buy anything more. The judge called Discover's behavior "unconscionable" and threw out the case. Discover said that it turned the case over to a lawyer only after repeated unsuccessful efforts to reach Ms. Owens.[38]

Debtors are properly expected to repay what they owe, but critics claim debtors often are wrongly pursued. U.S. Senator Sherrod Brown (D-OH) explained:

> It's hard enough when families aren't able to make enough to pay their bills, but it's tragic that families who are struggling to make ends meet are hounded to make payments on debts that they have already paid off or that they never owed in the first place.[39]

Furthermore, collectors reportedly call at all hours of the night, spewing obscenities, contacting family members or employers and falsely threatening property seizures or imprisonment.[40] Perhaps not surprisingly, the big banks—so broadly criticized for their roles in the financial meltdown—are likewise accused of involvement in unlawful debt-collection practices. At this writing in 2013, the state of California has sued the nation's largest bank, JPMorgan Chase, for having run a "massive debt collection mill" seeking wage garnishments and default orders against about 100,000 credit cardholders from 2008 to 2011. The complaint also accuses JPMorgan of practicing "sewer service" where the bank claims to have properly provided notice to the defendant-consumer of a debt-collection lawsuit when, in fact, notice was not provided.[41] Since about one in ten Americans is dealing with debt collectors,[42] and the consequences can be so destructive, both state and federal governments have developed extensive legal protections for debtors.

Debt Collection Law

The federal Fair Debt Collection Practices Act (FDCPA) is designed to shield debtors from unfair debt collection tactics by debt collection agencies and attorneys who routinely operate as debt collectors. FDCPA does not extend to creditors who are themselves trying to recover money owed to them. Often employing very aggressive tactics, several thousand debt collection agencies nationwide pursue those who are delinquent in their debts.

The FDCPA protects consumers by forbidding, among others, the following practices:

- Use of obscene language.
- Contact with third parties other than for the purpose of locating the debtor. (This provision is an attempt to prevent harm to the debtor's reputation.)
- Use of or threats to use physical force.

- Contact with the debtor during "inconvenient" hours. For debtors who are employed during "normal" working hours, the period from 9 PM to 8 AM would probably be considered inconvenient.
- Repeated phone calls with the intent to harass.
- Contacting the debtor in an unfair, abusive, or deceptive manner.

The Federal Trade Commission and the Consumer Financial Protection Bureau jointly enforce the FDCPA. The CFPB also has supervisory authority over the largest debt collectors—about 175 firms. Under that authority, the CFPB provides a consumer complaint–dispute resolution process and determines whether debt collectors have harassed or deceived consumers along with assuring that debt collectors provide accurate information and fully disclose who they are and how much the consumer owes. In addition to federal and state regulatory protection, wronged consumers may sue for damages. [For more details about the FDCPA, see **www.ftc.gov/os/statutes/fdcpajump.shtm**]. The case that follows suggests some of the confusion that can arise in the debt collection process.

LEGAL BRIEFCASE

Williams v. OSI Educational Services 505 F.3d 675 (7th Cir. 2007)

Circuit Judge Ripple

Sandra Williams . . . sought relief under the Fair Debt Collection Practices Act ("FDCPA"). The district court granted the defendant, OSI Educational Services, Inc., ("OSI"), summary judgment. Ms. Williams then filed a timely appeal to this court.

I. BACKGROUND

A

Ms. Williams is a consumer whose debt was incurred for personal, family or household purposes. OSI is a debt collection agency; it was hired by Great Lakes Higher Education Guaranty Corp. ("Great Lakes") to collect its debts. OSI sent Ms. Williams a letter and a debt validation notice, dated March 28, 2005. The letter sought to collect a sum of $807.89 labeled as "Total Due," which was the outstanding balance owed to Great Lakes. The letter breaks down the amount owed as follows:

Date:	03/28/05
Principal:	$683.56
Interest:	16.46
Fees:	107.87
Total Due:	$807.89

The letter further states:

> The balance may not reflect the exact amount of interest which is accruing daily per your original agreement with your creditor. Contact us to find out your exact payout balance.

B

The district court . . . determined that the letter apprised Ms. Williams of the total amount due, including the amount of the principal, interest and fees due. The district court stated that, . . . the letter clearly advises that additional interest is accruing on a daily basis and that, therefore, additional interest may be added. Comparing this case to *Taylor v. Cavalry Investment, L.L.C.*, the district court took the view that the letter complied with the statute because OSI's "letter states the amount of the debt clearly enough so that an unsophisticated recipient would not misunderstand it."

II. DISCUSSION

Ms. Williams submits that there is an issue of material fact as to whether OSI's letter clearly states the amount of the debt, as required by the FDCPA. In examining that contention, we begin with the wording of the statute. The FDCPA requires that debt collectors state "the amount of the debt" that they are seeking to collect from the consumer. The debt collector's letter must state the amount of the debt "clearly enough that the recipient is likely to understand it." *Chuway v. Nat'/Action Fin.Servs. Inc.* To ensure that this statutory command is implemented properly, we must evaluate the letter to determine whether it causes any "confusion" or "misunderstand[ing]" as to the amount due. In making this determination, we evaluate the letter from the perspective of an "unsophisticated consumer or debtor." The unsophisticated consumer is "uninformed, naive, [and] trusting," but possesses "rudimentary knowledge about the financial world, is wise enough to read collection notices with added care, possesses 'reasonable intelligence,' and is capable of making basic logical deductions and inferences." *Pettit v. Retrieval Masters Creditors Bureau, Inc.* Notably, we have rejected explicitly the notion that we should employ the *least* sophisticated debtor standard, the "very last rung on the sophistication ladder" *Pettit.*

* * * * *

Our past cases indicate that summary judgment may be avoided by showing that the letter, on its face, will "confuse a substantial number of recipients." We also have said that, absent a showing that the face of the letter will precipitate such a level of confusion, the "plaintiff must come forward with evidence beyond the letter and beyond [her] own self-serving assertions that the letter is confusing in order to create a genuine issue of material fact for trial." *Durkin v. Equifax Checking Servs* (noting that evidence may consist of "carefully designed and conducted consumer survey[s]" or expert witnesses).

Ms. Williams chooses to base her case on the first of these options. She focuses on the following language from OSI's letter:

> The balance may not reflect the exact amount of interest which is accruing daily per your original agreement with your creditor. Contact us to find out your exact payout balance.

In her view, there are three reasons why OSI's letter would confuse a substantial number of recipients. We shall examine each.

First, Ms. Williams argues that the language in OSI's letter is more confusing than that in *Chuway,* which we held could "confuse a substantial number of recipients." *Chuway.* In that case, the letter stated the "balance" and also contained the following language: "Please remit the balance listed above in the return envelope provided. To obtain your most current balance information, please call [phone number]." We held that the letter violated the FDCPA. There, the confusion arose because the letter did not state why the "current balance"

would be different than the stated "balance." The plaintiff could have thought that "the reference to the 'current balance' meant that the defendant was trying to collect an additional debt [without] telling her how large an additional debt and thus violating the statute." In contrast, the language in OSI's letter links the difference between the "total due" and the "exact payout balance" to the "interest which is accruing daily per your original agreement with your creditor." OSI's letter thus provides the information that created the confusion in the *Chuway* letter.

Ms. Williams' second and third arguments are best treated together. She submits that the letter's language leaves open the possibility that the actual amount due is less than the amount stated on the letter. She further suggests that the sentence's use of the present tense makes it possible to conclude that the stated amount due was not accurate on the date that the letter was written. In our view, both these contentions are based on a strained reading of the sentence. It would be "unrealistic, peculiar, [and] bizarre" to read OSI's letter in this way. *Durkin.* The common sense reading of the letter is that the balance is accurate as of the date the letter is written, but that the amount due will increase because of interest that is accruing daily. This construction is supported by the letter's itemization of "PRINCIPAL," "INTEREST," "FEES" and "TOTAL DUE" in a box with, and immediately below, the "DATE." Under a natural reading, the language conveys, even to an unsophisticated consumer, that interest will accrue after the letter is sent and therefore that the consumer should call to find out the "*exact* payout balance."

As we said in *Chuway,* "It is impossible to draft a letter that is certain to be understood by every person who receives it; only if it would confuse a significant fraction of the persons to whom it is directed will the defendant be liable."

We believe that the language in this letter is closer to the language in *Taylor* than to the language in *Chuway.* In *Taylor,* the letter similarly set forth the total due and broke down that total into principal and interest. If further stated: "[I]f applicable, your account may have or will accrue interest at a rate specified in your contractual agreement with the original creditor." Three plaintiffs in *Taylor* had submitted affidavits stating that this sentence confused them about the amount of debt that the debt collector was trying to collect. We held that the language was "entirely clear on its face." . . .

As we noted earlier, in opposing summary judgment, Ms. Williams relied solely on OSI's letter. She submitted no other evidence to support her view that OSI's letter is confusing. Without more, Ms. Williams' unsupported assertion that OSI's letter is confusing is insufficient to create a genuine issue of fact as to confusion.

* * * * *

CONCLUSION

The letter set forth the amount of the debt with sufficient clarity and accuracy to comply with the requirements of the statute.

Affirmed.

Questions

1. *a.* A debt collection letter must be evaluated to determine whether it causes confusion or misunderstanding for the consumer. What level of consumer sophistication was employed by the court to determine whether the debt collection letter to Williams caused confusion or misunderstanding?

   b. Is confusion on the part of an individual consumer conclusive evidence of a violation of the Fair Debt Collection Practices Act? Explain.

   c. Describe the two ways by which a plaintiff/consumer can establish that a debt collection letter caused an impermissible level of confusion or misunderstanding.

2. Miller owed $2,501.61 to the Star Bank of Cincinnati. Payco attempted to collect the debt by sending a one-page collection form to Miller. The front side of the form included, among other words, in very large capital letters a demand for IMMEDIATE FULL PAYMENT, the words PHONE US TODAY, and the word NOW in white letters nearly two inches tall against a red background. At the bottom of the page in the smallest print on the form was the message: NOTICE: SEE REVERSE SIDE FOR IMPORTANT INFORMATION. The reverse side contained the validation notice required under the FDCPA. Does the form conform to FDCPA requirements? Explain. See *Miller v. Payco-General American Credits, Inc.,* 943 F.2d 482 (4th Cir. 1991).

3. Why shouldn't debt collectors be able to use aggressive tactics to encourage payment of legitimate bills?

Foreclosure Fraud?

The mortgage industry, already buried in bad loans and worse publicity, faced another scandal in 2010 when the news emerged that some or perhaps many banks and individuals had not followed proper legal procedures in pursuing foreclosure orders against borrowers (commonly, the situation in which a homeowner fails to make mortgage payments and loses the home). Broadly, the scandal involved allegations that lenders bent rules to speed up the foreclosure process. Sloppy record keeping and outright errors apparently were routine. In a process now called "robo-signing," bank employees sometimes signed thousands of foreclosure affidavits in a single day, clearly never carefully examining them as expected. Critics now believe banks often cannot prove the facts necessary to achieve a lawful foreclosure. In some instances, the sloppy and perhaps negligent record keeping may even prevent banks from proving they are the legal owners of the properties being foreclosed on. Foreclosure proceedings were halted all over the country as bank and government officials reviewed records to see how common these problems were. Hundreds of thousands of homeowners now believe they were foreclosed on unlawfully.

State and federal officials and the five biggest mortgage servicing banks (e.g., JPMorgan Chase, Citigroup, and Ally Financial) reached a 2012 settlement totaling $25 billion in penalties to compensate for robo signing, faulty loan processing, and wrongful mortgage foreclosure practices. At least $17 billion of the settlement will go directly to homeowners. Many, many complaints remain, however, and at this writing, the New York state attorney general has indicated that he intends to sue Bank of America and Wells Fargo for failing to fulfill the settlement requirements.

Sources: Associated Press, "Foreclosure Class Actions Pile Up Against Banks," *The Des Moines Register,* November 18, 2010, p. 7B; Associated Press, "Iowa Attorney General: Mortgage Industry Problems Broad," *The Des Moines Register,* November 17, 2010, p. 7B; and Editorial, "Banks Still Behaving Badly," *The New York Times,* May 8, 2013 [**www .nytimes.com/**].

Part Four—Bankruptcy

Fresh Start? Should we lend a hand to those subprime borrowers and others who are down on their luck? Bankruptcy law was specifically designed to provide a fresh start for those whose financial problems were insurmountable. We believed that both the debtor and society benefited from the new beginning. As bankruptcy filings skyrocketed, however, we downsized the fresh start by reforming federal bankruptcy law in 2005 to force more bankrupt parties to repay their creditors. Following the reform, bankruptcies did fall somewhat in 2006 to about 618,000, then rose to a recession-era high of 1.6 million in 2010 before falling back in 2012 to about 1.2 million.[43] Of course, those tough times are often of our own making. At this writing in 2013, American consumers owed $2.8 trillion in non-mortgage debt, an average of $8,900 for every person in the nation.[44]

> American consumers owed an average of $8,900 for every person in the nation.

Thus, we have millions of Americans deep in debt and facing a troubled economy. Does our bankruptcy system provide the rescue we intend for those people? A recent study concludes that the system falls short. Just one year following a declaration of bankruptcy, one in four debtors continues to struggle to pay routine bills and one in three reports a financial condition much the same or worse than was the case prior to the bankruptcy filing.[45] Without steady, sufficient income, the study finds that "bankruptcy is an incomplete tool to rehabilitate those in financial distress."[46]

Bankruptcy Rules

Bankruptcy in the United States is governed exclusively by federal law; the states do not have the constitutional authority to enact bankruptcy legislation, but they do set their own rules within the limits provided by Congress. Our attention will be limited to the principal federal statute, the Bankruptcy Reform Act of 1978, as amended.

Bankruptcy is an adjudication relieving a debtor of all or part of his/her/its liabilities. Any person, partnership, or corporation may seek debtor relief. Three forms of bankruptcy action are important to us:

1. **Liquidation** (**Chapter 7** of the Bankruptcy Act), is used by both individuals and businesses. Most debts are forgiven, all assets except exemptions are fairly distributed to creditors, and debtors receive a "fresh start."
2. **Reorganization** (**Chapter 11**), used by both individuals and businesses, keeps creditors from the debtor's assets while the debtor, under the supervision of the court, works out a financial reorganization plan and continues to pay creditors.
3. **Adjustment of debts** of an individual with regular income (**Chapter 13**), in which individuals with limited debts are protected from creditors while paying their debts in installments. [For frequently asked bankruptcy questions and links to bankruptcy sites on the Internet, see **www.lawtrove.com/bankruptcy**].

Liquidation

A Chapter 7 liquidation petition can be *voluntarily* filed in federal court by the debtor, or creditors can seek an *involuntary* bankruptcy judgment. A Chapter 7 liquidation is commonly called a "straight" bankruptcy.

In a voluntary action, the debtor files a petition with the appropriate federal court. The court then has jurisdiction to proceed with the liquidation, and the petition becomes the *order for relief.* The debtor need not be insolvent to seek bankruptcy.

Creditors often can compel an involuntary bankruptcy. The debtor may challenge that bankruptcy action. The court will enter an order for relief if it finds the debtor has not been paying his or her debts when due or if most of the debtor's property is under the control of a custodian for the purpose of enforcing a lien against that property.

After the order for relief is granted, voluntary and involuntary actions proceed in a similar manner. Creditors are restrained from reaching the debtor's assets. An interim bankruptcy trustee is appointed by the court. The creditors then hold a meeting, and a permanent trustee is elected. The trustee collects the debtor's property and converts it to money, protects the interests of the debtor and creditors, may manage the debtor's business, and ultimately distributes the estate proceeds to the creditors. Debtors are allowed to keep exempt property, which varies from state to state but typically includes a car, a homestead, some household or personal items, life insurance, and other "necessities." Normally a dollar maximum is attached to each.

The debtor's nonexempt property is then divided among the creditors according to the priorities prescribed by statute. Secured creditors are paid first. If funds remain, "priority" claims, such as employees' wages and alimony/child support, are paid. Then, funds permitting, general creditors are paid. Each class must be paid in full before a class of lower priority will be compensated. Any remaining funds will return to the debtor.

When distribution is complete, the bankruptcy judge may issue an order discharging (relieving) the debtor of any remaining debts except for certain statutorily specified claims. Those include, for example, taxes and educational loans. Thus, as noted above, the debtor is granted a "fresh start."

Reorganization

Under Chapter 11, the debtor may voluntarily seek reorganization, or the creditors may petition for an involuntary action. When a reorganization petition is filed with the court and relief is ordered, one or more committees of creditors are appointed to participate in bankruptcy procedures. Typically in the case of a business, the debtor continues operations, although the court may appoint a trustee to replace the debtor if required because of dishonesty, fraud, or extreme mismanagement. The company, its bankers, and its suppliers will meet to work out a method for continuing operations. A plan must be developed that will satisfy the creditors that their interests are being served by the reorganization. Perhaps new capital is secured, or perhaps creditors receive some shares in the company. The plan must be approved by the creditors and confirmed by the court. The company is then required to carry out the plan.

GM Bankruptcy/Bailout

General Motors, in 2009, was forced to enter Chapter 11 bankruptcy as part of a federal government-directed, prepackaged bailout of the failing firm. GM had gone from being one of the most prominent corporations in the world to a sprawling, dysfunctional failure. GM reported $82.29 billion in assets and $172.81 billion in debts. The federal government put $49.5 billion into the bailout and took a 60 percent equity stake in the new General Motors, although the company retained control of its day-to-day affairs.

Achieving a remarkable comeback, General Motors is now consistently profitable, has been restored to the Standard & Poor's 100 (after being kicked off), and is healthier than it has been in decades. In December 2013, the U.S. Treasury sold the government's remaining GM holdings. Taxpayer loss on the GM bailout totaled about $10 billion.

The rescue of GM, Chrysler, and their financing units saved an estimated 1 million jobs. According to a study by the Center for Automotive Research, had those jobs been lost, the cost to the government in reduced taxes and other negatives would have been nearly $29 billion. Thus, on balance, the Obama administration views the bailout as a significant financial and social welfare success. Critics argue, however, that the deal was a dangerous abandonment of market principles. Some of those arguments include:

- The bailout encouraged future risky behavior by conveying the message that the government will always be there as a backup.
- Private investors would have moved in to cut costs and restore a new, trimmer GM.
- The $50 billion of taxpayer money could have been better spent elsewhere or not spent at all.

Question

Was the federal government wise to bail out General Motors, or should GM have been left to face the force of the market and the decisions of the Chapter 11 bankruptcy judge?

Sources: John Lott, "GM's Bailout Is a Financial Disaster," FoxNews.com, November 18, 2010 [**www.foxnews.com**]; Mark Guarino, "With Big GM Stock Offering, Vindication for the Government Bailout?" *Christian Science Monitor,* November 19, 2010 [**www.csmonitor.com/2010/**]; and Drew Winter, "Dear Taxpayer: Your Auto Bailout Loan Is Repaid, with Interest," *Wards Auto,* June 10, 2013 [**http://wardsauto.com/**].

Adjustment of Debts

Under Chapter 13, individuals (not partnerships or corporations) can seek the protection of the court to arrange a debt adjustment plan. Chapter 13 permits only voluntary bankruptcies and is restricted to those with steady incomes and somewhat limited debts. The process can begin only with a voluntary petition from the debtor. Creditors are restrained from reaching the debtor's assets. The debtor develops a repayment plan. If creditors' interests are sufficiently satisfied by the plan, the court may confirm it and appoint a trustee to oversee the plan. The debtor may then have three to five years to make the necessary payments. [For an extensive bankruptcy law database, see **www.law.cornell.edu/wex/Bankruptcy**]

Bankruptcy Critique

The stigma that had historically attached to filing for bankruptcy dissipated somewhat in the "greed is good" 1980s, and bankruptcy became a more acceptable way of dealing with debts.[47] In an effort to benefit all by reducing unjustified and sometimes fraudulent bankruptcy filings, the federal Bankruptcy Abuse Prevention and Consumer Protection Act of 2005 has forced many debtors to seek bankruptcy through the challenging Chapter 13 process rather than the more forgiving Chapter 7. Debtors found to have some money (according to a means test) to apply to debts are required to take the Chapter 13 route, which requires a repayment plan rather than the much more attractive "fresh start" of Chapter 7.

Supporters of the 2005 reform argue that it reduces the cost of credit for all Americans, but opponents see the changes as a punitive assault on those already down on their luck.

For individuals, the reform made the process much more complicated, and the average cost of filing more than doubled to more than $2,000.[48] During the recession, homeowners behind on their house payments often found mortgage foreclosure more attractive than bankruptcy. Thus, many borrowers simply walked away from their "underwater" homes, leaving lenders with mountains of troubled properties. (Rising home values and banks' mortgage modification decisions have recently reduced the number of underwater homes.)

PRACTICING ETHICS   Bankruptcy—Who Is to Blame?

Commenting on the 2005 bankruptcy reform law, Todd Zywicki, a George Mason University law professor, said, "This is a matter of morality and personal responsibility." Consumer advocates, on the other hand, say the bankruptcy problem lies with the "enablers"—the credit card companies and mortgage lenders who encourage deeper and deeper indebtedness.

Question

Who bears the moral blame for America's bankruptcy struggles? Explain.

Source: Michael Schroeder and Suein Hwang, "Sweeping New Bankruptcy Law to Make Life Harder for Debtors," *The Wall Street Journal*, April 6, 2005, p. A1.

Internet Exercise

Go to the Center for Auto Safety website [**www.autosafety.org/**], click the lemon laws button and find your state's lemon law. Read the brief summary of the law of your state. Read the summary for the states of Texas, Virginia, and West Virginia.

a. Explain the differences among the state laws you reviewed.

b. Which of those three or four states, in your view, provides the "fairest" protection considering the viewpoints of both consumers and dealers?

Chapter Questions

1. A group of parents sued Gerber claiming its "Fruit Juice Snacks" product packaging was misleading. The words "Fruit Juice" appeared on the package beside images of fruits such as peaches and cherries. In fact, the only fruit juice in the "Snacks" was white grape from concentrate. A side panel statement said the product was made "with real fruit juice and other all natural ingredients," but the primary ingredients were corn syrup and sugar. The side panel also displayed the statement, "one of a variety of nutritious Gerber Graduates foods and juices that have been specifically designed to help toddlers grow up strong and healthy." The actual ingredients were correctly listed in "small print" on the side of the box. Is a "reasonable consumer" "likely to be deceived" by the Gerber packaging? Explain. See *Williams v. Gerber Products,* 523 F.3d 934 (9th Cir. 2008).

2. San Francisco Bay area consumers Wanda Greenwood, Ladelle Hatfield, and Deborah McCleese each signed up for an Aspire Visa credit card marketed by CompuCredit Corp. of Atlanta, Georgia. The card was advertised as a means of rebuilding cardholders' credit histories as well as providing $300 in immediate credit, with no down

payment. The consumers claimed that fees hidden in the fine print of this "fee harvester" agreement claimed much of the $300 with the result that they were misled about the card agreement's capacity to help restore their credit. The agreement also included language requiring both the consumer and the company to resolve disputes using binding arbitration. The federal Credit Repair Organizations Act (CROA) requires credit repair organizations to provide a disclosure statement to consumers saying: "You have a right to sue a credit repair organization that violates the [Act]." The three consumers brought a class-action lawsuit against CompuCredit alleging a violation of CROA which, among other things, forbids deceptive practices in credit repair.

a. CompuCredit argued that the lawsuit was barred because of the arbitration provision. As you look at the facts, do you think the consumers can sue CompuCredit, or must they turn to binding arbitration? Explain.

b. Recalling our discussion of arbitration in Chapter 4 and elsewhere in this text, in your judgment does arbitration provide an effective, efficient substitute for litigation in this CompuCredit case? Explain.

c. How might a ruling favoring arbitration encourage fraud by credit card companies? See *CompuCredit Corp. v. Wanda Greenwood, et al.,* 132 S.Ct. 665 (2012).

3. DeSantis sued a debt collection agency, Computer Credit. DeSantis apparently owed $319.50 to Dr. Jeffrey A. Stahl, who assigned the debt to CC for collection. On April 27, 2000, CC sent the following collection letter to DeSantis:

> This notice will serve to inform you that your overdue balance with Dr. Jeffrey A. Stahl has been referred to Computer Credit, Inc., a debt collector. *[The] doctor insists on payment or a valid reason for your failure to make payment.* The law prohibits us from collecting any amount greater than the obligation stated above. Unless you notify us to the contrary, we will assume the amount due is correct. This communication is sent to you in an attempt to collect this debt. Any information obtained will be used for that purpose. *In the absence of a valid reason for your failure to make payment, pay the above debt or contact the doctor to settle this matter.* Payment can be sent directly to the doctor. [Italics added.]

The Fair Debt Collection Practices Act specifies that the consumer may dispute the alleged debt, in which case the debt collector must desist from collection until the debt collector obtains verification regarding the amount of the debt, if any. Given that statutory requirement, was the FDCPA violated by the italicized sentences in the collection letter? Explain. See *DeSantis v. Computer Credit, Inc.,* 269 F.3d 159 (2d Cir. 2001).

4. A *New York Times* editorial argued that college students are taken advantage of by credit card companies:

> The credit card industry has made a profitable art of corralling consumers into ruinous interest rates and hidden penalties that keep even people who pay their bills permanently mired in debt. The companies are especially eager to target freshly minted college students, who are naïve in money matters and especially vulnerable to credit card offers that are too good to be true.[49]

a. Do you think beginning college students are often "vulnerable" to manipulation by credit card companies?

b. Are you vulnerable to that alleged manipulation?

   c. Should the federal government provide more protection against credit card deception? Explain.

5. Phusion Projects was accused by the Federal Trade Commission of mislabeling its flavored malt drink Four Loko. The FTC investigated the company's implied claims that consumers could safely drink one 23.5-ounce can at a sitting and that each can contained the alcoholic equivalent of one to two 12-ounce beers and concluded that those claims were misleading. The FTC found that a single Four Loko can had as much alcohol as four to five beers and that drinking one can on a single occasion would amount to binge drinking. Several states banned the drink and Phusion removed the caffeine and other stimulants. In 2013, the FTC ordered Phusion to put on the back of Four Loko cans containing more than two servings (a "serving" equals 0.6 ounces of alcohol) an "Alcohol Facts" panel that discloses alcohol content, serving size and the number of servings per can. Resealable containers are required for Four Loko drinks containing more alcohol than the equivalent of two and one-half servings.

   a. Many public comments to the FTC called for banning Four Loko from the market. Should the FTC do so? Explain.

   b. From the FTC point of view, what consumer benefit was achieved by the order?

   c. How would you have handled the Four Loko situation?

6. Millions of Americans are "underwater" on their home mortgages; that is, they owe more than their homes are worth. Many of those families could simply walk away from their mortgage, rent a similar home, and save thousands of dollars per year. Doubtless many decline to abandon their mortgages because they fear the consequences for their credit records and they want to avoid the cost of changing homes, but surely some continue to make payments simply because they believe defaulting would be immoral. While serving as U.S. Treasury Secretary, Henry Paulson said that anyone who walks away from his or her mortgage is "simply a speculator—and one who is not honoring his obligation."[50]

   a. Make the argument that deliberately walking away from an underwater home mortgage situation is immoral.

   b. Make the argument that walking away is not immoral.

   c. What would you do? Explain. See Richard H. Thaler, "Underwater, but Will They Leave the Pool?" *The New York Times,* January 24, 2010 [**www.nytimes.com**]; and Brent T. White, "Buyers Have No Moral Duty to Lenders," *Arizona Republic,* April 25, 2010 [**www.azcentral.com/arizonarepublic/viewpoints/articles/2010/04/25/2 0100425white25.htm**].

7. William Cohan, writing in *The New York Times,* objected to the federal government's consumer protection efforts in the Dodd–Frank Wall Street Reform and Consumer Protection Act, including the creation of the Consumer Financial Protection Bureau. Explain why Cohan and other critics would object to the government's efforts to protect consumers from "devious credit-card companies" and "dishonest mortgage lenders." See William D. Cohan, "The Elizabeth Warren Fallacy," *The New York Times,* September 30, 2010 [**http://opinionator.blogs .nytimes.com/**].

8. Recent studies suggest that consumer bankruptcies are much more common in some states than others. Aside from income levels, what socioeconomic factors would you expect to be closely correlated with high bankruptcy rates?

9. Playtex manufactured the market-leading spill proof cup for children, which a child uses by sucking on a spout to cause a valve to open. Gerber introduced its own version and ran ads showing an unnamed competitor's product and claiming that "Gerber's patented valve makes our cup more than 50 percent easier to drink from than the leading cup." Gerber's claims for the superiority of its cup were backed by tests from an independent laboratory. Playtex said the unnamed cup obviously was its brand and that the superiority claims were false and misleading. Playtex sought an injunction to block the Gerber ads. Would you grant that injunction? Explain. See *Playtex Products v. Gerber Products,* 981 F.Supp. 827 (S.D.N.Y. 1997).

10. Maguire, a credit card holder at Bradlees Department Store, fell behind in her payments. She received a series of dunning letters from Citicorp, which managed Bradlees' accounts, demanding that she pay the overdue amount. Later Maguire received a letter from "Debtor Assistance," which said that "your Bradlees account has recently [been] charged off." Debtor Assistance is a unit of Citicorp, but was not identified as such in the letter, beyond the phrase "a unit of CRS." The back of each Bradlees' account statement includes a notice that Citicorp Retail Services was the creditor that handled Bradlees' accounts. In general, creditors are not subject to the requirements of the Fair Debt Collections Practices Act, but Maguire sued claiming the Debtor Assistance letter violated the FDCPA. Is she correct? Explain. See *Maguire v. Citicorp Retail Services, Inc.,* 147 F.3d 232 (2d Cir. 1998).

11. A door-to-door salesman representing Your Shop at Home Services, Inc., called on Clifton and Cora Jones, who were welfare recipients. The Jones couple decided to buy a freezer from the salesman for $900. Credit charges, insurance, and so on were added to that $900 base so that the total purchase price was $1,439.69. Mr. and Mrs. Jones signed a sales agreement that accurately stipulated the price and its ingredients. The Joneses sued to reform the contract on unconscionability grounds. They had paid $619.88 toward the total purchase price. At trial, the retail value of the new freezer at the time of purchase was set at approximately $300.

    a. What is the issue in this case?

    b. Decide. Explain. See *Jones v. Star Credit Corp.,* 298 N.Y.S.2d 264 (1969).

12. Roseman resigned from the John Hancock Insurance Company following allegations of misuse of his expense account. He reimbursed the account. Subsequently he was denied employment by another insurance firm after that firm read a Retail Credit Company credit report on him. The credit report included accurate information regarding Roseman's resignation. Was Retail Credit in violation of the Fair Credit Reporting Act in circulating information regarding the resignation? Explain. See *Roseman v. Retail Credit Co., Inc.,* 428 F.Supp. 643 (Pa. 1977).

13. Once the government decided to intervene in the free market on behalf of consumers, two broad product safety options presented themselves: (a) the government could have limited its effort to generating and distributing information to consumers, or (b) the government could have set safety standards for all products. Assuming the government

was forced to choose one or the other but not elements of both, which option should it have chosen? Explain.

14. Consumers sometimes abuse sellers. One familiar technique is shoplifting. Of course, shoplifting is a crime. However, the criminal process is cumbersome and often does not result in monetary recoveries for sellers. As a result, at least 43 states now have laws permitting store owners to impose civil fines, the collection of which is usually turned over to a lawyer or collection agency with a threat to sue in civil court, file criminal charges, or both if payment is not forthcoming. Fines may range from $50 to $5,000 or more, depending on the value of the item stolen.

    a. Defense lawyers say this civil fine system is unfair. Why?

    b. On balance, is the civil fine approach to shoplifting a good idea? Explain.

    c. Cite some other examples of consumers abusing businesspeople.

15. Goswami failed to pay her $900 credit card bill. A collection agency, ACEI, mailed her a collection letter with a blue bar across the envelope saying "Priority Letter." The letter did not, in fact, constitute priority mail. The purpose of the bar was to encourage Goswami to open the envelope. Was the bar a deceptive practice in violation of the Fair Debt Collection Practices Act? Explain. See *Goswami v. American Collections Enterprise, Inc.,* 377 F.3d 488 (5th Cir. 2004); cert. den. 2005 U.S. LEXIS 5511.

Notes

1. Walter Hamilton, "For-Profit Colleges Face Federal Crackdown," *latimes.com,* February 6, 2011 [**www.latimes.com/business/la-fi-for-profit-colleges-20110206,0,1109616.story**].

2. "Community College Funding Shrinks, For-Profit Enrollment Grows," *HuffPost College,* December 26, 2012 [**www.huffington.com/**].

3. Justin Pope, "Enrollment Falls at For-Profit Colleges, after Years of Growth," *Des Moines Register,* October 20, 2012, p. 8A.

4. Amer Madhani, "New Federal Rules Target For-Profit Colleges," *USA Today,* March 17, 2014 [**http://www.usatoday.com/story/news/politics/2014/03/13/obama-for-profit-college-regulations/6386565/**]. For a journalistic account of the 2012 federal court ruling and a broader discussion of the "gainful employment" rules, see Tamar Lewin, "Judge Strikes Main Element of For-Profit College Rules," *The New York Times,* July 1, 2012 [**www.nytimes.com/**].

5. James Rainey, "Truth in Advertising Meets the Blogosphere," *latimes.com,* October 7, 2009 [**www.latimes.com/**].

6. Brent Kendall, "Skechers to Pay $50 Million to Settle Ad Suit," *The Wall Street Journal,* May 17, 2012, p. B3.

7. Jeffrey D. Knowles et al., "FTC Survey Estimates Fraud Affected 25.6 Million Americans in 2011," *LEXOLOGY,* April 25, 2013 [**www.lexology.com/**].

8. J. Craig Anderson, "Identity Theft Growing, Costly to Victims," *The Arizona Republic,* April 14, 2013 [**www.azcentral.com/business/consumer/articles/20130401identity-theft-growing-costly.html**].

9. Ibid.

10. Ibid.

11. Ibid.

12. Adam Levin, "Identity Theft in 2013: The Battle for Your Data," *ABC News,* December 23, 2012 [**http://abcnews.go.com/**].

13. Pete Yost, "Gov't: 1 in 14 Fell Prey to Identity Theft in 2012," *boston.com,* December 12, 2013 [**www.boston.com/**].

14. Alex Byers, "Privacy Issues at Top of Edith Ramirez's Federal Trade Commission Agenda," *Politico,* March 11, 2013 [**http://dyn.politico.com/**].

15. Ibid.

16. Monica Hesse, "Barbie Tells CPSC to Get the Lead Out in Viral Video," *Washington Post,* November 24, 2007, p. C01.

17. Associated Press, "New Crib Rules Toughest in World," *The Des Moines Register,* June 30, 2011, p. 7B.

18. Christopher Doering, "Surge in Products Being Recalled May Be Numbing Consumers," *USA TODAY,* June 20, 2012 [**usatoday30.usatoday.com**]

19. Ibid.

20. Jonathan V. O'Steen and Van O'Steen, "The FDA Defense: Vioxx and the Argument Against Federal Preemption of State Claims for Injuries Resulting from Defective Drugs," 48 *Arizona Law Review* 67 (2006).

21. Duff Wilson, "Merck to Pay $950 Million over Vioxx," *The New York Times,* November 22, 2011 [**www.nytimes.com/**].

22. P. J. Huffstutter, "Amid Mounting Safety Concerns, Technology Helps Track Food from Farm to Table," *latimes.com,* October 3, 2010 [**www.latimes.com**].

23. Neela Banerjee and Alana Semuels, "FDA Proposes Sweeping New Food Safety Rules," *Los Angeles Times,* January 4, 2013 [**http://articles.latimes.com/**].

24. Anna Edney and Catherine Larkin, "Drug Approvals Reach 15-Year High on Smoother FDA Reviews," *Bloomberg,* January 2, 2013 [**www.bloomberg.com**].

25. Andrew Zajac, "Most Recalled Medical Devices Received Speedy FDA Review," *latimes.com,* February 15, 2011 [**latimes.com/health/la-na-medical-devices-20110215,0,4206876.story**].

26. Thomas Philipson and Andrew von Eschenbach, "FDA Reform Can Lift U.S. Economy," *Bloomberg,* February 28, 2013 [**www.bloomberg.com/**].

27. Ibid.

28. Ibid.

29. JP, "Are Student Loans Ruining the Economy?" *U.S. News & World Report,* May 29, 2013 [**money.usnews.com/**].

30. Joshua Eferighe, "College Students More Wary of Credit Card Debt," *Washington Times,* April 1, 2013 [**www.washingtontimes.com/**].

31. Andrew Martin, "On Campus, New Deals with Banks," *The New York Times,* May 30, 2012 [**www.nytimes.com/**].

32. Ibid.

33. Associated Press, "Positive Results Seen from Credit Card Law," *Waterloo/Cedar Falls Courier,* May 10, 2011, p. B7.

34. Jennifer Liberto, "Bank Critic Praises Credit Card Companies," *CNNMoney.com,* February 22, 2011 [**http://money.cnn.com/fdcp?1298396190777**].

35. This summary of FCRA requirements was drawn largely from the FTC document, "A Summary of Your Rights under the Fair Credit Reporting Act" [**www.ftc.gov/bcp/conline/edcams/fcra/summary.htm**].

36. Editorial Board, "Taking Credit Scores Seriously," *The Washington Post,* February 16, 2013 [**www.washingtonpost.com/**].

37. Ibid.

38. John Collins Rudolf, "Pay Garnishments Rise as Debtors Fall Behind," *The New York Times,* April 1, 2010 [**www.nytimes.com**] and *Washington Post,* "Punitive Charges Dog Credit Card Users," *Waterloo/Cedar Falls Courier,* March 7, 2005, p. A1.

39. "Brown Calls on CFPB to Enact Rules to Rein in Debt Collection Agencies and End Consumer Abuses," press release, June 5, 2013 [**www.brown.senate.gov/**].

40. Editorial, "When a Stranger Calls," *The New York Times,* July 9, 2006 [**www.nytimes.com**].

41. Danielle Douglas, "California Suing JPMorgan Over Debt-Collection Practices," *The Washington Post,* May 9, 2013 [**www.washingtonpost.com/**].

42. Susan Tompor, "Reining in Debt Collectors," *USA TODAY,* November 1, 2012, p. 5B.

43. "Latest Bankruptcies for the 12 Months Ended December 31, 2012," *BankruptcyAction.com,* June 11, 2013 [**www.bankruptcyaction.com/**].

44. "Average American Owes $8,900 in Consumer Debt and Does Not Use a Budget," *The Central Banker,* March 20, 2013 [**www.thecentralbanker.com/**].

45. Katherine Porter and Deborah Thorne, "The Failure of Bankruptcy's Fresh Start," 92 *Cornell Law Review* 67 (2006).

46. Ibid.

47. John Greenya, "Bankruptcy Reform's Poor Legacy," *Pacific Standard,* October 2, 2008 [**www.psmag.com/**].

48. John Collins Rudolf, "Pay Garnishments Rise as Debtors Fall Behind," *The New York Times,* April 1, 2010 [**www.nytimes.com/2010/04/02/**].

49. Editorial, "The College Credit Scam," *The New York Times,* August 27, 2007 [**www.nytimes.com**].

50. Richard H. Thaler, "Underwater, but Will They Leave the Pool?" *The New York Times,* January 24, 2010 [**www.nytimes.com**].

CHAPTER SIXTEEN

International Ethics and Law

After completing this chapter, students will be able to:

1. Discuss the role of the World Trade Organization (WTO) in reducing global trade barriers.

2. Compare and contrast an American firm's social responsibility to its host country with its social responsibility to its home country.

3. Discuss the interrelationship of religion, culture, and legal rules with comparisons to American and Islamic viewpoints.

4. Evaluate arguments in favor of global social responsibility standards.

5. Describe the basic forms of global business expansion.

6. Compare and contrast treaties, custom, and comity and give illustrations of each.

7. Describe examples of the law governing international business in sales of goods, trade in-services, and employment.

8. Identify and describe the four main forms of intellectual property covered in the text and the international agreements that govern them.

9. Discuss how and why nations regulate imports and exports.

10. Describe the purposes and effects of the General Agreement on Tariffs and Trade (GATT) and the General Agreement on Trade in Services (GATS).

11. Identify and evaluate the means for resolving international disputes.

12. Explain the act of state doctrine.

13. Describe the doctrine of sovereign immunity and its exceptions as codified under the Foreign Sovereign Immunities Act (FSIA).

14. Discuss the recent use of the Foreign Tort Claims Act against corporate defendants.

15. Identify some challenges to the enforcement of foreign judgments.

Introduction

The preceding chapters have addressed law and ethics primarily in an American context. However, ours is undeniably a global economy, as painfully evidenced by the global economic recession triggered in 2008 and its continuing repercussions.

> Globalization is the breaking down of national boundaries to allow free interchange of people, communications, services, goods, businesses, investments, and ideas.

The process of globalization is the breaking down of national boundaries and rules to allow free interchange around the world—the free interchange of people, communications, services, goods, businesses, investments, and ideas. Evidence of the global economy is everywhere. Travel the world and you can readily access automated teller machines (ATMs) for local currency that will be instantaneously debited from your domestic bank account. You will see such American logos as Starbucks, McDonalds, and Deloitte adorning shops and buildings. Back at home, on streets and in malls, you can see branches and outlets for HSBC (formerly the Hongkong and Shanghai Banking Corporation, now one of the world's largest banks, headquartered in London), Godiva Chocolatier (founded in Brussels), Hyundai cars (Korean), and H&M clothing stores (Swedish). As for the interchange of people, in addition to the millions of international temporary business and pleasure travelers, there are some 215 million first-generation migrants, 40 percent more than in 1990.[1]

But how is business practice affected by this networked global economy? Which laws govern company behavior? The laws of the "home" country? The laws of the "host" country? The laws where the company's suppliers or customers reside? What happens if the laws of the host country and the home country conflict? And what happens when a corporation changes its home country? When the German corporation, Daimler Benz, merged with Chrysler, becoming Daimler Chrysler, did the laws to which Chrysler was subject change? Did those changes have to be unwound when Daimler later sold Chrysler to Cerberus Capital Management, an American private equity fund, in 2007? As of this writing, the Italian automaker Fiat owns a majority of Chrysler. What law governs the company now? As firms become companies of the world, rather than of one nation, difficult issues of ethics and law arise.

The International Environment

Ever since Adam Smith wrote *The Wealth of Nations* in 1776, many have argued that it is axiomatic that a decrease in trade barriers between any number of countries will stimulate the total world economy, not simply the economies of the countries involved in the specific trade agreement. Belief in this principle is affirmed each time a new nation joins the World Trade Organization (WTO). With the addition of six new countries in 2012 and 2013, including Russia, 159 countries are members. Afghanistan and Yemen are likely to have joined by the time this edition is in print, bringing the total to 161. A fundamental principle set forth in the preamble to the 1994 Marrakesh Agreement, which established the WTO effective January 1, 1995, is that "substantial reduction of tariffs and other barriers to trade" will contribute to the objectives of "raising standards of living, ensuring full employment and a large and steadily growing volume of real income."[2] Member countries in the WTO represent a diverse array of the world's governments: from communist to socialist to capitalist, from Buddhist to Jewish to Christian to Muslim, and from all points around the globe. Thus, belief in the benefits of decreasing trade barriers is widely shared in the international community. [The WTO maintains an extensive online presence, including full text documents, through its website at **www.wto.org**]

Trade Agreements

The desire to reach a common legal ground in international business is not a recent development. As early as 1778, U.S. commercial treaties have regulated shipping and trading rights and rules between U.S. citizens and those of other countries. Such agreements can be relatively simple—involving only two countries and only a few commodities—or more complex, multilateral agreements involving three or more countries and broad areas of their trading relationships, such as the North American Free Trade Agreement (NAFTA) among Canada, the United States, and Mexico. The more countries involved and the more topics on the table, the more complex the agreement. The WTO is the prototypical multilateral agreement. As previously noted, the vast majority of countries are members and conceivably any trade-related topic could become a topic for negotiation. In principle, the greatest economic stimulation would come from involving the maximum number of state actors and addressing the universe of possible trade issues. As a practical matter, that ideal may be very difficult to effectuate, as was manifestly illustrated by the WTO negotiations which concluded in December 2013.[3]

Those negotiations, known as the Doha Round after the city in Qatar where the round was initiated, began in 2001 and collapsed in 2008. Sticking points included the continuation of substantial agricultural subsidies for farmers in the United States and Europe, which negatively impact the competitive strength of agricultural products originating in other countries, and the relatively high import tariffs on manufactured goods imposed by some emerging economies, such as China and India. Another impediment to its conclusion was the dramatic change in the global trading environment over the thirteen years the negotiations continued. Not only have major industrialized countries suffered substantial recessions, but emerging economies began contributing dramatically to the global growth in gross domestic product (GDP)—accounting for two-thirds of it in 2008.[4] Both realities have contributed to a shift in the economic balance of power. The December 2013 agreement reflects a substantially modified agenda compared to that envisioned in 2001 and focuses primarily on the streamlining of international customs rules and procedures.

In light of the limited recent negotiating successes under the auspices of the WTO, the fear is that there will be a return to less comprehensive regional and bilateral negotiations in which the imbalance of power between rich and poor nations will be more pronounced. Regional trade agreements do seem to be on the rise. As of this writing, the United States is negotiating two major regional compacts: one with the European Union (the Transatlantic Trade and Investment Partnership or TTIP) and the other with 11 countries circling the Pacific (the Trans-Pacific Partnership or TPP). Successful conclusions to either or both would certainly lead to a decrease in trade barriers for the participants, but perhaps not for nonparticipants. Two points are worthy of note. The first is that the negotiating focus of both the TTIP and the TPP is on reducing *nontariff barriers,* particularly by promoting regulatory convergence through the adoption of common standards on such wide-ranging issues as food safety, government procurement rules, restrictions on state-owned enterprises, licensing standards, Internet freedom, and the protection of intellectual property, as well as labor and environmental standards. The second noteworthy point is that none of the major emerging economies—Brazil, Russia, India, and China (BRIC)—are participants of either of these nascent regional compacts. It has been observed that these talks "give the U.S. and the EU a chance to shape global rules in a wide range of industries" and therefore "pressure … large developing countries to adopt any harmonized rules" which result.[5]

> None of the major emerging economies—Brazil, Russia, India, and China (BRIC)—are participants in either the TTIP or TPP.

European Union

One of the most well-known, and most developed, trade agreements is that of the European Union. It is also quite significant for our purposes because the EU is the United States' largest trading partner, and vice versa. The EU is made up of 28 member countries, with five candidate countries: Montenegro, Serbia, Macedonia, Turkey, and Iceland. The EU population far surpasses the United States' (508 million compared with 316 million, as of this writing) and its combined gross domestic product is roughly equivalent to that of the United States' GDP (both just under $16 trillion). Like the United States, the European Union has a robust domestic regulatory regime that impacts foreign companies seeking to do business there. But their regulatory philosophies differ: Europe tends to take a precautionary approach, disallowing new products and technologies until they are proven safe, whereas the United States tends to weigh costs and benefits, even while recognizing that unknowns exist.[6] These differing approaches will challenge both sides' TTIP negotiators and may, in fact, prove insurmountable.

Like the WTO, the European Union is currently facing considerable challenges. When the financial crisis that began in 2008 spread around the world through the web of global financial and economic ties, not only were weak banks revealed, but also weak countries. The very success of the EU in increasing trade and other economic ties among its member countries became a weakness: The economically weaker countries acted as a further drag on the stronger economies. Some of the strongest economic ties in the European Union are those that link the 17 countries that have adopted the euro as their common currency. In the usual course, as a national economy deteriorates, its currency is devalued in relation to other currencies and the economic hardship stays primarily a domestic problem. However, within the eurozone, for example, Greece's currency can't fall to reflect the degree of its economic difficulties because the value of the euro is tied to perceptions of the total group of eurozone countries. But when the world sees weakness not just in Greece, but also in Spain, Portugal, Ireland, and Italy, even the economically strong eurozone countries suffer the downward revaluation of the currency. For those countries the issue becomes, if they provide the support to prop up the weaker economies, whether the recipient countries can and will make changes domestically to strengthen their economies and prevent future negative impacts on the euro. If the stronger economies do not have faith in future change, and cannot compel such change as a condition of their support, they may determine that the better choice for the long run is to abandon the euro. That step could lead to the disintegration of the European Union itself.[7] [EUROPA is the portal site of the European Union, found at **europa.eu/index_en.htm**]

Globalization and Countervailing Forces

Recall our definition of globalization: the breaking down of national boundaries to allow free interchange of people, communications, services, goods, businesses, investments, and ideas. Understanding what globalization is not may be as important as knowing what it is: It is not homogenization. The goal is not to make us all the same. But the goals do include increased choice through the sharing of diversity, as well as appropriate protection of historical, social, and cultural identities. It is also not just about free trade. Consider again some of the issues on the table in the TTIP and TPP negotiations, such as standards for food safety, of Internet freedom, for labor, and for acceptable environmental practices. The WTO's own website acknowledges, "[T]he WTO is not just about liberalizing trade, and in some circumstances its rules support maintaining trade barriers—for example, to protect consumers or prevent the spread of disease. ... The system's overriding purpose is to help trade flow as freely as possible—so long as there are no undesirable side-effects."[8]

> Globalization has not been uniformly beneficial.

What has also become clear is that the process of globalization has not been uniformly beneficial. "The real question isn't whether free markets are good or bad. It is why they are producing such wildly different results in different countries."[9] One reason for disparate results may be whether the local government develops in tandem with the economy and is able to and does capture an appropriate portion of the wealth created to put to use on behalf of its population. Where that is not occurring, it has been argued that "multinationals—which account for the bulk of direct cross-border investment and one third of trade—have social responsibilities in nations where the rule of law is weak. And this view dispenses with the erroneous notion that open markets will magically produce prosperity in all conditions."[10] The global impact of multinationals is a thread that runs throughout this chapter.

Questions

1. Consider the critics from the United States and elsewhere who have expressed concern about continued globalization. What do you think they are most concerned about—the free interchange of people, businesses, goods, services, investments, communications, or ideas? Explain.

2. If multinational corporations have affirmative social responsibilities in "nations where the rule of law is weak," who should select and impose those responsibilities? If you believe that it is a matter for corporate management, what forces might cause management to act more responsibly? What forces exist that might impede more corporate social responsibility on the part of multinationals? On the other hand, if you believe that social responsibilities should be imposed on multinationals, what body should do so? How will that body obtain the power to legislate and enforce such responsibilities?

The Intercultural Environment: Ethics Across International Borders

The September 11, 2001 World Trade Center attack focused light on ethical and legal tensions between the American and Islamic cultures. America's long presence in Iraq and Afghanistan kept these cultural divisions in the public eye. The public protests of the Arab Spring in 2011, however, may have demonstrated that Islamic cultures are no more homogeneous than America's. Many issues triggering the protests—such as human-rights violations, unemployment, and extreme poverty—are issues about which the American public could be sympathetic. [For more on the Arab Spring, see **en.wikipedia.org/wiki/Arab_ Spring**] Bridging cultural differences is an essential first step in creating an effective working relationship.

> In Islamic countries, religion is the basis for many legal, as well as ethical, standards.

Religion often provides the foundation for a culture's ethical structure. Thus, two countries with different religious heritages are likely to have divergent ethical and legal norms. For example, separation of church and state is a basic legal precept in the United States. By contrast, in Islamic countries, religion is the basis for many legal, as well as ethical, standards. In reading the following article, consider what human rights you believe to be "fundamental." Keep in mind that cultures differ in their judgments about which rights are so important that they should be protected.

READING   Islamic Law: Myths and Realities

Dennis J. Wiechman, Jerry D. Kendall, and Mohammad K. Azarian

In order to protect the five important indispensables in Islam (religion, life, intellect, offspring, and property), Islamic Law has provided a worldly punishment in addition to that in the hereafter. Islam has, in fact, adopted two courses for the preservation of these five indispensables: the first is through cultivating religious consciousness in the human soul and the awakening of human awareness through moral education; the second is by inflicting deterrent punishment, which is the basis of the Islamic criminal system. Therefore "Hudoud," Retaliation (Qesas), and Discretionary (Tazir) punishments have been prescribed according to the type of the crime committed.

Islamic Law and Jurisprudence are not always understood by the Western press. Although it is the responsibility of the mass media to bring to the world's attention violations of human rights and acts of terror, many believe that media stereotyping of all Muslims is a major problem. The [1993] bombing at the World Trade Center in New York City is a prime example. The media often used the term "Islamic Fundamentalists" when referring to the accused in the case. They also referred to the Egyptian connections in that case as "Islamic Fundamentalists." The media have used the label of "Islamic Fundamentalist" to imply all kinds of possible negative connotations: terrorists, kidnappers, and hostage takers. Since the media do not use the term "Fundamentalist Christian" each time a Christian does something wrong, the use of such labels is wrong for any group, Christians, Muslims, or Orthodox Jews.

A Muslim who is trying to live his religion is indeed a true believer in God. This person tries to live all of the tenets of his religion in a fundamental way. Thus, a true Muslim is a fundamentalist in the practice of that religion, but a true Muslim is not radical, because the Quran teaches tolerance and moderation in all things. When the popular media generalize from the fundamentalist believer to the "radical fundamentalist" label they do a disservice to all Muslims and others.

NO SEPARATION OF CHURCH AND STATE
To understand Islamic Law one must first understand the assumptions of Islam and the basic tenets of the religion. The

meaning of the word *Islam* is "submission or surrender to Allah's (God's) will." Therefore, Muslims must first and foremost obey and submit to Allah's will. Mohammed the Prophet was called by God to translate verses from the Angel Gabriel to form the most important book in Islam, the Quran, Muslims believe.

* * * * *

The most difficult part of Islamic Law for most Westerners to grasp is that there is no separation of church and state. The religion of Islam and the government are one. Islamic Law is controlled, ruled, and regulated by the Islamic religion. The theocracy controls all public and private matters. Government, law, and religion are one. There are varying degrees of this concept in many nations, but all law, government, and civil authority rest upon it and it is a part of Islamic religion. There are civil laws in Muslim nations for Muslim and non-Muslim people. Sharia [Islamic law] is only applicable to Muslims. . . . The U.S. Constitution (Bill of Rights) prohibits the government from "establishing a religion." The U.S. Supreme Court has concluded in numerous cases that the U.S. Government can't favor one religion over another. That concept is implicit, for most U.S. legal scholars and many U.S. academicians believe that any mixture of "church and state" is inherently evil and filled with many problems.

* * * * *

Islamic Law is very different from English Common Law or the European Civil Law traditions. Muslims are bound to the teachings of the Prophet Mohammed whose translation of Allah or God's will is found in the Quran. Muslims are held accountable to the Sharia Law, but non-Muslims are not bound by the same standard (apostasy from Allah). Muslims and non-Muslims are both required to live by laws enacted by the

various forms of government such as tax laws, traffic laws, white-collar crimes of business, and theft. These and many other crimes similar to Common Law crimes are tried in modern "Mazalim Courts." The Mazalim Courts can also hear civil law, family law, and all other cases. Islamic Law does have separate courts for Muslims for "religious crimes" and contemporary nonreligious courts for other criminal and civil matters.

Questions

1. Is it important to you that our laws protect "religion, life, intellect, offspring, and property"? How do our laws protect these values? Explain.

2. Do any of our laws "rest upon" religious principles found in Judaism or Christianity? Explain.

3. Another law over which countries have profound differences of opinion is capital punishment. At the time of this writing, a 56-year-old British woman was facing death by firing squad for smuggling about 10 pounds of cocaine into Bali. Nearly 100 countries have abolished capital punishment. According to Amnesty International, 682 confirmed executions were carried out worldwide in 2012 (excluding thousands in China, however, because accurate information is unavailable). The five countries with the highest numbers are China, Iran, Iraq, Saudi Arabia, and the United States. Develop brief arguments both for and against capital punishment. **Source:** "Not Dead Yet," *The Economist,* April 13, 2013; and **http://amnesty.org/en/death-penalty/death-sentences-and-executions-in-2012.**

Source: Office of International Criminal Justice, Criminal Justice International Online, 12, no. 3 (May 1996) [**www.iol.ie/~afifi/Articles/law.htm**]; reprinted by permission of Criminal Justice International Online.

Laws and Social Norms Regarding Free Speech

Standards for appropriate speech are regulated both by societal norms and, in many cases, by local law. The bounds of free speech vary considerably from country to country. The Internet magnifies the issue because its inherent nature allows speech to flow freely divorced from political boundaries. Although Chapter 18 will cover the Internet and free speech under U.S. law, here we look at the issue from an international perspective, not with regard to the speaker, but rather to the service provider that facilitates transmission of the contested speech.

Because service providers such as Google, Facebook, and Twitter store the speech of others on their servers, one issue is whether such a provider can, should, or must remove content that is offensive to portions of its audience, particularly after the provider has been notified of the specific content found objectionable. For example, in 2011 Google received more than 1,900 requests from governments for the removal of various content, many of which were honored by blocking access from those countries under Google's policy of complying with lawful requests. Which country's requests topped the list? Brazil with 418; the United States was second with 279. This is not as surprising as it might seem when one factors in that countries where less free speech is tolerated block content more directly. China's "Great Firewall" is a case in point. What speech draws a red flag in Brazil? Racial issues, but also some political speech. Brazil "has strict electoral laws that limit criticism of candidates in the runup to elections."[11] In Spring 2013, Facebook angered a considerable number of its U.S. constituents with regard to content that glorified violence against women. Groups concerned with women's rights have repeatedly reported offensive content, with mixed satisfaction. Frustrated, they used one medium to get the attention of another: They "asked Facebook users to use [a particular] Twitter hashtag . . . to call on companies to stop advertising on Facebook if their ads [had] been placed alongside" pages with names such as "Violently Raping Your Friend Just for Laughs." In a very short time the effort had garnered 224,000 supporters on a petition at change.org and Facebook publically stated that its "systems to identify and remove hate speech have failed to work as effectively as we would like, particularly around issues of gender-based hate."[12]

Perhaps even more challenging are requests from governments for service providers to turn over information revealing the identity of the content poster. France has antihate laws that proscribe anti-Semitic speech. Twitter had already removed at least some of the content at issue when a French court in a civil suit brought by a citizen's group ordered Twitter to identify the individuals who had posted the content. Although its policy is to provide such information only in response to a valid order of a U.S. court, ultimately Twitter agreed to provide the information to French authorities that were seeking to prosecute the posters under their antihate laws. In deciding to cooperate, Twitter may have been concerned that the employees of its Paris offices would be subject to prosecution.[13]

Question

Acceptable speech varies not just by country but also over time. Today's Internet content issues can be seen as a modern version of TV broadcast censorship. In the early years of TV, bedrooms of spouses could be shown only if they contained two beds. TV censorship varied somewhat by the time of day of the broadcast, but language and dress had some restrictions applicable at all times. As discussed in this section, sensitive topics can also be based on local history and conditions. Additional examples include Thailand's prohibitions against insults to its monarchy and India's fears about content that could spark religious violence. Hate speech is widely restricted. Try developing a substantive rule that an Internet provider could use to determine when a request to remove content should be acted upon, regardless of the country of origin. If your rule references hate speech, it will be important to indicate what speech meets the criteria.

Social Responsibility to Host Country

When doing business abroad, does a firm have social responsibilities to the host country beyond those required by the market and the law of that country? This issue has arisen in many contexts, including factory labor conditions. Not infrequently, corporations have been chastised for allowing working conditions in their foreign operations or in their suppliers' plants that Western cultures consider substandard. Such *sweatshops* pose a host of commercial, economic, ethical, political, and social questions. For example, on April 24, 2013, 1,129 people died when a multistory building collapsed in a suburb of Dhaka, the capital of Bangladesh. Only a day earlier, cracks had been discovered in the building, which housed retailers on the lower floors and a number of clothing factories on the top floors. In response to the discovery, the retailers immediately closed, but the owners of the factories on the higher floors insisted their workers continue to produce the clothing that was destined for European and American consumers. As evidenced by the over 5,000 garment factories employing more than 3.2 million workers, low labor costs have attracted nearly every major clothing company to Bangladesh, where unsafe factory facilities have long been a problem. Only five months earlier, a fire in a similar factory killed 112 workers after which importers, including Walmart, pledged to do more to ensure worker safety, but little was achieved. The call for Western buyers to take effective action came loudly and immediately following the loss of life in April 2013. Despite the renewed outcry, real reform does not appear to be on the near horizon.[14]

Traditionally, free-market economists have believed that sweatshops are necessary and beneficial. Sweatshops allow the economies of developing countries to improve because their export sectors expand and consumers in global markets are better off because they pay less for the products they buy. This faith in the market is based on the concept of comparative advantage: that developing countries typically have a comparative competitive advantage in cheap labor while developed countries have comparative advantages in such things as an educated workforce, manufacturing infrastructure and expertise, certain particularly well-developed industries, and so on. These economists argue that sweatshops have been an element of every developed country's transformation from an agrarian society to an urban-based, highly industrialized economy. If poor countries want to develop, a sweatshop stage is necessary, they say. The expected progression holds that, as exports from a developing country rise, its local economy grows, generating funds that can be used in part to increase the overall standard of living and to invest in education and infrastructure, which, in turn, will allow the country to compete on other bases.

Other economists disagree that all developing countries must necessarily endure a sweatshop phase. A pure free market, or hands-off economy, does not exist either in industrialized countries or in the developing world. Governments often play a role in creating comparative advantages. For example, in Bangladesh the government has set the minimum wage at $37 per month; it prohibits many workers from organizing labor unions and workers in industries which may be unionized face rules that make success challenging; it has set building standards, but does not effectively enforce them. In addition, the increase in national wealth referenced by free-market economists, often created by poor laborers, may for a considerable time find its way primarily into the hands of industry heads and government employees.[15]

[For journalist John Stossel's 2004 overview of sweatshop protests followed by his defense of low-wage jobs, see **www.youtube.com/watch?v=0VaHmgoB10E**]

Question

If you were the vice president for supply chain management for a large manufacturer or retailer, what type of labor standards would you impose on suppliers from other countries, if any?

Social Responsibility to Home Country?

We have noted a potential responsibility to a host country, but does a firm have any special obligation to its home country? Social responsibility to a home country might necessitate operating in accord with the values of one's home country even when doing business abroad. Microsoft and other U.S. companies, for example, have had difficulties with software piracy in foreign countries. Russia, supported by Microsoft lawyers, has taken some action to crackdown on such piracy. However, Russian human rights and environmental organizations have alleged that the government selectively investigates the use of illegal software in order to muzzle opposition voices while government allies are rarely if ever investigated. In late 2010, Microsoft initiated a new policy of providing blanket software licenses to advocacy groups in Russia so as to limit the government's ability to use software piracy as a pretext for government censorship or harassment.[16]

The United States exports its values structure in a variety of ways, including through the *extraterritorial* application of its laws. When the U.S. Supreme Court declared that antidiscrimination provisions of U.S. statutes such as Title VII of the Civil Rights Act of 1964 did not apply extraterritorially,[17] Congress reversed the decision with its 1991 Amendments to Title VII. Extraterritorial application is considered essential because over five million Americans work abroad. Accordingly, American firms that do not maintain certain Title VII standards abroad may be subject to liability in the United States. For instance, if a firm conducts operations in Saudi Arabia, where the circumstances under which women are allowed to work are considerably circumscribed, that firm is still held to Title VII's prohibition against gender discrimination. Compliance with American civil rights laws is not required, however, where doing so would violate the host country's laws.

The Foreign Corrupt Practices Act (FCPA)

Consider the problem of bribery and other forms of corruption. Some nations argue that bribery is acceptable behavior, whereas others criticize it severely. In July 2013, the Chinese minister who had overseen a substantial modernization of China's railways was sentenced to death (although reduction to a life sentence was possible) for accepting $10.5 million in bribes.[18] How would you define bribery? What problems are created by a culture of bribery?

For years, U.S. firms have dealt with bribery issues in America and abroad. Congress has attempted to respond harshly to corruption in other governments and to support U.S. firms that do not participate in foreign corruption. As we saw in Chapter 2, the FCPA prohibits businesses from making certain payments or gifts to government officials for the purpose of influencing business decisions. In recent years the United States has stepped up its enforcement of the FCPA, both through criminal suits brought by the Department of Justice and through civil cases brought by the Securities Exchange Commission.[19] Recent FCPA investigations have involved the following companies:

- GlaxoSmithKline: Both the United States and China are investigating bribes of nearly $500 million alleged to have been paid by the British company through Chinese travel agencies to doctors and hospital personnel for boosting their prescriptions of GSK pharmaceuticals, as well as to government officials and Chinese GSK executives. Allegedly, one travel agency "was handling about $16 million worth of Glaxo business a year. . . .

How the small agency [which also had other foreign drug companies as clients] secured business with many of the world's biggest drug makers remains a mystery."[20]

- Hollywood movie studios: In spring 2012, the SEC began an investigation of five companies, including 20th Century Fox, DreamWorks Animation, and Disney, into whether studios were gaining access to Chinese movie theaters for their films by paying bribes to Chinese officials.[21]

- Microsoft: Also under investigation are allegations by tipsters of kickbacks paid by Microsoft to foreign officials, resellers, and consultants for the purpose of securing contracts in five countries—China, Italy, Pakistan, Romania, and Russia.[22]

- Walmart: The government has been investigating Walmart with regard to alleged bribery, particularly in Mexico, to obtain approvals for a widescale expansion of its store sites, as well as an internal attempt to cover it up. A substantial report on its actions in Mexico was published by *The New York Times* in 2012; many executives holding critical positions, including the chief administrative officer in the U.S. and the general counsel of its Mexican division, have since left the company. [23]

Although well intentioned, some critics argue that the FCPA unduly restricts American companies operating abroad and prevents them from competing effectively. However, the biggest settlements under the FCPA have actually been paid by foreign companies, a consequence of the Act's application to any company that has securities listed on a U.S. stock exchange or does business in the United States.[24] Others argue the United States should not use foreign trade to unilaterally impose its sense of morality around the globe. Many other countries, however, are enforcing similar antibribery measures. [For more information on FCPA enforcement actions, see **www.fcpablog.com**]

Question

Is it ethical for the U.S. Congress to impose federal laws on the operations of U.S. corporations abroad? Why or why not?

Social Responsibility to Humanity?

Are we evolving toward a set of common international ethical standards that can be supported and implemented globally? Would international ethical standards simply represent a natural progression from national standards? At one time, agreements were achieved only at a city level, but state-level agreements followed, and those, in turn, evolved to agreements among federated states. Is a similar progression to global standards inevitable? Does a framework that divides ethical issues between those of the "host" country and those of the "home" country remain a useful analytical tool?

> If we are moving toward global social responsibility, can we do so without sacrificing the existence of wonderfully diverse and unique cultures?

If we are moving toward global social responsibility, can we do so without sacrificing the existence of wonderfully diverse and unique cultures? Do we have to become ever more uniform in our beliefs and practices? Can we agree on fundamentals, but still appreciate diversity?

Consider the evidence. Not only are businesses interacting with stakeholders of ever more diverse nationalities (investors/owners/shareholders, customers/clients, suppliers, general citizenry impacted by business decisions), but the cultural identity of businesses themselves may be unclear. Consider the example of Chrysler's changing ownership in the chapter introduction.

We have growing evidence of voluntary international cooperation to establish acceptable business practices, such as the establishment of October 14 as World Standards Day to honor the work of many nongovernmental international bodies that have established a wide range of voluntary standards addressing global production and trade. Other evidence includes:

- As far back as 1948, the U.N. General Assembly adopted its Universal Declaration of Human Rights. Inherent in the structure of the declaration is a recognition of the connection between work (and business, by extension) and the protection of fundamental human values. Article 23 declares that everyone has a right "to just and favourable conditions of work" and "to just and favourable remuneration ensuring for himself and his family an existence worthy of human dignity."[25]

- In 2000, the United Nations launched a voluntary initiative to promote corporate social responsibility globally. The 10 principles of the *Global Compact* address human rights, labor standards, the environment, and corruption. Over 7,000 businesses from 145 countries have joined the Compact. [For more on the Global Compact, see **www .unglobalcompact.org**]

- Social Accountability International has developed SA8000, a social accountability standard based on international norms (such as the Universal Declaration of Human Rights previously mentioned) that companies can adopt to develop and assure an equitable and safe workplace for their employees and those of their suppliers. A verification system was simultaneously developed so results are auditable. As of this writing, more than 3,100 facilities with 1.8 million employees in 69 countries are certified. [For more on SAI and SA8000, see **www.sa-intl.org** and **www.saasaccreditation.org**]

PRACTICING ETHICS Individual Social Responsibility to Humanity?

Consider the following excerpt from a speech delivered September 28, 2001, by Jose Ramos-Horta, Nobel Peace Prize Laureate (1996) and Minister for Foreign Affairs and Cooperation for the East Timor Transition Government:

There is no dispute that abject poverty, child labor, and prostitution are a moral indictment of all humanity.

However, poverty should not only touch our conscience: It is also a matter of peace and security because it destabilizes entire countries and regions. In turn it threatens the integration of the global economy that is vital if the rich are to stay rich or if the poor are to move up, if only an inch.

Peace will be illusory as long as the rich ignore the clamor of the poor for a better life, as long as hundreds of millions of people live below the poverty line, cannot afford a meal a day, do not have access to clean water and a roof.[26]

Questions

Should most of us, not just active international businesses, accept a social responsibility to humanity? If we answer yes to this question, how might our actions as students, educators, employees, employers, and investors change?

Laws Governing Cross-Border Business

All businesses must, of course, follow the laws of the countries in which they are physically present and operating. (Whether a business with no physical presence but which solicits or performs business in a foreign country electronically must follow the laws of the foreign country will be examined in Chapter 18.) Foreign firms often wish to establish operations in the United States, in part because Americans are more inclined to buy goods made in this country. Doing business in the United States brings with it the requirement to comply with U.S. laws and regulations.

Conversely, when U.S. businesses operate abroad, they are required to follow the law of the host country. In 2006 when Google began operating its search engine in China it accepted the government's requirement that it filter results to remove material the government deemed unsuitable for its citizens. In March 2010, Google ceased that practice and automatically redirected search requests coming from China to its uncensored site in Hong Kong. China then threatened Google with the loss of its license (to provide other online services such as its music, mapping, and translation). The license was renewed when Google proposed to stop automatically redirecting search requests and instead simply present would-be searchers with a clickable link to **google.com.hk**.[27]

Businesses may also be required, even in their foreign operations, to continue to follow certain laws of their home country, as previously discussed. Interestingly, although there is a presumption against the extraterritorial application of U.S. criminal law, where Congress has clearly indicated an intent to cover actions outside of the United States, U.S. citizens can be held accountable in America for their criminal actions abroad.[28]

Finally, businesses operating across national borders will also be subject to international law. The foundation and some examples of international business law will be discussed soon, but first it will be useful to explore some of the different forms of business available to companies wishing to expand their operations into foreign countries.

Forms of Global Business Expansion

Multinational Enterprise (MNE)

The term *multinational enterprise* traditionally refers to a company that conducts business in more than one country. Any of the following operations, except for a direct contract with a foreign purchaser, may qualify a company as an MNE.

Direct Contract

A firm may expand its business across territorial borders using a variety of methods. The simplest, from a contractual perspective, occurs where a firm in one country enters an agreement with a person in another country. For example, a firm may contract to sell its product to a purchaser in another country. This is called a *direct sale* to a foreign purchaser. The parties simply agree on the terms of the sale and record them in a contract.

Where the contract is silent as to a term of the sale, the law that will apply to the missing term will be the law specified in the contract; where none is specified, the applicable law will depend on the country in which the court is located. Some courts will employ the *vesting of rights doctrine,* applying the law of the jurisdiction in which the rights in the contract vested. Other courts may apply the *most significant relationship doctrine,* applying the law of the jurisdiction that has the most significant relationship to the contract and the parties. Finally, some courts will apply the *governmental interest doctrine,* applying the law of the jurisdiction that has the greatest interest in the issue's outcome.

Payment is one of the most complicated issues pertaining to direct sales. The seller should and usually does require an *irrevocable letter of credit,* which the buyer obtains from a bank after paying that amount to the bank (or securing that amount of credit). The bank then promises to pay the seller the contract amount after conforming goods have been shipped. The "irrevocable" component prohibits the bank from revoking the letter of credit without the consent of both the buyer and the seller. The seller is protected because the buyer has already provided adequate funds for the purchase, confirmed by a bank. The buyer is protected because the funds are not turned over to the seller until it has been determined that the goods conform to the contract. It is important to the buyer, however, that the letter of credit be specific as to the conformance of the goods because the bank will only ensure that the goods conform to the letter of credit and not to the contract itself.

> Payment is one of the most complicated issues pertaining to direct sales.

Foreign Representation A second type of foreign expansion is a sale through a distributor, agent, or other type of representative in the foreign country. A firm may decide to sell through an *agent*—that is, the firm hires an individual who will remain permanently in the foreign country, negotiate contracts, and assist in the performance of the contracts. Agents are generally compensated on a commission basis. On the other hand, the firm may act through a *representative,* who may solicit and take orders but, unlike an agent, may not enter into contracts on behalf of the firm. In some countries laws may substantially restrict the actions a representative may take. For example, in China a representative may generally only gather information and market research, but no direct business activities may be undertaken.[29]

Distributors purchase goods from the seller, then negotiate sales to foreign buyers on their own behalf. In so doing, a distributor may be more likely to invest resources to develop the foreign market for the goods. *Exclusive dealing agreements* with distributors, where a distributor agrees to sell only the goods of one manufacturer and the manufacturer agrees to sell only to that distributor in a particular geographic area, are generally not allowed abroad, although they often are legal in the United States.

Export trading companies specialize in acting as the intermediary between a domestic business and foreign purchasers. The trading company will take title to the goods being sold and then complete the sale in the foreign country. *Export management companies,* on the other hand, merely manage the sale but do not take title to the goods; consequently, they do not share any of the risk associated with the sale.

Joint Venture Foreign expansion may also occur through a *joint venture* agreement between two or more parties. This type of agreement usually covers one or several specific projects and is in effect for a specified period. For instance, Toyota and General Motors operated a joint venture at a plant in Fremont, California, from 1984 to 2009. Toyota currently has a joint venture with Subaru in Lafayette, Indiana.

Branch Office or Subsidiary A *branch office* is simply an extension of a foreign corporation into the host country. A *subsidiary,* however, is a legally separate entity formed under the laws of the host country and substantially owned by the foreign parent company. For example, an Indian paper company may open a branch office in London to market and sell its products. That office would be a mere extension of the offices already established in India. On the other hand, the Indian firm could create a British subsidiary to handle its British business from its London offices. Either a subsidiary or branch office relationship could also be established through acquisition of an existing firm in the host country.

The distinction between a subsidiary, which is a legal entity separate from its foreign parent, and a branch office, which is not, has a number of ramifications. For example, many countries may require a local subsidiary to have in-country directors and/or shareholders. On the other hand, setting up a branch office will likely subject the parent company to taxation in the host country. Indeed, the parent company is legally liable for all obligations of a branch office. In contrast, when a subsidiary is sued, the parent company is not generally liable. For example, in *U.S. v. Philip Morris, Inc.*,[30] the U.S. district court dismissed British American Tobacco (BAT) from the federal government's suit against various cigarette manufacturers for recovery of health care expenses. BAT was the British parent of the U.S. company, Brown & Williamson. The subsidiary, B&W, remained a part of the suit.

Licensing   Where a company has no interest in commencing operations in a foreign country but instead merely wants to have its product or name in that market, the company may decide to license the rights to the name or to manufacture the product to a company in the target market. The benefit to this type of relationship is that the licensor (holder of the right) has the opportunity to enter the foreign market, but the licensee assumes all of the obligations and risks of running the business.

Franchising   In a franchise agreement the franchisee pays the franchisor for a license to use trademarks, formulas, and other trade secrets. The difference between a franchising agreement and a licensing contract is that a franchise agreement is usually made up of a number of licensing arrangements, as well as other obligations. For instance, in a typical fast-food franchise agreement the franchisor will license to the franchisee the right to use its trademark, name, logo, recipes, menus, and other recognized resources. Ben & Jerry's offers franchise opportunities in Europe, Asia, Australia, Canada, and Mexico.

Question

Assume that you are interested in importing silk blouses from Bangkok, Thailand, to France. What facts might persuade you to enter into an agency agreement with a Thai blouse manufacturer rather than a distributorship or vice versa?

Foundations of International Law

What law would apply to this situation? Argentinean? Thai? French?

A firm with manufacturing plants in Argentina and Thailand, and corporate headquarters in Bangkok, enters into a contract with a French firm to distribute its products produced in the Argentinean plant. The French firm is not satisfied with the quality of the products being sent. What law would apply to this situation?

Argentinean? Thai? French? Or are there, perhaps, specific provisions of international law that will govern? The answer to this question is not simple, even for seasoned lawyers; yet the firms involved will be greatly affected by the result.

The source of law applicable to an international dispute depends in part on the issue involved. In general, private parties are free to form agreements in whatever manner they wish. The parties to the agreement can determine, for instance, which nation's law will govern the contract, where disagreements in connection with the contract will be settled, and even in which language the transactions will be made. This is referred to as the *private law* of contracts. Whenever the parties to a transaction from different jurisdictions are involved in a lawsuit, the court will start by looking at the agreement of the parties themselves to resolve these issues. Where the contract is silent as to the choice of law, jurisdiction, and other questions, the court must decide. Generally, the law of the jurisdiction in which the transaction occurred is applied. If the transaction is consummated through some form of cross-border communication, as are many international trade negotiations, most often the law of the jurisdiction of the seller's place of business will apply. Remember, however, that the parties may always contract for a different result.

Public law, on the other hand, includes those rules of each nation that regulate the contractual agreement between the parties—for instance, import and export taxes, packaging requirements, and safety standards. In addition, public law regulates the relationships among nations.

Public law derives from a number of sources. The most familiar source of international public law is a *treaty* or *convention* (essentially a contract between nations). For example, the United States, Canada, and Mexico have entered into the North American Free Trade Agreement (NAFTA), a convention regarding trade among those countries. Some treaties and conventions are self-executing, which means that once a country has ratified them, a business can rely on and directly enforce treaty terms in court. The United Nations Convention on Contracts for the International Sale of Goods (CISG), which will be discussed soon, is an example of a self-executing convention. On the other hand, some treaties and conventions apply only to government signatories and not directly to private parties. Such a convention may, for example, require an adopting country such as the United States to amend its domestic law to accomplish the purposes of the convention.

Public law is also found in *international custom* or *generally accepted principles of law*. These terms refer to practices that are commonly accepted as appropriate business or commercial practices among nations. For instance, sovereign immunity, discussed later in this chapter, is an accepted principle of international law. A *custom* is derived from consistent behavior over time that is accepted as binding by the countries that engage in that behavior.

Piracy on the High Seas

In recent years events off the coast of Somalia have raised public awareness of modern-day piracy. One might think that the international law against piracy would be clear given that piracy has existed as a threat to security since well before Britain's Royal Navy returned to port in 1718 with the severed head of Blackbeard. A 2010 federal case in Virginia, as well as attempts to prosecute raiders in other countries, suggested otherwise. What is clear is that generally accepted principles of international law give any country the right to capture pirates on the high seas. U.S. law merely states that "whoever on the high seas, commits the crime of piracy as defined by the law of nations . . . shall be imprisoned for life."

The Virginia court had before it several Somali men who by skiff had approached a U.S. amphibious dock landing ship in the Gulf of Aden in the early morning hours of July 7, 2010. One man shot an AK-47 rifle at the *USS Ashland*, which returned fire, sank the skiff, and then took the assailants into custody. The U.S. government argued that piracy under the law of nations does not require the active taking of property and that any unauthorized armed assault or direct violent act on the high seas is enough. The defense argued the charge could not stand because the defendants "did not board, take control, or otherwise rob the *USS Ashland*." Relying on an 1820 U.S. Supreme Court decision defining piracy as robbery on the high seas and holding that contemporary international law is unsettled on the definition of piracy, the court dismissed the piracy charge.

The case was appealed, as was a later federal district court opinion that upheld piracy charges against five other men who attacked another U.S. vessel off the coast of Somalia. Those defendants were sentenced to life in prison plus 80 years for piracy. The Fourth Circuit affirmed the latter sentences, vacated the *USS Ashland* decision, and held that the 1820 decision did not foreclose conduct other than robbery, including acts of violence committed for private ends against persons on the high seas, from qualifying as piracy.[31]

The Development of Customs

Historically, merchants followed certain accepted *customs* or principles in connection with the sale of goods. These customs or manners of dealing between merchants were often recognized and applied in court decisions and later in the United States became codified in the Uniform Commercial Code (UCC) Article 2 that regulates the sale of goods generally as well as sales between merchants. In this way, customs or practices traditionally followed by merchants have become accepted principles of law throughout the United States (except Louisiana).

In the international legal arena customary practices are still evolving. For instance, the practice had been that personal information moved freely between countries to encourage efficient information exchange in the business world. However, the European Union in 1998 established minimum standards for the protection of personal data. Any country receiving information from an EU country must comply with those standards. (See Chapter 18 for more on the European Union's Directive on Data Protection.)

Two factors are used to determine whether an international custom exists: (1) consistency and repetition of the action or decision and (2) recognition by nations that this custom is binding. The first merely holds that the action or decision must be accepted by a number of nations for a time long enough to establish uniformity of application. The second dictates that the custom be accepted as binding by nations observing it. If the custom is accepted as merely persuasive, it does not rise to the level of a generally accepted principle of law. Through persistent objections, any nation may ensure that such custom is not applied to cases in which it is involved.

Generally, once a contract has been created it is enforceable according to its terms by all parties to the contract. In the following case, read carefully to see what law the judge applied. He considered first the *private* law of the parties (that is, the express terms of the contract); then he looked to *custom;* and finally he applied the concept of *commercial impracticability*.

Transatlantic Financing Corporation v. United States

363 F.2d 312 (D.C. Cir. 1966)

Judge J. Skelly Wright

[In 1956, Transatlantic Financing, a steamship operator, contracted with the United States to ship wheat from Texas to Iran. Six days after the ship left port for Iran, the Egyptian government was at war with Israel and blocked the Suez Canal to shipping. The steamer therefore was forced to sail around the Cape of Good Hope. Transatlantic accordingly sued the United States for its added expenses as a result of this change of circumstances. Transatlantic contended that it had contracted only to travel the "usual and customary" route to Iran and that the United States had received a greater benefit than that for which it contracted. The district court held for the United States; Transatlantic appealed.]

Transatlantic's claim is based on the following train of argument. The charter was a contract for a voyage from a Gulf port to Iran. Admiralty principles and practices, especially stemming from the doctrine of deviation, require us to [infer] into the contract the term that the voyage was to be performed by the "usual and customary" route. The usual and customary route from Texas to Iran was, at the time of contract, via Suez, so the contract was for a voyage from Texas to Iran via Suez. When Suez was closed this contract became impossible to perform. Consequently, appellant's argument continues, when Transatlantic delivered the cargo by going around the Cape of Good Hope, in compliance with the Government's demand under claim of right, it conferred a benefit upon the United States for which it should be paid on quantum meruit.

The contract in this case does not expressly condition performance upon availability of the Suez route. Nor does it specify "via Suez" or, on the other hand, "via Suez or Cape of Good Hope." Nor are there provisions in the contract from which we may properly [infer] that the continued availability of Suez was a condition of performance. Nor is there anything in custom or trade usage, or in the surrounding circumstances generally, which would support our constructing a condition of performance. The numerous cases requiring performance around the Cape when Suez was closed indicate that the Cape route is generally regarded as an alternative means of performance. So the implied expectation that the route would be via Suez is hardly adequate proof of an allocation to the promisee of the risk of closure. In some cases, even an express expectation may not amount to a condition of performance. The doctrine of deviation supports our assumption that parties normally expect performance by the usual and customary route, but it adds nothing beyond this that is probative of an allocation of the risk.

If anything, the circumstances surrounding this contract indicate that the risk of the Canal's closure may be deemed to have been allocated to Transatlantic. We know or may safely assume that the parties were aware, as were most commercial men with interest affected by the Suez situation, that the Canal might become a dangerous area. No doubt the tension affected freight rates, and it is arguable that the risk of closure became part of the dickered terms. We do not deem the risk of closure so allocated, however. Foreseeability or even recognition of a risk does not necessarily prove its allocation. Parties to a contract are not always able to provide for all the possibilities of which they are aware, sometimes because they cannot agree, often simply because they are too busy. Moreover, that some abnormal risk was contemplated is probative but does not necessarily establish an allocation of the risk of the contingency which actually occurs. In this case, for example, nationalization by Egypt of the Canal Corporation and formation of the Suez Users Group did not necessarily indicate that the Canal would be blocked even if a confrontation resulted. The surrounding circumstances do indicate, however, a willingness by Transatlantic to assume abnormal risks, and this fact should legitimately cause us to judge the impracticability of performance by an alternative route in stricter terms than we would were the contingency unforeseen.

We turn then to the question whether occurrence of the contingency rendered performance commercially impracticable under the circumstances of this case. The goods shipped were not subject to harm from the longer, less temperate Southern route. The vessel and crew were fit to proceed around the Cape. Transatlantic was no less able than the United States to purchase insurance to cover the contingency's occurrence. If anything, it is more reasonable to expect owner–operators of vessels to insure against the hazards of war. They are in the best position to calculate the cost of performance by alternative routes (and therefore to estimate the amount of insurance required), and are undoubtedly sensitive to international troubles that uniquely affect the demand for and cost of their services. The only factor operating here in appellant's favor is the added expense, allegedly $43,972.00 above and beyond the contract price of $305,842.92, of extending a 10,000-mile voyage by approximately 3,000 miles. While it may be an overstatement to say that increased cost and difficulty of performance never constitute impracticability, to justify relief there must be more of a variation between expected cost and the cost of performing by an available alternative than is present in this case, where the promisor can legitimately be presumed to have accepted some degree of abnormal risk, and where impracticability is urged on the basis of added expense alone.

We conclude, therefore, as have most other courts considering related issues arising out of the Suez closure, that performance of this contract was not rendered legally impossible.

Affirmed.

Questions

1. *a.* What did the court find with respect to the private law of the parties?

   b. What did it find with respect to the application of custom?

2. Would the result in this case be different if the shipment had been tomatoes as opposed to wheat? Explain.

3. Would the result in this case be different if the United States and Transatlantic agreed by contract that shipment was to arrive in Iran within a period of time that was only possible if the shipper used the canal route? Explain.

4. What do you think it would take for a court to render a contract commercially impracticable? In this case, the shipper was forced to spend almost $44,000 more than it had expected to spend in performing the $306,000 contract. What if the added cost had amounted to $100,000? Would you be persuaded that the contract was then commercially impracticable? What if the closing of the canal doubled the price of the contract? Explain.

Comity

The unique aspect of public international law is that countries are generally not subject to law in the international arena unless they consent to such jurisdiction. For instance, a country is not bound by a treaty unless that country has signed the treaty. A country is not bound by international custom unless it has traditionally participated in that custom. Prior judicial decisions are only persuasive if a country is convinced by and accepts these decisions as precedent. Perhaps the most critical element in understanding international law is recognizing that it is not "law" in the way we generally think of that term. Countries are not bound to abide by it except through *comity*. Comity is the concept that countries should abide by international custom, treaties, and other sources of international direction because that is the civil way to engage in relationships. Nations must respect one another and respect some basic principles of dealing in order to have effective relationships. Although some believe that the origins of law are in religion and its commandments, others argue that law derives from a natural tendency to prevent chaos. International law is an attempt to prevent chaos in the international arena through the application of universal or widely held principles. Comity is the means by which those principles are encouraged.

The concept of comity also includes the respect one country gives to the actions another country takes in its own territory. Specifically, as stated by the Second Circuit in *Finanz AG Zurich v. Banco Economico S.A.*,[32] comity includes "the recognition which one nation allows within its territory to the legislative, executive, or judicial acts of another nation." Under this principle U.S. courts "ordinarily refuse to review acts of foreign governments and defer to proceedings taking place in foreign countries." Thus, the *Finanz* court held that a creditor could not sue in the United States to collect a debt that was subject to the jurisdiction of a bankruptcy proceeding in Brazil.

Regulation of International Trade

As we have just seen, there is no such thing as one body of international law per se that regulates international contracts and trade. Instead, a contract between firms in different countries may be subject to the laws of one country or the other, depending on (1) whether it is a sales contract subject to the U.N. CISG, discussed below, (2) whether the contract itself stipulates the applicable law and forum in which a dispute will be heard, and (3) the rules regarding conflict of laws in each jurisdiction.

In addition, every country has domestic laws that regulate business conducted within its borders and that sometimes regulate its domestic firms outside of its borders. These laws govern the areas of employment-related activities and discrimination, product liability, intellectual property, antitrust and trade practices, and import taxes, to name a few. Consequently, a business owner may actually decide to market a good in one country over another simply because of that country's laws relating to the particular good or to commercial contracts in general. What follows is a brief look at several specific examples of the law governing international business. [For an extensive international trade law database, see **www.jus.uio.no/lm**]

U.N. Convention on Contracts for the International Sale of Goods (CISG)

In 1988, 10 nations signed and became bound by the U.N. Convention on Contracts for the International Sale of Goods. At this writing the CISG is enforceable in 77 nations. The CISG applies to contracts between parties of countries that have signed the convention and provides uniform rules for the sale of goods.

The CISG contains rules regarding the interpretation of contracts and negotiations and the form of contracts. Many obligations of the parties are enunciated by the CISG. For instance, the seller is required to deliver the goods and any documents relating to the goods, as well as to make sure that the goods conform to the contract terms. The buyer, on the other hand, is required to pay the contract price and to accept delivery of the goods. [For the Pace University CISG database, see **cisgw3.law.pace.edu**]

The Convention, however, does not answer all questions that may arise in a transaction. For instance, questions of a contract's validity are left to national law. As we saw in Chapter 6, under American law, an enforceable contract requires five elements:

- *Capacity* to enter the contract.
- *Offer and acceptance* of the terms of the contract.
- *Consideration* for the promises in the contract.
- *Genuineness of assent.*
- *Legality of purpose* of the contract.

Countries with civil law systems do not, however, require consideration for a valid contract.

International Trade in Services

Services, as opposed to goods, are the largest component of the world's gross domestic product, accounting for 63.4 percent in 2012.[33] In the United States, this percentage is even higher—services were 79.7 percent of gross national product (GNP) in 2012.[34] Furthermore, trade in services represents about 29 percent of the total dollar value of U.S. exports.[35] The United States isn't the only country exporting services. The popular press continues to report on the "outsourcing" and "offshoring" of U.S. service-sector jobs. Outsourcing generally refers to the contracting by U.S. companies of such services as call centers, accounting, and customer services to foreign companies located in low-wage markets.

Offshoring refers to U.S. companies setting up their own offices in foreign low-wage markets to perform services previously done by U.S. employees. Economists argue about whether the net effect on jobs in the United States is negative (through the direct loss of jobs) or positive (through corporate and consumer cost savings that permit job growth in the United States).[36]

What international agreements exist to regulate trade in services? Although international trade in goods has been the subject of international agreement since shortly after WWII, until 1994 no similar agreement existed covering international trade in services. This was remedied with the creation of the General Agreement on Trade in Services (GATS), which is now one of the foundation agreements along with the General Agreement on Tariffs and Trade (GATT) to which all member countries of the World Trade Organization (WTO) must subscribe. [The foundation agreements can be found at the WTO website, in the document area, at **www.wto.org**]

The GATS agreement, still in its infancy, sets forth the general principles for the future of trade in services across borders, but at this time requires very little of member countries in moving toward the realization of those principles. Rather, it sets the stage for future negotiations to reduce barriers to trade in services. The services covered by GATS, and therefore by such negotiations, are broad: "any service in any sector except services supplied in the exercise of governmental authority."[37]

Two important general principles that govern international services negotiations are:

• *Most favored nation (MFN) status.* WTO members get treatment by the host country no less favorable than that given to suppliers from any other country, whether or not the other country is a member of the WTO.

• *National treatment.* The national treatment standard calls for a comparison of the treatment accorded to suppliers from WTO member countries with the treatment accorded to domestic suppliers. As a general rule, the treatment is to be "no less favorable" than that received by domestic suppliers.

Question

The WTO member nations have only recently turned their consideration to the barriers between nations that impede the flow of services across boundaries. In the professions, such as medicine, law, and accounting, substantial barriers currently exist. Some barriers are in the form of domestic licensure requirements, which in turn often require a particular educational background for the applicant. Would establishing a clearinghouse for educational equivalencies around the world and requiring WTO members to honor the educational achievements received by applicants in other member countries be a good idea? Why or why not?

Employment-Related Regulations

Social responsibility principles such as those in the U.N. Universal Declaration of Human Rights set aspirational goals for countries and business managers, but they are not enforceable laws. In the absence of enforceable global labor standards, MNEs are left with the obligation to apply substantially varying laws to their employees in different jurisdictions, as well as perhaps having to adhere to their home country laws that have extraterritorial application, such as Title VII for U.S. companies. That said, globalization has transformed workplace governance worldwide, both for good and for ill. A government seeking to improve domestic labor conditions can look to policies and practices that have been successful in other countries, but a government more focused on developing a competitive advantage may specifically exploit its lower labor standards, such as low wages, to attract direct investment by foreign businesses, as seems to be the case for Bangladeshi garment workers as previously discussed.

Even within countries with protective labor regimes, responsible MNEs may be challenged by legal compliance requirements. Not only do substantive laws differ (for example, Germany requires a company either to hire the disabled or pay for an exclusion), but required procedures governing employer-employee relationships vary tremendously. For example, as a result of the recent global recession, an MNE might reasonably determine that a reduction in force across its operations is prudent. Managing such a decision equitably and effectively could be a daunting task. In many countries, nearly all employees may be covered by a works council or trade union with whom the MNE might be required to negotiate a reduction, whereas in the United States less than 10 percent of employees outside the public sector are covered by collective bargaining agreements.[38] In the Netherlands the government must approve most layoffs; in Venezuela, Japan, and China a successful reduction in force might require either agency or court approval. In Europe, an employer even considering such a reduction must consult in good faith with employees about avoiding or mitigating such an action, even if the reduction policy was set by the board of directors at its foreign headquarters.[39] Similar issues can face MNEs involved in international mergers or acquisitions.

Compulsory Retirement

In late 2007, the European Court of Justice ruled that the European Framework Directive on Equal Treatment, which prohibits unjustified age discrimination in the workplace, applied to national laws requiring age-based compulsory retirement. The case challenged a Spanish law permitting employers to impose a compulsory retirement age. Although the Court held the Directive applied to the Spanish law, it nevertheless ruled that the Spanish legislation was a lawful, appropriate means of achieving a legitimate government aim. The law had been passed during a period of high unemployment in Spain and was intended to further a national policy for a better distribution of work between generations.

In the United States, the Age Discrimination in Employment Act (ADEA) prohibits discrimination on the basis of age against individuals who are 40 or older. It applies to decisions to hire or fire, as well as to discriminatory compensation or other terms or conditions of employment. Interestingly, a narrow exception allows universities to require retirement of tenured faculty who reach the age of 70. The ADEA specifically applies to American citizens employed overseas by American companies.

Questions

1. A U.S. corporation operates a branch in Spain. Consistent with Spanish law, it adopts a compulsory retirement age of 62. Is this a violation of the ADEA?

2. Which policy do you favor—the Spanish or the American approach to compulsory retirement? Why? Is this an issue over which countries should be allowed to differ?

Intellectual Property Regulations

Intellectual property, most broadly, refers to creations of the mind. As used here, it refers more specifically to creations of the mind for which legal protection is given, especially trade secrets, trademarks, patents, and copyrights. It is a form of personal property or *personalty,* which is the legal term used to denote all forms of property, both tangible and intangible, other than real property or realty. *Realty* is comprised only of land or real estate and items permanently affixed to the land, such as buildings.

The commercial significance of intellectual property has grown tremendously; by one estimate, "70% of the value of publicly traded corporations is estimated to be in 'intangible assets.'"[40] Theft of intellectual property has also grown tremendously; dollar losses amount to hundreds of billions annually. Clearly then, understanding the legal protections available for intellectual property is of significant importance to business managers. The greatest losses are suffered by U.S., European, and Japanese business; the largest threats originate from China, India, and Russia. Even though cybersecurity issues are often in the news, a lot of theft occurs in other manners, such as when "[hard] drives are either duplicated on site or physically stolen by bribed employees; employees . . . leave and illegally share proprietary information; products are dissected, re-engineered, and sold without permission or payment of royalties; . . . [and] phones are tapped for the purpose of obtaining trade secrets."[41] A *trade secret* can be almost any information that has economic value because it is not generally known which a business makes reasonable efforts to keep secret to secure an advantage over its competition.

[For more information on the theft of intellectual property, see the report of the Commission on the Theft of American Intellectual Property, which can be found at **http://ipcommission.org**]

Trademarks

A *trademark* distinguishes the source of a particular good or service, whether that is accomplished by a trade name, packaging, logo, or other distinguishing mark. When the law protects a trademark, it grants to the holder of the mark a limited monopoly: No one else may use that mark without the holder's permission. Under the Tariff Act of 1930, it is unlawful to import goods bearing a trademark registered with the Patent and Trademark Office that is "owned by a citizen of, or by a corporation or association . . . organized within the United States" without the permission of the mark holder.

This provision safeguards a U.S. trademark holder's rights in the United States from infringement by foreign actors. But what about an American company that wants to obtain trademark protection in other countries? Each country has distinct trademark regulations and offers different levels of protection to marks registered in other countries. For example, a battle that lasted nearly a century ended in early 2013 when the EU General Court in Luxembourg ruled that the Czech brewer, Budvar, could not assert exclusive use of either "Bud" or "Budweiser" throughout the EU because its use of the names was not sufficiently widespread. Anheuser-Busch InBev had claimed use of the Budweiser name as early as 1876, almost 20 years before Budvar was formed.[42]

As of this writing, 174 countries including the United States are parties to a treaty that provides protection for trademarks, known as the *Paris Convention*. More formally called the International Convention for the Protection of Industrial Property, it was originally signed by 11 countries in 1883. According to the Paris Convention, subject to several exceptions, member countries ensure trademark protection to marks registered in other member countries. The convention also provides for *national treatment,* which requires that any individual claiming infringement must have the same protection as would a national of that country. A member country may not favor its own nationals over foreigners. Another treaty, the Madrid Agreement Concerning the International Registration of Marks, attempts to create an international trademark system. If a holder registers a trademark with the World Intellectual Property Organization (WIPO) in Switzerland, that mark is protected in all member countries requested by the holder. A 1989 Protocol relating to the Madrid agreement aimed to render the Madrid system more flexible and more compatible with the domestic legislations of certain countries which had not been able to accede to the Agreement."[43] The United States is a party to the Protocol but has not acceded to the Agreement. [For extensive information on WIPO, see **www.wipo.int**]

That said, trademark issues still arise between countries, both even if are parties to the Paris Convention and the Madrid Agreement or Protocol. For example, after two French courts found Google guilty of infringing on the Louis Vuitton trademark, the highest French court sought a ruling under EU trademark law from the European Court of Justice (ECJ). At issue was Google's AdWords service, pursuant to which Google sold ad space to a Vuitton competitor next to the search results returned any time Louis Vuitton was entered as a search phrase. The ECJ determined that Google had not impermissibly "used" the Louis Vuitton trademark if its role proved to be "merely technical, automatic and passive," and it had not been active in "drafting the commercial message" displayed by the competitor.[44]

Patents

A *patent* is a monopoly on a product, process, or device where the item or process claimed is an innovation, unique and inventive, and useful. The Paris Convention covers patents as well as trademarks; however, it does not establish a network of protection, even among member countries. Patents granted in different member countries for the same invention are independent of each other. However, the convention does establish a *right of priority,* which gives a patent applicant filing in one member nation one year from the original filing to file in other member countries and have the subsequent filings treated as if made on the date of the first filing. Nevertheless, because a patent must be original to be registered in any country, many countries hold that patents previously awarded in other countries automatically preclude additional patent registration.

Other issues have made the international enforcement of a patent quite challenging. For example, the United States has long awarded patents on a first-to-create basis, whereas most other nations have used a first-to-file rule in cases of multiple applicants. Following the passage of the America Invents Act in 2011, effective March 16, 2013, the United States adopted the first-to-file rule. Europe also seems on the brink of simplifying the patent process across most of the European Union. In late 2012, the European Parliament voted in favor of the creation of a single patent, recognized automatically in 25 EU countries (Italy and Spain have not joined in) without the need to file separately in each country, accompanied with a translation into that country's national tongue.[45]

Copyrights

A *copyright* is a government grant giving the copyright holder exclusive control over the reproduction of a literary, musical, or artistic work. Most developed nations provide copyright protection within their borders, but many also belong to international copyright protection pacts. The Berne Convention of 1886 and the Universal Copyright Convention (UCC) of 1952 both provide a measure of international protection against the unauthorized reproduction of books, photos, drawings, movies, and the like. Copyright protection extends for a period provided by national law. For example, in the United States a copyright currently spans the author's life plus 70 years. The United States is a party to the UCC and the Berne Convention.

The case below points out that formal accession to an international treaty does not necessarily lead to satisfactory compliance in the view of other signatories.

LEGAL BRIEFCASE

Golan v. Holder
132 S.Ct. 873 (2012)

Justice Ginsburg

The Berne Convention . . . is the principal accord governing international copyright relations. Latecomer to the international copyright regime launched by Berne, the United States joined the Convention in 1989. To perfect U.S. implementation of Berne, . . . Congress, in 1994 [through enactment of] § 514 of the Uruguay Round Agreements Act (URAA) [, extended] copyright protection to preexisting works of Berne member countries, protected in their country of origin, but lacking protection in the United States for any of three reasons: The United States did not protect works from the country of origin at the time of publication; the United States did not protect sound recordings fixed before 1972; or the author had failed to comply with ... formalities Congress no longer requires as prerequisites to copyright protection.

The URAA accords no protection to a foreign work after its full copyright term has expired, causing it to fall into the public domain, whether under the laws of the country of origin or of this country. Works encompassed by § 514 are granted the protection they would have enjoyed had the United States maintained copyright relations with the author's country or removed formalities incompatible with Berne. Foreign authors, however, gain no credit for the protection they lacked in years prior to

§ 514's enactment. They therefore enjoy fewer total years of exclusivity than do their U.S. counterparts. As a consequence of the barriers to U.S. copyright protection prior to the enactment of § 514, foreign works "restored" to protection by the measure had entered the public domain in this country. . . .

Petitioners include orchestra conductors, musicians, publishers, and others who formerly enjoyed free access to works § 514 removed from the public domain. They maintain that the Constitution's Copyright and Patent Clause, Art. I, § 8, cl. 8, and First Amendment both decree the invalidity of § 514. [All further reference to petitioners' First Amendment argument has been omitted.-ed.] Under those prescriptions of our highest law, petitioners assert, a work that has entered the public domain, for whatever reason, must forever remain there.

[W]e conclude that § 514 does not transgress constitutional limitations on Congress' authority. . . .

I

Members of the Berne Union agree to treat authors from other member countries as well as they treat their own. . . . Each country, moreover, must afford at least the minimum level of protection specified by Berne. The copyright term must span the author's lifetime, plus at least 50 additional years, whether or not the author has complied with a member state's legal formalities. And, as relevant here, a work must be protected abroad unless its copyright term has expired in either the country where protection is claimed or the country of origin.

A different system of transnational copyright protection long prevailed in this country. Until 1891, foreign works were categorically excluded from Copyright Act protection. Throughout most of the 20th century, the only eligible foreign authors were those whose countries granted reciprocal rights to U.S. authors and whose works were printed in the United States. For domestic and foreign authors alike, protection hinged on compliance with notice, registration, and renewal formalities.

The United States became party to Berne's multilateral, formality-free copyright regime in 1989. Initially, Congress adopted a "minimalist approach" to compliance with the Convention. The Berne Convention Implementation Act of 1988 (BCIA) . . . accorded no protection for "any work that is in the public domain in the United States." . . . Congress indicated, however, that it had not definitively rejected "retroactive" protection for preexisting foreign works; instead it had punted on this issue of Berne's implementation, deferring consideration until "a more thorough examination of Constitutional, commercial, and consumer considerations is possible."

The minimalist approach essayed by the United States did not sit well with other Berne members. . . . Mexican authorities complained about the United States' refusal to grant protection . . . to Mexican works that remained under copyright domestically. The Register of Copyrights also reported "questions" from Turkey, Egypt, and Austria. Thailand and Russia balked at protecting U.S. works, copyrighted here but in those countries' public domains, until the United States reciprocated with respect to their authors' works.

Berne, however, did not provide a potent enforcement mechanism. . . .

The landscape changed in 1994. The Uruguay round of multilateral trade negotiations produced the World Trade Organization (WTO) and the Agreement on Trade–Related Aspects of Intellectual Property Rights (TRIPS). The United States joined both. TRIPS mandates, on pain of WTO enforcement, implementation of Berne's first 21 articles. The WTO gave teeth to the Convention's requirements: Noncompliance with a WTO ruling could subject member countries to tariffs or cross-sector retaliation. The specter of WTO enforcement proceedings bolstered the credibility of our trading partners' threats to challenge the United States for inadequate compliance with Article 18.

Congress' response to the Uruguay agreements put to rest any questions concerning U.S. compliance with Article 18. Section 514 of the URAA extended copyright to works that garnered protection in their countries of origin, but had no right to exclusivity in the United States for any of [the previously listed] three reasons. . . .

. . . Copyrights "restored" under URAA § 514 "subsist for the remainder of the term of copyright that the work would have otherwise been granted . . . if the work never entered the public domain." Prospectively, restoration places foreign works on an equal footing with their U.S. counterparts; assuming a foreign and domestic author died the same day, their works will enter the public domain simultaneously. . . .

The URAA's disturbance of the public domain hardly escaped Congress' attention. Section 514 imposed no liability for any use of foreign works occurring before restoration. In addition, anyone remained free to copy and use restored works for one year following § 514's enactment. . . .

In 2001, petitioners filed this lawsuit challenging § 514. . . .

II

We first address petitioners' argument that Congress lacked authority, under the Copyright Clause, to enact § 514. The Constitution states that "Congress shall have Power . . . [t]o promote the Progress of Science . . . by securing for limited Times to Authors . . . the exclusive Right to their . . . Writings."

Art. I, § 8, cl. 8. Petitioners find in this grant of authority an impenetrable barrier to the extension of copyright protection to authors whose writings, for whatever reason, are in the public domain. We see no such barrier in the text of the Copyright Clause, historical practice, or our precedents.

. . . Petitioners' contrary argument relies primarily on the Constitution's confinement of a copyright's lifespan to a "limited Tim[e]." "Removing works from the public domain," they contend, "violates the 'limited [t]imes' restriction by turning a fixed and predictable period into one that can be reset or resurrected at any time, even after it expires."

Our decision in *Eldred* [*v. Ashcroft*] is largely dispositive of petitioners' limited-time argument. There we addressed the question whether Congress violated the Copyright Clause when it extended, by 20 years, the terms of existing copyrights [in the Copyright Term Extension Act (CTEA)]. Ruling that Congress acted within constitutional bounds, we declined to infer from the text of the Copyright Clause "the command that a time prescription, once set, becomes forever 'fixed' or 'inalterable.' " "The word 'limited,' " we observed, . . . is best understood to mean "confine[d] within certain bounds," "restrain[ed]," or "circumscribed." . . .

The terms afforded works restored by § 514 are no less "limited" than those the CTEA lengthened. In light of *Eldred*, petitioners do not here contend that the term Congress has granted U.S. authors—their lifetimes, plus 70 years—is unlimited. Nor do petitioners explain why terms of the same duration, as applied to foreign works, are not equally "circumscribed" and "confined." . . .

The difference, petitioners say, is that the limited time had already passed for works in the public domain. What was that limited term for foreign works once excluded from U.S. copyright protection? Exactly "zero," petitioners respond. We find scant sense in this argument, for surely a "limited time" of exclusivity must begin before it may end. . . .

Historical practice corroborates our reading of the Copyright Clause to permit full U.S. compliance with Berne. . . .

On occasion . . . Congress has seen fit to protect works once freely available. Notably, the Copyright Act of 1790 granted protection to many works previously in the public domain. Before the Act launched a uniform national system, three States provided no statutory copyright protection at all. Of those that did afford some protection, seven failed to protect maps; eight did not cover previously published books; and all ten denied protection to works that failed to comply with formalities. The First Congress, it thus appears, did not view the public domain as inviolate. . . .

Congress has also passed generally applicable legislation granting patents and copyrights to inventions and works that had lost protection. An 1832 statute authorized a new patent for any inventor whose failure, "by inadvertence, accident, or mistake," to comply with statutory formalities rendered the original patent "invalid or inoperative." An 1893 measure similarly allowed authors who had not timely deposited their work to receive "all the rights and privileges" the Copyright Act affords, if they made the required deposit by March 1, 1893. And in 1919 and 1941, Congress authorized the President to issue proclamations granting protection to foreign works that had fallen into the public domain during World Wars I and II. . . .

Installing a federal copyright system and ameliorating the interruptions of global war, it is true, presented Congress with extraordinary situations. Yet the TRIPS accord, leading the United States to comply in full measure with Berne, was also a signal event. Given the authority we hold Congress has, we will not second-guess the political choice Congress made between leaving the public domain untouched and embracing Berne unstintingly.

Petitioners' ultimate argument as to the Copyright and Patent Clause concerns its initial words. Congress is empowered to "promote the Progress of Science and useful Arts" by enacting systems of copyright and patent protection. . . .

The "Progress of Science," petitioners acknowledge, refers broadly to "the creation and spread of knowledge and learning." They nevertheless argue that federal legislation cannot serve the Clause's aim unless the legislation "spur[s] the creation of . . . new works." . . .

. . . In *Eldred*, . . . we held that the Copyright Clause does not demand that each copyright provision, examined discretely, operate to induce new works. Rather, we explained, the Clause "empowers Congress to determine the intellectual property regimes that, overall, in that body's judgment, will serve the ends of the Clause." . . .

. . . Congress rationally could have concluded that adherence to Berne "promotes the diffusion of knowledge." A well-functioning international copyright system would likely encourage the dissemination of existing and future works. Full compliance with Berne, Congress had reason to believe, would expand the foreign markets available to U.S. authors and invigorate protection against piracy of U.S. works abroad, thereby benefitting copyright-intensive industries stateside and inducing greater investment in the creative process.

. . . Congress determined that exemplary adherence to Berne would serve the objectives of the Copyright Clause. We have no warrant to reject the rational judgment Congress made.

Affirmed.

Questions

1. What does it mean to say that a work is in the "public domain"?

2. *a.* If you were a Canadian composer in 1950 with a new orchestral piece, fully protected under the copyright laws of Canada (a Berne signatory), what would you have had to do to protect your work in the United States (based on the law as it is presented in *Golan*)?

   b. If you were a Canadian composer in 2005 under similar facts?

3. Before Congress passed § 514 of the URAA what could petitioners do that, after the legislation, was no longer legal?

4. In the words of the Court, why did "Congress have reason to believe" that full compliance with the Berne Convention "would expand the foreign markets available to U.S. authors and invigorate protection against piracy of U.S. works abroad"? Explain.

Agreement on Trade-Related Aspects of Intellectual Property

As should now be readily apparent, a solid international system for effective protection of intellectual property does not yet exist. That said, the Agreement on Trade-Related Aspects of Intellectual Property (TRIPS) agreement mentioned by the Court in *Golan v. Holder* is having a positive effect. As one of the foundation agreements to which all WTO member countries must subscribe, the provisions of TRIPS are enforceable through the WTO Dispute Settlement Body, which is discussed later in this chapter. TRIPS establishes certain minimum levels of protection for copyrights, trademarks, and patents, and also requires WTO members to adopt effective enforcement measures. Whether members are effectively enforcing its provisions remains an issue regularly raised in WTO settings.

Regulation of Multinational Enterprises (MNEs)

With globalization, the number of MNEs has vastly expanded. Precisely because MNE operations span the globe, regulating their activities has become quite difficult. For example, despite the proven health risks from smoking tobacco and the 177 signatories to the Framework Convention on Tobacco Control, which addresses controls on ingredients, packaging, marketing, cessation programs, and smoke-free spaces (all proven to reduce smoking), tobacco companies "are aggressively recruiting new customers in developing nations."[46] Philip Morris sued Uruguay claiming that its regulations were excessive. The Convention was negotiated under the auspices of the World Health Organization, whose head of its Tobacco Free Initiative stated, "They're using litigation to threaten low- and middle-income countries."[47] Philip Morris's annual sales are twice Uruguay's gross domestic product. [For more on the Convention, see **www.who.int/fctc/en**]

In the absence of effective international regulatory regimes, which do not currently exist, MNEs also face challenges in trying to comply with many different overlapping, often contradictory, national regulatory schemes. Countries that impose regulatory requirements on MNEs may, in any given circumstance, be viewed with approval or be accused of "regulatory imperialism"[48] or be charged with domestic protectionism.[49] One of the growing issues impacting the effective regulation of MNEs is the growth of state-owned companies, both in number and size. They make up 19 of the world's 100 largest MNEs and 28 of the top 100 emerging market companies, and are found in almost every industry.[50] Many are effectively monopolies at home; many are very active abroad. How they will and can be effectively regulated outside of their home countries is unknown.

We now consider five additional areas of governmental oversight: securities regulation, imposition of financial accounting and auditing standards, anticompetitive restraints of trade, mergers, and import and export restrictions. The U.S. law covering most of these areas was presented in Chapters 9 through 11. Here we will look at their international dimensions, particularly with regard to overseeing the behavior of MNEs.

Securities Regulation

Most people in the business world are aware of numerous corporate financial scandals that rocked the world around the turn of the millennium: Enron and WorldCom in the United States, Barings Bank in the United Kingdom, HIH Insurance in Australia, and Parmalat in Italy, to name a few. In the United States, the Securities and Exchange Commission (SEC) has long played a major role in uncovering and pursuing financial corporate wrongdoing. But it also has a reputation outside the United States, as one commentator

> The SEC has been "the cop on the beat for the world's securities markets."

put it, "as the cop on the beat for the world's securities markets."[51] The SEC has a broad reach because of its jurisdiction to regulate all companies that choose to list their equity or debt securities on any U.S. securities market, such as the New York Stock Exchange. But its reach has long been thought to stretch even further, through the extraterritorial application of the fraud provisions in U.S. securities laws. The application of those laws to foreign companies that list their securities on a U.S. exchange is not an extraterritorial application because those companies have voluntarily availed themselves of U.S. capital markets. But what about foreign companies not so listed that act wrongfully (in light of U.S. law) such that their conduct has a substantial negative effect in the United States or upon U.S. citizens? In a 2010 case, the Supreme Court held the fraud provisions were only intended to apply within the United States.[52] Within a month, however, Congress passed the Dodd–Frank Act, making clear the extraterritorial enforcement powers of the SEC and the U.S. Department of Justice. From Chapter 9, you know that another powerful tool for the enforcement of our securities laws is the ability of harmed investors to bring private suits against violators. Congress has not counteracted the Supreme Court interpretation in that regard.

Accounting Standards

An important component of securities regulation is the establishment of the financial accounting standards that underlie financial statements provided to the public. In the United States, accounting standards are under the authority of the SEC. Internationally, however, the growth in the number of MNEs and the integration of the world's capital markets have propelled the development of financial accounting standards that could be applied transnationally. In 2001, one set of such standards, International Financial Reporting Standards (IFRS), was offered for adoption by the International Accounting Standards Board (IASB) based in London. Over 100 countries, including the entire European Union, have implemented these standards, although many have adopted local variations. In 2006, the IASB and the SEC initiated a harmonization project, generally referred to as convergence, between U.S. Generally Accepted Accounting Principles (GAAP) and IFRS. The process was intended to eliminate major differences so that investors could more readily make comparative evaluations among companies regardless of their home country. Whether there will be universal adoption of either system seems highly unlikely as of this writing.[53] However, the European Union permits U.S. companies to file GAAP financial statements without requiring reconciliation to IFRS, and the SEC permits foreign corporations to file IFRS financial statements (so long as there are no local variations), without reconciliation to GAAP.

The establishment of accounting standards is only one aspect necessary for reliable disclosure to make it into the hands of current and future investors. Independent audits of companies' books also need to be done and by auditors with appropriate credentials. This is not difficult for American companies with audit firms that practice in the United States. However, when foreign companies are listed on a U.S. stock exchange, U.S. investors need to know that the financial statements of those companies are reliable. Accounting fraud at Chinese companies has been much in the news for several years. The headline of one *Wall Street Journal* article in 2012 began, "Accounting fraud and China have become synonymous for many investors."[54] Accounting firms auditing foreign companies need to be registered with and regularly inspected by the U.S. Public Company Accounting Oversight Board (PCAOB). For Chinese companies listed on U.S. exchanges, this was commonly accomplished by having audits done by Chinese affiliates of the Big Four auditing firms. Then China changed its regulations and required that such affiliates be owned by a majority of Chinese partners, while refusing to allow the PCAOB to inspect the Chinese firms. In May 2013, some progress was made when China agreed to give the PCAOB access to documents from the Chinese firms which are necessary for the Board to fulfill its oversight responsibilities. The agreement does not, however, allow the PCAOB into China to inspect the Chinese audit firms, nor does it allow the SEC to obtain documents relevant to its fraud investigations.[55] For the time being, investors in Chinese companies still need to take to heart the adage, "buyer beware." [For more information on the IASB and IFRS, see **www.ifrs.org**]

Choice of Nationality?

In today's world, a corporation is generally free to choose its "nationality"—that is, its home country, the country in which it will establish its legal existence or, using U.S. terminology, the country in which it will incorporate. That nation's laws will govern the relationship between the entity and its owners—that is, the corporate governance rules it must follow—as well as the accounting standards with which it must comply. If incorporated outside of the United States, it will only become subject to U.S. securities laws if it chooses to list its securities on a U.S. exchange. Unlike other countries, the United States taxes U.S. corporations on their worldwide income, not just the income earned in the United States. Thus, if a business incorporates outside the country, it may avoid significant U.S. taxes, substantial U.S. regulation, and the extraterritorial application of U.S. laws.

Consider Michael Kors Holdings: its corporate headquarters are in Hong Kong; its clothes are manufactured primarily in Asia; its largest office is in New York; it receives about 95 percent of its revenues from U.S. and Canadian sales. But it is incorporated in the British Virgin Islands, where it had no operations. Although it launched its initial public offering (IPO) of stock in the United States, as a foreign corporation its financial reporting requirements are much less than those discussed in Chapter 9. Financial reporting for foreign corporations has been deliberately lessened, precisely to make listing securities more attractive to foreign businesses. Although much of its income is currently taxed in the United States, if it grows its international sales, those sales will not be so taxed.[56]

Consider too a company's choice of place of incorporation for its subsidiaries. For some businesses, a significant source of profits derives from royalty and licensing fees generated by its intellectual property. Thus, a common tax strategy is to incorporate subsidiaries to hold valuable intellectual properties, like patents, in low-tax jurisdictions. Thus, Apple has subsidiaries in Ireland, the Netherlands, Luxembourg, and the British Virgin Islands. "When customers across Europe, Africa or the Middle East ... download a song, television show or app, the sale is recorded" in Luxembourg.[57] Quite legally, 70 percent of Apple's profits are allocated to its non-U.S. entities. "Although technology is now one of the [United States'] largest and most valued industries, many tech companies are among the least taxed."[58]

Question

Michael Kors and Apple are acting legally and advantageously by moving some of their income tax liabilities out of the United States. Is this a good trend? Is it equitable? Consider smaller companies without the resources for such sophisticated tax advice. What about profit-comparable companies which suffer higher taxes because their revenues come from physical sales? Is it equitable to countries which provide the infrastructure for high-tech development? What about the countries that now can collect taxes from businesses that have little physical presence other than an office with a mailing address? If there are inequities, what might bring them back into balance?

Anticompetitive Restraints

Many countries regulate anticompetitive behaviors such as collusion among competitors and abuse of monopoly power. Two prominent examples involve Microsoft and Google, both of which have been challenged for anticompetitive behaviors in both the United States and Europe.

Microsoft has repeatedly been charged with abusing its monopoly market power in computer operating systems (Windows) to provide an advantage for its browser (Internet Explorer), media player, and servers. In the United States alone, Microsoft faced three successive bouts of litigation brought by the U.S. Department of Justice, as well as numerous suits by private plaintiffs, resulting in payment of substantial settlement sums and long-term government oversight. Microsoft's actions have also been scrutinized by the European Commission for violations of the EU's Competition Law, suffering an adverse decision and substantial fines in 2004 in a dispute that began in 1998. Then again in 2008, the Commission opened another investigation, which was settled when Microsoft agreed to load a ballot box on all new Windows 7 computers sold in Europe that would allow purchasers to select any one of 12 competing browsers. Four years later, the Commission fined it $732 million for failure to live up to the agreement.

From the standpoint of fines, Google has fared much better than Microsoft, but it still had to undergo two years of investigation by the Federal Trade Commission and a hearing before the Senate antitrust panel over whether it had abused its dominant position in Internet search engines, in part by giving more prominent placement to its own services over its competitors in returning search results. The investigation by the European Commission covers abuse in both Internet search and advertising markets. As of the time of this writing, the investigation had not concluded; the Commission appeared to be seeking more significant changes in the way search results are displayed and threatening fines up to $5 billion.[59]

Mergers

In September 2012, the European Commission approved the takeover of EMI Music by Universal Music Group, already the dominant music company as gauged by the size of its collection of copyright holdings. The approval came with some strings; Universal was required to sell at least two-thirds of EMI's assets to a buyer with a "proven track record in the music industry" that will serve to act as a "credible competitor."[60] It is not uncommon for merger regulators to require accommodations to address antitrust national concerns before providing the required approval. Such national-level reviews and negotiations can be a significant cost for mergers and acquisitions involving MNEs. Although some bilateral agreements among countries are in place, the approximately 70 countries with merger review systems as yet do not have an agreement coordinating their processes—not even at the level of coordinating review thresholds, timetables, and required filings.[61]

Regulation of Trade

Import Tariffs

The General Agreement on Tariffs and Trade (GATT), now governed by the WTO, regulates import duties among signatory countries to reduce barriers to trade and to ensure fair treatment. Without GATT, it is argued, countries with stronger markets would be able to secure better deals on imports than would other countries. In addition, countries with strong market economies could use the threat of higher import taxes as a bargaining chip in other negotiations. To limit such discriminatory practices, the concepts of MFN status and national treatment are integral to GATT, just as they are to GATS as discussed earlier in the context of international trade in services. Thus, under GATT, a reduced tariff offered to one WTO member country must be offered to all WTO members and, once a good has been imported, it must be treated just as domestic goods are treated. That, at any rate, is the ideal. In practice GATT has not actually done away with nonconforming tariffs. Rather, it prohibits countries from moving further away from the ideal, while providing successive rounds of multilateral trade negotiations to encourage countries to collectively move forward on achieving these goals.

A Closer Look at U.S. Tariffs

In addition to the fact that the imposition of any tariffs runs counter to the avowed goal of free trade, little logic or defense seems to exist for the disparities across tariffs imposed by particular countries. For example, in the United States, an 8.5 percent duty is imposed on imported women's wool suits, but no duties are imposed on men's suits. Furthermore, when a broader view is taken that incorporates whether U.S.-imposed tariffs hit imports from all countries fairly or evenly, it is readily evident that they do not. In 2006, both France and Cambodia paid $367 million in duties to the United States; but for its payment,

France was able to import $36.8 billion in goods, whereas Cambodia paid the same duties for the importation of only $2.2 billion in goods.[62]

Questions

1. Who in the United States is hurt by the tariffs described above? Who in the United States is advantaged by them?
2. Why might U.S. tariffs be friendlier to French products than Cambodian goods?

Export Restrictions

Whereas imports are regulated to protect American businesses, exports by these businesses may be regulated for several purposes. The U.S. Export Administration Act of 1979 permits restrictions on goods and technology where exportation would harm national security, or where restriction would significantly advance U.S. foreign policy, prevent an excessive drain of scarce materials, or reduce serious inflationary impacts from foreign demand. [To learn more about U.S. import and export practices, see **www.cbp.gov/xp/cgov/trade**]

Rare Earth Elements

China controls 93 percent of the production of rare earth elements—metals less scarce than precious metals but still relatively rare. Many of these metals have turned out to be important to a wide range of green technologies, such as those used in wind turbines and in the electric motors for the Toyota Prius and Chevrolet Volt. They are also used in the electric motors in some U.S. missile guidance systems. China has been reducing production and exports of such metals to ensure it has an adequate supply for its own needs and to reduce environmental damage from the mines. [63] In 2011, a WTO panel held China's export control impermissible. It noted that the proffered environmental concerns had not resulted in reduced mine production.[64] The panel's decision was affirmed on appeal in 2012.[65]

Question

If these actions were being taken by the United States instead of China, do you think they would be defensible under the Export Administration Act? Why or why not?

Fair Trade Regulations: Dumping and Subsidies

To promote fair trade the WTO prohibits the practice of *dumping*. Dumping occurs when a manufacturer sells its goods in a foreign country for less than their normal value. If this practice causes or threatens material injury to a domestic or established foreign manufacturer in the foreign country, the act is prohibited. The price is considered less than normal value if it is less than the price charged in the producer's home country. A firm may want to dump its goods in a foreign market for two reasons. First, its home market may be saturated and cannot support any further supply. Second, a firm might sell its goods in a foreign market at a price below other competitors and support that price with higher prices in its home country in an effort to establish itself and perhaps drive other firms out of the foreign market. After its competitors are forced out, the producer may raise prices to the normal level or above. GATT permits retaliatory duties to be imposed on countries that have dumped goods in other member countries.

The WTO also prohibits the payment of *unfair subsidies* by governments. This occurs when a government, perhaps in an effort to encourage growth in a certain industry, offers subsidies to producers in that industry. The producers are therefore able to sell their goods at a price lower than the prices of their worldwide competitors. Subsidies are considered unfair when governments use them to promote export trade that harms another country. When unfair subsidization is found, the WTO permits the harmed country to impose countervailing duties on those products in an amount sufficient to counteract the effect of the offending subsidy. If a country feels such *countervailing duties* have been illegally imposed, it must either sue in the courts of the country imposing the duties based on that country's law or take the dispute through the adjudication process provided by the WTO, discussed later in this chapter.

An ongoing dispute over solar panels illustrates many of these fair trade regulations. In what has been called "the world's largest antidumping and antisubsidy trade cases,"[66] both the United States and the European Union contend that China has become the world's dominant producer of solar panels through the provision of subsidies in the form of favorable loans from state-owned banks and incentives provided by local and provincial governments to Chinese manufacturers.[67] They also argue that China is dumping its panels into Western markets at prices below its cost of production, resulting in more than 20 American and European manufacturers cutting back production or going bankrupt. In response, both the United States and the European Union imposed substantial tariffs on the importation of Chinese panels. China responded with a tariff of its own—on the importation of polysilicon, one of the main raw materials in the production of the panels. This was a move that didn't particularly harm Chinese panel producers because of the existence of an abundance of other sources for the polysilicon. As of this writing, the countries are in negotiations to find a solution to the increasing trade barriers and tensions, and it looks like the European Union and China may be nearing a bilateral solution.

Question

Why do developed countries such as the United States regulate trade through the mechanisms described in this section? Why might a less developed country do so?

Trade Restrictions—A Tangled Web

Even if all could agree that as a whole the world would be better off if all national trade restrictions were ended, it does not follow that all countries or that all persons would be better off, certainly not in the short run. International trade has never been free of national barriers in modern times. WTO negotiations start with existing historical protections and member countries agree not to increase barriers and commit to participating in multilateral trade negotiations with the goal of lessening restrictions over time. New countries are admitted to the WTO only after sometimes prolonged negotiations with existing members over modifications of their existing trade-related barriers deemed necessary before they can be admitted. Every country has companies and industries that benefit directly from existing barriers, businesses whose profits rely on, and sometimes depend on, protection. Each of these businesses in turn have employees, suppliers, and communities that indirectly benefit from those protections. Thus, any change in a nation's trade policies will have a negative effect on some segment of its economy,

> Every country has companies and industries that benefit directly from existing barriers

even if it can be demonstrated that a change would produce a positive effect on the total economy.

Take a specific example: The United States has had an ongoing dispute with China over its protection of and trade in intellectual property. Recently a WTO dispute resolution panel ruled that China must permit foreign companies to sell music online in China. The panel said China's prohibition on downloaded music violates a promise China made on joining the WTO to open access to foreign mass-produced art. China responded that it never promised to open markets in the electronic distribution of sound recordings in a nonphysical form and that the restriction was necessary to protect China's "public morals."[68] Interestingly, only once has the public morals defense previously been used before the WTO—by the United States when it argued in support of its ban on Internet gambling over the objections of Antigua. The United States lost. To succeed, a proponent has to be able to show that the restriction is "necessary" to defend public morals.

Now consider more broadly the trade relationship between the United States and China. What other forces influence the resolution of a particular dispute? Consider, for example, that China exports to the United States $4.46 of goods for every $1 of goods that the United States exports to China, which would suggest that China is more dependent on trade with the United States than the reverse.[69] Conversely, in significant part because of China's large positive trade balance with the United States, China invests its abundance of U.S. dollars in U.S. Treasury bonds. China's demand for treasuries keeps the interest rates the United States pays on those bonds significantly lower than they would otherwise be, thus reducing the cost of borrowing by the United States.

The United States also has an ongoing trading dispute with Brazil. Brazil forced the United States into the WTO dispute resolution process arguing that the $3 billion per year the United States has been paying to cotton growers (mostly large agribusinesses in the South) constitutes an unfair subsidy. United States companies account for about 40 percent of cotton exports globally. The WTO ruled in favor of Brazil and ultimately authorized the imposition of countervailing duties. In order to avoid the imposition of those duties, the United States negotiated a settlement that permits the United States to keep paying the $3 billion in subsidies, at least until Congress passes a new farm bill, so long as the United States also pays Brazil $147.3 million per year in the interim.[70]

Questions

1. How would you challenge China's assertion that prohibiting music downloads is necessary to protect public morals in China? What facts might you look for to support your argument?

2. Is it ethical for the United States to dispute China's protectionist policies while itself spending years defending subsidies for a well-developed U.S. industry? Explain.

International Dispute Resolution

As we have seen to this point, international business relationships are highly complex. Disputes are inevitable. International dispute resolutions often face roadblocks. Three significant international dispute resolution bodies presently exist: the International Court of Justice, the European Court of Justice, and the WTO Dispute Settlement Body.

International Court of Justice

The only court devoted entirely to hearing cases of international public law is the International Court of Justice (ICJ) in the United Nations. The ICJ is made up of 15 judges from 15 different member countries. It may issue two types of decisions. It has advisory jurisdiction where the United Nations asks the court for an opinion on a matter of international law. These opinions do not bind any party. It has contentious jurisdiction where two or more nations (not individual parties) have consented to its jurisdiction and have requested a binding opinion. Such opinions are not, however, precedent for the ICJ in later cases. [For more information about the ICJ, see **www.icj-cij.org**]

How Binding Are ICJ Decisions?

Just how binding an ICJ contentious case decision actually is on U.S. state and federal courts has been called into question by the 2008 U.S. Supreme Court decision in *Medellin v. Texas*.[71] The Court, in a 6–3 decision, held that a Texas court did not have to give effect to an ICJ ruling in spite of the fact that the case was submitted to the ICJ pursuant to a treaty obligation specifying that the ICJ has "compulsory jurisdiction" for all "disputes arising out of the interpretation or application" of the treaty. In the view of the majority, the "most natural reading" of the "compulsory jurisdiction" language is "as a bare grant of jurisdiction. . . . The [treaty] says nothing about the effect of an ICJ decision and does not itself commit signatories to comply with an ICJ judgment." In his dissent, Justice Breyer observed:

> In the majority's view, the [treaty] simply sends the dispute to the ICJ . . . and the U.N. Charter contains no more than a promise to "undertak[e] to comply" with that judgment. Such a promise, the majority says, does not as a domestic law matter . . . "operat[e] of itself without the aid of any legislative provision." Rather, here (and presumably in any other ICJ judgment rendered pursuant to any of the approximately 70 U.S. treaties in force that contain similar provisions for submitting treaty-based disputes to the ICJ for decisions that bind the parties) Congress must enact specific legislation before ICJ judgments entered pursuant to our consent to compulsory ICJ jurisdiction can become domestic law. . . . In my view . . . we must look instead to our own domestic law, in particular, to the many treaty-related cases interpreting the Supremacy Clause. Those cases . . . lead to the conclusion that the ICJ judgment before us is enforceable as a matter of domestic law without further legislation.[72]

European Court of Justice

The European Court of Justice (ECJ) hears cases involving European Community law. Although not required, one judge from each member nation traditionally sits on the ECJ. At first glance, the ECJ may not seem a particularly important court for American business. But in an age of MNEs, its decisions can be very important. The ECJ ruled on whether, under EU trademark law, Google's AdWord service violated the Louis Vuitton trademark when Google sold an ad to a Vuitton competitor next to search results returned any time Louis Vuitton was entered as a search phrase.[73] The court held, with certain caveats, that it was not a violation. [For information on the ECJ, see **curia.europa.eu/jcms/jcms/Jo2_6999/**]

WTO Dispute Settlement Body

Although the WTO Dispute Settlement Body (DSB) is not a true court, it is a significant forum for the resolution of international trade disputes between WTO members. The DSB is made up of all member governments, usually represented by ambassadors or the equivalent. The DSB establishes a panel to hear a particular dispute brought by a member state. The panel then reports back to the DSB, which can either accept or reject the panel's findings. Either side can then appeal to the WTO Appellate Body. Again, the DSB can either accept or reject the appeals report. If a WTO member fails to comply with the final decision of the DSB, the opposing party may seek compensation. If compensation is not agreed on between the parties within 20 days, the complaining party can seek authorization for retaliation—that is, the suspension of favorable trade concessions to the noncompliant party. The reality of this power was demonstrated by the DSB's authorization of import duties against U.S. goods by Brazil as previously discussed. [For more information on the WTO dispute resolution function and dispute documents, see **www.wto.org/english/tratop_e/dispu_e/dispu_e.htm**]

Other International Fora

In addition to the three institutions just discussed, particular treaties may implement specific dispute resolution processes for disputes arising under that treaty between its signatories. For example, NAFTA provides for special tribunals before which corporations can, and have, brought complaints against governments for actions perceived to be unfair or inequitable to them as foreign investors. Of concern to some commentators is that a tribunal under NAFTA can, as a practical matter, operate as a further review of a decision of a domestic court. Thus, after the U.S. Supreme Court declined to review a Massachusetts case brought by a Canadian real estate company, the company took its dispute to a NAFTA tribunal (which decided that Massachusetts had not violated international law).[74] [For information on proceedings before NAFTA tribunals against the governments of Canada, Mexico, and the United States, see the U.S. State Department site at **www.state.gov/s/l/c3439.htm**, as well as a private site, **www.NaftaClaims.com**]

National courts also rule on matters of international law and on matters involving business in international settings. In fact, because of the absence of any international courts of general jurisdiction, national courts are where most international business disputes are heard. When the underlying dispute seems to have little association with the forum state, but that state's national court agrees to rule on the substantive claim, legal commentators may lay charges of "judicial imperialism."[75] The principle of comity previously discussed also applies to the exercise of a national court's jurisdiction.

The Long Road through Court

In the summer of 2007, 12 banana plantation workers from Nicaragua got their day or, rather, their four months in a California federal district court.

The workers were employed by Dole Food Co. on banana plantations in Nicaragua, where a pesticide known as DBCP, manufactured by Dow Chemical Co., was used to increase the weight of the banana harvest and help with rodent and pest control. In 1977 the U.S. government suspended the use of the chemical after complaints arose of sterility in California workers. When Dow informed Dole that it would no longer be producing the chemical, the two companies agreed that Dow would sell to Dole, for use in Central America, the more than 500,000 gallons that had been returned to it by other purchasers.

The plaintiffs were some of the workers who were exposed to DBCP while working for Dole in Nicaragua, workers who then became sterile.

After a successful suit was brought in the United States in the early 1980s on behalf of affected California workers, U.S. law firms began suing in U.S. courts on behalf of workers from other countries. Nearly every case ended when American courts ruled that the principle of forum non conveniens required the lawsuits to be maintained in the countries where the workers had suffered their injuries. Their view was that Nicaragua was a more appropriate forum for the dispute. So the workers tried again at home. After lengthy delays and, ultimately, a change in Nicaraguan law to facilitate the DBPC lawsuits, in 2002 a Nicaraguan court awarded nearly $490 million in damages and other judgments followed. But so far Dole and Dow have successfully blocked all enforcement of the judgments in U.S. courts. The new laws in Nicaragua have meant, however, that Dole and Dow have ceased invoking the forum non conveniens argument against new suits in the United States.

After a month of deliberations in the 2007 case in California, the jury awarded six of the Nicaraguan workers a total of $3.3 million. Following a number of post-trial motions, the companies successfully reduced the award to $1.58 million to be shared among four of the plaintiffs. The jury decision as to one plaintiff was overturned and Dole was granted a new trial as to another.[76] In the years following, Dole filed post-trial motions to have the jury verdict thrown out; in 2011, the judgment was vacated. At the same time, each side accused the other of fraud, including fraud instigated by the opposing attorneys, but the California State Bar is no longer pursuing investigations of those attorneys.[77]

Questions

1. Why do you think Dole and Dow did not object to the new suits brought in the United States after the plaintiffs' successful suit in Nicaragua?

2. Do you think the Nicaraguan judgments should be enforceable in the United States? Why or why not?

3. Apart from whether Dole or Dow Chemical or both are liable for health issues associated with exposure to DBCP, was it ethical for Dole to use and Dow to supply DBCP for use in Nicaragua and elsewhere after the chemical was banned in the United States? Explain.

Arbitration

In light of the difficulty of litigation between parties of diverse nationalities and the desire for more certainty and expediency in business transactions, parties to an international contract may prefer to insert a clause that calls for the international arbitration of any dispute. As discussed in Chapter 4, arbitration is a nonjudicial means to settle a conflict where the parties agree to a hearing in front of a neutral third party who will issue a binding award decision. [For more information on international arbitration, see **www.arbitration-adr.org** and **www.i-a-a.ch**]

Government Defenses

"Some evil acts don't violate international law unless they are performed by someone acting with government authority."[78] Even where government action is the source of the wrong, two additional doctrines, accepted as general principles of international law, may pose barriers to the judicial enforcement of a party's rights: the *act of state doctrine* and the *doctrine of sovereign immunity*.

Act of State Doctrine

It is generally accepted that a country has absolute rule over what occurs within its borders. Consequently, the act of state doctrine holds that a judge in one country does not have the authority to examine or challenge the acts of another country within that country's borders. For instance, an American court may not declare invalid the acts of the British government taken within its own jurisdiction because it is presumed that the foreign country, Britain, acted legally within its own territory.

One government action that has caused a great deal of dispute in connection with the act of state doctrine is *expropriation*. Expropriation is the taking by a national government, without adequate compensation, of property and/or rights of a foreign person within that government's borders. The United States contends that international law requires compensation for the taking. Not all governments agree with the United States' position. In 2012, Argentina nationalized YPF, an affiliate of a Spanish oil company. Shortly before the government acted, YPF had discovered what may be the world's largest deposits of natural gas. Before its privatization in 1999, YPF had been Argentina's state energy corporation. The reason given for the 2012 nationalization was that YPF's production had fallen, causing Argentina to become a net importer of energy.[79]

Doctrine of Sovereign Immunity

The doctrine of sovereign immunity is based on the concept that "the king can do no wrong." In other words, if the king makes the rules, how could the king ever be wrong? As Chief Justice Marshall explained in *The Schooner Exchange v. McFaddon*,[80] "The jurisdiction of the nation within its own territory is necessarily exclusive and absolute. It is susceptible of no limitation not imposed by itself; deriving validity from an external source would imply a diminution of its sovereignty to the extent of the restriction, and an investment of that sovereignty to the same extent in that power which could impose such restriction."

The doctrine has been codified in the United States by the Foreign Sovereign Immunities Act of 1976 (FSIA), which provides that foreign countries may not be sued in American courts, subject to several exceptions. Accordingly, U.S. citizens usually would not be allowed to sue Britain in the U.S. courts, unless the claim falls into one of the following FSIA exceptions:

- The foreign country has waived its immunity (that is, it has consented to be sued in another country's courts).
- The legal action is based on a commercial activity by the foreign country in the United States or outside the United States but having a direct effect in the United States.
- The legal action is based on personal injuries "caused by an act of torture, extrajudicial killing, aircraft sabotage, hostage taking, or the provision of material support or resources" for such acts.[81]

Thus, a country that conducts a commercial activity in a foreign country may not hide behind sovereign immunity if sued, while a country acting on its own behalf and not for a commercial purpose would be able to avail itself of the protection. In 2010 the Supreme Court further clarified the FSIA, holding that it provides immunity only to a foreign state and not to a foreign official, even if that official is acting on behalf of the state.[82]

The "restrictive theory of immunity" recognized and applied by the United States is to be contrasted with the policies of some countries that contend that immunity is absolute— no exceptions exist. The following case examines sovereign immunity.

Butters v. Vance International, Inc.
225 F.3d 462 (4th Cir. 2000)

LEGAL BRIEFCASE

Chief Judge Wilkinson

Appellant Nyla Butters brought suit against her employer, Vance International, claiming that Vance discriminated against her on the basis of gender. The district court held that Vance was entitled to immunity from Butters' suit under the Foreign Sovereign Immunities Act because Vance's client, the Kingdom of Saudi Arabia, was responsible for Butters not being promoted.

I

Vance International, headquartered in Oakton, Virginia, provides security services to corporations and foreign sovereigns. In October 1994, Saudi Arabia hired Vance to augment the security provided to Princess Anud, a wife of Saudi King Fhad, while the Princess was undergoing medical treatments in California. The Saudi military was responsible for protecting Princess Anud. The Princess' residence in Bel Air, California, was referred to as "Gold." Saudi Arabian Colonel Mohammed Al-Ajiji supervised all security at the site—three Saudi military officers and the Vance agents. . . . The Saudi government paid Vance for its services.

In August 1995, Vance hired Nyla Butters as a part-time, at-will security agent. From 1995 until April 14, 1998 . . . [on] several occasions, Butters temporarily worked in Gold's command post.

In early April 1998, Vance supervisors at Gold recommended that Butters serve a full rotation in the command post. . . . Gregg Hall, the Vance detail leader, spoke with Mohammed. Colonel Mohammed denied Hall's request for Butters to

serve a rotation in the command post. Colonel Mohammed told Hall that such an assignment was unacceptable under Islamic law, and Saudis would consider it inappropriate for their officers to spend long periods of time in a command post with a woman present. This in turn could have political ramifications at home for the Saudi royal family. Mohammed also informed Hall that the Princess and her contingent wanted to speak only to male officers when they called the command post. In total, three Vance supervisors recommended Butters for the assignment. Saudi military officers denied every request.

* * * * *

On May 28, 1998, Butters filed a charge of gender discrimination with the California Department of Fair Employment and Housing. On October 15, 1998, Butters filed suit . . . for discriminatory constructive termination, retaliatory constructive termination, and wrongful constructive termination in violation of public policy under California's Fair Employment and Housing Act. Vance filed a motion for summary judgment with respect to these counts.

On July 30, 1999, the district court granted Vance's motion, finding Vance immune from Butters' suit under the Foreign Sovereign Immunities Act (FSIA). . . . The district court held that derivative FSIA immunity attached to Vance because it was "acting under the direct military orders of Colonel Mohammed when [it] did not allow the plaintiff to work a full rotation in the command center." Butters appeals.

II

Butters first contends that FSIA immunity does not attach to Vance because the action here was a "commercial activity." . . .

The FSIA defines "commercial activity" as "a regular course of commercial conduct or a particular commercial transaction or act. The commercial character of an activity shall be determined by reference to the nature of the course of conduct or particular transaction or act, rather than by reference to its purpose." . . . The Court elaborated on the distinction: "[A] state engages in commercial activity . . . where it exercises 'only those powers that can also be exercised by private citizens,' as distinct from those 'powers peculiar to sovereigns.'"

The relevant act here—a foreign sovereign's decision as to how best to secure the safety of its leaders—is quintessentially an act "peculiar to sovereigns." . . . Indeed, it is difficult to imagine an act closer to the core of a nation's sovereignty. Providing security for the royal family in this country is not a commercial act in which the state is acting "in the manner of a private player within the market." . . .

* * * * *

III

Butters next argues that Vance is not entitled to immunity since Vance, as opposed to the Saudi officials, was responsible for the decision not to promote Butters.

A

If Vance was following Saudi Arabia's orders not to promote Butters, Vance would be entitled to derivative immunity under the FSIA. . . .

. . . To abrogate immunity would discourage American companies from entering lawful agreements with foreign governments and from respecting their wishes even as to sovereign acts. Under the circumstances here, imposing civil liability on the private agents of Saudi Arabia would significantly impede the Saudi government's sovereign interest in protecting its leaders while they are in the United States.

* * * * *

IV

Any type of governmental immunity reflects a trade-off between the possibility that an official's wrongdoing will remain unpunished and the risk that government functions will be impaired. FSIA immunity presupposes a tolerance for the sovereign decisions of other countries that may reflect legal norms and cultural values quite different from our own. Here Saudi Arabia made a decision to protect a member of its royal family in a manner consistent with Islamic law and custom. The Act requires not that we approve of the diverse cultural or political motivations that may underlie another sovereign's acts, but that we respect them. We thus affirm the judgment.

Questions

1. Why did the court hold that Vance, a U.S. corporation, could avoid Butters's claim of discrimination based on a claim of sovereign immunity? Why did Butters argue that sovereign immunity should not apply?

2. How do you feel about the end result of this decision? Did Butters suffer discrimination? Explain.

Subjecting MNEs to Compliance with the Law of Nations

The largest MNEs have economic strength equaling or exceeding that of some countries. In this chapter, we have seen how challenging it can be to effectively regulate their activities. That makes it worth asking whether MNEs should be held liable if, in furtherance of their economic objectives, they either (1) take advantage of foreign government actors willing to subdue a local population or (2) are complicit in a foreign government's perpetuation of its own dominance where the action of the foreign government violates the law of nations.

Some foreign plaintiffs are attempting to hold MNEs liable under such circumstances in suits brought in U.S. federal courts under the Alien Tort Statute. In one sentence this statute authorizes foreign nationals to file civil suits in the United States against those who violate "the law of nations or a treaty of the United States." Enacted in 1789, in the 1990s the statute began to be used to sue major corporations for alleged complicity in crimes violating human rights by foreign governments, including torture, extrajudicial killings, and war crimes.

Many such suits have withstood motions to dismiss by corporate defendants. In some cases, juries have found against the plaintiffs; a number of suits have been settled, subject generally to a restriction that the settlement terms not be publicly disclosed. An exception to such nondisclosure was a 2009 settlement for $15.5 million of claims against Royal Dutch Shell for its role in the Nigerian government's execution of local activists who protested the environmental damage caused by oil drilling in the Niger delta.[83]

Other plaintiffs did not settle. On April 17, 2013, the U.S. Supreme Court foreclosed their claims, holding that the Alien Tort Statute was subject to the traditional presumption against extraterritorial application, but suggesting that cases that "touch and concern the territory of the United States" might "displace the presumption."[84] U.S. courts may not hear claims of foreign plaintiffs against foreign companies on foreign soil, but other claims—such as those of foreign plaintiffs against U.S. companies on foreign soil—perhaps are still viable.[85]

Under EU law, a European company can be sued "at home for complicity in human-rights violations committed anywhere in the world."[86]

Enforcement of Decisions

As we have seen, even if a harmed party in an international dispute successfully initiates a judicial proceeding, many procedural hurdles are likely to be encountered. Recall the *forum non conveniens* principle that initially kept the Nicaraguan workers from obtaining substantive hearings in U.S. courts. But what happens after the successful conclusion of such a suit? Do challenges arise in the enforcement of the court's decision?

The answer is yes, particularly in those cases where the losing defendant has insufficient or no assets located in the same jurisdiction as the court awarding the plaintiff monetary relief. In those cases, the plaintiff may need to present the judgment to a court in a country where assets of the defendant are located and seek local enforcement. This is an added cost, in time and money, for successful plaintiffs. Furthermore, enforcement may be difficult or impossible to obtain.

Enforcing Foreign Judgments   When a plaintiff is successful in a California court, but the defendant's assets are in New York, the plaintiff may have to seek enforcement from a New York court. In that situation, the U.S. Constitution requires the New York court to give "full faith and credit" to the decision of the California court. No such broad policy exists in U.S. law with respect to decisions of foreign courts; nor does such a broad policy exist in international law. Instead, the court from which enforcement is being requested is likely to consider whether the original foreign judgment violates local notions of justice and morality, or is otherwise contrary to public policy, so as not to be entitled to enforcement. This is also true of foreign arbitration awards if the losing party has refused to satisfy the award—even if both countries are among the 142 current signatories of the United Nations Convention on the Recognition and Enforcement of Foreign Arbitral Awards (also known as the New York Convention). [Current information on the status of the convention, as well as additional information, can be found at **www.uncitral.org/uncitral/en/uncitral_texts/arbitration/NYConvention.html**]

To illustrate, consider the previously discussed Nicaraguan banana plantation workers. After U.S. courts largely refused to allow substantive hearings in the 1980s based on *forum non conveniens,* the workers took their claims back to Nicaragua, which was exactly what U.S. courts had told them to do. Although resolution of claims in Nicaragua took a long time, some plaintiffs obtained substantial judgments there. In response to plaintiffs' applications to U.S. courts for recognition and enforcement of these Nicaraguan judgments, however, the defendant U.S. corporations have thus far been successful in avoiding the requested enforcement.

Enforcing U.S. Judgments   Similar problems can arise when a U.S. citizen obtains a judgment from a U.S. court against a foreign national, which judgment is then sent for enforcement to the home courts of the foreign national. Consider the case of an Alabama 15-year-old, who died in an accident when the buckle of his motorcycle helmet failed. The helmet was made by an Italian company. His mother sued in an Alabama court and won a $1 million judgment. The Italian company refused to pay and the mother presented the judgment to an Italian court for enforcement. The Italian Supreme Court found the award of punitive damages so offensive to its notion of justice that it refused to enforce any of the award. Many countries share the Italian court's distaste for punitive damages in such situations. [87]

Question

On balance, do you think it would be better for countries to agree mutually to simply enforce judgments in favor of private citizens (nationals or nonnationals) obtained from foreign courts, respecting the effort and delay the plaintiff has already undergone in obtaining the judgment and without applying culturally based notions of justice? Why or why not? If not, try generating a list of principles you think should permit a court to refuse enforcement of a foreign judgment.

Internet Exercise

Identify a multinational firm that conducts business with suppliers in developing countries. Find its code of vendor conduct on its website and evaluate the areas of enforcement that might prove to be the most difficult.

Chapter Questions

1. Thomas Friedman in his 2005 book, *The World Is Flat: A Brief History of the Twenty-First Century,* argues that countries with connected manufacturing supply chains won't go to war with one another. He offers an example of Dell's multicountry supply chain for the manufacture of its laptops. On balance, do you think globalization is a catalyst for bringing world peace or a tinderbox that may set international disputes on fire through the collision of differing ideals? Explain.

2. *a.* Why do you think China, one of the most communist of nations, wanted to join the WTO?

   b. Would it surprise you to learn that Iraq, Iran, and Syria, while not currently WTO members, are all formally enrolled as observer countries? This means they are (or are considering) pursuing accession negotiations to become WTO member states. Why might they be interested in joining the WTO?

3. From 2010 through 2012 many state legislatures considered or passed laws outlawing aspects of Islamic or Shariah law. Some of them would have prohibited the enforcement of private contracts in which a "butcher would no longer be able to enforce his contract for halal meat—contracts that, like deals for kosher or other faith-sanctioned

foods, are regularly enforced around the country. Nor could a Muslim banker seek damages for violations of a financial instrument certified as 'Sharia compliant' since it pays no interest."[88]

a. Develop an argument that laws prohibiting enforcement of such contracts would be unconstitutional.

b. What historical parallels exist in which laws in the United States were seen to deny equal protection to a subgroup of American citizens?

4. Different countries and cultures have different norms for dress. In the United States, for example, some restaurants require men to wear jackets and state law generally prohibits even partial public nudity. Public schools often have enforceable dress codes. In the 1960s, those codes often prohibited female students from wearing pants. Consider the following:

- In 2010, the French Parliament passed a law forbidding people from concealing their faces in public, punishable by fines. Higher fines and prison sentences up to one year could be imposed on individuals who encouraged others to ignore the ban. Although freedom of religion is constitutionally protected in France, it is generally acknowledged that the purpose of the law was to prohibit Muslim women from wearing traditional head coverings and full-body robes. It has been estimated that fewer than 2,000 women in France, most of whom are French nationals, wear them. Some supporters of the ban have said that such robes are a means of forcing women to be submissive and are a sign of enslavement or debasement. Some of the wearers say that the dress is a method to concentrate on their religious faith.[89]

- Also in 2010, one province in Indonesia, the world's most populous Muslim-majority nation, banned Muslim women from wearing revealing clothes such as tight skirts and pants. After their third violation, women could be subject to two weeks' detention. Shopkeepers violating restrictions on selling inappropriate clothing could lose their business licenses.[90]

a. Do the laws discussed in the sections above seem logical to you? On what basis should you judge them?

b. Would conflicts with cultural issues, such as those addressed by the local laws above, impact your decision as a manager about where to conduct your business? *Should* they impact your decisions? Explain.

c. If your job required you to live in a country that had laws with which you disagreed on moral grounds, would you follow those laws? Explain.

5. America has embraced fast food. This may be part of the reason that obesity, in the United States, has risen at an epidemic rate during the past 20 years. According to the Centers for Disease Control and Prevention, currently one-third of the adults in the United States are considered obese. Seventeen percent of those between 2 and 19 are obese.

a. Should other countries be concerned about the influx of American fast-food chains? Why or why not?

b. What about countries that provide universal health care?

c. If a country is concerned about its citizens' dietary changes, what actions should it take in response? Explain. [For more on obesity in the United States, see the website for the Centers for Disease Control and Prevention, **www.cdc.gov/obesity/index.html**]

A group called the Hindu Jagran Manch, or the Hindu Awakening Platform, said Valentine's Day was an affront to Indian traditional culture and warned against Feb. 14 celebrations in the city. Many conservative segments of Indian society view the day—a celebration of romantic love—as indecent.

"Valentine's Day, Mother's Day, and Father's Day . . . these are all the gimmicks of multinational companies to market their products. Valentine's Day is against the culture and ethics of Indian society," said Vinay Tewari, a Manch leader.[91]

6. As a result of threatened attacks by Manch, many shopkeepers in India's largest state closed for Valentine's Day. A nation's cultural values can sometimes conflict with "outside" values spread through the process of globalization. Consider the following:
   a. Should the shopkeepers have closed their doors?
   b. Do you understand how a celebration of "romantic love" might be offensive to some?
   c. Do you think that Valentine's Day and other U.S. holidays are promoted more for their commercial value than to further the stated purpose for the day? Explain. Consider the dates when Halloween, Thanksgiving, and Christmas decorations go up in U.S. stores.

7. Judge Leo Strine, the Vice Chancellor of the Delaware Court of Chancery (the Delaware Court with original jurisdiction over state corporate law cases), has suggested that effective regulation of corporate behavior will require nations to give up some of their sovereignty to international institutions in exchange for regulation of the global product and financial markets in which multinational corporations conduct their business.[92]
   a. Do you agree?
   b. Will some form of corporate global regulation be necessary to protect all of the stakeholders of such corporations?

8. *a.* What are the relative advantages and disadvantages of each form of doing business in a foreign country?
   b. Why would a firm choose one form over another?

9. What may look to one observer like the application of objective standards may appear to another observer as improper protectionism. Originally signed in the mid-1990s, NAFTA calls for an open border for commercial truck traffic among Canada, the United States, and Mexico. But in early 2005, Mexican trucks were still not allowed into the United States, due in part to litigation brought by environmental and labor groups. Their claim was that the United States hadn't appropriately considered the environmental impact of letting Mexican trucks roll on American roads because there are no standardized emissions rules for commercial vehicles. On balance, does this argument sound to you more like a principled objection or like protection for U.S. jobs? Why? See *Dept. of Transportation v. Public Citizen*, 541 U.S. 752 (2004).

10. Original Appalachian Artworks (OAA) was the manufacturer and license holder of Cabbage Patch Kids dolls. Granada Electronics imported and distributed Cabbage Patch Kids dolls to the United States that were made in Spain by Jesmar under a license from OAA. Jesmar's license permitted manufacture and distribution of the dolls in Spain, the Canary Islands, Andorra, and Ceuta Melilla. Under the license, Jesmar

agreed not to make, sell, or authorize any sale of the dolls outside its licensed territory and to sell only to those purchasers who agreed not to use or resell the licensed products outside the territory as well. Jesmar's argument that Granada's sales did not constitute "gray market" sales was that OAA's dolls sold in the United States had English-language adoption papers, birth certificates, and instructions while Granada's dolls came equipped with Spanish-language adoption papers, birth certificates, and instructions. In addition, Granada argued that the role of trademark law was to prevent an infringer from passing off its goods as being those of another. Such was not the case here. Are these sales prohibited? Explain. See *Orig. Appalachian Artworks v. Granada Electronics,* 816 F.2d 68 (2d Cir. 1987); cert. den. 484 U.S. 847 (1987).

11. Camel Manufacturing imported nylon tents to the United States. The tents held nine people and weighed over 30 pounds. The tents' floors ranged from 8 feet by 10 feet to 10 feet by 14 feet. The tents were to be used as shelter during camping. The importer categorized the goods as "sports equipment," which carried a 10 percent import duty, whereas the U.S. Customs Service considered the tents "textile articles not specifically provided for," with a duty of $.25 per pound plus 15 percent import duty. The importer appealed the decision. What should be the result? Explain. See *Camel Manufacturing Co. v. United States,* 686 F.Supp. 912 (C.I.T. 1988); aff'd 861 F.2d 1266 (Fed. Cir. 1988).

12. Should a Mexican citizen who bought a Chrysler vehicle in Mexico be allowed to sue the manufacturer in a U.S. court under U.S. product liability laws when the plaintiff's three-year-old son was killed when the passenger-side air bag deployed during an accident in Mexico? See *Gonzalez v. Chrysler Corp.,* 301 F.3d 377 (5th Cir. 2002); cert. den. 538 U.S. 1012 (2003).

13. Prior to 1941, Kalmich owned a business in Yugoslavia. In 1941, the Nazis confiscated his property as a result of Kalmich's Jewish heritage and faith. Bruno purchased the business from the Nazis in 1942 without knowledge of the potential unlawful conversion. Kalmich contended that because the confiscation was in violation of well-defined principles of international law prior to the German occupation, the transfer to Bruno was ineffective. Kalmich sought to apply a 1946 Yugoslavian law called "Law Concerning the Treatment of Property Taken Away from the Owner." That law provided that where property is taken from its owners, the owner may bring an action against "responsible persons" for recovery.
    a. Did the act of state doctrine apply in this case?
    b. If not, what should be the result in an American court? Explain. See *Kalmich v. Bruno,* 450 F.Supp. 227 (N.D. IL 1978).

14. Zedan received a telephone call from a Saudi Arabian organization offering him an engineering position at a construction project in Saudi Arabia. The Ministry of Communications, an agency of the government, guaranteed payment to Zedan for any work he performed there, whether for the government or for a nonsovereign third party. After three years, Zedan left the country without being fully paid. After he returned to the United States, he filed an action in federal court seeking to enforce the ministry's guarantee. The ministry argued that it was protected under the Foreign Sovereign Immunities Act.

a. Was Zedan's recruitment in the United States a commercial activity as required by the act?

b. Did this action have a direct effect in the United States as required by the act? Explain. See *Zedan v. Kingdom of Saudi Arabia,* 849 F.2d 1511 (1988).

15. From time to time courts are called on to determine the enforceability of an arbitration clause contained in a contract. One such case was *DiMercurio v. Sphere Drake Insurance,* 202 F.3d 71 (1st Cir. 2000). DiMercurio was injured in 1994 when the commercial fishing vessel in which he was working sank. The vessel was owned by R&M, which was found by a court to be liable to DiMercurio for his injuries and ordered to pay $350,000 in compensation. However, because R&M had no other assets, it assigned to DiMercurio all the rights it had against Sphere Drake, the London-based insurer of the fishing vessel. When DiMercurio looked to Sphere Drake for payment, it denied the claim and invoked the arbitration clause in its insurance policy with R&M, which required the arbitration to take place in England. Should DiMercurio be required to pursue his claim through arbitration in England? Explain.

Notes

1. "Weaving the World Together," *The Economist,* November 19, 2011.
2. "Marrakesh Agreement Establishing the World Trade Organization," [**http://www.wto.org/english/docs_e/legal_e/04-wto_e.htm**].
3. "Trade Talks Produce a Deal," *The New York Times,* December 12, 2013.
4. "When Giants Slow Down," *The Economist,* July 27, 2013.
5. Sudeep Reddy, Matthew Dalton, and Joann Lublin, "Broad Trade Deal on Table," *The Wall Street Journal,* February 13, 2013; see also "The Other Conclave," *The Economist,* March 16, 2013.
6. "A Transatlantic Tipping Point," *The Economist,* April 27, 2013.
7. "Europe's Choice," *The Economist,* May 26, 2012.
8. **www.wto.org/english/thewto_e/whatis_e/tif_e/fact1_e.htm**.
9. Pete Engardio, "Global Capitalism: Can It Be Made to Work Better," *BusinessWeek,* November 6, 2000, p. 72.
10. Ibid.
11. Craig Timberg and Paula Moura, "In Brazil, Google Is in the Middle of a Battle over Free Speech," *The Washington Post,* October 3, 2012.
12. Tanzina Vega, "Facebook Says It Failed to Bar Posts With Hate Speech," *The New York Times,* May 28, 2013.
13. Eric Pfanner and Somini Sengupta, "In a French Case, a Battle to Unmask Twitter Users," *The New York Times,* January 24, 2013; Somini Sengupta, "Twitter Yields to Pressure in Hate Case in France," *The New York Times,* July 12, 2013.
14. Steven Greenhouse, "U.S. Retailers See Big Risk in Safety Plan for Factories in Bangladesh," *The New York Times,* May 22, 2013; Julfikar Ali Manik and Jim Yardley, "Building Collapse in Bangladesh Leaves Scores Dead," *The New York Times,* April 24, 2013.
15. Steven Greenhouse, "Under Pressure, Bangladesh Adopts New Labor Law," *The New York Times,* July 16, 2013; Jim Yardley, "Garment Trade Wields Power in Bangladesh," *The New York Times,* July 24, 2013.

16. Clifford J. Levy, "Microsoft Changes Policy Over Russian Crackdown," *The New York Times,* September 13, 2010.

17. *EEOC v. Arabian American Oil Co., 499 U.S. 244 (1991).*

18. "The World This Week," *The Economist,* July 13, 2013.

19. Dionne Searcey, "Watergate-Era Law Revitalized in Pursuit of Corporate Corruption," *The Wall Street Journal,* October 15, 2010.

20. David Barboza, "Files Suggest a Graft Case in China May Expand," *The New York Times,* July 21, 2013; "Bitter Pill," *The Economist,* July 20, 2013; Laurie Burkitt, "China Releases Details of Glaxo Bribery Allegations," *The Wall Street Journal,* July 15, 2013.

21. Edward Wyatt, Michael Cieply, and Brooks Barnes, "S.E.C. Asks if Hollywood Paid Bribes in China," *The New York Times,* April 24, 2012.

22. Christopher M. Matthews and Shira Ovide, "Microsoft Bribe Probe Reaches into Pakistan, Russia Deals," *The Wall Street Journal,* August 21, 2013.

23. Elizabeth A. Harris, "After Bribery Scandal, High-Level Departures at Walmart," *The New York Times,* June 4, 2014; David Barstow, "Wal-Mart Hushed Up a Vast Mexican Bribery Case," *The New York Times,* April 21, 2012.

24. Leslie Wayne, "Foreign Firms Most Affected by a U.S. Law Barring Bribes," *The New York Times,* September 3, 2012.

25. A copy of the Declaration can be found in the University of Minnesota's Human Rights Library [**www1.umn.edu/humanrts/instree/b1udhr.htm**].

26. Jose Ramos-Horta, "Speech to the Northern Medical Foundation Tribute to Military Medicine and Lt-Gen. P. Cosgrove," Sydney, Australia, September 28, 2001. Copy with author's work papers.

27. Amir Efrati and Andrew Batson, "Google to Alter Access to Its China Site," *The Wall Street Journal,* June 30, 2010, p. B3; "China Renews Google's License," *The Waterloo/Cedar Falls Courier,* July 9, 2010, p. A11.

28. See, for example, *U.S. v. Kim,* 246 F. 3d 186 (2d Cir. 2001), where a New York resident was convicted of wire fraud while working for the United Nations in Croatia.

29. Mayer Brown JSM, *Guide to Doing Business in the PRC* (2010), p. 9.

30. 116 F. Supp. 2d 116 (D.D.C. 2000).

31. *U.S. v. Said,* 757 F.Supp 2d 554 (E.D. Va. 2010), *vacated by* 680 F.3d 374 (4th Cir. 2012); *U.S. v. Dire,* 680 F.3d 446 (4th Cir. 2012).

32. 192 F. 3d 240 (2d Cir. 1999).

33. From the CIA's World Factbook [**https://www.cia.gov/library/publications/the-world-factbook/geos/xx.html**].

34. From the CIA's World Factbook [**https://www.cia.gov/library/publications/the-world-factbook/geos/us.html**].

35. From the U.S. Census Bureau, Foreign Trade Division [**www.census.gov/foreign-trade/statistics/historical/gands.pdf**].

36. Michael Schroeder, "Outsourcing May Create U.S. Jobs," *The Wall Street Journal,* March 30, 2004, p. A2.

37. GATS, Art. I, para. 3(b).

38. Donald C. Dowling, Jr. and Oliver Brettle, "Globally Aligning Collective Bargaining Strategy," *White & Case LLP,* June 1, 2010 [**www.lexology.com/library/detail.aspx?g=3f66a46b-d041-4d66-82d6-ac611b8bbfd6**].

39. Donald C. Dowling, Jr., "Reductions-in-Force Outside the US," *White & Case LLP,* December 1, 2008 [**www.lexology.com/library/detail.aspx?g=36c0b923-0d90-4e11-8eac-e524a21314cc**].

40. Commission on the Theft of American Intellectual Property, "The IP Commission Report," May 22, 2013 [**http://ipcommission.org**].

41. Ibid.

42. "When You Say 'Bud'," *ABA Journal,* July 2013, p. 12.

43. **www.wipo.int/treaties/en/**.

44. *Google Inc. v. Louis Vuitton Malletier SA*, European Court of Justice C-236/08, March 23, 2010.

45. "Yes, ja, oui, no, no," *The Economist*, December 15, 2012.

46. Duff Wilson, "Cigarette Giants in Global Fight on Tighter Rules," *The New York Times*, November 13, 2010.

47. Ibid.

48. Michael Schroeder and Silvia Ascarelli, "New Role for SEC: Policing Companies beyond U.S. Borders," *The Wall Street Journal*, July 30, 2004, p. A1.

49. "European Imperialism," *The Wall Street Journal*, October 31, 2007, p. A20.

50. "The Company That Ruled the Waves," *The Economist*, December 17, 2011.

51. Schroeder and Ascarelli, "New Role for SEC," p. A1.

52. *Morrison v. National Australia Bank Ltd*, 130 S.Ct. 2689 (2010).

53. Floyd Norris, "Accounting Détente Delayed," *The New York Times*, July 19, 2012.

54. David Reilly and Duncan Mavin, "Chinese Accounting Earns Tough Stance," *The Wall Street Journal*, August 7, 2012.

55. Michael Rapoport, "U.S., China Set Pact On Auditor Access," *The Wall Street Journal*, May 24, 2013.

56. Steven M. Davidoff, "The Benefits of Incorporating Abroad in an Age of Globalization," *The New York Times*, December 20, 2011.

57. Charles Duhigg and David Kocieniewski, "How Apple Sidesteps Billions in Taxes," *The New York Times*, April 28, 2012.

58. Ibid.

59. James Kantor, "Google's European Antitrust Woes Are Far From Over," *The New York Times,* June 22, 2014; James Kanter and Claire Cain Miller, "In European Antitrust Fight, Google Needs to Appease Competitors," *The New York Times*, July 17, 2013.

60. Ben Sisario, "U.S. and European Regulators Approve Universal's Purchase of EMI," *The New York Times*, September 21, 2012.

61. For a good comparison of U.S. and E.U. merger analysis and enforcement, see Cento Veljanovski, "EC Merger Policy after GE/Honeywell and Airtours," *Antitrust Bulletin* 49 (Spring 2004), p. 153.

62. Editorial, "The Other Boot," *The New York Times,* May 4, 2007.

63. Keith Bradsher, "China Tightens Grip on Rare Minerals," *The New York Times*, September 1, 2009.

64. "Hands Slapped," *The Economist*, July 9, 2011.

65. Paul Geitner, "U.S., Europe and Japan Escalate Rare-Earth Dispute with China," *The New York Times*, June 27, 2012.

66. Keith Bradsher, "U.S. and Europe Prepare to Settle Chinese Solar Panel Cases," *The New York Times*, May 20, 2013.

67. James Kantor and Keith Bradsher, "Europe and China Agree to Settle Solar Panel Fight," *The New York Times,* July 27, 2013.

68. "Hollywood Upstages Beijing," *The Wall Street Journal,* August 13, 2009, p. A1.

69. Keith Bradsher, "China Moves to Retaliate Against U.S. Tire Tariff," *The New York Times*, September 14, 2009.

70. "Brazil's Victory in Cotton Trade Case Exposes America's Wasteful Subsidies," *The Washington Post,* June 3, 2010, p. A16.

71. 128 S.Ct. 1346 (2008).

72. Ibid., 1377.

73. *Google v. Louis Vuitton Malletier SA,* ECJ C-236-08 (March 23, 2010).

74. Adam Liptak, "NAFTA Tribunals Stir U.S. Worries," *The New York Times,* April 18, 2004.

75. Klaus-Heiner Lehne, "Hands Off Our Torts," *The Wall Street Journal,* November 18, 2003, p. A20.

76. Based on information from T. Christian Miller, "Plantation Workers Look for Justice in the North," *Los Angeles Times,* May 27, 2007; Justin Rebello, "U.S. District Court in Calif. Rules against Dow Chemical in Pesticide Exposure Case," *Lawyers USA,* December 2007; "Dole Food Co. Inc. Wins Court Rulings," *Business Wire,* March 10, 2008.

77. Based on information from Victoria Kim, "Judge Throws Out Verdict Awarding Millions to Dole Workers," *Los Angeles Times*, July 16, 2010; Business Wire, "Dole Food Company Announces that Court Enters Final Order Vacating Judgment, Dismissing Fraudulent Lawsuit Brought by Nicaraguans Claiming to Have Been Banana Workers," press release, March 15, 2011 [**www.thestreet.com/story/11046743/1/dole-food-company-announces-that-court-enters-final-order-vacating-judgment-dismissing-fraudulent-lawsuit-brought-by-nicaraguans-claiming-to-have-been-banana-workers.html**]; Amada Bronstad, "California Bar Drops Complaint Against Dole's Lawyers," February 28, 2011 [**www.law.com**]; "Juan Dominguez Cleared of any Wrongdoing by State Bar," March 17, 2011 [**www.bananasthemovie.com**].

78. Steve Garmisa, "U.S. Courts Handle International Law," *Chicago Sun-Times,* September 24, 1997.

79. Juan Forero, "Seizure of Repsol Affiliate in Argentina Stuns Oil Markets," *The Washington Post,* April 26, 2012.

80. 11 U.S. (7 Cranch) 116 (1812).

81. *Sutherland v. Islamic Republic of Iran,* 151 F. Supp. 2d 27 (D.D.C. 2001).

82. *Samantar v. Yousuf,* 130 S.Ct. 2278 (2010).

83. Based on information from Brent Kendal, "High Court Rejects Pfizer Appeal in Nigeria Drug-Trial Case," *The Wall Street Journal,* June 29, 2010; Nathan Koppel, "Arcane Law Brings Conflicts from Overseas to U.S. Courts," *The Wall Street Journal,* August 27, 2009; Jad Mouawad, "Shell to Pay $15.5 Million to Settle Nigerian Case," *The New York Times,* June 9, 2009; Jad Mouawad, "Oil Industry Braces for Trial on Rights Abuses," *The New York Times,* May 22, 2009; Russell Gold, "Chevron Case Weighs Extent of Overseas Liability," *The Wall Street Journal,* December 1, 2008; Warren Richey, "U.S. High Court Allows Apartheid Claims Against Multinationals," *The Christian Science Monitor,* May 13, 2008.

84. *Kiobel v. Royal Dutch Petroleum Co.*, 133 S.Ct. 1659 (2013). For a similar ruling by the Supreme Court in 2014 regarding alleged human rights violations against Argentinian workers by the German company Daimler AG, see Jess Bravin and Brent Kendall, "Supreme Court Bars Rights Suits Against Daimler in California," *The Wall Street Journal,* January 14, 2014.

85. Mark Walsh, "Global Warning," *ABA Journal,* July 2013, p. 17.

86. "Law's Long Arm," *The Economist,* October 6, 2012.

87. Adam Liptak, "Foreign Courts Wary of U.S. Punitive Damages," *The New York Times,* March 26, 2008.

88. Aziz Huq, "Defend Muslims, Defend America," *The New York Times,* June 19, 2011. See also, Eliyahu Stern, "Don't Fear Islamic Law in America," *The New York Times,* September 2, 2011.

89. David Gauthier-Villars and Charles Forelle, "Burqa Is Banned in France," *The Wall Street Journal,* September 15, 2010.

90. Fakhrurradzie Gade, "Indonesia's Aceh Province Enacted a Strict Muslim Law Thursday: A Tight Pants Ban," *The Christian Science Monitor,* May 27, 2010.

91. Rupan Bhattacharya, "Valentine's Day Menace Causes Shop Closings," *Des Moines Register,* February 14, 2001, p. 2A.

92. Leo E. Strine, "Human Freedom and Two Friedmen: Musings on the Implications of Globalization for the Effective Regulation of Corporate Behavior," *University of Pennsylvania Law School Law and Economics Research Paper Series,* November 1, 2007.

CHAPTER SEVENTEEN

Environmental Protection

After completing this chapter, students will be able to:

1. Identify some of the ways market incentives can be used to prevent and correct environmental problems.

2. Evaluate particular environmental problems using the concepts of causation and correlation, cost-benefit analysis, future impacts, and identification of costs imposed.

3. Describe the National Environmental Policy Act (NEPA).

4. Identify duties of the Environmental Protection Agency (EPA).

5. Describe the uses of the Clean Air Act (CAA), including its application to greenhouse gas emissions.

6. Describe the uses of the Clean Water Act (CWA).

7. Describe the legal issue involving the reach of the CWA.

8. Identify some of the major federal laws that address land pollution.

9. Discuss the purpose and effect of the Comprehensive Environmental Response, Compensation, and Liability Act of 1980 (CERCLA), commonly known as "the Superfund."

10. Identify penalties and other enforcement mechanisms under federal and state regulations.

11. Describe some of the challenges to protecting a species under the Endangered Species Act.

12. Describe the primary common law remedies for environmental damage.

13. Evaluate both the strengths and weaknesses of a global process for addressing climate change.

14. Give concrete examples of environmental degradation in the United States and globally.

Introduction

From local decisions—such as routing a new highway around a wetland or allowing the use of wood stoves—to colossal fears such as global climate change, environmental issues mark our lives in a manner that was unimaginable a few decades ago. From the moment a firm begins to produce, service, manufacture, or create, its operations affect the environment. Imagine all the small decisions made by a company: Does it pack its glassware in plastic bubbles or corrugated wrapping? Does it publish a catalog in paper or only through the Internet? Does it meet with the community before choosing a disposal system? Each decision will have an impact on our physical world, so it is critical to understand the legal and ethical dimensions of each such decision.

A Global View

Environmental issues are complex: One action can have variable impacts on the environment—reducing emission of greenhouse gases (GHG) and at the same time adversely affecting water quality. Environmental issues are complex: The consequences of action in one location may only manifest themselves at substantial distances, both in space and time. Environmental issues are complex: Scientific methodology requires time to establish causation with a sufficient coefficient of probability to offset countervailing economic harm arguments. Environmental issues are complex: The Earth is a closed, complex, and unique system. No computer program can model it; no lab can test possibilities under lifelike conditions. Environmental issues are complex: No international body has the jurisdiction or credibility to make enforceable decisions to balance competing national interests and protect against devastating harms to the world's peoples and ecosystem.

What observable evidence of this complexity do we have? Consider the following:

- In June 2013, the air pollution in both Singapore and southern Malaysia peaked, with the former issuing face masks and the latter declaring a state of emergency. The cause? The intentional burning of forests and peat wetland across the Strait of Malacca in Indonesia in favor of expanding palm oil plantations. Indonesia is one of the world's largest emitters of carbon, primarily because of its clearing of forests. The fires burned in spite of Indonesia's pledge to cut its carbon emissions by at least 26 percent by 2020 and a $1 billion agreement with Norway in support of a UN program to reduce deforestation. Both forest and wetlands are "huge absorbers of carbon," and the forests are home to Indonesia's endangered orangutans.[1]

> For 86 days oil spewed out of British Petroleum's Macondo well.

- For 86 days in 2010, oil spewed out of British Petroleum's Macondo well in the Gulf of Mexico. The long-term impacts on sea life, shorelines, and coastal communities from the roughly 200 million gallons spilled, as well as the effects of the nearly 2 million gallons of chemical dispersants used to combat the spill, areu nknown.[2] By volume it was far larger than the 1989 *Exxon Valdez* spill in Prince William Sound, Alaska. Globally, these are not isolated events. For example, in the Niger delta where Royal Dutch Shell, Chevron, and ExxonMobil have significant drilling operations, over the last 50 years as many as 546 million gallons of oil have leaked into the waters,[3] averaging annually the rough equivalent of the *Exxon Valdez* spill. [For a copy of the Oil Spill Commission's final report, see **http://oscaction.org/resource-center/commission-reports-papers**]

- On Saturday, January 12, 2013, an air-quality monitor at the U.S. Embassy in Beijing topped off at 755, referred to as "Beyond Index" because 500 is supposed to be the top of the scale. The monitor measures particles 2.5 microns in diameter or less, which are the most dangerous; they are fine enough to enter the lungs and the bloodstream. Vehicles, factories, and power plants are the source of the pollution, which resulted in the city being deemed unsafe more than 60 percent of the days in the first half of 2013. The national average during the same six months was nearly 50 percent. Recent air pollution studies are disturbing: As a result of more widespread use of coal, northern Chinese on average live five fewer years than their southern Chinese countrymen and "children with prenatal exposure to high levels of air pollutants exhibit signs of slower mental development and of behavior disorders."[4]

- Two-and-a-half years after the earthquake and tsunami that crippled its Fukushima plant, Japan turned off the last of its 50 nuclear reactors, with no date for returning any of them to service. As of the time of this writing, flow of groundwater into the buildings at Fukushima had not been stopped; the plan is to try to seal off the buildings "behind a mile-long subterranean wall of ground frozen by liquid coolant."[5] Until the groundwater issue is resolved, the plant will continue to produce 400 tons per day of contaminated water, used to cool the damaged reactors, all of which is stored on site. In July 2013, 300 tons of this water was discovered to have drained into the sea. Another looming issue is the need to remove the reactors' fuel cores to safer, long-term storage. Robotic removal is complex. "Molten fuel not only piled up like wax from a candle on the vessel floor . . . but ran through cracks into the piping and machinery below. . . . [I]t may even have found its way into the ground beneath the buildings."[6] Yet another issue is the cleanup of the radioactive contamination that spread through the environment at the start of the disaster. At an elementary school about 12 miles distant, "[f]or eight hours a day, construction workers blast buildings with water, cut grass and shovel dirt and foliage into big black plastic bags—which, with nowhere to go, dot . . . the landscape like funeral mounds."[7] The central government is in charge of cleanup efforts in the most heavily contaminated areas, but the rest is left for local governments to handle.

- According to the World Health Organization, about 1.2 billion people or almost one-fifth of the world's population live in areas where water is physically scarce and 10 percent consume food that has been irrigated with wastewater potentially contaminated with chemicals and disease-causing organisms.[8]

- In 2010, a report for the academic journal *Science* analyzed the danger level for 25,000 species, classifying 13 percent of birds as threatened with extinction, 25 percent of mammals, and 41 percent of amphibians.[9]

PRACTICING ETHICS   Global Environmental Justice

The concept of *environmental justice* includes the expectation that environmental risks and hazards should be equally distributed when measured against wealth or race. Studies in the United States have shown that at least some risks, such as proximity to hazardous waste disposal sites, are not equally distributed.[10] Is the concept of equally distributed environmental risks a useful tool in assessing global environmental hazards? Consider the following:

- The Niger delta provides 10 percent of U.S. oil imports and routinely suffers substantial oil spills, as noted above.

- Eighty percent of Nigeria's government revenue comes from the Niger delta, but life expectancy in the delta is the lowest in Nigeria.[11]

Question

Are oil companies guilty of unethical behavior if their drilling procedures off the coast of Africa do not take environmental precautions equivalent to those they take when drilling in U.S. or European waters? Explain.

Part One—A Return to Fundamentals: The Market, Government Regulation, and Self-Regulation

The first three chapters of this text set up a framework for analyzing the substantive law topics that have followed: (1) consideration of how well market forces achieve the goals we have for our society; (2) a brief investigation of whether government intervention can bring us closer to those societal goals; and (3) reflection on the role that self-regulation, through ethical decision making and corporate social responsibility, can and does play in realizing our goals. This framework is also useful in evaluating the relationship between business and our natural environment.

Market Failure?

Without regulation, a firm may consider that dumping its garbage into a nearby canal is no big deal. In fact, perhaps the slight amount of garbage the firm dumps is no big deal. However, if every firm were allowed to dump that amount, the canal might become thoroughly polluted. Or consider the possibility that we may all prefer less costly cars that pollute more. Would future generations concur?

As discussed in Chapter 8, these examples of water and air pollution would be categorized by economists as *negative externalities*. Wilfred Beckerman, a British economist, described the analysis as follows:

> [T]he costs of pollution are not always borne fully, if at all, by the polluter. . . . Naturally, he has no incentive to economize in the use [of the environment] in the same way that he has for other factors of production that carry a cost, such as labor or capital. . . . This defect of the price mechanism needs to be corrected by governmental action in order to eliminate excessive pollution.[12]

Thus environmentalists claim the market has failed to protect us from pollution, so rules are necessary. The public and Congress have apparently agreed: A substantial number of environmental laws have been enacted since the early 1970s—laws that address pollution of our air and waterways, that regulate use, disposal, and cleanup of hazardous and toxic wastes, and that protect rare plant and animal species. Many of these laws will be discussed in Part Two.

But as we shall see, our conceptualization of the problems we face may be too simplistic. The bulk of our environmental laws and regulations were drafted to address compartmentalized and discrete issues—clean air or clean water or hazardous waste; particular contaminants, point sources, or individual species. They may be inadequate to address the interrelationships that characterize both our environment and our social and political structures.

Elinor Ostrom, a Nobel laureate in economics, was a leading scholar of common-pool resource management before her death in 2012. She studied how communities develop effective rules for governing depletable resources such as water, fishing grounds, and the atmosphere. Her conclusion, "Trying to find the best set of rules . . . . there isn't one best set."[13] All arrangements—"government-controlled, privatized, or owned by a community—work in some places but not in others. The success or failure of a specific approach hinges on the match of the specific institutional arrangement, local culture, and particular problems involved, as well as how the approach is implemented. . . . [P]olicies for common resources should be considered experiments within complex systems."[14]

Market Incentives

One approach federal regulation has taken is to dictate standards with which businesses must comply. Such legislation has led to steady, and at times even spectacular, strides forward in environmental protection in the United States. But this progress has not dispelled the view, particularly among economists and businesspeople, that standard-setting regulation may not be the best approach to remedy environmental problems. They believe that pollution control is not so much a matter of law as of economics. It follows that, with proper incentives, the market will in some instances prove superior to traditional regulation in preventing and correcting environmental problems. Some examples of market incentives follow.

Cap-and-Trade Programs

The concept behind cap-and-trade incentives is that a government sets a cap on the total emissions of a particular pollutant, a cap lower than the existing level of emissions. It then issues pollution credits to the most significant emitters of that pollutant. Credit recipients can either reduce their discharges to within their credit limit or buy credits from other companies who have reduced their emissions below their own credit amounts. Such programs, therefore, allow the most cost-effective pollution reduction methods to be used to reach the desired environmental goals. The United States was very successful using this approach to reduce sulfur dioxide emissions that were a major factor in the creation of acid rain.[15] By 1999, electric utilities produced about 41 percent more electricity than they had in 1980 while emitting 25 percent fewer tons of sulfur dioxide.[16] In 2007, total sulfur dioxide emissions dropped below the long-term goal, ahead of the 2010 statutory deadline.[17] In 2009, the House of Representatives passed a cap-and-trade bill to address greenhouse gas (GHG) emissions, but the Senate declined to act on it. Independently, however, a coalition of nine Northeast and Mid-Atlantic states set up such a program for carbon emissions from power plants in their jurisdictions, which in its first three years cut the average annual emissions by 23 percent.[18] As part of its program to cut GHG emissions to 1990 levels by 2020, California began running its own carbon cap-and-trade program on January 1, 2013, the second-largest such program in the world, following only the European Union's.[19]

Valuing Ecosystem Services

The GHG cap-and-trade programs are more complex than the acid rain program in the United States in that there are many, many different sources of GHG emissions and many varied ways to reduce global GHG. For example, forests and peat wetlands act as carbon sinks—naturally capturing atmospheric carbon and locking it up. Thus, a GHG emitter could cause global GHG emissions to decrease by paying a country such as Indonesia to prevent deforestation that would otherwise occur. Such an approach to controlling global GHG emissions raises complex valuation and verification issues. If country A pays country B to protect its forests, how many GHG credits should country A receive? How much carbon is captured by a square mile of Indonesian forest? How long should country B be required to protect that forest for a particular payment?

Some ecologists and economists are working to establish an analytical framework that would facilitate targeted conservation investments yielding the highest ecological returns by systematically inventorying and valuing the services nature performs, such as carbon absorption. Others, such as foresters, chemists, and accountants, are developing ways to verify and audit such factors as the amount of carbon stored by a particular stand of trees.

This approach to control of GHG has raised ethical issues. One commentator has argued that, "farmers should not be paid to reduce their water pollution any more than I should be paid to stop mugging people." In contrast, another sees the possibility of a hybrid "stoplight" approach. "The red part is: Here's some things you can do to your land that are so bad that we're gonna take you to prison. The yellow light is: Here's . . . some minimal stuff that you really ought to do. Then the green light is: Here's some stuff that's above and beyond the stewardship obligation, and we're going to pay you for doing it, because it's to the benefit of society."

Sources: Matt Jenkins, "Mother Nature's Sum," *Pacific Standard,* October 2008 [**www.psmag.com/business -economics/mother-nature-s-sum-4226**]; and Felicity Barringer, "A Grand Experiment to Rein In Climate Change," *The New York Times,* October 13, 2012.

Question

If burning fossil fuels is a major catalyst of global climate change, then the developed world is the major cause. But citizens of the least developed countries will suffer the most severe consequences. If you already suffer food and water insecurity, any further disruption is catastrophic. "Because hunger and misery cannot afford to make the distinctions of the well-fed—to choose between cutting a tree or saving it—poverty is among the greatest environmental threats in the world."[20] Does this reasoning provide a response to the argument that farmers should not be paid to reduce their water pollution? Explain.

Tax Laws

Tax provisions can also affect behavior, either by encouraging particular behavior through tax incentives or by discouraging other behavior through additional taxes. For example, there are or have been credits against one's federal income taxes for solar installations, production of power from wind turbines, and purchasing certain new fuel-efficient cars, such as hybrids. Conversely, many in the United States favor the imposition of a new federal tax on carbon, such as a specified tax per ton of carbon dioxide emitted. Proponents argue such a tax would motivate emitters to reduce their emissions while simultaneously raising revenues, which could be used for one or more of the following: reduce the federal deficit, lower corporate tax rates to make U.S. companies more competitive, or compensate lower-income citizens on whom the tax would fall more heavily (through higher gas and heating bills). The Congressional Budget Office has estimated that the poorest 20 percent of Americans spend 21.4 percent of their income on gas and utilities, whereas the richest 20 percent spend only 6.8 percent. Further, 34 of the richest industrialized countries collect an average of $68.4 per ton of carbon dioxide, while the United States collects federal taxes on energy (including the federal gas tax) amounting to $6.30 per ton.[21]

Other Incentives

Other targeted market incentives also have been employed to address environmental issues. Direct subsidies in the nature of rebates were used in the 2009 federal Cash for

> Cash for Clunkers.

Clunkers program. Nearly 678,000 clunkers with a mean miles per gallon (MPG) of 15.7 were traded in for new vehicles with a mean MPG of 24.9. The estimated annual reduction in oil consumption is about 800,000 barrels and in greenhouse gas (GHG) emissions is approximately 360,000 metric tons.[22] Government agencies have also subsidized particular activities through guaranteed loan programs. An Energy Department program created in 2005 to encourage application of new pollution-reducing technologies helped fund the electric cars produced by Tesla Motors. On a $34 billion loan portfolio administered the Department, the government has lost only about $800 million (including the loan to solar cell company Solyndra, the bankruptcy of which created a political storm in 2011). That loss is only a small fraction of the $10 billion Congress set aside to cover program losses.[23]

Ethical Business Decision Making

On a particularly busy corner in a suburb of Auckland, New Zealand, the proprietors of a small café, Triniti of Silver, do a brisk breakfast, lunch, and coffee trade. Their menu declares their philosophy: "Only organic eggs of free-range chickens are used here; only paddock-reared pigs; only certified organic beef—we do not feel happy to encourage the inhumane treatment of animals." Just one example of grassroots, intentional, ethical business decision making.

But what level of environmental concern can we expect from managers of publicly held corporations? Can we identify examples of environmental corporate social responsibility? The answer is a resounding yes—all one has to do is review a sampling of corporate websites. Why are corporate giants voluntarily doing now what they haven't done in the past? In part, the answer may be that the market has changed and market forces are operating to reward corporate responsibility. For example, managers may believe that being "green," or being seen as being green by consumers and investors, will improve the corporate bottom line. Or a manager may believe that a proactive approach may lessen the likelihood of fu-

> Pay-now-or-pay-later

ture regulation on an issue that is becoming increasingly visible.[24] This is one example of a pay-now-or-pay-later analysis. Managers may take a more environmentally responsible approach now because they think the future cost of not doing so could be enormously larger—in negative publicity or in the cost of more stringent future regulation—than the present actual cost of the action.

> Green growth

Does the market actually reward sound environmental practices? As a general proposition, that has not been shown, but successful *green growth* examples are multiplying—concrete illustrations that economic growth and environment protection are not mutually exclusive. By 1994, 60-year-old Ray Anderson had grown his 15-person carpet-tile company,

Interface Inc., into the world's largest carpet-tile maker, but customers were pushing for the company to develop an environmental strategy. Anderson did. His goal for his company? By 2020, to produce no GHG emissions and no waste and to consume no raw materials that could not be rapidly replenished. As of 2010, GHG emissions were down 35 percent, water usage by 82 percent, fossil fuel consumption by 60 percent. Interface carpet is increasingly made out of carbohydrate polymers, rather than petroleum, and old-carpet sludge is recycled into pellets that are then used for carpet backing. Seventy-four thousand tons of used carpet has been reclaimed from landfills. Company sales increased by 64 percent, and its earnings have more than doubled.[25] [For many examples of environmentally responsible actions of business, see **www.bsr.org/en/about/in-the-news**]

Question

"The single most important and pervasive moral obligation facing mankind is to ensure survival of a healthy planet for our grandchildren and theirs."[26] Do you agree? Why or why not?

Part Two—Laws and Regulations

Having reviewed both market forces and ethical business decision making, we turn now to government regulation as an approach for meeting our environmental goals. The United States has developed a wide variety of environmental protection laws and remedies, some of which are covered in this section. In evaluating a particular regulation, it will be helpful to keep in mind the following concepts:

- **Cost–Benefit Analysis.** Environmental protection can be expensive. How much as a society are we willing to pay? Do we want clean air at any cost? We may (or may not) be able to estimate the cost of a particular pro-environment action, but we also need to consider its benefits, including its economic benefits. How do we value human life, represented by a statistical decrease in deaths or illness from exposure to environmental pollutants or by decreased productivity? When does environmental protection cause the sacrifice of short-term economic development? Are there offsetting long-term economic benefits? Can these costs and benefits be measured? These are not easy questions. The answers will necessarily be inexact and require subjective judgments and the use of estimates. More attention, however, is being directed at the effort. A project was initiated in 2007 by the G-8 nations (Canada, France, Germany, Italy, Japan, Russia, the United Kingdom, and the United States) to study environmental monetary values. It has estimated that environmental degradation costs the world economy between $2.5 and $4 trillion annually, or up to 5 percent of global GDP.[27]

How do we value human life?

- **Impact on Future Generations.** When performing a cost–benefit analysis, how do we evaluate the cost to future generations of our not taking action? How can we measure the value to those generations if we do take action? In some cases, future generations will bear the brunt of the decision, whatever choice we make. For example, how do we measure the impact of climate change on future generations? This is a complex question about which there is no scientific or economic consensus.

- **Proving Causation.** If event A occurs and event B follows, is it necessarily true that event A *caused* event B? It could simply be a coincidence that first A was observed and then B. Or there could, in fact, be a *correlation* between events A and B, but no actual causation. For example, event Z might cause both A and B, but no causal link may exist between A and B. In the environmental area, issues of coincidence, correlation, and causation may be extremely difficult to determine. Does exposure to secondhand smoke cause lung cancer in some nonsmokers? Did the observed increase in greenhouse gases contribute to global warming such that sea levels rose, increasing the intensity of Hurricane Katrina, in turn causing property damage to a degree that would not otherwise have occurred?[28] If, in the example of Z, A, and B, we spend a lot of effort trying to stop A to prevent B from occurring, we will be wasting our money. On the other hand, how long can we wait to determine definitively whether a causal link exists between A and B? Our answer may depend on the severity of the harm we believe is associated with B.

- **Who Pays?** If we decide to correct an environmental problem, who should pay for the correction? If we require corporate America to invest in pollution control devices, the cost may be shared between consumers (through increased prices) and investors (through a reduced corporate profit). If habitats of endangered species are to be preserved, current landowners may simply lose all or a portion of their investment and workers employed on the land may lose their jobs. Who should pay? Sometimes the issue is where a particular facility, such as a hazardous waste disposal site, should be located. Not surprisingly, a common response of citizens near a proposed location is, "yes, it's necessary, but *not in my backyard!*" This response is so common, that it is now referred to as NIMBY.

> "Not in my backyard!"

- **Politics.** Environmental protection in the United States is not just a matter of science, cost assessment, and social policy; it is also a matter of politics. California, for example, has historically received permission from the Environmental Protection Agency (EPA) to impose stricter vehicle emission standards than federal law requires. California sought similar permission in 2005, in part to add greenhouse gases to the emissions regulated. After delaying the decision for two years, on the day in 2007 when President Bush signed into law the federal 35 miles per gallon standard, the EPA denied California's request. California responded by taking the EPA to court. A year later, in his first month in the White House, President Obama directed the EPA to reconsider California's application, signaling a sharp break with the Bush administration's less aggressive stance on climate change. The waiver was approved in June 2009.[29]

Question

What environmental issue do you care about most? Greenhouse gases? Deforestation? Drinkable water for the world's population? Protection of the polar bear? Select an issue you care about. (If it's climate change, select a particular possible response to it, such as sharing environmental technologies with developing countries, increasing mileage requirements, requiring the use of energy-efficient lightbulbs, etc.) Do some online research for related data and then explore your issue in light of the five concepts discussed above.

The Federal Role

The federal government has long maintained a role in the protection of the environment—some argue too great a role. As early as 1899, Congress enacted a law that required a permit to discharge refuse into navigable waters. When it became apparent that private, state, and local environmental efforts were not adequate to address the burgeoning problems, Congress began taking more aggressive legislative steps in the early 1970s.

National Environmental Policy Act

The 1970 National Environmental Policy Act (NEPA) established a strong federal presence in the promotion of a clean and healthy environment. NEPA represents a general commitment by the federal government to "use all practicable means" to conduct federal affairs in a fashion that both promotes "the general welfare" and operates in "harmony" with the environment.

NEPA established the Council on Environmental Quality (CEQ), which serves as an adviser to the president. The CEQ is a watchdog of sorts. It is required to conduct studies and collect information regarding the state of the environment. The council then develops policy and legislative proposals for the president and Congress. [For more on the CEQ, see **www.whitehouse.gov/ceq**]

NEPA's primary influence, however, results from its *environmental impact statement* (EIS) requirements. With few exceptions, "proposals for legislation and other major federal action significantly affecting the quality of the human environment" must be accompanied by an EIS explaining the impact on the environment and detailing reasonable alternatives. Completing an EIS requires undertaking a cost–benefit analysis. It also requires consideration of cause-and-effect links. Major federal construction projects (highways, dams, nuclear reactors) would normally require an EIS, but less visible federal programs (ongoing timber management or the abandonment of a lengthy railway) may also require EIS treatment. Although the focus here is on federal actions, thus exempting solely private acts from this scrutiny, a major private-sector action supported by federal funding or by one of several varieties of federal permission may also require an EIS. Hence private companies receiving federal contracts, funding, licenses, and the like may be parties to the completion of an EIS.

> NEPA's primary influence results from its environment impact statement (EIS) requirements.

Questions

Should a state be required to prepare an EIS if it wants to use federal funds to promote statewide tourism? Does it matter which state it is? Consider Iowa and then consider Hawaii.[30]

Environmental Protection Agency

The private sector was not left without regulation or constraint. The Environmental Protection Agency (EPA) was created in 1970 to mount a coordinated attack on environmental problems. EPA duties include, among other things, (1) gathering information, particularly by surveying pollution problems, (2) conducting research on pollution problems, (3) assisting state and local pollution control efforts, and (4) administering many of the federal laws directed to environmental concerns. [For the EPA home page, see **www.epa.gov**]

A Cautionary Tale

As previously mentioned, many of our environmental laws and regulations were drafted to address compartmentalized and discrete issues. This means that, outside of federal action triggering the requirement of an EIS, there may be no forum for an activity that may raise multiple issues to be evaluated based on its full environmental impact. Consider hydraulic fracturing, commonly referred to as fracking, in which a mixture of sand, fluids, and chemical additives are pumped under high pressure into wells to fracture shale rock, thereby releasing natural gas for extraction. Substantial reserves of natural gas have been found in North America—enough that the United States could overtake Russia as the world's largest producer of oil and gas, a potential global political game-changer. Approximately 13,000 new wells are being drilled each year in the United States. If this newly accessible gas is used to produce electricity, allowing coal-fired plants which emit twice the carbon dioxide as gas to be retired, our total carbon dioxide emissions should decrease.

However, whether GHG emissions are actually reduced or whether substantial other environmental issues are created by the fracking process are questions worth considering. At least one report suggests that such issues may well be economically feasible to remediate, but for the most part companies are not currently required to do so. Specific issues that have been raised, but which remain partly or wholly unaddressed, include the following:

- Three to five million gallons of water are used to extract the gas from each well, approximately 15 percent of which is returned to the surface as "flowback." The flowback can release methane (a GHG 70 times more potent than carbon dioxide) and other toxins into the atmosphere, depending in part on whether best available well-completion technology is employed. Such technology will not be federally required until 2015, so a substantial number of existing wells do not, and will not be required to, use such technology.

- A report released in 2012 by three members of Congress indicates that between 2005 and 2009, 750 chemicals had been used in the fracking process, some of which were extremely toxic, such as benzene and lead. The only fracking fuel additive required by federal law to be disclosed is diesel fuel, in part owing to a 2005 exemption placed in the Safe Drinking Water Act.

- Numerous concerns have been raised with regard to the impact of fracking on local water resources, including concerns that some of the natural gas released may migrate out of the wells and negatively affect drinking, surface, and groundwater. These water resources may also be endangered by escape of the fracking fluid or by the flowback water. The volume of water necessary for the fracking process may also have a negative impact on local water supplies.

- When not actually in use, both the fracking fluid and flowback waters will require environmentally sound storage and disposal. Approximately 60 percent of the flowback water is recycled by transportation to storage and treatment locations via pipelines or trucks and, after treatment (often only by dilution), discharged into surface water. The rest may be injected back into the ground, raising some concerns that this deep injection process may trigger earthquakes.

- Once extracted, the gas itself requires transportation to refineries by rail or pipeline, raising additional environmental issues. Extensions of existing pipelines require regulatory approvals, but most rail transport does not.

Sources: Joe Nocera, "A Fracking Rorschach Test," *The New York Times,* October 4, 2013; Abbi L. Cohen and John M. Ix, "What's the Deal with Fracking?" *Association of Corporate Counsel,* July 18, 2012 [**www.lexology.com**]; "Natural Gas, by the Book," *The New York Times,* June 9, 2012; John M. Broder, "U.S. Caps Emissions in Drilling for Fuel," *The New York Times,* April 19, 2012, p. A20; "The Need to Be Seen to Be Clean," *The Economist,* May 14, 2011, p. 37.

Regulation of Air Pollution

In the United States we depend on (indeed, we emotionally embrace) the automobile. In doing so, we have opened vistas of opportunity not previously imagined. However, motor vehicles also discharge carbon monoxide, nitrogen oxide, and hydrocarbons as by-products of the combustion of fuel, thus fouling our air. Today we know those vehicles also are significant emitters of greenhouse gases. Industrial production, manufacturing, generation of electricity, and the combustion of fossil fuels in homes and workplaces are also significant contributors to the dilemma of dirty air and greenhouse gases.

Clean Air Act of 1990

Early clean air legislation in 1963 and 1965 afforded the government limited authority. The Clean Air Act (CAA) amendments of 1970 and 1977 gave the EPA the power to set air quality standards and to ensure that those standards are achieved according to a timetable prescribed by the agency. Politics brought clean air to the fore in 1990 and the Clean Air Act of 1990 followed. It phased in new standards over a period of years, generally required tougher auto emission controls, cleaner-burning gasoline, and new equipment to capture industrial and business pollution, all of which worked toward the general goal of reducing airborne pollutants by about 50 percent. Under the CAA, air quality standards are set federally, but the states are required to establish implementation plans to achieve and maintain those standards.

In recent years, there has been considerable high-profile litigation over clean air standards. The Supreme Court's decision in *Massachusetts v. EPA,* presented below, has had the most profound effect. In this case a number of states, cities, and private organizations joined as petitioners to argue that the EPA had abdicated its responsibility under Section 202(a)(1) of the CAA to "prescribe . . . standards applicable to the emission of any air pollutant" when it refused to regulate greenhouse gas emissions from new motor vehicles.

LEGAL BRIEFCASE

Massachusetts v. Environmental Protection Agency 127 S.Ct. 1438 (2007)

Justice Stevens

A well-documented rise in global temperatures has coincided with a significant increase in the concentration of carbon dioxide in the atmosphere. Respected scientists believe the two trends are related. For when carbon dioxide is released into the atmosphere, it acts like the ceiling of a greenhouse, trapping solar energy and retarding the escape of reflected heat. It is therefore a species—the most important species—of a "greenhouse gas."

Calling global warming "the most pressing environmental challenge of our time," a group of states, local governments, and private organizations, alleged . . . [that the] EPA has abdicated its responsibility under the Clean Air Act to regulate the emissions of four greenhouse gases, including carbon dioxide. Specifically, petitioners asked us to answer two questions concerning . . . the Act: whether EPA has the statutory authority to regulate greenhouse gas emissions from new motor vehicles; and if so, whether its stated reasons for refusing to do so are consistent with the statute.

I

Section 202(a)(1) of the Clean Air Act . . . provides:

> The [EPA] Administrator shall by regulation prescribe (and from time to time revise) . . . standards applicable to the emission of any air pollutant from any class or classes of new motor vehicles or new motor vehicle engines, which in his judgment cause, or contribute to, air pollution which may reasonably be anticipated to endanger public health or welfare. . . .

The Act defines "air pollutant" to include "any air pollution agent or combination of such agents, including any physical, chemical, biological, radioactive . . . substance or matter which is emitted into or otherwise enters the ambient air." "Welfare" is also defined broadly: among other things, it includes "effects on . . . weather . . . and climate."

* * * * *

II

On October 20, 1999, a group of 19 private organizations filed a rulemaking petition asking EPA to regulate "greenhouse gas emissions from new motor vehicles under Section 202 of the Clean Air Act." . . . As to EPA's statutory authority, the petition observed that the agency itself had already confirmed that it had the power to regulate carbon dioxide. In 1998, Jonathan Z. Cannon, then EPA's General Counsel, prepared a legal opinion concluding that "CO[2] emissions are within the scope of EPA's authority to regulate," even as he recognized that EPA had so far declined to exercise that authority. Cannon's successor, Gary S. Guzy, reiterated that opinion before a congressional committee just two weeks before the rulemaking petition was filed.

* * * * *

On September 8, 2003, EPA entered an order denying the rulemaking petition. The agency gave two reasons for its decision: (1) that contrary to the opinions of its former general counsels, the Clean Air Act does not authorize EPA to issue mandatory regulations to address global climate change; and (2) that even if the agency had the authority to set greenhouse gas emission standards, it would be unwise to do so at this time.

* * * * *

Having reached that conclusion, EPA believed it followed that greenhouse gases cannot be "air pollutants" within the meaning of the Act. . . . The agency bolstered this conclusion by explaining that if carbon dioxide were an air pollutant, the only feasible method of reducing tailpipe emissions would be to improve fuel economy. But because Congress has already created detailed mandatory fuel economy standards subject to Department of Transportation (DOT) administration, the agency concluded that EPA regulation would either conflict with those standards or be superfluous.

Even assuming that it had authority over greenhouse gases, EPA explained in detail why it would refuse to exercise that authority. The agency began by recognizing that the concentration of greenhouse gases has dramatically increased as a result of human activities, and acknowledged the attendant increase in global surface air temperatures. EPA nevertheless gave controlling importance to the [National Resource Council] Report's statement that a causal link between the two cannot be unequivocally established. Given that residual uncertainty, EPA concluded that regulating greenhouse gas emissions would be unwise.

The agency furthermore characterized any EPA regulation of motor-vehicle emissions as a "piecemeal approach" to climate change and stated that such regulation would conflict with the president's "comprehensive approach" to the problem. That approach involves additional support for technological innovation, the creation of nonregulatory programs to encourage voluntary private-sector reductions in greenhouse gas emissions, and further research on climate change—not actual regulation. According to EPA, unilateral EPA regulation of motor-vehicle greenhouse gas emissions might also hamper the president's ability to persuade key developing countries to reduce greenhouse gas emissions.

V [III–IV omitted-ed.]

* * * * *

[We] "may reverse any such action found to be . . . arbitrary, capricious, an abuse of discretion, or otherwise not in accordance with law."

VI

On the merits, the first question is whether Section 202(a)(1) of the Clean Air Act authorizes EPA to regulate greenhouse gas emissions from new motor vehicles in the event that it forms a "judgment" that such emissions contribute to climate change. We have little trouble concluding that it does. . . .

The statutory text forecloses EPA's reading. The Clean Air Act's sweeping definition of "air pollutant" includes "*any* air pollution agent or combination of such agents, including *any* physical, chemical . . . substance or matter which is emitted into or otherwise enters the ambient air. . . . " On its face, the definition embraces all airborne compounds of whatever stripe, and underscores that intent through the repeated use of the word "any." Carbon dioxide, methane, nitrous oxide, and hydrofluorocarbons are without a doubt "physical [and] chemical . . . substance[s] which [are] emitted into . . . the ambient air." The statute is unambiguous.

* * * * *

EPA finally argues that it cannot regulate carbon dioxide emissions from motor vehicles because doing so would require it to tighten mileage standards, a job (according to EPA) that Congress has assigned to DOT. But that DOT sets mileage standards in no way licenses EPA to shirk its environmental responsibilities. EPA has been charged with protecting the public's "health" and "welfare," a statutory obligation wholly independent of DOT's mandate to promote energy efficiency. The two obligations may overlap, but there is no reason to think the two agencies cannot both administer their obligations and yet avoid inconsistency.

* * * * *

VII

The alternative basis for EPA's decision—that even if it does have statutory authority to regulate greenhouse gases, it would be unwise to do so at this time—rests on reasoning divorced from the statutory text. While the statute does condition the exercise of EPA's authority on its formation of a "judgment," that judgment must relate to whether an air pollutant "cause[s], or contribute[s] to, air pollution which may reasonably be anticipated to endanger public health or welfare." Put another way, the use of the word "judgment" is not a roving license to ignore the statutory text. It is but a direction to exercise discretion within defined statutory limits.

If EPA makes a finding of endangerment, the Clean Air Act requires the agency to regulate emissions of the deleterious pollutant from new motor vehicles. . . . EPA no doubt has significant latitude as to the manner, timing, content, and coordination of its regulations with those of other agencies. But once EPA has responded to a petition for rulemaking, its reasons for action or inaction must conform to the authorizing statute. Under the clear terms of the Clean Air Act, EPA can avoid taking further action only if it determines that greenhouse gases do not contribute to climate change or if it provides some reasonable explanation as to why it cannot or will not exercise its discretion to determine whether they do. To the extent that this constrains agency discretion to pursue other priorities of the administrator or the president, this is the congressional design.

EPA has refused to comply with this clear statutory command. Instead, it has offered a laundry list of reasons not to regulate. For example, EPA said that a number of voluntary executive branch programs already provide an effective response to the threat of global warming, that regulating greenhouse gases might impair the president's ability to negotiate with "key developing nations" to reduce emissions, and that curtailing motor-vehicle emissions would reflect "an inefficient, piecemeal approach to address the climate change issue."

Although we have neither the expertise nor the authority to evaluate these policy judgments, it is evident they have nothing to do with whether greenhouse gas emissions contribute to climate change. Still less do they amount to a reasoned justification for declining to form a scientific judgment. . . .

Nor can EPA avoid its statutory obligation by noting the uncertainty surrounding various features of climate change and concluding that it would therefore be better not to regulate at this time. If the scientific uncertainty is so profound that it precludes EPA from making a reasoned judgment as to whether greenhouse gases contribute to global warming, EPA must say so. That EPA would prefer not to regulate greenhouse gases because of some residual uncertainty . . . is irrelevant. The statutory question is whether sufficient information exists to make an endangerment finding.

In short, EPA has offered no reasoned explanation for its refusal to decide whether greenhouse gases cause or contribute to climate change. Its action was therefore "arbitrary, capricious, . . . or otherwise not in accordance with law." . . . [Reversed and remanded.]

Questions

1. Under what conditions did the Supreme Court say it had the power to reverse the EPA's decision not to regulate the carbon dioxide emissions of new vehicles?

2. What did the petitioners, including the State of Massachusetts, want the EPA to do?

3. The EPA said that, even if it had the authority to regulate greenhouse gas emissions from motor vehicles, it would not do so. What reasons did the EPA give for this refusal? What did the Supreme Court say about those reasons?

4. Following this decision of the Supreme Court, what was the EPA required to do? Was the EPA required to set a standard for greenhouse gas emissions from new vehicles?

5. Look back at the discussion about proving causation at the start of Part Two of this chapter. Did the Supreme Court say that greenhouse gas emissions from vehicles caused global warming? What did the Court observe about causation?

AFTERWORD

Despite the Court's 2007 ruling in *Massachusetts v. EPA*, not until President Obama took office did the EPA rule that GHG emissions are pollutants that threaten public health. Built on the foundation of its initial endangerment finding, the EPA then promulgated rules establishing fuel economy and greenhouse gas emission standards for cars and light trucks covering model years 2012–2016, as well as a timetable for controlling GHG emissions from power plants and other stationary sources and targeting those controls to cover only the largest emitters. Quickly, the EPA found itself back in court with various industry groups and 14 states, arguing in part that the EPA had impermissibly relied on scientific findings from the UN Intergovernmental Panel on Climate Change, the National Research Council, and the U.S. Global Change Research Program. In a sharply worded opinion, the federal circuit court for the District of Columbia ruled on June 26, 2012, that:

> [the] EPA had before it substantial record evidence that anthropogenic emissions of greenhouse gases "very likely" caused warming of the climate over the last several decades. ... Relying again upon

substantial scientific evidence, EPA determined that anthropogenically induced climate change threatens both public health and public welfare. It found that extreme weather events, changes in air quality, increases in food-and water-borne pathogens, and increases in temperatures are likely to have adverse health effects. The record also supports EPA's conclusion that climate change endangers human welfare by creating risk to food production and agriculture, forestry, energy, infrastructure, ecosystems, and wildlife. Substantial evidence further supported EPA's conclusion that the warming resulting from the greenhouse gas emissions could be expected to create risks to water resources and in general to coastal areas as a result of expected increase in sea level.

The Supreme Court granted *certiorari* and on June 23, 2014 held that the EPA could regulate GHG emissions from stationary sources which were already subject to regulation based on their emissions of conventional pollutants.[31]

Greenhouse Gas Regulations

Although many have argued that no GHG regulation will be as effective as a federal climate bill would be, Congress has thus far chosen not to act. The Obama administration, however, has made curbing GHG emissions a priority for his second term and intends to do so through administrative rule making. The most far-reaching element in the plan will restrict carbon dioxide emissions at power plants—both new plants and existing plants. In September 2013, the proposed regulations applicable to new power plants were announced. By all accounts, the standards will effectively ban new coal-fired plants unless carbon capture and storage (CCS) technology is installed. Coal, although cheap and plentiful, produces substantially more GHG when used in power production than either oil or gas. GHG regulations applicable to existing plants were published in a proposed form in June 2014. These regulations set a goal of a 30 percent reduction in carbon dioxide from 2005 levels by 2030. The states are to develop plans to reduce their emissions and could, but are not required to, include cap-and-trade arrangements which would allow more efficient plants to sell their excess credits to less efficient plants, allowing attainment of the required GHG reduction to be achieved as cost-effectively as possible for the state as a whole.[32]

Non-GHG Air-Quality Regulations

Greenhouse gases are, of course, not the only air pollutant hazardous to health. A 2012 report from the American Lung Association noted that 41 percent of our population lives in counties that exceeded standards set for ozone and particulates from 2008 to 2010.[33] In recent years, the EPA has issued stricter standards governing such pollutants as ozone, which is a substantial contributor to smog; fine particulate matter, also known as soot, which can enter the lungs and bloodstream and cause respiratory and heart ailments; and sulfur dioxide, which contributes to acid rain and smog. Another persistent problem that the EPA has attempted to address is air pollution traveling into downwind states and impairing their capacity to attain federally mandated air standards. The Cross-State Air Pollution Rule (CSAPR) would have taken effect on January 1, 2011 had it not been challenged in court by nearly 40 separate petitioners, including cities, states, power companies, and various trade organizations. CSAPR would require power plants in 28 states to install new pollution controls or buy pollution credits under a limited cap-and-trade system. In 2012, the federal circuit court for the District of Columbia held that the EPA had exceeded its statutory authority in the design of CSAPR's provisions, a decision overturned by the Supreme Court, in April 2014.[34]

Even without the new GHG regulations applicable to coal-fired plants and with the delayed CSAPR regulations discussed above, tighter regulation of traditional air pollutants working in concert with price competition from abundant natural gas, has been reducing coal-fired plants' contribution to power generation. At its peak in 1988, coal provided 60 percent of our electricity, but by 2012 its share had dropped almost in half.[35]

Motor Vehicle Emission Standards

Accompanying the financial crisis, responding to higher gas prices and realizing benefit from gradually increasing vehicle mileage, the total gallons of gas consumed has gradually decreased since its peak in 2007. Consumption in 2012 was about 6 percent below the 2007 peak and roughly on par with usage in 2003.[36] Continued improvement should result from the steady increase in average fuel economy mandates—29 miles per gallon (MPG) in 2012 rising to 54.5 MPG for the 2025 model year, standards that have been supported by most major auto manufacturers. The latest regulations also incorporate for the first time express GHG emission standards, which is particularly significant in that light-duty vehicle emissions account for roughly 17 percent of GHG emissions in the United States.[37] On average, European vehicles are 30 percent more fuel-efficient than American vehicles, except with regard to light-duty vehicles, where U.S. standards are tougher, and heavy-duty vehicles, for which Europe sets no fuel-efficiency requirements.[38]

Regulation of Water Pollution

As with the air, we often treat our water resources as free goods. Rather than paying the full cost of producing goods and services, we have simply dumped a portion of that cost into the nearest body of water. The results range from smelly to dangerous to tragic. The evidence can be found in our local rivers and lakes, but also in our global gulfs, seas, and oceans.

BP's oil spill in the Gulf of Mexico has done and will do untold damage, but the waters of the Gulf before the spill were hardly pristine. Ninety percent of America's offshore drilling occurs there, drilling that has gone on for over 60 years and that provides tens of thousands of jobs. Since 1964, more than 300 spills releasing over a half million barrels of oil have occurred, not to mention the thousands of tons of "produced water"—a by-product of drilling that includes oil, grease, and heavy metals—that are dumped annually. After World War II, the Gulf was even used by the government to dispose of surplus mines, bombs, and ammunition.[39]

The debris of our modern lives—including lightbulbs, bottle caps, toothbrushes, and all manner of plastics—also shows up in our oceans.[40] In both the Atlantic and Pacific oceans, "garbage patches" involving millions of square miles exist, composed primarily of microplastics broken down from larger items, but also including larger objects such as those already mentioned. We have ample evidence of the consequences for fish and other aquatic life. As one observer who has worked on the Gulf his whole life noted, "You can fool people, but you can't fool the fish."[41] [For more on the Great Pacific Garbage Patch, see **http://education.nationalgeographic.com/education/encyclopedia/great-pacific-garbage-patch/?ar_a=1**]

> "You can fool people, but you can't fool the fish."

Federal Policy

The 1972 Clean Water Act (CWA), designed to "restore and maintain the chemical, physical, and biological integrity of the nation's waters," established two national goals: (1) achieving water quality sufficient for the protection and propagation of fish, shellfish, and wildlife and for recreation in and on the water and (2) eliminating the discharge of pollutants into navigable waters. The states have primary responsibility for enforcing the CWA, but the EPA is empowered to assume enforcement authority if necessary.

There is no doubt the CWA has resulted in enormous improvements, but there are problems as well. The EPA conducts national surveys to evaluate water quality, sediment quality, coastal habitats, and fish-tissue contaminants. Its 2012 report rated the West Coast as fair to good; the Northeast, Southeast, and Gulf coasts as fair; and the Great Lakes as poor.[42] The goals of the Act are implemented primarily by imposing limits on the amount of pollutants that may lawfully enter U.S. waters from any "point source" (typically a pipe). The National Pollutant Discharge Elimination System (NPDES) requires all dischargers to secure a permit, most often from the EPA, but at times from some other government agency, before pouring effluent into a navigable stream. The permit specifies maximum permissible levels of effluent and typically also mandates the use of a particular pollution control process or device to ensure that level is not exceeded. It also requires the permit holder to monitor its own performance and report the results to the state or the EPA.

But regulation of point sources leaves many pollutants unmonitored. Surface water runoff is polluted with our lawn fertilizer, pet waste, and grease and oil from vehicles. In spite of rules put in place in 1999, surface water is also polluted by runoff from large row crop, hog, cattle, and poultry farms. Nitrogen from fertilizers finds its way into the Mississippi River from sources hundreds of miles from the Gulf— 1.5 million tons of it yearly. As a result, in the Gulf there is a dead zone larger in size than Connecticut, in which little life can exist.[43]

> In the Gulf there is a dead zone larger in size than Connecticut.

Discouragingly, even sources covered by the NPDES nevertheless violate the terms of their permits, often with impunity. *The New York Times* published a series of articles over the fall of 2009 based on records received in response to Freedom of Information Act requests made to every state and the EPA. In them, journalist Charles Duhigg presented an alarming picture of CWA violations rising steadily across the nation.

Many violations were relatively minor but about 60 percent were deemed to be in "significant noncompliance." Fewer than 3 percent resulted in fines or other substantial punishment. Some, but not all, of the rise is attributable to insufficient enforcement resources. The number of regulated facilities more than doubled in a 10-year span, but state enforcement budgets remained essentially flat. The EPA made promises to regulate the discharge of such toxic substances as arsenic, lead, and cadmium, but has never done so. [To read the articles in this series, go to **www.nytimes.com/toxicwaters**]

How Did Your State Respond?

The New York Times website provides the data it received from responding states regarding CWA permits, violations, and enforcement actions. The *Times* also provides information from each state on staffing and budgets related to oversight of water pollution. What information was provided from your state? See **http://projects.nytimes.com/toxic-waters/polluters /state-data**

Covered Waters

Decades after CWA enactment, it remains unclear exactly what waters are actually covered by the act and therefore subject to EPA regulation. In the 2001 *Northern Cook County* case that follows, the Supreme Court looked at what qualifies as "navigable waters" for purposes of the CWA. Only a bare majority (five) of the justices agreed with this decision; the remaining four dissented. In 2006, the Supreme Court again looked at the issue. That decision will be discussed following *Northern Cook County.*

LEGAL BRIEFCASE

Solid Waste Agency of Northern Cook County v. U.S. Army Corps of Engineers   531 U.S. 159 (2001)

Chief Justice Rehnquist

Section 404(a) of the Clean Water Act (CWA or Act) regulates the discharge of dredged or fill material into "navigable waters." The United States Army Corps of Engineers (Corps) has interpreted Section 404(a) to confer federal authority over an abandoned sand and gravel pit in northern Illinois that provides habitat for migratory birds. We are asked to decide whether the provisions of Section 404(a) may be fairly extended to these waters, and, if so, whether Congress could exercise such authority consistent with the Commerce Clause. We answer the first question in the negative and therefore do not reach the second.

Petitioner, the Solid Waste Agency of Northern Cook County (SWANCC), is a consortium of 23 suburban Chicago cities and villages that united in an effort to locate and develop a disposal site for baled nonhazardous solid waste. The Chicago Gravel Company informed the municipalities of the availability of a 533-acre parcel, . . . which had been the site of a sand and gravel pit mining operation for three decades up until about 1960. Long since abandoned, the old mining site eventually gave way to a successional stage forest, with its remnant excavation trenches evolving into a scattering of permanent and seasonal ponds of varying size (from under one-tenth of an acre to several acres) and depth (from several inches to several feet).

The municipalities decided to purchase the site. . . .

Section 404(a) grants the Corps authority to issue permits "for the discharge of dredged or fill material into the navigable waters at specified disposal sites." The term "navigable waters" is defined under the Act as "the waters of the United States, including the territorial seas." The Corps has issued regulations defining the term "waters of the United States" to include.

> waters such as intrastate lakes, rivers, streams (including intermittent streams), mudflats, sandflats, wetlands, sloughs, prairie potholes, wet meadows, playa lakes, or natural ponds, the use, degradation or destruction of which could affect interstate or foreign commerce.

In 1986, in an attempt to "clarify" the reach of its jurisdiction, the Corps stated that Section 404(a) extends to intrastate waters

a. Which are or would be used as habitat by birds protected by Migratory Bird Treaties; or

b. Which are or would be used as habitat by other migratory birds which cross state lines; or

c. Which are or would be used as habitat for endangered species; or

d. Used to irrigate crops sold in interstate commerce.

This last promulgation has been dubbed the "Migratory Bird Rule."

The Corps initially concluded that it had no jurisdiction over the site. . . . However, after the Illinois Nature Preserves Commission informed the Corps that a number of migratory bird species had been observed at the site, the Corps reconsidered and ultimately asserted jurisdiction over the balefill site pursuant to subpart (b) of the "Migratory Bird Rule." The Corps found that approximately 121 bird species had been observed at the site, including several known to depend upon aquatic environments for a significant portion of their life requirements. . . .

* * * * *

[The] Corps refused to issue a Section 404(a) permit. The Corps found that SWANCC had not established that its proposal was the "least environmentally damaging, most practicable alternative" for disposal of nonhazardous solid waste; that SWANCC's failure to set aside sufficient funds to remediate leaks posed an "unacceptable risk to the public's drinkingwater supply"; and that the impact of the project upon area-sensitive species was "unmitigatable since a landfill surface cannot be redeveloped into a forested habitat."

Petitioner filed suit. . . . Petitioner argued that respondents had exceeded their statutory authority in interpreting the CWA to cover nonnavigable, isolated, intrastate waters based upon the presence of migratory birds. . . .

The Court of Appeals [held] that respondents' "Migratory Bird Rule" was a reasonable interpretation of the Act.

We granted certiorari. . . .

Congress passed the CWA for the stated purpose of "restoring and maintaining the chemical, physical, and biological integrity of the Nation's waters." In so doing, Congress chose to "recognize, preserve, and protect the primary responsibilities and rights of States to prevent, reduce, and eliminate pollution, to plan the development and use (including restoration, preservation, and enhancement) of land and water resources, and to consult with the Administrator in the exercise of his authority under this chapter." Relevant here, Section 404(a) authorizes respondents to regulate the discharge of fill material into "navigable waters," which the statute defines as "the waters of the United States, including the territorial seas." Respondents have interpreted these words to cover the abandoned gravel pit at issue here because it is used as habitat for migratory birds. We conclude that the "Migratory Bird Rule" is not fairly supported by the CWA.

This is not the first time we have been called upon to evaluate the meaning of Section 404(a). In *United States v. Riverside Bayview Homes, Inc.,* 474 U.S. 121 (1985), we held that the Corps had Section 404(a) jurisdiction over wetlands that actually abutted on a navigable waterway. In so doing, we noted that the term "navigable" is of "limited import" and that Congress evidenced its intent to "regulate at least some waters that would not be deemed 'navigable' under the classical understanding of that term." But our holding was based in large measure upon Congress' unequivocal acquiescence to, and approval of, the Corps' regulations interpreting the CWA to cover wetlands adjacent to navigable waters. We found that Congress' concern for the protection of water quality and aquatic ecosystems indicated its intent to regulate wetlands "inseparably bound up with the 'waters' of the United States."

It was the significant nexus between the wetlands and "navigable waters" that informed our reading of the CWA in

Riverside Bayview Homes.... In order to rule for respondents here, we would have to hold that the jurisdiction of the Corps extends to ponds that are *not* adjacent to open water. But we conclude that the text of the statute will not allow this.

Indeed, the Corps' *original* interpretation of the CWA, promulgated two years after its enactment, is inconsistent with that which it espouses here. Its 1974 regulations defined Section 404(a)'s "navigable waters" to mean "those waters of the United States which are subject to the ebb and flow of the tide, and/or are presently, or have been in the past, or may be in the future susceptible for use for purposes of interstate or foreign commerce." The Corps emphasized that "it is the water body's capability of use by the public for purposes of transportation or commerce which is the determinative factor." Respondents put forward no persuasive evidence that the Corps mistook Congress' intent in 1974.

* * * * *

We hold that [the regulations], as clarified and applied to petitioner's balefill site pursuant to the "Migratory Bird Rule," [exceed] the authority granted to respondents under Section 404(a) of the CWA. The judgment of the Court of Appeals for the Seventh Circuit is therefore
Reversed.

Questions

1. Summarize the arguments made by the Army Corps of Engineers for finding that the government had the power to regulate this site under the CWA.

2. Explain the Supreme Court's response to each of the Army Corps of Engineers' arguments previously identified.

3. Did the Supreme Court hold that the government could not regulate this type of site or only that Congress had not in fact sought to extend its regulation to this type of site?

4. In your view, should the federal government be able to regulate bodies of water that are of significant use by migratory birds? Explain.

AFTERWORD

In the *Northern Cook County* case the Supreme Court evaluated a regulation of the Army Corps of Engineers and determined that the Corps exceeded its scope of authority under the CWA. All nine justices agreed that the term "navigable waters" should be interpreted more broadly than its literal meaning, but only four of the justices would have approved the Corps' expansive reading of the statute.

In the 2006 case, *Repanos v. United States,* the Supreme Court once again reviewed the term "navigable waters."[44] The same four justices dissented, arguing that the revised, but still broad authority asserted by the Corps was permissible under the statute. This time, however, the remaining five justices did not agree on the reach of the CWA, but only agreed that the Corps was still asserting an authority broader than allowable. The result was that the case was remanded for "further proceedings" but without a standard on which to base those proceedings. The bottom line was that the government was required once again to define the scope of its regulatory authority.

In the meantime, enforcement under the Act has been substantially hampered. "In drier states, some polluters say the act no longer applies to them and are therefore refusing to renew or apply for permits, making it impossible to monitor what they are dumping." A case in point—Cannon Air Force Base in New Mexico has informed the EPA that it "no longer considers itself subject to the act." According to *The New York Times,* it "dumps wastewater—containing bacteria and human sewage—into a lake on the base."[45] In April 2011 the EPA announced new guidelines,[46] which will no doubt be challenged in court.

> In drier states, some polluters say the act no longer applies to them.

Regulation of Land Pollution

Pollution does not fit tidily into separate compartments (air, water, land) as might seem to be suggested by the divisions of this chapter. Acid rain debases air and water as well as the fruits of water and land such as fish and trees. So too, the problems of land pollution addressed in this section can seep into the soil, polluting groundwater, and harming plants and animals directly and indirectly. This section addresses the laws governing how we dispose of waste—solid, hazardous, and toxic.

Toxic Substances Control Act

Because our disposal laws vary based on the classification of the materials being disposed, the primary law governing classification is a good place to start. In 1976, Congress approved the Toxic Substances Control Act (TSCA) to identify toxic chemicals, assess their risks, and control dangerous chemicals. Under the terms of TSCA, the EPA is empowered to review and limit or stop the introduction of new chemicals. Companies must notify the EPA before manufacturing or importing new industrial chemicals, but they need not provide any safety data unless the data they have suggest the substance poses a "substantial risk." The EPA has only 90 days to block the chemical and can only suspend review and request company data if the EPA can show a potential risk from the chemical.

The structure of TSCA results in a "safe until proven dangerous" presumption. Only a small fraction of 85,000 industrial chemicals in use today have been tested for safety.[47] Some that have been tested, such as formaldehyde, which is used in a wide range of products—from nail polish and hair straighteners to many building materials—are still in wide use. The Department of Health and Human Services identified formaldehyde as a known carcinogen in June 2011, but as of this writing the EPA still listed it as a "probable human carcinogen."[48] Perhaps more disconcerting, the names and physical properties of nearly 20 percent of the chemicals in use are secret from all but a handful of EPA employees who are required by law to protect the trade secrets of the manufacturers.[49] That protection prohibits disclosure to other federal officials, state health and environmental regulators, and physicians, as well as the public. Although many of these unknown chemicals are likely harmless, in just one month "more than half of the 65 'substantial risk' reports filed" with the EPA by manufacturers "involved secret chemicals." Only Congress can change the law and until it does we are all trading knowledge in exchange for "ensuring the long-term competitiveness of the U.S. [chemical] industry."[50] [For more on programs under TSCA, see **www.epa.gov/opptintr/index.html**]

Pollution in the Movies

Perhaps surprisingly, toxic pollution has provided the central theme in two major Hollywood movies: *Erin Brockovich* and *A Civil Action*. The 2000 movie *Erin Brockovich* tells the story of a California community's battle against Pacific Gas & Electric for allegedly causing groundwater pollution resulting in extensive illness. [For more information on the pollutant at issue in the movie, the carcinogen hexavalent chromium, see **www.atsdr.cdc .gov/csem/csem.asp?csem=10&po=4**]

In the 1998 Disney movie *A Civil Action,* John Travolta played a plaintiff's lawyer based on a true story about some middle-class families who sued two corporate giants, Beatrice Food and W. R. Grace & Co., for allegedly polluting the groundwater in East Woburn, Massachusetts, where eight children died of leukemia. [For more information on this pollutant, Trichloroethylene, see **www.atsdr.cdc.gov/phs/phs.asp?id=171&tid=30**]

Question

Look back at the discussion of proving causation at the start of Part Two. Using that terminology, describe the causation issues that had to be addressed in the real-life counterparts to these movies.

Resource Conservation and Recovery Act

By 1976, the dangers of hazardous substances were becoming apparent to all, and Congress complemented the TSCA with the Resource Conservation and Recovery Act (RCRA). The act addresses both nonhazardous and hazardous solid wastes. Its provisions for nonhazardous wastes are more supportive than punitive in tone and approach. The federal government is authorized, among other strategies, to provide technical and financial assistance to states and localities; to prohibit future open dumping; and to establish cooperative federal, state, local, and private-enterprise programs to recover energy and valuable materials from solid waste.

Subtitle C of the RCRA is designed to ensure the safe movement and disposal of hazardous solid wastes. The generator of the waste must determine if that waste is hazardous under EPA guidelines. If so, the waste generator must then create a manifest to be used in tracking the waste from its creation to its disposal. Along the cradle-to-grave path, all those with responsibility for it must sign the manifest and safely store and transport the waste. Once the waste reaches a licensed disposal facility, the owner or manager of that site signs the manifest and returns a copy of it to the generator. Disposal sites must be operated according to EPA standards, and remedial action must be taken should hazardous wastes escape from the sites. [For more information, see the EPA website at **www.epa.gov /epawaste/hazard/tsd/index.htm**]

A preliminary requirement for cradle-to-grave tracking to apply is the statutory requirement that, to be solid waste, the material must be "discarded." The U.S. Court of Appeals for the District of Columbia has ruled that "discarded" means "disposed of," "abandoned," or "thrown away" and has repeatedly held various versions of the EPA's rules to have been too broad because they improperly covered recycling practices when the materials were not discarded within the meaning of the statute.[51] Thus, *recycled* hazardous materials are not covered by RCRA, although they may be subject to other EPA regulations.[52]

Household Recycling

Our lifestyles result in mountains of waste that grow higher every year. On average each of us produce 7.1 pounds of garbage daily. This number is a lot higher than 4.3, the number in the prior edition of this text. The difference? It is from real-world data based in part on measurements now done at landfills, instead of the estimates and simulations of the EPA's materials flow analysis.[53] Of course, we pay an immediate price to dispose of all the leftovers of our lives, but the long-term concern is that the waste will come back to haunt us.

Even state-of-the-art landfills can leak, with the result that toxic elements can enter our groundwater. Seventy percent of the toxic waste in our landfills comes from electronics. The United States is the only industrialized country that has not ratified the Basel Convention, a treaty prohibiting export or trafficking in toxic e-waste. The solution, of course, is to "reduce, reuse, recycle."

> Seventy percent of the toxic waste in our landfills comes from electronics.

Recycling turns materials that would otherwise become waste into usable resources, which can reduce dependence on new materials (reducing deforestation, for example). It is now cheaper to recycle an aluminum can than it is to make one from new materials. The same is true of plastic bottles.[54] The EPA reports that 85 million tons of material was recycled in 2010.[55] A growing number of large food and beverage companies in the United States is voluntarily taking on the costs of recycling the consumer packaging of their goods, a process known as "extended producer responsibility." A subsidiary of Coca-Cola has taken on the goal of recycling all of its cans and bottles in North America by 2015, establishing factories to do just that. Customers in 18 percent of Starbucks stores can deposit their cups for recycling, on the way to reaching 100 percent in 2014. The cups from its Chicago-area stores are trucked to a Wisconsin recycling facility where they are turned into paper napkins for the store. Stonyfield Farm, which produces organic yogurt, now has bins in Whole Foods stores for the recycling of No. 5 plastic containers—the plastic it uses for its yogurt which most cities do not recycle.[56] Europe has required packaged goods companies to take financial responsibility for package recycling for many years.

> **Freegans attempt to live totally on free goods found in dumpsters and at "freemeets."**

The ultimate recycling approach, however, may be that taken by a group of anticonsumerists who call themselves freegans (as compared with vegans)—who attempt to live totally on free goods found in dumpsters and at "freemeets."[57] [For sites identifying the availability of free goods, see **www.craigslist.org** (select "free" from the for sale menu), and **www.freecycle.org**]

Of course, the most cost-effective, environmentally friendly practice of all is to simply *reduce* consumption. [For a fun, interactive lesson in garbology, see **www.naturebridge.org/garbology.php**]

Superfund—Comprehensive Environmental Response, Compensation, and Liability Act of 1980

The Comprehensive Environmental Response, Compensation, and Liability Act of 1980 (CERCLA), more commonly known as the Superfund, was enacted for the purpose of identifying and cleaning up abandoned hazardous waste sites. The process involves the assessment and ranking of proposed sites, followed by the development and implementation of cleanup plans for sites added to the National Priorities List. Cleanups may be carried out by the EPA or private parties, either of which may seek reimbursement of costs from those liable under the Act. Potentially responsible parties include present owners of the site as well as past owners who operated the site when the hazardous wastes were deposited; parent firms can be liable for actions of subsidiaries; and transferors (successive owners of businesses discharging hazardous wastes) are also liable. Any parties found to be responsible are strictly liable—that is, liability attaches without proof of either intent or negligence.

> **Any parties found to be responsible are strictly liable.**

Cleanup tends to be very expensive and generally requires considerable time to accomplish. The first listed Superfund site, Love Canal in Niagara Falls, New York, was finally clean enough to be delisted in 2004.[58] Originally cleanup costs were paid from a trust fund created by taxes on chemicals and petroleum, but that taxing authority lapsed in 1995. The Superfund program has since been running on annual appropriations and reserve funds. According to a recent Government Accountability Office report, that funding is likely to be inadequate for the foreseeable future. The annual estimated remediation costs for the five years ending in 2014 run from $335 to $681 million, but from 2000 to 2009 the highest funding received was only $267 million.[59] As of October 23, 2013, there are 54 proposed new Superfund sites, 1,314 sites currently on the national priorities list, and only 371 sites that have been delisted.[60]

How Does Your Community Compare?

Thirty-three years after the passage of CERCLA, some of the country's most hazardous sites remain toxic. Until the earthquake and tsunami in Japan, the biggest nuclear waste hazard in the Western world was located in southeast Washington—the Hanford nuclear facility, a 586-square-mile site constructed as part of the Manhattan project to produce weapons-grade plutonium in nine nuclear reactors along the banks of the Columbia River. The highly toxic waste is currently stored in underground tanks, where it will continue to wait until at least 2019 when it is projected that a specialized waste-treatment plant will commence transforming the waste into still-radioactive glass logs that will be more suitable for long-term storage.[61] [For maps and some aerial pictures of Hanford, explore the site beginning at its home page, **http://yosemite.epa.gov/r10/cleanup.nsf/sites/hanford**]

What do you know about the pollution in your community? Find out by logging onto **www.scorecard.org** and inserting your zip code. Then visit the EPA's site and discover any Superfund sites near you on its maps at **www.epa.gov/superfund/sites/npl/where.htm.**

Questions

1. Are there any Superfund sites in or near your community?
2. How does your home town rate with regard to the industrial release of toxic chemicals?
3. How does your air quality stack up with other communities in the United States?
4. How clean are your rivers and lakes?

Small Business Liability Relief and Brownfields Revitalization Act

There has been considerable dissatisfaction over CERCLA for a number of reasons, including the percentage of Superfund dollars that have gone to administration expenses and litigation, as well as the slow remediation process at most sites. Worried about liability risks, developers were often reluctant to buy and improve brownfield sites, but that problem was alleviated with the passage of the 2002 Small Business Liability Relief and Brownfields Revitalization Act (Brownfields Act). This law provides liability protection for prospective purchasers and contiguous property owners and authorizes increased funding for state and local programs that assess and clean up brownfields. [For more on brownfields, see **www.epa.gov/brownfields/index.html**]

PRACTICING ETHICS Environmentally Aware Decision Making

Imagine you have just been hired as the business manager for a chain of restaurants in your state. During the interview process you were told that part of your responsibilities would be to develop more environmentally friendly practices to be implemented at all 10 locations, while making sure that the changes overall either have a neutral or a positive impact on the business's bottom line. A local business school professor is interested in having her students do semester projects on the feasibility of various green projects for local businesses. Develop a list of possible practices your restaurants could implement to share with the professor for further development by her students.

Part Three—Penalties and Enforcement under Federal Law

Many environmental statutes require companies to monitor their own environmental performance and report that information, including violations, to the government. As noted above in discussing the Clean Water Act, such disclosure does not necessarily lead to any form of corrective or enforcement action. Government agencies also have broad authority to conduct environmental inspections of both plants and records as necessary, although they must obtain search warrants if criminal prosecutions are anticipated.

A broad array of enforcement actions are available to both state and federal agencies. Often violators initially are simply warned and a compliance schedule may be prescribed. If corrective action is not forthcoming, sterner measures may follow, including an administrative order to comply. Such orders may be somewhat less effective in the future, given the Supreme Court's 2012 decision in *Sackett v. EPA*.[62] There the Court held the issuance of a compliance order under the Clean Water Act, requiring the Sacketts to restore the wetlands on their property and subjecting them to a $75,000 per day penalty for any noncompliance, was a final agency action entitling them to immediate judicial review for declaratory relief. It can be expected that the ruling will impact the effectiveness of compliance orders under many other environmental programs as well.

Alternatively, the government may resort to litigation. It may seek an injunction to prevent continued or future violations or to require the polluter to remediate the environmental damage that has occurred. Monetary civil penalties and fines may be imposed under most environmental statutes. Governments that have incurred cleanup costs responding to the violation may also seek recovery of those costs. Although many suits are brought, most are settled rather than litigated. Settlement opens the possibility of somewhat more creative solutions, sometimes including Supplemental Environmental Projects (SEPs). Such projects involve the violator undertaking some environmental "good work" or community service project. For example, in two separate settlements, Scotts Miracle-Gro agreed to pay $500 million in contributions to various charities dedicated to the protection of bird populations and $2 million to acquire and protect 300 acres to prevent runoff of agricultural chemicals into nearby waterways.[63] [To find other examples of SEPs, explore the database maintained by the EPA at **www.epa-echo.gov/echo/about_sep.html**]

Many environmental laws also provide for the imposition of criminal penalties, as well as imprisonment. Individual corporate officers can be held criminally liable if they either had actual knowledge of the criminal action or they are held to be a "responsible person" under the appropriate law. So, for example, in 2012, Discount Computers, Inc. pleaded guilty to violating RCRA by failing to obtain a permit to dispose of hazardous substances for exporting used computer monitors containing hazardous wastes to foreign countries, including Egypt. Discount Computers was fined $2 million (the estimated value of the monitors) and its owner was sentenced to 30 months in prison and assessed a $10,000 fine.[64] Of course, the importance and effectiveness of any enforcement measure depends to a significant degree on the extent to which it is both sought and imposed. According to one study of sentences imposed after convictions were obtained, the "bark" of federal sentencing guidelines for environmental crimes "remains considerably worse than their bite."[65]

BP Gulf Oil Spill: A Case Study of Costs

The cost to BP as a result of the Gulf oil spill may well exceed the $40 billion that BP has publicly expected. Here is an estimate of what BP may pay:

- As of mid-2013, BP had already spent $14 billion to plug the Macondo well and clean up spilled oil.
- In November 2012, BP pleaded guilty to 14 criminal charges and agreed with the Justice Department to pay $4.5 billion over five years in fines and other penalties.
- Under the Clean Water Act, BP is subject to civil fines, based in part on the volume of oil spilled as well as the level of BP's culpability. As of this writing, fines could total anywhere from $3.5 to $17.1 billion.
- State and local governments around the Gulf are also pursuing compensation for environmental damage suffered. BP has already agreed to provide an initial $1 billion for some restoration projects.
- BP set up a $20-billion compensation fund in August 2010 to address damages suffered by individuals and businesses. In 2012, BP reached a settlement with tens of thousands of Gulf Coast businesses and individuals for economic and property loss. That settlement set up standards for establishing claims but did not set a cap on the total payments. By July 2013, BP indicated that $19.7 billion of the total had been committed. It also stated that there could be another $4.5 billion in payments due on claims already submitted. New claims could be submitted until April 2014.
- BP will also have legal fees, estimated by one account at $2 billion, including fees of experts necessary to pursue and defend the various legal actions.

BP may, however, recoup some of these costs if it is successful in any of its suits against its minority partners or the rig owner, Transocean Ltd.

Sources: Justin Scheck, Tom Fowler, and Selina Williams, "BP Says Spill Fund Is Running on Fumes," *The Wall Street Journal*, July 30, 2013; "Deepwater, Deep Pockets," *The Economist*, July 13, 2013, p. 59; Clifford Krauss and Stanley Reed, "Leaner BP Blanches at Bill for Cleanup," *The New York Times*, July 11, 2013; Clifford Krauss and Barry Meier, "As Oil Spill Trial Opens, Push for a Deal Continues," *The New York Times*, February 25, 2013; "Gulf of Mexico Oil Spill, 2010," *The New York Times*, April 25, 2011; Associated Press, "Tallying the Spill's Cost," *The Des Moines Register*, December 30, 2010, p. 8B.

Citizen Suits

In addition to the aforementioned mechanisms, many environmental statutes allow citizen suits, in which individuals may challenge government environmental decisions, such as the granting of a permit, and generally demand both governmental and private-sector compliance with the law. *Massachusetts v. EPA*, the Clean Air Act case above, was brought by a group of states, local governments, and private organizations as a citizen suit.

Citizens suits have often been brought under the Endangered Species Act (ESA), which provides a federal program for the protection of threatened and endangered species and their habitats. Such suits may either seek greater protection for a species or argue that proposed protections exceed that which is necessary. The two cases that follow illustrate both types of concerns. In the first, more protection for the Cook Inlet beluga whale was sought; in the second, plaintiffs argued that too large an area had been designated for the protection of the Mexican spotted owl in the southeastern United States. In both cases petitioners lost. When reading the cases, pay attention to the process required of the government in listing a species as threatened or endangered and in defining its protected habitat.

LEGAL BRIEFCASE

Cook Inlet Beluga Whale v. Daley 156 F.Supp.2d 16 (D.C.D.C. 2001)

Judge James Robertson

The Cook Inlet Beluga Whale . . . is a genetically distinct, geographically isolated marine mammal with a remnant population that inhabits Cook Inlet from late April or early May until October or November. NMFS [National Marine Fisheries Service] estimates that in the mid-1980s, between 1,000 and 1,300 whales inhabited the inlet. Today, the population is estimated at between 300 and 400 whales. It is not disputed that the single most significant factor in the population decline has been Native American hunting. . . . That is why, in March 1999, the plaintiffs filed a petition to list the Cook Inlet Beluga Whale under the Endangered Species Act (ESA).

The Endangered Species Act delegates to the Secretary of Commerce the authority to determine whether fish, wildlife, or plant species should be listed as endangered or threatened. A species is "endangered" when it is in "danger of extinction throughout all or a significant part of its range," and it is "threatened" when it is "likely to become an endangered species within the foreseeable future." The Secretary's ESA determination is made on the basis of five statutorily prescribed factors, any one of which is sufficient to support a listing determination.

Within 30 days of plaintiffs' request for an ESA listing, the NMFS published formal notice that action under the ESA "may be warranted." That notice triggered a one-year status review

period. On October 19, 1999, the NMFS published a proposed rule, not under the ESA, but under the Marine Mammal Protection Act (MMPA), to list the whale as "depleted." . . . Under the MMPA, the Secretary can designate a species as "depleted" . . . if the Secretary determines that the stock is below its Optimum Sustainable Population. Once a marine mammal has been listed as "depleted," the Secretary is authorized to promulgate regulations limiting takings by Native Americans, but a listing under the MMPA does not have the regulatory, economic, and environmental fallout of a listing as "threatened" or "endangered" under the ESA.

On June 22, 2000, the NMFS determined that an ESA listing was "not warranted." It is that determination which, in plaintiffs' submission, was "arbitrary, capricious, an abuse of discretion, or otherwise not in accordance with law."

ARGUMENT

"In exercising its narrowly defined duty . . . , the Court must consider whether the agency acted within the scope of its legal authority, adequately explained its decision, based its decision on facts in the record, and considered the relevant factors." Plaintiffs argue that the agency decision in this case improperly applied the law and facts to the five-factor determination; failed to apply the best scientific and commercial data available; and improperly considered political and economic factors.

I. Statutory Factors

A decision whether or not to list a species shall be made "solely on the basis of the best scientific and commercial data available . . . after conducting a review of the status of the species and after taking into account those efforts, if any, being made by any State or foreign nation." Applying this standard, the Secretary must list a species as endangered or threatened if "any of Section 1533(a)(1)'s five factors are sufficiently implicated." Each of the five factors is considered below.

(A) The Present or Threatened Destruction, Modification, or Curtailment of the Species' Habitat or Range   The agency's conclusion that "no indication exists that the range has been, or is threatened with being modified or curtailed to an extent that appreciably diminishes the value of the habitat for both survival and recovery of the species," was not arbitrary or capricious. There is no dispute that the Cook Inlet, the whale's habitat, has changed over time in response to the increasing demand of municipal, industrial, and recreational activities, but there is no record basis for concluding that these changes have had a deleterious effect on the whale. Plaintiffs can point only to the fact that the whales have increasingly inhabited the upper inlet in recent decades. The agency concedes that this change in whale behavior might be in response to human activities, but no data suggest that the change threatens extinction. The agency is not required to conduct further testing to determine the effect of various environmental factors, such as oil drilling, on the whale population. "The 'best available data' requirement makes it clear that the Secretary has no obligation to conduct independent studies."

(B) Overutilization   All agree that Native American harvesting has been the most significant factor in the declining whale population. The agency has found "that a failure to restrict the subsistence harvest would likely cause CI beluga whales to become in danger of extinction in the foreseeable future." But the agency has also concluded that "overutilization" does not support ESA listing because it has been stopped—by designating the whale as "depleted" under the MMPA. Plaintiffs attack that conclusion as unreasonable.

If the moratorium fails to control Native American harvesting in the future, ESA listing will be warranted. That much is agreed. But plaintiffs have been unable to point to anything in the record indicating that the current whale population is unsustainable if the harvest is indeed restricted successfully. . . .

[There] is no reason to believe that the MMPA's enforcement mechanisms, which are identical to those of the ESA, will be less effective in controlling illegal takings. Plaintiffs' concerns are reasonable, and enforcement should be carefully monitored, but the record contains support for the agency's conclusion that future takings will be minimal and that the current population is sustainable.

(C) Disease or Predation   The agency concedes that both disease or predation "occur in the CI beluga population and may affect reproduction and survival," but it has concluded that these factors are not causing the stock to be threatened or endangered. Plaintiff has not shown that conclusion to be arbitrary or capricious. . . .

(D) Inadequacy of Existing Regulatory Mechanisms   We have found nothing in the record, and plaintiff has identified nothing, showing that there are inadequacies in existing regulatory mechanisms or, if there were, what the effects of such inadequacies would be. Plaintiffs argue that the MMPA is inadequate to ensure that illegal hunting does not occur . . . , but that argument simply asserts plaintiffs' policy preference for a remedy under the ESA and begs the question of whether ESA listing is required.

(E) Other Natural or Manmade Factors Affecting Its Continued Existence   Plaintiffs argue that there are many other factors—strandings, oil spills, takings through commercial fishing, effects of pollutants, ship strikes, noise, urban runoff, etc.—that put the species at risk and that it was arbitrary and capricious for the agency to determine that "the best available information . . . indicates that these activities, alone or cumulatively, have not caused the stock to be in danger of extinction and are not likely to do so in the foreseeable future." . . .

It is true that the absence of "conclusive evidence" of a real threat to a species does not justify an agency's finding that ESA listing is not warranted. But neither is listing required simply because the agency is unable to rule out factors that could contribute to a population decline. It was not arbitrary or capricious for the agency to place its principal reliance on the cessation of Native American hunts and the [study that concluded] that the Cook Inlet Beluga Whale population could sustain itself, even accounting for stochastic events.

[Plaintiffs' remaining arguments have been omitted.]

Ordered that defendant's motion for summary judgment is granted.

Questions

1. Why did the plaintiffs want the Cook Inlet Beluga Whale listed as endangered under the ESA?

2. What was the standard of review that the court applied to the agency's decision?

3. What five factors are to be considered in the listing of a species as endangered under the Endangered Species Act?

Judge Betty B. Fletcher

Litigation History

In 1993 the Mexican Spotted Owl was listed as a threatened species under the Endangered Species Act ("ESA"). The listing decision prompted a series of lawsuits alternately seeking to compel the FWS [U.S. Fish and Wildlife Service] to designate critical habitat for the owl and, following the FWS's designation of habitat, attacking that designation.

The first such lawsuit was in 1995 to compel the FWS to designate critical habitat and resulted in the FWS's issuing a final rule designating 4.6 million acres of critical owl habitat, a designation that was quickly challenged in court and then revoked in 1998. After another lawsuit was filed to compel the FWS to designate habitat, the FWS proposed a rule in 2000 to designate 13.5 million acres of critical habitat and in 2001 the agency promulgated a final rule that again designated 4.6 million acres. That rule was later struck down and . . . the FWS reopened the comment period on the rule it proposed in 2000. In 2004 the FWS designated approximately 8.6 million acres of critical habitat. It is this designation, the 2004 Final Rule, that Arizona Cattle challenges in the current action.

Arizona Cattle moved for summary judgment to set aside the 2004 Final Rule. . . . The District Court rejected Arizona Cattle's arguments. . . .

THE 2004 FINAL RULE

The FWS relied on three types of habitat management areas . . . as a starting point for the 2004 Final Rule: protected areas, restricted areas, and other forest and woodland types. Protected areas are those areas containing known owl sites, termed Protected Activity Centers ("PACs"); "steep slope" areas meeting certain forest conditions; and legally and administratively reserved lands. "PACs include a minimum of 600 acres . . . that includes the best nesting and roosting (i.e., resting) habitat in the area . . . and the most proximal and highly used foraging areas." However, PACs contain only 75% of necessary foraging areas for the owl. Restricted areas include non-steep slope areas with appropriate forest conditions that are "adjacent to or outside of protected areas." "Areas outside of PACs, including restricted areas, provide additional habitat appropriate for foraging." . . .

* * * * *

THE ESA AND THE DEFINITION OF "OCCUPIED"

The ESA defines a species' critical habitat as . . . "the specific areas within the geographical area occupied by the species, at the time it is listed. . . ."

The statute thus differentiates between "occupied" and "unoccupied" areas. . . . [We] face the preliminary issue of what it means for an area to be "occupied" under the ESA.

It is useful to unpack this inquiry into two components: uncertainty and frequency. Uncertainty is a factor when the FWS has reason to believe that owls are present in a given area, but lacks conclusive proof of their presence. Frequency is a factor when owls are shown to have only an intermittent presence in a given area. Occasionally, both factors will play a part in determining whether an area is "occupied." Because the ESA permits only one of two possible outcomes for this inquiry-occupied or unoccupied- . . . we must determine the scope of the FWS's authority to categorize as "occupied" those areas that may not fit neatly into either pigeonhole.

We have ample guidance on the "uncertainty" issue. The ESA provides that the agency must determine critical habitat using the "best scientific data available." This standard does not require that the FWS act only when it can justify its decision with absolute confidence. . . .

Turning to the "frequency" component, Arizona Cattle asserts that the word "occupied" is unambiguous and must be interpreted narrowly to mean areas that the species "resides in." In the context of the owl, they argue that such areas consist only of the 600-acre PACs. The FWS argues . . . that where a geographic area is used with such frequency that the owl is likely to be present, the agency may permissibly designate it as occupied. FWS contends that, at a minimum, this includes the owl's "home range" and may include other areas used for intermittent activities.

We cannot agree that "occupied" has an unambiguous, plain meaning as Arizona Cattle suggests. The word "occupied," standing alone, does not provide a clear standard for how frequently a species must use an area before the agency can designate it as critical habitat. Merely replacing the word "occupied" with the word "resides" does not resolve this ambiguity. . . . Viewed narrowly, an owl resides only in its nest; viewed more broadly, an owl resides in a PAC; and viewed more broadly still, an owl resides in its territory or home range. Determining whether a species uses an area with sufficient regularity that it is "occupied" is a highly contextual and fact-dependent inquiry. . . . Such factual questions are within the purview of the agency's unique expertise and are entitled to the standard deference afforded such agency determinations.

* * * * *

The FWS has authority to designate as "occupied" areas that the owl uses with sufficient regularity that it is likely to be present during any reasonable span of time. This interpretation is sensible. . . . Arizona Cattle's "reside in" interpretation would make little sense as applied to nonterritorial, mobile, or migratory animals-including the owl-for which it may be impossible to fix a determinate area in which the animal "resides." Such a narrow interpretation also would mesh poorly with the FWS's authority to act in the face of uncertainty.

* * * * *

It is possible for the FWS to go too far. Most obvious is that the agency may not determine that areas unused by owls are occupied merely because those areas are suitable for future occupancy. Such a position would ignore the ESA's distinction between occupied and unoccupied areas. . . . The fact that a member of the species is not present in an area at a given instant does not mean the area is suitable only for future occupancy if the species regularly uses the area.

Having thus framed the inquiry, we turn to the primary issue before the court: whether the FWS included unoccupied areas in its critical habitat designation.

THE FWS DID NOT DESIGNATE UNOCCUPIED AREAS AS CRITICAL HABITAT

* * * * *

. . . PACs are explicitly defined with reference to frequent owl presence, and non-PAC protected areas and restricted areas are "devised around" and "adjacent to" PACs. More to the point, we note significant record support for owl occupancy of these areas in the form of studies correlating the habitat characteristics of protected and restricted areas with owl presence.

The agency did not stop there. [Its] analysis proceeds, unit by unit, through the addition of areas to the critical habitat proposal on the basis of information about known owl locations. . . .

A point of recurring significance to our analysis is that PACs reflect only known owl sites. Although the 2004 Final Rule identified 1,176 PACs, owl populations have been estimated to be significantly greater than the maximum 2,352 owls reflected by this number of PACs. . . . Efforts by the FWS to identify other evidence of owl presence when it is unable to fix the location of a PAC with certainty are, therefore, highly significant.

Even more significant is the fact that the FWS excluded areas with evidence of few or no owls. . . . Finally, we note that . . . the FWS excluded the vast majority of critical habitat units that contained no PACs and refined the boundaries of the critical habitat units to exclude large areas that are distant from PACs.

The FWS's process for designating critical habitat gives us a strong foundation for our conclusion that the agency did not arbitrarily and capriciously treat areas in which owls are not found as "occupied." . . .

THE AMOUNT OF LAND DESIGNATED IS NOT DISPROPORTIONATE TO THE NUMBER OF OWLS

Arizona Cattle also argues that even using the owl's substantially larger home range as the appropriate measure for the territory occupied by the owl, the FWS has designated a grossly disproportionate amount of land compared to the amount the owl occupies. It ties this argument to a seemingly simple calculation: multiplying the 1,176 PACs by the maximum estimated home range size of the owl of 3,831 acres, the resultant area is only approximately 4.5 million acres, in contrast to the 8.6 million acres designated. This calculation, however, rests on a faulty assumption that the PACs represent all extant owls. We have already explained that PACs reflect only known owl sites and that there is record support for the existence of substantially greater numbers of owls and undiscovered sites. . . . Arizona Cattle's argument does not overcome the strong evidence that the FWS was focused on designating areas occupied by owls.

* * * * *

We find no fault with the FWS's designation of habitat for the Mexican Spotted Owl. . . .

Affirmed.

Questions

1. Identify the statutory language the court had to interpret to resolve this case.
2. How did the FWS select the areas included in its designation of 8.6 million acres as critical habitat for the owl?
3. What contrary arguments were made by Arizona Cattle?
4. What was the standard of review that the court applied to the agency's decision?
5. How many years elapsed between the first lawsuit over the designation of the Mexican spotted owl and the decision in this case?

Endangered Species Act

The combination of the *Cook Inlet Beluga Whale* and *Arizona Cattle Grower's Ass'n* decisions illustrate how complicated and time-consuming the legal process is for the protection of species. It is also costly—for citizen groups on both sides, for the government (and therefore all of us as taxpayers), for those whose lives and livelihoods may be substantially altered by the protections extended, and also for the species and our world in the event protections are not extended, if needed, or are not effective.

Consider what may be on the horizon. The International Union for the Conservation of Nature has 4,224 species listed as critically endangered.[66] The U.N. Intergovernmental Panel on Climate Change indicates temperature increases this century could put 20 to 30 percent of the world's plants and animals in danger of extinction.[67] From 2008 through 2011, environmental groups requested more than 1,230 species be listed under the ESA as threatened or endangered, compared with prior annual averages of about 20 species. This forced the FWS, in its 2012 budget request, to point out that it had neither the personnel nor budget to meet the time constraints for final listing decisions required by law.[68] These facts set the context for a 2011 settlement with two environmental groups in which the FWS pledged to make listing determinations on all backlogged species by 2018. When the backlog is addressed, then 550 other potential candidates will be evaluated. The ultimate result may be that the endangered list could increase by as much as 60 percent.[69] From 2010 to present, 198 species have been newly listed as either threatened or endangered, compared to a total of 27 in the prior four years.[70] [For photos of some endangered or threatened species in the United States, see **www.nytimes.com/interactive/2013/03/06 /science/earth/endangered-species.html?ref=earth#index**]

Part Four—Common Law Remedies

Most of the remedies discussed in Part Three are based on *statutory* claims. But long before federal or state governments became actively involved in environmental issues, courts were grappling with the problem and fashioning *common law* remedies. As early as the 1500s, city officials were ordered by a court to keep the streets clean of dung deposited by swine allowed to run loose; the air was said to be "corrupted and infected" by this practice. Legal arguments have typically revolved around the extent of a person's right to use and enjoy private property if such usage causes harm to a neighbor's property or the use of public property. More recently, tort actions of negligence and strict liability have been pursued by injured individuals. Successful plaintiffs may recover monetary damages for the harm suffered or obtain an injunction to prevent similar conduct (and therefore harm) by the defendant in the future, or both.

Nuisance A private nuisance is a substantial and unreasonable invasion of the private use and enjoyment of one's land; a public nuisance is an unreasonable interference with a right common to the public. Harmful conduct may be both a public and private nuisance simultaneously; the case law distinctions between the two are often blurred. A classic nuisance dispute is the 1970 New York case *Boomer v. Atlantic Cement Co.*[71] Neighboring landowners sued the operator of a cement plant for injury to their properties from the plant's dirt, smoke, and vibration. The court recognized the wrong done and ordered the operator to pay damages.

In the last decade, a number of nuisance cases were initiated in federal courts against emitters of significant greenhouse gases. In one, *Connecticut v. American Electric Power Co.,* several states, New York City, and three land trusts sued operators of coal-fired power plants claiming their carbon emissions were a nuisance under federal common law and seeking an order requiring the utilities to cap and then reduce their carbon dioxide emissions. A unanimous Supreme Court ruled against the plaintiffs in 2011 finding that the Clean Air Act and EPA rule making authority displaced any common law right to sue to curb carbon dioxide emissions from power plants.[72] The decision affirms the power of the EPA under the CAA and encourages a single nationwide standard for addressing carbon emissions rather than multiple court-imposed remedies. According to some commentators, it may also foreclose the use of the common law cause of action of nuisance for many other environmental harms under federal law. Some further believe it may prevent success under state law based on arguments that, where federal law exists, federal environmental laws preempt state law causes of action.

Trespass   A trespass occurs and liability is imposed on any intentional invasion of an individual's right to the exclusive use of his or her own property. For example, in a 1959 Oregon case, *Martin v. Reynolds Metals Co.,* the plaintiffs successfully sued in trespass for damages caused by the operation of an aluminum reduction plant, which caused certain fluoride compounds in the form of gases and particulates to become airborne, settle on the plaintiffs' land, contaminate their forage and water, and poison their cattle.[73]

Negligence   The elements of negligence have been previously discussed in Chapter 7. In 2010, the Florida Supreme Court held that fishermen were entitled to recover for the damages they suffered when defendants' wastewater storage pond spilled into the Tampa Bay, killing fish, crabs, and other marine life. Defendants' negligence "interfered with the special interest of the commercial fishermen to use the public waters to earn their livelihood."[74] Particularly troubling causation issues can and have arisen in negligence cases based on environmental pollution, such as when a plaintiff claims injury from a toxic substance manufactured or otherwise supplied by a defendant. Recall the discussion of causation at the start of this chapter, as well as the factual basis for the movies *Erin Brockovich* and *A Class Action.* Think of the factual difficulties of proving that a particular substance causes certain medical conditions, that it was the cause of a particular individual's injury, and that the substance is traceable back to a particular defendant. An organic compound, MTBE, is used around the world as an additive to gas. However, at least half of U.S. states have banned its use, and the EPA has classified it as a possible human carcinogen. Many lawsuits have been brought against oil companies by municipalities and other governmental bodies to recoup the costs of cleaning up water supplies contaminated with MTBE. New Hampshire brought such a suit against 16 oil companies, all of which except ExxonMobil settled with the state for a total of $136 million. In April 2013, a jury returned a verdict for the state finding Exxon negligent for putting the additive in its gas and without warning the state of its risks. Exxon is appealing.[75]

Strict Liability   Certain activities, such as the use of toxic chemicals, may be seen as so abnormally dangerous as to give rise to a strict liability claim (previously discussed in Chapter 7). In an environmental law context, strict liability has been considered where crop dusting contaminated adjacent properties,[76] toxic chemicals were improperly disposed of,[77] and oil contaminated a nearby water well.[78]

Several of the above claims can sometimes be triggered by the same set of facts. In a 2007 West Virginia case, a jury found DuPont negligent in its use of a 112-acre site that for 90 years had been a zinc-smelting plant. The jury also found DuPont had created both a public and a private nuisance, had committed trespass, and should be held strictly liable for exposing local residents to various toxic substances. Residents and property owners had sued, claiming that the company had deliberately dumped toxic heavy metals, particularly zinc, on the site. The medical problems caused by such toxins include cancer, damage to internal organs, and decreased fertility.[79]

Part Five—Global Climate Change

Global climate change has been described as "among the handful of most important public policy issues of our time,[80] "one of the greatest challenges the world faces,"[81] and the "greatest market failure the world has ever seen."[82] At issue is the projected overall increase in surface and ocean temperatures around the globe, substantially caused by the release into the atmosphere of manmade carbon dioxide and other greenhouse gases, largely through the burning of fossil fuels, especially in gasoline engines and coal-fired plants.

Both the politics and the science of global climate change have been controversial—a particularly potent and poignant example of the issues of coincidence, correlation, and causation discussed at the beginning of Part Two. The fifth assessment report of the Intergovernmental Panel on Climate Change (IPCC) will be complete in October 2014. The first part, on the physical science basis for climate change, states that it is "extremely likely that human influence has been the dominant cause of the observed warming since the mid-20th century" and that human influence "has been detected in warming of the atmosphere and the ocean, in changes in the global water cycle, in reductions in snow and ice, in global mean sea level rise, and in changes in some climate extremes." In the report's terminology, "extremely likely" refers to a probability of 95 to 100 percent.[83] Also apparent from the report is that, from 1998 to 2012, global average surface temperatures have not appreciably risen (despite significant global GHG emissions). Some commentators have recommended a hiatus in the implementation of emission reduction policies while we "see if the non-warming trend continues."[84] Others have pointed out that the "current pause is consistent with numerous prior pauses" and that "it is a mistake to interpret a landing as the end of the climb."[85] [The first part of the IPCC Fifth Assessment Report can be found at **www.ipcc. ch/report/ar5/wg1/#.Um0UDBCJ0nc;** all prior assessment reports, and the full Fifth Assessment Report when complete, can be found at **www.ipcc.ch/publications_and_data/ publications_and_data_reports.shtml#.Um0UOBCJ0nc**]

Scholar and activist Bill McKibben has argued that we no longer live on the same planet on which our parents grew up, and that climate change has passed the tipping point.

"The planet we inhabit has a finite number of huge physical features. Virtually all of them seem to be changing rapidly."[86] Consider the following:

- On September 16, 2012, the Arctic ice sheet shrank to a record low—half of what it was in 1979. The sheet is getting thinner as well—a quarter of what it was in 1979.[87] Gla-

> On September 16, 2012, the Arctic ice sheet shrank to half of what it was in 1979.

ciers in the Alps, the Andes, the Rocky Mountains, and New Zealand are melting. The ice on the Tibetan plateau and its surrounding mountains, including the Himalayas, is the source of 10 major rivers, and 1.5 billion people live in the basins of those rivers. Less researched than the Earth's poles, in 2009, scientists in China, the United States, and Germany began a long-term program called the Third Pole Environment to study the area. Its initial findings are that glaciers in the eastern Himalayas and the eastern Tibetan plateau are retreating fast.[88] [For an award-winning 2012 Sundance Film Festival documentary recording receding glaciers throughout the world using time-lapse photography, see **www.chasingice.com**]

- "The oceans, which cover three-fourths of the Earth's surface, are distinctly more acid and their level is rising; they are also warmer, which means the greatest storms on our planet, hurricanes and cyclones, have become more powerful."[89] Acidification of the oceans weakens shells, which means fewer shelled organisms. It may also endanger such commercially important species as marlin, mackerel, and tuna.[90] The lowest country in the world, the island nation of the Maldives in the Indian Ocean, is creating a reserve fund to allow the population to resettle in Sri Lanka, India, or Australia in the event they lose their homelands to the sea.[91] In early 2012, the island states of Palau and Grenada requested that the UN General Assembly seek an advisory opinion from the International Court of Justice "on the responsibilities of States under international law to ensure that activities carried out under their jurisdiction or control that emit greenhouse gases do not damage other States."[92]

- Deliberate burning of forests in the Amazon and Indonesia reduces the world's carbon sink capacity, as well as releasing previously captured carbon into the atmosphere. Deforestation in Indonesia is substantially related to its production of palm oil for export—to be used as biodiesel fuel in European vehicles. Forests are natural carbon sinks, but some may be near their carbon saturation point. It may take a binding agreement on forest management for European forests to continue offsetting carbon emissions from other sources. Better forest management may also be necessary to offset the impact worldwide from such natural, but increasing, devastation from beetles (western U.S. and British Columbia), drought (Colorado's aspens and the Amazon), heat (South Africa's euphorbia trees, Algeria's cedars, and Australia's eucalyptus), and fires (Siberia and Southwest United States).[93]

The Kyoto Protocol

In 1997 the governments of the world, realizing that global action would be required to have any significant impact on overall emissions, adopted the Kyoto Protocol. Specifically, the protocol called for a 5 percent reduction from 1990 levels of greenhouse gas emissions to be achieved by 2012. The protocol acknowledged that developed countries were principally responsible for the GHG levels at that time. These countries agreed to legally binding emission reductions; developing countries did not take on binding reductions and were allowed to grow consistent with their development needs. It became binding when ratified by 180 countries, on Russia's ratification in late 2004. The United States never ratified the protocol.

In achieving its fundamental objective, the protocol has been a complete failure. In 1990, approximately 31 million metric tons of carbon dioxide equivalents were emitted globally; by 2010 that number had risen to roughly 50 million metric tons.[94] China is now the largest GHG emitter, and the United States is the only developed country in the list of top four emitters. India and Russia are in third and fourth place, respectively. The EU, however, has met and surpassed its goal under the protocol and is on track to reach its further goal of a 20 percent reduction over 1990 by 2020. In contrast, emissions from the United States were 8 percent higher in 2012 than in 1990. The Obama administration set a national goal, independently of Kyoto, to reduce emissions 17 percent over 2005 by 2020. Achieving that goal would amount to an approximately 3.4 percent reduction over our 1990 emissions.[95]

The Kyoto Protocol was recognized from the start as only the first step in the development of a global emission reduction program to stabilize greenhouse gases. Formal discussions for a post-Kyoto international framework began in Bali, Indonesia, in December 2007. They were expected to last through 2009. Despite annual climate conferences under the auspices of the UN, as of this writing there is still no post-Kyoto agreement. Technically, the Kyoto Protocol was extended to 2017 by the EU's agreement to undertake a second round of emissions reductions, but it in fact agreed to no more than it is already legally required to do under EU law. In return, 194 countries have agreed to agree by 2015 on how to reduce GHG through commitments from developing, as well as developed, countries. The stated goal of Kyoto to keep climate change below a 3.6 degrees Fahrenheit increase seems further off than ever. On the table for the new agreement will likely be consideration of "loss and damage" from climate change, as well as mitigation and adaptation. The new agreement is to take effect in 2020.[96]

Giving the last word to science, we go back to the first part of the IPCC's Fifth Assessment Report, the part that addresses the physical science basis for climate change. In the September 2013 report, for the first time, the participating scientists endorsed an upper limit of carbon dioxide that can be produced if the 3.6 degree increase is to be avoided: no more than 1 trillion metric tons. According to one of the report's authors, "Just over a half-trillion tons have already been burned since the beginning of the Industrial Revolution, and at the rate energy consumption is growing, the trillionth ton will be burned sometime around 2040."[97] The full report will be out by October 2014, including its recommendations for mitigation. Perhaps politics will take notice.

PRACTICING ETHICS   Voluntarily Reduce Greenhouse Gas Emissions?

Although the United States has not been a party to the Kyoto Protocol, many U.S. multinationals will be subject to its provisions because they do business in ratifying countries. Other U.S. businesses have chosen to voluntarily adopt emission reduction strategies.

Question

Imagine that you are a vice president of a corporation that burns significant fossil fuels in the production process but operates solely in the United States. What stance would you take on global climate change? Why?

Internet Exercise

One indication of how much global climate change has become a grassroots issue in the United States is the entry of carbon footprint considerations into everyday conversation. A carbon footprint is a measurement of how much carbon dioxide is emitted into the atmosphere as the result of a particular product, activity, or lifestyle. It is a way to measure the carbon "cost" of a particular activity or the carbon "savings" of changing that activity.

What's your carbon footprint? Find out from **www.bp.com/en/global/corporate /sustainability/bp-energy-lab/calculator.html.** Compare that with your ecological footprint—that is, how many Earths we would have to have if everyone lived as you do. Go to **www.earthday.org/footprint-calculator.**

Chapter Questions

1. Economist B. Peter Pashigian:

   It is widely thought that environmental controls are guided by the public-spirited ideal of correcting for "negative externalities"—the pollution costs that spill over from private operations. This view is not wrong by any means. But it is suspiciously incomplete. After all, there are numerous studies of regulatory programs in other fields that show how private interests have used public powers for their own enrichment.[98]

   In addition to correcting negative externalities, what forces might be influencing federal pollution control?

2. How might the government's ever-increasing environmental regulations, along with the public's call for a new environmental consciousness, favor big business interests over those of small business owners?

3. "The Aral Sea is going, gone. Once the world's fourth largest inland body of water, the Aral has shriveled to half its former area and a third of its volume. As for the region's drinking water, even the local vodka has a salty tang."[99] The Aral is the victim of the former Soviet Union's central planners, who decreed that the area would be the nation's main source of cotton. To achieve that goal, intense irrigation was required, with the result that only a trickle of fresh water was left to feed the Aral. Refilling the Aral would require tremendous dislocations in the agriculture of the vast region. If you were a member of a commission charged with developing a plan for the future of the Aral Sea, what issues would you cover?

4. Professor and business ethics scholar Norman Bowie:

   Environmentalists frequently argue that business has special obligations to protect the environment. Although I agree with the environmentalists on this point, I do not agree with them as to where the obligations lie. Business does not have an obligation to protect the environment over and above what is required by law; however, business does have a moral obligation to avoid intervening in the political arena in order to defeat or weaken environmental legislation.[100]

   a. Explain Professor Bowie's reasoning.
   b. Do you agree with him? Explain.

5. Mexico is quickly running short of water:

   85 percent of Mexico's economic growth and 75 percent of its 100 million people are in the north, and the water is far to the south. . . . [P]oliticians facing elections are reluctant to ask voters to spend more on any utility, let alone water. Agriculture uses 80 percent of the

water and pays nothing, although it only ranks seventh in contribution to the gross national product. . . . Less than half of the capital's wastewater is treated. The rest sinks into underground lakes or flows toward the Gulf of Mexico, turning rivers into sewers. . . . Well over half of irrigation water is lost to evaporation or seepage.[101]

Brainstorm as many possible contributions to the solution of Mexico's water problem as you can.

6. Because of the spread of the West Nile virus in the state of New York, an insecticide spraying program was implemented to control the mosquitoes responsible for spreading the virus. Several groups sued, arguing that the spray was a pollutant that damaged waters in violation of the Clean Water Act. What criteria should the court use to decide the outcome? See *No Spray Coalition, Inc. v. The City of New York,* 2000 U.S. Dist. LEXIS 13919, 51 ERC (BNA) 1508 (S.D.N.Y. 2000).

7. Ott Chemical Co. polluted the ground at its Michigan plant. CPC International created a wholly owned subsidiary to buy Ott, which was accomplished in 1965. CPC retained the original Ott managers. Pollution continued through 1972 when CPC sold Ott. In 1981 the U.S. EPA began a cleanup of the site. To recover some of the tens of millions in cleanup costs, the EPA sued CPC (called Bestfoods) among other potentially responsible parties. The Superfund law places responsibility on anyone who "owned or operated" a property when pollution was deposited. The district court held that CPC was liable because of its active participation in Ott's business and its control of Ott's decisions in that it selected the Ott board of directors and placed some CPC managers as executives at Ott.

   a. Do you think CPC should be held liable? Why or why not?

   b. What test would you employ to determine whether a parent corporation should be liable for a subsidiary's pollution? See *United States v. Bestfoods,* 524 U.S. 51 (1998).

8. William Tucker:

   [Environmentalism is] essentially aristocratic in its roots and derives from the land and nature-based ethic that has been championed by upper classes throughout history. Large landowners and titled aristocracies . . . have usually held a set of ideals that stresses "stewardship" and the husbanding of existing resources over exploration and discovery. This view favors handicrafts over mass production and the inheritance ethic over the business ethic.[102]

   Tucker went on to argue that environmentalism favors the economic and social interests of the well-off. He said people of the upper middle class see their future in universities and the government bureaucracy, with little economic stake in industrial expansion. Indeed, such expansion might threaten their suburban property values. Comment.

9. Americans' commitment to the car obviously raises serious environmental problems. The vast spaces required to park those cars are themselves a significant environmental hazard. Explain some of the environmental problems created or encouraged by parking lots.

10. The Endangered Species Act provides that all federal agency actions are to be designed so that they do not jeopardize endangered or threatened species. The act had been interpreted to reach federal agency work or funding in foreign countries, but

the federal government changed that interpretation in 1986 to limit the act's reach to the United States and the high seas. A group labeled Defenders of Wildlife filed suit, seeking to reinstate the original interpretation. The case reached the U.S. Supreme Court, where Justice Scalia wrote that Defenders of Wildlife would have to submit evidence showing that at least one of its members would be "directly" affected by the interpretation. In response, one member of Defenders of Wildlife wrote that she had visited Egypt and observed the endangered Nile crocodile and hoped to return to do so again but feared that U.S. aid for the Aswan High Dam would harm the crocodiles.

Do you think Defenders of Wildlife should have been permitted to sue? Why or why not? See *Lujan v. Defenders of Wildlife,* 112 S.Ct. 2130 (1992).

11. Economist Robert Crandall:

> [O]ur best chances for regulatory reform in certain environmental areas, particularly in air pollution policy, come from the states. Probably, responsibility for environmental regulation belongs with the states anyway, and most of it ought to be returned there.[103]

   a. What reasoning supports Crandall's notion that responsibility for environmental regulation belongs with the states?
   b. How might one reason to the contrary?
   c. If the power were yours, would environmental regulation rest primarily at the state, federal, or international level? Explain.

12. The United States seems to be quite enamored with sport utility vehicles (SUVs), in spite of the fact that their gas mileage is considerably poorer than most sedans. To graphically bring home the environmental irresponsibility of SUV owners, two men in the San Francisco Bay area dreamed up a scheme to address what they perceived to be a market failure. Uninvited, they stuck homemade bumper stickers on hundreds of SUVs. The bumper stickers read, "I'm changing the environment! Ask me how!"[104]
   a. What effect do you think these self-appointed environmental police sought from their actions?
   b. What effect do you think they actually had?

13. Airplanes are a significant contributor to greenhouse gases. Comment on the following proposal: Each person receives an annual allowance for flights, fuel, gas, and electricity. If a person's use exceeds the allowance, he will have to purchase "carbon points" from someone under their limit.[105]

Notes

1. "Unspontaneous Combustion," *The Economist,* June 29, 2013, p. 39; "Logging the Good News," *The Economist,* May 25, 2013, p. 40; "REDDY at Last," *The Economist,* December 8, 2012, p. 43.
2. "Gulf of Mexico Oil Spill (2010)," *The New York Times,* updated April 25, 2011; Henry Fountain, "Gulf Spill Sampling Questioned," *The New York Times,* August 19, 2013.
3. Adam Nossiter, "Far From Gulf, a Spill Scourge 5 Decades Old," *The New York Times,* June 16, 2010; "A Desperate Need for Reform," *The Economist,* October 20, 2012.
4. Edward Wong, "Life in a Toxic Country," *The New York Times,* August 3, 2013; Chris Buckley, "Silver Lining in China's Smog as It Puts Focus on Emissions," *The New York Times,* August 31,

2013; "Something in the Air?" *The Economist,* January 19, 2013, p. 47; Edward Wong, "On Scale of 0 to 500, Beijing's Air Quality Tops 'Crazy Bad' at 755," *The New York Times,* January 12, 2013.

5. Martin Fackler, "Errors Cast Doubt on Japan's Cleanup of Nuclear Accident Site," *The New York Times,* September 3, 2013. See also, "Power Struggle," *The Economist,* September 21, 2013, p. 45.

6. Ibid.

7. Hiroko Tabuchi, "In Japan, a Painfully Slow Sweep," *The New York Times,* January 7, 2013.

8. **www.who.int/features/factfiles/water/water_facts/en/index2.html** and **www.who.int/features/factfiles/water/water_facts/en/index7.html**.

9. Ariel Zirulnick, "The Extinction Risk for Birds, Mammals, and Amphibians," *The Christian Science Monitor,* October 27, 2010.

10. Amy Littlefield, "EPA Looks at Effects of Waste Plants on Minorities, Poor," *Los Angeles Times,* July 27, 2009.

11. Adam Nossiter, "Far From Gulf, a Spill Scourge 5 Decades Old." *The New York Times,* June 16, 2010.

12. Wilfred Beckerman, cited in Robert Solomon, *The New World of Business* (Lanham, MD: Rowman & Littlefield, 1994), p. 319.

13. "The Science of Sharing," *NYU Law Magazine* 2012, p. 106.

14. Ibid.

15. Susan Lee, "How Much Is the Right to Pollute Worth?" *The Wall Street Journal,* August 1, 2001, p. A15.

16. Mark Golden, "Dirty Dealings," *The Wall Street Journal,* September 13, 1999, p. R13.

17. **www.epa.gov/airmarkt/progress/arp07.html**.

18. Peter Shattuck and Daniel L. Sosland, "Northeast Faces Stark Choice on Climate Pollution," *The New York Times,* January 24, 2013.

19. "Gold and Green," *The Economist,* March 16, 2013, p. 29.

20. Jeff Gersh, "Seeds of Change," *Amicus Journal* 21, no. 2 (Summer 1999), p. 36.

21. Eduardo Porter, "In Energy Taxes, Tools to Help Tackle Climate Change," *The New York Times,* January 29, 2013.

22. **www.cars.gov/files/official-information/CARS-Report-to-Congress.pdf**.

23. Diane Cardwell, "U.S. Revives Aid Program for Clean Energy," *The New York Times,* September 19, 2013.

24. Jon J. Fialka and Jeffrey Ball, "Companies Get Ready for Greenhouse-Gas Limits," *The Wall Street Journal,* October 26, 2004, p. A2.

25. "Ray Anderson," *The Economist,* September 10, 2011, p. 99; The Ray C. Anderson Foundation [**www.raycandersonfoundation.org/bio-ray-anderson**].

26. Bill Leonard, "Someday We'll Regret Damage to Our Planet," *The Des Moines Register,* September 20, 2004, p. 7A.

27. Katy Daigle, "Putting a Price on Clean Environment," *The Des Moines Register,* June 18, 2012, p. 6A.

28. This was the essence of plaintiffs' nuisance suit against various large greenhouse emitters in *Comer v. Murphy Oil USA,* 2007 WL 6942285 (D.C. Miss. 2009). The district court dismissed; a three-judge panel for the 5th Circuit reversed. When defendants sought an en banc rehearing,

a number of the circuit judges recused themselves but the remaining quorum granted the request and vacated the panel decision. Another judge then recused herself, leaving the court without a quorum. It determined the rehearing could not proceed, nor could the panel decision be reinstated. Thus, the district court's dismissal is the final decision.

29. John M. Broder and Peter Baker, "Obama's Order Is Likely to Tighten Auto Standards," *The New York Times,* January 26, 2009; Editorial, "Cleaner Cars," *The New York Times,* October 5, 2010.

30. Ellen Goodman, "Can Tourists Love a Place to Death?" *The Des Moines Register,* March 31, 2001, p. 7A.

31. *Utility Air Regulatory Group v. E.P.A.,* __ S.Ct. __ (June 23, 2014), an appeal of *Coalition for Responsible Regulation, Inc. v. EPA,* 684 F.3d 102, 121 (DC Cir. 2012).

32. Coral Davenport, "Obama to Take Action to Slash Coal Pollution," *The New York Times,* June 1, 2014.

33. David Erickson and Mark Anstoetter, "ALA Report Says U.S. Air Quality Improving," *Association of Corporate Counsel,* May 4, 2012 [**www.lexology.com**].

34. *EPA v. EME Homer City Generation,* 134 S.Ct. 1584 (2014).

35. "The Mixed Fortunes of a Fuel," note 32.

36. Janet Larsen, "Falling Gasoline Use Means United States Can Just Say No to New Pipelines and Food-to-Fuel," *Earth Policy Institute,* March 28, 2013 [**www.earth-policy.org/data_highlights/2013/highlights38**].

37. Bill Vlasic, "U.S. Sets Higher Fuel Efficiency Standards," *The New York Times,* August 28, 2012; Juliet Eilperin, "EPA Issues New Fuel-Efficiency Standard," *The Washington Post,* August 28, 2012.

38. Elisabeth Rosenthal, "Life After Oil and Gas," *The New York Times,* March 23, 2013; Zack Colman, "U.S. Fuel-Efficiency Standards on Trucks Stricter Than Europe, Canada," *The Hill's Energy & Environment Blog,* September 20, 2012 [**http://thehill.com/blogs/e2-wire/e2-wire/250627-reports-us-gets-good-marks-on-fuel-efficiency-policy**].

39. Campbell Robertson, "Gulf of Mexico Has Long Been Dumping Site," *The New York Times,* July 29, 2010.

40. Lindsey Hoshaw, "Afloat in the Ocean, Expanding Islands of Trash," *The New York Times,* November 9, 2009.

41. Robertson, "Gulf of Mexico Has Long Been Dumping Site."

42. David Erickson and Mark Anstoetter, "EPA Rates U.S. Coastal Waters as 'Fair,'" *Association of Corporate Counsel,* May 4, 2012 [**www.lexology.com**].

43. "Blooming Horrible," *The Economist,* June 23, 2012, p. 36; Robertson, "Gulf of Mexico Has Long Been Dumping Site."

44. 547 U.S. 715 (2006).

45. Charles Duhigg and Janet Roberts, "Rulings Restrict Clean Water Act, Foiling E.P.A.," *The New York Times,* February 28, 2010.

46. Juliet Eilperin, "EPA Proposes Stricter Controls on Water Pollution," *The Washington Post,* April 27, 2011.

47. Ian Urbina, "Think Those Chemicals Have Been Tested?" *The New York Times,* April 13, 2013.

48. **www.niehs.nih.gov/health/materials/formaldehyde_508.pdf** and **www.epa.gov/iris/subst/0419.htm**.

49. Lyndsey Layton, "Use of Potentially Harmful Chemicals Kept Secret under Law," *The Washington Post,* January 4, 2010, p. A01.

50. Ibid.

51. See, for example, *Safe Food and Fertilizer v. EPA,* 350 F.3d 1263 (D.C. Cir. 2003).

52. **www.epa.gov/epawaste/hazard/recycling/regulations.htm**.

53. Edward Humes, "Grappling with a Garbage Glut," *The Wall Street Journal,* April 14–15, 2012, p. C3.

54. Stephanie Strom, "Companies Pick Up Used Packaging, and Recycling's Cost," *The New York Times,* March 23, 2012.

55. **http://waste.supportportal.com/link/portal/23002/23023/Article/19159/Is-recycling-worth-while**.

56. Stephanie Strom, "Companies Pick Up Used Packaging, and Recycling's Cost."

57. Steven Kurutz, "Not Buying It," *The New York Times,* June 21, 2007.

58. Anthony DePalma, "Love Canal Declared Clean, Ending Toxic Horror," *The New York Times,* March 18, 2004, p. A1.

59. David Erickson and James Neet, "CERCLA: GAO Report Says Remediation Funds Insufficient," *Association of Corporate Counsel,* July 2, 2010 [**www.lexology.com**].

60. **www.epa.gov/superfund/sites/npl/index.htm**.

61. "From Bombs to $800 Handbags," *The Economist,* March 19, 2011, p. 40.

62. 132 S.Ct. 1367 (2012).

63. May Wall and John Fehrenbach, "Scotts Miracle-Gro to Pay $10 Million in Criminal Fines and Civil Penalties, and Spend $2.5 Million on Environmental Projects, for Violations of Federal Pesticide Laws," *Association of Corporate Counsel,* September 10, 2012.

64. *U.S. v. Mark Glover and Discount Computers, Inc.,* Case No. 12-CR-20282 (E.D. Mich. 2012).

65. Michael M. O'Hear, "Bark and Bite: The Environmental Sentencing Guidelines after Booker," 2009 *Utah L. Rev.* 1151.

66. "Hang On," *The Economist,* September 14, 2013, p. 13.

67. Moises Velasquez-Manoff, "Ecosystems Respond Well to Restoration," *The Christian Science Monitor,* July 13, 2009.

68. Todd Woody, "Wildlife at Risk Face Long Line at U.S. Agency," *The New York Times,* April 20, 2011.

69. Michael Wines, "Endangered or Not, but at Least No Longer Waiting," *The New York Times,* March 6, 2013.

70. **http://ecos.fws.gov/tess_public/pub/speciesCountByYear.jsp**.

71. 257 N.E.2d 870 (N.Y. 1970).

72. *American Electric Power Co., Inc. v. Connecticut,* 131 S.Ct. 2527 (2011).

73. 342 P.2d 790 (Or. 1959).

74. *Curd v. Mosaic Fertilizer LLC,* 39 So.3d 1216 (Fla. 2010).

75. Julian Harrell, "Is Gasoline a Defective Product?" *Association of Corporate Counsel,* April 23, 2013 [**www.lexology.com**]; **http://doj.nh.gov/media-center/press-releases/2013/20130410-exxon-mtbe.htm**.

76. *Valicopters, Inc.,* 567 P.2d 218 (Wash. 1977).

77. *State Dep't of Envtl. Prot. v. Ventron,* 468 A.2d 150 (N.J. 1983).

78. *Branch v. W. Petroleum, Inc.,* 657 P.2d 267 (Utah 1982).

79. Associated Press, "DuPont Found Negligent in Waste-Site Lawsuit," *The Wall Street Journal,* October 3, 2007.

80. David Markell and J. B. Ruhl, "An Empirical Survey of Climate Change Litigation in the United States," 40 *Environmental Law Rptr.* 10644 (2010).

81. Intergovernmental Panel on Climate Change, "Summary for Policymakers of the Synthesis Report of the ICC Fourth Assessment Report" (2007), p. 1 [**www.ipcc.ch/publications_and_data/ publications_and_data_reports.shtml**].

82. "Carbon Taxes Cut Debt, Cool Planet," *Bloomberg,* August 14, 2012 [**www.bloomberg.com/ news/print/2012-08-14/carbon-taxes-cut-debt-cool-planet.html**].

83. Summary for Policymakers, Climate Change 2013: The Physical Science Basis, IPCC Fifth Assessment Report, September 2013 [**www.ipcc.ch/report/ar5/wg1/#.Um0UDBCJ0nc**].

84. "Climate of Uncertainty," *The Wall Street Journal,* October 1, 2013.

85. Richard A. Muller, "A Pause, Not an End, to Warming," *The New York Times,* September 25, 2013.

86. Bill McKibben, *eaarth* (New York: Henry Holt, 2010), p. 45.

87. "Tequila Sunset," *The Economist,* February 9, 2013, p. 76.

88. "Pole-land," *The Economist,* May 11, 2013, p. 84.

89. McKibben, *eaarth,* p. 45.

90. "A Look Into the Ocean's Future," *The New York Times,* July 15, 2011.

91. Randeep Ramesh, "Paradise Almost Lost: Maldives Seek to Buy a New Homeland," *The Guardian,* November 10, 2008.

92. Department of Public Information, "Press Conference on Request for International Court of Justice Advisory Opinion on Climate Change," United Nations, February 3, 2012 [**www.un.org/ News/briefings/docs/2012/120203_ICJ.doc.htm**].

93. Mark Kinver, "European Forests Near 'Carbon Saturation Point'," *BBC News,* August 18, 2013; Justin Gillis, "With Deaths of Forests, a Loss of Key Climate Protectors," *The New York Times,* October 1, 2011.

94. **www.epa.gov/climatechange/science/indicators/ghg/global-ghg-emissions.html**; UN Environment Programme, The Emissions Gap Report, November 2012, p. 1 [**www.unep.org/ pdf/2012gapreport.pdf**].

95. Russell Gold, "Rise in U.S. Gas Production Fuels Unexpected Plunge in Emissions," *The Wall Street Journal,* April 18, 2013; EPA, "Inventory of U.S. Greenhouse Gas Emissions and Sinks: 1990–2011—Executive Summary," April 2013, p. ES-4 [**www.epa.gov/climatechange/gh-gemissions/usinventoryreport.html**].

96. "What Doha Did," *The Economist,* December 15, 2012; "A Deal in Durban," *The Economist,* December 17, 2011.

97. Justin Gillis, "U.N. Climate Panel Endorses Ceiling on Global Emissions," *The New York Times,* September 27, 2013.

98. B. Peter Pashigian, "How Large and Small Plants Fare under Environmental Regulation," *Regulation,* March–April 1983, p. 19.

99. Hugh Pope, "Uzbeks Manage to Endure Amid Ruins of the Aral Sea," *The Wall Street Journal,* February 5, 1998, p. A18.

100. Norman Bowie and Kenneth Goodpaster, "Corporate Conscience, Money and Motorcars," *Business Ethics Report, Highlights of Bentley College's Eighth National Conference on Business Ethics* (Ed. Peter Kent 1989), pp. 4, 6.

101. "Profligate Past, Poor Planning Created Mexican Water Crisis," *Associated Press,* August 22, 2002.

102. "Tucker Contra Sierra," *Regulation,* March–April 1983, pp. 48–49.

103. Robert Crandall, "The Environment," in "Regulation—The First Year," *Regulation,* January–February 1982, pp. 19, 29, 31.

104. "'Mad Taggers' Leave Their Mark on SUV Culture," *Waterloo/Cedar Falls Courier,* December 26, 2000, p. B5.

105. "Save the Planet: Stop Flying," *Parade,* January 7, 2007, p. 22.

CHAPTER EIGHTEEN

Internet Law and Ethics

After completing this chapter, students will be able to:

1. Explain the ethical dilemmas referred to as the digital divide and net neutrality.

2. Apply the requirements of personal jurisdiction to a dispute arising in cyberspace, both where the parties are residents of different states and where they are residents of different countries.

3. Identify free speech issues that arise in the context of the Internet and present the competing interests that make each particular issue difficult to resolve.

4. Provide examples of online activities that raise privacy concerns.

5. Explain the differences in online privacy protection between the United States and the European Union.

6. Describe several Internet-related crimes, including cyberstalking and cybersecurity.

7. Explain the impact of the Electronic Signatures in Global and National Commerce Act (E-SIGN).

8. Discuss the legal effect of click-wrap agreements.

9. Discuss standard-essential patents and give an example.

10. Explain the copyright doctrines of fair use and first sale.

11. Explain the trademark issues described in the text affecting Google and eBay.

12. Identify and discuss the basic tax issue that arises from cyberspace transactions.

Introduction: The Internet and Globalization

> Over 2.4 billion of the world's 7 billion inhabitants have Internet access.

The Internet has changed our lives. Over 2.4 billion of the world's 7 billion inhabitants have Internet access.[1] That number has been made possible, in part because of the relatively cheap access offered by cell phones in comparison with the cost of computers. The extraordinary power of this nearly instantaneous global communication system has produced remarkable new opportunities and challenges, creating and facilitating relationships (whole new "communities" of interest) among individuals, businesses, and governments that could never have occurred without it. The Internet is itself a catalyst for continuing globalization, breaking down national boundaries and rules to allow free interchange of communications, ideas, goods, and services around the world.

This global communication system raises yet another opportunity to consider such fundamental issues as what substantive law we want to govern the world's Internet activities and what process we should use to establish global standards for this global medium. Consensus is necessary on everything from the assignment of domain names to when and what cyberattacks are allowable as weapons of war.[2]

The most interesting question raised by our now pervasive Internet relationships may be what process will evolve to determine and implement substantive laws governing the Internet. Can national governments legitimately impose standards and sanctions? Will international forums, such as the U.N. Internet Governance Forum, be necessary to resolve issues that have global ramifications? Will international bodies be able to act fast enough and have enough legitimacy to secure national acquiescence? Might international enforcement tools need to be developed? Will grassroots use of the Internet among individuals, business, and government drive the development of this new medium so vigorously that it will be a force driving a fundamental restructuring of our global relationships?

Part One—The Market, Law, and Ethics

The roots of the Internet date to the late 1960s when a small group of researchers sought a way to freely exchange digital information with colleagues at other institutions. By the end of the 1980s, a backbone system of networked computers had been created and e-mail use reached the general public. In the mid-1990s the first browser was released and the World Wide Web was born.[3] Since then the cost of both technology and access has dropped sufficiently to make the Internet a truly public, and international, space.

Policy makers, users, and posters are all concerned about the degree to which we can, need to, or will impose the force of law on the Internet. Originally, it was an open-access forum only lightly touched by regulation. The growth in users and uses, in needs and desires, has created arguably the most diverse community imaginable—nearly as diverse as the human race itself. The combination of volume and diversity brings conflict with it. Peaceful and dependable conflict solutions require the existence of an established dispute resolution mechanism. Some conflict is resolvable by developing norms of conduct—such as e-mail and Internet etiquette. Some conflict is resolvable by the establishment of site principles to be applied by a site administrator. But some conflicts will end up in courts because they are our established structural mechanism for peaceful dispute resolution.

> The growth in users and uses ... has created arguably the most diverse community imaginable.

To be accepted by the disputants, judicial decisions need to be based on shared principles. Likewise we have developed legislative processes for the creation of rules to govern behavior. No existing judicial or legislative body, however, has obvious or natural jurisdiction over the Internet in its entirety. "[T]herein lies the central truth of globalization today: We're all connected and nobody is in charge."[4]

What choices do we have in this difficult situation? On one end of the spectrum, one might argue for the establishment and enforcement of globally applicable principles and processes. On the other end of the spectrum, one might predict complete balkanization with countries enforcing national standards by creating isolated domestic internets. As with most aspects of our globalized world, the more likely result will fall in the middle: global standards where uniformity is critical to the functioning of the whole system, national regulation where fundamental cultural values and political choices vary and, perhaps, also the establishment of physically separate national internets, as Iran has proposed.[5]

Market Forces and Government Regulation

A discussion of regulating business conducted through the Internet must begin with the impact the market has in developing (or, put another way, "regulating") appropriate business behavior. For example, the photo- and video-sharing social network Instagram triggered a public outcry late in 2012 by announcing a change in its terms of use that would allow it to use posted photos for advertising purposes without specific permission of the poster and without providing a general opt-out mechanism. Within a day, the provision was removed.

In regulating the functioning of the Internet and its component parts, global norms are required. At present many norms, such as the assignment of top-level domain names (.com, .org, and so forth) and the system for routing digital traffic, are set by the United States. The European Union and Brazil in particular have argued matters of Internet governance should be globalized, instead of continuing to rest with the United States. In April 2014, Brazil hosted a conference, In March 2014, the United States indicated a willingness to relinquish its control over the Internet, and several international meetings are scheduled over the next few years to seek a consensus solution.[6]

One function of the Internet is as a mass communications system. Much like the traditional broadcast systems of radio and TV, the Internet can deliver the same content to an infinite number of users. Most, if not all, countries regulate content delivered by traditional broadcast systems. This will likely continue to be true for content delivered through the Internet, as we will further discuss in Part Three.

The Internet also delivers private communications between particular users, much as a phone system. In general, Western governments do not censor private communications, but they do at times seek information from carriers about the existence of participants in private communications. Governments also seek access to the content of private communications sent through public networks as, for example, through phone wiretaps. In the digital world, the content of private communications can be stored for substantial lengths of time as data on the equipment of the service provider, making a much larger volume of such communications subject to government access. Again, market forces have little bearing on government access to such information, although the political maelstrom raised by Edward Snowden's disclosures about U.S. surveillance programs does seem likely to result in significant changes to some of the government's practices. Such government access rules vary significantly among countries. Service providers subject to the jurisdiction of a particular country must comply with those rules, although at times a provider may elect not to do business in a particular country rather than subject itself to access demands with which it disagrees.

Internet Access

As we have seen in other areas, market forces and legal regulation will blend in some uncertain, emerging formula to provide the security and confidence necessary for effective e-commerce. But ethics, too, will play a part. The speed, the traffic volume, the surface anonymity, and the global reach of the Internet suggest very difficult, and new, ethical issues, as well as old problems in a new venue. We turn now to two access issues.

The Digital Divide

The divide in the United States is not just along economic lines, but also along race, age, and geographic lines. Seventy-six percent of white households are connected, but only 57 percent of African-American households; 75 percent of those under 65 use the Internet, but only about 50 percent of those 65 and older; and the lowest Internet usage is in Mississippi, Alabama, and Arkansas. Although nearly 98 percent of American households are located where broadband is available, 20 percent of American adults are not connected—not at home, at work, through public access points such as libraries, or through a smartphone. Availability of service is not the problem; the cost of connecting and digital literacy are. But presumptions about availability exacerbate the disadvantages of the unconnected, as job announcements and applications, public school homework assignments, government services information and applications, among many other things, migrate to the web.[7]

An even greater access imbalance exists at the global level. For example, only 15.6 percent of Africa's citizens have access, compared with 78.6 percent in North America. Worldwide, it is estimated that just over one-third of the population is connected. But the number of connections is growing by less than 9 percent annually.[8] As in the United States, one issue of access is availability, another is user cost, and another is training. But each of these issues is more intransigent outside of the United States. For example, only 24 percent of the population in sub-Saharan Africa has access to electricity. In most of these countries, the gross domestic product per capita is under $2,000. A group of seven well-known high-tech companies announced in 2013 the start of an Internet access project to address the two-thirds of the world's population that is on the other side of the divide, but it is too early to tell if significant improvement will result.[9] [For current statistics on world Internet usage, see **www.internetworldstats.com/stats.htm**]

Questions

1. Can you think of any imaginative ways to provide widespread Internet access in developing countries? For one approach, watch the video at **www.ted.com/talks/aleph_molinari_let_s_bridge_the_digital_divide.html.**

2. How would you deal with the reality that most Internet content is in English?

Net Neutrality

In general, if someone in the United States wishes to connect to the Internet, they contract with a commercial Internet service provider (ISP) (such as AT&T, Comcast, or Verizon) and pay a fee for the type (such as dial-up or broadband) and level of service (such as speed, data volume, and length of term) they desire. They then have access to any content provider (such as Amazon, Craigslist, Google, and YouTube). This uniform access is referred to as *net neutrality*. It implies that ISPs will not discriminate against the traffic of any legal content provider. Some ISPs would like the right to change that—for example, by charging certain content providers for access or for enhanced transmission speeds to the ISP's subscribers. Their argument is that bandwidth is not infinite and they need to be able to manage traffic during periods of congestion to prevent performance degradation over the entire system. Specifically, ISPs want to charge content providers with heavy traffic, such as sites where users download music and videos, for the substantial bandwidth used to access their sites, products, and services. The consequence of nonpayment would be either blocked access at certain times or degraded speed at which access is provided.

Vigorous arguments have been raised against such fees, including:

- ISP subscribers already pay for the distribution system (and pay higher fees for various types and levels of service).
- Some ISPs compete with content providers (for example, cable companies provide content as well as access) and might discriminate either in price or speed to favor their own content.
- Variable pricing might make it difficult for new content providers to succeed. (Amazon.com had high-volume traffic long before it became profitable.)

In December 2010, the Federal Communications Commission (FCC) issued new rules on net neutrality to address these issues. For wired broadband services, the rules prohibited blocking of "lawful content, applications, services, or non-harmful devices" and compelled disclosure regarding network performance and the principles that would be used to manage network congestion. Wireless providers were subject to the same disclosure rules but were granted more leeway with regard to equal access. Blocking of consumer access to "lawful websites" and "applications that compete with the provider's voice or video telephony services" was prohibited. Thus, AT&T would not be allowed to block or slow access to Skype, but would be allowed to block downloads from Netflix even while allowing access to an official AT&T video player.

These regulations were challenged by Verizon; in mid-January 2014, the federal Court of Appeals for the District of Columbia Circuit held that the FCC's equal access rules were unsustainable, but the disclosure requirements were both severable and enforceable. The Court found that the FCC could impose antidiscrimination rules on broadband providers only if those providers were subject to common carrier regulation under the Telecommunications Act of 1996. After the passage of that Act, the FCC continued to classify broadband Internet service furnished over telephone lines as "telecommunications services" subject to common carrier regulation. Four years later, however, the FCC changed the classification and determined that broadband providers were instead "information services," which, under the Act, are not subject to common carrier regulation. The Court in *Verizon v. FCC* found that the antidiscrimination provisions were common carrier regulations and, thus, were not valid if broadband services were classified by the FCC as information services.[10] After announcing that it would not appeal the Court's ruling, in the spring of 2014 the FCC issued proposed rules for public comment that opened the door to arrangements whereby content providers could pay for enhanced services. The FCC also invited comment on whether it should change the classification of broadband services so as to make them subject to regulation as common carriers.[11]

Questions

The issue of net neutrality raises the question of whether regulation is either appropriate or necessary to restrict unwanted behavior. Would you favor imposing the same rules on wired and wireless ISPs? If so, which approach would you prefer? The 2010 FCC rules for wired providers? The rules for wireless providers? The post-*Verizon v. FCC* position? Or would you prefer to leave it to the market to determine which ISPs will be successful? Explain your responses.

Part Two—Jurisdiction to Adjudicate

Business in the cyberworld raises puzzling new legal problems. The Internet, after all, is borderless. We can and do communicate and engage in transactions around the world. When a dispute arises from one of those billions of communications and transactions, where will that dispute be litigated? If an American website provides child pornography viewed by a resident of Germany, which nation will have the authority to prosecute the offense?[12] If a Massachusetts resident posts an arguably libelous article on an Internet bulletin board sited in New York, may the Texas resident who claims harm from the libel sue the author and the bulletin board host in a Texas court?[13] These are *jurisdictional* questions. The party filing suit must take its claim to a court that has both *subject-matter jurisdiction* (the authority to address the particular kind of legal problem raised) and *personal jurisdiction* (the power to compel the defendant to respond). (For a general discussion of jurisdiction, see Chapter 4.)

In the United States, where the plaintiff and defendant are both residents of the forum state, personal jurisdiction ordinarily is not an issue. However, personal jurisdiction over nonresidents depends on the constitutional requirement of *due process*. In practice, the test is one of *minimum contacts*: Did the defendant have sufficient contact with the forum state that being sued there would be fair and just? Put another way, was the defendant's contact with the forum state of such a nature that it should expect to be subject to the state's courts? Thus, the more business a defendant does in a state, the more likely personal jurisdiction will be found. Internet business raises special problems because the "contacts" are often electronic and fleeting.

> Did the defendant have sufficient contact ... that being sued there would be fair and just?

Several cases have arisen in the United States that begin to answer these personal jurisdiction questions. In one the Fifth Circuit held in a case of alleged copyright violation that Texas did not have personal jurisdiction over a Vermont corporation merely because the corporation's website was accessible from Texas.[14] It reached this conclusion, in part, because there was no specific connection between the existence of the corporation's website and the harm complained of by the plaintiff. Thus, the Vermont corporation could be sued in Texas only if it had contacts with Texas that were sufficiently "continuous and systematic" as to subject the corporation to suit in Texas generally. A passive website was insufficient to do this. When the defendant has more contact with the forum state than the existence of a passive website reachable by forum state computer users, the due process analysis becomes more complex and hinges on an evaluation of the defendant's specific additional contacts with the state. The existing decisions are often hard to reconcile and many cases have been reversed on appeal, indicating that judgments as to personal jurisdiction are challenging and uncertain.[15]

Question

The operator of the dating service be2.com sued the CEO of the competing dating service be2.net for trademark infringement. The suit was brought in a federal district court in Illinois. Defendant was a New Jersey resident. The only evidence of his contact with Illinois was a list of 20 Illinois members of be2.net. After the court granted a default judgment when the defendant did not respond to the complaint, defendant moved to vacate the judgment for lack of personal jurisdiction.[16] Should Illinois courts have jurisdiction? Explain.

Jurisdiction in International Suits

Similar jurisdictional issues arise across national boundaries. In 2010, an Italian court convicted three U.S.-based Google executives in absentia of violating Italian privacy laws based on a video posted by third parties on Google's system. The video showed three teenage boys harassing an autistic boy. Italian law holds executives responsible for company actions.[17] Google appealed and the decision was overturned. The appellate court found that Google had not performed an editorial function. Under EU law, mere hosting of user-generated content does not make the hosting service responsible for the content.[18]

In international contexts it may be useful to distinguish among three types of jurisdiction: jurisdiction to prescribe (legislate), jurisdiction to adjudicate (judicial personal jurisdiction), and jurisdiction to enforce.[19] Most countries have long had laws that prohibit or regulate some forms of commerce, such as pornography, gambling, and alcohol. When a country seeks to apply those laws to foreigners, the question is whether the country has jurisdiction to adjudicate. The Restatement (Third) of Foreign Relations Law attempts to identify the circumstances under which countries have exercised their jurisdiction to adjudicate. It enumerates, among other circumstances: (1) when a person is present in the territory, other than transitorily; (2) when a person is domiciled, a resident, or a national of that country; (3) when a person regularly carries on business in that country; (4) when a person has carried on an activity in the country and that activity is the subject of the dispute; and (5) when a person has done something outside the country that has a "substantial, direct, and foreseeable effect within" the country and that effect forms the subject of the suit. Based on those standards, do you think the Italian courts have jurisdiction over Google's American executives?

> Most countries have long had laws that prohibit or regulate some forms of commerce, such as pornography, gambling, and alcohol.

Consider both the French court's approach and the U.S. district court's approach to the issue of jurisdiction to adjudicate in the following dispute.

LEGAL BRIEFCASE

YAHOO! v. La Ligue Contre Le Racisme Et L'Antisemitisme
169 F.Supp.2d 1181 (N.D. Cal. 2001)

Judge Jeremy Fogel

I. PROCEDURAL HISTORY

[Defendant] La Ligue Contre Le Racisme Et L'Antisemitisme ("LICRA") [is a French nonprofit organization] dedicated to eliminating anti-Semitism. Plaintiff Yahoo!, Inc. ("Yahoo!") is a corporation organized under the laws of Delaware with its principal place of business in Santa Clara, California. . . . Yahoo! services ending in the suffix ".com," without an associated country code as a prefix or extension (collectively, "Yahoo!'s

U.S. Services"), use the English language and target users who are residents of, utilize servers based in, and operate under the laws of the United States. Yahoo! subsidiary corporations operate regional Yahoo! sites and services in 20 other nations, including, for example, Yahoo! France, Yahoo! India, and Yahoo! Spain. Each of these regional websites contains the host nation's unique two-letter code as either a prefix or a suffix in its URL. Yahoo!'s regional sites use the local region's primary language, target the local citizenry, and operate under local laws.

Yahoo! provides a variety of means by which people from all over the world can communicate and interact with one another over the Internet. . . . As relevant here, Yahoo!'s auction site allows anyone to post an item for sale and solicit bids from any computer user from around the globe. Yahoo! records when a posting is made and after the requisite time period lapses sends an e-mail notification to the highest bidder and seller with their respective contact information. Yahoo! is never a party to a transaction, and the buyer and seller are responsible for arranging privately for payment and shipment of goods. Yahoo! monitors the transaction through limited regulation by prohibiting particular items from being sold (such as stolen goods, body parts, prescription and illegal drugs, weapons, and goods violating U.S. copyright laws or the Iranian and Cuban embargos). . . . Yahoo! informs auction sellers that they must comply with Yahoo!'s policies and may not offer items to buyers in jurisdictions in which the sale of such item violates the jurisdiction's applicable laws. Yahoo! does not actively regulate the content of each posting, and individuals are able to post, and have in fact posted, highly offensive matter, including Nazi-related propaganda and Third Reich memorabilia, on Yahoo!'s auction sites.

On or about April 5, 2000, LICRA sent a "cease and desist" letter to Yahoo!'s Santa Clara headquarters informing Yahoo! that the sale of Nazi and Third Reich–related goods through its auction services violates French law. LICRA threatened to take legal action unless Yahoo! took steps to prevent such sales within eight days. Defendants subsequently utilized the United States Marshal's Office to serve Yahoo! with process in California and filed a civil complaint against Yahoo! in the Tribunal de Grande Instance de Paris (the "French Court").

The French Court found that approximately 1,000 Nazi and Third Reich–related objects, including Adolf Hitler's *Mein Kampf, The Protocol of the Elders of Zion* (an infamous anti-Semitic report produced by the Czarist secret police in the early 1900s), and purported "evidence" that the gas chambers of the Holocaust did not exist, were being offered for sale on Yahoo.com's auction site. Because any French citizen is able to access these materials on Yahoo.com directly or through a link on Yahoo.fr, the French Court concluded that the Yahoo.com auction site violates Section R645-1 of the French Criminal Code, which prohibits exhibition of Nazi propaganda and artifacts for sale. On May 20, 2000, the French Court entered an order requiring Yahoo! to (1) eliminate French citizens' access to any material on the Yahoo.com auction site that offers for sale any Nazi objects, relics, insignia, emblems, and flags; (2) eliminate French citizens' access to Web pages on Yahoo.com displaying text, extracts, or quotations from *Mein Kampf* and *Protocol of the Elders of Zion;* (3) post a warning to French citizens on Yahoo.fr that any search through Yahoo.com may lead to sites containing material prohibited by Section R645-1 of the French Criminal Code, and that such viewing of the prohibited material may result in legal action against the Internet user; (4) remove from all browser directories accessible in the French Republic index headings entitled "negationists" and from all hypertext links the equation of "negationists" under the heading "Holocaust." The order subjects Yahoo! to a penalty of 100,000 Euros for each day that it fails to comply with the order. . . .

The French Court also provided that penalties assessed against Yahoo! Inc. may not be collected from Yahoo! France. Defendants again utilized the United States Marshal's Office to serve Yahoo! in California with the French Order.

Yahoo! subsequently posted the required warning and prohibited postings in violation of Section R645-1 of the French Criminal Code from appearing on Yahoo.fr. Yahoo! also amended the auction policy of Yahoo.com to prohibit individuals from auctioning:

> Any item that promotes, glorifies, or is directly associated with groups or individuals known principally for hateful or violent positions or acts, such as Nazis or the Ku Klux Klan. Official government-issue stamps and coins are not prohibited under this policy. Expressive media, such as books and films, may be subject to more permissive standards as determined by Yahoo! in its sole discretion.

Notwithstanding these actions, the Yahoo.com auction site still offers certain items for sale (such as stamps, coins, and a copy of *Mein Kampf*) which appear to violate the French Order. . . .

Yahoo! claims that because it lacks the technology to block French citizens from accessing the Yahoo.com auction site to view materials which violate the French order or from accessing other Nazi-based content of websites on Yahoo.com, it cannot comply with the French order without banning Nazi-related material from Yahoo.com altogether. Yahoo! contends that such a ban would infringe impermissibly upon its rights under the First Amendment to the United States Constitution. Accordingly, Yahoo! filed a complaint in this Court seeking a declaratory judgment that the French Court's orders are neither cognizable nor enforceable under the laws of the United States.

Defendants immediately moved to dismiss on the basis that this Court lacks personal jurisdiction over them. That motion was denied. . . .

II. OVERVIEW

As this Court and others have observed, the instant case presents novel and important issues arising from the global reach of the Internet. Indeed, the specific facts of this case implicate issues of policy, politics, and culture that are beyond the purview of one nation's judiciary. Thus it is critical that the Court define at the outset what is and is not at stake in the present proceeding.

This case is *not* about the moral acceptability of promoting the symbols or propaganda of Nazism. Most would agree that such acts are profoundly offensive. By any reasonable standard of morality, the Nazis were responsible for one of the worst displays of inhumanity in recorded history. . . .

Nor is this case about the right of France or any other nation to determine its own law and social policies. A basic function of a sovereign state is to determine by law what forms of speech and conduct are acceptable within its borders. . . .

What *is* at issue here is whether it is consistent with the Constitution and laws of the United States for another nation to regulate speech by a United States resident within the United States on the basis that such speech can be accessed by Internet users in that nation. In a world in which ideas and information transcend borders and the Internet in particular renders the physical distance between speaker and audience virtually meaningless, the implications of this question go far beyond the facts of this case. The modern world is home to widely varied cultures with radically divergent value systems. There is little doubt that Internet users in the United States routinely engage in speech that violates, for example, China's laws against religious expression, the laws of various nations against advocacy of gender equality or homosexuality, or even the United Kingdom's restrictions on freedom of the press.

* * * * *

The French order prohibits the sale or display of items based on their association with a particular political organization and bans the display of websites based on the authors' viewpoint with respect to the Holocaust and anti-Semitism. A United States court constitutionally could not make such an order. The First Amendment does not permit the government to engage in viewpoint-based regulation of speech absent a compelling governmental interest, such as averting a clear and present danger of imminent violence.

* * * * *

Comity

No legal judgment has any effect, of its own force, beyond the limits of the sovereignty from which its authority is derived. . . . The extent to which the United States, or any state, honors the judicial decrees of foreign nations is a matter of choice, governed by "the comity of nations." United States courts generally recognize foreign judgments and decrees unless enforcement would be prejudicial or contrary to the country's interests.

As discussed previously, the French order's content and viewpoint-based regulation of the Web pages and auction site on Yahoo.com, while entitled to great deference as an articulation of French law, clearly would be inconsistent with the First Amendment if mandated by a court in the United States. . . . The reason for limiting comity in this area is sound. "The protection to free speech and the press embodied in [the First] amendment would be seriously jeopardized by the entry of foreign judgments granted pursuant to standards deemed appropriate in [another country] but considered antithetical to the protections afforded the press by the U.S. Constitution." Absent a body of law that establishes international standards with respect to speech on the Internet and an appropriate treaty or legislation addressing enforcement of such standards to speech originating within the United States, the principle of comity is outweighed by the Court's obligation to uphold the First Amendment.

* * * * *

CONCLUSION

Yahoo! seeks a declaration from this Court that the First Amendment precludes enforcement within the United States of a French order intended to regulate the content of its speech over the Internet. . . . Accordingly, the motion for summary judgment will be granted.

AFTERWORD

On appeal in 2006 the Ninth Circuit Court of Appeals ruled by a vote of eight to three that the California district court had personal jurisdiction over the French defendants, but six judges also held that Yahoo! could not pursue its declaratory judgment action. Three of those six said the declaratory judgment action was not "ripe" for decision, while the other three were the minority that held that the court had no personal jurisdiction.[20] The Supreme Court declined to review the decision.[21]

Questions

1. We cannot tell from this opinion why the French court believed it had jurisdiction to adjudicate against Yahoo!, as opposed to Yahoo! France. Look back at the discussion of the Restatement (Third) of Foreign Relations Law immediately before this case. Why might the French court have had jurisdiction over Yahoo! France? Over Yahoo!?

2. If you were sitting on the Ninth Circuit, how would you have decided the jurisdiction question? Consider both the U.S. rule of minimum contacts and the Restatement provision.

3. Notice the Court's conclusion that the principle of comity is outweighed by its constitutional obligation to uphold the freedom of speech. Is this approach to the requirements of comity consistent with the discussion of comity in Chapter 16?

Part Three—Constitutional Law: Speech and Privacy

Speech

The district court opinion in *Yahoo! v. La Ligue Contre Le Racisme et L'Antisemitisme* illustrates one of the free speech issues the Internet raises. Internet content has also raised free speech issues here at home. The Internet's seeming anonymity, ease of use, relatively low costs, and global reach make it a natural vehicle for transporting speech messages. As we saw in Chapter 5, the First Amendment protects us from government restraints on the *content* of speech, although reasonable restraints on the *context* (time, place, and manner) of that speech are sometimes constitutionally permissible. Thus, a court will not restrain free speech by enjoining someone from posting defamatory or copyrighted material, but the damaged party may, of course, sue for defamation or copyright infringement after the posting.[22] [For articles on cyberlaw free speech, search for "free speech" at **http://repository.jmls.edu/jitpl/all-issues.html**]

One of the most troublesome Internet free speech issues is whether and how children can be protected from online pornography while maintaining adult access to constitutionally protected content. In a 2007 survey, 34 percent of Internet users aged 10 to 17 experienced "unwanted exposure to online pornography."[23] But Congress has been unsuccessful in its repeated attempts to enact constitutional legislation that would still effectively eliminate access by minors. In 1997, the Supreme Court held critical provisions of the Communications Decency Act of 1996 were overbroad and therefore violated the First Amendment.[24] Then in 2007, a federal district court found the Child Online Protection Act of 1998 unconstitutional and permanently enjoined its enforcement. In refusing to hear the government's appeal in 2009, the Supreme Court effectively left the permanent injunction in place.[25]

> Thirty-four percent of Internet users aged 10 to 17 experienced "unwanted exposure to online pornography."

Somewhat more successfully, Congress has also addressed a slightly different problem—the exploitation of children in the making of child pornography and its online accessibility to predators of children. Its first attempt was held unconstitutional by the

Supreme Court,[26] but in 2008 the Court upheld the PROTECT Act of 2003. Nevertheless, child pornography remains one of the Internet's most intractable challenges, "too large for law enforcement, policy makers and child protection groups to handle on their own."[27] (For more on child online protection, see Chapter 5.)

Anonymous Speech

"[An] author's decision to remain anonymous, like other decisions concerning omissions or additions to the content of a publication, is an aspect of the freedom of speech protected by the First Amendment."[28]

A unique characteristic of the Internet and electronic communication through the Internet is the ease with which a poster or sender can be anonymous and remain so without "fear of economic or official retaliation . . . [or] social ostracism."[29] Anonymity makes it more likely that individuals will feel free to say things about which they would otherwise keep silent. Thus, it can promote "the robust exchange of ideas."[30] Anonymity may, however, make individuals bolder about asserting untruths—misleading, fraudulent, or otherwise unprotected speech. For example, sites containing "revenge porn" have proliferated; these are sites on which ex-boyfriends, ex-husbands, and ex-lovers can post explicit photos of their former partners, at times along with disparaging remarks, information on where the women work and live, and links to their Facebook pages.

The victim of such a post can request the hosting site remove the material; indeed, hundreds of thousands of content complaints (for many different reasons) are received by Facebook, Google, and Twitter each week.[31] But it is largely up to the hosting site whether the content will actually be removed. Even if the offending material is removed from the originating site, there is a significant chance that it has been copied and could reappear in other locations at any time. The Communications Decency Act makes it very unlikely that the hosting website will be held liable for such postings, particularly if it removes the material when requested to do so. The law rests liability on the "information content provider," and courts have generally held that website owners are not content providers on these facts. Some lower courts seem willing to consider that some actions of a hosting website may result in liability—such as itself supplying responsive comments supportive of the original post or by naming the site in such a way as to encourage offensive, damaging, or defamatory posts.[32]

With regard to the original poster, there is very little state law that would criminalize the posting of such material. Victims occasionally have brought civil suits for damages, depending on the facts based on harassment, invasion of privacy, copyright infringement, or child pornography claims. [For more on revenge porn, see **www.endrevengeporn.com**]

Before a victim of revenge porn or other forms of online harassment, defamation, and invasion privacy can sue the content provider, the victim has to be able to prove who that is. Seeking the release of that information from the website or the ISP of the poster triggers First Amendment claims to anonymity on behalf of the original poster. In the case that follows, a Yahoo! poster argues the First Amendment prohibits Yahoo! from responding to a subpoena from Immunomedics, a corporation claiming the anonymous poster is or was an employee who violated the company's confidentiality agreement by posting company information on a Yahoo! message board.

Judge Fall

Defendant Jean Doe, a/k/a "moonshine_fr," appeals from an order . . . denying her motion to quash a subpoena issued to Yahoo! by plaintiff, Immunomedics, Inc., seeking all personally identifiable information relating to the person or identity who posted messages on the Yahoo! Finance Message Board under the identifier "moonshine_fr" which may identify or lead to the identification of that person or entity.

Immunomedics is a publicly held biopharmaceutical Delaware corporation . . . focused on the development, manufacture, and commercialization of diagnostic imaging and therapeutic products for the detection and treatment of cancer and infectious diseases.

Yahoo! is an Internet Service Provider (ISP) that maintains a Web site that includes a section called Yahoo! Finance. Yahoo! Finance maintains a message board for every publicly traded company, including Immunomedics. Visitors to the Immunomedics site can obtain up-to-date information on the company, and can post and exchange messages about issues related to the operation or performance of the company.

On October 12, 2000, Immunomedics filed a complaint against Jean Doe, also known by the computer screen name "moonshine_fr" ("Moonshine"). The complaint alleged that Moonshine had "posted a message on Yahoo! Finance." Immunomedics claimed that message contained information confidential and proprietary to Immunomedics. As a result, Immunomedics asserted it had sustained injury and that Moonshine should be held liable under theories of breach of contract, breach of duty of loyalty, and negligently revealing confidential and proprietary information.

* * * * *

Of the two messages in question, the first, with Moonshine describing herself as "[a] worried employee," stated that Immunomedics was "out of stock for diagnostic products in Europe" and claimed that there would be "no more sales if [the] situation [did] not change." The second message, allegedly posted by Moonshine after the initial complaint was filed, reported that Chairman of the Company Dr. Goldenberg was going to fire the Immunomedics "european manager." In her certification to the trial court, Immunomedics' Executive Vice President and Chief Operations Officer Cynthia L. Sullivan admitted that the statements were true, but that, as an employee, Moonshine had violated the company's confidentiality agreement and "several provisions" of the company's Employee Handbook.

On or about October 20, 2000, Immunomedics served a subpoena on Yahoo!, seeking discovery of Moonshine's true identity. Yahoo!, in turn, contacted Moonshine. In response, Moonshine filed a motion to quash the subpoena on or about November 15, 2000.

. . . After considering the arguments, the judge denied Moonshine's motion, stating, in pertinent part,

> We have two issues here. We have an issue, she's an employee, she signed a confidential document saying that she was not going to speak freely about information she learned at the company. So she contracted away her right of free speech if she's an employee. Number two, free speech, anonymous, but if it harms another individual, that is another way that we have a little bit of a dent in our rights for free speech.

* * * * *

Moonshine contends the motion judge erred in denying her motion to quash the subpoena, as anonymous speech is constitutionally protected and Immunomedics' complaint is insufficient to warrant a breach of that anonymity. Immunomedics argues that, while anonymous speech is constitutionally protected, that protection can be overcome if a defendant uses that freedom in an unlawful manner. . . .

In another case involving an application for expedited discovery to disclose the identity of an anonymous user of an ISP message board, we concluded that courts must decide such applications by striking a balance between the First Amendment right of an individual to speak anonymously and the right of a company to protect its proprietary interest in the pursuit of claims based on actionable conduct by the ISP message board user.

* * * * *

We hold that . . . the trial court should first require the plaintiff to undertake efforts to notify the anonymous posters that they are the subject of a subpoena or application for an order of disclosure, and withhold action to afford the fictitiously named defendants a reasonable opportunity to file and serve opposition to the application. These notification efforts should include posting a message of notification of the identity discovery request to the anonymous user on the ISP's pertinent message board.

The court shall also require the plaintiff to identify and set forth the exact statements purportedly made by each anonymous poster that plaintiff alleges constitute actionable speech.

The complaint and all information provided to the court should be carefully reviewed to determine whether plaintiff has set forth a prima facie cause of action against the fictitiously named anonymous defendants. In addition to establishing that its action can withstand a motion to dismiss for failure to state a claim upon which relief can be granted, the plaintiff must produce sufficient evidence supporting each element of its cause of action, on a prima facie basis, prior to a court ordering the disclosure of the identity of the unnamed defendant.

Finally, assuming the court concludes that the plaintiff has presented a prima facie cause of action, the court must balance the defendant's First Amendment right of anonymous free speech against the strength of the prima facie case presented and the necessity for the disclosure of the anonymous defendant's identity to allow the plaintiff to properly proceed.

The application of these procedures and standards must be undertaken and analyzed on a case-by-case basis. The guiding principle is a result based on a meaningful analysis and a proper balancing of the equities and rights at issue.

. . . Here, Immunomedics' cause of action is based on Moonshine's status as an employee and her alleged violation of a confidentiality agreement, and Moonshine's alleged breach of her common law duty of loyalty. . . .

Applying the procedure and test outlined, we conclude Judge Zucker-Zarett properly analyzed the disclosure issue, and we affirm substantially for the reasons articulated by the judge in her oral opinion. . . . We add the following. Immunomedics presented sufficient evidence that Moonshine is, or was, an employee of Immunomedics. Ms. Sullivan indicated in her certification that "all employees are bound by several Company policies and a confidentiality agreement." Within its "Confidentiality and Assignment Agreement," Immunomedics includes the following language:

> This Agreement and any disputes arising under or in connection with it shall be governed by the laws of the State of New Jersey and each of the parties hereto hereby submits to the jurisdiction of any Federal or state court sitting in the State of New Jersey over any such dispute.

Accordingly, Immunomedics clearly established a prima facie cause of action for breach of the confidentiality agreement founded on the content of Moonshine's posted messages.

In balancing Moonshine's right of anonymous free speech against the strength of the prima facie case presented and the necessity for disclosure, it is clear that the motion judge struck the proper balance in favor of identity disclosure. With evidence demonstrating Moonshine is an employee of Immunomedics, that employees execute confidentiality agreements, and the content of Moonshine's posted messages providing evidence of the breach thereof, the disclosure of Moonshine's identity, which can be reasonably calculated to be achieved by information obtained from the subpoena, was fully warranted. Although anonymous speech on the Internet is protected, there must be an avenue for redress for those who are wronged. Individuals choosing to harm another or violate an agreement through speech on the Internet cannot hope to shield their identity and avoid punishment through invocation of the First Amendment.

* * * * *

Affirmed.

Questions

1. In your opinion, should employers, victimized individuals, and others who have been damaged by anonymous postings be able to obtain the identity of the poster from the hosting site or the poster's ISP? Explain.

2. An FBI agent monitored an AOL chat room suspected of being a site for exchanging child pornography. The agent did not participate in the chat room conversations. Charbonneau allegedly distributed child pornography to the chat room participants, including the FBI agent. Charbonneau was arrested. Did Charbonneau have a First Amendment free speech right to transmit child pornography online? Explain. See *U. S. v. Kenneth Charbonneau,* 979 F.Supp. 1177 (S.D. Ohio 1997).

3. Having read these materials on freedom of speech and the limits on the right to anonymity, what would you advise a friend who was a regular blogger? A classmate posting comments on **www.ratemyprofessors.com**? Your middle school cousin who is an avid Facebook user? Explain.

Commercial Speech

Remember from Chapter 5 that commercial speech has been accorded reduced but significant First Amendment protection. Thus, online advertising is subject to the same kinds of government oversight as that in print and on television. One form of online commercial message receiving special attention is so-called *spam* (mass e-mails). This electronic junk mail may be a legitimate form of commercial message at times, but it may also be an annoyance or a threat to the efficiency of the Internet because of its volume. It may also be deceptive, or fraudulent, or contain objectionable content, such as obscenity or viruses. Globally, about 70 percent of all e-mail is spam.[33]

The federal CAN-SPAM Act of 2003 establishes both civil and criminal penalties for violations of its provisions. The Federal Trade Commission (FTC), charged with enforcing the Act, won a substantial victory in 2008 when it obtained a court order freezing the assets of and shutting down a spam network that was capable of sending 10 billion e-mail messages a day and was responsible at one point for one-third of all spam. The group based its websites in China, processed credit cards payments through Cyprus and the former Soviet republic of Georgia, and in one month cleared $400,000 in credit card charges from sales of replica watches, as well as pharmaceuticals for weight loss and for the enhancement of the male anatomy.[34] In 2013, a court in Moscow convicted two Russians of designing and controlling a botnet—a network of infected computers that can be harnessed to take coordinated action, such as sending spam. Most hijacked infected computers are located in developing countries where users often cannot afford virus protection software. This particular botnet, known as Festi outside of Russia, for a three-month period in 2012 generated a third of all spam e-mail messages circulating globally.[35] [To file a complaint with the FTC about spam you receive, go to **https://www.ftccomplaintassistant.gov**]

Privacy

Most individuals probably do not fully appreciate the amount of their personal information that is available online, how it may be used, or the degree to which it may be misused. This is likely still the case, even after the 2013 disclosures precipitated by Edward J. Snowden of the extent to which the National Security Administration has routinely collected data on U.S. citizens. Most of the outcry following Snowden's disclosures addressed the legality of the government's actions under the Fourth Amendment's search and seizure restrictions and probable cause warrant requirements. Our focus here is different—this section looks at privacy concerns stemming from the way the Internet facilitates broad availability and accessibility of users' personal data, in ways that are often unintended and sometimes harmful.

The Internet has brought with it an explosion of accessible data, including personal data. Some of the information now available online has in fact been public for decades, but most people were not aware that it was public, did not know how to obtain it, or simply never bothered, a reality sometimes referred to as "practical obscurity."[36] For example, local governments keep property, tax, criminal, and court records, often housed in the local courthouse but not easily searchable. Now local governments are making much of these data available online and accessible to those who are simply curious.[37] Similarly, governmental agencies responsible for professional and occupational licensing may now have websites with membership lists, complaints filed, and disciplinary actions taken. Marketing firms, of course, have long collected all of this information and more, including home and work addresses, phone numbers, profession, income information, credit scores, bankruptcies, home ownership, mortgage amounts, vehicle and boat registrations, hunting licenses, bridal and birth registries, warranty cards, magazine and newspaper subscriptions, and even dog licenses. But maintaining current data was costly and the resulting profiles were not available to the general public. With the advent of the Internet that has changed. At Criminal-Searches.com, a site supported by advertising, anyone can look up neighbors, babysitters, teachers, plumbers, or their children's friends for free, which the site encourages one to do. Many other sites will provide similar information for a fee to anyone willing to pay. How long will it be before jurors are tempted to look up the criminal record of the defendant?

A simple browser search can turn up much more information from the public pages of social media sites, both self-disclosed and posted by friends, family, and acquaintances. Consider the following information, which is readily available or which you yourself may be unwittingly providing:

- Satellite and street views of your home, your work, and your children's school. Scouting a location or stalking someone has never been easier.

- Candid pictures and videos of you and your family, while attending your daughter's school Halloween party or at a business lunch or making a quick dash into your local convenience store or sitting at your MacBook surfing the Internet. Digital cameras are cheap, tiny, and potentially anywhere. Most cell phones come with built-in cameras. Several vendors sell miniature, high-definition Wi-Fi cameras for under $200, which one such company promotes "with easy setup in 60 seconds" and "continuous cloud recording." In early 2014, that company was uploading 1,000 hours of video per minute, 10 times the amount uploaded to YouTube.[38] Then there's Google Glass—a small computer worn on a person's face, which connects wirelessly to a smartphone and can do much of what a cell phone can do, including take pictures and videos of persons without their knowledge or consent. Finally, we have learned that laptop webcams are susceptible to hacking. A paper by researchers at Johns Hopkins explains how to reprogram a MacBook webcam to record without triggering the LED indicator that is supposed to alert the user that the camera is on. "There is only really one solution that can guarantee no one is spying on you: a piece of tape stuck over your computer camera."[39]

- Facebook confessions of indiscretions or, worse, crimes that find their way into police reports, school and job application files, and credit evaluations, as well as Instagram pictures that show up in divorce and child custody proceedings. Social media is having a wider impact than most people imagine, and the legal system may be having a hard time keeping up. Lawyers are turning to blog posts and online profiles to evaluate potential jurors; jurors have been "caught tweeting during testimony, polling Facebook friends for input on the verdict," and doing online research related to crimes with which the defendant has been charged. Some judges now require all electronic devices to be left outside the courtroom and, presumably, the jury room.[40]

> Jurors have been caught tweeting during testimony, polling Facebook friends for input on the verdict.

Data Mining

Now consider the amount of information residing in the databases of institutions with whom we regularly deal: credit card companies, online vendors, membership organizations, schools, pharmacies, medical service providers, our ISPs, phone companies, and so forth. Data mining is the process of building profiles of individuals by organizing all the disparate pieces of information collected in the normal course of business. Those profiles can be used to provide better services to repeat customers—from the pizza outlet that knows what you ordered last time (and how often, as well as how much you spend and, possibly, whether you tip) to Netflix that knows all your historical downloads and rentals (and how you rated them), as well as everything listed in your queue, and from that information can give you tailored recommendations for other movies you might like. Significant efficiencies can be achieved from the use of mined data, but there are downsides as well.

Personalized responses can also permit price discrimination. An investigation by the *Wall Street Journal* discovered such "dynamic pricing" used by Staples.com—the same stapler offered for $14.29 and $15.79. From a sampling of visits from more than 42,000 zip codes, "statistically speaking, by far the strongest correlation involved the distance to a rival's store from the center of a zip code."[41] That is, if the query came from a shopper close to a brick-and-mortar Office Depot or Office Max, the online price of the stapler was lower. This can replicate discrimination that mimics offline shopping: higher prices in locations with less competition, including rural and poor areas. Visit a comparison shopping site before going to your chosen vendor and the offered price may drop; "click too quickly from home-page to product page to checkout, and the seller can conclude that you have already decided to buy—so why offer you a discount?"[42]

Visit your favorite news or bookstore or streaming video site and you may get recommendations based on your prior viewing history. A convenience? Perhaps. But it may also steer you away from news stories, books, and movies that don't fit the profile labels the filtering algorithms have decided your online history reveals. If the algorithm concludes a user is likely to be a shopaholic or financially overextended, payday lender ads may start appearing on the screen. Not only are many users not aware of the extent of personalization occurring, but even if they are, there is no process for correcting these hidden profiles that influence one's online experience nor right to delete them.

To achieve this degree of personalization, the data collected on users go significantly beyond an individual site mining the data provided while a user browses its site. Users of a site may also knowingly give the merchant personal information to complete their transaction. Amazon.com identifies the following as examples of information customers provide: "your name, address, and phone numbers; credit card information; people to whom purchases have been shipped, including addresses and phone number; … e-mail addresses of your friends and other people; … and financial information, including Social Security and driver's license numbers."[43] Profiles built by one online vendor, including both browsing history and user-provided information, may also be provided to or aggregated with information gathered by affiliated businesses or by third-party advertisers. Or the business that compiles the profiles may sell them to marketing firms and others.

Cross-Device Tracking

Instead of one vendor, consider for a moment the source of the user-specific data available to certain iconic Internet businesses, such as Facebook, Google, Apple, and Microsoft. When repeat customers use Staples' website, they are likely to browse the site for desired items and then proceed to checkout, entering their username and password to do so. When they have finished, they leave the site. Users of Facebook, on the other hand, log in and then are likely to have the program running for extended periods of time, using various apps, chatting with friends, and so on. Even when they go elsewhere on the Internet, they may "like" places they visit, connecting them back to their Facebook accounts. If the users also own a smartphone, they may also use it to access Facebook and have it running as they travel through their day. This allows Facebook to collect user-specific information across multiple devices (laptop, work computer, smartphone), from many other websites, over extended periods of time, and from many geographical locations.

Google, Apple, and Microsoft can also do cross-device tracking—Google by connecting its users through Google Plus, whether they are on its Chrome browser, Google search, gmail, Google maps, or its phones; Apple among its phones, its iPads, and laptops running its Safari browser, and its app stores; and Microsoft through its browsers, MSN, Hotmail, Outlook.com, Xbox, phones, and Bing. These companies are not only tracking across devices, but also across many different platforms.

All four of these companies can both develop extensive user profiles and reap substantial advertising dollars by facilitating targeted third-party ads to users manifesting specific attributes.

Aggregators

In this user-information market, will anyone be able to compete with these Internet giants? So far the answer remains yes—aggregators can and do.

An aggregator in our context is any person who takes data that are discrete at the level of the individual and aggregates them with individual-level data from one or more other sources. By itself, a data file containing the browsing history of 200 discrete individuals (each person's browsing history separately presented but with no information identifying whose history it is) may not seriously threaten the anonymity of those individuals. By combining data from various sources, however, an aggregator creates even more detailed individual profiles, thereby increasing the probability that the data reveal the identity of the person behind it.

Where does an aggregator obtain the data sets that it combines? One major source is to develop profiles of users' Web browsing habits by placing cookies, tiny pieces of code, on thousands of websites to track users' online movements. When a visitor to a site logs in, about 25 percent of the time the site passes along the user's name, e-mail address, and other personal information to any third-party company with its own cookie on the page.[44] In a study conducted in 2012, 6,485 cookies were found on the 100 most popular websites—a majority of which were placed by third-party trackers, not the websites themselves.[45]

Although cookies may work on mobile browsers, iPhone's mobile Safari blocks all third-party cookies, and cookies do not attach at all to mobile apps. However, third-party aggregators successfully take advantage of so-called leaky apps that transmit identifiable user data, including locational data, as smartphones surf the Web, send e-mails and texts, and make calls. Apparently, both the U.K. and U.S. governments have been able to collect considerable data when smartphone users send posts to such popular services as Facebook, Flickr, LinkedIn, and Twitter.[46]

Of considerable concern is that no state or federal law prohibits the collection or sharing of most data by third parties, and independent aggregators have no privacy agreements with the individuals who are profiled and may have no agreement with the data source to restrict the use of the data. Aggregators generally are in the business of selling these data.

Privacy Policies: Did Someone Say Privacy?

These days an online merchant is likely to have a privacy policy posted on its site that describes, among other things, what data it collects and how they are used. For example, Amazon.com's Privacy Notice states "Information about our customers is an important part of our business, and we are not in the business of selling it to others."[47] The information it automatically collects includes "login; e-mail address; password; computer and connection information such as browser type, version, and time-zone setting, browser plug-in types and versions, operating system, and platform; purchase history ...; the full Uniform Resource Locator (URL) clickstream to, through, and from our website, including date and time; cookie number; [and] products you viewed or searched for." It also receives information such as "account information, purchase or redemption information, and page-view information from some merchants with which we operate co-branded businesses." A partial list of such businesses includes "Starbucks, OfficeMax, American Apparel, Verizon Wireless, Sprint, T-Mobile, AT&T, J&R Electronics, PacSun, Eddie Bauer and Northern Tool + Equipment." The Notice further acknowledges that its site includes third-party advertising and links to other websites. It then states, "We do not have access to or control over cookies or other features that advertisers and third party sites may use, and the information practices of these advertisers and third-party websites are not covered by our Privacy Notice."

Having read the materials in this section on data mining, pause and think now about the vast amount of personal data you now know is compiled and stored by various entities—Internet vendors, social media sites, and aggregators, but also phone companies and such traditional institutions such as banks and employers. Now consider the ramifications of the fact that anything stored can likely be stolen. For example, Google is one of the strongest, most technically sophisticated Internet companies in the world, but even it cannot prevent covert cyberattacks on its systems. Neither can Facebook, Apple, Twitter, Yahoo!, LinkedIn, Bloomberg, the International Monetary Fund, the FBI or the Pentagon, all of which have acknowledged that their systems have suffered successful attacks. Indeed, the opening lines of a recent *New York Times* article were, "The question is no longer who has been hacked. It's who hasn't?"[48]

Question

How would you rate the privacy protections available to individuals who purchase items through Amazon.com? How safe are similar data of individuals who have never purchased an item through Amazon.com?

Privacy of Employees

As discussed in Chapter 12, whether and when employers can legally access e-mails sent from or received on office computers continues to be uncertain. In a 2010 case, the New Jersey Supreme Court held that an employee had an expectation of privacy in an e-mail sent from her office computer but through a personal, password-protected Web mail account, an expectation the employer violated when it forensically retrieved her e-mail off of office servers. The result might have been different if the employer's privacy policy had clearly advised employees that their e-mails, even those sent through personal Web mail accounts, could be reviewed by the employer.[49] On the other hand, a U.S. Supreme Court case held that a city's review of a police officer's text messages was a reasonable search under the Fourth Amendment when the texts were sent from a wireless pager provided to the officer by the city, even if the officer had had a reasonable expectation of privacy.[50]

In recent years, a number of states have passed laws prohibiting employers from requiring log-on information to employee social media accounts, such as Facebook and Twitter, as a condition for the employee to get or keep a job. Exceptions are provided if an employer has specific information about work-related employee misconduct occurring through the use of such accounts or an employee's unauthorized publication of the employer's proprietary information.

Today's software can be customized to look for such things as company officers' and competitors' names, as well as inappropriate language. Software is also available today that can "track every keystroke, file download, and Internet page that appears on an employee's computer screen."[51] It can also be customized to look for such things as company officers' and competitors' names, as well as inappropriate language in office e-mail traffic. In part, companies may adopt some of these strategies to protect themselves from lawsuits. Employers wishing to implement such monitoring programs should, however, expressly advise their employees of that fact and have all employees sign an acknowledgment so there is no question about whether an employee has any expectation of privacy on company systems.

Question

Explain why employers might want to monitor their employees' computer activities.

Regulation

The United States has no comprehensive privacy law addressing the Internet environment. Instead, the privacy of users has largely been left to the "self-regulation" of service and content providers, buffered primarily only by periodic public outcries over, for example, a company's unilateral change in its stated privacy policy and occasional civil suits based on existing legal principles, such as defamation.

Most online content is and has remained free to users, funded primarily by advertising dollars. To make that advertising more effective, and thus able to generate more revenue, advertisers and content providers have developed behavioral tracking to follow users' paths through the Internet, thereby allowing ads targeted to users' specific interests. In a very real sense, Google and Facebook and other advertising-driven business models sell their users' data to pay for the services they give without charge to their users. "Self-regulation" then puts users' privacy protection into the very hands that derive substantial revenue from the sale of personal information. This is an irreconcilable conflict of interest. Periodically, lawmakers have acted, but the resulting laws have largely addressed privacy issues in discrete areas, such as motor vehicle records, patient billing, or video rental records. California law requires websites and apps to have privacy policies, and the FTC has taken action against companies that violate their stated privacy policies, as it did with Google in 2012. But there are no laws governing the content of company privacy policies. Similarly, there has been substantial discussion over many years on "Do Not Track" rules. Most browsers now have a user-controlled setting to alert advertisers that they do not want their Web activities tracked. But engaging that setting is largely symbolic—online advertisers are not required to honor the user's wishes. A working group established by the World Wide Web Consortium has been arguing over Do Not Track standards for over two years, with little evidence that a consensus will be reached anytime soon.[52]

Child Privacy Online

The United States does have a separate law addressing the privacy of children online. The 1998 Children's Online Privacy Protection Act (COPPA) prohibits websites from collecting personal information from children under 13 without parental permission and requires that parents be allowed to review and correct any information collected about their children. The FTC is charged with primary enforcement of COPPA. In 2012, it updated its rules under COPPA in a number of ways: by expanding the definition of "personal information" to include not just names, phone numbers, home and e-mail address, but also mobile phone serial numbers, and extending the rule's application to cover social media sites, interactive gaming sites, and smartphone and tablet apps. It also puts more substantial restrictions on the use of behavior-based online advertising. The information that triggers the need for parental consent now includes photos, video, and the location of the child's mobile device.[53] [To take a look at the complaints, and other information, in cases brought by the FTC under COPPA, go to **www.business.ftc.gov/privacy-and-security/children's-online-privacy**]

Privacy in Europe

The European Union has taken quite a different tack than America's market-driven approach to online privacy. The European Union's 1998 Data Protection Directive basically allows individuals to decide how their collected data can be used. Thus, if a European consumer provides personal information such as an address when buying from an online store, that store cannot legally send an ad to the purchaser without first seeking permission.[54] The directive also prohibits the transfer of data to countries outside the European Union that do not have "adequate" privacy rules.[55] The United States was one of the nations deemed inadequate, but by June 2000, European and U.S. negotiators had reached an agreement shielding U.S. companies from prosecution by EU governments for violation of the Data Protection Directive as long as the companies comply with a list of "safe harbor" privacy principles.[56] Following the revelations in 2013 of the extent of U.S. digital surveillance activities in Europe, there have been many calls in the European Union to reconsider the terms of this safe harbor. At the time of this writing, no such steps had been taken.[57] However, a substantial revision of the 1998 Directive is underway and may be enacted as early as mid-2014.[58] The revision might force a renegotiation of the safe harbor with the United States.[59]

The philosophical chasm separating U.S. and EU data privacy policies was dramatically illustrated when it became public that Google occasionally collected e-mails and passwords from residential Wi-Fi networks while its cars were driving city streets taking photos for its Street View mapping service. In the United States the FTC ended its inquiry when Google pledged to stop gathering that information. In Europe, Google has agreed to destroy the data collected in Austria, Britain, Denmark, France, and Ireland, and then in 2012 acknowledged that it had not actually done so. The Czech Republic banned Google from expanding its mapping program; Google was sued by an association of Internet users in Spain; and in 2013 authorities in Germany imposed close to the maximum fine its law allowed, although that was just shy of $190,000.[60]

Part Four—Crime

Crimes facilitated by the Internet include both truly new types and some old, familiar crimes in somewhat new clothing. Some statutes previously discussed, such as the CAN-SPAM and PROTECT acts, provide criminal penalties. Other laws criminalize specific online behavior, such as the Computer Pornography and Child Exploitation Prevention Act of 1999, which makes it unlawful to use a computer to solicit, lure, or entice a child or otherwise engage in sexual offenses with a child. The Computer Fraud and Abuse Act of 1986 bars individuals from accessing networked computers without authorization or obtaining information the individual is not authorized to take. Violation can result in substantial jail time and fines. There is considerable difference among the federal circuits as to the breadth of its reach: The Ninth and Fourth Circuits read the law narrowly, limited to unauthorized access of computer systems,[61] while the First, Fifth, Seventh, and Eleventh Circuits have taken a broader view. For example, the Seventh Circuit found that an employee who had been given access could still violate the law if the employee used that access to take unauthorized actions, such as deleting stored information.[62] Judge Kozinski of the Ninth Circuit, concerned with vast expansion in the reach of the law, queried: "Many employers have adopted policies prohibiting the use of work computers for nonbusiness purposes. Does an employee who violates such a policy commit a federal crime?"

Many of our long-standing, pre-Internet criminal laws can be applied to both online and offline behavior. For example, in February 2013, over just a few hours, digital thieves stole $45 million from thousands of ATM machines in New York City.[63] Fundamentally, this is no different from an old-fashioned bank robbery but using modern-day tools. Likewise, it is a federal crime to transport stolen property across state lines, even if the property is an intangible such as a detailed litigation strategy e-mailed by a law firm's employee to opposing counsel in another state.[64]

So too, fraud can be perpetrated with or without the aid of computers and the Internet. Recently hatched schemes include:

- Ransomware, which locks a user's computer and sends a fake police warning charging the user with abusive use of the Internet and imposing a fine to get the computer unlocked.[65]

- Bogus tech support calls, in which a person who receives a call, allegedly from a company such as Microsoft, is told that their computer has reported a virus. If given remote access to the computer, the caller will download a program onto the computer and then show the owner a file that displays a warning message. The caller then offers to remove the virus immediately for a specified fee.[66]

- Malware delivered to Apple computers through a security breach in a Java program which co-opts the computer into a botnet controlling thousands of such computers to perpetrate click fraud that, alternatively, can cause the computers to click repeatedly on ads for a particular business, causing its advertising bill to skyrocket, or to click repeatedly on ads appearing on a host website earning revenue for that site for getting potential customers to the advertiser's site.[67]

- Fake reviews on Yelp, Google, Citysearch, and similar sites posted by reputation enhancement companies on behalf of client restaurants, dentists, lawyers, and others, for the purpose of directing business to them based on fictitious experiences.[68]

Yet some existing criminal laws describe the prohibited behavior in terms that often prevent their application to cyber-versions of what is, at its essence, the same bad act, such as between physical stalking and *cyberstalking*. In a 2005 Illinois case, a former electronics store employee was sentenced to four years in prison for sending lewd photos and threatening e-mail and phone messages to a 22-year-old woman who had taken her computer in for repair.[69] This is *cyberstalking*—the repeated use of electronic media (such as e-mail or chat rooms) to harass or threaten another person. Every state has laws criminalizing traditional physical stalking. Most of these laws require that the perpetrator make a credible threat of violence for the action to be a violation; many do not expressly include cyberstalking, although under appropriate facts it might be covered.

In recent years, the biggest stories in cybercrime have not been crimes targeted at specific individuals or even major crimes such as the New York City bank heist. Instead what has dominated the news is organized, widespread criminal activity directed at major institutions, both commercial and governmental, which raises an issue unique to our newly digital world—cybersecurity.

Cybersecurity

We live in the age of information. With the near complete infiltration of digital technology into the basic fabric of our lives, much of our most valuation information is stored on computers, with vast quantities of information available even on single computer systems, enticing a whole new category of thieves—*hackers*. Thanks to the Internet, hackers can break into our computers from the privacy of their own home, even if that home is a three-room apartment in St. Petersburg, Russia.[70] Hacking can be simply malicious—destroying data or whole computer networks.[71] Or computing power can be the object of the theft, as is true with botnets which were used in conjunction with the spam attacks previously discussed.

On the other hand, the goal of some hacks is the theft of personal data from, at times, millions of individuals simultaneously. In 2012, the tax records of 3.8 million individuals and 850,000 businesses were stolen from the South Carolina Department of Revenue's database, records that contained information ranging from Social Security numbers to bank account information.[72] From late November through mid-December 2013, thieves hacked into the cash registers at Target stores, stealing tens of millions of payment card numbers.[73] By some estimates, 12.6 million people in the United States were victims of identity theft in 2012 alone.[74]

As devastating as identity theft can be for the individual whose identity has been stolen, from a societal point of view it gets worse. Of considerable concern has been the rise of cyber-espionage—both industrial and military espionage for the purpose of stealing military and economic secrets and intellectual property. The perpetrators can strike from U.S. soil or from foreign nations; there has been considerable speculation that such attacks have sourced from governments, including China, Iran, North Korea, and the United States.[75] The United States has expressed concern that its critical infrastructure is being targeted, such as its electricity grids, water supplies, computer and cell phone networks, and banks.[76]

The cost of all this cybercrime, which includes the spending to defend against it, has been estimated at $1 trillion. But more recently, a study undertaken in part by the Center for Strategic and International Studies, a nonprofit based in Washington, D.C., estimated the cost at $100 billion per year.[77] That said, Congress has not addressed the problem with legislation and the Obama administration issued only voluntary cybersecurity guidelines for certain crucial industries, such as banks and utilities.[78]

International Computer-Facilitated Crime

As is obvious from the foregoing, any truly effective response to cybercrime would be substantially aided by an international, coordinated approach. The Council of Europe has proffered the Convention on Cybercrime as an international effort to address computer-facilitated crime. It has been signed by 44 member states and four nonmember states, although only 40 states have ratified it.[79] The convention went into force July 1, 2004, for the original ratifying states. It requires "the criminalization of a long list of computer activities—everything from breaking into a computer to the 'deterioration' of computer data. . . . It also requires countries to make sure they can snoop through Internet data in real time. And it obliges nations to assist each other's investigations by monitoring Net communications."[80]

Each country's decisions to criminalize certain behaviors reflect that country's moral attitudes and historical experiences. Some proscribed behaviors such as murder are fairly universal, but other behaviors are acceptable in some countries while criminalized in others. Where such crimes are facilitated by the Internet, international disputes over the appropriate reach of such laws have arisen. We have already seen one example in the *Yahoo! v. La Ligue Contre Le Racisme et L'Antisemitisme* case in Part Two of this chapter, where France sought to enforce its ban on the sale of Nazi memorabilia to French citizens.

Both the United Kingdom and Germany have enforced criminal laws based on pornographic materials posted on websites outside their geographic boundaries. The United Kingdom convicted one of its citizens operating out of his home in the United Kingdom of "publication" of pornographic materials on websites located in the United States.[81] Germany originally convicted the German head of CompuServe, a U.S. company, for allowing German citizens access to pornographic websites hosted outside Germany, despite the fact that CompuServe had no feasible technological way to block access.

(Block-ing access would have required the U.S. corporation to block access to all of its customers worldwide.) The conviction was overturned a year later.[82]

Part Five—Commercial Law

Contracts and Uniform Laws

Internet sales have grown significantly, but for the Internet to reach its commercial potential a routine, well-settled contracts structure is essential. The basic ingredients of a binding contract, as we saw in Chapter 6, also apply to Internet transactions.

- **Capacity** to enter the contract.
- **Offer and acceptance** of the terms of the contract.
- **Consideration** for the promises in the contract.
- **Genuineness** of assent.
- **Legality** of purpose of the contract.

Thus, an e-mail exchange fulfilling the traditional contract requirements should result in an enforceable agreement. But what if acceptance is indicated only by providing an "electronic signature" (a digital code unique to an individual), downloading some information, opening a shrink-wrap package, or clicking an "Accept" button?

E-Signature   Electronic signatures can take a variety of forms (voice prints, distinctive marks, mathematical codes), but they share a common purpose—to have the same legal effect as a signature affixed by hand. On June 30, 2000, President Clinton signed into law the Electronic Signatures in Global and National Commerce Act (E-SIGN), giving electronic signatures the same legal stature as handwritten ones, at least for most commercial purposes.[83] Consumers, however, cannot be forced to accept electronic signature agreements or to receive records and documents electronically rather than in paper form. [For a look at the digital signature laws of the United Nations, European Union, and the United Kingdom, see **http://law.richmond.edu/jolt/v11i2/article6.pdf**]

UCITA   In 1999, the National Conference of Commissioners on Uniform State Laws (NCCUSL) approved a model law designed to achieve uniformity across the United States in the law governing software and Internet transactions. The proposed law reaches all deals involving computer information or goods and is designed to address the special problems of the electronic market, including software licensure (right to use). The Uniform Computer Information Transactions Act (UCITA) addresses the substance of computer information transactions, rather than procedural aspects such as electronic signatures.

To this point, UCITA has been amended twice (2000 and 2002), but it has been adopted in only Maryland and Virginia.[84] Until it or some other such legislation is widely approved, the Uniform Commercial Code (UCC), other applicable state and federal laws, and the common law of contracts (judge-made law) will govern electronic contractual arrangements.

(The UCC, having been approved in 49 of the 50 states, is designed to provide nationwide consistency, predictability, and fairness in contract law where a sale of goods is involved.)

Click-Wrap Agreements   Today, software is typically downloaded with license terms provided onscreen during the installation process. Those terms often say that by using the software the buyer agrees to the terms. Whether all of those terms are enforceable in court is the subject of dispute. The likelihood is that many terms will be enforceable if the buyer has a reasonable opportunity to review those terms and can abort the installation (and the charge) if the terms are unacceptable. The court in *Caspi v. Microsoft Network,*[85] applying a traditional contract law analysis, ruled that the choice of forum provision in just such an online click-wrap agreement was enforceable.

Critics are increasingly concerned, however, about just how voluntary some provisions in such standard-form contracts are. That is, has the purchaser genuinely consented to the contract terms? It can appear that retailers are, perhaps deliberately, obscuring one-sided terms.[86] Who has not viewed with trepidation the presentation of contract terms in a 2-by-4-inch scrollable window with an "Agree" button prominently displayed below?

Intellectual Property

Continued expansion of electronic commerce depends to a significant extent on the business community's success in protecting its technology from theft, copying, infringement, and the like. Intellectual property, broadly, is composed of creative ideas that are the products of the human mind. Songs, computer programs, new medicines, a novel, and so on are forms of intellectual property. Recalling our discussion of market failure in Chapter 8, you may recognize that intellectual property, from an economics point of view, is a public good.

> Intellectual property, from an economics point of view, is a public good.

Intellectual property laws have been developed to provide a measure of protection from theft and exploitation to creators of such properties. The goal is to reward those whose ingenuity and hard work have produced tangible results (recordings, movies, and the like) as an incentive for them and others to continue doing so. At least that is the American and Western view of intellectual property. Some cultures remain reluctant to recognize property rights of this kind, but globalization seems certain to generate relatively consistent intellectual property standards for most of the world. Inclusion of the Agreement on Trade-Related Aspects of Intellectual Property Rights (TRIPS Agreement) as one of the WTO's foundation agreements supports this projection. [For more on intellectual property law, see **www.ipmall.info/hosted-resources/fplchome.asp**]

Patents   Exactly what role patents will play in the future development of the Internet is still somewhat uncertain. The grant of some early patents associated with basic methods of doing business online (such as Amazon.com's "one-click" method for making Internet purchases and Priceline.com's process of "reverse" auctions) raised considerable controversy, resulting in the announcement by the U.S. Patent and Trademark Office in 2000 that it was overhauling the way it processes and awards patents for many online processes.[87] [For more on business methods patents, see **www.uspto.gov/web/menu/pbmethod**]

The Patent Wars

In recent years, the most prominent Internet-related patent issues have arisen in disputes involving the thousands of patents associated with mobile devices such as smartphones and tablets, referred to as "a tsunami of patent-related lawsuits"[88] in courts all over the world, including Australia, Britain, Germany, Japan, South Korea, the Netherlands, and the United States. The disputes have focused on acceptable license fees for standard-essential patents and on patent infringement allegations with regard to design and functionality characteristics.

Standard-essential patents are those that address matters of basic communication and data handling which support and permit industrywide standards. For example, the technology behind wireless communication requires standardization so that smartphones made by any company can interact appropriately with Wi-Fi hotspots. Within the industry, companies that own standard-essential patents have generally agreed to license the technology to other companies and to charge rates that are fair, reasonable, and nondiscriminatory (FRAND). It is in the patent holders' interest for their patents to become industry standards because license fees then produce a continuing income stream. On the other hand, it is equally important that standard-essential patent holders not be allowed to abuse their monopoly power with high fees so as to impair their competitors' financial ability to compete. Complaints of overreaching rates have generated much litigation. In one such case, Microsoft argued Motorola's offered rate could cost Microsoft $4 billion annually; the judge ruled that the interest of the whole market had to be considered in resolving the dispute, not just the interests of the two litigants, and set a rate of just under $1.8 million a year. The court pointed out that at least 92 entities own standard-essential patents related to the operational standard at issue in the suit. "If each of these 92 entities sought royalties similar to Motorola's request of 1.15% to 1.73% of the end-product price, the aggregate royalty to implement [this operational standard] would exceed the total product price."[89]

Apple and Samsung, the industry leaders in the smartphone market, have been involved in an epic patent infringement battle that began in a California federal district court in April 2011 when Apple sued Samsung for copying patented aspects of Apple's iPhones, including their distinct look (a rectangle with rounded corners) and a number of their software and hardware features. Samsung counterclaimed charging Apple with violations of some of Samsung's standard-essential patents. They have pursued this battle, over these and other patents, not just in California where this first suit was filed, but also in Germany, South Korea, the Netherlands, and the United Kingdom. In August 2012, the jury in the California case found in favor of Apple and awarded $1 billion in damages (which was later somewhat reduced). Apple proceeded to pursue an injunction against Samsung continuing to produce its smartphone models that incorporated the infringed patents. While that issue was proceeding through motions and then appeals, Samsung pursued their fight in front of the U.S. International Trade Commission (ITC), which has the power to ban importation of items that it determines infringe others' patents. The ITC ruled in June 2013 that Apple infringed some of Samsung's patents with regard to wireless connectivity and banned importation of some older models of Apple's iPhones and iPads, which order was vetoed by the Obama administration in early August, on the basis that such bans were inappropriate where the infringement was related to standard-essential patents such as was the case with the Samsung patents at issue. A mere week later, the ITC issued another order banning importation, this time at Apple's request and against certain Samsung devices. This time no standard-essential patents were involved.

At the time of this writing, there has been no, and likely won't be any, clear winner in these battles between Apple and Samsung. But then, many observers have pointed out that these battles aren't really about patent protection, but rather represent a battle for dominance in the mobile device market, including smartphones and tablets. It is worthy of note that in other contexts, Apple and Samsung work in concert: Apple is the largest customer for components manufactured by Samsung.[90]

Copyrights

In America and much of the world, anyone who creates "original works of authorship," whether in print or digital form, is in most cases automatically protected by copyright laws if the "works" are original and are "fixed in tangible form" (written down on paper, for example). The author has exclusive rights to commercially exploit those works for a period of years. Virtually all of the information available online is protected by the U.S. Copyright Act and includes such intellectual creations as data, databases, literature, music, software, photos, and multimedia works. Although original works of authorship are automatically copyrighted, the fullest protection of the law can only be achieved by placing a copyright notice on the work (such as "copyright 2014 McGraw-Hill") and registering the copyright with the U.S. Copyright Office. International protection is provided by the principal copyright treaty, the Berne Convention. [Information on the U.S. Copyright Office can be found at **www.copyright.gov**]

The copyright holder possesses the exclusive right to (1) reproduce the copyrighted work, (2) prepare adaptations based on the copyrighted material, (3) distribute the material by sale or otherwise, and (4) perform or display the material. When anyone other than the copyright holder, or one acting with the holder's permission, makes use of one of those rights, the copyright has been infringed unless the use falls within a series of exceptions. Perhaps the most notable of those exceptions is the *fair use doctrine*, which allows use of copyrighted material without permission under some conditions, such as limited, nonprofit use in a classroom.

Another exception is the *first sale doctrine*, which provides that someone who owns a copy of a copyrighted work is free to resell it without infringing on the author's rights. The court in *Capitol Records v. ReDIGI* held that songs bought from Apple's iTunes and similar retailers cannot be resold by the original purchaser under the first sale doctrine because the doctrine protects only the owner of a particular copy, and no one can own a particular copy of a digital song—all copies are indistinguishable. It was also persuaded by the fact that physical copies degrade, whereas a digital copy could last forever.[91]

One of the most visible Internet copyright disputes has been the ongoing battle of the music recording industry to protect its copyrights. Music file sharing took off in the late 1990s through the use of the Napster website, where users could swap digital music. The recording industry successfully obtained an injunction against Napster's facilitation of such file sharing;[92] but the practice continued, aided by peer-to-peer computer programs such as KaZaA and Grokster, which are installed on users' computers. The recording industry sued Grokster and other file-sharing software distributors. The defendants prevailed at the district and circuit court levels.[93] Then, in the following unanimous Supreme Court decision, the recording industry achieved a major victory.

Metro-Goldwyn-Mayer Studios v. Grokster
125 S.Ct. 2764 (2005)

Justice Souter

I

A

Respondents, Grokster, Ltd., and StreamCast Networks, Inc., defendants in the trial court, distribute free software products that allow computer users to share electronic files through peer-to-peer networks, so called because users' computers communicate directly with each other, not through central servers. . . .

A group of copyright holders (MGM for short, but including motion picture studios, recording companies, songwriters, and music publishers) sued Grokster and StreamCast for their users' copyright infringements, alleging that they knowingly and intentionally distributed their software to enable users to reproduce and distribute the copyrighted works in violation of the Copyright Act.

* * * * *

Although Grokster and StreamCast do not know when particular files are copied, a few searches using their software would show what is available on the networks the software reaches. MGM commissioned a statistician to conduct a systematic search, and his study showed that nearly 90 percent of the files available for download on the FastTrack system were copyrighted works. Grokster and StreamCast dispute this figure. . . . They also argue that potential noninfringing uses of their software are significant in kind, even if infrequent in practice. Some musical performers, for example, have gained new audiences by distributing their copyrighted works for free across peer-to-peer networks, and some distributors of unprotected content have used peer-to-peer networks to disseminate files, Shakespeare being an example. . . .

But MGM's evidence gives reason to think that the vast majority of users' downloads are acts of infringement, and because well over 100 million copies of the software in question are known to have been downloaded, and billions of files are shared across the FastTrack and Gnutella networks each month, the probable scope of copyright infringement is staggering.

Grokster and StreamCast concede the infringement in most downloads, and it is uncontested that they are aware that users employ their software primarily to download copyrighted files, even if the decentralized . . . networks fail to reveal which files are being copied, and when. . . .

Grokster and StreamCast are not, however, merely passive recipients of information about infringing use. The record is replete with evidence that from the moment Grokster and StreamCast began to distribute their free software, each one clearly voiced the objective that recipients use it to download copyrighted works, and each took active steps to encourage infringement.

After the notorious file-sharing service, Napster, was sued by copyright holders for facilitation of copyright infringement, StreamCast gave away a software program of a kind known as OpenNap, designed as compatible with the Napster program and open to Napster users for downloading files from other Napster and OpenNap users' computers. Evidence indicates that "it was always [StreamCast's] intent to use [its OpenNap network] to be able to capture e-mail addresses of [its] initial target market so that [it] could promote [its] StreamCast Morpheus interface to them."

* * * * *

StreamCast developed promotional materials to market its service as the best Napster alternative. One proposed advertisement read, "Napster Inc. has announced that it will soon begin charging you a fee. That's if the courts don't order it shut down first. What will you do to get around it?" Another proposed ad touted StreamCast's software as the "#1 alternative to Napster" and asked "when the lights went off at Napster . . . where did the users go?"

* * * * *

In addition to this evidence of express promotion, marketing, and intent to promote further, the business models employed by Grokster and StreamCast confirm that their principal object was use of their software to download copyrighted works. Grokster and StreamCast receive no revenue from users, who obtain the software itself for nothing. Instead, both companies generate income by selling advertising space, and they stream the advertising to Grokster and Morpheus users while they are employing the programs. As the number of users of each program increases, advertising opportunities become worth more.

Finally, there is no evidence that either company made an effort to filter copyrighted material from users' downloads or otherwise impede the sharing of copyrighted files. . . .

B

The District Court . . . granted summary judgment in favor of Grokster and StreamCast as to any liability arising from distribution of the then current versions of their software.

Distributing that software gave rise to no liability in the court's view, because its use did not provide the distributors with actual knowledge of specific acts of infringement.

The Court of Appeals affirmed. In the court's analysis, a defendant was liable as a contributory infringer when it had knowledge of direct infringement and materially contributed to the infringement. But the court read [our decision in] *Sony Corp. of America v. Universal City Studios, Inc.* as holding that distribution of a commercial product capable of substantial noninfringing uses could not give rise to contributory liability for infringement unless the distributor had actual knowledge of specific instances of infringement and failed to act on that knowledge. The fact that the software was capable of substantial noninfringing uses in the Ninth Circuit's view meant that Grokster and StreamCast were not liable, because they had no such actual knowledge, owing to the decentralized architecture of their software. The court also held that Grokster and StreamCast did not materially contribute to their users' infringement because it was the users themselves who searched for, retrieved, and stored the infringing files, with no involvement by the defendants beyond providing the software in the first place.

II
A

* * * * *

The argument for imposing indirect liability in this case is . . . a powerful one, given the number of infringing downloads that occur every day using StreamCast's and Grokster's software. When a widely shared service or product is used to commit infringement, it may be impossible to enforce rights in the protected work effectively against all direct infringers, the only practical alternative being to go against the distributor of the copying device for secondary liability on a theory of contributory or vicarious infringement.

B

* * * * *

In *Sony Corp. v. Universal City Studios* this Court addressed a claim that secondary liability for infringement can arise from the very distribution of a commercial product. There, the product, novel at the time, was what we know today as the videocassette recorder or VCR. Copyright holders sued Sony as the manufacturer, claiming it was contributorily liable for infringement that occurred when VCR owners taped copyrighted programs because it supplied the means used to infringe, and it had constructive knowledge that infringement would occur. At the trial on the merits, the evidence showed that the principal use of the VCR was for "'time-shifting,'" or taping a program for later viewing at a more

convenient time, which the Court found to be a fair, not an infringing, use. There was no evidence that Sony had expressed an object of bringing about taping in violation of copyright or had taken active steps to increase its profits from unlawful taping. Although Sony's advertisements urged consumers to buy the VCR to "'record favorite shows'" or "'build a library'" of recorded programs, neither of these uses was necessarily infringing.

On those facts, with no evidence of stated or indicated intent to promote infringing uses, the only conceivable basis for imposing liability was on a theory of contributory infringement arising from its sale of VCRs to consumers with knowledge that some would use them to infringe. But because the VCR was "capable of commercially significant noninfringing uses," we held the manufacturer could not be faulted solely on the basis of its distribution.

* * * * *

Because the Circuit [Court of Appeals] found the StreamCast and Grokster software capable of substantial lawful use, it concluded on the basis of its reading of Sony that neither company could be held liable, since there was no showing that their software, being without any central server, afforded them knowledge of specific unlawful uses.

This view of *Sony,* however, was error. . . .

C

[Nothing] in *Sony* requires courts to ignore evidence of intent if there is such evidence. . . . Thus, where evidence goes beyond a product's characteristics or the knowledge that it may be put to infringing uses, and shows statements or actions directed to promoting infringement, *Sony's* . . . rule will not preclude liability. The classic case of direct evidence of unlawful purpose occurs when one induces commission of infringement by another, or "entices or persuades another" to infringe, as by advertising.

* * * * *

[The] inducement rule is a sensible one for copyright. We adopt it here, holding that one who distributes a device with the object of promoting its use to infringe copyright, as shown by clear expression or other affirmative steps taken to foster infringement, is liable for the resulting acts of infringement by third parties. We are, of course, mindful of the need to keep from trenching on regular commerce or discouraging the development of technologies with lawful and unlawful potential. Accordingly, just as *Sony* did not find intentional inducement despite the knowledge of the VCR manufacturer that its device could be used to infringe, mere knowledge of infringing potential or of actual infringing uses would not be enough here to subject a distributor to liability. Nor would ordinary acts incident to product distribution, such as offering customers technical support or product updates, support liability in themselves. The inducement rule, instead, premises liability on purposeful, culpable expression and conduct, and thus does nothing to compromise legitimate commerce or discourage innovation having a lawful promise.

III

A

The only apparent question about treating MGM's evidence as sufficient to withstand summary judgment under the theory of inducement goes to the need on MGM's part to adduce evidence that StreamCast and Grokster communicated an inducing message to their software users.

* * * * *

Here, the . . . record is replete with evidence that Grokster and StreamCast, unlike the manufacturer and distributor in *Sony*, acted with a purpose to cause copyright violations by use of software suitable for illegal use.

Three features of this evidence of intent are particularly notable. First, each company showed itself to be aiming to satisfy a known source of demand for copyright infringement, the market comprising former Napster users.

* * * * *

Second, this evidence of unlawful objective is given added significance by MGM's showing that neither company attempted to develop filtering tools or other mechanisms to diminish the infringing activity using their software.

Third, [it] is useful to recall that StreamCast and Grokster make money by selling advertising space, by directing ads to the screens of computers employing their software. . . .

B

In addition to intent to bring about infringement and distribution of a device suitable for infringing use, the inducement theory of course requires evidence of actual infringement by recipients of the device, the software in this case. As the account of the facts indicates, there is evidence of infringement on a gigantic scale, and there is no serious issue of the ade-

quacy of MGM's showing on this point. . . . There is substantial evidence in MGM's favor on all elements of inducement, and summary judgment in favor of Grokster and StreamCast was error.

[Vacated and remanded.]

Questions

1. *a.* Explain how the Court was able to hold software distributors like Grokster liable for the misconduct of others (those who actually used the peer-to-peer networks to download copyrighted materials).

   b. What does the Court mean by "contributory" and "vicarious" copyright infringement?

   c. Why did the Supreme Court overrule the Court of Appeals decision?

2. Has this decision effectively stopped illegal downloading of copyrighted material? Explain.

3. As a consequence of this decision, is peer-to-peer technology now unlawful? Explain.

4. In your judgment do Grokster and other peer-to-peer software distributors have a moral responsibility regarding the unlawful use of their products by third parties? Explain.

AFTERWORD

Concurrently with suing file-sharing facilitators such as Grokster and StreamCast, the recording industry pursued the file sharers as well—35,000 of them between 2003 and 2008 including many university students.[94] According to one source, in 2006 "college students illegally obtained two-thirds of their music and accounted for 1.3 billion illegal downloads."[95] Under the Digital Millennium Copyright Act (DMCA), copyright holders can subpoena ISPs, including universities, to obtain the identity of those believed to be infringing. Of the 35,000 identified file sharers mentioned above, 12,000 lawsuits were filed, with two ultimately proceeding to trial. In one, a jury set damages against a former graduate student of $22,500 per song. The $675,000 award became final after the Supreme Court declined to hear the student's petition in 2012.[96] Just one month later, the Eighth Circuit reinstated a jury verdict of $220,000 in the second case.[97]

Market Response

While record labels were pursuing copyright infringers, some of the largest online music stores changed policies to remove usage restrictions from downloaded files. In mid-2007, both Apple and Amazon.com announced that their music would no longer be locked to certain players or programs. Both have the support of EMI, one of the largest record labels. The restrictions against putting their downloads on multiple computers and mobile devices (restrictions that aren't imposed when a CD is purchased) had long annoyed consumers. It had also drawn the unfavorable attention of EU regulators, who saw it as a form of unfair competition.[98]

In 2013, Amazon and Apple once more seemed to be positioning themselves to lead the market. In January 2013, Amazon received a patent "to set up an exchange for all sorts of digital material."[99] And in March 2013, the U.S. Patent and Trademark Office published an application from Apple for a patent of its own for a digital marketplace for users to sell or give away various digital copyrighted material. Thus, both companies seem to be exploring the possibility of having the first sale doctrine apply to digital copies or perhaps lobbying for a statutory change to the DMCA.

Grokster Redux?

In 2007, Viacom sued Google's YouTube video-sharing service alleging willful facilitation of infringement on a massive scale of Viacom's copyrights from shows on Comedy Central, MTV, and Nickelodeon. Viacom claimed over $1 billion in damages.[100] The trial court granted YouTube's motion for summary judgment. The DMCA provides a safe harbor against copyright infringement claims for ISPs and host websites if the host site responds expeditiously to remove, or disable access to, the copyrighted material when notified of violations. The court pointed out that Viacom had invoked the DMCA safe harbor when it notified YouTube of 100,000 offending videos and, by the next business day, YouTube had removed virtually all of them.[101] The Second Circuit vacated the decision, stating that, at least with respect to "a handful of the offending clips," "a reasonable jury could conclude that YouTube had knowledge or awareness" of infringement. It also directed the lower court to consider whether YouTube had been "willfully blind" to the presence of infringing material on its site. On remand, the lower court was to "allow the parties to brief [the specified] issues, with a view to permitting renewed motions for summary judgment as soon as practicable."[102] A year later, the lower court once again granted YouTube's motion for summary judgment, in a two-sentence opinion presenting summary conclusions on the issues remanded by the Second Circuit without analysis.[103]

What should be clear at this point is that copyright infringement is rampant, and the Internet has caused its exponential growth. What is not at all clear is what can or should be done about it. On the one side, content owners individually have very little ability to stop infringement of their copyrights. On the other side, seeking to impose the cost of protection on payment processors, advertising services, and domain name registries, as the Stop Online Piracy Act (SOPA) and the PROTECT IP Act (both introduced in Congress in 2012) would have done, may be costly to those middlemen and, in the end, not much more effective. Costly because reviewing and removing all the potentially infringing material would be a herculean task. Likely ineffective because offending content could be posted from and in any part of the world and still be accessible in nearly any other part.[104] This problem lets us reconsider an issue we have seen repeatedly in this text—who has the power and the right to assert jurisdiction over what is a worldwide problem? At the moment, there really is no answer to that question.

Trademarks and Domain Names

Trademarks

Words, names, symbols, devices, or combinations thereof that are used to distinguish one seller's products from those of another are called *trademarks* when associated with products (like IBM, Coke, and Pepsi) and *service marks* when associated with service businesses (United Airlines). Having established a trademark (or service mark), the holder can prohibit any unauthorized use of the mark, thus ensuring consumers can trust the source of goods they are buying. The mark also protects mark owners by preventing loss of reputation and value, for example, when the unauthorized product is of poor quality. Mark owners are also protected from an increase in supply that dilutes the product's value. Infringement cannot occur unless, however, the marks are sufficiently similar that consumers could be confused.

The Internet has created new opportunities for confusion and, therefore, potential infringement. Recall the discussion of the dispute between Google and Louis Vuitton from Chapter 16. The issue was whether Google was infringing on Vuitton's trademarks by selling ad space to Vuitton's competitors at the top of Google's search results when individuals used Google's search engine looking for Vuitton products. The European Court of Justice said no. Another company that has had to defend repeated trademark infringement suits is eBay. Individuals sometimes try to sell counterfeit goods on eBay. At times, for some luxury goods manufacturers, the percentage of counterfeits available on the site had been quite high. The issue raised is the extent to which eBay has a duty to weed out counterfeit goods. After being sued, eBay improved its processes to greatly lessen the quantity of counterfeits sold, but it is also protected from liability by quickly removing any items when advised by the trademark holder that the goods are counterfeit.

Domain Names

The Internet address for a Web page is called its domain name. The Domain Name System (DNS) for the whole of the Internet is overseen by the Internet Corporation for Assigned Names and Numbers (ICANN), a nonprofit organization with its headquarters in California. Ordinarily, a business engaging in electronic commerce will want to use the simplest form of its name as its domain name. Rights to a domain name are secured simply by being the first to request a name and pay the registration fee. The 1999 Anticybersquatting Consumer Protection Act creates a cause of action if a trademark is infringed by another's registration of a domain name that Web searchers may confuse with that trademark. The Third Circuit has also held that registration of deliberate misspellings of famous marks is a violation of the act.[105]

In 1999, ICANN set up an arbitration process for the resolution of domain name disputes. Since then, more than 20,000 cases have been filed, of which 91 percent have been decided for the complainant.[106] Carmen Electra, Michael Crichton, Kevin Spacey, Pamela Anderson, Celine Dion, and Bruce Springsteen have all used the process to have domain name versions of their names transferred to them, all of which were previously registered by the same Canadian company.[107] [For information on the arbitration services available from the United Nations' World Intellectual Property Organization pursuant to ICANN's domain name arbitration policy, see **www.wipo.int/amc/en/domains**]

PRACTICING ETHICS) Top-Level Domain Name Sale

At this writing, more than a thousand new top-level domain names (TLDs) are just starting to go live. TLDs are the descriptors that follow the period in a Web address, such as .com, .org, and .gov. Up until 2014, there were 22 general TLDs and 280 country-specific ones.[108] Some of the new TLDs will be written in Arabic, Chinese, and Russian scripts; others are likely to be company names, such as .google or .amazon; still others will be generic terms, such as .blog or .pizza. Successful registrants will have the right to sell second-level domains (the portion of the address that precedes the TLD). Thus, popular TLDs could also be very lucrative to their holders. Verisign, which currently manages the .com and .net TLDs, reported $874 million in 2012 revenues. ICANN accepted proposals from applicants for both open-use TLDs and restricted TLDs, the use of which the successful applicant might reserve solely for itself. L'Oreal is seeking the TLD .beauty and has stated that it would reserve some second-level domains, such as personal.beauty for itself. Amazon indicated that all of the TLDs for which it applied will be closed, for its use only. ICANN has indicated, however, that it has not yet determined whether to allow "closed generic domains."[109] [For more on the new TLDs, see **http://newgtlds.icann.org/en**]

Questions

1. If you were a member of ICANN, who would you vote to give the TLD of .amazon to—Amazon.com or the consortium of Latin American countries through which the Amazon River runs?[110] Would you agree to the creation of such TLDs as .Jew, .Christian, .Muslim, .Baha'i, .Moses, .Jesus, and .Mohamad? Explain. Should community, cultural, historical interests—such as the use of a name—be in control of commercial interests and individual companies? Discuss.

2. Applicants were charged $185,000 for each TLD application they filed. They will incur another $25,000 annually for each TLD they retain.[111] Do these fees raise ethical issues in terms of who might have wanted to control a particular TLD, but were financially unable to pay these fees? Explain.

3. Donuts Inc. filed the most applications, 307, and paid $57 million for the privilege to do so.[112] It was the only applicant for 149 of them. Some have expressed concern with Donuts Inc. as an appropriate registrant because of its alleged ties to Demand Media, "a company with a well-documented history of providing services to spammers and other perpetrators of Internet abuses."[113] Demand Media has been a "host to sites that commit 'cybersquatting.'"[114] Would you vote to allow Donuts Inc. to control over a hundred new TLDs? Discuss.

4. As stated above, Donuts Inc. applied for 307 TLDs. Google applied for 101 TLDs; Amazon for 76.[115] Should one entity be permitted to control that many TLDs? Is it anticompetitive to give control over generic TLDs to private companies? Discuss.

Taxes

We close this chapter with an interesting public policy question raised by the remarkable confusion (and profusion) of the Internet. It is a policy issue, like many discussed in this chapter, that crosses traditional jurisdictional lines—both state boundaries in the United States and national boundaries around the world. Its resolution, either at the national level or at the international level, will require substantial negotiation, compromise and, ultimately, consensus building.

What is the issue? We start with a national example: If you buy a CD on the Internet, your neighborhood retailer will not receive your business and your state and local governments often will not receive sales taxes as they would have if you had made the purchase at a local store. In pre-Internet days the Supreme Court had ruled that an out-of-state vendor cannot be required to collect sales taxes for any state in which that vendor does not have some significant presence, including a physical presence.[116] The Court held that it would be an undue burden on interstate commerce for states to be able to require out-of-state vendors to comply with each unique set of state and local sales tax rules. Thus, many states joined an effort to streamline, simplify, and coordinate their sales tax laws. The idea is that, if state sales taxes are more uniform, the burden on interstate commerce from requiring the compliance of out-of-state vendors will be materially reduced.

As of this writing, a majority of states have been involved in the project, and 23 states and the District of Columbia have conformed their laws to the requirements of the negotiated agreement, which became operational in 2005. Participation on the part of vendors is voluntary, but many have registered and are now remitting taxes to member states. The primary incentive for voluntary participation is a grant of amnesty for any prior unpaid taxes that might have been owed.[117] [For more on the Multistate Tax Compact, see **www.mtc.gov**]

That said, many online businesses have not agreed to submit voluntarily to collection of state taxes in states where they have no physical presence. Seven states are attempting to push the point through state legislation that defines nexus more broadly than determined by the Supreme Court in 1992. New York has passed such a law and sought to enforce it by suing noncomplying Internet vendors. The highest state court ruled that the state could require Internet retailers to collect sales taxes "if a vendor is paying New York residents to actively solicit business in this state" and denied appeals from both Amazon.com and Overstock.com. With regard to the law's constitutionality under the prior Supreme Court decision, the New York judge wrote, "The world has changed dramatically in the last two decades and it may be that the physical presence test is outdated. An entity may now have a profound impact upon a foreign jurisdiction solely through its virtual projection via the Internet. That question, however, would be for the United States Supreme Court to consider."[118] That may be, but in December 2013 the Supreme Court declined to do so when it declined the companies' petitions for *certiorari*, leaving New York's ruling to stand, thus requiring collection of state sales taxes.[119]

The problem is just as complex, if not more so, on an international scale. Here the issue spans the whole range of taxes, paralleling both our income tax laws and our sales tax laws. In a nutshell, what nation is entitled to tax cross-border transactions? In the international arena, certain key principles were adopted in 1998 by the countries that comprise the Organization for Economic Cooperation and Development (OECD), including the principle that consumption taxes (like our sales taxes) should be collected by the jurisdiction where consumption takes place. But finding workable arrangements to effectuate the general principles has proven elusive. [For more on the OECD, see **www.oecd.org**]

Reprise: Who Governs Cyberspace?

We near the end of this chapter examining the same kinds of questions we have raised throughout this book: How much government do we need in our lives? To what extent should government restrain the explosive and stupendously successful cyberspace industry? Is the Internet a bit too much of a "Wild West" environment for the general good? Consider the story that follows:

Bitcoin: The Rise and Fall of a Virtual Currency

A paper published anonymously in 2008 outlined a method for creating a digital currency that could be exchanged on a peer-to-peer basis, but which would not be susceptible to unauthorized duplication. A year later the first Bitcoins were "mined" using an open-source program, which by design constrains how many digital coins can be created and at what intervals (currently 25 every 10 minutes, but dropping in half every four years, with a total cap of 21 million). Digital currencies, of which Bitcoin is just one example, although the one with the largest circulation thus far, are creatures of the Internet. They may have no issuing or governing body, can be self-authenticating, and are usable worldwide by members of the general public to engage in the same types of direct, one-to-one transactions that daily occur using government-issued currencies.

As a currency, a digital currency may have some advantages over other mediums of exchange. For example, merchants may prefer payment in Bitcoins because there is little or no transaction cost, in contrast to the 2 to 3 percent charged on most credit card transactions. Fees are charged on exchanges of Bitcoins into or out of a specific national currency, which is also true for any foreign-exchange transaction. But the global nature of Bitcoin makes such exchanges less necessary—or at least will make them less necessary if its fluctuation in value ultimately settles down. At present, however, its value can fluctuate tremendously. For example, as of early March 2013, one exchange showed its historical high closing at $1,147 on December 4, 2013, but on February 25, 2014, the closing was $535, following the announcement that the world's largest Bitcoin exchange, Mt. Gox in Japan, was likely to file for bankruptcy following its discovery of a large theft from its exchange. Just a week later, however, the price was hovering around $660.[120]

Another cause of its fluctuating price is that the currency has largely gone unregulated by the world's governments. The United States has exerted some authority over the regulation of exchanges that deal in Bitcoin, but the currency itself is largely free of governmental interference. If the currency is going to survive, that likely will change at least to some degree.

Question

The questions for digital currencies are, of course, should they be regulated and, if so, by whom? Based on Bitcoin's short history, what could regulation achieve? What might it impede?

Internet Exercise

Review the materials on privacy issues in this chapter and then log on to the website for an Internet vendor that you, or someone you know, has used. Can you find the vendor's privacy policy? Is it easy to find? Is it easy to access, read, and understand? How long is it? How complicated? Do any of its provisions surprise you? What control do you have over the use of your personal information by that vendor? Is that information easy to find? Can you tell when the policy was last updated and what changes were made in it? Has the policy received approval from TRUSTe.org (indicated by a seal displayed on the policy page)? Would you purchase again from this vendor?

Chapter Questions

1. The United Nations has warned that the worldwide growth of e commerce may constitute a threat to the well-being of the world's developing nations as well as parts of Europe. Explain the U.N. concerns.

2. Psychologists are worried that the Internet will make shopping too easy. Explain their concern.

3. In March 1992, Danish police seized the business records of BAMSE, a computer bulletin board system based in Denmark that sold child pornography over the Internet. The records included information that Mohrbacher, who lived in Paradise, California, had downloaded two graphic interface format (GIF) images from BAMSE in January 1992.

   In March 1993, police executed a search warrant at Mohrbacher's workplace and found, among other images, two files that had been downloaded from BAMSE, one of a nude girl and one of a girl engaged in a sex act with an adult; both girls were under 12. During the execution of the warrant, Mohrbacher was cooperative, confessing that he had downloaded the two images from BAMSE. Mohrbacher was charged with transporting or shipping images by computer as prohibited by 18 U.S.C. 2252(a)(1). Mohrbacher argued that downloading is properly characterized as receiving images by computer, which is proscribed by section 2252(a)(2). He was not charged under (a)(2).

   Should downloading from a computer bulletin board constitute shipping or transporting within the meaning of 18 U.S.C. section 2252(a)(1)? Explain. See *U.S. v. Mohrbacher,* 182 F.3d 1041 (9th Cir. 1999).

4. *a.* Should online bloggers be entitled to protection as journalists under the First Amendment with regard to the confidentiality of their sources?

   b. What if those sources have illegally revealed corporate trade secrets?[121]

5. America Online (AOL), an ISP, sued TSF Marketing and Joseph Melle, who founded TSF. AOL claimed that Melle and TSF sent spam to AOL subscribers. The e-mail contained the letters "aol.com" in the headers. AOL claimed that the e-mail totaled some 60 million messages over a 10-month period. Melle allegedly continued the mailings after he was notified in writing by AOL to stop. AOL received over 50,000 complaints from subscribers. AOL claimed, among other things, that Melle had diluted its trademark.[122] The case arose before the passage of the CAN-SPAM Act. Would Melle have been liable under that act? Explain.

6. McLaren was an employee of Microsoft Corporation. In December 1996, Microsoft suspended McLaren's employment pending an investigation into accusations of sexual harassment and "inventory questions." McLaren requested access to his electronic mail to disprove the allegations against him. According to McLaren, he was told he could access his e-mail only by requesting it through company officials and telling them the location of a particular message. By memorandum, McLaren requested that no one tamper with his Microsoft office workstation or his e-mail. McLaren's employment was terminated on December 11, 1996.

   Following the termination of his employment, McLaren filed suit against the company alleging as his sole cause of action a claim for invasion of privacy. In support of his claim, McLaren alleged that, on information and belief, Microsoft had invaded his privacy by "breaking into" some or all of the personal folders maintained on his office computer and releasing the contents of the folders to third parties. According to McLaren, the personal folders were part of a computer application created by Microsoft in which e-mail messages could be stored. Access to the e-mail system was obtained through a network password. Access to personal folders could be additionally restricted by a "personal store" password created by the individual user. McLaren created and used a personal store password to restrict access to his personal folders.

McLaren concedes in his petition that it was possible for Microsoft to "decrypt" his personal store password. McLaren alleges, however, that "[b]y allowing [him] to have a personal store password for his personal folders, [McLaren] manifested and [Microsoft] recognized an expectation that the personal folders would be free from intrusion and interference." McLaren characterizes Microsoft's decrypting or otherwise "breaking in" to his personal folders as an intentional, unjustified, and unlawful invasion of privacy.

Did Microsoft unlawfully invade McLaren's privacy? Explain. See *McLaren v. Microsoft,* 1999 Texas App. LEXIS 4103 (5th Dist., Dallas).

7. Bensusan Restaurant Corporation owns the famous New York City jazz club "The Blue Note," and in 1985 it registered the name as a federal trademark. Since 1980, King has operated a small club in Columbia, Missouri, also named "The Blue Note." Around 1993, Bensusan wrote to King demanding that he discontinue use of "The Blue Note" name. King's attorney responded by saying that Bensusan had no legal right to make the demand. In 1996, King created, in Missouri, a website for "The Blue Note," which also contained a hyperlink to the New York club's website. Bensusan then sued in the Southern District of New York, alleging Lanham Act and trademark violations, among other things. The New York court dismissed the case for lack of personal jurisdiction. Bensusan appealed. Decide. Explain. See *Bensusan Restaurant Corp. v. King,* 126 F.3d 25 (2d Cir. 1997).

8. Plaintiff Marobie-FL, Inc., released software of copyrighted clip art for use in the fire service industry. Robisheaux administered the National Association of Fire Equipment Distributors (NAFED) Web page. He received the clip art from a source that he could not remember. He placed the clip art on NAFED's Web page. At that point, the clip art could be readily accessed and downloaded by any Web user. Marobie claimed copyright infringement. Among other arguments, NAFED claimed that its display of the clip art constituted a fair use, within the meaning of federal copyright law. Decide. Explain. See *Marobie-FL v. National Ass'n of Fire Equip. Dist.,* 983 F.Supp. 1167 (N.D. Ill. 1997).

9. Journalist John Snell remarked, "Not long ago you couldn't turn around in cyberspace without bumping into a tech geek. Now you're no more than a mouse click away from a lawyer. Attorneys are everywhere."[123] What factors account for the dramatic increase in lawyers addressing Internet issues?

Notes

1. **www.internetworldwide.com/stats.htm**.
2. Duncan B. Hollis, "E-War Rules of Engagement," *Los Angeles Times,* October 8, 2007.
3. Anick Jesdanun, "As Internet Turns 40, Barriers Run Contrary to Creators' Aims," *The Des Moines Register,* August 31, 2009, p. 1A.
4. Thomas L. Friedman, "The Great Iceland Meltdown," *The New York Times,* October 19, 2008. Although this statement was offered in a somewhat different context—the financial crisis of 2008—it is equally applicable to this discussion of the Internet.

5. "The World Is What You Make It," *The Economist,* October 27, 2012, p. 20.

6. "Doing the ICANN-can," *The Economist,* March 22, 2014, p. 62.

7. Edward Wyatt, "Most of U.S. Is Wired, but Millions Aren't Plugged In," *The New York Times,* August 18, 2013.

8. Evelyn M. Rusli and Don Clark, "Facebook CEO Announces Internet Access Project," *The Wall Street Journal*, August 21, 2013.

9. Ibid.

10. *Verizon v. F.C.C.*, _ F.3d _, 2014 WL 113946 (D.C. Cir. 2014); Gautham Nagesh and Brent Kendall, "Appeals Court Strikes Down FCC's Net Neutrality Rules," *The Wall Street Journal*, January 14, 2014; Edward Wyatt, "Industry and Congress Await the F.C.C. Chairman's Next Moves on Internet Rules," *The New York Times*, February 9, 2014.

11. Edward Wyatt, "F.C.C. Backs Opening Net Neutrality Rules for Debate," *The New York Times,* May 15, 2014.

12. "Ex-CompuServe Chief's Conviction Overturned; German Case Involved Child Porn Sites," *Houston Chronicle,* November 18, 1999, p. 3. The head of CompuServe Germany was convicted in 1998 of violating German law by failing to block CompuServe's customers' access to child pornography websites. At the time the only technical way for CompuServe to comply was to block all of its worldwide users from access. The conviction was reversed in 1999.

13. See *Revell v. Lidov,* 317 F.3d 467 (5th Cir. 2002). Lidov posted an article he wrote on the "bombing of Pan Am Flight 103, which exploded over Lockerbie, Scotland, in 1988. The article alleges that a broad politically motivated conspiracy among senior members of the Reagan administration lay behind their willful failure to stop the bombing despite clear advance warnings. Furthermore, Lidov charged that the government proceeded to cover up its receipt of advance warning. . . . Specifically, the article singles out Oliver "Buck" Revell, then Associate Deputy Director of the FBI, for severe criticism, accusing him of complicity in the conspiracy and cover-up." The article was posted on an Internet bulletin board maintained by Columbia University's School of Journalism. "At the time he wrote the article, Lidov had never been to Texas, except possibly to change planes, or conducted business there, and was apparently unaware that Revell then resided in Texas." "Columbia, since it began keeping records, never received more than 20 Internet subscriptions to the *Columbia Journalism Review* from Texas residents." The Fifth Circuit found that neither general nor specific jurisdiction existed in the Texas courts.

14. *Mink v. AAAA Development,* 190 F.3d 333 (5th Cir. 1999).

15. See, for example, *Pavlovich v. DVD Copy Control Association.* A California appeals court held that a Texas resident was subject to California's jurisdiction for the knowing posting of trade secrets of a California company on an Indiana website. 91 Cal. App. 4th 409, 109 Cal. Rptr.2d 909 (Cal. Ct. App. 2001). But the California Supreme Court reversed. 58 P.3d 2 (Cal. 2002). See also *Gator.com Corp. v. L. L. Bean, Inc.,* where the district court held that L. L. Bean could not be sued in California where it had no stores or agents, although it did sell merchandise to California residents through its website. 2001 U.S. Dist. LEXIS 19373 (N.D. Cal. 2001). A three-judge panel of the Ninth Circuit reversed, finding in part that the volume of Internet business done by L. L. Bean with California residents made it subject to California's jurisdiction. 341 F.3d 1072 (9th Cir. 2003). That decision was vacated, however, when the Ninth Circuit decided to rehear the case en banc. 366 F.3d 789 (9th Cir. 2004). After oral argument on the rehearing, however, Gator.com and L. L. Bean settled their substantive dispute, and thus the Ninth Circuit dismissed the appeal because of the lack of a continuing case or controversy. 398 F.3d 1125 (2005).

16. Ryan Davis, "7th Circ. Lets Bulgarian Dating Site Off Hook in IP Row," *Law 360,* April 27, 2011 [**www.law360.com**].

17. Rachel Donadio, "Larger Threat Is Seen in Google Case," *The New York Times,* February 25, 2010.

18. Eric Pfanner, "Italian Appeals Court Acquits 3 Google Executives in Privacy Case," *The New York Times,* December 21, 2012.

19. Stephan Wilske and Teresa Schiller, "International Jurisdiction in Cyberspace: Which States May Regulate the Internet?" *Federal Communications Law Journal* 50 (December 1997), p. 117.

20. 433 F.3d 1199 (9th Cir. 2006).

21. 126 S.Ct. 2332 (2006).

22. *Obsidian Finance Group v. Cox,* _ F.3d _ , 2014 WL 185376 (9th Cir. 2014). At trial, a federal jury found a Montana-based blogger had defamed both an Oregon attorney and the finance firm of which he was a principal, awarding damages to both plaintiffs. In her blog, defendant had asserted the attorney, a court-appointed trustee in a bankruptcy proceeding, had committed tax fraud. The Ninth Circuit held that unlawful acts of a person in such a position was a matter of public concern. Thus, plaintiffs could not prevail simply by proving the assertion to be false, but were also required to prove negligence on plaintiff's part. In addition, any damage award would require proof of actual damages. The case was remanded for a new trial.

23. "42% of Youths Report Exposure to Porn on Web," *The Des Moines Register,* February 5, 2007, p. 5A.

24. *Reno v. ACLU,* 521 U.S. 844 (1997).

25. *ACLU v. Gonzales,* 478 F.Supp. 775 (E.D. Pa. 2007); *Mukasey v. ACLU,* 139 S.Ct. 1032 (2009).

26. *Ashcroft v. Free Speech Coalition,* 122 S.Ct. 1389 (2002).

27. Christine Arena, "Child Porn Too Big for Law Enforcement? Microsoft Steps In," *The Christian Science Monitor,* June 13, 2010.

28. *McIntyre v. Ohio Elections Comm'n,* 514 U.S. 334, 342 (1995).

29. Ibid.

30. *In re Anonymous Online Speakers v. U.S. Dist. Ct. for the Dist. of Nevada, Reno,* 2011 WL 61635 (9th Cir. 2011).

31. Somini Sengupta, "Free Speech in the Age of YouTube," *The New York Times,* September 22, 2012.

32. Robert L. Rogers III, "Two federal cases hold website 'responsible' for postings on thedirty.com," *Association of Corporate Counsel,* January 31, 2013 [**www.lexology.com**].

33. Andrew E. Kramer, "Online Attack Leads to Peek into Spam Den," *The New York Times,* September 2, 2013.

34. Brad Stone, "Authorities Shut Down Spam Ring," *The New York Times,* October 15, 2008.

35. Andrew E. Kramer, "Online Attack Leads to Peek Into Spam Den."

36. Brad Stone, "If You Run a Red Light, Will Everyone Know?" *The New York Times,* August 3, 2008.

37. Jim Stanton, "From Where Your House Is to How Much You Paid for It—It's All on the Internet for Anyone to See," *Waterloo/Cedar Falls Courier,* August 27, 2000, p. A1.

38. Quentin Hardy, "Webcams See All (Tortoise, Watch Your Back)," *The New York Times,* January 7, 2014.

39. Nick Bilton, "Researchers Hack Webcam While Disabling Warning Lights," *The New York Times*, December 19, 2013.

40. Ian Urbina, "Social Media, a Trove of Clues and Confessions," *The New York Times*, February 15, 2014.

41. Jennifer Valentino-Devries, Jeremy Singer-Vine, and Ashkan Soltani, "Websites Vary Prices, Deals Based on Users' Information," *The Wall Street Journal*, December 24, 2012.

42. "Caveat emptor.com," *The Economist*, June 30, 2012, p. 12.

43. Amazon.com Privacy Notice, February 22, 2014 (accessed through the Privacy Notice link at the bottom of its web pages) [**www.amazon.com**].

44. Jennifer Valentino-Devries and Jeremy Singer-Vine, "They Know What You're Shopping For," *The Wall Street Journal*, December 7, 2012.

45. Natasha Singer, "More Companies Are Tracking Online Data, Study Finds," *The New York Times*, November 12, 2012.

46. James Glanz, Jeff Larson, and Andrew W. Lehren, "Spy Agencies Tap Data Streaming from Phone Apps," *The New York Times*, January 27, 2014.

47. These statements from Amazon come from pages reached through the Privacy Notice link at the bottom of its Web pages. It was accessed on February 22, 2014.

48. Nicole Perlroth, "*Washington Post* Joins List of News Media Hacked by the Chinese," *The New York Times*, February 1, 2013.

49. *Stengart v. Loving Care Agency*, 990 A.2d 650 (N.J. 2010).

50. *City of Ontario v. Quon*, 130 S.Ct. 2619 (2010).

51. Pui-Wing Tam, Erin White, Nick Wingfield, and Kris Maher, "Snooping E-Mail by Software Is Now a Workplace Norm," *The Wall Street Journal*, March 9, 2005, p. B1.

52. Somini Sengupta and Natasha Singer, "'Do Not Track' Rules Come a Step Closer to an Agreement," *The New York Times*, July 15, 2013.

53. Natasha Singer, "New Online Privacy Rules for Children," *The New York Times*, December 19, 2012.

54. Glenn Simpson, "U.S., EU Negotiators Reach Agreement on Electronic-Commerce Privacy Rules," *The Wall Street Journal*, March 15, 2000, p. B4.

55. Carter Manny, "Privacy Controls on Trans-Border Flows of Personal Data from Europe," *Business Law Review*, Spring 2001, pp. 101–120.

56. "U.S., Europe Move to Net Privacy Pact," *Waterloo/Cedar Falls Courier*, June 5, 2000, p. B5.

57. Mark Scott, "Europe Urges U.S. to Handle Data Privacy With Care," *The New York Times*, November 27, 2013.

58. Natasha Singer, "An American Quilt of Privacy Laws, Incomplete," *The New York Times*, March 30, 2013.

59. Natasha Singer, "Data Protection Laws, an Ocean Apart," *The New York Times*, February 2, 2013.

60. Claire Cain Miller, "Stern Words, and a Pea-Size Punishment, for Google," *The New York Times*, April 2, 2013; Eric Pfanner, "Google Failed to Delete Street View Data in France," *The New York Times*, July 31, 2012; Cecilia Kang, "Satisfied with Google's Promise to Restrain Street View, FTC Drops Privacy- Breach Probe," *The Washington Post*, October 27, 2010; Raphael Minder, "Google Sued in Spain Over Data Collection," *The New York Times*, August 17, 2010.

61. *WEC Carolina Energy Solutions LLC v. Miller,* 687 F.3d 199 (4th Cir. 2012); *U.S. v. Nosal,* 676 F.3d 854 (9th Cir. 2012).

62. *International Airport Centers, LLC v. Citrin,* 440 F.3d 418 (7th Cir. 2006).

63. Nicole Perlroth, "Robbing a Gas Station: The Hacker Way," *The New York Times,* June 6, 2013.

64. *U.S. v. Farraj,* 142 F.Supp.2d 484 (S.D. N.Y. 2001).

65. Raphael Minder, "Cybercrime Network Based in Spain Is Broken Up," *The New York Times,* February 13, 2013.

66. Edward Wyatt, "Multinational Crackdown on Computer Con Artists," *The New York Times,* October 3, 2012.

67. Nicole Perlroth, "A New Variant of Malware Takes Aim at Mac Users," *The New York Times,* April 23, 2012.

68. David Streitfeld, "Give Yourself 5 Stars? Online, It Might Cost You," *The New York Times,* September 22, 2013.

69. "Former Worker Gets 4 Years for Cyberstalking," *Chicago Tribune,* March 18, 2005, p. 13.

70. Andrew E. Kramer, "Online Attack Leads to Peek Into Spam Den."

71. Spencer E. Ante and Brian Grow, "Meet the Hackers," *BusinessWeek,* May 29, 2006, p. 58.

72. "Let's Stay Together," *The Economist,* December 1, 2012, p. 34.

73. Nicole Perlroth, "Reporting from the Web's Underbelly," *The New York Times,* February 16, 2014.

74. "SIRF's Up," *The Economist,* November 30, 2013, p. 27.

75. Thom Shanker and David E. Sanger, "U.S. Helps Allies Trying to Battle Iranian Hackers," *The New York Times,* June 8, 2013; Jackie Calmes and Steven Lee Myers, "U.S. and China Move Closer on North Korea, but Not on Cyberespionage," *The New York Times,* June 8, 2013.

76. "War on Terabytes," *The Economist,* February 2, 2013, p. 63; David E. Sanger and Eric Schmitt, "Rise Is Seen in Cyberattacks Targeting U.S. Infrastructure," *The New York Times,* July 26, 2012; "The War on Terabytes," *The Economist,* December 31, 2011, p. 57.

77. Siobhan Gorman, "Annual U.S. Cybercrime Costs Estimated at $100 Billion," *The Wall Street Journal,* July 22, 2013.

78. Gautham Nagesh and Danny Yadron, "White House Releases Voluntary Cybersecurity Rules for Critical Infrastructure," *The Wall Street Journal,* February 12, 2014.

79. **http://conventions.coe.int/Treaty/Commun/ChercheSig.asp?NT=185&CM=& DF=&CL=ENG**.

80. Thomas Weber, "Treaty on Cybercrime Flew under the Radar Despite Potential Risks," *The Wall Street Journal,* December 3, 2001, p. B1.

81. Alan S. Reid and Nic Ryder, "The Case of Richard Tomlinson: The Spy Who E-Mailed Me," *Information & Communications Technology Law* 9 (March 2000), p. 61.

82. "Ex-CompuServe Chief's Conviction Overturned," p. 3.

83. P. Liddell, M. Moore, and R. Moore, "Just Sign on the Electronic Line," *Journal of the Academy of Marketing Science,* Winter 2001, p. 110.

84. **www.uniformlaws.org/Act.aspx?title=Computer%20Information%20Transactions%20Act**.

85. 732 A.2d 528 (N.J. Super. 1999).

86. Ronald J. Mann and Travis Siebeneicher, "Just One Click: The Reality of Internet Retail Contracting," *University of Texas Law, Law and Econ Research Paper* No. 104, May 2007 [**http://ssrn.com/abstract=988788**].

87. Anna Mathews, "U.S. Will Give Web Patents More Scrutiny," *The Wall Street Journal,* March 29, 2000, p. B1.

88. "Swipe, Pinch and Zoom to the Courtroom," *The Economist,* September 1, 2012.

89. *Micro Corp. v. Motorola Inc.,* 2013 WL 2111217 (W.D. WA 2013); Steve Lohr, "Court Ruling Takes a Stand on Essential High-Tech Patents," *The New York Times,* April 28, 2013.

90. In addition to the previously cited sources, the discussion of the patent wars also relies on the following: Daisuke Wakabayashi and Ian Sherr, "Jury Orders Samsung to Pay $119 Million to Apple in Patent Case," *The Wall Street Journal,* May 2, 2014; Brent Kendall and Don Clark, "U.S. Panel Orders Import Ban on Some Samsung Devices," *The Wall Street Journal,* August 10, 2013; Brian X. Chen, "Trade Commission Orders Ban on Some Samsung Products," *The New York Times,* August 9, 2013; Nick Wingfield and Brian X. Chen, "Patent Case Has Potential to Give Apple the Upper Hand," *The New York Times,* August 8, 2013; Ian Sherr and Jessica E. Lessin, "Ruling Blocks iPhone Sales," *The Wall Street Journal,* June 4, 2013; Jessica E. Vascellaro, "Apple Wins Big in Patent Case," *The Wall Street Journal,* August 25, 2012; Kevin J. O'Brien, "German Courts at Epicenter of Global Patent Battles Among Tech Rivals," April 8, 2012.

91. *Capitol Records v. ReDIGI,* 934 F.Supp.2d 640 (S.D.N.Y. 2013); Ben Sisario, "A Setback for Resellers of Digital Products," *The New York Times,* April 1, 2013.

92. *A&M Records, Inc. v. Napster, Inc.,* 284 F.3d 1091 (9th Cir. 2002); *A&M Records, Inc. v. Napster, Inc.,* 239 F.3d 1004 (9th Cir. 2001).

93. *Metro-Goldwyn-Mayer Studios, Inc. v. Grokster, Ltd.,* 380 F.3d 1154 (9th Cir. 2004).

94. Sarah McBride and Ethan Smith, "Music Industry to Abandon Mass Suits," *The Wall Street Journal,* December 19, 2008.

95. Amy Brittain, "Universities Strike Back in Battle over Illegal Downloads," *The Christian Science Monitor,* June 18, 2007.

96. Susan Neuberger Weller, "Are You Willing to Pay $22,500 to Download a Song?" *Association of Corporate Counsel,* August 28, 2012 [**www.lexology.com**]; Ben Sisario, "Supreme Court Passes on File-Sharing Case, but Still No End Is in Sight," *The New York Times;* May 21, 2012.

97. *Capitol Records v. Thomas-Rasset,* 692 F.3d 899 (8th Cir. 2012).

98. Rob Peoraro, "The Sound of Copy Restrictions Crashing," *The Washington Post,* May 17, 2007, p. D1; Michelle Quinn, Alana Semuels, and Dawn C. Chmielewski, "Apple Seeks to Unchain Melodies," *Los Angeles Times,* February 7, 2007.

99. David Streitfeld, "Imagining a Swap Meet for E-Books and Music," *The New York Times,* March 7, 2013.

100. Miguel Helft, "Judge Sides with Google in Viacom Video Suit," *The New York Times,* June 23, 2010.

101. *Viacom International Inc. v. YouTube, Inc.,* 718 F.Supp.2d 514 (S.D. N.Y. 2010).

102. *Viacom International Inc. v. YouTube, Inc.,* 676 F.3d 19 (2d Cir. 2012).

103. *Viacom International Inc. v. YouTube, Inc.,* 940 F.Supp.2d 110 (S.D. N.Y. 2013).

104. Michael Davis-Wilson, "The Burden of Online Misdeeds: Who Should Be Responsible?" *Association of Corporate Counsel,* March 19, 2012 [**www.lexology.com**]; "Stopping SOPA," *The Economist,* January 21, 2012.

105. *Shields v. Zuccarini,* 254 F.3d 476 (3d Cir. 2001).

106. Christy Roth, Marianne Dunham, and Jason Watson, "Cybersquatting; Typosquatting— Facebook's $2.8 Million in Damages and Domain Names," *Association of Corporate Counsel,* May 10, 2013.

107. "People: News/Gossip/Scoops," *St. Louis Post–Dispatch,* January 17, 2004, p. 41.

108. "The Name Game," *The Economist,* February 8, 2014, p. 59.

109. Natasha Singer, "When You Can't Tell Web Suffixes Without a Scorecard," *The New York Times,* August 17, 2013.

110. Eric Pfanner, "Amazon Rejected as Domain Name After South American Objections," *The New York Times,* July 18, 2013.

111. "The Name Game."

112. Singer, "When You Can't Tell Web Suffixes Without a Scorecard."

113. Craig Timberg and James Ball, "Donuts Inc.'s Major Play for New Web Domain Names Raises Fears of Fraud," *The Washington Post,* September 24, 2012.

114. Ibid.

115. John McKeown, "What Brand Owners Need to Do to Cope with the New Domain Names after Reveal Day," *Association of Corporate Counsel,* October 15, 2012.

116. *Quill Corporation v. North Dakota,* 504 U.S. 298 (1992).

117. Michelle Blackson, "Closing the Online Tax Loophole," *State Legislatures* 34, No. 4 (April 2008), p. 24.

118. Adam Liptak, "Justices Pass on Tax Case from Online Merchants," *The New York Times,* December 2, 2013.

119. *Amazon.com v. New York State Dept. of Taxation and Finance,* 134 S.Ct. 682 (2013); *Overstock.com v. New York State Dept. of Taxation and Finance,* 134 S.Ct. 682 (2013).

120. See the historical price information at **www.coindesk.com/price**.

121. Compare *Apple Computer v. Doe,* 205 WL 578641 (Cal. Superior 2005) (requiring disclosure) with *O'Grady v. Superior Ct.,* 44 Cal Rptr 3d 72 (Cal. App. 2006) (reversing on appeal).

122. See *America Online, Inc. v. IMS,* 24 F.Supp.2d 548 (E.D. Va. 1998).

123. John Snell, "Lawyers Drawn to Unsettled Internet; Lots of Legal Issues, Large and Small, Must Be Sorted Out," *Minneapolis Star Tribune,* November 29, 1999, p. 6D.

The Constitution of the United States of America

Preamble

We the People of the United States, in Order to form a more perfect Union, establish Justice, insure domestic Tranquility, provide for the common defence, promote the general Welfare, and secure the Blessings of Liberty to ourselves and our Posterity, do ordain and establish this Constitution for the United States of America.

Article I

Section 1. All legislative Powers herein granted shall be vested in a Congress of the United States, which shall consist of a Senate and House of Representatives.

Section 2. (1) The House of Representatives shall be composed of Members chosen every second Year by the People of the several States, and the Electors in each State shall have the Qualifications requisite for Electors of the most numerous Branch of the State Legislature.

(2) No Person shall be a Representative who shall not have attained to the Age of twenty-five Years, and been seven Years a Citizen of the United States, and who shall not, when elected, be an Inhabitant of that State in which he shall be chosen.

(3) Representatives and direct Taxes shall be apportioned among the several States which may be included within this Union, according to their respective Numbers, which shall be determined by adding to the whole Number of free Persons, including those bound to Service for a Term of Years, and excluding Indians not taxed, three fifths of all other Persons.[1] The actual Enumeration shall be made within three Years after the first Meeting of the Congress of the United States, and within every subsequent Term of ten Years, in such Manner as they shall by Law direct. The Number of Representatives shall not exceed one for every thirty Thousand, but each State shall have at Least one Representative; and until such enumeration shall be made, the State of New Hampshire shall be entitled to chuse three, Massachusetts eight, Rhode Island and Providence Plantations one, Connecticut five, New York six, New Jersey four, Pennsylvania eight, Delaware one, Maryland six, Virginia ten, North Carolina five, South Carolina five, and Georgia three.

[1]Refer to the Fourteenth Amendment.

(4) When vacancies happen in the Representation from any State, the Executive Authority thereof shall issue Writs of Election to fill such Vacancies.

(5) The House of Representatives shall chuse their Speaker and other Officers; and shall have the sole Power of Impeachment.

Section 3. (1) The Senate of the United States shall be composed of two Senators from each State, chosen by the Legislature thereof,[2] for six Years; and each Senator shall have one Vote.

(2) Immediately after they shall be assembled in Consequence of the first Election, they shall be divided as equally as may be into three Classes. The Seats of the Senators of the first Class shall be vacated at the Expiration of the Second Year, of the second Class at the Expiration of the fourth Year, and of the third Class at the Expiration of the sixth Year, so that one third may be chosen every second Year; and if Vacancies happen by Resignation, or otherwise, during the Recess of the Legislature of any State, the Executive thereof may make temporary Appointments until the next Meeting of the Legislature, which shall then fill such Vacancies.[3]

(3) No Person shall be a Senator who shall not have attained to the Age of thirty Years, and been nine Years a Citizen of the United States, and who shall not, when elected, be an Inhabitant of that State for which he shall be chosen.

(4) The Vice President of the United States shall be President of the Senate, but shall have no Vote, unless they be equally divided.

(5) The Senate shall chuse their other Officers, and also a President pro tempore, in the Absence of the Vice President, or when he shall exercise the Office of President of the United States.

(6) The Senate shall have the sole Power to try all Impeachments. When sitting for that Purpose, they shall be on Oath or Affirmation. When the President of the United States is tried, the Chief Justice shall preside: And no Person shall be convicted without the Concurrence of two thirds of the Members present.

(7) Judgment in Cases of Impeachment shall not extend further than to removal from Office, and disqualification to hold and enjoy any Office of honor, Trust, or Profit under the United States: but the Party convicted shall nevertheless be liable and subject to Indictment, Trial, Judgment, and Punishment, according to Law.

Section 4. (1) The Times, Places and Manner of holding Elections for Senators and Representatives, shall be prescribed in each State by the Legislature thereof; but the Congress may at any time by Law make or alter such Regulations, except as to the Places of chusing Senators.

(2) The Congress shall assemble at least once in every year, and such Meeting shall be on the first Monday in December, unless they shall by Law appoint a different Day.[4]

Section 5. (1) Each House shall be the Judge of the Elections, Returns, and Qualifications of its own Members, and a Majority of each shall constitute a Quorum to do Business; but a smaller Number may adjourn from day to day, and may be authorized to compel the Attendance of absent Members, in such Manner, and under such Penalties as each House may provide.

[2]Refer to the Seventeenth Amendment.

[3]Ibid.

[4]Refer to the Twentieth Amendment.

(2) Each House may determine the Rules of its Proceedings, punish its Members for disorderly Behavior, and, with the Concurrence of two thirds, expel a Member.

(3) Each House shall keep a Journal of its Proceedings, and from time to time publish the same, excepting such Parts as may in their Judgment require Secrecy; and the Yeas and Nays of the Members of either House on any question shall, at the Desire of one fifth of those Present, be entered on the Journal.

(4) Neither House, during the Session of Congress, shall, without the Consent of the other, adjourn for more than three days, nor to any other Place than that in which the two Houses shall be sitting.

Section 6. (1) The Senators and Representatives shall receive a Compensation for their Services, to be ascertained by Law, and paid out of the Treasury of the United States. They shall in all Cases, except Treason, Felony and Breach of the Peace, be privileged from Arrest during their Attendance at the Session of their respective Houses, and in going to and returning from the same; and for any Speech or Debate in either House, they shall not be questioned in any other Place.

(2) No Senator or Representative shall, during the Time for which he was elected, be appointed to any civil Office under the Authority of the United States, which shall have been created, or the Emoluments whereof shall have been encreased during such time; and no Person holding any Office under the United States, shall be a Member of either House during his Continuance in Office.

Section 7. (1) All Bills for raising Revenue shall originate in the House of Representatives; but the Senate may propose or concur with Amendments as on other Bills.

(2) Every Bill which shall have passed the House of Representatives and the Senate, shall, before it becomes a Law, be presented to the President of the United States; If he approve he shall sign it, but if not he shall return it, with his Objections to the House in which it shall have originated, who shall enter the Objections at large on their Journal, and proceed to reconsider it. If after such Reconsideration two thirds of that House shall agree to pass the Bill, it shall be sent together with the Objections, to the other House, by which it shall likewise be reconsidered, and if approved by two thirds of that House, it shall become a Law. But in all such Cases the Votes of both Houses shall be determined by yeas and Nays, and the Names of the Persons voting for and against the Bill shall be entered on the Journal of each House respectively. If any Bill shall not be returned by the President within ten Days (Sundays excepted) after it shall have been presented to him, the Same shall be a Law, in like Manner as if he had signed it, unless the Congress by their Adjournment prevent its Return in which Case it shall not be a Law.

(3) Every Order, Resolution, or Vote, to Which the Concurrence of the Senate and House of Representatives may be necessary (except on a question of Adjournment) shall be presented to the President of the United States; and before the same shall take Effect, shall be approved by him, or being disapproved by him, shall be repassed by two thirds of the Senate and House of Representatives, according to the Rules and Limitations prescribed in the Case of a Bill.

Section 8. (1) The Congress shall have Power To lay and collect Taxes, Duties, Imposts and Excises, to pay the Debts and provide for the common Defence and general Welfare of the United States; but all Duties, Imposts and Excises shall be uniform throughout the United States;

(2) To borrow money on the credit of the United States;

(3) To regulate Commerce with foreign Nations, and among the several States, and with the Indian Tribes;

(4) To establish a uniform Rule of Naturalization, and uniform Laws on the subject of Bankruptcies throughout the United States;

(5) To coin Money, regulate the Value thereof, and of foreign Coin, and fix the Standard of Weights and Measures;

(6) To provide for the Punishment of counterfeiting the Securities and current Coin of the United States;

(7) To Establish Post Offices and Post Roads;

(8) To promote the Progress of Science and useful Arts, by securing for limited Times to Authors and Inventors the exclusive Right to their respective Writings and Discoveries;

(9) To constitute Tribunals inferior to the Supreme Court;

(10) To define and punish Piracies and Felonies committed on the high Seas, and Offenses against the Law of Nations;

(11) To declare War, grant Letters of Marque and Reprisal, and make Rules concerning Captures on Land and Water;

(12) To raise and support Armies, but no Appropriation of Money to that Use shall be for a longer Term than two Years;

(13) To provide and maintain a Navy;

(14) To make Rules for the Government and Regulation of the land and naval Forces;

(15) To provide for calling forth the Militia to execute the Laws of the Union, suppress Insurrections and repel Invasions;

(16) To provide for organizing, arming, and disciplining, the Militia, and for governing such Part of them as may be employed in the Service of the United States, reserving to the States respectively, the Appointment of the Officers, and the Authority of training the Militia according to the discipline prescribed by Congress;

(17) To exercise exclusive Legislation in all Cases whatsoever, over such District (not exceeding ten Miles square) as may, by Cession of particular States, and the Acceptance of Congress, become the Seat of the Government of the United States, and to exercise like Authority over all Places purchased by the Consent of the Legislature of the State in which the Same shall be, for the Erection of Forts, Magazines, Arsenals, dock-Yards, and other needful Buildings;—And

(18) To make all Laws which shall be necessary and proper for carrying into Execution the foregoing Powers, and all other Powers vested by this Constitution in the Government of the United States, or in any Department or Officer thereof.

Section 9. (1) The Migration or Importation of Such Persons as any of the States now existing shall think proper to admit, shall not be prohibited by the Congress prior to the Year one thousand eight hundred and eight, but a Tax or duty may be imposed on such Importation, not exceeding ten dollars for each Person.

(2) The privilege of the Writ of Habeas Corpus shall not be suspended, unless when in Cases of Rebellion or Invasion the public Safety may require it.

(3) No Bill of Attainder or ex post facto Law shall be passed.

(4) No Capitation, or other direct, Tax shall be laid, unless in proportion to the Census or Enumeration herein before directed to the taken.[5]

[5]Refer to the Sixteenth Amendment.

(5) No Tax or Duty shall be laid on Articles exported from any state.

(6) No Preference shall be given by any Regulation of Commerce or Revenue to the Ports of one State over those of another; nor shall Vessels bound to, or from, one State be obliged to enter, clear, or pay Duties in another.

(7) No money shall be drawn from the Treasury, but in Consequence of Appropriations made by Law; and a regular Statement and Account of the Receipts and Expenditures of all public Money shall be published from time to time.

(8) No Title of Nobility shall be granted by the United States; And no person holding any Office of Profit or Trust under them, shall, without the Consent of the Congress, accept of any present, Emolument, Office or Title, of any kind whatever, from any King, Prince, or foreign State.

Section 10. (1) No State shall enter into any Treaty, Alliance, or Confederation; grant Letters of Marque and Reprisal; coin Money; emit Bills of Credit; make any Thing but gold and silver Coin a Tender in Payment of Debts; pass any Bill of Attainder, ex post facto Law, or Law impairing the Obligation of Contracts, or grant any Title of Nobility.

(2) No State shall, without the Consent of the Congress, lay any Imposts or Duties on Imports or Exports, except what may be absolutely necessary for executing its inspection Laws: and the net Produce of all Duties and Imposts, laid by any State on Imports or Exports, shall be for the Use of the Treasury of the United States; and all such Laws shall be subject to the Revision and Controul of the Congress.

(3) No State shall, without the Consent of Congress, lay any Duty of Tonnage, keep Troops, or Ships of War in time of Peace, enter into any Agreement or Compact with another State, or with a foreign Power, or engage in War, unless actually invaded, or in such imminent Danger as will not admit of delay.

Article II

Section 1. (1) The executive Power shall be vested in a President of the United States of America. He shall hold his Office during the Term of four Years, and, together with the Vice President, chosen for the same Term, be elected as follows:

(2) Each State shall appoint, in such Manner as the Legislature thereof may direct, a Number of Electors, equal to the whole Number of Senators and Representatives to which the State may be entitled in the Congress; but no Senator or Representative, or Person holding an Office of Trust or Profit under the United States, shall be appointed an Elector.

(3) The Electors shall meet in their respective States, and vote by Ballot for two Persons, of whom one at least shall not be an Inhabitant of the same State with themselves. And they shall make a list of all the Persons voted for, and of the Number of Votes for each; which List they shall sign and certify, and transmit sealed to the Seat of the Government of the United States, directed to the President of the Senate. The President of the Senate shall, in the Presence of the Senate and House of Representatives, open all the Certificates, and the Votes shall then be counted. The Person having the greatest Number of Votes shall be the President, if such Number be a Majority of the whole Number of Electors appointed; and if there be more than one who have such Majority, and have an equal Number of Votes, then the House of Representatives shall immediately chuse by Ballot one of them for President; and if no Person have a Majority, then from the five highest on the List the said

House shall in like Manner chuse the President. But in chusing the President, the Votes shall be taken by States, the Representation from each State have one Vote; A quorum for this Purpose shall consist of a Member or Members from two thirds of the States, and a Majority of all the States shall be necessary to a Choice. In every Case, after the Choice of the President, the Person having the greater Number of Votes of the Electors shall be the Vice President. But if there should remain two or more who have equal Votes, the Senate shall chuse from them by Ballot the Vice President.[6]

(4) The Congress may determine the Time of chusing the Electors, and the Day on which they shall give their Votes; which Day shall be the same throughout the United States.

(5) No person except a natural born Citizen, or a Citizen of the United States, at the time of the Adoption of this Constitution, shall be eligible to the Office of President; neither shall any Person be eligible to that Office who shall not have attained to the Age of thirty-five Years, and been fourteen Years a Resident within the United States.

(6) In case of the removal of the President from Office, or of his Death, Resignation or Inability to discharge the Powers and Duties of the said Office, the Same shall devolve on the Vice President, and the Congress may by Law provide for the Case of Removal, Death, Resignation or Inability, both of the President and Vice President, declaring what Officer shall then act as President, and such Officer shall act accordingly, until the Disability be removed, or a President shall be elected.[7]

(7) The President shall, at stated Times, receive for his Services, a Compensation, which shall neither be encreased nor diminished during the Period for which he shall have been elected, and he shall not receive within that Period any other Emolument from the United States, or any of them.

(8) Before he enter on the Execution of his Office, he shall take the following Oath or Affirmation: "I do solemnly swear (or affirm) that I will faithfully execute the Office of President of the United States, and will to the best of my Ability, preserve, protect, and defend the Constitution of the United States."

Section 2. (1) The President shall be Commander in Chief of the Army and Navy of the United States, and of the militia of the several States, when called into the actual Service of the United States; he may require the Opinion, in writing, of the principal Officer in each of the executive Departments, upon any Subject relating to the Duties of their respective Offices, and he shall have Power to grant Reprieves and Pardons for Offenses against the United States, except in Cases of Impeachment.

(2) He shall have Power, by and with the Advice and Consent of the Senate, to make Treaties, provided two thirds of the Senators present concur; and he shall nominate, and by and with the Advice and Consent of the Senate, shall appoint Ambassadors, other public Ministers and Consuls, Judges of the supreme Court, and all other Officers of the United States, whose Appointments are not herein otherwise provided for, and which shall be established by Law; but the Congress may by Law vest the Appointment of such inferior Officers, as they think proper, in the President alone, in the Courts of Law, or in the Heads of Departments.

[6]Refer to the Twelfth Amendment.

[7]Refer to the Twenty-Fifth Amendment

(3) The President shall have Power to fill up all Vacancies that may happen during the Recess of the Senate, by granting Commissions which shall expire at the End of their next Session.

Section 3. He shall from time to time give to the Congress Information of the State of the Union, and recommend to their Consideration such Measures as he shall judge necessary and expedient; he may, on extraordinary Occasions, convene both Houses, or either of them, and in Case of Disagreement between them, with Respect to the Time of Adjournment, he may adjourn them to such Time as he shall think proper; he shall receive Ambassadors and other public Ministers; he shall take Care that the Laws be faithfully executed, and shall Commission all the Officers of the United States.

Section 4. The President, Vice President and all civil Officers of the United States, shall be removed from Office on Impeachment for, and Conviction of, Treason, Bribery, or other high Crimes and Misdemeanors.

Article III

Section 1. The judicial Power of the United States, shall be vested in one supreme Court, and in such inferior Courts as the Congress may from time to time ordain and establish. The Judges, both of the supreme and inferior Courts, shall hold their Offices during good Behaviour, and shall, at stated Times, receive for their Services a Compensation, which shall not be diminished during their Continuance in Office.

Section 2. (1) The judicial Power shall extend to all Cases, in Law and Equity, arising under this Constitution, the Laws of the United States, and Treaties made, or which shall be made, under their Authority;—to all Cases affecting Ambassadors, other public Ministers and Consuls;—to all Cases of admiralty and maritime Jurisdiction;—to Controversies to which the United States shall be a Party;—to Controversies between two or more States;—between a State and Citizens of another State,[8]—between Citizens of different states;—between Citizens of the same State claiming Lands under the Grants of different States, and between a State, or the Citizens thereof, and foreign States, Citizens or Subjects.

(2) In all Cases affecting Ambassadors, other public Ministers and Consuls, and those in which a State shall be a Party, the supreme Court shall have original Jurisdiction. In all the other Cases before mentioned, the supreme Court shall have appellate Jurisdiction, both as to Law and Fact, with such Exceptions, and under such Regulations as the Congress shall make.

(3) The trial of all Crimes, except in Cases of Impeachment, shall be by Jury; and such Trial shall be held in the State where the said Crimes shall have been committed; but when not committed within any State, the Trial shall be at such Place or Places as the Congress may by Law have directed.

Section 3. (1) Treason against the United States, shall consist only in levying War against them, or, in adhering to their enemies, giving them Aid and Comfort. No Person shall be convicted of Treason unless on the Testimony of two Witnesses to the same overt Act, or on Confession in open Court.

---

[8]Refer to the Eleventh Amendment.

(2) The Congress shall have Power to declare the Punishment of Treason, but no Attainder of Treason shall work Corruption of Blood, or Forfeiture except during the Life of the Person attainted.

Article IV

Section 1. Full Faith and Credit shall be given in each State to the public Acts, Records, and judicial Proceedings of every other State. And the Congress may by general Laws prescribe the Manner in which such Acts, Records and Proceedings shall be proved, and the Effect thereof.

Section 2. (1) The Citizens of each State shall be entitled to all Privileges and Immunities of Citizens in the several States.

(2) A Person charged in any State with Treason, Felony, or other Crime, who shall flee from Justice, and be found in another State, shall on demand of the executive Authority of the State from which he fled, be delivered up, to be removed to the State having Jurisdiction of the Crime.

(3) No Person held to Service or Labour in one State, under the Laws thereof, escaping into another, shall, in Consequence of any Law or Regulation therein, be discharged from such Service or Labour, but shall be delivered up on Claim of the Party to whom such Service or Labour may be due.[9]

Section 3. (1) New States may be admitted by the Congress into this Union; but no new State shall be formed or erected within the Jurisdiction of any other State; nor any State be formed by the Junction of two or more States, or Parts of States without the Consent of the Legislatures of the States concerned as well as of the Congress.

(2) The Congress shall have Power to dispose of and make all needful Rules and Regulations respecting the Territory or other Property belonging to the United States; and nothing in this Constitution shall be so construed as to Prejudice any Claims of the United States, or of any particular State.

Section 4. The United States shall guarantee to every State in this Union a Republican Form of Government, and shall protect each of them against Invasion; and on Application of the Legislature, or of the Executive (when the Legislature cannot be convened) against domestic Violence.

Article V

The Congress, whenever two thirds of both Houses shall deem it necessary, shall propose Amendments to this Constitution, or, on the Application of the Legislatures of two thirds of the several States, shall call a Convention for proposing Amendments, which, in either Case, shall be valid to all Intents and Purposes, as part of this Constitution, when ratified by the Legislatures of three fourths of the several States, or by Conventions in three fourths thereof, as the one or the other Mode of Ratification may be proposed by the Congress; Provided that no Amendment which may be made prior to the Year One thousand eight hundred and eight shall in any Manner affect the first and fourth Clauses in the Ninth Section

[9]Refer to the Thirteenth Amendment.

of the first Article; and that no State, without its Consent, shall be deprived of its equal Suffrage in the Senate.

Article VI

(1) All Debts contracted and Engagements entered into, before the Adoption of this Constitution shall be as valid against the United States under this Constitution, as under the Confederation.

(2) This Constitution, and the Laws of the United States which shall be made in Pursuance thereof; and all Treaties made, or which shall be made, under the Authority of the United States, shall be the supreme Law of the Land; and the Judges in every State shall be bound thereby, any Thing in the Constitution or Laws of any State to the Contrary notwithstanding.

(3) The Senators and Representatives before mentioned, and the Members of the several State Legislatures, and all executive and judicial Officers, both of the United States and of the several States, shall be bound by Oath or Affirmation, to support this Constitution, but no religious Test shall ever be required as a Qualification to any Office or public Trust under the United States.

Article VII

The Ratification of the Conventions of nine States shall be sufficient for the Establishment of this Constitution between the States so ratifying the Same.
[Amendments 1 to 10, the Bill of Rights, were ratified in 1791.]

Amendment I

Congress shall make no law respecting an establishment of religion, or prohibiting the free exercise thereof; or abridging the freedom of speech, or of the press; or the right of the people peaceably to assemble, and to petition the Government for a redress of grievances.

Amendment II

A well regulated Militia, being necessary to the security of a free State, the right of the people to keep and bear Arms, shall not be infringed.

Amendment III

No Soldier shall, in time of peace be quartered in any house, without the consent of the Owner, nor in time of war, but in a manner to be prescribed by law.

Amendment IV

The right of the people to be secure in their persons, houses, papers, and effects, against unreasonable searches and seizures, shall not be violated, and no Warrants shall issue, but upon probable cause, supported by Oath or affirmation, and particularly describing the place to be searched, and the persons or things to be seized.

Amendment V

No person shall be held to answer for a capital, or otherwise infamous crime, unless on a presentment or indictment of a Grand Jury, except in cases arising in the land or naval forces, or in the Militia, when in actual service in time of War or public danger; nor shall any person be subject for the same offence to be twice put in jeopardy of life or limb; nor shall be compelled in any criminal case to be a witness against himself, nor be deprived of life, liberty, or property, without due process of law; nor shall private property be taken for public use, without just compensation.

Amendment VI

In all criminal prosecutions, the accused shall enjoy the right to a speedy and public trial, by an impartial jury of the State and district wherein the crime shall have been committed, which district shall have been previously ascertained by law, and to be informed of the nature and cause of the accusation; to be confronted with the witness against him; to have compulsory process for obtaining witnesses in his favor, and to have the Assistance of Counsel for his defence.

Amendment VII

In Suits at common law, where the value in controversy shall exceed twenty dollars, the right of trial by jury shall be preserved, and no fact tried by jury, shall be otherwise re-examined in any Court of the United States, than according to the rules of the common law.

Amendment VIII

Excessive bail shall not be required, nor excessive fines imposed, nor cruel and unusual punishments inflicted.

Amendment IX

The enumeration in the Constitution, of certain rights, shall not be construed to deny or disparage others retained by the people.

Amendment X

The powers not delegated to the United States by the Constitution, nor prohibited by it to the States, are reserved to the States respectively, or to the people.

Amendment XI [1798]

The Judicial power of the United States shall not be construed to extend to any suit in law or equity, commenced or prosecuted against one of the United States by Citizens of another State, or by Citizens or Subjects of any Foreign State.

Amendment XII [1804]

The Electors shall meet in their respective states and vote by ballot for President and Vice-President, one of whom, at least, shall not be an inhabitant of the same state with themselves; they shall name in their ballots the person voted for as President, and in distinct ballots the person voted for as Vice-President, and they shall make distinct lists of all persons voted for as President, and of all persons voted for as Vice-President, and of the number of votes for each, which lists they shall sign and certify, and transmit sealed to the seat of the government of the United States, directed to the President of the Senate;—The President of the Senate shall, in the presence of the Senate and House of Representatives, open all the certificates and the votes shall then be counted;—The person having the greatest number of votes for President, shall be the President, if such number be a majority of the whole number of Electors appointed; and if no person have such majority, then from the persons having the highest numbers not exceeding three on the list of those voted for as President, the House of Representatives shall choose immediately, by ballot, the President. But in choosing the President, the votes shall be taken by states, the representation from each state having one vote; a quorum for this purpose shall consist of a member or members from two-thirds of the states, and a majority of all the states shall be necessary to a choice. And if the House of Representatives shall not choose a President whenever the right of choice shall devolve upon them before the fourth day of March next following, then the Vice-President shall act as President, as in the case of the death or other constitutional disability of the President.[10]—The person having the greatest number of votes as Vice-President, shall be the Vice-President, if such number be a majority of the whole number of Electors appointed, and if no person have a majority, then from the two highest numbers on the list, the Senate shall choose the Vice-President; a quorum for the purpose shall consist of two-thirds of the whole number of Senators, and a majority of the whole number shall be necessary to a choice. But no person constitutionally ineligible to the office of President shall be eligible to that of Vice-President of the United States.

Amendment XIII [1865]

Section 1. Neither slavery nor involuntary servitude, except as a punishment for crime whereof the party shall have been duly convicted, shall exist within the United States, or any place subject to their jurisdiction.

Section 2. Congress shall have power to enforce this article by appropriate legislation.

[10]Refer to the Twentieth Amendment.

Amendment XIV [1868]

Section 1. All persons born or naturalized in the United States, and subject to the jurisdiction thereof, are citizens of the United States and of the State wherein they reside. No State shall make or enforce any law which shall abridge the privileges or immunities of citizens of the United States; nor shall any State deprive any person of life, liberty, or property, without due process of law; nor deny to any person within its jurisdiction the equal protection of the laws.

Section 2. Representatives shall be apportioned among the several States according to their respective numbers, counting the whole number of persons in each State, excluding Indians not taxed. But when the right to vote at any election for the choice of electors for President and Vice President of the United States, Representatives in Congress, the Executive and Judicial officers of a State, or the members of the Legislature thereof, is denied to any of the male inhabitants of such State, being twenty-one years of age,[11] and citizens of the United States, or in any way abridged, except for participation in rebellion, or other crime, the basis of representation therein shall be reduced in the proportion which the number of such male citizens shall bear to the whole number of male citizens twenty-one years of age in such State.

Section 3. No person shall be a Senator or Representative in Congress, or elector of President and Vice President, or hold any office, civil or military, under the United States, or under any State, who having previously taken an oath, as a member of Congress, or as an officer of the United States, or as a member of any State legislature, or as an executive or judicial officer of any State, to support the Constitution of the United States, shall have engaged in insurrection or rebellion against the same, or given aid or comfort to the enemies thereof. But Congress may by a vote of two thirds of each House, remove such disability.

Section 4. The validity of the public debt of the United States, authorized by law, including debts incurred for payment of pensions and bounties for services in suppressing insurrection or rebellion, shall not be questioned. But neither the United States nor any State shall assume or pay any debt or obligation incurred in aid of insurrection or rebellion against the United States, or any claim for the loss or emancipation of any slave; but all such debts, obligations and claims shall be held illegal and void.

Section 5. The Congress shall have power to enforce, by appropriate legislation, the provisions of this article.

Amendment XV [1870]

Section 1. The right of citizens of the United States to vote shall not be denied or abridged by the United States or by any State on account of race, color, or previous condition of servitude.

Section 2. The Congress shall have power to enforce this article by appropriate legislation.

[11]Refer to the Twenty-Sixth Amendment.

Amendment XVI [1913]

The Congress shall have power to lay and collect taxes on incomes, from whatever source derived, without apportionment among the several States, and without regard to any census or enumeration.

Amendment XVII [1913]

(1) The Senate of the United States shall be composed of two Senators from each State, elected by the people thereof, for six years; and each Senator shall have one vote. The electors in each State shall have the qualifications requisite for electors of the most numerous branch of the State legislatures.

(2) When vacancies happen in the representation of any State in the Senate, the executive authority of such State shall issue writs of election to fill such vacancies: *Provided,* That the legislature of any State may empower the executive thereof to make temporary appointments until the people fill the vacancies by election as the legislature may direct.

(3) This amendment shall not be so construed as to affect the election or term of any Senator chosen before it becomes valid as part of the Constitution.

Amendment XVIII [1919]

Section 1. After one year from the ratification of this article the manufacture, sale, or transportation of intoxicating liquors within, the importation thereof into, or the exportation thereof from the United States and all territory subject to the jurisdiction thereof for beverage purposes is hereby prohibited.

Section 2. The Congress and the several States shall have concurrent power to enforce this article by appropriate legislation.

Section 3. This article shall be inoperative unless it shall have been ratified as an amendment to the Constitution by the legislatures of the several States, as provided in the Constitution, within seven years from the date of the submission hereof to the States by the Congress.[12]

Amendment XIX [1920]

(1) The right of citizens of the United States to vote shall not be denied or abridged by the United States or by any State on account of sex.

(2) Congress shall have power to enforce this article by appropriate legislation.

Amendment XX [1933]

Section 1. The terms of the President and Vice President shall end at noon on the 20th day of January, and the terms of Senators and Representatives at noon on the 3rd day of

---

[12]Refer to the Twenty-First Amendment.

January, of the years in which such terms would have ended if this article had not been ratified; and the terms of their successors shall then begin.

Section 2. The Congress shall assemble at least once in every year, and such meeting shall begin at noon on the 3rd day of January, unless they shall by law appoint a different day.

Section 3. If, at the time fixed for the beginning of the term of the President, the President elect shall have died, the Vice President elect shall become President. If the President shall not have been chosen before the time fixed for the beginning of his term or if the President elect shall have failed to qualify, then the Vice President elect shall act as President until a President shall have qualified; and the Congress may by law provide for the case wherein neither a President elect nor a Vice President elect shall have qualified, declaring who shall then act as President, or the manner in which one is to act shall be selected, and such person shall act accordingly until a President or Vice President shall have qualified.

Section 4. The Congress may by law provide for the case of the death of any of the persons from whom the House of Representatives may choose a President whenever the right of choice shall have devolved upon them, and for the case of the death of any of the persons from whom the Senate may choose a Vice President whenever the right of choice shall have devolved upon them.

Section 5. Sections 1 and 2 shall take effect on the 15th day of October following the ratification of this article.

Section 6. This article shall be inoperative unless it shall have been ratified as an amendment to the Constitution by the legislatures of three-fourths of the several States within seven years from the date of its submission.

Amendment XXI [1933]

Section 1. The eighteenth article of amendment to the Constitution of the United States is hereby repealed.

Section 2. The transportation or importation into any State, Territory, or possession of the United States for delivery or use therein of intoxicating liquors, in violation of the laws thereof, is hereby prohibited.

Section 3. This article shall be inoperative unless it shall have been ratified as an amendment to the Constitution by conventions in the several States, as provided in the Constitution, within seven years from the date of the submission hereof to the States by the Congress.

Amendment XXII [1951]

Section 1. No person shall be elected to the office of the President more than twice, and no person who has held the office of President, or acted as President, for more than two years of a term to which some other person was elected President shall be elected to the office of President more than once. But this Article shall not apply to any person holding the office of President when this Article was proposed by the Congress, and shall not prevent any person who may be holding the office of President, or acting as President, during the term within which this Article becomes operative from holding the office of President or acting as president during the remainder of such term.

Section 2. This article shall be inoperative unless it shall have been ratified as an amendment to the Constitution by the legislatures of three-fourths of the several States within seven years from the date of its submission to the States by the Congress.

Amendment XXIII [1961]

Section 1. The District constituting the seat of Government of the United States shall appoint in such manner as the Congress may direct:

A number of electors of President and Vice President equal to the whole number of Senators and Representatives in Congress to which the District would be entitled if it were a State, but in no event more than the least populous state; they shall be in addition to those appointed by the states, but they shall be considered, for the purposes of the election of President and Vice Prisident, to be electors appointed by a state; and they shall meet in the District and perform such duties as provided by the twelfth article of amendment.

Section 2. The Congress shall have power to enforce this article by appropriate legislation.

Amendment XXIV [1964]

Section 1. The right of citizens of the United States to vote in any primary or other election for President or Vice President, for electors for President or Vice President, or for Senator or Representative in Congress, shall not be denied or abridged by the United States or any State by reason of failure to pay any poll tax or other tax.

Section 2. The Congress shall have power to enforce this article by appropriate legislation.

Amendment XXV [1967]

Section 1. In case of the removal of the President from office or of his death or resignation, the Vice President shall become President.

Section 2. Whenever there is a vacancy in the office of the Vice President, the President shall nominate a Vice President who shall take office upon confirmation by a majority vote of both Houses of Congress.

Section 3. Whenever the President transmits to the President pro tempore of the Senate and the Speaker of the House of Representatives his written declaration that he is unable to discharge the powers and duties of his office, and until he transmits to them a written declaration to the contrary, such powers and duties shall be discharged by the Vice President as Acting President.

Section 4. Whenever the Vice President and a majority of either the principal officers of the executive departments or of such other body as Congress may by law provide, transmit to the President pro tempore of the Senate and the Speaker of the House of Representatives their written declaration that the President is unable to discharge the powers and duties of his office, the Vice President shall immediately assume the powers and duties of the office as Acting President.

Thereafter, when the President transmits to the President pro tempore of the Senate and the Speaker of the House of Representatives his written declaration that no inability exists, he shall resume the powers and duties of his office unless the Vice President and a majority of either the principal officers of the executive departments or of such other body as Congress may by law provide, transmit within four days to the President pro tempore of the Senate and the Speaker of the House of Representatives their written declaration that the President is unable to discharge the powers and duties of his office. Thereupon Congress shall decide the issue, assembling within forty-eight hours for that purpose if not in session. If the Congress, within twenty-one days after receipt of the latter written declaration, or, if Congress is not in session, within twenty-one days after Congress is required to assemble, determines by two-thirds vote of both Houses that the President is unable to discharge the powers and duties of his office, the Vice President shall continue to discharge the same as Acting President; otherwise, the President shall resume the powers and duties of his office.

Amendment XXVI [1971]

Section 1. The right of citizens of the United States, who are eighteen years of age or older, to vote shall not be denied or abridged by the United States or by any State on account of age.

Section 2. The Congress shall have power to enforce this article by appropriate legislation.

Amendment XXVII [1992]

No law, varying the compensation for the services of the Senators and Representatives, shall take effect, until an election of Representatives shall have intervened.

Uniform Commercial Code 2000 Official Text, Article 2

Table of Sections

Article 2. Sales

Part 1. Short Title, General Construction, and Subject Matter

Section

Part 2. Form, Formation, and Readjustment of Contract

Article 2. Sales

Part 1. Short Title, General Construction, and Subject Matter

§ 2–101. Short Title

This Article shall be known and may be cited as Uniform Commercial Code—Sales.

§ 2–102. Scope; Certain Security and Other Transactions Excluded from This Article

Unless the context otherwise requires, this Article applies to transactions in goods; it does not apply to any transaction which although in the form of an unconditional contract to sell or present sale is intended to operate only as a security transaction; nor does this Article impair or repeal any statute regulating sales to consumers, farmers, or other specified classes of buyers.

§ 2–103. Definitions and Index of Definitions

(1) In this Article unless the context otherwise requires

    (a) "Buyer" means a person who buys or contracts to buy goods.

    (b) "Good faith" in the case of a merchant means honesty in fact and the observance of reasonable commercial standards of fair dealing in the trade.

    (c) "Receipt" of goods means taking physical possession of them.

    (d) "Seller" means a person who sells or contracts to sell goods.

(2) Other definitions applying to this Article or to specified Parts thereof, and the sections in which they appear, are:

"Acceptance"	Section 2–606.
"Banker's credit"	Section 2–325.
"Between merchants"	Section 2–104.
"Cancellation"	Section 2–106(4).
"Commercial unit"	Section 2–105.
"Confirmed credit"	Section 2–325.
"Conforming to contract"	Section 2–106.
"Contract for sale"	Section 2–106.
"Cover"	Section 2–712.
"Entrusting"	Section 2–403.
"Financing agency"	Section 2–104.
"Future goods"	Section 2–105.
"Goods"	Section 2–105.
"Identification"	Section 2–501.
"Installment contract"	Section 2–612.
"Letter of credit"	Section 2–325.
"Lot"	Section 2–105.
"Merchant"	Section 2–104.
"Overseas"	Section 2–323.
"Person in position of seller"	Section 2–707.
"Present sale"	Section 2–106.
"Sale"	Section 2–106.
"Sale on approval"	Section 2–326.
"Sale or return"	Section 2–326.
"Termination"	Section 2–106.

(3) The following definitions in other Articles apply to this Article:

"Check"	Section 3–104.
"Consignee"	Section 7–102.
"Consignor"	Section 7–102.
"Consumer goods"	Section 9–102.
"Dishonor"	Section 3–502.
"Draft"	Section 3–104.

(4) In addition Article 1 contains general definitions and principles of construction and interpretation applicable throughout this Article.

§ 2–104. Definitions: "Merchant"; "Between Merchants"; "Financing Agency"

(1) "Merchant" means a person who deals in goods of the kind or otherwise by his occupation holds himself out as having knowledge or skill peculiar to the practices or

goods involved in the transaction or to whom such knowledge or skill may be attributed by his employment of an agent or broker or other intermediary who by his occupation holds himself out as having such knowledge or skill.

(2) "Financing agency" means a bank, finance company, or other person who in the ordinary course of business makes advances against goods or documents of title or who by arrangement with either the seller or the buyer intervenes in ordinary course to make or collect payment due or claimed under the contract for sale, as by purchasing or paying the seller's draft or making advances against it or by merely taking it for collection whether or not the documents of title accompany the draft. "Financing agency" includes also a bank or other person who similarly intervenes between persons who are in the position of seller and buyer in respect to the goods (Section 2–707).

(3) "Between merchants" means in any transaction with respect to which both parties are chargeable with the knowledge or skill of merchants.

§ 2–105. Definitions: "Transferability"; "Goods"; "Future" Goods; "Lot"; "Commercial Unit"

(1) "Goods" means all things (including specially manufactured goods) which are movable at the time of identification to the contract for sale other than the money in which the price is to be paid, investment securities (Article 8), and things in action. "Goods" also includes the unborn young of animals and growing crops and other identified things attached to realty as described in the section on goods to be severed from realty (Section 2–107).

(2) Goods must be both existing and identified before any interest in them can pass. Goods which are not both existing and identified are "future" goods. A purported present sale of future goods or of any interest therein operates as a contract to sell.

(3) There may be a sale of a part interest in existing identified goods.

(4) An undivided share in an identified bulk of fungible goods is sufficiently identified to be sold although the quantity of the bulk is not determined. Any agreed proportion of such a bulk or any quantity thereof agreed upon by number, weight, or other measure may to the extent of the seller's interest in the bulk be sold to the buyer who then becomes an owner in common.

(5) "Lot" means a parcel or a single article which is the subject matter of a separate sale or delivery, whether or not it is sufficient to perform the contract.

(6) "Commercial unit" means such a unit of goods as by commercial usage is a single whole for purposes of sale and division of which materially impairs its character or value on the market or in use. A commercial unit may be a single article (as a machine) or a set of articles (as a suite of furniture or an assortment of sizes) or a quantity (as a bale, gross, or carload) or any other unit treated in use or in the relevant market as a single whole.

§ 2–106. Definitions: "Contract"; "Agreement"; "Contract for Sale"; "Sale"; "Present Sale"; "Conforming" to Contract; "Termination"; "Cancellation"

(1) In this Article unless the context otherwise requires "contract" and "agreement" are limited to those relating to the present or future sale of goods. "Contract for sale" includes both a present sale of goods and a contract to sell goods at a future time. A

"sale" consists in the passing of title from the seller to the buyer for a price (Section 2–401). A "present sale" means a sale which is accomplished by the making of the contract.

(2) Goods or conduct including any part of a performance are "conforming" or conform to the contract when they are in accordance with the obligations under the contract.

(3) "Termination" occurs when either party pursuant to a power created by agreement or law puts an end to the contract otherwise than for its breach. On "termination" all obligations which are still executory on both sides are discharged, but any right based on prior breach or performance survives.

(4) "Cancellation" occurs when either party puts an end to the contract for breach by the other, and its effect is the same as that of "termination" except that the cancelling party also retains any remedy for breach of the whole contract or any unperformed balance.

§ 2–107. *Goods to Be Severed from Realty: Recording*

(1) A contract for the sale of minerals or the like (including oil and gas) or a structure or its materials to be removed from realty is a contract for the sale of goods within this Article if they are to be severed by the seller; but until severance a purported present sale thereof which is not effective as a transfer of an interest in land is effective only as a contract to sell.

(2) A contract for the sale apart from the land of growing crops or other things attached to realty and capable of severance without material harm thereto but not described in subsection (1) or of timber to be cut is a contract for the sale of goods within this Article whether the subject matter is to be severed by the buyer or by the seller even though it forms part of the realty at the time of contracting, and the parties can by identification effect a present sale before severance.

(3) The provisions of this section are subject to any third party rights provided by the law relating to realty records, and the contract for sale may be executed and recorded as a document transferring an interest in land and shall then constitute notice to third parties of the buyer's right under the contract for sale.

Part 2. Form, Formation, and Readjustment of Contract

§ 2–201. *Formal Requirements; Statute of Frauds*

(1) Except as otherwise provided in this section, a contract for the sale of goods for the price of $500 or more is not enforceable by way of action or defense unless there is some writing sufficient to indicate that a contract for sale has been made between the parties and signed by the party against whom enforcement is sought or by his authorized agent or broker. A writing is not insufficient because it omits or incorrectly states a term agreed upon, but the contract is not enforceable under this paragraph beyond the quantity of goods shown in such writing.

(2) Between merchants, if within a reasonable time a writing in confirmation of the contract and sufficient against the sender is received and the party receiving it has reason to know its contents, it satisfies the requirements of subsection (1) against such party unless written notice of objection to its contents is given within 10 days after it is received.

(3) A contract which does not satisfy the requirements of subsection (1) but which is valid in other respects is enforceable

    (a) if the goods are to be specially manufactured for the buyer and are not suitable for sale to others in the ordinary course of the seller's business and the seller, before notice of repudiation is received and under circumstances which reasonably indicate that the goods are for the buyer, has made either a substantial beginning of their manufacture or commitments for their procurement; or

    (b) if the party against whom enforcement is sought admits in his pleading, testimony, or otherwise in court that a contract for sale was made, but the contract is not enforceable under this provision beyond the quantity of goods admitted; or

    (c) with respect to goods for which payment has been made and accepted or which have been received and accepted (Section 2–606).

§ 2–202. Final Written Expression: Parol or Extrinsic Evidence

Terms with respect to which the confirmatory memoranda of the parties agree or which are otherwise set forth in a writing intended by the parties as a final expression of their agreement with respect to such terms as are included therein may not be contradicted by evidence of any prior agreement or of a contemporaneous oral agreement but may be explained or supplemented

    (a) by course and dealing or usage of trade (Section 1–205) or by course of performance (Section 2–208); and

    (b) by evidence of consistent additional terms unless the court finds the writing to have been intended also as a complete and exclusive statement of the terms of the agreement.

§ 2–203. Seals Inoperative

The affixing of a seal to a writing evidencing a contract for sale or an offer to buy or sell goods does not constitute the writing a sealed instrument and the law with respect to sealed instruments does not apply to such a contract or offer.

§ 2–204. Formation in General

(1) A contract for sale of goods may be made in any manner sufficient to show agreement, including conduct by both parties which recognizes the existence of such a contract.

(2) An agreement sufficient to constitute a contract for sale may be found even though the moment of its making is undetermined.

(3) Even though one or more terms are left open a contract for sale does not fail for indefiniteness if the parties have intended to make a contract and there is a reasonably certain basis for giving an appropriate remedy.

§ 2–205. Firm Offers

An offer by a merchant to buy or sell goods in a signed writing which by its terms gives assurance that it will be held open is not revocable, for lack of consideration, during the time stated or if no time is stated for a reasonable time, but in no event may such period of irrevocability exceed three months; but any such term of assurance on a form supplied by the offeree must be separately signed by the offerer.

§ 2–206. Offer and Acceptance in Formation of Contract

(1) Unless otherwise unambiguously indicated by the language or circumstances

(a) an offer to make a contract shall be construed as inviting acceptance in any manner and by any medium reasonable in the circumstances;

(b) an order or other offer to buy goods for prompt or current shipment shall be construed as inviting acceptance either by a prompt promise to ship or by the prompt or current shipment of conforming or nonconforming goods, but such a shipment of nonconforming goods does not constitute an acceptance if the seller seasonably notifies the buyer that the shipment is offered only as an accommodation to the buyer.

(2) Where the beginning of a requested performance is a reasonable mode of acceptance, an offerer who is not notified of acceptance within a reasonable time may treat the offer as having lapsed before acceptance.

§ 2–207. Additional Terms in Acceptance or Confirmation

(1) A definite and seasonable expression of acceptance or a written confirmation which is sent within a reasonable time operates as an acceptance even though it states terms additional to or different from those offered or agreed upon, unless acceptance is expressly made conditional on assent to the additional or different terms.

(2) The additional terms are to be construed as proposals for addition to the contract. Between merchants such terms become part of the contract unless

(a) the offer expressly limits acceptance to the terms of the offer;

(b) they materially alter it; or

(c) notification of objection to them has already been given or is given within a reasonable time after notice of them is received.

(3) Conduct by both parties which recognizes the existence of a contract is sufficient to establish a contract for sale although the writings of the parties do not otherwise establish a contract. In such case the terms of the particular contract consist of those terms on which the writings of the parties agree, together with any supplementary terms incorporated under any other provisions of this Act.

§ 2–208. Course of Performance or Practical Construction

(1) Where the contract for sale involves repeated occasions for performance by either party with knowledge of the nature of the performance and opportunity for objection to it by the other, any course of performance accepted or acquiesced in without objection shall be relevant to determine the meaning of the agreement.

(2) The express terms of the agreement and any such course of performance, as well as any course of dealing and usage of trade, shall be construed whenever reasonable as consistent with each other; but when such construction is unreasonable, express terms shall control course of performance and course of performance shall control both course of dealing and usage of trade (Section 1–205).

(3) Subject to the provisions of the next section on modification and waiver, such course of performance shall be relevant to show a waiver or modification of any term inconsistent with such course of performance.

§ 2–209. Modification, Rescission, and Waiver

(1) An agreement modifying a contract within this Article needs no consideration to be binding.

(2) A signed agreement which excludes modification or rescission except by a signed writing cannot be otherwise modified or rescinded, but except as between merchants such a requirement on a form supplied by the merchant must be separately signed by the other party.

(3) The requirements of the statute of frauds section of this Article (Section 2–201) must be satisfied if the contract as modified is within its provisions.

(4) Although an attempt at modification or rescission does not satisfy the requirements of subsection (2) or (3) it can operate as a waiver.

(5) A party who has made a waiver affecting an executory portion of the contract may retract the waiver by reasonable notification received by the other party that strict performance will be required of any term waived, unless the retraction would be unjust in view of a material change of position in reliance on the waiver.

§ 2–210. Delegation of Performance; Assignment of Rights

(1) A party may perform his duty through a delegate unless otherwise agreed or unless the other party has a substantial interest in having his original promisor perform or control the acts required by the contract. No delegation of performance relieves the party delegating of any duty to perform or any liability for breach.

(2) Except as otherwise provided in Section 9–406, unless otherwise agreed all rights of either seller or buyer can be assigned except where the assignment would materially change the duty of the other party, or increase materially the burden or risk imposed on him by his contract, or impair materially his chance of obtaining return performance. A right to damages for breach of the whole contract or a right arising out of the assignor's due performance of his entire obligation can be assigned despite agreement otherwise.

(3) The creation, attachment, perfection, or enforcement of a security interest in the seller's interest under a contract is not a transfer that materially changes the duty of or increases materially the burden or risk imposed on the buyer or impairs materially the buyer's chance of obtaining return performance within the purview of subsection (2) unless, and then only to the extent that, enforcement actually results in a delegation of material performance of the seller. Even in that event, the creation, attachment, perfection, and enforcement of the security interest remain effective, but (i) the seller is liable to the buyer for damages caused by the delegation to the extent that the damages could not reasonably be prevented by the buyer, and (ii) a court having jurisdiction may grant other appropriate relief, including cancellation of the contract for sale or an injunction against enforcement of the security interest or consummation of the enforcement.

(4) Unless the circumstances indicate the contrary a prohibition of assignment of "the contract" is to be construed as barring only the delegation to the assignee of the assignor's performance.

(5) An assignment of "the contract" or of "all my rights under the contract" or an assignment in similar general terms is an assignment of rights and unless the language or the circumstances (as in an assignment for security) indicate the contrary, it is a delegation of performance of the duties of the assignor and its acceptance by the assignee constitutes a promise by him to perform those duties. This promise is enforceable by either the assignor or the other party to the original contract.

(6) The other party may treat any assignment which delegates performance as creating reasonable grounds for insecurity and may without prejudice to his rights against the assignor demand assurances from the assignee (Section 2–609).

Part 3. General Obligation and Construction of Contract

§ 2–301. General Obligations of Parties

The obligation of the seller is to transfer and deliver and that of the buyer is to accept and pay in accordance with the contract.

§ 2–302. Unconscionable Contract or Clause

(1) If the court as a matter of law finds the contract or any clause of the contract to have been unconscionable at the time it was made the court may refuse to enforce the contract, or it may enforce the remainder of the contract without the unconscionable clause, or it may so limit the application of any unconscionable clause as to avoid any unconscionable result.

(2) When it is claimed or appears to the court that the contract or any clause thereof may be unconscionable the parties shall be afforded a reasonable opportunity to present evidence as to its commercial setting, purpose, and effect to aid the court in making the determination.

§ 2–303. Allocation or Division of Risks

Where this Article allocates a risk or a burden as between the parties "unless otherwise agreed," the agreement may not only shift the allocation but may also divide the risk or burden.

§ 2–304. Price Payable in Money, Goods, Realty, or Otherwise

(1) The price can be made payable in money or otherwise. If it is payable in whole or in part in goods each party is a seller of the goods which he is to transfer.

(2) Even though all or part of the price is payable in an interest in realty the transfer of the goods and the seller's obligations with reference to them are subject to this Article, but not the transfer of the interest in realty or the transferor's obligations in connection therewith.

§ 2–305. Open Price Term

(1) The parties if they so intend can conclude a contract for sale even though the price is not settled. In such a case the price is a reasonable price at the time for delivery if

(a) nothing is said as to price; or
(b) the price is left to be agreed by the parties and they fail to agree; or

(c) the price is to be fixed in terms of some agreed market or other standard as set or recorded by a third person or agency and it is not so set or recorded.

(2) A price to be fixed by the seller or by the buyer means a price for him to fix in good faith.

(3) When a price left to be fixed otherwise than by agreement of the parties fails to be fixed through fault of one party the other may at his option treat the contract as cancelled or himself fix a reasonable price.

(4) Where, however, the parties intend not to be bound unless the price be fixed or agreed and it is not fixed or agreed there is no contract. In such a case the buyer must return any goods already received or if unable so to do must pay their reasonable value at the time of delivery and the seller must return any portion of the price paid on account.

§ 2–306. Output, Requirements, and Exclusive Dealings

(1) A term which measures the quantity by the output of the seller or the requirements of the buyer means such actual output or requirements as may occur in good faith, except that no quantity unreasonably disproportionate to any stated estimate or in the absence of a stated estimate to any normal or otherwise comparable prior output or requirements may be tendered or demanded.

(2) A lawful agreement by either the seller or the buyer for exclusive dealing in the kind of goods concerned imposes unless otherwise agreed an obligation by the seller to use best efforts to supply the goods and by the buyer to use best efforts to promote their sale.

§ 2–307. Delivery in Single Lot or Several Lots

Unless otherwise agreed all goods called for by a contract for sale must be tendered in a single delivery and payment is due only on such tender; but where the circumstances give either party the right to make or demand delivery in lots the price if it can be apportioned may be demanded for each lot.

§ 2–308. Absence of Specified Place for Delivery

Unless otherwise agreed

(a) the place for delivery of goods is the seller's place of business or if he has none his residence; but

(b) in a contract for sale of identified goods which to the knowledge of the parties at the time of contracting are in some other place, that place is the place for their delivery; and

(c) documents of title may be delivered through customary banking channels.

§ 2–309. Absence of Specific Time Provisions; Notice of Termination

(1) The time for shipment or delivery or any other action under a contract if not provided in this Article or agreed upon shall be a reasonable time.

(2) Where the contract provides for successive performance but is indefinite in duration it is valid for a reasonable time but unless otherwise agreed may be terminated at any time by either party.

(3) Termination of a contract by one party except on the happening of an agreed event requires that reasonable notification be received by the other party and an agreement dispensing with notification is invalid if its operation would be unconscionable.

§ 2–310. Open Time for Payment or Running of Credit; Authority to Ship under Reservation

Unless otherwise agreed

  (a) payment is due at the time and place at which the buyer is to receive the goods even though the place of shipment is the place of delivery; and

  (b) if the seller is authorized to send the goods he may ship them under reservation, and may tender the documents of title, but the buyer may inspect the goods after their arrival before payment is due unless such inspection is inconsistent with the terms of the contract (Section 2–513); and

  (c) if delivery is authorized and made by way of documents of title otherwise than by subsection (b) then payment is due at the time and place at which the buyer is to receive the documents regardless of where the goods are to be received; and

  (d) where the seller is required or authorized to ship the goods on credit the credit period runs from the time of shipment, but postdating the invoice or delaying its dispatch will correspondingly delay the starting of the credit period.

§ 2–311. Options and Cooperation Respecting Performance

(1) An agreement for sale which is otherwise sufficiently definite (subsection (3) of Section 2–204) to be a contract is not made invalid by the fact that it leaves particulars of performance to be specified by one of the parties. Any such specification must be made in good faith and within limits set by commercial reasonableness.

(2) Unless otherwise agreed specifications relating to assortment of the goods are at the buyer's option and except as otherwise provided in subsections (1) (c) and (3) of Section 2–319 specifications or arrangements relating to shipment are at the seller's option.

(3) Where such specification would materially affect the other party's performance but is not seasonably made or where one party's cooperation is necessary to the agreed performance of the other but is not seasonably forthcoming, the other party in addition to all other remedies

  (a) is excused for any resulting delay in his own performance; and

  (b) may also either proceed to perform in any reasonable manner or after the time for a material part of his own performance treat the failure to specify or to cooperate as a breach by failure to deliver or accept the goods.

§ 2–312. Warranty of Title and Against Infringement; Buyer's Obligation Against Infringement

(1) Subject to subsection (2) there is in a contract for sale a warranty by the seller that

  (a) the title conveyed shall be good, and its transfer rightful; and

(b) the goods shall be delivered free from any security interest or other lien or encumbrance of which the buyer at the time of contracting has no knowledge.

(2) A warranty under subsection (1) will be excluded or modified only by specific language or by circumstances which give the buyer reason to know that the person selling does not claim title in himself or that he is purporting to sell only such right or title as he or a third person may have.

(3) Unless otherwise agreed a seller who is a merchant regularly dealing in goods of the kind warrants that the goods shall be delivered free of the rightful claim of any third person by way of infringement or the like; but a buyer who furnishes specifications to the seller must hold the seller harmless against any such claim which arises out of compliance with the specifications.

§ 2–313. Express Warranties by Affirmation, Promise, Description, Sample

(1) Express warranties by the seller are created as follows:

(a) Any affirmation of fact or promise made by the seller to the buyer which relates to the goods and becomes part of the basis of the bargain creates an express warranty that the goods shall conform to the affirmation or promise.

(b) Any description of the goods which is made part of the basis of the bargain creates an express warranty that the goods shall conform to the description.

(c) Any sample or model which is made part of the basis of the bargain creates an express warranty that the whole of the goods shall conform to the sample or model.

(2) It is not necessary to the creation of an express warranty that the seller use formal words such as "warrant" or "guarantee" or that he have a specific intention to make a warranty, but an affirmation merely of the value of the goods or a statement purporting to be merely the seller's opinion or commendation of the goods does not create a warranty.

§ 2–314. Implied Warranty: Merchantability; Usage of Trade

(1) Unless excluded or modified (Section 2–316), a warranty that the goods shall be merchantable is implied in a contract for their sale if the seller is a merchant with respect to goods of that kind. Under this section the serving for value of food or drink to be consumed either on the premises or elsewhere is a sale.

(2) Goods to be merchantable must be at least such as

(a) pass without objection in the trade under the contract description; and

(b) in the case of fungible goods, are of fair average quality within the description; and

(c) are fit for the ordinary purposes for which such goods are used; and

(d) run, within the variations permitted by the agreement, of even kind, quality, and quantity within each unit and among all units involved; and

(e) are adequately contained, packaged, and labeled as the agreement may require; and

(f) conform to the promises or affirmations of fact made on the container or label if any.

(3) Unless excluded or modified (Section 2–316) other implied warranties may arise from course of dealing or usage of trade.

§ 2–315. Implied Warranty: Fitness for Particular Purpose

Where the seller at the time of contracting has reason to know any particular purpose for which the goods are required and that the buyer is relying on the seller's skill or judgment to select or furnish suitable goods, there is unless excluded or modified under the next section an implied warranty that the goods shall be fit for such purpose.

§ 2–316. Exclusion or Modification of Warranties

(1) Words or conduct relevant to the creation of an express warranty and words or conduct tending to negate or limit warranty shall be construed wherever reasonable as consistent with each other, but subject to the provisions of this Article on parol or extrinsic evidence (Section 2–202) negation or limitation is inoperative to the extent that such construction is unreasonable.

(2) Subject to subsection (3), to exclude or modify the implied warranty of merchantability or any part of it the language must mention merchantability and in case of a writing must be conspicuous, and to exclude or modify any implied warranty of fitness the exclusion must be by a writing and conspicuous. Language to exclude all implied warranties of fitness is sufficient if it states, for example, that "There are no warranties which extend beyond the description on the face hereof."

(3) Notwithstanding subsection (2)

(a) unless the circumstances indicate otherwise, all implied warranties are excluded by expressions like "as is," "with all faults," or other language which in common understanding calls the buyer's attention to the exclusion of warranties and makes plain that there is no implied warranty; and

(b) when the buyer before entering into the contract has examined the goods or the sample or model as fully as he desired or has refused to examine the goods there is no implied warranty with regard to defects which an examination ought in the circumstances to have revealed to him; and

(c) an implied warranty can also be excluded or modified by course of dealing or course of performance or usage of trade.

(4) Remedies for breach of warranty can be limited in accordance with the provisions of this Article on liquidation or limitation of damages and on contractual modification of remedy (Sections 2–718 and 2–719).

§ 2–317. Cumulation and Conflict of Warranties Express or Implied

Warranties whether express or implied shall be construed as consistent with each other and as cumulative, but if such construction is unreasonable the intention of the parties shall determine which warranty is dominant. In ascertaining that intention the following rules apply:

(a) Exact or technical specifications displace an inconsistent sample or model or general language of description.

(b) A sample from an existing bulk displaces inconsistent general language of description.

(c) Express warranties displace inconsistent implied warranties other than an implied warranty of fitness for a particular purpose.

§ 2–318. Third Party Beneficiaries of Warranties Express or Implied

Note: *If this Act is introduced in the Congress of the United States this section should be omitted. (States to select one alternative.)*

Alternative A   A seller's warranty whether express or implied extends to any natural person who is in the family or household of his buyer or who is a guest in his home if it is reasonable to expect that such person may use, consume, or be affected by the goods and who is injured in person by breach of the warranty. A seller may not exclude or limit the operation of this section.

Alternative B   A seller's warranty whether express or implied extends to any natural person who may reasonably be expected to use, consume, or be affected by the goods and who is injured in person by breach of the warranty. A seller may not exclude or limit the operation of this section.

Alternative C   A seller's warranty whether express or implied extends to any person who may reasonably be expected to use, consume, or be affected by the goods and who is injured by breach of the warranty. A seller may not exclude or limit the operation of this section with respect to injury to the person of an individual to whom the warranty extends.

§ 2–319. F.O.B. and F.A.S. Terms

(1) Unless otherwise agreed the term F.O.B. (which means "free on board") at a named place, even though used only in connection with the stated price, is a delivery term under which

(a) when the term is F.O.B. the place of shipment, the seller must at that place ship the goods in the manner provided in this Article (Section 2–504) and bear the expense and risk of putting them into the possession of the carrier; or

(b) when the term is F.O.B. the place of destination, the seller must at his own expense and risk transport the goods to that place and there tender delivery of them in the manner provided in this Article (Section 2–503);

(c) when under either (a) or (b) the term is also F.O.B. vessel, car, or other vehicle, the seller must in addition at his own expense and risk load the goods on board. If the term is F.O.B. vessel the buyer must name the vessel and in an appropriate case the seller must comply with the provisions of this Article on the form of bill of lading (Section 2–323).

(2) Unless otherwise agreed the term F.A.S. vessel (which means "free alongside") at a named port, even though used only in connection with the stated price, is a delivery term under which the seller must

(a) at his own expense and risk deliver the goods alongside the vessel in the manner usual in that port or on a dock designated and provided by the buyer; and

(b) obtain and tender a receipt for the goods in exchange for which the carrier is under a duty to issue a bill of lading.

(3) Unless otherwise agreed in any case falling within subsection (1)(a) or (c) or subsection (2) the buyer must seasonably give any needed instructions for making delivery, including when the term is F.A.S. or F.O.B. the loading berth of the vessel and in an appropriate case its name and sailing date. The seller may treat the failure of needed instructions as a failure of cooperation under this Article (Section 2–311). He may also at his option move the goods in any reasonable manner preparatory to delivery or shipment.

(4) Under the term F.O.B. vessel or F.A.S. unless otherwise agreed the buyer must make payment against tender of the required documents and the seller may not tender nor the buyer demand delivery of the goods in substitution for the documents.

§ 2–320. C.I.F. and C. & F. Terms

(1) The term C.I.F. means that the price includes in a lump sum the cost of the goods and the insurance and freight to the named destination. The term C. & F. or C.F. means that the price so includes cost and freight to the named destination.

(2) Unless otherwise agreed and even though used only in connection with the stated price and destination, the term C.I.F. destination or its equivalent requires the seller at his own expense and risk to

    (a) put the goods into the possession of a carrier at the port for shipment and obtain a negotiable bill or bills of lading covering the entire transportation to the named destination; and

    (b) load the goods and obtain a receipt from the carrier (which may be contained in the bill of lading) showing that the freight has been paid or provided for; and

    (c) obtain a policy or certificate of insurance, including any war risk insurance, of a kind and on terms then current at the port of shipment in the usual amount, in the currency of the contract, shown to cover the same goods covered by the bill of lading and providing for payment of loss to the order of the buyer or for the account of whom it may concern; but the seller may add to the price the amount of the premium for any such war risk insurance; and

    (d) prepare an invoice of the goods and procure any other documents required to effect shipment or to comply with the contract; and

    (e) forward and tender with commercial promptness all the documents in due form and with any endorsement necessary to perfect the buyer's rights.

(3) Unless otherwise agreed the term C. & F. or its equivalent has the same effect and imposes upon the seller the same obligations and risks as a C.I.F. term except the obligation as to insurance.

(4) Under the term C.I.F. or C. & F. unless otherwise agreed the buyer must make payment against tender of the required documents and the seller may not tender nor the buyer demand delivery of the goods in substitution for the documents.

§ 2–321. C.I.F. or C. & F.: "Net Landed Weights"; "Payment on Arrival"; Warranty of Condition on Arrival

Under a contract containing a term C.I.F. or C. & F.

(1) Where the price is based on or is to be adjusted according to "net landed weights," "delivered weights," "out turn" quantity or quality, or the like, unless otherwise agreed the seller must reasonably estimate the price. The payment due on tender of the documents called for by the contract is the amount so estimated, but after final adjustment of the price a settlement must be made with commercial promptness.

(2) An agreement described in subsection (1) or any warranty of quality or condition of the goods on arrival places upon the seller the risk of ordinary deterioration, shrinkage, and the like in transportation but has no effect on the place or time of identification to the contract for sale or delivery or on the passing of the risk of loss.

(3) Unless otherwise agreed where the contract provides for payment on or after arrival of the goods the seller must before payment allow such preliminary inspection as is feasible; but if the goods are lost delivery of the documents and payment are due when the goods should have arrived.

§ 2–322. Delivery "Ex-Ship"

(1) Unless otherwise agreed a term for delivery of goods "ex-ship" (which means from the carrying vessel) or in equivalent language is not restricted to a particular ship and requires delivery from a ship which has reached a place at the named port of destination where goods of the kind are usually discharged.

(2) Under such a term unless otherwise agreed

   (a) the seller must discharge all liens arising out of the carriage and furnish the buyer with a direction which puts the carrier under a duty to deliver the goods; and

   (b) the risk of loss does not pass to the buyer until the goods leave the ship's tackle or are otherwise properly unloaded.

§ 2–323. Form of Bill of Lading Required in Overseas Shipment; "Overseas"

(1) Where the contract contemplates overseas shipment and contains a term C.I.F. or C. & F. or F.O.B. vessel, the seller unless otherwise agreed must obtain a negotiable bill of lading stating that the goods have been loaded on board or, in the case of a term C.I.F. or C. & F., received for shipment.

(2) Where in a case within subsection (1) a bill of lading has been issued in a set of parts, unless otherwise agreed if the documents are not to be sent from abroad the buyer may demand tender of the full set; otherwise only one part of the bill of lading need be tendered. Even if the agreement expressly requires a full set

   (a) due tender of a single part is acceptable within the provisions of this Article on cure of improper delivery (subsection (1) of Section 2–508); and

   (b) even though the full set is demanded, if the documents are sent from abroad the person tendering an incomplete set may nevertheless require payment upon furnishing an indemnity which the buyer in good faith deems adequate.

(3) A shipment by water or by air or a contract contemplating such shipment is "overseas" insofar as by usage of trade or agreement it is subject to the commercial, financing, or shipping practices characteristic of international deep water commerce.

§ 2–324. *"No Arrival, No Sale" Term*

Under a term "no arrival, no sale" or terms of like meaning, unless otherwise agreed,

(a) the seller must properly ship conforming goods and if they arrive by any means he must tender them on arrival but he assumes no obligation that the goods will arrive unless he has caused the nonarrival; and

(b) where without fault of the seller the goods are in part lost or have so deteriorated as no longer to conform to the contract or arrive after the contract time, the buyer may proceed as if there had been casualty to identified goods (Section 2–613).

§ 2–325. *"Letter of Credit" Term; "Confirmed Credit"*

(1) Failure of the buyer seasonably to furnish an agreed letter of credit is a breach of the contract for sale.

(2) The delivery to seller of a proper letter of credit suspends the buyer's obligation to pay. If the letter of credit is dishonored, the seller may on seasonable notification to the buyer require payment directly from him.

(3) Unless otherwise agreed the term "letter of credit" or "banker's credit" in a contract for sale means an irrevocable credit issued by a financing agency of good repute and, where the shipment is overseas, of good international repute. The term "confirmed credit" means that the credit must also carry the direct obligation of such an agency which does business in the seller's financial market.

§ 2–326. *Sale on Approval and Sale or Return; Rights of Creditors*

(1) Unless otherwise agreed, if delivered goods may be returned by the buyer even though they conform to the contract, the transaction is

(a) a "sale on approval" if the goods are delivered primarily for use, and

(b) a "sale or return" if the goods are delivered primarily for resale.

(2) Goods held on approval are not subject to the claims of the buyer's creditors until acceptance; goods held on sale or return are subject to such claims while in the buyer's possession.

(3) Any "or return" term of a contract for sale is to be treated as a separate contract for sale within the statute of frauds section of this Article (Section 2–201) and as contradicting the sale aspect of the contract within the provisions of this Article on parol or extrinsic evidence (Section 2–202).

§ 2–327. *Special Incidents of Sale on Approval and Sale or Return*

(1) Under a sale on approval unless otherwise agreed

(a) although the goods are identified to the contract the risk of loss and the title do not pass to the buyer until acceptance; and

(b) use of the goods consistent with the purpose of trial is not acceptance but failure seasonably to notify the seller of election to return the goods is acceptance, and if the goods conform to the contract acceptance of any part is acceptance of the whole; and

    (c) after due notification of election to return, the return is at the seller's risk and expense but a merchant buyer must follow any reasonable instructions.

  (2) Under a sale or return unless otherwise agreed

    (a) the option to return extends to the whole or any commercial unit of the goods while in substantially their original conditions, but must be exercised seasonably; and

    (b) the return is at the buyer's risk and expense.

§ 2–328. Sale by Auction

(1) In a sale by auction if goods are put up in lots each lot is the subject of a separate sale.

(2) A sale by auction is complete when the auctioneer so announces by the fall of the hammer or in other customary manner. Where a bid is made while the hammer is falling in acceptance of a prior bid the auctioneer may in his discretion reopen the bidding or declare the goods sold under the bid on which the hammer was falling.

(3) Such a sale is with reserve unless the goods are in explicit terms put up without reserve. In an auction with reserve the auctioneer may withdraw the goods at any time until he announces completion of the sale. In an auction without reserve, after the auctioneer calls for bids on an article or lot, that article or lot cannot be withdrawn unless no bid is made within a reasonable time. In either case a bidder may retract his bid until the auctioneer's announcement of completion of the sale, but a bidder's retraction does not revive any previous bid.

(4) If the auctioneer knowingly receives a bid on the seller's behalf or the seller makes or procures such a bid, and notice has not been given that liberty for such bidding is reserved, the buyer may at his option avoid the sale or take the goods at the price of the last good faith bid prior to the completion of the sale. This subsection shall not apply to any bid at a forced sale.

Part 4. Title, Creditors, and Good-Faith Purchasers

§ 2–401. Passing of Title; Reservation for Security; Limited Application of This Section

Each provision of this Article with regard to the rights, obligations, and remedies of the seller, the buyer, purchasers, or other third parties applies irrespective of title to the goods except where the provision refers to such title. Insofar as situations are not covered by the other provisions of this Article and matters concerning title become material the following rules apply:

(1) Title to goods cannot pass under a contract for sale prior to their identification to the contract (Section 2–501), and unless otherwise explicitly agreed the buyer acquires by their identification a special property as limited by this Act. Any retention or reservation by the seller of the title (property) in goods shipped or delivered to the buyer is limited in effect to a reservation of a security interest. Subject to these provisions and to the provisions of the Article on Secured Transactions (Article 9), title to goods passes from the seller to the buyer in any manner and on any conditions explicitly agreed on by the parties.

(2) Unless otherwise explicitly agreed title passes to the buyer at the time and place at which the seller completes his performance with reference to the physical delivery of the goods, despite any reservation of a security interest and even though a document of title is to be delivered at a different time or place; and in particular and despite any reservation of a security interest by the bill of lading

    (a) if the contract requires or authorizes the seller to send the goods to the buyer but does not require him to deliver them at destination, title passes to the buyer at the time and place of shipment; but

    (b) if the contract requires delivery at destination, title passes on tender there.

(3) Unless otherwise explicitly agreed, where delivery is to be made without moving the goods.

    (a) if the seller is to deliver a document of title, title passes at the time when and the place where he delivers such documents; or

    (b) if the goods are at the time of contracting already identified and no documents are to be delivered, title passes at the time and place of contracting.

(4) A rejection or other refusal by the buyer to receive or retain the goods, whether or not justified, or a justified revocation of acceptance revests title to the goods in the seller. Such revesting occurs by operation of law and is not a "sale."

§ 2–402. Rights of Seller's Creditors Against Sold Goods

(1) Except as provided in subsections (2) and (3), rights of unsecured creditors of the seller with respect to goods which have been identified to a contract for sale are subject to the buyer's rights to recover the goods under this Article (Sections 2–502 and 2–716).

(2) A creditor of the seller may treat a sale or an identification of goods to a contract for sale as void if as against him a retention of possession by the seller is fraudulent under any rule of law of the state where the goods are situated, except that retention of possession in good faith and current course of trade by a merchant–seller for a commercially reasonable time after a sale or identification is not fraudulent.

(3) Nothing in this Article shall be deemed to impair the rights of creditors of the seller

    (a) under the provisions of the Article on Secured Transactions (Article 9); or

    (b) where identification to the contract or delivery is made not in current course of trade but in satisfaction of or as security for a preexisting claim for money, security, or the like and is made under circumstances which under any rule of law of the state where the goods are situated would apart from this Article constitute the transaction a fraudulent transfer or voidable preference.

§ 2–403. Power to Transfer; Good-Faith Purchase of Goods; "Entrusting"

(1) A purchaser of goods acquires all title which his transferor had or had power to transfer except that a purchaser of a limited interest acquires rights only to the extent of the interest purchased. A person with voidable title has power to transfer a good title to a good-faith purchaser for value. When goods have been delivered under a transaction of purchase the purchaser has such power even though

    (a) the transferor was deceived as to the identity of the purchaser, or

(b) the delivery was in exchange for a check which is later dishonored, or

(c) it was agreed that the transaction was to be a "cash sale," or

(d) the delivery was procured through fraud punishable as larcenous under the criminal law.

(2) Any entrusting of possession of goods to a merchant who deals in goods of that kind gives him power to transfer all rights of the entruster to a buyer in ordinary course of business.

(3) "Entrusting" includes any delivery and any acquiescence in retention of possession regardless of any condition expressed between the parties to the delivery or acquiescence and regardless of whether the procurement of the entrusting or the possessor's disposition of the goods have been such as to be larcenous under the criminal law.

(4) The rights of other purchasers of goods and of lien creditors are governed by the Articles on Secured Transactions (Article 9). [Bulk Transfers/Sales (Article 6)* and Documents of Title (Article 7)].

Part 5. Performance

§ 2–501. *Insurable Interest in Goods; Manner of Identification of Goods*

(1) The buyer obtains a special property and an insurable interest in goods by identification of existing goods as goods to which the contract refers even though the goods so identified are nonconforming and he has an option to return or reject them. Such identification can be made at any time and in any manner explicitly agreed to by the parties. In the absence of explicit agreement identification occurs

(a) when the contract is made if it is for the sale of goods already existing and identified;

(b) if the contract is for the sale of future goods other than those described in paragraph (c), when goods are shipped, marked, or otherwise designated by the seller as goods to which the contract refers;

(c) when the crops are planted or otherwise become growing crops or the young are conceived if the contract is for the sale of unborn young to be born within 12 months after contracting or for the sale of crops to be harvested within 12 months or the next normal harvest season after contracting, whichever is longer.

(2) The seller retains an insurable interest in goods so long as title to or any security interest in the goods remains in him; and where the identification is by the seller alone he may until default or insolvency or notification to the buyer that the identification is final substitute other goods for those identified.

(3) Nothing in this section impairs any insurable interest recognized under any other statute or rule of law.

§ 2–502. *Buyer's Right to Goods on Seller's Insolvency*

(1) Subject to subsections (2) and (3) and even though the goods have not been shipped, a buyer who has paid a part or all of the price of goods in which he has a special property under the provisions of the immediately preceding section may on making

and keeping good a tender of any unpaid portion of their price recover them from the seller if

> (a) in the case of goods bought for personal, family, or household purposes, the seller repudiates or fails to deliver as required by the contract; or
> (b) in all cases, the seller becomes insolvent within 10 days after receipt of the first installment on their price.

(2) The buyer's right to recover the goods under subsection (1)(a) vests upon acquisition of a special property, even if the seller had not then repudiated or failed to deliver.

(3) If the identification creating his special property has been made by the buyer he acquires the right to recover the goods only if they conform to the contract for sale.

§ 2–503. Manner of Seller's Tender of Delivery

(1) Tender of delivery requires that the seller put and hold conforming goods at the buyer's disposition and give the buyer any notification reasonably necessary to enable him to take delivery. The manner, time, and place for tender are determined by the agreement and this Article, and in particular

> (a) tender must be at a reasonable hour, and if it is of goods they must be kept available for the period reasonably necessary to enable the buyer to take possession; but
> (b) unless otherwise agreed the buyer must furnish facilities reasonably suited to the receipt of the goods.

(2) Where the case is within the next section respecting shipment tender requires that the seller comply with its provisions.

(3) Where the seller is required to deliver at a particular destination tender requires that he comply with subsection (1) and also in any appropriate case tender documents as described in subsections (4) and (5) of this section.

(4) Where goods are in the possession of a bailee and are to be delivered without being moved

> (a) tender requires that the seller either tender a negotiable document of title covering such goods or procure acknowledgment by the bailee of the buyer's right to possession of the goods; but
> (b) tender to the buyer of a nonnegotiable document of title or of a written direction to the bailee to deliver is sufficient tender unless the buyer seasonably objects, and receipt by the bailee of notification of the buyer's rights fixes those rights as against the bailee and all third persons; but risk of loss of the goods and of any failure by the bailee to honor the nonnegotiable document of title or to obey the direction remains on the seller untill the buyer has had a reasonable time to present the document or direction, and a refusal by the bailee to honor the document or to obey the direction defeats the tender.

(5) Where the contract requires the seller to deliver documents

> (a) he must tender all such documents in correct form, except as provided in this Article with respect to bills of lading in a set (subsection (2) of Section 2–323); and

    (b) tender through customary banking channels is sufficient and dishonor of a draft accompanying the documents constitutes nonacceptance or rejection.

§ 2–504. Shipment by Seller

Where the seller is required or authorized to send the goods to the buyer and the contract does not require him to deliver them at a particular destination, then unless otherwise agreed he must

    (a) put the goods in the possession of such a carrier and make such a contract for their transportation as may be reasonable having regard to the nature of the goods and other circumstances of the case; and

    (b) obtain and promptly deliver or tender in due form any document necessary to enable the buyer to obtain possession of the goods or otherwise required by the agreement or by usage of trade; and

    (c) promptly notify the buyer of the shipment.

Failure to notify the buyer under paragraph (c) or to make a proper contract under paragraph (a) is a ground for rejection only if material delay or loss ensues.

§ 2–505. Seller's Shipment under Reservation

    (1) Where the seller has identified goods to the contract by or before shipment,

    (a) his procurement of a negotiable bill of lading to his own order or otherwise reserves in him a security interest in the goods. His procurement of the bill to the order of a financing agency or of the buyer indicates in addition only the seller's expectation of transferring that interest to the person named.

    (b) a nonnegotiable bill of lading to himself or his nominee reserves possession of the goods as security but except in a case of conditional delivery (subsection (2) of Section 2–507) a nonnegotiable bill of lading naming the buyer as consignee reserves no security interest even though the seller retains possession of the bill of lading.

    (2) When shipment by the seller with reservation of a security interest is in violation of the contract for sale it constitutes an improper contract for transportation within the preceding section but impairs neither the rights given to the buyer by shipment and identification of the goods to the contract nor the seller's powers as a holder of a negotiable document.

§ 2–506. Rights of Financing Agency

    (1) A financing agency by paying or purchasing for value a draft which relates to a shipment of goods acquires to the extent of the payment or purchase and in addition to its own rights under the draft and any document of title securing it any rights of the shipper in the goods including the right to stop delivery and the shipper's right to have the draft honored by the buyer.

    (2) The right to reimbursement of a financing agency which has in good faith honored or purchased the draft under commitment to or authority from the buyer is not impaired by subsequent discovery of defects with reference to any relevant document which was apparently regular on its face.

§ 2–507. *Effect of Seller's Tender; Delivery on Condition*

(1) Tender of delivery is a condition to the buyer's duty to accept the goods and, unless otherwise agreed, to his duty to pay for them. Tender entitles the seller to acceptance of the goods and to payment according to the contract.

(2) Where payment is due and demanded on the delivery to the buyer of goods or documents of title, his right as against the seller to retain or dispose of them is conditional upon his making the payment due.

§ 2–508. *Cure by Seller of Improper Tender or Delivery; Replacement*

(1) Where any tender or delivery by the seller is rejected because nonconforming and the time for performance has not yet expired, the seller may seasonably notify the buyer of his intention to cure and may then within the contract time make a conforming delivery.

(2) Where the buyer rejects a nonconforming tender which the seller had reasonable grounds to believe would be acceptable with or without money allowance the seller may if he seasonably notifies the buyer have a further reasonable time to substitute a conforming tender.

§ 2–509. *Risk of Loss in the Absence of Breach*

(1) Where the contract requires or authorizes the seller to ship the goods by carrier

    (a) if it does not require him to deliver them at a particular destination, the risk of loss passes to the buyer when the goods are duly delivered to the carrier even though the shipment is under reservation (Section 2–505); but

    (b) if it does require him to deliver them at a particular destination and the goods are there duly tendered while in the possession of the carrier, the risk of loss passes to the buyer when the goods are there duly so tendered as to enable the buyer to take delivery.

(2) Where the goods are held by a bailee to be delivered without being moved, the risk of loss passes to the buyer

    (a) on his receipt of a negotiable document of title covering the goods; or

    (b) on acknowledgment by the bailee of the buyer's right to possession of the goods; or

    (c) after his receipt of a nonnegotiable document of title or other written direction to deliver, as provided in subsection (4)(b) of Section 2–503.

(3) In any case not within subsection (1) or (2), the risk of loss passes to the buyer on his receipt of the goods if the seller is a merchant; otherwise the risk passes to the buyer on tender of delivery.

(4) The provisions of this section are subject to contrary agreement of the parties and to the provisions of this Article on sale on approval (Section 2–327) and on effect of breach on risk of loss (Section 2–510).

§ 2–510. *Effect of Breach on Risk of Loss*

(1) Where a tender or delivery of goods so fails to conform to the contract as to give a right of rejection the risk of their loss remains on the seller until cure or acceptance.

(2) Where the buyer rightfully revokes acceptance he may to the extent of any deficiency in his effective insurance coverage treat the risk of loss as having rested on the seller from the beginning.

(3) Where the buyer as to conforming goods already identified to the contract for sale repudiates or is otherwise in breach before risk of their loss has passed to him, the seller may to the extent of any deficiency in his effective insurance coverage treat the risk of loss as resting on the buyer for a commercially reasonable time.

§ 2–511. Tender of Payment by Buyer; Payment by Check

(1) Unless otherwise agreed tender of payment is a condition to the seller's duty to tender and complete any delivery.

(2) Tender of payment is sufficient when made by any means or in any manner current in the ordinary course of business unless the seller demands payment in legal tender and gives any extension of time reasonably necessary to procure it.

(3) Subject to the provisions of this Act on the effect of an instrument on an obligation (Section 3–310), payment by check is conditional and is defeated as between the parties by dishonor of the check on due presentment.

§ 2–512. Payment by Buyer before Inspection

(1) Where the contract requires payment before inspection nonconformity of the goods does not excuse the buyer from so making payment unless

  (a) the nonconformity appears without inspection; or
  (b) despite tender of the required documents the circumstances would justify injunction against honor under this Act (Section 5–109(b)).

(2) Payment pursuant to subsection (1) does not constitute an acceptance of goods or impair the buyer's right to inspect or any of his remedies.

§ 2–513. Buyer's Right to Inspection of Goods

(1) Unless otherwise agreed and subject to subsection (3), where goods are tendered or delivered or identified to the contract for sale, the buyer has a right before payment or acceptance to inspect them at any reasonable place and time and in any reasonable manner. When the seller is required or authorized to send the goods to the buyer, the inspection may be after their arrival.

(2) Expenses of inspection must be borne by the buyer but may be recovered from the seller if the goods do not conform and are rejected.

(3) Unless otherwise agreed and subject to the provisions of this Article on C.I.F. contracts (subsection (3) of Section 2–321), the buyer is not entitled to inspect the goods before payment of the price when the contract provides

  (a) for delivery "C.O.D." or on other like terms; or
  (b) for payment against documents of title, except where such payment is due only after the goods are to become available for inspection.

(4) A place or method of inspection fixed by the parties is presumed to be exclusive but unless otherwise expressly agreed it does not postpone identification or shift the place for delivery or for passing the risk of loss. If compliance becomes impossible, inspection

shall be as provided in this section unless the place or method fixed was clearly intended as an indispensable condition, failure of which avoids the contract.

§ 2–514. *When Documents Deliverable on Acceptance; When on Payment*

Unless otherwise agreed documents against which a draft is drawn are to be delivered to the drawee on acceptance of the draft if it is payable more than three days after presentment; otherwise, only on payment.

§ 2–515. *Preserving Evidence of Goods in Dispute*

In furtherance of the adjustment of any claim or dispute

> (a) either party on reasonable notification to the other and for the purpose of ascertaining the facts and preserving evidence has the right to inspect, test, and sample the goods including such of them as may be in the possession or control of the other; and
>
> (b) the parties may agree to a third-party inspection or survey to determine the conformity or condition of the goods and may agree that the findings shall be binding upon them in any subsequent litigation or adjustment.

Part 6. Breach, Repudiation, and Excuse

§ 2–601. *Buyer's Rights on Improper Delivery*

Subject to the provisions of this Article on breach in installment contracts (Section 2–612) and unless otherwise agreed under the sections on contractual limitations of remedy (Sections 2–718 and 2–719), if the goods or the tender of delivery fail in any respect to conform to the contract, the buyer may

> (a) reject the whole; or
>
> (b) accept the whole; or
>
> (c) accept any commercial unit or units and reject the rest.

§ 2–602. *Manner and Effect of Rightful Rejection*

(1) Rejection of goods must be within a reasonable time after their delivery or tender. It is ineffective unless the buyer seasonably notifies the seller.

(2) Subject to the provisions of the two following sections on rejected goods (Sections 2–603 and 2–604),

> (a) after rejection any exercise of ownership by the buyer with respect to any commercial unit is wrongful as against the seller; and
>
> (b) if the buyer has before rejection taken physical possession of goods in which he does not have a security interest under the provisions of this Article (subsection (3) of Section 2–711), he is under a duty after rejection to hold them with reasonable care at the seller's disposition for a time sufficient to permit the seller to remove them; but
>
> (c) the buyer has no further obligations with regard to goods rightfully rejected.

(3) The seller's rights with respect to goods wrongfully rejected are governed by the provisions of this Article on Seller's remedies in general (Section 2–703).

§ 2–603. *Merchant Buyer's Duties as to Rightfully Rejected Goods*

(1) Subject to any security interest in the buyer (subsection (3) of Section 2–711), when the seller has no agent or place of business at the market of rejection a merchant buyer is under a duty after rejection of goods in his possession or control to follow any reasonable instructions received from the seller with respect to the goods and in the absence of such instructions to make reasonable efforts to sell them for the seller's account if they are perishable or threaten to decline in value speedily. Instructions are not reasonable if on demand indemnity for expenses is not forthcoming.

(2) When the buyer sells goods under subsection (1), he is entitled to reimbursement from the seller or out of the proceeds for reasonable expenses of caring for and selling them, and if the expenses include no selling commission then to such commission as is usual in the trade or if there is none to a reasonable sum not exceeding 10 percent on the gross proceeds.

(3) In complying with this section the buyer is held only to good faith and good-faith conduct hereunder is neither acceptance nor conversion nor the basis of an action for damages.

§ 2–604. *Buyer's Options as to Salvage of Rightfully Rejected Goods*

Subject to the provisions of the immediately preceding section on perishables if the seller gives no instructions within a reasonable time after notification of rejection the buyer may store the rejected goods for the seller's account or reship them to him or resell them for the seller's account with reimbursement as provided in the preceding section. Such action is not acceptance or conversion.

§ 2–605. *Waiver of Buyer's Objections by Failure to Particularize*

(1) The buyer's failure to state in connection with rejection a particular defect which is ascertainable by reasonable inspection precludes him from relying on the unstated defect to justify rejection or to establish breach

   (a) where the seller could have cured it if stated seasonably; or

   (b) between merchants when the seller has after rejection made a request in writing for a full and final written statement of all defects on which the buyer proposes to rely.

(2) Payment against documents made without reservation of rights precludes recovery of the payment for defects apparent on the face of the documents.

§ 2–606. *What Constitutes Acceptance of Goods*

(1) Acceptance of goods occurs when the buyer

   (a) after a reasonable opportunity to inspect the goods signifies to the seller that the goods are conforming or that he will take or retain them in spite of their nonconformity; or

   (b) fails to make an effective rejection (subsection (1) of Section 2–602), but such acceptance does not occur until the buyer has had a reasonable opportunity to inspect them; or

(c) does any act inconsistent with the seller's ownership; but if such act is wrongful as against the seller it is an acceptance only if ratified by him.

(2) Acceptance of a part of any commercial unit is acceptance of that entire unit.

§ 2–607. Effect of Acceptance; Notice of Breach; Burden of Establishing Breach after Acceptance; Notice of Claim or Litigation to Person Answerable Over

(1) The buyer must pay at the contract rate for any goods accepted.

(2) Acceptance of goods by the buyer precludes rejection of the goods accepted and if made with knowledge of a nonconformity cannot be revoked because of it unless the acceptance was on the reasonable assumption that the nonconformity would be seasonably cured; but acceptance does not of itself impair any other remedy provided by this Article for nonconformity.

(3) Where a tender has been accepted

(a) the buyer must within a reasonable time after he discovers or should have discovered any breach notify the seller of breach or be barred from any remedy; and

(b) if the claim is one for infringement or the like (subsection (3) of Section 2–312) and the buyer is sued as a result of such a breach he must so notify the seller within a reasonable time after he receives notice of the litigation or be barred from any remedy over for liability established by the litigation.

(4) The burden is on the buyer to establish any breach with respect to the goods accepted.

(5) Where the buyer is sued for breach of a warranty or other obligation for which his seller is answerable over

(a) he may give his seller written notice of the litigation. If the notice states that the seller may come in and defend and that if the seller does not do so he will be bound in any action against him by his buyer by any determination of fact common to the two litigations, then unless the seller after seasonable receipt of the notice does come in and defend he is so bound.

(b) if the claim is one for infringement or the like (subsection (3) of Section 2–312) the original seller may demand in writing that his buyer turn over to him control of the litigation including settlement or else be barred from any remedy over and if he also agrees to bear all expense and to satisfy any adverse judgment, then unless the buyer after seasonable receipt of the demand does turn over control the buyer is so barred.

(6) The provisions of subsection (3), (4), and (5) apply to any obligation of a buyer to hold the seller harmless against infringement or the like (subsection (3) of Section 2–312).

§ 2–608. Revocation of Acceptance in Whole or in Part

(1) The buyer may revoke his acceptance of a lot or commercial unit whose nonconformity substantially impairs its value to him if he has accepted it

(a) on the reasonable assumption that its nonconformity would be cured and it has not been seasonably cured; or

(b) without discovery of such nonconformity if his acceptance was reasonably induced either by the difficulty of discovery before acceptance or by the seller's assurances.

(2) Revocation of acceptance must occur within a reasonable time after the buyer discovers or should have discovered the ground for it and before any substantial change in condition of the goods which is not caused by their own defects. It is not effective until the buyer notifies the seller of it.

(3) A buyer who so revokes has the same rights and duties with regard to the goods involved as if he had rejected them.

§ 2–609. Right to Adequate Assurance of Performance

(1) A contract for sale imposes an obligation on each party that the other's expectation of receiving due performance will not be impaired. When reasonable grounds for insecurity arise with respect to the performance of either party the other may in writing demand adequate assurance of due performance and until he receives such assurance may if commercially reasonable suspend any performance for which he has not already received the agreed return.

(2) Between merchants the reasonableness of grounds for insecurity and the adequacy of any assurance offered shall be determined according to commercial standards.

(3) Acceptance of any improper delivery or payment does not prejudice the aggrieved party's right to demand adequate assurance of future performance.

(4) After receipt of a justified demand failure to provide within a reasonable time not exceeding 30 days such assurance of due performance as is adequate under the circumstances of the particular case is a repudiation of the contract.

§ 2–610. Anticipatory Repudiation

When either party repudiates the contract with respect to a performance not yet due the loss of which will substantially impair the value of the contract to the other, the aggrieved party may

(a) for a commercially reasonable time await performance by the repudiating party; or

(b) resort to any remedy for breach (Section 2–703 or Section 2–711), even though he has notified the repudiating party that he would await the latter's performance and has urged retraction; and

(c) in either case suspend his own performance or proceed in accordance with the provisions of this Article on the seller's right to identify goods to the contract notwithstanding breach or to salvage unfinished goods (Section 2–704).

§ 2–611. Retraction of Anticipatory Repudiation

(1) Until the repudiating party's next performance is due he can retract his repudiation unless the aggrieved party has since the repudiation cancelled or materially changed his position or otherwise indicated that he considers the repudiation final.

(2) Retraction may be by any method which clearly indicates to the aggrieved party that the repudiating party intends to perform, but must include any assurance justifiably demanded under the provisions of this Article (Section 2–609).

(3) Retraction reinstates the repudiating party's rights under the contract with due excuse and allowance to the aggrieved party for any delay occasioned by the repudiation.

§ 2–612. "Installment Contract"; Breach

(1) An "installment contract" is one which requires or authorizes the delivery of goods in separate lots to be separately accepted, even though the contract contains a clause "each delivery is a separate contract" or its equivalent.

(2) The buyer may reject any installment which is nonconforming if the nonconformity substantially impairs the value of that installment and cannot be cured or if the nonconformity is a defect in the required documents; but if the nonconformity does not fall within subsection (3) and the seller gives adequate assurance of its cure the buyer must accept that installment.

(3) Whenever nonconformity or default with respect to one or more installments substantially impairs the value of the whole contract there is a breach of the whole. But the aggrieved party reinstates the contract if he accepts a nonconforming installment without seasonably notifying of cancellation or if he brings an action with respect only to past installments or demands performance as to future installments.

§ 2–613. Casualty to Identified Goods

Where the contract requires for its performance goods identified when the contract is made, and the goods suffer casualty without fault of either party before the risk of loss passes to the buyer, or in a proper case under a "no arrival, no sale" term (Section 2–324) then

(a) if the loss is total the contract is avoided; and

(b) if the loss is partial or the goods have so deteriorated as no longer to conform to the contract the buyer may nevertheless demand inspection and at his option either treat the contract as voided or accept the goods with due allowance from the contract price for the deterioration or the deficiency in quantity but without further right against the seller.

§ 2–614. Substituted Performance

(1) Where without fault of either party the agreed berthing, loading, or unloading facilities fail or an agreed type of carrier becomes unavailable or the agreed manner of delivery otherwise becomes commercially impracticable but a commercially reasonable substitute is available, such substitute performance must be tendered and accepted.

(2) If the agreed means or manner of payment fails because of domestic or foreign governmental regulation, the seller may withhold or stop delivery unless the buyer provides a means or manner of payment which is commercially a substantial equivalent. If delivery has already been taken, payment by the means or in the manner provided by the regulation discharges the buyer's obligation unless the regulation is discriminatory, oppressive, or predatory.

§ 2–615. Excuse by Failure of Presupposed Conditions

Except so far as a seller may have assumed a greater obligation and subject to the preceding section on substituted performance,

(a) delay in delivery or nondelivery in whole or in part by a seller who complies with paragraphs (b) and (c) is not a breach of his duty under a contract for sale if performance as agreed has been made impracticable by the occurrence of a contingency the nonoccurrence of which was a basic assumption on which the contract was made or by compliance in good faith with any applicable foreign or domestic governmental regulation or order whether or not it later proves to be invalid.

(b) where the causes mentioned in paragraph (a) affect only a part of the seller's capacity to perform, he must allocate production and deliveries among his customers but may at his option include regular customers not then under contract as well as his own requirements for further manufacture. He may so allocate in any manner which is fair and reasonable.

(c) the seller must notify the buyer seasonably that there will be delay or nondelivery and, when allocation is required under paragraph (b), of the estimated quota thus made available for the buyer.

§ 2–616. Procedure on Notice Claiming Excuse

(1) Where the buyer receives notification of a material or indefinite delay or an allocation justified under the preceding section he may by written notification to the seller as to any delivery concerned, and where the prospective deficiency substantially impairs the value of the whole contract under the provisions of this Article relating to breach of installment contracts (Section 2–612), then also as to the whole,

(a) terminate and thereby discharge any unexecuted portion of the contract; or

(b) modify the contract by agreeing to take his available quota in substitution.

(2) If after receipt of such notification from the seller the buyer fails so to modify the contract within a reasonable time not exceeding 30 days the contract lapses with respect to any deliveries affected.

(3) The provisions of this section may not be negated by agreement except in so far as the seller has assumed a greater obligation under the preceding section.

Part 7. Remedies

§ 2–701. Remedies for Breach of Collateral Contracts Not Impaired

Remedies for breach of any obligation or promise collateral or ancillary to a contract for sale or not impaired by the provisions of this Article.

§ 2–702. Seller's Remedies on Discovery of Buyer's Insolvency

(1) Where the seller discovers the buyer to be insolvent he may refuse delivery except for cash including payment for all goods therefore delivered under the contract, and stop delivery under this Article (Section 2–705).

(2) Where the seller discovers that the buyer has received goods on credit while insolvent he may reclaim the goods upon demand made within 10 days after the receipt, but if misrepresentation of solvency has been made to the particular seller in writing within three months before delivery the 10-day limitation does not apply. Except as provided in this subsection the seller may not base a right to reclaim goods on the buyer's fraudulent or innocent misrepresentation of solvency or of intent to pay.

(3) The seller's right to reclaim under subsection (2) is subject to the rights of a buyer in ordinary course or other good-faith purchaser under this Article (Section 2–403). Successful reclamation of goods excludes all other remedies with respect to them.

§ 2–703. Seller's Remedies in General

Where the buyer wrongfully rejects or revokes acceptance of goods or fails to make a payment due on or before delivery or repudiates with respect to a part or the whole, then with respect to any goods directly affected and, if the breach is of the whole contract (Section 2–612), then also with respect to the whole undelivered balance, the aggrieved seller may

    (a) withhold delivery of such goods;

    (b) stop delivery by any bailee as hereafter provided (Section 2–705);

    (c) proceed under the next section respecting goods still unidentified to the contract;

    (d) resell and recover damages as hereafter provided (Section 2–706);

    (e) recover damages for nonacceptance (Section 2–708) or in a proper case the price (Section 2–709);

    (f) cancel.

§ 2–704. Seller's Right to Identify Goods to the Contract Notwithstanding Breach or to Salvage Unfinished Goods

    (1) An aggrieved seller under the preceding section may

        (a) identify to the contract conforming goods not already identified if at the time he learned of the breach they are in his possession or control;

        (b) treat as the subject of resale goods which have demonstrably been intended for the particular contract even though those goods are unfinished.

    (2) Where the goods are unfinished an aggrieved seller may in the exercise of reasonable commercial judgment for the purposes of avoiding loss and of effective realization either complete the manufacture and wholly identify the goods to the contract or cease manufacture and resell for scrap or salvage value or proceed in any other reasonable manner.

§ 2–705. Seller's Stoppage of Delivery in Transit or Otherwise

    (1) The seller may stop delivery of goods in the possession of a carrier or other bailee when he discovers the buyer to be insolvent (Section 2–702) and may stop delivery of carload, truckload, planeload, or larger shipments of express or freight when the buyer repudiates or fails to make a payment due before delivery or if for any other reason the seller has a right to withhold or reclaim the goods.

    (2) As against such buyer the seller may stop delivery until

        (a) receipt of the goods by the buyer; or

        (b) acknowledgment to the buyer by any bailee of the goods except a carrier that the bailee holds the goods for the buyer; or

        (c) such acknowledgment to the buyer by a carrier by reshipment or as warehouseman; or

        (d) negotiation to the buyer of any negotiable document of title covering the goods.

(3) (a) To stop delivery the seller must so notify as to enable the bailee by reasonable diligence to prevent delivery of the goods.

   (b) After such notification the bailee must hold and deliver the goods according to the directions of the seller, but the seller is liable to the bailee for any ensuing charges or damages.

   (c) If a negotiable document of title has been issued for goods, the bailee is not obliged to obey a notification to stop until surrender of the document.

   (d) A carrier who has issued a nonnegotiable bill of lading is not obliged to obey a notification to stop received from a person other than the consignor.

§ 2–706. Seller's Resale Including Contract for Resale

(1) Under the conditions stated in Section 2–703 on seller's remedies, the seller may resell the goods concerned or the undelivered balance thereof. Where the resale is made in good faith and in a commercially reasonable manner the seller may recover the difference between the resale price and the contract price together with any incidental damages allowed under the provisions of this Article (Section 2–710), but less expenses saved in consequence of the buyer's breach.

(2) Except as otherwise provided in subsection (3) or unless otherwise agreed resale may be at public or private sale including sale by way of one or more contracts to sell or of identification to an existing contract of the seller. Sale may be as a unit or in parcels and at any time and place and on any terms but every aspect of the sale including the method, manner, time, place, and terms must be commercially reasonable. The resale must be reasonably identified as referring to the broken contract, but it is not necessary that the goods be in existence or that any or all of them have been identified to the contract before the breach.

(3) Where the resale is at private sale the seller must give the buyer reasonable notification of his intention to resell.

(4) Where the resale is at public sale

   (a) only identified goods can be sold except where there is a recognized market for a public sale of futures in goods of the kind; and

   (b) it must be made at a usual place or market for public sale if one is reasonably available and except in the case of goods which are perishable or threaten to decline in value speedily the seller must give the buyer reasonable notice of the time and place of the resale; and

   (c) if the goods are not to be within the view of those attending the sale the notification of sale must state the place where the goods are located and provide for their reasonable inspection by prospective bidders; and

   (d) the seller may buy.

(5) A purchaser who buys in good faith at a resale takes the goods free of any rights of the original buyer even though the seller fails to comply with one or more of the requirements of this section.

(6) The seller is not accountable to the buyer for any profit made on any resale. A person in the position of a seller (Section 2–707) or a buyer who has rightfully rejected or justifiably revoked acceptance must account for any excess over the amount of his security interest, as hereinafter defined (subsection (3) of Section 2–711).

§ 2–707. "Person in the Position of a Seller"

(1) A "person in the position of a seller" includes as against a principal an agent who has paid or become responsible for the price of goods on behalf of his principal or anyone who otherwise holds a security interest or other right in goods similar to that of a seller.

(2) A person in the position of a seller may as provided in this Article withhold or stop delivery (Section 2–705) and resell (Section 2–706) and recover incidental damages (Section 2–710).

§ 2–708. Seller's Damages for Nonacceptance or Repudiation

(1) Subject to subsection (2) and to the provisions of this Article with respect to proof of market price (Section 2–723), the measure of damages for nonacceptance or repudiation by the buyer is the difference between the market price at the time and place for tender and the unpaid contract price together with any incidental damages provided in this Article (Section 2–710), but less expenses saved in consequence of the buyer's breach.

(2) if the measure of damages provided in subsection (1) is inadequate to put the seller in as good a position as performance would have done then the measure of damages is the profit (including reasonable overhead) which the seller would have made from full performance by the buyer, together with any incidental damages provided in this Article (Section 2–710), due allowance for costs reasonably incurred and due credit for payments or proceeds of resale.

§ 2–709. Action for the Price

(1) When the buyer fails to pay the price as it becomes due the seller may recover, together with any incidental damages under the next section, the price

    (a) of goods accepted or of conforming goods lost or damaged within a commercially reasonable time after risk of their loss has passed to the buyer; and

    (b) of goods identified to the contract if the seller is unable after reasonable effort to resell them at a reasonable price or the circumstances reasonably indicate that such effort will be unavailing.

(2) Where the seller sues for the price he must hold for the buyer any goods which have been identified to the contract and are still in his control except that if resale becomes possible he may resell them at any time prior to the collection of the judgment. The net proceeds of any such resale must be credited to the buyer, and payment of the judgment entitles him to any goods not resold.

(3) After the buyer has wrongfully rejected or revoked acceptance of the goods or has failed to make a payment due or has repudiated (Section 2–610), a seller who is held not entitled to the price under this section shall nevertheless be awarded damages for nonacceptance under the preceeding section.

§ 2–710. Seller's Incidental Damages

Incidental damages to an aggrieved seller include any commercially reasonable charges, expenses, or commissions incurred in stopping delivery, in the transportation, care, and custody of goods after the buyer's breach in connection with return or resale of the goods, or otherwise resulting from the breach.

§ 2–711. Buyer's Remedies in General; Buyer's Security Interest in Rejected Goods

(1) Where the seller fails to make delivery or repudiates or the buyer rightfully rejects or justifiably revokes acceptance then with respect to any goods involved, and with respect to the whole if the breach goes to the whole contract (Section 2–612), the buyer may cancel and whether or not he has done so may in addition to recovering so much of the price as has been paid

> (a) "cover" and have damages under the next section as to all the goods affected whether or not they have been identified to the contract; or
>
> (b) recover damages for nondelivery as provided in this Article (Section 2–713).

(2) Where the seller fails to deliver or repudiates the buyer may also

> (a) if the goods have been identified recover them as provided in this Article (Section 2–502); or
>
> (b) in a proper case obtain specific performance or replevy the goods as provided in this Article (Section 2–716).

(3) On rightful rejection of justifiable revocation of acceptance a buyer has a security interest in goods in his possession or control for any payments made on their price and any expenses reasonably incurred in their inspection, receipt, transportation, care, and custody and may hold such goods and resell them in like manner as an aggrieved seller (Section 2–706).

§ 2–712. "Cover"; Buyer's Procurement of Substitute Goods

(1) After a breach within the preceding section the buyer may "cover" by making in good faith and without unreasonable delay any reasonable purchase of or contract to purchase goods in substitution for those due from the seller.

(2) The buyer may recover from the seller as damages the difference between the cost of cover and the contract price together with any incidental or consequential damages as hereinafter defined (Section 2–715), but less expenses saved in consequence of the seller's breach.

(3) Failure of the buyer to effect cover within this section does not bar him from any other remedy.

§ 2–713. Buyer's Damages for Nondelivery or Repudiation

(1) Subject to the provisions of this Article with respect to proof of market price (Section 2–723), the measure of damages for nondelivery or repudiation by the seller is the difference between the market price at the time when the buyer learned of the breach and the contract price together with any incidental and consequential damages provided in this Article (Section 2–715), but less expenses saved in consequence of the seller's breach.

(2) Market price is to be determined as of the place for tender or, in cases of rejection after arrival or revocation of acceptance, as of the place of arrival.

§ 2–714. Buyer's Damages for Breach in Regard to Accepted Goods

(1) Where the buyer has accepted goods and given notification (subsection (3) of Section 2–607) he may recover as damages for any nonconformity of tender the loss resulting

in the ordinary course of events from the seller's breach as determined in any manner which is reasonable.

(2) The measure of damages for breach of warranty is the difference at the time and place of acceptance between the value of the goods accepted and the value they would have had if they had been as warranted, unless special circumstances show proximate damages of a different amount.

(3) In a proper case any incidental and consequential damages under the next section may also be recovered.

§ 2–715. Buyer's Incidental and Consequential Damages

(1) Incidental damages resulting from the seller's breach include expenses reasonably incurred in inspection, receipt, transportation, and care and custody of goods rightfully rejected, any commercially reasonable charges, expenses, or commissions in connection with effecting cover, and any other reasonable expense incident to the delay or other breach.

(2) Consequential damages resulting from the seller's breach include

(a) any loss resulting from general or particular requirements and needs of which the seller at the time of contracting had reason to know and which could not reasonably be prevented by cover or otherwise; and

(b) injury to person or property proximately resulting from any breach of warranty.

§ 2–716. Buyer's Right to Specific Performance or Replevin

(1) Specific performance may be decreed where the goods are unique or in other proper circumstances.

(2) The decree for specific performance may include such terms and conditions as to payment of the price, damages, or other relief as the court may deem just.

(3) The buyer has a right of replevin for goods identified to the contract if after reasonable effort he is unable to effect cover for such goods or the circumstances reasonably indicate that such effort will be unvailing or if the goods have been shipped under reservation and satisfaction of the security interest in them has been made or tendered. In the case of goods bought for personal, family, or household purposes, the buyer's right of replevin vests upon acquisition of a special property, even if the seller had not then repudiated or failed to deliver.

§ 2–717. Deduction of Damages from the Price

The buyer on notifying the seller of his intention to do so may deduct all or any part of the damages resulting from any breach of the contract from any part of the price still due under the same contract.

§ 2–718. Liquidation or Limitation of Damages; Deposits

(1) Damages for breach by either party may be liquidated in the agreement but only at an amount which is reasonable in the light of the anticipated or actual harm caused by the breach, the difficulties of proof of loss, and the inconvenience of nonfeasibility of otherwise obtaining an adequate remedy. A team fixing unreasonably large liquidated damages is void as a penalty.

(2) Where the seller justifiably withholds delivery of goods because of the buyer's breach, the buyer is entitled to restitution of any amount by which the sum of his payments exceeds

(a) the amount to which the seller is entitled by virtue of terms liquidating the seller's damages in accordance with subsection (1), or

(b) in the absence of such terms, 20 percent of the value of the total performance for which the buyer is obligated under the contract or $500, whichever is smaller.

(3) The buyer's right to restitution under subsection (2) is subject to offset to the extent that the seller establishes

(a) a right to recover damages under the provisions of this Article other than subsection (1), and

(b) the amount or value of any benefits received by the buyer directly or indirectly by reason of the contract.

(4) Where a seller has received payment in goods their reasonable value or the proceeds of their resale shall be treated as payments for the purposes of subsection (2); but if the seller has notice of the buyer's breach before reselling goods received in part performance, his resale is subject to the conditions laid down in this Article on resale by an aggrieved seller (Section 2–706).

§ 2–719. *Contractual Modification or Limitation of Remedy*

(1) Subject to the provisions of subsections (2) and (3) of this section and of the preceding section on liquidation and limitation of damages,

(a) the agreement may provide for remedies in addition to or in substitution for those provided in this Article and may limit or alter the measure of damages recoverable under this Article, as by limiting the buyer's remedies to return of the goods and repayment of the price or to repair and replacement of nonconforming goods or parts; and

(b) resort to a remedy as provided is optional unless the remedy is expressly agreed to be exclusive, in which case it is the sole remedy.

(2) Where circumstances cause an exclusive or limited remedy to fail of its essential purpose, remedy may be had as provided in this Act.

(3) Consequential damages may be limited or excluded unless the limitation or exclusion is unconscionable. Limitation of consequential damages for injury to the person in the case of consumer goods is prima facie unconscionable but limitation of damages where the loss is commercial is not.

§ 2–720. *Effect of "Cancellation" or "Rescission" on Claims for Antecedent Breach*

Unless the contrary intention clearly appears, expressions of "cancellation" or "rescission" of the contract or the like shall not be construed as renunciation or discharge of any claim in damages for an antecedent breach.

§ 2–721. *Remedies for Fraud*

Remedies for material misrepresentation or fraud include all remedies available under this Article for non-fraudulent breach. Neither rescission or a claim for rescission of the contract for sale nor rejection or return of the goods shall bar or be deemed inconsistent with a claim for damages or other remedy.

§ 2–722. Who Can Sue Third Parties for Injury to Goods

Where a third party so deals with goods which have been identified to a contract for sale as to cause actionable injury to a party to that contract

(a) a right of action against the third party is in either party to the contract for sale who has title to or a security interest or a special property or an insurable interest in the goods; and if the goods have been destroyed or converted a right of action is also in the party who either bore the risk of loss under the contract for sale or has since the injury assumed that risk as against the other;

(b) if at the time of the injury the party plaintiff did not bear the risk of loss as against the other party to the contract for sale and there is no arrangement between them for disposition of the recovery, his suit or settlement is, subject to his own interest, as a fiduciary for the other party to the contract;

(c) either party may with the consent of the other sue for the benefit of whom it may concern.

§ 2–723. Proof of Market Price: Time and Place

(1) If an action based on anticipatory repudiation comes to trial before the time for performance with respect to some or all of the goods, any damages based on market price (Section 2–708 or Section 2–713) shall be determined according to the price of such goods prevailing at the time when the aggrieved party learned of the repudiation.

(2) If evidence of a price prevailing at the times or places described in this Article is not readily available the price prevailing within any reasonable time before or after the time described or at any other place which in commercial judgment or under usage of trade would serve as a reasonable substitute for the one described may be used, making any proper allowance for the cost of transporting the goods to or from such other place.

(3) Evidence of a relevant price prevailing at a time or place other than the one described in this Article offered by one party is not admissible unless and until he has given the other party such notice as the court finds sufficient to prevent unfair surprise.

§ 2–724. Admissibility of Market Quotations

Whenever the prevailing price or value of any goods regularly bought and sold in any established commodity market is in issue, reports in official publications or trade journals or in newspapers or periodicals of general circulation published as the reports of such market shall be admissible in evidence. The circumstances of the preparation of such a report may be shown to affect its weight but not its admissibility.

§ 2–725. Statute of Limitations in Contracts for Sale

(1) An action for breach of any contract for sale must be commenced within four years after the cause of action has accrued. By the original agreement the parties may reduce the period of limitation to not less than one year but may not extend it.

(2) A cause of action accrues when the breach occurs, regardless of the aggrieved party's lack of knowledge of the breach. A breach of warranty occurs when tender of

delivery is made, except that where a warranty explicitly extends to future performance of the goods and discovery of the breach must await the time of such performance the cause of action accrues when the breach is or should have been discovered.

(3) Where an action commenced within the time limited by subsection (1) is so terminated as to leave available a remedy by another action for the same breach such other action may be commenced after the expiration of the time limited and within six months after the termination of the first action unless the termination resulted from voluntary discontinuance or from dismissal for failure or neglect to prosecute.

(4) This section does not alter the law on tolling of the statute of limitations nor does it apply to causes of action which have accrued before this Act becomes effective.

A

absolute privilege   In libel and slander law, situations where a defendant is entirely excused from liability for defamatory statements because of the circumstances under which the statements were made.

acceptance   The actual or implied receipt and retention of that which is tendered or offered.

accord and satisfaction   A legally binding agreement to settle a disputed claim for a definite amount.

accredited investors   Financially sophisticated and/or wealthy individuals and institutions who understand and can withstand the risk associated with securities investments.

act of state doctrine   The view that a judge in the United States or another country does not have the authority to challenge the legality of acts by a foreign government within that foreign government's own borders.

actus reus   Wrongful act or omission.

ad substantiation   Under Federal Trade Commission policy, product claims for which reasonable evidentiary support does not exist. Constitute unfair and deceptive trade practices.

ad valorem   According to value. Hence an ad valorem tax would be based on the value of the item in question rather than, for example, a fixed rate for all such items.

adjudication   The formal pronouncement of a judgment in a legal proceeding.

adjustment of debts   Individuals with limited debts are protected from creditors while paying their debts in installments (Chapter 13 bankruptcy).

administrative agency   An agency of the government charged with administering particular legislation.

administrative law   That branch of public law addressing the operation of the government's various agencies and commissions. Also the rules and regulations established by those agencies and commissions.

administrative law judge   An officer who presides at the initial hearing on matters litigated before an administrative agency. He or she is independent of the agency staff.

Administrative Procedure Act   A federal statute specifying the procedural rules under which the government's agencies and commissions conduct their business.

adverse impact   An employee may make a prima facie case for adverse impact where the employer's facially neutral rule may result in a different impact on one protected group than on another.

adverse possession   Open and notorious possession of real property over a given length of time that denies ownership in any other claimant.

advisory jurisdiction   Power of the International Court of Justice (ICJ) to hear a dispute and to render an advisory opinion on the matter. The opinion is not binding on any party.

affidavit   A written statement sworn to by a person officially empowered to administer an oath.

affirmative action   A government or private-sector program, springing from the civil rights movement, designed to actively promote the employment or educational opportunities of protected classes rather than merely forbidding discrimination.

affirmative defense   A portion of a defendant's answer to a complaint in which defendant presents contentions that, if proved true, will relieve the defendant of liability even if the assertions in the complaint are correct.

agent   A person entrusted by a principal to act on behalf of that principal; one who is authorized to carry out the business of another.

agreement   A meeting of the minds based on an offer by one party and acceptance by another.

alternate dispute resolution   The growing practice of employing strategies other than conventional litigation to solve conflicts. Those strategies include negotiation, arbitration, and mediation with variations such as "mini-trials" and "rent-a-judge" arrangements.

amicus curiae   A "friend of the court" who, though not a party to the case, files a brief because of a strong interest in the litigation.

annual percentage rate (APR)   The rate of interest charged for borrowing money as expressed in a standardized, yearly manner allowing for comparison among lenders' fees.

annual percentage yield (APY) The rate of interest paid on a deposit as expressed in a standardized, yearly manner allowing for comparison of returns among institutions.

answer The defendant's first pleading in a lawsuit, in which the defendant responds to the allegations raised in the plaintiff's complaint.

anticipatory breach A contracting party's indication before the time for performance that he cannot or will not perform the contract. Also referred to as **anticipatory repudiation.**

appeal The judicial process by which a party petitions a higher court to review the decisions of a lower court or agency to correct errors.

appellant The party filing an appeal.

appellee The party against whom an appeal is filed.

appraisal Assessment of the value of property by one with appropriate qualifications for the task.

appropriation Making commercial use of an individual's name or likeness without permission.

arbitrary trademark A trademark that is a new word or a common word that bears no relation to the product to which it is applied.

arbitration An extrajudicial process in which a dispute is submitted to a mutually agreeable third party for a decision.

arraignment A criminal law proceeding in which a defendant is brought before a judge to be informed of the charges and to file a plea.

articles of incorporation Document filed with a state to create a corporation.

assault A show of force that would cause reasonable persons to believe that they are about to receive an intentional, unwanted, harmful physical touching.

assignee A person to whom an assignment is made.

assignment A transfer of property, or some right or interest therein, from one person to another.

assignor The maker of an assignment.

assumption of risk An affirmative defense in a negligence case in which the defendant seeks to bar recovery by the plaintiff by showing that the plaintiff knowingly exposed himself or herself to the danger that resulted in injury.

attachment As to secured transactions, the process by which a security interest in the property of another becomes enforceable.

at-will employee An individual not under contract for a specified term and therefore, under the general rule, subject to discharge by the employer at any time and for any reason.

B

bait-and-switch advertising An unlawful sales tactic in which the seller attracts buyer interest by insincerely advertising a product at a dramatically reduced price while holding no genuine intent to sell the product at that price. The seller then disparages the "bait" and diverts the buyer's attention to a higher-priced product (the switch), which was the sales goal from the first.

barriers to entry Economic or technological conditions in a market making entry by a new competitor very difficult.

battery An intentional, unwanted, harmful physical touching.

beyond a reasonable doubt The level of proof required for conviction in a criminal case.

bilateral contract A contract formed by an offer requiring a reciprocal promise.

blacklists Lists of union organizers or participants in labor activities circulated to companies to dissuade the companies from hiring the listed individuals.

blue laws Laws forbidding certain kinds of business on Sundays.

blue sky laws Statutes regulating the sale of stocks and other securities to prevent consumer fraud.

bona fide In good faith; honestly.

bona fide occupational qualification (BFOQ) A defense in a discrimination claim where the employer argues that a particular religion, sex, or national origin is a necessary qualification for a particular job.

boycott A confederation or conspiracy involving a refusal to do business with another or an attempt by the confederation to stop others from doing business with the target person or organization.

breach of contract Failure, without legal excuse, to perform any promise that forms the whole or part of a contract.

breach of warranty Failure, without legal excuse, to fulfill the terms of the guarantee.

bribe Anything of value given or taken with the corrupt intent to influence an official in the performance of her or his duties.

brief A written document setting out for the court the facts, the law, and the argument of a party to the lawsuit.

burden of proof The party with the burden of proof (normally the plaintiff in a civil suit and the state in a criminal case) is required to prove the truth of a claim or lose on that issue.

business judgment rule A rule protecting business managers from liability for making bad decisions when they have acted prudently and in good faith.

bylaws A document that governs the maintenance and operation of an organization.

C

cap-and-trade incentives A situation in which a government sets a cap on the total emissions of a particular pollutant that is lower than the existing level of emissions.

capacity The ability to incur legal obligations and acquire legal rights.

capitalism Private ownership of the means of production with a largely unrestricted marketplace in goods and services.

cause of action The legal theory on which a lawsuit is based.

cause in fact The actual cause of an event. One of the required elements in a negligence claim.

caveat emptor Let the buyer beware.

cease and desist order An instruction from an agency instructing a party to refrain from a specified goal.

certificate of incorporation An instrument from the state bestowing the right to do business under the corporate form of organization. Also referred to as **charter.**

certiorari A legal procedure affording an appellate court the opportunity to review a lower court decision. Also a writ asking the lower court for the record of the case.

choice of law rule A rule of law in each jurisdiction that determines which jurisdiction's laws will be applied to a case. For instance, one state may have a choice of law rule that says that the law of the jurisdiction where the contract was signed shall govern any dispute, while another state may apply a different rule.

civil law The branch of law dealing with private rights. Contrast with criminal law.

class action A legal action brought by one on behalf of himself or herself and all others similarly situated.

Clean Air Act Amended in 1990, establishes air quality standards and enforcement procedures for the standards.

Clean Water Act Establishes standards for water quality relating to the protection of water life as well as for safe recreation, and the enforcement of those standards.

closed-end loan Credit arrangement where a specified sum is borrowed and a repayment plan usually is established.

closely held corporation A corporation with relatively few shareholders, the stock of which is not publicly traded. Also referred to as a **close corporation.**

closing date The date on which a transfer of property is made.

Code of Federal Regulations A compilation of final federal agency rules.

codetermination German corporate governance and labor law system in which board representation by labor unions is required.

Colgate doctrine Sellers may lawfully engage in resale price maintenance if they do nothing more than specify prices at which their products are to be resold and unilaterally refuse to deal with anyone who does not adhere to those prices.

collateral Property pledged as security for satisfaction of a debt.

comity Courtesy. Nations often recognize the laws of other nations not because they must do so but because of the tradition of comity: that is, goodwill and mutual respect.

Commerce Clause The portion of the U.S. Constitution that provides for federal regulation of foreign and interstate trade.

commercial impracticability The standard used by the Uniform Commercial Code (UCC) to relieve a party of his or her contract obligations because of the occurrence of unforeseeable, external events beyond his or her control.

commercial speech Speech directed toward a business purpose. Advertising is an example of commercial speech. Such speech is protected by the First Amendment, but not to the degree that we protect other varieties of speech.

Commodity Futures Trading Commission (CFTC) Federal regulatory agency responsible for overseeing futures trading.

common law Judge-made law. To be distinguished from statutory law as created by legislative bodies.

common shares Most universal type of corporate stock.

community property Property acquired during marriage through the labor or skill of either spouse.

comp time   Compensatory time. Giving an employee time off from work in place of cash for hours of overtime worked.

comparable worth   The legal theory that all employees should be paid the same wages for work requiring comparable skills, effort, and responsibility and having comparable worth to the employer.

comparative negligence   Defense in a negligence suit in which the plaintiff's recovery is reduced by an amount equivalent to her contribution to her own injury.

compensatory damages   Damages that will compensate a party for actual losses due to an injury suffered.

complaint   The first pleading filed by the plaintiff in a civil lawsuit.

concerted activity   Organizing, forming, joining, or assisting labor organizations, bargaining collectively through representatives of the employees' choosing, or other activities taken for the purpose of collective bargaining or other mutual aid or protection.

concurrent conditions   When each party's obligation to perform under a contract is dependent on the other party's performance.

condemning   To appropriate land for public use.

conditions precedent   Conditions that operate to give rise to a contracting party's duty to perform.

conditions subsequent   Conditions that operate to discharge one from an obligation under a contract.

condominium or cooperative ownership   An interest in property where owners retain individual control and specific ownership over a precise segment of real estate, but own common areas as tenants in common.

confession of judgment clause   A clause stipulating that the lessee grants judgment in any action on the contract to the landlord without the formality of an ordinary proceeding.

conglomerate merger   A merger between firms operating in separate markets and having neither buyer–seller nor competitive relationships with each other.

conscious parallelism   Conduct by competitors that is very similar or identical but that is not the product of a conspiracy and thus is not, in and of itself, illegal.

consent decree   A settlement of a lawsuit arrived at by agreement of the parties. Effectively, an admission by the parties that the decree is a just determination of their rights.

consent order   The order administrative agencies issue when approving the settlement of an administrative action against some party.

consequential damages   Damages that do not flow directly and immediately from an act but rather flow from the results of the act.

consideration   A required element in an enforceable contract. The thing of value passing between the parties that results in a benefit to the one making the promise or a detriment to the one receiving the promise.

conspiracy   An agreement between two or more persons to commit an unlawful act.

constructive eviction   A breach of duty by the landlord that makes the property uninhabitable or otherwise deprives the tenant of the benefit of the lease and gives rise to the tenant's right to vacate the property and to terminate the lease.

consumer goods   Under the Uniform Commercial Code (UCC), goods used or bought primarily for personal, family, or household purposes.

contentious jurisdiction   Power of the International Court of Justice (ICJ) to hear a dispute and to render a binding opinion on the issue and the parties involved. All parties must give prior consent to contentious jurisdiction.

contingent fee   An arrangement wherein an attorney is compensated for his or her services by receiving a percentage of the award in a lawsuit rather than receiving an hourly wage or specified fee.

contingent workers   Workers that do not have an implicit or explicit contract for ongoing employment.

contract   An agreement that is legally enforceable by the courts.

contract of adhesion   One in which all the bargaining power (and all the contract terms) are unfairly on one side. This often occurs when buyers have no choice among sellers of a particular item, and when the seller uses a preprinted form contract.

contract bar rule   The National Labor Relations Board (NLRB) prohibits an election during the term of a collective bargaining agreement, for a maximum of three years.

contract firm workers   Workers employed by a company that provides them or their services under contract or leases. Usually are assigned to only one customer and work at the customer's worksite.

contributory negligence   A defense in a negligence action wherein the defendant attempts to demonstrate that the plaintiff contributed to the harm on which the litigation was based. Contrast with **comparative negligence.**

conversion   Wrongfully exercising control over the personal property of another.

copyright   The creator's (artist, author, or the like) right to control the copying and distribution of his or her work for a period of time specified by statute.

corporate opportunity   A doctrine that prevents corporate officials from personally appropriating an opportunity that belongs to the corporation.

corporation   A form of business organization that is owned by shareholders who have no inherent right to manage the business, and is managed by a board of directors elected by the shareholders.

Council on Environmental Quality   Serves as an adviser to the president in connection with the preparation of the annual Environmental Quality Report.

counterclaim   A cause of action filed by the defendant in a lawsuit against the plaintiff in the same suit.

counteroffer   Response by the offeree that, in its legal effect, constitutes a rejection of the original offer and proposes a new offer to the offeror.

countervailing duties   Duties imposed by a government against the products of another government that has offered subsidies to its own producers.

covered disabilities   A physical or mental impairment that substantially limits one or more major life activities of an individual; a record of such impairment or being regarded as having such impairment.

creditor   A person to whom a debt is owed.

creditor beneficiary   Person who has given consideration, who is an intended beneficiary of a contract though not a party, and thus is entitled to enforce the contract.

crime   A public wrong, an act punishable by the state.

criminal law   Wrongs against society that the state has seen fit to label as crimes and that may result in penalties against the perpetrator(s). Contrast with **civil law.**

cumulative voting   A procedure for voting for directors that permits a shareholder to multiply the number of shares he or she owns by the number of directors to be elected and to cast the resulting total of votes for one or more directors.

curtesy interest   The right of a husband upon the death of his wife to receive all of the wife's real property as long as the two had a child between them.

D

d.b.a.   Doing business as.

de facto   In fact. Actually. As in *de facto* school segregation, which is caused by social and economic conditions rather than by government act.

de jure   Legitimate. Lawful. Of right. As in *de jure* school segregation, which is caused by government order and thus is legally correct even if morally wrong.

debenture   Any long-term debt instrument, such as a bond, issued by a company or institution, secured only by the general assets of the issuer.

deceit   A tort involving intentional misrepresentation to deceive or trick another.

deception   Trade claim that is either false or likely to mislead the reasonable consumer and that is material to the consumer's decision making.

deceptive advertising   Advertising practices likely to mislead the reasonable consumer where the practice in question is material in that it affected consumer choice.

decertification petition   Election petition stating that a current bargaining representative no longer has the support of a majority of the employees in the bargaining unit.

declaration   A document that defines the rights, responsibilities, and powers of property owners in a condominium.

declaratory judgment or order   A judicial or agency action expressing an opinion or articulating the rights of the parties without actually requiring that anything be done.

deed   An instrument transferring title to property.

deed of trust   A three-party instrument used to create a security interest in real property in which the legal title to the real property is placed in one or more trustees to secure the repayment of a sum of money or the performance of other conditions.

defamation   A false and intentional verbal or written expression that damages the reputation of another.

default   A party fails to pay money when due or when lawfully demanded.

default judgment   A judgment entered by the court in favor of the plaintiff because the defendant failed to respond to the plaintiff's complaint.

defeasible fee simple   A title to property that is open to attack, that might be defeated by the performance of some act, or that is subject to conditions.

defendant   The party in a civil suit against whom the cause of action was brought and, in a criminal case, the party against whom charges have been filed.

delegatee   The one to whom a duty is delegated.

delegator   The one who delegates a duty.

deontological ethics   The rightness of an action depends on its conformance with duty, obligation, and moral requirements regardless of outcome.

deposition A discovery procedure wherein a witness's sworn testimony is taken out of court, prior to trial, for subsequent use at trial.

deregulation Returning authority to the free market by shrinking government bureaucracies and reducing government rules.

derivative suit A lawsuit by a stockholder on behalf of the corporation where the corporation declines to act to protect the organization's rights against the conduct of an officer, director, or outsider.

derivatives Specialized trading contracts tied to underlying assets such as bonds or currencies.

descriptive mark A trademark that is merely descriptive of the product or its qualities.

dicta Statements in a judicial opinion that are merely the views of the judge(s) and are not necessary for the resolution of the case.

directed verdict A party to a lawsuit makes a motion asking the judge to instruct the jury to reach a particular decision because reasonable minds could not differ about the correct outcome of the case.

discharged Released from liability.

disclaimer As to warranties, a contract term wherein a party attempts to relieve itself of potential liability under that contract.

discovery Legal procedures by which one party to a litigation may obtain information from the other party. Depositions and interrogatories are examples of discovery procedures.

disparate impact Employment discrimination theory in which a facially neutral employment practice (such as requiring a high school diploma for new hires) results in an unfair and adverse impact on a protected class.

disparate treatment Theory of employment discrimination wherein an individual or group is intentionally disfavored via actual discriminatory policies and practices.

dissolution In partnership law, the change in the relation of the partners caused by any partner ceasing to be associated with the carrying on of the business.

diversity of citizenship One standard by which federal courts may gain jurisdiction over a lawsuit. Plaintiffs and defendants must be from different states and more than $75,000 must be at issue.

divestiture In antitrust law, a remedy wherein the court orders a defendant to dispose of specified assets.

dividend A shareholder's earnings from his or her stock in a corporation.

doctrine of sovereign immunity Principle that a foreign nation may not be sued in American courts, with certain exceptions.

dominant estate The property accessed through an easement appurtenant or implied easement.

donee beneficiary Person who has not given consideration, but is an intended beneficiary of a contract, though not a party, and is entitled to enforce the contract.

double jeopardy The U.S. Constitution provides that the same individual may not be tried twice in the same tribunal for the same criminal offense.

dower interest The right of a wife upon the death of her husband to receive a life estate in one-third of her husband's real property.

dramshop law State laws imposing liability on the seller of intoxicating liquors when a third party is injured as a result of the intoxication of the buyer where the sale has caused or contributed to that intoxication.

due care and diligence Corporate officers and directors must act in good faith and in a prudent manner.

due diligence A defense against a securities violation claim where the defendant used ordinary prudence and still failed to find an error or omission in the registration statement.

due process A constitutional principle requiring fairness in judicial proceedings and that government laws and conduct be free of arbitrariness and capriciousness.

dumping The commercial practice of selling goods in a foreign market at a price substantially beneath that charged in the domestic market.

duress Overpowering of the will of a person by force or fear.

duty of due care Standard of conduct expected of a reasonable, prudent person under the circumstances.

E

easement The right to use property without taking anything away from the property.

easement or profit appurtenant The right of an owner of adjacent land to enter or to enter and take away from property next to it.

economies of scale Expansion of a firm or industry's productive capacity resulting in a decline in long-run average costs of production.

efficiencies   A defense to an otherwise unlawful merger in which costs of production are reduced because of the merger.

election year or certification year bar   The National Labor Relations Board (NLRB) prohibits an election for 12 months following a prior election.

elective share   Legislative mandate that a spouse receive a specific percentage interest in a deceased spouse's estate.

embargo   Government order prohibiting importation of some or all products from a particular country.

embezzlement   The fraudulent and unauthorized taking of the money of another while charged with the care of that money.

Emergency Planning and Community Right-to-Know Act of 1986   Amended Superfund requiring companies to inform the government upon release of any hazardous chemicals into the environment and to provide to the government an inventory of their hazardous chemicals. The act also requires states to establish emergency procedures for chemical discharges.

eminent domain   The state's power to take private property for public use.

employer identification number   Number issued to employer by federal and state governments for the purpose of record keeping associated with income and Social Security tax collections.

en banc   All of the judges hearing a case as a group rather than individually or in panels.

enabling legislation   Law that establishes an administrative agency and grants power to that agency.

enjoin   To require. A court issues an injunction requiring a certain act or ordering a party to refrain from a certain act.

enterprise law   Legal doctrine treating all companies in a corporate group as one giant organization rather than a collection of smaller, independent units.

entity law   Legal doctrine treating each company in a corporate group as a separate, independent unit.

environmental impact statement   Statement of the anticipated impact on the environment of legislation or other major federal action, and suggestions for reasonable alternatives.

Environmental Protection Agency   Created in 1970 to gather information relating to pollution and to assist in pollution control efforts and sanctions.

equal protection   The Fourteenth Amendment to the U.S. Constitution provides that all similarly situated individuals are entitled to the same advantages and must bear the same burdens under the law.

equitable remedies   Injunction, specific performance, restraining orders, and the like, as opposed to money damages.

equity   Fairness; a system of courts that developed in England. A chancellor presided to mete out fairness in cases that were not traditionally assigned to the law courts headed by the king.

essential functions of a position   Those tasks that are fundamental, as opposed to marginal or unnecessary, to the fulfillment of the position's objectives.

Establishment Clause   The First Amendment to the U.S. Constitution forbids the U.S. government from creating a government-supported church or religion.

estate   An interest in land or property owned by a decedent at the time of her or his death.

estate *pur autre vie*   A life estate that is measured by the life of someone other than the possessor.

estoppel   A legal doctrine providing that one may not assert facts that are in conflict with one's own previous acts or deeds.

eviction   Depriving a tenant of the possession of leased premises.

excise taxes   Taxes imposed at both the state and federal levels on the sale of particular commodities, especially alcohol, tobacco, and gasoline.

exclusive dealing   Agreement to deal only with a particular buyer or a particular seller.

exculpatory clause   Portion of a contract that seeks to relieve one of the parties to the contract from any liability for breach of duty under that contract.

executed   In contract law, full performance of the terms of the bargain.

executed contract   Performances are complete.

executory contract   Not yet fully performed or completed.

exemplary damages   Same as **punitive damages.**

exempt property   Specified classes of property that are unavailable to the creditor upon default of the debtor.

exempt security   Certain kinds of securities and certain transactions involving securities are not required to meet federal registration requirements under the 1933 Securities Act.

existentialism A philosophy emphasizing the individual's responsibility to make herself what she is to become. Existence precedes essence.

express authority Corporate officers' powers as expressed in the bylaws or conferred by the board of directors.

express authorization In contract law, offeror specifies a means of communication by which the offeree can accept.

express conditions Conditions within contracts that are clear from the language.

express contract Contract whose terms are clear from the language.

express warranty A guarantee made by affirmation of fact or promise, by description of the goods, or by sample or model.

expropriation A government's taking of a business's assets, such as a manufacturing facility, usually without just compensation.

extraterritoriality The application of U.S. laws on persons, rights, or relations beyond the geographic limits of this country and even though the parties involved are not American citizens.

F

failing company doctrine A defense to an otherwise unlawful merger in which the acquired firm is going out of business and no other purchaser is available.

fair use A doctrine that permits the use of copyrighted works for purposes such as criticism, news reporting, training, or research.

false imprisonment Tort of intentionally restricting the freedom of movement of another.

false light Falsely and publicly attributing certain characteristics, conduct, or beliefs to another such that a reasonable person would be highly offended.

featherbedding A labor law term describing the practice where workers were paid even though they did not perform any work. Featherbedding is a violation of federal labor law.

federal question Litigation involving the federal constitution, statutes, and treaties. The federal courts have jurisdiction over cases involving federal questions.

Federal Register Daily publication of federal agency regulations and other legal materials coming from the executive branch of government.

federal sentencing guidelines Standards established by the U.S. Sentencing Commission that rank the seriousness of individual and organizational federal crimes and provide sentences that, with little flexibility, must be applied to those crimes.

Federal Trade Commission Agency of the federal government responsible for promoting fair trade practices in interstate commerce.

federalism The division of authority between the federal government and the states to maintain workable cooperation while diffusing political power.

fee simple A form of land ownership that gives the owner the right to possess and to use the land for an unlimited period of time, subject only to governmental or private restrictions, and unconditional power to dispose of the property during his or her lifetime or upon death.

felony A crime of a serious nature ordinarily involving punishment by death or imprisonment in a penitentiary.

fiduciary One who holds a relationship of trust with another and has an obligation to act in the best interests of the other—for example, one who manages property on behalf of another.

fiduciary duty The responsibility of one in a position of trust with another to act in the best interests of the other.

financing statement Document notifying others that the creditor claims an interest in the debtor's collateral. Must be filed as provided for by law to perfect a security interest.

firm offer Under the Uniform Commercial Code (UCC), a signed, written offer by a merchant containing assurances that it will be held open, and which is not revocable for the time stated in the offer, or for a reasonable time if no such time is stated.

fixture A thing that was originally personal property and that has actually or constructively affixed to the soil itself or to some structure legally a part of the land.

foreclose To terminate the mortgagor's rights in the property covered by the mortgage.

forum non conveniens A legal principle under which a court may refuse to hear a case where it determines that another jurisdiction would provide a more appropriate location for the trial.

franchise A marketing arrangement in which the franchisor permits the franchisee to produce, distribute, or sell the franchisor's product using the franchisor's name or trademark.

franchisee   A holder of a franchise.

franchisor   A party granting a franchise.

fraud   An intentional misrepresentation of a material fact with intent to deceive where the misrepresentation is justifiably relied on by another and damages result.

fraud-on-the-market theory   Misleading statements distort the market and thus defraud a securities buyer whether the buyer actually relies on the misstatement or not. Based on the assumption that the price of a stock reflects all of the available information about that stock.

Free Exercise Clause   First Amendment provision guaranteeing all Americans the right to pursue their religious beliefs free of government intervention (with limited exceptions).

free riders   Those who lawfully benefit from goods or services without paying a share of the cost of those goods or services.

Full Faith and Credit Clause   Provision of the U.S. Constitution requiring each state to recognize the laws and judicial decisions of all other states.

futures   Contracts to deliver or take delivery of specified quantities of commodities at a previously specified price.

G

G8   An association embracing eight of the world's leading industrial powers (Canada, France, Italy, Germany, Japan, Russia, the United Kingdom, and the United States) designed to improve worldwide economic and political conditions.

garnishment   Action by a creditor to secure the property of a debtor where that property is held by a third party.

General Agreement on Tariffs and Trade (GATT)   A World Trade Organization foundational document that establishes and regulates import duties among signatory countries.

General Agreement on Trade in Services (GATS)   A World Trade Organization foundational document that sets forth principles for reducing barriers to international trade in services.

general duty   An OSHA provision requiring that employers furnish to each employee a place of employment free from recognized hazards that cause or are likely to cause death or serious physical harm to the employee.

general warranty deed   A deed that carries with it certain warranties or guarantees.

generic mark   A trademark employing a common descriptive name for a product.

genuineness of assent   In contract law, the parties knowingly agreed to the same thing.

going private   Used to describe a transaction in which private investors buy all of the equity securities of a public corporation, such that the corporation ceases to be a public corporation.

going public   A reference to the first time a company sells its shares on the open market.

good faith   Honesty; an absence of intent to take advantage of another.

goods   All things that are movable at the time of identification to the contract for sale except the money in which the price is to be paid, investment securities, and so forth.

grand jury   A body of people convened by the state to determine whether the evidence is sufficient to bring a criminal indictment (formal accusation) against a party.

grant deed   A deed that does not have the warranties contained in a warranty deed.

gray market   Transactions conducted outside the usual supplier-approved channels of distribution. These transactions (unlike *black market* sales) are lawful but are often discouraged by suppliers. The gray market operates parallel to the "officially" authorized chain of distribution.

grease   Payments to low-ranking authorities for the purpose of facilitating business in another nation. Not forbidden by the Foreign Corrupt Practices Act if legal in the host nation.

greenhouse gas (GHG)   Any gas that when released in the atmosphere acts like the ceiling of a greenhouse to trap solar energy, thereby contributing to global climate change. The most common greenhouse gas is carbon dioxide. Other greenhouse gases include methane, nitrous oxide, hydrofluorocarbons, perfluorocarbons, and sulfur hexafluoride.

greenmail   Takeover defense involving the target corporation's repurchase of a takeover raider's stock at a premium not offered to other shareholders.

group boycott   An agreement among traders to refuse to deal with one or more other traders.

guarantor   A person who promises to perform the same obligation as the principal if the principal should default.

H

Herfindahl–Hirschman Index (HHI)   Calculation used by the Justice Department to determine the degree of economic concentration in a particular market and to determine the degree to which a proposed horizontal merger would further concentrate that market. Computed by squaring the market share of each firm in a market and summing those totals.

holdover lease   The tenancy that exists where a tenant subject to a term lease is allowed to remain on the premises after the term has expired.

horizontal divisions of the market   Competitors agree to share their market geographically or to allocate customers or products among themselves.

horizontal merger   Acquisition by one company of another company competing in the same product and geographic markets.

hostile environment   A form of sexual harassment in which sexual conduct, sexual remarks, sexual depictions, and the like render the workplace offensive and intimidating such that performance is affected even though no tangible employment action has occurred.

hostile takeover   The acquisition of a formerly independent business where the acquired business resists the union.

I

Immigration Reform and Control Act (IRCA)   Enacted by Congress, IRCA's purpose is to discourage the entry of illegal aliens to the United States.

implied authority   Corporate officers' powers to take actions that are reasonably necessary to achieve their express duties.

implied authorization   In contract law, where the offeror's behavior or previous dealings with the offeree suggest an agreeable means of communicating an acceptance.

implied easement   Also called easement by prescription or way of necessity. An interest created where someone has openly used an adjoining piece of property for access with no complaint from the owner for a statutorily determined period of time.

implied warranty of fitness for a particular purpose A warranty that arises by operation of law and promises that the good warranted is reasonably useful for the buyer's purpose where the buyer was relying on the seller's expertise in making the purchase.

implied warranty of habitability   Implied warranty arising in lease or sale of residential real estate that the property will be fit for human habitability.

implied warranty of merchantability   A warranty that arises by operation of law and promises that the good warranted is at least of average, fair, reasonable quality.

implied-in-fact conditions   Conditions derived from the parties' conduct and the circumstances of the bargain.

implied-in-fact contract   Contract whose terms are implicitly understood based on the behavior of the parties.

implied-in-law conditions or constructive conditions Conditions imposed by the court to avoid unfairness.

in personam jurisdiction   The power of the court over a person.

incidental beneficiary   Person who is not a party to a contract, who benefits indirectly from the contract, who was not contemplated by the parties, and who may not enforce the contract.

incidental damages   Collateral damages that are incurred because of a breach; damages that compensate a person injured by a breach of contract for reasonable costs incurred in an attempt to avoid further loss.

incorporators   Those who initiate a new corporation.

indemnification   Corporate policy to compensate officers and directors for losses sustained in defending themselves against litigation associated with their professional duties where those duties were performed with reasonable business judgment.

indemnify   Reimburse one who has suffered a loss.

indenture   Agreement governing the conditions under which bonds are issued.

indenture trustee   Person or institution holding legal title to trust property and charged with carrying out the terms of the indenture.

independent contractor   A person who contracts with a principal to perform some task according to his or her own methods, and who is not under the principal's control regarding the physical details of the work.

indictment   A grand jury's formal accusation of a crime.

industry guides   Published advice to industry and the public providing Federal Trade Commission interpretations of the likely legality of specific marketing practices.

information   A prosecutor's formal accusation of a crime.

initial public offering (IPO) A security offered for sale to the public for the first time.

injunction A court order commanding a person or organization to do or not do a specified action.

injurious falsehood Intentional tort based on a false statement made with malice that disparages the property of another.

innocent misrepresentation An unintentional misrepresentation of material fact where the misrepresentation is justifiably relied on by another and damages result.

insider In securities law, anyone with a fiduciary duty who has knowledge of material facts not available to the general public.

insider trading Trading securities while in possession of material nonpublic information, in violation of a fiduciary duty.

intellectual property Intangible personal property, generally in the nature of copyrights, patents, and trademarks.

intent A conscious and purposeful state of mind.

intentional infliction of emotional distress Intentional tort based on outrageous conduct that causes severe emotional distress in another.

intentional tort Voluntary civil wrong causing harm to a protected interest.

interference with contractual relations Improperly causing a third party to breach or fail to perform its contract with another.

interference with prospective advantage Improperly causing a third party not to enter a prospective contractual relationship.

interpretive rules In administrative law, an agency's view of the meaning of statutes governing agency action.

interrogatories An ingredient in the discovery process wherein one party in a lawsuit directs written questions to another party in the lawsuit.

intrastate offerings Registration exemption for securities sold only to residents of the state in which the issuer is organized and doing business.

intrusion Wrongfully entering on or prying into the solitude or property of another.

invasion of privacy Violation of the right to be left alone.

invitee One who comes on the premises of another by invitation of the owner, in connection with the owner's business, and for the benefit of the owner or for the mutual benefit of the invitee and the owner.

J

joint liability Liability of a group of persons in which, if one of these persons is sued, he can insist that the other liable parties be joined to the suit as codefendants, so that all must be sued collectively.

joint and several liability Liability of a group of persons in which the plaintiff may sue all members of the group collectively or one or more individuals for the entire amount.

joint tenancy An estate held by two or more jointly with an equal right in all to share in the enjoyment of the land during their lives.

joint venture A form of business organization essentially identical to a partnership, except that it is engaged in a single project, not carrying on a business.

judgment notwithstanding the verdict (judgment n.o.v.) A judge's decision overruling the finding of the jury.

judgment proof Describes those against whom money judgments will have no effect because they are insolvent or their assets are beyond the reach of the court.

judicial review A court's authority to review statutes and, if appropriate, declare them unconstitutional. Also refers to appeals from administrative agencies.

jurisdiction The power of a judicial body to adjudicate a dispute. Also the geographical area within which that judicial body has authority to operate.

jurisprudence The philosophy and science of law.

jury instructions A judge's directions to the jury explaining the law that must be applied in the case at hand.

K

keiretsu Japanese cartels of vertically related firms working together in a collaborative fashion.

L

land contract Typically, an installment contract for the sale of land wherein the purchaser receives the deed from the owner on payment of the final installment.

landlord/lessor A party to a lease contract who allows a tenant to possess and to use his or her property in return for rent payments.

latent defects Imperfections that are not readily apparent upon reasonable inspection.

lease A contract for the possession and use of land or other property, including goods, on one side, and a recompense of rent or other income on the other.

leasehold estate A right to occupy and to use land pursuant to a lease or contract.

legal detriment Any act or forbearance by a promisee.

legal impossibility A party to a contract is relieved of his or her duty to perform when that performance has become objectively impossible because of the occurrence of an event unforeseen at the time of contracting.

legality of purpose The object of the contract does not violate law or public policy.

legitimate nondiscriminatory reason (LNDR) An employer's justification for taking adverse action against an employee or applicant where the basis for the action is something other than the individual's membership in a protected class (such as termination for dishonesty or theft).

lemon laws State statutes providing remedies for those buying vehicles that turn out to be so thoroughly defective that they cannot be repaired after reasonable efforts.

letter of credit A statement from a financial institution such as a bank guaranteeing that it will pay the financial obligations of a particular party.

libel Tort of defaming or injuring another's reputation by a published writing.

license A contractual right to use property in a certain manner.

licensee A person lawfully on land in possession of another for purposes unconnected with business interests of the possessor.

licenses Government-granted privileges to do some act or series of acts. Authorization to do what, without a license, would be unlawful. Also referred to as **permits.**

lien A claim against a piece of property in satisfaction of a debt; the financial interest of the lienholder in the property as a result of a debt or other obligation of the landowner.

life estate A property interest that gives a person the right to possess and to use property for a time that is measured by her or his lifetime or that of another person.

life tenant The possessor of a life estate interest.

limited liability Maximum loss normally limited to the amount invested in the firm.

limited liability company (LLC) Hybrid of limited partnership and corporation receiving partnership tax treatment with the operating advantages of a corporation.

limited liability partnership A special partnership form providing some of the advantages of limited liability.

limited partnership A form of business organization that has one or more general partners who manage the business and have unlimited liability for the obligations of the business and one or more limited partners who do not manage and have limited liability.

liquidated damages Damages made certain by the prior agreement of the parties.

liquidation "Straight" bankruptcy action in which all assets except exemptions are distributed to creditors (Chapter 7 bankruptcy).

lockout defense Takeover defense where the target company manipulates its assets, shares, and so on, to make the company unattractive as a takeover candidate.

lockouts Where employees are kept from the workplace by the employer. Where the landlord deprives the tenant of the possession of the premises by changing the locks on the property.

long-arm statute A state enactment that accords the courts of that state the authority to claim jurisdiction over people and property beyond the borders of the state as long as certain "minimum contacts" exist between the state and the people or property.

M

mailbox rule Rule holding that a mailed acceptance is effective upon dispatch when the offeror has used the mail to invite acceptance; the rule has been expanded to include the use of any reasonable manner of acceptance.

malice A required element of proof in a libel or slander claim by a public figure. Proof of a defamatory statement expressed with actual knowledge of its falsity or with reckless disregard for the truth would establish malice.

malicious prosecution Criminal prosecution carried on with malice and without probable cause with damages resulting.

malpractice Improper or negligent conduct in the performance of duties by a professional such as a doctor or lawyer.

market failure Economic theory arguing that the free market works imperfectly because of certain allegedly inherent defects such as monopoly, public goods, and so forth.

market foreclosure   In vertical mergers, the concern that the newly combined firm will close its doors to potential suppliers and purchasers such that competition will be harmed.

market share liability   Product liability action by which plaintiffs may be able to recover against manufacturers of defective products based on those manufacturers' market shares even though proof of causation cannot be established.

material breach   In contract law, performance that falls beneath substantial performance and does not have a lawful excuse.

mechanic's lien or materialman's lien   A claim created by law for the purpose of securing a priority of payment of the price or value of work performed and materials furnished in erecting or repairing a structure.

mediation   An extrajudicial proceeding in which a third party (the mediator) attempts to assist disputing parties to reach an agreeable, voluntary resolution of their differences.

mens rea   Evil intent.

merger   The union of two or more business organizations wherein all of the assets, rights, and liabilities of one are blended into the other with only one firm remaining.

misappropriation   In securities law, taking material, nonpublic information and engaging in insider trading in violation of a fiduciary duty.

misdemeanor   A criminal offense less serious than a felony normally requiring a fine or less than a year in a jail other than a penitentiary.

misrepresentation   The innocent assertion of a fact that is not in accord with the truth.

mitigation   Obligation of a person who has been injured by a breach of a contract to attempt to reduce the damages.

Model Business Corporation Act (MBCA)   Drafted by legal experts, the MBCA is designed to improve corporate law and to serve as a model for state legislatures in drafting their corporate laws.

mommy track   An employment track, whether formally or informally instituted, in some firms that allows for slower upward mobility for mothers who must divide their attention between their positions and their families.

monopoly   Market power permitting the holder to fix prices or exclude competition.

monopsony   Only one buyer to purchase the output of several sellers. A "buyer's monopoly."

moot   An issue no longer requiring attention or resolution because it has ceased to be in dispute.

moral hazard   Individuals feel a reduced incentive to guard against risk when they know themselves to be protected from the consequences of that risk.

mortgage   An interest in land formalized by a written instrument providing security for the payment of a debt.

mortgagee   One who receives a mortgage to secure repayment of a debt.

mortgagor   One who pledges property for a particular purpose such as security for a debt.

most favored nation status (MFN)   Preferential status offered to certain countries under the GATT or WTO, which allows the MFN country to obtain the lowest applicable tariff on goods.

motion   A request to a court seeking an order or action in favor of the party entering the motion.

motion for a directed verdict   A request by a party to a lawsuit arguing that the other party has failed to prove facts sufficient to establish a claim and that the judge must, therefore, enter a verdict in favor of the moving party.

multinational enterprise   A company that conducts business in more than one country.

mutual mistake   Where both parties to the contract are in error about a material fact.

N

National Environmental Policy Act   Requires that the government "use all practicable means" to conduct federal affairs in harmony with the environment.

National Pollutant Discharge Elimination System   Requires that all who discharge pollutants obtain an EPA permit before adding pollutants to a navigable stream.

National Priorities List   A list of hazardous dump or spill sites scheduled to be cleaned using Comprehensive Environmental Response, Compensation, and Liability Act (CERCLA) funds.

national treatment   Concept that requires that, once goods have been imported into a country, they must be treated as if they were domestic goods (that is, no tariff may be imposed other than that at the border).

nationalization   A country taking over a private business often without adequate compensation to the ex-owners.

necessaries   That which is reasonably necessary for a minor's proper and suitable maintenance.

negative externality   A spillover in which all the costs of a good or service are not fully absorbed by the producer and thus fall on others.

negligence   Failure to do something that a reasonable person would do under the circumstances, or an action that a reasonable and prudent person would not take under the circumstances.

negligence *per se*   Action violating a public duty, particularly where that duty is specified by statute.

negligent tort   Unintentional, civil wrong causing harm to a protected interest. Injury to another resulting from carelessness.

nolo contendere   A no-contest plea in a criminal case in which the defendant does not admit guilt but does submit to such punishment as the court may accord.

nominal damages   Small damages, oftentimes $1, awarded to show that there was a legal wrong even though the damages were very slight or nonexistent.

noncompetition clause   Employee agrees not to go into business in competition with employer.

nonpossessory interest   An interest in real property that is not sufficient to be an ownership or possessory interest.

nonprice restraints   Resale limitations imposed by manufacturers on distributors or retailers in any of several forms (such as territorial or customer restraints) that do not directly affect price.

nonreversionary interest   The interest held by the **remainderman.** It is called *nonreversionary* because it does not revert to the original grantor.

nonvoting stock   Owners of nonvoting stock participate in firm profits and dividends but may not vote at shareholder meetings.

novation   A mutual agreement between all parties concerned for the discharge of a valid existing obligation by the substitution of a new valid obligation on the part of the debtor or another, or a like agreement for the discharge of a lessee to a landlord by the substitution of a new lessee.

nuisance   A class of wrongs that arises from the unreasonable, unwarrantable, or unlawful use by a person of his or her property that produces material annoyance, inconvenience, discomfort, or hurt.

O

obligee   A person to whom another is bound by a promise or other obligation; a promisee.

obligor   A person who is bound by a promise or other obligation; a promisor.

offer   A proposal by one person to another that is intended to create legal relations on acceptance by the person to whom it is made.

offeree   One to whom an offer is made.

offeror   One making an offer.

oligopoly   An economic condition in which the market for a particular good or service is controlled by a small number of producers or distributors.

on-call workers   Workers who report to work only when called.

open-end loan   Credit arrangement not involving a lump sum but permitting repeated borrowing where payment amounts are not specified.

option contract   A separate contract in which an offeror agrees not to revoke her or his offer for a stated period in exchange for some valuable consideration.

ordinance   A law, rule, or regulation enacted by a local unit of government (such as a town or city).

output restriction   An agreement to limit production, which is a per se violation of the Sherman Act and may have the effect of artificially stabilizing or raising prices.

over-the-counter securities   Stocks, bonds, and like instruments sold directly from broker to customer rather than passing through a stock exchange.

P

parol evidence   When the written document is intended as the parties' final expression of their contract, oral evidence of prior agreements or representations cannot be used to vary the terms of the document.

partial ownership interest   An interest that may revert back to the original grantor.

partition   A legal proceeding that enables joint tenants or tenants in common to put an end to thetenancy and to vest in each tenant a sole estate in specific property or an allotment of the lands and buildings. If division is impossible, the estate may have to be sold and the proceeds divided.

partnership   An association of two or more persons where they agree to work together in a business designed to earn a profit.

past consideration   Performance that is not bargained for and was not given in exchange for the promise.

patent   A right conferred by the federal government allowing the holder to restrict the manufacture, distribution, and sale of the holder's invention or discovery.

patent defects   Imperfections that are visible and obvious.

Patient Protection and Affordable Care Act (ACA)   The health care act also known as *Obamacare*.

per curiam   By the court. Refers to legal opinions offered by the court as a whole rather than those instances where an individual judge authors the opinion.

per se   By itself; inherently.

per se **doctrine**   Certain antitrust violations are considered so harmful to competition that they are always unlawful and no proof of actual harm is required.

peremptory challenge   An attorney's authority to dismiss prospective members of the jury without offering any justification for that dismissal.

perfection   Process by which a secured party obtains a priority claim over other possible claimants to certain collateral belonging to a debtor.

periodic tenancy   The tenancy that exists when the landlord and tenant agree that the rent will be paid in regular successive intervals until notice to terminate is given but do not agree on a specific duration of the lease.

personal jurisdiction   The authority of a particular court over the parties to a lawsuit.

personal property   Movable property. All property other than real estate.

piercing the corporate veil   Holding a shareholder responsible for acts of a corporation due to a shareholder's domination and improper use of the corporation.

plaintiff   One who initiates a lawsuit.

pleadings   The formal entry of written statements by which the parties to a lawsuit set out their contentions and thereby formulate the issues on which the litigation will be based.

police power   The government's inherent authority to enact rules to provide for the health, safety,and general welfare of the citizenry.

political action committee   A legally defined lobbying group that uses funds and activities to support certain political views.

possibility of reverter   An interest that is uncertain or may arise only upon the occurrence of a condition.

precedent   A previously decided lawsuit that may be looked to as an authoritative statement for resolving current lawsuits involving similar questions of law.

predatory pricing   Selling of goods below cost for the purpose of harming competition.

preemption doctrine   Constitutional doctrine providing that the federal government "preempts the field" where it passes laws in an area, thus denying the states the right to pass conflicting laws or, in some cases, denying the states the right to pass any laws in that area.

preemptive right   A shareholder's option to purchase new issuances of shares in proportion to the shareholder's current ownership of the corporation.

preexisting duty   Prior legal obligation or commitment, performance of which does not constitute consideration for a new agreement.

preferred shares   Shares having dividend and liquidation preferences over other classes of shares.

pretext   After an employee has established a prima facie case of discrimination and the employer has articulated a bona fide occupational qualification (BFOQ) or legitimate nondiscriminatory reason (LNDR), the employee must show that the proffered defense is pretextual—that is, the BFOQ is not bona fide (or not applied in all situations) or that the LNDR has been applied differently to this individual compared to another.

price discrimination   Selling goods of like grade and quality to different buyers at different prices without justification where competitive harm results.

price fixing   An agreement among competitors to charge a specified price for a particular product or service. Also any agreement that prevents a seller from independently setting a price or from independently establishing the quantity to be produced.

prima facie **case**   A litigating party may be presumed to have built a prima facie case when the evidence is such that it is legally sufficient unless contradicted or overcome by other evidence.

principal   In agency law, one under whose direction an agent acts and for whose benefit that agent acts.

private law   Individually determined agreement of the parties relating to choice of laws, where disagreements shall be settled, and the language of the transactions.

private placements   Securities sold without a public offering, thus excusing them from Securities and Exchange Commission (SEC) registration requirements.

privatization   The many strategies for shifting public-sector activities back to private enterprise. Those strategies include contracting out government work to private parties, raising the user fees charged for public services, selling state-owned property and enterprises, and returning government services such as garbage collection to the private sector.

privity of contract   The legal connection that arises when two or more parties enter a contract.

procedural due process   Constitutional principle requiring that the government ensure fundamental fairness to all in the execution of our system of laws.

procedural rules   In administrative law, an agency's internal operating structure and methods.

product liability   Refers to legal responsibility of manufacturers and sellers to compensate buyers, users, and, in some cases, bystanders for harm from defective products.

profit à prendre   The right to enter property and to take something away from it, such as crops.

promisee   The person to whom a promise is made.

promisor   A person who makes a promise to another.

promissory estoppel   An equitable doctrine that protects those who foreseeably and reasonably rely on the promises of others by enforcing such promises when enforcement is necessary to avoid injustice.

promoter   A person who incorporates a business, organizes its initial management, and raises its initial capital.

prospectus   A communication, usually in the form of a pamphlet, offering a security for sale and summarizing the information needed for a prospective buyer to evaluate the security.

proximate cause   Occurrences that in a natural sequence, unbroken by potent intervening forces, produce an injury that would not have resulted in the absence of those occurrences.

proxy   Written permission from a shareholder to others to vote his or her share at a stockholders' meeting.

public disclosure of private facts   Public disclosure of private facts where disclosure of the matter in question would be highly offensive to a reasonable person.

public goods   Goods or services usually provided by government when not sufficiently by markets.

public law   Rules of national law that regulate transactions between parties, as well as the relationships between nations.

public policy   That which is good for the general public, as gleaned from a state's constitution, statutes, and case law.

publicly held corporation   A corporation with publicly traded shares. Also referred to as a **public corporation.**

puffing   An expression of opinion by a seller not made as a representation of fact.

punitive damages   Damages designed to punish flagrant wrongdoers and to deter them and others from engaging in similar conduct in the future.

purchase money security interest   A security interest that is (1) taken or retained by the seller of collateral to secure all or part of its purchase price or (2) taken by a debtor to acquire rights in or the use of the collateral if the value is so used.

Q

qualified person with a disability   An individual with a covered disability who can perform the essential functions of her or his position, with or without reasonable accommodation.

qualified privilege   In libel and slander law, situations where a defendant is excused from liability for defamatory statements except where the statements were motivated by malice.

quantum meruit   As much as he deserves. Describes a plea for recovery under a contract implied by law. Fair payment for work performed.

quasi-contract   The doctrine by which courts imply, as a matter of law, a promise to pay the reasonable value of goods or services when the party receiving such goods or services has knowingly done so under circumstances that make it unfair to retain them without paying for them.

quid pro quo   Exchanging one thing of value for another. In sexual harassment law, quid pro quo cases are those where employment benefits are conditioned on the subordinate's submission to sexual advances.

quitclaim deed   A deed conveying only the right, title, and interest of the grantor in the property described, as distinguished from a deed conveying the property itself.

R

ratified   The adoption or affirmance by a person of a prior act that did not previously bind her or him.

ratify   Adopting or affirming a prior, nonbinding act.

real property   Land, buildings, and things permanently attached to land or buildings.

real property or real estate The earth's crust and all things firmly attached to it.

reasonable accommodation An accommodation to an individual's disability or religion that does not place an undue burden on the employer, which may be determined by looking to the size of the employer, the cost to the employer, the type of employer, and the impact of the accommodation on the employer's operations.

reasonable expectations test Measure of negligence holding that a product is negligently designed if it is not safe for its intended use and also for any reasonably foreseeable use.

reasonable person Fictitious being the law constructs to determine whether a person's behavior falls short of what a "reasonable person" would do under the circumstances.

red herring A preliminary securities prospectus that provides information but does not constitute an offer to sell.

redlining Most commonly, the practice of refusing to make loans in economically unstable areas with the result that minorities are sometimes discriminated against in securing credit.

reformation An equitable remedy in which a court effectively rewrites the terms of a contract.

registration statement Document filed with the Securities and Exchange Commission (SEC) upon issuance of a new security detailing the information investors need to evaluate that security.

Regulation Z Rules of the Federal Reserve Board implementing provisions of the Federal Truth-in-Lending Act.

release Agreement to relinquish a right or a claim. Sometimes labeled a *waiver* or a *hold harmless clause.*

remainderman One who is entitled to the remainder of the estate after a particular estate carved out of it has expired.

remand To send back. For example, a higher court sends a case back to the lower court from which it came.

rent The consideration paid by a lessee to a lessor in exchange for the right to possess and to use property.

rent-strike statutes Legislation that allows a tenant to deduct from the rent payment the cost of property repairs that are otherwise the responsibility of the landlord.

reorganization A bankruptcy action in which creditors are kept from the debtor's assets while the debtor, under court supervision, works out a repayment plan and continues operations (Chapter 11 bankruptcy).

res A thing, object, or status.

res ipsa loquitur The thing speaks for itself. Rule of evidence establishing a presumption of negligence if the instrumentality causing the injury was in the exclusive control of the defendant, the injury would not ordinarily occur unless someone was negligent, and there is no evidence of other causes.

res judicata A thing decided. A doctrine of legal procedure preventing the retrial of issues already conclusively adjudicated.

resale price maintenance Manufacturer's effort to restrict the price at which its product is resold.

rescission Canceling a contract; its effect is to restore the parties to their original position.

Resource Conservation and Recovery Act Authorizes the federal government to provide assistance to states and localities in connection with solid waste, to prohibit open dumping, and to establish programs to recover energy and valuable materials from solid waste.

respondeat superior Let the master answer. Doctrine holding employers liable for acts (especially negligent acts) committed by employees while in the course of employment.

Restatement of Contracts A collection of the rules of contract law created by the American Law Institute to provide guidance to lawyers and judges.

restitution A remedy whereby one is able to obtain the return of that which she has given the other party, or an equivalent amount of money.

restraints of trade Contracts, combinations, or conspiracies resulting in obstructions of the marketplace, including monopoly, artificially inflated prices, artificially reduced supplies, or other impediments to the natural flow of commerce.

restrictive covenant An agreement restricting use of real property.

retaliation Various statutes, including Title VII of the Civil Rights Act of 1964, forbid employers from punishing employees who legitimately exercise their legal rights.

reverse Overturn the decision of a court.

RICO The Racketeer Influenced and Corrupt Organizations Act, federal organized crime law making it illegal to acquire or operate an enterprise by a pattern of racketeering behavior.

right of survivorship   A feature of a joint tenancy that causes a co-owner's interest in property to be transferred on her or his death to the surviving co-owner(s).

right-of-way   Where an easement appurtenant refers to the right to physically cross property.

right-to-know laws   Federal and state laws and regulations requiring employers to assume the affirmative responsibility of acquainting employees with hazardous substances and conditions in the workplace.

risk–utility test   Measure of negligence holding that a product is negligently designed if the benefits of that product's design are outweighed by the risks that accompany that design.

RM petition   Employer-filed request to the National Labor Relations Board (NLRB) seeking an election to demonstrate that a union is no longer supported by a majority of the employees.

rule of reason   For antitrust purposes, reviewing an agreement in its specific factual setting, considering its pro- and anticompetitive features, to determine if it is harmful to competition.

runaway shop   An employer closes in one location and opens in another to avoid unionization.

S

S corporation   See **subchapter S corporation** below.

scienter   Intent to commit a legal wrong. Guilty knowledge.

scope of employment   Limitation on master's liability to only those torts that a servant commits while "about the master's business."

scorched earth defense   Takeover defense where the target corporation takes on new debt, sells assets, and so on in an effort to make itself a less attractive target.

secondary boycott   Typically a union strategy that places pressure not on the employer with whom the union has a dispute but rather with a supplier or customer of that employer in the hope that the object of the boycott will persuade the employer to meet the union's expectations.

Securities and Exchange Commission (SEC)   Federal regulatory agency responsible for overseeing the securities markets.

security   A stock, bond, note, or other investment interest in an enterprise designed for profit and operated by one other than the investor. As to loans, refers to lien, promise, mortgage, or the like, given by a debtor to assure payment or performance of her debt.

security interest   A lien given by a debtor or her creditor to secure payment or performance of a debt or obligation.

self-employment tax   A Social Security tax on people who are self-employed.

separate property   Property held by either spouse at the time of marriage or property received by either spouse through a gift or inheritance.

separation of powers   The strategy of dividing government into separate and independent executive, legislative, and judicial branches, each of which acts as a check on the power of the others.

service mark   A word, mark, symbol, design, picture, or combination thereof that identifies a service provider.

servient estate   The property subject to an easement appurtenant or implied easement.

sexual harassment   Unwelcome sexual advances, requests for sexual favors, and other unwanted physical or verbal conduct of a sexual nature.

shareholder   One holding stock in a corporation. Also referred to as a **stockholder.**

shareholder derivative suit   Suit brought on behalf of a harmed corporation by a shareholder, usually for wrongs done to the corporation by directors or officers.

shark repellant   Various kinds of corporate behaviors designed to make a company unattractive to potential acquirers.

shelf registration   Initial public offering (IPO) registration that permits the issuer to hold the securities for sale until favorable market conditions emerge or the issuer needs the proceeds.

short-swing profits   Profits made by an insider through sale of company stock within six months of acquisition.

slander   A defamatory statement orally communicated to at least one third party.

slander per se   Category of oral defamation not requiring proof of actual harm to recover.

small claims courts   Courts of limited powers designed to hear cases involving modest sums of money (typically limited to $2,000–$7,500, but some states permit recoveries of $15,000 or more) in hearings free of many of the formalities and burdens associated with the more conventional judicial process.

small issues   Registration exemption for securities issued in small amounts.

sole proprietorship   A form of business under which one person owns and controls the business.

sovereign immunity   The government's right to exclude itself from being sued for damages in all but those situations where it consents to be sued. In international law, sovereign immunity permits a nation to decline to be sued in the courts of other nations.

specific performance   A contract remedy whereby the defendant is ordered to perform precisely according to the terms of her contract.

standing   A stake in a dispute sufficient to afford a party the legal right to bring or join a litigation exploring the subject of the dispute.

stare decisis   Let the decision stand. A doctrine of judicial procedure expecting a court to follow precedent in all cases involving substantially similar issues unless extremely compelling circumstances dictate a change in judicial direction.

state action   Situation of a sufficiently close relationship between the state and the action in question that the action can reasonably be treated as that of the state itself.

statute   A legislative enactment.

statute of frauds   A statute specifying that certain contracts must be in writing to be enforceable.

statute of limitations   A statute requiring that certain classes of lawsuits must be brought within defined limits of time after the right to begin them accrued or the right is lost.

straight voting   A form of voting for directors that ordinarily permits a shareholder to cast a number of votes equal to the number of shares he or she owns for as many nominees as there are directors to be elected.

strict liability   Civil wrong springing from defective and "unreasonably dangerous" products where responsibility automatically attaches without proof of blame or fault.

subchapter S corporation   A close corporation whose shareholders have elected to be taxed similarly to the way partners are taxed under federal income tax law. They are also known as *sub S corporations* or, more succinctly, just as *S corporations*.

subject-matter jurisdiction   The authority of a particular court to judge a particular kind of dispute.

sublease   A transfer of some but not all of a tenant's remaining right to possess property under a lease.

subpoena   An order from a court or administrative agency commanding that an individual appear to give testimony or produce specified documents.

substantial performance   Performance with minor, unimportant, and unintentional deviation.

substantive due process   The Due Process Clause of the Constitution requires that a statute be fair and reasonably related to a legitimate government purpose so that persons are not improperly deprived of their property rights.

suggestive mark   A trademark that suggests the product or its qualities; one that is more than merely descriptive.

summary judgment   A judicial determination prior to trial finding that no factual dispute exists between the parties and that, as a matter of law, one of the parties is entitled to a favorable judgment.

summons   A document originating in a court and delivered to a party or organization indicating that a lawsuit has been commenced against him, her, or it. The summons constitutes notice that the defendant is expected to appear in court to answer the plaintiff's allegations.

sunset legislation   A statute providing that a particular government agency will automatically cease to exist as of a specified date unless the legislative body affirmatively acts to extend the life of the agency.

Superfund/CERCLA   Comprehensive Environmental Response, Compensation, and Liability Act (CERCLA), established to help pay for the cleanup of hazardous dumps and spills.

Supremacy Clause   An element of the U.S. Constitution providing that all constitutionally valid federal laws are the paramount law of the land and, as such, are superior to any conflicting state or local laws.

surety   A person who promises to perform the same obligation as the principal and is jointly liable with the principal for that performance.

suretyship   A third party agrees to answer for the debt of another.

T

takeover bid   A tender offer designed to assume control of a corporation.

teleological ethics   The rightness of an action depends on its contribution to an end; often the maximum good.

temporary workers   Workers paid by a temporary help or staffing company.

tenancy by the entirety A form of co-ownership of property by a married couple that gives the owners a right of survivorship.

tenancy in partnership The manner in which partners co-own partnership property, much like tenancy in common, except that partners have a right of survivorship.

tenancy at sufferance The leasehold interest that occurs when a tenant remains in possession of property after the expiration of a lease.

tenancy at will A leasehold interest that occurs when a property is leased for an indefinite period and is terminable at the will of either party to the lease.

tenant/lessee A party to a lease contract who pays rent in return for the right to possess and to use property.

tenants in common Co-owners of real property who have undivided interests in the property and equal rights to possess it.

tender offer A public bid to the shareholders of a firm offering to buy shares at a specified price for a defined period of time.

term tenancy The tenancy that exists where a landlord and tenant have agreed to the terms of the lease period and a specific termination date for the lease.

test of nonobviousness Determines whether the development described in a patent application would have been obvious to an ordinary skilled worker in the art at the time the invention was made.

third-party beneficiaries People who are not parties to a contract but who have the right to enforce it because the contract was made with the intent to benefit them.

thrust upon Company holds a monopoly innocently because of superior performance, the failure of competition, or changing market conditions.

tippee In securities law, one who receives inside information from another.

tipper In securities law, one who conveys inside information to another.

tombstone ad A securities advertisement that does not constitute an offer and that usually appears in the financial press set inside heavy black borders suggestive of a tombstone.

tort A civil wrong, not arising from a contract, for which a court will provide a remedy.

totalitarianism A rigid, undemocratic government according power to a particular political group and excluding all others from access to political influence.

The Soviet Union, Nazi Germany, and Fascist Italy were totalitarian states.

Toxic Substances Control Act Requires chemical manufacturers to report information relating to chemicals that pose a "substantial risk" and allows the EPA to review and limit, or to stop, the introduction of new chemicals.

Trade Regulation Rules Directives from the Federal Trade Commission interpreting the will of Congress and specifying those practices that the commission considers unfair or deceptive.

trademark A word, name, packaging, logo, or other distinctive mark registered with the government and used exclusively by the owner to identify its goods or services.

trademark infringement Unauthorized use of the trademark of another.

treaty or convention A contract between nations.

treble damages An award of damages totaling three times the amount of actual damages, authorized by some statutes in an effort to discourage further wrongful conduct.

trespass Entering the property of another without any right, lawful authority, or invitation.

trespasser A person who enters the property of another without any right, lawful authority, or invitation.

tying arrangement Dealer agrees to sell or lease a product (the tying product) only on the condition that the buyer also purchases or leases another product (the tied product).

U

UETA The Uniform Electronic Transactions Act, a uniform act, widely adopted by state legislatures, giving electronic records and signatures the same legal power as paper documents and manually signed signatures.

ultra vires Corporate conduct beyond the scope of activities provided for under the terms of incorporation.

unconscionable A contract so one-sided and oppressive as to be unfair.

underwriter Professional who helps sell new securities or buys those securities for the purpose of resale.

undivided share A share of the interest in property that is not subject to division into parts.

undue hardship A burden imposed on an employer by accommodating an individual's disability or religion that would be too onerous for the employer to bear. See reasonable accommodation.

undue influence   Dominion that results in a right to rescind a contract.

unemployment taxes   Federal and state (most) taxes paid by employers as a percentage of the total payroll to fund benefits for those who have lost their jobs.

unenforceable contract   Meets basic requirements, but remains faulty.

unfair labor practice   Activities identified by Congress that employers might use to thwart workers' attempts to unionize and to undermine the economic power that would come from the workers' right to concerted activities and to unionize.

unfair subsidies   Subsidies offered to producers in a certain industry by a government to spur growth in that industry. These subsidies are considered unfair if they are used to promote export trade that harms another country.

Uniform Partnership Act (UPA)   Original uniform act for creation and operation of partnerships.

unilateral contract   A contract wherein the only acceptance of the offer that is necessary is the performance of the act.

unilateral mistake   Where one party to a contract is in error about a material fact.

union shop   In labor law, the situation where all employees of a company must join a union to retain employment. Forbidden in right-to-work states.

unjust enrichment   An unearned benefit knowingly accepted.

unsecured   Refers to a loan not backed by some kind of security.

use taxes   Normally, taxes imposed on the use, storage, or consumption of tangible personal property bought outside of the state imposing the taxes.

usury   Charging an interest rate exceeding the legally permissible maximum.

V

valid contract   Effective; sufficient in law.

venture capital funds   Organizations designed to invest in new and often risky business enterprises.

venue   The specific geographic location in which a court holding jurisdiction should properly hear a case, given the convenience of the parties and other relevant considerations.

verdict   The jury's decision as to who wins the litigation.

vertical merger   A union between two firms at different levels of the same channel of distribution.

vesting rights   The right of an individual to a present or future fixed benefit.

vicarious liability   Legal responsibility for the acts of another person because of some relationship with the person; for example, the liability of an employer for the acts of an employee.

void contract   Entirely null; no contract at all.

voidable contract   Capable of being made void; enforceable but can be canceled.

voir dire   The portion of a trial in which prospective jurors are questioned to determine their qualifications, including absence of bias, to sit in judgment in the case.

voting stock   Owners of voting stock have the right to vote at shareholder meetings.

W

waiver   Relinquishing a legal right—as in the situation where one agrees not to sue if injured while participating in a particular activity, such as attending a baseball game.

warranty   Any promise, expressed or implied, that the facts are true as specified. For example, in consumer law, the warranty of merchantability is a guarantee that the product is reasonably fit for the general purpose for which it was sold.

watered stock   Inadequate consideration received for stock.

whistle-blower   An informant, often an employee, who chooses to report misconduct within an organization to an authority figure or the public.

white-collar crime   Law violations by corporations or by managerial and executive personnel in the course of their professional duties.

white knight   In a takeover battle, a friendly company that rescues the target company from a hostile takeover. Often the rescue is accomplished by a merger between the target and the white knight.

winding up   In partnership and corporation law, the orderly liquidation of the business's assets.

without reserve   At an auction advertised as "without reserve," the seller is not free to withdraw an item before the high bid is accepted.

workers' compensation laws State statutes providing fixed recoveries for injuries and illnesses sustained in the course of employment. Under those statutes, workers need not establish fault on the part of the employer.

World Trade Organization (WTO) An international organization formed in 1995 for the purpose of establishing international trading principles and facilitating multilateral trade negotiations for the reduction of trade barriers.

wrongful discharge Tort of dismissing another from employment in violation of public policy or for other illegal reasons.

Y

yellow dog contract An employment agreement by an employee not to become a member of a union.

Z

zoning Restriction on the use of land as a result of public land use regulation.

zoning ordinances Dividing a city or a county into geographical areas of restriction—for example, only residential housing would be permitted in an area zoned R.

CASE INDEX